The Common Law of Obligations

The Common Law of Obligations

Third Edition

John Cooke LLB MPHIL
Barrister; Principal Lecturer in Law, Liverpool John Moores University

Professor David Oughton
Department of Law, De Montfort University

Butterworths
London, Edinburgh, Dublin
2000

United Kingdom	Butterworths, a Division of Reed Elsevier (UK) Ltd, Halsbury House, 35 Chancery Lane, LONDON WC2A 1EL and 4 Hill Street, EDINBURGH EH2 3JZ
Australia	Butterworths, a Division of Reed International Books Australia Pty Ltd, CHATSWOOD, New South Wales
Canada	Butterworths Canada Ltd, MARKHAM, Ontario
Hong Kong	Butterworths Asia (Hong Kong), HONG KONG
India	Butterworths India, NEW DELHI
Ireland	Butterworth (Ireland) Ltd, DUBLIN
Malaysia	Malayan Law Journal Sdn Bhd, KUALA LUMPUR
New Zealand	Butterworths of New Zealand Ltd, WELLINGTON
Singapore	Butterworths Asia, SINGAPORE
South Africa	Butterworths Publishers (Pty) Ltd, DURBAN
USA	Lexis Law Publishing, CHARLOTTESVILLE, Virginia

A CIP Catalogue record for this book is available from the British Library.

ISBN 0 406 90414 6

Printed in Great Britain by Cromwell Press, Trowbridge, Wiltshire

Visit Butterworths LEXIS *direct* **at: http://www.butterworths.com**

Preface

The aim of this book is to seek to illustrate and assess the complimentary nature of the various strands of the common law of obligations. It is principally designed for use by law degree students in English and Welsh universities, although we also hope that it will prove to be of value to postgraduate students, practitioners and others concerned with aspects of the legal process.

Academic work in both the United Kingdom and the United States of America has demonstrated that there is an overlap between contract law and tort law, and has laid the foundations of a developing theory of restitution. The latter still needs to be worked out fully, but scholars and members of the judiciary are beginning to map out the scope of the law of restitution, which cuts across the boundaries of common law and equity.

Where textbooks are used for the purposes of a course or module, they have tended to be traditionally dedicated to the issues of the law of contract, the law of tort and pioneers of the law of restitution have begun to place their ideas on the market. The more adventurous of these authors have sought to make reference to the most obvious areas of overlap between the various strands of the law of obligations, such as the issues of liability for misleading statements and remoteness of loss; however, it is argued that the underlying connecting principles are not fully examined.

In considering the historical roots of the law of obligations and the interests protected by common law rules and related equitable principles, we hope that it will be possible to identify the underlying themes on which protection of the expectation, reliance and restitution interests of a plaintiff are based.

A book which covers all the topics traditionally covered by textbooks on contract, tort and restitution would be of unmanageable proportions. We have therefore attempted to explain the general principles governing the creation of obligations, negation of liability and the remedies available in the event of a breach of duty. The second part of the book seeks to illustrate those general principles by reference to selected areas of common law liability where the different aspects of common law liability interrelate.

In this edition there have been some structural changes. In particular the separate chapter on liability for statements in part two of the book has disappeared, the material from which has been incorporated in a new chapter on the protection of economic interests. The rapid pace of change on the matter of tortious liability for negligent misstatement has necessitated consideration of the role of voluntary assumption of responsibility for statements and the role of the former requirement of reasonable reliance.

As in previous editions, we have sought to clarify the distinction between exchange and non-exchange relationships through a discussion of the three cardinal interests protected by common law rules and by examining the different treatment applied to consumer and business dealings. In this edition we have considered the effect of a number of important statutory rules and their effect on common law liability. In particular the changes brought about by the Human Rights Act 1998, the Contracts (Rights of Third Parties) Act 1999 and the Unfair Terms in Consumer Contracts Regulations 1999 have been given extensive treatment. As ever, the pace of change in the higher appellate courts has been considerable, and throughout this edition account has been taken of relevant case law developments.

The authors would like to acknowledge the assistance and co-operation of colleagues at Liverpool John Moores University and De Montfort University who have assisted us in this enterprise. In particular we would like to extend our thanks to Tony Harvey and Lorie Charlesworth in Liverpool and Martin Davis, Veronica Matthew and Chris Willett at De Montfort University for their advice and comments on aspects of previous editions of this book. Thanks also have to go to the students at both universities who have endured our teaching and experimentation.

Special thanks must go to the staff at Butterworths Tolley for their diligence in reading the manuscript and preparing it for publication. Their patience in waiting for the final copy of the manuscript was remarkable.

Last, but by no means least, very special thanks must go to our families. Sue, Emma, Gareth, Matthew and Karen have had to put up with a lot during the protracted preparation of this edition. Their patience, good humour and willingness to put up with the amount of time spent hunched over a word processor is very much appreciated.

We have endeavoured to state the law as it stood on 1 July 2000.

PJ Cooke
DW Oughton

July 2000

Contents

Section D

Negation of liability

Part II

Specific obligations

Table of statutes

Table of cases

H

I

PAGE

S

T

X

Y

Z

Part I

General principles

Section A

The common law in context

CONTENTS

Chapter 1

Historical background to the common law

The modern common law of obligations is divided into three parts. Contractual liability is based on breach of promise. Tortious liability is based on wrongful conduct. Unjust enrichments may be reversed in an action for restitution. The present division is based on concepts found in Roman law but their transmission into English law was a tortuous business.

1. ROMAN LAW CONCEPTS

The organisation of law into systematic categories has usually been the task of academic lawyers. Practising lawyers have historically been concerned with particular cases rather than systems.

The origin of obligations as a category of law lies in Roman law. This branch of law was concerned with civil relationships between persons (in personam) rather than between persons and things (in rem). The latter relationship was governed by the law of property rather than the law of obligations.

In Roman law the 'obligatio' was two-sided. It involved a personal right to claim on one side and a right to performance on the other. In the case of a debt for example, obligation referred to either the right of the creditor to the money or the duty of the debtor to pay. For reasons which are not clear English law has adopted a one-sided view of obligation. In the above example the obligation is simply the duty of the debtor to pay.

The most enduring contribution of the Roman law of obligations to English obligations has been the categories it adopted. Obligations were divided into contract, delict, quasi-contract and quasi-delict.[1]

The major distinction was between contract and delict[2] and is thought to have been borrowed from a distinction made by Aristotle between voluntary and involuntary transactions.[3] A similar distinction has been drawn in English law between contract

---

1   Justinian, Inst III, 13, 2.
2   Institutes, Gai III 88.
3   Kaser, *Das Romische Privatrecht*, (Munich, 1971) 2nd edn, ch I p 522.

and tort and for present purposes delict and tort will be treated as interchangeable.[4] Both contract and delict are civil wrongs affecting individuals, as opposed to criminal acts which are public wrongs affecting the state. The distinction between contract and delict is an extremely difficult one to make and in many modern legal systems has become blurred. Different legal systems have adopted different analysis of factual situations. For example, a claim against a manufacturer by a consumer of his product is dealt with by tort (delict) in England and by contract in France. In England, a person who is a victim of a negligent statement has a remedy in tort, whereas in Germany the remedy is in contract. Considerable academic debate has concentrated on whether the distinction should be maintained.[5] One of the objectives of this book is to see if there is a modern alternative classificatory system.

That two categories were not sufficient is apparent from the case of unjustified enrichment. If A owes money to B and by mistake pays it to C, how is he to get it back? There is no contract between A and C, and C has committed no wrong (tort or delict). A third category, in Roman law called quasi-contract, is needed to deal with this type of case. In modern England these types of claim are dealt with by the law of restitution. The problem of trying to work with only two categories is apparent from the English attempt to accommodate unjustified enrichment within contract by virtue of an 'implied promise'.[6]

The fourth category of quasi-delict has had an unhappy history. Only four classes of case came within it[7] and it was difficult to see what principle underlay quasi-delict. One possibility was that these cases were examples of what we would now call strict liability. If so, then the virtual disappearance of quasi-delict from modern European legal systems represents a lost opportunity. Retention of this category would have avoided the modern problem of finding a natural home for strict liability and rationalised the old strands such as cattle trespass and the modern ones forged from the Industrial Revolution.[8]

2.   THE TRANSMISSION OF ROMAN LAW INTO CIVILIAN SYSTEMS

The history of the transmission and synthesis of Roman law into modern legal systems is complex and controversial.[9] A warning note should be sounded at this point. There is always a temptation to look at the past through modern eyes. What would be described as contract at one time in history may not have the same meaning now. Certain functions performed by what we now call contract may have been regulated by different means in other societies.[10] The purpose of this history is to trace the history of categories and not to closely analyse the contents of those categories at different stages in history.

What we would regard as the beginnings of a general law of contract appear to have emerged in the sixteenth century. This was achieved by a group known as the 'late

---

4   Markesinis (1977) 93 LQR 78.
5   Fridman (1977) 93 LQR 422; Smith (1984) 18 Univ of British Columbia LR 95; Gilmore *The Death of Contract* (1974); Atiyah *Rise and Fall*; Burrows (1983) 99 LQR 217; Fried *Contract as Promise*; Markesinis (1987) 103 LQR 354.
6   See *Sinclair v Brougham* [1914] AC 398 at 415 (per HALDANE LC).
7   A judge who through breach of his official duty caused damage to another person. Anyone from whose dwelling something was thrown into the street so as to injure another person or from whose building objects placed on an eave fell and endangered traffic. Sea carriers, innkeepers and stable-keepers whose employees had stolen or damaged the property of customers.
8   See ch 12.
9   See Zimmermann *The Law of Obligations* (Juta, 1990).
10 See Adams and Brownsword *Understanding Contract Law*, ch 10.

scholastics' achieving a synthesis between Roman law and Aristotelian philosophy. Concepts such as the efficacy of promise keeping; consent as the basis of contractual obligation; and the doctrines of duress, fraud and mistake are present.[11] In order to be enforceable a promise had to be made for a sufficient reason (causa), being either the receipt of a performance in return for one's own or 'liberality'. This was based on the Aristotelian distinction between commutative justice and liberality. Liberality for Aristotle was giving wealth away to the right people, in the right amount and at the right time. Commutative justice was an exchange so that neither party was unjustly enriched at the expense of the other.

These doctrines were adopted by the natural lawyers such as Grotius, Pufendorf and Barbeyrac and popularised by authors such as Domat and Pothier. The drafters of the French Civil Code borrowed extensively from Pothier and Domat.

3.   THE ENGLISH ISOLATION?

Mainland Europe gradually established a highly developed legal system based on Roman law. One reason for this borrowing of Roman concepts may have been the relatively late development of the single nation state in Europe. In contrast, one effect of the Norman invasion and conquest of England in the eleventh century was to produce a single state with a centralised government. One aspect of this government was the development of a centralised legal system with its own characteristics. Chief among these were the development of the writ system and jury trial. This meant that England was to a large extent isolated from developments in mainland Europe.

The extent of this isolation is a matter of some controversy and some Roman law ideas appear to have penetrated the common law, particularly with the idea of consideration (motive) for a promise. It should also be remembered that the Chancellors until the time of Henry VIII were clergymen who would be knowledgeable in Roman and Canon law.[12]

What is clear is that the adoption of the writ system prevented the development of categories of law such as contract or tort. English categories were defined during the writ period by the appropriate form of action rather than the Roman classification. The distinction between contract and tort would have to wait until the forms of action lost their hold in the nineteenth century.

4.   THE ENGLISH WRIT SYSTEM[13]

Although an extensive system of local courts existed in England,[14] the early history of the common law was concerned with the establishment of central courts and a procedure to make them effective. By 1307, the three central courts of common law, namely King's Bench, Common Pleas and Exchequer had become permanent institutions based in London.[15]

It was necessary that the central courts should have a warrant to act in order to give justice. This warrant was the writ, specifying the complaint and demanding that the defendant should appear before the court to answer the complaint. Initially, writs were

---

11   See Gordley *The Philosophical Origins of Modern Contract Doctrine* (Clarendon, 1991) pp 69–112.
12   Simpson *History* p 400.
13   Baker *An Introduction to English Legal History* (3rd edn, 1990) ch 4; Milsom *Historical Foundations of the Common Law* (2nd edn, 1980) pp 33–37; Maitland *Forms of Action at Common Law* (1909).
14   Baker pp 1–9; Milsom pp 11–22.
15   Baker ch 2; Milsom pp 23–32.

issued on an individual basis but, as certain factual situations recurred, they fell into certain classes and came to have fixed wording. Examples of these were the writ of debt to recover money owed, the writ of detinue to recover personal property and the writ of covenant to enforce a promise. By the fourteenth century covenant had acquired the formality that it had to be under seal, which limited its usefulness.

The writ system had its defects. If a person chose the wrong writ, his action would fail. Some writs were subject to the procedure known as wager of law. This required a party to bring as many witnesses as possible to swear to the truth of his case. This procedure led to debt and detinue becoming unpopular with plaintiffs as they were subject to wager of law.

The establishment of the writs of debt, detinue, covenant and account[16] left gaps in the common law of obligations. There was no action to enforce an informal, unsealed agreement without wager of law. Nor was there an action for misfeasance in the sense of performing an obligation badly, as opposed to non-feasance in the sense of not performing at all. These actions would have been available in the local courts and the next step in the development of the common law was their admission to the central courts.

5.   TRESPASS AND CASE[16a]

Trespass signified a wrong. To be admitted to the central courts, the trespass had to be committed *vi et armis*. This enabled the court to gain jurisdiction over the case on the grounds that the act complained of was contrary to the king's peace. *Vi et armis* became no more than a formula and was used in cases where there was no such force. Actions in assault, battery and false imprisonment continued to contain the *vi et armis* clause, but actions which local custom classified as wrongs were admitted to the central courts without the need for the *vi et armis* clause. These were known as actions on the case. Examples included failure to carry out a duty to repair sea walls and actions by owners of markets and fairs against persons defrauding them of tolls by selling secretly in their own houses. Trespass lost its original meaning and became identified with *vi et armis*.

6.   ASSUMPSIT AND THE ORIGINS OF CONTRACT[16b]

The modern law of contract may stem from a form of case known as assumpsit. From this writ, the common law developed an action for breach of informal promises.

The action of assumpsit appeared in the mid-fourteenth century. The plaintiff alleged that the defendant had entered into an informal agreement with him and by misconduct, caused damage in a way not envisaged by the transaction. In an early case,[17] the plaintiff sought a cure for ringworm from the defendant doctor. He alleged that the doctor undertook (assumpsit) to cure him in return for a sum of money previously paid, and that the defendant had so negligently performed the cure as to cause damage. Assumpsit proceeded on the basis that the defendant had voluntarily assumed an obligation. An exception to this principle were the 'common callings'. These included persons such as innkeepers, blacksmiths and surgeons. Here there was both a voluntary undertaking and a public policy element as it was of benefit to the community that these people carried out their duties without negligence. The first reported case in which the idea

---

16   See Milsom ch 10; Ibbetson 24–30.
16a   Ibbeston 39–56.
16b   Ibbetson 126–145.
17   *Skyrne v Butolf* (1367) YB 2 Ric 2, 223.

that the common callings were to exercise care in the performance of their duties was the *Humber Ferry* case.[18] The action was brought against a ferryman who had accepted a mare for carriage across the river. He overloaded the ferry with the result that the mare was lost. The action was brought in trespass and the defendant's plea that the correct action was that of covenant failed. In modern terms, the appropriate question would be whether the action lay in contract or in tort. There was a breach of contract because the mare was not carried across the river, but the carrier was liable in tort by causing the death of the mare.

In 1533, assumpsit was extended from cases of misfeasance to those of non-feasance.[19] The outstanding problem became the overlap between assumpsit and the praecipe writs such as debt and detinue. Assumpsit was popular with plaintiffs as it was tried by jury and they could avoid wager of law. In 1602, in *Slade's Case*,[20] the triumph of assumpsit was confirmed. The plaintiff now had a choice between assumpsit and the praecipe actions. There was also a principle upon which any undertaking was actionable. The defendant was sued for breach of promise, tried by jury and the remedy for breach was compensatory damages.

When assumpsit became established as an action for breach of promise, this raised the difficult problem encountered by all legal systems, namely to decide which promises should be enforced. The common law's answer to this lay in the doctrine of consideration. A consideration was a motivating reason for a promise. Whether a promise was enforceable depended upon that reason.[1] A promise given without a proper motive or reason was not binding, as it could not have been seriously intended.

What was a proper motive in the sixteenth century is obscure and uncertain. It is clear that the basis of the enforceability of an assumpsit action was consideration and not some other theory such as benefit or detrimental reliance.[2] Benefit and detriment had become facets of consideration rather than alternatives to it.

It should not be assumed that the only enforceable promises were those supported by consideration. A promise made in the form of a deed under seal was enforceable in the writ of covenant. Such formalities would have been unpopular with traders who required a swift informal mechanism for transactions but provided an alternative mechanism to enforce promises made in a more formal setting. Where a promise was couched in the form of a deed no consideration was necessary to support the promise. The formalities took the place of consideration and provided evidence of the seriousness of the promise. A logical development from this would have been to enforce only those promises made in writing. The fact that a promisor has taken the trouble to reduce his promise to writing could be taken to indicate the seriousness of the promise. LORD MANSFIELD attempted to introduce this idea in 1765 when he held that a written commercial contract not supported by consideration was not *nudum pactum*.[3] However, this view was decisively rejected in 1778.[4]

The most strongly argued alternative to the requirement of consideration is that the presence of some benefit or detriment justifies the enforcement of a promise. If the promisor has been paid or otherwise recompensed for his promise, then holding him to his word can be justified in order to prevent unjust enrichment. This has nothing to do with the promisor's motive in making the promise. The promisor may also induce the promisee to rely on the promise and to alter his position in a way in which he

---

18   *Buckton v Tounesende* (1348) YB 22 Ass, p 141. See Kiralfy *The Action on the Case* (1951) p 187.
19   *Pickering v Thoroughgood* (1533) 93 Selden Society 4.
20   (1602) 4 Co Rep 91a. See Baker [1973] CLJ 51; Ibbetson (1984) 40 JLS 295.
1   Simpson *History* pp 322–323, 391–394, 485–486.
2   St Germain's *Doctor and Student* (1530). Dial 2, c 24; 91 Selden Society 230. Cf Atiyah *Rise and Fall* ch 6.
3   *Pillans and Rose v Van Mierop and Hopkins* (1765) 3 Burr 1664.
4   *Rann v Hughes* (1778) 7 Term Rep 350n.

would otherwise not have done. The promisor may then be held to his promise or be obliged to compensate for loss suffered.

Both benefit and detriment were incorporated into the doctrine of consideration in a confused manner. A detriment to the promisee emerged as good consideration but it was not necessarily the motive for the promise. If a doctor was promised money to heal a sick person, the doctor's work was induced by the promise, but was not the *motive* for the promise.[5] Professor Simpson has commented:[6]

> In a tidy and more intelligible scheme of thought, induced injurious reliance as a ground for actionability would have been presented not as an aspect of the doctrine of consideration but as an alternative to it.
>
> The common law's adoption of consideration as the sole test for the enforceability of promises is described as an example of its 'tendency towards a sort of doctrinal monism'.[7]

(1)   CONSIDERATION AND ASSUMPSIT[7a]

A crucial step in the development of promissory liability was the adoption of consideration as the test for the enforceability of promises. The effect was to give an extremely flexible doctrine to the common law. What initially sufficed as consideration reflected the ideas previously accepted by the law. The flexibility of the doctrine meant that what was 'good' consideration could change with time and accepted practice.

(i)   Benefit as consideration

The payment of money was good consideration for a promise to repay it. If A lent B £10, then the promise was enforceable because of the benefit conferred on B. The promise provided evidence that the money was a loan and not a gift.

In the case of non-monetary benefits, it was a question for the jury to decide whether the benefit had to be paid for. Whether a promise to pay had been made was a secondary matter providing evidence of the benefit. In modern contract law, the promise is the basis of the obligation to recompense the promisee for the benefit. A benefit conferred in the absence of a promise is treated as part of the law of restitution.

(ii)   Detrimental reliance as consideration

Detrimental reliance probably entered English law through delict. If goods were entrusted to a person exercising a common calling, then this constituted an act of reliance. By the 1560s, it was clear that the person exercising the common calling was liable 'in contract' rather than in delict.[8]

(iii)   Past consideration and requests

During the seventeenth and eighteenth centuries, the doctrine of consideration became complicated by the notion of the request. A benefit could only be good consideration for a promise if the benefit was supplied *after* the promise. A benefit conferred before the promise was a past consideration and was not a good consideration as it was not requested. This rule ensured that the promisor did not have to pay for something which did not really benefit him. For example, if services were rendered and the recipient

5   Simpson pp 324–325.
6   Ibid at p 325.
7   Ibid.
7a   Ibbetson 141–145.
8   Ibbetson [1982] 41 CLJ 142 at 153; cf Atiyah *Rise and Fall* pp 181–184.

later promised to pay for the service, the promisor would not be bound. It was assumed that the promise on its own was insufficient evidence of a benefit to the promisor.

Exceptions to this rule did develop. In some instances a request would be implied and in cases of emergency, no request was necessary.[9]

(iv)   The role of the jury

It is a mistake to look for any coherent contractual theory in the assumpsit action in the sixteenth and seventeenth centuries. Many of the features of modern contract law were missing. Rules on offer and acceptance, mistake and remoteness of damage were unknown. Illegality and discharge of contract started to emerge in quasi-contract in the eighteenth century. Any attempt to find a rational theory of consideration acceptable to the modern lawyer is doomed to founder in the contradictions in the reports.

The reason for the absence of detailed legal rules was the use of the jury in civil cases. In most cases of assumpsit, the defendant would plead that he had not assumed responsibility and the issue then had to be decided on its factual merits by the jury.[10] What was a good motive or consideration for a promise was quite simply a matter for the jury to decide. A body of law only came to be established when this question was removed from the jury and left to the judges as a question of law. This movement started with LORD MANSFIELD in the eighteenth century,[11] and in the late eighteenth and early nineteenth centuries the familiar principles of modern contract law were shaped by the courts as 'counsel increasingly took advantage of the procedures for raising detailed questions of law *in banc*'.[12]

In a sense English law grew up in isolation as a result of the writ system. This system encouraged practical pleading around the writs, rather than the development of legal concepts such as contract or tort. It was only with the gradual disintegration of the writ system that the need for other categories of law was felt. At this stage English lawyers looked to the continent where the Roman categories had survived and were transmitted into codes. The modern development of a law of obligations is the story of these categories being adopted, modified and grafted onto the existing writ system.

7.   THE DEVELOPMENT OF TORT LAW

(1)   THE EARLY DEVELOPMENT OF TRESPASS AND CASE[12a]

It has been seen how the action of assumpsit developed, based on promise and consideration. This opened the way for what we would now call contract. Assumpsit had developed from case, and case itself from trespass. The courts found it necessary to distinguish assumpsit from other types of case.[13] It was the non-assumpsit varieties of trespass and case which led to the development of the modern law of tort.

In the sixteenth century, there was no clear concept of tort or contract. Certain actions which would be identifiable to the modern reader as tortious did exist. For example, detinue was actionable as a praecipe writ, and conversion (trover) and nuisance were actionable as actions on the case. Apart from these specific actions, liability for 'wrongdoing' other than breach of promise was remedied through trespass *vi et armis*

9   See *Church v Church* (1665) T Raym 260; 83 ER 133. See also Gilmore *The Death of Contract* (1974) pp 74–76.
10   Baker ch 19.
11   Baker ch 5.
12   Baker p 400.
12a   Ibbetson 39–56.
13   *Bosun v Landford* (1689) 1 KB 101; *Carter v Fossett* (1623) Palm 329.

and case. The history of the modern law of tort is to be found in the development of these actions. In the specific actions the identifying feature was the type of harm caused. In detinue, the harm was the detention of the plaintiff's goods rather than any fault on the part of the defendant.

(i)   Trespass

The trespass *vi et armis* action extended much further than present day battery. The details of the action are concealed behind the procedure used. It has already been seen that the '*vi et armis*' clause rapidly became a fiction to enable the case to be heard by the Royal Courts. The standard plea was always that the defendant 'assaulted with force and arms', whatever the facts of the case. The defendant would then enter a plea of 'not guilty' and explain his case to the jury who would then enter a verdict. This procedure prevented any substantive law on accidents from developing for centuries.

The case of *Weaver v Ward*[14] is instructive as to such law as there was in these cases. The plaintiff was injured when the defendant's weapon was discharged during an exercise of trained bands. The defendant pleaded that the wounding was accidental and against his will. This was held to be a bad plea, but the court indicated what would be an acceptable defence. It was said that the defendant could plead that his act was involuntary,[15] that the plaintiff was responsible for the damage by failing to take precautions to avoid the loss,[16] or that there had been an inevitable accident. The third plea has caused great problems to legal scholars and has led to the theory that liability in trespass was strict. The preferable view is that this was not the case.[17] The nature of the writ of trespass suggested 'deliberate wickedness',[18] but as the plaintiff could not be required to prove the acknowledged fiction in the writ, he was therefore obliged only to show that the defendant had done the harm. The defendant's plea would then be 'not guilty', which indicated that he had not harmed the plaintiff. If the defendant had inflicted harm on the plaintiff, he then had to prove that it was not his fault. The jury would then decide the case and the real issue would remain hidden, as it would not appear in the report.

(ii)   Action on the case

Actions for wrongful conduct causing harm where there was a pre-existing relationship between the parties were brought in case. The writ would allege that the defendant had undertaken to do something for the plaintiff and had done it carelessly (*negligenter*). The essence of the action was not in doing the act as in trespass *vi et armis*, but in performing it carelessly. The likes of bailees, surgeons and carriers undertook to do a particular job, but they did not undertake to perform it to a particular standard. 'The obligation to use care was imposed by law rather than by contract.'[19] Whether the work had been performed to a required standard was a question for the jury.

Assumpsit was a species of case, but was there any difference between an action on the case for assumpsit and one for undertaking? By the end of the sixteenth century, the distinction was that in the former there had to be consideration, and in the latter there had to be negligence. Other actions were allowed in case where there was no pre-existing relationship between the parties, provided no attempt was made to use

14   (1616) 80 ER 284. See Kretzmer (1984) 4 OJLS 46 at 69.
15   See *Gibbon v Pepper* (1695) 91 ER 922.
16   See Holdsworth *A History of English Law* (4th edn, 1956) vol 8, p 459 et seq.
17   See Baker pp 458–459; Kretzmer (1984) 4 OJLS 46 at 124–125.
18   Milsom p 394.
19   Baker p 460.

case instead of existing available actions. In 1520, for example, a mill keeper was sued for breach of his duty to control a mill sluice. The duty was imposed in order to prevent flooding.[20]

The first indications of what we would now call negligence appeared in the seventeenth century. This was due to an increase in road traffic and the number of running down cases. These actions were brought in case for negligence in order to avoid trespass *vi et armis*, which carried certain disadvantages for the plaintiff.[1] *Michell v Allestry*[2] has been subsequently interpreted as crucial. The defendant was liable for creating a danger when he took horses into a busy area. The action succeeded despite the absence of force, undertaking or custom of the realm. However, the court did not fully appreciate the effect of its decision. The judges seemed only to be conscious of having made a slight enlargement of the *scienter* principle.

(2)   TRESPASS AND CASE IN THE NINETEENTH AND TWENTIETH CENTURIES[2a]

The large number of running down cases[3] raised the problem of how to distinguish between trespass and case. The distinction originally arose when trespass with its special formula was admitted to the central courts, but actions on the case still continued to be heard in the local courts. Eighteenth-century lawyers came to distinguish between direct or forcible injury (trespass) and indirect or consequential injury (case). This caused practitioners a number of problems which were eased by a clear rule emerging in *Williams v Holland*.[4] The court recognised that there was an overlap between trespass and case. If the plaintiff had an action in trespass for a direct and physical wrong, he could also sue in case if he could prove negligence. Trespass came to be associated with intentional or wilful injuries, and case with negligence. The negligence had to be expressly pleaded and proved. Running down cases could now be brought in case, and the issue was to decide which driver had been negligent. Questions of risk-generation and loss-avoidance were therefore merged.[5]

Nineteenth-century developments led to negligence becoming the basis of the collision cases. It remained to be seen whether trespass had any role to play in other personal injuries cases. The abolition of the forms of action[6] caused the courts to consider for the first time the purpose served by the substantive law of trespass. The courts were able to distinguish between cases where the defendant alone created the risk of injury, and those where both parties generated the risk. An example of the former arose in accidental shooting cases. The latter category was exemplified by the collision cases, where the issue was to decide which of two people was at fault.

In *Rylands v Fletcher*,[7] the House of Lords took the view that trespass was a tort of strict liability. Accidents on the highway were an exception to this rule. In such cases, the plaintiff might have assumed the risk of injury, therefore negligence had to be proved.[8] There was no authority to compel the House to lay down a strict liability rule for trespass. The question arose directly for decision in *Stanley v Powell*,[9] where the

20   *Fynamore v Clifford* (1520) 94 SS 229.
1   See Baker pp 464–465.
2   (1676) 1 Vent 295, 86 ER 190.
2a   Ibbetson 153–199.
3   See Fifoot *History and Sources of the Common Law* (1949) p 185.
4   (1833) 10 Bing 112, 131 ER 848. Pritchard [1964] CLJ 234–253.
5   Kretzmer (1984) 4 OJLS 46 at 79f.
6   Common Law Procedure Act 1852 and Judicature Acts 1873–5.
7   (1868) LR 3 HL 330.
8   See also *Holmes v Mather* (1875) LR 10 Exch 261; Goodhart (1933) 49 LQR 359.
9   [1891] 1 QB 86.

defendant fired his own gun. The bullet ricocheted off a tree and struck the plaintiff. The jury found no negligence, and DENMAN J entered judgment for the defendant. The case has generated considerable controversy, but has now stood for nearly a century and been approved by the Court of Appeal.[10] The significance of the case was that it dispensed with the centuries-old risk-generation and loss-avoidance questions of determining liability. Instead, the defendant's conduct was seen as the basis of tort liability.

One final matter remained unresolved, namely where did the burden of proof lie in a trespass action? In negligence, the burden is on the plaintiff. In *Fowler v Lanning*,[11] the plaintiff's writ claimed damages for trespass to the person, alleging that 'the defendant shot the plaintiff.' It was held that this disclosed no cause of action as it neither alleged fault nor gave particulars of negligence.[12] As the burden of proof in trespass was on the plaintiff, the eclipse of trespass as a tort protecting against personal injuries by negligence was confirmed. The case was approved by the Court of Appeal,[13] although this may have been obiter. The burden of proof distinction has been maintained in commonwealth countries.[14]

(3)   CASE AND NEGLIGENCE

The nineteenth century saw the beginnings of the modern tort of negligence. Two concepts had to be fused in order to produce this. These were liability for positive acts causing damage, known as misfeasance, and liability for neglect of a duty to act, known as non-feasance. In the eighteenth century, these were actionable as case for misfeasance and case for negligence respectively.[15] The action for non-feasance covered the neglect to perform various duties which were imposed by law, and included duties imposed by undertakings, and customs of the realm, local custom and those arising out of an office. The development of the action for misfeasance outside of pre-existing relationships was limited and was largely confined to road accidents, which were classified as actions on the case (negligence) because of the assumption of risk theory.[16]

Development in negligence liability was stifled by the new law of contract being fashioned by the judges in the early years of the nineteenth century and by the doctrine of *laissez-faire*. The abolition of the writ system saw a clear distinction emerge between three branches of the common law of obligations, with contract emerging as the strongest partner because of the prevailing economic and philosophical influences. This dominance of contract restricted and closely defined the emergence of tort and restitution. The Industrial Revolution increased the likelihood of accidents arising out of industrial construction and the operation of the railways.[17]

Although the judges rapidly developed a unified theory of contract, there was nothing to unite the various negligence actions until an authoritative statement in 1932 by LORD ATKIN in *Donoghue v Stevenson*.[18] This was the famous 'neighbour test', which required a man to take 'reasonable care to avoid acts or omissions which he can reasonably foresee would be likely to injure his neighbour'.[19] In answer to the question, 'Who is

---

10   *National Coal Board v JE Evans & Co (Cardiff) Ltd* [1951] 2 All ER 310.
11   [1959] 1 QB 426.
12   Dworkin (1959) 22 MLR 538.
13   *Letang v Cooper* [1965] 1 QB 232.
14   *Cook v Lewis* [1952] 1 DLR 1 (Canada); *McHale v Watson* (1964) 111 CLR 384 (Australia).
15   Sir John Comyns *Digest of the Laws of England* (1762).
16   *Williams v Holland* (1833) 10 Bing 112 and *Holmes v Mather* (1875) LR 10 Exch 261.
17   See Cornish and Clark, ch 7.
18   [1932] AC 562, [1932] All ER Rep 1.
19   See Baker at p 473.

a neighbour?' LORD ATKIN's answer was, 'persons who are so closely and directly affected by my act that I ought reasonably to have them in contemplation as being so affected when I am directing my mind to the acts or omissions which are called into question'.[20] This test was not the first attempt to articulate a general theory of duty in negligence, but it was the first one to gain general acceptance.[1]

In the nineteenth century, a right to due care was seen as something which a man had to pay for.[2] Where there was a pre-existing relationship between the parties, the action was seen to have a contractual flavour. The tendency had been to restrict liability within the newly-defined contractual parameters. The judiciary may have been reluctant to stifle the development of nascent industries by imposing on employers and manufacturers liability to compensate an injured plaintiff. At that time, there was no strong insurance market, accordingly liability was generally only imposed where there was a pre-existing relationship of some kind between the plaintiff and the defendant.

The 'neighbour test' did not explain why certain duties were recognised but not others. At this time, there was no liability for pure non-feasance in the absence of a pre-existing relationship between the parties. Certain positive acts which caused damage to others were not actionable in negligence. If a person ruined another financially by legitimate trade competition, then there was no liability. The duty only extended to physical damage to the person or property, and not to 'pure' economic harm which might be caused.

(4)   THE PRIVITY OF CONTRACT FALLACY

The approach of the courts in the nineteenth century to the question of liability for manufactured goods is illustrated by *Winterbottom v Wright*.[3] The user of a carriage with a defective wheel was not allowed to recover for his injuries as he had no contract with the manufacturer. The court appears to have been swayed by policy considerations in reaching its decision. To allow the action would have opened the floodgates to numerous potential plaintiffs and would enable the contract between the manufacturer and the plaintiff's employers to be 'ripped open' by an action in tort.[4] The relevant economic argument was that the manufacturer would have calculated the price of the carriage by reference to factors such as his potential liability towards persons with whom he had contracted and that others would not have been considered. If a third party was allowed to recover, this might upset price calculation. However, if manufacturers knew that they would be liable to third parties, they could price accordingly.

The case introduced the privity of contract fallacy which provided that if there was a contract to which the injured person was not a party, that person could not sue in contract or in tort. The fallacy proved to be an inhibiting factor in the development of the tort of negligence for the best part of a century. The *ratio* in *Winterbottom v Wright* strengthened the emerging doctrine of privity of contract.[5] Contrary to the impression of some judges, it did not establish a rule that a person not a party to the contract could not sue in tort. The *ratio* of the case was that as the only wrong alleged was the breach of contract and as the plaintiff was not a party to the contract, he had no case. In contrast, LORD ABINGER's *dictum* was much wider and accordingly mistaken.

---

20   [1932] AC 562 at 580.
1   See *Heaven v Pender* (1883) 11 QBD 503 at 509 (per LORD BRETT MR).
2   Atiyah *Rise and Fall* (1979) p 501.
3   (1842) 152 ER 402.
4   Ibid at 405 (per ABINGER CB).
5   See ch 6.

In the case of manufactured products, the fallacy was destroyed in *Donoghue v Stevenson*. The argument is still heard, albeit unsuccessfully, in the case of attempts to sue solicitors.[6]

---

6   *White v Jones* [1995] 1 All ER 691. *Ross v Caunters* [1979] 3 All ER 580. See also *Groom v Crocker* [1938] 2 All ER 394; *Clark v Kirby-Smith* [1964] 2 All ER 835; *Midland Bank Trust Co Ltd v Hett, Stubbs & Kemp (a firm)* [1979] Ch 384.

Chapter 2

The intellectual background to the classical contract theory

1. INTRODUCTION

The present dominance of contract in the law of obligations stems from the development by the judiciary of the 'classical' law of contract. No precise date can be fixed for the commencement of this development, but it is generally thought to be the end of the eighteenth century.

The most profound change in the English law of obligations came with the development of a general theory of contract in the nineteenth century. The reasons for such a change are a matter of acute controversy. One school of thought, represented by Atiyah in England[1] and Horwitz in the United States,[2] have identified the development with the growth of industrial capitalism in the period 1770–1870. They identify a shift of emphasis from relationships such as reliance or the receipt of benefits, to a consensual basis founded on executory agreements. Such agreements take the form of bargains which create expectations. The content of such bargains was almost entirely a matter for the parties. The role of the court was, where necessary, to enforce those bargains with an award of expectation damages. Unfairness in the bargain was not a matter for the court. This change in emphasis is said to mark a change from an essentially paternalistic agrarian society in the eighteenth century to an aggressive entrepreneurial industrial society in the nineteenth century. The values reflected in the general theory of contract were those of *laissez faire* and economic liberalism rather than those of an earlier, more protective society.

These views have come under criticism from a legal history perspective. According to Simpson[3] and Barton,[4] the features of contract theory which Horwitz and Atiyah trace to the period 1770–1870 were all there long before. Executory contracts, inequality in exchange and damages for expectation losses can all be traced to the reports in the sixteenth and seventeenth centuries.

The difficulty for any researcher looking for ideological shifts, is that there was very little law of contract in the modern sense before the nineteenth century. One effect of

---

1 *Rise and Fall.*
2 *The Transformation of American Law* (1977) ch 6.
3 (1979) 46 Univ Chicago Law Rev 533–601.
4 (1987) 103 LQR 118.

the forms of action was to conceal legal principle behind pleading formalities, and the decision of questions by the jury as matters of fact meant that there was no machinery for producing contract law.

What is clear is that a general theory of contract did emerge in the nineteenth century. A number of institutional factors appear to have been responsible for this. An increasing number of commercial cases were coming before the central courts and some of these were of increasing complexity. Jury decisions were notoriously unpredictable and lawyers needed rules to enable their clients to reach settlements. What had previously been questions of fact for the jury became questions of law for the judge. It is possible that the judges were embarrassed by the chaotic picture that English law presented and wanted to make it more scientific, in the manner of emerging disciplines such as economics. This process was assisted by the emergence of textbooks on law and the teaching of the subject to undergraduates.

This chapter seeks to examine some of the philosophical and socio-economic influences which may have affected the development of this general theory.

2. POLITICAL THEORY AND THE SOCIAL CONTRACT

To the modern mind, the relationship between the government and the governed, and the relationship between contracting individuals appear to have little in common. The philosophical theories of the seventeenth and eighteenth centuries on the social contract provided the theoretical background to, and justification for, the 'Glorious Revolution' of 1689. These also opened the way for the development of a private law of contract theory based on free choice. Both the social contract and private contract involved relationships in which mutual rights and duties were created. What was new about social contract theory was the break from the Aristotelian theory which dominated medieval times. This saw man compulsorily entangled in a network of communal and social relationships. In contrast, social contract theory saw man as an individualist in a society where political communities only existed through the free choice of individuals. Mutual rights and duties existed in medieval theory, where the ruler owed duties to God and also to his subjects, but the new theory stressed the right of the individual freely to choose the nature of his relationship with his fellow men and also with his ruler.

The social contract in its various forms gave an alternative to the divine origin of government, in which God bestowed power on certain persons, and rebellion was not only treason, but sacrilege. In the political sphere, it marked part of a larger movement, whereby man had a choice as to how his life was lived, instead of being born into a fixed system where his role was defined by immemorial custom.

(1) HOBBES (1588–1679)

Hobbes's major work, *The Leviathan*, was published in 1651. He depicted a pre-political stage called the state of nature. In this state of nature, life was 'nasty, brutish and short',[5] and men were in a state of perpetual warfare. To escape from the state of nature, men would combine into communities by means of a social contract. Each community would be subject to a central authority. A number of people came together and agreed to choose a sovereign (body) which would exercise authority over them and put an end to the universal war. The purpose of the restraint men put upon themselves was self-preservation. The contract (or covenant, as Hobbes called it) was not with the ruling

5   *Leviathan* ch 13.

power, but with other members of the community to obey such ruling power as the majority chose. Once chosen, their political power was at an end. There was no right of rebellion, and the ruler was not bound by any contract, whereas his subjects were.

This theory had little appeal to the Parliamentarians of the seventeenth century, but his thought foreshadowed bourgeois economic liberalism. In this world, men retained freedom on all things not prohibited by the sovereign. The function of the sovereign (state) was envisaged as being the upholding of rights of property and regulating a private market economy.

(2) LOCKE (1623–1704)

John Locke is widely regarded as the founder of empiricism,[6] and was the apostle of the 1689 revolution. His political theories received wide recognition and were influential in England until the twentieth century. They are also embedded in the United States' constitution.

Locke also had a state of nature, but a very different one to that of Hobbes. Locke's philosophy was dominated by the idea of property. In his state of nature, men were busy acquiring property and not continuously at war. Everyone had at least one piece of property — his own person: 'This nobody has any right to but himself.'[7] Any property acquired by the labour of a man's body or hands was to be his. By this method, the hardworking would acquire the most property.[8] This theory forced Locke to confront the fact that most property was owned by those who did the least labour. He answered the problem with the concept of scarcity and the invention of money. A man offended against the common law of nature by acquiring so much property that it rotted before he could use it. But with the invention of money, people could store wealth without fear of it rotting. Inequalities of wealth could therefore grow up.[9]

In Locke's state of nature, men had the right to defend their own property. This raised the problem of each man being his own judge. Political societies were therefore set up to provide impartial judges and penalties to deal with disputes over property.[10] Offences had to be defined, which was the task of the legislature. Court judgments had to be enforced, which became the task of the executive.

Locke agreed with Hobbes that civil society was created by consent, but differed on certain points. The most important of these was that if the government failed to perform its function, then rebellion was justified.[11] He also differed on the vexed question of consent obtained by fear. Hobbes believed that such consent was valid, but Locke thought that a consent obtained by fear was not a true consent.[12] This stricture applied to fear imposed by the government to extract a consent or promise: 'Supreme power cannot take from any man any part of his property without his own consent.'[13]

Locke's views on consent eased the way to the acceptance of consent as a valid source of legal or political obligation. This view was easier to accept where the consent was freely given.[14]

---

6   Philosophical doctrine that all our knowledge is derived from experience.
7   *Second Treatise on Government* (1690) Section 26.
8   Ibid, Section 33. The labour theory of value which some attribute to Karl Marx and others to Ricardo is to be found in Locke's work.
9   Ibid, Section 48.
10 'The great end for which men entered into society was to secure their property'; *Entick v Carrington* (1765) 19 State Tr 1029 at 1066 (per PRATT CJ); cf Locke *Second Treatise on Government* para 12.
11 *Second Treatise on Government* (1690) Section 176.
12 Ibid, Section 186.
13 Ibid, Section 138.
14 Atiyah *Rise and Fall* p 50.

(3)   HOBBES, LOCKE AND ECONOMIC LIBERALISM

Early liberalism was a product of protestantism. It was marked by religious tolerance valuing commerce and industry, and favouring the middle class rather than the aristocracy and monarchy. It also had respect for rights of property.[15] It was individualistic in a way that Plato and Aristotle were not, and was first represented in modern Western philosophy by Descartes.[16]

Hobbes and Locke laid the theoretical background in England for the economic liberalism which was to grow in strength during the eighteenth century and reach its peak during the nineteenth century. The profound effects of the social contract upon men's attitudes towards the political world marked the transition from the medieval world to the modern world. This transition was from a world in which one's obligations were defined by custom, and in which property was not generally freely alienable,[17] to a world in which man was believed to have entered a political (civil) society, with a view to protection of property. The effect of this freedom to act, combined with man's innate selfishness, gave rise to the need for a strong government or sovereign. This government would lay down rules as to property ownership, and would enforce contracts.[18] Professor McPherson found the essentials of economic liberalism flowing naturally from this political view.[19] As man was now a free agent who selfishly and voluntarily entered into relationships with others, he had property in his own person. This gave him the freedom to dispose of his labour by contract, and to dispose of his goods.

This change in the view of society was dramatic. Instead of being born into a static world, man came into a world where his society consisted of a series of market relationships. Atiyah has argued that this is why contract was so important to Hobbes: 'Not only is it contract which creates civil society in the first place, but one of the primary purposes of that society, once created, is to enforce contracts.'[20]

(4)   HUME (1711–1776)

David Hume was a philosopher who was well ahead of his time, yet his ideas had very little direct influence during his lifetime. His major work, *The Treatise on Human Nature*, was published in 1739–40 and had an indirect but immeasurable influence, through the work of Adam Smith and Jeremy Bentham.

The Treatise was a critique of Locke which firmly rejected social contract ideas. There never had been a state of nature, and society was not formed by a promissory-based social contract.[1] In Hume's opinion, civil society was based on man's awareness of the benefits that flow from mutual association. The duty of allegiance to the state was based on self-interest, and could be justified by the protection given by the state.[2] The state's purpose was seen as utilitarian, and could be overturned by the people if it ceased to perform its function.[3] During the eighteenth century, his political theory had very little impact, and the dominant theory continued to be that most practically

15   See Russell *History of Western Philosophy* ch XII.
16   Russell, p 579.
17   For a discussion of the ideas of *Gemeinschaft* and *Gesellschaft* in relation to property, see Gray and Symes *Real Property and Real People* (1981) pp 15–20.
18   McPherson *The Political Theory of Possessive Individualism* (1962) pp 97–98.
19   Ibid.
20   Atiyah *Rise and Fall* p 71.
1   *Treatise on Human Nature* Book III, Part II, Section II.
2   Ibid.
3   Ibid, Book III, Part II, Section IX.

influential philosopher, Locke. Eventually, through Smith and Bentham, his political theory came to be almost universally accepted and social contract theory rejected.

Hume's view of private contract theory was largely utilitarian. To Hume, anything remotely resembling the then undeveloped 'will theory' was unacceptable.[4] Instead, the obligation to perform a promise was seen by Hume as based on self-interest, in much the same way as the citizen's unconnected obligation to obey the sovereign.[5]

If a person merely expressed an intention to do something, then no obligation was created. The will theory[6] posited that if this expression of intent was made in a certain form of words, then this created an obligation. Hume ridiculed this idea by comparing it to transubstantiation or superstition: 'We feign a new act of the mind which we call the willing of an obligation; and on this we suppose the morality to depend.'[7] As the mind cannot will something, it could not be the will itself, but the manifest expression of the will that created the obligation.

The classical theory rested the source of legal obligation in the promise. But Hume argued that a promise merely served as an expression of the maker's resolution to do something, combined with a form of words which can be recognised by others.[8] The promise, in other words, served as evidence of the promisor's seriousness of intent. It did not show us the source of the promisor's obligation.

Hume distinguished between 'an agreement' and 'making an agreement'. The former connoted common action or doing something with a common purpose, resulting in reciprocal obligations. The latter involved an exchange of promises. In the case of an agreement, the parties' obligations arose out of what was done, and did not rest totally on consent. If consent had to be invoked here, it had to be an implied consent. In the case of the making of an agreement, the obligations arose out of what was said, and were based on express consent.[9]

Although Hume was eventually successful in destroying the idea of consent in the area of the social contract, consent became the basis of obligation in law. Based on the idea of free choice, all legal obligations were thought to be based on:

> a deliberate and conscious choice of a man who made a promise; and by 1770 this was already beginning to lead to the conclusion that all legal obligations arose from free choice — which, if it was not expressed, must then be implied.[10]

3.   THE RISE OF ECONOMIC LIBERALISM

The profound changes which the social contractarians had made in the way in which men conceived the political scene was mirrored by the rise of economic liberalism in the eighteenth and nineteenth centuries. The roots of economic liberalism go back into the seventeenth century, and Coke is seen by many to be one of its earliest adherents. He despised monopolies because of the stifling effect they had on freedom of trade, and argued against restrictions on the freedom of an individual to work where he pleased.

---

4   Atiyah *Rise and Fall* p 53.
5   Hume *Treatise on Human Nature* Book III, Part II, Section VIII.
6   See ch 3.
7   Hume *Treatise on Human Nature* Book III, Part III, Section V.
8   Ibid, Book III, Part II, Section V.
9   Hume *Treatise on Human Nature*, Book III, Part II, Section II.
10   Atiyah *Rise and Fall* p 57.

(1)   ADAM SMITH (1723-1790)

Smith is seen as the father of nineteenth-century economic liberalism by virtue of his book *The Wealth of Nations*, published in 1776. His views were based on natural law principles and he believed that positive laws should reflect natural laws as closely as possible. There was an underlying order in the social world, just as there was in the physical world, which could be deduced and used to formulate positive laws.

Smith assumed that man was a rational, pleasure-seeking being who, if left to his own devices, would choose to maximise his own happiness. What gave one man happiness was not necessarily what made another man happy, but each person was his own best judge of what brought him happiness or pleasure. Smith accepted that not everyone would immediately perceive what was in his best interests. He therefore believed that people had to be taught what was best for them. Protective legislation was counter-productive, as it prevented people from learning by their own experience.

Smith's man was similar to Locke's. He was a property-collecting person, who lived in a society the job of which was to protect that property. In order to maximise his happiness, he had to be able to exchange goods of which he had a surplus for others of which he had a dearth.

(i)   The market

The exchange process was inexorably governed by the law of supply and demand. If a commodity was in short supply, its price would rise in the market. In the short term, consumer demand would be reduced to the level supplies could meet. In the long term, producers would increase supply to meet demand if they thought they could make higher profits. This process benefited everyone. To increase production, the producer would borrow money at higher rates of interest because prices were high, which benefited the capitalist. Labourers would move to the area where they could earn the highest wages. If supply exceeded demand, the price of the commodity would fall, and capital and labour would be moved to an area where there was demand. The advantages of this system were said to be that everyone followed their self-interest, and the consumer got the goods he wanted.

Goods were said to have a 'natural price' which, if the market was allowed to operate freely, they would reach, allowing for short-term fluctuations. What was a 'natural price' depended on the 'theory of value'. Each product had a use value and an exchange value, which were not proportionate. As the use value did not determine the exchange value or price, Smith theorised that the price was determined by the cost of production. The problem of use value and exchange value was not solved until economists developed the theory of marginal utility nearly one hundred years later.

The idea that prices are fixed by the market meant that a price agreed by the parties to a contract (the market price) was not always a 'just price'. Smith supported this position because, if a product was in short supply, consumers would not otherwise have an incentive to reduce consumption, nor producers to increase production. It was therefore in the public interest for prices to rise and fall, although it might operate to the disadvantage of an individual in a particular transaction.

(ii)   Market failures

The market would only function properly if it was free and competitive. Any interference with the market created a form of monopoly. Smith's idea of a monopoly was very wide, and covered anything which interfered with free trade.

Import prohibitions benefited the home supplier, and export prohibitions benefited the home buyer by distorting the market price. The Apprenticeship Laws were also opposed, as they gave a monopoly in a particular type of work to persons who had served their apprenticeship. The Settlement Laws prevented labourers moving to areas where work was available. These were seen by Smith as an interference with the free movement of labour.

All these were legally created monopolies, but private monopolies also existed. These included restrictive practices by producers to limit output, fix prices or fix maximum wages. Combinations by workmen to achieve a minimum wage were also opposed on the ground that they might lead to market failure. The successful operation of the market depended on competition, and it would not work with a monopoly supplier of one product.

One step Smith refused to advocate was the reform of the Usury Laws controlling the lending of money at interest. These had a long history, and it was left to Bentham in 1790 to advocate their repeal.

As the market was self-regulating, any changes would be made by the market itself. If an attempt was made to hold prices down when a product was scarce then, in the short term, producers would have no incentive to step up supply, or consumers to reduce consumption. In the long term, as suppliers would be unwilling to sell at the regulated price, they would withold supplies from the market, and a black market would develop.

(iii)   The role of the state

A limited role was envisaged by Smith for the state. Its function was to protect society from external enemies, to protect citizens from oppression, force and fraud, to administer justice, and to erect public works and institutions which were too expensive to be provided by individuals. In this last category fell roads, harbours and canals etc. It is clear that Smith was not advocating total *laissez-faire*. The enforcement of contracts by the state, the control of interest rates and laws to prevent monopolies were all inconsistent with such a regime.

(2)   BENTHAM AND THE UTILITARIANS

The nineteenth century was dominated by two schools of thought: the classical economists and the utilitarians. Both schools of thought shared a belief in individualism, but Bentham also believed in government interference if it was for the good of the public. For Bentham, there were no natural laws. Laws were man-made so that they would lead to the greatest happiness for the greatest number of people. The job of the law-maker was to create and adjust laws to manipulate an artificial harmony of interests. Adam Smith assumed an outer framework of laws within which competition and the pursuit of self-interest could be left alone. In contrast, Bentham believed that there was no artificial line to be drawn between an outer framework of laws and an inner circle of freedom. The line between intervention and freedom was to be drawn where utility demanded, so as to provide for the greatest happiness of the greatest number of people.

Both the classical economists and the utilitarians stressed the importance of freedom of contract, but accepted that the law must provide for enforcement of contracts. The classical economists were unable to explain why this was not a form of government intervention. To the utilitarians, it was an application of the greatest happiness principle. It is likely that both were thinking of simultaneous exchanges (executed contracts).

However, lawyers may have taken these theories to mean that executory exchanges ought to be enforced. When opposition was raised to legislative interference with freedom of contract, the arguments on the principle of interference were meaningless, as interference already existed in the form of enforcement.

4.   CRITICISM OF *LAISSEZ-FAIRE*

The principle of *laissez-faire* was adopted by the common lawyers of the nineteenth century, and the theories of the classical economists were shaped into the classical theory of contract. However, *laissez-faire* and the principles of the classical economists came under increasing criticism during the nineteenth century. The criticism of *laissez-faire* came from the utilitarians and a later generation of economists known as the neo-classicists. The utilitarians shared the methodology of the classical economists, but differed in their objectives. The neo-classical economists preferred to test their rules empirically rather than to deduce general principles as the classical economists had done. By acting in this way, the neo-classical economists turned their backs on other disciplines. In turn, the lawyers of the nineteenth and twentieth centuries ignored the new economic theories, and largely contented themselves with the out-of-date theories of the classical economists.

(1)   EXTERNALITIES

The utilitarians criticised the classical economists for their failure to come to terms with the problem of externalities. If a contract was viewed as a private exchange between two parties, then there was no need to consider its effects on third parties. The utilitarians pointed out that a cost may be imposed or a benefit given to a third party to a contract. If these were not for the public good, then they should be avoided. An example arose in the form of contracts of employment. If the employee was injured at work, then he would have to be treated at public expense. In order to shift the cost, the employer should be made liable to the employee for his injuries.[11]

One answer to the problems posed by externalities was government interference to give subsidies to those who gave benefits to others, and to levy taxes on those who imposed costs on others. In legal terms, this was marked by the rise in importance of the law of restitution, which required benefits to be paid for, and tort law, which stressed the need to compensate when harm has been caused.

(2)   DISTRIBUTION

Classical theory was concerned with production, and did not concern itself with distribution. It was assumed that free competition would lead to fair distribution. The gap between rich and poor was seen as the inevitable outcome of the laws of political economy about which nothing could be done. This was exemplified by the gloomy theories of Malthus, who attacked the Poor Law which guaranteed a minimum wage. Malthus argued that if there was a guaranteed minimum wage, then population would outstrip food supplies. Only the threat of starvation would educate people to be careful about the size of their families. Applying the law of supply and demand to the population, Malthus concluded that the prosperity of the masses could never be improved, as

---

11   See also Atiyah *Rise and Fall* pp 333–334 and Inglis *Property and the Industrial Revolution* (1961) pp 205–220.

population would always outstrip food supplies, driving wages down and food prices up.

The doctrine of freedom of contract tended to perpetuate inequalities in wealth, as it was not concerned with distribution. This lack of concern meant that inequality of bargaining power, now one of the main arguments against freedom of contract, was of no concern to the classical economists. The utilitarian approach was that in the pursuit of the greatest happiness for the greatest number, taxation of the rich could be justified to provide a fairer distribution of wealth. This conflicted with the ideal of freedom of contract, as it could only be achieved by state intervention, which would distort the market.

(3) MONOPOLIES

The classical economists held the view that monopolies would be eliminated by competition between individuals. This did not happen, and the growth of monopolies squeezed competition and distorted the market. The failure by lawyers to appreciate the problem posed by monopolies is illustrated by *Mogul Steamship Co Ltd v McGregor, Gow & Co.*[12]

(4)   MARGINAL UTILITY

The old problem of the relationship between use value and exchange value was not solved until economists developed the theory of marginal utility at the end of the nineteenth century. This stated that each good of a particular kind acquired by an individual was of less use to that individual than the previous one so acquired. In political terms, the theory justified the provision of public services by the government. This was because the total aggregate of utility of a society could only be achieved by sharing out wealth between members of that society.

---

12 [1892] AC 25, HL.

Chapter 3

Classical law of contract

1. INTRODUCTION[1]

During the nineteenth century the judiciary and the treatise writers fashioned what are known as the rules of classical contract. The motivation for this has already been stated.[1a] What was missing in English law was the conceptual material. To preserve continuity, the action was fashioned around the action of assumpsit for breach of promise which had developed in the sixteenth and seventeenth centuries.[2] What emerged was radically different from assumpsit and drew on Continental sources which had been influenced by Roman law and Natural law concepts and theories.[3] Where English law had been lacking in a conceptual basis, such a basis was already present elsewhere.

At the time Blackstone wrote,[4] there was scarcely any contract theory or doctrine. There were specific writs such as covenant and assumpsit and vague grounds for relief from contracts given by courts of equity. Beginning with Powell[5] a series of treatise writers[6] borrowed from the French writer Robert Pothier's work *Traité des Obligations* to fashion a theory. Whether the judges were aware of this work is unknown and the relative contributions of the treatise writers and judges is a matter for speculation at present. The values espoused by this contract doctrine, such as sanctity of bargain, freedom of dealing and the advantage of the market over government intervention were undoubtedly attractive to many judges of the nineteenth century. It would be wrong to oversimplify the picture and equity maintained a jurisdiction to grant relief in contractual issues throughout this period. This jurisdiction was exercised on a different basis to the common law rules and even among the common law judges there were differences of opinion.

The classical theory has had a mesmerising grip on the English law of obligations. The emphasis given to consent as the basis of obligation had a stultifying effect on the growth of modern negligence and restitution during the nineteenth century and early

1   Ibbetson 202-214.
1a   See ch 2.
2   See ch 1.
3   See ch 1.
4   *Commentaries* 1761–1765.
5   *Essay upon the Law of Contracts* (London, 1790).
6   Eg Chitty, *A Practical Treatise on the Law of Contracts* (1826); Pollock *Principles of Contract* (1876); Anson *Principles of the English Law of Contract* (1879).

twentieth century. The elements of this 'monstrous machine'[7] still hold sway in the textbooks and law courses and between 1983 and the mid-1990s appeared to have revived and stifled the rapid expansion made by negligence in the period 1963–1983.[8]

2.   OUTLINES OF THE CLASSICAL THEORY OF CONTRACT

The typical classical contract has been defined as:

> A bilateral executory agreement. It consists of an exchange of promises; the exchange is deliberately carried through by the process of offer and acceptance, with the intention of creating a binding deal. When the offer is accepted, the agreement is consummated, and a contract comes into existence before anything is actually done by the parties. No performance is required. ... The contract is binding because the parties intended to be bound. ... When the contract is made, it binds each party to performance, or, in default, to a liability to pay damages in lieu. *Prima facie* these damages represent the value of the innocent party's disappointed expectations.[9]

This model has been said to represent market economic theory and to involve market principles.[10] These principles are that each person relies on his own skill and judgment in the market and the parties bargain or negotiate with each other. In contract law, this is reflected in the rules of offer, counter offer and acceptance, which, in classical theory, are essential to the formation of a binding contract. Neither party owes a duty to volunteer information, and the only limitation on bargaining is that there must be no fraud or misrepresentation. Once the parties have reached their agreement, then any mistakes are irrelevant unless they affect the voluntary assent needed to reach agreement. The contents of the contract are up to the parties to agree, and the court has no active role to play unless the agreement has been broken. The court cannot make or unmake a bargain for the parties, or question its fairness, as this would be interference with the market. If a party does not perform his side of the bargain, then he must pay damages.

3.   THE ELEMENTS OF THE CLASSICAL THEORY

(1)   THE AGREEMENT

(i)   The will theory[11]

Classical contract theory attributed the creation of a contract and its attendant legal obligations to the will of the parties. What was intended by the parties was said to arise from a '*consensus ad idem*', or meeting of the minds. In its pure form, the will theory was too theoretical to gain much of a hold in the common law.[12] It required the court to determine what the contracting parties intended at the time they made their contract. What subsequently came to matter was the existence of external signs of agreement rather than subjective intentions.[13] If the parties appeared to the reasonable man to

---

7   Gilmore *The Death of Contract* p 17.
8   See ch 4. However, recent developments in negligence appear to have breathed new life into this area. See ch 10.
9   Atiyah *Essays*. Essay No 2, pp 11–12.
10   Atiyah *Rise and Fall* pp 402–403.
11   See Gordley *The Philosophical Origins of Modern Contract Doctrine* (1991) pp 161–229; Ibbetson 220–244.
12   Cf *British and American Telegraph Co v Colson* (1871) LR 6 Exch 108, (per Bramwell B).
13   Spencer [1973] CLJ 104.

have assented to do something, this was deemed to be the essence of their agreement.[14] These external signs were classified as an offer by one party which was accepted by the other party. The objective test of agreement is also illustrated by the parol evidence rule, under which a written contract could not be varied by oral evidence to the effect that it did not correctly represent the intentions of the parties.[15]

(ii)   Offer and acceptance

A purely subjective test of when consent gave rise to a contractual obligation would have been unworkable. Instead, English law settled on the objective concepts of offer by one party and acceptance of that offer by the other party, ideas which originated in Pothier's *Treatise*. In the nineteenth century the rules on offer and acceptance were superimposed on the doctrine of consideration as the elements of a binding contract.

This marked an important change from a promise broken to a contract broken and imposed restrictions on the enforceability of promises. The new doctrine was concerned with bilateral relations and bargain promises. Unilateral offers, for example the promise of a reward, were to give rise to severe doctrinal problems, as were non-bargain promises.

The notion of offer and acceptance is sometimes said to have been first used by the courts in *Payne v Cave*,[16] but in bilateral contracts its first recognition was in *Adams v Lindsell*.[17] Offer and acceptance was used to solve the problems caused by contracts made through correspondence.

This chapter will examine the basic principles of offer and acceptance as applied by the courts. Subsequent chapters will look at the difficulties created by attempting to force all promissory liability into one format and put forward alternative theories for these situations.

(iii)   The offer

An offer is an expression of willingness to contract on certain terms, made with the intention that a binding contract will exist once the offer is accepted.

(a)   *Offers and invitations to treat*   The offer must be clear and be made with the intention that it should be binding. As such, it must be distinguished from an invitation to treat. An offer, once accepted, forms a binding contract. An invitation to treat means that a person is merely seeking to initiate negotiations.

The distinction between an offer and an invitation to treat is said to depend on the intention of the parties, although the actual wording of the statement will not be conclusive. In practice the distinction is not easy to make and a number of reasons can be advanced for decisions in particular cases.

In bilateral agreements an advertisement is usually classified as an invitation to treat unless it comes from a manufacturer.[18] The reason normally put forward for this is that if an advert was held to be an offer to sell then each order would be an acceptance and a concluded contract would arise. A manufacturer would be able to produce goods to demand. This reasoning does not really hold up if one considers that the advert could be made subject to specific stocks being available. Further, is there really any distinction between a manufacturer in the traditional sense and a major retail chain such as

---

14   See *Raffles v Wichelhaus* (1864) 159 ER 375.
15   *Goss v Lord Nugent* (1833) 110 ER 713.
16   (1789) 3 Term Rep 148, 100 ER 502.
17   (1818) 1 B & Ald 681, 106 ER 250.
18   *Partridge v Crittenden* [1968] 2 All ER 421; cf *Grainger & Son v Gough* [1896] AC 325.

Sainsburys? In the case of unilateral contracts, an advert, properly worded, is capable of being an offer providing the offeror has the requisite contractual intent.[19] For example, an 'offer' of a reward for a lost dog will be construed as a legal offer to be accepted by the return of the correct dog.

The retail display of goods is classed as an invitation to treat. In *Fisher v Bell*[20] a flick knife was displayed in a shop window and the shopkeeper prosecuted for the criminal offence of offering the knife for sale. It was held that the display of the knife was an invitation to treat. In supermarket sales the offer is made by the customer taking the goods to the check-out where the offer can be accepted or rejected.[1] This means that at common law the shop does not have to sell at the advertised price.

In the case of auction sales, the auctioneer's call for bids is an invitation to treat. Each bid is an offer and acceptance is signified by the fall of the auctioneer's hammer.[2] This means that the item can be withdrawn from sale by the auctioneer if it does not reach its reserve price, unless the auction is held 'without reserve,' when the auctioneer is obliged to sell to the highest bidder.[3] The auction sale is indicative of the fact that the common law does not require an express promise. An implied promise can be deduced where the court can find a consensual element or it is pragmatic to find a contract. Why must the auctioneer sell to the highest bidder in a 'without reserve' sale? In *Warlow v Harrison*[4] it was stated, obiter, that there was a collateral contract between the auctioneer and the highest bidder. The auctioneer in calling for bids is offering to accept the highest bid and this offer is accepted by bidding. To say that this strains the concept of offer and acceptance is an understatement but within classical contract this was the only way a contract could be found.

Tenders also provide an example of the distinction. A statement that goods are to be sold by tender or an invitation to tender for the supply of goods or services is normally not an offer.[5] The tender will then be an offer which can be accepted or rejected. This rule can give rise to problems where the person placing the invitation to tender does not comply with his stated rules for compliance with the tender. This may force the court to recognise that compliance with the invitation to tender may give rise to legally binding obligations based on reasonable reliance.[6]

The question of referential bids has posed a difficulty for the courts in the area of tenders. A referential bid is made when a person tenders £X or £1 higher (or lower) than the highest (or lowest) tender. In *Harvela Investments Ltd v Royal Trust Co of Canada (CI) Ltd*,[7] two people were invited to submit 'offers' to buy shares. The defendant agreed to accept the highest offer. The plaintiff bid $2,175,000, while the other bid was $2,100,000 or $10,000 in excess of the highest bid received. The House of Lords held that referential bids would defeat the idea of confidential competitive tendering and were unacceptable unless specifically invited.

(b)   *Offers and requests for information*   The classical contract view was that the bargaining period should not give rise to legal liability. But in the case of sales of land where

---

19   *Carlill v Carbolic Smoke Ball Co* [1892] 2 QB 484.
20   [1961] 1 QB 394.
1   *Pharmaceutical Society of Great Britain v Boots Cash Chemists (Southern) Ltd* [1952] 2 All ER 456; affd [1953] 1 All ER 482.
2   *Payne v Cave* (1789) 3 Term Rep 148; 100 ER 502; *McManus v Fortescue* [1907] 2 KB 1.
3   *Warlow v Harrison* (1859) 120 ER 502.
4   Ibid.
5   *Spencer v Harding* (1870) LR 5 CP 561.
6   See *Blackpool and Fylde Aero Club Ltd v Blackpool Borough Council* [1990] 3 All ER 25.
7   [1986] AC 207.

information was requested problems could arise. In *Harvey v Facey*[8] the appellants telegraphed the respondents; 'will you sell us Bumper Hall Pen? Telegraph lowest cash price.' The respondents replied: 'lowest price for Bumper Hall Pen, £900.' The appellants replied; 'we agree to buy Bumper Hall Pen for £900 asked by you. Please send us your title deeds ...' No reply was received and the appellants brought an action for specific performance. It was held that the second telegram was not an offer to sell but was a mere request for information. The final telegram was an offer to buy which was not accepted.[9]

(c)   *Withdrawal of offer*   The offer may normally be withdrawn at any time before it is accepted. The withdrawal must reach the offeree before he has accepted.[10] It need not be the offeror that communicates the withdrawal but should be by someone the offeree is entitled to trust.[11]

(iv)   Acceptance

An acceptance is an unqualified expression of assent to all the terms of an offer.

(a)   *Counter offers*   If a purported acceptance attempts to introduce new terms it will be classed as a counter offer, which has the effect of destroying the original offer. In *Hyde v Wrench*[12] the defendant offered to sell his farm for £1,000. In reply the plaintiff said he would pay £950 for it. The defendant refused to sell at this price. The plaintiff then wrote to the defendant agreeing to pay £1,000. It was held that there was no contract as the plaintiff's counter offer had destroyed the original offer which was no longer capable of being accepted.

If the response is merely a request for further information or clarification it will not be classed as a counter offer and the original offer will still be open to acceptance unless it has been withdrawn.[13]

In practice this rule may prove too rigid for businessmen and has led to problems with the 'battle of the forms'. This occurs where two parties exchange their own standard terms of contracting. It will be difficult, if not impossible, for the court to find a contract on the basis of offer and acceptance, although commercial reality may dictate that there should be one.[14] This is one example of where modern business practice (standard form contracts) has posed severe conceptual problems for a system devised in the nineteenth century when commercial practices were very different.

(b)   *Communication of acceptance*   The general rule is that an acceptance must be communicated to the offeror before a contract comes into effect. Acceptance may be by words or conduct[15] but mere silence is insufficient.[16]

Unilateral contracts do not fit this pattern. If the offeror's promise stipulates a prescribed act, is commencement or completion of the act the acceptance? The courts

8   [1893] AC 552.
9   See also *Clifton v Palumbo* [1944] 2 All ER 497; *Bigg v Boyd Gibbins Ltd* [1971] 2 All ER 183; *Gibson v Manchester City Council* [1979] 1 WLR 294; *Storer v Manchester City Council* [1974] 3 All ER 824.
10   *Byrne & Co v Van Tienhoven* (1880) 5 CPD 344.
11   *Dickinson v Dodds* (1876) 2 Ch D 463.
12   (1840) 3 Beav 334.
13   *Stevenson, Jaques & Co v McLean* (1880) 5 QBD 346.
14   See *Butler Machine Tool Co Ltd v Ex-Cell-O Corpn Ltd* [1979] 1 All ER 965.
15   *Brogden v Metropolitan Rly Co* (1877) 2 App Cas 666.
16   *Felthouse v Bindley* (1862) 11 CBNS 869.

have stated that the act must be completed.[17] Does this mean that the offeror can withdraw the offer once the offeree has commenced performance?[18]

The rule that acceptance must be communicated is applicable to telephone messages, and telex messages.[19] However, different rules apply to contracts made by post. Here the acceptance is complete at the time the letter is posted, not when it arrives.[20] This rule applies even when the letter is delayed or lost in the post.[1] In order for the rule to apply it must have been reasonable to use the post as a means of acceptance.[2] The rule provides an early example of *consensus ad idem* being abandoned in favour of a pragmatic solution, penalising the offeror.

(c)   *Knowledge of the offer*   Is it possible for a person to accept an offer of which he has no knowledge? This is most likely to occur in unilateral contracts where a person performs an act or service for the offeror without knowing of the offer of reward. There is clearly no *consensus ad idem*[3] but it has been held that there is a contract in such circumstances[4] although an Australian case has held that knowledge of the offer is necessary.[5]

(v)   Defective assent, duress and mistake

The origins of duress and mistake lie in actions to recover money paid. The plaintiff alleged that the money was paid under force (duress) or by mistake. With the move to executory contracts, the two doctrines became reduced almost to extinction.

The view of force adopted by the common lawyers was that of Locke. Physical force rendered assent defective, but no other type of pressure would suffice. As the contract action was now based on agreement, duress was seen as a question of defective assent, or an unfree will. In *Skeate v Beale*,[6] the court refused to accept that economic duress or duress of goods was available to show that assent was defective. This concurred with current ideas that economic pressure was to be expected but not physical pressure.

The doctrine of mistake has been an area of acute controversy in contract law since the nineteenth century. There are several reasons for this, and the question has not been made any easier by the differing approaches of common law and equity to the problem. Whether a broadly-based doctrine of mistake was applicable depended on whether mistake was related to agreement or not. If it was, then a narrow approach would be taken if an objective approach was taken to consensus, but a much broader one if a subjective approach was taken.

All these elements can be seen at play in the confusion surrounding the nineteenth century mistake cases. The subjective approach to *consensus ad idem* led to the decision in *Cundy v Lindsay*,[7] but the objective approach based on the sense in which the promisor thought that the promisee understood the promise succeeded in *Smith v Hughes*.[8]

The alternative approach to either subjective or objective consensus was based on implied conditions, and had some success in the early nineteenth century. The parties

17 *Daulia Ltd v Four Millbank Nominees Ltd* [1978] 2 All ER 557.
18 See *Errington v Errington and Woods* [1952] 1 KB 290; cf *Luxor Ltd v Cooper* [1941] AC 108.
19 *Entores Ltd v Miles Far East Corpn* [1955] 2 QB 327.
20 *Adams v Lindsell* (1818) 1 B & Ald 681, 106 ER 250.
1 *Household Fire and Carriage Accident Insurance Ltd v Grant* (1879) 4 Ex D 216.
2 *Holwell Securities v Hughes* [1974] 1 All ER 161.
3 See ch 7.
4 *Gibbons v Proctor* (1891) 64 LT 594.
5 *R v Clarke* (1927) 40 CLR 227.
6 (1840) 113 ER 688.
7 (1878) 3 App Cas 459.
8 (1871) LR 6 QB 597.

were treated as having reached agreement. That agreement was subject to an implied condition that some state of affairs existed. If that state of affairs did not exist, then there was no contract.[9] A conflict between the consensus and implied condition approaches can be seen in *Raffles v Wichelhaus*.[10]

The success of the consensus theory of mistake was confirmed in *Bell v Lever Bros Ltd*.[11] The difficulty is stating exactly what mistakes will negate or nullify consent. In theory, classical contract law should have been hostile to mistake. The executory contract was an exercise in risk-planning by the parties, and risks should have been identified and taken into account in the terms of the contract. Unexpected events should not have been allowed to upset a freely-made bargain.[12]

(vi)   Unilateral contracts

A unilateral contract consists of a promise in return for an act. As such, it is principally concerned with a breach of promise. The classical theory so emphasised the bilateral contract thereby turning the action from one for breach of promise to one for breach of contract. In this environment, the unilateral contract came to be regarded as anomalous.

The problem with unilateral contracts was that they did not appear to be based on agreement at all. As there was only one model of contract, they had to be forced to fit that model. In the classic reward case, eg where a man is promised money to walk to York,[13] it is necessary to ask when the offer is accepted. Does this happen when the man commences his journey, or when he completes it? If it is the former, can the offer be withdrawn after the man sets out but before he reaches his destination?[14]

A more practical example of this problem is shown by the case of the commission agent. A modern example of this breed is an estate agent. If X instructs Y to sell his house, and agrees to pay Y a fee when the sale is effected, is X entitled to revoke his offer before Y effects a sale? This question illustrates as well as the rules on formation of contracts, the interests protected by the contract. In classical theory, reasonable expectations generated by the contract were protected. At the high point of classical theory, it was established that a binding executory contract came into existence when agreement was reached. In our example, the contract created an expectation in Y, and he was entitled to damages if that expectation remained unfulfilled.[15]

An alternative interest worthy of protection is the reliance interest, but protection of this interest would not protect the promisee's expectations. The House of Lords in *Luxor Ltd v Cooper*[16] has held, in effect, that the expectation is not capable of protection in unilateral contract cases. In this case, it was held that X could withdraw from the arrangement before the sale was effected.[17]

(2)   *CAVEAT EMPTOR* AND THE WARRANTY DOCTRINE

The principle of *caveat emptor*, or let the buyer beware, was, in theory, one of the cornerstones of the classical theory. It was asserted by nineteenth-century writers as a

9   See *Couturier v Hastie* (1856) 5 HL Cas 673.
10   (1864) 2 H & C 906, 33 LJ Ex 160.
11   [1932] AC 161 at 217.
12   Atiyah *Rise and Fall* pp 436–437.
13   *Rogers v Snow* (1572) Dal 94.
14   *Williams v Carwardine* (1833) 1 B & Ad 621; see also *Carlill v Carbolic Smoke Ball Co* [1893] 1 QB 256 at 269 (per BOWEN LJ).
15   See *Inchbald v Western Neilgherry Coffee, Tea & Cinchona Plantation Co* (1864) 144 ER 293.
16   [1941] AC 108.
17   See also *Errington v Errington and Woods* [1952] 1 KB 290.

general principle.[18] Neither party was under a duty to volunteer information to the other concerning the contract. If a person wanted a warranty that the goods he was buying were sound, then, in theory, he had to insist on an express warranty.[19] This he would have to pay for, and the giving of the warranty would be reflected in the price of the goods.

Caveat emptor was consistent with the principles of self-reliance, freedom of contract and *laissez-faire*,[20] and as late as 1871 it was held that the passive acquiescence of the seller in the self-deception of the buyer did not allow the buyer to avoid the contract.[1] All-important was the express warranty.

Even in the nineteenth century *caveat emptor* was not blindly adhered to, and there appeared to be differences of approach according to which members of the judiciary heard the action. BEST CJ in Common Pleas was more likely to take the buyer's side than PARKE B or ABINGER CB. The most direct contradiction of *caveat emptor* came in the development of the implied warranties of quality and fitness.[2] The implication of such terms, to a large extent, reflected the increase in the number of manufactured goods coming onto the market in the nineteenth century. But it also reflected the view that the payment of a sound price implied a sound commodity.[3] Eventually, *caveat emptor* came to be restricted to those cases where the buyer had purchased specific or identified goods and had exercised his own judgment prior to purchase.[4] The important question was whether the buyer had relied on the seller or on his own inspection of the goods sold.

Caveat emptor had a stronger hold in the case of real property transactions, where the purchaser was expected to survey or otherwise ascertain the suitability of the property he acquired. Thus it was once said, 'There is no law against the letting of a tumbledown house.'[5]

Warranties and misrepresentations

Where a person committed himself to a statement, either orally or in writing, *caveat emptor* had no application. Normally, a contracting party has the right to remain silent, and non-disclosure will not usually give rise to damages or rescission.[6] A statement could be treated as a term of a contract, as a warranty or as a misrepresentation. Warranties gradually came to be treated as contractual terms in the nineteenth century.[7]

Aside from warranties and the doctrine of *caveat emptor*, a limited form of relief was offered where a person was induced to enter a contract by an untrue statement of fact which was not a term of the contract. Relief was restricted to rescission of the contract in equity or damages for fraudulent misrepresentation through the tort of deceit. However, in *Derry v Peek*,[8] the House of Lords defined fraud within the narrowest possible grounds,[9] in a judgment that conformed to the spirit of *laissez-faire*. In the absence of criminal conduct (fraud), only bargained-for reliance within contractual limits was legally enforceable. A person who relied on a non-contractual promise did so at his

18   *Benjamin on Sale* (1st edn, 1868), (2nd edn, 1873); Anson *Law of Contract* (2nd end, 1901) p 231.
19   *Baglehole v Walters* (1811) 3 Camp 154, 170 ER 1338; *Parkinson v Lee* (1802) 2 East 314, 102 ER 389.
20   See Atiyah *Rise and Fall* pp 464–479. See also Hobbes *Leviathan* Part I, ch 15, p 208.
1   *Smith v Hughes* (1871) LR 6 QB 597 at 603 (per COCKBURN J).
2   See now Sale of Goods Act 1979, s 14(2) and (3) respectively.
3   *Jones v Bright* (1829) 5 Bing 533; *Parkinson v Lee* (1802) 2 East 314.
4   *Bigge v Parkinson* (1862) 7 H & N 955; *Jones v Just* (1868) LR 3 QB 197.
5   *Robbins v Jones* (1863) 15 CBNS 221; cf *Smith v Marrable* (1843) 11 M & W 5.
6   See ch 10.
7   See ch 10.
8   (1889) 14 App Cas 337.
9   See ch 10.

own risk. Equity was somewhat more generous in its relief, and extended the remedy of rescission to all types of misrepresentation. Equity was unable to award damages, and could only give an indemnity to the plaintiff.[10] The bars to rescission,[11] coupled with the limited nature of the indemnity and common law relief, caused hardship in some cases. This hardship was only removed by developments in the 1960s,[12] when remedies were made available for misstatements which were not contractual terms.

The fact that liability for statements was effectively restricted to contractual terms demonstrates the dominance of contract law in the nineteenth and early twentieth centuries. The old *laissez-faire* approach was characterised by *Derry v Peek*,[13] and the decision in *Heilbut, Symons & Co v Buckleton*.[14] In the latter case, the House of Lords held that it was necessary to consider the intentions of the parties in order to decide whether a statement should attract liability or not. In contrast, the alternative view of equity was reflected in misrepresentation cases such as *Redgrave v Hurd*,[15] where persons with means of knowledge were held liable. Whether or not the statement was intended to have contractual effect seemed not to matter. Full development of this idea was restricted until the 1960s.[16]

(3)   CONSIDERATION

(i)   Introduction

The establishment of the rules on offer and acceptance as the basis for contractual obligation meant that if there were mutual promises, then by definition there was good consideration. The receipt of a promise in return for a promise given was proof of the beneficial nature of those promises.[17]

It would have been possible by this stage to abolish the doctrine of consideration. From its key position in the eighteenth century, it had been reduced to a role where its only obvious purpose was to exclude liability on unilateral, gratuitous promises.[18] This opportunity was rejected in 1840 in *Eastwood v Kenyon*.[19]

The doctrine of consideration was retained, principally to rebut LORD MANSFIELD's moral obligation doctrine.[20] On this view, if a person is under a moral obligation to pay money and then promises to pay, the pre-existing moral duty provides consideration for the promise: 'The ties of conscience upon an upright mind are a sufficient consideration.'[1] By retaining the doctrine of consideration, some promises were legally enforceable, others were not. Nineteenth-century attempts to define consideration in terms of benefit to the promisor or detriment to the promisee were unsatisfactory. It was clear that certain benefits conferred were unprotected. Likewise, unbargained-for reliance would not constitute a good consideration. What emerged was the 'bargain theory' of consideration. To be enforceable, a promise had to be 'bought' by the promisee.

---

10   See ch 18.
11   See ch 18.
12   See chs 10.
13   (1889) 14 App Cas 337.
14   [1913] AC 30.
15   (1881) 20 Ch D 1.
16   See ch 10.
17   *Haigh v Brooks* (1839) 113 ER 119, affd sub nom *Brooks v Haigh* (1840) 113 ER 124.
18   Cf Simpson (1975) 91 LQR 247 at 263.
19   (1840) 113 ER 482.
20   *Hawkes v Saunders* (1782) 1 Cowp 289.
1   Ibid.

An act or forebearance of one party, or the promise thereof, is the price for which the promise of the other is bought, and the promise thus given for value is enforceable.[2]

In classical theory, the parties were left to judge their own bargain and the courts would not intervene to correct one which was unfair in the absence of fraud or duress.[3] In practice, however, the courts have used consideration as a policy lever and the 'rules' of consideration conceal the true motives behind the decision.

(ii)   Past consideration

The rule is that consideration may be executed or executory but may not be past. Executory consideration is furnished where a promise is exchanged for a promise of future performance. Executed consideration involves a simultaneous exchange, for example, a sale in a shop. Past consideration is given where the act alleged to constitute consideration is performed before the date the promise to pay by the other party is made. As the element of bargain is missing there is said to be no consideration and therefore no contract.[4] If someone saves a person from drowning and that person subsequently promises to pay him for his efforts, that promise is apparently unenforceable as it is supported by past consideration.

In certain cases there is an exception to the rule on past consideration where a promise to pay can be implied at the time the act is performed. For example, in *Re Casey's Patents*[5] the owners of certain patent rights promised a person who had carried out managerial services on their behalf that he would be given a third share in those patent rights. It was held that the fact of a past service can raise an implication that at the time it was rendered it should be paid for. If the performer of the same service is subsequently told that he will be paid for what he has done, this promise can be treated either as evidence of an obligation to pay for the service, or as a positive bargain which fixes the amount of a reasonable remuneration.[6] But in either event, an important factor is that a benefit has been received. The rule has been reasserted in *Pao On v Lau Yiu Long*[7] where it was stated that:[8]

> An act done before the giving of a promise to make a payment or to confer some other benefit can sometimes be consideration for the promise. The act must have been done at the promisor's request; the parties must have understood that the act was to be remunerated by a payment or the conferment of some other benefit and the payment or conferment of the benefit must have been legally enforceable had it been promised in advance.

This case involved a complex share deal in which a promise by the respondent to guarantee the value of certain shares was said to be supported by an earlier promise by the appellant eventually to sell those shares to a subsidiary of the respondent. An important factor would have been that the respondent would eventually obtain the benefit of the whole transaction.

---

2   Pollock's definition adopted by the House of Lords in *Dunlop Pneumatic Tyre Co Ltd v Selfridge & Co Ltd* [1915] AC 847 at 855. See also definition contained in the *American Restatement of Contracts* (2d) para 75.
3   See *Thomas v Thomas* (1842) 2 QB 851.
4   *Roscorla v Thomas* (1842) 3 QB 234; *Re McArdle* [1951] Ch 669.
5   [1892] 1 Ch 104. See also *Lampleigh v Brathwait* (1615) Hob 105.
6   See also Supply of Goods and Services Act 1982, s 15 and see ch 26.
7   [1980] AC 614.
8   Ibid at 629 (per LORD SCARMAN).

(iii)   Consideration must move from the promisee[9]

This rule developed from the idea that contracts were bilateral arrangements resulting in a bargain. If the promisee could not show that he had furnished consideration, how could he show that he was a party to the alleged bargain? This rule is also closely related to the requirement of privity of contract.[10]

Although the consideration must move from the promisee, it is not necessary that it move to the promisor.

(iv)   Consideration must be sufficient but need not be adequate

The bargain theory of consideration produced the rule that something of value had to be exchanged. What was required was a quid pro quo. The parties themselves were treated as the arbiters of what was of value, which reflected the nineteenth century value of the freedom of the individual to make whatever arrangement he liked. This was reflected in the rule that consideration need not be adequate.[11]

To a certain extent this rule still applies today, since it would be impossible to remove from individuals the right to decide what value they place upon an article or service they might wish to acquire. It has been said that no bargain will be upset which is the ordinary interplay of forces.[12] A person may therefore be bound by a contract to grant a six month option to purchase property where the agreed payment is only £1.[13] Likewise, a company may be bound by an agreement to pay the equivalent of less than 8p plus three chocolate wrappers in return for a record seemingly worth much more.[14]

In theory the thing exchanged must have some economic value which means that a promise made in return for natural love and affection has been held to be unenforceable.[15] Likewise a son's promise to stop boring his father with complaints was held unenforceable.[16] In practice however the doctrine of adequacy appears to have been stretched to the point where a purely nominal consideration, if requested, can suffice to render a promise enforceable. In *Ward v Byham*[17] a promise to pay maintenance was held to be enforceable where the promisor asked a mother to keep a child well looked after and happy. Arguably all the mother provided was no more than natural love and affection. The trend appears to have been to give effect to a promise if the promisor has got that which he requested,[18] even if the thing furnished as consideration might not appear to comply with the rules of consideration.

Although the consideration need not be adequate it must be sufficient. This means that the alleged consideration must be capable of being recognised as such by law. The rule appears to have been developed to prevent a person using that which he was already obliged to do by law or private contract as consideration. This 'rule' has therefore always had overtones of public policy.

Where a person is obliged by law to perform a duty, can performance of this duty amount to sufficient consideration? In *Collins v Godefroy*[19] the plaintiff was subpoenaed to give evidence in a trial. The defendant promised to pay him six guineas if he gave

9   *Price v Easton* (1833) 4 B & Ad 433.
10   See *Tweddle v Atkinson* (1861) 1 B & S 393.
11   *Haigh v Brooks* (1839) 10 Ad & El 309.
12   *Lloyds Bank Ltd v Bundy* [1975] QB 326 at 336, per LORD DENNING MR.
13   *Mountford v Scott* [1975] Ch 258. See also *Midland Bank Trust Co Ltd v Green* [1981] AC 513.
14   *Chappell & Co Ltd v Nestlé Co Ltd* [1960] AC 87.
15   *Bret v JS* (1600) Cro Eliz 756.
16   *White v Bluett* (1853) 23 LJ Ex 36.
17   [1956] 2 All ER 318.
18   See Smith (1979) 13 Law Teacher 73.
19   (1831) 1 B & Ad 950.

evidence. It was held that no consideration was given for this promise as the plaintiff was already obliged by law to give evidence. In *Glasbrook Bros Ltd v Glamorgan County Council*[20] the House of Lords held that where a person did more than they were obliged to do by law, sufficient consideration was provided for a promise. In doing so they drew on the nineteenth century case of *England v Davidson*,[1] where it was held that a policeman was entitled to a reward offered for information leading to the conviction of a criminal.[2]

A similar issue arises where the plaintiff alleges that his consideration is the performance of an existing contractual duty with either the defendant or a third party. The courts have held that the latter is good consideration.[3] The former category has given rise to considerable case law, mostly concerned with variation of contractual obligations. Any 'rule' to the effect that performance of an existing contractual duty is not good consideration for a promise is said to come from *Stilk v Myrick*.[4] The captain of a ship promised the crew extra wages if they brought a ship back short-handed from the Baltic. An action to enforce the promise failed. In an earlier case, *Harris v Watson*,[5] it was held that a promise to pay extra wages when the ship was in danger was unenforceable on grounds of the rule and policy of maritime law. The two reports of *Stilk v Myrick* differ noticeably. One reporter[6] has the case decided on the same grounds as *Harris v Watson*, with no mention of consideration theory. The other reporter[7] has the case decided on the ground of want of consideration. The case was clearly distinguishable from *Harris v Watson*, as the ship was safe in port and therefore in no danger. LORD ELLENBOROUGH, wishing to decide the case against the plaintiff, had to turn to a different ground for his decision. From *Stilk v Myrick* emerged the 'rule' that performance of an existing contractual duty is not good consideration unless the plaintiff does something above and beyond his duty.[8] This rule has since caused problems in cases of re-negotiation of contracts.[9]

The question has also arisen in the context of part-payment of debts. In *Pinnel's Case*[10] it was said that part-payment of a debt is not consideration for a promise by the creditor to release the debtor from the balance. In *Foakes v Beer*,[11] Mrs Beer had obtained judgment against Dr Foakes. After Dr Foakes had paid the debt by instalments, Mrs Beer sued for the interest on the debt. Dr Foakes pleaded an agreement that, if he paid the debt, Mrs Beer would not 'take any proceedings whatsoever on the judgment'. The House of Lords gave judgment for Mrs Beer on the ground that the agreement lacked consideration.[12] There is no doubt that the decision was in keeping with the spirit of the times, but it was historically unsupportable.[13]

The history of the 'rules' on sufficiency casts doubt on whether the body of case law as a whole supported such 'rules'.[14] Certainly the rules are at odds with business

---

20   [1925] AC 270.
1   (1840) 11 Ad & El 856.
2   See also *Harris v Sheffield United Football Club Ltd* [1987] 2 All ER 838.
3   *New Zealand Shipping Co Ltd v AM Satterthwaite & Co Ltd, The Eurymedon* [1975] AC 154. See also *Shadwell v Shadwell* (1860) 9 CBNS 159; *Chichester v Cobb* (1866) 14 LT 433; *Scotson v Pegg* (1861) 6 H & N 295.
4   (1809) 2 Camp 317, 170 ER 851.
5   (1791) Peake 102, 170 ER 94.
6   (1809) 6 Esp 129.
7   (1809) 2 Camp 317.
8   See *Hartley v Ponsonby* (1857) 7 E & B 872; *North Ocean Shipping Co Ltd v Hyundai Construction Co Ltd* [1979] QB 705, [1978] 3 All ER 1170.
9   See chs 6 and 13.
10   (1602) 5 Co Rep 117a.
11   (1884) 9 App Cas 605.
12   Thereby upholding the rule in *Pinnel's Case* (1602) 5 Co Rep 117a.
13   See Ames 12 HLR (1899) at 521 et seq.
14   See Gilmore *Death of Contract* pp 22–28.

practice. This problem was recognised by LORD BLACKBURN in his prepared dissenting judgment in *Foakes v Beer*.

> All men of business ... every day recognise and act on the ground that prompt payment of a part of their demand may be more beneficial to them than it would be to insist on their rights and enforce payment of the whole.[15] This problem has now been recognised by the courts and dealt with by a variety of methods. In the public duty cases a promise to perform an existing public duty will usually be good consideration unless this is contrary to public policy.[16]
>
> In existing contractual duty cases the Court of Appeal has apparently recognised business practice in the renegotiation of contracts[17] and doctrines such as economic duress and estoppel have been developed to control the fairness of such alterations.[18]

(v) Detriment and benefit

The influence of market theory and *laissez-faire* on the development of contract law in the nineteenth century meant that if a person wished to legally protect himself, he had to 'buy' the right to such protection by paying a price for a promise. One effect of a contract doctrine based on agreement supported by consideration was that unbargained-for reliance and unbargained-for benefits fell outside the law of contract altogether.

In *Jorden v Money*,[19] it was held that a representation by a creditor that she would not enforce a bond was not binding. A promise or a representation of future conduct acted on or relied on by the promisee or representee was not enforceable unless it was binding as a contract. The effect of this decision was to exclude unbargained-for reliance from common law until it reappeared in the guise of estoppel and in the law of tort. The narrow definition of contract necessitated these two developments.[20]

So far as benefits were concerned, the action of *indebitatus assumpsit* had allowed both claims for money had and received, and other non-pecuniary benefits conferred on the defendant. The form of the pleading involved a fictional promise to repay money. The Roman expression, *quasi ex contractu*, led the common lawyers to believe that these actions belonged in the law of contract, based on implied promises.[1] An attempt was made by LORD MANSFIELD in *Moses v Macferlan*[2] to explain the juristic basis of the action on the grounds of unjust enrichment. Blackstone's influence was dominant, and when the forms of action were abolished in the nineteenth century, the cases were stated to be based on an 'implied contract'.[3] This fiction was caused by the clear division which had appeared between tort and contract with the abolition of the forms of action. As the quasi-contract cases were not based on any form of wrongdoing by the defendant, then they had to be based on agreement, as the classification of actions into contract and tort was rigid and exclusive. As the actions were not based on any genuine consent, then they must rest on an implied consent or agreement. This palpable nonsense survived because in cases of unjust enrichment, it was seen to be in the interests of justice that

---

15 (1884) 9 App Cas 605 at 622.
16 *Ward v Byham* [1956] 1 WLR 496 at 498, per DENNING LJ; *Williams v Williams* [1957] 1 WLR 148 at 150, per DENNING LJ.
17 See *Williams v Roffey Bros & Nicholls (Contractors) Ltd* [1990] 1 All ER 512. See ch 6.
18 See chs 6 and 23.
19 (1854) 5 HL Cas 185, 10 ER 868.
20 See ch 6 and *American Restatement of Contracts* (2d) para 90. See also Gilmore *Death of Contract* (1974) p 60 et seq.
1 See Birks and Mcleod (1986) 6 OJLS 46.
2 (1760) 2 Burr 1005.
3 See *Sinclair v Brougham* [1914] AC 398 (per LORD SUMNER at 452 and LORD HALDANE at 415).

many benefits conferred on a person should be paid for by the beneficiary. These cases could not be treated as contractual in the classical sense, as there was no bargain, so normal contractual remedies were not available. But there was no alternative juristic device to order restitution.[4]

(4)   DAMAGES

Because a jury was used to assess damages prior to the nineteenth century, what law there was, was obscure.[5] Rules on the assessment of damages had emerged in relation to particular types of contract in the first half of the nineteenth century.

In cases where the vendor of land had failed to make a good title, the buyer was restricted to the cost of his reliance on the vendor. This meant that he could only recover his actual expenditure incurred in searching title.[6] Damages were not available for the 'fancied goodness of the bargain which he (the plaintiff) supposes he has lost'.[7]

In contracts for the sale of goods, the seller's damages were restricted to the difference between the contract price and the market price of the goods at the date and place of delivery.[8] In 1837, an action was refused when the plaintiff bought a horse which was warranted to be sound and re-sold it at a profit with a similar warranty. The plaintiff was obliged to take the horse back. He sued his supplier for his lost profit, but the action failed.[9]

In the case of a contract to lend money, the creditor's sole action was to recover that sum, unless the contract expressly stipulated that interest should be payable.[10] The consequential loss suffered by the creditor as a result of late payment of the debt could be recovered.[11]

The common thread linking these rules was that expectation damages for loss of profits or consequential losses from the breach of contract were not recoverable. Where no established rule existed, it was for the jury to decide what damages should be awarded. Because of this, it would be rash to say that expectation or consequential losses were not compensated in contract actions.

The modern law on contract damages begins with the decision in *Hadley v Baxendale*.[12] The plaintiff mill owners contracted with the defendant carriers to have a broken crankshaft transported to Greenwich. Delay on the part of the defendant caused the plaintiffs' mill to be closed for several days longer than would otherwise have been the case. The plaintiffs sued to recover the profits lost by the delay. The jury gave a verdict for the plaintiffs for £25 which was reversed by the Court of Exchequer.

ALDERSON B laid down a general rule for the recovery of damages in a breach of contract action:

Where two parties have made a contract which one of them has broken, the damages which the other party ought to receive in respect of such breach of contract should be such as may fairly and reasonably be considered as either arising naturally, that is according to the usual course of things, from such a breach of contract itself, or such as may be reasonably

4   See ch 11.
5   *Hadley v Baxendale* (1854) 9 Exch 341 at 346 (per PARKE B).
6   *Flureau v Thornhill* (1776) 2 Wm Bl 1078, 96 ER 635.
7   Ibid at 635 (per DE GREY CJ).
8   *Gainsford v Carroll* (1824) 107 ER 516.
9   *Clare v Maynard* (1837) 7 C & P 741.
10   *Robinson v Bland* (1760) 96 ER 141.
11   See now *Wadsworth v Lydall* [1981] 2 All ER 401, [1981] 1 WLR 598.
12   (1854) 9 Exch 341, 23 LJ Ex 179. Danzig (1975) 4 JLS 249; Barton (1987) 7 OJLS 40.

supposed to have been in the contemplation of both parties, at the time they made the contract, as the probable result of the breach of it.[13]

The judgment went on to say that if there were 'special circumstances' which took the case out of the 'usual course of things', those special circumstances could only be considered if the defendant was aware of them at the time the contract was made. If the special circumstances were within the defendant's contemplation, he would be liable for the special damages. The reason the mill was closed was that the crankshaft was broken. This was thought to be a special circumstance of which the defendant was not aware. Accordingly, the plaintiffs were not entitled to recover their lost profits.

The case has both a negative and a positive aspect. The negative aspect was of most immediate importance, as it was useful as a device for controlling jury verdicts on damages. As there was now a test for damages, the question became one of law and not fact, and was reviewable on appeal. This was part of the process of removing issues from the jury and transferring them to the judge. This, in turn, allowed a contract doctrine to develop.

The positive aspect of this decision has been of lasting importance. Damages were no longer limited to the value of the thing contracted for. Consequential loss in the form of loss of profits could now be recovered. This aspect of the decision was initially treated with some hostility. In *British Columbia Saw-Mill Co Ltd v Nettleship*,[14] the 'special circumstances' rule was interpreted to mean that such circumstances had to be communicated to the defendant and he must have contracted to bear the loss likely to be suffered.[15]

The notion which prevailed in English law was that of *foresight* of damage, and *Hadley v Baxendale* survived, although the process was not completed until *The Heron II*.[16] In this case, the House of Lords allowed an action for damages for loss of market. The defendant shipper had delivered a cargo late, with the result that the cargo was worth less on arrival than if it had been delivered on time. The difference between the resale value of the cargo and what it should have realised was recoverable as normal loss, occurring in the ordinary course of things. The shipper could have foreseen that, if the ship arrived late, the cargo owner would have suffered some financial loss.[17]

Hadley v Baxendale effectively terminated a theory that damages might depend on the defendant's *conduct* in breaking the contract. The theory was that if the contract was broken fraudulently, the consequential losses would be recovered, but not where it was broken negligently. The theory was laid to rest after *Hadley v Baxendale*,[18] and after 1875 the matter was not raised, as by then 'the judgment of ALDERSON B had attained its present canonical status.'[19]

(5)   CONCLUSION

The approach to contract formation adopted by English law has created substantial problems:

> English law, having committed itself to a rather technical and schematic doctrine of contract, in application takes a practical approach, often at the cost of forcing the facts to fit uneasily into the marked slots of offer, acceptance and consideration.[20]

13   (1854) 9 Exch 341 at 354.
14   (1868) LR 3 CP 499.
15   See also *Horne v Midland Rly Co* (1873) LR 8 CP 131.
16   *Koufos v C Czarnikow Ltd, The Heron II* [1969] 1 AC 350.
17   See ch 16.
18   *British Columbia Saw-Mill Co v Nettleship* (1868) LR 3 CP 499; *Smith v Green* (1875) 1 CPD 92.
19   Barton (1987) 7 OJLS 40 at 43.
20   *New Zealand Shipping Co Ltd v AM Satterthwaite & Co Ltd* [1975] AC 154 at 167 (per LORD WILBERFORCE).

The rules on offer and acceptance have produced a mass of case law, much of it irreconcilable, in the attempt to fit cases into the slots. Atiyah has argued that the cases of implied contract illustrate the courts' willingness to protect reasonable reliance which was not contracted for.[1] As the courts had come to regard contractual obligations as resting on consent, there was no way they could protect the reliance interest without also finding a contract and protecting the plaintiff's expectation interest. Promises contingent on a person's marriage can be seen in this light.[2] Where the promisee had, or might have, changed his position in reliance on a promise, the court was willing to find a contract. The effect of this was to protect the promisee's full expectation interest, that is the value of the promise, rather than his reliance interest, namely the extent to which the promise had actually been relied on.

4.   EFFECTS OF THE CLASSICAL MODEL

The adoption by the common law of this model of contract had profound implications which still shape legal thinking. Emphasis was moved from acts to agreements. In legal terms, this meant a shift of emphasis from the consideration to the promise. The result was that the executory contract, rather than the executed contract, became the paradigm contract of the day. The effect of this change can be illustrated by reference to contracts to lend money and to purchase goods.

In the case of a loan of money, the debtor was now obliged to repay the money, not because he had received it, but because he had 'promised' to repay it. In pre-classical law, the 'promise' to repay was merely evidence of the legal duty to repay, and helped to show that the money was not a gift. In the case of a sale of goods, the buyer was obliged to pay for the goods, not because he had received something of benefit, but because he had 'promised' to pay for the goods. Goods displayed in a shop window were now said to be an invitation to treat. The customer made the offer to buy and this could be accepted or rejected by the retailer. If the offer was accepted, then a contract came into existence.

The classical model of contract based on the executory contract was designed for businessmen dealing at arm's length and negotiating a future exchange. Its advantage was said to be that it enabled businessmen to plan ahead, and that it protected reasonably engendered expectations. However, with what has been described as the common law's tendency towards monism,[3] the model came to be applied to all contracts, regardless of subject matter or parties, and marked a move from a law of contracts to a law of contract. What had previously been a law of bailment, employment, carriage, sale etc became a uniform system to which market theory was applicable. The same principles were even applied to agreements to marry. Once the agreement had been made, damages had to be paid if the promise was not fulfilled.[4] In adopting this monolithic system the common law, in a sense, sowed the seeds for its own destruction. What was appropriate for businessmen of theoretically equal bargaining power was singularly inappropriate for employers and employees, retailers and customers. Although the contract law textbooks which appeared in the nineteenth century[5] depicted contract law as uniform, this was probably never the case in practice. Legislative interference with freedom of contract was commonplace during the nineteenth century. Even as the courts were embarking on the construction of the classical model, Parliament, although basically

---

1   Atiyah *Rise and Fall* pp 460–461.
2   See *Shadwell v Shadwell* (1860) 142 ER 62.
3   *Simpson* p 325. See also ch 1.
4   *Hall v Wright* (1858) 120 ER 688.
5   See Pollock *The Law of Contract* (1st edn, 1875); Anson *The Law of Contract* (1st edn, 1879); Chitty *Contracts* (1st edn, 1826).

supportive of the doctrine of freedom of contract, was busy intervening with paternalistic legislation in the form of the Factories Acts, Passenger Acts and Truck Acts. It was soon found that the classical theory did not work in practice. Where this was so, Parliament intervened and such changes were then treated as if they no longer belonged to the law of contract. During the nineteenth and twentieth centuries, this process resulted in most of the commonplace areas of contract being placed in specialist categories such as Employment law.

Classical theory led to contract being reified as a thing. The contract was separate from anything done by the parties. Once agreement was reached, a contract existed and was independent of any prior or subsequent acts by the parties. This helped draw a line between contract and tort. Tort was concerned with what the parties did, and duties were imposed in law. Contract was what the parties promised they would do, and any duties were voluntarily assumed by the parties.

One effect of the Judicature Acts 1873–5, was to place more common lawyers than Chancery in the High Court and the appellate courts. This meant that common law rather than equitable principles prevailed[6] and the classical theory became more embedded with little restraining influence.

---

6   Eg *Derry v Peek* (1889) 14 App Cas 337; *Britain v Rossiter* (1879) 11 QBD 123; *Heilbut, Symons & Co v Buckleton* [1913] AC 30.

Chapter 4

Changing values

1. INDIVIDUALISM TO COLLECTIVISM

In the second half of the nineteenth century, state intervention came to be seen as an effective way of resisting some of the worst social evils of the day, such as poverty and drunkenness. The extension of the vote between 1832 and 1870, leading to universal male suffrage, also produced a change of attitude towards government. The government no longer belonged to a small clique, who saw it as 'their government'. As people voted for policies which opposed the wealth distribution of the early nineteenth century, it was inevitable that freedom of contract would become less important.

A substantial growth in the size of businesses had led to the danger of monopoly power. But at the same time combinations of employees, the forerunner of the modern trade union, had emerged with the express remit to provide representation in negotiations over wages and working conditions. The government started to pay its employees on the same daily wage rate, regardless of market rates. Large companies also adopted a similar approach.

The late nineteenth century and more particularly the twentieth century saw the emergence and growth of the consumer society. In the retailing sector, a move towards the use of fixed charges discouraged haggling over prices. Moreover there was a move against the casual provision of credit. In the production sector, companies grew larger and their relationship with consumers became more impersonal. Goods were produced pre-packaged so that pre-purchase inspection became difficult or impossible. Some retailers pursued a policy of taking back unsatisfactory goods. However, the consumer was very much at a disadvantage as a contracting party, especially in the light of business use of standard form contracts which eliminated the possibility of bargaining and negotiation of terms.

With the development of a mixed economy, there was an increase in governmental intervention. Moreover the twentieth century development of the welfare state further undermined free market principles, by striking at the method by which resources were allocated.

These changes were reflected in the common law of obligations. Although the skeleton structure of classical contract principles was retained, in practice there was a softening of the effect of some of the rules. In tort law, a process of protection against physical harm was developed through the development of clearer rules on negligence set against a background of insurance cover. What we would now call the law of restitution had been treated, in substance, as an outgrowth from the law of contract, being based on the notion of the implied promise. But as the twentieth century progressed a separate set of principles based on the reversal of unjust enrichments came to be recognised. These drew on a wide variety of sources and straddled the boundaries of a number of traditional subject areas.

Nineteenth century values had encouraged the view that obligations could only be voluntarily assumed through the free choice of individuals. There was little room for legally imposed obligations, such as the modern tort of negligence or legally compelled restitution. For example nineteenth century employment relationships were largely governed by the contract between the parties, but given the employee's weak bargaining position he would be unlikely to have secured the employer's agreement to bear responsibility for an accident at work. Initially the courts were reluctant to impose tortious duties on the employer to protect the employee's safety because this would be inconsistent with the contract which did not allocate responsibility. Devices used to secure this end included the doctrines of common employment and *volenti non fit injuria*. So intractable was the common law on this issue that legislative intervention was necessary to provide an insurance scheme for injured workmen.[1]

The market–individualist ideology prevalent in the nineteenth century had as its counterpart the principle of freedom of contract. The growing industrial society required businesses to be able to plan ahead, and this could be best facilitated by emphasising the enforceability of promises, including those which were entirely executory and had not resulted in any steps towards performance. As a result, an action for an anticipatory breach of contract was permitted where there had been no detrimental reliance on a promise.[2]

The values of the twentieth century differed. We have seen the emergence of the welfare state. We now live in a consumer-orientated society. The assumption of equality of bargaining power made in the nineteenth century is not always possible. Twentieth-century values placed more emphasis upon egalitarianism. The idea of self-regulation by contract has, in part, given way to statutory controls imposed on businesses and a greater judicial willingness to police unfair contracts. The shift is also illustrated in the emergence of the modern law of negligence and the greater willingness of the courts to order that benefits received should be paid for. These changes can be put down to an alteration in the values which govern modern social relations. Individualism and the preservation of personal freedoms coupled with minimal market regulation were the order of the day in the nineteenth century. But we can now say that the values of the twentieth century are those of paternalism, fairness and co-operation. Society can be said to impose conditions on the privilege of contract making.

While there is a difference between the values of the nineteenth and twentieth centuries, there has been a resurgence of political belief in the workings of the free market. This has led, in particular, to the emergence of a powerful body of academic opinion which argues for greater individual choice.[3]

1   Cornish & Clark *Law & Society in England* 1750–1950 (1989) ch 7. Bartrip & Burman *The Wounded Soldiers of Industry* (1983).
2   *Hochster v De La Tour* (1853) 2 E & B 678.
3   See Kronman and Posner *The Economics of Contract Law* (1979); Burrows and Veljanovski *The Economic Approach to Law* (1981); Ogus and Veljanovski *The Economics of Law and Regulation* (1982).

2.   CONSUMER–*WELFARISM*[4]

The change in values from those of the nineteenth century to those of the twentieth century were well illustrated by the growth of consumer–welfarism. As an ideology this is not as straightforward as market–individualism but it stands for consumer protection and fairness and reasonableness in contractual dealings. In order to provide for reasonableness of result, especially in consumer contracts, it is considered necessary for the courts and the legislature to provide a set of rules which police the bargain. In these circumstances, the free choice of the individual and market principles have little or no role to play.

A detailed discussion of consumer–welfarism is not possible in a book of this type and it is necessary to simplify the concepts involved. The major divide in economic practice in the twentieth century was between centrally planned (socialist) and market-based (capitalist) economies. In a centrally planned economy production is directed by the state according to objectives set by the state. In a market economy production is dictated by the market according to the economic principles of supply and demand and the principle of marginal utility.[5] In practice raw capitalism with an unfettered market is unacceptable in a democracy. To soften the edges, consumerism has dictated intervention in the market in the form of legislation and case law redressing the imbalance between producer and consumer. In a competitive economy, the less efficient firms may go out of business, leaving people unemployed. Here the state will intervene, providing unemployment benefit and income support. In theory, where there is healthy competition and provided there is no market distortion through the presence of monopoly power, the consumer should get the goods he wants at the price he wants to pay.[6] But reasons for protecting consumers still remain. First, fraudulent and dangerous practices must be controlled. This view has been widespread for some time and explains many of the older common law rules on public nuisance and deceit as well as aspects of the criminal law. Beyond this, consumer protection is politically controversial. It is attacked from the right as interference with the market and from the left as a 'band-aid on the malignancy of capitalism.'[7] Within the political centre there is broad agreement that consumer protection is a requirement which according to the Molony Committee[8] should seek to achieve certain ends. First, the law should seek to give assurances as to the quality and safety of goods offered for sale.[9] Secondly, it should provide sufficient information about goods to allow the consumer to judge for himself whether or not they will satisfy his requirements. Thirdly, provision should be made for the assessment by independent agencies, of the merits of goods offered for sale. Fourthly, adequate means of obtaining fair redress should be made available. Fifthly, misdescriptions of goods and services should be restrained as should any other objectionable sales promotion practice, whether in the form of advertisements or otherwise, if they are calculated to divert the shopper from a proper judgment of his best interests.

To a large extent these modest objectives have been achieved by a variety of methods, including case law developments, legislation, codes of practice, complaints systems and the advance of groups such as the Consumers Association to give independent advice. Recent developments have included a move to extend consumer protection to services[10] and more radical intervention such as powers to reopen extortionate credit bargains.

---

4   *See Adams & Brownsword* pp 189–194.
5   See ch 2.
6   Control of monopolies is a complex issue and is dealt with by national and EC legislation.
7   Goldring, 6 Federal Law Rev 288.
8   Cmnd 1781 (1962), para 16.
9   See Sale of Goods Act 1979, ss 14(2) and (3) and see ch 25; Consumer Protection Act 1987, Part II.
10   See ch 26.

In contract law, the major advance of consumer–welfarism has come with the statutory control of exclusion clauses in consumer transactions. Such clauses seek to limit, restrict or exclude the rights or remedies of weaker parties. Within the market–individualist framework of classical contract law, some judges sought to protect consumers from what they saw as unfair exclusion clauses through the use of rules of construction, such as the doctrine of fundamental breach and the *contra proferentem* rule. But the need for such judicial ingenuity has evaporated with the enactment of legislation which provides a framework of protection for consumers and persons dealing on another party's written standard terms.[11] In other areas of contract law where there has been no legislative intervention, members of the judiciary have been split between those adopting a consumer–welfarist stance and those preferring to apply market-based rules. Examples can be seen in the areas of implied terms,[12] economic duress[13] and undue influence.[14]

In tort, the major development has been in the tort of negligence. Beginning in 1932, and against a background of widely available indemnity insurance, the judiciary fashioned a remedy for physical harm caused by fault. The catalyst for this development was the neighbour test established by Lord Atkin in *Donoghue v Stevenson*.[15] Although slow to be adopted by the judiciary, this test for whether one person owed another a duty to take reasonable care has had a remarkable history. In terms of consumer protection it provided a remedy for those persons who had no contractual protection, such as donees. In doing this it was filling a gap left by the rigidity of the contractual doctrines of consideration and privity. However successful negligence was in dealing with compensation for physical harm, it has great difficulties in providing a remedy for economic loss. The courts have regarded economic loss caused by negligent acts as the proper province of contract law and with rare exceptions have refused a remedy in negligence. This process is illustrated in the defective buildings cases[16] where no remedy lies in tort against careless builders and building supervisors whose negligence has resulted in structural defects in property owned by the consumer. The loss to the building owner has been regarded by the courts as pure economic loss which is actionable only where there is a contract between the parties.

Whatever the doctrinal problems of negligence, it has created severe difficulties for consumers seeking a remedy. The expense and time of litigating and the difficulties of proving negligence are sufficient to deter all but the most determined plaintiff. The common law's partial success in this area has been to provide a legal framework against which producers and providers of services can work out self-regulatory codes of practice and complaints procedures, often in conjunction with the Office of Fair Trading. A good example is the Association of British Travel Agents code, under which, initially, a dissatisfied customer does not have to take legal proceedings but can go through a relatively swift and inexpensive complaints procedure.

3.   THE RISE OF RELIANCE AND BENEFIT-BASED LIABILITIES

The value of paternalism may explain the rise in the importance of reliance and benefit-based liabilities. It is arguable that the principles of compensating wrongful harm and of reversing unjust enrichments have taken on an increased importance at the expense of

11   See ch 24.
12   See ch 7.
13   See ch 24.
14   See ch 24.
15   [1932] AC 562 at 580. See ch 8.
16   See eg *Murphy v Brentwood District Council* [1990] 2 All ER 908.

the principle in favour of protecting individual expectations. This shift has led to the argument that the reason why promises are enforceable is that the promisor has either received some valuable benefit or has induced an act of reliance on the part of some other person, which justifies the imposition of a legal obligation to fulfil the promise.[17]

Reliance is a factor in some aspects of the modern tort of negligence, but it is increasingly an important factor in deciding whether a contractual obligation is owed. Unjust enrichment as a sub-category of a wider benefit-based liability is the cornerstone of the law of restitution, but an obligation to perform a contractual promise may also arise where the promisor has received a valuable benefit. Moreover, it has been argued that reliance also plays a part in restitutionary claims, especially where the 'benefit' to the recipient is elusive, as may be the case where services have been supplied under a failed contract.[18] The importance of these changes is that where a duty is imposed because of an act of reliance or because of the conferment of a valuable benefit, the court is concentrating on what the parties have done rather than upon the content of their promises.

Concentration upon a person's actions or conduct is something more closely associated with legally imposed obligations than with those supposedly concerned with free choice and consent. For example, the tort of negligence is principally concerned with what has been done. The point of emphasis is the harm inflicted upon the plaintiff by the defendant. Likewise, in cases of unjust enrichment, a crucial consideration is whether the defendant has become enriched at the expense of the plaintiff. Increasingly in contract cases, what the parties have done becomes important, rather than what has been promised. For example, there is a greater willingness on the part of the courts to construct a contract where one person has relied on the statement of another and has incurred expenditure. Similarly, if the parties have used uncertain language, but one person has performed his side of the 'contract', the court will make a greater effort to 'find an agreement'.[19]

The value of co-operation may also explain certain other changes. According to the classical theory, legal relations were entered into by antagonistic, pleasure-seeking individuals. A result of this was that contractual relationships were seen to be essentially two-sided.[20] However, many modern contractual relationships involve a large number of parties, not all of whom will be in a direct contractual relationship with other members of the arrangement.[1] In these multipartite relationships, it is important that all participants co-operate to ensure they mutually benefit from the arrangement. The receipt of a benefit may justify the imposition of an obligation to fulfil an implied promise,[2] or the fact that one person relies on another to keep his word may also have like effect.[3]

17   See Atiyah *Essays* Essay No 2 pp 42–43 and see chs 6 and 10.
18   Beatson *The Use and Abuse of Unjust Enrichment* (1991) pp 21–44.
19   See ch 7.
20   See ch 3.
1   See chs 6.
2   See *New Zealand Shipping Co Ltd v AM Satterthwaite & Co Ltd* [1975] AC 154 and see ch 7.
3   See ch 6.

Section B

Principles of the law of obligations

CONTENTS

Chapter 5

The strands of the common law of obligations

1. COMMON LAW AND EQUITY

Strictly, the title of this book, *The Common Law of Obligations*, is misleading. It is essential that common law rules are considered alongside rules of equity, first developed in the Court of Chancery.[1] There is a close interaction between the two sets of rules and often where the common law cannot provide a suitable remedy, rules of equity will be at hand to provide a solution.

Generally, equitable rules are of more importance to the parties to a contractual or exchange relationship and to the issue of restitutionary remedies than to the issue of tortious liability. In particular, rules of equity are often used to release one of the parties from what would otherwise be a binding contractual relationship under common law rules. For example, rules which were equitable in origin have a pervasive influence on the issues of mistake,[2] misrepresentation,[3] duress and undue influence.[4] Equitable jurisdiction is also important in relation to remedies. For example, where the common law remedy of damages is inappropriate, the court has a discretion to grant a decree of specific performance of a contract or to grant an injunction to prevent the commission of a wrong, whether it be a tort or a breach of contract.[5] As a pure generalisation, equity is more flexible than the common law and sometimes can be used in a creative way to develop the law in areas in which it has not previously been used. For example, the use of the doctrine of equitable estoppel to enforce certain types of promise[6] and the development of a seemingly separate jursidiction in relation to mistake, whether this relates to a contractual or restitutionary issue[7] are cases in point.

---

1   This is not the place to discuss the detailed relationship between the two systems of law which are now administered in the same courts following the creation of a unified court system by the Judicature Acts 1873–1875. The reader is referred to standard texts on the History of English Law, in particular Simpson *History*; Baker *An Introduction to English Legal History* (2nd edn, 1979); Milsom *Historical Foundations of the Common Law* (2nd edn, 1980); Cornish & Clark *Law & Society in England 1750–1950* (1989) pp 215–226.
2   See chs 7 and 23.
3   See chs 10 and 18.
4   See ch 24.
5   See ch 14.
6   See ch 6.
7   See chs 11, 18 and 23.

2.   NINETEENTH, TWENTIETH AND TWENTY-FIRST CENTURY VALUES

Much of the difficulty associated with identifying the respective roles of the law of contract, the law of tort and the law of restitution can be traced to the nineteenth century. In that period classical contract theorists enshrined the executory contract as the paradigm variety of contract. They deduced that obligations could only be voluntarily assumed through the free choice of individuals. From this developed the theory that contracts were bargains negotiated through the process of offer and acceptance and enforced only if there was some valuable consideration.[8] There was little room for obligations imposed by law, such as the modern tort of negligence or the emerging law of restitution. These appeared not to be justifiable in terms of voluntarily assumed liability. Such liability as did exist in this area tended to be explained in terms of voluntary choice, but explanations of this type tended to produce anomalies.[9] In more recent years, common law rules have developed along more communitarian lines. Rules of the law of contract, in particular, now take account of the value of co-operation, most recently recognised in the conferment of rights of enforcement by third parties under the Contracts (Rights of Third Parties) Act 1999, recognising the notion of the network contract. Furthermore, rules of contract and tort also take account of the position of weaker parties, evidenced in the mass of twentieth and twenty-first century consumer protection measures.

3.   EXCHANGE AND NON-EXCHANGE RELATIONSHIPS

The common law of obligations is comprised of three principal strands, namely, the law of contract, the law of tort and the law of restitution. Contract law can be viewed in both a narrow and a broad sense. In narrow terms, it is concerned with identifying those exchange undertakings or promises which the law will enforce, the obligations created by those undertakings and the remedies of the parties in the event of a breach of undertaking. In broader terms, it is also concerned with the law which relates to contracts generally and in this sense it overlaps with the other branches of the law of obligations. For example misleading statements which cause a person to enter into a contract may amount to a tort and the careless performance of a contractual obligation may cause harm to a third party which is actionable in tort and may give rise to a restitutionary remedy. Moreover, an actionable mistake or a subsequent frustrating event or a serious breach of contract may result in an unjust enrichment, giving rise to restitutionary consequences where it is unjust for the benefit to be kept.

The law of tort is primarily concerned with compensating a person who has been harmed by the unacceptable conduct of another. Often the parties to the action will be total strangers, unlike the parties to a contract who will have some sort of relationship from which their obligations derive. But owing to the recognition that a person may be concurrently liable in contract and tort, where the facts of the case permit this, there is an overlap between contractual and tortious principles, particularly in relation to economic losses.

For the purposes of the relationship between tort and restitution, it is necessary to think in terms of a tort being a variety of a wider species known as 'wrongs' including both wrongs at law and in equity.[10] The wrong may be done both with and without

---

8   See ch 3.
9   See ch 3.
10   *Birks* p 39.

fault[11] on the part of the defendant and normally it will give rise to a right to compensation or may be remedied by means of an injunction. But wrongs can give rise to a monetary or other quantifiable gain on the part of the wrongdoer. For example where the defendant is guilty of conversion, the plaintiff may elect to 'waive' his right to compensation and claim restitution of the value of the thing converted.

(1)   CONTRACT AND TORT

A number of distinctions between contract and tort can be offered, but it remains the case that there are still substantial areas of overlap between these two strands of common law liability. At best, it can be said that there are differences between contractual and tortious obligations, but that the two interact and complement each other and in many instances they overlap.

(i)   Legally imposed and voluntarily assumed obligations

One of the most commonly offered distinctions is that tortious duties are fixed by law whereas the contractual obligations of the parties are fixed by the parties themselves, but like most generalisations, this is apt to mislead. For example, many contractual obligations are legally imposed, not the least of which is the duty not to break a promise which forms the basis for a remedy for breach of contract. In addition to this there are a number of contractual duties which can only be described as arising by operation of law. For example, in the field of product liability, terms are implied in contracts for the supply of goods which owe little to voluntary choice.[12] Likewise, the courts are able to imply terms into contracts so as to make sense of the arrangement. Ostensibly the purpose of such implication is to give effect to the presumed intent of the parties,[13] but one might be forgiven for taking the view that the court is actually legislating[14] by imposing duties upon the parties to the contract. Sometimes, a court may 'create' a contract for the parties.[15] In such cases, the court would appear to have imposed an obligation upon the 'promisor'. Frequently it will be found that the collateral contract device is used to fill a gap which has appeared in the law. For example, it was used to create liability in damages for negligent misrepresentations before the Misrepresentation Act 1967 was passed.[16] It was also used to render liable the supplier of goods under a hire purchase contract for statements made by him during the course of negotiations.[17] An explanation of these cases is that the court used the collateral contract as a means of disapproving of the defendant's conduct by ordering him to compensate the plaintiff for the loss he had suffered. In this way, the court effectively imposed an obligation upon the defendant.

One final matter which merits consideration is what is meant by agreement. To the classical scholar, a contract could only exist when there was an agreement.[18] The point at which agreement is reached is now decided objectively,[19] and the court will look at

---

11   For example, the tort of conversion.
12   Sale of Goods Act 1979, ss 12–15; Supply of Goods and Services Act 1982, ss 2–5, 7–10; Supply of Goods (Implied Terms) Act 1973, ss 8–11 and see ch 25.
13   See *Shirlaw v Southern Foundries (1926) Ltd* [1939] 2 KB 206 and see chs 7 and 12.
14   See Williams (1946) 61 LQR 401.
15   See ch 7.
16   *Esso Petroleum Co Ltd v Mardon* [1976] QB 801.
17   *Brown v Sheen and Richmond Car Sales Ltd* [1950] 1 All ER 1102; *Andrews v Hopkinson* [1957] 1 QB 229. See now Consumer Credit Act 1974, s 56.
18   See ch 3.
19   See ch 7.

all the available evidence and decide whether there appears to be an agreement between the parties. Sometimes, the impression is given that the court has found an agreement where none really exists, and the facts of the case may be forced to fit uneasily in the slots marked offer and acceptance[20] so as to justify the conclusion. This objective approach to the meaning of agreement has been used by some to argue that contract is dead.[1]

Just as it is misleading to say that contractual obligations are voluntarily assumed, it is also a mistake to ignore the relevance of voluntary choice when considering the issue of tortious liability. Some tortious duties arise out of a relationship which has been voluntarily entered into. For example, the duties owed by an employer to his employees[2] and that owed by an occupier of premises[3] is partly dependent on the relationship between the parties. Moreover, liability for economic loss caused by negligently prepared advice[4] will involve a consideration of the relationship between the adviser, the advisee and any relevant third party and it will be necessary to take account of any contractual undertaking that might have been given. While tortious duties are imposed by law, it does not always follow that they are immovable since it is possible for such duties to be modified by an agreement between the parties.[5]

(ii)   Strict and fault-based liability

A further generalisation is that contractual liability is strict, whereas tortious liability is fault-based.[6] Although it is true that many contractual duties are strict, there are many that require the defendant to exercise reasonable care and are therefore fault-based. Many tortious duties are said to be fault-based, but the problem is to decide what is meant by fault. It is clear that the word 'fault' has different meanings. For example, very rigorous standards are imposed in areas where liability insurance is compulsory. Furthermore, there are a number of strict liability torts in which it is not necessary to show that the tortfeasor is blameworthy in causing harm to the plaintiff.

(iii)   The interest protected when granting a remedy

The common law recognises a number of interests which it regards as deserving of protection. Traditionally, the fulfilment of expectations[7] is perceived to be the function of the law of contract with the result that an award of contract damages is supposed to put the plaintiff in the position he would have occupied had the defendant's undertaking been fulfilled. The plaintiff's expectations may be protected in other ways, for example where a defaulting buyer is ordered to pay for goods he has agreed to purchase, or if the court grants a decree of specific performance. Compensating a plaintiff for wrongfully inflicted harm[8] is seen to be the role of the law of tort and requires the plaintiff to be returned to the position he was in before the defendant's wrong was done. Accordingly, in general terms, tort damages are not supposed to take account of what would have

---

20   *New Zealand Shipping Co Ltd v AM Satterthwaite & Co Ltd* [1975] AC 154 at 167 (per LORD WILBERFORCE).
1   See Gilmore *The Death of Contract* (1974). See also Atiyah *Rise & Fall*; Atiyah *Essays* Essay No 2. Cf Burrows (1983) 99 LQR 217.
2   See ch 27.
3   See ch 28.
4   See ch 10 .
5   See ch 22.
6   For more detailed consideration of this distinction see ch 12.
7   See ch 6.
8   See chs 8 and 9.

happened to the plaintiff. Instead damages are assessed on the 'out of pocket' principle. But these distinctions are apt to mislead and it is important not to say that only the law of contract is concerned with expectations, and that only the law of tort is concerned with compensating wrongful harm. In some instances the so-called 'contract measure' is relevant in a tort action, for example where the plaintiff in a personal injuries case is awarded damages for loss of future earnings or where a solicitor has negligently drafted a will depriving the beneficiaries of their bequest.[9] Frequently the 'tort measure' applies to an action for breach of contract in the sense that full expectation recovery is denied under rules on mitigation of loss and remoteness of damage.[10]

Not all common law remedies fit within these interests. For example, some interests are regarded as so fundamental that nominal damages may be awarded where no actual loss has been suffered. It is sufficient that the interest has been infringed. Examples include cases of trespass actionable *per se*. Furthermore, a person's interest in his reputation may be protected by an action for defamation, which is actionable without proof of damage in the case of a libel and some varieties of slander. A court may occasionally award punitive damages so as to punish the defendant for his behaviour rather than to compensate the plaintiff.[11]

(iv)   Concurrent contractual and tortious liability

Some contractual duties require the exercise of reasonable care and since liability for the tort of negligence is based on the exercise of reasonable care and skill, it came to be recognised that there are circumstances in which the liability of the defendant may sound in both contract and tort, for example where the defendant negligently performs a contract to supply a service.[12] At one stage, the distinction between contract and tort tended to be minimised[13] to the extent that tortious duties might be imposed upon the parties to a contract in the absence of a contractual provision dealing with the loss suffered by the plaintiff. If taken too far, underplaying the role of contract law might lead to the conclusion that virtually any negligent breach of contract could amount to the commission of a tort.

In what appears to have been a massive over-reaction to some of the less desirable consequences of the 'tort-trumps-contract' approach, the courts became more circumspect about imposing tortious obligations on the parties to a contract, particularly one of a commercial nature. Thus it was observed in *Tai Hing Cotton Mill Ltd v Liu Chong Hing Bank Ltd*[14] that nothing to the advantage of the law's development is to be found in searching for liability in tort when the parties are in a contractual relationship.[15] The problem with this approach was that it cast doubt on the principle of concurrent liability, although none of the concurrent liability cases were referred to in the Privy Council opinion.

The law on concurrent liability was settled by the House of Lords in *Henderson v Merrett Syndicates Ltd*.[16] Underwriting members of Lloyd's (Names) sued their managing

---

9   *White v Jones* [1995] 2 AC 207.
10   See ch 16.
11   See ch 15.
12   *Midland Bank Trust Ltd v Hett, Stubbs & Kemp (a firm)* [1979] Ch 384; *Forsikringsaktieselskapet Vesta v Butcher* [1988] 2 All ER 43 at 52 (per O'CONNOR LJ) and see chs 10 and 26.
13   See *Junior Books Ltd v Veitchi Co Ltd* [1983] 1 AC 520 at 545 (per LORD ROSKILL).
14   [1986] AC 80.
15   Ibid at 107 (per LORD SCARMAN).
16   [1995] 2 AC 145.

agents. In some cases the Names had a contract with their agents but this was held not to preclude the existence of a duty of care in tort. The names could pursue either their remedy in contract or tort where the agent had made a voluntary assumption of responsibility to the Name.

The law on concurrent liability in contract and tort gives a good insight into the interplay between the two areas of law and their similarities and differences. Under the post-*Henderson* regime no distinction is made between duty of care and breach of duty, although the separate rules on issues such as limitation of actions and remoteness of damage continue to apply. Thus, a professional who contracts to carry out work for a client with reasonable skill and care will be liable for breach of an express or implied term of the contract or breach of the duty of reasonable care in the tort of negligence.

Clearly concurrent liability will not apply in all cases where a contract exists between the parties. First it is necessary that the contractual duty is one which requires the exercise of reasonable care rather than one which imposes strict liability and therefore most cases of concurrent liability are likely to arise in the provision of services rather than goods, where duties tend to be strict.[17] Secondly, the tortious duty must be co-extensive with the contractual duty and freestanding, in the sense that a claimant cannot build on the existence of a contract to establish a duty where no tortious duty is recognised. At present, no duty of care is imposed on a builder in tort to avoid pure economic loss to a person who acquires the building. The fact that there was a contract between the parties does not mean that a duty of care will be imposed. Similarly, a person is not generally liable for the acts of their independent contractor in negligence[18] but a contract can stipulate that a person shall be liable for the acts of an independent contractor. If the loss has been caused by the negligence of the defendant's independent contractor, the only possible action would be in contract.[19] Although the tortious duty must be freestanding, the contract may have an effect on the tortious duty in the form of an exclusion or limitation clause affecting liability for negligence. Such a clause may attempt to limit liability for negligence and thus preclude any tortious duty, subject to the operation of the Unfair Contract Terms Act 1977 and the Unfair Terms in Consumer Contracts Regulations 1999.[20]

The freestanding nature of the tortious duty is further illustrated by the fact that it may be possible for the tortious duty to be more extensive than the contractual duty. This could occur where a professional gives advice which is outside the scope of his retainer.[1]

In practical terms the bonus for a claimant in concurrent liability is that it enables him to take advantage of the more favourable rules on limitation of actions[2] and remoteness of loss[3] in tort. For a defendant, the main advantage in being sued in tort is the availability of a defence of contributory negligence. However, by suing in contract the claimant cannot deprive the defendant of that defence.[4]

---

17   See ch 25.
18   See ch 27.
19   See *Aiken v Stewart Wrightson Members Agency Ltd* [1995] 1 WLR 1281.
20   See ch 24.
1   See *Holt v Payne Skillington* [1996] PNLR 179.
2   See ch 19.
3   See ch 16.
4   *UCB Bank plc v Hepherd Winstanley & Pugh* [1999] Lloyds Rep PN 963. On contributory negligence see ch 20.

(2) RESTITUTION, CONTRACT AND TORT

The restoration of unjust enrichments[5] is regarded as the province of the law of restitution. The guiding principle is that if the defendant is enriched at the expense of the plaintiff in a manner which can be regarded as unjust, the enrichment may be reversed in an action for restitution of the benefit received by the defendant.

(i) Legally imposed and voluntarily assumed obligations

Like the duty to compensate for wrongfully caused harm, the duty to restore an undeserved gain is one imposed by operation of law. It is the fact of the unjust enrichment of the defendant at the plaintiff's expense which triggers the restitutionary remedy. In contrast, it is said that where a benefit is conferred under a contract, it is the exchange undertaking which justifies payment for the benefit received. A tortious remedy is granted by operation of law, but the main purpose served by a tortious remedy is to compensate the plaintiff for the wrong he has suffered at the hands of the defendant. In contrast, the gist of a restitutionary remedy is thought not to be based on the fact that the defendant may have done a wrong but that it is unjust for him to be enriched and that the enrichment is at the expense of the plaintiff.

The nineteenth-century notion of quasi-contract justified the availability of a restitutionary remedy on the basis of an implied promise by the recipient of the benefit to pay for what he had received. But it has been seen that this was palpable nonsense.[6] The better view is that the remedy was made available 'as if there was a contract',[7] not because there was an implied promise to pay. But this should not be taken to mean that voluntary choice is irrelevant to restitution. For example, a number of restitutionary claims can be justified on the ground that the defendant has freely accepted the benefit conferred on him when, as a reasonable man, he should have known that a person in the position of the plaintiff would expect to be paid and the defendant did not take a reasonable opportunity to reject the benefit.[8]

Although restitutionary remedies may be said to be conferred by operation of law, both a restitutionary claim and a contractual action can arise from the same facts. For example, if X asks Y to perform a service without there being any reference to the cost of the work, X is contractually bound to pay a reasonable price.[9] If the work is completed, Y may also recover the value of the benefit by means of a restitutionary action for *quantum meruit*.[10] Also, many restitutionary claims arise because a contract has failed, for example on the grounds of illegality, mistake[11] or is for some other reason unenforceable. Similarly restitutionary remedies may be available where the obligation to perform a contract has been discharged on the grounds of frustration or anticipatory repudiation.[12] In these circumstances, it is the unjust enrichment of the defendant that justifies a claim for restitution and not the agreement of the defendant to pay.

It is also arguable that the avoidance of unjust enrichment is, in part, one of the objectives of the law relating to contracts.[13] For example, where a remedy is given for

5   See ch 11.
6   See ch 3.
7   The noun 'quasi-contract' was an anglicisation of the phrase *quasi ex contractu*: see *Birks* pp 29–30.
8   Jones in *Essays on the Law of Restitution* (ed Burrows, 1991) p 4. See also ch 11.
9   Supply of Goods and Services Act 1982, s 15 and see ch 26.
10 See ch 11.
11 See ch 23.
12 See ch 18.
13 See Waddams in *Essays on the Law of Restitution* (ed Burrows, 1991) pp 197–213.

fraudulent misrepresentation[14] part of the justification for doing so is that the defendant should not be allowed to benefit from a statement which he admits to be false.[15] The notion of unconscionability is important in identifying when an enrichment is unjust[16] but it is equally important in determining whether a party to an exchange relationship is entitled to be freed from the consequences of the contract he has entered into on the grounds of undue influence or duress.[17] Moreover, since the concept of economic duress is closely entangled with the question of whether there is sufficient consideration to support a promise to vary the terms of an existing contract, unconscionability, a restitutionary concept, is again relevant.[18]

(ii)   Interests protected when granting a remedy

In addition to the expectation and status quo interests, common law rules also protect the restitution interest. If the plaintiff has conferred some benefit upon the defendant, the court may force the defendant to disgorge the benefit.[19] The important factor in this instance is the benefit or the gain to the defendant at the plaintiff's expense. This should not be taken to mean that in all cases where a benefit is conferred that benefit will have to be returned. For example, in most cases a gift is not returnable to the donor. Likewise, if some 'officious intermeddler' decides that a person's car is dirty and needs to be washed and acts accordingly, he will not entitled to payment for the service.

If unjust enrichment is regarded as part of a wider benefit-based liability, it will be found that more than just the law of restitution becomes relevant. Where a benefit is conferred on a party to an exchange relationship, the fact of this benefit may be treated as good consideration for that party's promise. For example, a buyer's promise to pay for goods must be supported by the seller's delivery of the goods. In such a case, the action will lie in contract. However, where there is a failure to agree, or where the duty to perform the contract is discharged, for example where there is a frustrating event or a repudiatory breach of contract, an action for restitution may lie.

In a further set of circumstances, a court may order restitution of an unjust enrichment made by the defendant as a result of a wrong he may have committed. This wrong might prove to be a tort or a breach of contract, but the plaintiff may elect to protect his restitution interest by recovering the benefit gained by the defendant. Generally, this will be done by allowing the plaintiff to recover the value received by the defendant. This method of recovery will always involve an action *in personam* and the principal actions are for moneys had and received, for *quantum meruit*[20] or for *quantum valebat*.[1] Although all of these amount to an obligation to repay the value received by the defendant, in some instances the measure of restitution will be the value surviving, that is what the defendant has left. Actions *in rem* to recover property provide a good example of this, as does the remedy of tracing whereby, in equity, a beneficiary may follow misappropriated assets to which he is entitled.

14   Which also involves the commission of the tort of deceit.
15   *Redgrave v Hurd* (1881) 20 Ch D 1 at 12 (per Sir George Jessel MR).
16   See ch 11.
17   See ch 24.
18   See ch 6.
19   Fuller and Perdue (1936/37) 46 Yale LJ 52.
20   As much as he deserves.
1   As much as it is worth.

(iii) Restitution and compensation

Both restitution and compensation are responses to a particular event. The event which brings about compensation is generally a wrong of some kind, whether it be a tort or a breach of contract. The person who suffers as a result of the wrong will be compensated by an award of damages. The event which triggers restitution is an unjust enrichment of the defendant.

Restitution appears to have more than one meaning. In one sense it involves the restoration of a person to a previous state of affairs. This interpretation of restitution is, in fact, a matter concerned with compensation in the sense that losses incurred must be paid for. Thus where a person is compensated so as to return him to the position he was in before the defendant's negligence, then it is his status quo interest that the law protects. The way restitution should be properly understood is that in certain circumstances a thing may be restored to a person because it has been taken from him by someone else.

Wrongs normally give rise to compensation. But it is also possible to ask for a restitutionary remedy in respect of a wrong in which case, the plaintiff is said to 'waive' the tort in order to bring the restitutionary claim. Where the defendant commits the tort of conversion, the plaintiff can choose between specific restitution of the converted goods, recovery of the value of the converted goods or damages.[2] The remedy in these circumstances is tortious, but the plaintiff may elect for a restitutionary remedy and relieve the defendant of the gain he has made at the plaintiff's expense. Where this occurs, it is not the fact of the wrong which justifies the restitutionary remedy but that the defendant has unjustly gained something at the plaintiff's expense. If an agent takes a bribe, his principal may recover the amount of the bribe from the briber or the bribed agent in an action for restitution or he may sue for tort damages representing the loss he has suffered by entering into the transaction which was induced by the giving of the bribe,[3] and it may also be the case that the bribe can be recovered even where the principal has suffered no loss at all.[4]

In other instances, the loss suffered by the plaintiff may be non-existent but the gain suffered by the defendant substantial. In such a case, the plaintiff's action in tort will allow only the recovery of nominal damages.[5] Whether in like circumstances there is a restitutionary action has not been decided. Unfortunately, the Privy Council has not been prepared to take the opportunity to lay down a clearly principled approach to the question whether an award of damages should be based on restitutionary or compensatory principles. In *Inverugie Investments Ltd v Hackett*[6] the issue was whether a tenant was able to recover 'mesne profits' under a lease of hotel apartments following the commission of the tort of trespass by the landlord. In deciding that the tenant should recover a reasonable rent in respect of the 15 years of trespass, LORD LLOYD opined that there was no issue of principle as to whether damages were compensatory or restitutionary, since the 'user principle' combines elements of both.[7] This failure to give guidance could cause problems. For example, it might lead to a situation in which a person could recover the equivalent of substantial damages for nuisance or defamation, based on the gain made by the defendant, when no loss on the part of the plaintiff can

2 Torts (Interference with Goods) Act 1977, s 3(2).
3 *Mahesan s/o Thambiah v Malaysia Government Officers' Co-operative Housing Society Ltd* [1979] AC 374.
4 *Reading v A-G* [1951] AC 507.
5 *Stoke-on-Trent City Council v W & J Wass Ltd* [1988] 3 All ER 394.
6 [1995] 1 WLR 713.
7 Ibid at 718.

be proved.[8] Whether this is undesirable is a different matter, but a precedent does exist in relation to actions for breach of confidence where an exploiter must account for the profit he makes, regardless of the loss suffered by the plaintiff.[9]

8   *Stoke-on-Trent City Council v W & J Wass Ltd* [1988] 3 All ER 394 at 401 (per NOURSE LJ).
9   *Peter Pan Manufacturing Corpn v Corsets Silhouette Ltd* [1964] 1 WLR 96. See also *A-G v Guardian Newspapers Ltd (No 2)* [1990] 1 AC 109.

Chapter 6

Promissory liability in exchange relationships

1. THE PROTECTION OF EXPECTATIONS

(1) INTRODUCTION

One of the standard generalisations of the common law of obligations is that the law of contract protects a person's expectations by putting him into the position he would have been in had those expectations been fulfilled. Since, in an exchange relationship, the parties are known to each other, the relevant expectations are those generated by a promise voluntarily given by the promisor to the promisee. We are not concerned, here, with 'general' expectations such as the expectation of life or enjoyment or expected future earnings. If these 'expectations' are dented by the defendant's wrong the harm suffered is treated as a variety of status quo loss,[1] in which case the plaintiff is put into the position he was in before the wrong was committed – so far as a money payment of damages can do this. The importance of promise-based expectations is that the promise creates the expectation and breach of that promise causes the expectation to be unfulfilled. In contrast, 'general' expectations exist independently of the actionable wrong which damages them.

There has been a certain amount of criticism of the view that the law of contract does, in fact, protect the promisee's expectation interest. For example, it has been argued that what is protected is not so much the 'expectation interest' but rather the 'performance interest',[2] in other words what is protected is the promisee's expectation that the promisor will perform his contractual obligations.

The protection of expectations raises two principal issues. First, it must be considered on what grounds can we justify the protection of expectations, which is considered in this chapter. Secondly, it must be considered how legitimately created expectations are to be protected. This second issue is pursued in more detail in section C on remedies. But for present purposes, the main methods of protecting expectations are an order compelling performance of contractual obligations[3] and an action for expectation

---

1   Cf *Treitel* pp 873–874.
2   See Friedmann (1995) 111 LQR 628. See also Burrows *Understanding the Law of Obligations* (Hart Publishing, 1998) essay 1.
3   See ch 14.

damages.[4] But it should not be assumed that where the basis of the obligation is the protection of expectations that one of these remedies will necessarily be given, since expectations are also protected in other ways.

In classical terminology, expectations are created by bargain promises, namely those given in return for something of value moving from the promisee, thereby introducing a test of enforceability based on reciprocity.[5] But this thing of value is said to include not just benefits actually conferred on a person or detriments suffered or undertaken but also the simple promise voluntarily to do or refrain from doing something. Accordingly, the promise is treated as a commodity which can be traded in.

The idea that promises are enforceable only if they have been traded for something of identifiable legal value is one which has been attacked. If these challenges are well-founded, it may mean that the basis upon which the doctrine of consideration is founded is unsafe. For example it has been argued by Professor Atiyah that the courts never set out to create a doctrine of consideration, but have always been more concerned with the much more practical problem whether, in a given case, a particular promise should be enforced.[6] Professor Atiyah also adds that what the courts will look for is a sufficient reason for enforcing a promise and if a sufficient reason can be found, the promise will be enforced, whether or not there was a bargain.[7] Moreover, there are also signs that the judiciary do not regard a rigid doctrine of consideration based on the reciprocity of mutual promises to be either necessary or desirable. Instead, what they will look for are the true intentions of the parties, especially in commercial transactions.[8]

It should also be noted that expectations may arise in circumstances other than through a mutual exchange of promises. For example, a misrepresentation can create an expectation, but here the plaintiff only recovers his status quo loss.[9] For example, if X agrees to sell Y a car, but delivers something so defective that it is incapable of self-propulsion, the legal response is that X has broken his promise to supply a car. Y's expectation that he will receive some means of transport has not been fulfilled and he may be compensated so as to put him into the position he would have been in had the promise been fulfilled. Conversely, if X represents that the car has travelled only 35,000 miles when it has, in fact, travelled 60,000, X's statement is likely to be treated as a misrepresentation and his damages will represent the difference in value between a car that has travelled 35,000 miles and one which has travelled 60,000 miles.

So, what is it about a promise that justifies the recovery of expectation loss? An answer is that a promise involves the appearance of accepting an obligation to do, or refrain from doing, a particular thing,[10] whereas a representation is an assertion of fact that does not assume such an obligation. A deterrence theory can also be applied to promises in the sense that the legal enforcement of a promise can deter a person from breaking a promise in the future. In contrast, a deterrence argument cannot work in relation to false factual statements. If a green car is misrepresented to be blue, the statement is false and there is nothing that can be done to change the colour of the car.

---

4   See ch 17 but note the limitations on an award of full expectation damages in ch 16.
5   See ch 3.
6   Atiyah *Consideration – A Restatement* in Atiyah *Essays on Contract* (OUP).
7   Cf Treitel pp 64–69.
8   See *KH Enterprise v Pioneer Container, The Pioneer Container* [1994] 2 All ER 250 at 256 (per LORD GOFF); *Williams v Roffey Bros & Nicholls (Contractors) Ltd* [1991] 1 QB 1 at 18 (per RUSSELL LJ). See also *Vantage Navigation Corpn v Suhail, The Alev* [1989] 1 Lloyd's Rep 138 at 147 (per HOBHOUSE J) where consideration is described as just a matter of formality and Lord Steyn, *Contract Law: Fulfilling the Reasonable Expectations of Honest Men* (1997) 113 LQR 433 at 437.
9   See ch 10.
10   Burrows (1983) 99 LQR 217 at 245. See also Fried *Contract as Promise* (1981) p 9.

(2)   REASONS FOR PROTECTING EXPECTATIONS

In recent years the premise that expectations are deserving of protection has been attacked.[11] The executory contract, in which there is no performance but merely a mutual exchange of promises, has been the principal focus of this challenge. It has been observed that there has been a decline in the importance of the executory contract at the expense of performance-based obligations in line with the co-operation and fairness-based values of the twentieth century. Atiyah, in particular, argues that a more acceptable and unifying conceptual structure for the law of obligations can be built around the relationship between reciprocal benefits, acts of reasonable reliance and voluntary human conduct.[12] If this shift is accurately observed, the courts will tend to look in greater depth at what the parties to an exchange relationship have done rather than at what has been promised in deciding whether an obligation is owed at common law.

There are both moral and economic reasons for the protection of expectations. Morally, it is right that promises should be kept, but it is not the case that all promises are legally enforceable. Moreover it has been argued that promises will usually be made in order to get something and that they tend to encourage acts of reliance. If the promisor gets what he seeks or if there is an act of reliance by the promisee, this enhances the case for enforcing the promise.[13] If the promisee's expectation interest is protected, this serves as an encouragement to the promisor to fulfil his promise, thereby upholding the operation of the market economy. In this way, the protection of the expectation interest encourages the efficient movement of resources to the person who values them most.[14] If only the status quo or reliance interest were to be protected, there would be no incentive to contracting parties to perform. But if the expectation interest is protected, such an incentive does then arise. A further economic justification for protecting the expectation interest is that an exchange of promises may act as a deliberate risk-allocation device which allows a business to shift the risk of a particular loss to someone who is better able to take the risk or avoid it in some way. However, such risks may not always be capable of being absorbed by the person to whom they are transferred. In such a case, judicial or parliamentary intervention in favour of the weaker party may be justified.[15] Sometimes a promise may be kept for reasons other than legal compulsion. For example, it has been shown by empirical research that promises may be kept by businessmen because they deal frequently with a particular business and do not wish to lose that business relationship for the future.[16]

The protection of the expectation interest upholds the operation of the market economy. But the market must operate fairly within the constraints of twentieth and twenty-first century values. As a result, contracting parties in a position of disadvantage may escape from the consequences of a contract they have entered more easily than was the case in the nineteenth century and it appears that modern developments have restricted the extent to which a person's expectations may be protected. For example, there are now signs that some executory consumer contracts do not always create enforceable expectations. Consumers have been led to believe that they may cancel some otherwise binding contractual arrangements before the date of performance. The

11   See Gilmore *The Death of Contract* (1974) and the work of Professor Atiyah, notably *Rise and Fall; Introduction; Promises, Morals and Law* (1981); *Essays* Essay No 2.
12   Atiyah *Essays* Essay No 2 pp 42–43.
13   Atiyah *Essays* Essay No 2 p 44.
14   See Fuller and Perdue (1936/37) 46 Yale LJ 52 and Posner *Economic Analysis of Law* (1977); Beale *Remedies for Breach of Contract* (1980) pp 159–164; Burrows *Remedies* pp 17–21.
15   See chs 23 and 24.
16   See Macaulay (1963) 28 Am Soc Rev 55; Beale and Dugdale (1975) 2 Brit J of L & S 45.

Consumer Credit Act 1974 permits the cancellation of certain credit transactions.[17] Moreover, outside the field of credit provision, a wider range of consumer contracts entered into following doorstep selling are now subject to a provision allowing for cancellation[18] and a cooling-off period of fourteen days is now granted to both cash and credit purchasers of timeshare holidays.[19] Moreover, in the future, consumers will be given additional cancellation rights under distance selling contracts by virtue of further European Community initiatives.[20]

There are also similar signs in some non-consumer transactions. Many airlines adopt a deliberate policy of allowing for 'no-shows', that is people who book a flight but fail to turn up. In such a case, the 'no-show' is not charged for his booking.[1] Also, some empirical work shows that, in executory agreements made between general and special building contractors, contracts are not regarded as binding, at least until the general contractor secures the main contract.[2]

2.   THE BASIS OF PROMISSORY EXCHANGE LIABILITY

(1)   INTRODUCTION

It is necessary to consider which promises the common law will enforce. The classical response to this question is that only a bargain promise, that is a promise given in exchange for a valuable consideration[3] is enforceable,[4] although this begs the question, what is a valuable consideration? On a 'classical' analysis of the requirement of consideration, the promise must be exchanged for something of value in order to be enforceable. The 'rules' of the doctrine of consideration, such as those on sufficiency, past consideration and that the consideration should move from the promisee[5] all emanate from this concept of bargain, since if nothing of legal value is given in return for a promise, there is no bargain, merely the promise of a gratuitous benefit. However, it must be questioned how far the performance of something one is already obliged to do or the prior performance of a beneficial act fail to confer something of value on a promisor, especially where the relevant performance has been requested by the promisor.

The doctrine of consideration has always reflected the values and policies of the day and has never involved a mechanical or systematic application of concrete rules. Many of the cases illustrative of the doctrine of consideration were decided in the nineteenth century and reflect the idea that the individual is free to make whatever bargain he pleases. One result of this is the rule that the court will not enquire into the adequacy of the consideration. However, as values change, such rules may come to be regarded as anomalous.

---

17   Consumer Credit Act 1974, s 67. See also Package Travel, Package Holidays and Package Tours Regulations 1992 (SI 1992/1942); *Revised Proposals for Legislation on Credit Marketing* (DTI, December 1991).
18   Consumer Protection (Cancellation of Contracts Concluded away from Business Premises) Regulations 1987, SI 1987/2117, SI 1988/958 and SI 1998/3050. See also the Financial Services (Cancellation) Rules 1989.
19   Timeshare Act 1992.
20   Directive 97/7/EC OJ No L144/19 and see also the proposed Directive on Distance Selling of Financial Services, COM 98 0469, OJC 385 11.12.98, p 11.
1   See *British Airways Board v Taylor* [1976] 1 All ER 65, [1976] 1 WLR 13.
2   Lewis (1982) Brit Jo of L & S 153.
3   See ch 3.
4   Gratuitous promises made under seal are enforceable, but in the absence of the formal requirement of a deed, a gratuitous promise is unenforceable due to the absence of consideration.
5   See ch 3.

It is clear from the case law that non-bargain promises are enforced by the courts. The continuing hold of the classical contract theory in some textbooks has severely strained the doctrine in order to fit these cases into the mould created in the nineteenth century. A more satisfactory analysis is to say that in certain circumstances, reliance by the promisee or the receipt of a valuable benefit by the promisor will be sufficient to justify enforcement of a promise, even where there is no obvious exchange, provided there has been a prior request that the benefit be provided or that the promisee should suffer the detriment. In many instances, the receipt of a benefit and the fact of reliance will correspond, so that there is a true exchange relationship. For example, if a person returns a lost dog to its owner in response to an offer of reward, a benefit is conferred on the owner and the finder has acted in reliance on the offer of reward.

The varieties of non-bargain promise are numerous and can be found in standard contract textbooks under the headings estoppel, collateral contracts and negligent misstatement. While these cases sit uneasily with a traditional analysis, it is suggested that common threads run through these areas of the law.

The first part of the framework requires voluntary conduct on the part of the promisor. It follows from this that a promise made under duress is not enforceable.[6] Secondly, the promise must be supported by either reasonable reliance on the part of the promisee or the conferment of a valuable benefit on the promisor. In some circumstances it may also be sufficient that the promisor simply avoids some disbenefit as a result of what is done by the promisee. Even stronger grounds for enforcement of the promise will exist where the act of reasonable reliance and the conferment of the benefit coincide, but that will not always be the case.

If A contracts to do work for B in return for payment of £5,000, but due to circumstances beyond A's control he is unable to complete the work for that amount, he may approach B and ask for an increase in the contract price to £6,000. If B promises to pay £6,000 then in classical terms, the promise is unenforceable for want of consideration on the ground that A has done no more than he is already contractually bound to do. However, A has reasonably relied on the promise of extra reward, and in the absence of unfair pressure on A's part, there are strong grounds for regarding B's promise as enforceable, especially if the 'bird-in-the-hand' received by B is regarded as being of benefit to him. This will be even more the case where B has made some specific request that A should complete the work originally contracted for.[7]

This analysis takes into account the prevalent late twentieth-century values of fairness and co-operation. If B had not wanted to pay the extra money to A, he could have terminated the contract and engaged someone else to finish the work. But it will probably be cheaper and easier for B to pay A the extra £1,000 than to engage a new contractor, which will involve him in the time and expense of additional transaction costs. Moreover, to renege on the promise, having made it voluntarily, would be unfair to A, unless A was guilty of seeking to impose unfair pressure.

It will be seen from the remainder of this chapter that more than one value may have to be taken into account by the court. In business transactions, it is frequently asserted that certainty is important. Accordingly, the individualist ideals of the nineteenth century and the classical theory may sometimes appear to triumph since their application may provide the certainty required in business transactions. In the case of consumer transactions, including those between businessmen of unequal bargaining strength, issues such as fairness of exchange and the protection of the weaker party are more likely to dominate with the result that decisions in this area may appear to be more interventionist.

---

6   See ch 24.
7   See the discussion of *Williams v Roffey Bros & Nicholls (Contractors) Ltd* [1990] 1 All ER 512 below.

(2)   THE CLASSICAL NOTION OF GOOD CONSIDERATION

The classical idea of exchange requires a good consideration for a promise before that promise can be enforced. Consideration has been defined as, 'an act or forbearance or the promise thereof which is the price for which the promise of the other is bought, and the promise thus given for value is enforceable.'[8] This test also has the effect of conflating the rules relating to consideration with those on offer and acceptance[9] since if a definite promise is made by the offeror which is reponded to positively by the promisee, prior to the date on which there has been a purported revocation of the offer, then there is both objective evidence of an agreement and if what is promised or done in return by the promisee is of legal value, there is also consideration for the promise made by the offeror.

The idea that the promise has to be exchanged for something of value is the basis for a large number of the rules forming the doctrine of consideration.[10] For example, the rule that consideration must be sufficient imports a requirement that the thing given in return for the promise must have some legal value so that the exchange of something of no such value should not amount to a good consideration. Likewise the rule that consideration should move from the promisee is overtly bargain-based, assuming that the paradigm contractual relationship is bilateral and that the person to whom the promise is made should give something in return for it. Similarly, in a typical bargain, the promise comes first and the consideration for it should follow, resulting in the classical denial of the validity of past consideration.

In deciding what is a good consideration, the court will take account of the values and policies of the day. Accordingly, if values and policies change, it is likely that a legal rule reflecting the values of another age may come to be regarded as anomalous. This problem surrounds many of the rules of consideration which originated in the nineteenth century. For example, the classical theory is generally based on the freedom of the individual to make what bargain he pleases, with the result that the classical statement of the doctrine of consideration informs us that the courts will not enquire into the adequacy of what is given in return for the promise.

(3)   PROMISSORY EXCHANGE LIABILITY AND BENEFITS

Where a person makes a promise, he will often derive some benefit from doing so. In the classical sense, if the promise is given in order to ensure receipt of that benefit, there is a good consideration for the promise, which renders it enforceable. But the promise and the benefit do not always need to be 'traded' in the classical sense in order for a promise to be enforceable so that a voluntary promise, if coupled with an express or implied request that the benefit be conferred, which brings about the conferment of that benefit may suffice to render the promise enforceable.

(i)   Bare promises and unrequested benefits

It is a general principle of English law that a bare promise, unless given under seal, is not binding upon the promisor. Thus a simple promise to pay £20,000 to church funds in

---

8   Pollock *Principles of the Law of Contract* (13th edn, 1950) p 133 approved in *Dunlop Pneumatic Tyre Co Ltd v Selfridge & Co Ltd* [1915] AC 847. See also US Restatement, *Contracts,* 2d § 71. Generally, by taking on board the notion of executory consideration, this test is regarded as preferable to other definitions, such as that in *Currie v Misa* (1875) LR 10 Exch 153 at 162 which concentrates on executed consideration, not taking account of the fact that an exchange of promises can suffice to evidence an enforceable contract.

9   See ch 7.

10   See further ch 3.

five annual instalments of £4,000, is unenforceable against the estate of the promisor after his death, unless the promise was formalised in the form of a deed.[11] It is generally thought that bare promises of this kind may be made rashly and that there is no reason for enforcing them unless the formality of a deed has been employed.[12] Just as a person who gratuitously confers a benefit on another cannot be sued on his promise, so also the donee will not be able to sue for the value of what he has given. The general rule is that the 'officious intermeddler' cannot sue in contract or for restitution. Thus it has been said, that if one cleans another's shoes, what can the other do but put them on.[13] The simple fact of the conferment of a benefit, standing alone, does not create an obligation to pay for the benefit received. It is a principle of English law that liabilities are not forced upon people behind their backs.[14]

Other problematic cases include those where a promise by one person is merely conditional on the occurrence of a particular event. If control over this event does not lie with the promisee, it seems reasonable to assume that the promise is dependent on a condition which may or may not occur and will not be regarded as an enforceable contractual promise. Conversely, if there is an express or implied promise on the part of the promisee to do something or to refrain from doing something, there may be a sufficient consideration. Thus in *Dunton v Dunton*[15] a promise by a man to make financial provision for his ex-wife so long as she was prepared to behave in a virtuous fashion and with sobriety was held to be enforceable on the basis that the former spouse had impliedly promised that she would behave in the manner suggested in the 'offer' of financial provision.

Where the relevant event is within the control of the promisee, there is usually less difficulty in finding that there is something of value given in return for the promise, unless it can be shown that there has been no promise to bring about the event in question.

(ii)   Mutual promises

It is a well-settled rule of English law that the simple exchange of promises is just as enforceable as a promise which has resulted in the conferment of a benefit or an act of reasonable reliance.[16] As such, a promise to deliver a hire car for use in one week's time in return for a promise to pay the hire charges is a binding contract. Each promise stands as consideration for the promise of the other party and also evidences an agreement. The problem with this view is that where mutual promises are exchanged, there is no reliance and no immediate benefit until one of the promises is performed, although the element of voluntary human conduct is present in the sense that the promisor has freely indicated his willingness to do something in the future. This difficulty has led to the argument that a mutual exchange of promises is less worthy of recognition as a source of obligation than a promise which has induced reliance or resulted in the conferment of a benefit or both. Moreover, particularly in consumer transactions, there are legislative developments which allow for the cancellation of otherwise valid executory exchanges.[17]

Since the elements of benefit or reliance are not immediately present, there is a similarity between mutual promises, bare promises and unrequested benefits, namely that there is only the constant element of voluntary human conduct which justifies a

11   *Re Hudson, Creed v Henderson* (1885) 54 LJ Ch 811.
12   *Morley v Boothby* (1825) 3 Bing 107.
13   *Taylor v Laird* (1856) 25 LJ Ex 329 at 332 (per POLLOCK CB).
14   *Falcke v Scottish Imperial Insurance Co* (1886) 34 Ch D 234 at 249 (per BOWEN LJ).
15   (1892) 18 VLR 114.
16   Simpson *History* pp 459–470.
17   Discussed above p 63.

decision that the promise should be enforceable. In addition, where the promise is made in a commercial context, there may be an additional reason for enforcing it since a businessman who makes a promise expects to have to keep it and he too can expect the same of the other party.[18]

(iii)   Voluntary conduct and related benefit

Where the voluntary conduct of the promisor is related to the conferment of a benefit upon him, there is a stronger reason for enforcing his promise, in that two of the key elements are present. In many of the cases involving the conferment of a benefit, it is often difficult to identify a bargain in the classical sense, namely an exchange of something of legal value in return for the promise of the other party. But provided the promise secures some indirect benefit to the promisor, this should suffice. Thus in *Chappell & Co Ltd v Nestlé Co Ltd*[19] a promise to supply a gramophone record to any person who sent in to the promisor three chocolate bar wrappers was held to be enforceable. It was clear that the motive behind the offer was to increase sales,[20] but a majority of the House of Lords found it possible to treat the indirect benefit of possible increased sales as a sufficient reason for enforcing the promise despite the fact that sending the wrappers could hardly be seen as a detriment to the promisee.[1] It should also be noted that historical research on the doctrine of consideration demonstrates that either benefit to the promisor or detriment to the promisee were, independently, sufficient to establish the existence of a good consideration.[2]

In some instances, a different view may be taken for reasons of policy. Thus in contrast to the decision in *Chappell v Nestle* it was decided in *Lipkin Gorman v Karpnale Ltd*[3] that where a gaming club supplied a customer with gaming chips in return for money paid to the club by that customer, there was no consideration, on the basis that the chips were 'worthless'. Clearly, this was an instance in which the court was not prepared to invent consideration, but it would appear that this was the case because the money paid to the club by the customer had been stolen, and the club was attempting to defeat a claim to the money by the true owner.

(a) *Specific requests*   It has been asserted that a good consideration can be found where there has been a specific request which results in the conferment of a benefit.[4] If a promisor requests that a certain thing be done and that request is satisfied, the promise ought to be enforced, unless there is some policy factor which dictates otherwise.

The importance of benefit-based liability has been emphasised in the context of the performance by a promisee of an existing contractual obligation. Although the conventional rule is that if there is a new promise made by one of the parties to an existing contractual relationship and all the promisee does in return is the continued performance of an existing contractual obligation owed to the promisor, there is an insufficient consideration.[5] However more recently in *Williams v Roffey Bros & Nicholls*

---

18   *Treitel* p 66.
19   [1960] AC 87.
20   But traditional theory informs us that motive and consideration are distinct: *Thomas v Thomas* (1842) 2 QB 851.
1   The minority thought otherwise preferring to regard the requirement that wrappers be sent in as a mere condition of the supply of the record, but not consideration for the promise. See also *Shadwell v Shadwell* (1860) 9 CBNS 159 for another example of a split decision on the same issue.
2   Simpson *A History of the Common Law of Contract* (1975).
3   [1991] 2 AC 548.
4   See Smith (1979) 13 Law Teacher 73.
5   See *Stilk v Myrick* (1809) 2 Camp 317, 6 Esp 129.

(Contractors) Ltd,[6] the Court of Appeal made substantial inroads into this rule, emphasising the importance of specific requests coupled with the conferment of some identified benefit. In *Williams v Roffey Bros & Nicholls (Contractors) Ltd* it was asserted that,

> ...the law on this subject can be expressed in the following propositions:
> (i)   if A has entered into a contract with B to do work for, or to supply goods or services to, B in return for payment by B and (ii) at some stage before A has completely performed his obligations under the contract B has reason to doubt whether A will, or will be able to, complete his side of the bargain and (iii) B thereupon promises A an additional payment *in return for A's promise to perform his contractual obligations on time* and (iv) as a result of *giving his promise B obtains in practice a benefit, or obviates a disbenefit,* and (v) B's promise is not given as a result of economic duress or fraud on the part of A, then, (vi) the benefit to B is capable of being consideration for B's promise, so that the promise will be legally binding.[7]

In *Williams v Roffey* a sub-contractor had agreed to complete carpentry work on a development of flats in respect of which the defendants were the main contractors. The agreed fee for the sub-contract work was a fixed price of £20,000, but it became apparent that this would not cover the sub-contractor's costs since he had already been paid over 80% of the agreed fee, but had only completed some 50% of the work at that stage. At the specific request of the main contractor and in return for a promise to increase the fee by £10,300, the sub-contractor promised to complete the carpentry work on time. This had the effect of allowing the main contractor to fulfil his contractual obligations to the owner of the building on time, thereby avoiding the imposition of penalties under that contract. This increase in price was stated to be payable at a rate of £575 per flat completed. The plaintiffs completed eight flats after that date, but had received no payment with the result that they ceased work and claimed damages for breach of contract. The defendants resisted that claim on the ground that there was no consideration for their promise to pay the extra amount. The Court of Appeal held that there was consideration for the promise to pay the extra amount, since the main contractor had received the practical benefits of getting the work completed on time, thereby avoiding the disbenefit of having to pay liquidated damages and had avoided the need to look for replacement sub-contractors. More specifically, RUSSELL LJ observed that the main contractors also received the benefit of the replacement of a 'haphazard method of payment' with one which was more formalised, involving the payment of a specified sum on the completion of each flat.[8]

The principle applied in *Williams v Roffey* is important in that it seems to be consistent with the views expressed by DENNING LJ in *Ward v Byham*[9] and *Williams v Williams*[10] that there need not be reciprocal benefit and detriment[11] and that if the promisor gets the benefit for which he has stipulated, he ought to honour his promise.[12] Accordingly, there seems to be an additional rule on what constitutes a sufficient consideration over and above the accepted principle that if a promisee does more than his existing duty this will suffice to support a promise to make a further payment beyond that originally promised.[13]

6   [1990] 1 All ER 512. See Hooley [1991] JBL 19, Adams & Brownsword (1990) 53 MLR 536.
7   Ibid at 521–522 (per GLIDEWELL LJ). Emphasis added.
8   Ibid at 524.
9   [1956] 1 WLR 496.
10   [1957] 1 WLR 148.
11   See also *Bolton v Madden* (1873) LR 9 QB 55.
12   *Ward v Byham* [1956] 1 WLR 496 at 498. See also *Williams v Williams* [1957] 1 WLR 148 at 151.
13   As to which see ch 3 and, in particular, *Glasbrook Bros Ltd v Glamorgan County Council* [1925] AC 270 (existing public duty); *Hartley v Ponsonby* (1857) 7 E & B 872 (existing contractual duty owed to the promisor).

The difficulty with the principle established in *Williams v Roffey* is to ascertain how far it extends. It is undoubtedly a very important development, having been described extra-judicially as a 'landmark' decision,[14] and having been accepted as correct in later decisions.[15] However, as the rule is stated it may go further than is justified by the request/valuable benefit principle. The language used by GLIDEWELL LJ in *Williams v Roffey* indicates that the promisor will be bound where the promisee either performs his existing contractual obligations or promises to do the same. In this latter case there is no actual performance and therefore a benefit in kind has not yet been conferred on the promisor. Indeed the facts of *Williams v Roffey* itself illustrate the point, since in that case, the subcontractor in fact ceased work after he had completed a further eight flats following the main contractor's promise to pay the additional sum of £10,300 and therefore did not fulfil his promise to complete all of the flats on time. However, there may be some oblique support for the approach adopted in *Williams v Roffey* in the form of the decision in *Ward v Byham*,[16] since, on the facts of that case, consideration for the promise of the father of an illegitimate child to pay maintenance was supported by the promise of the child's mother to keep the child happy. In Australia, the position seems to be slightly different, although the basic principle in *Williams v Roffey* has been accepted as correct. In *Musumeci v Winadell Pty Ltd*[17] SANTOW J reformulated the rule in *Williams v Roffey* by appearing to place greater emphasis on the requirement that the promisee should have performed his existing contractual duty, although he did also repeat the view expressed in *Williams v Roffey* that a promise to perform would also suffice.[18] However, SANTOW J also emphasised that regard should be had to the question whether what has been obtained by the promisor is more valuable to him than any likely remedy he would obtain if he were to decide to commence legal proceedings against the defaulting promisee.[19]

The language used by GLIDEWELL LJ in *Williams v Roffey* suggests other limitations on the application of the principle. In the first place it is stated to be applicable only where there is a contract for the supply of goods or services. From this it follows that where the contract is one to pay money, the principle may not apply. This conclusion was confirmed in *Re Selectmove Ltd*[20] in which it was observed that so far as contracts of debt are concerned, the guiding principle remains that established by the House of Lords in *Foakes v Beer*[1] namely that the part payment of a debt is not satisfaction of the whole with the result that even if a creditor freely requests payment of a lesser sum than that owed by the debtor, there will be nothing to prevent the creditor from suing for the outstanding balance unless one of the recognised exceptions to the rule applies.[2] The rationale for this rule appears to be that the creditor is performing no more than he is legally bound to pay.[3] The difficulty with this view is that the underlying principle in *Foakes v Beer,* that payment of less than the amount owed to a creditor is not satisfaction of the whole debt, has the same basis as the so-called rule in *Stilk v Myrick* that the performance of an existing contractual obligation owed to the promisor is not good consideration for a promise made by the promisor. If performance of what one is already obliged to do is insufficient, then performance of less than one is obliged to do must

---

14   LORD STEYN (1997) 113 LQR 433 at 437.
15   See *Anangel Atlas Compania Naviera SA v Ishikawajima-Harima Heavy Industries Co Ltd (No 2)* [1990] 2 Lloyd's Rep 526; *Simon Container Machinery Ltd v Emba Machinery AB* [1998] 2 Lloyd's Rep 429.
16   [1956] 2 All ER 318.
17   (1994) 34 NSWLR 723.
18   Ibid at 747.
19   Ibid.
20   [1995] 2 All ER 531.
1   (1884) 9 App Cas 605.
2   *Pinnell's case* (1602) 5 Co Rep 117a.
3   *Ferguson v Davies* [1997] 1 All ER 315.

also be insufficient in the eyes of the law. Despite this, the Court of Appeal in *Williams v Roffey* has been able to develop the special rule applicable to contracts for the supply of goods and services while also asserting that the basic principle established in *Stilk v Myrick* is correct. At the same time, the Court of Appeal in *Re Selectmove*, obviously constrained by the fact that there was an unfortunate majority decision of the House of Lords standing in their way, felt unable to recognise that a creditor who agrees to take a smaller payment than was agreed, or as in *Re Selectmove* itself, agrees to re-schedule the terms of repayment of the debt over a longer period of time than was originally agreed, has received a valuable benefit in the form of avoiding the possible bankruptcy or insolvency of the debtor. This remains the case despite the obvious benefit to a creditor in staving off the possible bankruptcy of his debtor by promising to take a smaller payment. Indeed, the commercial benefit to a creditor in making such a promise was clearly recognised by Lord Blackburn in *Foakes v Beer*. Thus in *Re Selectmove*[4] a promise by a tax official that a company could reschedule its tax liabilities over a longer period of time than was provided for by law was considered to be unenforceable on the basis of the majority rule in *Foakes v Beer* despite the fact that by holding the company to its fiscal responsibilities forced it into liquidation, thereby depriving the Treasury of future payments on the assumption that the company would continue trading into the future.

Clearly what exists in this area of contract law is an absolute mess, consisting of unconvincing attempts to reconcile irreconcilable decisions and principles. It seems that the only answer lies in a trip to the House of Lords on the earliest possible occasion in order to sort out the conflicting rules and the proper scope of the principle laid down in *Williams v Roffey*. As the rule stands at present, it would appear to apply only to the renegotiation of a contract for the supply of goods or services in return for the payment of a sum of money. The rule will come into play where the promisor has reason to believe that the promisee will not be able to complete his side of the bargain, whereupon the promisor promises an additional payment in return for a promise by the other party to complete his obligations on time. In such circumstances the promise is enforceable unless there is evidence of fraud or economic duress on the part of the promisee.

Since the principle established in *Williams v Roffey* does not apply to the repayment of debts, other means of circumventing the rule in *Foakes v Beer* may have to be found. It is well established that there is consideration for a promise to accept a smaller amount, if, at the request of the creditor, the debtor repays in kind or if he repays the debt at an earlier time or in a different place to that required by the original contract.[5] Moreover, for the purposes of the rule in *Foakes v Beer*, the creditor's claim must not be doubtful, since if there is any doubt as to the amount owed, the creditor's acceptance of any amount in settlement will be regarded as consideration for the promise.[6] Furthermore, the facts of a given case may also reveal that the creditor has received some other benefit capable of amounting to consideration. For example, the debtor may perform obligations under his contract with the creditor other than the obligation to repay the debt, in which case, that additional performance might be regarded as conferring a sufficient practical benefit on the creditor. For example in *Anangel Atlas Compania Naviera SA v Ishikawajima Harima Heavy Industries Co Ltd (No 2)*[7] a shipbuilder agreed to a price reduction in return for the promise of the buyer to accept delivery on the day originally agreed between the parties. In the circumstances, since the buyers were considered to

4   [1995] 2 All ER 531.
5   *Pinnel's Case* (1602) 5 Co Rep 117a.
6   *Anangel Atlas Compania Naviera SA v Ishikawajima Harima Heavy Industries Co Ltd (No 2)* [1990] 2 Lloyd's Rep 526.
7   [1990] 2 Lloyd's Rep 526.

be 'core customers' of the builders, they were taken to have given consideration for the promised price reduction, since other customers might otherwise cancel their orders. It is also established that part payment of a debt by a third party is an exception to the general rule, since it would be a fraud on the third party if the creditor were to go back on his promise to accept the lesser payment.[8] Since the passing of the Contracts (Rights of Third Parties) Act 1999 it also appears to be the case that the debtor may be able to establish that the contract between the creditor and the third party was intended to be for his benefit, in which case the debtor will have rights regardless of whether there is any consideration for the promise to accept the lesser sum. General principles of insolvency law may also provide means by which the rule in *Foakes v Beer* may be circumvented. For example, it is well established that a written composition agreement between the creditors of a declared bankrupt will be bound by their joint agreement to accept payment of a pro rata percentage of the debt owed to them. Moreover, voluntary arrangements under the Insolvency Act 1986 Parts I and VIII can also bind a creditor, even where he has not attended the meeting of creditors or has dissented from the majority decision of the other creditors.[9]

On the basis that the principle only applies to a pre-existing relationship, it would appear to have limited application, since it will be of no use in cases where there is no existing contractual relationship between the parties, such as will be the case with the maintenance promises made in *Ward v Byham* and *Williams v Williams*. More difficult to ascertain is whether the principle can apply outside of cases involving the performance of an existing contractual duty owed to the promisor. The principle stated in *Williams v Roffey* appears to be confined to such cases, but GLIDEWELL LJ, in formulating the principle, drew heavily on cases involving the performance of a public duty, such as that imposed by statute in *Ward v Byham*.

Applying the request principle, if the promisor expressly requests the performance of an act, he has acted voluntarily, but that alone is not a sufficient reason for enforcing his promise. It is the performance of what is requested that provides consideration for the promise. Thus if a person offers a reward should a certain act be performed, it is the fact that a valuable benefit is conferred on the promisor which justifies the enforcement of the promise. These unilateral contract cases pose serious problems for the classical theory because it is difficult to say that the promise is the basis of the obligation. In *Gibbons v Proctor*,[10] the plaintiff was able to recover a reward of which he had no knowledge. In classical terms, the decision is problematic since the reciprocity principle requires the promisee to react in response to the promise and on these facts the promisee could not have had an expectation of reward. All that could be said was that he had conferred a valuable benefit on the promisor. But it was a benefit which had been expressly and voluntarily requested by the promisor and he received the benefit he desired.

The entitlement of a commission agent to payment for services rendered is equally benefit related. Thus it has been held that a person employing an estate agent can withdraw from the contract at any time before the event justifying payment of the commission takes place.[11] In the case of an estate agent, the relevant event is the introduction of a person ready, willing and able to purchase the client's property. In view of these circumstances, the promise to pay commission seems to carry little weight.

---

8   *Hirachand Punamchand v Temple* [1911] 2 KB 330. Although the ethics of this decision, on the facts, seem a little questionable, since the third party (a relative of the debtor and a high ranking British military officer in India) placed considerable pressure on the creditor (an Indian moneylender) to accept the lesser sum.

9   Insolvency Act 1986, ss 5(2) and 260(2) and see also *Johnson v Davies* [1998] 2 All ER 649.

10   (1891) 64 LT 594. Cf Hudson (1968) 84 LQR 503.

11   *Luxor Ltd v Cooper* [1941] AC 108.

What triggers the obligation to pay commission is the conferment of a benefit by the estate agent on his client.

(b) *Is detriment to the promisee a requirement?*   In all of these cases, provided there is no policy justification for refusing to enforce the promise, the thing requested will be a good consideration and the promisor will be bound to fulfil his promise. It follows that even a purely nominal consideration, if requested, may suffice to render a promise enforceable. In classical theory, it has been asserted that the consideration for a promise must be of value in the eyes of the law. Thus it has been held that natural love and affection cannot be good consideration for a promise[12] and that the performance of an existing duty owed in law[13] or to the other party to the bargain[14] cannot support a fresh promise. However, in *Ward v Byham*,[15] the father of an illegitimate child promised to pay maintenance to the child's mother if she would agree to keep the child well looked after and happy. Arguably, all the mother provided was no more than natural love and affection, but there was an undoubted benefit to the father which justified the enforcement of the promise to pay. There were other, less convincing grounds for the decision in that the majority were able to discern additional benefits to the promisor which would not have been derived had the mother done no more than she was legally obliged to do and that this additional performance might be regarded as a detriment to her.[16] Moreover, there is sufficient in the decision in *Williams v Roffey* to suggest that both a practical benefit to the promisor and a practical detriment to the promisee will be sufficient to render a promise enforceable, even if the benefit or detriment would not necessarily suffice to satisfy the requirements of a legal consideration.

In the light of the suggestion that there might have been a detriment to the promisee in *Ward v Byham*, the real test of the benefit principle must come in cases where there is no detriment to the promisee but in which the promisor derives a benefit or obviates a disbenefit. Such was the case in *Williams v Roffey Bros & Nicholls (Contractors) Ltd*.[17] In *Stilk v Myrick*[18] it had been held that the performance of what one is already contractually bound to do is not a good consideration. In terms of the classical notion of exchange, the performance of an existing duty or the promise to do so is sterile because the promisee suffers no legal detriment. However, in cases of this kind the importance of policy considerations comes to the fore, particularly where there is a possibility of coercion.[19] But this did not prevent the Court of Appeal in *Williams v Roffey* from holding that by promising to pay the extra amount, the defendants secured valuable benefits.[20] But these are all benefits the defendants would have received had the plaintiff performed the contract as originally planned.[1] On this basis, if there is no additional benefit conferred on the promisor, there can be no detriment to the promisee with the result that there is no element of reciprocation. But where a benefit is conferred on each party in

---

12   *Bret v J S* (1600) Cro Eliz 756. See also *White v Bluett* (1853) 23 LJ Ex 36 and *Mansukhani v Sharkey* [1992] 2 EGLR 105.
13   *Collins v Godefroy* (1831) 1 B & Ad 950.
14   *Stilk v Myrick* (1809) 170 ER 1168.
15   [1956] 2 All ER 318.
16   Ibid at 498–499 (per MORRIS LJ).
17   [1990] 1 All ER 512. See also *North Ocean Shipping Co Ltd v Hyundai Construction Co Ltd, The Atlantic Baron* [1979] QB 705.
18   (1809) 170 ER 1168. See also ch 3.
19   See Fairness of exchange, considered below.
20   *Williams v Roffey Bros & Nicholls (Contractors) Ltd* [1990] 1 All ER 512 at 518 and 522 (per GLIDEWELL LJ) and at 524 (per RUSSELL LJ).
1   See Hooley [1991] JBL 19, 25.

circumstances in which one of the parties has suffered no detriment, there can still be a sufficient consideration.[2]

Stilk v Myrick was not overruled in *Williams v Roffey*, indeed it was referred to as a cornerstone of English contract law.[3] But it was also described as rigid[4] and undesirable[5] and should be limited to the simple proposition that bare promises are not enforceable in English law.[6] But the two cases are fundamentally at odds with each other. *Williams v Roffey* proceeds on the basis that a bird in the hand is worth more than one in the bush[7] whereas *Stilk v Myrick* appears to work on the basis that keeping the bird in the hand is of no benefit at all to the promisor. What remains of the decision in *Stilk v Myrick* is now open to question. At one level, it could be said that it represents the rule that where there is no legal consideration for a promise, that promise should remain unenforceable, but *Williams v Roffey* now challenges what should be regarded as a sufficient legal consideration by suggesting that, in certain circumstances, the conferment of a practical benefit or the sufferance of a practical detriment may suffice to render a promise enforceable in the absence of any reciprocation between the parties. Perhaps all that *Stilk v Myrick* now decides is that a promise which is potentially capable of having been elicited by duress or fraud should not be enforceable, although the reports of that case are equivocal on the point, one basing the decision on the grounds of insufficiency of consideration[8] and the other being based on the possibly preferable policy ground.[9]

(c) *Implied requests*   In the cases considered so far, there has been a specific request that the promisee should do something which benefits the promisor. But there are also cases in which the courts must have resort to an implied promise to pay for a benefit received. However, it will remain the case that the performance alleged to constitute consideration will have been specifically requested. Typically this problem arises where the alleged consideration for the promise is past, that is the benefit conferred on the promisor precedes the promise to which it relates.

Although the general rule is that a past consideration will not suffice to make a promise enforceable, there are exceptions to the general rule, which are all premised on the fact that there has been a specific request by the promisor which is followed by an act of performance on the part of the promisee followed by a subsequent promise to pay for the past act. In terms of the bargain principle, the benefit provided has been donated and there is no reason to enforce the subsequent bare promise to pay for that benefit. Thus a guarantee of goods given after the sale is complete is not supported by a good consideration[10]. If there is no prior request, it is unlikely that a court will see reason to depart from the general rule that past consideration will not suffice. Thus if A moves into a house jointly owned by A and B (with B's permission) and carries out unrequested refurbishment work on the property, a subsequent promise by B to pay part of the cost of the work will be unenforceable on the basis that the act alleged to amount to consideration occurred before the date on which the promise was made and was not

---

2   *Williams v Roffey Bros & Nicholls (Contractors) Ltd* [1990] 1 All ER 512 at 527 (per PURCHAS LJ).
3   Ibid at 525 (per PURCHAS LJ).
4   Ibid at 520 (per GLIDEWELL LJ) and at 524 (per RUSSELL LJ).
5   Ibid at 524 (per RUSSELL LJ).
6   Ibid at 524 (per RUSSELL LJ) and at 525 (per PURCHAS LJ).
7   See Corbin, *Contracts* (1963) vol 1A, s 172.
8   *Stilk v Myrick* (1809) 2 Camp 317.
9   *Stilk v Myrick* (1809) 6 Esp 129. However, it should be noted that Espinasse, as a law reporter, was not regarded with any high esteem, on the basis that he was often tempted to report a case as he believed it ought to have been decided rather than on the basis of the actual decision.
10   *Roscorla v Thomas* (1842) 3 QB 234. But cf Directive 1999/44/EC On Certain Aspects of the Sale of Consumer Goods and Associated Guarantees, 25 May 1999, OJL171, 7/7/99 pp12–16.

requested by the promisor.[11] However, this should not be taken to mean that severance payments offered to an employee on leaving his employment are unenforceable, since the employee will have been paid, not for his services, but for his giving up existing rights as an employee.[12] Moreover, it may be possible to get round the subsequent guarantee rule by implying a promise to give a guarantee at the time the purchase is made.

Where there is a specific prior request that the relevant act be performed it is more likely that the promise will be enforceable on the basis that there was an implied promise to pay for the work at the time it was requested. Thus in *Pao On v Lau Yiu Long*[13] it was observed that,

> An act done before the giving of a promise to make a payment or confer some other benefit can sometimes be consideration for the promise. The act must have been done at the promisors' request: the parties must have understood that the act was to be remunerated either by a payment or the conferment of some other benefit: and payment, or the conferment of a benefit, must have been legally enforceable had it been promised in advance.[14]

Thus if work is specifically requested such as repairs to a central heating system by a plumber and subsequently the customer promises to pay for the work, it seems unlikely that a tradesman would do work for nothing, in which case it should be possible to infer that there was an intention that the work be paid for. Moreover, if there is nothing which would render the promise to pay unenforceable had it been made in advance of the work, it should follow that there is an obligation to pay for the work in question. In *Re Casey's Patents, Stewart v Casey*[15] the owners of certain patent rights promised a person who had carried out managerial services on their behalf that he would be given a third share in those patent rights. It was held that the fact of a past service can raise an implication that at the time it was rendered it should be paid for. If the performer of the same service is subsequently told that he will be paid for what he has done, this promise can be treated either as evidence of an obligation to pay for the service, or as a positive bargain which fixes the amount of a reasonable remuneration.[16] But in either event, an important factor is that a benefit has been received.

The cases referred to so far state the rule in terms of prior acts, but a benefit can be provided in a number of ways, including a promise of future performance. For example in *Pao On v Lau Yiu Long*[17] there was a complex share deal in which a promise by the respondent to guarantee the value of certain shares was said to be supported by an earlier promise by the appellant eventually to sell those shares to a subsidiary of the respondent. An important factor would have been that the respondent would eventually obtain the benefit of the whole transaction.

The past consideration cases are not the only cases to employ artificial reasoning such as the implied promise device. In *New Zealand Shipping Co Ltd v AM Satterthwaite & Co Ltd*,[18] a similar artificiality of reasoning could be found in relation to a case raising the question whether the performance of an existing duty owed to a third party was a sufficient consideration. In this case, a series of contracts were made to ensure that the

11   *Re McArdle* [1951] Ch 669.
12   *Bell v Lever Bros Ltd* [1932] AC 161. Cf *Wyatt v Kreglinger and Fernau* [1933] 1 KB 793.
13   [1980] AC 614. See also *Lampleigh v Brathwait* (1615) Hob 105.
14   Ibid at 629 (per LORD SCARMAN).
15   [1892] 1 Ch 104.
16   See also Supply of Goods and Services Act 1982, s 15.
17   [1980] AC 614.
18   [1975] AC 154. See also *The Antwerpen* [1994] 1 Lloyd's Rep 213; *The Mahkutai* [1996] 3 All ER 502.

buyer's property was shipped to and unloaded at its destination. The question which arose was whether the stevedores who unloaded the ship were entitled to the protection of an exclusion clause contained in a contract between the consigners of the cargo and the shippers. The Privy Council constructed a collateral contract between the buyer of the cargo and the stevedores under which the owners had impliedly promised to extend to the stevedores the benefit of an exemption clause contained in the bill of lading. The consideration furnished by the stevedores was said to be their performance of the contractual obligations they owed to the carrier of the goods. As LORD WILBERFORCE pointed out:[19]

> An agreement to do an act which the promisor is under an existing obligation to a third party to do may quite well amount to a valid consideration . . . the promisee obtains the benefit of a direct obligation which he can enforce.

In these cases involving the promise to perform or the performance of an existing duty owed to a third party, there is a valuable benefit to the other party in the form of a directly enforceable action against the promisor. Moreover, there is also detriment to the person who promises to perform, since he has now exposed himself to two actions, should he fail to perform his existing duty. As a result, in cases of this kind there is voluntary conduct and reciprocal benefit and detriment.

(iv)   Voluntary conduct and reciprocal benefit and detriment

The coincidence of the three key elements of voluntary human conduct, detriment and reasonable reliance provides the strongest case for enforcing a promise. If the promisor voluntarily undertakes to do something for the promisee and in so doing derives a valuable benefit and where the promisee incurs some detriment in the sense that he does more than he was previously obliged to do, then in the absence of strong policy reasons to the contrary, the promise should be enforced. It is this situation which most closely resembles the classical requirement of reciprocity of exchange or the truly bargained for promise.

The case law tradition of the common law requires that new circumstances are dealt with according to the existing structure of the common law. But, given that many of the rules of the doctrine of consideration have their origin in the nineteenth century, this can often be problematic in the sense that the values of the nineteenth century differ from those of today. However, the formalist judge is keen to apply existing rules in order to secure consistent development.[20] Often, this will involve artificial reasoning in order to achieve a particular result within the framework set up by the established rules.

The problems of the formalist approach are often encountered when applying the doctrine of consideration in order to determine whether a promise is enforceable and this is very evident in cases in which it is claimed that the performance of an existing duty is a sufficient consideration for a promise. It has been seen that the classical rule is that the performance of an existing duty is sterile, since nothing new is undertaken by the promisee. But if it can be shown that the promisee has done something in excess of his existing duty, there is no difficulty in regarding that additional performance as a good consideration since the promisor derives something of benefit to him and the extra performance is a detriment to the promisee. It follows that if the promisee is obliged

---

19   Ibid at 168.
20   See Adams & Brownsword *Understanding Contract Law* (1994), ch 8; Adams & Brownsword (1988) 8 Legal Studies 205 at 213–215.

to work a ship to its destination and back to its home port, but on the return journey undertakes additional duties, he provides consideration for a promise of additional remuneration.[1] Similarly, where the existing duty is one owed in law, such as the duty of the police to preserve law and order, an undertaking to do more than is legally necessary may be regarded as a sufficient consideration for a promise to pay for those policing services.[2] Moreover, the Police Act 1964, section 15(1) allows for payment in respect of special services provided at the request of the promisor and this includes the situation in which the request can be implied from conduct such as putting on an event which by its nature requires special policing services, such as a league football match.[3]

Given the nature of the rule on additional detriment to the promisee, it has been possible to use it to circumvent the strictness of the classical principle on existing duties. But it is often the case that the additional performance is difficult to discern. For example in *Ward v Byham*[4] a promise by the father of an illegitimate child to pay for its maintenance was said to be supported by an undertaking by the child's mother to keep the child well looked after and happy. This was said to exceed the mother's legal duty to maintain the child.[5] But the problem this reasoning creates is that the mother was providing little more than natural love and affection which is traditionally regarded as an insufficient reason for enforcing a promise.[6] Similarly artificial reasoning has been used in relation to existing contractual duties owed to the promisor. In *North Ocean Shipping Co Ltd v Hyundai Construction Co Ltd, The Atlantic Baron*[7] a promise to pay 10% more than the agreed price for the construction of a ship was held to be enforceable against the promisor because the promisee had changed the figures in a letter of credit arranged by him with his financial backers. Again, it is difficult to regard this additional performance as being of any serious detriment to the promisee, but the case is illustrative of the contrived use of an established exception to the rule on performance of an existing duty in order to justify the enforcement of a promise which it is not unfair to enforce. A better explanation of the case can be found in the 'bird-in-the-hand' approach adopted in the Court of Appeal decision in *Williams v Roffey Bros & Nicholls (Contractors) Ltd*,[8] in that there was a voluntary undertaking which was of substantial benefit to the promisor in ensuring that the ship was completed on time so that a valuable arrangement to charter the ship on its completion was not lost. The fact that there was no significant detriment to the promisee was, in fact, immaterial. It has been observed that the notion of bargain consideration was the basis of a number of nineteenth-century rules. The idea of a bargain suggests that contracts are bilateral arrangements resulting in a voluntary exchange of resources under which the promisee does, or undertakes to do, something or to forbear from doing a particular thing in return for the promisor's undertaking, which in many cases results in a benefit to the promisor.

(4)   PROMISSORY EXCHANGE LIABILITY AND RELIANCE

It is suggested that as in the case of benefits received, a satisfactory framework for the enforcement of obligations can be based around the notions of voluntary conduct on

1   *Hartley v Ponsonby* (1857) 119 ER 1471; *North Ocean Shipping Co Ltd v Hyundai Construction Co Ltd, The Atlantic Baron* [1979] QB 705; *Vantage Navigation Corpn v Suhail, The Alev* [1989] 1 Lloyd's Rep 138. Cf *Raggow v Scougall and Co* (1915) 31 TLR 564.
2   *Glasbrook Bros Ltd v Glamorgan County Council* [1925] AC 270. See also *Williams v Williams* [1957] 1 WLR 148 concerning a very different kind of duty owed in law.
3   *Harris v Sheffield United Football Club Ltd* [1988] QB 77.
4   [1956] 2 All ER 318.
5   Ibid at 320 (per MORRIS LJ).
6   *Bret v J S* (1600) Cro Eliz 756.
7   [1979] QB 705.
8   [1990] 1 All ER 512.

the part of the promisor and reasonable reliance on the part of the promisee. As has been observed above, the strongest case for the enforcement of a promise can be found where the elements of voluntary conduct, benefit to the promisor and reasonable reliance on the part of the promisee all coincide. But there are also a number of cases in which this bilateral exchange of valuable resources is not immediately apparent and in which the voluntary conduct of the promisor has induced some act of reliance on the part of the promisee.[9]

It is proposed to consider the reliance model of liability under three broad headings. First, it is necessary to ask what kinds of voluntary conduct are capable of inducing an act of reliance. Secondly, it must be considered what conditions of reliance must be satisfied in order that an exchange-based obligation should arise and thirdly, the effects of reliance must be taken into account.

(i)   Voluntary conduct capable of inducing reasonable reliance

In the course of an exchange relationship, a number of statements may be made, including promises or warranties of future performance, statements of intent, not intended to bind the maker and simple factual statements, amounting to representations, which if false, may give rise to an action for misrepresentation. All are capable of inducing acts of reliance, but it does not necessarily follow that a failure to comply with the content of the statement will always have the same result. In terms of traditional classification a breach of contractual promise potentially gives rise to full protection of the expectation interest[10] in the form of damages which place the promisee in the position he would have been in had the promise been performed. Conversely, a false statement of fact or misrepresentation and the failure to carry out a non-promissory statement of intention may trigger a remedy with a *restitutio* effect in the sense that the plaintiff is returned to the position he was in before the statement was made. In these circumstances, the defendant may have damaged the plaintiff's expectations, but what is protected is usually the status quo or restitution interest. Moreover, where promissory exchange liability is based on the notion of reliance, the plaintiff is not confined to compensation for harm to his reliance or status quo interest only. It is possible for a plaintiff to be put in a better position than before the promise was made. It may be said in these circumstances that the reliance model of liability can protect the plaintiff's expectation interest to the limited extent that the English law does protect a person's full expectations of performance.

(a) *Contractual promises and other statements of intention* Apart from the doctrine of consideration, English law has developed a second set of rules which serve to identify those promises or statements of future intention which give rise to promissory exchange liability, in the form of the doctrine of intention to create legal relations. Whether or not a separate doctrine of intention to create legal relations is necessary has been doubted,[11] and it may be that the rules developed under this head are more concerned with issues of contractual certainty[12] or with a general policy consideration in the form of trying to reduce the number of informal domestic or social disputes being dealt with by commercial courts.

---

9   See also United States *Restatement, Contracts* (2d) para 90. Cf para 75.
10   Subject to the limitations on an award of expectation damages discussed in ch 16.
11   See Hepple (1970) CLJ 122; Hedley 5 OJLS 391.
12   See *Carlill v Carbolic Smoke Ball Co* [1893] 1 QB 256 in which the argument whether there was an intention to create legal relations was decided on the basis that the defendant's offer was sufficiently clear in its terms to be legally binding, if accepted.

As a general rule, in commercial transactions, there will be few cases in which a promise made in a business context is not enforceable, unless the circumstances in which it is made expressly show that there was no intention to be contractually bound, for example where a promise is clearly stated to be binding in honour only.[13] In other commercial transactions other phrases have been used with a view to demonstrating that there was no intention to create legal relations, but with less success. For example, it has been held that an express provision to the effect that one of the parties was 'fixed in good faith' only, was considered not to negative a contractual intention.[14] Similarly, in the context of an arbitration agreement, a clause to the effect that the contract should be treated as 'an honourable engagement rather than as a legal obligation' was not enough to negative an intention to create legal relations.[15] It is often said that it would be contrary to the general purposes of the common law to place unnecessary hurdles in the way of a person wishing to enforce a seriously made commercial transaction.

Reliance is a crucial issue in relation to the matter of intention to create legal relations, since if a promise is made but is qualified by a clear statement that it is binding in honour only, it would not be reasonable for the promisee to expect anything of it while the arrangement between the parties remains purely executory. The same is true of letters of intent and letters of comfort where the language used by the parties may suggest that reliance on the promise is unreasonable. Letters of intent may be worded in such a way as to negative any intention to be contractually bound with the result that should a dispute arise, the court may conclude that there is no contract between the parties,[16] in which case it may be necessary to pursue a restitutionary remedy if there is any element of unjust enrichment.[17] Generally, a letter of intent may have one of three different meanings. First, it may be construed as an offer of a bilateral contract; secondly, it may be regarded as an offer of a unilateral contract under which no contract comes into existence until the requested act is performed. Thirdly, it may be construed as having no contractual effect at all. In order to ascertain which approach will be applied, it will be necessary to have close regard to the wording of the letter. The bilateral contract conclusion is an unlikely event, since in most cases, the nature of a letter of intent is such that the person to whom it is addressed ought to be aware that there is no intention, at the time of issue, to enter into any particular contractual relationship. However, there are exceptional circumstances in which this is a possibilty.[18] The more likely construction is that there is an offer of a unilateral contract, since this will mean that no contract comes into existence until there has been an act of reliance in the form of performance of the requested act. As *British Steel Corpn v Cleveland Bridge Engineering Co Ltd* demonstrates, there may also be circumstances in which no contract exists at all. This is most likely to be the case where there is no semblance of agreement between the parties on the essential terms of the suggested contract, such as those relating to price, or where the letter of intent expressly states that it is to have no contractual effect.[19]

Advertising jargon, albeit used in a commercial context, cannot be taken with any degree of seriousness and is therefore unlikely to give rise to any sort of contractual

---

13   *Rose and Frank Co v JR Crompton and Bros Ltd* [1925] AC 445; *County Ltd v Girozentrale Securities* [1996] 3 All ER 834. Similar provisions can be found on football pool coupons: *Jones v Vernon's Pools Ltd* [1938] 2 All ER 626. Whether it is unreasonable to do this has been considered under Scots law: *Ferguson v Littlewoods Pools Ltd* 1997 SLT 309.

14   *The Mercedes Envoy* [1995] 2 Lloyd's Rep 559.

15   *Home Insurance Co v Administratia Asigurarilor de Stat* [1983] 2 Lloyd's Rep 674.

16   *British Steel Corpn v Cleveland Bridge and Engineering Co Ltd* [1984] 1 All ER 504.

17   See chs 11 and 18 and Ball (1983) 99 LQR 572.

18   *Turriff Construction Ltd v Regalia Knitting Mills Ltd* (1971) 222 Estates Gazette 169.

19   See *Drake and Scull Engineering Ltd v Higgs and Hill (Northern) Ltd* (1994) 11 Const LJ 214.

relationship between the advertiser and purchaser.[20] For example, no reasonable person would regard as binding a statement that a certain salad dressing is the only one not to cause sticks of celery to recoil in horror on the plate or that consuming a certain brand of lager will have untold beneficial effects on one's personal performance. However, in contrast, more serious statements made in advertisements which are capable of being relied upon may lead to a different conclusion.[1]

Where there are commercial dealings betwen the parties, the person alleging a lack of intention to create a legally binding relationship bears the onus of proof, which is extremely difficult to discharge,[2] although the issue is essentially one of fact. If a statement has been made which is intended to be relied upon by the other party and there is evidence of such reliance, an intention to create legal relations is likely to be found. For example, an advertisement which clearly induces reliance on the part of a customer may form the basis of a binding contract,[3] particularly where the advertiser stands to derive a substantial commercial advantage.[4] Moreover, even in the case of a promise expressed to be binding in honour only, if action in reliance on the promise, in the form of performance takes place, the transaction will give rise to ordinary legal rights.[5] Similarly, a letter of intent which has been open for a considerable time and has resulted in acts of detrimental reliance may form the basis of a collateral contract.[6] The mere fact that, in practice, the terms of an agreement might not be enforced between the parties because they are members of the same group of companies is also insufficient to negative the existence of a contractual intention.[7]

(b) *Promises and statements of fact*   Generally, a statement of fact, a typical example of which is a misrepresentation, will not give rise to contractual liability unless it has become incorporated as a term of the contract to which it relates. Moreover, where the statement starts life as a misrepresentation, but later becomes incorporated as a term of the contract, it may still only allow the recovery of status quo loss, if it is construed as nothing more than a representation that reasonable care will be taken. In this case, the plaintiff is put back into the position he was in before the statement was made.[8]

Both promises and statements of fact are likely to be relied upon, but with potentially different consequences. In *Kleinwort Benson Ltd v Malaysia Mining Corpn Bhd*[9] the plaintiffs had made a loan facility available to a subsidiary of the defendants. Initially, the plaintiffs had asked for a guarantee of the subsidiary company's debts, which had been declined by the defendants. Instead they issued a letter of comfort in which they stated that it was their policy, at all times, to ensure that the subsidiary was in a position to meet its debts in return for a small increase in the commission payable to the plaintiffs. Subsequently, the subsidiary company went into liquidation and the plaintiff sought to recover the amount of the loan from the defendants, who refused to pay. The Court of Appeal held that the statement of policy was not a contractual promise, but was a factual statement of the defendants' present intention. Oddly, despite the presence of the words 'at all times' it was not regarded as a promise that the policy would continue

---

20   *Lexmead (Basingstoke) Ltd v Lewis* [1982] AC 225 at 262.
1   See *Carlill v Carbolic Smoke Ball Co* [1893] 1 QB 256; *Bowerman v ABTA* [1995] NLJR 1815.
2   *Edwards v Skyways Ltd* [1964] 1 All ER 494 at 500 (per MEGAW J).
3   *Carlill v Carbolic Smoke Ball Co* [1893] 1 QB 256.
4   *Esso Petroleum Ltd v Customs and Excise Comrs* [1976] 1 All ER 117.
5   *Rose and Frank Co v JR Crompton and Bros Ltd* [1925] AC 445 at 455 (per LORD PHILLIMORE).
6   *Trollope & Colls Ltd v Atomic Power Constructions Ltd* [1963] 1 WLR 333; *Turriff Construction Ltd v Regalia Knitting Mills Ltd* (1971) 222 Estates Gazette 169.
7   *The Marine Star (No 2)* [1994] 2 Lloyd's Rep 629.
8   See eg *Esso Petroleum Co Ltd v Mardon* [1976] QB 801.
9   [1989] 1 All ER 785. See Brown [1990] JBL 281; Davenport [1988] LMCLQ 290.

into the future.[10] Moreover, the fact that the loan facility was made available in reliance on the letter of comfort might properly be regarded as action in reliance giving rise to ordinary legal rights.[11] In other circumstances, it is possible that a statement of present intention may impliedly represent that the intention is genuinely held at the time it was made.[12] Moreover, it will be important to construe the language used by the parties to determine whether there is an intention to be bound. Thus if the agreement gives a very wide discretion to one or other of the parties as to whether he is required to perform, it is more likely that there will be no intention to be bound,[13] whereas an agreement couched in terms of compulsory performance is more likely to be construed as to give rise to a contractual intention.[14] In *Kleinwort Benson,* since the statement was merely one of fact, it would only give rise to liability in respect of losses suffered through relying on the expression of policy after the policy had changed.[15] Since the plaintiffs had made no further advances after the change of policy, there was no point in pursuing such a claim.

As an alternative to an action for damages for breach of contract or for negligent misstatement, both promises and factual statements may be subject to rules on estoppel. The varieties of estoppel include estoppel by representation, a common law rule, proprietory estoppel and promissory estoppel, both of which have their origins in equity.[16] An estoppel is an evidential device which applies where a person has used words or conduct which lead another person to believe in a particular state of affairs and which cause that other person to alter his position in reliance upon his belief. In such a case, the person who allowed the belief in the represented state of affairs to come about may be prevented from going back on his word.[17]

The common law doctrine of estoppel by representation applies to statements of fact only. Thus in *Jorden v Money,*[18] Money owed a debt of £1,200 which was secured on a bond which Mrs Jorden was in a position to enforce. She had frequently said that she would never enforce the bond and had made such assertions to Money's prospective parents-in-law. In reliance on these statements, Money married his fiancee and then sought an order that the debt had been abandoned. The House of Lords held that Mrs Jorden's statements could not be construed as assertions of fact. They were promises which were not the subject of the doctrine of estoppel by representation. The dividing line between a promise and a statement of fact is narrow,[19] for example, it could be argued that Jorden said she had released the debt.

In contrast, the equitable varieties of estoppel do apply to promises. Promissory estoppel requires a promise which is intended to create legal relations and which, to the knowledge of the promisor, will be and is, in fact, acted upon. Where these conditions are satisfied, the promise is binding, despite the absence of consideration.[20] In the *High Trees* case,[1] in view of wartime conditions, a landlord had gratuitously promised to reduce

10   Ibid at 792 (per RALPH GIBSON LJ).
11   *Rose and Frank Co v JR Crompton and Bros Ltd* [1925] AC 445 at 455 (per LORD PHILLIMORE).
12   *Re Atlantic Computers plc* [1995] BCC 696.
13   *Wyatt v Kreglinger and Fernau* [1933] 1 KB 793.
14   *Wilson Smithett & Cape (Sugar) Ltd v Bangladesh Sugar and Food Industries Corpn* [1986] 1 Lloyd's Rep 378.
15   Under the rule in *Hedley Byrne & Co Ltd v Heller & Partners Ltd* [1964] AC 465: [1989] 1 All ER 785 at 790 (per RALPH GIBSON LJ).
16   Although these are all called estoppels, it has been asserted that they are subject to different rules and that there is no single principle under which they can all be subsumed: *First National Bank plc v Thompson* [1996] Ch 231 at 236 (per MILLETT LJ).
17   See *Maclaine v Gatty* [1921] 1 AC 376 at 386 (per LORD BIRKENHEAD).
18   (1854) 5 HL Cas 185.
19   *Salisbury v Gilmore* [1942] 2 KB 38 at 52 (per MACKINNON LJ). Cf *Spence v Shell UK Ltd* (1980) 256 Estates Gazette 55.
20   *Central London Property Trust Ltd v High Trees House Ltd* [1947] KB 130 at 135 (per DENNING J).
1   Ibid.

the rent payable by his tenant. The promise was held by DENNING J to be enforceable so long as the promise was acted upon and until such time as the landlord chose to revert to the higher rent charged before the promise was made. The basis on which DENNING J proceeded was that the equitable principle established in *Hughes v Metropolitan Rly Co*[2] could be applied to promises as well as to actions leading another person to believe in a particular state of affairs. In *Hughes v Metropolitan Rly* it was stated that:

> ...(I)f parties who have entered into definite and distinct terms involving certain legal results – certain penalties or legal forfeiture – afterwards by their own act or with their own consent enter upon a course of negotiation which has the effect of leading one of the parties to suppose that the strict rights arising under the contract will not be enforced, or will be kept in suspense, or held in abeyance, the person who otherwise might have enforced those rights will not be allowed to enforce them where it would be inequitable, having regard to the dealings which have thus taken place between the parties.[3]

On the face of it, this principle appeared to be based on the notion of forfeiture of a lease, since what had prompted the principle was the fact that the parties had commenced negotiations for sale of the lease to the tenant. These negotiations caused the tenant not to carry out certain repairs to the premises as the lease required, since the tenant believed he was soon to become the freehold owner of the property. Subsequently, those negotiations broke down and the landlord sought to enforce a term of the lease allowing forfeiture for non-compliance with a requirement that repairs should be completed within six months of receipt of notice. The effect of the principle stated above was that the landlord was estopped from relying on his right of forfeiture until the expiry of six months from the date of the cessation of negotiations, rather than from the date of service of the original notice.

From the rule established in *Hughes*, DENNING J in *High Trees* derived a somewhat different principle based on the potential enforceability of promises which were not supported by consideration in the legal sense and in circumstances which had nothing to do with forfeiture of a lease. In brief, DENNING J summed up the principle as one to the effect that,

> ...A promise, intended to be binding, intended to be acted on and in fact acted on, is binding so far as its terms properly apply.[4]

The importance of the principle established in *High Trees* is that it applies to a promise by a creditor to accept a smaller payment in satisfaction of a debt owed to him, thus providing a means of evading the rule in *Foakes v Beer* that a promise to accept a lesser payment is, generally, not supported by consideration. In *Re Selectmove Ltd*[5] a debtor claimed that his creditor had agreed to accept repayment of a debt by instalments and that the creditor was estopped from going back on his promise. In the event, it was decided that the representation by the creditor was not sufficiently clear to be binding on the creditor and that even if a representation had been made, it would not be inequitable to allow the creditor to resile on his promise, since the debtor had not started to make repayments under the new arrangement. However, the implication is that had these requirements been satisfied, the doctrine of promissory estoppel would have applied so as to postpone the debtor's obligation to repay, but not to extinguish it altogether.

---

2   (1877) 2 App Cas 439.
3   Ibid at 448 (per LORD CAIRNS LC).
4   *Central London Property Trust Ltd v High Trees House Ltd* [1947] KB 130 at 136 (per DENNING J).
5   [1995] 2 All ER 531.

There are limitations on the doctrine, which mean that it will never completely replace the requirement of consideration in English contract law. In order to bring the equitable doctrine into operation, the promise must be clear and unambiguous, and must indicate that the representor will not insist on his strict legal rights,[6] although it can be implied from conduct.[7] However, mere inaction will be insufficient to invoke the doctrine since silence is equivocal.[8] However, there may be very unusual exceptional circumstances in which the law may impose a duty to disclose certain facts or to clarify a legal relationship.[9] If the promise is vague or uncertain, it is unlikely to bring the doctrine of promissory estoppel into operation.[10] Furthermore, it seems that before the doctrine can be invoked, it must be equitable for the court to intervene and grant relief. Usually, if the promisee has relied on a promise, it will be equitable to enforce the promise. But if the party seeking to plead estoppel in his defence has acted with some improper motive or has come to equity without 'clean hands', relief is unlikely to be granted.[11]

It is also possible to enforce promises under the doctrine of proprietory estoppel. The principal reason for enforcement is that the promisor has induced an act of reliance in relation to an interest in land.[12] For example, in *Dillwyn v Llewelyn*[13] a father purported to present his son with a farm by means of a written, but ineffective memorandum. The son relied on the promise by building a house valued at £14,000. It was held that the incomplete gift could be perfected, although the reasons for the decision are not wholly clear. The case can be explained on the grounds of unjust enrichment, in that if the the father had been able to repossess the land he would unjustly receive the benefit of the work done by his son. Alternatively, the decision may be justified on the basis of an induced reasonable expectation as the subsequent expenditure of the son coupled with the 'approbation of the father supplied a valuable consideration . . .'[14] Moreover, it may even be argued that the alternative explanations amount to the same thing.[15] Generally, the unjust enrichment argument seems to be more acceptable in the view of a number of recent cases, on the basis that liability is based on the existence of an implied or constructive trust.[16]

(ii)   The varieties of reliance

The simple fact that a person relies on a promise or statement made in the course of negotiations leading to an exchange of valuable resources cannot, of itself, justify the imposition of an obligation to perform. The nature of the reliance must be qualified and general policy issues must be addressed, in particular it must be considered whether the person who relied on the promise or other statement was justified in doing so.

---

6   *Woodhouse AC Israel Cocoa Ltd SA v Nigerian Produce Marketing Co Ltd* [1972] AC 741 at 757 (per LORD HAILSHAM LC).

7   *Hughes v Metropolitan Rly Co* (1877) 2 App Cas 439; *The Kanchenjunga* [1990] 1 Lloyd's Rep 391 at 399 (per LORD GOFF).

8   *Allied Marine Transport Ltd v Vale do Rio Doce Navegacao SA, The Leonidas D* [1985] 2 All ER 796 at 805 (per ROBERT GOFF LJ).

9   *Petrotrade Inc v Stinnes Handel GmbH* [1995] 1 Lloyd's Rep 142.

10   *The Winson* [1980] 2 Lloyd's Rep 213 (reversed on other grounds in [1982] AC 939).

11   *D & C Builders Ltd v Rees* [1966] 2 QB 617 at 625 (per LORD DENNING MR).

12   *A-G of Hong Kong v Humphreys Estate Ltd* [1987] 2 All ER 387 at 392 (per LORD TEMPLEMAN).

13   (1862) 4 De GF & J 517.

14   Ibid at 522 (per LORD WESTBURY LC). This might indicate that unrequested reliance can be a good consideration, where justice so requires. See Atiyah *Essays* Essay No 8, pp 232–233.

15   *Gillies v Keogh* [1989] 2 NZLR 327. Cf Birks 'In Defence of Free Acceptance', in Burrows (ed) *Essays on the Law of Restitution* 1991, p 109.

16   See *Sen v Headley* [1991] Ch 425; *Lloyds Bank plc v Carrick* [1996] 4 All ER 630.

Generally, a promise is more likely to induce an act of reliance than is a statement of fact. The nature of a promise is such that the promisor gives a guarantee of a certain future state of affairs which the promisee can assume will come to fruition. In these circumstances, it is entirely understandable that the promisee may alter his position on the assumption that the promise will be performed. More caution is necessary in the case of a statement of fact or a promise implied from conduct, but if the reliance is reasonable and justified, this will provide a good reason for holding the promisor to his word or compensating the promisee for loss suffered in consequence of his reliance.

Reliance can be divided into a number of sub-categories. First it may be unreasonable, secondly it may be reasonable but not detrimental and thirdly, it may be reasonable and detrimental. Generally, it is fair to assume that unreasonable reliance whether detrimental or not should not give rise to liability on the part of the promisor, but where the reliance is reasonable and justified, there are strong reasons for enforcing the promise.

(a) *Unreasonable reliance*   If the promisee acts on a promise in a manner which is wholly unreasonable it is unlikely that this will be regarded as a sufficient reason for enforcing the promise. But in a deliberately bargained for exchange, reliance on the promisor's promise is not likely to be unreasonable where the act of reliance is part of the exchange. If a promise has been given and some action on the part of the promisee has been requested and performed, it seems perfectly reasonable to expect the promisor to keep his word. Unreasonable reliance is more likely to be found outside of exchange relationships such as where a financial statement has been issued by an auditor or where an official 'watch-dog' has impliedly suggested that a company is a sound investment.[17]

(b) *Voluntary conduct and reasonable, detrimental reliance*   If the promisee reasonably relies on a voluntarily given promise and changes his position there are good reasons for enforcing that promise, particularly if the act of reliance has been bargained for. The detriment suffered by the promisee may consist of expense incurred or in taking on additional obligations. Thus where there is a promise to grant an interest in property if the promisee will perform the covenant obligations of the promisor,[18] or will pay outstanding amounts due under a mortgage there is a good consideration for the promise.

The notion of detrimental reliance in the form of expense incurred also explains many of the exceptional cases in which the courts are prepared to admit the existence of an intention to create legal relations in the event of a domestic dispute. While it is generally the rule that commercial courts will not entertain a contractual dispute between family members, it is clear that the dispute will be heard if the arrangement between the parties was seriously intended and that they were operating at arm's length. Such an intention can be found where there is evidence of reasonable detrimental reliance on the part of the promisee. For example, an arrangement between estranged spouses whereby the freehold interest in the matrimonial home will be transferred if the transferee will assume responsibility for mortgage payments does give rise to an intention to create legal relations.[19] Conversely, where such reliance as there might have been has evaporated, the court may return to the conventional view that contractual liability should not attach. In *Jones v Padavatton*,[20] a mother induced her daughter to give up her job and move to London to study for the bar examinations. It was agreed that the mother would buy a house and allow her daughter to live in it. The daughter took up occupation, subsequently married and, after five years, had made no progress towards qualifying for

---

17   See ch 10.
18   *Johnsey Estates Ltd v Lewis and Manley (Engineering) Ltd* [1987] 2 EGLR 69.
19   *Merritt v Merritt* [1970] 1 WLR 1211. See also *Errington v Errington and Woods* [1952] 1 KB 290.
20   [1969] 1 WLR 328.

the bar. While the decision turned on an absence of an intention to create legal relations, the issue of reliance was important. If the validity of the arrangement had been tested when the daughter first arrived, there probably would have been a binding contract. But the promise to allow the daughter to use the house only lasted for a reasonable time after the expiry of which the mother could retake possession of the property.[1]

Detriment can also be found where the promisee forgoes a benefit or gain which might otherwise have been available. Thus not enforcing a valid claim, such as a forbearance to sue,[2] or abandoning a defence or a remedy[3] will also amount to a good consideration provided what is given up is not known to the parties to be bad in law.

The cases so far considered have involved an element of exchange, but there are also cases in which the element of reciprocity is absent but in which an act of detrimental reliance provides a good reason for enforcing the voluntary promise of the other party. For example, in *Shadwell v Shadwell*,[4] the defendant, when he heard of his nephew's intended marriage, promised to pay him a sum of money per year. It was held that there was consideration for the promise in that the nephew had adopted a material change in his position and that the marriage could be regarded as a benefit to the defendant in the sense that the marriage was an object of interest to a close relative.[5] However, it seems somewhat artificial to say that the defendant bargained for the marriage of his nephew. In truth, the defendant was probably doing no more than expressing his contentment that his nephew had become engaged to be married.[6] However, an important factor was that the promise might have induced a change of position by the nephew which would have resulted in financial embarrassment had the defendant's promise not been enforced.[7]

Detrimental reliance is also a key feature where a collateral contract or warranty is inferred from the conduct or words of the promisor. The title collateral contract suggests that the contract or warranty should sit beside another contract and that there should be some contractual intent. This explains the description of a collateral warranty as 'a contract the consideration for which is the making of some other contract'.[8] Thus if a manufacturer warrants his product suitable for a particular use and the person to whom the warranty is given then purchases the product from another source, in reliance on the assertion of suitability, there is consideration for that assertion in making the contract with the retail supplier.[9] However, there are also signs that the courts are not over-diligent in their search for a contractual intent in every case.[10]

In the case of unilateral contracts, involving an act done in response to an offer of reward, it is often the fact of detrimental reliance which justifies the enforcement of the promise. For example, in *Errington v Errington and Woods*,[11] a promise by a father to allow the plaintiff, his daughter-in-law, to live in the house which he had partly paid for so long as she continued to pay the outstanding mortgage debt was held to be

---

1   Ibid at 335 (per SALMON LJ).
2   *Greene v Church Comrs for England* [1974] Ch 467.
3   *Allied Marine Transport Ltd v Vale do Rio Doce Navegacao SA, The Leonidas D* [1985] 2 All ER 796.
4   (1860) 9 CBNS 159. See also *Scotson v Pegg* (1861) 30 LJ Ex 225; *Chichester v Cobb* (1866) 14 LT 433.
5   Ibid at 174 (per ERLE CJ).
6   Ibid at 177 (per BYLES J (dissenting)).
7   Ibid at 174 (per ERLE CJ).
8   *Heilbut, Symons & Co v Buckleton* [1913] AC 30 at 47 (per LORD MOULTON). See also *Lexmead (Basingstoke) Ltd v Lewis* [1982] AC 225.
9   *Shanklin Pier Ltd v Detel Products Ltd* [1951] 2 KB 854; *Wells (Merstham) Ltd v Buckland Sand and Silica Ltd* [1965] 2 QB 170.
10 *De Lassalle v Guildford* [1901] 2 KB 215; *Schawel v Reade* [1913] 2 IR 81; *Couchman v Hill* [1947] KB 554; *Andrews v Hopkinson* [1957] 1 QB 229; *Dick Bentley Productions Ltd v Harold Smith (Motors) Ltd* [1965] 1 WLR 623. See also chs 7 and 10.
11 [1952] 1 KB 290.

enforceable after the father's death while ever the plaintiff continued to pay the necessary instalments. An important factor was that the occupant had acted upon the promise, therefore it followed that no-one could eject her in disregard of the action in reliance.[12]

Even in the absence of a specific request, reasonable detrimental reliance can be used as a justification for the enforcement of a promise. For example in *Jorden v Money*,[13] frequent public assertions by a creditor that she would not enforce a bond on which a debt was secured induced the debtor to marry his fiancee. There had been no request by the creditor that the debtor should act in this way, but there are indications that had the promise in consideration of marriage complied with formal requirements[14] there would have been a good contract.[15] This has led Atiyah[16] to argue that the debtor's reliance on the creditor's promise could be seen as a good consideration even though the act of reliance had not been requested by the promisor.

Reasonable detrimental reliance is also an important requirement in cases involving the application of principles of proprietary estoppel, according to the majority of the case law on the subject.

(c) *Voluntary conduct and reasonable, non-detrimental reliance*　According to the classical rules, a promise will only be enforceable where the promisee's reliance is to his detriment in the sense that he has done something over and above that already required of him. If the promisee does no more than his existing duty he has not given anything of value in the eyes of the law. Moreover, in terms of reliance, if the promisee does no more than he is already bound to do, he cannot be said to have relied to his detriment on the promise of the other party. Typically, this issue will arise in the context of ongoing transaction adjustments, namely, where the parties to an existing contract seek to modify or vary the terms of their original contract. In these circumstances, where the court is unable to find consideration for the promise to modify, the doctrine of promissory estoppel may assist as a limited means of enforcing the promise. It has been seen above that the doctrine is securely based on the notion of reliance, but it would appear that detriment is not necessarily a requirement.

In cases of proprietory estoppel detrimental reliance is a requirement.[17] Moreover, there are also statements to the effect that detrimental reliance is a requirement of promissory estoppel.[18] In contrast, there are also supporters of the view that simple reliance without detriment is sufficient for the purposes of promissory estoppel.[19] The fact that simple reliance is regarded as sufficient would appear to support the view that the expectation interest is protected. The reliance of the promisee upon the promisor has generated a reasonable expectation that the promise will be performed.

Where the issue of reliance arises in a context other than the variation of an existing contractual obligation, detriment may be a requirement. In *Waltons Stores (Interstate) Ltd*

12　Ibid at 300 (per DENNING LJ).

13　(1854) 5 HL Cas 185.

14　The Statute of Frauds 1677 required such promises to be proved in writing.

15　(1854) 5 HL Cas 185 at 214–217 (per LORD CRANWORTH).

16　*Essays* Essay No 8, pp 233–238. Cf Treitel (1976) 50 Aust LJ 439.

17　*A-G of Hong Kong v Humphreys Estate Ltd* [1987] 2 All ER 387 at 392 (per LORD TEMPLEMAN); *Grant v Edwards* [1986] 2 All ER 426 at 439 (per BROWNE WILKINSON VC); *Lloyds Bank plc v Rossett* [1990] 1 All ER 1111 at 1118–1119 (per LORD BRIDGE).

18　*Tool Metal Manufacturing Co Ltd v Tungsten Electric Co Ltd* [1955] 1 WLR 761 at 764 (per VISCOUNT SYMONDS); *Ajayi v RT Briscoe (Nigeria) Ltd* [1964] 1 WLR 1326 at 1331 (per LORD HODSON).

19　*Central London Property Trust Ltd v High Trees House Ltd* [1947] KB 130 at 135 (per DENNING J); *Tool Metal Manufacturing Co Ltd v Tungsten Electric Co Ltd* [1955] 1 WLR 761 at 799 (per LORD COHEN); *WJ Alan & Co Ltd v El Nasr Export and Import Co* [1972] 2 QB 189 at 213 (per LORD DENNING MR); *Brikom Investments Ltd v Carr* [1979] QB 467 at 484 (per Lord Denning MR).

v Maher[20] a builder was led to believe that he was to be awarded a contract to erect a supermarket. He was allowed to commence demolition work on the intended building site at a time when the appellants were having second thoughts about the deal. At no stage was the builder given any indication that the appellants might not proceed with the contract. A majority of the High Court of Australia held that the builder had acted on the assumption that a contract would be entered into and that a promissory estoppel prevented the appellants from denying the existence of such a contract. It was said that the object of the doctrine of estoppel was not to make good the expectations engendered by the promise, but to avoid the detriment to the promisee which would follow from the unconscionable departure of the promisor from the terms of the promise.

(iii)   The effects of reliance

(a) *Defence or cause of action?*   It has been seen above that an act of reliance may satisfy the requirements stipulated for a sufficient consideration or may be relevant in the context of a plea of estoppel. The importance of the distinction lies in the more limited effects of a promise which the court holds has not been supported by consideration. In theory, the breach of a contractual promise will trigger the range of remedies associated with harm to expectations.[1] Moreover, where a promise is supported by consideration, it creates rights which did not previously exist, so that in contract there is a distinct cause of action which allows enforcement of the promise.

The fact that an estoppel is an evidential device suggests that it may operate only as a defence, so that the doctrine of promissory estoppel can be used only as a 'shield' and not as a 'sword',[2] that is it prevents a person from unjustly insisting on his strict legal rights but it cannot be used to create a new cause of action.[3] Thus in *Combe v Combe*,[4] the appellant had promised to pay the respondent maintenance of £100 per year, as a result of which the respondent did not apply for judicial maintenance. It was held that the respondent could not use the doctrine of promissory estoppel in order to enforce the promise as this would involve creating a cause of action where none previously existed. Conversely, it has been observed that it is not a bar to raising estoppel as a defence where the effect of doing so is to enable a party to enforce a cause of action which would not otherwise exist.[5] Accordingly, it may be asserted that if the parties have conducted dealings on the basis of an underlying assumption, neither will be permitted to go back on his word and if one of them does so, such remedy as the equities of the case demand may be granted.[6]

Cases of proprietory estoppel also run against the view that an estoppel operates as a shield not a sword. In such cases, a person has detrimentally relied on the reasonably held belief that he has acquired, or will acquire, rights in or over the land of another. The doctrine of proprietory estoppel and perhaps the doctrine of promissory estoppel can be used to confer rights on a person where such rights did not previously exist. The underlying principle is one of unconscionability,[7] which demonstrates that it can

---

20   (1988) 76 ALR 513. See Duthie (1988) 104 LQR 362.
1   See chs 16 and 17.
2   See *Hiscox v Outhwaite (No 3)* [1991] 2 Lloyd's Rep 524. Cf the position in the USA where *Restatement, Contracts* (2d), para 90 provides that estoppel may found a cause of action where justice so requires.
3   *Combe v Combe* [1951] 1 All ER 767 at 769 (per DENNING LJ).
4   Ibid. See also *Argy Trading Development Co Ltd v Lapid Developments Ltd* [1977] 3 All ER 785; *Syros Shipping Co SA v Elaghill Trading Co, The Proodos C* [1981] 3 All ER 189.
5   *Amalgamated Investment and Property Co Ltd v Texas Commerce International Bank Ltd* [1982] QB 84 at 105–108 (per ROBERT GOFF J).
6   Ibid at 122 (per LORD DENNING MR).
7   *Amalgamated Investment and Property Co Ltd v Texas Commerce International Bank Ltd* [1982] QB 84 at 105–108 (per ROBERT GOFF J); *Pacol Ltd v Trade Lines Ltd, The Henryk Sif* [1982] 1 Lloyd's Rep 456 at 467–468 (per WEBSTER J). See also ch 24.

be used flexibly to meet the equities of a particular case. However, at present, there seems to be little indication that English courts are prepared to use principles of 'equitable' estoppel in the broad sense employed by the High Court of Australia in *Waltons Stores (Interstate) Ltd v Maher,* discussed elsewhere.[8]

One person may have either actively encouraged another to believe that he has acquired some right over land, or may have passively acquiesced in some mistake as to entitlement made by that other. If in such cases it would be unconscionable to deny the second person's right over the land where he has incurred some expense,[9] or has in some other way acted to his detriment,[10] then the doctrine of estoppel can be used to create such a right. Where an equity is created in relation to particular property, a third party who has knowledge of the equity will also be bound by it.[11]

Whether the doctrine of promissory estoppel is properly restricted to cases of defence only, is subject to doubt in other parts of the common law world. For example, in *Waltons Stores (Interstate) Ltd v Maher*[12] a builder had been led to incur expense following the promise of a property developer to award a contract to build a supermarket to the builder. Although there was no existing contractual relationship between the parties, the doctrine of promissory estoppel was held to apply, despite the fact that to do so would confer on the builder rights which did not previously exist. As a result the High Court of Australia awarded damages in lieu of specific performance of the contract, although it is difficult to establish precisely the basis on which the decision was reached since the reasoning of the various members of the court differs substantially. GAUDRON J appears to have reached her decision on the basis that the developers would have been unjustly enriched if they had been allowed to deny the existence of a contract and that they could be prevented from saying that contracts had not been exchanged on the basis of a common law estoppel. While not invoking principles of unjust enrichment, DEANE J also appears to apply principles of common law estoppel. In contrast MASON CJ, WILSON J and BRENNAN J took the view that there was no representation of fact, which would seem to suggest that an essential requirement of common law estoppel had not been complied with. Instead, the essence of their (majority) decision appears to have been that there was a promise that contracts would be exchanged, thereby invoking principles of promissory estoppel so as to give rise to a new cause of action. The only English case to get anywhere close to this proposition is *Williams v Roffey Bros & Nicholls (Contractors) Ltd*[13] although, as has been seen above, this was done via the creation of an exception to the rule in *Stilk v Myrick,*[14] that the promise of performance of an existing duty owed to the promisor may be a sufficient consideration for the promise if the promisor derives some practical benefit or obviates some practical disbenefit as a result of making his promise. In *Williams v Roffey* at least two members of the court[15] made it clear that they would have been more than happy to have received an argument from counsel to the effect that the main contractors were estopped from going back on their statement of existing fact that they intended to make the additional payment to the subcontractor.

---

8   See *Pridean Ltd v Forest Taverns Ltd* (1996) 75 P & CR 447. (No estoppel where there was no evidence of a concluded agreement).
9   *Dillwyn v Llewelyn* (1862) 4 De GF & J 517; *Inwards v Baker* [1965] 2 QB 29; *Hussey v Palmer* [1972] 1 WLR 1286.
10 *Crabb v Arun District Council* [1976] Ch 179.
11 *Lloyds Bank Ltd v Carrick* [1996] 4 All ER 630.
12 (1988) 164 CLR 387.
13 [1990] 1 All ER 512.
14 (1809) 2 Camp 317.
15 [1990] 1 All ER 512 at 523 (per RUSSELL LJ) and at 520 (per GLIDEWELL LJ). See also academic argument to the effect that *Williams v Roffey* ought to have been dealt with on the basis of the doctrine of promissory estoppel: Phang (1991) 107 LQR 21; Hird & Blair [1996] JBL 254.

There are ways in which the enforcement of a promise through the use of rules on estoppel differ from the enforcement of a contractual promise. For example, rules on promissory and proprietory estoppel will reflect the equities of the case and may not afford the same protection which is, in theory, available to the victim of a breach of contract. Moreover, the general effect of a contractual promise is that where supported by consideration it is fully binding. However, a promise to vary existing contractual obligations under the doctrine of promissory estoppel may be binding only temporarily, pending the giving of notice of an intention to return to the status quo. In *Hughes v Metropolitan Rly Co*,[16] a landlord gave his tenant six months' notice to effect certain repairs to the leased premises. During the course of the six months' notice, the landlord and tenant commenced negotiations for the sale of the lease. These negotiations continued for two months and, during that time, the tenant did nothing towards the fulfilment of his covenant to repair because he reasonably believed that the premises would be sold to him. Exactly six months after service of the original notice to repair, the landlord claimed that the lease was forfeited and sought to eject the tenant. The House of Lords held that the landlord had impliedly promised that so long as negotiations for the sale of the lease continued, he would not enforce the notice to repair. It was reasonable to expect the tenant to rely on this promise and the effect of the estoppel was to temporarily suspend the commencement of the notice to repair until after the negotiations had failed. Accordingly, the tenant was entitled to equitable relief against forfeiture.

The case has led to the view that the doctrine of estoppel serves only to suspend the right of the promisor to return to the terms of the original contract and not to extinguish that right altogether.[17] Conversely, there are cases which suggest that the doctrine of promissory estoppel may serve to extinguish the promisor's right to return to the status quo altogether.[18] For example, it has been said that if a creditor intends to take a part payment in full settlement of a debt and this is made abundantly clear, he will be permanently bound by his promise.[19] Furthermore, if it becomes impossible to perform the original contract, the promisor may find himself in a position whereby his new promise becomes permanently binding.[20]

In *Brikom Investments Ltd v Carr*,[1] a series of leases of flats provided that the tenants should contribute towards expense incurred by the landlords in repairing the roof. The landlords had asserted that they would undertake such repairs at their own cost. The majority of the Court of Appeal treated this as a binding collateral contract between the original tenants and the landlords. However, some difficulty arose over the position of the tenants who were assignees from the original tenants. LORD DENNING MR took the view that the doctrine of promissory estoppel was applicable, and that it operated to extinguish the right of the landlords to return to the original contract and ask the tenants to contribute to the cost of roof repairs. However, the majority treated this as a case of waiver,[2] which has been interpreted to mean a variation supported by consideration.[3] On this basis, the extinction of the landlords' right to return to the

---

16 (1877) 2 App Cas 439.
17 See *Refineries Ajayi v RT Briscoe (Nigeria) Ltd* [1964] 3 All ER 556 at 559 (per LORD HODSON).
18 *Motor Oil Hellas SA v Shipping Corpn of India, The Kanchenjunga* [1990] 1 Lloyd's Rep 391 at 399 (per LORD GOFF).
19 *Central London Property Trust Ltd v High Trees House Ltd* [1947] KB 130 at 134 (per DENNING J); *D & C Builders Ltd v Rees* [1966] 2 QB 617 at 624 (per LORD DENNING MR). Cf *Foakes v Beer* (1884) 9 App Cas 605.
20 *Ajayi v RT Briscoe (Nigeria) Ltd* [1964] 3 All ER 556, [1964] 1 WLR 1326.
1   [1979] QB 467.
2   Ibid at 488 (per ROSKILL LJ) and at 490 (per CUMMING-BRUCE LJ).
3   *Treitel*, pp 121–122.

original contract is justified because new expectations have been generated in the promisee.

A preferable, academic view of the cases in this area is that regard should be had to the manner in which a promissory estoppel works, and to distinguish between the effect of a representation made while a contract is still executory and a representation made after a breach of contract has already occurred.[4] Promissory estoppel can work in three different ways. It may be used to vary the terms of a contract; it may operate to exclude a specific type of remedy; or it may prevent a remedy of any sort from being obtained.[5] In deciding whether estoppel suspends or extinguishes rights, it is necessary to consider at what stage the promise is made. If the promise is made before any breach, then the estoppel will serve to suspend the rights of the promisor. But he may serve notice of his wish to return to his original contractual position. However, if there has been a breach of contract and the promisor accepts the breach, it is unlikely that he would be allowed to insist on remedies provided in the original terms of the contract. Viewed in this way, the promisor's right to insist on a particular remedy is extinguished.[6]

(b) *What interest is protected?*   A highly misleading view of reliance-based promissory liability is that merely the status quo interest is protected.[7] This would have the effect of returning the promisee to the position he was in before he relied on the words or conduct of the promisor. Contractual promises create legitimate expectations of performance, but other statements may also create expectations in the person to whom they are made. Similarly, a promise enforced by means of one of the varieties of estoppel is just as likely to have engendered expectations in the promisee as a promise supported by consideration. In this last respect, much difficulty is caused by the insistence that estoppel can be used only as a shield and not as a sword,[8] but it has been seen that there are critics of this view and that to a limited extent, estoppels can be used to enforce rights which would not otherwise have been enforceable.

Where new rights are created, it may be argued that these are expectations engendered in the promisee through an act of reasonable reliance upon the promise.[9] Certainly the dispute as to whether promissory estoppel serves to suspend or extinguish rights seems to be a dispute over what interest is protected. If the promisor's rights are extinguished, this points to the protection of the expectation interest. The promisee has relied upon the promise and has come to expect fulfilment of that promise. In such circumstances, the promisor may be prevented from going back on his promise even though there is no consideration. But, it must be emphasised that we are here concerned with an equitable remedy and not every act of reliance will lead to the enforcement of a promise. If an expectation is very clearly defined, it is likely that it will be enforced in full. For example, in *Pascoe v Turner*[10] a man promised the woman with whom he had cohabited that she could keep the house they had previously occupied. She was not wealthy but, in reliance on the promise, she spent over £200 of her own money on repairs and improvements to the property. The Court of Appeal held that the man should convey the legal estate in the property to the woman. An important consideration was the man's ruthlessness in trying to evict his partner. If the court had sought to protect her status quo interest only, this could have been done by granting her an irrevocable licence to occupy the house. However, the court went further in protecting the legitimate

---

4   Dugdale and Yates (1976) 39 MLR 680; Thompson (1983) 42 CLJ 257.
5   Thompson (1983) 42 CLJ 257 at 261.
6   Dugdale and Yates (1976) 39 MLR 680.
7   See Duncanson (1976) 39 MLR 268. See also Fried *Contract as Promise* (1981) p 25.
8   *Combe v Combe* [1951] 1 All ER 767.
9   Burrows (1983) 99 LQR 217 at 241–244; Thompson [1983] 42 CLJ 257 at 275–277.
10   [1979] 1 WLR 431.

expectation of the promisee that a legal interest in the property would be conveyed to her.

The result achieved in this case does not mean that a person's expectations will always be fully protected. It might not be equitable to go so far as to fully protect a person's expectation interest.[11] Thus, in appropriate circumstances, it may be that the promisee is confined to damages representing his expenditure incurred in reliance upon the promise.[12]

The controversy over the type of reliance required in cases of promissory estoppel also relates to the variety of interest protected. Those who take the view that reliance as opposed to detrimental reliance is required are in favour of the proposition that the expectation interest is protected. Thus in those cases of variation in which the promisee does no more than he is already bound to do, the promisee relies on the promise in the sense that he expects it to be fulfilled. In these cases, there is often no detriment but if the promise is enforced, it is because of a desire to satisfy the promisee's expectation of performance.

Conversely, a promise can be enforced so as to avoid the detriment the promisee would suffer as a result of an unconscionable departure from the terms of that promise rather than to make good the expectations engendered by the promise.[13] Where this is the case, the reason for the enforcement of the promise appears to be to remedy the denial of a future right, which is just as much part of the promisee's status quo interest as incurring expenditure in reliance on a promise. But the equitable nature of the remedy provided does not mean that any promise can be enforced in this way. It will only be enforced to the extent that this is necessary in avoiding possible detriment.

Similarly, in cases of proprietory estoppel, there is a requirement of detriment, and because the remedy provided is equitable, the impression may be given that more than the status quo interest is protected. In some instances, the promisee may recover no more than the expenditure he has incurred.[14] However, if the equities so demand, the promisee's expectations may be fully or partially satisfied.[15]

3.   UNDERPINNING VALUES AND POLICIES

The simple presence of a voluntary promise or act combined with reasonable reliance on the part of the promisee or the receipt of a benefit by the promisor does not provide the whole answer in determining when promissory exchange liability will arise. It is also necessary to consider the values and policies which assist in determining the liability of the parties. It is argued here that the most important considerations are those of fairness of exchange and co-operation. Moreover, where appropriate, regard may also be had to the public interest in the proper administration of civil justice.

(1)   FAIRNESS OF EXCHANGE

(i)   Value for money

It has been seen that the classical view of contractual relations was that provided consideration had some value in the eyes of the law, it did not matter that it was

---

11   See *Crabb v Arun District Council* [1976] Ch 179 at 199 (per SCARMAN LJ).

12   See *Dodsworth v Dodsworth* (1973) 228 Estates Gazette 1115.

13   *Waltons Stores (Interstate) Ltd v Maher* (1988) 76 ALR 513. See also *Hoffman v Red Owl Stores Inc* 133 NW 2d 267 (1965).

14   *Dillwyn v Llewelyn* (1862) 4 De GF & J 517; *Dodsworth v Dodsworth* (1973) 228 Estates Gazette 1115.

15   *Crabb v Arun District Council* [1976] Ch 179; *Pascoe v Turner* [1979] 1 WLR 431.

inadequate when compared to the value of the thing given in return. In other words, because of the principle of *caveat emptor* (let the buyer beware) the law was in no way concerned with value for money. This rule must also hold today in a considerable number of transactions since it cannot be possible to remove from individuals the right to decide what value they place upon an article or a service they might wish to acquire. Thus it is said that no bargain will be upset which is the ordinary interplay of (market) forces.[16] It follows that a person may be bound by a contract to grant a six-month option to purchase property where the agreed payment is only £1.[17] Moreover, a mistake in the valuation of the subject matter of a contract, provided it is not wrongly induced by the other party, will not be a ground for relief at common law,[18] although in equity the position is different where rescission of the contract is an available remedy, subject to the imposition of terms which attempt to do justice between the parties.[19] The adequacy principle is also preserved by the Unfair Terms in Consumer Contracts Regulations 1999[20] which make it clear that in a consumer contract, a term cannot be considered to be unfair where it concerns the adequacy of the price or remuneration, as against the goods or services which are the subject matter of the contract.[1] The only exception to this principle arises where the relevant term is not expressed in 'plain and intelligible language'. Thus, if a term in a consumer contract which relates to the adequacy of consideration is not comprehensible, the relevant term may be treated as unenforceable.[2]

Despite the general rule and because of a greater interest in the fairness of the exchange process, there are examples of a willingness to consider the adequacy of the consideration where this is justified. This may not always be done under the auspices of the doctrine of consideration. For example, an important factor in deciding whether goods are of satisfactory quality for the purposes of the Sale of Goods Act 1979, section 14(2A) is how much has been paid. The buyer can expect value for his money. The purchaser of a Rolls Royce can expect a better car for his money than the purchaser of a 'budget' family vehicle.[3]

Where a person seeks to avoid liability on a contract on the grounds of duress, undue influence or inequality of bargaining power, the court must consider whether the bargain is fair,[4] or whether the consideration is grossly unfair and inadequate.[5] Moreover, the general rule in equity is that 'equity will not assist a volunteer' with the effect that where a person has received property, for example, without making any payment, the court is not prepared to order specific performance or grant an injunction in favour of the volunteer. This will be especially the case where there is evidence of improper conduct on the part of the defendant or a mistake on the part of the plaintiff.[6]

In addition to these common law and equitable departures from the general rule on the adequacy of consideration, there are a number of statutory departures from the rule, particularly applicable to consumers entering into credit arrangements.[7] Furthermore,

---

16   *Lloyds Bank Ltd v Bundy* [1975] QB 326 at 336 (per Lord Denning MR).
17   *Mountford v Scott* [1975] Ch 258. See also *Chappell & Co Ltd v Nestlé Co Ltd* [1960] AC 87.
18   *Leaf v International Galleries* [1950] 2 KB 86.
19   *Grist v Bailey* [1967] Ch 532 and see ch 23.
20   SI 1999/2083.
1   Ibid reg 6(2)(b).
2   Ibid reg 6(2).
3   *Rogers v Parish Ltd* [1987] 2 All ER 232 at 237 (per Mustill LJ). See also *Shine v General Guarantee Corpn* [1988] 1 All ER 911.
4   *Pao On v Lau Yiu Long* [1980] AC 614 at 634 (per Lord Scarman).
5   *Lloyds Bank Ltd v Bundy* [1974] 3 All ER 757 at 765 (per Lord Denning MR). See ch 24.
6   *Falcke v Gray* (1859) 29 LJ Ch 28.
7   See in particular, the provisions of the Consumer Credit Act 1974, ss 137–139 in relation to the reopening of extortionate credit bargains.

in insolvency law, a court has a power to set aside certain transactions entered into at an undervalue, if made with a view to defrauding creditors.[8]

(ii)   Taking unfair advantage

The classical values of individualism and freedom of contract saw contracting parties as antagonistic defenders of their own position. Each party was encouraged to do the best for himself and the extent of legal intervention in dealings between individuals was minimal. In contrast, modern contractual relationships have a distinct co-operative base. It is no longer sufficient to leave it to the parties to decide what is best and basic guarantees of co-operation within the exchange relationship must be established.[9] In general terms this co-operation is provided for by the remedies for breach of contract and the ability of the parties to negotiate with each other against the background of those remedies.

A further feature of the value of social co-operation is that a contracting party should not be allowed to take unfair advantage of the person with whom he deals. The clearest manifestation of this is the growth of common law, equitable and statutory rules which recognise the inequality of bargaining power that exists between consumer purchasers and the businesses with whom they have to deal. In general, the common law has progressed on a piecemeal basis, through rules on misrepresentation,[10] negligent misstatement,[11] fraud, mistake,[12] duress and undue influence[13] and has found it unnecessary to develop any general principle of inequality of bargaining power or a duty to contract in good faith,[14] considering this to be the role of Parliament. Nevertheless, the way the various common law rules associated with fairness of exchange have developed shows an increasing awareness of the value of social co-operation. In particular, a person will not be allowed to take unfair advantage of a superior position and through the medium of rules on consideration, a person will not be allowed to benefit from what amounts to extortion.

Where a person is in a position of responsibility or influence, and he takes unfair advantage of that position, it is possible for existing common law rules on consideration to be used so as to reverse the effects of that advantage having been taken. For example, in *Warlow v Harrison*[15] an auction sale was advertised as being 'without reserve', indicating that lots would be sold to the highest bona fide bidder. The auctioneer allowed the owner to bid when it appeared that his property might be sold at a low price, but it was held that the auctioneer was in breach of a contract to sell to the highest bona fide bidder. In classical terms, it could hardly be said that there was a bargain under which good consideration had been given, but the policy basis of the decision is clear. A similar willingness to defeat unfair dealing can also be found where a person uses an illegitimate threat as a means of securing advantage. While cases of this kind should now be dealt with under rules on duress and associated developments in equity,[16] earlier cases confronted with this problem tended to deal with the issue by recourse to rules on consideration. In *D & C Builders Ltd v Rees*[17] the parties were in dispute over the value

---

8   Insolvency Act 1986, s 423.
9   See further the discussion of co-operation below.
10   See ch 10.
11   See ch 10.
12   See ch 23.
13   See ch 24.
14   *National Westminster Bank plc v Morgan* [1985] 1 All ER 821 at 830 (per LORD SCARMAN) and see ch 24.
15   (1859) 1 E & E 309.
16   See ch 24.
17   [1966] 2 QB 617.

of work done by the plaintiffs for the defendants. At the time, the plaintiffs were in some financial difficulty and the defendant's wife offered a sum considerably less than the £480 outstanding. In effect, she said 'accept £300 or nothing at all' and was said to have held the plaintiffs to ransom.[18] It was considered not to be inequitable for the creditor to insist on his strict legal rights and since there was no true accord under which the creditor voluntarily agreed to accept the lesser amount, the creditor could sue for the remaining balance.[19]

The same general approach has also been taken in relation to the performance of an existing duty as consideration and where appropriate, courts have refused to enforce the promise on the ground that to do so would be contrary to public policy. It has been seen that the classical view was that the performance of an existing duty is a sterile consideration for a promise since the promisee suffers no detriment[20] unless there is some additional performance over and above that required by the existing duty. But this disguises the policy issues which also justify the same result. The performer of the existing duty may have secured the promise of the other party by means of some illegitimate threat.

In *Stilk v Myrick*,[1] a promise by a ship's captain to share the wages of deserting crew members among those who remained loyal was held to be unenforceable for want of consideration since the crew did no more than they were already obliged to do. However, in *Harris v Watson*,[2] a similar promise was held to be unenforceable on the ground that the master might be held to ransom by the crew. These policy issues are identical to those now taken into account in determining whether a promise has been secured by way of a threat of economic duress.[3]

Where there is no suggestion of extortion, there now appears to be no objection to the enforcement of the promise given in return for the performance of an existing duty, provided it arises in the context of a contract to supply goods or services. Thus if the terms of a contract are renegotiated at the suggestion of the promisor and the renegotiation gives the promisor a benefit or allows him to obviate some disbenefit, the promise is enforceable provided there is nothing contrary to public policy in doing so.[4] Moreover, the question of consideration has been described as a mere formality in the light of the policy developments in respect of economic duress and that in the absence of a threat, there is no justification for failing to recognise the existence of some consideration even if it is insignificant or where there is no mutual bargain between the parties.[5]

The equities of the case are also an important consideration in cases of promissory and proprietary estoppel. It is clear that a court of equity will not grant relief to a person who has himself acted inequitably.[6] Thus it might be suggested that a promisor who changes his mind very quickly, seeking to return to the original terms of the contract, has acted inequitably. However, this will not always be the case. For example in *The Post Chaser*[7] a change of mind only two days after the promise to vary the terms of the

---

18 Ibid at 625 (per LORD DENNING MR).
19 Ibid.
20 *Stilk v Myrick* (1809) 2 Camp 317.
1 Ibid.
2 (1791) Peake 102.
3 See *North Ocean Shipping Co Ltd v Hyundai Construction Co Ltd, The Atlantic Baron*, [1979] QB 705 and see ch 24.
4 *Williams v Roffey Bros & Nicholls (Contractors) Ltd* [1990] 1 All ER 512 at 518 and 522 (per GLIDEWELL LJ) and at 524 (per RUSSELL LJ). See also *Ward v Byham* [1956] 1 WLR 496 at 498 (per DENNING LJ); *Williams v Williams* [1957] 1 WLR 148 at 150 (per DENNING LJ).
5 *Vantage Navigation Corpn v Suhail, The Alev* [1989] 1 Lloyd's Rep 138 at 147 (per HOBHOUSE J).
6 See eg *D & C Builders Ltd v Rees* [1966] 2 QB 617.
7 [1981] 2 Lloyd's Rep 695. See also *Transcatalana de Commercio SA v Incobrasa Industrial* [1995] 1 Lloyd's Rep 215.

original contract was considered not to be inequitable, since in the short intervening period, the promisee had not suffered any prejudice as he was still in the same position as he had been previously.

(2)   CO-OPERATION

It is essential that in determining whether promises or other statements give rise to contractual liability the value of co-operation is taken into account. Modern society does not consist of vast numbers of antagonistic, self-interested individuals, but instead works on the basis of co-operation and inter-dependence.[8] It is necessary that the law should encourage the acceptance of responsibility towards others and allow for trust in others. This requirement of respect for the interests of others makes contract law just as much a social device as is the law of tort and reflects the increased importance of acts of reasonable reliance on the words and deeds of others as forming the basis for contractual liability. Similar reasoning also explains the growth in the number of exceptions to the individualism-driven doctrine of privity of contract,[9] recognising the conferment of benefits on third parties.

The value of co-operation is also an influence on business relationships. Many modern commercial transactions are long-term ventures which involve complex inter-relationships in which it is essential for the parties to co-operate with one another in order to ensure satisfactory completion for the benefit of all concerned. In these long-term ventures, there are often gaps in the planning process and the whole arrangement is geared towards flexibility rather than certainty.[10] Often, in these relationships, the parties find it necessary to refer disputes to arbitration by a third party rather than contract in advance for a particular result. In these circumstances, co-operation between the parties is essential. There is also evidence that, in practice, insistence upon fine details in a business contract is bad for continuing business relations.[11] Moreover, there are other long term relationships, such as employment relations and collective bargaining arrangements which are so alien to the classical model of contract law that they have been hived off as distinct subject areas with their own rules.[12]

Examples of these long term arrangements involving a number of parties include construction contracts in which there will be a number of sub-contractors engaged by the main or general contractor to carry out specialist functions in relation to the construction of a building. Similarly, in the case of the international sale of goods, a series of related contracts will come into existence in order to ensure that the goods sold ultimately reach their destination.[13] Each party in this complex of relationships relies on the others to carry out their respective duties but to talk of each party entering into an exchange relationship would appear somewhat misleading. In such cases, it has been said that evidence of a high degree of co-operation between the parties and practical acts of collaboration will be sufficient evidence of an implied contract and will provide the necessary consideration.[14] Often the use of classical rules to deal with issues of co-operation seem strained, but it must be remembered that English law has committed

---

8   *Collins* p 48.
9   See Range of liability, discussed below.
10   See Macneil (1978) 72 NW U L R 854, 865.
11   See Macaulay 'Non-Contractual Relations in Business' (1963) 28 Am Sociological Rev 45 abridged in Aubert (ed) *Sociology of Law* (1969) pp 195–209; Beale and Dugdale (1975) BJL & S 45; Tillotson *Contract Law in Perspective* (2nd edn, 1986) ch 5.
12   Macneil (1978) 72 NW U L R 854, 885.
13   See *New Zealand Shipping Co Ltd v AM Satterthwaite & Co Ltd* [1975] AC 154.
14   *Mitsui & Co Ltd v Novorossiysk Shipping Co, The Gudermes* [1991] 1 Lloyd's Rep 456 at 469–470 (per HIRST J). See also *Cia Portorafti Commerciale SA v Ultramar Panama Inc, The Captain Gregos (No 2)* [1990] 2 Lloyd's Rep 395 at 403 (per BINGHAM LJ).

itself to a technical doctrine of contract and that sometimes it may be necessary to force the facts of a case to fit uneasily in the marked slots of offer, acceptance and consideration.[15]

The value of co-operation is particularly important in commercial relationships and, as a general rule, the courts find it relatively easy to discover the existence of a valuable consideration sufficient to allow the enforcement of serious promises made in a commercial environment. This is particularly evident in cases in which there appears to have been little enquiry as to whether there was any consideration for a particular promise, for example cases in which there is clearly an agreement between two business contracting parties. However the fact of an agreement may be regarded as consideration in its own right, since there will have been an exchange of promises of sorts. Thus in *Brandt v Liverpool, Brazil and River Plate Steam Navigation Co Ltd*[16] a contract was found to exist between the carrier of goods and the consignee of those goods based on the consignee's presentation of the bill of lading, despite the fact that all direct dealings were between the carrier and the consignor. What is important in this context is that the parties have entered into a commercial relationship demonstrating a serious intent to contract, and it is this intention which is likely to influence the court in treating the arrangement as binding on the basis that the parties have conferred rights and obligations upon each other which were intended to be obtained and accepted.[17] What must be remembered is that in a commercial context, it is usually more important not to allow an existing contractual relationship to fail and that it will be desirable, in most cases, to find a compromise solution so as to allow the relationship to continue rather than running to the courts with a view to litigation. If disputes can be settled by a co-operative compromise then the courts are likely to sanction such a settlement. Thus in *Williams v Roffey* it was a sensible reaction to treat as consideration for the main contractor's promise to make an additional payment, the subcontractor's performance of his existing obligations owed to the main contractor.

(3)   ADMINISTRATION OF JUSTICE

A further policy issue which may affect the enforceability of a promise is the effect that enforcement would have on the proper administration of justice. For example, if the essence of the agreement is to obstruct proceedings in such a way as to adversely affect the way in which justice is administered, it may be an illegal contract.[18] Moreover, an agreement with one party to proceedings not to give evidence for another party may not be in the public interest.[19] A similar result can also be achieved through the use of rules on consideration. For example, if a witness is promised payment in return for giving testimony, it may be said that he has given no consideration for the promise to pay, since he has done no more than he is legally obliged to do.[20] However, the policy argument in such a case is plain to see. It would be contrary to public policy to allow a person to set his price for appearing as a witness.

The proper administration of justice may also be a factor in cases where there has been a promise to abandon a claim. Where a person does make such a promise and he is aware of the value of the claim he might have against the other party, there should be little problem in treating the promise of abandonment as consideration since there is a detriment to the promisee in giving up his claim and a benefit to the other party in

15   *New Zealand Shipping Co Ltd v AM Satterthwaite & Co Ltd* [1975] AC 154 at 167 (per LORD WILBERFORCE).
16   [1924] 1 KB 575.
17   See *The Aramis* [1989] 1 Lloyd's Rep 213 at 225 (per BINGHAM LJ).
18   *Elliott v Richardson* (1870) LR 5 CP 744.
19   *Harmony Shipping Co SA v Saudi Europe Line Ltd* [1979] 1 WLR 1380.
20   *Collins v Godefroy* (1831) 1 B & Ad 950.

knowing that the claim has been abandoned.[1] In contrast, in cases in which a claim is known to be bad in law, it can be said that the promisee suffers no detriment in promising to give up that claim. Moreover, it has also been said that it is *contra bonos mores* and certainly contrary to principles of natural justice that a man should institute proceedings against another when he is conscious that he has no good cause of action.[2]

A second policy issue related to the administration of justice is the 'floodgates' issue. This is particularly important in the context of domestic and social arrangements. If the arrangement is entirely trivial, it may be declared that there is no intention to create legal relations. However, there is almost certainly an unstated fear that to render such arrangements enforceable would result in a deluge of minor claims which would over-stretch the courts, with a corresponding adverse effect on the proper administration of justice. For example, in *Balfour v Balfour*,[3] the court was concerned with the enforceability of a promise by one spouse to the other and made within the marriage, to pay living expenses. It was held that there was no intention to create legal relations, but that view disguises the policy basis of the decision, namely that if agreements of this kind were to result in binding obligations, the small courts of the country would have to be multiplied one hundred fold.[4] It follows that the purpose of the doctrine of intention to create legal relations, in this context, is to keep the law of contract in its place, namely in the commercial sphere. Only in rare instances where, as a matter of policy, the court considers contractual rules to have a useful role to play will a domestic arrangement be held to create a legally binding relationship.[5]

4.   THE RANGE OF PROMISSORY EXCHANGE LIABILITY

(1)   INTRODUCTION

In an action on a contract, the doctrine of privity of contract states that only the parties to a contract can sue or be sued. The difficulty is to determine who is a party to the contract. Moreover, following the enactment of the Contracts (Rights of Third Parties) Act 1999, there are now limited circumstances in which a contract between A and B may be enforced by a third party, C, for whose benefit the contract was expressly or impliedly made.

A strict application of the doctrine of privity ignores the economic problem of externalities,[6] namely that an arrangement between two people can affect a third party. Moreover, the doctrine, having been developed in the nineteenth century, is heavily influenced by market individualist theory, assuming that contracts are essentially bilateral arrangements. But this tends to ignore the value of co-operation which engenders a greater respect for the interests of others, including third parties. For this reason, various methods have been adopted to circumvent the unfortunate effects of a strict application of the doctrine and in other quarters the doctrine has been attacked on the basis that there is no doctrinal, logical or other policy reason to justify its existence.[7] To say that a person cannot sue on a contract because he could not be sued is also misleading, since this is precisely the result achieved in cases involving unilateral contracts.

---

1   See *Bank of Credit and Commerce International SA v Ali* [1999] 2 All ER 1005.
2   *Wade v Simeon* (1846) 2 CB 548 at 564 (per TINDAL CJ).
3   [1919] 2 KB 571.
4   Ibid at 579 (per ATKIN LJ).
5   See Hedley (1985) 5 OJLS 391.
6   See ch 2.
7   *Darlington Borough Council v Wiltshier Northern Ltd* [1995] 1 WLR 68 at 76 (per STEYN LJ).

In other parts of the common law world, the need to reflect the value of co-operation in commercial dealings has also led to a number of head-on conflicts with the basic rule of privity. This has been particularly the case in relation to insurance arrangements made by, for example, a main building contractor wishing to extend the benefit of the insurance policy to his subcontractors[8] and cases in which it is intended that nominated third parties should be protected by an exemption clause in a contract between two other related parties, such as is often the case where goods subject to a contract of sale are stored in a warehouse[9] or are transported to their ultimate destination by a carrier.[10] In each of these cases, the contractual dealings of a third party may be based on the assumption that there is a provision in a contract between two other parties which is intended to protect him or provide him with some benefit. As a result of this the third party may be able to adjust his own contractual dealings, for example, by reducing the price he charges for his services, on the assumption that he is to be benefited in some other way by co-operation with the other parties to a related contract. As will be seen below, some of these relationships, although not all, will be covered by the provisions of the Contracts (Rights of Third Parties) Act 1999 and may more easily be regarded as giving rise to enforceable contractual rights in favour of a third party.

Numerous statutory provisions stand as outright exceptions to the doctrine. All of these can be treated as having been motivated by positive policy considerations in favour of extending the benefit of a contract to a reasonably foreseeable plaintiff. Also, in some instances, a third party may be subject to the burden of a contract made between others, for reasons of public policy.

(2)   PRIVITY OF CONTRACT – THE GENERAL RULE

The general rule stipulates that a person who is not a party to the contract cannot sue on the contract or be subject to the obligations imposed by the contract. The rule as stated in *Price v Easton*[11] was couched in terms of two principles, namely that there is no privity between a contracting party and a third party,[12] and that the third party does not give any consideration for the promise.[13] It may be objected that the confusion of the doctrines of privity and consideration is unfortunate. The doctrine of consideration is concerned with those promises the law is prepared to enforce, whereas the doctrine of privity of contract is concerned with the range of contractual liability.[14] Nevertheless there are close affinities between the two doctrines, since in classical terms, if no consideration has moved from the promisee, it is difficult to say that he is a party to the alleged bargain. However, the fact that there is such a close relationship between the doctrine of privity and the rule that consideration should move from the promisee could give rise to difficulty. It will be seen below that the Contracts (Rights of Third Parties) Act 1999 creates an exception whereby a third party may be given the right to enforce a term of a contract between two other parties where that term expressly or by implication is intended to benefit the third party. But, on the face of it, this merely relaxes the rules on privity of contract and not those relating to consideration. The answer to this problem seems to turn on the reasoning employed by the Law Commission[15] on whose report the provisions of the 1999 Act are based. The Law

8   See *Trident General Insurance Co Ltd v McNiece Bros Pty Ltd* (1988) 165 CLR 107.
9   See *London Drugs Ltd v Kuehne and Nagel International Ltd* [1993] 1 WWR 1.
10   See *New Zealand Shipping Co Ltd v AM Satterthwaite & Co Ltd, The Eurymedon* [1975] AC 154.
11   (1833) 4 B & Ad 433. See also *Tweddle v Atkinson* (1861) 1 B & S 393.
12   Ibid at 434 (per LITTLEDALE J).
13   Ibid (per Lord DENMAN CJ).
14   See *Collins* p 289.
15   *Privity of Contract: Contracts for the Benefit of Third Parties,* Law Comm No 242, Cm 3329, 1996.

Commission expressed the view that the consideration question related only to the relationship between the original parties to the contract and should not apply also to the third party, since this would only raise questions of enforceability and would have no bearing on whether or not there was a bargain.[16] Had the reasoning in the report stopped there, there would have been little difficulty. However, in a later section of the report there are further views that the 1999 Act may have the effect of relaxing rules on consideration in certain respects.[17] In particular this view was arrived at on the ground that the effect of the 1999 Act will be to treat a third party more favourably than the way in which the law has hitherto treated a gratuitous promisee. Neither of these provides consideration, yet the former may be able to enforce the terms of a contract made for his benefit, but the latter will not be in a position to enforce a promise made to him due to want of consideration. This prompted the Law Commission to the view that rules on consideration might have become relaxed. However, this ignores the earlier reasoning of the Law Commission that rules on privity are not concerned with the question of whether there is an enforceable bargain. In the case of a gratuitous promisee there is no bargain, whereas in the case of a third party there will be an enforceable bargain between the two contracting parties and all the 1999 Act will do is to give the third party a right to enforce those terms expressed to be for his benefit.

For good reasons, the rule has been subject to much hostile criticism, but it was confirmed as a rule of English law by the House of Lords in *Dunlop Pneumatic Tyre Co Ltd v Selfridge & Co Ltd*,[18] in which it was held that English law knows nothing of a *jus quaesitum tertio* arising by way of contract.[19] According to this general rule, contractual provisions cannot be enforced for the benefit of a third party, even if it is abundantly clear, as in *Dunlop*, that the stipulation is intended for the benefit of that third party. However, what was said in *Dunlop* about privity of contract is strictly obiter, as the *ratio* of the decision is based on the rule that consideration must move from the promisee.

(i)   The parties to the agreement

In classical terms, the parties to a contract are the two parties to a bilateral arrangement whose communications with each other form the basis of the contract. If a third party were allowed to sue on the contract, this would serve to fetter the contracting parties' ability to vary or rescind an agreement.[20] However, difficulties may arise where there is a network of related contractual arrangements involving more than two parties.[1] In these circumstances the need for co-operation between the various parties and regard for the interests of others is much greater and it becomes more difficult to justify the strict privity approach.

The strict effects of the doctrine can be avoided if communications between the plaintiff and defendant form the basis of a collateral contract between them. Thus if a manufacturer warrants the suitability of a product which a consumer later purchases from a retail supplier, the consumer will have recourse to the manufacturer should the product prove to be qualitatively defective.[2] The same device may also be employed in relation to a contract for the provision of services, where the service is clearly provided

---

16   See generally the discussion in part VI of the report.
17   See the report, para 6.13.
18   [1915] AC 847. See also *Beswick v Beswick* [1968] AC 58 and *The Pioneer Container* [1994] 2 AC 324 at 335.
19   Ibid at 853 (per LORD HALDANE).
20   *Re Schebsman* [1944] Ch 83.
1   See Adams & Brownsword (1990) 10 Legal Studies 12.
2   *Shanklin Pier Ltd v Detel Products Ltd* [1951] 2 KB 854; *Wells (Merstham) Ltd v Buckland Sand and Silica Ltd* [1965] 2 QB 170. See also *Andrews v Hopkinson* [1957] 1 QB 229 and see ch 25.

for the benefit of a third party.[3] The relationship which arises in these circumstances is triangular, in the sense that the manufacturer contracts with the supplier of the product and the supplier contracts with the consumer. What the court does is to draw the third line of the triangle by finding a collateral contract between the manufacturer and the consumer. The relationship seems remarkably similar to that which arose in *Junior Books Ltd v Veitchi Co Ltd*,[4] in which the same triangle joined the owner, the main contractor and the sub-contractor. This serves to illustrate the view that the third party is often a reasonably foreseeable plaintiff. Similar reasoning also seems to apply to the use of a credit card by a consumer. In *Re Charge Card Services Ltd*[5] it was held that when a consumer uses a credit card as the means of payment for goods or services, in effect, three separate bilateral contracts come into existence. First there is the contract of supply; secondly there was a contract of debt under which the consumer undertook to repay the amount borrowed from the credit card company; and lastly, there was a contract between the credit card company and the goods or service supplier under which the credit card company undertook to pay the supplier in respect of the subject matter of the contract. On this reasoning, where the credit card company became insolvent, customers who had bought goods or services were not liable for the price of the goods and services purchased by them, since this was a matter which related to the contract between the suppliers and the credit card company.

A number of these collateral contract cases may well be covered by the provisions of the Contracts (Rights of Third Parties) Act 1999,[6] since in many such cases there will be an express or implied intention to confer a contractual right on a third party. For example in cases like *Charnock v Liverpool Corporation* it is relatively easy to see that the contractual arrangements between the insurance company and the garage effecting repairs on the plaintiff's car were intended to confer a right on the plaintiff as owner of the car.

A person may be deemed to contract on behalf of others, for example, where one member of a family books a ferry crossing on behalf of himself and his family, all members of the family are contracting parties.[7] Likewise, a meal booked at a restaurant by one person for a large group is said to create a contract between the restaurateur and each member of the group.[8] Although this does raise the problem of how a court would approach the case if one member of the dinner party was a young child and might not be contractually capable. It seems likely that the court might still be prepared to overcome the doctrine of privity by treating the 'host' as having contracted on behalf of everyone in the group. For example, it has been held that a railway ticket bought by the mother of a child in arms was purchased on behalf of the mother and the child.[9]

(ii)   The parties to the consideration

As the doctrine of privity of contract and the rule that consideration should move from the promisee appear to achieve the same result, it has been argued that they amount to the same rule.[10] The argument is that a contract is a bargain, and that a person who is not a party to the bargain is not a party to the contract. Accordingly, it has been held that it would be a monstrous proposition to say that a person was a party to a contract

3   *Charnock v Liverpool Corpn* [1968] 3 All ER 473 and see ch 26.
4   [1983] 1 AC 520.
5   [1987] Ch 150.
6   Under s 1(1)(b).
7   *Daly v General Steam Navigation Co Ltd, The Dragon* [1980] 2 Lloyd's Rep 415.
8   *Lockett v A & M Charles Ltd* [1938] 4 All ER 170. See also ch 25.
9   *Austin v Great Western Rly Co* (1867) 2 QB 442.
10   See Furmston (1960) 23 MLR 373 at 382–384. Cf *Kepong Prospecting Ltd v Schmidt* [1968] AC 810.

for the purposes of suing on it but not a party to it for the purpose of being sued.[11] This presents two reasons for denying the third party action. First, there is a lack of reciprocity[12] and secondly the third party might receive something for nothing and should be treated as if he were a gratuitous beneficiary. However, in this type of case, there is a bargained for exchange between the two contracting parties made with the object of benefiting the third party on which that third party has probably relied.[13] The effect of the doctrine, then, is to allow a person to snap his fingers at a bargain deliberately made which is not unfair and in which the third party has a legitimate interest.[14] Moreover, the promisor has broken his promise, albeit to the other contracting party, and it seems only fair that he should pay for the damaged expectations of the third party. If in this type of case, the third party cannot enforce a promise made for his own benefit, one ends up with the equally monstrous result that the only person with a valid claim has suffered no loss and the person who has suffered has no valid claim.[15]

That the doctrines of consideration and privity are separate is illustrated in cases where a person is a contracting party and has provided no consideration. For these purposes, it seems that it is possible to regard consideration as being provided by one person on his own and a third party's behalf, so that the third party may sue on that contract.[16]

(iii)   The operation of the doctrine of privity

The general effect of the doctrine is that a third party, subject to exceptions, is not able to enforce a contract made for his benefit, and that a third party is not subject to burdens arising out of a contract between others. But this does not mean that the contract is ineffective as between the promisor and the promisee. Some of the remedies available to the promisee may serve to assist the third party for whose benefit the contract is made. This possibility means that the relationship between the third party and the promisee is crucial, since the third party may want the promisee to take action on his behalf.

(a) *The promisee's action to compel performance*   The promisee may be able to secure performance of the promisor's obligations through a decree of specific performance, by obtaining an injunction or by bringing an action for an agreed sum.[17]

In cases where a contract is intended to benefit a third party, an award of damages to the promisee might be nominal only, since the actual loss to the promisee is likely to be negligible.[18] However a contrary view has been expressed where the promisee would be in a position in which he would have to make good the failure of the promisor to fulfil his promise. In this last case, substantial damages could be awarded.[19] Moreover, it is possible that the promisor might be unjustly enriched by his failure to confer the agreed benefit on the third party,[20] in which case there could be an action for restitution.[1] But the award of a decree of specific performance would also reverse the

11   *Tweddle v Atkinson* (1861) 1 B & S 393 at 398 (per CROMPTON J).
12   But in other areas the lack of reciprocity argument is wearing thin: *Price v Strange* [1978] Ch 337.
13   Cf *Shadwell v Shadwell* (1860) 9 CBNS 159 at 174 (per ERLE CJ).
14   *Dunlop Pneumatic Tyre Co Ltd v Selfridge & Co Ltd* [1915] AC 847 at 855 (per LORD DUNEDIN). See also Law Revision Committee 6th Interim Report (1937) Cmnd 5449.
15   *Ross v Caunters* [1979] 3 All ER 580 at 583 (per MEGARRY VC).
16   *Coulls v Bagot's Executor and Trustee Co Ltd* (1967) 119 CLR 460.
17   See ch 14.
18   *Beswick v Beswick* [1968] AC 58 at 102 (per LORD UPJOHN).
19   Ibid at 88 (per LORD PEARCE).
20   *Trident General Insurance Co Ltd v McNiece Bros Pty Ltd* (1988) 165 CLR 107 at 175–176 (per GAUDRON J).
1   Whether this is consistent with general principles of unjust enrichment is doubtful. See ch 11.

enrichment and enforce the promise in favour of the third party. In *Beswick v Beswick*,[2] it was agreed that a business would be sold to the appellant by his uncle, provided the appellant would pay an annuity to his aunt and uncle during their joint lives. After the uncle died, the appellant refused to make further payments to the aunt. It was held that, while the aunt could not enforce payment in her personal capacity, she could enforce the promise in her capacity as the administratrix of her deceased husband's estate. Accordingly, a decree of specific performance was ordered.

Specific performance may not always be available in these situations, as, generally, the bars to such an award will still apply. However, it has been suggested that the adequacy of damages rule might not be relevant where enforcement in favour of a third party is considered appropriate.[3] It is highly unlikely, however, that the remedy would be granted where the promisor agrees to provide a service for the benefit of the third party.

If specific performance is not available and the promisor is in breach of a negative stipulation, the court may be able to grant an injunction. For example, if A breaks a promise to B that he will not compete in business with T the court may grant an injunction to enforce A's promise. Similarly, if A breaks a promise to B that he will not sue T, B may be joined as a party to the action between A and T to enforce A's promise, provided B has a sufficient interest in the enforcement of A's promise.[4] This requirement is satisfied if, as a result of A's breach, B would be exposed to legal liability to T. However, it appears that the requirement of sufficient interest may be dispensed with or ignored in appropriate cases. In *Snelling v John G Snelling Ltd*,[5] three brothers who were directors of a family business lent money to the company on condition that should any of them resign his directorship, he would forfeit his right to recover the loan from the company. One of the brothers did resign, and sought to recover the amount of his loan. The other brothers were joined as defendants and were able to obtain a stay of proceedings against the company. The plaintiff's action was dismissed, despite the fact that the defendant brothers appeared not to be under any legal liability to the company if the money lent by the plaintiff were to be recovered. However, the reasoning in this case seems to accord with the sentiment implied in *Beswick v Beswick* that, where the promisee does take steps to enforce a contract on behalf of a third party, such remedy as is appropriate should be granted.

A third method of compelling the promisor's performance is an action for an agreed sum. The difficulty with this action is that it is brought by the promisee and it may be an objection that the promisor should not be bound to pay the promisee when he has agreed to pay the third party only.[6] However, where the agreed sum is payable to the third party, it may be possible for payment to be enforced by means of a decree of specific performance.[7] This would remain the case, despite the fact that an action for the agreed sum itself would be more appropriate in an action between the promisee and the promisor.

(b) *The promisee's action for damages*   The compensatory principle which applies to an action for damages means that the promisee can normally recover only in respect of his own losses. If the contract is intended wholly for the benefit of a third party, it is possible that the promisee's loss will be nominal only. If, for some reason, the promisee also suffers loss as a result of the failure to perform, substantial damages may be awarded, but the damages are intended to compensate the promisee, not the third party.

---

2   [1968] AC 58.
3   Ibid at 88 (per LORD PEARCE).
4   *Gore v Van der Lann* [1967] 2 QB 31.
5   [1973] QB 87.
6   See *Coulls v Bagot's Executor and Trustee Co Ltd* [1967] ALR 385.
7   See *Gurtner v Circuit* [1968] 2 QB 587.

If the loss suffered by the third party is treated as loss incurred by the promisee it may be recoverable. For example, in *Jackson v Horizon Holidays Ltd*,[8] damages for disappointment suffered by an entire family following a disastrous holiday were recoverable by the plaintiff. It was assumed that the plaintiff's wife and children were not parties to the contract,[9] but damages were awarded on the basis that the distress suffered by the plaintiff was exacerbated by witnessing the distress of his wife and children,[10] or because the plaintiff had contracted for the benefit of the entire family.[11] The latter aspect of the decision was based on a *dictum* relevant only to cases in which the contract creates a trust in favour of a third party.[12]

The same matter was reconsidered by the House of Lords in *Woodar Investment Development Ltd v Wimpey Construction (UK) Ltd*.[13] The plaintiffs agreed to sell land to the defendants for £850,000 under terms which required the defendants to pay £150,000 to a third party. The plaintiffs claimed damages for a repudiation when the defendants failed to proceed with the contract. On the issue of privity it was said obiter that LORD DENNING's judgment in *Jackson* was incorrect, although it was thought that the right result might have been achieved by the other members of the court. The issue of damages in *Woodar* was said to be one of great difficulty, but it has been suggested that whether the defendant would have to compensate the plaintiff in respect of the third party's loss would depend on whether the plaintiff was under a legal obligation to ensure that the third party was paid.[14] Although the implication behind the decision in *Woodar* is that, as a general rule, the promisee will not be able to recover damages on behalf of the third party. However, to that general rule there are a number of admitted exceptions, which have recently been interpreted in such a way as to open up greater possibilities for the recovery of damages on behalf of a third party.

First, there is an accepted rule that a trustee may recover substantial damages suffered by the *cestui que trust*.[15] Alternatively, the law of agency contains a clear principle to the effect that an agent may recover substantial damages on behalf of an undisclosed principal on whose behalf he is acting with authority.[16] Furthermore, it has been held that a local authority, in certain circumstances, may recover damages on behalf of their residents, where the only persons to have suffered loss are the residents rather than the local authority.[17] Perhaps the most important exception relates to the right of a shipper of goods to recover substantial damages on behalf of a person to whom those goods have been sold.[18] However, for this exception to apply, the buyer of the goods must not have acquired the right to sue the carrier under the terms of the Carriage of Goods by Sea Act 1992, section 2(4), since in this last case, the buyer will have an independent contractual right not dependent on the ability of the seller to recover damages on his behalf.[19]

More recently, the list of exceptions to the rule appears to have been extended. In *Linden Gardens Trust Ltd v Lenesta Sludge Disposals Ltd*[20] a building contract entered into

---

8   [1975] 1 WLR 1468.
9   Cf *Daly v General Steam Navigation Co Ltd, The Dragon* [1980] 2 Lloyd's Rep 415.
10   [1975] 1 WLR 1468 at 1474 (per JAMES LJ).
11   Ibid (per LORD DENNING MR).
12   *Lloyds' v Harper* (1880) 16 Ch D 290 at 331 (per LUSH LJ). See also *Beswick v Beswick* [1968] AC 58 at 88 (per LORD PEARCE) and *Coulls v Bagot's Executor and Trustee Co Ltd* [1967] ALR 385.
13   [1980] 1 WLR 277. See also ch 14.
14   *Treitel* pp 549–550.
15   See below.
16   See below.
17   *St Albans City and District Council v International Computers Ltd* [1996] 4 All ER 481.
18   *Dunlop v Lambert* (1839) 6 Cl & Fin 600.
19   *The Albazero* [1977] AC 774.
20   [1994] 1 AC 85.

between parties who described themselves as employer and contractor required the contractor to develop a site of shops, offices and flats. Later the site, but not the benefit of the contract, was transferred by the employer to a third party, who discovered that the work done by the contractor was defective and required a considerable amount of remedial work. Some of these defects also came into existence after transfer of the site. The employer sued the contractor, but the latter argued that since only the third party had suffered loss, the employer was not entitled to substantial damages. LORD GRIFFITHS considered that the employer had suffered loss since he was required to spend money in order to obtain the benefit he had expected to receive from the contractor.[1] Although he added, as a rider, that the court will want to be satisfied that the repairs in respect of which substantial damages are given have been or are likely to be carried out.[2] The majority in *Lenesta* based their reasoning on a slightly narrower ground, namely that the loss was suffered by the third party rather than the employer, but that the case fell within the reasoning employed in *Dunlop v Lambert*. On this basis, it became necessary to ask whether property and risk had passed to the third party purchaser and it was essential that the third party had acquired no independent contractual rights of his own. In these circumstances, it is reasonable to assume that the parties to the initial contract of carriage have made that contract with the intention of benefiting all third parties who might be expected to acquire an interest in the goods. Similarly, in *Lenesta,* it is reasonable to assume that both the employer and the contractor had intended that the site be sold off to third parties when it was ready to be occupied.

Since *Lenesta* there have been further decisions which appear to take the exception still further. In *Darlington BC v Wiltshier Northern Ltd*[3] a local authority intended to develop land which it already owned, but was not in a position to borrow money due to government restrictions on local authority spending. As a result of this the council entered into two parallel agreements, namely, a building contract under which a bank prepared to lend the required money was the employer and the defendants were the building contractors. Alongside this, there was a second contract under which the bank agreed to procure the building, to pay all amounts due under the building contract and to assign to the council the benefit of any rights they had against the defendant. This contract also provided that the bank would not be liable to the council for any incompleteness in the building work. Since this second contract operated by way of an assignment, the clause relating to incompleteness of the building work gave rise to difficulties. Normally, the rule is that an assignee will not be allowed to recover any more than the assignor could have done. As a result, it was argued on behalf of the builders that the council could not sue in respect of incompleteness since the bank was not liable for any incompleteness. The Court of Appeal, however, rejected this argument holding that the bank could have recovered substantial damages from the defendants, apparently on the basis that this case was covered by the principle established by *Dunlop v Lambert* and extended to contracts of all kinds in *Lenesta*. However, it would appear that there are differences between *Darlington BC v Wiltshier* since in the earlier cases it was assumed to be a requirement that the original contracting parties always envisaged a transfer of property in the thing which was the main subject matter of the contract. In contrast, in the *Darlington* case ownership of the land remained with the council throughout. STEYN LJ's reasoning in this case seems to be based more on pragmatic grounds than on a strict application of legal principle, since he makes the point that but for an application of the principle in *Lenesta* an otherwise meritorious claim would have

1   Ibid at 97.
2   Ibid. But cf contra *Darlington Borough Council v Wiltshier Northern Ltd* [1995] 1 WLR 68.
3   [1995] 1 WLR 68. See also *Alfred McAlpine Construction Ltd v Panatown Ltd* (1998) 58 Con LR 46.

disappeared down a legal black hole,[4] but this was a black hole created by the parties themselves due to the clause relieving the bank of any liability for incompleteness.

(c) *The relations between third party and promisee.*   It is clear that in certain circumstances, the promisee may be able to enforce the contract on behalf of the third party, or possibly recover damages in respect of the third party's loss. Accordingly, the relations between the two are important. No problem arose in *Beswick v Beswick*,[5] since the promisee and the third party were the same person. However, the issue may arise whether the third party can require the promisee to seek an order for specific performance or an injunction, or whether he can require the promisee to hand over the damages he has been awarded. In the Court of Appeal in *Beswick v Beswick*,[6] LORD DENNING suggested that it might be possible for the third party to sue the promisor and join the promisee as co-defendant.[7] However, this was denied by the other members of the Court of Appeal. So far as damages are concerned, if they are recoverable, the promisee would appear to hold them as money had and received for the use of the third party.[8] Accordingly, they may be recovered in a restitutionary action. Similarly, in the growing number of cases in which it has been recognised that a promisee may sue for substantial damages on behalf of a third party, it seems to be well established that what is received is held by the promisee on trust for the benefit of the third party.[9]

(3)   CIRCUMVENTION OF THE DOCTRINE OF PRIVITY OF CONTRACT

The doctrine of privity merely provides that a third party cannot enforce benefits or be subject to burdens arising under a contract to which he is not a party. Accordingly, rights may be conferred on a third party otherwise than under a contract. For example, such rights and burdens may arise by way of tort, trust, agency or assignment.

(i)   Circumvention of the doctrine of privity: benefits

In finding ways of conferring benefits on a third party, thereby developing means of avoiding the harsher effects of the doctrine of privity, it is necessary to consider the different issues which will arise. Two main questions need to be considered where there is a contract between A and B under which T seeks rights:
(1)   Can T enforce the terms of a contract between A and B which is expressed to be for the benefit of T?
(2)   Can T claim to set up a defence contained in the contract between A and B in an action brought against him by A or B?

(a) *The tort of negligence*   A contract between A and B may also impose on the promisor a duty to take care in relation to a third party. For example, a contract for the supply of a service may require the supplier to exercise reasonable care in relation to a third party. Thus a contract between a main building contractor and a sub-contractor may require the sub-contractor to exercise reasonable care in relation to the main contractor's client.[10]

---

4   Ibid at 79.
5   [1968] AC 58.
6   [1966] Ch 538.
7   Ibid at 557.
8   *Jackson v Horizon Holidays Ltd* [1975] 1 WLR 1468 at 1473 (per LORD DENNING MR).
9   *The Albazero* [1977] AC 774 at 845; *Linden Gardens Trust Ltd v Lenesta Sludge Disposals Ltd* [1994] 1 AC 85.
10   *Junior Books Ltd v Veitchi Co Ltd* [1983] 1 AC 520.

In order for a duty of care to be owed, it is necessary that the harm suffered by the third party is reasonably foreseeable. This will require a close relationship of proximity between the promisor and the third party.[11] However, it was noted in *Balsamo v Medici*[12] that unless certain limits are placed upon the principle established in *Junior Books*, the effect would be to abrogate the concept of privity of contract.

The difficulty with duties of care arising in this context is that they are usually concerned with the issue of economic loss, in the form of diminution in the value of a defective building which is said to be rarely recoverable in a tortious action.[13] Moreover, even where the third party suffers physical harm to his property, he might not be able to maintain an action against the promisor where the third party is not the legal owner or a person with possessory title to the goods damaged.[14]

In consequence of the relationship between tortious rules on proximity and the various methods of circumventing the doctrine of privity of contract, it may be argued that there is a common law doctrine of the foreseeable plaintiff.[15] It is established that contractual and tortious duties may exist concurrently. Accordingly, the recipient of a defective product or service may proceed against his supplier in contract or in tort where there has been a failure to exercise reasonable care. Cases in which there is said to be a collateral contract can be compared with cases of negligence in which three or more parties are closely linked by a series of contracts.[16] Unpaid-for negligent advice is normally actionable in tort, but it is possible for such a case to give rise to a contractual action if the court is prepared to manufacture a consideration for the promise to exercise reasonable care. Furthermore, commercial practice may dictate that a person who is not directly linked to another by means of a contract may still acquire contractual rights. For example, a banker is liable to the seller of goods under a commercial credit.

In the area of negligent advice, it is well established that a duty of care may be owed by the giver of the advice under the principles set out in *Hedley Byrne & Co Ltd v Heller & Partners Ltd*[17] as qualified by a number of later decisions of the House of Lords. The basis of the tortious liability imposed in such cases is largely that the claimant has reasonably relied upon the advice given by the defendant, who has knowledge that the advice will be relied upon; that there is a sufficiently close relationship of proximity between the parties; that it is just and reasonable to impose a duty of care; and in appropriate circumstances there may be an additional requirement that the defendant should have voluntarily assumed responsibility for the accuracy of his statement by freely entering into the relationship with the claimant.[18] Thus in *White v Jones*[19] a solicitor undertook to advise his client on the preparation of an effective will which was intended to confer a benefit on the plaintiff, with whom the solicitor had no contractual relationship. Because of this state of affairs, it was clear that there was no privity of contract as between the solicitor and the intended beneficiaries, but because the solicitor had voluntarily entered into a relationship with the client, he had undertaken obligations to the intended beneficiaries which lay in the tort of negligence, on the basis that they had reasonably relied upon him to advise his client properly and that the solicitor could be taken to be aware of that reliance; that they might foreseeably suffer loss if he were not

11   See chs 8 and 10.
12   [1984] 2 All ER 304 at 311 (per WALTON J).
13   See *Murphy v Brentwood District Council* [1990] 2 All ER 908; *D & F Estates Ltd v Church Comrs for England* [1988] 2 All ER 992.
14   *Leigh and Sillivan Ltd v Aliakmon Shipping Co Ltd* [1986] 2 All ER 145. But cf Carriage of Goods by Sea Act 1992, s 2(4).
15   See *Collins* pp 119–127.
16   *Charnock v Liverpool Corpn* [1968] 3 All ER 473; *Junior Books Ltd v Veitchi Co Ltd* [1983] 1 AC 520.
17   [1964] AC 465.
18   For further discussion of the parameters of this duty of care see ch 10.
19   [1995] 1 All ER 691. See also *Carr-Glynn v Frearsons* [1998] 4 All ER 225.

to give advice as would be expected of a reasonable solicitor; and that it was just and reasonable to impose liability in the circumstances. Earlier case law[20] had raised the question whether voluntary assumption of responsibility was a proper issue to raise in the context of tortious duties of care, since the accepted view is that tortious duties are imposed by law rather than by virtue of any voluntary acceptance of responsibility towards the plaintiff. However, this was answered in *White v Jones* by holding that the defendant did not voluntarily assume the duty of care, since this was imposed by law, but he did voluntarily enter into a relationship with his client and this led to the acceptance of a responsibility towards persons who might be forseeably affected by his actions or omissions. What can be seen from this is that, in appropriate circumstances, a person who gives advice may owe a duty of care to a third party, despite the fact that there is no contractual connection with that person, but it is important to empasise that the duty lies in tort rather than in contract. Moreover, even following the introduction of new means of side-stepping the doctrine of privity in the Contracts (Rights of Third Parties) Act 1999, cases such as *White v Jones* will not come to be regarded as actions in contract, since it must be the contract betwen the relevant contracting parties which expressly or impliedly confers a benefit on the third party, and in *White v Jones* it was the will rather than the contract which conferred the relevant benefit.

In other circumstances, it has become clear that the necessary ingredients of a tortious duty of care may not be satisfied where advice has been given negligently, although the reason for this may be policy driven. In particular, it is necessary to have regard to the extent of possible liability which may be imposed on a defendant and the range of possible claimants who may be owed a duty of care and whether in all the circumstances it would be just and reasonable to impose liability. Thus on this last count, it is often necessary to consider if there is some other available avenue of legal redress, such as a public law action or one in contract which might otherwise have been available.

The second question, above, asks if T can claim to set up a defence contained in the contract between A and B in an action brought against him by A or B. This raises two issues considered elsewhere. The first of these is whether under the principle of vicarious immunity,[1] a party to a network of related contracts can rely on an exclusion clause contained in a contract entered into between two other parties to the network. In *Elder Dempster* the bill of lading which formed the basis of the contract between the carriers and the sellers of a consignment of palm oil exempted the carriers from liability for bad stowage. The carriers had chartered a ship from the defendant owners for the purpose of fulfilling their contract. The buyers of the palm oil brought an action against the owners in respect of damage caused by bad stowage. Although there was no direct contract between the owners of the ship and the buyers, the owners were nevertheless held to be protected by the exemption clause for two reasons. First the carriers had acted as agents for the owners of the ship since the bill of lading did specifically refer to them. Secondly, there was a 'bailment on terms' represented by the presentation of the goods for carriage and the acceptance of those goods by the captain of the ship as a representative of the owner. The most contentious possible justification of the decision is based on the notion of vicarious immunity, namely that if a person employs an agent to perform a contract on his behalf that agent is entitled to any immunity which would otherwise be available to his principal (the employer). On this basis, the ship owners were entitled to the protection of the exemption clause since they were the agents of the carriers in performing the contract of carriage between the carriers and the buyers. The difficulty with this concept of vicarious immunity is that subsequent to the decision

20   See *Smith v Eric S Bush (a firm)* [1990] 1 AC 831.
1   See *Elder, Dempster and Co Ltd v Paterson, Zochonis and Co Ltd* [1924] AC 522; *New Zealand Shipping Co Ltd v AM Satterthwaite & Co Ltd* [1975] AC 154, and see ch 22.

in *Elder Dempster* the House of Lords in *Scruttons Ltd v Midland Silicones Ltd*[2] denied the existence of such a doctrine, holding that the principle of vicarious immunity did not form part of the *ratio* in that case. Furthermore, none of the other reasons for the decision in *Elder Dempster* applied to the facts of *Scruttons v Midland Silicones* in which a firm of stevedores sought to rely on an exemption clause in the bill of lading which formed the basis of the contract of carriage between a seller and a carrier. In particular, there was no evidence that the carrier intended to act as an agent on behalf of the stevedores. Furthermore the decision in *Scruttons* may have been heavily influenced by policy factors, since the firm of stevedores admitted that they had committed a tort and it was stated that such a person should not be allowed to hide behind a document which is 'no concern of his'.[3] Subsequently, more detailed drafting of such clauses has revealed the possibility that a sufficient intention to protect a third party can be established. In particular, it is relevant that in *Scruttons,* the exemption clause did not refer specifically to the stevedores as protected parties. However in *New Zealand Shipping Co Ltd v AM Satterthwaite & Co Ltd, The Eurymedon*[4] there was a much closer connection between the stevedores and the carriers since they were part of an associated group of companies with the result that when the buyer presented the bill of lading to the stevedore he was taken to have made an offer of a unilateral contract to the stevedore, the terms of which included the extension of the exemption of liability to the stevedore, despite the fact that the exemption clause actually appeared in a contract made by two other parties. The fact that this close connection between the carrier and the stevedore existed might be taken to mean that there should always be a connecting factor of this kind sufficient to invoke the principle in *Satterthwaite.* However this seems not to be the case and there have been instances in which someone in the position of the stevedores has been able to rely on an exemption clause in a contract to which he was not a party despite evidence of previous authorisation.[5]

The scope of the principle in *Satterthwaite* is important to define, since the stevedores may cause damage in circumstances in which they are not protected. In *Satterthwaite,* it was important that the stevedores were assisting in the performance of the contract in which the exemption clause was to be found. Thus if the damage complained of had occurred before performance of the main contract had commenced[6] or occurred after performance of that contract had been completed, the stevedores would not have been protected. It is also important to examine closely the wording of the clause relied on. For example in *The Mahkutai*[7] the third party was entitled to the benefit of 'all exceptions, limitations, provisions and liberties' in the main contract. This language was construed to apply only to terms which benefited one of the parties, so that any contractual provisions included for the mutual benefit of all parties, such as an exclusive jurisdiction clause, did not apply to the third party sub-contractor.

A further privity issue is whether a court is permitted to consider the wider contractual setting in which T, A and B have dealt with each other in order to enable T to rely on a restriction of liability contained in the contract between A and B. Recent authorities suggest that this can be done and that if the contract between A and B makes it clear that A is to accept responsibility for a certain type of damage and insure accordingly, T may take the benefit of that provision.[8]

---

2   [1962] AC 446
3   *Wilson v Darling Island Stevedoring and Lighterage Co Ltd* [1956] 1 Lloyd's Rep 346 at 359.
4   [1975] AC 154. See also *Alder v Dickson* [1955] 1 QB 155.
5   See *The Pioneer Container* [1994] 2 AC 324, although on the facts of this case the third party was able to rely on the terms of a sub-bailment to which he was a party.
6   See *Burke Motors Ltd v Mersey Docks and Harbour Co* [1986] 1 Lloyd's Rep 155.
7   [1996] AC 650.
8   See *Norwich City Council v Harvey* [1989] 1 All ER 1180; *Southern Water Authority v Carey* [1985] 2 All ER 1077 and see ch 22.

(b) *Assignment of contractual rights*   A contractual right, such as a debt, can be assigned by the creditor to a third party so that the latter is entitled to sue the debtor. The basis on which the assignment operates is that there has been an immediate transfer of an existing proprietary right, whether vested or contingent, from the assignor to the assignee.[9] Thus it becomes necessary to identify property which is the subject matter of the assignment. In the case of contracts, it is said that it is the rights created by the contract which are assigned. Strictly, there is no conflict between rules on assignment and those regarding privity of contract, since an assignment does not create a relationship of privity between the assignee and the obligor.

At common law, assignments were generally not recognised, unless the debtor agreed to the assignment, as in the case of a novation, where the third party's right is based on the agreement with the debtor.[10] Alternatively, a debtor can create third party rights by way of an acknowledgment that a debt has been transferred.[11] In equity, there was a greater willingness to recognise an assignment of contractual rights, which were treated as property rights.[12] An assignment can also be effected due to certain statutory provisions. For example, a life assurance or a marine insurance policy is assignable. Likewise, a debt or other legal *chose in action* can be assigned in writing by virtue of the Law of Property Act 1925, section 136(1). This assignment must be absolute, therefore assignment of part of a debt,[13] as opposed to the balance of a debt,[14] is not assignable. An assignment not in writing may still be enforceable in equity,[15] but it must be communicated to the assignee by the assignor, and the debtor must be aware of the assignment.

(c) *Negotiability.*   A negotiable instrument such as a bill of exchange, a cheque or a promissory note, may be negotiated to another person. The holder of the bill of exchange is treated as a holder for value if consideration for the bill has, at any time, been given. Accordingly, the holder can enforce the bill against the person responsible to make payment.

(d) *Agency*[16]   An agency relationship arises where a principal authorises a willing agent to act on his behalf in the making of contracts and the transfer of property. The effect of an agency relationship is that the third party with whom the agent deals may acquire rights and be subject to obligations. While agency is not an exception to the doctrine of privity, it is a useful means of avoiding the harsher effects of that doctrine, where one person is deemed to be the agent of another. For example, agency is employed in order to allow a stranger to a commercial contract to take the benefit of an exclusion clause in a contract between others.[17]

A contract of agency may arise by express agreement under which the agent's authority to act may be expressly stated or implied from the circumstances of the case or by reference to trade custom.[18] Alternatively, agency may be without agreement giving rise to an ostensible authority on the part of the agent. Such an agency is based on estoppel. For example, the principal may have allowed the agent to give the impression

---

9   *Norman v Federal Comr of Taxation* (1963) 109 CLR 9 at 26 (per WINDEYER J.).
10   See *Rasbora Ltd v JCL Marine Ltd* [1977] 1 Lloyd's Rep 645.
11   See *Shamia v Joory* [1958] 1 QB 448.
12   See *Crouch v Martin* (1707) 2 Vern 595.
13   *Forster v Baker* [1910] 2 KB 636.
14   *Durham Bros v Robertson* [1898] 1 QB 765.
15   Ibid. Cf *Milroy v Lord* (1862) 4 De GF & J 264.
16   See Fridman *Law of Agency* (7th edn, 1996); Markesinis and Munday *Outline of the Law of Agency* (4th edn, 1997).
17   See *New Zealand Shipping Co Ltd v A M Satterthwaite & Co Ltd* [1975] AC 154 and see ch 21.
18   See *Watteau v Fenwick* [1893] 1 QB 346.

that he has authority to act when this is not the case,[19] or he may have failed to advise the third party that the agent's authority is in some way restricted.[20] The necessary ingredients of an estoppel are that there has been a factual representation by the principal to the third party; that the agent has authority to act; that the third party has relied on the representation, and that the reliance has resulted in an alteration in the position of the third party.[1] In some instances, an agent may perform an unauthorised act which finds favour with the principal. The principal can ratify the agent's act, so that binding obligations arise between the principal and the third party.

Where a contract of agency exists, the agent can make contracts on the principal's behalf which are binding on the principal and the third party. This is also the case, subject to exceptions, where the principal is undisclosed, that is, where the third party is unaware of the principal's existence. The right of the undisclosed principal to sue is independent[2] of the right of the agent to sue. The agent is also liable on the contract.[3] The principal is also liable on a contract made by his agent, except where circumstances show that the agent has accepted personal responsibility.[4]

(e) *Trusts*   A trust is an equitable device which allows a person to pass property to a trustee subject to a requirement that he should hold that property for the benefit of a third person, the beneficiary. The beneficiary is able to enforce the terms of the trust for his benefit. It is important that there is an intention to create a trust.

The most significant use of the trust in the context of the doctrine of privity is where a trust of contractual rights comes into existence. In such a case, one party declares himself to be a trustee on behalf of a third party in respect of the right to the contractual performance of the other party to the contract. While the trust concept is concerned with property interests, it has been possible, in equity, to regard a promise to pay money as a property interest.[5] Accordingly, it was held in *Walford's* case[6] that a clause in a charterparty which provided for payment of a commission to a broker by the shipowner could be enforced. The charterer, to whom the promise was made, was regarded as a trustee for the promise, which allowed the broker to enforce the promise against the shipowner.

While this device would appear to be a useful means of evading the harsh effects of the doctrine of privity, subsequent developments show that there are limitations upon its use. First, it must be shown that there is an intention to create a trust on the part of the promisee. This intention is established if the words trust or trustee are used, but their use is not essential.[7] A major difficulty with the trust of contractual rights is that it creates a third party interest which will prevent the parties to the contract from varying or rescinding the contract.[8] Accordingly, there is often an unwillingness on the part of the courts to infer an intention to create a trust in favour of a third party.

A second limitation is that there must be an intention to benefit the third party. If it is clear that the promisee intends to take the benefit of the promised performance himself, no trust will be created in favour of the third party. Thus, if the promise is designed to protect against harm that the third party will not suffer, no trust will come

---

19   See *Freeman and Lockyer v Buckhurst Park Properties (Mangal) Ltd* [1964] 2 QB 480.
20   See *Watteau v Fenwick* [1893] 1 QB 346.
1   See *Rama Corpn Ltd v Proved Tin and General Investments Ltd* [1952] 2 QB 147 at 149 (per SLADE J).
2   *Pople v Evans* [1969] 2 Ch 255.
3   *Sims v Bond* (1833) 5 B & Ad 389.
4   *Basma v Weekes* [1950] AC 441.
5   *Tomlinson v Gill* (1756) Amb 330.
6   *Affréteurs Réunis SA v Leopold Walford (London) Ltd* [1919] AC 801.
7   *Re Flavell* (1883) 25 Ch D 89.
8   *Re Schebsman* [1944] Ch 83.

into existence.[9] However, if there is clear evidence that the promisee does not intend to take the benefit of the promise for himself, a trust may be said to exist.[10]

The third limitation is that the intention to benefit the third party must be irrevocable. Thus, if the promisee has the ability to divert the benefit of the promise to himself, no trust will arise. Thus, in *Re Schebsman*,[11] the contracting parties were held to have intended to keep alive their common law right to vary the terms of their contract. Such an intention was inconsistent with an intention to irrevocably benefit the third party.

Where a trust in favour of a third party does arise, its effect is to allow the third party to sue the promisor and keep the money payable. However, the promisee should be joined as a party to the action unless the promisor waives this requirement, as in *Walford's* case.[12] If the promisee is unwilling to enforce the promise, the third party can commence proceedings in his own name and subsequently join the promisee as a party to the action.[13]

(ii)   Circumvention of the doctrine of privity: burdens

In some instances, the burden of contractual performance can be imposed on a third party, although the circumstances in which this will be done are limited. As with the consideration of the conferment of benefits on a third party, it is necessary to identify the main privity issues concerned with imposing burdens on a third party. Where there is a contract between A and B, the two principal questions are:

(1)   Can A or B set up a defence based on a term in their contract in an action brought against T?

(2)   Can A or B enforce the terms of their contract against T?

While imposing burdens on a third party is something the law will not do lightly, it should be remembered that if a third party derives a benefit from the contractual dealings of A and B, in the interests of justice, it may be right for that third party to be subject to burdens imposed by the contract between A and B.

(a) *Setting up a defence*   Particularly in the case of contract networks,[14] in which there are a number of contracting parties working together to secure the purpose set out in a principal contract, a person may be subject to the burden of an exclusion clause in a contract entered into between other parties to the network. Construction contracts and contracts for the international shipment of goods are examples in that in each case there is a principal contract (the main building contract or the contract of sale) which spawns other contracts, such as sub-contracted work in equipping the finished building or a contract with a stevedore to secure the unloading of the cargo. If the principal contract between A and B contains terms which limit the liability of B, this may be set up by B to defeat an action brought by T in respect of damage he may claim to have suffered.[15] This matter has been considered elsewhere.[16]

(b) *Enforcing the terms of a contract against T*   Rules of agency may serve to impose a burden on a third party, particularly where there is an undisclosed principal. It has been observed

9   *West v Houghton* (1879) 4 CPD 197.
10   *Lyus v Prowsa Developments Ltd* [1982] 1 WLR 1044.
11   [1944] Ch 83. See also *Re Sinclair's Life Policy* [1938] Ch 799.
12   [1919] AC 801.
13   *Vandepitte v Preferred Accident Insurance Corpn of New York* [1933] AC 70.
14   See Adams & Brownsword (1990) 10 Legal Studies 12.
15   See *Elder, Dempster and Co Ltd v Paterson Zochonis and Co Ltd* [1924] AC 522; *Pyrene Co Ltd v Scindia Navigation Co Ltd* [1954] 2 QB 402.
16   See ch 22.

already that the effect of the doctrine of the undisclosed principal is to allow the principal or the agent to sue the third party in circumstances in which the third party was initially unaware of the principal's existence.

On rare occasions, the burden of a contract may be assigned, but this assignment requires the consent of the promisee. For example, performance of a contractual undertaking to supply a service can be delegated to another, provided the task delegated does not require the exercise of skill or the personal qualities of the main contractor.[17]

(iii)   Exceptions to the doctrine of privity

(a) *Property interests*   The vendor of land may attach to the land sold a restrictive covenant. Under the rule in *Tulk v Moxhay*,[18] the effect of such a covenant is to pass with the land. Accordingly, a subsequent purchaser of the protected property is entitled to the benefit of the covenant. It is also the case that the burden of a covenant passes to a subsequent purchaser of the land which is subject to that covenant. At one stage, a similar principle was applied to movable property. In *Lord Strathcona Steamship Co Ltd v Dominion Coal Co Ltd*,[19] it was held that the charterer of a ship had a sufficient interest in the ship so that he could enforce that interest against a person who had purchased the ship from the previous owner. The rule was said to depend upon the subsequent purchaser's notice of the existence of the charterparty. However, the decision was not followed in *Port Line Ltd v Ben Line Steamers Ltd*,[20] where the purchaser of a ship did not have actual notice of the precise extent of the charterer's rights under the charterparty. The difficulty with the *Strathcona* case was that it introduced the uncertainty of applying the doctrine of constructive notice to commercial dealings. What the decision in *Port Line* does not establish is that a third party can always disregard property rights in respect of a chattel. For example, the economic torts considered below may serve to prevent an interference with a person's contractual rights.

An important statutory provision which affects property interests is the Law of Property Act 1925, section 56(1). This provides that:

> A person may take an immediate or other interest in land or other property, or the benefit of any condition, right of entry, covenant or agreement over or respecting land or other property, although he may not be named as a party to the conveyance or other instrument.

At one stage, it was argued that this section amounted to a statutory repeal of the doctrine of privity of contract. This view was based on the statutory definition of property, which includes any thing in action and any personal property.[1] Accordingly, it was arguable that a third party could acquire an interest in property, taken in this wide sense, where it was conferred on him by a contract made between others. Thus, the Court of Appeal in *Beswick v Beswick*[2] held that the widow had a personal right to sue for the annuity promised by her nephew. However, this interpretation of section 56 was rejected in the House of Lords,[3] where it was considered that the section applies to land, and that it does not dispense with the doctrine of privity of contract.

---

17   See *Griffith v Tower Publishing Co Ltd* [1897] 1 Ch 21.
18   (1848) 2 Ph 774.
19   [1926] AC 108.
20   [1958] 2 QB 146.
1   Law of Property Act 1925, s 205(1)(xx).
2   [1966] Ch 538.
3   [1968] AC 58.

(b) *Insurance*   A strict application of the doctrine of privity to insurance policies would create havoc in the insurance industry, since the avowed intent of many contracts of insurance is to confer a benefit on a third party. The effects of the doctrine of privity have been mitigated by the use of the law of agency and by the application of the concept of the trust. Furthermore, there are a number of statutory exceptions to the rule.

The Married Women's Property Act 1882, section 11 provides that, where a person insures his or her life for the benefit of a spouse and children,[4] the policy creates a trust in favour of the persons named therein. The provision does not apply to dependants other than spouses or children. Accordingly, an informally adopted child will not be able to recover.[5]

In relation to motor vehicle insurance, an injured third party can recover against an insurer once he has obtained judgment against the insured. Likewise, a person driving an insured motor vehicle with the consent of the owner can enforce the policy against the insurer, if he is a person entitled, by virtue of the policy, to drive the car.[6]

(c) *The Contracts (Rights of Third Parties) Act 1999.*   In the light of continued criticism of the the effects of the doctrine of privity of contract, the matter of reform of the doctrine was referred to the Law Commission[7] who concluded that in certain circumstances a third party should be given the right to enforce terms of a contract to which he is not a party, provided those terms are expressed to be for the benefit of the third party. Accordingly the extent of the reform is such that it will apply only to benefits and will not relax the current rules applicable to burdens under a contract and their effect on third parties. The difficulty with this approach is that in some instances it may be difficult to properly distinguish between benefits and burdens. The question whether a third party can enforce a term of a contract expressed to be for his benefit and the question whether a third party can rely on an exemption clause in a contract entered into by two others both raise issues of benefit. Conversely, the question whether A can enforce the terms of his contract with B against T clearly raises the issue of burden. However, there are other cases in which A seeks to set up a defence based on the terms of his contract with B in order to defeat a claim made against him by T.[8] The view expressed by the Law Commission initially seems to suggest that this last group of cases raises the issue of burden,[9] but there may be instances in which the contract between A and B confers a benefit on T, subject to a condition. The Law Commission give the example of a contract between A and B which confers on T a right of way, subject to a condition that T should keep it in a good state of repair.[10] Similar problems might also arise where a benefit is conferred on T but is subject to an exemption clause which limits T's ability to sue A in respect of the benefit conferred. On this matter the Law Commission state that T's right to enforce the benefit must be read subject to the exemption clause.[11] If the 1999 Act is to apply in such a case it would appear that the burden element will have to be conflated with the related benefit conferred by A and B on T.

---

4   Including illegitimate children: Family Law Reform Act 1969, s 19(1).
5   *Re Clay's Policy* [1937] 2 All ER 548.
6   Road Traffic Act 1988, s 148(7); *Digby v General Accident Fire and Life Assurance Corpn Ltd* [1943] AC 121. See also Third Parties (Rights against Insurers) Act 1930, s 1; Road Traffic Act 1988 ss 151–153; Policy Holders Protection Act 1975, s 7.
7   *Privity of Contract: Contracts for the Benefit of Third Parties,* Law Comm No 242, Cm 3329, 1996.
8   See *Scruttons Ltd v Midland Silicones Ltd* [1962] AC 446.
9   Law Comm No 242 para 2.1
10   Ibid para 10.26–10.27.
11   Ibid para 10.30.

The general effect of the 1999 Act is to make the right of a third party to enforce a term intended to benefit him subject to the intentions of the main contracting parties. Under section 1(1) the third party may enforce such a term in his own right if, (a) the contract expressly provides that he may or (b) the relevant term purports to confer a benefit on him. However, in this last case, the right of T is subject to the proviso in section 1(2) that if, on a proper construction of the contract, it appears that the parties to the contract did not intend the term to be enforceable by the third party, T will have no right of enforcement.

Under section 1(1)(a) a third party may enforce a term of a contract between A and B if the parties to that contract have expressly provided for this. Thus a case such as *Tweddle v Atkinson*,[12] in which two relatives of a couple intending to get married entered into an agreement to pay a specified sum of money each to the third party on the occasion of his marriage, would now give the third party a right to enforce the respective promises of the two relatives, since it was their joint intention to benefit the third party. Similarly, section 1(1)(a) would also appear to apply to cases in which a third party seeks to rely on an exemption clause contained in a bill of lading forming the basis of a contract betwen a consignor and a shipper. In these cases, discussed above, it is a requirement that the protected third party be named, in which case there will be an express intention to confer a benefit on the third party. This view follows from the provisions of section 1(6) which defines the word 'enforcing' as including 'availing himself of the exclusion or limitation'.

Unlike the position before the 1999 Act, there will be no need to employ devices to allow the third party to sue such as creating a trust of the promises of the contracting parties or by making the third party a joint promisee. Furthermore, since the third party has a direct right to enforce the promise(s), he will not need to join the promisee as a party to his action.

Under section 1(1)(b) the third party may enforce a term of a contract entered into between A and B if the term purports to confer a benefit on him. However, this is subject to the proviso that there will be no such right of enforceability if, on a proper construction of the contract, it was not the intention of A and B to confer such a right. It would appear that cases such as *Beswick v Beswick*[13] would fall within this provision. In that case there was no express provision in the contract between the uncle and his nephew that the uncle's spouse had a right to enforce the contract. Nevertheless, it was clear on the facts of the case that the contract did purport to confer a right to an annuity on Mrs Beswick. Likewise, in the holiday cases, such as *Jackson v Horizon Holidays Ltd*[14] it is likely that provided the person ordering the holiday names the other members of the party when making the booking that those third parties will be considered to have a right of enforcement. In contrast, if a person were to rent a holiday cottage from an owner who advertises the availability of the property in a national newspaper, without specifying the names of the members of his family who are to accompany him, there would appear to be little basis on which a joint intention to benefit those others could be inferred.

It is also important to emphasise that under section 1(1)(b) it must be the contractual term which purports to confer the right of enforceability. Thus in cases such as *White v Jones*[15] in which a client asked his solicitor to assist in the preparation of a will intended to benefit the claimant, it was the will which purported to confer the benefit on the third party rather than the contract between the client and his solicitor. Moreover, in

---

12   (1861) 1 B & S 393.
13   [1968] AC 58.
14   [1975] 3 All ER 92.
15   [1995] 2 AC 207.

other tort cases such as *Junior Books Ltd v Veitchi Co Ltd*[16] it is likely that the 1999 Act will have no effect since even if the sub-contract named T (the owner) as an intended beneficiary of the sub-contractor's expected performance, a probable interpretation of the contract between the main contractor and the sub-contractor is that it was intended to regulate the relationship between the principal contracting parties rather than to confer a benefit on the owner of the building. Moreover, it is common to find that in cases of construction contracts, there may be an express provision that one of the parties has an alternative contractual right of enforceability other than against the party he is seeking to render liable. In these circumstances, there ought to be a strong presumption against enforceability of a contract other than the one under which he has been given specific rights.

The proviso in section 1(2) is likely to give rise to substantial litigation, since it will be crucial to ascertain what were the true intentions of the parties to the contract in determining whether the third party has a direct right of enforceability. It might be argued that if there is no specific provision in the contract conferring such a right on a third party, then the parties did not intend the third party to have such a right. For these purposes, it seems that there is a rebuttable presumption of enforceability and it will be up to the party contesting liability to prove that there was no intention to confer a benefit on the third party.[17] In seeking to rebut this presumption, it is important to emphasise that what section 1(2) provides is that it must be demonstrated that the parties to the contract did not intend to confer a benefit on T. Thus, it will be insufficient for a contracting party to show that he, personally, did not intend to confer a benefit on T. Instead, it must be established that A *and* B did not intend to confer that benefit.

For the purposes of section 1(2), it is important to emphasise that the relevant term must purport to confer a benefit on the third party. Thus it will not be sufficient for the third party to demonstrate simply that the relevant term does, in fact, confer a benefit on him. For example, if A employs B to 'cut the hedge adjoining T's land', T would undoubtedly benefit from B's performance, but there is nothing in the relevant contractual term which purports to confer a benefit on T.[18] A more difficult case, however might arise where A contracted with B to perform some service specifically referable to T's property, since in such a case there might be a strong presumption that the contract was intended to benefit T even though there was no specific right of enforceability conferred on T. Thus in cases like *Linden Gardens Trust Ltd v Lenesta Sludge Disposals Ltd*[19] there is clear evidence that the work to be done would ultimately benefit the owner of the land, when property was eventually transferred. However, it would be difficult to argue that the relevant term of the contract was intended to confer a benefit on the ultimate owner, which he was entitled to enforce. One way in which A and B can make their position clear would be by way of some specific provision in their contract to the effect that either T has or does not have a right to enforce the term of the contract which purports to benefit him. Difficulties will arise, however, in cases in which A and B do not make it clear what their intentions are.

Under section 1(3) of the Contracts (Rights of Third Parties) Act 1999 it is provided that the third party must be expressly identified by name, as a member of a class or as answering to a particular description. However, there is no need for that person to be in existence at the time the contract between A and B is entered into. Thus T will have no right of enforceability simply on the basis that he or the class to which he

16   [1983] 1 AC 520.
17   See Law Comm No 242 para 7.46. dealing with the facts of *Beswick v Beswick*. Their conclusion was that the nephew would not have been able to rebut the presumption.
18   See *Treitel* p 601.
19   [1994] 1 AC 85.

belongs is intended to be benefited by implication. On the other hand, a contract between A and B which makes specific reference to the children of a specified third party will be enforceable by those children, even if they were not born at the time the contract between A and B was entered into. A similar approach will also be taken in relation to future spouses or limited companies which have not yet been formed.

In cases where there is no express identification of the third party, the 1999 Act will be of no assistance. Thus in *Scruttons Ltd v Midland Silicones Ltd*[20] the fact that the third party was not specifically referred to in the bill of lading would prove to be crucial under the 1999 Act. In contrast, in those cases such as *New Zealand Shipping Co Ltd v Satterthwaite & Co Ltd*[1] a different result would be likely to obtain because of the specific identification of employees, agents and sub-contractors as intended beneficiaries of the exemption clause.

Under the provisions of section 1(5), it is specified that T will have a direct right of enforcement. This avoids the problem of T having to rely on the right of enforcement being transferred to him via either A or B. However, in doing this, section 1(5) does employ the fiction of transfer of rights, since it is specified that T will have such rights as would have been available to him had he been a party to the contract betwen A and B. It follows from this that T will be able to pursue all remedies which would have been available to B, such as seeking an order for injunction, specific performance or expectation damages, despite the fact that he was not a party to the bargain. But since general principles of contract law will apply, presumably T's remedies will also be limited by rules on remoteness of loss, mitigation of damage and the general restrictions on the availability of specific relief. The difficulty with this is that since, by definition, T is not a party to the bargain, he may not have had the opportunity to state his concerns over the appropriate allocation of particular losses, in which case under rules on remoteness of loss, he may find himself in a position whereby the requirements of *Hadley v Baxendale*[2] are not satisfied.

The Contracts (Rights of Third Parties) Act 1999 also deals specifically with the issue of rescission or variation of the main contract. It should be observed that one of the common law objections to third party rights has been that to create such a right would interfere with the right of the principal contracting parties to vary the terms of their contract. Section 2(1) of the 1999 Act provides generally that if T has acquired the right to enforce a term of a contract made between A and B under section 1 then it follows that A and B cannot vary the terms of their contract so as to extinguish or alter T's entitlement without T's consent, provided the requirements of section 2 are satisfied. Clearly to extinguish T's rights would be wrong, but it should be noted that an 'alteration' may be either beneficial or prejudicial to T, but the Act appears to make no distinction between the two forms of alteration. Clearly, in the case of beneficial alterations, it is likely that T will immediately consent. For example if an alteration were to increase payments which would otherwise have been made to T, it is unlikely that he would object.

Where T has communicated his assent[3] to the term in the contract between A and B which confers a benefit upon him, it will not be possible for the terms of the original contract to be varied. But it is important that T's assent is communicated to the promisor. Furthermore, communication of assent to the promisee will not suffice.[4] For these purposes, the 'postal rule' applicable to communication of acceptance of an offer does

---

20   [1962] AC 446.
1   [1975] AC 154.
2   (1854) 9 Exch 341.
3   This may be by words or conduct: Contracts (Rights of Third Parties) Act 1999, s 2(2)(a).
4   Ibid s 2(1)(a).

not apply with the result that the assent has to be received by the promisor.[5] Difficulties may arise in this context where T has 'sent' notification of his assent in the form of a letter by post or where he has sent a message by facsimile or electronic mail and the message has arrived, but has not been read by the addressee. Logic would seem to suggest that in such circumstances, the courts are likely to apply a fault principle similar to that used in relation to rules on offer and acceptance. Thus if the message is sent at a time when it would be expected that no one would be present to receive it, the communication would not become effective until the promisor's business has been open and operative for a reasonable time.[6]

The right of the promisor (A) to rescind or vary his contract with the promisee (B) is also lost where A is aware that T has relied upon the term of the contract or where A could reasonably have been aware of such reliance which has actually occurred.[7] For these purposes, given the provisions in section 1(5) regarding remedies, it would appear to be the case that T will have a right to ask for promised performance and to recover damages in respect of any loss suffered in reliance upon that promise, subject to the avoidance of possible double recovery.

There may be circumstances in which the parties to the main contract rescind or vary that contract without the consent of T. The way in which the provisions of the 1999 Act are worded, T may choose to ignore the purported rescission or variation and seek to treat it as being ineffective.[8] However, there may be circumstances in which this is not an option since the effect of the rescission may be that further performance of the contract for the benefit of T becomes impossible. In this instance it would seem to be appropriate to allow T to maintain an action for damages in respect of quantifiable loss he has suffered.

Since the basis of the provisions of the 1999 Act is the intention of the parties to the main contract, there are provisions in section 2(3)(a) to the effect that the main contract may still be cancelled or varied without the consent of T, if the contract expressly so provides. In these circumstances if the contract makes such express provision, it will make no difference whether T consents to the variation or cancellation and it will be irrelevant that T has in fact relied on the promise to confer a benefit upon him. Moreover, by virtue of section 2(3)(b) an express term of the main contract may also require the consent of T in any circumstance other than those specified in section 2(1). For example it would be open to the contracting parties to specify the form in which the consent is to be given, in which case T's consent would be ineffective unless given in the form specified by A and B.

In certain circumstances, the court has a discretion to dispense with the requirement of consent. Under section 2(4) the court may, on an application by A and B, order that T's consent is not necessary. The first of these is where T cannot be found and the second where T is mentally incapable of giving consent. Likewise, under section 2(5) the requirement of T's consent may be waived where it cannot reasonably be ascertained whether T has, in fact, relied on the terms in the contract between A and B. In these circumstances, the court has a power to award compensation to T.

The 1999 Act provides for a number of defences to an action brought by a third party. Under section 3(2) where T seeks to enforce a term expressed to be for his benefit against the promisor (A), A may rely by way of defence or set off 'any matter that arises from or in connection with the contract and is relevant to the term'. For these purposes the relevant defence must be one which would have been available to A in proceedings

---

5 Ibid s 2(2)(b).
6 See eg *The Brimnes* [1975] QB 929.
7 Contracts (Rights of Third Parties) Act 1999, s 2(1)(b) and (c) respectively.
8 Ibid s 2(1).

brought by the promisee (B).[9] Thus A would be able to rely on any exemption clause in the main contract or would be able to pursue relief in respect of an actionable mistake or misrepresentation. The general rule established by section 3(2) can be displaced by an express provision in the contract between A and B. Thus it would be open to the parties to the main contract to narrow or widen the defences or set-offs available to A or to exclude the availabilty of such defences altogether.[10] The Act also envisages the possibility that there may be defences which can be pleaded against T which would not have been available in an action between A and B. For example there may be circumstances in which T owes obligations to A under another contract. In these circumstances, it is provided that A may rely on these defences as if T had been a party to the contract.[11]

Section 6 of the 1999 Act provides for a number of exceptional cases in which section 1 of the Act will not apply. These include contracts on negotiable instruments, contracts for the carriage of goods by sea and the contract which binds a company and its members under the terms of the memorandum and articles of association. In each case, there is separate provision for these varieties of contract under other legislation.

Apart from the provisions of the 1999 Act, the third party's rights arising under some other rule of law will remain unaffected.[12] Thus if an existing common law or equitable exception to the doctrine of privity of contract applies in favour of T he may rely on that instead of invoking the provisions of the 1999 Act. This will be particularly important in cases in which T is unable to prove that he has relied on the term in the contract between A and B or in any other case in which the restrictive provisions of section 1 and section 2 might work against T. Thus if T can establish the existence of a trust of the promise made in his favour or if he has an action in the tort of negligence or if some other statutory exception applies in his favour, T will still be able to avail himself of that alternative route. Although section 7(1) only refers to T's right under section 1, it must follow that the provisions of section 2 and 3 are also inapplicable, since both of these provisions expressly state that they apply where T has relied on section 1.

It has been seen above that at common law there is nothing to prevent the promisee from enforcing a term expressed to be for the benefit of the third party, if he wishes to do so. This position is preserved under section 4 of the 1999 Act.

---

9   Contracts (Rights of Third Parties) Act 1999, s 3(2)(b).
10   Ibid s 3(3); s 3(5).
11   Ibid s 3(4).
12   Ibid s 7(1).

Chapter 7

The ascription of responsibility in exchange relationships

1. INTRODUCTION

The rules on consideration and related issues discussed in the previous chapter are concerned with identifying those promises which the law is prepared to enforce, but in an exchange relationship, it is also necessary to consider, amongst other issues, when exchange liability comes into existence. Four elements have been identified in the process of ascribing contractual responsibility. These are, first, to decide what conditions need to be fulfilled before an obligation may be ascribed. Secondly, it becomes necessary to decide when responsibility commences. Thirdly, the content of the obligation must be established and, finally, the range of responsibility must be decided. The last of these matters has already been considered elsewhere.[1]

In the nineteenth century, all four matters were established by the single concept of agreement. Thus it followed that voluntary acts of consent led to the ascription of responsibility, liability commenced when the parties were in agreement, the content of the obligation was represented by the joint intentions of the parties, and the range of liability was generally restricted to those who were parties to a bilateral agreement.

Prominent features in the process of discovering an agreement were the rules on offer and acceptance coupled with an identified consideration so as to point to a bargain. But it may be objected that the intermixing of the doctrine of consideration with rules on offer and acceptance tends to confuse the separate issues of which promises are enforceable and when liability on a promise should arise.

It has been commented that the paradigm nineteenth-century contract tends to conjure up the image of an eastern bazaar rather than a modern consumer transaction.[2] The rules of offer and acceptance require a clear offer to be communicated to the offeree. The offeree then has to accept the offer by means of a clear, unequivocal, communicated acceptance. However, it is fairly clear that there are many modern transactions which do not work on this basis.[3] In particular, the modern consumer transaction frequently involves a simultaneous exchange which is difficult to explain in

---

1   See ch 6.
2   Atiyah *Introduction* p 60 cites *Pollock on Contract* (13th edn, 1950) pp 4–5, as an example.
3   See *New Zealand Shipping Co Ltd v AM Satterwaite & Co Ltd* [1975] AC 154 at 167 (per LORD WILBERFORCE).

terms of the process of negotiation which was envisaged by the classical model of contract formation.

All this should not be taken to mean that agreement is now totally irrelevant, as there are undoubtedly cases in which the parties have reached an agreement. This might suggest that the classical theory can be used to explain why a contractual relationship has come into existence. But, the claim of the classical model was that it applied to all contracts, which is simply not the case.[4]

It is suggested that a better structure can be built around the three key notions of voluntary human conduct, reasonable reliance and benefit. Undoubtedly, there are cases where the parties have reached an express, but executory, agreement, but other factors are also relevant. For example, where there has been an exchange of promises, it is reasonable for a promisee to rely on the promisor to perform his promise. This reliance is more pronounced where the promisee has altered his position in the belief that the promise of the other will be performed. Finally, if the actions of the promisee have conferred a valuable benefit on the promisor, there is an even stronger reason for finding a binding agreement giving rise to contractual obligations. Apart from the notions of reliance and benefit, regard may also be had to the type of transaction under consideration. Generally, it can be said that in relation to business transactions, courts will tend to apply rules which promote certainty so that the parties and their legal advisers know where they stand. Conversely, where the courts are faced with a transaction involving a consumer, rules based on fairness and reasonableness tend to become dominant, so as to take account of the apparent difference in bargaining power which may exist.

2.   CONDUCT JUSTIFYING THE ASCRIPTION OF RESPONSIBILITY

(1)   EXPRESS AND IMPLIED CONSENT

Where the parties' consent to be bound is express, contractual liability is seemingly based on agreement. Thus, in the case of an executory contract in which there has been no performance and where the parties have overtly expressed their intention to be bound, the requirements of offer and acceptance are apparently satisfied. But it should be appreciated that such executory arrangements are a means of rational planning. Accordingly, an agreement of this kind may well induce later acts of reliance in the form of business expansion plans which may result in benefits being conferred on the promisor or in some detriment to the promisee.

According to the classical theory, there are three principal elements in the process of reaching an agreement.[5] There must be a definite offer which is unconditionally accepted and that acceptance must be communicated to the offeror. It is important to appreciate that the rules of offer and acceptance are simply a mechanism for deciding when to ascribe responsibility on a contract and that difficulties may be encountered in attempting to fit all cases within the framework set up by these rules. On the other hand, the rules do provide a starting point for determining when liability attaches and also provide an important measure of certainty for the courts, contracting parties and their legal advisers.

The agreement required for the imposition of contractual liability does not have to be expressly given. From a fairly early stage in the nineteenth century, it was realised that to judge agreement by reference to the subjective intent of the parties was

---

4   Campbell in a review of the first edition of this book (1989) *Law Teacher* 334, 340.
5   See ch 3.

impossible,[6] since the Devil himself knows not the intent of man.[7] What developed was an objective theory under which the court decided what the parties had agreed to by reference to the available external evidence. Thus relevant factors to consider will be matters such as whether one of the parties has signed a document indicating his assent to the terms proposed by the other party.[8] Furthermore, the courts have come to look at what the parties have done in order to decide whether there was a binding contract. Thus it has been observed that it is a mistake to think that all contracts can be analysed in terms of offer and acceptance. Instead it is necessary to look at the correspondence, as a whole, which has taken place between the parties and the conduct of the parties in order to determine whether they have come to an agreement.[9] What matters are the reasonable expectations of sensible businessmen, not unexpressed mental reservations.[10] In *Brogden v Metropolitan Rly Co*,[11] coal had been supplied by the appellant to the respondents over a number of years under an informal arrangement. Later a draft agreement was drawn up by the respondents which was approved by the appellant, without further steps being taken towards execution of the contract. Orders for coal were made and fulfilled throughout this period but when a dispute arose the appellant argued that there was no contract. The House of Lords held that if both parties had acted upon the contents of the draft agreement, then it was binding upon them. As the terms of the draft agreement had been proposed by one party and had been marked 'approved' by the other, it is easy to see how this was objectively viewed as a binding contract. Perhaps what is important in cases of this kind is that the parties had acted as if they had entered into a contract, in which case, the courts are very likely to seek to find an agreement.[12] Just as the act of supplying goods in response to a request that they be supplied can be treated as an acceptance by conduct, similarly, if a supplier receives a request for the supply of services and he commences performance of the service, that act may be regarded as an acceptance.[13] Sometimes, it may be the case that the conduct of the party appearing to 'accept' relates not to the draft contract sent by the other party, but to some other set of terms, for example those forming the basis of an oral arrangement between the parties, in which case the objective test of agreement would seem to suggest that the relevant terms are those of the earlier arrangement rather than the written draft.[14]

Implying agreement from actions is one thing but to do the same in the event of inaction is a different matter. As a general rule English law will not ascribe responsibility on a contract in the event of mere silence or inaction.[15] Thus in arbitration cases, it is unlikely that failure to go to arbitration will be treated as an offer to abandon a contract,[16]

---

6   See ch 3.
7   Anon (1478) YB 17 Ed, 4 (per Brian CJ).
8   *L'Estrange v F Graucob Ltd* [1934] 2 KB 394; *Butler Machine Tool Co Ltd v Ex-Cell-O Corpn Ltd* [1979] 1 All ER 965.
9   *Butler Machine Tool Co Ltd v Ex-Cell-O Corpn Ltd* [1979] 1 All ER 965 at 968 (per Lord Denning MR). Cf contra *Gibson v Manchester City Council* [1979] 1 All ER 972 at 969 (per Lord Diplock)
10   *G Percy Trentham Ltd v Archital Luxfer Ltd* [1993] 1 Lloyd's Rep 25 at 27 (per Steyn LJ).
11   (1877) 2 App Cas 666.
12   See also *G Percy Trentham Ltd v Archital Luxfer Ltd* [1993] 1 Lloyd's Rep 25.
13   *The Kurnia Dewi* [1997] 1 Lloyd's Rep 552.
14   *Jayaar Impex Ltd v Toaken Group Ltd* [1996] 2 Lloyd's Rep 437; *UK Safety Group Ltd v Heane* [1998] 2 BCLC 208.
15   *Unisys International Services Ltd v Eastern Counties Newspapers Ltd* [1991] 1 Lloyd's Rep 538 at 553 (per Parker LJ).
16   *Paal Wilson & Co A/S v Partenreederei, The Hannah Blumenthal* [1983] 1 AC 854; *Allied Marine Transport Ltd v Vale do Rio Doce Navegacao SA, The Leonidas D* [1985] 2 All ER 796. See now Arbitration Act 1996, s 41.

unless that failure is joined with action which suggests abandonment.[17] In those cases in which an agreement to abandon a contract is inferred from silence, it will usually be because the court considers it 'necessary' to do so or where it is an inevitable inference from the circumstances.[18] For these purposes, the court effectively 'invents' a contract by means of a pure legal fiction.[19] It can be seen that the authorities in this area are not particularly helpful in ascertaining whether there has been an agreement to abandon a contract, with the result that the whole process has been described as 'largely useless in practice.'[20]

The problem of silence and acceptance may also arise in the context of a wrongful repudiation by one party followed by inaction on the part of the 'innocent' party. This may result in a judicial application of the maxim 'silence is pregnant with meaning' if the circumstances are such that some positive act could have been expected in the circumstances. Thus if the seller of goods is expected to obtain an export licence and the buyer subsequently behaves in a manner capable of amounting to a repudiation of the contract, if the seller then says nothing but also fails to take any steps to obtain the required licence, his silence may amount to an acceptance of the buyer's repudiation.[1]

(2)   VOLUNTARY CONDUCT AND RELATED BENEFIT

Where a person has deliberately accepted the benefit of the performance of another this may justify the imposition of an obligation to pay for the benefit received. While the classical response is that agreement justifies the ascription of responsibility, there are cases which tend to stretch the notion of agreement beyond its limits and which might be better explained on some other ground. Important considerations in these cases are that the contract is part-executed when the benefit is conferred, and that benefit has been voluntarily received by the recipient. Moreover, the person who confers the benefit is also likely to have acted in a manner which is to his detriment so that where there is a convergence of the elements of benefit, detriment and voluntary acceptance, there will be greater reason for the court to ascribe contractual responsibility.

A number of recurring situations have posed difficulties for an agreement-based rule. These include the classical bilateral contract, unilateral contracts and simultaneous exchanges.

(i)   Bilateral transactions

A rule based on executory agreements and forward planning breaks down when the parties fail to reach an agreement, or the language they use is vague but in either case there has been performance on one side. This performance may well confer a benefit on the other party. If this benefit is voluntarily received, then there are good reasons for saying that it should be paid for. The classical doctrine can be stretched to the point of ridicule in order to explain these cases or they can be analysed in terms of benefit voluntarily received.

---

17   *The Multitank Holsatia* [1988] 2 Lloyd's Rep 486 at 493 (per PHILLIPS J). See also *The Boucraa* [1994] 1 AC 486.

18   See *The Hannah Blumenthal* [1983] 1 AC 854 at 914 (per LORD BRANDON); *Rust v Abbey Life Assurance Co Ltd* [1979] 2 Lloyd's Rep 334 at 340 (per BRANDON LJ).

19   *Thai-Europe Tapioca Service Ltd v Seine Navigation Co Inc, The Maritime Winner* [1989] 2 Lloyd's Rep 506 at 515 (per POTTER J).

20   *The Boucraa* [1994] 1 AC 486 at 521.

1   See eg *Vitol SA v Norelf Ltd* [1996] AC 800. There might also be a trade custom or usage to the effect that some sort of positive act could be expected: *Minories Finance Ltd v Afribank Nigeria Ltd* [1995] 1 Lloyd's Rep 134.

Generally, the rule applied at common law is that where the parties still have further negotiation to undertake, there is no agreement. Traditional agreement-based analysis regards the parties as having postponed liability to some later date. Thus where the parties have reached an agreement 'subject to contract' there is taken to be no binding contract.[2] From this it follows that even if one of the parties has incurred expense in the expectation that a finalised agreement will be reached, he may find that the expenditure is not recoverable,[3] although in this instance, there may be a reason to look for a different solution. Indeed there are instances in which the courts have departed from the general rule that an agreement 'subject to contract' is not binding on the parties, particularly where the parties have proceeded to deal with each other in a manner which suggests that agreement has been reached and especially where the vendors have accepted payment of a deposit and have therefore benefited from the arrangement they have entered into. Thus in *Michael Richards Properties Ltd v Corpn of Wardens of St Saviour's Parish, Southwark*[4] the parties entered into an agreement to sell certain property, following the submission of the highest tender by the plaintiffs. In error the defendants marked their acceptance of the tender, 'subject to contract' but both parties continued to deal with each other as if they had reached a finalised agreement, the plaintiffs paying their deposit and the defendants seeking approval of the transaction from the Charity Commission, as required by the contract. Subsequently, the plaintiffs failed to complete and the defendants sought forfeiture of the deposit, arguing that there was no binding contract. In the circumstances, it was considered that the use of the phrase 'subject to contract' was meaningless and that the parties had reached a binding agreement to sell the property in question.

Similar problems of uncertainty may also arise where a person is invited to start work on a project and the party issuing a letter of intent states that it is his intention to enter into a contract at some future stage.[5] If work has commenced, the sender of the letter of intent may have received a benefit, and he may be required to pay for the service rendered. For example, if work is commenced under a letter of intent and a contract is later drawn up, the contract will be held to give legal effect to the actions which took place before the agreement was reached. Thus, in *Trollope & Colls Ltd v Atomic Power Constructions Ltd*[6] a letter of intent had been issued requesting that work on a nuclear power station should proceed. Much of the work was completed before a contract was drawn up. MEGAW J held that the contract operated retrospectively so as to apply to all work done pursuant to the letter of intent. While this type of problem can be explained in terms of a retrospective acceptance a very important consideration must have been the undeniable benefit received by the defendants. The principle which can be said to lie behind cases of this kind is that of free acceptance,[7] in that the defendant has chosen to take the benefit of the plaintiff's performance. In view of this, it is not surprising to find that there is an alternative restitutionary solution to the same problem. For example, in both *Peter Lind & Co Ltd v Mersey Docks and Harbour Board*[8] and *British Steel Corpn v Cleveland Bridge and Engineering Co Ltd*[9] work had commenced under the terms of a letter of intent and was completed while the parties were still trying to reach an agreement. In both cases, no contract was held to exist, but the party in receipt of the benefit of performance was required to pay for the work done on a quantum meruit.

2   *Winn v Bull* (1877) 7 Ch D 29; *Chillingworth v Esche* [1924] 1 Ch 97; *Eccles v Bryant* [1948] Ch 93.
3   See *Regalian Properties plc v London Docklands Development Corpn* [1995] 1 All ER 1005.
4   [1975] 3 All ER 416. See also *Alpenstow Ltd v Regalian Properties plc* [1985] 2 All ER 545.
5   See Ball (1983) 99 LQR 572.
6   [1963] 1 WLR 333.
7   See ch 11.
8   [1972] 2 Lloyd's Rep 234.
9   [1984] 1 All ER 504.

Of the two solutions, finding a contract is to be preferred, since any terms of the contract can be used to produce a detailed and flexible relationship. In contrast, where a restitutionary solution is adopted, the court will be concerned solely with the unjust enrichment of the defendant. For example, in *British Steel Corpn v Cleveland Bridge Engineering* [10] ROBERT GOFF J was concerned only with the value of the steel nodes supplied to the defendant. No account could be taken of the terms of delivery, so the defendant's counter-claim that the nodes were delivered late was ignored. If it had been possible to construct a contract, this problem might have been resolved. [11]

The cases considered above illustrate the position where the parties are aware that there was never any agreement. But there are other cases in which the parties believe they have reached an agreement, in which it later transpires that the language they have used is excessively vague or uncertain or where vital terms have been omitted. It is suggested that in these circumstances, the decision of a court that a contractual obligation is owed will depend on the issue of part performance. If the contract remains executory throughout, with no performance on either side, then the court will have little reason to strain to discover the meaning of the language used by the parties. But if one of the parties has performed his obligations under the alleged contract, thereby conferring a benefit on the other, that other may be required to pay for the work and the court will have to justify this by finding some meaning in the language used, and may imply a term resolving any uncertainty in the language used by the parties. [12]

In *British Bank for Foreign Trade Ltd v Novinex Ltd* [13] the Court of Appeal approved the general rule stated by DENNING J that: [14]

> The principle to be deduced from the cases is that if there is an essential term which has yet to be agreed and there is no express or implied provision for its solution, the result in point of law is that there is no binding contract. In seeing whether there is an implied provision for its solution . . . there is a difference between an arrangement which is wholly executory on both sides and one which has been executed on one side or the other.

In this case, the defendants had been introduced to clients by the plaintiffs and a contract between the clients and the defendants had followed. The defendants further agreed to pay an unspecified commission to the plaintiffs in respect of any follow-up orders which might be attributable to the initial introduction. Follow-up orders were placed, but the defendants denied liability to pay commission on the ground that there was no legally enforceable agreement because the language used was too vague. The Court of Appeal held that there was an implied agreement to pay a reasonable commission, the consideration for which was the plaintiffs' rendering of a valuable service. Another way of putting this is that the plaintiffs had conferred a valuable benefit on the defendants.

In contrast, in *Bushwall Properties Ltd v Vortex Properties Ltd* [15] there was an executory agreement to sell land for £500,000, the price to be paid in three instalments of £250,000, £125,000 and £125,000. It was further agreed that a proportionate part of the land would be released at each date of payment. The parties had made no provision for the allocation of the proportionate parts, and the Court of Appeal held that the agreement

---

10   Ibid. See also Howarth (1987) JBL 122.
11   Cf *G Percy Trentham Ltd v Archital Luxfer Ltd* [1993] 1 Lloyd's Rep 25.
12   *G Percy Trentham Ltd v Archital Luxfer Ltd* [1993] 1 Lloyd's Rep 25 at 27–28 (per STEYN LJ).
13   [1949] 1 KB 623.
14   Ibid at 629.
15   [1976] 2 All ER 283. See Emery [1976] CLJ 215. See also *Courtney and Fairbairn Ltd v Tolaini Bros (Hotels) Ltd* [1975] 1 All ER 716; *F and G Sykes (Wessex) Ltd v Fine Fare Ltd* [1967] 1 Lloyd's Rep 53 at 57–58 (per LORD DENNING MR); *G Scammell and Nephew Ltd v Ouston* [1941] AC 251.

was void for uncertainty. No actual benefit would have been conferred on either party, therefore there was no urgent need to look for an implied solution.

Where a court seeks to impose liability on a contract, it may take into account trade customs so as to complete a contract where vague language has been used.[16] Alternatively, the vague term may be ignored, the rest of the terms being given effect.[17]

(ii) Offers of a unilateral contract

A unilateral contract comes into existence when the promisor gives an undertaking to do something if the promisee will do or refrain from doing something in return. Typical examples of these 'if' contracts include certain types of guarantee, options to purchase land for a valuable consideration, contracts of estate agency and offers of reward.

Unilateral offers have always caused problems of analysis. At a simple level the reward cases illustrate the difficulties. If A offers £300 for the return of his lost dog and B returns the dog in ignorance of the offer, is B entitled to the reward? Classical analysis of unilateral offers would suggest that the person responding to the offer of a reward in the above example is not entitled to the reward, as there is no agreement where a person is unable to consent to an offer of which he is not aware.[18] However, the offeror of the reward has received the benefit he desires and has offered to pay for it. If this is the case, it is arguable that there should be an obligation to pay for the return of the lost dog on the ground that there has been a voluntary offer and a related receipt of a desired benefit.[19] The relevant principle is similar to that of free acceptance which operates in cases of restitution.[20]

Moreover, even where the offeror is aware of the offer of reward, application of the classical rules on acceptance can create problems. For example it may be difficult to determine when the offer has been accepted since it is unlikely that the offeree will inform the offeror that he is about to commence performance of the act which has been requested. However, if the act has resulted in the conferment of some positive benefit on the offeror, this, too, may justify the imposition of an obligation to carry out the offer to pay for the benefit received.[1] One way in which the normal requirement of communication of acceptance can be side-stepped is by importing a fiction that the offeror has waived the need for communication. This is especially the case where the offer is addressed to the public in the form of an advertisement,[2] This analysis may also apply where a bank issues a credit card on terms which allows its customer to purchase goods or services on credit from a supplier. The simple act of acceptance of the card by the retailer constitutes acceptance of the bank's offer, despite the fact that there is no communication to the bank at the time,[3] but it is evident that in these circumstances, the bank derives the benefit of being able to charge interest on the loan to the customer.

Other difficulties which may arise include the identification of what has been undertaken by the offeror and the question of revocation of the offer once it has been made. Generally, what the offeror has undertaken to do will require a close scrutiny of the language of the offer itself. In some instances there may be a form of standing offer which can be accepted over and over by performance of the required act, whereas in

---

16   See *Hillas & Co Ltd v Arcos Ltd* (1932) 147 LT 503.
17   See *Nicolene Ltd v Simmonds* [1953] 1 QB 543.
18   See *Fitch v Snedaker* 38 NY 248 (1868); *R v Clarke* (1927) 40 CLR 227; cf Hudson (1968) 84 LQR 503.
19   Cf *Gibbons v Proctor* (1891) 64 LT 594.
20   See ch 11.
1   See *Morrison Shipping Co Ltd v R* (1924) 20 Ll L Rep 283.
2   See *Carlill v Carbolic Smoke Ball Co* [1893] 1 QB 256.
3   *First Sport Ltd v Barclays Bank plc* [1993] 1 WLR 1229 at 1234–1235.

other cases there may be a single offer which will only crystallise into one binding contractual relationship.

So far as revocation is concerned, the principal difficulty will arise in cases in which the required performance on the part of the offeree takes time to complete. Applying normal rules of offer and acceptance, the offeror can revoke his offer at any time before it has been unequivocally accepted, but there would be obvious injustice if the offeror were to wait until just before the final act of completion before seeking to revoke his offer. Similarly, the first step towards performance of the required act cannot be regarded as full acceptance otherwise the offeree would be able to commence performance but not complete it and still claim to have accepted the offer.

This problem can be dealt with in a number of different ways. For example, it has been suggested that the offeror accepts the offer by commencing performance, but does not supply consideration for the promise until he completes performance.[4] Alternatively, a number of authorities approach the question on the basis that there are two separate offers. Under the first of these, the offeror makes the principal offer, and under the second he offers not to revoke the principal offer before the offeree has had a chance to complete the requested performance.[5] What may prove crucial in these cases is any agreed allocation of risk between the parties. For example in estate agency contracts, there is widely accepted to be a unilateral contract under which the estate agent is entitled to payment of his commission only when he produces the required result on behalf of the vendor of the property up for sale. In *Luxor (Eastbourne) Ltd v Cooper*[6] it was agreed between the parties that the estate agent would be paid commission on 'completion of the sale', but was prevented from achieving this result when the vendor withdrew his property from the market and later sold to a purchaser by private treaty. In declining to imply a term to the effect that the vendor would not prevent the agent from earning his commission, the House of Lords had very close regard to the fact that the estate agent appeared to have taken the risk that a sale might not materialise, but that if one did, the agent would stand to receive handsome remuneration. On this basis, it can be said that although the vendor received the benefit of the estate agent's performance, the agreed allocation of risk indicated that the vendor had not undertaken to pay the agent until a specified event occurred.

At a more complex level, voluntary acceptance of a conferred benefit may be used to explain some of the shipping cases such as *New Zealand Shipping Co Ltd v AM Satterthwaite & Co Ltd*.[7] Here there was a contract to carry a drill from Liverpool to the consignee's place of business in New Zealand. The contract made between the carrier and the consignor of the goods contained an exclusion clause which purported to exempt from liability any person involved in the process of discharging the contract. The carrier engaged a firm of stevedores to unload the cargo and, in the course of unloading, the consignee's drill was damaged. The Privy Council took the view that if the carrier had executed the contract of carriage, including unloading, he would have been exempt from liability. It followed that if unloading was executed by a firm of stevedores, they too, were exempt from liability. A collateral contract was said to exist between the consignee and the stevedores. The justification for this was that the carrier acted as an agent for the stevedores, and that there was a unilateral contract between the consignee and the stevedores (made through the carrier as agent) which became a full contract when the stevedores unloaded the ship. The performance of this task consisted of the

4   See Pollock, *Contract* (13th ed, 1950), p 19.
5   *Harvela Investments Ltd v Royal Trust Co of Canada Ltd* [1986] AC 207; *Blackpool and Fylde Aero Club Ltd v Blackpool Borough Council* [1990] 3 All ER 25.
6   [1941] AC 108.
7   [1975] AC 154.

conferment of a valuable benefit upon the consignee.[8] This, in turn, could be said to be of benefit to the consignee, accordingly the stevedores were entitled to the protection of the exclusion clause. Under Lord Wilberforce's analysis there was a unilateral offer on the part of the consignee which crystallised into a full contract when the stevedores commenced unloading. However, more recently, the type of contract created has been described as bilateral.[9] The difficulty with this line of reasoning, however, is that if there is a bilateral contract then it ought to follow that if the offer of exemption from liability is accepted by the stevedores then whether the stevedores actually unload the vessel or not, they remain exempt from liability. In contrast, under the unilateral contract approach, the stevedores will not be exempt from liability until the commencement of performance of the requested act.

(iii)   Simultaneous exchange

Many everyday consumer transactions may be explained as cases in which the consumer has deliberately received a benefit. For example, the act of boarding a bus has been tortuously explained in terms of agreement,[10] but, surely, an easier and more palatable explanation is that the passenger has boarded the bus and, in doing so, has accepted the benefit of the operator's service. Similarly, purchases made in a supermarket are ostensibly based on an agreement between the parties made through the process of offer and acceptance. However, these transactions are better described as simultaneous exchanges[11] in which the consumer is obliged to pay for what he has received because it is of benefit to him. It is as if a person has been loaned an amount of money. On receipt of the benefit of the loan, the recipient is obliged to pay for the benefit received.

Other modern phenomena associated with everyday consumer transactions are equally problematical in terms of their precise analysis under rules of offer and acceptance. The underlying rationale of the rules of offer and acceptance is that an agreement is reached between two individual contracting parties. However, in a number of typical consumer contracts, this so-called agreement is reached with minimal human involvement on the part of the supplier. For example, it is common for a motorist to park his car in a car park, having first obtained a ticket from a vending machine. Subsequently, the parking ticket is fed into a machine which reads the time of entry and indicates the charge payable, which amount is then fed into the machine by the customer. In these circumstances, it appears that the owner of the car park makes an offer through the machine, which is accepted by the customer when he takes the ticket from the machine.[12] More recently, consumers have been able to scan their purchases made in a supermarket into a hand-held device which records the purchases made. Subsequently, the scanner is presented and connected to a computer which indicates the price payable. Traditional analysis of supermarket transactions indicates that the retailer does not offer to sell goods displayed in the store, but merely invites an offer from the consumer.[13] However, this new form of shopping might be better analysed as an offer by the retailer to sell at the price indicated by the computer.

8   Ibid at 167–168 (per LORD WILBERFORCE).
9   *The Mahkutai* [1996] AC 650
10   See *Wilkie v London Passenger Transport Board* [1947] 1 All ER 258 at 259 (per LORD GREENE MR).
11   See Atiyah *Essays* Essay No 2, pp 19–20.
12   *Thornton v Shoe Lane Parking Ltd* [1971] 2 QB 163.
13   *Pharmaceutical Society of Great Britain v Boots Cash Chemists (Southern) Ltd* [1952] 2 QB 795.

(3)   VOLUNTARY CONDUCT AND REASONABLE RELIANCE

It has been said that there is a general principle of English law that injurious reliance upon that which another person has done may be a source of legal rights against the person inducing the reliance.[14] This reasonable reliance may be either that of the offeree when he relies to his detriment on the words or conduct of the offeror, or it may be reliance by a third party which justifies a finding of contractual responsibility.

(i)   Reliance by the offeree

If by his words or conduct, the offeror has led another to believe that he has undertaken to perform a particular act, the court may hold that there is a binding contract.[15] This principle of injurious reliance may be used to explain a number of cases which are difficult to explain in terms of agreement.

In 'Battle of the Forms' cases, in which the buyer and seller may use standard form documents which contain conflicting terms, it can be difficult to establish if a contract is made where an agreement-based analysis is applied. In general terms, the classical contract theory regards an offer followed by a counter offer as having been rejected by the offeree who puts in the counter offer.[16] Thus if the buyer insists on a fixed price but the seller's terms of contracting contain a price variation clause, to take account of raw material costs, it will be difficult to identify any agreement as to the means of ascertaining the price payable for the goods sold. But, if one of the parties has signed a delivery note or an order form, that signature will usually be treated as a reason for holding the signatory to be bound by the contract terms suggested by the other party.[17] The signature may be said to induce the performance of the other party. What is clear from these 'battle of the forms' cases is that where possible, the courts will strain to find a contract, particularly in circumstances where there has been an act of reliance in the form of performance of the contract. The courts have suggested a number of possible solutions to the problem. Perhaps the closest of these to classical contract analysis is the 'last shot' doctrine, under which the person who makes the most recent reference to his terms is treated as the offeror and provided the other party has given some objective sign of assent to those terms, for example, in the form of delivering goods contracted for or taking delivery of those goods, then a contract is made on the terms of the person delivering the 'last shot.'[18] Other factors which may also be relevant include whether the parties have had a previous consistent course of dealing, in which case, agreement based on that course of dealing may be inferred.[19] Alternatively, as in *Butler* itself, there may be a significant act, such as placing a signature on a document submitted by the other party and containing his terms of contracting, in which case the signature will be regarded as an objective indication of the assent of the signatory of the terms put forward by the other party. Moreover, it has also been controversially suggested that the courts might construct a contract based on the common elements of agreement between the

---

14   *Paal Wilson & Co A/S v Partenreederei, The Hannah Blumenthal* [1983] 1 AC 854 at 916 (per LORD DIPLOCK). See also Howarth (1987) JBL 122.

15   See *Hardwick Game Farm v Suffolk Agricultural and Poultry Producers Association Ltd* [1966] 1 WLR 287 at 339 (per DIPLOCK LJ) sub nom *Henry Kendall & Sons v William Lillico & Sons Ltd* [1969] 2 AC 31 at 113 (per LORD PEARCE). See also *The Hannah Blumenthal* [1983] 1 AC 854 at 916 (per LORD DIPLOCK).

16   *Hyde v Wrench* (1840) 3 Beav 334. Cf *Stevenson, Jaques & Co v McLean* (1880) 5 QBD 346 in which the language of the offeree was construed as a mere request for information, not destroying the original offer.

17   *Butler Machine Tool Co Ltd v Ex-Cell-O Corpn (England) Ltd* [1979] 1 All ER 965. See also *British Road Services Ltd v Arthur V Crutchley & Co Ltd* [1968] 1 All ER 811.

18   *British Road Services Ltd v Arthur V Crutchley & Co Ltd* [1968] 1 All ER 811.

19   Ibid.

parties or upon what can be reasonably inferred from those common elements.[20] However, this approach has been criticised on the ground that while it produces flexibility, it also introduces excessive uncertainty into the law of business contracts.

Reliance is also a key feature in the case of unilateral contracts in which the offer has induced the performance of the other party. These promises in return for an act, have always caused difficulty for the classical notion of agreement[1] and this is particularly so where the act constituting acceptance is commenced without the knowledge of the promisor.

In *Errington v Errington and Woods*,[2] a father's promise to allow his son and daughter-in-law to occupy a house provided they continued to pay the outstanding mortgage debt was irrevocable since the promisee had commenced performance. It was held that the father's estate was not bound to convey the estate to the daughter-in-law immediately, since final conveyance would be dependent on all outstanding mortgage debts being paid off, but assuming the full debt was eventually settled, the daughter-in-law, in time, would be entitled to transfer. Once she and her husband had started to repay the mortgage debt, as agreed, it was too late for the offeror to withdraw his offer.

In these cases once the act in reliance on the offer is performed, it is too late for the offer to be withdrawn. How this conclusion is justified may be explained in a number of different ways. On the one hand, it may be that there is an implied promise on the part of the offeror that he will not revoke his offer while the offeree is in the process of completing the act amounting to acceptance.[3] The difficulty with this approach is that an implied term will take effect as part of the main contract, whereas, in order to prevent the offeror from revoking his offer, this particular implied term will have to take effect before the main contract comes into existence. Alternatively, it may be that the offer becomes irrevocable once the offeree commences performance, without the need for any implied promise. [4] This would seem to suggest that perhaps the most plausible explanation of the position in respect of offers of a unilateral contract is that there are two separate offers, namely the principal offer and a subsidiary offer not to revoke the first. However, in any case, a fairly obvious rationale, in these circumstances, is that the promisee has injuriously relied upon the promise and can expect to be given time to fulfil the requirements of the offeror.

The reliance principle is also dominant in cases in which the courts are prepared to construct a contract for the parties using the device of the collateral contract.[5] It has been objected that these are merely examples of the law of contract being used to fill gaps in other areas of the law.[6] However, the fact that a contractual solution is possible in such cases would appear to demonstrate that there are common principles underlying the common law of obligations.

If an agent represents that he has authority to act on behalf of another, this is very likely to induce an act of injurious reliance on the part of the person to whom the representation is addressed, in which case the agent is liable in damages to that person.[7] The justification for this view is that the agent has caused the plaintiff to rely upon his representation in much the same way as a person relies upon advice given in the course

20 *Butler Machine Tool Co Ltd v Ex-Cell-O Corpn (England) Ltd* [1979] 1 All ER 965 (per LORD DENNING MR).
1   See McGoveney (1914) 27 Harv LR 644 and ch 3.
2   [1952] 1 KB 290.
3   Ibid at 293 (per SOMERVELL LJ). See also *Daulia Ltd v Four Millbank Nominees Ltd* [1978] 2 All ER 557 at 561 (per GOFF LJ).
4   *Daulia Ltd v Four Millbank Nominees Ltd* [1978] 2 All ER 557 at 561 (per GOFF LJ).
5   See Atiyah *Introduction* ch 4; Wedderburn [1959] CLJ 58.
6   Vorster (1987) 103 LQR 274 at 282.
7   *Collen v Wright* (1857) 8 E & B 647.

of a special relationship under the rule in *Hedley Byrne & Co Ltd v Heller & Partners Ltd*.[8] However, while there are similarities between the doctrine of breach of warranty of authority and the principle in *Hedley Byrne* it would appear that they are not exactly the same. It is true that both are based heavily on the notion of reasonable reliance, but it is also clear that the doctrine of breach of warranty of authority imposes a stricter form of liability on an agent and is clearly founded on the fact that the agent has given a guarantee that he is authorised to act on behalf of his principal. In *Penn v Bristol and West Building Society* [9] a firm of solicitors was held to be in breach of their waranty of authority where they had believed they purported to act on behalf of a married couple, unaware of the fact that the wife's consent to the transaction had been vitiated by the fraud of her husband. On discovering the fraud, the wife sought a declaration against the defendant building society that the charge created over the family home was null and void. On a counter-claim, the building society argued that the solicitors had warranted themselves to have an authority which they did not, in fact, possess. Despite the fact that there was no fault on the part of the solicitors, it was still held that there was a breach of warranty of authority. The ingredients of the action were considered to consist of an express or implied promise that the agent had authority to act on behalf of the principal and evidence of reliance on the promise so as to satisfy the requirement of consideration, although that consideration did not need to consist of entering into a transaction with the principal, but could include entering into a transaction with a third party (in this case, the building society). It is also clear from the requirement of reliance that there is a close affinity between cases of breach of warranty of authority and the rule in *Hedley Byrne v Heller,* but there are differences. In particular, earlier case law demonstrates that an agent may be in breach of his warranty of authority where he has knowingly, fraudulently or negligently represented himself to have an authority he does not, in fact, possess. However, it is equally the case that an agent may be liable where he has no knowledge of his lack of authority, for example, where his principal becomes of unsound mind without his knowledge. [10] Accordingly, there is no requirement that fault on the part of the agent should be established.

In supply of goods cases the collateral warranty device has been used to circumvent the effects of the doctrine of privity by allowing a customer who has been induced to purchase a defective product by a manufacturer's assurance of quality.[11] However, the extent to which the courts are prepared to go is limited by the insistence in some cases that there must be a contractual intent before a collateral warranty can be inferred.[12] Conversely, other cases have not involved much of a search for this intent, although most of these have been cases in which there was a misrepresentation at a time when the common law did not allow an action for damages for misrepresentation.[13]

(ii)   Third party reliance

The objective theory of agreement requires the court to have regard to the external appearance of an agreement rather than the subjective intentions of the parties. Thus if

8   [1964] AC 465 and see ch 10.
9   [1997] 3 All ER 470. See also *Yonge v Toynbee* [1910] 1 KB 215.
10   *Yonge v Toynbee* [1910] 1 KB 215.
11   *Carlill v Carbolic Smoke Ball Co* [1893] 1 QB 256; *Shanklin Pier Ltd v Detel Products Ltd* [1951] 2 KB 854; *Wells (Merstham) Ltd v Buckland Sand and Silica Ltd* [1965] 2 QB 170; *Bowerman v ABTA Ltd* [1995] NLJR 1815 and see ch 25.
12   *Heilbut, Symons & Co v Buckleton* [1913] AC 30; *Lambert v Lewis* [1980] 1 All ER 978 (reversed on other grounds [1981] 1 All ER 1185).
13   *De Lassalle v Guildford* [1901] 2 KB 215; *Schawel v Reade* [1913] 2 IR 64; *Couchman v Hill* [1947] KB 554; *Andrews v Hopkinson* [1957] 1 QB 229; *Dick Bentley Productions Ltd v Harold Smith (Motors) Ltd* [1965] 2 All ER 65 and see ch 10.

a person has acted in a way which is likely to induce an act of reasonable reliance on the part of a third party, an agreement may be held to have been entered into. For example, where a person signs a standard form contractual document without reading its contents, he may be said to have agreed to the terms contained in it. In *L'Estrange v F Graucob Ltd*,[14] the plaintiff signed a contract for the sale of a slot machine which contained an onerous exclusion clause. The Divisional Court held that, in the absence of fraud or misrepresentation, that signature was binding. It might be argued that the decision was harsh and that the defendant was probably aware that, had the plaintiff read the document, she would not have agreed to such onerous terms, which is a more likely result in consumer transactions,[15] but the act of signature does tend to induce reliance.

The importance of a signature is particularly great when a third party is presented with a document signed by the plaintiff. In *Gallie v Lee*,[16] the plaintiff, an old lady with failing eyesight, had signed a document which she believed to be an assignment of a leasehold interest to her nephew. In fact, the fraudulently prepared document had the effect of transferring the relevant interest to the defendant. The House of Lords held that the plaintiff was bound by her signature and was not entitled to raise the defence of *non est factum* (not my deed), because she had been negligent in failing to read the document. She could have fetched a pair of spectacles, but preferred to rely on an oral explanation of the effect of the document. An important factor in this case was that a building society had advanced money to the defendant in reliance upon the plaintiff's signature. Accordingly, she was not allowed to disavow her signature.[17]

The injurious reliance principle might also explain the rule, in practice, that once opened, a bankers' commercial credit is binding upon the bank.[18] The process by which such a credit comes into existence is that a foreign seller requires the buyer of goods to open up an irrevocable credit, for a specified period of time, in favour of the seller. The buyer then makes an arrangement with his bank, whereby the bank will open this credit so long as the buyer will reimburse the bank. The buyer's bank then notifies the foreign seller that an irrevocable credit has been opened in his favour, and that the credit can be drawn on presentation of the relevant shipping documents. According to Lord Cairns in *Morgan v Larivière*,[19] the banker states that he will act as paymaster only if the seller can show that the goods have been delivered to their customer. Various theories have been put forward to justify the binding nature of the relationship between the bank and the seller, with varying degrees of success.[20] However, if there is a general principle that injurious reliance upon that which another person has done may be a source of legal rights against the performer, then the instance of the irrevocable credit may fall within that principle. In such a case, the seller acts to his detriment by making over to the buyer the documents which signify ownership of the goods and by allowing shipment to commence. He does so in reliance upon the irrevocability of the credit.

14   [1934] 2 KB 394.
15   *Tilden Rent-a-Car Co v Clendenning* (1978) 83 DLR (3d) 400 and see also Spencer [1973] CLJ 103.
16   [1971] AC 1004, sub nom *Saunders v Anglia Building Society*. See Stone (1972) 88 LQR 190.
17   Ibid at 1036 (per LORD PEARSON).
18   *Dexters Ltd v Shenker & Co* (1923) 14 Ll L Rep 586.
19   (1875) LR 7 HL 423 at 432.
20   See Gutteridge and Megrah *The Law of Bankers Commercial Credits* (7th edn, 1984) ch 3; Ellinger *Documentary Letters of Credit* (1989).

3.   THE MOMENT OF CONTRACTUAL RESPONSIBILITY

(1)   THE CLASSICAL RULES OF OFFER AND ACCEPTANCE

In classical terminology, the parties to a contract are not bound until they are in agreement, which requires an acceptance corresponding with and made in response to an offer to be communicated to the offeror. In practice, these rules are not always adhered to, and it has been argued that the courts appear to set the moment of contractual responsibility when it seems reasonable to do so.[1]

Brief consideration of the rule that an acceptance should be communicated reveals that there are many exceptions to it and, curiously, few examples of the operation of the rule itself. Undoubtedly, the general rule plays an important role in preventing a contract from arising where a person privately decides to accept an offer without informing the offeror of this fact. However, if an acceptance is sent by post,[2] it is effective from the moment it is posted, and there is no need for it to reach the offeror.[3] A similar rule applies to telegrams or telemessages.[4] What the position is in relation to more modern means of electronic communication is not wholly clear. What seems to be developing is a fault-based principle under which it will be important to consider whether the recipient could have done more to ensure that he has received and understood the message. Thus there are dicta which suggest that a facsimile message sent at a time when it would be reasonable to expect the recipient not to be operating normal working hours will not be regarded as communicated the second it arrives in the in-tray.[5] Instead, a reasonable construction would appear to be that if the message is received outside normal working hours, it will only be considered to have been received at the beginning of the next working day.[6] Likewise with e-mail messages, it is common to experience some delay before the message is sent from one server to another and then on to the intended recipient thereafter. As a result, it would be fair to assume that these modern means of communication are not instantaneous. However, it is suggested that simply because of this fact it should not follow that the postal rule applies in these cases. It should be noted that what now forms the postal rule was only one of three possible options which could have been adopted in the nineteenth century and for no apparent reason the rule came to be that a posted letter of acceptance became effective as from the date of sending rather than receipt. This had no logical justification, but was simply a rule of pragmatic convenience and there is no reason why the same approach should be adopted for the purposes of electronic communication.

Expressly or impliedly, the terms offered may waive the need for communication of acceptance and, where there is a unilateral offer, communication of acceptance would appear to be unnecessary.[7]

Where the offer and acceptance do not correspond, it is difficult to argue that agreement indicates the time when a contract comes into existence. Instead, it is suggested that the courts have regard to the actions of the parties and may look for evidence of reasonable reliance or the fact of a beneficial part performance.

---

1   Collins p 109.
2   For the complexities of the postal rule see Treitel ch 2.
3   *Adams v Lindsell* (1818) 1 B & Ald 681; *Household Fire and Carriage Accident Insurance Co Ltd v Grant* (1879) 4 Ex D 216. See also ch 3 and Winfield (1939) 55 LQR 499; Simpson (1975) 91 LQR 247.
4   *Bruner v Moore* [1904] 1 Ch 305.
5   *Tenax Steamship Co Ltd v Reinante Transoceania Navegacion SA, The Brimnes* [1975] QB 929.
6   See *The Pamela* [1995] 2 Lloyd's Rep 249 at 252; *The Petr Schmidt* [1998] 2 Lloyd's Rep 1.
7   *Carlill v Carbolic Smoke Ball Co* [1893] 1 QB 256.

(2) BENEFICIAL PART PERFORMANCE OR REASONABLE RELIANCE INDICATING THE MOMENT OF RESPONSIBILITY

If one of the parties has rendered a service or has provided something of tangible benefit, the court will be under pressure to hold that there is a contract. Similarly, if a person induces an act of reliance, the court may set the moment of responsibility by reference to the time of reliance. For example, if the plaintiff is induced by the defendant to incur expense, the court may treat the time at which that expenditure is incurred as the moment when the contract comes into existence.

It has been seen already that, in the case of unilateral contracts, once performance has commenced, the offeror cannot withdraw his offer. One justification for this is that the performance may be of some benefit to the offeror.[8] Equally, if a unilateral offer induces a person to act to his detriment, the offeror will be bound from the moment of reliance.[9]

The importance of performance and reliance is also illustrated in the 'battle of the forms' cases which are difficult to reconcile with the classical rules of offer and acceptance.[10] These create the legal equivalent of the irresistible force meeting the immovable object.[11] In such instances, the rule that an offer and acceptance must correspond tends to be ignored, but some of the cases may be explained on the basis that there has been an act of reliance or a part performance which confers a benefit on the other party. In a typical battle of the forms, each party will have used his own printed contract forms. The buyer may have enquired as to the availability of the goods he wishes to purchase. The seller will respond on his standard form, citing his conditions of sale. The buyer may then place his order using his own standard order form, which may contain his conditions of purchase. The seller may then return a confirmation note in which he refers back to his conditions of sale. Finally, the buyer will take delivery of the goods. It can be seen that traditional offer and acceptance analysis may encounter some difficulty in ascertaining when a contract comes into existence. A brief consideration of these circumstances might suggest that there is no contract, since the early thrusts in the process of correspondence are a succession of counteroffers, each of which has the effect of cancelling any earlier offer.[12] One way of resolving the problem is to ask which of the parties has put in the last shot,[13] namely, the last clear reference to a particular set of terms. Under this approach, the last shot is the offer, and the court must consider whether or not that offer has been accepted. However, an examination of the cases reveals that this approach is not always taken, and that an important factor is whether one party has led the other to rely on him. This may be the case where one of the parties signs a document leading the other party to believe that the signatory is prepared to contract on the other's terms. For example, in *Butler Machine Tool Co Ltd v Ex-Cell-O Corpn Ltd*[14] a process of correspondence similar to that outlined above involved a conflict in the standard forms over the issue of price variation. An examination of the various responses revealed that the seller had put in the last shot. But, the contract was held to be made on the buyers' terms because the seller, at an earlier stage, had signed and returned to the buyers a confirmation of their order. The seller's signature was held to be a positive and unequivocal act on his part.[15]

8   See *Morrison Shipping Co Ltd v R* (1924) 20 Ll L Rep 283.
9   See *Errington v Errington and Woods* [1952] 1 KB 290.
10 See Hoggett (1970) 33 MLR 518; Adams (1983) JBL 297; Jacobs (1985) 34 ICLQ 297.
11 See *Re Doughboy Industries Inc* 233 NYS 2d 488 (1962).
12 *Hyde v Wrench* (1840) 3 Beav 334.
13 *British Road Services Ltd v Arthur V Crutchley & Co Ltd* [1968] 1 All ER 811; *Butler Machine Tool Co Ltd v Ex-Cell-O Corpn (England) Ltd* [1979] 1 All ER 965.
14 [1979] 1 All ER 965.
15 Ibid at 969 (per Lord DENNING MR) and at 971 (per BRIDGE LJ).

In *Butler* the thing contracted for was a piece of machinery which the seller had already manufactured. It might be said that, if the dispute had arisen at a time when the machine was still to be made, the parties would not have proceeded with the contract. However, the seller had manufactured the machine and the buyer needed it. The court therefore felt obliged to look for some solution. In these circumstances, a number of different solutions might be adopted.[16] A contract could be said to have been made either on the seller's terms or on the buyer's terms. Alternatively a contract might be made according to the terms that the common law would imply in such circumstances. A further suggestion is that a contract could be based on an amalgam of the buyer's and seller's terms of contracting. If the parties have dealt with each other in the past, then the previous dealings between them might also be considered so as to resolve any dispute.[17] In the last resort, if the language used by the parties is thought insufficient to point to a contract, a restitutionary remedy might be granted so as to allow the plaintiff to recover from the defendant the value of any benefit received.[18]

A third situation where a reliance analysis is more convincing than one based on agreement is where the courts infer a collateral warranty. If a person gives an assurance that a wrecked ship can be found in a particular location, and the person to whom the assurance is addressed incurs expense in setting up a salvage operation, the date that expense is incurred will be treated as the date on which the collateral contract comes into existence.[19] An attempt to apply traditional agreement-based analysis in these circumstances will inevitably create difficulties.

4.   UNDERPINNING VALUES AND POLICIES

The rules of offer, counteroffer, rejection and acceptance as a means of determining when a contractual obligation comes into being have been the subject of much criticism, having been described as out of date.[20] The difficulty with alternative formulations, such as looking at the conduct of the parties alone,[1] is that they may tend to create uncertainty which would be undesirable, especially in business transactions. Accordingly, the rules of offer and acceptance are repeatedly used as a mechanism for determining when a contractual obligation arises,[2] despite the fact that they have been admitted to be defective in many respects.

The reason why the mechanism of offer and acceptance cannot provide a full answer to the question of when a contractual obligation arises is that the rules are a product of the classical model, under which the value of individualism was given pride of place. To understand the modern approach, it is necessary to apply the rules on agreement in the light of the different values and policies which apply in the twentieth and twenty-first centuries. In particular, it is necessary to consider matters such as social co-operation, fairness in exchange relationships and the different approaches which may be taken when dealing with consumer transactions as opposed to dealings between businessmen.

16   Ibid at 968–969 (per LORD DENNING MR).
17   *Henry Kendall & Sons v Lillico & Sons Ltd* [1969] 2 AC 31.
18   See *Peter Lind & Co Ltd v Mersey Docks and Harbour Board* [1972] 2 Lloyd's Rep 234; *British Steel Corpn v Cleveland Bridge and Engineering Co Ltd* [1984] 1 All ER 504.
19   *McRae v Commonwealth Disposals Commission* (1950) 84 CLR 377.
20   *Butler Machine Tool Co Ltd v Ex-Cell-O Corpn Ltd* [1979] 1 All ER 965 at 968 (per LORD DENNING MR).
1   *The Aramis* [1989] 1 Lloyd's Rep 213 at 224 (per BINGHAM LJ).
2   See *Hispanica de Petroleos SA v Vencedora Oceanica Navegacion SA, The Kapetan Markos NL (No 2)* [1987] 2 Lloyd's Rep 321 at 331 (per MUSTILL LJ).

(1)   SOCIAL CO-OPERATION [3]

The classical view of contracting parties as antagonistic individuals seeking the best for themselves is consistent with the idea that the majority of contracts are discrete transactions entered into between parties who are probably unknown to each other. But this view has to be qualified in a number of respects. First, where one of the parties is a consumer, the view of the contract as a discrete transaction is probably accurate, but because of the disparity of bargaining power between business and consumer contractors, it is difficult to regard the consumer as someone able to negotiate the best deal for himself.

The idea that all contracts are discrete transactions is also a matter which must be qualified. The difficulty which the classical rules of offer and acceptance give rise to is that they envisage a contract as a one-off transaction in which agreement is reached on-the-spot when terms satisfactory to both parties have been negotiated. In particular, the rule that an acceptance must be absolute and unconditional does not go down well in terms of business practice, since it quite frequently fails to meet the need of the business community for flexibility. The rule that an acceptance should be without any sort of qualification can sometimes prove to be far too rigid a requirement.[4]

There are many contracts of a relational nature such as employment contracts and other long-term business relationships in which alterations arise out of day-to-day operations, there are gaps in the planning process, there may be agreements to agree, and in order to deal with possible future disputes, there may be an agreement to refer the dispute to a third party such as an arbitrator.[5] Moreover, it is arguable that even in the nineteenth-century market economy, the idea that all contractual relations were based on discrete transactions was not a complete description of the wider range of contractual relations which existed at the time.[6] For example, ongoing relationships were readily discoverable in contracts relating to the production and distribution of goods and long-term employment relationships in a wide variety of different markets. What is important to emphasise in these long-term relationships and multipartite transactions, such as will arise where a series of contracts is entered into with a view to producing and distributing goods to their ultimate market, is that the parties develop a relationship of mutual dependence and will seek to encourage reciprocity in performance of the various obligations undertaken. Furthermore, it has been argued that in such relationships 'opportunistic behaviour' such as reneging on the agreement or taking advantage of unanticipated events is discouraged.[7]

In the case of a long-term relationship what becomes important is the ability of the parties to co-operate with each other. For example in *Sim v Rotherham Metropolitan Borough Council*[8] the question arose whether a teacher could refuse to provide cover for absent colleagues. In ascertaining what the contract was, it was necessary to look at the actions of the parties and the background circumstances.[9] It was accepted that the job of a teacher cannot be confined to imparting knowledge, but was required to obey the reasonable directions of the head teacher as the circumstances of the case might dictate. No surprise was expressed that the teacher's contract failed to spell out in detail her specific obligations.[10] Moreover many commercial dealings involving networks of inter-

3   See Adams & Brownsword *Key Issues in Contract* (Butterworths, 1995), ch 9.
4   See Howarth (1987) JBL 122.
5   See Macneil (1978) 72 Northwestern University LR 854, 865; Macneil (1985) Wisconsin LR 483, 505.
6   See Macneil (1986) 96 Ethics 567, 591–2.
7   See Lorenz 'Neither Friends nor Strangers' in Thompson, Frances, Levacic and Mitchell (eds) *Markets, Hierarchies and Networks* (London, Sage Publications, 1991) p 186.
8   [1986] 3 All ER 387.
9   Applying *Liverpool City Council v Irwin* [1977] AC 239 at 252–253 (per Lord WILBERFORCE).
10   *Sim v Rotherham Metropolitan Borough Council* [1986] 3 All ER 387 at 403 (per SCOTT J).

related contracts are better described as relational contracts rather than as transactions. They involve complex inter-relationships in which the parties may be more interested in flexibility than in certainty.

In practice, there is evidence that businessmen do not always insist on fine details in their contracts as this can be bad for continuing business relations.[11] In many instances, there will be widely accepted conventions within a particular area of business. All businesses within that area will abide by those conventions, and there will be no need to spell out the fine details of the contract.[12]

Even in the case of discrete transactions, the rules on what is an offer capable of giving rise to a binding contractual relationship also lend themselves to co-operation between the parties. For example the court may recognise that negotiations between the parties can spread over a considerable period of time. In such circumstances, the parties may appear to have come to an agreement. However, the court may consider that more time is required for the purposes of gathering information or to reflect on the commitment which is to be made. As a matter of policy, the court may provide the necessary room for manoeuvre by regarding a statement as an invitation to treat rather than as an offer.

A response to an invitation to treat is not regarded as the acceptance of an offer. Thus, an invitation for tenders is generally regarded as an invitation to make an offer,[13] since the parties need to ascertain the terms of the contract to supply the goods requested. However, in some instances, the request for tenders may be so specific in its language that no further negotiation is necessary, in which case the invitation may be construed as an offer to supply on the conditions specified. Thus in *Harvela Investments Ltd v Royal Trust Co of Canada (CI) Ltd*[14] an invitation to make an offer to purchase shares was taken to have been worded in such a way as to indicate that what was expected from each bidder was a fixed offer to purchase at the highest price the bidder was prepared to pay. As a result, when one of the bidders submitted a fixed bid and a referential bid claiming that the bidder was prepared to buy the shares at a price of $101,000 more than any other bid received, the referential bid was held not to comply with the conditions specified in the invitation. Moreover, this may also be seen as an example of the court taking account of the value of co-operation in a relational setting by ruling out the opportunistic behaviour of the referential bidder.

A similar policy in favour of allowing time for reflection seems to underlie the rule on agreements 'subject to contract'. Where an agreement for the sale of a house is made, the use of the formula 'sold subject to contract' indicates that there is no binding contract between the parties.[15] The use of this formula is essentially a paternalistic device designed to protect a person from committing himself until he has had time to consult a solicitor. For example, the purchaser may need to obtain the necessary finance to purchase the property or have it surveyed before any legal commitment is made.

(2)   FAIRNESS IN EXCHANGE NEGOTIATIONS

The classical theory had little room for notions of fairness of exchange, except in so far as some unfair tactics might serve to prevent a true agreement from being made. Thus with the exception of rules on mistake, misrepresentation and duress concerning the

---

11   See Macaulay *Non-Contractual Relations in Business* (1963) 28 Am Sociological Rev 45 abridged in Aubert (ed) *Sociology of Law* (1969) pp 195–209; Beale and Dugdale (1975) BJL & S 45; Tillotson *Contract Law in Perspective* (2nd edn, 1986) ch 5.
12   Beale and Dugdale (1975) BJL & S 45 at 48.
13   *Spencer v Harding* (1870) LR 5 CP 561.
14   [1986] AC 207.
15   *Winn v Bull* (1877) 7 Ch D 29; *Eccles v Bryant* [1948] Ch 93.

issue of procedural unfairness, there was little in the classical theory requiring the exercise of good faith in contract negotiations. However, a feature of the value of social co-operation is that the parties to contract negotiations should deal with each other in good faith. Of course the danger with a general duty of good faith is that it may tend to produce undesirable uncertainty[16] although this has not prevented other jurisdictions from embracing a general duty of good faith.[17] In general terms, the arguments in favour of a doctrine of good faith are first that it would tend to encourage transparency in the law by allowing a court to do justice quite openly rather than have to resort to 'bending' an existing rule of law to fit the circumstances of the case. Secondly, it could operate as a means of filling gaps where they become apparent, without disturbing established principles. Thirdly, it is arguable that a doctrine of good faith would be more responsive to the different expectations which may arise in different contracting contexts. Thus if it were to be recognised that certain contracting environments are essentially competitive[18] then the application of principles of good faith could be rolled back, but in other contexts, it could be applied with greater vigour, as the context demands. Finally, it may be argued that a doctrine of good faith would give the parties greater security and flexibility in the way in which they deal with each other. For example, if the contracting parties are aware from the start that they will both be required by the law to act co-operatively, then this is likely to cause them to act in a different way than they might have done if they worked on the assumption that the law encourages opportunism and exploitation.

To an extent, English law is beginning to see the emergence of principles of good faith, both in the context of relational contracting and, to a lesser extent, in the context of negotiations leading to discrete transactions. The developing doctrine of economic duress[19] which applies particularly to attempts to vary the terms of an existing relationship attempts to distinguish between the acceptable inducement to agree to a variation and an illegitimate threat. Similarly, in *Williams v Roffey Bros & Nicholls (Contractors) Ltd*[20] what appears to lie behind the approach of the court to the issue of performance of an existing duty as consideration seems to be a desire to see fair dealing between the parties to a contract renegotiation. While it would be wrong to say that English law has never embraced the idea of contracting in good faith, it should be observed that the common law notion is more one of not contracting in bad faith, with the result that most examples of a good faith doctrine tend to turn on the negative aspects of the defendant's conduct in dealing with the claimant.

In general terms, English courts are opposed to the introduction of a broad duty of good faith. It has been said that broad concepts of honesty and fair dealing are too uncertain a guide when seeking to determine the existence of an obligation [1] and that the repudiation by one of the parties of his moral responsibility is not a matter for the courts.[2] Similarly, it has also been observed by a member of the House of Lords that 'the concept of a duty to carry on negotiations in good faith is inherently repugnant to the adversarial position of the parties when involved in negotiations.' [3] Generally, the

---

16   See McLean (1988) CLJ 172.
17   See French Civil Code art 1134; German Civil Code art 242; *Hoffman v Red Owl Stores* 26 Wis 2d 683, 133 NW 2d 267 (1965) (USA); *Waltons Stores Ltd v Maher* (1988) 76 ALR 513; cf *Holman Construction Ltd v Delta Timber Co Ltd* [1972] NZLR 1081, all of which enact or point to a duty of care in contract negotiations.
18   For example, the commodities market.
19   See chs 6 and 24.
20   [1990] 1 All ER 512. See also ch 6 and Hooley (1991) JBL 19.
1   *Banque Financière de la Cité SA v Westgate Insurance Co Ltd* [1989] 2 All ER 952 at 990 (per SLADE LJ).
2   *Kleinwort Benson Ltd v Malaysia Mining Corpn Bhd* [1989] 1 All ER 785 at 797 (per RALPH GIBSON LJ).
3   *Walford v Miles* [1992] 1 All ER 453 at 460 (per LORD ACKNER).

arguments against the adoption of a duty to contract in good faith are that it would undermine the individualist basis of the common law by requiring contracting parties to think about the legitimate interests of others. Secondly, in commercial transactions, such a doctrine would create unacceptable uncertainty. Thirdly, if such a doctrine were to be adopted, it would require an inquiry into the state of mind of the parties at the time of contracting so as to ascertain their reasons for acting in a particular way. Fourthly, it would restrict the autonomy of the parties to a contract, which has prompted courts to decline to give relief even where enforcement of the contract might be unconscionable, since to do so would set aside an express provision which the parties could expect to be enforced .[4] But this has not prevented the courts from recognising bad faith where it exists and from dealing with it accordingly.

Whether or not there is a general duty to contract in good faith depends, in part, on principles which are to be found outside the rules which traditionally form part of a contract law course. But the law in this area is not strictly 'the law of contract' but 'the law relating to the making of contracts'. Thus the parties to a contractual relationship may owe each other a duty to take reasonable care in the course of contract negotiations. Thus it follows that negligent advice given during the course of negotiations may be actionable under the Misrepresentation Act 1967 or may attract liability in the tort of negligence.[5] These cases have all been ones in which a finalised contract has followed the negotiations, but the test of a general duty to contract in good faith must come from those cases in which the negotiations have not resulted in finalised contractual dealings between the parties.

Recent cases at appellate level seem to be moving towards the position in which contracting parties are required to behave decently towards each other, to warn each other of risks and not to take unfair advantage of a stronger position. It has been observed that a duty to contract in good faith involves more than just a duty not to deceive, but is a principle of fair and open dealing.[6] This duty, it appears, extends to drawing the attention of the other party to the fact that a very high price is payable for borrowing hired goods for longer than the agreed period of hire.[7] Moreover, the same general principle also lies behind the rules on giving explicit notice of a particularly onerous exclusion clause.[8] In this area in particular, English law has tended to ask whether in all the circumstances, it is fair to regard a person as bound by the term in question, which produces a result very similar to that which would be obtained by an application of the civil law principle of good faith.[9]

There are also indications that good faith is a relevant factor in other areas such as agreements to lock oneself out of negotiations with another person and in relation to invitations to tender. For example a person who invites others to submit a tender for the operation of pleasure flights from an airport, specifying that tenders should be received by a particular date and time, at least owes a duty to consider all tenders received by that time and will be liable in damages for a failure to consider a conforming tender.[10] While this duty does not oblige the person issuing the invitation to accept a particular tender, regard was had to the fact that the procedure was heavily weighted in favour of the invitor.[11] Similar considerations also apply to the issue of letters of intent which are

---

4   See *Union Eagle Ltd v Golden Achievement Ltd* [1997] 2 All ER 215 at 218–219 (per LORD HOFFMANN).
5   *Esso Petroleum Co Ltd v Mardon* [1976] QB 801 and see ch 10.
6   *Interfoto Picture Library Ltd v Stiletto Visual Programmes Ltd* [1988] 1 All ER 348 at 352 (per BINGHAM LJ).
7   Ibid.
8   *J Spurling Ltd v Bradshaw* [1956] 2 All ER 121 at 125 (per DENNING LJ): the so called 'red hand' test, and see ch 22.
9   *Interfoto Picture Library Ltd v Stiletto Visual Programmes Ltd* [1988] 1 All ER 348 at 357 (per BINGHAM LJ).
10   *Blackpool and Fylde Aero Club Ltd v Blackpool Borough Council* [1990] 3 All ER 25.
11   Ibid at 30 (per BINGHAM LJ).

capable of inducing acts of reliance on the part of the addressee. Reliance losses in the form of expenditure incurred in the belief that a contract will be made may be recovered if assurances in the letter of intent can be treated as the basis of a collateral contract.[12] Moreover, in *Crabb v Arun District Council*[13] the council had led the plaintiff to believe that he would be granted a right of access on to a road adjoining his land. The Court of Appeal held that the plaintiff was entitled to the right of access because he had relied to his detriment on the belief that such a right of way would be granted by selling other land of his to a third party. In one way, it can be said that this case goes further than other cases because the council did not actively encourage the plaintiff to sell his land.

Where contract negotiations have commenced, for example for the sale of a business, the vendor may encounter others who show an interest in purchasing the business. In these circumstances, assurances may be made by the vendor which encourage one of the potential purchasers to incur expense. Here it is necessary to consider whether those assurances have contractual force. It has been seen that the classical response to such a situation is that if there is no concluded agreement, no contractual obligations will arise. But the application of principles of good faith may invite a different conclusion. Generally if the assurances given by the vendor amount to an agreement to negotiate, no contractual obligation will arise,[14] unless they have resulted in some definite expenditure on the part of the person to whom they were addressed in the expectation that a contract will be entered into.[15]

In contrast, the principle of good faith in negotiation may have some limited force in relation to an agreement not to deal with a particular person if it is sufficiently definite. In *Walford v Miles*[16] the defendants had been negotiating with X for the sale of a business, but were dissatisfied with the price offered. Subsequently they entered into negotiations with the plaintiffs who provided a letter of comfort from their bankers to the effect that credit of £2 million was available should the plaintiffs decide to purchase the business. In return, the defendants agreed not to give further consideration to any alternative proposal and that they would cease to deal with X. At all times the defendants kept in contact with X and subsequently sold the business to him after his offer had been raised to £2 million. The House of Lords held that the defendants were liable in damages to the limited extent that they had agreed to lock themselves out of negotiations with others for a specified period of time.[17] It is important to emphasise that the remedy given was one for damages in respect of the costs incurred following the encouragement of an expectation that a contract may materialise. What *Walford* does not decide is that the 'lock out' clause obliges the parties to contract with each other. Accordingly, all the claimant will receive will be reliance damages and a request to grant an injunction to prevent breach of the lock out clause will be refused.[18] However, a lock out clause is recognised in law and it can be used as a means of preventing the defendant from raising the asking price for property to the level of a higher offer received from a third party during the period of 'lock out'.[19]

In *Walford v Miles* it was also held that English law does not recognise a contract to negotiate on the ground that this amounts to an unspecific agreement to deal with the

12   *Turriff Construction Ltd v Regalia Knitting Mills Ltd* (1971) 222 Estates Gazette 169.
13   [1976] Ch 179. See ch 6.
14   *Walford v Miles* [1992] 1 All ER 453; *Courtney and Fairbairn Ltd v Tolaini Bros (Hotels) Ltd* [1975] 1 All ER 716.
15   *Trollope & Colls Ltd v Atomic Power Constructions Ltd* [1963] 1 WLR 333.
16   [1992] 1 All ER 453. See Neill (1992) 108 LQR 405; Brown (1992) JBL 353.
17   Ibid at 461–462 (per Lord Ackner).
18   *Tye v House* [1997] 41 EG 160.
19   *Pitt v PHH Asset Management Ltd* [1993] 4 All ER 961.

other party in good faith, which lacks the necessary certainty required by English law.[20] Conversely, an undertaking to use best endeavours to negotiate an agreement with the other party was held to be sufficiently certain to be enforceable.[1]

The difficulty which *Walford* creates is that while the House of Lords has denied the existence of a general duty to negotiate in good faith, they have still recognised a limited requirement of good faith. To say that a person may validly lock himself out of dealings with others does not lock him in to negotiations with the person to whom the assurance is addressed,[2] but an agreement to use best endeavours to negotiate an agreement with the other party surely imports a requirement of good faith. Where a person agrees to use his best endeavours to reach an agreement, there must be circumstances in which those best endeavours come to nought. This undertaking to use best endeavours is presumably broken where in bad faith the defendant fails to attempt to reach an agreement. In having recognised one variety of duty to negotiate in good faith, the bare assertion that a general duty to negotiate in good faith is unenforceable on the grounds of lack of certainty becomes very unconvincing. This is especially so if the courts can use their power to imply terms into the contract to make it more specific. For example, an implied term to the effect that the attempt at negotiations will last for a reasonable time would not be excessive.[3]

(3)   BUSINESS AND CONSUMER TRANSACTIONS

In determining when a contractual obligation arises, regard may be had, expressly or impliedly, to the nature of the transaction. In particular, it is necessary to consider the respective bargaining positions of the parties. The fact that one of the parties is a consumer and therefore presumed likely to be in a weak position vis-à-vis the other may be a reason for using the rules of offer and acceptance in such a way as to provide some means of protection for the weaker party. In contrast, in dealings between businessmen, there may be a desire to develop rules which provide at least some measure of certainty so as to allow for forward planning.

(i)   Consumer transactions

Since the notion of protecting a weaker party is not wholly consistent with classical rules, it is reasonable to expect decisions motivated by a desire to protect consumers to be at odds with many of the rules of offer and acceptance. However, this is not universally the case, since it may be possible by employing a purely formalist approach to legal rules to achieve the desired effect.[4]

The rule that the terms of an offer must be clearly communicated to the other party before they can properly form the basis of a contract has been used on a number of occasions as an instrument of consumer protection, particularly in the context of the validity of an exclusion clause contained in a standard form document.[5] If a person is to be bound he must be aware of the existence of the exclusion. Thus, a notice on a hotel bedroom wall making reference to a purported exclusion of liability on the part of the hotel owners will not be effective, since the offer and acceptance occur when

---

20   Ibid at 460 (per LORD ACKNER).
1   Ibid.
2   Ibid at 461 (per LORD ACKNER).
3   See *Walford v Miles* [1991] 2 EGLR 185 at 188 (per BINGHAM LJ).
4   See Adams & Brownsword (1987) 7 Legal Studies 205 at 214; Adams & Brownsword *Understanding Contract Law* (Fontana, 2nd edn, 1994) ch 8.
5   See also ch 22.

the guest is booked into the hotel.[6] Moreover, for the proferens to be able to rely on the exclusion it may be advisable for him to make the consumer aware of the content of the exclusion.[7] Even where there are previous dealings between the parties, if the person seeking to rely on the exclusion clause has failed to make his intentions clear on the particular occasion, he may find that the judicial response is that he has failed to take sufficient steps to communicate the terms of his offer to the consumer.[8]

Generally, decisions reached with a desire to protect the consumer are more likely to fly in the face of classical rules, since they are concerned with discouraging bad faith, the prevention of injurious reliance and general principles of reasonableness and fairness.

The classical view of how contracts are made is often distinctly at odds with the way modern consumer transactions are entered into. For example the idea that contracting parties negotiate with each other until they reach a mutually beneficial outcome does not tally with the consumer transaction as a simultaneous exchange relationship. Yet we are told that shop and supermarket displays[9] and advertisements[10] are merely invitations to treat and that it is the consumer buyer who offers to purchase the goods displayed or advertised. While the position in respect of advertisements may be justified since it may be necessary to obtain further information before proceeding with a purchase, the same cannot always be said of retail displays since the purchaser is faced with the option of purchasing at the price stated by the retailer or not purchasing at all. It would not be too difficult to imply an offer on the part of the retailer which lasted only so long as supplies lasted.[11] In any event, most modern retailing giants have such sophisticated stock control procedures that it is unlikely that they would find themselves in a position whereby they could not meet the necessary demand. However, there is an alternative rationale for the rule on retailers' invitations to treat which, itself, has the interests of consumers in mind. The normal justification for treating the display of goods as an invitation to treat is that without such a rule, the consumer would be bound from the time of selecting goods from the shelf if he were to be taken to have accepted an offer. As a result the general rule allows the consumer to change his mind prior to making the final commitment at the check-out.

In the case of advertisements, although the general rule is that they will amount to no more than an invitation to treat, there may be circumstances in which the advertisement offers something specific and, in the interests of consumer protection, may be regarded as an offer capable of acceptance. Thus a misleading advertisement by a manufacturer of a patent medicine offering a reward should a consumer purchase and use his product in accordance with instructions supplied with the product may be taken to have made an offer.[12] Similarly, the placement of advertisements in travel agents' shops proclaiming the benefits of a bonding scheme offered by a trade association may be taken to offer something specific to consumers to the extent that the advertisement becomes an offer capable of acceptance.[13]

6   *Olley v Marlborough Court Ltd* [1949] 1 KB 532.
7   *Thornton v Shoe Lane Parking Ltd* [1971] 2 QB 163.
8   *McCutcheon v David MacBrayne Ltd* [1964] 1 WLR 125.
9   *Timothy v Simpson* (1834) 6 C & P 499; *Pharmaceutical Society of Great Britain v Boots Cash Chemists (Southern) Ltd* [1952] 2 QB 795; affd [1953] 1 QB 401; *Fisher v Bell* [1961] 1 QB 394. See also Unger (1953) 16 MLR 369.
10   *Partridge v Crittenden* [1968] 2 All ER 421. Cf *Grainger & Son v Gough* [1896] AC 325.
11   See *Lefkowitz v Great Minneapolis Surplus Stores* 86 NW 2d 689 (1957).
12   *Carlill v Carbolic Smoke Ball Co* [1893] 1 QB 256.
13   *Bowerman v ABTA Ltd* [1995] NLJR 1815.

(ii)   Business transactions

Since the rules of the classical model, by and large, leave the contracting parties in little doubt as to what is required, the necessary measure of certainty is provided. On this basis, if a court wishes to reach a decision which achieves the necessary degree of certainty for the purposes of business transactions, it will normally be able to do so by applying classical rules. But, it has already been observed that there are business relationships which do not strive for the same degree of certainty as may be required in discrete transactions. Accordingly, there may be a preference for rules which allow for the flexibility needed in these relational contracts. Moreover, where commercial practice suggests a conclusion which is at variance with an application of classical rules, it may be necessary to bend those rules in order to justify the conclusion the court desires to reach.[14]

5.   THE CONTENT OF CONTRACTUAL OBLIGATIONS

Classical theory based the content of a contractual obligation upon the notion of agreement, that is the content of the contract was represented by what the parties had agreed. But, it must be understood that this agreement is judged on an objective basis, taking account of the circumstances surrounding the contracting parties and the way in which they have acted towards each other and how those actions are to be reasonably understood from the outside.

(1)   THE OBJECTIVE THEORY OF INTENTION

In order to circumvent the problem of the apparent lack of agreement, the courts have adopted an objective test of intention under which all available evidence is taken into account.[15] Thus in *Smith v Hughes*[16] it was stated that:

> If what a man's real intention may be, he so conducts himself that a reasonable man would believe that he was assenting to the terms proposed by the other party upon that belief enters into the contract with him, the man thus conducting himself would be equally bound as if he had intended to agree to the other party's terms.

This objective theory requires the court to look at what the parties have done rather than at what they might subjectively intend. The orthodox rule is that words or actions are to be interpreted as they were reasonably understood by the person to whom they were addressed.[17] On the basis that what matters is the reasonable understanding of the addressee, it may be argued that this amounts to little more than a version of the reliance-based rules on estoppel.[18] Certainly, both the objective theory of intention and

---

14   *New Zealand Shipping Co Ltd v AM Satterthwaite & Co Ltd* [1975] AC 154 at 167 (per Lord Wilberforce).

15   See Spencer [1973] CLJ 104; Howarth (1984) 100 LQR 265; Vorster (1987) 103 LQR 274; Smith and Thomas *A Casebook on Contract* (10th edn, 1996) pp 108-136.

16   (1871) LR 6 QB 597 (per Blackburn J).

17   *McCutcheon v David MacBrayne Ltd* [1964] 1 WLR 125 at 128; *Henry Kendall & Sons v William Lillico & Sons Ltd* [1969] 2 AC 31 at 33; *Ashington Piggeries Ltd v Hill Ltd* [1972] AC 441 at 502; *The Hannah Blumenthal* [1983] 1 AC 854 at 914; *Allied Marine Transport Ltd v Vale do Rio Doce Navegacao SA, The Leonidas D* [1985] 2 All ER 796 at 805; *Harvela Investments Ltd v Royal Trust Co of Canada Ltd* [1986] AC 207 at 225.

18   Indeed much of Blackburn J's inspiration for the principle espoused in *Smith v Hughes* was derived from the estoppel case of *Freeman v Cooke* (1848) 2 Exch 654. Further support can also be derived from many of the abandonment cases considered above: See inter alia, *The Hannah Blumenthal* [1983] 1 AC 854.

promissory estoppel have been regarded as examples of 'injurious reliance'.[19] Alternatively, it may be regarded as a manifestation of principles of good faith. Thus what matters are the 'reasonable expectations of honest men'.[20]

It is said to be important not to apply too objective a test,[1] for it might be possible to reach a conclusion which forces upon both parties to a contract a result which neither of them wants.[2] However it has been argued that if a wholly objective view is taken and a compromise between two extreme views is taken you are more likely to have got close to the truth than if the agreement is viewed from one side of the contract or the other.[3]

What is meant by objectivity has given rise to a difference of opinion. On the one hand it might mean that one considers the understanding of a reasonable man in the position of the maker of the statement under consideration. However, this appears not to be supported by judicial opinion. In the majority of cases, the court will judge the actions and words of the two parties and decide which party to the contract has acted most reasonably. This will normally be judged from the perspective of a reasonable man in the position of the person to whom the statement in question was addressed.[4] Invariably, the contract will be made on the basis of the understanding of the party with the most reasonable belief. However, in some cases the court has adopted a hard objective test whereby the issue of agreement is judged in a detached manner employing a 'fly-on-the-wall' test.[5]

A product of the objective theory of agreement is the parol evidence rule which provides that, where the terms of a contract have been reduced to writing, parol or extrinsic evidence cannot be admitted to add to, vary or contradict the written terms. However, rigid adherence to a rule of this sort may be criticised,[6] since it may involve ignoring evidence which a reasonable man might wish to consider. Because of this, there are a large number of 'exceptions' to the rule which serve the interests of justice by admitting extrinsic evidence to supplement or vary contract terms which have been reduced to writing.[7] However, it may be inaccurate to refer to these as 'exceptions' since they would all appear to evidence circumstances in which the parol evidence rule could not have been applied.

Some of the more important exceptions to the parol evidence rule, such as the variation[8] and estoppel exceptions,[9] and the rule on collateral contracts,[10] involve the imposition of an obligation to perform a promise where there has been an act of misplaced

---

19 See *The Hannah Blumenthal* [1983] 1 AC 854.
20 *Trentham Ltd v Archital Luxfer Ltd* [1993] 1 Lloyd's Rep 25 at 27 (per STEYN LJ) and see also LORD STEYN (1997) 113 LQR 433.
1 Cf Holmes *The Common Law* (1881) (ed Howe, 1963) p 242.
2 See Spencer [1973] CLJ 104 at 113.
3 Atiyah *Essays*, Essay No 5 p 110.
4 See *Smith v Hughes* (1871) LR 6 QB 597; *The Hannah Blumenthal* [1983] 1 AC 854 at 915 (per Lord DIPLOCK).
5 See *Solle v Butcher* [1950] 1 KB 671 at 691 (per DENNING LJ); *Frederick E Rose Ltd v William H Pim Jnr & Co Ltd* [1953] 2 QB 450 at 461 (per DENNING LJ); *Storer v Manchester City Council* [1974] 1 WLR 1403 at 1408 (per LORD DENNING MR); *Hornal v Neuberger Products Ltd* [1957] 1 QB 247 at 261 (per DENNING LJ); *Eyre v Measday* [1986] 1 All ER 488 at 493 (per SLADE LJ). See also Howarth (1984) 100 LQR 265 at 275 et seq.
6 See Law Commission Report No 154 (1986) Cmnd 9700 on the Parol Evidence Rule (para 2.7).
7 See *Treitel* pp 175–183 for a catalogue of these exceptions.
8 See *Morris v Baron & Co* [1918] AC 1; *Goss v Nugent* (1833) 5 B & Ad 58.
9 *Central London Property Trust Ltd v High Trees House Ltd* [1947] KB 130.
10 See *City and Westminster Properties (1934) Ltd v Mudd* [1959] Ch 129; *Mendelssohn v Normand Ltd* [1970] 1 QB 177; *J Evans & Son (Portsmouth) Ltd v Andrea Merzario Ltd* [1976] 1 WLR 1078; *Brikom Investments Ltd v Carr* [1979] QB 467. See also Law Commission No 154 para 2.32–2.36 and McLauchlan (1976) 3 Dalhousie LJ 136.

reliance upon the words of the promisor by the promisee.[11] In this respect, the court is still concentrating heavily on the conduct of the promisor in much the same way that the actions of the defendant are the focal point in cases of negligence.

A relatively recent development has been the use of what are called 'entire contracts clauses' which, in effect, amount to the use of an express term of the contract to produce the effect of an application of the parol evidence rule. Where operative, these terms may have the effect of expressly excluding from the contract, statements and misrepresentations which are not embodied in a written contract. Clauses purporting to have this effect tend to be couched in terms which provide that 'this agreement sets forth the entire agreement...' and that 'the purchaser acknowledges that it has not been induced to enter into this agreement by any representation or warranty other than the statements contained or referred to in schedule 6'.[12] Clearly, the effect of such a clause may be that a contracting party is prevented from relying on remedies he might otherwise have had as a result of being induced to enter a contract following a misrepresentation. However, the courts have taken a dim view of such provisions and have generally adopted the position that clauses of this nature amount to exemption clauses subject to challenge under the Unfair Contract Terms Act 1977 and the Unfair Terms in Consumer Contracts Regulations 1999.

That the courts consider which of the parties has acted most reasonably is illustrated by a pair of cases involving a mistake as to the terms of a contract, where there was a dispute as to the content of a seller's promise. In *Tamplin v James*,[13] the defendant bid for a plot of land which he believed included a garden which had been used by a previous tenant. If the defendant had consulted plans showing what was for sale, he would have discovered that it did not include the garden. It was held that specific performance could be granted and the defendant could be compelled to purchase the land exclusive of the garden which was the subject of the defendant's mistake. In *Denny v Hancock*[14] the defendant had consulted a plan of property for sale by auction. A reasonable construction of the plan was that the property for sale included all land up to an iron fence on the western side of the property. In fact, the vendor did not own all the land up to the fence. It was held that the mistake made by the defendant was one that any reasonable prospective purchaser might make,[15] therefore the court refused to grant specific performance of the contract. The difference between the two cases appears to be that the vendor's understanding of the contract was seen as more reasonable in the first case, whereas the purchaser's understanding was more reasonable in the second.

Similar reasoning may also be applied where ambiguous language is used by the promisor. The test to apply is that of the understanding of the reasonable man in the position of the person to whom the promise was addressed.[16] If ambiguous language is used, it is foreseeable that the reasonable man might misinterpret it.

Where the court does adopt an objective view of a contract based on the understanding of a reasonable man in the position of the person to whom words or actions are addressed, inevitably this may involve the imposition of an obligation upon someone who is not happy to comply.[17] The same result is also achieved if the court

---

11   See also ch 6.
12   See eg *Thomas Witter Ltd v TBP Industries Ltd* [1996] 2 All ER 573.
13   (1880) 15 Ch D 215. See also *Hartog v Colin and Shields* [1939] 3 All ER 566 and *McMaster University v Wilchar Construction Ltd* (1971) 22 DLR (3d) 9.
14   (1870) 6 Ch App 1.
15   Ibid at 11 (per JAMES LJ).
16   *Falck v Williams* [1900] AC 176.
17   A willingness to construct a contract in the absence of agreement does exist. See chs 6 and 10. See also Atiyah *Introduction* ch 4.

applies a 'fly on the wall' test, and looks at the contract in a detached manner, independent of the viewpoint of either party. In the case of a test of detached objectivity, there is greater scope for judicial imposition of contractual obligations although, if the court wishes to remain within the traditional rules on contract formation, it may adopt a non-contractual solution. For example, where a benefit has been conferred, a restitutionary remedy may be granted and where words or conduct have led to an act of misplaced reliance, it may be decided that there is a breach of duty of care.[18]

(2)   IMPLIED TERMS[19]

The perceived role of the court, in classical terminology, is to act as an umpire and to give effect to what the parties to a contract have agreed. However, the parties to a contract frequently fail to define all their duties. In these circumstances, the court has the power to imply terms into the contract. Such terms may fall into one of three categories, namely, terms implied in law, terms implied in fact and terms implied by virtue of some customary usage or business practice. The use of the terminology 'implied term' conjures up a picture of the court reading into a contract what is logically implied in the language used by the parties. On other occasions, the court may read into a contract a term that the parties may have contemplated but did not express. Alternatively, the court can imply a term which the parties would have accepted if the matter had been brought to their attention. Finally, a term can sometimes be implied where the court thinks this is desirable in the interests of justice and fairness. To talk in terms of agreement in all these cases is likely to lead to anomalies. This is particularly so where terms have been implied in the interests of justice and fairness.

(i)   Terms implied in fact

These are terms implied on a one-off basis so as to give effect to the presumed intention of both parties. A number of different tests have been put forward to explain when such a term will be implied. One such test is often referred to as the 'officious bystander' test which requires the term to be implied to be so obvious a requirement that, if an officious bystander suggested the term should be implied, both parties would immediately agree to its implication.[20] It is apparently insufficient that the term sought to be implied is a reasonable one.[1]

Other tests used by the courts include the 'business efficacy' test under which it is necessary to consider whether a term must be implied so as to make business sense of the transaction. In some cases an additional requirement of necessity has also been imposed.[2] However, this probably adds little to the business efficacy test.[3] What is clear is that the courts are not happy with the idea of implying a term simply because it is reasonable to do so. If the court were to do this, it would be tantamount to making the contract for the parties. Thus a term will not be implied if its contents would conflict with an express term in the contract.[4] Similarly, there are judicial statements to the

---

18   See ch 10.
19   See Phang (1990) JBL 394.
20   *Shirlaw v Southern Foundries (1926) Ltd* [1939] 2 KB 206; affd [1940] AC 701. See also *North Sea Energy Holdings NV v Petroleum Authority of Thailand* [1997] 2 Lloyd's Rep 418 at 431. Cf *Marcan Shipping Ltd v Polish Steamship Co, The Manifest Lipkowy* [1989] 2 Lloyd's Rep 138.
1   *Reigate v Union Manufacturing Co (Ramsbottom) Ltd* [1918] 1 KB 592; *Trollope & Colls Ltd v North West Metropolitan Regional Hospital Board* [1973] 2 All ER 260; *Liverpool City Council v Irwin* [1977] AC 239; *Shell UK Ltd v Lostock Garage Ltd* [1977] 1 All ER 481.
2   *Baker v Black Sea and Baltic General Insurance Co Ltd* [1998] 1 WLR 974 at 980
3   See *Luxor (Eastbourne) Ltd v Cooper* [1941] AC 108 at 137 (per LORD WRIGHT).
4   *Duke of Westminster v Guild* [1985] QB 688 at 700.

effect that judicial implication of a term should not facilitate an improvement in the contract, however desirable that improvement might be.[5]

Since both parties must readily agree to the term implied, unawareness of relevant facts may prove fatal, since both parties must be capable of assenting to the term. In *K C Sethia (1944) Ltd v Partabmull Rameshwar*,[6] the sellers of a quantity of Indian jute were unable to perform the contract of sale because they had failed to obtain a quota for sale to Italy. The Italian buyers were unaware of any regulations imposing quotas, therefore it was held that no term could be implied that the contract was subject to quota. Although knowledge of the relevant facts is important, it is also necessary to consider what type of knowledge is required. In some instances the facts demonstrated that one of the parties did not have actual knowledge of the facts required to allow the implication of a term.[7] But there are judicial inferences to the effect that in certain circumstances, it may be possible to infer a common intention in the absence of actual knowledge of the relevant facts.[8]

If the term is one which one of the parties probably would not have agreed to, then it is not likely to be implied, even if it appears reasonable to do so. For example, in *Shell UK Ltd v Lostock Garage Ltd*[9] the defendants had agreed to obtain their supplies of petrol and oil solely from Shell. During a petrol price war, Shell gave subsidies to some of its garages, but not to the defendants. The defendants obtained supplies of petrol from another source. In an action by Shell to obtain an injunction, the defendants argued that a term should be implied that Shell would not abnormally discriminate against them. It was held that, as desirable as such a term might seem, one could not be implied, because Shell probably would not have agreed to it had it been suggested by an officious bystander. Likewise in *Luxor (Eastbourne) Ltd v Cooper*[10] it was inherently unlikely that an owner of property who had agreed to pay commission to an estate agent only on 'completion of the sale' would agree to a term to the effect that he would not sell to anyone other than a person introduced by the estate agent.

An alternative to the officious bystander test is one to the effect that a term may be implied in order to give business efficacy to the transaction.[11] Whether there is a difference between the two tests is a moot point. It has been said that the bystander test is broader than the efficacy test in that the former involves an objective, reasonable man approach and that the latter is a more stringent test, operating only in order to make a contract workable.[12] Conversely, the view has been expressed that the two tests are the same, namely that in order to give business efficacy to the contract a term may be implied where the parties as reasonable men would have agreed to its implication without hesitation.[13] However, there are differences between the tests since the efficacy test appears to have little to do with the intentions of the parties.

5   *Trollope & Colls Ltd v North West Metropolitan Regional Hospital Board* [1973] 1 WLR 601 at 609.
6   [1950] 1 All ER 51; affd [1951] 2 Lloyd's Rep 89.
7   See eg *Spring v National Amalgamated Stevedores and Dockers Society* [1956] 1 WLR 585.
8   See *Star Shipping AS v China National Foreign Trade Transportation Corpn, The Star Texas* [1993] 2 Lloyd's Rep 445 at 451 (per STEYN LJ).
9   [1977] 1 All ER 481. See also *Wilson v Best Travel Ltd* [1993] 1 All ER 353.
10   [1941] AC 108. See also *Kumar v AGF Insurance Ltd* [1998] 4 All ER 788 at 793.
11   *The Moorcock* [1886–90] All ER Rep 530 at 534 (per BOWEN LJ); *Luxor (Eastbourne) Ltd v Cooper* [1941] AC 108 at 137 (per LORD WRIGHT); *Barrett v Lounova (1982) Ltd* [1989] 1 All ER 351 at 357 (per KERR LJ).
12   *Associated Japanese Bank (International) Ltd v Crédit du Nord SA* [1988] 3 All ER 902 at 908–909 (per Steyn J).
13   *Liverpool City Council v Irwin* [1977] AC 239 at 258 (per LORD CROSS); *Bank of Nova Scotia v Hellenic Mutual War Risks Association, The Good Luck* [1989] 3 All ER 628 at 665 (per MAY LJ).

It seems that if either test is satisfied, a term may be implied.[14] However, the difficulty here is that the officious bystander test is based on the presumed intention of both parties, whereas to make a contract workable under the efficacy test involves consideration of what the reasonable person considers necessary and involves imposing an obligation, despite the intentions of the parties.[15]

What does appear to flow from both tests is that a term cannot be implied simply because it is reasonable. However, the language used by the courts sometimes suggests that reasonable terms may be implied. In *The Moorcock*,[16] the plaintiff's ship was badly damaged in the course of unloading at the defendant's wharf when it was grounded on an uneven river bed at low tide. The defendant could have ascertained the state of the river bed, but had done nothing and the contract did not provide for this event. The Court of Appeal implied a term that the defendant should have taken reasonable care to see that the berth was safe and, if it was not safe, that the plaintiff should be warned accordingly.[17] BOWEN LJ stated that:[18] 'An implied warranty or . . . a covenant in law . . . is . . . founded on the presumed intentions of the parties and upon reason. It is an implication which the law draws . . . with the object of giving efficacy to the transaction and preventing such a failure of consideration as cannot have been within the contemplation of either of the parties.'

By referring to a covenant in law and to the implication of terms on the grounds of reason, BOWEN LJ was not exclusively concerned with the intention of the parties. In the circumstances, it would be difficult to say that the officious bystander test had been satisfied, since one of the parties might not have agreed to the implication of such a term. From this, it follows that the parties' intentions are not always crucial in deciding what obligations should be implied. Instead, it seems that, in appropriate circumstances, a term can be implied where it is reasonable to do so, for example, to give business efficacy to a transaction. Certainly, the term implied in *The Moorcock* was regarded by BOWEN LJ as a reasonable modification to the arrangements made by the parties.[19]

Evidence that a court may sometimes imply a reasonable term in a contract can be found in cases where the parties to a contract cannot agree on the price to be paid for the thing sold. For a long time, there was a rule to the effect that, if a contract provided for a method of ascertaining the price but that method could not be put into effect, the court would not substitute an alternative method, [20] even where one of the parties was at fault.[1] In *Sudbrook Trading Estate Ltd v Eggleton*,[2] an option to purchase the reversion of a number of leases provided that the price payable should be determined by valuers, one to be nominated by each of the parties. The lessors refused to appoint a valuer. The House of Lords held that, on its true construction, the contract was for a sale at a fair and reasonable price. Provided all other necessary preconditions had been satisfied, the court could substitute its own machinery so as to ascertain a fair and reasonable price. It was considered important that the parties had chosen to have the price assessed by professional valuers who would apply objective standards in coming to their assessment.[3]

---

14   *Marcan Shipping Ltd v Polish Steamship Co, The Manifest Lipkowy* [1989] 2 Lloyd's Rep 138 at 143 (per MAY LJ).

15   *Barrett v Lounova (1982) Ltd* [1989] 1 All ER 351 at 357 (per KERR LJ).

16   [1886–90] All ER Rep 530.

17   Ibid at 534 (per LORD ESHER MR) and at 536 (per BOWEN LJ).

18   Ibid at 534.

19   Ibid at 536.

20   *Morgan v Milman* (1853) 3 De GM & G 24.

1   See *Agar v Macklew* (1825) 2 Sim & St 418 and *Vickers v Vickers* (1867) LR 4 Eq 529. Now overruled by *Sudbrook Trading Estate Ltd v Eggleton* [1983] 1 AC 444.

2   [1983] AC 444.

3   Ibid at 479 (per LORD DIPLOCK) and at 483–484 (per LORD FRASER of Tullybelton). Cf LORD RUSSELL of Killowen at 486.

The notion of the reasonable price is also something that may be invoked in cases where a benefit has been conferred, but where the contract itself has broken down. In such circumstances, it may be open to the court to make a restitutionary award on the basis of a quantum meruit. Such award as may be made has to be valued objectively, since it may be difficult to place any subjective value upon the work done.[4]

Where the language used by the parties is particularly clear, this would appear to make the implication of reasonable terms much more difficult. If a builder agrees to construct the walls of a house using nine-inch brick and he complies with the contract specification, a term that the house will be reasonably fit for habitation may not be implied.[5] The reason for this is that the implication of such a term would be inconsistent with the express terms of the contract.[6] However, consistent with what was said in *The Moorcock*, the builder may be under a duty to warn the plaintiff that the design of the house is defective.[7] Furthermore, if there is no express provision in the contract, a court may be willing to imply a term to the effect that a building is fit for habitation.[8]

(ii)   Terms implied in law

Many contractual obligations arise out of rules of law imposed upon the parties either by statute or by the court acting out of necessity. In these circumstances, any resort to the notion of agreement as an explanation of the source of the obligation is unhelpful, since these obligations are imposed by operation of law. While the process of implying a term in fact is taken to be a recognised gap-filling mechanism, where a term is implied in law, they are setting minimum standards for the type of relationship under consideration. In the United States this is referred to as a 'standardised default rule.'[9]

The clearest examples of legally imposed contractual obligations can be found in statutory provisions. For example, in sale of goods transactions, sections 12 to 15 of the Sale of Goods Act 1979[10] imply terms relating to title, description, quality and fitness. Similarly, if there is no agreement as to the price payable for goods, the Sale of Goods Act 1979, section 8(2) allows the court to determine what is a reasonable price. If the contract is one for the supply of a service, there are implied terms concerning the exercise of reasonable care and skill, the charge payable and the time taken to render the service.[11]

In addition to express statutory provisions, terms may be implied where they are a necessary incident of a particular type of relationship. Thus, there are terms which necessarily arise out of the relationship between the supplier and the consumer of goods and services, an employer and an employee, a landlord and a tenant, and a builder and the person who commissions the building. In cases of this kind, the court examines earlier authorities to decide what obligations the law imposes. The main difficulty in this regard is whether the contract entered into is one which is of a defined type. For example, the contract may be one between banker and customer but at the same time

---

4   See *Planché v Colburn* (1831) 8 Bing 14 and see chs 11 and 18.
5   *Lynch v Thorne* [1956] 1 All ER 744.
6   *Johnstone v Bloomsbury Health Authority* [1991] 2 All ER 293 at 302 (per LEGGATT LJ). Cf 298 (per STUART-SMITH LJ).
7   *Brunswick Construction Ltd v Nowlan* (1974) 21 BLR 27; *EDAC v William Moss Ltd* (1984) 2 Con LR 1.
8   *Basildon District Council v J E Lesser (Properties) Ltd* [1985] 1 All ER 20.
9   See *Society of Lloyd's v Clementson* [1995] CLC 117 at 131 (per STEYN LJ).
10   Identical terms are implied in hire-purchase contracts by the Supply of Goods (Implied Terms) Act 1973, ss 8–11 and the Consumer Credit Act 1974, Sch 4, para 35, and in contracts for the transfer of ownership in goods by the Supply of Goods and Services Act 1982, ss 2–5. Similar but not identical terms are implied in contracts of hire by the Supply of Goods and Services Act 1982, ss 7–10. See also chs 25 and 26.
11   Supply of Goods and Services Act 1982, ss 13–15 and see ch 26.

is so carefully drawn up on a one-off basis that it falls outside the general class.[12] But there appears to be an alternative approach to the problem in that new fact situations may be promoted to the status of a defined type of contract. Thus a contract for the sale and purchase of travellers' cheques has been described as self-evidently such a contract[13] although the issue of whether a solus agreement was of a defined class seemed to cause much greater difficulty some 13 years earlier.[14]

In the case of the employer/employee relationship, it is regarded as a legal incident of the contract that the employee is reasonably skilled,[15] that the employee will act in good faith[16] and will faithfully serve his employer,[17] that the employee will not act against his employer's interests,[18] and that he will indemnify his employer against liabilities incurred due to his wrongful act.[19] In return, the employer is under a duty not to ask his employee to perform an illegal act,[20] and to provide a safe place of work.[1]

The legal incidents of the landlord/tenant relationship[2] consist of, inter alia, a covenant that the tenant will enjoy quiet possession;[3] that a furnished property will be reasonably fit for habitation;[4] that the landlord will not frustrate the use of the land for the purpose for which it was let,[5] and that the landlord will keep any common areas in a reasonable state of repair.[6] The tenant also owes certain obligations which are referred to as implied terms. For example, he must not commit waste,[7] and he must keep the premises in a good state of repair.[8]

After an examination of earlier authorities, it may be discovered that there is no guidance on whether a particular term can be implied. Here the court may imply terms on the basis of necessity,[9] but implying a term because it is reasonable to do so, is not permitted.[10]

It has been seen above that when seeking to imply a term in fact, the courts sometimes use the language of necessity, but it seems that necessity in the context of a term implied in law has a different meaning. In *Scally v Southern Health and Social Services Board*[11] a distinction was drawn between 'the search for an implied term necessary to give business

---

12   *National Bank of Greece SA v Pinios Shipping Co, The Maira* [1989] 1 All ER 213 at 219 (per LLOYD LJ).
13   *El Awadi v Bank of Credit and Commerce International SA Ltd* [1989] 1 All ER 242 at 253 (per HUTCHISON J).
14   *Shell (UK) Ltd v Lostock Garage Ltd* [1977] 1 All ER 481.
15   *Harmer v Cornelius* (1858) 5 CBNS 236.
16   *Robb v Green* [1895] 2 QB 315.
17   *Hivac Ltd v Park Royal Scientific Instruments Ltd* [1946] Ch 169.
18   *Wessex Dairies Ltd v Smith* [1935] 2 KB 80.
19   *Lister v Romford Ice and Cold Storage Co Ltd* [1957] AC 555.
20   *Gregory v Ford* [1951] 1 All ER 121.
1   *Matthews v Kuwait Bechtel Corpn* [1959] 2 QB 57.
2   See also ch 28.
3   *Markham v Paget* [1908] 1 Ch 697; *Lavender v Betts* [1942] 2 All ER 72.
4   *Collins v Hopkins* [1923] 2 KB 617; *Smith v Marrable* (1843) 11 M & W 5.
5   *Browne v Flower* [1911] 1 Ch 219.
6   *Liverpool City Council v Irwin* [1977] AC 239.
7   This covers pulling down or altering property (*Marsden v Edward Heyes Ltd* [1927] 2 KB 1); opening a mine and allowing the property to fall into a state of decay.
8   *Cheetham v Hampson* (1791) 4 Term Rep 318.
9   *Liverpool City Council v Irwin* [1977] AC 239.
10   Ibid at 266 (per LORD EDMUND-DAVIES). See also *Shell UK Ltd v Lostock Garage Ltd* [1977] 1 All ER 481 at 487–488 (per LORD DENNING MR) and *Trollope & Colls Ltd v North West Metropolitan Regional Hospital Board* [1973] 2 All ER 260. Cf *Liverpool City Council v Irwin* [1977] AC 239 at 258 (per Lord CROSS), 'the court will naturally ask itself whether the term…would be one which it was reasonable to insert.'
11   [1992] 1 AC 294.

efficacy to a particular contract and the search, based on wider considerations, for a term which the law will imply as a necessary incident of a definable category of contractual relationship.'[12] To further emphasise the difference, if a term is implied for reasons of business efficacy it is to make the contract workable, but it would be quite possible for a contract of sale to be workable even if the implied terms as to satisfactory quality and fitness for purpose were not present. Accordingly, the necessity referred to in this context is more likely to be some policy driven necessity such as protection of a weaker contracting party.

In *Liverpool City Council v Irwin,* [13] the local authority had let a flat in a tower block to the appellant. The tenancy agreement consisted of a list of tenants' obligations with no corresponding landlord's duties. Due to the actions of vandals, certain common areas, including lifts, stairways and rubbish chutes, became either inoperative or unsafe to use. As a protest against these conditions, the defendant refused to pay his rent and the council sought to regain possession of the flat. The council had sent workmen on a regular basis to repair damage caused to the common areas, but they were unable to keep pace with the damage caused. The appellant asked for the implication of a term that he would have quiet enjoyment of the property. The House of Lords held that the nature of the contract implicitly required the landlord to exercise reasonable care to maintain the common areas.[14] However, nothing more than this was necessary, therefore the council was not under an absolute obligation to maintain the services concerned.

In deciding what terms are necessary, the court will take into account general policy considerations. To this extent, the court does consider what is reasonable in the circumstances. It may be argued that the House of Lords' insistence that a term must be necessary before it will be implied is simply resorting to the pure fiction that courts will not make a contract for the parties. Certainly, there can be no doubt that, in cases where the court enquires what the general incidents of a particular relationship are, it is quite possible that the officious bystander test will not be satisfied.[15]

If the court is engaged in a process of taking considerations of justice and social policy into account, it is asking is whether a legal duty should be imposed upon one of the parties to a contract. For example, in *Lister v Romford Ice and Cold Storage Co Ltd*[16] the appellant was employed by the respondents as a lorry driver. In the course of his employment, he negligently injured his father, a fellow employee. The father successfully sued the respondents, who sued the appellant for his breach of contract. The appellant argued that there should be an implied term that the respondents should indemnify him against liability he might incur in the course of his employment if they were insured against the risk concerned. The House of Lords decided in favour of the respondents, holding that, while an employee impliedly undertakes to use reasonable care and skill, no term could be implied on the part of the employer that he would grant an indemnity to the employee. Some of the justifications for this decision were couched in terms of the officious bystander test. For example, it was said that both parties would not have agreed to the term.[17] However, this was not the real issue. An argument which was

12   Ibid at 307. See also *Mahmud v Bank of Credit amd Commerce International* [1998] AC 20 at 45.
13   Ibid. See MacIntyre [1977] CLJ 15.
14   Ibid at 257 (per LORD WILBERFORCE).
15   Ibid at 258 (per LORD WILBERFORCE).
16   [1957] AC 555.
17   Ibid at 578 (per VISCOUNT SIMONDS).

particularly persuasive was that it would be undesirable to allow a driver to be indemnified by his employer because he might then drive less carefully. In this respect, the court was not concerned with terms implied in fact, but rather with the question of whether a term in law should be implied. But if this is the case, the policy issue is perhaps one which ought to be resolved by Parliament rather than the courts.[18]

(iii)   Terms implied by custom or out of business practice

In addition to implied terms imposed on the parties by operation of law and those apparently representing the intention of the parties, terms may also be implied by virtue of custom or usage. To regard customary practice as being based on the presumed intention of the parties is somewhat unrealistic. If a custom is regarded as reasonable, it will bind the parties, even though they might not have been aware of it.[19] The process adopted by the courts is that 'if there is a uniform practice...so well defined and recognised that the parties must have had it in their minds when they contracted', a term based on that usage may be implied. [20] If the express terms of a contract are inconsistent with some customary practice, then the custom will not be binding, and will be regarded as unreasonable.

Trade usage may be referred to in order to ascertain the content of the contract. For example, trade associations may produce standard form documents for use by members. These standard forms may be taken to represent business practice, thereby containing the relevant contract terms in the event of a dispute.[1]

18   See *Reid v Rush & Tompkins Group plc* [1990] 1 WLR 212.
19   *Reynolds v Smith* (1893) 9 TLR 494.
20   *Vitol SA v Phibro Energy AG, The Mathraki* [1990] 2 Lloyd's Rep 84 at 88 (per EVANS J.). See also *Fyffes Group Ltd v Reefer Express Lines Pty Ltd, The Kriti Rex* [1996] 2 Lloyd's Rep 171.
1   See *British Crane Hire Corpn Ltd v Ipswich Plant Hire Ltd* [1975] QB 303 at 311 (per LORD DENNING MR).

Chapter 8

Compensation for wrongful harm — general principles

1. CONDUCT, NEEDS, FAIRNESS AND RIGHTS

It is generally accepted that wrongfully caused harm should give rise to a duty to compensate in the absence of any policy considerations to the contrary, but it is necessary to identify the varieties of harm which may give rise to a duty to compensate.

(1) NEEDS AND CONDUCT

A person who has been harmed 'needs' compensation, particularly where that harm consists of personal injury and the victim may be unable to work. He has suffered some injury in respect of which amends need to be made. Frequently it is the case that the person who causes the injury is not in a financial position to adequately compensate the injured person. Accordingly, the law may allocate responsibility not according to blameworthiness[1] but according to the ability of a person to spread the loss as fairly as possible.[2] Thus an employer is made vicariously liable for the harm caused by his employees if they are acting within the course of their employment. The employer is in the best position to absorb the cost of compensating the injured individual because he can spread that loss amongst the consumers of the product or service he provides. A similar principle lies behind the idea of insurance against possible risk of injury to others. While the imposition of vicarious liability is an example of 'vertical' loss spreading, in many instances those required to take out insurance are those who have created the risk of injury in the first place. For example, employers must hold an employer's liability policy by law. It is compulsory for motor vehicle drivers to hold insurance against third party risks. Solicitors must now be insured against professional negligence. All of those required to insure are the risk creators but, in turn, they may spread the loss still further. The employer, if he produces an end product, will reflect his insurance premiums in the price charged for his produce. The solicitor will increase his scale of charges for the service he provides. The driver is not in the same fortunate position. If he is the 'consumer' at the end of a 'chain of distribution', he is unable to pass on his insurance costs elsewhere. But given the statistical inevitability that road traffic accidents will occur, it is considered

---

1 This process is called loss shifting.
2 This process is called loss spreading.

necessary to require those who engage in such a potentially dangerous activity to bear the risk of injury to other road users.

These methods can be seen as satisfying the need of the injured person for compensation. However, it is still necessary to examine the causes of the action in the first place. The cardinal principle of compensating harm wrongfully caused requires the injured person to be returned to the position he was in before the harm was caused, so far as this is possible. This may be described as restoring the status quo,[3] and may involve repaying expenses incurred, compensating for lost opportunities, compensating economic or physical harm suffered and compensating expenses incurred in rectifying the effects of the harm. Alternatively, the status quo interest may be protected by granting an injunction ordering that the harmful activity should cease.

One factor underlying protection of the status quo interest, particularly where there is pure economic loss, is that of reliance.[4] This is justified on the basis that a person has reasonably relied on what another has said or done and is illustrated by the rules on misrepresentation and is one basis of liability for misstatement, under which a person can incur common law liability for failing to take reasonable care in the giving of advice which is reasonably and detrimentally relied upon by the person to whom it is made. Reliance in this sense is not the answer in all cases in which the status quo interest is protected and the courts have increasingly begun to make use of the concept of whether a person has voluntarily assumed responsibility for his conduct. In this sense it would be appropriate to ask whether a solicitor has voluntarily assumed responsibility to a beneficiary when he drafts a will and whether the writer of a reference has assumed responsibility to the subject of the reference. It would also be difficult to argue that a pedestrian relies on a motorist not to run into him, or that a person relies on his neighbour not to pollute the atmosphere, or that an extreme right-wing political activist relies on a person of a different political persuasion not to threaten him or vice versa. Different interests are at stake in these circumstances.

(2)   FAIRNESS AND CONDUCT

The person who complains of his neighbour's activities is asking the court to balance his interests as a property owner against those of his neighbour. It may be said that torts such as those of private nuisance and the rule in *Rylands v Fletcher*[5] are based on a notion of fairness. The underlying rationale of these torts is that the courts must achieve a fair distribution of the benefits and burdens of social activity. Liability under the rule in *Rylands v Fletcher* can be based on the view that the defendant benefits from the use of his land and that he should therefore bear the costs imposed on his neighbours by such use. Likewise, in nuisance, liability is fairness-based. What the court must do is to balance the competing interests of two or more land users. In this context, it does not matter whether the defendant has taken reasonable precautions or not to avoid the interferences caused by his activities.[6] Historically, nuisance and the rule in *Rylands v Fletcher* are not based on the conduct or fault of the defendant. Instead, they are concerned with the reasonableness or otherwise of the activity carried on by the defendant on his own land. Sometimes, this may give the impression that these torts involve the imposition of strict liability.[7] However, the advance of negligence has had an impact in this area. The defendant's conduct is now increasingly considered by the courts. For example, an

---

3   See Burrows (1983) 99 LQR 217; cf Fuller and Perdue (1936/37) 46 Yale LJ 52 and 373 who in the context of contract actions, speak of the reliance interest.
4   See ch 10.
5   (1868) LR 3 HL 330 and see ch 29.
6   See *Miller v Jackson* [1977] QB 966; cf *Kennaway v Thompson* [1981] QB 88.
7   See ch 12.

important consideration in *Rylands v Fletcher* cases is whether the defendant has exercised reasonable care in guarding against the risk of escape of the thing accumulated on his land. The considerations taken into account by the court are similar to those which apply in negligence cases when deciding whether reasonable precautions have been taken. The court will examine what the defendant did, where he did it, what precautions were taken, and the social utility of the defendant's conduct.[8] It is also necessary that the kind of damage which occurred could be reasonably foreseen by the defendant.[9]

Likewise, the conduct of the defendant is important in nuisance cases involving material property damage. While there is a requirement in nuisance that there should be an unreasonable state of affairs giving rise to an interference with the plaintiff's interest, increasingly the courts now concentrate on the conduct which causes damage to the plaintiff. Thus a landowner may be liable for continuing a nuisance created by the act of a stranger,[10] or an act of nature.[11] But in these circumstances it should be appreciated that a fault-based rule is surely inevitable where one is concerned with holding a person liable for external events such as the act of a third party.

(3)   RIGHTS AND CONDUCT

One who complains that he has been struck or threatened by another is seeking to defend rights the law should rightly protect. The basis of the action is the right to be free from unjustified interference. Similarly one has a right to the legal protection of one's reputation. Torts such as trespass, actionable *per se*, conversion and defamation[12] are examples of this rights based liability. In such torts, a lack of awareness of the unlawful nature of one's acts is irrelevant, although a lack of awareness of the very act complained of may not involve the commission of a tort. Unawareness apart, a person can only avoid liability if he can show that he has a right which is more deserving of protection than that of the plaintiff. Thus if the defendant can show that he acted in self-defence or that he acted with statutory authority, he may not be liable for the alleged trespass. Likewise, in defamation cases the right to freedom of expression, through the operation of defences such as justification, absolute and qualified privilege and fair comment, may take precedence over the right of the plaintiff to keep his reputation intact.

However, conduct-based liability is making inroads into this area too, particularly in respect of trespass causing personal injuries. If one pleads direct forcible injury without pleading either intention or negligence, the action will fail.[13] Moreover, an action is likely to be treated as one for negligence whenever unintentionally inflicted personal injury is alleged.[14]

The conduct of the defendant plays an important part in determining liability for wrongfully caused harm. This conduct may take a number of forms. It may be an intentional act, it may be a negligent act, or it may amount to a breach of contract. The consequence of the act may be to cause personal injury, property damage, or economic loss. No tangible loss may be caused by the wrongful act but as some actions, such as trespass to the person, have a wider function than the protection of the plaintiff against physical harm, the tort also serves to protect the inviolability of the person and to guard against the infringement of civil liberties.

8   See *Mason v Levy Auto Parts of England Ltd* [1967] 2 QB 530 and see also ch 12.
9   *Cambridge Water Co Ltd v Eastern Counties Leather plc* [1994] 1 All ER 53.
10   See *Sedleigh-Denfield v O'Callaghan* [1940] AC 880.
11   *Leakey v National Trust for Places of Historic Interest or Natural Beauty* [1980] QB 485; *Goldman v Hargrave* [1967] 1 AC 645.
12   And the tort of injurious falsehood, to the extent that malice and damage can be proved: see eg *Joyce v Sengupta* [1993] 1 WLR 337.
13   *Stanley v Powell* [1891] 1 QB 86.
14   *Letang v Cooper* [1965] 1 QB 232 and see also ch 1.

2.   COMPENSATION FOR HARM CAUSED BY NEGLIGENT CONDUCT

Negligence constitutes the breach of a legal duty to take care which results in damage, undesired by the defendant, to the plaintiff. Negligence consists of three elements, namely (i) the existence of a duty of care owed by the defendant to the plaintiff; (ii) a breach of that duty by the defendant;[15] and (iii) damage to the plaintiff, which is not too remote and has been caused by the defendant's breach of duty.[16] Here it is proposed to consider the elements which make up a duty situation, thereby forming the basis for the defendant's obligation to compensate for the harm suffered.

(1)   THE INGREDIENTS OF A DUTY SITUATION

If no duty to take care is owed, there is no liability for negligence. The principal criterion of liability is that of foresight of harm. It must be foreseeable to the defendant that his conduct might cause injury to the plaintiff if he fails to exercise reasonable care. Ordinarily, this is more likely to be the case where the defendant is guilty of a positive act which causes physical harm to the plaintiff's person or property.

(i)   Established duty situations

Established duty situations exist as between the manufacturer and consumer of a defective product, an employer and his employees in respect of the workplace and an occupier of premises to his visitors in respect of the safety of those premises. But these well established duty situations appear to depend more on status than anything else and their existence does not assist in identifying the characteristics of a duty situation which might arise in a novel situation. Over and above these specific duties, there is a general duty not to act carelessly. The best known statement of this general duty is to be found in *Donoghue v Stevenson*[17] where the plaintiff consumed part of a bottle of ginger beer manufactured by the defendant. The bottle had been bought by a friend, so there was no action in contract and the opaque bottle allegedly contained a decomposed snail,[18] as a result of the presence of which the plaintiff contracted gastro-enteritis. The House of Lords held, assuming the facts alleged to be true, that the manufacturer owed to the plaintiff a duty to take care that his product did not contain anything which might cause injury to those who might ordinarily be expected to come into contact with it.

(ii)   The neighbour principle

In addition to the specific duty applicable to manufacturers,[19] there were *dicta* in *Donoghue v Stevenson* laying down a more general principle consisting of a duty to take reasonable care. LORD ATKIN said:[20]

> ... Rules of law arise which limit the range of complainants and the extent of their remedy. The rule that you are to love your neighbour becomes in law, you must not injure your neighbour; and the lawyer's question, who is my neighbour? receives a restricted reply. You must take reasonable care to avoid acts or omissions which you can reasonably foresee

---

15   See ch 12.
16   See ch 16.
17   [1932] AC 562.
18   See Heuston (1957) 20 MLR 2.
19   See ch 25.
20   [1932] AC 562 at 580.

would be likely to injure your neighbour. Who then, in law, is my neighbour? The answer seems to be — persons who are so closely and directly affected by my act that I ought reasonably to have them in contemplation as being so affected when I am directing my mind to the acts or omissions which are called into question.

Taken at face value, this means that a duty of care is owed to anyone who can be foreseen as likely to be injured by the defendant's carelessness. But the rule disguises more than it says. The immediate judicial reaction to this statement was to continue to find negligence only in those established relationships in which a duty of care had been previously recognised.[1] A convenient way of ignoring the general duty was to treat passages such as those from LORD ATKIN's judgment as not representing the *ratio* of *Donoghue v Stevenson*. But new duty situations did begin to emerge, such as that owed by the manufacturer of a product which was not food.[2] However, in other cases, the existence of a duty of care was denied. Initially, no duty was owed in respect of carelessly uttered statements.[3] Likewise, a builder of a house was said not to owe a duty of care to the purchaser or a subsequent owner of the house.[4] All of this went on despite the declaration that the 'categories of negligence are never closed'.[5]

(iii)   Development of the neighbour principle

During the period between 1970 and 1983 the neighbour rule was seen as a statement of general principle, with the result that there grew up a body of case law to the effect that foresight of harm should be the key criterion in determining when a duty of care was owed, unless there was some valid reason for its exclusion.[6] This view was subsequently enshrined in the House of Lords 'two-stage test' in *Anns v Merton London Borough Council*,[7] in which LORD WILBERFORCE said that there was no need now to bring the facts of a novel situation within those of previous cases in which a duty of care has been held to exist.[8] Instead the matter could be approached by asking whether carelessness on the part of the wrongdoer is reasonably likely to cause harm to the injured party. If such harm is foreseeable, it then had to be asked whether any policy considerations existed which served to negative, reduce or limit the scope of the duty of care, or the class of people to whom the duty was owed, or the damages which could be awarded in respect of the breach. Thus policy considerations were promoted to the position of a 'long stop' so as to prevent the test of reasonable foreseeability from having socially undesirable consequences.[9]

The breadth of this 'two-stage test' gave rise to problems of how to delimit the scope of the tort of negligence, especially when it was extended to cover foreseeable economic loss, whether caused by acts or statements. It became increasingly apparent that a simple test of reasonable foresight of harm tended to omit essential considerations but also included non-essential factors in determining when or if a duty of care should be owed, ultimately resulting in the decision in *Anns* being overruled in *Murphy v*

---

1   See *Otto v Bolton and Norris* [1936] 2 KB 46 at 54–55 (per ATKINSON J).
2   See *Grant v Australian Knitting Mills Ltd* [1936] AC 85.
3   See now *Hedley Byrne & Co Ltd v Heller & Partners Ltd* [1964] AC 465 .
4   See also chs 10 and 28.
5   *Donoghue v Stevenson* [1932] AC 562 at 619 (per LORD MACMILLAN). Cf *The Aliakmon* [1986] 2 All ER 145 at 154–155 (per LORD BRANDON).
6   *Home Office v Dorset Yacht Co Ltd* [1970] AC 1004 at 1027 (per LORD REID). See also LORD MORRIS at 1034 and LORD PEARSON at 1035.
7   [1978] AC 728.
8   Ibid at 751.
9   See Williams and Hepple *Foundations of the Law of Tort* (2nd edn, 1984) p 102 and see 'policy' below.

Brentwood District Council.[10] Even at the height of popularity of the 'two–stage test' if a case fell within previously stated principles to the effect that no duty was owed, there was some reluctance to depart from the established rule.[11]

Later statements of principle showed that LORD WILBERFORCE's remarks should not be regarded as being of a definitive character.[12]

In considering the duty issue, it is important to appreciate that there is a world of difference between extending an existing and established duty situation by reference to what is reasonably foreseeable and taking the tort of negligence into new and, as yet, untested waters. The problem with the 'two–stage test' was that potentially it applied to either situation, with the result that it was used to open up new duty situations in respect of types of loss not previously seen as the province of the law of tort. The high water mark of these developments was probably the decision of the House of Lords in *Junior Books Ltd v Veitchi Co Ltd*[13] in which a duty of care was held to exist in respect of pure economic loss suffered as a result of the negligent performance of a contractual duty owed to a third party. By analogy, this decision could also be extended to economic losses suffered in consequence of the supply of a defective product or the negligent construction of a building. In a reaction to this development, it was complained that it had become fashionable for a plaintiff to allege negligence on the assumption that we are all neighbours, and that someone solvent must be liable in damages.[14]

(iv)   The reaction to the *Anns* test

The reaction to the less desirable aspects of the decision in *Anns*[15] resulted in it being overruled in so far as it established that a local authority owes a duty of care in respect of pure economic losses suffered by a building owner flowing from the negligent exercise of a building inspection,[16] but the process of resiling from *Anns* had started at an earlier stage.

Instead, it is now necessary to consider a number of related factors forming part of a composite test, taking into account the whole of the necessary relationship which exists between the parties.[17] Moreover, the preferred approach is now to develop the law of negligence incrementally, and by analogy with existing, established categories rather than to take massive sweeps into the unknown, based on a test of reasonable foresight of harm qualified only by indefinable policy considerations.[18] It follows that for the future, whether a duty of care is owed in a particular set of circumstances requires a pragmatic approach, which is suited to gradual development requiring most careful analysis.[19]

The factors which must be considered in this process are first whether the harm suffered by the plaintiff is foreseeable, secondly whether there exists between the plaintiff

---

10   [1990] 2 All ER 908.
11   *Candlewood Navigation Corpn Ltd v Mitsui OSK Lines Ltd, The Mineral Transporter* [1986] AC 1; *Leigh and Sillavan Ltd v Aliakmon Shipping Co Ltd, The Aliakmon* [1986] 2 All ER 145 overruling *Schiffahrt und Kohlen GmbH v Chelsea Maritime Ltd, The Irene's Success* [1982] QB 481.
12   See *Governors of the Peabody Donation Fund v Sir Lindsay Parkinson & Co Ltd* [1985] AC 210 at 240 (per LORD KEITH); *Leigh and Sillavan Ltd v Aliakmon Shipping Co Ltd, The Aliakmon* [1986] 2 All ER 145 at 153 (per LORD BRANDON); *Yuen Kun Yeu v A-G of Hong Kong* [1987] 2 All ER 705 at 710 (per LORD KEITH).
13   [1983] 1 AC 520.
14   *CBS Songs Ltd v Amstrad Consumer Electronics plc* [1988] 2 All ER 484 at 497 (per LORD TEMPLEMAN).
15   See generally Smith & Burns (1983) 46 MLR 147; Kidner (1987) 7 Legal Studies 319.
16   *Murphy v Brentwood District Council* [1990] 2 All ER 908.
17   *Yuen Kun Yeu v A-G of Hong Kong* [1987] 2 All ER 705 at 710 (per LORD KEITH).
18   *Sutherland Shire Council v Heyman* (1985) 60 ALR 1 at 43–44 (per BRENNAN J).
19   *Rowling v Takaro Properties Ltd* [1988] 1 All ER 163 at 172 (per LORD KEITH).

and the defendant a sufficient relationship of proximity, thirdly, whether it is just and equitable to impose liability and finally, but as a last resort, there may be cases in which pure policy considerations must be considered in determining whether it is proper to subject the defendant to a duty to take reasonable care.[20] While the courts have attempted to devalue the role of policy,[1] there would appear to be little difference between the policy issues in mind in *Anns* and the requirement of justice and equity insisted on in more recent cases.

The combination of these various elements does not simplify the duty issue at all, since it must be appreciated, from the outset, that all of the elements are part of a composite test and that what is foreseeable will depend on the proximity of relationship between the parties and on what is just and equitable and, where relevant, on policy issues.[2] Thus the greater the foreseeability of the harm to the plaintiff, the more likely it is that there will be a necessary relationship of proximity and the more likely it will be that it is just and equitable to subject the defendant to a duty to take care. Generally, where the plaintiff complains of physical harm, it will rarely be necessary to consider the issue of proximity as the fact of the physical damage itself will provide the necessary limiting factor.[3] However, even in the case of physical damage there is no universal duty of care.[4] But more difficult considerations will arise where the harm complained of consists of economic loss, since this type of loss has the potential to be very widespread. In contrast, physical harm to the person or to property rarely spreads from the person to whom it is caused. However, where there is a danger of possible indeterminate liability, or possible 'gold-digging' claims, it may be necessary to consider other matters. For example in *Bourhill v Young*,[5] a woman who did not witness a traffic accident involving a motor cycle ridden by the defendant and was in no physical danger could not recover in respect of the psychiatric damage or nervous shock she suffered on hearing the collision and later seeing blood on the road. Strictly, the harm she suffered was foreseeable in a general sense, but no duty of care was owed by the deceased rider of the motor cycle, since one is expected to show some reasonable signs of fortitude.

(v)   Foresight of harm and proximity

The answer to the question whether there is a duty of care depends on the extent to which a reasonable man could foresee harm to the plaintiff and on the proximity of relationship which exists between the parties. The degree of foresight required is that of the reasonable man, but this on its own does not take the enquiry any further, especially since what is foreseeable to one person may not be so to another. Conversely, the reasonable foresight test is useful when used in the sense of a 'duty in fact' in determining whether this defendant owes this plaintiff a duty of care.[6] For example, there may be circumstances in which the defendant's actions, in ordinary circumstances, may fail to reveal a duty situation, but because of peculiarities affecting one or other of the parties a duty of care may be owed. Thus the fact that the plaintiff is blind in one eye may point to the need for special precautions on the part of his employer when asking him to use welding equipment.[7] Similarly, the fact that the plaintiff is completely

---

20   *Caparo Industries plc v Dickman* [1990] 1 All ER 568 at 573–574 (per Lord Bridge); *Al Saudi Banque v Clark Pixley (a firm)* [1989] 3 All ER 361 at 365 (per Millett J).
1   See eg *Yuen Kun Yeu v A-G for Hong Kong* [1987] 2 All ER 705 at 712 (per Lord Keith).
2   See *Caparo Industries plc v Dickman* [1990] 1 All ER 568 at 585 (per Lord Oliver).
3   *Al Saudi Banque v Clark Pixley (a firm)* [1989] 3 All ER 361 at 366 (per Millett J).
4   *Marc Rich & Co AG v Bishop Rock Marine Co Ltd (The Nicholas H)* [1996] AC 211.
5   [1943] AC 92.
6   See *Goodwill v British Pregnancy Advisory Service* [1996] 1 WLR 1397.
7   *Paris v Stepney Borough Council* [1951] AC 367.

blind may also affect the position of the parties where the defendant digs a hole or leaves some other obstruction in the road.[8]

The proximity looked for is not to be understood in the sense of physical proximity, otherwise a duty of care would rarely be owed in respect of economic losses, since the parties may be thousands of miles apart when the loss is suffered. Instead, the variety of proximity looked for is legal proximity, which has been described as a highly elusive element.[9] But while physical proximity is not always necessary, it may be a vital consideration in some cases. For example, in *Home Office v Dorset Yacht Co Ltd*,[10] the defendants were liable for damage caused when borstal inmates under their control escaped and caused damage to the plaintiffs' property. An important factor was that the plaintiffs were physical neighbours. If the plaintiffs' property had been situated some miles away, then it seems likely that no action would have been available.[11]

Beyond cases of physical proximity, the test is one of reasonable foresight qualified by the other ingredients of the duty test. It must be asked whether the plaintiff is someone 'so closely and directly affected by my act that I ought reasonably to have them in contemplation'.[12] This does not require the plaintiff to be specifically identifiable by the defendant, but there are a wide range of other factors to consider, especially where the plaintiff has suffered economic loss.[13]

(vi)   Justice, equity and policy

The requirement that it should be just and equitable or reasonable to impose a duty of care appears to do little more than was done by the residual policy element in the *Anns* two-stage test. It is there as a filter to prevent a duty from being owed in circumstances in which it would be unfair on the defendant to hold him liable. It follows that general policy considerations will be relevant here. Thus it will be necessary to ask whether the finding of a duty situation will tend to lead to indeterminate liability, thereby opening the floodgates of litigation. Moreover, it will be necessary to consider if there is or should be some alternative means by which the plaintiff's claim could have been pursued and whether there is some other policy motive for denying the existence of a duty of care. In this light, it is misleading to talk in terms of the existence of a duty of care, since the real issue is whether the defendant should be held liable for the harm he has caused, based on the demands of society for protection from the carelessness of others.[14]

In this sense policy is the central issue in the decision as to whether to impose a duty of care on the defendant and the discrediting of the *Anns* reasoning on duty of care is somewhat unnecessary.[15]

(a)   *The floodgates argument*   The fear that lies behind the use of negative policy considerations in restricting the circumstances in which a duty of care is owed is that unless the court is circumspect, the floodgates of litigation might be opened. The fear is expressed by asserting that the court will strive to avoid liability in an indeterminate

8   *Haley v London Electricity Board* [1965] AC 778.
9   *Murphy v Brentwood District Council* [1990] 2 All ER 908 at 934 (per LORD OLIVER).
10   [1970] AC 1004.
11   Ibid at 1032 (per LORD REID). See also *Lamb v Camden London Borough Council* [1981] QB 625.
12   *Donoghue v Stevenson* [1932] AC 562 at 580 (per LORD ATKIN).
13   See ch 10.
14   *Hedley Byrne & Co Ltd v Heller & Partners Ltd* [1964] AC 465 at 536 (per LORD PEARCE).
15   (See eg *Caparo Industries plc v Dickman* [1990] 2 AC 605; *Spring v Guardian Assurance plc* [1995] 2 AC 296; *White v Jones* [1995] 2 AC 207; *Marc Rich & Co AG v Bishop Rock Marine Co Ltd (The Nicholas H)* [1996] AC 211.)

amount for an indeterminate time to an indeterminate class.[16] Generally, the fear is greatest where the court is concerned with potential liability for economic losses. For example, a negligent misstatement can be read by large numbers of people and it might be unfair to saddle the defendant and his insurer with liability.[17] Alternatively, if a person carelessly causes an accident which results in the closure of the Mersey tunnel, many people may be prevented from reaching work. In such a case, the harm suffered by those people may be technically foreseeable, but, for policy reasons, an action for negligence may be denied. Thus, it has been said that disguises such as the test of remoteness or duty should be discarded and that the proper test should be whether, in the circumstances of the case, as a matter of policy, economic loss should be recoverable or not.[18]

(b)   *Fairness to the defendant*   Whether or not it is fair and reasonable to hold the defendant liable will be a crucial factor. Thus if the plaintiff has effectively brought the harm on himself, it would not be in the interests of justice to impose a duty of care on the defendant. For example, even before the decision in *Murphy v Brentwood District Council*[19] it had been held that a local authority owes no duty of care, arising out of its powers of building inspection, to a building contractor who through his own failure to take care has brought upon himself financial losses by failing to comply with the requirements laid down by the Building Regulations.[20]

Similar considerations will also apply where the plaintiff ought to have pursued an alternative remedy. This could be a contractual remedy, whether against the same defendant or another person. Arguably this was the case in *Junior Books Ltd v Veitchi Co Ltd*[1] since the plaintiff appears to have compromised a claim in contract which he would otherwise have had.[2] Similar considerations apply in the case of a public law remedy such as an appeal against a government officer's decision[3] or an action for judicial review.[4] Moreover, where the plaintiff and defendant are both parties to a wider network of related contracts, it would be unfair to the defendant to impose upon him a duty of care in respect of losses which he can reasonably expect the plaintiff to insure against.[5]

(c)   *The effect of a decision to impose a duty of care*   It has been observed that it sometimes helps to assess the merits of a decision by first noting its likely results.[6] Thus, if a decision to impose liability might result in the success of an unmeritorious action, no duty of care will be owed.[7]

The insurance implications of a particular decision are pertinent. If the scope of liability for negligence, in particular, expands, the risks faced by an insurer are increased. It may be that some risks of loss become too great to insure against, with the result that insurance cover is no longer available in respect of those risks. This, in turn, may lead to the

16   *Ultramares Corpn v Touche* 255 NY 170 (1931) at 444 (per CARDOZO CJ).
17   See further ch 10.
18   *Spartan Steel & Alloys Ltd v Martin & Co (Contractors) Ltd* [1973] QB 27 at 37 (per LORD DENNING MR).
19   [1990] 2 All ER 908.
20   *Governors of the Peabody Donation Fund v Sir Lindsay Parkinson & Co Ltd* [1985] AC 210.
1   [1983] 1 AC 520
2   See Atiyah *Introduction* pp 382-383.
3   *Jones v Department of Employment* [1988] 1 All ER 725. See also *X v Bedfordshire County Council* [1995] 2 AC 633.
4   *Rowling v Takaro Properties Ltd* [1988] 1 All ER 163; *Stovin v Wise* [1996] AC 923.
5   *Norwich City Council v Harvey* [1989] 1 All ER 1180. See also *Pacific Associates Inc v Baxter* [1989] 2 All ER 159 and *Greater Nottingham Co-operative Society Ltd v Cementation Piling and Foundations Ltd* [1988] 2 All ER 971.
6   *ICI Ltd v Shatwell* [1965] AC 656 at 675 (per VISCOUNT RADCLIFFE).
7   Ibid at 675–676 (per VISCOUNT RADCLIFFE).

abandonment of beneficial, high-risk activities, resulting in a net loss to the community.[8] Furthermore, extending tortious liability will result in an increase in insurance premiums generally, which might have an inflationary effect on costs and prices,[9] particularly if the expansion is widespread.

A decision to impose a duty of care can also have other undesirable effects which may be mitigated by recourse to policy considerations. In some instances, the spectre of tortious liability might have a deleterious effect on the performance of a person. For example, the imposition on the police of a general duty to exercise care in relation to their crime prevention or detection functions might have undesirable effects. It might lead to police functions being carried out in a defensive manner,[10] every citizen would be able to ask a court to investigate the performance of police officers,[11] and closed investigations might be indiscriminately reopened involving increased expense and pressure on police time.[12]

However, the exclusionary rule laid down in *Hill* has now been successfully challenged in the European Court of Human Rights.[13] The court held that the rule breached Article 6(1) of the European Convention on Human Rights as it constituted a disproportionate restriction on the applicant's right of access to a court. This means that cases of negligence against the police will have to be tried on their merits rather than being struck out as disclosing no reasonable cause of action. In Convention terms the rule was legitimate in its aims but not proportional, as it failed to weigh the public policy concerns of access to court with police needs. The court noted that the proximity test that had to be satisfied was sufficiently rigid to narrow the number of negligence cases against the police which could successfully go to trial. Whether a later Court of Appeal decision that police immunity is not total and has to be balanced against other public policy principles for Convention compliance is sufficient remains to be seen.[14]

Similar considerations also apply to arbitrators[15] and judges.[16] If such persons owed a duty of care in respect of their judicial functions the proper administration of justice might be adversely affected. In *Rondel v Worsley*,[17] it was held that a barrister owed a duty to the court to present his client's case properly, and to make a barrister liable for negligence might impair the performance of his duty to the court.[18] However, a more convincing justification for the immunity was that without it many cases would be retried at the instance of disappointed and unsuccessful litigants, which would be harmful to the administration of justice.[19] Conversely, the barrister's previous immunity was criticised on the ground that, if he were to be liable for his negligence, the quality of legal services might well be enhanced.[20] The *Osman* decision meant that blanket immunity on the grounds of policy contravened Article 6 and the barristers' immunity could not withstand a challenge in its previous form.

---

8   See Oughton (1989) Geneva Papers on Risk and Insurance (No 53) pp 331–346.
9   *Morgans v Launchbury* [1973] AC 127 at 143 (per LORD PEARCE).
10   *Hill v Chief Constable of West Yorkshire* [1988] 2 All ER 238 at 243 (per LORD KEITH). See also *Skinner v Secretary of State for Transport*, (1995) Times, 3 January — coastguards.
11   Ibid at 245 (per LORD TEMPLEMAN). See also *Ancell v McDermott* [1993] NLJR 363 at 364 (per BELDAM LJ).
12   Ibid at 244 (per LORD KEITH).
13   *Osman v United Kingdom* [1999] Crim LR 82, ECHR. See also *KL v United Kingdom (Application 29392/95)* (1998) 26 EHRR CD 113.
14   *Swinney v Chief Constable of Northumbria Police Force* [1996] 3 All ER 449; Sprince & Cooke (1999) 15 PN 228.
15   *Sutcliffe v Thackrah* [1974] AC 727; *Arenson v Casson, Beckman, Rutley & Co* [1977] AC 405.
16   *Sirros v Moore* [1975] QB 118.
17   [1969] 1 AC 191.
18   Ibid at 227–228 (per LORD REID).
19   Ibid at 230 (per LORD REID).
20   Veljanovski and Whelan (1983) 46 MLR 700.

The previous extent of the barrister's immunity was not entirely clear, but was not absolute. In *Saif Ali v Sydney Mitchell & Co*,[1] it was held that a barrister's failure to advise his client to resettle a claim for personal injuries was actionable. It was held that the immunity would extend to pre-trial work intimately connected with the conduct of a case, but pure paperwork unconnected with litigation was not subject to protection from an action for negligence. Much greater emphasis was placed on the public policy need to avoid relitigation.[2] The immunity attracted a considerable amount of litigation in relation to barristers and solicitor advocates.[3] Door of the court settlements were covered by the immunity[4] but not necessarily settlements approved by a judge unless the settlement was made at the court room door.[5] The House of Lords has now abolished advocate's immunity and reversed *Rondel*.[6] The problem of relitigation of cases will be dealt with by the principle of collateral challenge.[7]

(d)   *The type of harm inflicted*   Where physical harm is suffered as a result of the defendant's negligent act, generally few policy issues arise. Difficulties have been encountered in relation to psychological harm, particularly in deciding who should be allowed to maintain an action for negligence and in what circumstances recovery should be allowed.[8]

Policy issues are also relevant to novel actions for medical negligence where moral and ethical issues are important. For example, recent attempts to establish an action for wrongful life have failed on policy grounds.[9] Similarly, an action for wrongful birth has been denied.[10] The argument that an unwillingness to allow an action in such circumstances might lead to an increase in late abortions was rejected.[11]

(2)   ACTS AND OMISSIONS

A distinction drawn in the common law of obligations is that which exists between doing something badly (misfeasance) and failing to act (non-feasance).[12] The dominant philosophy of *laissez-faire* coupled with the ideal of individualism in the nineteenth century meant that non-feasance related problems were regarded as primarily the province of the law of contract. The attitude was that if A wished B to do something for him, B had to be paid for his services and, if after payment (or the promise thereof), B failed to perform the service, he was in breach of contract.

This stance had not always been taken. Before the establishment of a unified law of contract, actions had been admitted to the courts on the basis of the forms of action. There were numerous examples of liability for failure to act where a person had 'undertaken' to perform a service for another. In these cases, there was also a legally

1   [1980] AC 198.
2   Ibid at 214–215 (per LORD WILBERFORCE), and at 222–223 (per LORD DIPLOCK).
3   See Courts and Legal Services Act 1990, s 62.
4   *Kelley v Corston* [1997] 4 All ER 466. See also *Hall & Co v Simon* [1999] 1 FLR 536, CA; Williams (1999) 15 PN 75.
5   *Griffin v Kingsmill* [1998] PIQR P24.
6   *Hall & Co v Simons* (2000) Times, 21 July.
7   See *Hunter v Chief Constable of West Midlands Police* [1982] AC 529.
8   See 'Mental distress', below.
9   *McKay v Essex Area Health Authority* [1982] QB 1166.
10   *McFarlane v Tayside Health Board* [1999] 4 All ER 961.
11   Ibid.
12   On the distinction see Smith and Burns (1983) 46 MLR 147.

imposed duty to act positively for the benefit of another, such as in the case of innkeepers or where the holder of an office was obliged to act on another person's behalf.

While the neighbour principle in *Donoghue v Stevenson*[13] requires a person to refrain from acts or omissions which will foreseeably cause harm to others,[14] it does not follow that this covers every failure to act which results in harm to another. It is true that if foreseeability of harm alone were to be considered, there would be liability in negligence on the part of a person who sees another about to walk over a cliff with his head in the air, and forbears to shout a warning,[15] but the omission to which LORD ATKIN referred in *Donoghue* was an omission in the course of conduct. Thus if a driver fails to apply the brake to a moving car, he will owe a duty of care to other road users.[16] Likewise, a manufacturer who fails to inspect goods he has produced, owes a duty of care to the consumer of that product.

The distinction between acts and omissions can produce some strange results. For example, if a person sees a man drowning in a river and fails to throw a lifebelt to him, no legal obligation is incurred. If he saves the man from the water, but leaves him on the river bank where he dies of hypothermia, he has made the man's position worse and may owe him a duty of care.[17] It follows that the priest and the Levite in the parable of the Good Samaritan obviously had good legal advice, but the Good Samaritan had exposed himself to potential liability if his intervention were to cause additional harm to the traveller.

Returning to the drowning man — if he were to offer someone £5 to throw him a lifebelt and he failed to do so, having accepted his offer, then he is in breach of contract. Liability might also arise if a relationship between the rescued man and the rescuer is recognised in law. For example, a parent may be obliged to take positive action to save his child from harm. If a lawful visitor is on an occupier's land, or if a passenger is on board a ship, the occupier and the captain respectively may be obliged to effect a rescue if the other person is endangered.[18] An employer may be held liable for failure to take positive steps to protect his employee's safety.[19]

Judicial response to the acts and omission distinction has been mixed. LORD GOFF, whilst upholding the rule, felt that it would have to be considered at some stage.[20] However, the rule was upheld by the House of Lords on 'sound reasons' in *Stovin v Wise,*[1] where a local authority had resolved to improve a road junction and then did nothing. The plaintiff's claim that the local authority owed a duty to road users in this respect failed.

Arguments against the imposition of liability for omissions include the view that an obligation to act is more burdensome than a duty not to cause harm and also that the defendant has not identified himself as the person who has caused the injury. However, it is arguable that in most cases where liability is imposed for an omission, the defendant is a person who has put himself forward as one to whom liability may be attached.[2]

---

13   [1932] AC 562.
14   Ibid at 580 (per LORD ATKIN).
15   *Yuen Kun Yeu v A-G of Hong Kong* [1987] 2 All ER 705 at 710 (per LORD KEITH).
16   *Kelly v Metropolitan Rly Co* [1895] 1 QB 944.
17   See *The Ogopogo* [1970] 1 Lloyd's Rep 257; affd [1971] 2 Lloyd's Rep 410 on other grounds.
18   Ibid.
19   See *Barrett v Ministry of Defence* [1995] 1 WLR 1217. Atiyah, *The Damages Lottery* (Oxford) 1997, pp 40–1.
20   *Smith v Littlewoods Organisation Ltd* [1987] AC 241, 247.
1   [1996] AC 923; Harris (1997) 113 LQR 398.
2   See Atiyah *Accidents* pp 60–68.

(i)   Voluntary conduct

In the nineteenth century, duties to act positively came to be seen as the province of the law of contract. This was because most voluntary dealings were seen as market relationships involving the shifting of resources to a person who valued them most. However, the concept of the non-contractual duty did not completely disappear. For the defendant to be liable for an omission other than one committed in the course of conduct, he must owe to the plaintiff a duty to act.[3]

The duty may arise in a number of ways. There may be a contractual or fiduciary duty on the plaintiff to act. A failure to act may give rise to an action for breach of contract either on an express or implied term of the contract. Alternatively the defendant may be liable for a breach of fiduciary duty such as within a solicitor–client relationship.[4] It is now established that the defendant may be liable in negligence where there is a negligent breach of contract[5] on the basis that there has been an assumption of responsibility by the defendant to the plaintiff.[6]

The concept of voluntary assumption of responsibility may also apply where there is no contractual or fiduciary relationship. A solicitor who negligently fails to amend a will in accordance with the testator's wishes may be liable in negligence to the intended beneficiary.[7] The circumstances in which such a voluntary assumption of responsibility can be found in the absence of a contractual or fiduciary duty are controversial[8] and have been criticised as undermining the doctrine of consideration.[9] The concept may be used in conjunction with a principle of detrimental reliance but it is now clear that this is not necessary for a duty to be found. Clearly, however, there must be some detriment for damage to be established.

Most of the litigation on voluntary conduct has been concerned with the special problem of economic loss but it is now clear that if A gives a non-contractual undertaking to perform a certain act for B and then fails to perform, B can recover in respect of his loss if he has relied to his detriment on A's undertaking. For example, if a doctor stops to give assistance to an injured person, the doctor may be liable for his failure to administer first aid, although the principles on which liability is based are unclear. It appears that there should be an identifiable act of reliance. In *The Ogopogo*[10] it was held that a rescuer could be liable for leaving the rescued person worse off than he was before the rescue attempt commenced. In these circumstances, the rescuer has crossed the line between non-feasance and misfeasance by making the plaintiff's position worse.

(ii)   Statutory powers

An area which has attracted much litigation is that of statutory powers[11] conferred on regulatory authorities and government officers. The defendant authority may have failed to properly carry out an optional act which it has voluntarily decided to perform. The courts are concerned with powers rather than duties, in these circumstances. However, a breach of a statutory duty may be a tort in its own right.[12]

---

3   *Zoernsch v Waldock* [1964] 1 WLR 675 at 685 (per Willmer LJ).
4   See *Nocton v Lord Ashburton* [1914] AC 932.
5   *Henderson v Merrett Syndicates Ltd* [1995] AC 145.
6   See also *Barclays Bank plc v Fairclough Building Ltd (No 2)* [1995] IRLR 605.
7   *White v Jones* [1995] 2 AC 207.
8   See Barker (1993) 109 LQR 461.
9   Whittaker (1997) LS 169.
10   [1970] 1 Lloyd's Rep 257; affd [1971] 2 Lloyd's Rep 410 on other grounds.
11   See McLean (1988) 8 OJLS 442; Brodie (1998) 18(1) LS 1.
12   See ch 26.

In *Anns v Merton London Borough Council*,[13] the defendant local authority was held liable for an inadequate inspection of the foundations of a building subsequently purchased by the plaintiff. The House of Lords assumed that there had been an inspection pursuant to bye-laws introduced by the council. The foundations were so poor, not having been taken down to a sufficient depth by the builder, that the building had to be demolished. The cause of the inadequate foundations was the fault of the builder, but the council was held liable for the failings of their inspector when he omitted to notice the inadequacies of the foundations. The decision has been criticised for its failure to distinguish between acts causing harm and omissions.[14] It could be said that the decision creates a duty to help one's neighbour in addition to the duty not to harm one's neighbour. But it should be observed that recent authorities have served to limit the scope of the decision in *Anns*.

Generally, since the court is concerned with powers created by statute, the intention of Parliament will be important. Thus if the statute specifically omits to provide a remedy for breach of the power under consideration, the court may conclude that it should not be the role of the common law to fill the gap.[15]

In *Stovin v Wise*[16] the defendant local authority had a statutory power to remove obstructions to visibility on the highway. They resolved to remove an obstruction but then 'went to sleep' for nearly a year before an accident in which S was injured. S recovered against W, who sought an indemnity from the local authority. The House of Lords held against W as the statute itself gave rise to no liability and its breach could not be the basis of a liability at common law. According to Lord Hoffmann there was no way that a statutory 'may' could be turned into a common law 'ought.'[17] The majority, however, said that a common law duty of care could arise in the context of a statutory power if it would have been irrational not to exercise the power and that there were exceptional grounds for holding that the policy of the statute requires compensation to be paid to persons injured by its non-exercise.[18] It was suggested that a duty of care in such circumstances could be found where there was 'general reliance, in the sense of a general dependance on performance with due care', as in the case of air traffic control.[19]

The *Anns* decision could perhaps be justified on this basis but the signs are that the courts are resisting its incorporation into English law. Fire brigades have been held to be under no common law duty to respond to a call and were only liable where they attended and made the situation worse.[20] The principle was said to have 'little, if any, support in English law....'[1]

Moreover, where the power is wide and affects large numbers of potential plaintiffs, the court is unlikely to impose liability on policy grounds because of the fear of indeterminate liability. Thus a regulatory agency empowered to license public listed companies owes no duty of care to potential investors in a company which has been

13 [1978] AC 728. Although this case has been overruled in one respect, the House of Lords in *Murphy v Brentwood District Council* [1990] 2 All ER 908 left open the question whether a local authority might owe a duty of care in respect of the failure to comply with a statutory power.
14 See Smith and Burns (1983) 46 MLR 147; Weir [1985] CLJ 26; Fleming *Introduction* pp 40–41. Cf *East Suffolk Rivers Catchment Board v Kent* [1941] AC 74.
15 *Yuen Kun Yeu v A-G of Hong Kong* [1987] 2 All ER 705.
16 [1996] AC 923.
17 Ibid at 948.
18 Ibid at 953.
19 See *Sutherland Shire Council v Heyman* (1985) 60 ALR 1 at 30 per MASON J. See also *Pyrenees Shire Council v Day* (1998) 151 ALR 147.
20 *Capital & Counties plc v Hampshire County Council* [1997] QB 1004. Cf *Kent v Griffiths* [2000] 2 All ER 474, CA (ambulance service)
1   Ibid at 344.

listed.[2] However, if the class of plaintiffs is small there may be less difficulty in imposing a duty of care. Thus a government minister who has a public interest power to require an undertaking from an individual that he will not take a shareholding above a specified percentage in a named company owes a duty to release the undertaking when it is no longer required in the public interest.[3]

(iii)   Special relationships

In some instances, the status of a person may justify the imposition of liability for an omission. An occupier of premises owes a duty of care to his lawful visitors, which includes a duty not to cause harm by reason of anything done or omitted to be done on the premises concerned.[4] Thus a patron of a public house may be entitled to the protection of the landlord from other rowdy patrons.[5] A landowner may also owe a duty of care to a neighbouring landowner in respect of dangers created by a third party,[6] or by an act of nature.[7]

The fact that the courts are dealing with non-feasance as opposed to misfeasance can sometimes result in a concession as to the meaning of reasonable care. Generally, the law imposes an objective standard, but in *Goldman v Hargrave*,[8] the Privy Council injected subjective overtones into the requirement of reasonable care. It was said to be necessary to consider the wealth of the occupier. What is reasonable for a company to do might not be reasonably expected of a private individual.[9]

Liability for an omission to act may also be imposed where one person has a particular responsibility for another. A parent may omit to protect his or her child and may be guilty of a failure to take care.[10] The decision in *The Ogopogo*[11] can also be explained on the grounds that the rescuer was the ship's captain, and that he owed a particular responsibility to his passengers. Similarly, an employer[12] may be liable for an omission which adversely affects his employee, or a doctor may owe a duty of care in respect of his omission to give proper medical care.[13] The police may be under a duty to prevent harm, including self inflicted harm, to persons in custody.[14] Some of these relationships may well be contractual in which case problems may be avoided by implying a term in the contract to the effect that reasonable care will be exercised. Thus a privately paid-for doctor may undertake to carefully advise his patient of the risks inherent in a medical procedure.[15]

In *Stansbie v Troman*,[16] a decorator was held to have assumed responsibility for the loss of the plaintiff's valuables when he failed to lock up her house on leaving and a

2   Ibid.
3   *Lonrho plc v Tebbitt* [1992] 4 All ER 280.
4   Occupiers' Liability Act 1957, s 1(1) and see ch 28.
5   Fleming *Introduction* p 45 asks whether a bank must hand over money to a robber so as to avert the danger of a shoot-out.
6   *Sedleigh-Denfield v O'Callaghan* [1940] AC 880.
7   *Goldman v Hargrave* [1967] 1 AC 645; *Leakey v National Trust for Places of Historic Interest or Natural Beauty* [1980] QB 485 and see ch 29.
8   [1967] 1 AC 645.
9   See also Occupiers' Liability Act 1984, s 1(3) and see ch 28.
10   *Surtees v Kingston upon Thames Borough Council* [1992] PIQR P101.
11   [1970] 1 Lloyd's Rep 257.
12   See ch 27.
13   *Barnett v Chelsea and Kensington Hospital Management Committee* [1969] 1 QB 428 and see ch 26.
14   *Kirkham v Chief Constable of Greater Manchester Police* [1990] 2 QB 283; *Reeves v Metropolitan Police Comr* [2000] 1 AC 360.
15   *Thake v Maurice* [1986] 1 All ER 497.
16   [1948] 2 KB 48. Cf *Lamb v Camden London Borough Council* [1981] QB 625 at 638 (per LORD DENNING MR).

thief entered the house. Presumably a similar principle could also be applied to a person left alone on premises as a non-contractual licensee.[17]

(iv)   Control of third parties

Where the defendant fails to exercise control over a third party, with the result that the plaintiff suffers harm, exceptionally, a duty may be owed. It has been seen that a person in a special relationship with another may owe that other a duty of care. Likewise, if the special relationship involves the exercise of control over a third party, and failure to control that person results in harm to the plaintiff, the plaintiff may have an action. For example, a parent or some person *in loco parentis* may owe a duty of care to a third person in respect of physical injury caused by the failure to control a child.[18] Similarly, a prison[19] or borstal[20] authority or a mental hospital[1] may owe a duty of care in respect of harm caused by an inmate of the establishment.

In these cases the damage caused by the person under control must be something very likely to happen if the defendant fails to exercise the required degree of control.[2] But it must also be borne in mind that human conduct can be highly unpredictable,[3] and that the controller will only be responsible for the reasonably foreseeable consequences of the escaping child or inmate. Thus in *Home Office v Dorset Yacht Co Ltd*,[4] the defendants were liable for their failure to control inmates at a borstal institution with the result that a neighbour's yacht was damaged. If, however, the inmates had escaped and caused harm some 200 miles away, it seems highly unlikely that such harm would have been regarded as foreseeable.

The classic example of liability for harm caused by a person under one's control is, of course, that of vicarious liability, where an employer is responsible for the acts of his employee performed in the course of his employment.[5] However, in these circumstances, the fault of the employer is not in issue. Vicarious liability is a variety of strict liability in the sense that there is no need to prove the negligence of the employer in selecting or supervising his workforce. If the employee is not acting in the course of his employment, it may be possible to hold the employer in breach of his duty of care if he has failed to control his employee.[6]

A second possible ground for the imposition of liability for failing to prevent harm caused by another may arise where the defendant himself has created a danger. In such a case, it may be reasonably foreseeable that some other person might interfere and cause damage by sparking off the danger created by the defendant.[7] For example, in *Haynes v Harwood*,[8] the defendant left a horse and cart unattended, with the result that a child was able to throw stones at the animal, causing it to bolt. The plaintiff, a policeman, was injured when he tried to prevent the horse from running into a nearby group of women and children. The action of the boy in throwing the stone was

---

17   See *Smith v Littlewoods Organisation Ltd* [1987] 1 All ER 710 at 730 (per LORD GOFF).
18   *Carmarthenshire County Council v Lewis* [1955] AC 549.
19   *Ellis v Home Office* [1953] 2 All ER 149.
20   *Home Office v Dorset Yacht Co Ltd* [1970] AC 1004.
1   *Holgate v Lancashire Mental Hospitals Board* [1937] 4 All ER 19. Cf *Home Office v Dorset Yacht Co Ltd* [1970] AC 1004 at 1062 (per LORD DIPLOCK).
2   *Home Office v Dorset Yacht Co Ltd* [1970] AC 1004 at 1030 (per LORD REID).
3   *Lamb v Camden London Borough Council* [1981] QB 625 at 642 (per OLIVER LJ).
4   [1970] AC 1004.
5   See ch 27.
6   *Hudson v Ridge Manufacturing Co Ltd* [1957] 2 QB 348.
7   *Smith v Littlewoods Organisation Ltd* [1987] 1 All ER 710 at 730 (per LORD GOFF). Cf *CBS Songs Ltd v Amstrad Consumer Electronics plc* [1988] 2 All ER 484 at 497 (per LORD TEMPLEMAN).
8   [1935] 1 KB 146.

something that the defendant might reasonably have foreseen and ought to have guarded against. However, if the defendant could not reasonably have been aware of the danger, then no duty of care will be found to exist. For example in *Smith v Littlewoods Organisation Ltd*,[9] the defendants bought an old cinema which they left unoccupied for a short period of time prior to its intended demolition. During that period, vandals broke into the unguarded premises and lit a fire which spread to the plaintiff's premises, thereby causing damage. Littlewoods were unaware of a general reputation of the particular area for acts of vandalism. Furthermore, specific acts of vandalism which had come to light had not been reported to Littlewoods by the police. In the circumstances, it was held by the House of Lords that while there was a general duty to exercise reasonable care to ensure that the condition of occupied premises is not a source of danger to neighbouring property, that duty did not extend to a case such as this where the defendants could not have been aware of the event which caused the harm to the plaintiff.[10] Likewise, a bus company that leaves a bus unattended with the key in the ignition is not liable for damage caused by a third party who steals the bus.[11]

A third reason for holding a defendant liable for the act of some other person is that he may be aware (or ought to be aware) that that other has created a risk and that he (the defendant) has failed to take reasonable steps to abate the risk.[12] For example, failure to properly abate the danger created by the burning tree in *Goldman v Hargrave*[13] might be seen as an example of this. Similarly, if in *Smith v Littlewoods Organisation Ltd*[14] there had been a known and substantial threat to neighbouring property due to vandalism on a large scale, the position may have been substantially different.[15] However, if there is no effective precaution that can be taken to deal with the act of the third party, then no duty of care will be held to exist.[16]

(3)   VARIETIES OF HARM

A third factor which may influence the decision of whether or not a duty of care is owed is the nature of the injury inflicted on the plaintiff. In this context, it is strange that the law speaks in terms of duty. It would appear to be the case that the courts are not concerned with duties at all. Instead, the court is more concerned with the injury to the plaintiff than with what is expected from a defendant.[17] The court will concentrate not on whether the defendant has broken some obligation, but on whether it is right that the plaintiff should be compensated for the particular harm he has suffered. The importance of the plaintiff is illustrated by those cases in which the defendant is liable for injury suffered by a 'thin skulled' plaintiff.[18] The exercise of reasonable care in such cases may require the taking of special precautions, but the problem is usually dealt with by saying that there has been no breach of the duty of care.

---

9   [1987] 1 All ER 710.
10   See also *P Perl (Exporters) Ltd v Camden London Borough Council* [1983] 3 All ER 161.
11   *Topp v London Country Bus (South West) Ltd* [1993] 1 WLR 976.
12   *Smith v Littlewoods Organisation Ltd* [1987] 1 All ER 710 at 731 (per LORD GOFF).
13   [1967] 1 AC 645.
14   [1987] 1 All ER 710.
15   See *Thomas Graham & Co Ltd v Church of Scotland General Trustees* 1982 SLT (Sh Ct) 26.
16   See *King v Liverpool City Council* [1986] 3 All ER 544; *P Perl (Exporters) Ltd v Camden London Borough Council* [1983] 3 All ER 161.
17   See *Voli v Inglewood Shire Council* [1963] Qd R 256 at 257 (per WINDEYER J).
18   See *Smith v Leech Brain & Co Ltd* [1962] 2 QB 405; *Paris v Stepney Borough Council* [1951] AC 367; *Haley v London Electricity Board* [1965] AC 778.

3.   THE HUMAN RIGHTS ACT 1998 AND NEGLIGENCE

(1)   INTRODUCTION

The Human Rights Act 1998 will come into force on 4 October 2000. The Act provides that wherever possible legislation must be interpreted in a way which is compatible with the rights in the European Convention on Human Rights[19] and that it is unlawful for a public authority to act in a way which is incompatible with a Convention right.[20]

A court is classified as a 'public authority'[1] and a judge adjudicating on a claim must consider compatibility with Convention rights and attempt to ensure consistency between the common law and Convention rights. However, Convention rights are in addition to and not in substitution for rights and freedoms which already exist at common law.[2] A Convention right is directly enforceable against a public authority and an individual who thinks that his Convention rights have been violated may sue for damages.[3] In many cases a Convention right will already be protected by the common law, in which case the claimant will probably sue for breach of the relevant duty and the court will interpret that right in accordance with the jurisprudence of the European Court of Human Rights. This may require a different approach from the one which English courts are used to. Many Convention rights include a derogation from the right but this derogation has to be interpreted on a proportional basis, balancing the relevant interests. For example Article 10 (1) gives a right of freedom of speech but Article 10 (2) allows freedom of speech to be restricted for certain purposes such as the protection of reputation. However, a court has to carry out a balancing exercise between the two competing interests. In some areas of English common law this will be a new approach for the courts who are used to taking a different approach.

It appears that the Human Rights Act will affect English common law in two ways. Firstly, if there is no right recognised by English common law but there is a Convention right. In this case, if the defendant is a public authority, the claimant will proceed directly against the public authority under the Act. This could be the case in privacy claims where it is arguable that there is no recognised common law right. Secondly, there may be a restriction on the claimant's common law right such as a policy immunity bar to suing the police for negligence in the investigation of crime. This will be dealt with below.   At the time of writing it appears likely that four Convention rights will be particularly relevant. These are Article 6 (the right to a hearing), Article 2 (the right to life), and Article 8 (the right to privacy and a family life) and Article 10 (freedom of speech).

(2)   PUBLIC POLICY IMMUNITIES

The immunities given in certain areas of negligence are likely to come under immediate challenge unless the English courts have sufficiently redefined them by the relevant time. Challenges will be mounted on the basis of Article 6 which states that in the determination of their civil rights and obligations everyone is entitled to a fair and public hearing.

---

19   See s 3.
20   See ss 6–8. A Convention right means Articles 2–12 and 14 of the Convention, Articles 1–3 of the First Protocol and Articles 1 and 2 of the Sixth Protocol.
1   See s 6(3)(a).
2   See s 11.
3   See ss 7–8.

Immunity was given to the police in respect of the investigation of crime in *Hill v Chief Constable of West Yorkshire*[4] and actions brought against the police in this respect would be struck out on a preliminary application without a full hearing of the case. This happened in *Osman v Ferguson*[5] where the case was said by the Court of Appeal to be doomed to failure because of the *Hill* immunity, although there was arguably sufficient proximity between the claimant and the police. The allegation was that police negligence had led to a child's death after a campaign of harassment against the child by the killer. However, the European Court of Human Rights, while accepting that there was a legitimate justification for the immunity, held that it had to be open to a domestic court to have regard to other public interest considerations, as a failure to do so would mean that there would be no distinction between degrees of negligence or consideration of the justice of a particular case.[6] The failure of the Court of Appeal to consider competing public interests was held to be a disproportionate response to the aim of maintaining police effectiveness and had deprived the plaintiff of the right to a fair hearing under Article 6.

There is now a clear line of English authorities where the courts have considered competing public interests before reaching a decision, rather than simply applying a blanket immunity.[7] However, in the case of *Brindle v Comr of Police of Metropolis*,[8] the plaintiff was injured whilst being used as bait by the police but had his action struck out under the *Hill* immunity. As there was no consideration of the merits, this would appear to be a clear breach of Article 6.

Similar principles operate in respect of the immunity of participants in legal proceedings. The immunity of an advocate in respect of work done in connection with the conduct of the case in court has now been abolished[9] by the House of Lords and although Article 6 is not stressed in the judgments it was fairly clear that the practice of striking out actions against advocates on the ground of public policy immunity was contrary to Article 6.[10]

The immunity which was granted to social work and education services in *X v Bedfordshire County Council*[11] will require a similar merits approach and again it is clear that the courts are already moving towards this.[12]

(3)   THE RIGHT TO LIFE

Article 2 of the Convention gives a right to life. This could be invoked in a number of areas, including actions against the police and the rescue services. Article 2 was invoked in *Osman v United Kingdom*[13] and the European Court of Human Rights found that it implied, in certain well defined circumstances, a positive obligation to take protective operational measures to protect a person whose life is at risk from the criminal acts of another individual. In order to be in breach, the authorities must have known of the existence of a real and immediate risk to the life of an identified individual and failed to take measures within the scope of their powers, which judged reasonably, might have

4   [1989] AC 53.
5   [1993] 4 All ER 344.
6   *Osman v United Kingdom* [1999] Crim LR 82 (ECHR).
7   *Swinney v Chief Constable of Northumbria Police Force* [1997] QB 464; *Costello v Chief Constable of Northumbria Police* [1999] 1 All ER 550.
8   5 June 1998, unreported.
9   *Hall & Co v Simons* (2000) Times, 21 July.
10   *See* Sprince & Cooke (1999) 15 (4) PN 228.
11   [1995] 2 AC 633.
12   *Barrett v Enfield London Borough Council* [1999] 3 All ER 193; *Phelps v Hillingdon London Borough Council* [1999] 1 All ER 421.
13   [1999] Crim LR 82 (ECHR).

been expected to avoid that risk. On the facts, given the presumption of innocence, the police were found to have reasonably held the view that they lacked the required standard of suspicion to use their powers. However, the decision in *Brindle*,[14] where the police set a trap, rather than warning the victim of an attempted assassination attempt, would appear to be in breach of Article 2.

Similar principles would apply to the rescue services where life, as opposed to property, is in danger. English law would appear, at present, to be in breach of Article 2 in this respect.[15]

The combination of Articles 2 and 6 and section 6 of the Human Rights Act 1998, which gives the Convention direct effect against public authorities, may mean that the courts have to reconsider the whole question of omissions in the context of public authorities, in particular, the law of negligence relating to the rescue services. In the absence of such developments, a claimant will have an action under the Human Rights Act for failure to uphold a Convention right.

(4)   THE RIGHT TO PRIVACY AND A FAMILY LIFE

This right is given by Article 8 and may have an effect in the area of liability for psychiatric damage.[16] As the law stands at present there is no claim for psychiatric damage caused by gradual attacks on the nervous system accumulated over a period of time.[17] Therefore, when a known abuser was placed as a foster child with a fostering family, the Court of Appeal struck out a claim by the parents for shock at abuse of their natural children.[18] It is certainly arguable that this rule and the rejection of secondary victim claims by siblings deprive the parties of full respect for their family life.

---

14   *Brindle v Comr of Police of Metropolis* 5 June 1998, unreported.
15   See *Capital & Counties plc v Hampshire County Council* [1997] QB 1004; *Stovin v Wise* [1996] AC 923. Cf *Kent v Griffiths* [2000] 2 All ER 474.
16   See ch 9.
17   See *W v Essex County Council* [1998] 3 All ER 111.
18   Ibid.

Chapter 9

Compensation for wrongful harm — physical damage

The central feature in *Donoghue v Stevenson* was that the defendant produced, by his negligent act, a product which was dangerous and which caused physical harm to the plaintiff. As a result of this, it became readily acceptable that physical harm to a person or his property caused by positive negligent conduct should be compensated. The troublesome cases arose in areas outside this category. For example, it has become necessary to consider whether damages may be awarded for mental distress, or for economic loss. Problem cases have also arisen where the harm suffered has resulted from an omission to act rather than from positive conduct.

The most commonly encountered varieties of negligent conduct causing physical harm or death are road accident and industrial injury cases. The dangers involved at work[1] or on the road are now so obvious that it would be pointless to try to argue that no duty of care is owed by a careless driver or an employer. Indeed the dangers presented by these two activities have prompted Parliament to intervene and insist that drivers are insured against third party risks and that employers are insured against risks of injury to employees whilst at the workplace. Such is the influence of insurance in this area that it is arguable whether the common law has any further role to play. Conceivably, it might be possible to introduce a system of private insurance to cover all personal injury claims.[2]

These two instances clearly involve the restoration of the status quo in that the plaintiff is compensated so as to return him to the position he was in before the injury was suffered, so far as money can do this. Beyond these cases, most examples of physical harm occur in a direct or indirect relational setting such as that of manufacturer and consumer, retailer and consumer, or occupier and visitor. In each of these cases, the plaintiff may suffer physical harm because he has been supplied with a defective product or has encountered some unreasonable risk whilst on the other person's premises.

In the case of defective products, the consumer may have bought the goods himself[3] or he may have been a donee,[4] but in either case he is entitled to damages so as to

---

1   See ch 27.
2   See ch 11.
3   *Godley v Perry* [1960] 1 WLR 9 (loss of expectation of life); *Grant v Australian Knitting Mills Ltd* [1936] AC 85 (pain and suffering).
4   *Donoghue v Stevenson* [1932] AC 562.

restore him to the position he was in before the injury was suffered. The damages awarded may cover pain and suffering and loss of life expectancy. A person who is injured because of the defective performance of a service is also entitled to be compensated in respect of that injury, whether he is someone who has contracted for that service[5] or whether he is a bystander foreseeably within the area of risk,[6] or a donee.[7]

In the case of occupiers and visitors, the Occupier's Liability Act 1957 specifies that the occupier owes his lawful visitors a common duty of care.[8] This duty is owed to any person lawfully on the premises and therefore covers contractual visitors, invitees or persons deemed to have authority to be on the premises. Any such person is entitled to be compensated in respect of foreseeable physical injury suffered whilst on the premises.[9] A duty of reasonable care is also owed to a trespasser to premises in certain circumstances.[10]

1.   PSYCHIATRIC DAMAGE[11]

English law has experienced some difficulty in deciding how to deal with psychical harm as opposed to physical harm. It has been pointed out that the public draws a distinction between the cripple and the neurotic.[12] Thus if a person loses his leg due to the defendant's negligence or his breach of contract, that loss is remediable, provided the harm suffered is not too remote. But the same is not true where distress, grief or nervous shock is suffered. At one stage, the common law denied an action for damages for shock even where the plaintiff feared for his own personal safety.[13] A return to such a position has been advocated.[14]

(1)   MERE DISTRESS

It is said that grief, disappointment and distress are normal human emotions.[15] They are part of everyday life and a person of normal disposition is expected to cope with such emotions. As an exception, the spouse of a deceased person or the parents of a deceased unmarried minor may recover damages for bereavement.[16] If two parents seek damages for bereavement, the fixed sum will be split equally between them.[17]

A similar approach is also adopted in actions for breach of contract. Thus damages will not be awarded for injured feelings if a person is dismissed in an insulting or demeaning way.[18]

---

5   *Kimber v William Willett Ltd* [1947] KB 570.
6   *Stennett v Hancock and Peters* [1939] 2 All ER 578.
7   *White v John Warrick & Co Ltd* [1953] 1 WLR 1285.
8   Occupiers' Liability Act 1957, s 2(2) and see ch 28.
9   See *Thornton v Shoe Lane Parking Ltd* [1971] 2 QB 163 (contractual visitor); *Lowery v Walker* [1911] AC 10 (invitee); *Hartley v Mayoh & Co* [1954] 1 QB 383 (fireman entering premises in the course of his duty).
10 Occupiers' Liability Act 1984, s 1(3) and (4).
11 See Law Commission No 249 (1998).
12 Weir, (7th edn) p 88.
13 *Victorian Railways Comrs v Coultas* (1888) 13 App Cas 222. Cf *Dulieu v White & Sons* [1901] 2 KB 669.
14 Stapleton (ed Birks) *The Frontiers of Liability* Vol 2 (OUP, 1994) pp 83–84.
15 *McLoughlin v O'Brian* [1983] 1 AC 410 at 431 (per LORD BRIDGE).
16 Fatal Accidents Act 1976, s 1A. The award of damages is set at a fixed sum of £7,500 which may be increased by statutory instrument.
17 Ibid, s 1A(4).
18 *Addis v Gramophone Co Ltd* [1909] AC 488; See also *Hayes v James & Charles Dodd (a firm)* [1990] 2 All ER 815 and *Bliss v South East Thames Regional Health Authority* [1985] IRLR 308 overruling *Cox v Philips Industries Ltd* [1976] 3 All ER 161.

Conversely, in some cases, the plaintiff may have contracted to 'buy' peace of mind and he may be disappointed. For example, a holiday maker may recover damages for distress and disappointment suffered when his holiday is ruined.[19] Likewise a person employs a surveyor to give him peace of mind when purchasing a house.[20] Moreover where a client asks a solicitor to obtain a non-molestation order and nothing is done towards that end, the distress suffered by virtue of the harassment of a former spouse may be compensated.[1]

The type of loss suffered in these cases appears to relate to consumer expectations and what is compensated is the value placed on the product or service over and above its market value.[2] However, these distress and disappointment cases all involve the provision of a service, in which case, there is an implied contractual term that the provider of the service will exercise reasonable care and skill.[3] If the provider of the service, in the performance of the contract, fails to exercise that required degree of skill, he is guilty of a failure to exercise reasonable care. The plaintiff is contracting for a result in much the same way as a patient expects a surgeon to exercise reasonable care in the conduct of a medical operation. In such a case, there is an implied term that the surgeon will exercise reasonable care.[4] Furthermore, such expectations as are raised in these cases can be described as general expectations similar to cases in which damages are awarded for loss of amenity or pain and suffering.[5] Viewed in this way, it may be said that the disappointment suffered by the plaintiff is a consequence of a defendant's failure to take care. If the plaintiff is compensated, he is given sufficient to restore him to the position he was in before the 'harm' was inflicted. What must be decided in these cases is whether the non-pecuniary loss suffered by the plaintiff is reasonably foreseeable as likely to result from the breach of contract.[6] Furthermore, if one regards the disappointment as a variety of physical harm, suffered as a consequence of the defendant's conduct, then there is some authority for the view that the remoteness test is the same in contract as it is in tort.[7]

(2)   PSYCHIATRIC ILLNESS

English law normally requires some definite and identifiable psychiatric illness[8] before damages for psychiatric damage will be awarded. Any recognisable psychiatric illness will suffice. Damages have been awarded for post traumatic stress disorder;[9] pathological grief disorder;[10] morbid depression;[11] chronic fatigue syndrome;[12] and hysterical personality disorder.[13] This may include an anxiety neurosis, reactive depression or some

---

19   *Jarvis v Swans Tours Ltd* [1973] 1 All ER 71; *Jackson v Horizon Holidays Ltd* [1975] 3 All ER 92. See also
      Diesen v Samson 1971 SLT 49 (wedding photographs lost by photographer).
20   *Perry v Sidney Phillips & Son* [1982] 1 WLR 1297 at 1302–1303 (per LORD DENNING MR) (tort damages
      for vexation).
1   *Heywood v Wellers* [1976] 1 All ER 300.
2   Otherwise known as the 'consumer surplus'. See Harris, Ogus and Phillips (1979) 95 LQR 581. See
      Ruxley Electronics and Construction Ltd v Forsyth [1996] AC 344.
3   Supply of Goods and Services Act 1982, s 13 and see ch 25.
4   *Thake v Maurice* [1986] 1 All ER 497; *Eyre v Measday* [1986] 1 All ER 488.
5   See Harris, Ogus and Phillips (1979) 95 LQR 581 at 596. Cf Burrows (1983) 99 LQR 217 at 221 n (10).
6   *Koufos v C Czarnikow Ltd, The Heron II* [1969] 1 AC 350. Cf Jackson (1977) 26 ICLQ 502 and see
      ch 15.
7   *H Parsons (Livestock) Ltd v Uttley Ingham & Co Ltd* [1978] QB 791 and see also ch 16.
8   See *Hinz v Berry* [1970] 2 QB 40; *McLoughlin v O'Brian* [1983] 1 AC 410 at 431 (per LORD BRIDGE);
      Sprice (1998) 18(1) LS 59.
9   *Alcock v Chief Constable of South Yorkshire Police* [1991] 4 All ER 907.
10   *Vernon v Bosley (No 1)* [1997] 1 All ER 577.
11   *Hinz v Berry* [1970] 2 QB 40.
12   *Page v Smith* [1996] AC 155.
13   *Brice v Brown* [1984] 1 All ER 997.

other recognisable psychiatric condition. For the most part, whether such a condition is present will be established by medical evidence. However, there would appear to be something called 'non-psychiatric' shock which is identifiable by the judge and which does not have to be established by medical evidence.[14] This is more than emotional distress or worry but does not amount to a psychiatric illness. The decision is usually regarded as an aberration.[15]

Traditionally, the term 'nervous shock' has been used in negligence actions, but this has been described as 'misleading and inaccurate'[16] and the term 'psychiatric damage' is preferred to describe all relevant forms of mental illness, neurosis and personality change.[17]

The fact that a person suffers nervous shock as a result of the defendant's negligence does not necessarily mean that he will be compensated. It may be that the defendant causes an accident with particularly gruesome consequences. Is he to be required to compensate everyone who suffers distress at observing the accident? Let us suppose that the organiser of a motor cycle stunt carelessly fails to take precautions for the safety of the cyclist, with the result that the cyclist is killed in front of 100,000 spectators at Wembley Stadium. Is the organiser to compensate everyone in the crowd in respect of their feelings of revulsion? Suppose the cyclist comes from a very large family and he has many brothers, sisters, aunts and uncles, none of whom are sufficiently bothered to see their relative perform. Is the organiser to compensate these relatives if they are distressed at the news of the cyclist's death? This example illustrates that limits have to be set upon the extent to which a person is liable for causing harm of this sort. In this regard, English law looks for the foreseeable plaintiff. If a contractual relationship exists and the defendant's breach of contract causes the plaintiff to suffer nervous shock, damages can be awarded in respect of that harm, provided shock was foreseeable, at the time of the contract, as a probable consequence of the breach.[18]

In non-contractual relationships, the common law asks whether the defendant owed the plaintiff a duty to take care in order to determine whether he is liable for psychiatric damage suffered by the plaintiff.[19] The problem with the use of the concept of duty is that it has a number of meanings. It can be used to describe the circumstances in which a duty of care is said to exist; whether it was reasonably foreseeable that the plaintiff would suffer harm in a given set of circumstances; or whether a duty was owed in respect of a particular kind of loss.[20]

Until the House of Lords decision in *Page v Smith*[1] it was understood that what had to be reasonably foreseeable was psychiatric injury caused by shock.[2] Initially the plaintiff had to be within the possible area of impact[3] and thus in fear for their own safety.[4] This was extended to fear for the safety of others as the courts realised that shock was a specific kind of damage, different to standard cases of personal injury.[5] The basis of liability therefore became foreseeability of injury by shock.[6]

14   *Whitmore v Euroways Express Coaches Ltd* (1984) Times, 4 May.
15   Law Commission 259 (1998) para 2.5 fn 15.
16   *Attia v British Gas plc* [1987] 3 All ER 455 at 462 (per BINGHAM LJ); *Alcock v Chief Constable of South Yorkshire Police* [1991] 4 All ER 907 at 922–923 (per LORD OLIVER).
17   Ibid.
18   *Cook v Swinfen* [1967] 1 WLR 457 at 461 (per LORD DENNING MR).
19   Cf the position where shock is caused intentionally. See *Wilkinson v Downton* [1897] 2 QB 57; *Janvier v Sweeney* [1919] 2 KB 316.
20   See Smith *Liability in Negligence* (1984) p 115. See also Dias [1967] CLJ 62.
1   [1996] AC 155.
2   See Mullany & Handford *Tort Liability for Psychiatric Damage* (1993) pp 69–70.
3   *Dulieu v White & Sons* [1901] 2 KB 669.
4   See also *McFarlane v EE Caledonia Ltd* [1994] 2 All ER 1; *Schneider v Eisovitch* [1960] 1 All ER 169.
5   *Hambrook v Stokes Bros* [1925] 1 KB 141.
6   *King v Phillips* [1953] 1 QB 429, 441 per DENNING LJ, approved in *Overseas Tankship (UK) Ltd v Morts Dock & Engineering Co Ltd (The Wagon Mound)* [1961] AC 388, 426 per VISCOUNT SIMON.

In the majority of cases, the psychiatric damage complained of flows from conduct that has caused physical harm. As was pointed out by LORD BRIDGE in *McLoughlin v O'Brian*:[7]

> ... it is well to remember that we are concerned only with the question of liability of a defendant who is, ex hypothesi, guilty of fault in causing the death, injury or danger which has, in turn, triggered the psychiatric illness.[8]

The danger referred to by LORD BRIDGE may or may not have manifested itself in physical injury. For example, it may be that a person suffers shock as a result of seeing or eating adulterated food. In such a case, it can be said that there is a risk of physical harm which has not yet been realised.[9] It follows that the defendant has already been 'negligent' in the sense that he has created a risk of physical harm. The issue whether the plaintiff is entitled to damages for nervous shock then becomes one of reasonable foresight of harm. It must be asked if it is a foreseeable consequence of the defendant's negligence that a reasonable man in the position of the plaintiff would suffer in the way in which the plaintiff suffered. It is important to stress that the plaintiff will only recover if the reasonable man, possessed of a strong nerve or customary phlegm,[10] would have suffered from shock. This operates as a policy restriction to prevent 'gold-digging' claims which might be made by hypersensitive plaintiffs. However, if the reasonable man might have suffered from shock, then the defendant is liable for the full extent of the plaintiff's injury, even if the plaintiff is possessed of some unusual personality disorder.[11]

Where there is no physical injury to the plaintiff, the same principle applies that the defendant can assume the plaintiff is a person of normal fortitude or 'customary phlegm.'[12] Once it is established that a person of normal fortitude would suffer some psychiatric illness, then a sensitive or susceptible plaintiff can recover for the full extent of the illness.[13] In determining what is normal fortitude, English law has no equivalent of the American 'firemans' rule, whereby a member of the professional rescue services is unable to claim as they are expected to to deal with stressful sights.[14]

In looking at what kind of damage has to be reasonably foreseeable it is now necessary to determine whether the plaintiff was a primary or a secondary victim of the plaintiff's negligence. This distinction has its origins in dicta by LORD OLIVER in *Alcock*.[15]

> ... two categories, that is to say those cases in which the injured plaintiff was involved, either mediately or immediately as a participant, and those in which the plaintiff was no more than the passive and unwilling witness of injury caused to others.

Involvement as a participant means that the plaintiff is a primary victim and what needs to be reasonably foreseeable is personal injuries. There is no need to distinguish between physical injury and psychiatric illness.[16] In *Page v Smith*[17] the plaintiff was involved in a traffic accident of moderate severity and suffered no physical injury.

---

7   [1983] 1 AC 410. See Hutchinson and Morgan (1982) 45 MLR 693; Owen [1983] CLJ 41; Teff (1983) 99 LQR 100.
8   Ibid at 441.
9   *Taylor v Weston Bakeries Ltd* [1976] WWD 165, 1 CCLT 158; *Negro v Pietro's Bread Co Ltd* [1933] OR 112, 1 DLR 490.
10   *Bourhill v Young* [1943] AC 92.
11   *Brice v Brown* [1984] 1 All ER 997. See Gearty [1984] CLJ 238.
12   *Bourhill v Young* [1943] AC 92, 117 per LORD PORTER.
13   *Brice v Brown* [1984] 1 All ER 997.
14   *White v Chief Constable of South Yorkshire Police* [1999] 1 All ER 1, 49 per LORD HOFFMANN.
15   *Alcock v Chief Constable of South Yorkshire Police*. [1992] 1 AC 310, 406.
16   *Page v Smith* [1996] AC 155.
17   Ibid.

However, as a result of the accident he suffered a recurrence of chronic fatigue syndrome (M.E.). The House of Lords, by a majority, held that a duty of care was owed to the plaintiff in respect of the damage. The plaintiff was a primary victim within LORD OLIVER's definition and as some damage was reasonably foreseeable as a result of the accident, the defendant's were liable for the full extent of the M.E. The special control mechanisms applicable to secondary victims (see below) did not apply.

The change from reasonable foreseeability of shock to reasonable foreseeability of physical injury (including shock) has proved controversial.[18] It has also been criticised on the grounds that it is contrary to well established authority and misunderstands the so-called 'egg-shell skull rule' relating to sensitive plaintiffs and treated it as having general application, thereby creating a wider principle of liability. Where the plaintiff can be classified as a primary victim it is therefore not necessary to ask whether the plaintiff is of customary phlegm.

(i)   Secondary victims and control devices

The primary/secondary victim distinction is the most recent attempt to rationalise this area of law. For some time a test of foreseeability was applied in a robust way but this led to discrepancies in the results of cases.[19] English law then came close to applying a literal test of foreseeability. In *McLoughlin v O'Brian*,[20] two members of the House of Lords[1] adopted a test of principle based on reasonable foresight of harm. But LORDS WILBERFORCE and EDMUND-DAVIES qualified the reasonable foresight test with policy considerations substantially based on the 'floodgates' argument. The difference between the two approaches should not be overstated since, in the majority of cases, the same result is likely to be achieved.[2] The *policy* argument advanced by LORD WILBERFORCE[3] identified three main issues, namely who can sue, where they must be at the time of the accident, and what was the means by which the shock was caused?

At one stage, it was thought that those whose claims could be recognised would be confined to close family relationships such as that between husband and wife or parent and child. However, in the leading House of Lords decision in *Alcock v Chief Constable of South Yorkshire Police*[4] the shackles of the relationship rule were dispensed with. Instead, it was held that the proper test to apply at this stage was to consider whether it was reasonably foreseeable that psychiatric damage might be suffered.[5] Ordinarily, the required degree of foresight would be established by the existence of a close tie, based on care, between the plaintiff and the victim of the defendant's negligence,[6] but other more remote relationships, including a mere bystander, could not be ruled out.[7] Thus it follows that sibling relationships, aunts and uncles, friends, engaged couples should all be recognised as potential claimants. However, it will be for the plaintiff to prove that the required relationship of care exists. Moreover, while that relationship can be presumed in the case of close family members, the presumption is rebuttable.[8] It follows

---

18   See LORD GOFF's dissenting judgment in *White v Chief Constable of South Yorkshire Police* [1999] 1 All ER 1. See also Handford (1996) Tort Law Rev 5; Trinidade (1996) 112 LQR 22; Sprince (1995) 11 PN 124. For a supporting view see Law Commission 249 (1998) para 5.12.
19   See *White v Chief Constable of South Yorkshire Police* [1999] 1 All ER 1 at 40 per LORD HOFFMANN.
20   [1983] 1 AC 410.
1   LORDS BRIDGE and SCARMAN.
2   Smith *Liability in Negligence* (1984) pp 156–157.
3   Stated to be the leading judgment in *Alcock v Chief Constable of South Yorkshire Police* [1991] 4 All ER 907 at 912 (per LORD KEITH).
4   [1991] 4 All ER 907.
5   Ibid at 919 (per LORD ACKNER).
6   Ibid.
7   Ibid.
8   Ibid.

that a mother who gave up her child at birth for adoption would probably not be able to establish the caring relationship required in order to have standing to sue. Similarly in *Alcock* itself, a brother and a brother-in-law were considered not to have proved the existence of the caring relationship required to satisfy the test. The Law Commission[9] recommended that legislation should be introduced to lay down a list of relatives where a close tie of love and affection would be deemed to exist. This would include spouses, parents, children, brothers and sisters. Anyone in a relationship outside this list would need to prove the requirement.

It is also possible for a claim to succeed where there is no danger to life at all. In this property-owning democracy, it seems to be foreseeable that a person whose family home is destroyed by a negligently caused fire may suffer psychiatric harm.[10] However, this principle has not yet been extended to include favourite pet animals.

The most restrictive element in LORD WILBERFORCE's analysis in *McLoughlin* is that those entitled to sue are limited to those who are proximate to the accident in time and space. Thus in order to sue successfully, the plaintiff must see or hear the accident or come upon its immediate aftermath as in *McLoughlin*[11] itself, where the plaintiff had been told of a traffic accident, caused by the defendant's negligence, which had caused the death of one of her children and left the rest of her family in need of hospital treatment. She attended the hospital some two hours after the event and saw the extent of the injuries to her family. She suffered from organic depression and a personality change. The House of Lords held, unanimously, that the plaintiff was entitled to damages in respect of the shock suffered as a result of witnessing the aftermath of the accident, since at the time of her arrival, the members of her family had not been cleaned up.

Until the decision in *Alcock* arising out of the Hillsborough football stadium tragedy, some cases had suggested an extension of the aftermath doctrine, based on the reasonable foresight principle. This would have allowed recovery on the part of a mother who was told of the death of her son, but did not see his body[12] and a father who saw the undisfigured body of his favourite son in a mortuary some three hours after an accident caused by the defendant's negligence.[13] But it is clear that neither of these cases can stand with the strict requirement of proximity in time and space to the accident in which the victim is killed or injured.

It follows from the above that a close relative of the victim who is told of an accident by a friend,[14] or who reads about the accident and suffers shock as a result of what he hears or reads, would be denied the right to sue. This conclusion certainly follows from the decision of the House of Lords in *Alcock v Chief Constable of South Yorkshire Police*[15] in which various relatives of spectators crushed to death or seriously injured at a football match which had been televised live claimed damages for psychiatric harm caused as a result of witnessing events which were admitted to have been caused by the negligence of the police. Most of these claimants were not present at the ground, and all within this category were denied recovery on the basis that the plaintiff must suffer shock as a result of actually seeing or hearing the accident with his own senses or come upon the immediate aftermath of the accident. Even live television viewers did not fall within this category, since they would be viewing events not through their own eyes, but through the eyes of the television director. Moreover, when considering whether the plaintiff can succeed, regard must be had to the proximity of relationship between the plaintiff and the defendant. In *Alcock* the police could reasonably foresee that relatives

9   (1998) No 249.
10   *Attia v British Gas plc* [1987] 3 All ER 455.
11   [1983] 1 AC 410.
12   *Ravenscroft v Rederiaktiebolaget Transatlantic* [1991] 3 All ER 73; revsd [1992] 2 All ER 470 (note).
13   *Hevican v Ruane* [1991] 3 All ER 65.
14   *Hambrook v Stokes Bros* [1925] 1 KB 141.
15   [1991] 4 All ER 907.

of the deceased would be watching the live event on television, but the defendant would also be aware of the television code of ethics which did not allow pictures of suffering by recognised individuals to be portrayed. Had the television company breached this code, their intervention would have been a novus actus interveniens.[16] But as the code had been complied with the police could reasonably expect that no such detailed pictures would be shown, thereby preventing the necessary relationship of proximity between the parties from arising.[17]

The Law Commission[18] recommended that the time and space proximity requirement be abolished by legislation as this requirement was artificial and arbitrary and a close relationship between plaintiff and immediate victim was sufficient.

(ii)   Primary victims

The control devices have been said not to apply in primary victim cases.[19] The difficulty however, is determining who is a primary victim. It could be that the plaintiff would have to be within the range of foreseeable physical injury in order to be a primary victim[20] or that reasonable foreseeability of psychiatric harm to a participant was sufficient.[1] The distinction is crucial in cases involving employees, rescuers and participant cases such as *Dooley v Cammell Laird & Co Ltd*.[2]

These issues were raised in *White v Chief Constable of South Yorkshire Police*.[3] Claims were made for psychiatric damage suffered by police officers on duty at Hillsborough at the time of the disaster. The claims rested on the plaintiff's status as employees of the defendant and the fact that they were rescuers. The employer-employee claim rested on the Chief Constable owing a duty to take reasonable care not to expose them to an unnecessary risk of injury, including psychiatric injury. The majority found that the duty owed by an employer to an employee was not a separate tort with its own rules, but an aspect of the general law of negligence. The relationship of employer-employee tells us that the duty of care is owed but nothing about the circumstances in which an employer will be liable for a particular type of injury. That is governed by the general law, in this case the law applicable to psychiatric damage. The plaintiffs here were secondary victims with no relationship to the victims and were therefore owed no duty of care in respect of that type of damage. A contrast was made[4] with *Walker v Northumberland County Council*[5] where the plaintiff was not a secondary victim. Walker's breakdown was caused by the work which his employer had compelled him to do, not for fear of someone else's safety.

As to the claim based on rescuers, Lord Hoffmann stated that rescuers do not form a special class and can be accommodated by the general law of negligence.[6] The question was therefore whether injury to the rescuer was foreseeable. Presumably what is meant by injury here is physical injury.

---

16   Ibid at 921 (per Lord Ackner).
17   Ibid.
18   No 249 (1998) para 6.16.
19   *Page v Smith* [1996] AC 155.
20   Ibid at 197 per Lord Lloyd .
1   *White v Chief Constable of South Yorkshire Police* [1999] 1 All ER 1 at 19 per Lord Goff; See also *Robertson v Forth Road Bridge Joint Board* [1995] SC 364; *Young v Charles Church (Southern) Ltd* (1997) Transcript; *Hunter v Duncan* 39 BMLR 146.
2   [1951] 1 Lloyd's Rep 271.
3   [1999] 1 All ER 1.
4   Ibid at 43 per Lord Hoffmann.
5   [1995] 1 All ER 737.
6   *White v Chief Constable of South Yorkshire Police* [1999] 1 All ER 1 at 47. See also Lord Steyn at 38.

The refusal of the majority to use incrementalism and create a class of rescuers was based on the difficulties of defining rescuers and also that it would offend the public's notions of distributive justice to favour one class while the bereaved relatives received nothing. The previous case of *Chadwick v British Rly Board*[7] survives on the basis that physical injury to the plaintiff rescuer who assisted at the scene of a rail crash, was reasonably foreseeable.

No attempt was made by the House to defend the control devices as LORD HOFFMANN felt that 'the search for principle was called off in *Alcock*'[8] and agreed with the comment of Professor Stapleton that, 'once the law has taken a wrong turning or otherwise fallen into an unsatisfactory state in relation to a particular cause of action, incrementalism cannot provide the answer.'[9]

(iii)   Shock

The requirement that psychiatric damage as a result of fear for others be caused by shock, rather than by an accumulation of assaults on the brain, was expressed in *Alcock* by LORD ACKNER[10] although shock is clearly not a requirement in cases of psychiatric illness induced through stress at work. The requirement had led to some harsh decisions.[11] The Law Commission[12] has recommended that the shock requirement be abolished but the House of Lords decision in *White* appears to strengthen the requirement for shock and it will probably require legislation to bring order to this whole area of law. A further consideration is the means by which the shock is caused. It is clear from *Alcock* that it is the assault on the plaintiff's senses which violently agitates the mind that matters most.[13] Accordingly psychiatric damage caused by the accumulation of a series of gradual assaults will not suffice. It follows that damage suffered by the plaintiff through caring for a seriously brain–damaged child will not suffice for present purposes.

(3)   HARM TO PROPERTY

In the same way that personal injuries may be compensated by an award of damages, so also may a person recover in respect of foreseeable property damage or loss whether the action lies in contract or in tort. If a person's car is damaged or 'written off' as a result of the negligent driving of the defendant, he may be compensated in respect of property damage suffered. The purchaser[14] or user[15] of a defective product may be entitled to compensation in respect of damage caused to other property by the defective product. Likewise, a person whose property is damaged due to the careless performance of a service is able to recover the loss he suffers in this regard.[16] Similarly, property damage is recoverable by a lawful visitor to the defendant's premises.[17] Most of the problems in this area tend to arise out of the issue of quantification of damages and will be dealt with elsewhere.[18]

---

7   [1967] 1 WLR 912.
8   At 48.
9   *Frontiers of Liability* Vol 2 (1994) ed Birks at 87.
10   [1991] 4 All ER 907 at 918.
11   *Sion v Hampstead Health Authority* [1994] 5 Med LR 170; *Taylorson v Shieldness Produce Ltd* [1994] PIQR P329.
12   No 249 (1998) para 5.33. See Jones [1995] 4 Web JCL 1; Teff (1996) 4 Tort Law Rev 44, 46–47.
13   Ibid at 918 (per LORD ACKNER).
14   *Wilson v Rickett, Cockerell & Co Ltd* [1954] 1 QB 598.
15   *Vacwell Engineering Co Ltd v BDH Chemicals Ltd* [1969] 3 All ER 1681.
16   *Stewart v Reavell's Garage* [1952] 2 QB 545.
17   Occupiers' Liability Act 1957, s 1(3)(b). Cf Occupiers' Liability Act 1984, s 1(8).
18   See ch 17.

Chapter 10

Damage to economic interests

1. INTRODUCTION

Where the loss suffered by the plaintiff as a result of a breach of duty by the defendant is economic rather than physical, particular problems are created for the legal system.

(1) FLOODGATES

While physical damage is limited by the laws of nature in its extent, this is not so with economic loss. It is said that the imposition of liability would place too heavy a burden on defendants and lead to people not practising in professions where the likelihood of economic loss claims was high and to a waste of resources in bankrupting defendants. The first of these arguments does not appear to hold up in practice as the present law exposes certain professions to a wide range of negligence liability and this does not appear to have had any noticeable detrimental effect on these professions. The most obvious are surveyors/valuers [1] who do have a duty of care imposed on them. Also, the mere fact that a duty is imposed does not mean that there is liability, as the plaintiff also has to establish breach and causation. The second argument states that it is more efficient for the market to spread costs than for the law to allocate them to a single defendant. However, it is possible for cases of physical damage to result in bankruptcy and it is possible for a potential defendant in an economic loss case to spread losses by insuring against them.

(2) CONTRACTUAL NEXUS

Many cases of economic loss arise within a network of contracts but where the plaintiff and defendant have no direct contractual relationship. If tortious liability was imposed, would this disturb a freely negotiated contractual nexus between the various parties?

Either the financial harm may be a direct consequence of a negligent act which causes physical harm to the plaintiff's property, a matter dealt with elsewhere, or, the loss may be an indirect result of reliance on the act of the defendant, often in the form of the breach of a contract made between the defendant and a third party. A typical

---

1 See *Smith v Bush* [1990] 1 AC 831.

example of this indirect economic loss arises where there is a network of contracts designed to achieve a common purpose, such as the construction of a building or the delivery of goods to a foreign buyer. In each of these examples, a number of subsidiary contracts will exist in order to secure the object of the principal contract. Thus, in the case of the construction of a building, there will be a main construction contract between A and B, but B, the main contractor, will also enter into contracts with sub-contractors C, D, E etc in order to carry out specialist functions. If C negligently causes A financial loss through his performance of his contract with B, the question arises whether C owes A a duty of care. This kind of economic loss is described in civilian systems as damage par ricochet. If the tort of negligence is used to compensate damage par ricochet, usually it will be found that the reason for doing so is to avoid anomalies which would arise due to the rigidity of the law of contract.[2] The main problem was the third party beneficiary rule which stated that A was not entitled to take a benefit from a contract between B and C, even if B and C intended A to take the benefit. Therefore, in a construction case where the sub-contractor's negligence (C) caused financial harm to the client (A) and the main contractor (B) became insolvent, A's only possible action would have been against C but this would depend on the courts fashioning a duty of care between A and C, which they have been reluctant to do. The Contracts (Rights of Third Parties) Act 1999 may well alleviate the contractual position.[2a]

In practice, the courts have found immense difficulty in holding that any duty situation is revealed in these circumstances. In the first place, the necessary relationship of proximity may not be sufficiently close. Secondly, there may be a 'floodgates' fear. Finally the courts may be reluctant to use tort law to intervene in a freely negotiated contractual agreement. In consequence, means have to be adopted to limit the scope of a duty of care. This fear does not apply to contract actions because one contracting party knows that his liability will be confined to those people treated as parties to the contract.

The harm suffered by the plaintiff may be of a type which ought to be recovered by other means such as suing for the breach of a relevant contract or taking out insurance to cover the risk. However, if a duty of care can be founded on a 'voluntary assumption of responsibility' by the defendant to the plaintiff, this may enable a court to negotiate these difficulties.

(3)   DIFFICULTY IN ASSESSING STANDARD OF PERFORMANCE

It has been alleged that if a duty was imposed in respect of economic loss it would be difficult to assess the required standard of the defendant's performance.[3] A contract is, in theory, a bargain and the plaintiff will have paid for a particular standard of performance from the defendant. As there is no requirement of consideration in negligence, it is argued that there is no yardstick by which to measure standard. However, where the plaintiff is a party to a network of contracts but not in direct contractual relationship with the defendant, the parties will normally have a common intention as to standard. For example, a contract between a main contractor and a sub-contractor will lay down the requirement for performance and this will be the standard which the client will be entitled to. Also, in many consumer transactions, the standard is not freely negotiable between the parties but is imposed by law.[4] In contracts for services there is a requirement that the service provider uses reasonable care and that standard is judged by the standards of that profession. In short, the standard of care required can usually be judged objectively but in a more limited way than contract as it is difficult to assess precisely what risks the defendant has voluntarily assumed responsibility for.

2   See Markesinis (1987) 103 LQR 354.
2a   See ch 6.
3   *Junior Books Ltd v Veitchi Co Ltd* [1983] 1 AC 520 , 551 per LORD BRANDON.
4   See the requirements imposed by the Sale of Goods Act.

2. HISTORICAL DEVELOPMENT OF RECOVERY FOR ECONOMIC LOSS

(1) CONTRACT AND MISREPRESENTATION

English law has historically regarded economic loss as the province of the law of contract as protection of economic interests had to be bargained and paid for. [5] Thus, a person who can establish that breach of an express or implied term of a contract has caused him economic loss, has an action for damages. These damages will represent either the plaintiff's damaged expectations under the contract or his status quo losses, depending on the nature of the term and the plaintiff's ability to satisfy the rules on damages. [6] A defendant who contracts to deliver a piece of machinery to the plaintiff by a certain date will therefore be liable for any lost profits that the plaintiff would have made with the machinery, provided the plaintiff can prove that he would have made a profit and the amount of the profit is not too remote.

A key distinction was between contract terms and representations. A contractual term or warranty may give rise to expectation damages for loss of bargain. Liability is for breach of promise and such liability may be strict. A representation, on the other hand, is a statement of fact which induces a person to enter a contract but which does not form part of the contract. Damages for a misrepresentation are reliance based, designed to put the plaintiff in the position he would have been in if the representation had not been made. The rules on remoteness of damage may differ from those on contractual terms [7] and liability is fault based.

(2) THE DISTINCTION BETWEEN TERMS AND REPRESENTATIONS

Classical contract distinguishes between a term and a representation by reference to the intention of the parties [8] judged from an objective viewpoint. If the maker of the statement did not intend it to have contractual force, it can only take effect as a representation. A more realistic approach is to ask whether it was reasonable, in the circumstances, for the recipient to rely on the statement. [9]

Where the statement is subsequently incorporated into a written contract between the parties, the statement will be a term and will be subject to contractual liability. However, most commercial and consumer dealings can not be conveniently packaged into one written document which constitutes an enforceable contract. In reality there will often be several oral or written exchanges between the parties leading up to the transaction which is called into question. The statement may be made at any stage and a court called upon to declare it a term or a representation. Three possible solutions have been evolved by the courts. The contract may be wholly contained in the written contract, the contract may be partly oral and partly written, or there may be a collateral contract in addition to the written instrument.

The key concept is reasonable reliance by the person to whom the statement is addressed on the statement's veracity, although the courts never developed a coherent doctrine of law in this respect. [10] At common law responsibility could be shifted by an

---

5   See ch 1.
6   See chs 16 and 17.
7   See ch 16.
8   *Heilbut, Symons & Co v Buckleton* [1913] AC 30.
9   The American Uniform Sales Act 1906, s 12 uses reliance rather than promissory intent as the test. See also *Esso Petroleum Co Ltd v Mardon* [1976] 2 All ER 5 at 13 (per LORD DENNING MR).
10   See *Dick Bentley Productions Ltd v Harold Smith Motors Ltd* [1965] 2 All ER 65; *Oscar Chess Ltd v Williams* [1957] 1 All ER 325. See also *Esso Petroleum Co Ltd v Mardon* [1976] 2 All ER 5 where the collateral warranty was used to create liability.

insistence that the recipient checked the information[11] and the recipient can make it clear that he relies on the statement by showing the importance he attaches to it.[12] Placing the risk on the person best able to discover the truth has also been said to be economically justified.[13]

The importance of the distinction between terms and representations has become of less importance since the implementation of the Misrepresentation Act 1967 as damages are now available for non-fraudulent misrepresentation.[14]

(3) REPRESENTATIONS

If a statement is not a contractual term, it can have effect as a representation. Representations can be divided into incorrect pre-contractual statements, which are known as misrepresentations, fraudulent statements, which are actionable in the tort of deceit, and negligent misstatements which are actionable in the tort of negligence. The latter two categories will be dealt with below.

A misrepresentation is an untrue statement of fact which induces a person to enter a contract. This is one area where the law has become bogged down in technicalities.

(i) Statements of Fact

A statement of fact is distinguished from a statement of opinion in that a statement of opinion may not amount to a misrepresentation where it is incapable of proof. In *Bisset v Wilkinson*,[15] the vendor of land not previously used for sheep farming stated that the land was capable of holding 2,000 sheep. This was held to be a statement of opinion and not a representation of capacity. However, in *Esso Petroleum Co Ltd v Mardon*,[16] *Bissett* was distinguished. A tenant was induced to take a lease of a petrol station by a statement made on behalf of Esso that the future annual turnover could be estimated at 200,000 gallons. This did not guarantee a turnover of 200,000 gallons, but neither was it merely a statement of opinion, as Esso had special knowledge and skill. Esso were therefore in a better position than Mardon to make a forecast[17] and were obliged to use reasonable care in making the estimate. Failure to do so made them liable for negligence at common law and for a breach of collateral warranty. Were the same facts to arise today, the tenant might have had an action for damages under section 2(1) of the Misrepresentation Act 1967.

Statements of intent also pose problems. Technically, if a person wishes to rely on a promise of future intent, the maker must have a contractual intent. But if the person making the statement knows that he cannot make that intention come true, he may be said to have made a statement of fact. Thus, where a prospectus invited loans from the public to extend a business but was intended to be used to discharge existing liabilities, it was held to be fraudulent misrepresentation.[18] The state of a man's mind is a much a fact as the state of his digestion.[19]

---

11   *Ecay v Godfrey* (1947) 80 Ll L Rep 286; *Schawel v Reade* [1913] 2 IR 81. Cf *Hopkins v Tanqueray* (1854) 15 CB 130, 139 ER 369.
12   *Bannerman v White* (1861) 10 CBNS 844.
13   Posner and Rosenfield (1977) 6 JLS 83 at pp 87–92.
14   The distinction is still appropriate, however. See *Independent Broadcasting Authority v EMI Electronics* (1980) 14 BLR 1.
15   [1927] AC 177.
16   [1976] QB 801. See also *Smith v Land and House Property Corpn* (1884) 28 Ch D 7.
17   Neither party in *Bisset* appears to have had superior knowledge.
18   *Edgington v Fitzmaurice* (1885) 29 Ch D 459. See also *British Airways Board v Taylor* [1976] 1 All ER 65; *Crédit Lyonnais Bank Nederland NV v Export Credits Guarantee Department* [1996] CLC 11.
19   Ibid at 483 (per BOWEN LJ)

(ii)   Duty of disclosure[20]

Although a person has a duty not to volunteer misleading information, there is no general duty of disclosure in English law. The general rule is that silence does not amount to a misrepresentation. The failure to disclose a material fact which might influence the mind of a prudent contractor does not give the right to avoid the contract.[1]

The general rule has always been subject to exceptions. If a person makes a representation which is initially true but which ceases to be true before the contract is made, he is under an obligation to disclose the change in circumstances. In *With v O'Flanagan*,[2] a doctor truthfully stated the income of his practice to be £200 per annum. Before the contract was completed, he became ill and his income fell to almost nothing. The contract was rescinded because of the doctor's failure to inform the purchaser of the change in circumstances.

A statement may be literally true but misleading. In *Nottingham Patent Brick and Tile Co v Butler*,[3] the purchaser of land asked the vendor's solicitor whether he knew of any restrictive covenants affecting the land. The solicitor's reply that he was not aware of any entitled the purchaser to rescind for misrepresentation. The solicitor had failed to inform him that he had not looked at the relevant documents.

Cases of liability for pure non-disclosure in English law are rare. Insurance contracts are known as contracts *uberrimae fidei,* or of the utmost good faith. The insured must disclose all such facts as a reasonable or prudent insurer might regard as material.[4] The definition of 'material' in the Marine Insurance Act 1906 has been held by the Court of Appeal to be applicable to all forms of insurance.[5] It follows that every circumstance 'which would influence' the prudent insurer in fixing the premium or determining whether he will take the risk[6] should be disclosed. The duty is mutual and an insurance policy can be avoided on the grounds of non-disclosure by the insurer.[7] However, no damages are avilable to the insured as a result of the breach of this duty, as the duty stems from equitable principles rather than from breach of an implied term at common law.[8] This is regrettable as the remedy of rescission may be appropriate to the insurer but not usually to the insured. In the United States a breach of good faith is a tort, sounding in damages, in the context of insurance. In Australia, a first instance court has refused summarily to dismiss a claim for damages for an insurers' breach of good faith.[9]

In cases of pure non-disclosure as opposed to misleading statements or statements later falsified, no remedy is available under sections 2(1) and (2) of the Misrepresentation Act 1967. The Act frequently uses the expression 'misrepresentation made', which would appear to refer to active misrepresentation rather than non-disclosure.

(iii)   Inducement

Liability for misrepresentation is based on reliance and it must be shown that the representee has relied upon the misrepresentation to the extent that he has been induced to enter a contract which he would not otherwise have made.

20   See Kronman (1978) 7 JLS 1.
1   *Bell v Lever Bros Ltd* [1932] AC 161 at 277 (per LORD ATKIN).
2   [1936] Ch 575.
3   (1886) 16 QBD 778.
4   *Lambert v Co-operative Insurance Society Ltd* [1975] 2 Lloyd's Rep 485.
5   *Locker and Woolf Ltd v Western Australian Insurance Co Ltd* [1936] 1 KB 408.
6   Cf Law Commission Report on Non-Disclosure and Breach of Warranty No 104 (1980) Cmnd 8064.
7   *Banque Financière de la Cité SA v Westgate Insurance Co Ltd* [1991] 2 AC 249, [1990] 2 All ER 947.
8   Ibid.
9   *Gibson v Parkes District Hospital* (1991) Austr Torts R 69, 321. See Fleming (1992) 108 LQR 357.

If the representee is unaware of the misrepresentation,[10] or does not allow it to affect his judgment,[11] he cannot rely on it as a ground for a remedy. A variation on this theme is that, if the representee has not relied on the representor's statements but has used his own sources of information on which to base his decision, no relief is available.[12]

As with any reliance-based rule, there has been debate over the extent of reliance required. Many commercial decisions are made for a variety of reasons and reliance on the information in question may not be the only relevant factor. There are objective and subjective elements involved. Subjectively the representee must actually have relied but objectively the subject matter of the misrepresentation must be such that it would have influenced a reasonable person.[13]

It has been established that the representation need not be the only,[14] or even the decisive factor inducing the representee to enter the contract.[15]

> As long as a misrepresentation plays a real and substantial part, though not by itself a decisive part, in inducing the plaintiff to act, it is a cause of his loss and he relies on it, no matter how strong or how many are the other matters which played their part in inducing him to act.[16]

One of the most remarkable of nineteenth century cases concerns reliance-based representations. In *Redgrave v Hurd*,[17] the plaintiff bought the defendant's house and solicitor's practice, relying on the defendant's assertions concerning the value of the practice and without examining the accounts. Rescission was granted, despite the fact that the plaintiff was given the opportunity of discovering the truth, but chose not to take it. The decision at the time was extraordinary, and 'even today may go too far',[18] particularly in the light of cases such as *Caparo Industries plc v Dickman*[19] which emphasise the reasonableness of the reliance, including taking account of alternative actions which could have been taken by the plaintiff. On whom should the loss fall in these cases? Both parties were careless, but both had the opportunity to check the facts. On present law a reduction for contributory negligence on the part of the plaintiff may be appropriate.[20]

The remedy available will depend on whether the statement was made fraudulently, negligently or innocently. Historically, pre-contractual statements were regarded as outside of contract and therefore subject to their own rules. Relief in the nineteenth century was limited to rescission of the contract in equity or common law damages in the tort of deceit for a fraudulent misrepresentation.[1] No damages were available for a negligent or innocent misrepresentation until the Misrepresentation Act 1967 permitted the award of damages for a negligent misrepresentation[2] and for damages to be awarded in lieu of rescission for an innocent misrepresentation.[3]

---

10   *Horsfall v Thomas* (1862) 1 H & C 90.
11   *Smith v Chadwick* (1884) 9 App Cas 187.
12   *Attwood v Small* (1838) 6 Cl & Fin 232.
13   *Pan Atlantic Insurance Co Ltd v Pine Top Insurance Co Ltd* [1994] 3 All ER 581.
14   *Edgington v Fitzmaurice* (1885) 29 Ch D 459.
15   *Reynell v Sprye* (1852) 1 De GM & G 660 at 709, approved in *Barton v Armstrong* [1976] AC 104 at 119. Cf *Atlantic Lines & Navigation Co Inc v Hallam Ltd, The Lucy* [1983] 1 Lloyd's Rep 188.
16   *JEB Fasteners Ltd v Marks, Bloom & Co (a firm)* [1983] 1 All ER 583 at 589 (per STEPHENSON LJ).
17   (1881) 20 Ch D 1.
18   Atiyah *Rise and Fall* p 772. Cf *Derry v Peek* (1889) 14 App Cas 337.
19   [1990] 2 AC 605.
20   See *Gran Gelato Ltd v Richcliff (Group) Ltd* [1992] 1 All ER 865. See also ch 20.
1   See *Derry v Peek* (1889) 14 App Cas 337.
2   S 2(1).
3   See ch 17 for damages for misrepresentation.

(4)   MISREPRESENTATION AND NEGLIGENCE

Because of the structure of the common law of obligations, there is an overlap between negligent misrepresentation and negligence[4] in relation to pre-contractual statements. The plaintiff has a choice of remedy. Damages for negligent misrepresentation will normally be claimed under the Misrepresentation Act 1967, section 2(1), although they can also be awarded under section 2(2) of the same Act, in lieu of rescission.

Actions for negligence and those for misrepresentation differ in certain important respects. Statements of opinion may be actionable in negligence if they induce reliance, but not in misrepresentation. In misrepresentation it is necessary that the parties to the statement enter a contract. In an action for damages under section 2(1) of the Misrepresentation Act 1967 the burden of proof is reversed and the representor will be liable unless he can prove that he had reasonable grounds for his belief. In negligence cases the plaintiff bears the burden of proof.

Assessment of damages in both actions is on tortious principles but in the statutory action the remoteness rule appropriate to deceit is applied rather than the reasonable foreseeability test appropriate to negligence.[5] This rule is based on the 'fiction of fraud' in section 2(1) but is subject to criticism as the defendant has been negligent but is treated as fraudulent. This may have the effect of making the plaintiff better off than is justified. Finally, the limitation periods are different for the two actions.

Doctrinal links between the two actions are reasonably clear. Reliance is a key element in tortious actions for negligence where a statement is involved and the loss is economic. An actionable misrepresentation also requires reliance by the representee in entering into a contract in reliance on the representors' statement of fact. Tortious actions for economic loss are frequently founded on a 'voluntary assumption of responsibility' by one person to another. This is reflected in the principle in misrepresentation that a positive statement may amount to a misrepresentation but generally silence does not. It is however conceivable that English law could found a principle of liability for silence in certain circumstances on the concept of voluntary assumption.

(5)   INTENTIONAL INFLICTION OF ECONOMIC LOSS AND THE ECONOMIC TORTS

Outside of contract law there were attempts to establish a general principle of liability for intentional interference with economic interests[6] but these have proved to be unsuccessful.[7] This leaves the difficult question as to why, if intentional interference with economic interests is prima facie lawful, should negligent interference with such interests be unlawful? The answer to this may may be that the rationale for the non-imposition of liability for intentional interference is so as not to interfere with free competition. However, where the interference is classed as 'unlawful' an action will lie, thus drawing a distinction between free and unfair competition. If Cooke has a fish and chip shop in a road and Oughton opens a similar establishment in the same road and undercuts Cooke's prices, this will not be actionable. However, if Oughton spreads false stories about the cleanliness of Cooke's product or threatens Cooke's customers, then an action will lie.

---

4   See below for the law on economic loss caused by negligence.
5   *Royscot Trust Ltd v Rogerson* [1991] 3 All ER 294. Cf *Smith New Court Securities Ltd v Citibank NA* [1997] AC 254 at 283 per LORD STEYN.
6   Eg *Keeble v Hickeringill* (1706) 11 East 574n.
7   *Allen v Flood* [1898] AC 1. See Carty (1988) LQR 250

A number of torts exist to deal with unfair competition[8] and it has been suggested that there is a 'genus' tort of unlawful acts which interfere with business.[9] On this basis negligence could be regarded as an 'unlawful act' and liability for negligently inflicted economic loss justified in certain circumstances.

(6)   NEGLIGENCE

In the nineteenth century, English law took the view that 'pure' economic loss could not be recovered in a negligence action.[10] This remained the position until the landmark case of *Hedley Byrne & Co Ltd v Heller & Partners Ltd,*[11] where the House of Lords created a general principle for careless statements causing economic loss. The plaintiff advertising agents asked their bankers to enquire as to the financial standing of one of the plaintiffs' clients, E Ltd, from E Ltd's bankers (the defendants). The defendants replied 'without responsibility', that E Ltd was 'good for its ordinary business engagements'. This information was incorrect. The plaintiffs relied on it, E Ltd went into liquidation, and the plaintiffs sued for negligence, alleging reliance losses of over £17,000. It was decided that, since the defendants had disclaimed liability, they could not be made responsible for the plaintiffs' losses. However, the House of Lords created a new form of liability for negligent misstatement where there was no such disclaimer.

The general duty principle laid down in *Donoghue v Stevenson*[12] was thought inappropriate, as it was believed that the law should treat negligent words differently from negligent acts.[13] LORD REID expressed a reason for this which corresponds to an economic model for statements:

> Another obvious difference is that a negligently made article will only cause one accident, and so it is not very difficult to find the necessary degree of proximity or neighbourhood between the negligent manufacturer and the person injured. But words can be broadcast with or without the consent or the foresight of the speaker or writer. It would be one thing to say that the speaker owes a duty to a limited class, but it would be going very far to say that he owes a duty to every ultimate consumer who acts on these words to his detriment.[14]

The judgments in the House of Lords were mainly concerned with the difficulties created by *Derry v Peek*[15] which had laid down that damages were not available for negligent misstatements. They are less concerned with the difficulties caused by the recovery of economic loss in negligence. With the benefit of hindsight, it is possible to say that LORD REID's distinction failed to take account of the fact that the type of loss in negligent misstatement cases is usually economic loss. This poses different problems to physical damage but these problems are not unique to statements cases. They also apply to cases where economic loss has been caused by a negligent act. However, one result of the case was that the law was now bedevilled by a distinction between statements and acts without any logical justification for this distinction.

---

8   Such as deceit, passing off, injurious falsehood, conspiracy and inducing a breach of contract. See Heydon *Economic Torts* (2nd edn).
9   *Merkur Island Shipping Corpn v Laughton* [1983] 2 AC 570.
10   *Cattle v Stockton Waterworks Co* (1875) LR 10 QB 453.
11   [1964] AC 465, [1963] 2 All ER 575. See Stapleton (1991) 107 LQR 249 at 259.
12   [1932] AC 562.
13   [1963] 2 All ER 575 at 580 (per LORD REID).
14   Ibid at 580–581.
15   (1889) 14 App Cas 337.

3.   CONSEQUENTIAL ECONOMIC LOSS

At this point it is necessary to point out a distinction between 'pure' economic loss and 'consequential' economic loss. The latter, strictly speaking, belongs with physical damage.

English law has had little difficulty in allowing a person to recover for economic loss suffered as a consequence of physical injury or property damage. Such recovery can be seen as protecting the status quo interest in the sense that the plaintiff is awarded, by way of damages, the cost of rectifying the direct effects of the physical harm caused by the defendant.

In contract cases, if the breach of contract causes physical harm, then any financial harm caused as a result of this may be recovered provided it is a natural consequence of the defendant's breach of contract.[16] Likewise, in tort cases, so long as the loss suffered is a foreseeable consequence of the breach of duty, then such loss may be recoverable. Thus, if the plaintiff is foreseeably injured as a result of the defendant's breach of duty, it follows that he will be able to recover damages in respect of his lost earnings if he is unable to work because of his injuries.

Likewise, if the plaintiff's property is harmed as a result of the defendant's act, direct consequential economic loss may also be recovered by the plaintiff, so as to rectify the immediate effects of the physical harm. Thus in *Spartan Steel & Alloys Ltd v Martin & Co (Contractors) Ltd*,[17] the defendant negligently damaged an electricity cable which supplied the plaintiffs' factory. A result of this was that the plaintiffs' machinery failed to operate and a quantity of molten metal in the process of preparation at the time had to be disposed of. Furthermore, during the time the furnaces were inoperative, four further melts could have been completed, and the plaintiffs accordingly suffered from a loss of profit. It was held by a majority of the Court of Appeal that the plaintiffs could only recover the profit lost on the metal in process at the time of the damage to the cable, and that nothing could be recovered in respect of future melts since this loss did not arise out of any physical damage.

The decision in *Spartan Steel* is very clearly dictated by policy considerations and it may be criticised on the ground that it can produce the anomalous result that a court must distinguish between different types of harm caused by a single incident. For example, suppose a driver causes a motor vehicle accident on a motorway, injuring the driver of the car he collides with and causing the motorway to become impassable. The driver must compensate the person he injures, but people who are unable to reach their place of work and thereby suffer foreseeable economic harm will be unable to recover anything at all on the *Spartan Steel* principle.

The Court of Appeal in *Spartan Steel* was not unanimous, as EDMUND-DAVIES LJ dissented on the ground that pure economic loss ought to be recoverable as long as it is foreseeable.[18] Furthermore, in *Hedley Byrne v Heller*, LORD DEVLIN was highly critical of the old rule that, before damages for loss resulting from a negligent misstatement could be recovered, there needed to be interposed some physical damage.[19]

Nevertheless, the rule remains at common law that only those economic losses directly consequent on damage to the plaintiff's property are recoverable. Moreover, it is an established rule at common law that the plaintiff must have a sufficient property interest in order to be able to sue. Thus while the law may protect an owner and a person with

---

16   *Hadley v Baxendale* (1854) 9 Exch 341 and see also ch 16.
17   [1973] QB 27. See also *Muirhead v Industrial Tank Specialties Ltd* [1985] 3 All ER 705; *SCM (UK) Ltd v Whittall (WJ) & Son Ltd* [1971] 1 QB 337.
18   [1972] 3 All ER 557 at 570.
19   [1964] AC 465 at 516–517.

possessory rights, such as one who holds a bill of lading which names him as a person with an interest in a cargo carried at sea,[20] it does not protect a person who has no such rights. Thus a person with a purely contractual interest in a ship, with no right of possession, such as a time charterer,[1] or the buyer of goods carried by sea, who because of the terms of his contract with the seller is neither the owner nor a person with a right to possession,[2] does not have a sufficient interest to sue at common law. However, this last result has caused serious harm to the shipping and insurance industries through the transfer of business elsewhere. In order to meet this problem, it is now provided by statute that an action may be maintained by a person who has rights of suit on behalf of the person with an interest or a right in relation to the goods carried by sea.[3] In *The Aliakmon*[4] the plaintiff had no possessory interest in the cargo, because he held the bill of lading as agent for the seller and the contract between the seller and the buyer provided that the buyer should bear the risk of damage in the course of transit. At common law, the buyer had no right of suit against the negligent carrier, but under the Carriage of Goods by Sea Act, section 4, the seller would be entitled to exercise his rights against the carrier on the buyer's behalf.

4.   DEVELOPMENT OF THE HEDLEY BYRNE PRINCIPLE

The decision in *Hedley Byrne & Co Ltd v Heller & Partners Ltd*[5] permitted the recovery of economic loss where, in certain circumstances, the defendant made a negligent statement to the plaintiff, resulting in loss to the plaintiff.

Having rejected reasonable foreseeability of damage alone as a sufficient criterion for imposing a duty, the House of Lords stated that for a duty to arise in giving advice there had to be a 'special relationship' between the giver and the recipient of the advice. Lord Morris stated:[6]

> My Lords, I consider that it follows and that it should now be regarded as settled that if someone possessed of a special skill undertakes, quite irrespective of contract, to apply that skill for the assistance of another person who relies on such skill, a duty of care will arise. Furthermore, if in a sphere in which a person is so placed that others could reasonably rely on his judgment or his skill or upon his ability to make careful inquiry a person takes it upon himself to give information or advice to, or allows his information or advice to be passed on to, another person who, as he knows, or should know, will place reliance upon it, then a duty of care will arise.

(1)   REQUIREMENTS OF THE TORT

The outcome of *Hedley Byrne* was that negligent misstatement was to be a sub-class of negligence with its own rules. The courts spent a considerable amount of time trying to lay down these rules.

First, there had to be a communication from the defendant or his agent to the plaintiff or his agent and the plaintiff had to make it clear that he was seeking considered advice and intended to act on it. The courts avoided the technical requirements of

---

20   *Brandt v Liverpool, Brazil and River Plate Steam Navigation Co Ltd* [1924] 1 KB 575. See also Carriage of
     Goods by Sea Act 1992, s 2(1).
1   *Candlewood Navigation Corpn Ltd v Mitsui OSK Lines Ltd, The Mineral Transporter* [1986] AC 1.
2   *Leigh and Sillivan Ltd v Aliakmon Shipping Co Ltd, The Aliakmon* [1986] 2 All ER 145.
3   Carriage of Goods by Sea Act 1992, s 4.
4   [1986] 2 All ER 145.
5   [1964] AC 465, [1963] 2 All ER 575.
6   Ibid at 492.

misrepresentation by not drawing a distinction between statements of fact and opinion.

Attempts were made to limit liability to professional advisers such as accountants, valuers and solicitors by a majority of the Privy Council.[7] However the minority view of LORDS REID and MORRIS prevailed.[8] A duty could arise where an enquirer consulted a businessman in the course of his business and made it clear that he was seeking considered advice and intended to act upon it in a particular way.

Liability will not normally arise for advice given on a social occasion[9] or impromptu advice given 'off the cuff over the telephone'.[10] But where the plaintiff asks the defendant for a specific fact which the plaintiff has no means of checking, this may indicate 'the gravity of the enquiry or the importance and influence attached to the answer.'[11]

The problems raised are illustrated by *Chaudhry v Prabhaker*.[12] The plaintiff knew nothing about cars and asked a friend, who had some knowledge, to look over one with a view to purchase. The plaintiff specifically stated that the car should not have been involved in an accident. The defendant recommended a car which the plaintiff bought. It was subsequently discovered that the car had been involved in an accident and was unroadworthy. Counsel for the defendant conceded that as a gratuitous agent he owed a duty of care but denied breach of duty. The Court of Appeal held the defendant liable. MAY LJ felt that counsel's concession was not rightly made.[13] STOCKER LJ[14] and STUART-SMITH LJ[15] would have held a duty to exist without the concession, as the relationship of principal and agent demonstrated that the occasion was not a purely social one.

The second requirement of the tort is that a 'special relationship' must exist between the parties. This requirement has been variously described as one 'equivalent to contract'[16] or where there has been a 'voluntary assumption of responsibility'.[17] A warning was, however, given against trying to seek a general principle.[18]

> … circumstances may differ infinitely and, in a swiftly developing field of law, there can be no necessary assumption that those features which have served in one case to create the relationship between the plaintiff and the defendant on which liability depends will necessarily be determinative of liability in the different circumstances of another case.

In some cases the courts concentrated on the purpose of the statement and the nature of the transaction in issue. This is particularly so in the cases involving allegedly negligent auditors. In other cases it is the relationship between the parties that is crucial.

Could a failure to speak give rise to liability? In *Banque Financière de la Cité SA v Westgate Insurance Co Ltd*,[19] the plaintiff banks made loans to a fraudster. The plaintiffs were also deceived by the manager of an insurance company which had arranged insurance cover

---

7   *Mutual Life and Citizens' Assurance Co Ltd v Evatt* [1971] AC 793.
8   *Esso Petroleum Co Ltd v Mardon* [1976] QB 801; *Howard Marine and Dredging Co Ltd v Ogden & Sons (Excavations) Ltd* [1978] QB 574.
9   *Mutual Life and Citizens' Assurance Co Ltd v Evatt* [1971] AC 793 (per LORDS REID and MORRIS).
10   *Howard Marine and Dredging Co Ltd v Ogden & Sons (Excavations) Ltd* [1978] QB 574, 591 (per LORD DENNING MR).
11   Ibid at 600 (per SHAW LJ).
12   [1988] 3 All ER 718.
13   Ibid at 725.
14   Ibid at 723.
15   Ibid at 721.
16   *Hedley Byrne & Co Ltd v Heller & Partners Ltd* [1964] AC 465 at 510 (per LORD DEVLIN) citing LORD SHAW in *Nocton v Lord Ashburton* [1914] AC 932 at 972.
17   See below.
18   *Caparo Industries plc v Dickman* [1990] 1 All ER 568 at 587 per LORD OLIVER.
19   [1990] 2 All ER 947.

for the loans. An employee of the insurance company was aware of the manager's dishonesty but failed to disclose it to the banks. In the Court of Appeal[20] it was held that there was no duty of care as there had been no assumption of responsibility by the defendants and no reliance by the plaintiffs. A failure to speak could in principle give rise to liability under *Hedley Byrne* principles in rare instances, but such a duty would not be allowed to disturb the contractual rule that there is no obligation to disclose material facts during pre-contractual negotiations in an ordinary commercial contract.

(i)   Advice given by a defendant to a plaintiff in the absence of a contract

This is the *Hedley Byrne* situation and the courts apply the 'course of business' test. LORD DEVLIN showed an awareness of this aspect of the problem in *Hedley Byrne*.

As a problem it is a by-product of the doctrine of consideration. If the respondents had made a nominal charge for the reference, the problem would not exist.

> If it were possible in English law to construct a contract without consideration ... the question would be, not whether on the facts of the case there was a special relationship, but whether on the facts of the case there was a contract.[1]

The cases so far considered involve statements made by A to B which are relied on by B to his detriment. Is there liability where the statement is made by A to B, who passes it on to C and C suffers loss by relying on it? In the A–B cases one problem is the link between contract and tort. In the A–B–C cases, more familiar tortious problems such as 'floodgates' are involved.

Where C is an identifiable person, one aspect of the 'floodgates' problem is avoided since there is not an indeterminate number of plaintiffs. Where A's advice relates to a specific piece of realty, the maximum extent of C's claim is limited to the value of the property. This situation has arisen where a valuation on a house has been made by a surveyor for a building society (B) and relied on by the purchaser (C). A first instance case held that A's advice is capable of giving rise to a duty of care,[2] and this was confirmed by the House of Lords.[3] Proximity in the cases of valuations on small houses was established by the overwhelming probability that the valuation would be relied on by the purchaser with the surveyor's knowledge. In over 90% of house purchases the buyer does not request a structural survey and so relies entirely on the valuation. The duty will only be owed to the purchaser for whom the valuation is made and probably no duty will be owed in the case of very expensive residential properties or commercial properties. Further factors in establishing the duty are that the plaintiff has paid a fee for the valuation (but has no contract with the surveyor) and the duty has been implicitly accepted by the presence of a disclaimer clause.

The practice of inserting disclaimer clauses in valuations raises the question whether a duty of care is capable of arising, given that a factor in the duty equation in the surveyor cases is reasonable reliance by the purchaser. The House of Lords held that the question of whether a duty arose has to be considered on the basis of whether a duty would exist 'but for' the disclaimer clause.[4] Given a positive answer to that question, the court must decide whether the disclaimer is reasonable.[5]

---

20   [1989] 2 All ER 952.
1   *Hedley Byrne & Co Ltd v Heller & Partners Ltd* [1963] 2 All ER 575 at 608 (per LORD DEVLIN).
2   *Yianni v Edwin Evans & Sons* [1982] QB 438.
3   *Smith v Eric S Bush; Harris v Wyre Forest District Council* [1989] 2 All ER 514. Chandler (1988) 51 MLR 377; Kaye (1989) 52 MLR 841.
4   See Unfair Contract Terms Act 1977, ss 11(3) and 13(1). See also *Phillips Products Ltd v Hyland* [1987] 2 All ER 620.
5   Ibid s 2(2).

More difficult problems arise when the statement is addressed to a class of persons rather than an identified person. The takeover boom of the mid-1980s raised this question in connection with an auditors' duty of care. In *Caparo Industries plc v Dickman*,[6] the appellants had audited the accounts of a public company. The annual audit of a public company is regulated by statute and the Companies Act 1985 laid down in detail what the statutory accounts had to contain. The respondents owned shares in the company and in reliance on the accounts, purchased further shares and made a successful takeover bid. The respondents alleged that the accounts were inaccurate and negligently prepared and that they had suffered loss as a result. The House of Lords held that a limited duty of care was owed by the auditors to shareholders to enable the shareholders to exercise proper control over the company. No duty was owed to an individual member of the company who relied on the accounts in a decision to buy additional shares. Whether such a duty existed in connection with a decision to sell shares was left open.

The effect of the decision was to prevent companies contemplating a takeover bid from relying on the annual audited accounts to determine the value of their bid. The bidder would have to make his own inquiries. Anyone who made an investment or lending decision in reliance on an unqualified opinion would not be able to sue the auditors for any losses suffered as a result. This would apply to shareholders, investors or institutional lenders.

Useful criteria were laid down by the Court of Appeal for determining when a statement may give rise to a duty of care:[7]

(i)   the purpose for which the statement was made. Was it made for the purpose of being communicated to the advisee or to another person for a different purpose (eg a statutory requirement)?

(ii) the purpose for which the statement was communicated. Was it requested by someone or was it given for information only?

(iii) the relationship between the adviser, the advisee and any relevant third party.

(iv) the size of any class to which the advisee belonged. In the case of a single advisee or a small class it may be easier to find a duty of care.

(v)   the state of knowledge of the adviser. This includes knowledge of the purpose for which the statement was made and the purpose for which it was communicated. This point may support an earlier decision imposing a duty of care on accountants[8] and *Morgan Crucible*.[9] Here, directors and financial advisors of a target company in a takeover bid made statements regarding the accuracy of financial statements and profit forecasts, intending that a bidder should rely on these forecasts. On an application for leave to amend the statement of claim, the Court of Appeal held that there was an arguable claim and that *Caparo* could be distinguished.[10]

(vi) reliance by the advisee. Did he in fact rely on the statement?[11] Was he entitled to rely on it or should he have sought independent advice?

The different economic markets may be one ground for distinguishing *Caparo* from the valuation cases. In the former the plaintiff is an entrepeneur taking high risks for high rewards and the cost to the defendant accountants could be catastrophic. In the latter, the plaintiff is likely to be a person of modest means and the effect of imposing liability on the defendant is relatively mild.

---

6   [1990] 1 All ER 568. Weir [1990] CLJ 212.
7   *James McNaughton Paper Group Ltd v Hicks Anderson & Co* [1991] 1 All ER 134; approved in *Morgan Crucible Co plc v Hill Samuel Bank Ltd* [1991] 1 All ER 148.
8   *JEB Fasteners Ltd v Marks Bloom & Co* [1983] 1 All ER 583.
9   *Morgan Crucible Co plc v Hill Samuel Bank Ltd* [1991] 1 All ER 148.
10   See also *Galoo Ltd v Bright Grahame Murray (a firm)* [1994] 1 WLR 1360.
11   See *JEB Fasteners Ltd v Marks Bloom & Co* [1983] 1 All ER 583; *Galoo Ltd v Bright Grahame Murray (a firm)* [1994] 1 WLR 1360.

(ii)   The problem cases

It can be seen from the above discussion that by 1990 the courts had developed *Hedley Byrne* into a sub tort which dealt with the problem of negligently given advice or information. The basis on which such liability was imposed was debatable but some form of reliance by the plaintiff on the defendant was necessary for a duty to be imposed. There was considerable debate as to the relevance and role of voluntary assumption of responsibility. However, some cases posed acute difficulties where advice was given by a defendant to a third party which resulted in loss to a plaintiff who did not rely on the defendant. This type of case was arguably not really within the ambit of the *Hedley Byrne* principle as then understood, as reliance was not involved. The position is illustrated by *Ross v Caunters*,[12] where the defendant solicitor negligently allowed a will to be witnessed by the spouse of an intended beneficiary. As a result, the plaintiff beneficiary was unable to take his bequest under the will. The only person to suffer loss was the plaintiff, but he had no contract with the solicitor and could not be said to have relied on him. MEGARRY VC nevertheless held the solicitor liable on basic negligence principles. He could have foreseen damage to the plaintiff, and there were no policy reasons for excluding a duty of care, as the only person who could have suffered loss was the plaintiff.

Another case which was said to fall into the same category was *Ministry of Housing and Local Government v Sharp*.[13] This case was decided on *Hedley Byrne* lines, however this was probably because of the principle of no recovery for economic loss in negligence outside the parameters of *Hedley Byrne*.

5.   DEVELOPMENT OF LIABILITY FOR ECONOMIC LOSS OUTSIDE THE HEDLEY BYRNE PRINCIPLE

The emphasis in *Hedley Byrne* on the distinction between economic loss caused by statements and economic loss caused by acts led to two different branches of law. Outside of liability for negligent statements, the judicial approach was generally hostile to the recovery of pure economic loss.

(1)   TRIPARTITE BUSINESS ARRANGEMENTS

Where businessmen embarked on a tripartite venture such as a building contract, protection was given by contract law. Problems of insolvency could give rise to attempts to circumvent the contractual chain by bringing an action in negligence.

In the case of building construction two common problems arise. The first is where the completed building is defective and the main contractor has become insolvent. The defect is due to sub-contractor 1's negligence. Sub-contractor 1 cannot be sued for breach of contract by the client unless the client has taken out a collateral contract or warranty with him. A similar situation would arise where the defect is due to sub-contractor 2's negligence and sub-contractor 1 has become insolvent. The main contractor cannot perform his contract with the client and has no contractual action against sub-contractor 2.

The highpoint of recovery of economic loss was reached in 1983 when the House of Lords upheld a claim that a duty of care was owed by a sub-contractor to the client.[14] The plaintiffs had contracted with the main contractors for the construction of a factory.

---

12   [1979] 3 All ER 580. See also *Clarke v Bruce Lance & Co (a firm)* [1988] 1 All ER 364.
13   [1970] 1 All ER 1009.
14   *Junior Books Ltd v Veitchi Co Ltd* [1983] 1 AC 520.

The defendants were specialist flooring sub-contractors. They were nominated by the plaintiffs but had no contract with them. The floor was defective and had to be re-laid. The plaintiffs brought an action in negligence against the sub-contractors, claiming the cost of re-laying the floor and loss of profit while this was being done. The House of Lords held that because of the close proximity between the parties, a duty of care was owed to the plaintiff. The key factor was that the plaintiff had nominated the defendants as sub-contractors.

> On the facts I have just stated, I see nothing whatever to restrict the duty of care arising from the proximity of which I have spoken ... I see no reason why what was called during the argument 'damage to the pocket' simpliciter should be disallowed when 'damage to the pocket' coupled with physical damage has hitherto always been allowed. I do not think that this development, if development it may be, will lead to untoward consequences.[15]

At the time the decision was thought to mark the end of the distinction between contract and tort actions. But the decision has not proved popular with the judiciary and although it survives as a precedent on its own particular facts, it has not been followed.

In *Simaan General Contracting Co v Pilkington Glass Ltd (No 2)*[16] the plaintiffs were the main contractors on a building project in Abu Dhabi. It was a term of the contract with the building owner that the curtain glass walling be a particular shade of green, as green is the colour of peace in Islam. The plaintiff engaged a firm to obtain and erect the glass. This firm ordered the glass from the defendants. The glass was of the wrong colour and this caused extra expense to the plaintiff in his performance of his contract with the building owner. The glass erectors went into liquidation, which prevented a contract action against them. The plaintiffs sued the defendants in negligence. The action failed as the plaintiffs were unable to show that the defendants had assumed any responsibility to them. The absence of a contract between plaintiff and defendant was fatal. The duty in a *Hedley Byrne* type of case was said to depend on the voluntary assumption of responsibility towards a particular party giving rise to a special relationship, but in the present case the court could see nothing whatever to justify a finding that Pilkington had voluntarily assumed a direct responsibility to Simaan for the colour and quality of Pilkington's glass panels. On the contrary, all the indications were the other way and showed that a chain of contractual relationships was deliberately arranged the way it was without any direct relationship between Simaan and Pilkington. Moreover, if in principle it were to be established in this case that a main contractor or an owner has a direct claim in tort against the nominated supplier to a sub-contractor for economic loss occasioned by defects in the quality of the goods supplied, the formidable question would arise, in future cases if not in this case, as to how far exempting clauses in the contract between the nominated supplier and the sub-contractor were to be imported into the supposed duty in tort owed by the supplier to those higher up the chain .[17]

(2)   ACQUISITION OF DEFECTIVE PROPERTY

A person who acquires defective property will have a primary claim in the law of contract. The friend who purchased the ginger beer in *Donoghue v Stevenson* could have sued the cafe owner for the cost of the ginger beer. In such consumer cases the Sale of Goods Act 1979 implies conditions of quality into the contract. Such an action depends on a contractual relationship existing, the defendant being solvent and there being no

---

15   Ibid at 546 per LORD ROSKILL.
16   [1988] QB 758
17   See also *Greater Nottingham Co-operative Society Ltd v Cementation Piling and Foundations Ltd* [1988] 2 All ER 971; *Pacific Associates Inc v Baxter* [1990] 1 QB 993.

exclusion clause in the contract. In theory any legal problems could be solved by a chain of contract actions but in practice there are problems. Insolvency by anyone in the chain could lead to the chain breaking down as it is not generally worthwhile suing an insolvent party. Attempts were therefore made to bring negligence actions to circumvent this problem.

Could the purchaser sue the manufacturer in negligence for supplying a defective, as opposed to a dangerous product? The recipient of a gift has of course no contractual protection as they have no contract with anyone. If the product causes physical damage then they will have a tort action against the manufacturer. But do they have any remedy if the product is simply of defective quality? Such a claim would be a claim for pure economic loss.

A logical extension of *Junior Books* would have been to apply it to the purchaser of defective property, provided there was sufficient proximity between manufacturer and purchaser. But in *Muirhead v Industrial Tank Specialities Ltd*[18] the Court of Appeal held that there was insufficient proximity between an ordinary purchaser of goods and the manufacturer of those goods to impose a duty of care in respect of economic loss.[19]

In the case of realty, the common law historically provided little protection to the purchaser.[20] The purchaser of a new house obtained limited contractual protection but the financial instability of the building trade sometimes rendered this of no value. If the builder became insolvent and the damage had been caused by the negligence of a sub-contractor, the purchaser has no contractual remedy. The local authority may also have a part to play in the construction by approving plans and checking the progress of buildings under construction. This work is done on the basis of statutory powers rather than contract. If the work is carried out negligently, would a person affected have a tort claim against the local authority? Purchasers of old houses obtained virtually no contractual protection because of the doctrine of 'caveat emptor.'

In the 1970s and early 1980s the common law began to provide protection in tort for the purchasers of defective realty. A duty of care would be owed by anyone involved in the building process to avoid a risk of physical damage to the health or safety of the occupier of the house. The damages in such cases were the cost of making the building safe.[1] Actions were brought against builders and also against local authorities. No floodgates problem existed in such cases, as only a residential owner could bring a claim and the extent of the claim was reasonably foreseeable.

Major statements of principle came from the House of Lords in the building cases as they tried to rein in the development unleashed by *Anns v Merton*. In *D & F Estates Ltd v Church Comrs for England*[2] the House of Lords held that a builder was not liable in negligence to a building owner for defects of quality. The builder was only liable where the defect caused personal injuries or damage to other property. LORD BRIDGE stated that economic loss would only be recoverable in a negligence action under the *Hedley Byrne* principles or where the unique proximity of *Junior Books* applied.

In *Murphy v Brentwood District Council*[3] a seven judge House of Lords was assembled and they overruled their own previous decision in *Anns v Merton*. The narrow ratio of the case was that a local authority is not liable in negligence to a building owner or occupier for the cost of remedying a dangerous defect, which resulted from the negligence of the authority in not ensuring that the building was erected in accordance

---

18   [1986] QB 507.
19   See ch 19.
20   See ch 28.
1   *Anns v Merton London Borough Council* [1978] AC 728.
2   [1988] 2 All ER 992.
3   [1990] 2 All ER 908.

with the building regulations.[4] The wider importance of the case is that it marked a contraction in the scope of duty of care in economic loss cases. Beyond this it is difficult to extract any general principles from the judgments. The case however provided a benchmark for some time to come in economic loss claims. Any plaintiff arguing for a duty to be owed in respect of economic loss which did not fall within *Hedley Byrne* principles, faced a well nigh impossible task.

Where did this leave *Junior Books*? In *Murphy*, the House of Lords cleared away the *Anns v Merton* precedent but left *Junior Books*. A number of judicial attempts have been made to explain away the case. In *Tate & Lyle Industries Ltd v Greater London Council*,[5] it was treated as a case of physical damage. In *D & F Estates* LORD BRIDGE thought that the case rested on unique proximity.[6] LORD OLIVER was of the opinion that it rested on the *Hedley Byrne* principle of reliance.[7]

Conclusions

The interlocking of contract and tort can clearly be seen in the above discussion and the major problem for the courts is the extent to which they should interfere with the contractual nexus by imposing a duty of care in negligence.

In some instances the plaintiff may have an alternative course of action in contract, in which case that course of action should be pursued.[8] In particular, regard must be had to the contractual nexus in which it is alleged that a duty of care exists. For example, where the plaintiff and defendant are parties to a network of related contractual relationships, as is common in the case of the construction of a building, regard must be had to the terms of the contracts made by each of the parties. Thus if the contract between the building owner and the main contractor clearly requires the former to insure the building against risk of fire damage, it may be unreasonable to expect a sub-contractor employed under a contract with the main contractor to owe the building owner a duty of care in respect of negligently caused fire damage when the sub-contractor is almost certainly aware of the insurance requirement in the main contract.[9] It follows that if the terms of the relevant contracts[10] rule out the possibility of a duty of care, any reliance on the defendant by the plaintiff is likely to be unreasonable.

Alternatively, the court may take the view that the plaintiff is well placed to insure against the risk of economic loss. This seems to have been in part the motivation behind the decision of the House of Lords in *Murphy v Brentwood District Council*[11] where it was implicit in LORD KEITH's view[12] that overruling *Anns v Merton London Borough Council*[13] would not significantly increase householders' insurance premiums and that he believed the householder to be the best insurer. However, it has been pointed out that the risk in *Murphy* was one which already existed at the time the householder took an interest in the property, in which case, it would be impossible to obtain insurance.[14] On this

---

4   See ch 28.
5   [1983] 2 AC 509.
6   [1988] 2 All ER 992 at 998, 1003.
7   Ibid at 1013.
8   Arguably this was the case in *Junior Books Ltd v Veitchi Co Ltd* [1983] 1 AC 520 in which the plaintiff should not have succeeded.
9   *Norwich City Council v Harvey* [1989] 1 All ER 1180. See also *Pacific Associates Inc v Baxter* [1989] 2 All ER 159.
10   This also includes any collateral contract found to exist by the court, *Greater Nottingham Co-operative Society Ltd v Cementation Piling and Foundations Ltd* [1988] 2 All ER 971.
11   [1990] 2 All ER 908.
12   Ibid at 923.
13   [1978] AC 728.
14   National Consumer Council *Murphy's Law* November 1991 PD31/91 R3, p 16.

basis, it seems unlikely that the plaintiff in *Murphy* was in a position to do very much to protect himself and that regarding his reliance as unreasonable may have been mistaken.

A further policy issue is whether protection is the role of Parliament. This policy argument has been used fairly frequently in cases which have a consumer protection flavour.[15] The argument has two consequences. First, if Parliament has already enacted legislation which protects the consumer and that legislation is intended to be exhaustive, it would be contrary to policy for the common law to go further. Secondly, in areas in which there has been no statutory intervention, it may be decided that proper controls are the province of the legislature rather than the courts. Where this is the case, the court may resort to the excuse that any reliance by the plaintiff on the act of the defendant is unreasonable.

6.   THE EXTENDED HEDLEY BYRNE PRINCIPLE

The rejection of economic loss claims outside the *Hedley Byrne* principle led to a concentration on what the principle was based on. The emphasis on reliance based statements causing economic loss effectively excluded negligent acts and gave very little scope for the recovery of economic loss caused by a negligently performed service. In the case of services, there could be a contract between the provider and the recipient, in which case principles of concurrent liability come into play,[16] or liability could be purely tortious, but on what basis?

Several other problems existed, such as the extent to which a tortious solution could compensate for disappointed expectations; the basis of liability for omissions; and the issue created by cases which had succeeded but were not obviously based on reliance.[17]

In these circumstances a reliance based principle had little scope but one based on voluntary assumption of responsibility did. However, the concept of voluntary assumption had a mixed history. In some cases it had been rejected as a basis of liability[18] and had been subjected to considerable academic criticism.[19] This has not prevented the House of Lords from attempting to shape the principle to provide a basis for extended *Hedley Byrne* liability through a series of cases which bring out many of the problems involved in imposing tortious liability for negligently performed services.

In *Spring v Guardian Assurance plc*,[20] the plaintiff sued his former employers in negligence for a reference which he claimed had prevented him from obtaining employment. The claim was for economic loss. The question for the House of Lords was whether an employer owed a duty of care in giving a reference on a past or present employee. The defendants argued public policy as a reason for not finding a duty of care. In the first place, to give a cause of action in negligence would distort and subvert the tort of defamation. If an action is brought in defamation regarding a reference, then the referee will normally have a defence of qualified privilege, which can only be defeated by malice on the part of the referee. The House decided that the two torts were different. Defamation exists in order to protect reputation and proof of actual financial loss is not necessary. To recognise a duty of care would be to extend defamation by removing the necessity for malice but would bring a different principle into play. This

---

15   *Murphy v Brentwood District Council* [1990] 2 All ER 908 at 923 (per LORD KEITH); at 931 (per LORD BRIDGE); at 938 (per LORD OLIVER) and at 943 (per LORD JAUNCEY). See also *D & F Estates Ltd v Church Comrs for England* [1988] 2 All ER 992 at 1007 (per LORD BRIDGE).

16   See ch 5.

17   Eg *Ross v Caunters* [1980] Ch 297, [1979] 3 All ER 580.

18   Eg *Smith v Bush* [1990] 1 AC 831, 865 per LORD GRIFFITHS.

19   Barker (1993) LQR 461; Hepple (1997) CLP 69.

20   [1995] 2 AC 296, [1994] 3 All ER 129.

would operate in a limited number of situations where foreseeability and proximity existed and negligent conduct would be required.

A second argument on public policy was that a person who makes a reference should be free to express their own views otherwise referees might be inhibited from giving frank references, or indeed any references at all. The House balanced this against the damage caused to the subject of the reference by negligence and came down in favour of a duty of care in certain situations. LORD KEITH dissented and specifically raised the question of people working with children and the need for free and frank disclosure in these circumstances.

Was this decision based on *Hedley Byrne* principles or on basic duty of care principles? The key distinction in the past had been the question of reliance. In order to bring the case within *Hedley Byrne*, it was necessary that the plaintiff had relied on the defendant's advice. The House was split on this issue. LORD GOFF based his decision on *Hedley Byrne* principles, where A undertook responsibility towards C and C relied on A to exercise skill and care. The other three judges in the majority based liability on a wider principle than *Hedley Byrne*. Economic loss to C was clearly foreseeable if A failed to use reasonable care and there was clearly proximity between A and C. As it was fair just and reasonable to impose a duty, then A as the employer owed a duty to give a careful reference. These three judges felt that it was irrelevant whether liability was founded on basic negligence or *Hedley Byrne* lines. LORD GOFF clearly felt that it did make a difference and was unhappy with broad negligence principles being invoked. His reasoning becomes clearer with the later case of *White v Jones*.

In *White v Jones*[1] a testator had quarrelled with his two daughters and instructed his solicitors, the defendants, to prepare a will cutting his daughters out of his estate. This was done. The testator then became reconciled with his daughters and instructed the defendants to prepare a fresh will leaving £9,000 to each of his daughters. The defendants did nothing for a month and then started to prepare a will. They arranged to visit the testator a month later but he died three days before the appointment.

The issue for the House of Lords was whether the defendants owed a duty of care to the daughters in respect of their lost legacies. It was held (LORD KEITH and LORD MUSTILL dissenting) that where a solicitor accepted instructions to draw up a will and as a result of his negligence an intended beneficiary under the will was reasonably foreseeably deprived of a legacy, the solicitor was liable for the loss of the legacy.

Although the House came to the same conclusion as MEGARRY V-C in *Ross v Caunters*[2] it did so on a very different conceptual basis. This was for two reasons. The House was faced with conceptual arguments which were not presented in *Ross* and the *Anns v Merton* approach to duty of care utilised in *Ross* has now been discredited.

The first conceptual difficulty was the contract 'fallacy' which was argued in *Donoghue v Stevenson*[3] and rejected. If A (solicitor) has bound himself to a contract with B, (testator) then A's liability in respect of the performance of the contract should be limited to B and not extend to third parties such as C, (beneficiary) to whom he has had no opportunity of limiting or excluding his liability. While accepting that it was generally true that a solicitor did not owe a duty of care to third parties while performing his duties to his client, this would leave the beneficiary with no claim because of a lacuna in the law. There is no claim in contract by the beneficiary as English law does not recognise a *ius quaesitum tertio*. There is no loss to the estate. This means that the only person who can suffer loss is the person who has no remedy unless a negligence action is granted.

1   [1995] 1 All ER 691.
2   [1979] 3 All ER 580.
3   [1932] AC 562.

A second difficulty was the type of loss suffered by the beneficiary. This was pure economic loss in the form of a loss of expectation. It was argued by the appellants that this type of loss fell within the exclusive zone of contractual liability and that only Parliament could create exceptions by extending contractual rights to persons who were not parties to the contract. LORD GOFF felt that damages for expectation losses could be recovered under the *Hedley Byrne* principle as they were recoverable for contractual negligence and no relevant distinction could be drawn between the two types of action.

The third problem was that this case involved an omission to act rather than a positive act on the part of the defendants and that as a general rule there is no liability in tortious negligence for an omission unless the defendant is under some pre-existing duty. Such liability, it has been argued, correctly belongs in contract. LORD GOFF, however, argued that the imposition of *Hedley Byrne* liability was based on an assumption of responsibility and the solicitor could be liable for negligent omissions as well as positive acts.

In *Henderson v Merrett Syndicates Ltd*[4] the defendants, who were managing agents, had undertaken, pursuant to a contract with a third party (the member's agents), the management of the underwriting affairs of the plaintiffs, who were Lloyd's names. The case was to clarify some of the issues of law involved in the litigation of the Lloyd's names against their managing agents to attempt to recoup part of their losses suffered on the insurance market. The facts of the action are complex but the basic question was whether the managing agents owed a tortious duty to take reasonable care in the management of the names business.

It was necessary to resolve the controversy of the co-extensive existence of liabilities in contract and tort. The House recognised that the fact that the parties had a contractual relationship did not prevent the plaintiff from suing in tort.[5]

The question of any tortious duty owed by the defendants required an examination of the *Hedley Byrne* principles and it was held that where a person assumed responsibility to perform professional or quasi-professional services for another who relied on those services, the relationship between the parties was sufficient, without more, to give rise to a duty of care. The fact that the parties were in a contractual relationship did not prevent this duty arising unless the contract prevented it from doing so.

The approach of LORD GOFF, who gave judgment in all three cases, makes it clear that he is attempting to solve the economic loss riddle within the framework of the *Hedley Byrne* principles. LORD BROWNE-WILKINSON in both *Henderson* and *White* pursued a somewhat different course by working from analogy with fiduciary duties to create a special relationship between the parties sufficient to found a duty.

The concept of voluntary assumption of responsibility was first raised by LORD REID in *Hedley Byrne* where he explained that a reasonable man who knew he was being trusted to give careful advice had three courses of action open: refuse to answer, answer with a disclaimer, or answer without a disclaimer.

> If he chooses the last course he must, I think, be held to have accepted some responsibility for his answer being given carefully, or to have accepted a relationship with the inquirer which requires him to exercise such care as the circumstances require.

The scepticism expressed on voluntary assumption of responsibility came under attack in the above three cases. In *Henderson*, LORD GOFF was clear that in that type of case, which was concerned with a situation equivalent to contract, an objective test should be applied. Once the defendant was found to have assumed responsibility there was no problem with the recovery of economic loss sustained from the negligent provision

4   [1995] 2 AC 145.
5   See ch 5.

of a service. Neither was there a problem with the question of liability for negligent omissions. In *Spring*, he argued that it was clear that *Hedley Byrne* extended beyond the giving of information or advice to include the provision of other services and that where the plaintiff has entrusted his affairs to the defendant, the defendant may be taken to have assumed responsibility to the plaintiff. The example given is the professional services rendered by a solicitor to his client.

In *White v Jones* LORD BROWNE-WILKINSON gave the most extensive explanation of the concept. He explained that the phrase 'assumption of reponsibility' was concerned with whether some duty of care existed, not with the extent of that duty, which would vary with the circumstances. The concept did not originate in *Hedley Byrne* but could be traced back to the cases on fiduciary duties. Such a duty came into existence not because of any mutual dealing between the parties, nor because there was a contract between them. Equity imposes the obligation because the defendant has assumed to act in the plaintiff's affairs. A trustee is under a duty to a beneficiary whether or not he has had any dealings with him. On this basis it is not necessary that there be reliance on the defendant, the important factor being that the defendant knows that the plaintiff's economic well-being depends on the plaintiff's careful conduct of his affairs. In the *Hedley Byrne* version of the special relationship, reliance was necessary, as damage is an essential element of the plaintiff's case. In cases of negligent statements, if the defendant could not foresee reliance by the plaintiff, there would be no cause of action. Assumption of responsibility was the key factor which gave rise to the duty, as by choosing to answer the inquiry the bank assumed to act and thereby created the special relationship. Assumption of responsibility meant assumption of responsibility for the task, not the assumption of legal responsibility. Was there a special relationship between a solicitor and an intended beneficiary which attracted a duty of care? The case did not fall within a fiduciary duty or a *Hedley Byrne* type duty. However, adopting the incremental approach to duty of care advocated in the influential Australian case of *Sutherland Shire Council v Heyman*[6] the category of special relationships could be increased to cover this situation.

The relevance of reliance to duty of care has had as chequered a history as that of voluntary assumption of liability. Some cases state that it is vital while others have denied its importance. What is understood by the term 'reliance' varies. There is detrimental and non-detrimental reliance. There are also concepts of specific and general reliance. Specific reliance will be present when the parties have communicated with each other, whereas general reliance will arise where the parties are more remote.

The classic *Hedley Byrne* case concerns the giving of advice or information and is based on specific reliance. This version operates as a check on liability becoming too wide. For example, in the surveyor cases the surveyor or valuer will only owe a duty to the person who has paid the building society for the valuation. If that person chose to show it to someone else, who relied on it, then no duty of care would arise.

General reliance operates in the sense that, the defendant had some power which could have been exercised carefully in the plaintiff's favour and the plaintiff was aware of that fact and 'relied' on the careful exercise of the power. An example of this is in the area of public authorities exercising statutory powers or duties in connection with building regulations. This approach has been rejected in England in this area.[7]

Reliance posed an acute problem in two of the cases under discussion here. In *Spring*, the specific reliance was by the potential employer on the past employer's reference. The reliance by the subject of the reference (the plaintiff) could more properly be described as general reliance and therefore outside the parameters of *Hedley Byrne* reliance as normally understood. This is what LORD GOFF meant when he stated:

6   (1985) 60 ALR 1.
7   *Murphy v Brentwood District Council* [1991] 1 AC 398.

... when the employer provides a reference to a third party in respect of his employee, he does so not only for the assistance of the third party, but also, for what it is worth, for the assistance of the employee ... Furthermore, when such a reference is provided by an employer, it is plain that the employee relies upon him to exercise due care and skill in the preparation of the reference before making it available to the third party.[8]

This use of reliance enables the parameters of the *Hedley Byrne* action to be broadened. Similarly in *Henderson* he stated;

... in the case of the provision of information and advice, reliance upon it by the other party will be necessary to establish a cause of action (because otherwise the negligence will have no causative effect), nevertheless there may be other circumstances in which there will be the necessary reliance to give rise to the application of the principle. In particular, as cases concerned with solicitor and client demonstrate, where the plaintiff entrusts the defendant with the conduct of his affairs, in general or in particular, he may be held to have relied on the defendant to exercise due skill and care in such conduct.[9]

LORD BROWNE-WILKINSON adopted a different approach to the problem posed by reliance. He drew an analogy with fiduciary duties owed by one person to another. No specific reliance is needed for these. For example, a fiduciary duty is owed by a trustee to a beneficiary. In cases of advice or information sought or given, specific reliance is necessary to create a special relationship on which the duty of care is based. Other special relationships could be created by the courts on an incremental basis and the facts in *White* were precisely such a situation.

It is clear that the House of Lords has moved away from the conservative position adopted in *Murphy* and is attempting to produce a more flexible formula to deal with the problems created by economic loss. The two judges who appear to have a consistent approach are LORD GOFF and LORD BROWNE-WILKINSON. LORD GOFF sees the way forward as being through *Hedley Byrne*, albeit on an extended basis. This is done by refining the concept of 'voluntary assumption of responsibility' and broadening the concept of reliance. The major problem of this approach is the vagueness of both concepts. They can be used flexibly but it is arguable that certainty is required in this area of law, if only to guide the indemnity insurance market.

LORD BROWNE-WILKINSON's approach is to use an equitable formula to determine the necessary relationship. This raises a number of problems, not least of which is that negligence is not a requirement in the equitable action for breach of fiduciary duty. The rules on remoteness and limitation are also considerably different.

Both approaches, with their stress on assumption of responsibility, have the advantage that there is no problem with negligent omissions and that there appears no logical reason why either approach should draw the present indefensible distinction between negligent acts and negligent statements.

The law was summarised in *Williams v Natural Life Health Foods Ltd*.[10] The plaintiff must establish that there is a special relationship within which the defendant has assumed responsibility for protecting the plaintiff's economic welfare and such a relationship will only arise where the plaintiff is identifiable as an individual or as a member of a class of persons for whom the defendant undertakes responsibility in the performance of a particular task. The role of negligence as gap-filling where contract or other torts fail to provide a solution is acknowledged. However, where the plaintiff suffers economic loss but is outside the extended *Hedley Byrne* principle, there is no recovery.

---

8   [1994] 3 All ER 129, 146.
9   [1994] 3 All ER 506, 520.
10 [1998] 2 All ER 577.

7.   SUMMARY

The area of recovery for economic loss is a fascinating but seemingly intractable one. It demonstrates the genius, flexibility and the chaos of the English common law.

The origins of the problem lie in the relatively early development of classical contract law with its emphasis on bargain promises stemming from economic liberalism.[11] Not surprisingly this period gave different priorities to different legally protected interests. The rise of protection of negligently inflicted physical damage probably owed a lot to the development of insurance, which gave the courts more leeway to expand the scope of protection. The emphasis of classical contract on paid-for protection of economic interests through the doctrine of consideration and the priority given to contract law at this period meant that protection of economic interests was primarily governed by the law of contract, in the absence of fraud on the part of the defendant. The doctrine of privity, however, restricted the number of persons who were able to take advantage of the contractual protection. Various contract failures, which are discussed above, combined with the stubborn refusal of commercial practice to conform with the common law's templates and the clash between market ideology and consumer welfarism,[12] led to pressures for change.

The House of Lords decision in *Hedley Byrne*[13] marked a breakthrough, by giving the law of negligence the opportunity to develop a principle for the recovery of economic loss. This development was hampered by the emphasis in the judgments on statements and led to the distinction between liability for negligent words and liability for negligent acts. However, developments in the common law in the 1990s gave the opportunity to overcome this artificial distinction. The re-shaping of the *Hedley Byrne* principle by the House of Lords[14] combined with the acceptance of concurrent liability in contract and tort[15] provided a springboard for development.

Where there is concurrent liability between the parties,[16] assumption of responsibility operates to provide a tortious remedy for the plaintiff and enables him to take advantage of more favourable tortious rules on matters such as limitation but also exposes him to a defence of contributory negligence.[17] The relationship between the contract action and the tort action is still a matter for speculation although if the contract is silent on a matter it appears that a party can succeed if he can prove that the other party assumed responsibility for that matter.[18] The duties in contract and tort may be concurrent but need not be co-extensive.[19] This principle is likely to cause difficulties however, as if assumption of responsibility means that a person agrees to do something, it will be difficult to find a person agreed to do something for the purposes of tort but not for the purpose of contract.

If there is no contract between the parties but there is an agreement, the 'broad principle' of *Hedley Byrne* appears to require only two elements. These are that the defendant agreed to perform a service for the plaintiff and held himself out as as having the necessary skill and knowledge in this respect. Where these conditions are satisfied the defendant will have voluntarily assumed responsibility to the other party to the

---

11   See chs 2 & 3.
12   See Adams & Brownsword *Understanding Contract Law* Fontana (1994) ch 8.
13   *Hedley Byrne & Co Ltd v Heller & Partners Ltd* [1964] AC 465, [1963] 2 All ER 575.
14   *Spring v Guardian Assurance plc* [1995] 2 AC 296; *White v Jones* [1995] 2 AC 207, [1995] 1 All ER 691; *Henderson v Merrett Syndicates Ltd* [1995] 2 AC 145; *Williams v Natural Life Health Foods Ltd* [1998] 2 All ER 577.
15   *Henderson v Merrett Syndicates Ltd* [1995] 2 AC 145. See ch 5.
16   See ch 5.
17   See *Barclays Bank plc v Fairclough Building Ltd (No 2)* [1995] IRLR 605.
18   *Holt v Payne Skillington* (1995) 77 BLR 51, [1996] PNLR 179.
19   Ibid (per Hɪʀsᴛ LJ).

agreement for the use of reasonable care in the performance of the task. If this view of voluntary acceptance of responsibility is accepted it provides a method of circumventing the doctrine of consideration and giving effect to consensual agreements. Consideration has been subjected to a considerable amount of criticism[20] but whether it should effectively be abolished in this manner is arguable.[1] It is even more arguable whether it should be circumvented only in certain circumstances such as the negligent performance of services and whether it should only apply in cases of agreements to act or should be extended to pure omissions.

The concept of voluntary assumption of responsibility appears to speak the language of contract rather than tort, as historically understood. The doctrine of consideration uses the concept of detriment and to an extent this is reflected in the role of reliance in the recovery of economic loss in tort. In the classic cases of negligent misstatement before the broad principle was introduced, the courts required that the plaintiff should have been entitled to rely on the defendant and did in fact so rely. The concept of reliance is closely linked to the idea that the defendant must possess a special skill. Does reliance have a role outside of the negligent misstatement cases where it is still a necessary condition of liability? In *White v Jones*[2] LORD GOFF acknowledged that liability would have to be imposed in the absence of reliance[3] and LORD BROWNE-WILKINSON stated that it was no longer necessary for the plaintiff to prove reliance.[4]

Doctrinal support for this flexible concept can be found in the equitable concept of fiduciary duties. This demonstrates the endless possibilities which exist in English law. A fiduciary duty is a flexible equitable concept which will arise where a person has assumed responsibility for another person's dealings. This duty does not arise because of any mutual dealings between the parties nor on any relationship similar to contract. It arises because one person has presumed to act in another's affairs and there need therefore be no reliance. For example, a solicitor has a number of fiduciary duties towards a client, such as the duty not to act for two principals. LORD BROWNE-WILKINSON in *White v Jones*[5] was able to find such a duty between solicitor and beneficiary on this basis and thus indicated a super-principle which fused law and equity and transcended contract and tort. It might be argued, however, that this decision was a 'one-off' to deal with a specific problem and that the broad principle will not, in general, be extended beyond the parties to an agreement.

That the concept can be used beyond the parties to the agreement is demonstrated by the fact that a solicitor drafting a will assumes responsibility not only to the testator but also to the beneficiary[6] and that a reference provider owes a duty to the subject of the reference.[7] At present it would appear that the concept of assumption of responsibility is relevant to the question of whether, in principle, a duty should be imposed on the defendant and issues of policy are not relevant to this question. The question of who that duty is owed to, if there is no agreement, is dependant on a number of factors and these will include policy issues of justice, reasonableness and fairness, such as whether a barrister should owe a duty to his client.

20 See ch 6.
1   See Burrows (1995) CLP 103. Whittaker (1997) LS 169.
2   [1995] 2 AC 207.
3   Ibid at 262.
4   Ibid at 272.
5   [1995] 2 AC 207.
6   *White v Jones* [1995] 2 AC 207, [1995] 1 All ER 691.
7   *Spring v Guardian Assurance plc* [1995] 2 AC 296.

The extent to which the courts use the 'broad principle' will be interesting. It is a flexible concept although it has the drawback of vagueness and development could be through this and the reform of the doctrine of privity effected by the Contracts (Rights of Third Parties) Act 1999.[8]

8   See ch 6.

Chapter 11

Non-exchange relationships and benefits received

The common law of obligations encompasses three broad areas, namely contract law, tort law and the law of restitution. The last of these three branches has existed for some considerable time, but has only been explicitly recognised in recent years. In many cases, the courts would employ a fiction that there was some implied contract between the parties that could justify restoration of benefits unjustly received by the defendant,[1] but the implied contract theory is unworkable in many instances. For example, should a company enter into a contract to repay a loan which is ultra vires the powers of the company, the contract is void and there can be no contractual solution. However, the fact that the loan has been made must indicate that the debtor has received a benefit which it would be unjust for it to keep, in which case the court may order restitution of the value of that benefit in an action for moneys had and received.[2]

Where a defendant has been unjustly enriched, a relevant factor will be the benefit he has received. But it is also evident that fault-based notions of reasonable reliance are also relevant, especially in determining whether there has been an enrichment of the defendant at the plaintiff's expense. On the other hand, the issue of unjustness appears to concentrate on the plaintiff's reasons for conferring the benefit. Two principal questions need to be answered. These are, what is an enrichment, and what is unjust?

1.   PRINCIPLES OF UNJUST ENRICHMENT[3]

(1)   ENRICHMENT

An enrichment is fairly easy to identify if it is in monetary form. In the typical case, money belonging to the plaintiff will have moved to the defendant. The defendant's enrichment will mirror the loss to the plaintiff. However, difficulties may arise where a benefit in kind, such as the provision of a service, has been conferred on the defendant since the recipient may not place any value on it thereby being able to claim that there has been no enrichment.[4] In particular, it is unlikely, in most cases, that a defendant

---

1   See *Sinclair v Brougham* [1914] AC 398.
2   *Westdeutsche Landesbank Girozentrale v Islington London Borough Council* [1996] AC 669.
3   See *Goff and Jones*; *Birks*.
4   See *BP Exploration Co (Libya) Ltd v Hunt (No 2)* [1979] 1 WLR 783; on appeal [1981] 1 WLR 232, CA; affd [1983] 2 AC 352, HL.

will be required to disgorge the value of a benefit in kind unless the conferment of that benefit has been requested by the claimant. In deciding whether there has been an enrichment, it is generally said that negative enrichments, such as savings made, do not lead to restitution.[5] However, this view has been criticised[6] and it is particularly difficult to accept that negative enrichments are not capable of leading to restitution in view of the decision in *Craven-Ellis v Canons Ltd.*[7]

(i)   The tests of enrichment

Defining enrichment is not easy. It is statutorily defined as the receipt of a valuable benefit,[8] which has been equated with the transfer of wealth.[9] But it has also been argued that an over-concentration on the notion of enrichment may serve to undervalue the relevance of reliance in determining whether a restitutionary remedy should be granted.[10]

In order to decide whether a benefit in kind, such as the provision of a service, is an enrichment, three tests may be employed, namely has there been a free acceptance, is there an incontrovertible benefit, and is it possible to make an objective valuation?

(a)   Free acceptance

It should be asked whether the defendant, as a reasonable man, should have known that a person in the position of the plaintiff would expect to be paid for the benefit which has been freely accepted by the defendant in circumstances in which the latter has declined to take a reasonable opportunity to reject the benefit.[11] Where a benefit in kind has been provided gratuitously, the recipient may subjectively devalue it. That is he may say that he did not wish to receive the benefit and that he should not be required to pay for it. Conversely, if it can be said that the recipient has requested the benefit, he will not be allowed to make a subjective devaluation. This would be the case where before any benefit is conferred, the intended recipient becomes aware of what the other intends to do and does nothing to prevent the benefit from being conferred. Here the basis for restitution appears to turn the enquiry into one which is fault-based.

The clearest example of an enrichment based on free acceptance comes where there has been a request that it should be provided. For example, if a letter of intent is issued, requesting the performance of work in the anticipation that a contract will be entered into and that work is carried out, there is an enrichment of the person who makes the request. Here restitution of the value of the work may be ordered if the anticipated contract does not materialise, but the order for restitution will not protect the plaintiff's full expectation interest, it will merely restore the reasonable value of the work done.[12] However, there may be circumstances in which the parties express an intention that should a contract not be concluded, both will be free to withdraw from the process of negotiation. In these circumstances, the intention of the parties indicates that there should be no recompense.[13]

---

5   *Phillips v Homfray* (1883) 24 Ch D 439.
6   *Birks* p 129.
7   [1936] 2 KB 403. Considered below.
8   Law Reform (Frustrated Contracts) Act 1943, s 1(3).
9   *Birks*, p 44.
10   Beatson *The Use and Abuse of Unjust Enrichment* (1991) p 21.
11   Jones 'The Law of Restitution: The past and future', in Burrows *Essays* p 4 and see below.
12   *British Steel Corpn v Cleveland Bridge and Engineering Co Ltd* [1984] 1 All ER 504; *Peter Lind & Co Ltd v Mersey Docks and Harbour Board* [1972] 2 Lloyd's Rep 234.
13   *Regalian Properties plc v London Dockland Development Corpn* [1995] 1 All ER 1005.

It does not always follow that a specific request is necessary, although here, the issue of reasonable reliance is an important factor. For example, in *Waltons Stores (Interstate) Ltd v Maher*[14] a building on the respondent's land was demolished and rebuilt in accordance with specifications given by the appellants who had led him to believe that they would require the site for the purposes of building a supermarket. In fact, the appellants were considering a change of mind, but took no steps to communicate this to the respondent, allowing him to proceed with the work on his own land. On this basis, the decision that the appellant was estopped from going back on his word is manifestly based on avoiding the detriment which would otherwise flow from the unconscionable failure of the appellant to keep his word.

(b)   Incontrovertible benefit[15]

There will be such a benefit if no reasonable man could say that the defendant was not enriched. For example, it could be said that *Upton-on-Severn RDC v Powell*[16] falls within this category. The defendant had called out the fire brigade, but his call was sent to a station which did not normally serve the area in which the defendant lived. Subsequently, he was asked to pay for the service. In fact the decision to require him to pay was uneasily based in contract, but no reasonable man could say that the defendant had not received a benefit. There is also an incontrovertible benefit in cases in which the defendant would have had to pay for the service if it had been provided by someone else. In *Craven-Ellis v Canons Ltd*,[17] the plaintiff worked as a managing director of the defendant company, mistakenly believing that he was employed under a valid contract. No such contract existed, but the plaintiff's claim for *quantum meruit* succeeded as, if he had not done the job, the defendants would have had to employ and pay someone else.

(c)   Objective valuation

It becomes necessary to ask what would the reasonable man pay for the benefit conferred. This test may well be applied in cases where there appears to be no subjective valuation of the work done. For example, in *Planché v Colburn*[18] the plaintiff agreed to write a book to be published in a series of children's titles. The publisher cancelled the series committing a repudiatory breach of contract. It would be difficult to say that a part-written book could have been freely accepted. Likewise, there was no incontrovertible benefit, yet the plaintiff's claim for *quantum meruit* was successful and he was entitled to the reasonable value of his part-performance. Perhaps a better way of viewing the case is to regard it as a case of reliance loss.[19] It is difficult to say that the defendant was enriched, since a part-written book has no intrinsic value, but if the defendant commissioned the work, it is clear that the ensuing work carried out by the plaintiff is done in reliance on the defendant's request. This is not to say that the plaintiff's expectations are protected since he will not receive the equivalent of royalties, but the reasonable value of his part-performance may be recovered.

14   (1988) 76 ALR 513.
15   Recognised in *Procter & Gamble Philippine Manufacturing Corpn v Peter Cremer GmbH & Co* [1988] 3 All ER 843 at 855 (per HIRST J). See also McKendrick (1989) LMCLQ 401.
16   [1942] 1 All ER 220.
17   [1936] 2 KB 403.
18   (1831) 8 Bing 14.
19   *Goff & Jones* p 53.

(ii)　Enrichment at the plaintiff's expense

An unjust enrichment on its own is insufficient, as it fails to identify a plaintiff.[20] It must be established that the enrichment of the defendant was at the expense of the plaintiff. If the defendant has gained wealth directly from the plaintiff, this requirement will be satisfied. But there are also cases in which the enrichment has been held to be at the plaintiff's expense where he has been denied the chance to make a gain.[1] Moreover, where the defendant has received wealth via a third party, enrichment at the plaintiff's expense is said to exist if he (the plaintiff) has a legal right to the wealth, or if the third party has stated that the defendant holds the wealth on the plaintiff's behalf.[2] If this problem arises in equity, the court will ask if there is an intention to create a trust.[3] If there is, the 'beneficiary' will be able to recover the wealth appropriated by the defendant under the doctrine of constructive trusts.

(iii)　Enrichment and the defence of change of position

In an action for restitution, there are two possible measures of recovery. The more common of the two is the value received by the defendant, namely the amount he has received at the expense of the plaintiff must be restored to that person. But it is also possible for the measure of restitution to be represented by the value surviving, for example where there has been a *bona fide* change of position following receipt of a benefit, in which case the amount which survives in the recipient's hands may be the measure of restitution, not taking account of sums which have been expended. In effect, the legitimate change of position reduces the extent to which the recipient has been enriched.

While a of change of position has been expressly recognised in other jurisdictions[4] for some time, the same was not true in English law until the decision of the House of Lords in *Lipkin Gorman (a firm) v Karpnale Ltd*.[5] The main reason for not recognising such a defence in the past has been the fear that, if recognised, the defence might apply to the mere expenditure of money after receipt.[6] Accordingly, where, in the past, a change of position has justified a limitation on the extent of recovery this has been effected by means of rules on estoppel.[7] But the difficulty here is that estoppel requires a representation, which is not a necessary requirement in cases of restitution for unjust enrichment. This is particularly the case where as in *Lipkin Gorman* the money has been stolen and paid to an innocent donee, since it can hardly be said that the true owner has represented to the donee that he is entitled to the money. Instead, the House of Lords held that if an innocent defendant's position is so changed that he will suffer an injustice if he is required to repay or to pay in full and that injustice outweighs the injustice of denying the plaintiff restitution, the defence of change of position is available.[8] This might cover a person who innocently receives money and gives it away to charity,[9] but it would not extend to a person who receives a windfall and subsequently disposes of it in bad faith and with knowledge of the plaintiff's right to restitution.[10]

20　*Chase Manhattan Bank NA v Israel-British Bank (London) Ltd* [1981] Ch 105.
1　*Seager v Copydex Ltd (No 2)* [1969] 2 All ER 718.
2　*Shamia v Joory* [1958] 1 QB 448.
3　*Re Schebsman* [1944] Ch 83 at 104 (per Du Parcq LJ).
4　See the United States *Restatement of Restitution* § 142.
5　[1992] 4 All ER 512.
6　Ibid at 534 (per Lord Goff).
7　*Avon County Council v Howlett* [1983] 1 All ER 1073.
8　*Lipkin Gorman (a firm) v Karpnale Ltd* [1992] 4 All ER 512 at 533 (per Lord Goff).
9　Ibid.
10　Ibid at 534 (per Lord Goff).

(2) UNJUST ENRICHMENT

Three principal grounds may be put forward for treating an enrichment as unjust. There may have been a non–voluntary transfer. Here, the reason for the restitution lies with the plaintiff in that he has made a transfer of wealth to a person whom he does not mean to have it. Alternatively, an enrichment may be unjust because of a free acceptance. Here the unjustness of the enrichment is defendant-related and is an example of a general move towards a variety of fault-based restitution. Thirdly, an enrichment may be regarded as unjust for policy reasons. In addition, an enrichment may be unjust because it is the result of a wrong committed by the defendant.

(i) Non–voluntary transfer

A transfer of wealth may be seen as unjust enrichment for a number of reasons. It may have been effected in ignorance, by mistake, under compulsion or by a person in a position of inequality. It may also have been made subject to a condition with the effect that the defendant's entitlement to the wealth is subject to qualification by later events.

(a) Ignorance

A transfer can be made in ignorance if some variety of theft is involved. Thus, a defendant who forges a cheque and thereby diverts funds from your bank account will be required to restore those funds.[11] However, a wrong is not necessary since any involuntary transfer may lead to restitution.[12] The wealth transferred will be restored by means of an action for money had and received.

(b) Mistake and misrepresentation

A distinction should be drawn between a mistake and a misprediction. For example, if a person does work preparing plans in the belief that he will be awarded a contract to develop a building site,[13] no action for restitution will lie. A similar result will obtain if a person spends money improving property which is jointly owned by him and the defendant, in the hope that the defendant will contribute to the cost of the improvements.[14] In each case, the plaintiff has only mispredicted the likely actions of the defendant.

The types of mistake which will permit an action for restitution are limited. One reason for this is that people frequently make mistakes, therefore to allow an action for restitution in every case might lead to a flood of litigation. Furthermore, the courts are wary of the problems which can be caused by trying to reverse a transaction which has already been partly performed. The result of these fears is that it has been held in *Aiken v Short*[15] that a plaintiff seeking restitution for a mistake will not be wholly ensured of success until he can show that he has made a mistake of fact which gives him the impression that he is legally liable to transfer a benefit to the defendant.

If an insurer pays a cargo owner on the mistaken assumption that his cargo is lost at sea, he may recover his indemnity.[16] If a bank receives an instruction from its client to pay a third party, it must pay so long as there are sufficient funds in the account. If the bank pays the third party by mistake, it appears that recovery of the payment from the third party is possible. These facts arose in *Barclays Bank Ltd v W J Simms, Son and Cooke (Southern) Ltd*.[17] Subsequently, the client discovered the payee had gone into receivership

11   *United Australia Ltd v Barclays Bank Ltd* [1941] AC 1.
12   *Moffatt v Kazana* [1968] 3 All ER 271.
13   *William Lacey (Hounslow) Ltd v Davis* [1957] 1 WLR 932.
14   *Re McArdle* [1951] Ch 669.
15   (1856) 1 H & N 210 (per BRAMWELL B). Cf *Sawyer and Vincent v Window Brace Ltd* [1943] 1 KB 32.
16   *Norwich Union Fire Insurance Society Ltd v Price Ltd* [1934] AC 455.
17   [1980] QB 677.

so he gave instructions to stop the cheque. The bank programmed its computer accordingly, but an employee mistakenly overlooked the instruction. The bank sought and gained restitution from the payee. Strictly, this does not fall within the rule in *Aiken v Short*,[18] as ROBERT GOFF J thought there was no mistake as to liability to pay.[19]

If there is no liability mistake, but it is desirable in policy terms, restitution may sometimes be allowed. In *Barclays Bank Ltd v W J Simms, Son and Cooke Ltd*, it was said that a mistake may allow restitution if it causes the payment to be made,[20] although the traditional view is that the mistake must be fundamental or overwhelming. For example, in *Greenwood v Bennett*,[1] the plaintiff improved a car which he believed to be his own. It had been sold to him by a thief. The county court ordered the return of the car to the defendant, the original owner, but allowed a claim by the plaintiff for restitution of the cost of improvement.[2]

If the plaintiff mistakenly believes he is contractually liable to the defendant when this is not so and he spends money in reliance on that belief, restitution may be allowed.[3] Thus in *Rover International Ltd v Cannon Film Sales Ltd (No 3)*[4] there was a recognisable mistake of fact where a company made a payment under a contract which was believed to be valid but which was, in fact, void on the ground that it has been made with an unformed company. Likewise, restitution may be possible where a person insures a ship which has already been seized by the enemy in time of war.[5]

To be an operative mistake, it must be fundamental. A causative mistake on its own is probably not sufficient. Thus in *Bell v Lever Bros Ltd*,[6] the respondents made payments to the appellants in the form of a 'golden handshake'. The appellants had committed breaches of duty as directors of the company and could have been dismissed. Unaware of this, the company nevertheless made the payments. They later sought to recover these on the ground that they had made a mistake. The mistake was not a liability mistake since Lever Bros only saw it as desirable to make the payments. Furthermore, the mistake was not sufficiently fundamental to justify allowing the recovery of the payments concerned.

In equity, less than fundamental mistakes can lead to the rescission of a contract subject to the imposition of terms. The amount recovered in these circumstances may not be a full restitution of the value received by the defendant. For example, in *Solle v Butcher*,[7] a lease was made under the mistaken belief that the property was not covered by rent control legislation. In fact there was a statutory maximum rent. The lease was set aside in equity provided the defendant would allow the plaintiff to stay on as a licensee until a new contract could be drawn up.

A further variety of mistake is that which has been induced by a misrepresentation. This, too, may lead to the restitution of transferred wealth on the grounds of unjust enrichment. As opposed to the position in respect of spontaneous mistakes, there is no need for an induced mistake to be fundamental. Instead, it is sufficient that the misrepresentation is an active inducement.[8] The relief granted is normally that of rescission in equity.[9]

---

18   (1856) 1 H & N 210.
19   [1980] QB 677 at 693.
20   Ibid at 695 (per ROBERT GOFF J).
1   [1973] QB 195.
2   See also Torts (Interference with Goods) Act 1977, s 6.
3   *Craven-Ellis v Canons Ltd* [1936] 2 KB 403.
4   [1989] 3 All ER 423.
5   *Oom v Bruce* (1810) 12 East 225.
6   [1932] AC 161. Cf *Sybron Corpn v Rochem Ltd* [1983] 2 All ER 707.
7   [1950] 1 KB 671. See also *Grist v Bailey* [1967] Ch 532. Cf *Leaf v International Galleries* [1950] 2 KB 86 and see ch 23.
8   See ch 10.
9   See chs 13 and 18.

If the mistake relates to comprehension of the legal position, the current state of English law is that a mistake of law is not actionable. However, there are circumstances in which it may be appropriate to allow such an action to succeed. As a result, it has been recommended by the Law Commission that the distinction between mistake of fact and mistake of law should be abolished.[10] Since then, the House of Lords has agreed with this stance and has abolished the mistake of law bar, as a blanket principle, but subject to any available defences which exist under the law of unjust enrichment.[11]

(c)   Compulsion

English law has developed a number of devices to counteract attempted compulsion. At common law, the rule was that only unlawful threats to the person or sometimes to goods could constitute duress.[12] It seems now that a threat to break a contract can amount to duress,[13] and that the court will determine whether a threat amounts to duress by asking whether illegitimate pressure has been applied.[14] Where a transfer of wealth has been made in such circumstances, a person may recover that wealth from the person guilty of applying duress. Moreover, in equity, a payment may be recovered if it has been made under actual undue influence.[15] What is necessary is that the defendant has acted with some degree of impropriety or fault.[16]

If a person makes a transfer of wealth on the grounds of moral compulsion, he may be regarded as an 'officious intermeddler' who will not be entitled to restitution.[17] However, this approach might only be adopted in respect of a person who acts in his own interests. If a person were to make some payment, for example, to avert a catastrophe likely to affect some other person, then it might be possible for a court to order restitution.[18]

(d)   Inequality

In equity, there is a rebuttable presumption of undue influence[19] where certain relationships exist. If the plaintiff has made a payment to someone in whom he places trust and confidence, that payment may be recovered if the presumption is not rebutted. If there is a potential for domination, the presumption operates.[20]

In some instances, a person may have entered a transaction which is capable of exploitation and may make a payment as a result of such exploitation. For example in *Kiriri Cotton Co Ltd v Dewani*,[1] the plaintiff entered into a lease of property. At the time, housing was in great demand and in short supply. The landlord asked for a payment of 10,000 Ugandan shillings as 'key money'. It was held that this money was recoverable by the tenant because the landlord had exploited those who needed a roof over their head.[2]

(e)   Qualification by later events

Where there has been a total failure of consideration, a transfer of wealth made on that basis is recoverable. What has happened is that a condition precedent to liability to pay

10   *Mistakes of Law and Ultra Vires Public Authority Receipts and Payments,* Law Comm No 227 (1994).
11   *Kleinwort Benson Ltd v Lincoln City Council* [1998] 4 All ER 513.
12   See ch 24.
13   *North Ocean Shipping Co Ltd v Hyundai Construction Co Ltd, The Atlantic Baron* [1979] QB 705. Cf *Pao On v Lau Yiu Long* [1980] AC 614.
14   *The Universe Sentinel* [1983] 1 AC 366.
15   *Williams v Bayley* (1866) LR 1 HL 200.
16   *Re Brocklehurst's Estate* [1978] Ch 14 at 39 (per BRIDGE LJ).
17   *Falcke v Scottish Imperial Insurance Co* (1886) 34 Ch D 234.
18   See *Scaramanga v Stamp* (1880) 5 CPD 295.
19   See ch 24.
20   See ch 24.
1   [1960] AC 192.
2   Ibid at 215 (per LORD DENNING).

has failed. The problem arises, in particular, where a contract fails on the grounds of frustration[3] or of repudiatory breach of contract.[4]

It is necessary to ask whether the promise can be performed or not,[5] and to ascertain whether the reason for the payment has failed to materialise or to remain in existence. If a payment is made on certain conditions and these conditions fail, then even in the absence of a contract the amount paid may be recovered. For example, if a donor were to write to a recently engaged couple congratulating them and enclosing a cheque for £1,000, 'to help you start your married life', and the couple later called off their engagement, the £1,000 could be recovered.[6] The reason for this is that the payment is clearly conditional on the event which did not take place, namely the marriage of the couple.

For there to be a total failure of consideration, it is generally said that the person making the payment should have received nothing at all in return. However, it appears that there may be circumstances in which a total failure of consideration exists despite the fact that some benefits have been received under the failed contract. In *Rover International Ltd v Cannon Film Sales Ltd (No 3)*[7] the appellants had paid instalments under a contract which was void. It was anticipated that under the contract, the appellants should have received the opportunity of a share of receipts due from the showing of films processed by them. But since the contract was void *ab initio*, the appellants had been deprived of the benefit of the contract they had made. However, some benefit did fall to the appellants on the delivery of films into their possession, but these benefits were merely incidental to the performance of the void contract and did not themselves form part of the bargain. As such, there could still be a total failure of consideration.[8]

While the use of the failed consideration has been confined, traditionally, to actions for money had and received, it has been argued that logically, similar considerations can apply to the recovery of the value of services or goods where the other party does not pay for the value received.[9] If this is the case, it serves to explain cases where the defendant has requested certain work, which has been provided by the plaintiff, but where the defendant has subsequently[10] declined to pay for the work.[11] Here identification of an unjust factor has proved difficult, principally on the ground that these cases have not easily fitted the description of a free acceptance, since at the time the benefit is received, the recipient may have intended to pay for it, and has unconscionably changed his mind at a later stage. But if a service or goods have been provided and received, but nothing is given in return for them, it is the failure of consideration which provides the necessary unjust element. In *Rover International Ltd v Cannon Film Sales Ltd (No 3)*[12] restitution was granted in respect of money paid and work carried out under a void contract. One of the parties who claimed only money was granted restitution specifically on the ground that there had been a total failure of consideration. In contrast, the appellants (Rover) claimed restitution in respect of both work done and money paid, which was allowed on the alternate grounds of payment under a mistake or failure of consideration and it has been argued that the failure of consideration must have been a valid reason for restitution in either case.[13]

---

3   See ch 18.
4   See ch 18.
5   *Fibrosa Spolka Akcyjna v Fairbairn Lawson Coombe Barbour Ltd* [1943] AC 32 at 48 (per VISCOUNT SIMON LC).
6   *Re Ames' Settlement* [1946] Ch 217.
7   [1989] 3 All ER 423.
8   Ibid at 433–434 (per KERR LJ). See also *Rowland v Divall* [1923] 2 KB 500.
9   Burrows (1988) 104 LQR 576.
10   On the distinction between subsequent and initial unconscionability, see Garner (1990) 10 OJLS 42, 48.
11   As in *Pavey & Matthews Pty Ltd v Paul* (1987) 162 CLR 221.
12   [1989] 3 All ER 423.
13   Birks 'In Defence of Free Acceptance' in Burrows *Essays* p 113.

The failure of consideration argument is also applicable to those cases in which there is a requested benefit, in the absence of any contractual relationship. This may arise where a letter of intent, requesting the commencement of specified work, is issued in anticipation of a contract which does not materialise.[14] Consideration for the purposes of restitution is the basis, in consideration of which the transfer was made.[15] In the letter of intent cases, the reason for the provision of services etc by the person claiming restitution is that he expects to be paid for what he has done and it would be unjust in the circumstances to deny him the reasonable value of that work.

More recently, the failure of consideration argument has been applied to instances in which local authorities have attempted to enter into interest rate swap agreements with financial institutions. The difficulty with many of these transactions was that they were ultra vires the powers of the local authority and therefore void transactions. In the circumstances it was held that these were personal actions for moneys had and received based on a total failure of consideration.[16]

In addition to the common law rule on total failure of consideration, there are now statutory provisions contained in the Law Reform (Frustrated Contracts) Act 1943 which allow for what may be called mutual restitution. Non-monetary benefits are recoverable. The maximum payable to the plaintiff is assessed by reference to the value of the benefit conferred on the defendant. The just sum payable by way of restitution depends upon the cost of the plaintiff's performance.[17] Money benefits paid before a frustrating event are recoverable, but the recipient may be entitled to recover performance expenses he may have incurred.[18]

(ii)   Free acceptance[19]

The notion of free acceptance finds the reason for restitution on the side of the defendant. He has freely accepted a benefit and he should therefore pay for it. But the notion is not without its critics since the fact that the defendant has freely accepted a benefit does not mean that the enrichment is unjust or that the defendant has been enriched in an unjust manner.[20] Instead, it may be argued that a better ground for regarding an enrichment as unjust is that there is a total failure of consideration,[1] particularly where the person receiving the benefit in respect of which restitution is granted has specifically requested that benefit. Conversely, there may be a stronger argument in favour of free acceptance in cases in which there is no request and the defendant has unconscientiously taken advantage of the benefit conferred on him.

The idea of free acceptance used to be explained by reference to contract. It was said that the defendant had impliedly agreed to pay for the benefit he received. However, this is inclined to produce very artificial reasoning in cases where there is clearly no contractual relationship. For example, if X confers a benefit on Y which Y keeps for himself, under the implied contract explanation X's right to recover that benefit is based on a promise by Y which is inferred from a request which, in turn, is inferred from the acceptance of the benefit. It has been observed already that such reasoning is palpable

---

14   *British Steel Corpn v Cleveland Bridge and Engineering Co Ltd* [1984] 1 All ER 504; *Peter Lind & Co Ltd v Mersey Docks and Harbour Board* [1972] 2 Lloyd's Rep 234. See also *William Lacey (Hounslow) Ltd v Davis* [1957] 1 WLR 932.
15   See *Birks* p 219 et seq.
16   *Westdeutsche Landesbank Girozentrale v Islington London Borough Council* [1996] 2 All ER 961.
17   Law Reform (Frustrated Contracts) Act 1943, s 1(3) and see *BP Exploration & Co Ltd v Hunt (No 2)* [1983] 2 AC 352 and ch 18.
18   Ibid, s 1(2).
19   See *Birks*, ch VIII; *Goff and Jones*, pp 17–23 and 369–374.
20   Burrows (1988) 104 LQR 576 at 577. See also Garner (1990) 10 OJLS 42. Cf Birks, 'In Defence of Free Acceptance', in Burrows *Essays* pp 106–146.
1   See 'Qualification by later events' above.

nonsense,[2] and the contractual explanation is now regarded as surplusage.[3] Instead, what matters is that the court should look at the facts and decide whether a promise to pay should be implied, irrespective of the views or intentions of the parties at the time when the work was done.[4]

An equitable variety of free acceptance can be found in the doctrine of acquiescence where, for example, a landowner freely accepts improvements done to his land by another. In *Ramsden v Dyson*,[5] there is a *dictum* to the effect that if a landowner allows a tenant at will to build on his land in the belief that a long lease will be granted and he is aware of that belief, the tenant is entitled to a remedy. The important factor in these circumstances is that an unrequested benefit has been conferred on the land owner and unconscientiously he has failed to take his opportunity to reject the benefit, preferring instead to keep it for himself.

(iii)   Restitution on the grounds of public policy

Occasionally, restitution will be permitted for policy reasons. For example, it is seen to be important to encourage rescue at sea. As a result, it is a root principle of salvage that seamen must be encouraged by awards of salvage to render assistance to property.[6]

Also, in order to ensure the protection of creditors, a creditor has the right to avoid a conveyance of property which has been made with an intent to defraud.[7]

(iv)   Restitution for wrongs

In most of the cases so far considered, the plaintiff has lost what the defendant has gained. But in the case of restitution for wrongs, it is the wrong of the defendant which justifies the action for restitution. It is necessary to establish which wrongs may give rise to an action for restitution. But restitution based on the conduct of the defendant appears to be an increasingly recognised concept, especially in the light of the cases on free acceptance considered above.

It is open to a plaintiff to waive his remedy for compensation for a tort and claim restitution instead. Once he makes his choice, he will not be able to revert to the original action. The victim of conversion may wish to recover the value of the article converted from the tortfeasor. In these circumstances, it must be remembered that the example given also falls within the meaning of an unjust enrichment at the plaintiff's expense already considered.

If it is the case that there is such a thing as a restitution giving wrong, then there must be no reason other than the wrong itself for the availability of an action for restitution. For example, in *Reading v A-G*[8] an army sergeant was bribed by smugglers. The Crown was able to recover the amount of the bribe. But for the wrong of the sergeant, there would have been no reason at all to order restitution.

---

2   See ch 4.
3   *William Lacey (Hounslow) Ltd v Davis* [1957] 1 WLR 932.
4   Ibid at 936 (per BARRY J).
5   (1866) LR 1 HL 129. See also *Willmott v Barber* (1880) 15 Ch D 96.
6   *The Telemachus* [1957] P 47.
7   Law of Property Act 1925, s 172.
8   [1951] AC 507.

Chapter 12

Standard of liability

1. INTRODUCTION

A distinction between tort and contract is said to be that tortious liability is fault-based, whereas contractual liability is strict. The purpose of this chapter is to examine the nature of fault and strict liability, and to determine the standard of liability applied in the various actions for breach of an obligation. The artificial contract/tort dichotomy renders this a difficult task. Modern law recognises an action for physical damage, which encompasses death, bodily injury and property damage. An action for such loss may sound in contract or in tort, but the doctrines of privity of contract and consideration may restrict the extent of contractual liability. For example, a person who purchases a defective product from a retailer may sue for a breach of the contract of sale. The liability of the retailer is said to be strict,[1] and it will cover physical harm suffered by the purchaser. A person who has not acquired the defective product pursuant to a contract must bring an action for negligence against the retailer or the manufacturer, and must prove fault unless the Consumer Protection Act 1987 applies.

If an action lies for economic loss, again, the doctrines of privity of contract and consideration may determine the nature of the action. A choice of action may exist, since there is now the potential for a tortious action for economic loss resulting from a negligent breach of contract. Where an action sounds in tort, the plaintiff may benefit from more favourable rules on limitation of actions and remoteness of damage. If negligence cannot be established, an action for breach of contract may be preferred. In practice, the strictness of contractual liability is circumscribed by the express or implied terms of the contract, by rules of law[2] or by the doctrines of mistake and frustration.

In certain cases, the plaintiff may be restricted to an action in tort,[3] in which case fault may have to be established. However, if there is an express executory or part-executed contract to which no statutory restrictions apply, then a strict liability action for breach of contract may lie.

---

1   Cf *Rogers v Parish (Scarborough) Ltd* [1987] 2 All ER 232.
2   See Unfair Contract Terms Act 1977 and Unfair Terms in Consumer Contracts Regulations 1999 SI 1999/2083.
3   See *Hedley Byrne & Co Ltd v Heller & Partners Ltd* [1964] AC 465.

2.   HISTORICAL DEVELOPMENT

The present division of the law of obligations into the categories of contract, tort and restitution dates from the nineteenth century. Contract law was considered dominant, and was perceived to be based on individual choice exercised in a market relationship. In order to function correctly, the market had to be free from interference. In a perfect market, value maximising exchanges would take place, ensuring that goods and services ended up where they were most valued. The basic law of supply and demand would ensure that the goods and services required were produced at the correct price. The operation of the market also assumed that persons contracting in it had perfect knowledge, and were antagonistic individuals seeking to maximise their resources. Any interference by the state, including the judiciary, would distort the market. The role of the court was therefore limited to determining whether a contract had been formed; whether it had been broken and, if so, what damages were to be paid. The judge was not concerned with the content of the obligation, as this was a matter for the parties to determine. The fairness of the exchange was a matter for the parties, and the court would not interfere to alter the bargain. In this way, contract law refused to concern itself with distribution of resources. A distinction can be drawn between procedural unfairness which was treated as a formation issue and dealt with by doctrines such as mistake and duress, and substantive unfairness, ie whether the transaction itself was fair. Substantive unfairness was not recognised in the nineteenth century but is widely recognised now.[4] One consequence of this was that contractual liability was perceived to be strict. Once a person had promised to do something, he was required to perform or, in default, pay damages. It did not matter that subsequent events rendered performance of the promise substantially different or even impossible. The contract was an exercise in forward planning, and would allocate the risks accordingly. Suppose that X contracted to supply to Y a quantity of Ruritanian widgets and war broke out in Ruritania and that X was unable to secure supplies of widgets. Under the classical theory, X would be liable for a breach of contract. Had X been more thoughtful, he would have insisted upon a term in the contract that war should terminate the contract. The judiciary would not terminate the contract, and the loss would educate X for his next contractual venture.

It should be noted that, although contractual liability is said to be strict, the notion of strict liability is essentially negative. Strict contractual liability only makes sense within the context of classical promissory theory. Once made, the promise had to be performed, or legal sanctions would be imposed. In sale of goods cases, the goods had to be delivered on the date stated, and the buyer had to pay the contract price, otherwise the party in breach would be held liable. No excuse would be entertained for such a failure to perform. The supplier of a medical service might also be strictly liable for a failure to provide a cure. However, an undertaking to guarantee success was regarded as unlikely and, in practice, the appropriate standard of care was fixed by the court.

The development of classical contract theory was facilitated in two ways, namely by the transformation of questions of fact to questions of law to be decided by the judge, and by the abolition of the forms of action. What had been concealed behind the forms of action and the jury verdict beame explicit. At the same time, the treatise writers attempted to systematise the apparent chaos of the common law, and to find distinguishing factors for the various actions. One of these factors was that contract law, based on bargain promises, imposed strict liability and gave rise to expectation damages. Non-contractual actions, such as those giving rise to restitution, were incorporated into contract law through the myth of quasi-contract.

---

4   See ch 24.

The remainder of the forms of action in the field of the law of obligations can be divided into two groups. The older writs such as detinue, nuisance and trover were based on the interest protected and the standard of liability had not been an issue. The general writs other than assumpsit were those of trespass and case. Whether liability for trespass was fault-based or not emerged as a problem in the late nineteenth century.[5] The action on the case covered a wide variety of situations which can now be described as cases of negligence. These included relational actions such as those by a patient against a doctor; situations where customary duties were imposed on persons, and cases of accident between strangers where the action on the case overlapped with trespass.[6] The rapid increase in the number of accidents that came with the industrial revolution,[7] both between strangers and at the work place, together with the procedural changes in the legal system, required a basis of liability. The answer to this problem was, in most cases, found in fault, since sound policy lets losses lie where they fall, except where a special reason can be shown for interference.[8]

The origins of fault in English civil law are complex and obscure. It was partly a moral concept which had its roots in the teaching of the Christian Church. This moral basis continued into the nineteenth century, and in the opinion of some writers, coincided with economic theories and operated as a hidden subsidy to the infant emerging industries.[9] The preferable view is that the emergence of classical contract law as the dominant branch of the law of obligations impeded and restricted the development of the law of tort in the early nineteenth century.[10] Many of the cases had a relational setting, such as employer-employee, passenger-carrier, and manufacturer-consumer, and these were seen as having a contractual flavour. Problems arose with these cases, particularly the railway passenger cases, where a passenger purchased a ticket from one company and then suffered injury due to the negligence of the servant of another company. This problem was not solved until 1880, when it was held that tort liability existed against a railway company in the absence of a contract.[11]

Accidents between strangers had not achieved the overwhelming statistical significance which was to become apparent in the twentieth century, and property damage caused by the emergent industries was mostly dealt with through the old tort of nuisance and later through an attempt to impose strict liability on non-natural uses of land causing damage by an escape. As potential accident situations increased, the courts came increasingly to rely on fault as the basis for the imposition of liability, and as a justification for shifting the loss from the plaintiff to the defendant when the latter was negligent.

3.   FAULT

Legal fault is divided into three main categories: intention, recklessness and negligence. Recklessness is also referred to as advertent negligence, and negligence itself as inadvertent negligence.

---

5   See ch 1.
6   See ch 1.
7   Between 1872 and 1875, 5,231 people were killed and 16,944 injured on the railway: Commissioners on Railway Accidents no C-1637 (1877) pp 25–27.
8   Holmes *The Common Law* (1923) p 50.
9   See Friedman *A History of American Law* (1973) pp 109–127; Horwitz *The Transformation of American Law 1780–1860* (1977) pp 67–108. Cf Schwartz (1981) 90 Yale LJ 1717.
10   See Atiyah *The Rise and Fall* p 50.
11   *Foulkes v Metropolitan District Rly Co* (1880) 5 CPD 157; *Hooper v London and North Western Rly Co* (1880) 50 LJQB 103.

(1)   INTENTION AND RECKLESSNESS

Intention consists of willing the result of an act or being aware of an omission and desiring the resultant consequences. A person may also intend a consequence where it is foreseen as the definitive result of an act or omission, although it may not be desired. For example, a surgeon who removes X's heart for the purposes of transplantation may not desire X's death, but death is an inevitable consequence of his conduct.

Emphasis should be placed on intended consequences rather than intentional acts. To qualify as an act, a movement needs to be willed. If the movement is automatous, or is the result of physical force applied by another person, it does not qualify as an act. But if an act is willed, for example where a motorist deliberately accelerates and strikes a pedestrian, the injuries cannot be said to have been intentionally inflicted unless the motorist desired this consequence.

A further refinement of the requirement of intention is that, in order for a defendant to be guilty of battery, he must intend to apply physical force in a hostile manner. It is not necessary that the defendant should intend to harm or injure the plaintiff. It follows that a schoolboy engaged in horseplay who injures a classmate is not guilty of battery.[12]

Recklessness, or advertent negligence, is normally classed as a variety of intention. Here, the consequence of the defendant's act or omission is neither desired nor certain, but is foreseen as possible. Since *Metropolitan Police Comr v Caldwell*[13] it may not be correct to refer to this as recklessness, since recklessness may now cover cases where the defendant does not advert to the consequences of his act.

Intention and recklessness give rise to many problems in criminal law, which have not troubled the courts much in civil cases. Intention or recklessness is rarely an essential requirement in a civil case. The requirement exists in the tort of deceit, malicious prosecution, and in certain economic torts such as inducement to a breach of contract. Intention also founds one basis of liability in trespass. It is also possible for an action to succeed in non-intentional trespass to the person,[14] but in cases involving personal injuries, it is difficult to see why a person would wish to proceed in trespass rather than negligence.

It may now be doubted whether there is any justification for retaining a category of liability based on intention. The negligence principle of imposing liability for unreasonably caused foreseeable harm may have become paramount. Although negligence appears to have swept all before it in personal injury cases, there are possibly grounds for retaining an action to protect a person against interference with basic liberties. While the compensation debate dominated tort thinking in the latter part of the twentieth century, it is also true that the law of tort does have more than one function.[15] In cases involving interference with civil liberties, the court may award exemplary damages where there have been oppressive, arbitrary or unconstitutional actions by servants of the government.[16] Whether this justifies the retention of intentional torts is arguable. One writer has indicated his preference for distinguishing states of mind only at the stage of awarding damages rather than for determining initial liability.[17]

---

12   *Wilson v Pringle* [1986] 2 All ER 440.
13   [1982] AC 341. This is a decision for the purposes of the criminal law.
14   *Fowler v Lanning* [1959] 1 QB 426; *Letang v Cooper* [1965] 1 QB 232.
15   *Weir* pp 331–336.
16   *Rookes v Barnard* [1964] AC 1129 at 1226 (per Lord Devlin).
17   Atiyah (1987) 7 OJLS 279 at 287.

(2)   NEGLIGENCE

Negligence may take two theoretical forms, namely advertent and inadvertent negligence. In the case of advertent negligence, the consequence of the defendant's action is foreseen but not desired. By contrast, inadvertent negligence consists of the defendant's failure to foresee and avoid a consequence of his actions.

As very few cases turn on intention, what is known as fault-based liability for most purposes consists of negligence. It is important to remember that what amounts to negligence, in civil law, is not a state of mind. When a court adjudges a defendant to be negligent, it is making an *ex post* assessment of his conduct. The person who totally disregards the safety of others but does not injure them, may be morally reprehensible, but is not guilty of negligence. Conversely, the person who tries his best and falls below socially required standards of behaviour and causes damage is legally liable.[18] This tells us that whatever its roots were in morality, the modern concept of negligence is now based on more practical concepts.

(i)   The reasonable man

Following the abolition of the forms of action in the nineteenth century, civil cases were still tried by jury. Greater control of the jury was exercised by the judge, but in the rapidly expanding number of accident cases, the question whether the defendant had been negligent was still for the jury to decide. Some form of directive to the jury was required to convey to them the applicable standard. A subjective enquiry into each person's capacities and ability would be inefficient. As a result, an objective standard judged by external manifestations of conduct was applied. The standard of conduct to be attained was described as that of the 'reasonable man'.[19]

The objective standard means that normally, no account is taken of individual disabilities or peculiarities. A high standard of care is used in judging highway accident cases. In *Nettleship v Weston*,[20] it was held that a learner driver would be judged by the standard of the average competent driver.

> The learner driver may be doing his best, but his incompetent best is not good enough. He must drive as well as a driver of skill, experience and care …[1]

If a person causes a car accident in a state of automatism, then he will not be negligent. But if he continues to drive after suffering a seizure which has impaired his ability to react, he will be liable.[2] In contrast, a person suffering from insane delusions as to the colour of traffic lights, will be found liable.[3]

To what extent should subjective factors be taken into account? The prevailing view is that, 'this notion of duty tailored to the actor, rather than to the act which he elects to perform, has no place in the law of tort.'[4] Applying this view to car drivers produces the approach in *Nettleship v Weston*.[5] What if the plaintiff got into a car with a driver who the plaintiff knew was drunk? The objective approach means that the standard by which the driver will be judged is that of the average driver, not the average drunken driver. The plaintiff's knowledge of the driver's particular characteristic is dealt

18   See *Nettleship v Weston* [1971] 2 QB 691 at 699 (per Lord Denning MR).
19   *Blyth v Birmingham Waterworks Co* (1856) 11 Exch 781 at 784, 156 ER 1047 at 1049 (per Alderson B). See Kidner (1991) 11 Legal Studies 1.
20   [1971] 2 QB 691.
1   Ibid (per Lord Denning at 699). Cf *Marshall v Osmond* [1983] QB 1034.
2   *Roberts v Ramsbottom* [1980] 1 WLR 823. See also *Mansfield v Weetabix Ltd* [1998] 1 WLR 1263.
3   See Fleming *Introduction* p 27.
4   *Wilsher v Essex Area Health Authority* [1987] QB 730 at 750 (per Mustill LJ).
5   [1971] 2 QB 691.

with by the defences to negligence.[6] The plaintiff may be held to have been contributorily negligent, thus reducing damages, or even *volens* to the risk of harm, denying any compensation at all. In contrast a view has been expressed in some Australian cases which suggests that known characteristics should be taken into account in assessing the standard of care.[7]

What if the driver of the car was a child? This poses theoretical problems as it is harsh to expect a child to come up to adult standards but a failure to do so may leave an injured plaintiff uncompensated. The standard of care to be expected from a child is that to be expected of a reasonable child of the same age, intelligence and experience.[8] Thus the standard of care is adjusted for the child's age but is otherwise objective. On this view the standard of care to be expected takes into account the factor of childhood. Why should childhood be a relevant factor and not others such as inexperience? It may be because children are not generally insured and a finding of negligence would impose a direct penalty.

The objectification of the test had the effect of permitting a flexible approach to a wide range of factual situations and to changing social ideals. Since jury verdicts on what constituted negligence did not create precedents, the law was not able to ossify at a particular stage in history. In theory, this still remains true, even though a finding of negligence is now made by the judge. But there are some indications that findings of negligence in discrete cases may be treated as precedents, a process which some eminent jurists favoured.[9]

As the judge gives reasons for his decision, the legal profession, in a subsequent case, may advise on the basis of a reported judgment. Although this process may have the advantage of encouraging settlements, it would be unfortunate if it was carried to its logical outcome of judicially defined standards. Given the sometimes stifling effect of the doctrine of precedent, judicially defined standards might have the effect of freezing the law and leaving little room for change. This problem does not arise in the United States as the jury is still commonly used in civil litigation, although damages awards may tend to be higher, resulting in increased insurance premiums.[10]

(ii)   Factors determining negligence

The reasonable man is, of course, a fictional character,[11] and is a disguise for the value judgment made by the judge.[12] If the failure to do what the reasonable man would do is negligence, can conformity with standard practice be accepted as absence of negligence? It may be standard practice and cost-efficient for industry to operate a production system which turns out 1% of its products in a dangerous condition, but this argument is unlikely to appeal to a court. Equally unlikely to succeed is the driver who persists in driving at excessive speed in a motorway contraflow system, even though he might claim that all drivers do the same. In both cases, the judge will decide how the defendant ought to have behaved in these circumstances. The standard of behaviour is decided on by the judge. There are, however, areas where standard practice will carry great weight with a court, such as medical negligence cases.

---

6   See chs 20 and 22.
7   See Kidner (1991) 11 Legal Studies 1, 12–14.
8   *Mullin v Richards* [1998] 1 All ER 920. See also *McHale v Watson* [1966] ALR 513.
9   See Holmes *The Common Law* (1881) pp 127–128.
10   Cf Priest (1987) 96 Yale LJ 1521.
11   See *Davis Contractors Ltd v Fareham UDC* [1956] AC 696 at 728 (per LORD RADCLIFFE). See also Herbert *Uncommon Law* (1969) p 4.
12   See Millner (1976) 92 LQR 131.

The judge is likely to take four factors into account in most cases.[13] These are the degree of probability that damage will be done; the magnitude of the harm likely; the utility of the object to be achieved, and the burden in time and trouble of taking precautions against the risk. It has been suggested that the test can be reduced to an economic formula.[14] In the United States, it has been stated that the defendant is negligent if the likelihood of injury multiplied by the gravity of the injury exceeds the burden of adequate precautions.[15] As the effect of a finding of negligence by a court is to shift the loss from the plaintiff to the defendant, the economic argument, based on efficiency, is that this is only justified where the cost of avoiding the accident is less than the accident costs. For example, if failure to have a safety device on a machine in a factory will lead to an accident once every thousand times the machine is used, and the accident cost will be £5,000, the expected cost of the accident will be £5 (£5,000 x 0.001). If the cost of the safety device is £10, its non-installation would not amount to negligence. If the accident cost were £20,000, the opposite would be true.

Economists now argue that a correct version of this theory should compare not total costs but marginal costs of accidents and accident prevention.[16] In the above example, if the machine operator could be given gloves at a cost of £2 and the accident cost would drop by half to £2,500, then this would be cost justified.

To someone conversant with legal reasoning, this is a bizarre way of looking at the question, as it ignores the issue of justice or fairness, and leaves out the third factor on the list, that of the utility of the object to be achieved. The approach has been severely criticised, particularly in the United Kingdom.[17] Many difficulties with the formula approach exist. The degree of probability of an accident in many cases cannot be calculated with any degree of accuracy. Furthermore, a court is not equipped to make such a calculation, and does not have assistance to assess the cost of prevention.[18] The utility factor would also appear to be inappropriate to mathematical calculation in money terms. How could the court assess the value of speed-boat racing, attempting to save life or putting a new drug onto the market? One advocate of the efficiency test has argued that 'judges can hardly avoid using some criterion of social welfare ... and efficiency is a more libertarian criterion than any other'.[19] Others[20] have attacked the efficiency test on the ground that it would impair individual freedom.

It is unlikely that this approach will prove to be a complete solution to the negligence problem, but it is helpful in illuminating at least one factor in the court's decision.

(a)   *The degree of probability that damage will be done*   Nearly every human action involves some risk of harm, but every risky act will not necessarily result in liability. Care must be taken in respect of a risk that is reasonably foreseeable.[1] It should be noted that foreseeability of damage caused is one relevant factor amongst others. Furthermore, foreseeability is a relative concept, not to be scientifically tested. Every event is foreseeable to a greater or lesser extent, but it is only at a certain level that the law will require a person to adjust his behaviour. In *Glasgow Corpn v Muir*,[2] negligence on the part of a tea-room manageress was alleged when she permitted members of a church

---

13   See Prosser *Torts* (4th edn, 1971) p 146 et seq.
14   Posner *Economic Analysis of Law* (2nd edn, 1977) p 122.
15   *United States v Carroll Towing Co Inc* 159 F (2d) 169 (2d Circ, 1947) at 173 (per LEARNED HAND J).
16   See Veljanovski 'The Economic Theory of Tort Liability' in *The Economic Approach to Law* (1981) (eds Burrows and Veljanovski) p 132.
17   Atiyah *Accidents* ch 18.
18   Cf *Haley v London Electricity Board* [1965] AC 778.
19   Posner *Economic Analysis of Law* (1973) p 17.
20   See Epstein (1973) 2 Jo LS 151.
1   *Fardon v Harcourt–Rivington* (1932) 146 LT 391 at 392 (per LORD DUNEDIN).
2   [1943] 2 All ER 44.

party to carry an urn of scalding tea down a corridor. For some unexplained reason, the urn slipped and children from another party were injured. It was held by the House of Lords that the manageress was not guilty of negligence, as she had no reason to anticipate that such an event would occur as a result of permitting the tea urn to be carried. It was reasonable to assume that the urn would be carried by responsible persons who would have regard for the safety of the children.[3]

The interaction of the various factors in the equation and the relative nature of foreseeability can be illustrated by contrasting two cases. In *Bolton v Stone*,[4] the plaintiff was struck by a cricket ball while she was standing outside her own house. Evidence was accepted that the occurrence was exceptional, since balls had been struck from the ground on only six occasions in thirty years. The defendants were found not liable, as the risk was so small that the reasonable man would have been justified in disregarding it. No precautions were necessary to eliminate the risk. In *Hilder v Associated Portland Manufacturers Cement Ltd*,[5] the defendants allowed children to play football on waste ground next to a road. Balls frequently went onto the road, and one caused a motor-cyclist to crash, killing him. Because of the degree of risk, the defendant was held liable.[6]

(b)   *Skill*   Where a person has held himself out as capable of attaining a certain standard of skill, whether in relation to the public in general, or to an individual, he is required to show the skill normally possessed by persons doing that work. Foreseeability may therefore depend on the knowledge which a person ought to possess. A doctor will be called upon to show the skill of the average doctor, not the skill of a layman.[7] To determine the standard required of a layman who undertakes a specialised or skilled task necessitates a consideration of all relevant circumstances. If he is compelled to act in an emergency, he will be judged by the standards of a reasonable person acting to avert a crisis. Thus, a mountaineer giving first-aid to an imperilled fellow climber will not be required to reach the same standard as a doctor. Conversely, where a person has a free choice whether to act or not, a higher standard will be imposed. In *Wells v Cooper*,[8] the defendant, a layman, badly fitted a door handle with the result that it came away in the plaintiff's hand. While the defendant was held not to have been negligent, the standard of care was said to be that required of a reasonably competent carpenter.[9]

(c)   *The magnitude of harm likely*   The greater the risk of injury, the greater will be the precautions required to avert the risk. In *Paris v Stepney Borough Council*,[10] a one-eyed welder, employed by the defendants, lost his sight because he was not provided with safety goggles. The defendants were liable because they were aware of his disability and should have taken greater care. But in *Withers v Perry Chain Co Ltd*,[11] the plaintiff was prone to suffer from dermatitis and was given the most grease-free job available. Despite this, she contracted dermatitis and sued her employers for causing or exacerbating

---

3   Ibid at 49 (per LORD MACMILLAN).
4   [1951] AC 850.
5   [1961] 3 All ER 709, [1961] 1 WLR 1434.
6   See also *Haley v London Electricity Board* [1965] AC 778, [1964] 3 All ER 185 and Disabled Persons Act 1981, s 1.
7   See *Bolam v Friern Hospital Management Committee* [1957] 2 All ER 118 at 121 (per MACNAIR J), approved in *Whitehouse v Jordan* [1981] 1 All ER 267; *Maynard v West Midlands Regional Health Authority* [1985] 1 All ER 635; *Sidaway v Board of Governors of the Bethlem Royal Hospital and the Maudsley Hospital* [1985] 1 All ER 643; *Bolitho v City and Hackney Health Authority* [1997] 4 All ER 771. See also *Roe v Minister of Health* [1954] 2 QB 66 and *Thake v Maurice* [1984] 2 All ER 513.
8   [1958] 2 QB 265.
9   Ibid at 271 (per JENKINS LJ). See also *Phillips v William Whiteley Ltd* [1938] 1 All ER 566.
10   [1951] AC 367.
11   [1961] 3 All ER 676, [1961] 1 WLR 1314.

it. The defendants were found not liable, as the only way of eliminating the risk was to dismiss her.

(d)   *The utility of the object to be achieved*   A frequent cause of anxiety in all developed countries is the toll of death and injuries caused by road accidents. This problem could be practically eliminated by imposing a speed limit of five miles per hour, but the consequences of this would be unacceptable in an industrialised economy.[12] As a result, a line must be drawn, indicating the point at which a person's conduct becomes socially unacceptable. This may be done by Parliament in the form of statutorily imposed speed limits, however, not every possibility can be legislated for. A court may be called upon to assess the utility of the defendant's conduct and the level of risk he was entitled to take. In *Watt v Hertfordshire County Council,*[13] a fireman was injured by the sudden movement of a heavy jack on a vehicle which was not adapted to carry it, but had been used in an emergency in an attempt to save life. The defendants were held not liable, as the objective of saving life justified the risk. However, had the risk been taken by a commercial enterprise, the plaintiff would have recovered.[14] Other values may be less easy to assess. It could be conjectured that the fact that the defendants were playing cricket had some effect on the decision in *Bolton v Stone.*[15] If the injury to the respondent had been caused by an unlawful activity, there is little doubt that the case would have been decided differently.

(e)   *The burden of taking precautions against the risk*   Once a risk is identified as reasonably foreseeable, the difficult question of whether the defendant should have taken precautions to protect the plaintiff against that risk arises. In *Latimer v AEC Ltd*[16] the floor of the defendants' factory became flooded after heavy rain. They took all possible steps to minimise the danger, short of closing the factory. The plaintiff slipped and was injured, but the defendants were found not liable. The court weighed the degree or extent of the risk against the cost of eliminating it.[17] Contrasting views have been expressed. In *Bolton v Stone,*[18] it was said that it would not be right to take into account the difficulty of carrying out remedial measures.[19]

It is not normally necessary to eliminate a risk altogether, as this would constitute insurance against the risk.[20] Conformity with standard and accepted practice may be sufficient to fulfil the standard of reasonable care but the courts are not always prepared to support professional practice. In *Lloyds Bank Ltd v EB Savory and Co,*[1] the defendants were held to be negligent, even though they had followed standard banking practice. In *Bolitho v City and Hackney Health Authority*[2] the House of Lords stressed that expert evidence in medical negligence cases had to be opinions whch had a logical basis and had weighed risks against benefits.[3] In industrial accidents, a clearly established practice

---

12   *Daborn v Bath Tramways Motor Co Ltd and Smithey* [1946] 2 All ER 333 at 336 (per Asquith LJ).
13   [1954] 1 WLR 835.
14   Ibid at 838 (per Denning LJ). See also *Daborn v Bath Tramways Motor Co Ltd and Smithey* [1946] 2 All ER 333.
15   [1951] AC 850. See also *Miller v Jackson* [1977] 3 All ER 338.
16   [1953] AC 643.
17   See also *Haley v London Electricity Board* [1965] AC 778.
18   [1951] AC 850.
19   Ibid at 867 (per Lord Reid).
20   Some risks are so great that insurance is essential. See Nuclear Installations Act 1965.
1   [1933] AC 201. See also *Edward Wong Finance Co Ltd v Johnson Stokes and Master* [1984] AC 296; *Re Herald of Free Enterprise* (1987) Independent, 18 December.
2   [1997] 4 All ER 771.
3   Ibid at 779 per Lord Browne-Wilkinson. See ch 26 for medical negligence.

will assist the defendant, but it is not conclusive.[4] And in cases of individual defendants, it has already been observed that conformity with standard practice, such as ignoring a stop sign on the highway, does not prevent a finding of negligence.

(iii)   Proof of fault

It may be necessary to prove fault on the part of a defendant, whether the action be framed in contract or in tort. The party seeking to establish fault may encounter difficulties presented by evidential rules.

(a)   *Burden and standard of proof*   The basic rule is that he who affirms must prove.[5] In civil cases, the burden of proof lies on the plaintiff to show that the defendant intended to cause damage, or fell below the required standard of care, and that this has caused damage. Where the defendant alleges contributory negligence on the part of the plaintiff, this must be proved by the defendant.[6]

This was not always so, and is not an axiom of all legal systems. In cases of trespass under the writ system, the plaintiff had to prove that the defendant had generated the risk of his being injured. The defendant then had to exonerate himself by proving that he was not responsible for the accident. This rule survives in trespass cases in Canada and Australia, but not in England.[7]

In England, there is one significant statutory exception to the rule on burden of proof. The Civil Evidence Act 1968, section 11 provides that the fact of conviction on a criminal charge is now admissible as evidence in a civil case based on the same facts. Where the defendant has been convicted of an offence in respect of conduct which is alleged to be negligent, a rebuttable presumption of liability is created.[8] To escape liability, the defendant must prove that he was not negligent.[9] If in a negligence action involving a car accident, the defendant has been convicted of a driving offence in connection with the accident, it will be up to him to show that he did not drive negligently. Although difficult, this may not be impossible. It may be a criminal offence to exceed the speed limit, but it is not necessarily the case that the driver is negligent.

In civil cases, a fact must be established on a balance of probabilities. In practice, the courts tend to impose high standards of care in certain areas. For example, high standards of proof may be applied where the defendant has to exculpate himself in employer-employee or road accident cases.[10]

(b)   *Judge and jury*   At one time, civil cases were normally tried by jury. This practice has now been eroded to the point where it is rare for a civil case to be heard with a jury.[11]

In negligence cases before a jury, it is necessary to ask if there is evidence of negligence and whether negligence has been proved. On the first issue, the judge must decide if there is sufficient evidence. If this is not so, the case may be withdrawn from the jury. Judicial error in this regard has, in the past, generated a number of appeals. Whether

---

4   See the 'Dunedin Formula' in *Morton v Dixon (William) Ltd* 1909 SC 807 as refined in *Morris v West Hartlepool Steam Navigation Co Ltd* [1956] AC 552 at 579.
5   *Abrath v North Eastern Rly Co* (1883) 11 QBD 440.
6   *Joseph Constantine Steamship Line Co Ltd v Imperial Smelting Corpn Ltd* [1942] AC 154.
7   *Cook v Lewis* [1952] 1 DLR 1 (Canada); *McHale v Watson* (1964) 111 CLR 384 (Australia). Cf *Fowler v Lanning* [1959] 1 QB 426 (England).
8   *Wauchope v Mordecai* [1970] 1 WLR 317.
9   *Stupple v Royal Insurance Co Ltd* [1970] 1 QB 50 at 71–73.
10   *Henderson v H E Jenkins & Sons and Evans* [1970] AC 282.
11   Administration of Justice (Miscellaneous Provisions) Act 1933, s 6. See also *Ward v James* [1966] 1 QB 273.

negligence is proved is a question of fact for the jury which would not involve a reasoned decision.

When trial is by judge alone, the two issues may be blurred, and whether or not there is evidence of negligence may seem to be less important. Instead, the judge will concentrate upon whether the defendant was negligent.

If an appeal court is called on to consider a judge's decision, it will normally accept his findings of primary fact, but may dispute the inferences to be drawn from these findings. In *Whitehouse v Jordan*,[12] the judge found that the defendant doctor had pulled too long and too hard. The House of Lords treated this as an inference from primary facts and open to re-assessment.

(c)   *Proof of fault*   The plaintiff must normally allege and prove specific acts or omissions which constitute negligent conduct. Not every fact need be proved, as the purpose of pleadings in a civil case is to isolate the issues which are in dispute between the parties. Thus, in a defective products case, it may be admitted that the plaintiff was a consumer, the defendant a manufacturer and that the injury was caused by the product. The defendant may then deny that he failed to take reasonable care, and this issue is joined between the parties.

In order to identify the difficulties of establishing fault, three cases may be examined. In *Ward v Tesco Stores Ltd*,[13] the plaintiff entered the defendants' supermarket and slipped on some yoghurt on the floor, suffering personal injuries. This was all she could prove, apart from the fact that, three weeks later, orange juice had remained on the floor of the same supermarket for fifteen minutes. The defendants gave evidence that the floor was brushed five or six times a day, and staff were instructed that, if they saw a spillage, they were to stay in that place and call someone to clean it up. The Court of Appeal, by a majority,[14] held that the plaintiff's evidence constituted a *prima facie* case of negligence, as the floor was under the defendants' management, and the accident was of such a kind as does not ordinarily happen if reasonable care is taken.[15] The defendants were therefore obliged to show that they had taken all reasonable care. This they had failed to do, and the plaintiff succeeded. In *Dulhunty v JB Young Ltd*,[16] the plaintiff slipped on a grape, but it was held that an essential part of the plaintiff's case was to show how long the grape had been on the floor.

In *Henderson v H E Jenkins & Sons*,[17] the plaintiff's husband was killed when the brakes on a lorry failed on a steep hill. The defendants pleaded that the failure resulted from a latent defect in the brake fluid pipe. They advanced evidence that they had cleaned and visually inspected the pipe, and the cause of failure was corrosion. This could only be detected by removing the pipe. This practice was not normally recommended by the manufacturers or the Ministry of Transport. The House of Lords, by a majority,[18] held that the plaintiff had raised an inference of negligence, and the defendants had failed to rebut this. They should have shown that nothing in the vehicle's life would have caused abnormal corrosion or called for special inspection.

In *Grant v Australian Knitting Mills Ltd*,[19] the plaintiff contracted dermatitis as a result of wearing long johns which were contaminated with a sulphur-based compound. He

12   [1981] 1 All ER 267. See also *Ratcliffe v Plymouth & Torbay Health Authority* [1998] Lloyd's Rep Med 162.
13   [1976] 1 WLR 810.
14   ORMROD LJ dissenting.
15   Relying on *Scott v London & St Katherine Docks Co* (1865) 3 H & C 596 at 601, Ex Ch.
16   (1975) 7 ALR 409.
17   [1970] AC 282, [1969] 3 All ER 756.
18   LORD GUEST and VISCOUNT DILHORNE dissenting.
19   [1936] AC 85, [1935] All ER Rep 209.

sued the manufacturers under the narrow rule in *Donoghue v Stevenson*[20] for their negligence and sued the retailers in contract. In the action against the manufacturers, it was held that, the appellant is not required to lay his finger on the exact person in all the chain who was responsible, or to specify what he did wrong. Negligence is found as a matter of inference from the existence of the defects, taken in connection with all the known circumstances.[1]

The evidence had shown that the manufacturers recognised the danger of excess sulphites, and had guarded against it. LORD WRIGHT was of the opinion that, if excess sulphites were in a garment, it could only be because someone was at fault.[2]

(d)   *Res ipsa loquitur*   It can be seen from the three cases referred to in the preceding section that the process of proof requires the plaintiff to adduce evidence on a balance of probabilities which raises an inference of negligence. If no such inference can be drawn, the plaintiff's case will fail. If the plaintiff is successful, the defendant must adduce evidence to dispel the inference. Strictly it is not possible to disprove a fact which has been proved but the defendant may call evidence which provides a plausible explanation for the accident. Alternatively, he may advance evidence which is equally consistent with negligence or absence of negligence on his part, thereby leaving the probabilities perfectly balanced. The fact situations which can give rise to an inference of negligence are infinite, and it is for the tribunal of fact to determine where the balance lies at the end of the evidence.

The issue of proof of fault has been bedevilled by the use of the phrase *res ipsa loquitur*, or the thing speaks for itself. The origin of the phrase lies in a statement by ERLE CJ:

> There must be reasonable evidence of negligence. But where the thing is shown to be under the management of the defendant or his servants, and the accident is such, as in the ordinary course of things, does not happen if those who have the management use proper care, it affords reasonable evidence, in the absence of explanation by the defendants, that the accident arose from want of care.[3]

This has since been referred to as *res ipsa loquitur*, but it has been judicially observed that it is not right to describe it as a doctrine,[4] and that its mystique is solely due to the fact that it is expressed in Latin.

The 'doctrine' is said to have two requirements. It has to be shown that the thing causing the damage was under the exclusive control of the defendant. This means that the mere occurrence of the accident should point to negligence on the part of the defendant and no-one else.[5] This could prove to be unduly restrictive, but the courts have shown some flexibility. In defective products cases, the 'control' lies in the manufacturing process, although the injury may be caused long after the product leaves the factory.[6] However, as Fleming states:

---

20 [1932] AC 562.
1   *Grant v Australian Knitting Mills Ltd* [1936] AC 85 at 101 (per LORD WRIGHT).
2   Ibid.
3   *Scott v London & St Katherine Docks Co* (1865) 3 H & C 596 at 601, Ex Ch, 159 ER 665 at 667.
4   *Lloyde v West Midlands Gas Board* [1971] 2 All ER 1240 at 1246 (per MEGAW LJ). See also *Roe v Minister of Health* [1954] 2 QB 66 at 87–88 (per MORRIS LJ).
5   See *Easson v London and North Eastern Rly Co* [1944] KB 421, [1944] 2 All ER 425. Cf *Gee v Metropolitan Rly Co* (1873) LR 8 QB 161. See also *The Kite* [1933] P 154, [1933] All ER Rep 234.
6   See *Grant v Australian Knitting Mills Ltd* [1936] AC 85, PC.

It would surely be at once more accurate and less confusing to abandon all reference to 'control' and postulate simply that the apparent cause of the accident must be such that the defendant would most probably be responsible for any negligence ...[7]

The second requirement is that the accident should be of a sort that does not normally happen in the absence of negligence. For example, sulphites are not normally present in woollen underwear;[8] stones do not normally form an ingredient in a bun;[9] and barrels do not normally fall from an upstairs window.[10] The advance of technology often makes it difficult for a plaintiff to prove what has happened. If an aircraft crashes or a car suddenly goes out of control or two railway trains crash, a probable explanation is a failure to exercise due care in maintenance or operation. This may not be true in the early stages of development of a new product. No doubt aeroplanes frequently crashed in the pioneer days of aviation, even when due care was exercised. It would have been impossible, then, to have drawn an inference of negligence from the fact of a crash, but now these are a rare event and require an explanation from those responsible for operation of aeroplanes.

A similar approach can be observed in medical practice. Initially, the courts were reluctant to draw an inference of negligence from the fact of a failed operation,[11] but the modern trend is for *res ipsa loquitur* to apply in simple situations, such as the plaintiff who goes into hospital with two stiff fingers and comes out with four stiff fingers[12] and a healthy patient who goes into cardiac arrest while under general anaesthesia.[13] One reason that *res ipsa loquitur* is not commonly raised in medical cases is that the parties will have the relevant evidence from medical records and expert medical opinion. The main question for the court will be how much weight to give to the evidence and whether an inference of negligence can be drawn.

Attempts have also been made to apply *res ipsa loquitur* in cases of economic loss. In *Stafford v Conti Commodity Services Ltd*,[14] the defendant commodity brokers were sued for negligence, and it was held that *res ipsa loquitur* had no application because of the volatile nature of the commodities market and that very strong evidence would be required from expert brokers to establish fault. *Res ipsa loquitur* is only applicable where there is no explanation for the accident. If all the facts are known, then the only question is whether or not negligence can be inferred. In *Barkway v South Wales Transport Co Ltd*,[15] a bus suddenly swerved and crashed. The cause of the accident was a burst tyre and, as all the facts were sufficiently known, the House of Lords held that *res ipsa loquitur* was inapplicable. But the fact that the defendants had not instructed their drivers to report heavy blows to tyres was found sufficient to establish negligence on the defendants' part.

When *res ipsa loquitur* is successfully raised by the plaintiff, two problems may arise. First, the phrase *res ipsa loquitur* may not even be mentioned by the court.[16] Accordingly, any further discussion of the proof of fault must proceed on the assumption that the plaintiff has proved, on a balance of probability, that the defendant is guilty of negligence. Secondly, the law of evidence can make matters more complex. The legal burden of proof lies on the plaintiff throughout a case, but the evidential burden of proof may

---

7   *Law of Torts* pp 305–306.
8   *Grant v Australian Knitting Mills Ltd* [1936] AC 85, PC.
9   *Chaproniere v Mason* (1905) 21 TLR 633.
10 *Byrne v Boadle* (1863) 2 H & C 722.
11 *Mahon v Osborne* [1939] 2 KB 14, [1939] 1 All ER 535, CA.
12 *Cassidy v Ministry of Health* [1951] 2 KB 343 at 365. *Roe v Minister of Health* [1954] 2 QB 66.
13 See *Glass v Cambridge Health Authority* [1995] 6 Med LR 91.
14 [1981] 1 All ER 691.
15 [1950] 1 All ER 392.
16 *Henderson v Henry E Jenkins & Sons* [1970] AC 282.

shift at various stages in the trial, because different issues may be involved. If a plaintiff raises an inference of negligence, the evidential burden shifts to the defendant. The difficulty is then to determine what the defendant must do to avoid liability. Two decisions of the House of Lords fail to clarify this issue.[17]

If the defendant can show how an accident has occurred, and that he has exercised reasonable care, he will escape liability. Similarly, if he can show that due care has been taken even though the exact cause of the accident cannot be established, liability will not be imposed. In *Barkway v South Wales Transport Co Ltd*,[18] the defendants would have been required to show that the burst tyre was either due to some specific cause unrelated to their negligence or, failing this, that they had used all reasonable care in the maintenance of their tyres. If these are the only methods by which the defendant can escape liability, it would appear that the effect of *res ipsa loquitur* is to shift the legal burden of proof.[19] However, in *Ng Chun Pui v Lee Chuen Tat*,[20] the Privy Council stated that the burden of proof does not shift.

An alternative view is that if the defendant can give an explanation of the accident equally consistent with negligence or absence of negligence on his part, the scales are tilted back in his favour:

> If the defendant can show a way in which the accident may have occurred without negligence, ... the fact of the accident by itself disappears, and the pursuer is left as he began, namely that he has to show negligence.[1]

This view is consistent with the speeches in *Colvilles Ltd v Devine*,[2] in which a pipe carrying oxygen exploded. The defendants suggested that this could have been caused by particles igniting. The court agreed that the defendants would not be required to prove this, and it could provide a non-negligent explanation for the explosion. On the facts, however, the defendants were liable, as they had not proved that filters to prevent particle entry were effective or had been checked. It has been suggested that the result in *Colvilles v Devine* is consistent with the alternative view that the defendant must prove no negligence.[3] This would also appear to be the effect of the result in *Henderson v Jenkins*.

It is considered by some writers that the effect of an application of *res ipsa loquitur* is to import a rule of strict liability into negligence cases.[4] This would appear to be particularly true in certain fields of accident law, where a high standard of care is called for as in the case of motor accidents, defective products and employer-employee relationships. Where the facts of the case bespeak negligence on the part of the defendant, there may be little he can do to dispel the inference or presumption that is raised. This is, however, a rather haphazard and unsatisfactory method of allowing a form of insurance to develop. The method is clearly incompatible with the theoretical framework of negligence liability, and ascribes to it an effect it was not intended to have. It is arbitrary in the sense that a plaintiff's chances of success in obtaining compensation will depend on the circumstances of his accident. Some accidents bespeak negligence and others do not. If strict liability is being smuggled in by the back door, it is irrational to deny or

---

17   Ibid. Cf *Colvilles Ltd v Devine* [1969] 1 WLR 475.
18   [1950] 1 All ER 392.
19   See *Moore v R Fox & Sons* [1956] 1 QB 596. See also the judgments of LORDS REID and DONOVAN in *Henderson v Henry E Jenkins & Sons and Evans* [1970] AC 282. LORD PEARSON refers to there being no change in the formal burden of proof. Ibid at 301.
20   [1988] RTR 298.
1   *Ballard v North British Rly Co* 1923 SC (HL) 43 at 54 (per LORD DUNEDIN).
2   [1969] 1 WLR 475.
3   Atiyah (1972) 35 MLR 337 at 344.
4   Millner *Negligence in Modern Law* (1967) pp 92–93; Fleming *Torts* pp 300–301.

grant compensation to a person because of the purely fortuitous circumstances in which he came by his injury.

The arbitrary and unjust method of compensating accident victims through the tort negligence system has led to many calls for reform. The most popular alternatives are a strict liability regime, or an insurance system of compensation.

(3)   FAULT AND ACCIDENT COMPENSATION[4a]

Accident compensation presents particular problems to any society. An accident causing personal injuries may have catastrophic consequences on a person's life and, in particular, on his ability to support himself. There are three ways in which the financial consequences of an accident may be ameliorated for its victim. The state may make provision through public insurance, the victim may take out insurance himself, or the person causing the accident can be made to compensate the victim. It is the latter with which the common law is concerned. Under what circumstances should liability be shifted from the victim to the person or organisation causing the accident? In order to answer this question, it is necessary to ask what purposes a liability rule is supposed to serve. The earliest purpose was to appease the victim and prevent him taking the law into his own hands. In the nineteenth century, ideas of individual moral responsibility provided a theoretical background to a system which had as its twin aims compensation and deterrence. Out of this came the principle that liability should be shifted when the accident causer was at fault.

(i)   Purposes of liability rules

(a)   *Appeasement*   One of the early purposes of both criminal and tort law was to provide a forum for the settlement of disputes arising from the infliction of injury. The victim was bought off by compensation which gave him satisfaction and vengeance on his aggressor.[5] Although we now accept this as self-evident, and that appeasement has received scant attention from theorists, it may still have some unconscious part to play in a court's decision to award compensation. The term 'demoralisation costs' has been coined in the context of public law compensation to describe the element in damages which commands respect in the community and pacifies any sense of outrage which might arise on the non-payment of damages.[6]

(b)   *Morality*[7]   Individual moral responsibility underpinned nineteenth-century fault-based tort liability. A person had to accept the responsibility for losses which fell upon him from risks which society inevitably created. If necessary, he could guard against these losses by taking out first party insurance. But where his losses were caused by another person's morally reprehensible conduct, then this was good reason for a rule shifting the loss to that person.

This kind of conduct was classified as fault and, while it may have been a useful theory in protecting fragile industries from the costs they imposed on others, it soon became divorced from any idea of moral fault. Fault has now become a socially convenient standard which is set for various activities. Where an activity is one backed by compulsory insurance, such as motor vehicle driving, the standard can be set so high as to preclude any moral standard. The morality theory failed to explain why some

---

4a   Atiyah *Accidents* ch 7.
5   Williams (1951) 4 CLP 137.
6   Michelman (1967) 80 HLR 1165 at 1217–1218. For its application to tort damages, see Ogus (1984) 37 CLP 29.
7   See Honore (1988) 104 LQR 530.

interests such as personal and property damage were protected by tort law, but not economic losses.

(c)   *Individual deterrence*   The idea of civil law as a deterrent appears to have been advanced by Bentham.[8] In its original form as individual deterrence, the infliction of a civil sanction would make the defendant change his behaviour and prevent him from causing a similar accident in the future. This aspect of civil law overlaps with criminal and public law, and the tide of academic and judicial opinion in the twentieth century has been against private civil law performing this function.

Part of this hostility comes from the statistical significance of motor vehicle accidents in modern tort law. The sheer volume of accidents in this area has perhaps led lawyers to think of the typical tort case as being a road accident causing personal injuries. It is precisely in this area that individual deterrence has the least effect. What is classed as negligence on the part of a driver may be unavoidable, even by those who are considered to be safe drivers.[9] If a person cannot avoid an error, he cannot be said to be deterred by a liability rule. The deterrent effect in driving cases is provided by the criminal law in the form of prosecutions for speed limit infringements, breathalyser tests etc. Even if the driver could accommodate his driving to this standard, he would be unlikely to be deterred by the civil sanction.[10] Any damages which are awarded against him will be paid by his insurance company, and his only loss will be his 'no-claims' bonus. A further reason for denying the deterrent effect of tort law is that damages are not assessed on the basis of the degree of culpability of the defendant. Instead, even the slightest degree of fault may give rise to enormous awards of damages where the extent of harm is great.

Outside of road accident cases, deterrence may have some part to play in torts such as defamation or nuisance, or in cases of professional negligence.

(d)   *Market or general deterrence*   English and American law has been primarily concerned with the compensation or loss distribution aspects of accident law. The deterrence argument returned to academic favour, mainly through United States' writings.[11] Market deterrence is not concerned with deterring individuals, but with reducing the costs of accidents to society by use of market mechanisms.[12] This approach involves: deciding what the accident costs of activities are and letting the market determine the degree to which, and the ways in which, activities are desired given such costs.[13]
Using this theory, decisions about loss allocation are made before the case is litigated. The cheapest 'cost-avoider', who is in a position to determine and minimise the accident costs of their activites, will bear the risk. If we can determine the cost of accidents and allocate them to the activities which cause them, the prices of activities will reflect their accident costs, and people, in deciding whether or not to engage in particular activities, will be influenced by the accident costs each particular activity involves.[14] The advantage of the theory is said to be that the market mechanism achieves the optimum allocation of resources, and that decisions are left to individual choice rather than being enforced by the state.

Two of Calabresi's examples may be taken to illustrate the theory. If a car manufacturer were to be charged the accident costs of cars in which seat belts were not installed, the

8   Williams (1951) 4 CLP 137.
9   *Driver Behaviour and Accident Involvement: Implications for Tort Liability* (1970) pp 177–178.
10   See Schwartz (1994) 42 UCLA Law Rev 377.
11   Calabresi *The Cost of Accidents* (1970). See also Posner (1972) 1 J Leg Studies 29, Schwartz (1978) 87 Yale LJ 697, and Atiyah *Accidents* ch 24.
12   See Atiyah *Accidents* ch 18.
13   Calabresi *The Costs of Accidents* (1970) p 69.
14   *Crisis in Car Insurance* (eds Keeton, O'Connell and McCord) (1968) pp 243–244.

price of cars without belts would reflect the accident costs. An individual would then have the choice of paying more for a car without seat belts, and a law compelling the installation of seat belts would be unnecessary. 'The question whether safety sells would be given a market answer ...'[15] Secondly, if the accident costs of teenage drivers were accurately reflected in the insurance premium they had to pay, then an individual teenage driver would have to decide whether driving at that price was worthwhile.

A number of problems are immediately apparent. For example, how can the cost of an activity be determined, and who is the cheapest cost-avoider? In the case of the installation of seat belts, it may be difficult to determine the cost of an accident, and it may not be possible to place an economic value on it. Factors such as the cost of calling out the emergency services and the cost of medical treatment to the victim have to be included. A second problem consists of identifying the 'activity' which causes the accident. Many defects or errors may cause a traffic accident. These might include the defective design of a car, a defective component produced by a supplier to the manufacturer, driver error, or the defective design of a road junction. In some accidents, all of these may be involved, in which case it is difficult to determine where the cost should be placed. At this stage, the theory clashes with English ideas of fault and morality. The cheapest 'cost-avoider' may be the injured person himself. His presence at the scene of the accident is a relevant factor even if, in legal terms, he was not at fault. If the victim is the cheapest 'cost-avoider', then, in economic terms, it may be efficient to allocate the risk to him, although this may ignore compensation objectives.

Further objections can be made to the theory in a society such as the United Kingdom, which operates a mixed economy. Activities may not be responsive to the price mechanism of the market in the same way that they are in a more private enterprise system such as the United States. Even where the market does operate freely, it is clear that not all activities are responsive to increased costs. It follows that allocating costs to such activities will not reduce the accident rate. Taxes imposed on motorists have not decreased the number of cars on the road. The reduction in the number of smokers is not due to increased taxation, but to public awareness of the health risks involved. This last point leads us to the final objection that a society might not wish all choices to be determined by the operation of the market. There are certain activities which we might want to prohibit outright, however much people might be willing to pay for them. Would, or should, a society sanction the sale of dangerous drugs such as heroin if the cost of its use were reflected in the price? From what we know of addiction, it is unlikely that a heroin user's habit would be responsive to pricing.

(e) *Standard of liability*[16] Calabresi's theory has led him to prefer strict liability to negligence. Once it has been decided to impose liability upon the cheapest cost avoider, this enterprise will be made to pay for the accident. The enterprise will be in the position of assuming, in advance, that it will have to pay, and there is an incentive to reduce the number of accidents.

When an accident does occur and litigation follows, two issues arise. It must be asked who is the cheapest cost-avoider. It is then necessary to determine whether such a person is in a position to avoid the costs of that particular accident. In Calabresi's view, this would avoid the arbitrary effects of a negligence rule. For example, if the costs of all accidents arising from the use of power drills were to be allocated to the manufacturer, litigation would be reduced, incentives for safe manufacture would exist and a climate of certainty would follow. However, such an approach would create no incentive for people to use products safely, and can be criticised on grounds of

15 Ibid.
16 Calabresi and Hirschoff (1972) 81 Yale LJ 1055 at 1060–1064.

efficiency.[17] This problem could be avoided by regarding the user as the cheapest cost-avoider in appropriate circumstances, but this might encourage the manufacturer to litigate more often. In such a case, the court would have to employ a balancing process which might be just as arbitrary as a negligence standard.

Further difficulties are created by the economist's view that people are rational utility-maximisers. At a corporate level, a product manufacturer might take the rational decision of making his product safer if it caused accidents, the costs of which he had to bear.[18] But it is most unlikely that this would apply to motor vehicle drivers, and the idea that motorists would avoid accidents worth avoiding has been described as 'fantastic'.[19]

(f)   *Compensation*   Generally, it has been accepted that a major aim of tort law is to compensate victims. There has been controversy over the type of loss which should be compensated, and how compensation should be achieved. Traditionally, tort law damages have been restricted to physical harm in the form of personal injury or damage to property. For the most part, a person who wished to recover economic losses would have to show the existence of a contract. It has been seen that this picture is no longer so simple. However, it still remains true that, in the majority of litigated cases where the plaintiff has been prejudiced by the defendant's conduct, the damage concerned is of a physical nature.

How compensation should be achieved has proved to be an even greater source of controversy. In physical damage cases, the common law has, generally, sought to shift losses by applying a negligence standard. The development of insurance and the discovery that costs could be passed on in higher prices for goods and services has meant that a finding of fault could result in a process of loss-spreading or loss-distribution. If an employer or product manufacturer is found to be negligent, a result is that the cost is passed on to the consumer in terms of higher prices, in order to reflect the higher insurance premiums the producer will have to pay.

Considerable criticism was directed at the use of a fault-based system to compensate the victims of accidents. In the twentieth century, the consensus of opinion seemed to favour a collective responsibility on the part of society for its members. This contrasts starkly with the individualism-based attitude of the nineteenth century, which helped to shape the fault-based system. From the time of Lloyd George's introduction of state pensions, the role of the state in the care of its citizens has grown, resulting in the flowering of welfarism in the period between 1945 and 1979. The provision of state benefits on the occurrence of economically disabling events, such as sickness and unemployment, sharply contrasted with the legal system's treatment of victims.

Three systems now co-exist to provide for accident victims. State or public insurance plays by far the biggest part in compensation. Direct payments may become due as a result of the injury, of which the most important are incapacity benefit,[20] sickness benefit or statutory sick pay.[1] These benefits are subject to contribution conditions under the National Insurance scheme. Where a person fails to qualify, he may be entitled to income support, which now provides the safety net of the welfare state. What distinguishes state payments from tort damages is that the former are payable on the occurrence of an event, according to need, whereas the latter are only payable on proof that a person caused an injury and was at fault in doing so.

---

17   Posner (1973) 2 J Leg Studies 205.
18   But doubt has been cast on whether corporations always act in a rational profit-maximising way. See Galbraith *The New Industrial State* (2nd edn, 1969).
19   Calabresi and Hirschoff (1972) 81 Yale LJ 1055 at 1057–1058.
20   See Atiyah *Accidents* ch 13.
1   See Atiyah *Accidents* ch 13.

The second system is that of private insurance. The most common form of this is life assurance, but policies may also cover fire damage,[2] loss or damage to household contents, personal accidents, motor vehicle accidents, loss of health and medical risks. These forms of insurance are referred to as first-party insurance, in order to distinguish them from third-party or liability insurance. The popularity of a particular type of insurance will depend on its expense, and the degree to which insurance is compulsory. Permanent health and personal accident insurance is expensive. The presence of the state scheme and occupational sick pay means that such policies are largely restricted to the self-employed, the well-off and those whose employers are prepared to provide health insurance benefits for their workforce. A distinction between first-party insurance and tort damages is that insurance is optional, and thereby gives freedom of choice and tends to promote premium competition between insurers. A person can decide for himself whether to bear the risk of a particular loss, or to spread it by means of insurance. As with state insurance, payment is triggered by the happening of an event rather than by the fault of the injurer.

The third system of compensation consists of an award of tort damages. In this case, a victim of harm must identify his injurer, prove that he is the cause of the injury and, usually, show that the injurer was negligent in doing so. In terms of the aim of compensation, the tort system can be criticised on the basis that it is very expensive to administer in comparison with a system of social security.[3] The tort system operates to the disadvantage of the plaintiff, both in terms of obtaining money[4] and the unpredictability of results. Because of this unpredictability, plaintiffs may be put under pressure to settle for less than they might have obtained had they successfully sued to judgment.[5]

There are two distinctions which can be made between social security payments and tort damages. First, social security payments tend to be paid periodically, whereas tort damages are paid in the form of a lump sum. Where a lump sum is paid, it is difficult to take account of inflation, to offset social security payments which might be made in the future, and to take account of any improvement or worsening of the plaintiff's medical condition. This last matter may be a significant factor in causing delays in settling some cases. An award of damages is supposed to put the plaintiff in the position he would have occupied had the accident not occurred, so far as this is possible through a monetary payment. In contrast, social security payments do not normally provide 'full' compensation.

(ii)   Proposals for reform

The multiplicity of systems of compensation for accident damage in England and the problems of double or non-compensation have led to demands for reform. At present, a distinction is drawn between accidents and natural diseases, and between those accidents caused by fault and those which are not. Where a person is injured by a fault-caused accident, he may be entitled to compensation from more than one system, and may be doubly compensated. A person who is the victim of a natural disease may receive no compensation at all. If the basis of compensation is perceived to be the victim's 'needs', then the existing systems can be seen to be arbitrary and unfair.

---

2   Fire insurance is widespread, but this may be because Building Societies and banks lending money under a mortgage insist on such insurance.
3   The Royal Commission on Civil Liability and Compensation for Personal Injury (1978) Cmnd 7054 (3 volumes) (hereafter called the Pearson Report) Vol 2, Table 116.
4   Pearson Report, Vol 2, Tables 114 and 115.
5   Pearson Report, Vol 2, Table 104.

Proposals for reform have generally taken the approach of either an extension of strict liability or an insurance system.

(a)   *Extension of strict liability*   At present, strict liability plays very little part in accident compensation, although there have been a number of proposals in favour of such a system, backed by insurance.[6] Under a strict liability regime, it would not be necessary to ask whose fault has caused an accident. Instead, the enquiry would be directed towards identifying the person who has generated the risk that an accident might occur. The risk creator would then be required to insure against that risk. If no one can be said to be responsible for a particular risk, the loss would have to fall on the victim, unless he is covered by first-party insurance.

This approach comes close to restating the problem without solving it. Why should the risk fall upon a particular person?[7] Liability could be based on causation, in which case a person whose activities normally cause accidents should incur the risk. It would then be necessary to ask whether a balancing mechanism should be provided, where the victim in a particular case happened to be the best risk-avoider. The person best able to take out insurance cover could be treated as the risk-bearer. As an alternative, some economic theory of efficiency could be applied. This would entail placing the risk where the most economically efficient allocation of resources could be obtained.[8]

(b)   *Insurance*[8a]   Insurance may be provided either privately or publicly. Examples of both systems already exist. Certain states in the United States operate no-fault schemes in relation to motor vehicle accidents. New Zealand operates a comprehensive public insurance scheme.

In those states of the United States[9] in which a private insurance system operates, the motorist is obliged to buy no-fault cover up to the amount required by the state legislation. Any person, including the driver, who is injured by the operation of the vehicle, may claim against the insurer for medical expenses, substitute services and loss of wages up to the statutory limit. The claims which may be made vary widely from state to state. The most generous, such as Michigan, place no time limit on loss of wages, but impose a maximum amount recoverable per month. Less generous schemes, such as South Carolina, impose a low maximum for all losses, thus removing small claims from the tort system. Non-pecuniary losses, such as pain and suffering, are not covered by any of the schemes and, in some states, no tort action is allowed for such losses unless the case passes a threshold test defined by the severity of the injury or medical expenses.

Since 1972, New Zealand[10] has operated an all-embracing public no-fault scheme. The scheme is run by the Accident Compensation Commission, and is financed from three sources. Injuries to the employed or self-employed are covered by a risk-rated levy on employers or the self-employed. Risks created by motor vehicle accidents are provided for by a levy on the use of such vehicles. All other accidents are provided for out of general taxation.

Compensation under the scheme is payable for personal injury by accident.[11] A victim makes a claim to the State Insurance Office. If they are satisfied, the victim will receive 80% of his pre-tax earnings up to the statutory limit, for loss of earnings and non-pecuniary loss up to the limit. The scheme originally provided for small payments for non-pecuniary

---

6   See Jolowicz [1968] CLJ 50 and *Accident Compensation After Pearson* (eds Allen, Bourn, Holyoak) (1979) p 33 et seq.
7   See Calabresi *The Cost of Accidents* (1970) and the discussion of 'market deterrence'.
8   Posner *Economic Analysis of Law* (1973).
8a Atiyah *The Damages Lottery* (Oxford: Hart, 1997).
9   Pearson Report, Vol 3, ch 2.
10 Pearson Report, Vol 3, ch 10; Harris (1974) 37 MLR 361.
11 This includes occupational disease.

loss but these were abolished in 1992 and replaced by independence allowance in cases of disability above 10%.

Rights of action in tort are abolished, as there can be no topping up from this source. It is difficult to draw accurate comparisons between this system, common law damages and a social security system. Under the New Zealand scheme, no one goes without compensation, but compensation is less generous than for a person who can prove fault and recover common law damages.

In the United Kingdom, the major appraisal of the way that compensation should be provided for personal injuries has come from the Pearson Commission.[12] The Commission was set up in response to the thalidomide drug tragedy, and was precluded from considering a comprehensive no-fault scheme by its terms of reference.[13] The major proposal was for the introduction of a no-fault scheme for motor vehicles, financed by a levy on petrol, providing compensation at rates equivalent to the industrial injuries scheme.[14] It was recommended that the right to sue for damages should remain, but that any payments received under the scheme should be offset against damages.

Some 188 proposals were made by the Commission, and it is doubtful if any reform can be traced directly to these. No action has been taken on the motor accident scheme by subsequent governments of various political persuasions. Some advance has been made in defective product law, with the introduction of the Consumer Protection Act 1987, but the impetus for this came from the EC. The Vaccine Damage Payments Act 1979 was prompted by the Report but is very different to proposals made in the Pearson Report.

(iii)   Justice

A school of thought between deterrence and compensation has emerged in response to the problems posed by the market deterrence theory. These problems are its complexity and the clash between justice and deterrence solutions. The new theories reject the application of economic theory, and emphasise the importance of 'corrective justice' in individual cases based on general standards of liability. The notion of justice is here based on justice between the parties without reference to the welfare of the community. The two leading exponents of this school are Professors Fletcher and Epstein.

Fletcher[15] puts forward a theory based on reciprocity of risks between parties. The party who subjects the other to the greater risk of injury must compensate him.[16] Where the risks are equal or reciprocal, no liability attaches,[17] and a balancing process is effected if the creator of a non-reciprocal risk can show that he created it through compulsion or ignorance.[18] This approach rejects foreseeability and reasonableness as criteria for assessing liability and in cases of non-reciprocal risks, is close to an 'act at peril' or strict liability standard.

Epstein[19] puts forward a complicated system of pleadings and presumptions not unlike the old writ system, and the standard of liability is strict. The system is based on causation, avoiding the 'but for' test. If the plaintiff can show that the defendant used direct force on him, frightened him, compelled another to use force or to frighten him, or exposed

---

12   See Fleming (1979) 42 MLR 249; *Accident Compensation After Pearson* (eds Allen, Bourn, Holyoak) (1979).
13   Pearson Report, Vol 1, ch 1.
14   Pearson Report, Vol 1, ch 18.
15   (1972) 85 Harv LR 537.
16   Ibid at 542.
17   Ibid.
18   Ibid at 553.
19   Epstein (1973) 2 J Leg Studies 151. See Simmons (1992) 51 CLJ 113.

the plaintiff to dangerous conditions, a presumption of liability in the plaintiff's favour is created. This could be rebutted by various defences such as assumption of risk or causation, and a reply to a defence could be given. For example, the defendant could deny intention to harm. The pleadings identify and narrow the issues at stake.

The system has the advantage of clearly identifying the issues involved and isolating them, thereby avoiding the notorious vagueness of tort tests such as that of reasonableness. What it does not do is to avoid the balancing of social interests, for which Epstein criticises negligence theory. In the case of a child trespasser, the child can create a presumption of liability once he shows he was harmed on the defendant's land. This presumption can be rebutted by showing that the child trespassed. The response would be that the plaintiff was an infant. But under Epstein's system, infancy is disregarded, with the result that the loss lies with the child. By ignoring infancy, a social judgment is made, in this case in favour of the autonomy of landowners.

The major distinction between Fletcher and Epstein is that, in cases where both parties are injured and the risks they have created are reciprocal, Fletcher would not impose liability. Epstein argues that 'even if two risks were reciprocal, it does not follow that neither party should have his action when injured.'[20]

The difficulty with both theories is that, for all their rigour, they do not seem to avoid the problems which negligence theory creates. Both attempt to avoid an individual case moving into the wider area of balancing social interest, and to confine the case to the precise issues between the parties, but neither succeeds in doing so.[1]

(iv)   Conclusion

The decision on liability rules and the choice of compensation systems for accident victims is ultimately a matter of political choice. Broadly speaking, a free market system will allow the market to determine where losses will fall and when compensation will be made. This is reflected in the faith of supporters of economic theories in allowing the market to perform this function. The results of such a system may seem harsh, but the advantage is said to be a reduction in the total costs of accidents achieved through individual choice rather than by state decree. A socialist system, on the other hand, would tend to lean in favour of an insurance system, in order to meet the needs of the victim. This has the advantage of ensuring some compensation is paid to all accident victims, and that compensation is not dependent on the sometimes arbitrary effect of legal liability rules. This approach is criticised, as there is said to be no incentive to avoid accidents. 'Social security "externalises" from activities that produce accidents, the costs of those accidents.'[2]

4.   STRICT LIABILITY

(1)   INTRODUCTION

Fault is a positive idea which tells us the pre-condition which must exist before liability can be imposed. Strict liability is a negative idea which informs us that liability can exist without fault, but it does not tell us on what liability is based. Thus, strict liability is not one possible alternative to liability for fault, but a collection of such alternatives.

The common thread which runs through the various forms of strict liability in the common law of obligations is that of risk allocation. Fault operates as a device for loss-

---

20   Epstein (1973) 2 J Leg Studies 151 at 165.
1   See also England (1980) 9 J Leg Studies 27; Cane (1982) 2 OJLS 30.
2   Calabresi (1967) 34 U Chic LR 239 at 243.

shifting and loss-spreading through a process of balancing different interests. Strict liability achieves the same ends by allocating the risk of damage in advance. The risk-bearer or risk-distributor is identified by law, and the requirement of fault on his part is eliminated. It may be difficult to identify who should be the risk-bearer. Furthermore, the criteria employed by the law to determine which activities should attract liability without fault may not be immediately obvious.

In order to determine who should be a risk-bearer, the traditional response is to look for a variety of voluntary conduct such as a contract, because the contract will identify the risk-bearer. The theory of the executory contract is based on rational forward planning, and the parties to the contract will identify risks and make provision for them. In cases where an obligation is imposed by law, for example tortious obligations, the dominant view in the nineteenth and twentieth centuries was against strict liability. In a few cases, strict tortious liability did exist in the nineteenth century, for example the *scienter* rule in respect of animals, but this was regarded as a relic of the past. New torts of strict liability, such as the rule in *Fletcher v Rylands*,[3] were viewed with hostility by most of the judiciary, and were gradually reduced to irrelevance.

The orderly and tidy picture that ought to have emerged was that contractual liability was strict, and tortious liability was based on fault. As life refuses to conform to the pedant's classifications, this was far from being the case. In contract law, the judiciary held back from imposing strict liability in contracts for services. The origins of this reluctance can perhaps be found in *Coggs v Barnard*.[4]

The concept of voluntary assumption of risks inherent in nineteenth-century classical contract theory has proved to be vulnerable to twentieth-century ideas of justice and inequality of bargaining power. The nineteenth-century paradigm contract involved two businessmen of equal bargaining power who would allocate the risks arising from the contract through contract terms. This idea of voluntary assumption of risk has also come under legislative and judicial attack. This is most obvious in relation to exclusion clauses in contracts. The effect of inequality of bargaining power and the use of standard form contracts was to allow the stronger party to shift risks onto the weaker one, which, given a free choice, he would not have accepted. The Unfair Contract Terms Act 1977 recognises this inequality, and intervenes to dictate where risks will fall in certain transactions.[5] Further evidence of legislative interference is shown by the Law Reform (Frustrated Contracts) Act 1943, which intervenes to allocate risk where a contract is frustrated. Finally, where the contract is silent as to risk allocation, the judge may imply a term into the contract. Although fictions have been employed to preserve the idea of freedom of choice, the judges have used the doctrine of frustration to allocate risk according to current notions of justice and policy.

It is now evident that large areas of promissory liability are not now subject to the free choice of the parties. In the case of businessmen dealing at arm's length, this freedom still exists and strict liability and allocation of risk by the contracting parties is still a reality. Elsewhere in contract law strict liability exists for different reasons. For example, the strict liability imposed on a seller in respect of the quality of the goods he supplies, can be justified, since he is able to pass on the cost up the chain of distribution to the manufacturer, unless the chain is broken by insolvency or an exclusion clause. In this case, the seller is the best risk-bearer, as he is easily identifiable by the plaintiff and the ultimate loss will fall on him.

3   (1865) 3 H & C 774 and see ch 29.
4   (1703) 2 Ld Ray 909, 92 ER 107.
5   See also the Unfair Terms in Consumer Contract Regulations 1999 SI 1999/2083. See ch 24.

In tort actions concerned with physical or economic harm, the dominant philosophy has been that of no liability without fault.[6] However, the appearance of fault-based liability has been distorted by the presence of a liability insurance market. Where a defendant is able to spread losses by means of insurance, the courts have been prepared to impose very high standards of care. For example, in the context of employers' liability, the presence of a compulsory insurance requirement has facilitated the development of an action for breach of statutory duty and the imposition of a high negligence standard. In the case of road traffic accidents, the standard required of a driver is set high precisely because the defendant should be insured and will not face the financial consequences of a large award of damages. Furthermore, in defective products cases, the use of *res ipsa loquitur* may place an almost impossible burden on a defendant to show that he was not negligent.[7]

The political move away from individualism towards collective responsibility which occurred in the twentieth century has created pressure to remove from the tort system liability involving personal injuries or death. Instead, such harm might be subjected to a form of compensation through insurance.[8] Collectivism, in the form of the consumer movement, has already forced reform in the area of products liability, and strict liability is now imposed by statute through the Consumer Protection Act 1987, although there is little doubt that without pressure from the EC, the Consumer Protection Act would not have been enacted.

(2)   STRICT LIABILITY AND MARKET EXCHANGES

Contract law has many functions, one of which is to control exchanges within a market economy. The exchange may take a number of forms. It may be simultaneous or executed. In such cases, legal control is confined to the quality of the thing exchanged. Alternatively the exchange may be over a period of time, or executory, and here, the law is concerned with the performance of the obligation by each party. Services, goods or labour may be exchanged.

The close link between the classical theory of contract and *laissez-faire* economics[9] dictated a judicial 'hands off' policy so far as contractual relations were concerned. The court's function was to act as an umpire and enforce the bargain made by the parties. Judicial activism was considered inappropriate, as it would tend to distort the market and constitute an infringement of personal liberty. A practical objection to intervention was the theory of marginal utility.[10] Under this theory, there is no such thing as an objectively valued price, and therefore, no way the court can substitute a price for that agreed by the parties. The classical theory dictated that, in the absence of duress, fraud, illegality or narrowly defined mistake, each person would be held to his bargain, however foolish or ill-judged it might seem to be.

Under this pure theory of contract, a risk will be assumed by the person on whom the loss will naturally fall, unless an express term of the contract shifts the loss onto another party. If Y contracts with X, a builder, to supply him with building materials and Y's supplier fails him, the loss will fall on Y, who will have to pay damages for non-delivery. If Y includes a contract term to the effect that he will be excused performance in the event of failure to obtain the goods, then any loss suffered will fall on X.

6   Cf cases of harm to a person's title to goods (conversion), or reputation (defamation) where liability is strict in the sense that, if the protected interest is interfered with, the defendant's intention or carelessness is irrelevant.
7   See *Grant v Australian Knitting Mills Ltd* [1936] AC 85.
8   See the Pearson Report.
9   See chs 2 and 3.
10   See ch 3.

Another way of looking at this issue is to say that contractual liability is strict, as the party who has assumed a risk must perform or pay damages. This differs from an enquiry into the standard of performance required from each party.

(3)   STRICT LIABILITY, RISK-BEARING AND INTERVENTION

The change in the nature of the relationship between the state and the governed, under which the state increasingly tended towards intervention in the late nineteenth and twentieth centuries, is sometimes described as a move from individualism to paternalism. Even as classical contract law and economic liberalism were at the height of their influence, the legislature was intervening to distort the market in the interests of fairness to weaker parties.[11] At first, this took the form of regulatory statutes in response to public or parliamentary outrage at shocking conditions in factories, mines or on migrant ships. The early twentieth century saw a more interventionist approach, with the introduction of pensions, control over prices and incomes, and sophisticated control of consumer sales and credit transactions.

This legislative lack of faith in an unrestrained market left a problem for the judiciary. In theory, they were non-interventionist, but in practice, they have exercised a considerable degree of control over the supposed autonomy of contracting parties. Difficulty is caused by the language used by the courts in an attempt to conceal the degree of their intervention.[12] Doctrine is strained and manipulated in a pretence of conforming with dogma, but a modern court has considerable scope to influence the distributive outcome of a contract, albeit with legislative assistance.[13]

One effect of the contract-tort dichotomy is that the judiciary has no need to conceal its interventionism when the case involves tortious issues. Nineteenth-century theory dictates that tortious obligations are imposed by law, and the courts have a free hand in defining the scope of such obligations. The present position in contract law is that a person is free to enter a contract,[14] but the terms of that contract and its performance are subject to judicial scrutiny.

(4)   THE CONTENT OF THE OBLIGATION

(i)   Gap-filling through implied terms[15]

The classical theory asserts that the content of a contract is for the parties to determine. In practice, there will be many gaps where the parties have not anticipated a particular event.[16] If the case is litigated, then the court may have to imply a term into the contract. These are known as terms implied in fact. But apart from these, the legal system has developed model contracts in the areas which involve recurring relationships and problems. Prominent among these are contracts of sale, hire, labour, leases, building works and carriage of goods. Where the contract is silent, then a term will be implied by law. This may be effected by statute or by precedent, and has nothing to do with the intentions of the parties.

---

11   See Atiyah *Rise and Fall* ch 16.
12   Similar problems were seen in negligence cases. See *Home Office v Dorset Yacht Co Ltd* [1970] AC 1004.
13   See *Collins* (1992) CLP 49.
14   Subject to persons under a disability such as some minors and the mentally ill.
15   See ch 7.
16   See Beale and Dugdale (1975) 2 Brit J Law & Society 45.

(ii)   Exclusion clauses

The primacy of the parties' intentions in classical theory is also illustrated by rules on exclusion clauses. Although the courts and the legislature might impose obligations on dominant contractual partners, it remained theoretically possible to contract out of these obligations by means of an express term. Thus, a seller of goods who wished to avoid the requirement that goods should be of merchantable quality, could do so by a suitably worded exclusion clause. The risk of the goods being defective was thereby returned to the buyer. There are numerous non-legal reasons why a dominant party would not wish to do this, not least being preservation of his business reputation. But a legal rule is designed to operate against the sharp practitioner, not the respectable businessman.

The response to contracting out can be viewed in two stages. First, the judiciary tended to construe exclusion clauses *contract proferentem*, that is against the party seeking to rely on the clause. By this method, the courts were able to retain the fiction of complying with the parties' intentions, but the weaker party could still be protected by means of a devious process of construction.[17]

The second stage consists of legislative interference with the contracting parties' powers of exclusion by insisting that exclusion clauses should not be unreasonable. An early example of this can be found in the Road Traffic Act 1960 which restricted the ability of owners of public service vehicles to exclude liability for death or bodily injury.[18] Reform was piecemeal, until the Unfair Contract Terms Act 1977 which imposes controls upon the use of exclusion clauses by persons acting in the course of a business, and the Unfair Terms in Consumer Contract Regulations 1994, which impose fairness requirements on all non-core terms in consumer contracts. The latter mark a change of emphasis as control is largely in the hands of the Office of Fair Trading and changes are usually made through negotiation rather than litigation.[19]

One effect of the Unfair Contract Terms Act is to complete the process of demolishing the notion of freedom of contract in cases of dependency. Not only are consumers protected, but it may also be the case that businessmen may find themselves in a position in which they must contract on the terms dictated by a stronger party.

(5)   PERFORMANCE OF THE OBLIGATION

Difficulties can arise apart from determining the content of the contractual obligation. Whatever the parties agreed, or thought they had agreed to, at the moment of responsibility may be affected by circumstances of which neither was then aware, or by a subsequent, unforeseen, change in the circumstances. The doctrines by which common law deals with such problems are those of common mistake and frustration. A further complication may arise, where the parties change the terms or conditions of performance of the obligation. These changes may not always be binding.[20]

(6)   STANDARD OF PERFORMANCE

The standard of contractual performance is usually thought to be strict, and it is true that many contractual duties are strict in the sense that the defendant may be liable where he is not at fault in failing to fully perform his contractual obligations.[1] In sale of

---

17   See ch 24.
18   Statutory controls in this area go back as far as 1854.
19   See ch 24.
20   See chs 13 and 23.
1   See *Congimex SARL v Continental Grain Export Corpn* [1979] 2 Lloyd's Rep 346. See also *Emanuel & Sons Ltd v Sammut* [1959] 2 Lloyd's Rep 629.

goods contracts, a retailer will be strictly liable for a failure to supply goods which are not of satisfactory quality or fit for their intended purpose.[2] This is the case even where a retailer could not have known of a defect because the produce is pre-packed in its defective state.[3] The justification for this is that the retailer can pass on the cost up the chain of distribution to the manufacturer, who is the person responsible for the defect.[4] Even in this area, there is some room for a standard of care to emerge. One of the factors used in determining whether goods are of satisfactory quality is the price.[5] If the item sold is a Range Rover costing £40,000, then a higher standard of quality will be imposed than in the case of a much cheaper car.[6]

The incongruities in a legal system which granted a remedy based on strict liability to a person with a contract but required others to prove fault were apparent for a long time, but this has been partly rectified by the Consumer Protection Act 1987, Part I, which imposes strict liability on the producers of defective products.[7]

Liability for defective products contrasts starkly with liability for defective services. Whether the action is framed in contract or in tort, the rule is that reasonable care must be exercised in the provision of a service.[8] The statutory rule is consistent with the fault-based liability imposed, at common law, on professional persons.[9] A result is, therefore, not guaranteed, although it is always possible, but improbable, that a person will expressly or impliedly contract to produce a specific result.[10] In the past, the distinction between goods and services has been capable of producing strange results. A garage which repairs a car is strictly liable for any parts which are supplied. But they are only liable for failure to take reasonable care in the installation of those parts. An anaesthetist who injects a patient with contaminated anaesthetic is only liable on proof of fault,[11] but a veterinary surgeon who innoculates cattle with contaminated serum is strictly liable.[12]

The reluctance to impose strict liability on suppliers of services appears to stem from their association with the professions and the court's refusal to accept that a doctor or lawyer could guarantee a result. This is difficult to reconcile with the idea that contract law is concerned with risk-allocation. Why should the professional person not accept the risk as does the retailer? Perhaps one answer is that the buck stops with the professional person or his insurer, whereas a retailer can pass the loss up the chain of distribution. But as liability insurance is also a method of loss-spreading, why is the distinction maintained?

A further anomaly arises in relation to statements. If a person makes a statement which is treated as a contractual term, he may be held strictly liable for a breach of that term. The maker guarantees the truth of the statement.[13] If the statement is a representation rather than a contractual term, the maker is merely under a duty to exercise reasonable

2   Sale of Goods Act 1979, s 14(2A) and (3).
3   *Frost v Aylesbury Dairy Co* [1905] 1 KB 608.
4   Cf *Lexmead (Basingstoke) Ltd v Lewis* [1982] AC 225, CA and HL.
5   Sale of Goods Act 1979, s 14(2A).
6   See *Rogers v Parish Ltd* [1987] 2 All ER 232; *Shine v General Guarantee Corpn Ltd* [1988] 1 All ER 911. And see also ch 25.
7   See ch 25.
8   Supply of Goods and Services Act 1982, s 13. See further ch 26.
9   *Clark v Kirby–Smith* [1964] Ch 506 (solicitors); *Bagot v Stevens Scanlon & Co Ltd* [1966] 1 QB 197 (architects); *Stafford v Conti Commodity Services* [1981] 1 All ER 691 (commodity brokers).
10 See *Hawkins v McGee* 84 NH 114, 146 A 641 (1929); *Greaves & Co (Contractors) Ltd v Baynham Meikle and Partners* [1975] 3 All ER 99. Cf *Thake v Maurice* [1986] QB 644, [1984] 2 All ER 513, and see further ch 26.
11 *Roe v Minister of Health* [1954] 2 QB 66.
12 *Dodd v Wilson* [1946] 2 All ER 691. And see also ch 26.
13 See *Bannerman v White* (1861) 10 CBNS 844. For an implied term based on reasonable care, see *Liverpool City Council v Irwin* [1977] AC 239.

care and to refrain from deceit.[14] The effect of this anomaly is somewhat reduced where the statement concerns the provision of information about a service, since reasonable care alone must be exercised. The court must interpret a contractual statement by asking what was promised.[15]

No coherent theme can be discovered in the decision whether to apply strict or fault-based liability. Paternalism, in the sense of helping the dependent party, and the presence of insurance may be two factors leading to a decision to impose strict liability. Balanced against these factors is the wish not to set the standard of liability so high as to discourage entry into transactions.

(7)   TORT AND STRICT LIABILITY

(i)   Introduction

The courts have been extremely reluctant to overtly impose strict liability in the traditional tortious areas of personal injuries and damage to property. In theory, the axiom of no liability without fault still holds good. It has already been observed that the fault requirement has been diluted in cases where one person is dependent on the care of another. Examples include the use of *res ipsa loquitur* in defective product cases and cases in which employees sue their employer for injuries suffered at work. Similar covert action is to be seen where a defendant is able to spread the loss through insurance. A high standard of care has been set for vehicle drivers and employers.

Despite this covert action, the fault principle is sometimes seen to stand in the way of an award of compensation in deserving cases, and has prompted legislative action. The effective campaign by parents of vaccine-damaged children led to the Vaccine Damage Payments Act 1979. The unprecedented risk posed to people by nuclear power stations led to the Nuclear Installations Act 1965. Pressure from the EC to harmonise product liability law within the Community has led to the Consumer Protection Act 1987, imposing a form of strict liability on producers of defective products for physical injury caused by their defective products.[16]

Despite the dominance of the fault principle in tort law, there are enclaves of strict liability to be found. No coherent theme links these areas and they represent useful historical relics and the common law's genius for pragmatism in the face of ideology. Some areas of strict liability are historic in origin, such as the rule on trespassing livestock.[17] It is unlikely that these would have escaped the attentions of a reform-minded nineteenth-century judiciary if some modern reason had not compelled their retention. In terms of risk-allocation, it makes sense to require the owners of livestock to fence in animals rather than to require their neighbours to fence them out.[18] The illogicality that this produces can be shown by the fact that a farmer will be strictly liable for his trespassing livestock, as will a zoo owner for an escaped tiger, but a road user injured in an accident caused by a stray dog must prove negligence. Far more damage is caused by stray dogs than by stray tigers or cattle.[19]

---

14   Misrepresentation Act 1967, s 2(1). See also *Esso Petroleum Co Ltd v Mardon* [1976] QB 801 and *Derry v Peek* (1889) 14 App Cas 337.
15   *Esso Petroleum Co Ltd v Mardon* [1976] QB 801.
16   Consumer Protection Act 1987, Part I.
17   See now Animals Act 1971, s 4.
18   Fleming *Introduction* p 153.
19   'Civil Liability for Animals' Law Com No 13 (1967) paras 36–38.

(ii) Interest protection and strict liability

Tort law originally tended not to concentrate upon the defendant's state of mind, instead, the nature of the plaintiff's interest seemed more important. Procedural changes in the nineteenth and twentieth centuries led to the development of fault-based liability, but the role of fault in the older, established tort actions is obscure. Indeed in some instances, there is liability without fault.

The tort of conversion protects a person's title to property. Conversion consists of the defendant's denial of the plaintiff's title. It is perfectly possible for the defendant to do this in good faith and without realising he is doing so. If a person buys a car from someone who has no title to it, the purchaser is guilty of conversion against the owner, even though the purchaser did not intend to deny the owner's title.[20]

A person's interest in his reputation is protected by the tort of defamation. In order to succeed, the plaintiff must show that the defendant published a defamatory statement which referred to him. It is not necessary for the plaintiff to show that the defendant was negligent in doing so, and it is no defence for the defendant to show that he took all reasonable care.

Interests in the peaceful use or enjoyment of land are protected by the tort of private nuisance. The plaintiff must prove that there has been an interference with the use or enjoyment of his land. To escape liability, the defendant must show that he acted reasonably. The modern obsession with negligence has led to a dispute over the meaning of the word 'reasonably', and whether nuisance is a fault-based tort or not. Certain branches of nuisance which developed in the twentieth century are similar to the tort of negligence. Where the nuisance is created by an act of nature or by a trespasser, the occupier is only liable on proof of fault.[1] Where the creator of the nuisance is sued personally, there is some confusion which has been caused by a tendency to consider the tort of nuisance as if it were a variety of negligence. Negligence is concerned with the way in which an activity is carried out. It is not a relevant issue to consider whether the activity can be carried on at all. In contrast, the tort of nuisance considers the activity of the defendant and it is asked whether or not that activity is reasonable. The fact that a person may have used all reasonable care in carrying out the activity does not provide a defence if the activity itself is unreasonable.[2]

(iii) Extra-hazardous activities

As a very rough rule of thumb, a strict liability rule may be applied to activities which are regarded as an undue threat or danger to society. The person who carries on the dangerous activity does so at his peril. What is a sufficient danger will vary from age to age. For example, in more primitive societies, the main dangers were seen to be fires and escaping animals. However, in a more industrialised society, the greatest danger was presented by industrial undertakings. But it did not follow that industry was subject to a strict liability rule in all cases, as this might have had the effect of crippling an emerging business with very heavy costs. However, some strict liability rules did emerge in the nineteenth century, particularly when it was recognised that liability insurance could be purchased which would enable enterprise to spread the cost of liability.

The most famous English attempt to impose enterprise liability can be found in *Rylands v Fletcher*,[3] in which the accumulation of water in large quantities for industrial purposes

---

20 *Hollins v Fowler* (1875) LR 7 HL 757.
1 See *Sedleigh-Denfield v O'Callaghan* [1940] AC 880; *Goldman v Hargrave* [1967] 1 AC 645; *Leakey v National Trust for Places of Historic Interest or Natural Beauty* [1980] 1 All ER 17.
2 See Atiyah *Accidents* ch 4.
3 (1868) LR 3 HL 330.

posed a threat to neighbouring landowners. In a brave departure from the emerging negligence principle, the House of Lords endorsed BLACKBURN J's principle of strict liability. To do this was not to suggest that it was negligent to embark on the operation in the first place. The public interest in the development of steam power precluded this. But it was apparent that even activities with a high social utility carried out with all reasonable care were still a risk. The person who would reap the benefit from the enterprise should also bear the risk of harm.

The *Rylands v Fletcher* doctrine has not proved a very hardy species faced with judicial ignorance of the principle and judicial hostility to strict liability. A combination of its application to normal, non-hazardous activities and a dilution of strict liability through use of concepts such as non-natural user and act of a stranger has made it rare for a plaintiff to succeed. In those cases where the rule is applied, it will invariably be found that the defendant is also guilty of negligence.[4]

At present, English law has no effective response to disasters caused by extra-hazardous activities. An injured person must undertake the usually onerous task of proving negligence against the operator. This problem has been recognised and discussed,[5] but no acceptable solution has been proposed. Part of the difficulty is that more injuries are caused by normal activities such as car driving than by abnormal ones such as mass production of chemicals. An abnormal activity is likely to be fairly closely controlled by regulatory statutes, and may therefore be safer than many normal activities. But when something does go wrong with an abnormal activity, the results can be catastrophic.[6] A further problem is the difficulty of deciding what is abnormal and what is a normal activity.

(iv) Loss spreading

The pragmatism of the common law can be seen in the concept of vicarious liability and the development of the action for breach of statutory duty. In both these areas, the fault principle has been abandoned and the risk of loss is placed on the person best able to insure against it. Ideology is jettisoned in favour of a practical solution, but lip service is still paid to the notion of fault.

The doctrine of vicarious liability makes an employer liable for the torts of an employee if committed in the course of his employment.[7] Its origins lie in the responsibility of a person for his servants. Where it is shown that the wrongdoer is an employee and that he was acting in the course of his employment, the employer will be liable without proof of any fault on his part. The employee also remains liable but, as the employer has the greater resources, the plaintiff will normally pursue him. As the employer is aware of his potential liability, he will insure himself against it and thereby spread the cost. As the accident will have occurred in pursuance of the enterprise's business, it is correct that it should be treated as a production cost.

To jurists wedded to the fault system, vicarious liability is unjust, and some would prefer a doctrine on the German lines, where the employer is only liable where he was at fault in selection or supervision of the employee.[8] In the case of industrial accidents, the judiciary has been able to develop the action for breach of statutory duty without fault forming a necessary requirement. Where a statute requires an employer to take

4   See *Cambridge Water Co v Eastern Counties Leather plc* [1994] AC 264 and see ch 29.
5   Law Commission Report on Civil Liability for Dangerous Things (1970) Law Com No 32; Pearson Report (1978) Cmnd 7054, Vol 1, ch 31.
6   This is the reason for the Nuclear Installations Act 1965.
7   See ch 27.
8   831 BGB. See Markesinis (1987) 103 LQR 354 at 358.

precautions for an employee's safety and the statute is broken resulting in injury, the employee may be able to sue for breach of statutory duty.[9] If the statutory duty is strict, the employer will be liable in the absence of negligence. The courts have been able to make this breach in the fault principle through the fiction that they are giving effect to the intention of Parliament.[10]

9   See ch 27.
10   See ch 27.

Section C

Remedies

CONTENTS

Chapter 13

Withholding contractual performance

1. INTRODUCTION

When faced with a breach of contract, a plaintiff will normally seek damages, an order for specific performance or an injunction. All of these remedies involve an enquiry into the nature of the defendant's conduct. However, it is also important for the plaintiff to know if he is still obliged to perform his contractual obligations despite the defendant's breach or any flaw in the making of the contract. In certain cases, the plaintiff will be entitled to withhold his performance of the contract and, if necessary, he may obtain a court order to this effect.

Two separate issues arise in the context of withholding performance. First, what was initially thought to be a valid contract may prove to be void or voidable. A contract may be void *ab initio* for reasons including a mistake at common law or by way of illegality. In such a case, there is no contract, and no performance is required. As there is no contract, no right to contractual damages can arise, and any monetary remedy sought must lie in the law of restitution.[1] A contract can be voidable in equity at the instance of the injured party, for example because it has been induced by fraud, misrepresentation or as the result of a mistake. In such a case, a contract exists, but it may be rescinded by the parties or the court. It can be said that these cases involve a flaw in the formation of the contract.

The second issue is that a valid contract may exist, but one of the parties has repudiated his obligations by means of an anticipatory breach of contract, or has rendered a seriously defective performance, amounting to a breach of a condition of the contract. In cases of defective performance, the innocent party may be discharged from further performance of his obligations. Two difficulties arise in this context. First, it must be decided which breaches will discharge further performance, and which will give rise to an action for damages. Secondly, the effect of the breach discharging performance must be determined. Before these issues can be considered, it is necessary to decide what is meant by the phrase contractual performance.

---

1   See chs 11 and 18.

2.   PERFORMANCE

Whether or not contractual obligations can be said to have been performed depends on the conditions of the contract. Conditions in this sense must be distinguished from conditions precedent to liability. In the case of a banker's commercial credit, the seller of goods may require the buyer to open a credit as a condition precedent to the formation of the contract. Alternatively, the provision of credit may be a term of the contract. In such a case, if the credit is not opened within the time stipulated, the seller will be discharged from his obligation to deliver due to a breach of a condition of the contract.[2] The condition here was a promissory condition rather than a condition precedent.

(1)   ORDER OF PERFORMANCE

A contract consists of a number of interrelated promises. It is necessary to determine the order in which these promises are to be performed. Three types of condition or covenant can be identified.[3] First, there may be an independent condition whereby a person is obliged to perform his side of the contract regardless of the breach of the other party. The common law has been reluctant to classify promises which relate to an important part of the bargain as independent. An example of such a condition is the duty of a tenant to pay rent despite the landlord's failure to comply with his covenant to repair the property.[4]

Secondly, there may be dependent conditions. In such a case, one party is not required to fulfil his contractual obligations until the other party has performed. The order of performance may be expressed by the terms of the contract,[5] or may be implied from the nature of the contract.[6] In a contract of employment, the employee must carry out his work before the employer is obliged to pay wages.[7] However, if the employer fails to provide work or tools, the employee may be able to claim his wages.[8] Where one party is obliged to perform first, he is, in effect, extending credit to the other. Where the courts have to determine the order of performance, it would appear that they decide which of the parties is the better credit risk. The origin of the 'work first, payment later' rule may be that the courts regarded the employer as the better credit risk.[9] In the United States, the performance of both parties is due simultaneously, unless one party's performance requires time for completion, or is contractually due at an earlier time.[10] This is thought to represent the English position.[11]

A third type of condition requires simultaneous performance of both parties' obligations. In these cases, neither party is able to sue, unless he has performed or is ready to perform his obligations. In a sale of goods contract, delivery and payment are due simultaneously, unless the contract provides otherwise.[12]

---

2   *Trans Trust SPRL v Danubian Trading Co Ltd* [1952] 2 QB 297.
3   *Kingston v Preston* (1773) 99 ER at 437 (per LORD MANSFIELD).
4   *Taylor v Webb* [1937] 2 KB 283. Cf *British Anzani (Felixstowe) Ltd v International Management (UK) Ltd* [1980] QB 137.
5   *Société Générale de Paris v Milders* (1883) 49 LT 55.
6   *Trans Trust SPRL v Danubian Trading Co Ltd* [1952] 2 QB 297.
7   *Wiluszynski v Tower Hamlets London Borough Council* [1989] IRLR 259; *Miles v Wakefield Metropolitan District Council* [1987] AC 539.
8   *Morton v Lamb* (1797) 7 Term Rep 125; *Cresswell v Board of Inland Revenue* [1984] ICR 508.
9   Patterson (1942) Columbia LR 903 at 917–920.
10   *American Restatement, Contracts* (2d) § 259.
11   Beale *Remedies for Breach of Contract* (1980) pp 28–29.
12   Sale of Goods Act 1979, s 28.

The rules on order of performance are mostly of common sense. Unless the contract stipulates otherwise, they give the court the opportunity to protect the weaker party by requiring the stronger party to perform first. In *Bentworth Finance Ltd v Lubert*,[13] a consumer debtor avoided liability for default in repayment, as the creditor was obliged to give him legal documents showing a change of ownership before the duty to pay arose.

(2) ENTIRE AND SEVERABLE OBLIGATIONS

The contract may expressly provide, or be construed by the court to provide, that A must perform the obligation completely before B is obliged to perform. In these cases, A's obligation is said to be entire. Alternatively, A's obligation may be sub-divided and, as each part of the total obligation is completed, B's obligation becomes due. In such a case, the obligations of the parties are described as severable.

The distinction between entire and severable obligations raises problems with both the order of performance and with the issue of defective performance. If A renders a defective performance and subsequently demands payment, whether or not B is obliged to pay will depend on whether A's obligation is entire or severable. If it is an entire obligation, B will not be required to pay. If it is a severable obligation, A may be able to claim payment for those parts of the work correctly performed.

Sale of goods contracts, for the most part, consist of entire obligations. If the seller does not deliver the contracted quantity of goods, the buyer may reject the entire consignment.[14] If the buyer accepts short delivery, he must pay at the contract rate for that which he has received. In some instances, the principle *de minimis non curat lex* may apply, and trivial discrepancies will be ignored.[15]

Where the contract is one for the delivery of goods by instalment and each instalment is to be separately paid for, the obligation is severable. Short delivery will not justify a refusal to accept future instalments. The strictness of the rule in most sale of goods cases may be explained on the ground that, since delivery and payment are simultaneous obligations, no extension of credit by either party is required.[16]

If the court holds an obligation to be entire, this may have a harsh effect on the plaintiff. In *Cutter v Powell*,[17] a sailor was contracted to assist in the working of a ship from Jamaica to Liverpool. He died two-thirds of the way through the voyage. The obligation was found to be entire, and the sailor's estate was not entitled to collect anything for his services. It may be significant that the contract provided for payment 'provided the sailor does his duty as second mate in the said ship from Jamaica to Liverpool', and that the wages were 30 guineas instead of the normal £8. On the facts, it was held that the sailor bore the risk of not completing the voyage. In *Taylor v Laird*,[18] a captain employed at a wage of £80 per month was entitled to claim payment for the months he worked before he gave up his command in the middle of a voyage. In some instances, the Apportionment Act 1870 may provide a solution. The Act provides that periodical payments in the nature of income are to be considered to accrue on a day-to-day basis, and may be apportioned accordingly.[19] However, the Act has no application

---

13 [1968] 1 QB 680, [1967] 2 All ER 810.
14 Sale of Goods Act 1979, s 30. See also *Re Moore and Co and Landauer and Co's Arbitration* [1921] 2 KB 519. But see *Reardon Smith Line Ltd v Hansen-Tangen* [1976] 1 WLR 989 at 998 (per LORD WILBERFORCE).
15 See *Shipton, Anderson & Co v Weil Bros Ltd* [1912] 1 KB 574. Cf *Arcos v Ronaasen & Sons* [1933] AC 470.
16 Treitel (1967) 30 MLR 139.
17 (1795) 6 Term Rep 320.
18 (1856) 1 H & N 266.
19 Apportionment Act 1870, s 2.

if it is expressly stated that apportionment is not to be permitted.[20] For this reason, the Act would not apply to a case like *Cutter v Powell*,[1] as it was agreed that a lump sum would be paid for a specific piece of work.

Cases involving payment for building work or other services also raise problems. If A undertakes to perform work for B and the obligation is entire, B need make no payment for the work until it is completed. If A fails to complete, B needs only to pay for a benefit which he could have returned but chose to keep.

In *Sumpter v Hedges*,[2] a builder performed £333's worth of a £565 building contract and subsequently abandoned the contract. The defendant finished the buildings himself with materials left on site. The builder could only recover in respect of the materials left on site. He could recover nothing in respect of his labour, which could not be accepted or rejected. A building contract may be worded so as to produce severable obligations on the part of the builder. Large building contracts will frequently provide for a valuation of and payment for work at different stages. Small building contracts may use phrases such as 'net cash as the work proceeds and balance on completion'. This phrase renders the obligation severable.[3]

A distinction is drawn between single obligations in a contract, which may be entire, and the contract as a whole, which may not impose entire obligations. This distinction helps to explain building cases in which the builder has completed the work in a defective manner. The obligation to complete, the obligation as to quantity, may be entire, but the obligation to provide a building of the required quality is not necessarily so.[4] However, it would appear that the courts will overlook minor omissions in the work and order payment, subject to a deduction in respect of defective performance.[5]

In practice, problems presented by such cases fall into two groups. In the case of large building contracts, the parties will be independently advised, and they will be able to expressly provide for such matters in the contract. Risks may be allocated by the contract, and appropriate insurance obtained. A different problem is presented by a householder employing a builder. If the work is not finished or is shoddily performed, the only effective sanction may be to demand completion or refuse payment.[6]

The principles so far stated apply to bilateral contracts, where the parties are usually dependent upon each other for the successful completion of the contract. The objective of the principles would appear to be to encourage co-operation in performance. In the case of unilateral contracts, the promisee must perform his side of the contract before any obligation to perform falls on the promisor.[7]

Where one party is in a stronger bargaining position, he may be able to impose advantageous terms as to performance. For example, he may stipulate that he is not required to perform until the obligations of the other party are completed. In such a case, the weaker party has extended credit to the stronger party. In instances of this kind, legislation may subject the terms imposed by the stronger party to a requirement of reasonableness.[8]

20   Ibid, s 7.
1   (1795) 6 Term Rep 320.
2   [1898] 1 QB 673.
3   *Hoenig v Isaacs* [1952] 2 All ER 176. See also *Dakin & Co Ltd v Lee* [1916] 1 KB 566; *Bolton v Mahadeva* [1972] 2 All ER 1322.
4   Ibid.
5   *Dakin & Co Ltd v Lee* [1916] 1 KB 566.
6   See also Law Commission No 121 (1983).
7   *Carlill v Carbolic Smoke Ball Co* [1893] 1 QB 256; *United Dominions Trust (Commercial) Ltd v Eagle Aircraft Services Ltd* [1968] 1 All ER 104.
8   See Unfair Contract Terms Act 1977, s 3(2)(b)(ii) and Unfair Terms in Consumer Contract Regulations 1999.

(3)   VARIATION OF THE OBLIGATION

Where performance of a contract runs over a period of time, it may be necessary to adjust or alter the original arrangements in the light of subsequent developments. The original contract may have made provision for alteration, but it is more likely that there is no such provision.[9]

The law must attempt to enable adjustments to be made smoothly and easily, but guard against the risk of one party exploiting the other to force an alteration in his favour. As the time for performance approaches, one party may be very heavily dependent on the performance of the other. If a ship, the subject of a construction contract, were to be urgently required by the buyer at the date fixed for completion, the seller could extort a higher price in return for completion on time.

It would appear that most adjustments are made outside the legal framework.[10] A party may well have strong commercial reasons for accepting a change in performance which may be disadvantageous to him in the short term. For example, if X takes a franchise to sell Y's widgets over a ten-year period, paying a monthly fee to Y, and X subsequently suffers temporary financial problems, it may suit Y to accept a reduced fee for a period of time. If he insists on his full contractual rights and terminates the franchise, he will then have the expense and trouble of finding a replacement for X.

It may be questioned whether common law rules facilitate commercial co-operation in cases of this kind. The classical view of variation (or 'waiver of breach') was to apply the same rules that were required for formation of a contract. The parties had to reach an agreement which was either in deed form or was supported by consideration.[11] The requirement of consideration was said to be justified so as to prevent unfair variations. It would prevent a debtor from taking advantage of his creditor when the creditor had agreed to accept less than the sum owed,[12] as payment of less could never be consideration for the full amount. This solution ignored the possibility that it may be to the creditor's advantage to accept less than the full debt. He may wish to take what he can get. A number of solutions were devised to cope with this problem, and consideration was said to exist where payment was in kind, or made at an earlier date than was provided by the contract. It is clear that modern law no longer applies these techniques. Agreement is not necessary, and the doctrine of estoppel allows variations unsupported by consideration. The courts will now give effect to variations which are not brought about by unfair pressure.[13] Unfair pressure is handled through the doctrines of undue influence and duress, particularly economic duress.[14]

A case illustrating both approaches is *D & C Builders v Rees*.[15] The builders did work for Mrs Rees, who owed them £482. Knowing that the builders were in financial difficulties, Mrs Rees offered £300 in full settlement, or nothing at all. The builders agreed to this, accepted a cheque and later successfully sued for the balance. On classic grounds, the decision is defensible under the rule in *Foakes v Beer*,[16] and because payment by cheque is not a sufficiently different mode of payment to constitute consideration. The modern approach is shown by LORD DENNING, who stated that the agreement to

9   Beale and Dugdale (1975) 2 Brit J of Law and Society 45.
10   Ibid.
11   For an alleged variation which failed for want of consideration, see *Stilk v Myrick* (1809) 2 Camp 317.
12   *Foakes v Beer* (1884) 9 App Cas 605, [1881–5] All ER Rep 106. See also *D & C Builders v Rees* [1966] 2 QB 617.
13   See *Williams v Roffey Bros & Nicholls (Contractors) Ltd* [1990] 1 All ER 512.
14   See *North Ocean Shipping Co Ltd v Hyundai Construction Co Ltd, The Atlantic Baron* [1978] 3 All ER 1170; *Pao On v Lau Yiu Long* [1980] AC 614. See also chs 6 and 24.
15   [1966] 2 QB 617.
16   (1884) 9 App Cas 605, [1881–5] All ER Rep 106.

accept less was destroyed by the debtor's intimidation in threatening to pay nothing. In more modern terms, this could be described as economic duress.

The decline of the importance of agreement in determining an effective variation is shown by *The Hannah Blumenthal*.[17] The case concerned a contract for the sale of a ship. Any dispute arising out of the sale was to be settled by arbitration. The buyers complained that the ship's engines were defective, and started proceedings under the arbitration clause in 1972. In 1980, the buyers proposed fixing a date for arbitration, but the sellers argued that the arbitration agreement was discharged on several grounds, including that of rescission. The House of Lords held that the arbitration would be abandoned if the sellers had acted in reliance on an express or inferred representation from the buyers to this effect. The representation could be inferred from the buyers' conduct, including inactivity. On the facts, it was held that there was no such inference as, by 1980, the sellers' solicitors were still trying to trace witnesses for the arbitration.[18]

The major contribution of estoppel in English contract law is in the area of variation of obligations.[19] The modern starting point for this development is *Central London Property Trust Ltd v High Trees House Ltd*.[20] The landlords agreed to take a reduction in rent to take account of wartime conditions when the tenants were unable to let the properties subject to the lease. It was stated, obiter, by DENNING J that the landlords could not recover the full rent during the war years, as the tenants had acted in reliance on the promise.

This principle has been developed by subsequent case law, and two main problems have emerged. The first is whether it is necessary for the promisee to have detrimentally relied on the promise. No clear position has emerged on this question due to the difficulties of distinguishing detriment from consideration. It would appear that any change of position on the part of the promisee or a failure by the promisee to take action for his own protection will be sufficient.[1] Secondly, it is not clear whether the effect of the representation is to suspend or to extinguish the promisor's rights. The question is somewhat illusory as is shown by *Charles Rickards Ltd v Oppenheim*.[2] In 1947, the defendant ordered a Rolls Royce chassis from the plaintiffs for delivery on a specified date. The work was not complete by that date, and the defendant agreed to wait another three months, by which time the chassis was still not complete. The defendant then gave notice that, if the chassis were not complete within four weeks, he would cancel, which he did. It was held that the defendant had waived his right to insist on delivery by the original contract date but had made time the essence of the contract by his notice requiring delivery within four weeks. The waiver operated to suspend the defendant's right to delivery by the contract date but, at the same time, it extinguished this right and replaced it with another.

The Privy Council in *Ajayi v RT Briscoe (Nigeria) Ltd*[3] has given guidance on this question. The promisor can revoke his promise and resume his original position, unless the promisee is unable to resume his original position.

---

17   [1983] 1 AC 854, [1983] 1 All ER 34.
18   See also ch 23.
19   See ch 6.
20   [1947] KB 130.
1   *W J Alan & Co Ltd v El Nasr Export and Import Co* [1972] 2 All ER 127; *Brikom Investments Ltd v Carr* [1979] 2 All ER 753. See further ch 6.
2   [1950] 1 All ER 420.
3   [1964] 3 All ER 556.

3. CONTRACTUAL TERMINATION AND THE RIGHT TO WITHHOLD PERFORMANCE

When one party is in breach of contract, the other party will always have the right to sue for damages. The innocent party may still be obliged to perform his obligations, as his failure to do so may constitute a breach of contract. However, he will be discharged from further performance where the guilty party has repudiated the contract, or is in breach of a condition of the contract.

(1) REPUDIATION

Where a party intimates by his words or conduct that he does not intend to perform his future contractual obligations, he is said to repudiate the contract. This is also described as an anticipatory breach of contract. The repudiation may be express, as in *Hochster v De La Tour*,[4] where the defendant agreed to employ the plaintiff as a courier on a tour commencing on 1 June but, in May, he indicated that he had changed his mind. Alternatively, the repudiation may be implied. In *Frost v Knight*,[5] the defendant agreed to marry the plaintiff when his father died. He broke off the engagement during his father's lifetime, and was held to be in breach of contract.

Where the contract is simple, consisting of one major obligation on each side, there is no great difficulty in determining whether the contract has been repudiated. In more complex transactions where a party has repudiated one or more of a series of obligations, the court must decide whether the innocent party has been substantially deprived of an adequate performance. The court will take into account the ratio which the breach bears to overall performance, and the degree of uncertainty which is created as to future performance. In *Decro-Wall International SA v Practitioners in Marketing Ltd*,[6] a company was appointed sole concessionaires for United Kingdom sales of a French company's product. The concessionaires frequently made late payments under the contract, and the French company appointed someone else as their concessionaire. It was held that termination of the contract was not justified, as the delays in payment were only slight and gave no reason to doubt that payment would be made. Termination was unnecessary, as damages were a perfectly adequate remedy.

Similar principles apply where the contract is to be performed in stages. For example, in an instalment contract, if there is a breach of contract relating to one instalment, the court must decide if it justifies termination of the whole contract. If a seller fails to deliver 1½ tons of a 100 ton order, the ratio which the breach bears to the contract as a whole is small, and will not lead to the conclusion that the breach is likely to be repeated.[7] However, a breach in relation to one instalment may be treated, occasionally, as a repudiation of the whole contract.[8]

A further problem may arise where a party takes steps which he believes are justified by the terms of the contract, but which amount to a breach of the contract. It must be decided whether the other party can treat this conduct as repudiation. In *Federal Commerce and Navigation Co Ltd v Molena Alpha Inc*,[9] a dispute arose between the owners of a ship and the plaintiff time charterers. The charterers had deducted the amount of a counterclaim against the owners from their periodic payments for hire. The owners had advised

---

4   (1853) 2 E & B 678.
5   (1872) LR 7 Exch 111. See now the Law Reform (Miscellaneous Provisions) Act 1970, s 1.
6   [1971] 1 WLR 361.
7   *Maple Flock Co Ltd v Universal Furniture Products (Wembley) Ltd* [1934] 1 KB 148. See also Sale of Goods Act 1979, s 31(2).
8   *Hong Kong Fir Shipping Co Ltd v Kawasaki Kisen Kaisha Ltd* [1962] 2 QB 26.
9   [1979] AC 757.

the ship's master not to issue freight pre-paid bills of lading, and had required that any future bills of lading be endorsed with the terms of the charterparty. The effect of this action was to prevent the charterers operating the ship, and the charterers claimed that the contract had been repudiated. This view was upheld by the House of Lords, who held that the seriously coercive effect of the owners' actions outweighed the fact that the owners believed they were entitled to take these steps. This decision stood, despite the fact that the owners still wished to continue with the contract, and had attempted to have the deductions dispute resolved by way of arbitration.

In *Woodar Investment Development Ltd v Wimpey Construction (UK) Ltd*,[10] a contract for the sale of land entitled the purchasers to withdraw from the contract in the event of a statutory authority commencing proceedings for compulsory purchase of the land. In fact, they were not entitled to do so, but it was held by a majority of the House of Lords that the purchaser's conduct did not amount to repudiation. Where a party purported to act under a term of the contract, the action had to be totally abusive or lacking in good faith in order to amount to a repudiation.[11] The decision is helpful, as it enables the parties to a contract to negotiate a settlement to their dispute. The minority view that the purchasers' conduct amounted to repudiation would have meant that, where a person mistakenly asserts what he believes to be his contractual rights, the other party is entitled to terminate the contract.

The two cases can be distinguished. In the *Molena Alpha*, there was a short interval between the alleged repudiatory conduct and performance under pressure. In *Woodar v Wimpey*, there was a considerable lapse of time between the purchasers' conduct and the date of performance. This enabled the parties to seek a resolution of the dispute. Both parties in *Woodar v Wimpey* were prepared to accept the decision of the court and wished to proceed with the contract, even if a decision in favour of the vendor was entered. In contrast, in the *Molena Alpha*, the charterers were reluctant, in any event, to proceed with the contract.

(2)   BREACH OF CONDITION

When a contract term is broken, it is important to be aware of the effect of the breach. It may give rise to the right to sue for damages to compensate for the effect of the breach, or it may entitle a person to treat the contract as discharged. Competing policy objectives may dictate which solution is most appropriate. The judicial quest for certainty in business transactions may insist that the parties should be aware of their contractual rights, with the result that minor breaches should not lead to a refusal to perform by the innocent party. However, a party who is legally well advised will be able to draft the contract in such a way as to enable him to avoid liability, if it so suits him, in the event of a minor breach by the other party.

The classical theory divides all contract terms into conditions, breach of which gives rise to a right to repudiate and warranties breach of which only gives rise to a right to damages. Applying the consensus theory, it should be open to the parties to decide for themselves what weight to give to a particular term. However, in practice, the courts have shown a willingness to intervene and emphasise the need for the parties to co-operate in performing the contract. In *L Schuler AG v Wickman Machine Tool Sales Ltd*,[12] the House of Lords refused to allow the designation of a term as a condition to give rise to the right to treat the contract as discharged. This would have meant that the failure of a party to carry out one visit out of 1,400 over four and a half years would

---

10   [1980] 1 All ER 571, [1980] 1 WLR 277.
11   Ibid at 576 (per LORD WILBERFORCE).
12   [1974] AC 235, [1973] 2 All ER 39.

entitle the other party to terminate the contract. However, the House of Lords has also stressed the need for certainty where the parties bargain at arms length, such as ship owners and charterers, in order that the parties to a contract can receive clear and confident legal advice.[13]

Given that the courts will not allow the parties to determine for themselves the weight to be attached to a term, how is this decided? In some cases, statute will dictate whether a term is a condition or a warranty.[14] However, the flexible approach of the common law has now to some extent been adopted by statute. If there is a slight breach of the implied terms of quality or quantity in a sale of goods contract and it would be unreasonable to reject them, the court may regard the breach as only giving rise to a right to damages.[15] This does not apply to consumer purchases and consumers will still be able to reject goods for minor defects.[16]

Otherwise two tests compete at common law. The first is derived from classical theory, under which the court looks at the contract at the time it is made, and infers the possible consequences of the breach.[17] The second test is to look at the effect of the breach rather than at the quality of the term broken. This is a more flexible approach, and means that the court can refrain from labelling a term as a condition or warranty and, instead, refer to it as an 'intermediate' or 'innominate' term.[18]

The use of 'innominate' terms allows the court to respect the parties' wishes where this produces a reasonable result. But it also allows intervention where a party is likely to be seriously prejudiced by not having the right to terminate, for example, where he needs to go into the market immediately to purchase a substitute, or where termination would be unfair to the party in breach, when the seriousness of the breach is weighed against its effect on the contract as a whole.

This kind of balancing process can be seen at work in the rules on failure to perform contractual obligations by a stipulated time. In *United Scientific Holdings Ltd v Burnley Borough Council*,[19] the House of Lords held that a failure to perform on time would not be treated as a breach of condition unless this was expressly stipulated by the contract,[20] or the nature of the subject matter of the contract (such as perishable goods), or the surrounding circumstances showed that time was to be of the essence. However, it would be open to a party subjected to unreasonable delay to give notice thereby making time of the essence once more.[1]

(3)   THE EFFECT OF REPUDIATION AND BREACHES OF CONDITION

The innocent party may waive the breach and choose to treat the contract as still remaining in force. In order to do this, he must have full knowledge of the facts. The contract remains in existence, and each party has the right to sue for damages for past and future breaches of contract. If the innocent party adopts this course, it may be that a supervening event has the effect of frustrating the contract, thereby relieving the defaulting party from all liability. In *Avery v Bowden*,[2] a chartered ship was required to

---

13   *Awilco A/S v Fulvia SpA di Navigazione, The Chikuma* [1981] 1 All ER 652, 658-9, per LORD BRIDGE.
14   See Sale of Goods Act 1979.
15   Sale of Goods Act 1979, s 15A(1) as amended by Sale and Supply of Goods Act 1994, s 4.
16   See Law Commission No 160, Cm 137 (1987).
17   See *Mihalis Angelos* [1971] 1 QB 164; see also *Bunge Corpn v Tradax SA* [1980] 1 Lloyd's Rep 294.
18   See *Hong Kong Fir Shipping Co Ltd v Kawasaki Kisen Kaisha Ltd* [1962] 1 All ER 474; see also *Cehave NV v Bremer Handelsgesellschaft MbH, The Hansa Nord* [1975] 3 All ER 739.
19   [1978] AC 904.
20   See *Union Eagle Ltd v Golden Achievement Ltd* [1997] AC 514.
1   See *Charles Rickards Ltd v Oppenheim* [1950] 1 KB 616.
2   (1855) 5 E & B 714.

carry a cargo from Odessa. Some time before the date for performance, the master was informed that no cargo would be available. The master decided to wait until the date of performance specified in the contract, but, before that date, the Crimean War broke out, thereby frustrating the contract.

Alternatively, the decision to treat the contract as valid can work to the advantage of the party not in breach. For example, in a sale of goods contract, if the repudiation is not accepted, there is no breach of contract, accordingly damages cannot be awarded at that stage, but may be awarded when performance is due. If the market price of goods of the type contracted for is rising, this will be to the buyer's advantage. However, if the market price of goods of that type is in decline, the buyer would be best advised to accept the repudiation and treat the contract as being at an end.

A further consequence of keeping the contract alive is that the original innocent party may subsequently be in breach himself, thus giving the other party the option to terminate. In *Fercometal SARL v Mediterranean Shipping Co SA (The Simona)*[3] a charterparty stated that if a ship was not ready to load by 9 July the charterers had the option of cancelling the contract. Before 9 July the charterer wrongfully attempted to repudiate the contract. The owners treated the contract as still alive but the ship was not ready to load on 9 July. The charterers cancelled the contract on the basis of the express right in the contract. The House of Lords upheld this action as the owner had kept the contract alive for the benefit of both parties.

Where the innocent party chooses to accept the repudiation or breach of condition, there is some dispute as to the effect of this on the contract. One view is that the contract is rescinded or discharged by the breach.[4] One reason for preferring this view is that an exclusion clause may be disposed of along with the other terms of the contract, if the court so desires. However, this approach may not be necessary in the light of legislation controlling exclusion clauses.

The general principles were stated by Dixon J in *McDonald v Dennys Lascelles Ltd*[5]

> When a party to a simple contract, upon a breach by the other contracting party of a condition of the contract, elects to treat the contract as no longer binding on him, the contract is not rescinded as from the beginning. Both parties are discharged from further performance of the contract, but rights are not divested or discharged which have already been unconditionally acquired. Rights and obligations which arise from partial execution of the contract and causes of action which have accrued from its breach alike continue unaffected.[6]

On this view the contract remains intact, but the innocent party is discharged from further performance. In *Heyman v Darwins Ltd*,[7] it was said that, by accepting the repudiation, the innocent party is discharged from further performance, and may bring an action for damages, but the contract is not rescinded.[8] The point was put in *Moschi v Lep Air Services Ltd*[9]

> When a contract is brought to an end by repudiation accepted by the other party all the obligations in the contract come to an end and they are replaced by operation of law by an obligation to pay damages. The damages are assessed by reference to the old obligations but the old obligations no longer exist as old obligations. Were it otherwise there would be

---

3   [1988] 2 All ER 742.
4   *Suisse Atlantique Société d'Armement Maritime SA v NV Rotterdamsche Kolen Centrale* [1967] 1 AC 361 at 398; *Moschi v Lep Air Services Ltd* [1973] AC 331 at 345–346 (per LORD REID).
5   (1933) 48 CLR 457, 476–7.
6   Approved by the House of Lords in *Johnson v Agnew* [1980] AC 367, 396, per LORD WILBERFORCE.
7   [1942] AC 356.
8   Ibid at 399 (per LORD PORTER).
9   [1973] AC 331 (the headnote).

in existence simultaneously two obligations, one to perform the contract and the other to pay damages.[10]

Some confusion exists over the use of the word rescission. In an action for rescission, in its properly understood sense, no action for damages under the contract will lie. Thus, if a contract is rescinded by reason of a misrepresentation, the only entitlement to damages lies under the Misrepresentation Act 1967. However, where there has been a breach of contract, an action for damages will still lie, thus it must be performance of the contract that is discharged rather than the contract as a whole.

The phrase 'rescission for breach' is the root cause of the confusion when it is used to describe discharge from performance. If it is accepted that the obligation to perform is discharged by breach, events arising after breach giving rise to an action for damages do not present a problem. For example, if A contracts to do four weeks' work for B at £10,000 per week and B repudiates after one week, A is discharged from further performance. However, his right to recover damages for three weeks' lost income is unaffected. This is best understood by considering the contract in terms of primary and secondary obligations. A primary obligation consists of a parties' promised performance. A secondary obligation is one which arises on breach. In the example above A's primary obligation is to do the work promised and B's is to pay the agreed amount. When B repudiates, A's primary obligation ceases and his damages are calculated in relation to the promised performance.[11] The existence of secondary obligations gives the contract a life beyond termination for breach and serves to distinguish termination for breach from rescission *ab initio*.[12]

Can the innocent party affirm and then change his mind and accept the repudiation, thereby bringing the the contract to an end and giving rise to a right to damages in respect of the anticipatory repudiation? A distinction appears to be drawn between; (a) a continuing actual breach ; (b) an actual breach which is no longer continuing and (c) an anticipatory breach.[13] In cases falling under (a) a claim for performance is not irrevocable. An example in this category is *Johnson v Agnew*.[14] The purchaser of land failed to complete even after specific performance had been ordered. The vendor applied for leave to sue for damages. It was held that, by choosing to ask for specific performance, the vendors had not made a final election, and were able to sue for damages. Cases falling in categories (b) and (c) have been said to be irrevocable.[15] Category (b) cases would cover a breach which cannot be put right such as a deviation in route by a ship. However, is there justification for treating affirmation in respect of anticipatory breaches as being irrevocable? The anticipatory breach may, of course be continuing or it may be one which cannot be cured. The authorities relied on by COLEMAN J do not appear to provide decisive support for this point and the main argument put forward for irrevocability of election is the need for certainty, in the sense that the guilty party needs to know whether the contract is still alive and whether he is under a duty to perform. The basis for this is whether the guilty party would suffer hardship if the innocent party was allowed to change his mind. Is the hardship hypothetical hardship or actual hardship? If it is hypothetical hardship then election to affirm would be irrevocable on most occasions. If it is actual hardship, this would involve the courts seeking factual evidence which might be difficult to prove. In the *Stocznia* case itself,

10 See also LORD DIPLOCK at 349–351.
11 *Photo Production Ltd v Securicor Transport Ltd* [1980] 1 All ER 556 at 567 (per LORD DIPLOCK).
12 See also *Hurst v Bryk* [1998] 2 WLR 269, 287 per HOBHOUSE LJ.
13 G. Treitel (1988) 114 LQR 22, 24.
14 [1980] AC 367.
15 *Stocznia Gdanska SA v Latvian Shipping Co* [1997] 2 Lloyd's Rep 228, 236 per COLEMAN J.

the House of Lords[16] overturned COLEMAN J's refusal to allow an amendment to the innocent party's pleadings seeking to repudiate and claim damages after affirming.

What is clear is that a party cannot unilaterally put an end to a contract by a repudiation or a breach of condition. The other party will have the right to waive the breach and continue with the contract.[17]

16   [1998] 1 All ER 883.
17   *Heyman v Darwins Ltd* [1942] AC 356; *Fercometal SARL v Mediterranean Shipping Co SA, The Simona* [1988] 2 All ER 742.

Chapter 14

Compelling performance

1. SPECIFIC PERFORMANCE AND INJUNCTIONS

(1) INTRODUCTION

The equitable remedies of specific performance and injunction have the effect of compelling a person to carry out his positive obligations or to cease a breach of a negative obligation. Ultimate enforcement of such orders is through the court's power to fine or imprison a person for contempt of court.

An order for specific performance compels performance of positive contractual obligations. It therefore protects the plaintiff's expectation interest.[1] An injunction may be mandatory, ordering the defendant to do something, or prohibitory, ordering the defendant not to do something. Either order may be made in a tort or a contract action. In English law, damages are regarded as the primary remedy, and compulsory performance is exceptional.[2] An order for specific performance or a mandatory injunction is subject to restrictions. The most important of these is that an award of damages must be inadequate before such an order will be given. The courts are careful to apply restrictions to the award of a prohibitory injunction, which has the effect of forcing the defendant to take positive action. In contrast, the prohibitory injunction is regarded as the primary remedy in a tort action, when the plaintiff's proprietary interest has been interfered with, for example in cases of trespass to land or nuisance.

A plaintiff may also seek an interlocutory injunction to temporarily preserve the status quo, pending settlement of the plaintiff's claim. Where harm is threatened but has not yet occurred, the plaintiff may seek a *quia timet* injunction.

(2) SPECIFIC PERFORMANCE, MANDATORY INJUNCTIONS AND DAMAGES

As contract law is said to support the expectation interest of the parties and a reliable system of market transactions, it would be natural to assume that the remedy for breach

---

1 See ch 6.
2 Cf Lawson *Remedies of English Law* (2nd edn, 1980) pp 223–224 and *Beswick v Beswick* [1968] AC 58.

of contractual undertakings would be an order for compulsory performance. However, as an award of damages appears to be the normal remedy, it has been necessary for classical lawyers to assert that financial compensation replaces compulsory performance.

The historical reason for this ambiguity lies in the fact that common law courts could only award damages. Specific performance and injunction, as equitable remedies, could only be awarded by Chancery courts. The political difficulties of competition were resolved by the rule that equitable remedies would only be awarded where the common law remedy of damages was inadequate. The courts have continued to pay lip-service to this rule, despite the fact that courts may now award common law or equitable remedies.

The test for whether specific performance can be awarded is the appropriateness of such relief.[3] There is an inherent tension between the moral concept of the sanctity of promises and economic ideas of efficiency.

The rules on damages are said to have the advantage of encouraging mitigation by the plaintiff, whereas specific performance gives no such encouragement, and may lead to a wasteful use of resources by the plaintiff. Linked to this is the economists' idea of an efficient breach of contract.[4] Economic efficiency is attained by moving resources to those who most value them. For example, A may contract to sell a grommet for £5,000 to B, who values it at £10,000. C, who values the grommet at £15,000, may induce A to break his contract with B and sell the grommet to C for £12,000. In such a case, an award of expectation damages of £5,000 to B will provide an efficient solution, but a decree of specific performance would lead to the grommet being transferred to B, who places a lower value on it.

The Coase Theorem[5] states that, in the absence of transaction costs, it does not matter what legal rights and remedies are available, because the parties, as rational maximisers of value, will negotiate around them to produce the most efficient result. Applying this to the example above, even if specific performance were to be ordered, A and B would negotiate for A to be released from his obligation to perform in return for a share of his profits on a sale to C. As A and B are not strangers, the negotiation costs should be small, and the most efficient result, namely a transfer to C, would be achieved.

Two objections to this theory can be made. First, the specific performance solution involves transaction costs which may be so high that they prevent release or, even if not prohibitive, produce a more expensive solution than would an award of damages. Secondly, the availability of an order for compulsory performance gives the plaintiff a considerable advantage in any subsequent negotiations.[6] The plaintiff could hold out for a sum of money in excess of any loss caused by non-performance and the purpose of contract law is not to punish the wrongdoer but to satisfy the expectations of the party entitled to performance.

It would appear that economic theory regards damages as producing the most efficient remedy. However, economic arguments are not wholly conclusive, since, in contracts of service, the courts have shown extreme reluctance to order compulsory performance, as this might be regarded as a form of slavery.

In favour of compulsory performance, it can be argued that it fulfils the morality of promise-keeping and protects interests which might not be covered by an award of

---

3   *Co-operative Insurance Society Ltd v Argyll Stores (Holdings) Ltd* [1998] AC 1.
4   Kronman (1978) 45 U of Chi LR 351; Schwartz (1979) 89 Yale LR 271; Goetz and Scott (1977) 77 Col LR 554.
5   Coase (1960) 3 J Law & Econ 1.
6   Tromans [1982] CLJ 87 at 105. *Isenberg v East India House Estate Co Ltd* (1863) De GJ & Sm 263, 273 per Lord Westbury; *Co-operative Insurance Society Ltd v Argyll Stores (Holdings) Ltd* [1997] 2 WLR 898, 305 per Lord Hoffman.

damages. For example, it can be used to prevent a person from making profits which might fall foul of the second principle of remoteness in *Hadley v Baxendale*.[7] Furthermore, compulsory performance may protect what is known as the consumer surplus.[8] The consumer surplus is the subjective value placed on goods or services over and above their market value, which may not be reflected by an award of damages. For example, A may contract to buy a picture from B for £1,000. The picture was painted by A's grandfather and has great sentimental value to A, who desperately wishes to acquire it. If B breaks the contract and the market value of the painting is £1,000, A's damages will be nominal. His subjective loss, however, will be enormous and protected by a decree of specific performance. Holiday cases such as *Jarvis v Swans Tours Ltd*,[9] would appear to indicate that it is possible to compensate the consumer surplus by an award of damages where the defendant knew, or ought to have known of the plaintiff's expectations. The House of Lords has also awarded damages in a defective building case based on the consumer surplus, rather than the normal diminution in value or cost of cure measures.[10]

It can be argued that specific performance is used on the basis of fairness and to control relationships of dependence. Cases involving specific performance of sale of goods contracts, those in which the defendant would be unjustly enriched by an award of damages[11] and cases in which the breach of a sole distribution agreement may lead to loss of reputation all appear to be based on fairness. Where one party to a continuing contract, such as a solus agreement in respect of a garage, is in a position of dependence, the courts may intervene by ordering the oil company to deliver petrol.[12] The order is not made to compensate the plaintiff, but to control the exercise of power established through the contractual agreement.

(3) THE BARS TO SPECIFIC PERFORMANCE

There are three so-called bars to an award of a decree of specific performance. These bars also apply to the award of an injunction where it is sought in such wide terms as to amount to specific performance. An order will not be made where damages are an adequate remedy; where performance of the obligation would require supervision, or where the order would compel the defendant to render personal services. As the order is equitable in origin and accordingly discretionary, standard equitable maxims may also be invoked by the court.

Whatever factor is invoked to justify granting or withholding the remedy, the test is the appropriateness of such relief and adequacy of damages is only one factor to be taken into account.[13]

(i) Adequacy of damages

It is said that specific performance will not be ordered where an award of damages is adequate. As the origin of the rule lies in a political compromise between the courts of common law and equity, it is not surprising that little sense can be made of it in the form in which it is traditionally framed. As the market places a value on virtually all

7   (1854) 9 Exch 341 and see ch 16.
8   Harris, Ogus and Phillips (1979) 95 LQR 581.
9   [1973] QB 233.
10   *Ruxley Electronics and Construction Ltd v Forsyth* [1996] AC 344.
11   See *Beswick v Beswick* [1968] AC 58.
12   *Sky Petroleum Ltd v VIP Petroleum Ltd* [1974] 1 WLR 576.
13   *Co-operative Insurance Society Ltd v Argyll Stores Ltd* [1997] 2 WLR 898, 903 per LORD HOFFMANN. See also the dissenting judgment of MILLETT LJ in the Court of Appeal [1996] Ch 286, 304.

contractual obligations, and the plaintiff can be compensated for all his losses, it might appear that damages will never be an inadequate remedy. However, in some cases, the loss suffered by the plaintiff may be too remote to be recoverable by way of an award of damages, or the plaintiff may have placed a subjective value on the subject matter of the contract which exceeds its market value. It is clear that English law allows the award of a decree of specific performance outside of these cases, and the decision of the House of Lords in *Beswick v Beswick*[14] appeared to have indicated that this bar to the availability of specific performance might be in decline. It was said that specific performance might be awarded to achieve a just result.[15] However, with rare exceptions,[16] the courts have continued to use traditional terminology, but have been able to widen the availability of specific performance as a remedy.

(a)   *Contracts for the sale of land*   In contracts of this type, specific performance is normally available on the ground that each parcel of land is regarded as unique. This is clearly not the case, as the order is available to the purchaser who intends to re-sell immediately and places no subjective value on the land. Specific performance is also available to the vendor, although his interest in the contract is purely financial. The traditional view is that the remedy is mutually available to both parties, and that both the vendor and the purchaser are entitled to the remedy of specific performance as a primary remedy, with the result that the adequacy of damages rule is ignored. It is also clear that the courts will refuse the order when it would cause severe hardship.[17] In *Patel v Ali*,[18] specific performance was refused where the defendant became disabled, bore two children and her husband was imprisoned after the date of sale. Because of these circumstances, the defendant became heavily dependent on her neighbours, and it would not be equitable to order performance, even in the absence of mistake or impossibility of performance.

(b)   *Contracts for the sale of goods*   The Sale of Goods Act 1979, section 52 gives the court a discretion to order specific performance of a contract to sell specific or ascertained goods. That section 52 is not a comprehensive statement of the law on this subject was demonstrated in *Sky Petroleum Ltd v VIP Petroleum Ltd*.[19] The plaintiffs were granted an interlocutory injunction to restrain the defendants from withholding supplies of unascertained goods consisting of petroleum products, which they had agreed to sell to the plaintiffs. This happened at a time when the market was in such an uncertain state that the plaintiffs would have been unlikely to obtain supplies elsewhere. In contrast, in *Re Wait*,[20] it was held that specific performance could not be awarded in a contract for the sale of unascertained goods. In general, the courts have not interpreted section 52 as affecting the adequacy of damages rule, and have refused specific performance on the ground that an award of damages enables a substitute to be bought in the market.

Where the goods are physically unique, the court may be prepared to order specific performance. In *Thorn v Public Works Comrs*,[1] specific performance was granted on a contract to sell stones from the old Westminster Bridge, which had been dismantled. On these grounds, specific performance may be granted on a contract to sell a ship

---

14   [1968] AC 58.
15   Ibid at 77 (per LORD REIN); at 88 (per LORD PEARCE) and at 102 (per LORD UPJOHN).
16   See *The Stena Nautica (No 2)* [1982] 2 Lloyd's Rep 336 at 346–347 (per MAY LJ).
17   *Denne v Light* (1857) 8 De GM & G 774 and see *Wroth v Tyler* [1974] Ch 30.
18   [1984] Ch 283.
19   [1974] 1 WLR 576.
20   [1927] 1 Ch 606. See also *Re London Wine Co (Shippers)* [1986] PCC 121.
1   (1863) 32 Beav 490. See also *Falcke v Gray* (1859) 4 Drew 651. Cf *Cohen v Roche* [1927] 1 KB 169.

with special characteristics.[2] While goods which are physically unique may be the subject of an order for specific performance, the most important issue is whether similar principles will also apply to goods which may be said to be commercially unique.[3] Failure to deliver such goods may be extremely disruptive to the buyer's business, particularly in the case of an ongoing contract such as an output and requirements contract. Although a monetary award may ultimately compensate for financial losses, some such losses may be irrecoverable due to difficulties in the assessment of damages. However, difficulties of this kind might not be a sufficient ground for granting specific performance.[4]

The status of commercial uniqueness in English law is uncertain.[5] *Sky Petroleum Ltd v VIP Petroleum Ltd*[6] recognises the concept, however the impact of this decision would appear to have been reduced as a result of *Société des Industries Metallurgiques SA v Bronx Engineering Co Ltd*.[7] In this case, an interlocutory injunction restraining the sellers from removing machinery from the jurisdiction of the court was refused, as there was no likelihood that the buyers would be granted an order for specific performance at the trial. Evidence was given that the buyers would suffer a nine- to twelve-month delay in obtaining substitute machinery. The case would appear to reject the notion of commercial uniqueness, even where the goods are specific.

Developments elsewhere would appear to indicate a greater commercial awareness. The Torts (Interference with Goods) Act 1977 gives the court a discretion to order delivery up of goods where the defendant tortiously interferes with them.[8] In *Howard Perry & Co Ltd v British Railways Board*,[9] the defendants refused to allow steel to be moved because of the fear of strike action. An interlocutory order for delivery up to the owner was made, as steel was not readily available because of a steelworkers' strike.[10] The *Bronx Engineering* case[11] was not referred to. However, the necessary requirements for an order for delivery up differ from those which apply to interlocutory injunctions and specific performance. In the case of the former, it is necessary to establish interference with a property right, whereas a breach of promise is a pre-condition to the grant of an order of specific performance or an injunction. Nevertheless, it is suggested that *Howard Perry & Co v British Railways Board*[12] represents the more accurate approach.

Both the buyer and seller of goods are subject to the apparent judicial reluctance to order specific performance.[13] However, it may be possible to assist the seller in a requirements contract by the grant of a prohibitory injunction preventing the buyer from purchasing supplies from a person other than the seller.[14]

(c)   *Contracts to pay money*   The general rule is that an award of damages is adequate compensation where there has been a breach of a promise to pay money. The doctrine of privity of contract can operate to the disadvantage of the plaintiff, resulting in only

2   See *Behnke v Bede Shipping Co Ltd* [1927] 1 KB 649. Cf *The Stena Nautica (No 2)* [1982] 2 Lloyd's Rep 336.
3   See Treitel (1966) JBL 211.
4   *Fothergill v Rowland* (1873) LR 17 Eq 132 at 140; *Société des Industries Metallurgiques SA v Bronx Engineering Co Ltd* [1975] 1 Lloyd's Rep 465 at 469–470. Cf *Decro-Wall International SA v Practitioners in Marketing Ltd* [1971] 1 WLR 361.
5   Cf The United States *UCC* 2–716(1). See also Kronman (1976) U of Chi LR 351.
6   [1974] 1 WLR 576.
7   [1975] 1 Lloyd's Rep 465.
8   See Torts (Interference with Goods) Act 1977, ss 3 and 4.
9   [1980] 1 WLR 1375.
10   See also Consumer Credit Act 1974, s 100(5).
11   [1975] 1 Lloyd's Rep 465.
12   [1980] 1 WLR 1375.
13   Cf *Elliott and H Elliot (Builders) Ltd v Pierson* [1948] 1 All ER 939.
14   *Clegg v Hands* (1890) 44 Ch D 503; *Metropolitan Electric Supply Co Ltd v Ginder* [1901] 2 Ch 799.

nominal damages being available. In *Beswick v Beswick*,[15] a coal merchant sold his business to his nephew, who promised to pay £5 a week to his uncle's widow. When the uncle died, the widow sought specific performance of the promise in her capacity as administratrix of her deceased husband's estate. The House of Lords held that, in this capacity, she was entitled to specific performance, as the estate would only have received nominal damages.

(ii)   Supervision

If the performance of contractual obligations is to be carried out over a period of time, it may be a bar to an order for specific performance, if the order would require the supervision of the court. In *Ryan v Mutual Tontine Westminster Chambers Association*,[16] specific performance was refused where it would have required the court to supervise the working habits of a resident porter who was required to be in constant attendance at the plaintiff's place of residence.

Whether the requirement of supervision alone is a satisfactory ground for refusing specific performance has always been in doubt,[17] as it is always open to the court to appoint an agent such as a receiver to act on its behalf.[18]

The supervision requirement was not specifically mentioned in *Beswick v Beswick*.[19] However the court did not regard it as a problem. The supervision of the periodical payments could be undertaken by the payee.

The trend towards loosening the supervision bar[20] was stopped by the House of Lords in *Co-operative Insurance Society Ltd v Argyll Stores Ltd*.[1] The case concerned a lessee's covenant to keep open a retail store in a large shopping centre. The covenant had nineteen years to run. Argyll were in financial trouble and decided to close down their less profitable supermarkets. The Co-Op sought an injunction to compel Argyll to keep the supermarket open, at least until a sub-letting or assignment. This was granted by the Court of Appeal[2] but reversed by the House of Lords as it was not the practice of courts to grant mandatory injunctions requiring a person to carry on business. LORD HOFFMANN explained the basis of the supervision bar as being one of wasted resources if the court had to give an indefinite series of rulings to clarify the terms of the order. The obligation in question was found to be too imprecise and concern was expressed that the only weapon of enforcement was the draconian one of contempt of court. A further factor was that the cost of compliance to the defendant would far outweigh any loss to the plaintiff. Balanced against this was the difficulty for the plaintiff of proving what loss it suffered as a result of Argyll's breach of covenant. However, a distinction is drawn between contracts requiring a person to carry on an activity over a period of time and a contract for results, such as a repairing covenant in a lease. In result contracts, indefinite applications to the court should not arise and it is likely that the contract will specify precisely what has to be done.

---

15   [1968] AC 58.
16   [1893] 1 Ch 116.
17   *Wolverhampton Corpn v Emmons* [1901] 1 KB 515.
18   Schwartz (1979) 89 Yale LJ 271, 291–294.
19   [1968] AC 58.
20   Eg *Posner v Scott-Lewis* [1987] Ch 25.
1   [1998] AC 1. See [1997] CLJ 488; (1998) LQR 43.
2   [1996] Ch 286.

(iii)   Contracts requiring personal services

The traditional rule is that contracts requiring the personal services of one of the parties are not specifically enforceable at the suit of the other party.[3] There are several reasons for this rule. Damages may be adequate compensation, or it may be difficult to determine exactly what had to be done under the contract. Once the relationship of trust and confidence often required by a contract of employment has broken down, it may be impossible to rebuild it by an order of specific performance. If the work requires a subjective appraisal such as that provided by an actor, it would be difficult to determine whether the work was being correctly performed. The most important reason is probably that the order would infringe personal liberty by transforming the contract into one of slavery.[4]

(a)   *The employee*   The rule against specific enforcement of a contract of employment is contained in the Trade Union and Labour Relations (Consolidation) Act 1992, section 236. The provision prohibits not just an order of specific performance,[5] but also an injunction restraining a breach of contract or a threatened breach of contract. However, where the contract contains an express negative covenant against working for another person, a prohibitory injunction may occasionally be granted to restrain a breach of that covenant. It is not possible for such a covenant to be implied from a positive obligation, even where the employee has undertaken to devote the whole of his time to his employer's business.[6]

Where an injunction is granted to enforce a negative covenant, it will not directly compel the employee to work for the employer, but it may have this effect indirectly. In *Lumley v Wagner*,[7] the defendant agreed to sing at the plaintiff's theatre and not to sing at any other theatre during that period. An injunction was granted to prevent the defendant singing at a rival opera house, but she could not have been restrained from taking any other form of employment.

The decision was followed in *Warner Bros Pictures Inc v Nelson*,[8] where the actress Bette Davis agreed to work exclusively for the plaintiffs as a film actress and not to work for any other film company. An injunction was granted preventing her from breaking the negative covenant, even though it effectively compelled her to work for the plaintiffs. The court resorted to the fiction that the defendant could take up alternative employment, but it is difficult to imagine Bette Davis washing dishes! The effect of the two cases was to compel performance of the contract of employment.

A more realistic approach is shown in *Page One Records Ltd v Britton*.[9] The Troggs pop group entered a five-year agreement with the plaintiff, under which he undertook to act as the group's manager. An application for an injunction to restrain a breach of the agreement by employing someone else was rejected, as it would have compelled specific performance of a contract for personal services. This approach has been followed generally by the courts. In *Warren v Mendy*[10] the Court of Appeal refused an application from Warren to prevent the boxer Nigel Benn employing Mendy as a manager. Benn had contracted with Warren not to employ anyone else as manager for a period of three years. The Court of Appeal took the view that to grant the injunction would be

---

3   *Britain v Rossiter* (1879) 11 QBD 123.
4   *De Francesco v Barnum* (1890) 45 Ch D 430 at 438 (per Fry LJ).
5   Trade Union and Labour Relations (Consolidation) Act 1992, s 236.
6   *Whitwood Chemical Co v Hardman* [1891] 2 Ch 416.
7   (1852) 21 LJ Ch 898, 1 De GM & G 604.
8   [1937] 1 KB 209.
9   [1968] 1 WLR 157.
10   [1989] 3 All ER 103.

to force Benn to employ the applicant, otherwise he could not use his special skills.[11] In *Evening Standard Co Ltd v Henderson*[12] the Court of Appeal did grant an injunction to prevent a newspaper production manager from working for a rival newspaper in breach of contract. However, the employers were willing to pay the employee even if he did not work and the employee had in fact continued to work for them with no breakdown in the relationship of trust and confidence. The injunction was limited to the period until the employee's period of notice expired.

(b)   *The employer*   There are statutory provisions which provide that an industrial tribunal may order the reinstatement of an employee who has been unfairly dismissed.[13] However, it would appear that this remedy is rarely used and, even where reinstatement is ordered but not complied with, the sanction is the payment of extra compensation. Statutory provisions apart, the general equitable rule is that no order will be granted which will compel the employer to employ the employee.[14] This is reflected in the unfair dismissal provisions, providing for increased compensation when an order for reinstatement is not complied with.

There is an exception to this rule, where an employer has failed to comply with the correct dismissal procedures. In *Hill v CA Parsons & Co Ltd*,[15] an interlocutory injunction was granted to restrain the employer from wrongfully dismissing an employee. The majority of the Court of Appeal thought that damages were inadequate, and that the granting of an injunction would preserve the contract of employment so that the employee could use the provisions of the Industrial Relations Act 1971, which protected an employee from dismissal if he did not join a trade union. Departure from the general rule was thought to be justified only where damages were inadequate and there was still complete confidence between employer and employee. The order only extended to the payment of wages, and did not allow the employee to attend at his place of work, nor did it compel the employer to provide work for the employee.

The case was initially regarded as exceptional.[16] However a basic principle with two exceptions has now emerged. The basic principle is that the contract of employment will not be specifically enforced. The first exception is where the order is only required to preserve the contract of employment. No relationship of trust and confidence between employer and employee is required as there is no question of the employee actually working.[17] The second exception is where the employee will continue to work. Here the order will only be made if there continues to be a relationship of confidence in the employee's ability to carry out the tasks of that employment and to work well with others.[18]

(iv)   Other bars[1]

The above are the classic bars to specific performance. As the remedy of specific performance is equitable, normal equitable principles will apply. It follows that an order

---

11   See also *Provident Financial Group plc v Hayward* [1989] 3 All ER 298.
12   [1987] ICR 588.
13   Employment Rights Act 1996.
14   *Scandinavian Trading Tanker Co AB v Flota Petrolera Ecuatoriana, The Scaptrade* [1983] 2 AC 694 at 701.
15   [1972] Ch 305.
16   *Chappell v Times Newspapers Ltd* [1975] 2 All ER 233, [1975] 1 WLR 482.
17   *Robb v London Borough of Hammersmith and Fulham* [1991] IRLR 72.
18   *Powell v London Borough of Brent* [1988] ICR 176.
1   Jones and Goodhart *Specific Performance* (1986) chs 2 and 3.

will be denied on the grounds of want of mutuality,[2] severe hardship,[3] absence of clean hands,[2] and where the plaintiff is not willing to do equity.[4]

(4)   DAMAGES IN LIEU OF SPECIFIC PERFORMANCE OR INJUNCTION

The Chancery Amendment Act 1858, section 2 gave Chancery the power to award damages in addition to, or in lieu of, specific performance. The Act has now been repealed, but the High Court retains this power, and may also allow a claim for common law damages to be combined with an action for specific performance.

There can be few advantages to a plaintiff in claiming equitable rather than common law damages. In *Johnson v Agnew*,[6] it was stated that the basis for assessment of equitable damages is the same as for common law damages. Only where common law damages are unavailable would equitable damages be advantageous. This might arise where specific performance of an oral contract for the sale of land has been ordered on the basis of proprietory estoppel.

(5)   INJUNCTIONS

(i)   Types of injunction

An injunction may be ordered in either a tort or a contract action. The injunction may be mandatory, ordering the defendant to do something, or prohibitory, ordering him not to do something. The distinction is one of substance, not of form and, where the defendant is obliged to take positive steps, the injunction should be mandatory.[7] This distinction may not be easy to apply. The courts will order a prohibitory injunction where the defendant is in breach of a negative covenant or other obligation and can comply with it without taking positive action, even though he will almost certainly take such positive steps. If the effect of the order is that the defendant must reduce the noise produced by his trade or cease trading, he will almost certainly take steps to reduce the noise.

Where no actionable wrong has yet been committed by the defendant but one is apprehended, then a *quia timet* injunction may be awarded. The injunction may be final or perpetual, awarded after a trial of the action, or interlocutory, being granted at an earlier stage of the proceedings. Such an order will last only until the trial. In cases of urgency, an interim injunction may be made. These differ from interlocutory injunctions only in that they do not last until the trial, but until counsel can be heard on the matter.

(a)   *Mandatory injunctions*   A mandatory injunction requires the defendant to undo that which he has done in breach of a tortious or contractual obligation. It is technically possible for a mandatory injunction to be granted to enforce a positive obligation. However, mandatory injunctions are rarely used to enforce tortious obligations, and a decree of specific performance fulfils the same function in relation to positive contractual obligations. As a result, the mandatory injunction is normally used to restore the plaintiff's infringed rights.

---

2   See *Price v Strange* [1978] Ch 337.
3   *Denne v Light* (1857) 8 De GM & G 774.
4   *Lamare v Dixon* (1873) LR 6 HL 414.
5   *Chappell v Times Newspapers Ltd* [1975] 2 All ER 233, [1975] 1 WLR 482.
6   [1980] AC 367. But see *Surrey County Council v Bredero Homes Ltd* [1993] 1 WLR 1361.
7   *Jackson v Normanby Brick Co* [1899] 1 Ch 438.

The principles for the award of a mandatory injunction were laid down in *Redland Bricks Ltd v Morris*.[8] There must be a strong probability of grave damage to the plaintiff, and damages must be an inadequate remedy. The court must consider the cost to the defendant of complying with the order, and it must be possible for the defendant to ascertain what it is he must do. Applying these principles, the court refused to uphold the mandatory injunction to take all reasonable steps to restore the plaintiff's land which had been granted by the trial judge. The initial order did not indicate what the defendant had to do. Furthermore, the cost of restoration by far exceeded the value of the land.

Unlike prohibitory injunctions, mandatory injunctions are not granted as a matter of course. Instead, they are granted very sparingly.[9] The court will take into account any hardship which would be caused to the defendant, and the nature of the defendant's behaviour. If the defendant has behaved reasonably but wrongly, the order may be refused.[10] Public interest may also be considered. For example, an application to compel the demolition of a housing estate built in breach of a restrictive covenant may be refused so as to avoid the waste of much-needed houses.[11] However, if the defendant has attempted to take advantage of the plaintiff, he can expect little sympathy. In *Daniel v Ferguson*,[12] the defendant attempted to complete a building before the plaintiff could obtain a court order. An injunction was granted, compelling the defendant to demolish those parts of the building which interfered with the plaintiff's right to light.

Whether the supervision bar to specific performance applies to mandatory injunctions is, at present, unclear but there is some support for it.[13]

(b)   *Prohibitory injunctions*[14]   Prohibitory injunctions are regarded as the primary remedy for the breach of a negative stipulation in a contract,[15] and to prevent continuing tortious misconduct. In tort cases, the order is usually granted at the final stage in order to protect the plaintiff's proprietary interest in actions for trespass to land and nuisance. However, prohibitory injunctions have also been granted where other torts have been committed, particularly those which can be repeated, such as defamation, trespass to the person and passing off.

The injunction may be refused if the harm suffered by the plaintiff is trivial. For example, in *Llandudno UDC v Woods*,[16] an injunction to prevent a clergyman holding services on the plaintiff's seashore was refused.

Where a prohibitory injunction is sought to prevent the breach of a negative stipulation in a contract, the order may be refused if to grant it would amount to specific performance where this would not otherwise be available. This rule applies with particular force to contracts of employment, but the courts have been prepared to exert pressure through prohibitory injunctions to perform other types of contract.[17]

The rationale which underlies the primacy of the prohibitory injunction is that the defendant should not be allowed to buy the right to inflict the damage.[18] Hardship to

---

8   [1970] AC 652.
9   Ibid at 665 (per LORD UPJOHN).
10   Ibid at 666 (per LORD UPJOHN).
11   *Wrotham Park Estate Co v Parkside Homes Ltd* [1974] 1 WLR 798. Cf *Charrington v Simons & Co Ltd* [1971] 1 WLR 598.
12   [1891] 2 Ch 27.
13   *Kennard v Cory Bros & Co Ltd* [1922] 2 Ch 1.
14   See also ch 29.
15   *Doherty v Allman* (1878) 3 App Cas 709.
16   [1899] 2 Ch 705. See also *Behrens v Richards* [1905] 2 Ch 614.
17   *Sky Petroleum Ltd v VIP Petroleum Ltd* [1974] 1 WLR 576; *Decro-Wall International SA v Practitioners in Marketing Ltd* [1971] 2 All ER 216.
18   *Shelfer v City of London Electric Lighting Co* [1895] 1 Ch 287 at 315–316 (per LINDLEY LJ).

the defendant will not prevent the making of the order,[19] nor will the public interest in the continuation of the defendant's activity.[20] However, in cases of hardship, the courts are prepared to suspend implementation of the injunction.[1]

There would appear to be a case for relaxing the rule that the prohibitory injunction should be regarded as the primary remedy, and that more use of an award of damages should be made.[2] This is particularly so when the defendant's activity is in the public interest, or where action by the plaintiff to avoid damage can easily be taken. There is a fear that the availability of the injunction may have shaped the substantive law. The courts may be reluctant to find that the defendant has infringed a legal right because of the drastic nature of the remedy.[3] An example of this is the wide interpretation given to the defence of statutory authority in nuisance cases.[4]

(c)   *Quia timet injunctions*   Where damage is only threatened, or the cause of action is not yet complete, the plaintiff may obtain a *quia timet* injunction, if he can show a high probability of substantial injury and that an award of damages would be inadequate. The plaintiff must show that the defendant threatens and intends to do acts which will cause him irreparable damage.

(d)   *Interlocutory injunctions*[5]   An interlocutory injunction is awarded during the course of court proceedings, and will not continue beyond the end of the trial. The injunction may operate as a mandatory, a prohibitory or a *quia timet* injunction. The interlocutory mandatory injunction is of the greatest importance in enforcing positive contractual obligations.

There are two conflicting views on what must be established in order to obtain an interlocutory injunction. In *American Cyanamid Co v Ethicon Ltd*,[6] the House of Lords held that an interlocutory injunction may be granted where there is a serious question to be answered, where damages would not be adequate and where the plaintiff's undertaking would compensate the defendant. Where there is doubt as to the adequacy of damages, the case will be decided on the balance of convenience, weighing the harm the defendant is likely to do against the damage which the defendant is likely to suffer.

The alternative approach is that the plaintiff must establish a *prima facie* case that the defendant was committing, or intended to commit, a wrong against the plaintiff.[7] If the plaintiff succeeded in this task, he would be entitled to a final injunction at the trial, if the balance of convenience favoured such an award. This approach involved a mini-trial of the merits of the case at the interlocutory stage. It was this aspect of the law that *American Cynamid v Ethicon Ltd* attempted to remove. The balance of convenience tended to be ignored, and the parties would be inclined to accept the interlocutory decision and not proceed to trial.[8]

American Cynamid v Ethicon Ltd attempted to prevent the interlocutory stage from being used as a mini-trial. However, the courts have been reluctant to follow the case,

19   *Redland Bricks Ltd v Morris* [1970] AC 652 at 664.
20   *Kennaway v Thompson* [1981] QB 88. Cf *Miller v Jackson* [1977] QB 966.
1   *Pride of Derby and Derbyshire Angling Association Ltd v British Celanese Ltd* [1953] Ch 149; *Woollerton and Wilson Ltd v Richard Costain Ltd* [1970] 1 WLR 411.
2   See Burrows *Remedies* pp 399–403. See also Calabresi & Melamed (1972) 85 Harv LR 1089 and Ogus and Richardson [1977] CLJ 284.
3   Tromans [1982] CLJ 87.
4   See *Allen v Gulf Oil Refining Ltd* [1981] 1 All ER 353 and Tromans [1982] CLJ 87 at 107.
5   Gray [1981] 40 CLJ 307.
6   [1975] AC 396.
7   *Stratford & Son Ltd v Lindley* [1965] AC 269.
8   See *Fellowes & Sons v Fisher* [1976] QB 122 at 133 (per LORD DENNING MR).

because the mini-trial has proved to be a swift and inexpensive means of settling disputes,[9] and often served to render a later trial unnecessary.

2.   THE ACTION FOR THE PRICE

One method of compelling performance of a contractual obligation is to bring an action for an agreed sum. The sum may be one fixed by the contract. Alternatively, the court may award a reasonable sum representing the value of goods sold[10] (*quantum valebat*), or reasonable remuneration in respect of services rendered[11] (*quantum meruit*). The agreed sum will become payable on the occurrence of an event expressly provided for by the contract or when the plaintiff has fulfilled, wholly or substantially, the obligation for which he claims payment.

This action differs from an action for damages, as it is for a liquidated sum and no questions of mitigation, remoteness or causation arise. The action is cheap, where no defence is entered, and is probably the commonest form of contractual action.[12] If a hire-purchase contract is repudiated by the debtor and the creditor successfully repossesses the goods, the creditor may wish to recover instalments which were payable prior to termination. The creditor will be able to bring an action for an agreed sum in respect of such payments, but he will have to bring an action for damages in respect of the failure to perform the remainder of the agreement.[13] After termination, the creditor will be obliged to take steps to mitigate his loss by attempting to re-hire the goods.

The innocent party may wish to continue with the contract after the guilty party's repudiation or breach of condition. In this case, the innocent party may elect to affirm the contract and seek specific performance or an injunction to compel performance. If these remedies are unavailable to him, he is restricted to an action for damages, and must then attempt to mitigate his losses, or he may be able to bring an action for the price, and thereby compel an unwanted performance by the contract breaker.

In sale of goods cases, it would appear that an action for the price is available, even where it leads to a wasteful use of resources. Normally, the obligation to pay the price arises when property in the goods passes to the buyer.[14] If property passes on delivery and the buyer refuses to accept the goods, the seller's only action is for damages.[15] If the contract provides for property in the goods to pass before delivery, the seller may sue for the price, if he is still in possession of the goods and the buyer refuses to accept them. Alternatively, the seller can accept the repudiation and sue for damages.[16] If the seller sues for the price, the buyer will be forced to take delivery. If the goods are not easily re-saleable, the rule makes sense but, in most cases, the seller will be able to find a substitute purchaser who places a greater value on them, thereby effecting a more efficient use of resources. The rule might be said to be based on the morality of promise-keeping and could be justified because it protects the seller's expectations.[17] However, it may also be described as an historical anomaly. In terms of efficiency, the comparable rule in the United States is preferable. This permits the seller to recover the price only

---

9   Wallington [1976] 35 CLJ 82.
10   Sale of Goods Act 1979, s 8(2).
11   Supply of Goods and Services Act 1982, s 15(1).
12   Beale *Remedies for Breach of Contract* (1980) p 144.
13   *Overstone Ltd v Shipway* [1962] 1 WLR 117.
14   Sale of Goods Act 1979, s 49(1).
15   *Colley v Overseas Exporters* [1921] 3 KB 302.
16   Sale of Goods Act 1979, s 50(1).
17   Burrows *Remedies* p 276.

if there is no reasonable prospect of his being able to resell the goods at a reasonable price.[18]

Outside of sale of goods cases, limitations have been introduced on a party's right to continue with performance and sue for the agreed price. In *White and Carter (Councils) Ltd v McGregor*,[19] the appellants made litter bins on which they displayed advertisements. The respondents contracted for their business to be advertised for three years, but repudiated the contract the same day. The appellants chose to affirm the contract, went ahead and displayed the advertisements and claimed the agreed price. The House of Lords, by a majority, upheld their claim as, if the injured party chose to affirm the contract, it remained in full effect.[20] LORD REID, however, suggested that:

> … it may well be that, if it can be shown that a person has no legitimate interest, financial or otherwise, in performing the contract, rather than claiming damages, he ought not to be allowed to saddle the other party with an additional burden with no benefit to himself.[1]

This has been used as an escape route from the wasteful effect of applying the decision of the majority. The difficulty is to determine what legitimate interest the appellants had in performing the contract rather than claiming damages. It would appear that LORD REID had a very narrow idea of 'no legitimate interest'.

The judicial trend since *White and Carter* has been largely hostile. It is clear that where the guilty party's co-operation is required to perform the contract, the *White and Carter* principle will be inoperative, and the innocent party will be restricted to damages. For example, where a landowner repudiates a building contract and refuses to allow the builder onto his land, the builder will be restricted to damages.[2] The courts have been prepared to stretch the definition of co-operation in order to distinguish *White and Carter*. In *Attica Sea Carriers Corpn v Ferrostaal*,[3] it was held that a charterparty required co-operation. However, this view has been subsequently rejected.[4] More recently, there would appear to be a move towards the minority decision in *White and Carter*. In *Clea Shipping Corpn v Bulk Oil International Ltd*,[5] LLOYD J, albeit constrained by precedent, held that the plaintiffs should accept the defendant's repudiation and claim damages. The charterers had repudiated the charterparty. The owners rejected the repudiation and kept the vessel at the disposal of the charterers until the expiry of the charter. Although the charterers paid the full cost of hire, they sought to recover it on the ground that the owner should have been restricted to damages and should have accepted the repudiation. It was held that the owners' conduct in refusing to accept the repudiation was wholly unreasonable, and they should be entitled to damages only. LLOYD J distinguished between merely unreasonable and wholly unreasonable conduct,[6] which is in line with *White and Carter*. However, it is difficult to reconcile his interpretation of 'wholly unreasonable' on the facts of the case with LORD REID's interpretation of 'no legitimate interest' in *White and Carter*.[7] The case would appear to mark a significant move away from the freedom of a person to enforce a contract.

---

18   *United States UCC* s 2–709.
19   [1962] AC 413.
20   See Goodhart (1962) 78 LQR 263; Neinaber [1962] CLJ 213.
1   [1962] AC 413 at 431.
2   *Hounslow London Borough Council v Twickenham Garden Developments Ltd* [1971] Ch 233.
3   [1976] 1 Lloyd's Rep 250.
4   *The Odenfeld* [1978] 2 Lloyd's Rep 357 and *Clea Shipping Corpn v Bulk Oil International Ltd* [1984] 1 All ER 129.
5   Ibid.
6   Ibid at 137.
7   [1962] AC 413 at 431.

If LLOYD J's interpretation is followed, the availability of the action for an agreed sum would appear to be limited, and with it the ability of a party to compel contractual performance. This would be in line with the rules on specific performance of a contract, which will not be ordered where damages are adequate. This can be viewed as a move away from the enforcement of promises to a more pragmatic approach based on economic efficiency through forcing the plaintiff to mitigate his losses.

3.   AGREED DAMAGES

(1)   INTRODUCTION

The parties to a contract may agree the amount of money which will be payable in the event of a specific breach of contract or other event. Where this sum of money is enforceable, it is the parties, rather than the court, that assess damages and it is a remedy which compels performance of a party's obligation to pay money. The courts, in exercising jurisdiction over agreed damages, have distinguished liquidated damages, which are enforceable, and penalty clauses, which are not enforceable.

This remedy is similar to the action for an agreed price, as it constitutes enforcement of a promise to pay a sum of money. In an action for agreed damages, it is the parties' agreed remedy that is enforced. Contractual limitation clauses operate in a similar fashion by allowing a person to limit to a specific sum the amount he has to pay in the event of a breach of contract. However, a limitation clause limits the liability of the party in breach to the actual loss caused, whereas where an agreed damages clause is enforced, the agreed sum will be payable, even where this amount exceeds the loss actually suffered.[8]

It has been observed that the courts have exercised jurisdiction over agreed prices and have the power to strike down limitation clauses under the Unfair Contract Terms Act 1977. In the same way, they have intervened with freedom of contract and have struck down onerous agreed damages clauses as penalty clauses. Such intervention may be to prevent an abuse of power by the stronger party, or to prevent upsetting the compensatory principle of damages. The EC Directive on Unfair Terms in Consumer Contracts may have an effect on penalty clauses. The list of terms which may be regarded as unfair includes a term which has the effect of 'permitting the seller or supplier to retain sums paid by the consumer where the latter decides not to conclude or perform the contract without providing for the consumer to receive compensation of an equivalent amount from the seller or supplier where the latter is the party cancelling the contract.'[9] Also, a term which has the effect of 'requiring any consumer who fails to fulfill his obligation to pay a disproportionately high sum in compensation.'[10]

(2)   LIQUIDATED DAMAGES AND PENALTY CLAUSES

Where an agreed damages clause is contested, the court must determine whether it is a genuine pre-estimate of likely loss or a penalty clause. If it is a genuine agreed or liquidated damages clause, the plaintiff will recover the agreed amount. In such a case, the issue of mitigation will not arise. However, this may prove wasteful in that a figure based on the assumption that the plaintiff will not mitigate his loss might over-compensate him if he has mitigated his loss as well. The issue of remoteness of damage would also

---

8   *Cellulose Acetate Silk Co Ltd v Widnes Foundry (1925) Ltd* [1933] AC 20.
9   Unfair Terms in Consumer Contract Regulations 1999, Sch 2 para 1(d).
10   Ibid, Sch 2 para 1(e).

appear to be irrelevant,[11] and the contracting parties have the advantage of planning their remedy according to their subjective circumstances. They do not need to rely on what they might regard as the somewhat arbitrary legal rules which apply to damages assessed by the court. For example, the parties may provide for losses, such as emotional disappointment, which may be compensated by a court with great difficulty.[12]

Where the clause is regarded as a penalty, the plaintiff will be limited to his actual loss on ordinary unliquidated damages principles. If the plaintiff's loss is greater than the agreed sum, it is unclear whether the plaintiff may have the clause struck down so that he can recover his actual loss.[13] In Canada, the option to recover actual losses in such a case is not available to the plaintiff.[14]

It is necessary to determine how the courts distinguish between a penalty clause and an agreed damages clause. Where the agreed figure is a genuine pre-estimate of the loss that will be caused to one party, it will be classified as an agreed damages clause. However, if the figure constitutes a threat to one party designed to ensure performance and punish him in the event of a breach of contract, it will be treated as a penalty clause. The classic test was laid down in *Dunlop Pneumatic Tyre Co Ltd v New Garage and Motor Co Ltd*,[15] in which a number of factors relevant to the distinction were identified. The onus of proving that a clause is penal lies on the person against whom recovery is sought. The fact that a clause is described as either a liquidated damages or a penalty clause is not conclusive. A clause is penal if it is extravagant and unconscionable in amount, in comparison with the greatest loss that could conceivably be proved to have followed from the breach. If the promisor's obligation is to pay a sum of money and the contract provides for him to pay a larger sum in default, the provision will be a penalty clause. Where the contract provides for the payment of a specified sum in the event of a single named breach, it is presumed that the provision is a liquidated damages clause. However, this must be read subject to the rule on extravagant amounts and the rule on payment of a greater amount than the contractual consideration. Furthermore, there is a presumption that a clause is penal if it provides for the payment of a single lump sum in the event of one or more or all of several events, some of which may occasion serious damage, and others of which may cause only trifling damage. This presumption will be weakened where it is impossible to prove the exact loss flowing from breaches of a number of terms of the contract.[16]

Application of these principles can be illustrated by the facts of the *Dunlop* case. Dunlop had supplied tyres to the defendant under a price maintenance agreement. The agreement included various terms, one of which was that tyres should not be sold below the listed price and that £5 liquidated damages should be paid for each tyre sold in breach of the agreement. The £5 sum was held to amount to a liquidated damages provision. The amount might have been disproportionate to the harm caused, but the damage to Dunlop's selling organisation would have been impossible to estimate. In contrast, in *Ford Motor Co Ltd v Armstrong*,[17] an agreed sum payable in the event of the breach of an obligation not to sell cars or car parts below the listed price was held to be a penalty. The size of the sum precluded the possibility that it could be treated as a genuine pre-estimate of the possible damage suffered as a result of the breach of contract.

---

11 *Robophone Facilities Ltd v Blank* [1966] 1 WLR 1428. Cf Law Commission Working Paper No 61, para 44.
12 See Goetz and Scott (1977) 77 Col LR 554; Beale and Dugdale (1975) 2 Brit J L & S 45.
13 *Robophone Facilities Ltd v Blank* [1966] 1 WLR 1428 at 1448 (per Lord Diplock); Hudson (1974) 90 LQR 31; (1975) 91 LQR 25; (1985) 101 LQR 480.
14 *Elsley v J G Collins Insurance Agencies Ltd* (1978) 83 DLR (3d) 1.
15 [1915] AC 79.
16 Ibid at 86–88 (per Lord Dunedin).
17 (1915) 31 TLR 267.

In *Phillips Hong Kong Ltd v A-G of Hong Kong*[18] the Privy Council were of the opinion that the courts should not be too ready to declare a clause as penal and that what the parties had agreed should normally be upheld. The actual loss suffered in the case could be taken into account in deciding whether the clause was penal, although the matter had to be judged at the time the contract was made. However, in assessing what could be reasonably expected, the actual loss (in this case greater than the agreed damages) was valuable evidence in assisting the court.

In hire-purchase contracts, it is common to find provisions for compensation for depreciation. If the agreement is terminated before completion by breach or death of the hirer, the hirer will have to pay an agreed sum. If this sum is penal in nature, it will be struck down by the court. A figure of two-thirds of the hire-purchase price payable on termination will be penal, as it provides a sliding scale of compensation, but a scale that slides in the wrong direction.[19] If the agreement were to be terminated after one instalment and the title remained with the creditor, he would be able to re-sell the goods almost new and receive two-thirds of their value from the hirer. This could not represent a genuine pre-estimate of loss.

(3)   CONCLUSION

Where an agreed damages clause is a genuine pre-estimate of loss, and therefore liquidated damages, it will reflect the compensatory principles of damages, and should bring advantages to the parties by avoiding the costs of litigation and encouraging timely performance. But Beale and Dugdale[20] have found that such clauses only appear in specifically negotiated contracts. In such contracts, a seller would be unlikely to be able to avoid any liability for delay and might prefer a liquidated damages clause, unless the buyer was unlikely to press for consequential losses because of a continuing relationship between the firms. Buyers tend not to favour liquidated damages clauses, preferring to preserve their common law rights. The buyer would often find the seller reluctant to accept a liquidated damages clause without a widely drafted 'force majeure' clause, depriving the buyer of much of the cost of delay, and a liquidated damages clause would impose high transaction costs on the buyer in keeping track of delays. In general, businessmen tend to view delay as a commercial problem rather than a legal problem which can be solved by contract planning.

Penalty clauses run counter to the compensatory aim of damages, as they are punitive rather than compensatory in nature. This probably constitutes the principal reason for refusing to uphold them.[1] A further argument is that they discourage efficient breaches of contract,[2] but this theory only holds up if the transaction costs of bargaining around the clause are too high.[3] For example, if a contract between A and B contains a penalty clause of £10,000 and B can make an efficient breach of contract by selling to C at a profit of £5,000 more than he would make by selling to A, the penalty clause would appear to discourage a breach. This ignores the possibility that A and B may negotiate around the penalty clause between A's valuation of the goods and the value which C places on the goods.

---

18   (1993) 9 Const LJ 202; 61 BLR 41
19   *Bridge v Campbell Discount Co Ltd* [1962] AC 600 at 623 (per LORD RADCLIFFE). Cf *Wadham Stringer Finance Ltd v Meaney* [1981] 1 WLR 39.
20   (1975) 2 Brit J L & S 45 at 55.
1   Burrows *Remedies* p 329.
2   Fenton (1975) 51 Ind LJ 189 at 191.
3   Goetz and Scott (1977) 77 Col LR 554.

Chapter 15

Non-compensatory damages

Where the defendant is in breach of a contractual or tortious obligation, the normal objective of an award of damages is to compensate the plaintiff for loss he has suffered as a result of the tort or breach of contract. Before the court assesses the amount to be awarded, it must consider the various factors which limit such an award.[1] These are that the damage has been caused by the breach of duty, that the damage is not too remote and that the plaintiff has taken reasonable steps to mitigate his loss.

In certain circumstances, the court may award non-compensatory damages in the form of nominal, contemptuous or exemplary damages.

1. NOMINAL DAMAGES

Nominal damages may be awarded for breach of contract,[2] or for a tort actionable *per se*.[3] They are not compensatory, as they are awarded for the wrong itself rather than any loss suffered by the plaintiff. It follows that an award of nominal damages recognises an infraction by giving a right to a verdict without giving the right to real damages.[4]

The amount awarded will be small, currently £10. The fact that a plaintiff has been awarded nominal damages does not mean that he should be regarded as a successful plaintiff for the purposes of costs.[5]

2. CONTEMPTUOUS DAMAGES

Contemptuous damages are normally only awarded in defamation cases by a jury. An award of contemptuous damages consists of the award of the least valuable coin of the realm, and acknowledges that the plaintiff's legal rights have been technically infringed,

---

1   See ch 16.
2   *Marzetti v Williams* (1830) 1 B & Ad 415.
3   *Constantine v Imperial Hotels Ltd* [1944] 1 KB 693.
4   *The Mediana* [1900] AC 113 at 116 (per LORD HALSBURY).
5   *Anglo-Cyprian Trade Agencies Ltd v Paphos Wine Industries Ltd* [1951] 1 All ER 873.

but expresses derision of his conduct in the matter.[6] It is unlikely that a plaintiff awarded contemptuous damages will recover his costs.

3. AGGRAVATED DAMAGES

Where damages are not limited to provable financial loss, the court may take into account the manner in which the tort was committed in assessing damages. This has been explained in a number of ways but amounts to the tort being committed in a malicious, insulting or oppressive manner.[7]

The Law Commission has recommended that aggravated damages should be renamed damages for mental distress and that such awards are compensatory.[8]

4. EXEMPLARY DAMAGES

Exemplary or punitive damages are a source of much controversy,[9] and there are a number of arguments both for and against their use.[10] The purpose of an award of exemplary damages is to punish the defendant for his wrongful conduct. This raises important questions concerning the role of civil law and whether it should attempt to perform a function traditionally reserved for the criminal law. In general, the common law has been hostile towards an award of exemplary damages.

(1) BREACH OF CONTRACT

Exemplary damages cannot be recovered for a breach of contract.[11] This is consistent with the principle that the plaintiff should not be put in a better position than if the contract had been performed.

Recent case law has been concerned with a landlord's breach of his covenant of quiet enjoyment.[12] The principle of non-recovery has been upheld but, where the breach is also a tort, exemplary damages may be awarded where they are permitted.[13]

(2) TORT

The basis of the law on exemplary damages in tort cases is now contained in *Rookes v Barnard*.[14] LORD DEVLIN was unhappy with the award of exemplary damages in civil cases, as it tended to confuse the role of civil and criminal law.[15] He considered that statute and precedent prevented the judicial abolition of an award of such damages, and was concerned to limit their application to three categories. That exemplary damages

---

6   See *Dering v Uris* [1964] 2 QB 669; *Pamplin v Express Newspapers Ltd (No 2)* [1988] 1 WLR 116n.
7   *Cassell & Co Ltd v Broome* [1972] AC 1027, 1085 per LORD REID. See also *Sutcliffe v Pressdram Ltd* [1990] 1 All ER 269, 288 per NOURSE LJ.
8   Report No 247 (1997)
9   Report No 247 (1997).
10 See Burrows *Remedies* pp 281–285; Gandhi (1990) 10 LS 182.
11 *Addis v Gramophone Co Ltd* [1909] AC 488.
12 *Perera v Vandiyar* [1953] 1 WLR 672; *Kenny v Preen* [1963] 1 QB 499.
13 *McMillan v Singh* (1984) 134 NLJ 1087.
14 [1964] AC 1129.
15 *Gray v Motor Accident Commission* (1999) 73 AJLR 45. See also A Beck [1997] Tort LR 85.

are confined to these three categories was confirmed by the House of Lords in *Cassell & Co Ltd v Broome*.[16]

(i)   Express authorisation by statute

The Reserve and Auxiliary Forces Act 1951, section 13(2) permitted an award of exemplary damages, but no other statutory examples were cited in *Rookes v Barnard*. Given the approach of the House of Lords and the suggestion that all references in statutes passed prior to *Rookes v Barnard* should be regarded as aggravated damages,[17] it would appear unlikely that any further cases will succeed on this basis.

(ii)   Conduct calculated to make a profit

Exemplary damages may be awarded where the defendant's conduct has been calculated to make a profit for himself which may exceed the compensation payable to the plaintiff.[18] In *Cassell & Co Ltd v Broome*,[19] a retired naval officer sued for libel the publishers of a book about a wartime convoy. The House of Lords upheld the jury award of £25,000 exemplary damages because of the profit the publishers would have made. The mere fact that the defendant committed the tort in the course of a profit-making business will not suffice, but it is not necessary that the defendant actually calculated that the profit to be made would exceed the damages he would have to pay. The appropriate principle is that the defendant has to be prepared to hurt somebody because he thinks he may well gain by doing so, even allowing for the risk that he may be liable to pay damages.[20] An award of this kind is not designed simply to reverse an unjust enrichment, it should also take into account the plaintiff's difficulties in litigating and that the damages awarded could be exceeded by the profit made by the defendant.[1]

Other cases where exemplary damages have been awarded for this reason include those where a tort has been committed by a landlord in order to encourage the departure of protected tenants, thereby increasing the value of the property,[2] and cases of tortious interference with the plaintiff's business.[3]

(iii)   Oppressive conduct by government servants

An award of exemplary damages can be justified where there has been oppressive, arbitrary or unconstitutional action by the servants of the government.[4] Servants of the government include persons purporting to exercise powers of government, central or local.[5] In *Bradford City Metropolitan Council v Arora*[6] a local authority was held liable to pay exemplary damages when it practised sexual or racial discrimination in the recruitment of its employees. However, the restrictive approach of the Court of Appeal in *AB v*

---

16   [1972] AC 1027. Accordingly public nuisance does not give rise to such damages: *AB v South West Water Services Ltd* [1993] 1 All ER 609.
17   *Rookes v Barnard* [1964] AC 1129 at 1133 (per Lord Devlin).
18   Ibid at 1226 (per Lord Devlin).
19   [1972] AC 1027. See also *John v MGN Ltd* [1996] 2 All ER 35 at 37 per Sir Thomas Bingham MR.
20   Ibid at 1094 (per Lord Morris).
1   Ibid at 1130 (per Lord Devlin).
2   *Drane v Evangelou* [1978] 2 All ER 437; *Mafo v Adams* [1970] 1 QB 548.
3   *Bell v Midland Rly Co* (1861) 10 CBNS 287.
4   [1964] AC 1129 at 1226 (per Lord Devlin).
5   Ibid at 1130 (per Lord Devlin). But this does not include the commercial operations of a privatised utility company: *AB v South West Water Services Ltd* [1993] 1 All ER 609.
6   [1991] 3 All ER 545.

South West Water Services Ltd,[7] to the effect that if a branch of law did not exist in 1964 then there could be no exemplary damages awarded in that area, has had an effect. The Employment Appeal Tribunal was led to conclude that there could be no exemplary damages in discrimination cases because there was no anti-discrimination law in 1964.[8]

One of the growth areas for the award of exemplary damages was in actions against police officers for trespass to the person and malicious prosecution.[9] In *Holden v Chief Constable of Lancashire*[10] it was held that this category covers wrongful arrest regardless of whether there was oppressive behaviour or aggravating circumstances. The court read the requirement of 'unconstitutional action' literally. However, the Court of Appeal has attempted to put a brake on these cases by restricting the amount of damages recoverable and the circumstances where exemplary damages will be recoverable in such actions.[11] It was stressed by LORD WOOLF MR[12] that there might be overcompensation as the jury would commonly award aggravated damages for injury to feelings. He stressed that the element of profit in cases within category (ii) was absent and that it was more difficult to justify the award where the defendant was the Chief Constable who was not himself the wrongdoer. Exemplary damages could be awarded where there was conduct (including oppressive or arbitrary behaviour) which deserved an exceptional remedy. The bracket for awards was set at between £5,000–£25,000, with a maximum of £50,000 where an officer of at least the rank of Superintendant was involved.

(3)   REFORM

The Law Commission[13] has produced recommendations on exemplary damages. These are that:
(i)   exemplary damages should be retained and renamed punitive damages;
(ii)   the question be raised of whether exemplary damages should be awarded and quantum should be assessed by a judge rather than a jury;
(iii) the 'categories' test from *Rookes v Barnard* and the 'cause of action' test from *AB v South West Water Services* should be abolished;
(iv)   there was no reason why outrageous conduct should not attract such an award even if not committed by government servants. The award should be available for any tort where deliberate and outrageous conduct disregarded the plaintiff's rights;
(v)   the award should not be available for breach of contract but should be in the case of equitable wrongs.

7   [1993] 1 All ER 609. See Howarth pp 598–601
8   *Deane v Ealing London Borough Council* [1993] ICR 329.
9   *White v Metropolitan Police Comr* (1982) Times, 24 April. See also *George v Metropolitan Police Comr* (1984) Times, 31 March; *Connor v Chief Constable of Cambridgeshire* (1984) Times, 11 April; *Taylor v Metropolitan Police Comr* (1989) Times, 6 December (£70,000).
10 [1987] QB 380.
11 *Thompson v Metropolitan Police Comr* [1997] 2 All ER 762.
12 Ibid at 772.
13 Report No 247 (1997).

Chapter 16

Compensatory damages I — factors limiting an award

1. INTRODUCTION

Once a plaintiff has established that the defendant is in breach of an obligation, he will normally seek damages to compensate for the loss flowing from the breach. Three major factors may limit or exclude the plaintiff's entitlement to damages. He must show that his loss was caused by the breach, that it was not too remote and that reasonable steps have been taken to mitigate the loss. In addition to these limiting factors, other matters may be relevant. For example, the contributory negligence of the plaintiff may reduce the amount of damages he receives.[1] Furthermore, the minimum contractual obligation of the defendant may limit the damages available to the plaintiff.[2] If the only obligation broken is a contractual duty to pay money, the sole remedy is to pay the agreed sum, and no additional expectation loss is compensatable by an award of compensatory damages.[3]

These principles have the effect of limiting an award of damages, with the result that the application of one or more of them may produce a similar result. However, the tendency of the court is to apply one rule only.[4]

2. FACTUAL CAUSATION

(1) INTRODUCTION

Whether an action is brought for a breach of contract or for breach of a tortious duty, the plaintiff must establish, on a balance of probabilities, that the damage he suffered was caused by the defendant's breach of duty. A relevant breach of tortious duty includes the simple commission of a tort actionable *per se*, or a breach of duty leading to actionable

---

1 See ch 20.
2 *Cockburn v Alexander* (1848) 6 CB 791 at 814 (per MAULE J); *Lavarack v Woods of Colchester Ltd* [1967] 1 QB 278 at 294 (per DIPLOCK LJ). See also Burrows *Remedies* pp 92–97.
3 *London, Chatham and Dover Rly Co v South Eastern Rly Co* [1893] AC 429. See Burrows *Remedies* pp 97–99.
4 *Compania Financiera Soleada SA v Hamoor Tanker Corpn Inc, The Borag* [1981] 1 All ER 856 at 864.

damage.[5] The issue of factual causation normally arises in tortious actions,[6] and usually causes the greatest difficulties in personal injury cases.

(2)   THE 'BUT FOR' TEST

A breach of duty is a cause of harm if that harm would not have occurred but for that breach of duty. This test usually excludes the defendant's breach of duty as a cause of harm suffered, but this is not always the case.[7] In *Barnett v Chelsea and Kensington Hospital Management Committee*,[8] the plaintiff's husband had complained of vomiting when he attended the defendant's hospital. No examination was ordered and he was referred to his own doctor. Five hours later, he died of arsenic poisoning. The defendants were in breach of duty by not examining the deceased, but tests showed that he would have died even if the doctor had examined him. Diagnosis and treatment would not have been effective in preventing the death. It was held that, since the deceased would have died regardless of the breach of duty, that breach was not a cause of the death. A further illustration is provided by *JEB Fasteners Ltd v Marks Bloom & Co*,[9] in which the defendant accountants carelessly overstated the value of a company's stock. The valuation was shown to the plaintiffs, who later purchased the company. The accountants' breach of duty was not a cause of the plaintiff's loss, as his decision to take over the company was based on factors other than the stock valuation.

The 'but for' test can create a number of difficulties in relation to the degree of probability of damage, negligent omissions, multiple causes of harm and economic loss.

(i)   Degree of probability of damage and 'loss of chance'

Where it is uncertain that the defendant's breach of duty has caused the damage complained of, it must be determined what degree of probability of harm must be established by the plaintiff. In cases of traumatic injury, such as physical harm caused to a pedestrian in a traffic accident, the mere presence of the car on the road will be treated as a cause of the pedestrian's injuries. More difficult issues arise where a disease is contracted or there is an omission to act. The plaintiff is required to prove, on the balance of probabilities, a causal connection between the defendant's breach of duty and the damage suffered.

On the 'all or nothing' approach of the common law in personal injuries cases, this means that if the evidence shows a 51% chance that the defendant's negligence was a cause of the damage, the plaintiff recovers in full for his loss. This is despite the fact that there is a 49% chance that the defendant's fault was not a cause of the damage. If the evidence shows a 49% chance of the fault causing the damage, the plaintiff recovers nothing.

Where all the sources of the risk are under the defendant's control, the courts have been prepared to find in the plaintiff's favour on causation even when he cannot cross the evidentiary gap. In *McGhee v National Coal Board*,[10] the medical evidence was unable to estimate the contribution of the breach of duty to the plaintiff's damage. However, the plaintiff was allowed to recover on the basis that the defendant's negligence had 'materially increased' the risk of the damage which occurred.[11]

5   See Stapleton (1988) 104 LQR 213.
6   Cf *Quinn v Burch Bros (Builders) Ltd* [1966] 2 QB 370; *Galoo Ltd v Bright Grahame Murray* [1995] 1 All ER 16.
7   See *Rouse v Squires* [1973] QB 889.
8   [1969] 1 QB 428. See also *The Empire Jamaica* [1957] AC 386.
9   [1983] 1 All ER 583. See also *Tate & Lyle Industries Ltd v Greater London Council* [1983] 1 All ER 1159.
10   [1973] 1 WLR 1; Weinrib (1975) 38 MLR 518.
11   See also *Bonnington Castings Ltd v Wardlaw* [1956] AC 613.

Where all the sources of the risk are not under the defendant's control, as is common in medical negligence cases, the courts have taken a firm line on causation. In *Wilsher v Essex Area Health Authority*[12] the House of Lords confirmed that the burden of proof remained on the plaintiff to establish a causative link between the defendant's negligence and the plaintiff's injury, although such a link could be inferred from the evidence, as in *McGhee*. Because of the background risk (alternative source) in medical negligence and disease cases, causation can be very difficult to establish. A plaintiff coming into contact with the medical profession will already be ill and may have suffered damage in the absence of medical intervention.

Proof of cause can be very difficult, especially where there is a 'new' illness and medical opinion is divided on whether it exists at all and if it does, how it is caused. The cause of an illness may be psychogenic (in the mind) rather than caused by the breach such as repetitive strain injury (RSI) and chronic fatigue syndrome (ME). In *Pickford v ICI plc*[13] the plaintiff was employed by the defendants as a typist and sued them for negligence on the basis that she had contracted RSI in the course of her employment. The argument on causation in the case was on whether the RSI was organic, in the sense of being caused by typing at high speed for long periods of time without proper breaks, or whether it was psychogenic. The medical evidence was split and the trial judge had rejected the defendant's evidence given in rebuttal that the cause was psychogenic. On that basis the Court of Appeal had found for the plaintiff but the House of Lords overturned this as the burden of proof was on the plaintiff who had failed to discharge that burden and establish on the balance of probabilities that the cause was organic.[14] This raises the interesting question of what would have happened if the plaintiff had pleaded the case in the alternative as having been organic in nature or psychogenic. In either case the defendant's breach may have been a cause of the damage. In contrast, in *Page v Smith (No 2)*[15] the plaintiff suffered a recurrence of ME after a traffic accident. The Court of Appeal[16] held that as there were a number of possible causes, the test was whether on the balance of probabilities the defendant's negligence had caused, or materially contributed (in the sense of being more than trivial or insignificant) to the plaintiff's damage. The test was *not* whether the plaintiff was exposed to an increased risk. In order to answer this question there were three factual points to be answered, which were all determined in the plaintiff's favour. These were, that ME existed; that it could be caused by 'an abstract entity of stress,' which included a road accident; and that the ME (on the basis of the medical evidence) was in fact caused by the road accident.

An attempt has been made to adopt the 'loss of chance' doctrine used in contract cases[17] to personal injuries cases. On the basis of this doctrine the plaintiff would receive damages in proportion to his lost chance rather than full compensation.[18] In *Hotson v East Berkshire AHA*[19] this argument succeeded at first instance and in the Court of Appeal but failed in the House of Lords. Failure to treat the plaintiff promptly had increased the chance that he would develop avascular necrosis. There was a 75% chance that had he been treated promptly he would still have suffered necrosis and on conventional causation principles the plaintiff failed. On the 'loss of chance' principle he would have

---

12   [1988] 1 All ER 871. Stapleton (1988) 104 LQR 389, 403–406.
13   [1998] 3 All ER 462.
14   Applying *Wilsher v Essex Area Health Authority* [1988] 1 All ER 871.
15   [1996] 3 All ER 272.
16   Applying *Bonnington Castings Ltd v Wardlaw* [1956] AC 613.
17   See *Chaplin v Hicks* [1911] 2 KB 786.
18   Stapleton (1988) 104 LQR 389; Hill (1991) 54 MLR 511; Scott (1992) 55 MLR 521; Stauch (1997) 17 OJLS 205.
19   [1987] AC 750.

recovered 25%. The balance of probability test for causation would have remained but the damage forming the 'gist' of the action would have been the lost chance rather than the physical damage. The House of Lords, however, held that on the balance of probabilities the injury was inevitable and the plaintiff had failed to establish a cause of action.

The decision leaves open the question of whether loss of chance could form the gist of an action in negligence. The House of Lords avoided this point by treating 'loss of chance' as an issue of quantification of damages, with the plaintiff first having to succeed on causation.

Whether 'loss of chance' should form a recoverable head of damage in personal injuries cases is controversial.[20] There are advantages in compensation and deterrence terms but there are 'formidable difficulties' in accepting it.[1]

In cases of economic loss it appears that the courts are awarding damages for loss of chance (see below).

(ii)   Omissions

Where the defendant's breach of duty consists of an omission to act (non-feasance) there is a hypothetical question of, 'what would have happened if ...?' The burden of proof on the plaintiff is to show that if the defendant had acted he would not have suffered the damage. This may involve looking at what the plaintiff would have done had the defendant acted.

In industrial safety cases where the defendant, in breach of duty, failed to supply safety equipment, would the plaintiff have used the safety equipment if it had been provided? If not, then the damage would have been suffered anyway and the defendant's breach of duty is not a cause.[2] One use of 'loss of chance' would be in such cases, calculating the chance that the employee would have used the equipment if provided and award damages on that basis.

The usual question in these cases is, 'would the plaintiff...?' However, the relevant question may be, 'would the defendant ...?' In some cases the 'would' may have to be combined with a 'should' and merge questions of breach and causation. In *Bolitho v City and Hackney Health Authority*[3] a doctor failed to attend a child patient who died. The child could have been saved if intubated. The doctor gave evidence that she would not have intubated if she had attended and the court found that a failure to intubate would not be a breach of the *Bolam* test for medical negligence. The doctor's failure to attend, which was a breach, was therefore not a cause of the child's death, as the child would have died even if the doctor had attended.

(iii)   More than one cause

Where the plaintiff's damage is the result of more than one cause, the 'but for' test would appear to provide no answer. Overlapping causes may be either concurrent or successive, but they must be independent, in that neither is a necessary condition of the occurrence of the other. If two fires are started independently by X and Y and both fires damage property owned by Z, both fires can be regarded as sufficient, concurrent causes of the harm suffered. An application of the 'but for' test to Y would result in no liability on his part, since the fire started by X would have damaged Z's

---

20   See Stapleton (1988) 104 LQR 389; Hill (1991) 54 MLR 511; Reece (1996) 59 MLR 188.
1   [1987] AC 750, 782 (per LORD BRIDGE).
2   *Cummings (or McWilliams) v Sir William Arrol & Co Ltd* [1962] 1 WLR 295.
3   [1998] AC 232.

property anyway. In cases of this kind, the 'but for' test is not applied, with the result that both X and Y are liable for the loss suffered.[4]

A similar principle applies where it is not certain which of two or more parties has caused the plaintiff's injuries. If guns are discharged simultaneously by A and B, and C is struck by a bullet, both A and B will be liable in the absence of proof that one or the other of the defendants fired the bullet that struck C.[5] The same approach can also be applied to a number of manufacturers who have produced drugs capable of harming the user by making the manufacturers liable in proportion to their share in the market for such drugs.[6]

Where causes are successive and the breach of duty of the second defendant causes the same damage as that of the first defendant, the 'but for' test will be applied in the action against the second defendant. In *Performance Cars Ltd v Abraham*,[7] the second defendant's car negligently collided with the plaintiff's car. The plaintiff claimed £75 as the cost of a respray, but, at the time of the accident, the car already required a respray as a result of a collision with the first defendant. The second defendant was not liable, as the need for the respray did not arise from his breach of duty.

A different approach is taken when the first defendant is sued and the second defendant has caused similar or increased damage to the plaintiff. In *Baker v Willoughby*,[8] the plaintiff suffered injuries to his left leg as a result of the first defendant's negligence. Before the trial, the plaintiff was shot in the left leg by the second defendant, who was engaged in an armed robbery. As a result, the leg had to be amputated. An application of the 'but for' test would have meant that the plaintiff would have been left uncompensated for his damaged leg after the robbery. Even if the second defendant could have been sued to judgment, an application of *Performance Cars* would have rendered him liable for depriving the plaintiff of a damaged leg. The plaintiff would have been left uncompensated for the difference between a sound leg and a damaged leg in respect of the period following the robbery. Faced with this problem, the House of Lords ignored the 'but for' test and held the first defendant liable for the full loss of use of the leg after the first injury, taking no account of the second injury.

Where the facts comprise a breach of duty followed by a natural event, the courts have used a 'vicissitudes of life' test. In *Jobling v Associated Dairies Ltd*,[9] the plaintiff's back was injured due to the defendant's negligence, and his earning capacity was reduced by 50%. Before the trial, he was found to have a spinal disease unrelated to the back injury, which rendered him totally unfit for work. The House of Lords applied the 'but for' test to restrict the defendant's liability for loss of earnings to the period before the onset of the disease. The reasoning in *Baker v Willoughby* was criticised, but the decision survives, on its own facts, where there are two successive torts rather than a tort followed by a disabling illness.[10]

Both *Baker* and *Jobling* are personal injury cases and, in this area, tort is not the only form of compensation available. In *Baker*, the plaintiff would probably have been entitled to compensation from the Criminal Injuries Compensation Board but only for losses brought about by the robbery.[11] The effect of *Baker* is to prevent a plaintiff falling

---

4   *Kingston v Chicago and NW Rail Co* 191 Wis 610 (1927). See also *Crossley and Sons Ltd v Lightowler* (1867) 2 Ch App 478.
5   *Cook v Lewis* [1952] 1 DLR 1. But see *Fowler v Lanning* [1959] 1 QB 426.
6   *Sindell v Abbott Laboratories* 449 US 912 (1980).
7   [1962] 1 QB 33.
8   [1970] AC 467.
9   [1982] AC 794.
10 See also *Malec v J C Hutton Pty Ltd* (1990) 64 AJLR 316.
11 Cf *Jobling v Associated Dairies Ltd* [1982] AC 794 at 803 (per LORD WILBERFORCE).

between two tortfeasors.[12] In *Jobling*, the plaintiff might have been able to claim social security benefits to partially compensate his losses, but it is also possible to fall between tort compensation and entitlement to social security payments.[13] The distinction seems to lie in the common law refusal to compensate for disease suffered in the absence of fault.

If the natural event happens before the breach of duty, the relevant issue is not one of causation, but one of assessment of damages. If the plaintiff suffers from a fatal disease at the time of breach of duty, damages will be assessed on the basis of the plaintiff's life expectancy before the date of the breach of duty.[14] A similar principle can be applied where the second cause is hypothetical. Where a person falls from a bridge to almost certain death, but strikes negligently maintained high voltage cables on the way down, causation is established, but damages are assessed on a life expectancy of a few seconds.[15]

(iv)   Economic loss

Where the loss is economic rather than physical, then to a certain extent the scope of the defendant's liability will be defined by the duty of care as the courts have been cautious in defining the precise extent of such liability.[16] In particular, a distinction has been made between giving advice and giving information. In advice cases the defendant will be responsible for all foreseeable consequences of the action taken by the advisee, whereas in information cases liability is simply for the consequences of the information being wrong.[17] However, it is clear that there are a number of causation issues to be determined in this area, however tightly the duty is defined.

The simple application of the 'but for' test has been rejected, except as a blunt instrument for ruling out non-operative causes. The fact that a case satisfies the 'but for' test does not mean that the plaintiff succeeds on causation. The breach of duty must be an 'effective cause' of the loss, rather than simply providing the opportunity for loss to be suffered.[18] Therefore an accountant who negligently states that a company is operating at a profit, when losses are being incurred, is not liable for the trading losses suffered by the company, as the accountant's negligence simply provides the opportunity for the losses to be suffered by the company remaining in business.[19]

Causation questions on economic loss tend to arise in professional negligence cases, where there is generally concurrent liability. The issue will be the causation barrier that has to passed by a plaintiff who has been given negligent advice or information (misfeasance), or, in breach of duty, has not been given advice or information (nonfeasance). It is not sufficient for the plaintiff simply to allege that he relied on the advice or information.[20] The plaintiff must prove that he would not have entered into the transaction he alleges caused him loss or would have done so on different terms. This applies to both misfeasance and nonfeasance claims, despite a statement in *Mothew* that this only applied in nonfeasance cases.[1] If a lender engages a solicitor to act in a mortgage transaction and the solicitor gives negligent information, or negligently fails

---

12   See McGregor and Strachen (1970) 33 MLR 378.
13   Harvey (1981) 97 LQR 210 at 211–212.
14   *Pickett v British Rail Engineering Ltd* [1979] 1 All ER 774.
15   *Dillon v Twin State Gas and Electric Co* NH 449 (1932).
16   See ch 10.
17   *South Australia Asset Management Corpn v York Montague Ltd* [1996] 3 All ER 365.
18   *Galoo Ltd v Bright Grahame Murray* [1995] 1 All ER 16.
19   Ibid applying *Alexander v Cambridge Credit Corpn Ltd* (1987) 9 NSWLR 310 and *March v Stramare Pty* (1991) 171 CLR 506.
20   *Bristol and West Building Society v Mothew* [1996] 4 All ER 698.
1   *Swindle v Harrison* [1997] 4 All ER 705.

to give information, resulting in loss to the lender from that transaction, the lender must prove that he would not have entered the transaction (or would have entered it on different terms) had he been in possession of the correct information.[2]

Where a professional has given, or failed to give, advice or information to a client, there will frequently be a hypothetical question. What would have happened if the correct information or advice had been given? In the solicitor-lender cases this can usually be established by reference to the lenders' standard practice. Is it possible, in cases where the outcome would have been uncertain, to award damages for the client's loss of chance? If a solicitor's negligence or breach of contract results in his client losing an action, but the outcome of the action was uncertain, can the client recover against the solicitor for his lost chance of success? If the client has lost some right of value, of reality and substance, he can recover.[3] If the lost chance is more than 50% then this does not pose causation problems, as the plaintiff will have passed the balance of probabilities test. However, what is the position where the chance of success of the original action was eg one in three? In conventional causation terms the action should fail, but the courts do allow such actions to succeed, in contrast to physical injury claims. In *Allied Maples Group v Simmons & Simmons*[4] it was held that although the lost chance must be real or significant it did not have to pass the 50% barrier.[5]

(3)   CAUSATION IN CONTRACT

The plaintiff must show that the loss was caused by the defendant's breach of contract. There is no formal test and the question rarely arises in contract cases. The Court of Appeal has stated that the test is the same in contract and tort where there is concurrent liability. The breach of contract must be the effective cause of the loss.[6]

3.   LEGAL CAUSATION

(1)   FACTORS CONSTITUTING A LEGAL CAUSE OF DAMAGE

Even where the defendant's breach of duty is a cause in fact of the plaintiff's damage, compensatory damages may be denied on the ground that the breach of duty was not the legal cause of the damage. Other expressions such as proximate cause, or *causa causans* are also used to describe legal causation. A number of factors may have been a factual cause of the damage, but a court has to allocate responsibility to the cause in law. It is necessary to attribute the damage to a particular cause, rather than to explain how the occurrence happened. Where a car crashes, thereby causing damage, the driver is likely to be regarded as the legal cause if his conduct is classified as negligent. Other factors may also have been 'causes' of the accident. The road surface may have been slippery, or the brakes on the car may have been inefficient in bad weather. Neither of these 'causes' will usually attract attention, as they would involve accident prevention measures, which are not normally regarded as the province of the common law.

The issue for remoteness of damage is to determine for what, if any, loss a wrongdoer should be liable for. Is it too harsh to impose liability for all consequences of the breach

2   See also *Bristol & West Building Society v Fancy and Jackson* [1997] 4 All ER 582. Sprince (1998) 14(1) PN 3

3   *Kitchen v RAFA* [1958] 2 All ER 241.

4   [1995] 1 WLR 1602.

5   Ibid at 1611–12 per STUART SMITH LJ. See also *Spring v Guardian Assurance plc* [1994] 3 All ER 129; *First Interstate Bank of California v Cohen Arnold & Co Ltd* [1995] EGCS 188; *Acton v Graham Pearce & Co* [1997] 3 All ER 909.

6   *Galoo v Bright Grahame Murray* [1994] 1 WLR 1360; *Monarch Steamship v Karlshamms Oljefabriker* [1949] AC 196; *Quinn v Burch Bros (Builders) Ltd* [1966] 2 QB 370.

on the defendant? If this is not done, however, the loss may fall on the plaintiff, unless it can be ascribed to a third party. Remoteness can be seen to have two aspects: should the defendant be responsible for any of the loss, and should he be liable for parts of it. The first part has largely been subsumed into duty of care in negligence. 'Sometimes I say: "there was no duty." In others I say: "the damage was too remote."'[7] The function performed by proximity in negligence performs the same function as remoteness relating to the whole of the loss. Duty has even claimed the function of allocating parts of loss in one area. In the negligent valuation cases the House of Lords avoided remoteness issues by framing the valuer's duty in terms of information as opposed to advice and only holding the valuer liable for the consequences of the valuation being wrong.[8] The effect of the valuer's breach is that the lender has less security for an advance than he thought. In this way losses caused by extraneous causes such as market falls are largely excluded, even though such falls are surely foreseeable. An incidental effect of the test is that it correlates degree of fault to damages payable.

(2)   CRITERIA FOR SELECTING A CAUSE OF DAMAGE

There are two views on the relevant criteria for selecting a legal cause. It may be that these criteria are to be found in the ordinary usage of speech.[9] Where A suffers damage and ordinary usage of speech would explain this as having been caused by B, B is the cause of A's damage. This would exclude liability where damage is a bizarre consequence of a series of events. This approach involves difficulties in formulating grounds for a decision, and also fails to distinguish between explanatory and attributive language. Ordinary usage of speech may explain B's conduct as the cause of the damage, in the sense that it explains how the damage came about. But this does not explain why liability is attributed to B.[10]

The second view is that policy factors should influence the issue of causation. Because of the part played by morality in common law development, the relevant policy applied is whether it is just to impose liability on a particular person because he is morally responsible. It follows that the contract breaker and the negligent driver or employer may be made liable on moral grounds. However, some limitation must be placed on liability. Limitations are effected by a number of devices which include the remoteness of damage principle and the notion of a break in the chain of causation. In cases involving a breach of statutory duty, a further limitation is imposed by asking whether the damage was of a type against which the defendant is required to take precautions.[11] In actions under the 'narrow' rule in *Donoghue v Stevenson*,[12] the causation enquiry is assisted by rules on intermediate examination and alternative cause. In actions under the rule in *Rylands v Fletcher*,[13] the defendant will not be liable if an escape is caused by the act of a third party.

The policy approach means that there is a close correlation between the issue of causation and that of breach of duty. In the majority of cases, once a person has been found to be in breach of duty, he will also be held to be the legal cause of the damage.

The moral policy approach has the unfortunate effect of failing to create an intelligible framework, particularly where the defendant is held not to be legally responsible for damage suffered. It also has the effect of obscuring other policy factors which may be

---

7   *Spartan Steel & Alloys Ltd v Martin & Co* [1973] QB 27,37 per LORD DENNING.
8   *South Australia Asset Management Corpn v York Montague Ltd* [1996] 3 All ER 365.
9   Hart and Honoré *Causation in Law* (2nd edn, 1985).
10   See also Harris et al *Compensation and Support for Illness and Injury* (1984) ch 4.
11   See *Gorris v Scott* (1874) LR 9 Exch 125 and see ch 27.
12   [1932] AC 562 and see ch 25.
13   (1868) LR 3 HL 330 and see ch 29.

important. The courts have acknowledged the part which is played by insurance,[14] and may wish to attribute liability to the best insurer. This factor is frequently obscured by the language of the decisions when the judge states that the damage was not caused by the breach of duty. Insurance is particularly important in fire damage cases. It is acknowledged that the most effective method of compensation is first-party insurance. Where A starts a fire destroying B, C and D's property, the court's decision not to shift the risk to A by finding him liable may be justified by saying that A did not cause the damage.

Many of the difficulties posed by legal causation, whatever theoretical underpinning may be used, can be attributed to an outdated conceptual structure. The major part of tort law is concerned with compensating for physical damage. The existing legal structure reflects nineteenth-century ideology, in the sense that liability is theoretically underpinned by moral responsibility for one's conduct. Modern emphasis has moved towards loss-spreading through insurance and accident prevention. In order to achieve these objectives, the courts are required to operate behind a cloak of rhetoric phrased in nineteenth-century language. Only the boldest members of the judiciary are prepared to explicitly state their objectives. The inefficiency of the system is starkly exposed by cases such as *Wilsher v Essex Area Health Authority*,[15] where the House of Lords was forced to the position of ordering the retrial of an action for negligence in respect of blindness suffered by a newborn baby, who was almost ten years of age by the time of the Lords' hearing.

When economic, as opposed to physical, damage is in question, the issue is clouded by the tort–contract divide and the policy issues at stake. Economic loss cases are concerned with risk-allocation. Where the parties have allocated the risk by the terms of their transaction, should the court intervene to take account of inequality of bargaining power? Where the risk has not been allocated, what factors should the court utilise in order to decide who is best placed to bear a particular item of loss?

(3)   PHYSICAL DAMAGE

(i)   Introduction

The expression 'physical damage' covers personal injuries, damage to property and consequential expenses. This form of loss is recoverable in both contract and tort cases, but the majority of such actions arise in the law of tort. The issue of information transfer is generally irrelevant in physical damage cases, except in so far as it relates to the initial question of liability.[16] For this reason, it is submitted that there is no valid reason for applying a different test of remoteness of damage to actions brought for breach of contract from that which applies to an action for a breach of a tortious duty.

In physical damage cases, the plaintiff is at an advantage. Once liability has been established, the defendant effectively becomes an insurer. All the plaintiff must show is that his injuries were of a kind likely to be suffered as a result of the defendant's breach of duty. The difficulty is to determine what is meant by such a kind of damage.

At one stage, it was sufficient that physical damage was a direct consequence of the defendant's breach of duty.[17] This was very generous to the plaintiff, but it should also be appreciated that the scope of potential tortious liability was relatively narrow at the time. The direct consequence test was considered by the Privy Council in *The Wagon*

---

14   See *Photo Production Ltd v Securicor Transport Ltd* [1980] AC 827; *Lamb v Camden London Borough Council* [1981] QB 625.
15   [1988] 1 All ER 871.
16   See *Paris v Stepney Borough Council* [1951] AC 367; Sale of Goods Act 1979, s 14(3).
17   *Re Polemis and Furness Withy & Co Ltd's Arbitration* [1921] 3 KB 560.

Mound (No 1).[18] The defendants negligently discharged fuel oil into Sydney Harbour. The oil spread to the plaintiff's wharf, where welding operations were in progress. A spark from a welding torch ignited the oil and caused considerable fire damage to the wharf. The oil also caused fouling to the wharf. The trial judge found that it was not foreseeable that fuel oil on water would catch fire, but that some foreseeable damage in the form of fouling was caused. It followed that there was a duty of care and a breach of that duty. By applying the direct consequence test, the defendants were held liable for the fouling of the wharf and the fire damage. However, the Privy Council held that the defendants were not liable for the fire damage. The test of remoteness applied was whether the type of damage suffered was a reasonably foreseeable consequence of the defendant's breach of duty.

The motivating factor behind the decision appears to have been an attempt to unify the tests for duty, breach and damage into one of reasonable foreseeability. It appeared illogical that a defendant's duty should depend on what he could have foreseen, but that he could be liable for types of damage which he could not have foreseen.[19] It is clear that the court was mistaken in this view, as foreseeability is only part of the formula for determining negligence.[20]

Although the courts have purported to apply the *Wagon Mound* test, the results of many cases appear to be similar to those which would have been achieved under a test of direct consequences.

(ii) Kind of damage

The key to the distinction between the direct consequence test and the *Wagon Mound* test is to determine what is meant by damage of a particular kind. In *Re Polemis*,[1] a plank was negligently dropped into the hold of a ship. Petrol vapour in the hold was ignited by a spark caused by the plank, which resulted in the destruction of the ship. The interpretation of the kind of damage covered both damage to property and to the person. In *The Wagon Mound*, the Privy Council attempted to place a narrower definition on the meaning of kind of damage by making a distinction between damage caused by fouling and that caused by fire.

This attempt to narrow the definition has been avoided by means of a number of devices. If the kind of damage suffered is reasonably foreseeable, it does not matter that the damage came about in an unforeseeable way. In *Hughes v Lord Advocate*,[2] Post Office employees erected a portable tent over an exposed manhole, and surrounded the tent with paraffin lamps. A child dropped one of the lamps down the hole, thereby causing an explosion which injured the child. Burning was a foreseeable kind of damage, even though the precise manner of burning might not have been foreseen. In *Doughty v Turner Manufacturing Co Ltd*,[3] the Court of Appeal distinguished burns caused by the eruption of a molten liquid from burns caused by the splashing of the molten liquid. This approach seems difficult to reconcile with *Hughes*, as the question which should have been asked was whether damage caused by burning was foreseeable.[4] In *Tremain v Pike*,[5] the plaintiff was not allowed to recover for damage caused by Weil's disease, a

---

18   Sub nom *Overseas Tankship (UK) Ltd v Morts Dock & Engineering Co Ltd* [1961] AC 388.
19   Ibid at 424 (per VISCOUNT SIMMONDS).
20   See ch 12 and Hart and Honoré *Causation in the Law* (2nd edn, 1985) ch IX.
1   [1921] 3 KB 560.
2   [1963] AC 837. See also *Bradford v Robinson Rentals Ltd* [1967] 1 All ER 267; *Jolley v Sutton London Borough Council* [1998] 6 All ER 559.
3   [1964] 3 QB 518.
4   Cf Atiyah *Accidents* p 104.
5   [1969] 1 WLR 1556.

rare disease contracted from rat's urine, as it was unforeseeable and different in kind from foreseeable consequences such as rat bites or food poisoning.[6]

Tremain could be regarded as a case on breach and based on the cost of taking precautions against a minimal risk. One way out of the kind of damage maze would be to treat kind of harm as 'injuries that would be prevented by the same precautions.'[7] In *Hughes,* the child's burns could have been avoided by taking simple precautions to guard the manhole. The courts however, do not seem to be moving in this direction. A curious purported application of *Hughes* was in *Jolley v Sutton London Borough Council.*[8] A boat was left on land owned by the defendants for two years. The plaintiff child jacked up the boat and started to repair it. The boat fell on the plaintiff. The Court of Appeal held that although the council were in breach of duty, the damage was too remote as the accident was of a different kind from that which could have been foreseen. Removing the boat would have been a cheap method of avoiding any accident involving the boat but the court was influenced by the plaintiff's actions in jacking the boat up.

Provided the kind of damage is foreseeable, it does not matter that it is more extensive than could have been foreseen. In *Vacwell Engineering Co Ltd v BDH Chemicals Ltd*[9] the defendants supplied a chemical but negligently failed to warn that it was liable to explode in contact with water. A scientist working for the plaintiffs placed the chemical in water, thereby causing a violent explosion which resulted in extensive damage. The defendants were held liable, even though the extent of the damage was unforeseeable.[10]

One particular example of the extent of damage principle is the rule that the defendant must take the plaintiff as he finds him, as regards his physical characteristics. This rule is sometimes referred to as the 'egg-shell skull' or 'thin skull' rule, and it is clear that it survives *The Wagon Mound*. In *Smith v Leech Brain & Co Ltd,*[11] a negligently inflicted burn caused an employee, whose lips were in a pre-malignant condition, to contract cancer. The defendants were liable for the damage resulting from death, even though death itself was not foreseeable. A similar principle also applies when the negligently caused injury is exacerbated by medical treatment to which the plaintiff is allergic.[12] What is not clear in civil law is whether the principle extends beyond physical characteristics. If a plaintiff suffers negligently inflicted injuries and dies because he refuses a blood transfusion on religious grounds, will the defendant be liable for the death?

Where the harm is psychiatric damage the courts have drawn a distinction between primary and secondary victims.[13] In the case of secondary victims the 'egg-shell skull' principle applies. If a reasonably strong-minded person might have suffered shock, a sensitive plaintiff can recover for the full extent of his shock.[14] It is, however, necessary that the defendant should have been able to foresee shock as a kind of harm. In the case of primary victims there is no distinction drawn in terms of foreseeability between psychiatric damage and physical damage simpliciter. If the defendant negligently causes a road accident in which the plaintiff suffers no physical injuries but does suffer the onset of a latent psychiatric condition , the foreseeability test is satisfied as physical injury was foreseeable.[15]

---

6   Cf *H Parsons (Livestock) Ltd v Uttley Ingham & Co Ltd* [1978] QB 791.
7   Howarth *Textbook on Tort* (Butterworths, 1995), p 155.
8   [1998] 6 All ER 559.
9   [1971] 1 QB 88.
10 See also *Muirhead v Industrial Tank Specialities Ltd* [1985] 3 WLR 993 at 1010 (per ROBERT GOFF LJ) and *Wieland v Cyril Lord Carpets Ltd* [1969] 3 All ER 1006 at 1009 (per EVELEIGH J).
11 [1962] 2 QB 405, [1961] 3 All ER 1159. See Rowe (1977) 40 MLR 377.
12 *Robinson v Post Office* [1974] 2 All ER 737, [1974] 1 WLR 1176. See Dias [1975] CLJ 15.
13 See ch 9.
14 *Brice v Brown* [1984] 1 All ER 997.
15 *Page v Smith* [1994] 4 All ER 522.

(iii)   Degree of likelihood of harm

There has been little discussion of the extent to which the kind of damage must be foreseeable under the *Wagon Mound* test. Such consideration as there has been suggests that a low degree of forseeability is required.[16]

The most important case on this issue is *The Wagon Mound (No 2)*.[17] This case concerned the same defendants and facts as *The Wagon Mound*, but the plaintiffs were the owners of two ships being repaired at the wharf and which were damaged by the fire. The action was brought in negligence and nuisance, and the trial judge found there was a bare possibility of fire, but this was so remote that it could be ignored. The Privy Council reversed the decision, stating that, as long as fire damage was foreseeable as a kind of damage, the degree of likelihood was irrelevant to the question of kind of damage suffered.

(iv)   Impecuniosity

The situation may arise where the plaintiff's loss is made greater by his financial inability to take steps to minimise the loss. The question arises as to whether the loss caused by the plaintiff's impecuniosity is too remote or not.

In *The Liesbosch Dredger*,[18] a dredger sank due to the negligence of the defendants. The owners required the dredger to complete a contract but, because of their impecuniosity, they were unable to buy a replacement dredger and had to hire one. The House of Lords held that the cost of hire was irrecoverable as an indirect consequence of the defendant's breach of duty.[19]

The *Liesbosch* decision has not proved popular, and has often been distinguished. In *Martindale v Duncan*,[20] the plaintiff delayed having his car repaired until it was clear that the defendants would pay the cost. He recovered the cost of hiring a substitute vehicle during that period. *The Liesbosch* was distinguished as the plaintiff's impecuniosity was not the sole reason he had delayed having the repairs done. He first wished to see whether he would be compensated for the repairs.[1]

(v)   Is *The Wagon Mound* a universal test?

It is now clearly settled that *The Wagon Mound* is the appropriate remoteness test in negligence, nuisance and *Rylands v Fletcher* cases.[2]

Where the defendant intends to do harm, the moral basis of the common law dictates that he should be more extensively liable than the merely negligent defendant.[3] The policy factors which restrict liability in negligence cases do not apply where harm is intentionally inflicted. However, issues of factual causation are still relevant. In deceit cases, the *Wagon Mound* test has not been applied, with the result that the defendant

---

16   *The Heron II* [1969] 1 AC 350; *H Parsons (Livestock) Ltd v Uttley Ingham & Co Ltd* [1978] QB 791.
17   Sub nom *Overseas Tankship (UK) Ltd v Miller SS Co Pty* [1967] 1 AC 617.
18   Sub nom *Owners of Dredger Liesbosch v Owners of Steamship Edison* [1933] AC 449.
19   Cf LORD WRIGHT ibid at 460.
20   [1973] 2 All ER 355. See also *Dodd Properties (Kent) v Canterbury City Council* [1980] 1 All ER 928; *Perry v Sidney Phillips & Sons* [1982] 3 All ER 705; *Mattocks v Mann* [1993] RTR 13; cf *Ramwade Ltd v WJ Emson & Co Ltd* [1987] RTR 72.
1   See also *Verderame v Commercial Union Assurance plc* [1992] BCLC 793.
2   *Cambridge Water Co v Eastern Counties Leather plc* [1994] 1 All ER 53.
3   See *Quinn v Leathem* [1901] AC 495 at 535 (per LORD LINDLEY).

may be liable for all the damage flowing from his fraud.[4] A similar test applies to actions for damages under section 2(1) of the Misrepresentation Act 1967.[5]

The so-called torts of strict liability present a more difficult problem. In the case of strict liability torts, foresight of damage is not necessary to establish liability, but foresight of the kind of harm suffered may be necessary for remoteness purposes. Furthermore, a defendant might not have foreseen any harm at all. Some commentators ask whether the damage should have been foreseen if the defendant was aware of the occurrence of the event causing that damage.[6] In *Galashiels Gas Co Ltd v O'Donnell*,[7] a lift on the defendants' premises was in perfect working order both before and after an accident which killed a person. The defendants were held liable for a breach of absolute statutory duty, despite the fact that they could not have foreseen the death. It must be asked whether the defendants were told of the failure of the lift and, if so, should they have foreseen the death?

That the question does not arise often is due to the extreme reluctance of the courts to impose strict liability at all, except where parliamentary language irrefutably requires this. Where a decision has been made to impose strict liability, the risk of harm lies with the defendant and can be insured against. The remoteness issue would appear to be whether the damage is within the scope of the risk,[8] rather than whether it could have been foreseen.

(vi)   A different test in contractual actions?

It is possible that a defendant may find himself liable to one person for a breach of contract giving rise to physical harm and to another person due to a breach of tortious duty.[9] For example, the manufacturer of a defective product, the occupier of premises or a doctor may all find themselves in this position. The defendant may also be concurrently liable for physical damage to a plaintiff in both contract and tort. Where economic loss has been suffered, there is no liability for abnormal losses, unless the defendant has been informed of special circumstances likely to give rise to those losses. However, there would appear to be no reason for this rule to apply to cases of physical damage. While a party to a contract might think of possible financial losses before making the contract, he is much less likely to contemplate the possibility of physical harm. The typical view is that, in tort cases, there is no opportunity for the injured party to protect himself.[10] However, this is not strictly true as, in many tort cases, the parties are known to each other and may even be in a contractual relationship. The better view would appear to be that physical harm is not something which is generally contemplated in any relationship, and that losses of this sort should be recoverable, so long as the harm suffered is not too remote. It would seem to follow that there is little justification for applying separate tests of remoteness in tortious and contractual actions for physical damage.

This was recognised in *Parsons v Uttley Ingham*,[11] where the plaintiff pig farmers bought a food storage hopper from the defendant manufacturers, who installed the hopper. The defendants failed to unseal a ventilator in the hopper, causing pignuts stored therein

---

4   *Smith New Court Securities Ltd v Scrimgeour Vickers (Asset Management) Ltd* [1996] 4 All ER 769; *Doyle v Olby (Ironmongers) Ltd* [1969] 2 QB 158; *Archer v Brown* [1984] 2 All ER 267.
5   *Royscot Trust Ltd v Rogerson* [1991] 3 All ER 294.
6   Burrows *Remedies* p 4; *Dias and Markesinis* p 138.
7   [1949] AC 275.
8   See *Gorris v Scott* (1874) LR 9 Exch 125.
9   See *H Parsons (Livestock) Ltd v Uttley Ingham & Co Ltd* [1978] QB 791 at 803 (per LORD DENNING).
10   *The Heron II* [1969] 1 AC 350 at 385–386 (per LORD REID).
11   [1978] QB 791.

to become mouldy. As a result of this, the plaintiff's pigs died of a rare intestinal disease caused by the presence of the bacterium, E Coli. It was held that the defendants' breach of contract was the cause of the pigs' death. In contractual loss of profit cases, *The Heron II*[12] provided for a strict test of remoteness, but the tortious remoteness test in *The Wagon Mound*[13] provided for a test more favourable to the plaintiff who suffered physical damage. LORD DENNING MR considered that the *Wagon Mound* test should be applied to all physical damage cases, regardless of whether the action was framed in contract or in tort.[14] Under this test, the defendants would be liable for the death of the pigs, if death could have been reasonably foreseen as a possible consequence, even if it was only a slight possibility.[15] The *Wagon Mound* test is concerned with the kind of damage suffered, that is the loss of the pigs, rather than with the extent of the damage or the way in which it came about. Applying this test, the defendants were liable.

The majority in the case rejected LORD DENNING's view, but considered that the defendants should reasonably have contemplated the serious possibility of the pigs becoming ill, and brought the case within the *Heron II* rule. SCARMAN LJ stated that it was the type and not the extent of the loss that must be contemplated,[16] but this places a heavy burden on the distinction between the type and the extent of the loss.[17]

It is submitted that LORD DENNING's approach is preferable, on the grounds that the courts are generally more willing to protect a plaintiff against physical damage than loss of profit, and it is unlikely that a contracting party will inform the other of the risk of 'abnormal' physical losses. Further, the extent of loss-shifting permitted in cases of physical damage is seriously limited by the Unfair Contract Terms Act 1977.[18]

If the common law takes a generous view of remoteness for the victims of tortious acts leading to physical damage, is there any valid reason why a party should be disadvantaged by a stricter remoteness test because he is a contracting party? In any case, the stricter contractual remoteness test could be avoided, in some instances, by framing the action in tort. One advantage of the tort action is that the defendant's knowledge of possible consequences may be more extensive at the time of the breach than at the time the contract was formed. What the defendant learned in the course of performance may alert him to consequences of a breach which he could not possibly have contemplated at the time of contracting.

(4)   NON-PHYSICAL DAMAGE

(i)   Introduction

Traditionally, non-physical or financial loss suffered by the plaintiff could only be recovered by means of an action for breach of contract but in limited circumstances may now be recovered in an action in the tort of negligence. In the paradigm action for physical damage, the defendant is likely to be insured against liability, as is the case where the defendant is a motorist, an employer, a doctor, a manufacturer, a carrier or an occupier of premises. However, the same cannot be assumed in cases involving financial loss, although certain professional persons, such as solicitors, architects and accountants, may well carry liability insurance. In commercial transactions, a party may

---

12   [1969] 1 AC 350.
13   [1961] AC 388.
14   [1978] QB 791 at 804.
15   Ibid.
16   Ibid at 813.
17   Cf *Victoria Laundry (Windsor) Ltd v Newman Industries Ltd* [1949] 2 KB 528 and see also *Wroth v Tyler* [1974] Ch 30.
18   See ch 24.

wish to seek to protect his position by seeking security against liability. He may do this by taking out insurance against a risk, by seeking to limit his liability by the use of a contractual limitation clause, or by charging a higher price for his product. In order to achieve this objective, the party needs to be informed as to the nature of the risks involved, that is, he needs to be aware of the consequences of his possible breach of duty.[19] The objective of remoteness rules should therefore be to avoid information asymmetry between the parties by encouraging disclosure of information.

Information disclosure will only be possible where the parties have a contractual or other relationship before the breach of duty. It will not be possible where they are strangers. This would suggest a remoteness rule applicable to both contract cases and tort cases where the parties are known to each other, and a separate rule for strangers.

Whether the case is framed in contract or in tort, or between strangers or not, it is clear that the emphasis on the kind of damage suffered in physical damage cases will cause problems in cases involving non–physical loss. Classifying the kind of damage as financial loss and then applying the rule that the extent of the damage need not be foreseeable results in too extensive a liability.[20] The only alternative to this test would be to break down financial losses into distinct categories. It may be preferable to ignore the distinction between the kind of damage and the extent of damage in loss of profit cases and concentrate instead on what the parties contemplated in each case, on the basis of the information available.

(ii)   Remoteness of damage in economic loss cases

Nineteenth–century law allowed recovery for non–physical or economic loss where there was a breach of contract. Until 1854, damages for breach of contract were assessed by jury, and such assessment depended on the type of contract involved.[1] The decision in *Hadley v Baxendale*[2] was part of a movement to convert questions of fact to be determined by a jury into questions of law decided upon by the court and, in this particular case, to establish a doctrine of remoteness of damage.[3] The test was based on the foresight of damage, and thus contract cases gradually adopted the language employed in tort cases.

In *Hadley v Baxendale*,[4] the plaintiff mill owners required the defendant carriers to transport a broken crankshaft to Greenwich. Due to delay on the part of the carriers, the plaintiffs' mill was closed for several days longer than would otherwise have been necessary. The plaintiffs sued to recover the profits lost by the delay. The jury gave a verdict for the plaintiffs which was reversed by the Court of Exchequer. ALDERSON B held that:

> Where two parties have made a contract which one of them has broken, the damages which the other party ought to receive in respect of such breach of contract should be such as may fairly and reasonably be considered arising naturally, that is according to the usual course of things from such breach of contract itself, or such as may reasonably be supposed to have been in the contemplation of both parties, at the time they made the contract, as the probable result of the breach of it.[5]

---

19   Cf *American Restatement, Contracts* (2d) s 351(3).
20   See *Islamic Republic of Iran Shipping Lines v Ierax Shipping of Panama, The Forum Craftsman* [1991] 1 Lloyd's Rep 81, 87. But see *Brown v KMR Services Ltd* [1995] 4 All ER 598.
1   See ch 4.
2   (1854) 9 Exch 341, 23 LJ Ex 179.
3   See ch 4.
4   (1854) 9 Exch 341.
5   Ibid at 354.

Damage was therefore divided into normal losses, which were recoverable, and abnormal losses, which were recoverable only if the defendant had knowledge of the special circumstances giving rise to the possibility of such loss at the time the contract was made. There is still controversy as to whether it is sufficient that the defendant knew of the special circumstances, or whether he was required to contract on the basis that he should bear the loss.[6] Later cases seem to suggest that knowledge alone is sufficient.[7]

In *Hadley v Baxendale*, since the plaintiff's loss was considered not to have followed naturally from the breach, as he might have had a spare mill shaft, and since the defendant was not aware of any special circumstances, the damage suffered was too remote.

The distinction between normal and abnormal losses is illustrated in *Victoria Laundry (Windsor) Ltd v Newman Industries Ltd.*[8] As a result of business expansion and in an attempt to secure lucrative dyeing contracts, the plaintiff launderers ordered a boiler from the defendants. The boiler was delivered late, and the plaintiffs claimed losses of profit amounting to £16 per week, which they claimed would have been earned from the expansion of their business. Furthermore, they claimed an additional £262 per week in respect of the loss of the dyeing contracts. They were held to be entitled to recover only their normal losses of £16 per week. The loss on the dyeing contracts was categorised as an abnormal loss and, since the defendants had no knowledge of the special circumstances giving rise to it, the loss was irrecoverable. It was said that a single rule could apply, namely that the defendant should be liable for loss which he foresaw, or ought to have foreseen, at the time of contracting.[9]

Foreseeability of a breach of contract is not in question, as the parties contemplate performance, not breach. The problem is to determine what kind of loss the parties would contemplate in the event of a breach. They are taken to have contemplated the normal kind of damage arising naturally, according to the usual course of things, but abnormal damage is only to be contemplated if the defendant had knowledge of the special circumstances.

The parties do not have to contemplate the precise detail of the damage nor the precise manner of its happening. If reasonable parties would have contemplated a particular type of loss they do not need to have in mind the extent of the loss. In *Brown v KMR Services Ltd,*[10] the Court of Appeal applied the extent of damage rule to economic loss. The plaintiff was a Lloyds' name who sued his agent for failing to advise against the consequences of over exposure on excess of loss syndicates. These are the syndicates that carry the heaviest losses during the bad years. Lloyds had suffered their worst trading period this century and the losses were unprecedented. The defendant's argument that the losses should be classified as abnormal under *Hadley v Baxendale* was rejected. The loss of ordinary business profits was different in kind from that flowing from a particular contract which gives rise to very high profits, the existence of the contract being unknown to the other contracting party. The problem with *Brown* is that there are two exceptions to the rule that extent of loss is irrelevant. These are where the normally expected amount of loss places a ceiling on recovery,[11] and negligent over-valuations.[12] It is difficult to see how *Victoria Laundry* was distinguished unless on the basis of a distinction between profits not made and losses incurred. *South Australia* was concerned with volatile markets (in that case the property market) and the decision was to exclude losses caused by

---

6   See *British Columbia Saw Mill Co Ltd v Nettleship* (1868) LR 3 CP 499; *Horne v Midland Rly Co* (1873) LR 8 CP 131.
7   *GKN Centrax Gears Ltd v Matbro Ltd* [1976] 2 Lloyd's Rep 555; *The Heron II* [1969] 1 AC 350 at 422.
8   [1949] 2 KB 528.
9   Ibid at 539 (per A*SQUITH* LJ).
10   [1995] 4 All ER 598.
11   See *Victoria Laundry (Windsor) Ltd v Newman Industries Ltd* [1949] 2 KB 528.
12   *South Australia Asset Management Corpn v York Montague Ltd* [1996] 3 All ER 365.

property market falls. *Brown* was concerned with volatile insurance markets but the defendant was liable for losses caused by market failure.

One difficulty is to determine the degree to which the defendant has to foresee damage, whether normal or abnormal. This issue was tackled by the House of Lords in *The Heron II*.[13] A chartered ship deviated, in breach of contract, with the result that it reached its destination nine days later than would otherwise have been the case. The market value of its cargo of sugar had fallen in the meantime. The defendant shipowners were held liable for this loss, which arose in the usual course of things.

Reasonable foreseeability, in the sense of the low degree of probability required in a tort action, was rejected as the test for remoteness in contract. A higher likelihood of loss was required in a contract action than in a tort action. Members of the House of Lords disagreed as to how this higher degree of foreseeability should be expressed. Phrases such as 'serious possibility',[14] a 'real danger'[15] or a 'very substantial' probability[16] of loss were used. The result of the decision in *The Heron II* is that a higher degree of probability of loss is required to satisfy the remoteness test in contract than in tort.

An illustration of the reasonable contemplation principle is given by *Balfour Beatty Construction (Scotland) Ltd v Scottish Power plc*.[17] The plaintiff was building an aqueduct and the defendant was supplying electricity. The defendant, in breach of contract, interrupted the electricity supply. The plaintiff's method of construction required a constant supply of concrete. The interruption meant that work already done had to be demolished. The cost of demolition and re-building were held too remote as the loss was not in the defendant's reasonable contemplation as he was unaware of the plaintiff's method of construction.[18]

Until this time, the courts had talked about the remoteness test in terms of whether the action was framed in contract or in tort. In *Parsons v Uttley Ingham*,[19] LORD DENNING injected a note of realism, and talked in terms of whether the damage was physical or non-physical. In his view, where there is physical damage, the *Wagon Mound* test applies, whether the action is framed in contract or in tort.[20] Where the action is in contract for non-physical loss, *The Heron II* applies. He remained silent on whether *The Heron II*, with its higher standard of foreseeability, would apply to tort actions for loss of profit.

(a)   *The rationale for the rule in* Hadley v Baxendale[1]   The rule that a party cannot be liable for unusual losses unless the risk is disclosed at the time of the contract has been described as fair and economically efficient.[2] It is fair in that it prevents a party who is in breach of contract from being responsible for unexpected amounts. A contracting party may raise his price to take account of a known or foreseeable risk, or limit his liability in respect of that risk. However, to do the same in respect of unusual or unlikely losses would not make economic sense. Furthermore, the rule is also economically sensible, as it encourages a party who is likely to suffer unusual losses to disclose relevant information. The other party can then safeguard his position by means of an exclusion

---

13 Sub nom *Koufos v Czarnikow Ltd* [1969] 1 AC 350.
14 Ibid at 414–415.
15 Ibid at 425.
16 Ibid at 388.
17 1994 SLT 807.
18 See also *Kpohraror v Woolwich Buiding Society* [1996] 4 All ER 119.
19 [1978] QB 791.
20 Ibid at 801.
1   See Beale *Remedies for Breach of Contract* (1980) pp 179–187.
2   See Beale *Remedies for Breach of Contract* (1980) p 180; Posner *Economic Analysis of Law* (2nd edn, 1977) pp 94–95.

of liability, subject to protective legislation.[3] Alternatively, he can insure against the possibility of loss. If a person were to be made responsible for unknown risks, it is unlikely that his efficiency would be increased in any way.[4] In contrast, the rule on normal losses requires no information disclosure. A party is taken to have contemplated such losses, as he is aware of normal business practice.[5]

(b)   *What rule should apply to tortious loss of profit cases?*   Where the parties are not strangers, information transfer should be encouraged, so as to allocate liability for normal losses. Contractual rules on remoteness would therefore appear to be the most appropriate. Where the parties are strangers, the issue has, so far, involved the question of whether a duty of care is owed. The test of proximity has been applied to determine liability. When a case arises which raises the issue of remoteness in the context of financial loss suffered by a stranger, the difficulty will be to determine the most appropriate test of remoteness of damage. Information transfer is not possible, with the result that the second rule in *Hadley v Baxendale* would be inappropriate. A single rule would have to be applied in order to determine the degree of foreseeability required. As the policy of the common law appears to be more generous to a plaintiff suffering physical harm as opposed to one suffering financial loss, the *Wagon Mound* rule might not be appropriate. The most likely rule would appear to be a version of the *Heron II* test involving the foreseeability of a loss to a substantial degree of probability.

4.   INTERVENING CAUSE

(1)   INTRODUCTION

The defendant's breach of duty may be a cause of the plaintiff's damage, in the sense that it satisfies the 'but for' test. However, some other factual cause, intervening after the breach, may be regarded as the sole cause of all, or part of, the plaintiff's damage. The courts frequently use the maxim *novus actus interveniens* to describe this phenomenon. Where the subsequent cause is held to be a *novus actus interveniens*, damage to the plaintiff occurring after the event, and caused by it, cannot be attributed to the defendant, and is said to be too remote.

   If A negligently runs over B, who is subsequently run over by C, C's action is unlikely to break the chain of causation, as this is a risk to which A's negligence had exposed B.[6] But what would be the position if C had stolen B's wallet? This might not be a risk to which A's breach of duty exposed B.[7]

(2)   JUDICIAL TESTS FOR IDENTIFYING AN INTERVENING CAUSE

Acts which may break the chain of causation are normally divided into natural events, acts of a third party and acts of the plaintiff. Given the multitude of factual situations which may be thrown up and the limited tools of reasoning available to the courts, it is not surprising that cogent principles have not been developed in order to determine what is an intervening cause. It has been said that judicial decisions in this respect are based on practical politics rather than upon logic, and that factors such as convenience,

3   See ch 24.
4   See Bishop (1983) 12 JLS 241.
5   *Victoria Laundry (Windsor) Ltd v Newman Industries Ltd* [1949] 2 KB 528 at 543 (per ASQUITH LJ).
6   See *Fitzgerald v Lane* [1988] 2 All ER 961; *Rouse v Squires* [1973] QB 889. Cf *Knightley v Johns* [1982] 1 WLR 349.
7   *Patten v Silberschein* [1936] 3 WWR 169.

public policy and justice shape the decision of the court.[8] The question the court must answer is the same as that which arises in the context of duty of care in negligence, namely, should the plaintiff go uncompensated for the harm he has suffered?

(i)   Policy considerations

Where justice suggests that the plaintiff should be compensated, it must be determined who is to make amends. Rules of causation and remoteness are methods of justifying the attribution of responsibility to a particular defendant. Reasoning on the basis of morality suggests that the person at fault should bear the loss. This may involve a comparison of the blameworthiness of the plaintiff's and the defendant's conduct.[9] A test of efficiency would require the court to determine who is the best risk-bearer. This person will frequently be the person in the best position to insure against the risk of loss.

Where there is an alternative source of liability, for example, where there is an intervening wrongful act of a third party, it may be easier to relieve the defendant of liability. In cases where the intervening act is a natural event or the non-culpable conduct of a third party, the courts may be reluctant to exonerate the defendant.[10]

Overt policy considerations were employed in *Lamb v Camden London Borough Council*,[11] in which the defendants' breach of duty caused the plaintiff's house to be left unoccupied. Squatters broke into the house and damaged it. LORD DENNING was of the opinion that the plaintiff had failed to mitigate her loss by ensuring that the house was securely boarded up. In broader terms, he regarded the plaintiff as the best insurer, and therefore the person on whom the risk should fall. One of the dangers of judicial policy-making is the lack of information the court has before it. It has been pointed out that, in fact, the defendants were the best insurers.[12]

(ii)   Formalistic reasoning

What the court is attempting to do may be obscured by formalistic reasoning. This may take the form of asking whether the intervening act was foreseeable or likely, or whether, in the case of human conduct, it was voluntary or involuntary.[13] The advantage of this type of reasoning is that it can give at least some guide as to whether an act is likely to break the chain of causation or not. The disadvantages are that many tests may be employed, and the judiciary appear to be unable to agree on the proper formulation of an appropriate test.

In *Home Office v Dorset Yacht Co Ltd*,[14] Lord Reid regarded the case as turning on the issue of remoteness of damage rather than upon that of duty of care. In order to determine whether the boys' acts broke the chain of causation, he said that they had to be something very likely to happen, otherwise they would not be regarded as *novus actus interveniens*.[15] On the facts of the case, it was very likely that, if the boys escaped as a result of the defendant's breach of duty, nearby yachts would be damaged. If the boys

---

8   *Palsgraf v Long Island Railroad Co* 284 NY 339 (1928) (per ANDREWS J).
9   See *Lamb v Camden London Borough Council* [1981] QB 625 at 636 (per DENNING MR). *McKew v Holland, Hannen & Cubbits Ltd* [1969] 3 All ER 1621.
10   See *Haynes v Harwood* [1935] 1 KB 146.
11   [1981] QB 625.
12   See Lee and Merkin (1981) 131 NLJ 965.
13   See *Haynes v Harwood* [1935] 1 KB 146; *Philco Radio and Television Corpn of Great Britain Ltd v J Spurling Ltd* [1949] 2 All ER 882.
14   [1970] AC 1004.
15   Ibid at 1030. See also *Paterson Zochonis & Co Ltd v Merfarken Packaging Ltd* [1986] 3 All ER 522 at 534 (per FOX LJ).

had fled to Carlisle and broken into a house there, damage might be likely, but no duty of care would be owed.

LORD REID's test was taken up and modified by OLIVER LJ in *Lamb v Camden London Borough Council*[16] where he said that the act should have been foreseen by a reasonable man as likely.[17] As the squatters' incursion was not foreseeable in this sense, the chain of causation was broken. An application of LORD REID's likelihood test may allow the court to distinguish between wrongful and non-wrongful conduct. Wrongful conduct is more likely to break the chain of causation, unless it is very likely to happen as a result of the defendant's breach of duty. For example, the wrongful conduct of the squatters in *Lamb* was not likely to happen, hence the break in the chain of causation. Yet in *Dorset Yacht*, the wrongful conduct of the escapees was likely in the circumstances. Non-wrongful conduct will rarely break the chain of causation,[18] unless the only contribution of the defendant's breach to the plaintiff's damage was to place the plaintiff or his property in a position whereby damage could be caused by the act of a third party.

(3)   NATURAL EVENTS

On policy grounds, the courts are reluctant to find that an intervening natural act breaks the chain of causation. This is because the plaintiff has no-one else to sue if the defendant is exonerated. If the natural event causes damage simply because the defendant's breach of duty has placed the plaintiff or his property in a position whereby that damage can be caused, the chain of causation is broken, unless the natural event is likely to happen. In *Carslogie SS Co Ltd v Royal Norwegian Government*,[19] the plaintiff's ship was damaged in a collision for which the defendant's ship was responsible. After temporary repairs, it set out for the United States on a voyage it would not have made had the collision not occurred. The ship suffered damage due to heavy weather conditions. The storm damage was not treated as a consequence of the collision, but as an intervening event in the course of an ordinary voyage. The only contribution of the breach of duty to the storm damage was that the ship was in the Atlantic Ocean at the time of the storm. It was important that the decision of the ship's owners to put to sea was voluntary.

Similar principles will apply if the plaintiff is injured by the defendant's breach of duty and subsequently suffers further harm when the ambulance conveying him to hospital is struck by a falling tree.[20] However, where the defendant negligently starts a fire and strong winds fan the blaze causing it to spread to the plaintiff's property, the winds do not break the chain of causation.

(4)   INTERVENING ACTS OF THIRD PARTIES

Where the defendant's breach of duty is followed by the act of a third party which is also a cause of the plaintiff's damage, or which exacerbates the harm to the plaintiff, it must be decided whether the defendant should be held responsible.

Where the defendant's duty is to guard the plaintiff or his property against damage from a third party, the third-party act will not relieve the defendant from the consequence of his breach of duty. In *Stansbie v Troman*,[1] the defendant decorator was employed in

---

16   [1981] QB 625.
17   Ibid at 642; cf LORD DENNING MR and WATKIN LJ at 634 and at 645.
18   See *Haynes v Harwood* [1935] 1 KB 146.
19   [1952] AC 292.
20   See *Hogan v Bentinck West Hartley Collieries (Owners) Ltd* [1949] 1 All ER 588 at 601 (per LORD McDERMOTT).
1   [1948] 2 KB 48.

the plaintiff's house and was told to lock the door if he went out. He failed to lock the door, and the plaintiff's jewellery was stolen. The thief's action was held not to be a break in the chain of causation, and the defendant was liable for the loss. The same issue has recently arisen in the context of a landowner's duty to secure his property against the entry of trespassers who may damage his neighbour's property.[2]

Where the defendant is not under a specific duty to guard against the damage suffered but he is in breach of his duty of care, the question is more problematical. The third party act must be independent of the defendant's breach of duty in order to break the chain of causation. In *The Oropesa*,[3] the defendant negligently caused a collision at sea. The captain of the other ship sent out a boat in heavy seas to discuss salvage. The boat overturned and a sailor was drowned. As the captain's action in sending the boat out was caused by and flowed from the collision, it was not independent and did not break the chain of causation. The case can also be explained on the ground that the captain acted in order to save lives. Accordingly, the act was not voluntary.[4] Where the third-party act is not independent of the defendant's breach of duty, the courts fall back on the policy considerations and formalistic reasoning considered at an earlier stage.

(5)   ACT OF THE PLAINTIFF

If both the plaintiff's lack of care for his own safety and the defendant's breach of duty are regarded as causes of the harm suffered, the plaintiff's act or omission will normally raise the issue of contributory negligence. Where the Law Reform (Contributory Negligence) Act 1945 applies, the court may reduce the plaintiff's damages according to his degree of blameworthiness. This avoids the all or nothing result achieved by the application of rules on causation.[5] However, there are circumstances in which the plaintiff's conduct may exonerate the defendant altogether. In tort cases, the plaintiff's conduct is treated as a *novus actus interveniens* and, in contract actions, it is said that the plaintiff has failed to mitigate his loss.[6]

Whether or not the plaintiff's act breaks the chain of causation depends on its reasonableness. In *McKew v Holland & Hannen & Cubbits (Scotland) Ltd*,[7] as a result of an accident caused by the defendant's negligence, the plaintiff occasionally lost control of his left leg. While holding his young daughter by the hand, the plaintiff attempted to descend a steep staircase with no hand-rail. His leg gave way and, after pushing his child back, he jumped to avoid falling and broke his ankle. By placing himself unnecessarily in a position whereby he might be confronted with such an emergency, he had acted unreasonably. The defendants were not liable for the broken ankle. However, in *Wieland v Cyril Lord Carpets Ltd*,[8] the plaintiff was unable to adjust her bi-focal spectacles as a result of a neck injury inflicted by the defendant's negligence. She fell downstairs, but, on the facts, was held to have acted reasonably in attempting to descend the stairs. Accordingly, her action did not break the chain of causation.

Once the defendant is held to be in breach of his duty, the plaintiff's obligation to act reasonably applies, whether the action is brought in contract or tort. In *Quinn v*

---

2   *P Perl (Exporters) Ltd v Camden London Borough Council* [1983] 3 All ER 161; *King v Liverpool City Council* [1986] 1 WLR 890; *Maloco v Littlewoods Organisation Ltd* [1987] AC 241. See also ch 28.

3   [1943] P 32.

4   Cf *Carslogie SS Co Ltd v Royal Norwegian Government* [1952] AC 292. See also Burrows *Remedies* pp 58–59.

5   See *The Calliope* [1970] P 172 and ch 20.

6   See *Banco de Portugal v Waterlow & Sons Ltd* [1932] AC 452.

7   [1969] 3 All ER 1621.

8   [1969] 3 All ER 1006. See also *Compania Naviera Maropan SA v Bowaters Lloyds Pulp and Paper Mills Ltd* [1955] 2 QB 68.

Burch Bros (Builders) Ltd,[9] the defendants, in breach of contract, failed to provide the plaintiff plasterer with a step-ladder. The plaintiff adapted a trestle for use as a ladder, but failed to secure it properly. As a result, the trestle slipped, causing the plaintiff to suffer injury. It was held that these injuries were caused entirely by the plaintiff's unreasonable conduct.

Whether or not conduct is reasonable is a matter to be judged on the facts of each case, but policy considerations may be relevant. For example, it may be unreasonable for a plaintiff to refuse to have an abortion in an action for 'wrongful birth'.[10] Policy issues also arise where the plaintiff is injured as a result of the defendant's breach of duty, and then commits suicide. The suicide could be viewed as a *novus actus interveniens*, on the grounds that it is an unreasonable act. In *Pigney v Pointers Transport Services Ltd*,[11] it was held, applying the direct consequence remoteness test, that suicide was not to be regarded as a break in the chain of causation. Accordingly, the widow of the deceased could recover damages in respect of the death. In a modern case, the *Wagon Mound* test of reasonable foreseeability may have to be applied, with arguably different results. Alternatively, the court might invoke the 'egg-shell skull' rule. The action will be brought by the estate of the deceased or by his dependants, which might affect the relevant test of remoteness of damage. Furthermore, it may be relevant how death came about. If the action is brought by the dependants under the Fatal Accidents Act 1976[12], the issue is whether the defendant has caused harm of a kind for which the law gives compensation.[12] In *Kirkham v Chief Constable of the Greater Manchester Police*[13] the widow of the deceased sued the police after her husband hanged himself in a remand centre. The deceased suffered from clinical depression and the police negligently failed to notify the remand centre of this fact. The suicide was held to be a foreseeable consequence of the breach of duty and not a *novus actus interveniens*, although it was a deliberate act. The decision was presumably made on the basis that as the duty was to guard against the act which occurred, the act itself could not break the chain of causation.[14] Whatever formalistic reasoning is employed, the root issue appears to be whether the court wishes to compensate the estate or the dependants of a suicide for the death. In *Kirkham* the suicide was not 'voluntary' as the deceased was depressed and not *volens* to the act. Even a 'sane' suicide will apparently not break the chain of causation.[15] As the suicide was the very act against which the defendant had been required to guard, the act did not constitute a new or intervening act.

5.   MITIGATION OF DAMAGE

(1)   INTRODUCTION

Subsequent to the defendant's breach of duty, the plaintiff is required to act reasonably so as to minimise his loss. The plaintiff's unreasonable conduct may be regarded as an intervening cause of his loss, or it may be that by failing to mitigate his loss, the plaintiff is denied recovery of damages in respect of that unmitigated loss. The expression 'the

9   [1966] 2 QB 370. See also *Sole v W J Hallt Ltd* [1973] QB 574; *Lexmead (Basingstoke) Ltd v Lewis* [1982] AC 225.
10   See *Emeh v Kensington and Chelsea and Westminster Area Health Authority* [1984] 3 All ER 1044 at 1053; *Rance v Mid-Downs Health Authority* [1991] 1 All ER 801. See also Grubb [1985] CLJ 30 and ch 25.
11   [1957] 1 WLR 1121.
12   See ch 17.
13   [1990] 2 QB 283.
14   See also *Stansbie v Troman* [1948] 2 KB 48.
15   *Reeves v Metropolitan Police Comr* [2000] 1 AC 360.

duty to mitigate' is often used, but this is misleading, as a failure to mitigate does not result in the imposition of liability upon the plaintiff. Where loss is caused partly by the defendant's breach and partly by the plaintiff's contemporaneous action, rules on contributory negligence[16] or causation may apply.

The doctrine of mitigation has the effect of significantly reducing the number of instances in which expectation damages are awarded for breach of contract. After breach, a plaintiff is not entitled to sit back, do nothing and sue for damages for the performance promised. He must take positive steps to reduce his losses by going into the market and seeking a replacement performance, where this is possible.

In determining the rules on mitigation, the courts are faced with a conflict between not depriving a party of a legal remedy and not encouraging a wasteful use of resources. The innocent party is entitled to reject an offer which requires him to surrender his right to damages, with the effect that he will not be in as good a position as if the contract had been performed.[17] However, he must not act unreasonably in refusing an offer if to accept it would have reduced his losses.[18]

As the courts work on a net loss basis for contract damages and mitigation is primarily, although not exclusively, a contract device, a plaintiff who has taken steps to mitigate and has in fact avoided potential loss, will have his damages assessed on actual loss suffered. This 'avoided loss' principle applies even if the plaintiff took greater steps to mitigate than were expected of him. Mitigation of loss takes two forms. First, the plaintiff must take reasonable steps to minimise his loss and put himself in as good a position as if the breach of duty had not occurred. For example, a wrongfully dismissed employee must attempt to find a comparable job, and where a seller fails to deliver goods, the buyer must go into the market to obtain substitute goods. Secondly, the plaintiff must not act unreasonably so as to increase his loss. This second rule only applies to expenses incurred after breach. Other unreasonable acts will be treated as an intervening cause of the harm suffered.

If the plaintiff terminates the contract on the grounds of the defendant's breach, this may release resources which the plaintiff would have used to perform his contract with the defendant. Should any benefit obtained by the plaintiff from an alternative use of his resources be taken into account if the opportunity to obtain the benefit arose only as a result of the defendant's breach? In principle the answer should be yes, however there are few cases in English law on this point. In *Lavarack v Woods of Colchester Ltd*,[19] a wrongful dismissal case, the plaintiff took a job with another company at a low salary but purchased half the shares in the company and stood to make a profit if the company did well. It was held that the profit on the shares was a concealed renumeration and part of it should be taken into account in reducing the plaintiff's damages. The reason for only a part deduction was that the plaintiff had probably used different skills and put in greater effort to the new job. Deduction of part also gives an incentive to re-deploy resources.

(2)   REASONABLE STEPS TO MINIMISE LOSS

What is reasonable is a question of fact in each case.[20] The party in breach may have offered a defective performance or, after the breach, may offer to cure the defect. The failure of the innocent party to accept a defective performance or a cured performance may amount to a failure to mitigate.

16   See ch 20.
17   *Shindler v Northern Raincoat Co Ltd* [1960] 2 All ER 239, [1960] 1 WLR 1038.
18   *Payzu Ltd v Saunders* [1919] 2 KB 581, [1918–19] All ER Rep 219.
19   [1967] 1 QB 268.
20   Ibid.

The court's approach to this issue involves a complex balancing of the wish not to deprive a party of a remedy, the desire to avoid a waste of resources, and subjective factors relevant to the particular case. Where a seller offers sub-standard goods at a reduced price, and the court insists on the buyer mitigating his loss by accepting the offer, it deprives the buyer of the right to reject the goods.[1] However, in *Payzu v Saunders*,[2] the court took the view that the best way to avoid the loss was to accept the defective performance. In that case, an instalment contract for the sale of silk provided for payment within one month of each delivery. The sellers wrongly insisted on cash on delivery. The buyers refused this offer and sued for the difference between the market price and the contract price on the date they accepted the repudiation. It was held that the buyers should have mitigated their loss by accepting the offer of cash on delivery terms.[3]

The decision in *Payzu v Saunders* can be distinguished from a case where there is an available market for the goods. In *Payzu v Saunders*, the market had risen and silk was not a readily available commodity. If there is no readily available market so as to allow the buyer to find a replacement and the buyer can be expected to put up with what is offered, he would appear to be obliged to accept.[4]

Subjective factors are particularly important in commercial contracts where business reputation is concerned. The innocent party will not be compelled to take steps which would ruin his reputation. In *London and South of England Building Society v Stone*,[5] a surveyor's valuation of property negligently failed to disclose subsidence damage, and the plaintiff building society refused to mitigate by enforcing a covenant to repair against the borrower. This refusal to act was held to be reasonable in order to protect the society's reputation.

In cases of wrongful dismissal, the question may arise whether the employee should accept an offer of renewed employment. Much will depend on the nature of the post offered compared with the old post, and whether the events leading up to the dismissal have destroyed the personal relationship between employer and employee.[6] A further subjective factor affecting the ability to mitigate may be a person's financial position. For example, a person may be unable to mitigate his loss because of his impecuniosity. Such impecuniosity is generally regarded as a valid reason for a failure to mitigate.[7]

Finally, the court will have regard to the fact that it is the defendant's breach that has forced the plaintiff to mitigate his loss. Generally, the plaintiff will not be compelled to take complex or difficult steps in this regard. In *Pilkington v Wood*,[8] title to property was found to be defective when the plaintiff came to sell his house. The plaintiff sued his solicitor, and it was held that he was not obliged to mitigate his loss by bringing an action against the vendor of the property for conveying a defective title. This step would have involved a complex process of litigation unwarranted in the circumstances.

In personal injury cases, similar issues arise where it is alleged that the plaintiff should have undergone an operation in order to improve his condition. The general view is that such a course of action will only be necessary where medical advice shows that the operation would be of positive benefit.[9]

1   *Heaven and Kesterton v Etablissements Francois Albiac & Cie* [1956] 2 Lloyd's Rep 316.
2   [1919] 2 KB 581. Cf *Strutt v Whitnell* [1975] 2 All ER 510, [1975] 1 WLR 870.
3   Bridge (1989) 105 LQR 398.
4   Cf United States *UCC* s 2–508(2).
5   [1983] 3 All ER 105. See also *James Finlay & Co Ltd v N V Kwik Hoo Tong* [1929] 1 KB 400.
6   *Yetton v Eastwoods Froy Ltd* [1967] 1 WLR 104. Cf *Brace v Calder* [1895] 2 QB 253.
7   *Robbins of Putney Ltd v Meek* [1971] RTR 345; *The Liesbosch Dredger* [1933] AC 449.
8   [1953] Ch 770.
9   *Selvanayagam v University of the West Indies* [1983] 1 All ER 824. Cf *McAuley v London Transport Executive* [1957] 2 Lloyd's Rep 500.

(3)   NOT INCREASING LOSSES

The plaintiff must not take unreasonable steps so as to increase his loss. If the plaintiff acts unreasonably in attempting to mitigate his loss, he cannot recover for the extra loss he suffers as a result. The courts will again take account of the fact that the plaintiff's position has been forced upon him by the defendant's breach of duty. Reasonable costs may be incurred so as to offset the effect of the breach of duty. For example, the plaintiff may recover interest incurred as a result of buying a replacement.[10] However, where the plaintiff incurs unreasonably high interest charges in mitigating his loss, these will be disallowed.[11]

The courts will also take account of the plaintiff's business reputation in deciding what is reasonable. In *Banco de Portugal v Waterlow & Sons Ltd*,[12] the defendants, in breach of contract, delivered a large number of bank notes to a criminal, who put them into circulation. The plaintiff bank had ordered the notes, and undertook to exchange them. This was held to be reasonable, bearing in mind the bank's commercial obligations to the public. The defendants were held liable for the full face value of the notes, rather than for the cost of printing alone.

What is reasonable is judged at the time the action is taken. The fact that the plaintiff's attempt to mitigate increases his loss rather than minimises it is irrelevant, provided that, at the time, his action was reasonable.[13] A buyer may therefore recover the costs of reasonably defending a claim brought by his sub-buyer, which is the result of a breach of contract committed by the seller. If the amount of costs is disputed they must be taxed on a standard basis.[14]

(4)   ANTICIPATORY BREACH OF CONTRACT

Where there is a breach of contract, both the right to damages and the obligation to mitigate arise. Where a party is guilty of an anticipatory repudiation of the contract, the innocent party is traditionally thought to be under a duty to mitigate his loss, if he accepts the repudiation.[15] However, if he rejects the repudiation and keeps the contract in existence, no duty to mitigate will arise.[16] The position in the United States would appear to be more sensible. The victim of a repudiation is not allowed to enhance his damages by unreasonably omitting action that would prevent harm.[17] It may be that English law is moving in this direction as a result of the decision in *Clea Shipping Corpn v Bulk Oil International Ltd*,[18] discussed at an earlier stage.[19] Where a party is found to have acted wholly unreasonably[20] in refusing to accept a repudiation, he will be limited to an action for damages, which will require the innocent party to mitigate his loss.

10   *Bacon v Cooper (Metals) Ltd* [1982] 1 All ER 397.
11   *Compania Financiera Soleada SA v Hamoor Tanker Corpn Inc, The Borag* [1981] 1 All ER 856.
12   [1932] AC 452.
13   *Lloyds and Scottish Finance Ltd v Modern Cars and Caravans (Kingston) Ltd* [1966] 1 QB 764.
14   *British Racing Drivers' Club v Hextall Erskine & Co* [1996] 3 All ER 667.
15   *Melachrino v Nickoll and Knight* [1920] 1 KB 693.
16   *Tredegar Iron and Coal Co Ltd v Hawthorn Bros and Co* (1902) 18 TLR 716; *White and Carter (Councils) Ltd v McGregor* [1962] AC 413.
17   *American Restatement, Contracts* (2d) s 388.
18   [1984] 1 All ER 129.
19   See ch 13.
20   *Clea Shipping Corpn v Bulk Oil International Ltd* [1984] 1 All ER 129 at 137 (per LLOYD J).

Chapter 17

Compensatory damages II — quantum of damages

1. DAMAGES FOR PERSONAL INJURIES, MENTAL DISTRESS AND DEATH

(1) INTRODUCTION

The term 'personal injury' includes physical harm to the person, disease and illness, the last of which encompasses recognised psychiatric illness.[1] Furthermore, damages may be awarded for the physical or mental effects of a rape or other sexual assault.[2] Since the Congenital Disabilities (Civil Liability) Act 1976, ante-natal injuries may now be regarded as a variety of personal injury.

Where a person suffers personal injuries as a result of the wrongful conduct of another, the objective of an award of damages is to compensate him for his loss. This is achieved, so far as is possible, by means of a monetary payment, by placing him in the position he would have occupied had the wrong not been committed. The majority of claims for personal injuries are based in the law of tort, but the same principle applies to actions for breach of contract, subject to the apparently different rules on remoteness of damage and possibly causation.

The reason for treating personal injury claims separately is that they raise problems not encountered in actions for other types of loss. In an action for financial loss, monetary compensation is adequate. Similarly, physical damage to property can be compensated by a monetary payment equivalent to the market value of the property damaged. But, where a person loses a leg or suffers pain, money is the only compensation available, but the market value of a leg or pain is impossible to ascertain. The concentration of English law on property rights appears to be to blame. As far as possible, the courts have treated personal injuries as depriving a person of a property right. This approach may work in some cases, but is inapplicable to subjective losses, such as pain, suffering and mental distress.

---

1   *Brice v Brown* [1984] 1 All ER 997 at 1005–1006 and see ch 9.
2   *W v Meah* [1986] 1 All ER 935.

(2) CLASSIFICATION OF DAMAGES

Damages for personal injuries are conventionally divided into pecuniary and non-pecuniary losses. A pecuniary loss is one that can be estimated in monetary terms. Into this category fall loss of earnings suffered as a result of injury, and medical and other expenses. This is not a problem-free area, as placing a monetary value on anything other than money involves difficulties. For example, the quantification of future loss of earnings involves guesswork as to future events. However, the essential principle is one of restitution. The plaintiff must be put into the financial position he would have been in had the injury not been inflicted. This head of damages is therefore essentially similar to any other head of restitutionary damages.

Conceptual difficulties are most acute in the case of non-pecuniary losses. English law has adopted a diminution in value approach. A competing approach is the functional one where damages are awarded as solace or comfort for the plaintiff's misfortune by enabling him to purchase substitute sources of satisfaction. Such damages are subjectively assessed and this approach is used in Canada[3] but was rejected by the English Law Commission as it would transform non-pecuniary losses into pecuniary ones and compel the abandonment of the tariff system.[4]

The standard heads of damage are loss of physical amenity and pain and suffering. Mental distress resulting from physical injury can normally be recovered as a variety of damages for pain and suffering, but is now recoverable without the need for proof of physical injury.[5]

The most sensible way to approach these items is to treat all non-pecuniary loss as a form of mental distress. The plaintiff who loses both legs in an accident will suffer distress at being unable to live the life he had enjoyed before, and at the pain and discomfort of the injury. A legal system which set out to codify damages in the twenty-first century would probably treat mental distress as one comprehensive head for all non-pecuniary losses. English law is fettered by precedent, and finds it difficult to come to terms with non-financial losses. Damages for mental distress are a relatively modern phenomenon and the judiciary are used to classifying and valuing proprietary interests. This is the approach taken to loss of amenity. Such loss is assessed objectively, without regard to the particular plaintiff.[6] However, the court may still refer to the effect of the plaintiff's loss of amenity on his ability to enjoy hobbies and other spare-time activities, which may result in an increased award of damages. The objective rule does have advantages in that it allows the court to compensate a comatose plaintiff who is unaware of his loss. In such cases, the lost amenity is regarded as a proprietary interest which must be compensated by a monetary payment. Pain and suffering is not susceptible to such an objective analysis. For example, a plaintiff who never recovers consciousness will not suffer any loss under this head. A more subjective approach is therefore taken by the courts, but uniformity is achieved by a tariff system.

(3) THE FORM AND BASIS OF THE AWARD

The abolition of jury trial in actions for personal injuries has required the judge, in a particular case, to itemise the award,[7] stating how much has been awarded for each item of loss. The reason for itemisation is that different rates of interest apply to non-

---

3   *Andrews v Grand & Toy Alberta Ltd* (1978) 83 DLR (3d) 452: *Arnold v Teno* (1978) 83 DLR (3d) 609; *Thornton v Board of School Trustees of School District No 57* (1978) 83 DLR (3d) 480.
4   Law Commission Consultation Paper 140 (1995) paras 2.3, 4.9, 4.10.
5   See *Attia v British Gas plc* [1987] 3 All ER 455.
6   *West v Shephard* [1964] AC 326.
7   *Jefford v Gee* [1970] 2 QB 130.

pecuniary and pecuniary losses.[8] The requirement of itemisation is advantageous in that it allows practitioners to be aware of the going rate for particular losses, thereby facilitating out-of-court settlements. However, it does not explain why a particular sum is considered appropriate.[9] There have been attempts to rationalise awards, but the courts still tend to assert that the award must be fair and reasonable in each case.[10] Whether it is preferable to let a relatively small number of people determine the going rate and achieve relative uniformity, or allow *vox populi,* in the form of the jury, to determine the issue and sacrifice uniformity is debatable.[11]

The basis of the damages award is full compensation. The plaintiff must be compensated for all pecuniary losses which he has suffered as a result of the wrong. This idea is so embedded in the common law that it is rarely questioned by the judiciary. However, it has been suggested that it might be unfair to award damages for loss of earnings to an unconscious plaintiff with no dependants to support.[12] The traditional view may not seem startling in the context of English common law damages, but it is unique compared to other methods of compensating for personal injuries such as social security.

While it might be impossible for the common law system of compensation for personal injuries to be drastically altered, a victim who can prove a legal wrong and recover damages receives markedly more generous treatment than other persons who suffer reduced living standards as a result of injury or illness. In other countries, the issue has been removed from the legal system and public insurance schemes established to compensate the victims of injury or illness.[13] Such a move in England appears unlikely following the non-implementation of the key recommendations in the Pearson Report.[14]

Two major criticisms can be made of the full compensation principle. It involves high cost for small claims, which could be reduced by excluding compensation for the first few days.[15] The principle also provides no incentive for a victim to recover and return to work.[16]

(i)   The lump sum

Once a plaintiff has litigated his case and obtained judgment, he will obtain damages paid in a lump sum. The award is made once and for all and, with one exception, the payment will not be increased if his condition turns out to be worse than was thought at the time of trial. Correspondingly, the defendant cannot ask for a reduction in damages if the plaintiff's condition transpires not to be as serious as was first believed to be the case. This method of awarding damages may make it difficult to assess likely loss of future earnings. The court will inevitably be engaged in a process of guesswork, which may turn out to be completely wrong.[17] The system is said to have the advantage of enabling the plaintiff to concentrate his mind on recovery without reducing his entitlement to compensation. Furthermore, he also has a large sum which he can use to

---

8   Cf *Wright v British Railways Board* [1983] 2 AC 773 and *Jefford v Gee* [1970] 2 QB 130.
9   See Ogus (1972) 35 MLR I and Atiyah *Accidents* p 184.
10   See *Gardner v Dyson* [1967] 1 WLR 1497 at 1501.
11   See Walker (1968) 84 LQR 400.
12   See *Lim Poh Choo v Camden Health Authority* [1979] QB 196 at 216–217 (per Lord Denning MR), disapproved in [1980] AC 174.
13   The best known is the New Zealand system. See Atiyah *Accidents* ch 19.
14   The Report of the Royal Commission on Civil Liability and Compensation for Personal Injuries (1978) Cmnd 7054.
15   Ibid, Vol 1, paras 467–495.
16   Atiyah *Accidents* pp 115–117.
17   See *Lim Poh Choo v Camden Health Authority* [1980] AC 174 at 183 (per Lord Scarman).

plan his life in order to suit any disability he may have suffered. It also means that the defendant, or his insurer, can pay and incur no further inconvenience. There is also no further intrusion on the plaintiff's life to enquire as to his condition.

The disadvantages of the lump sum are that the plaintiff may use his capital unwisely if he is unused to large sums of money. Also, if his medical condition deteriorates after trial or settlement, he may turn out to have been under-compensated, and the effects of inflation may diminish what was thought at the time to be fair compensation. The disadvantages of the lump sum are well illustrated in cases of fatal accidents where the widow claims as a dependant. The court used to be faced with the distasteful task of assessing the widow's chances of remarriage in order to determine what her loss might be. The Fatal Accidents Act 1976, section 3(3) now orders the court to ignore remarriage or prospects of remarriage in assessing damages. This may result in over-compensation where the widow has remarried by the time of the trial. The problem could be avoided by awarding the widow periodical payments subject to cessation or alteration when a change of circumstances such as remarriage takes place. Such a system operates in the matrimonial jurisdiction. Difficulties such as reluctance to remarry because it would terminate the award could be solved by use of a widow's dowry, which is used in the industrial injuries scheme to provide a lump sum on remarriage, thereby providing an incentive to the widow.

The Pearson Commission thought that the benefits of periodical payments outweighed the disadvantages for future pecuniary losses in cases of serious injury or death.[18] This would enable payments to be reviewed in line with the plaintiff's medical condition and average earnings. The Law Commission preferred retention of the lump sum on the ground that this was generally preferred by the plaintiffs, who would probably continue to settle out of court for a lump sum.[19] There is now a limited power to award periodical payments but only where both parties consent.[20] The court has no power to order such an arrangement.

The Law Commission did recommend that the court be empowered to award provisional damages, which has now been given statutory effect.[1] Where there is a serious and substantial chance that, at some future time, the injured person may develop some disease or suffer deterioration[2] in his physical or mental condition, he may be awarded damages based on the assumption that this will not occur, with a proviso that further damages will be given at a later date if it does occur. This provision must be pleaded by the plaintiff, who may opt for a higher award at the trial under the once and for all rule by not pleading the provision. The court may make a modest award to cover the risk of deterioration or further disease occurring. This is known as a 'risk award.'

Interim damages may be awarded at the interlocutory stage of proceedings, where the defendant admits liability but contests *quantum,* and the defendant is insured, or is a public authority, or is a defendant whose resources would enable him to make an interim payment.[3] This does not prevent the plaintiff obtaining a higher award at trial.

(ii) Structured settlements[4]

The tort system of awarding lump sum damages for personal injuries is defective in many ways. The plaintiff is at a disadvantage because of the difficulty in estimating the

---

18 Pearson Commission Report, Vol 1, ch 14.
19 Law Commission Report No 56 (1973) para 29.
20 Damages Act 1996, s 2.
1   Supreme Court Act 1981, s 32A. See Lewis (1997) 60 MLR 230.
2   *Willson v Ministry of Defence* [1991] 1 All ER 638.
3   Supreme Court Act 1981, s 32. See Lewis (1997) 60 MLR 230.
4   See Allen (1988) 104 LQR 448. See also Lewis (1991) 10 CJQ 212; Lewis (1993) 12 CJQ 251; Lewis (1993) OJLS 530; Law Commission Report 224 (1994).

award that will be awarded at trial. This, combined with the delay and stress of the litigation process, leads to plaintiffs accepting low figures in negotiated settlements.[5] One way of avoiding some of the problems associated with the lump sum is the structured settlement,[6] which provides pensions instead of lump sum damages for future losses.

A structured settlement works by the insurer buying an annuity which covers the liability involved and is held for the injured person. The pension can be varied and the payments structured over a period of time. The plaintiff obtains the benefit of income guaranteed against erosion by inflation and the money is paid free of tax, which increases by 25% the value of the lump sum paid by the insurer.

A structured settlement consists of a lump sum to cover financial losses up to the date of the settlement and a pension which will usually last for the rest of the plaintiff's life. Payments can be index-linked, which removes the problem of inflation. This pension covers future loss of income, non-pecuniary losses, medical expenses and the cost of future care. Moreover the settlement can take account of identified future needs, for example specialist care after the parents get too old, or after institutional care ends. There is still a lump sum element to allow for immediate costs such as house conversion.

The drawbacks to the structured settlement are that a court has no power to order one; they are only appropriate to future losses; and the amount involved must be at least £50,000 to make them worthwhile. The court must also calculate what the lump sum would be for the plaintiff in a conventional award before setting up the structured settlement.

(iii)   Pecuniary loss

(a)   *Loss of earnings*   Any loss of earnings suffered by the plaintiff before the trial must be pleaded as special damages. The plaintiff must show what his net loss has been as a result of his injury. The net loss is as at the date of assessment, not at the date of the injury.[7] Deductions such as taxation, national insurance contributions and pension payments must be made, but benefits such as the value of a company car may be claimed.

Future losses of earnings are claimed as general damages, and the court has the task of determining what the plaintiff's loss is likely to be. The starting point is the plaintiff's net annual loss, that is the difference between what he would have earned and what he is earning. This is known as the multiplicand. This figure will be adjusted to take account of factors such as promotion prospects. The court then applies a multiplier to this figure. The plaintiff should receive a sum which, when invested, will produce a figure equal to the lost income.

The multiplier is calculated by finding the number of years that the disability is likely to continue. This figure is then reduced to take account of the contingencies of life. The plaintiff might not have lived or worked until normal retirement age and he receives a capital sum, not income. An example was given by Lord Lloyd in *Wells v Wells*.[8] If the need was to provide £10,000 a year for twenty years, then a lump sum of £200,000 would be inappropriate as the £10,000 for year twenty would have been earning interest for nineteen years. On the basis of a net return of 5%, the discounted figure would be £148,800. In the case of a thirty-year-old man, the multiplier would until recently have

5   Genn *Out of Court Settlement in Personal Injury Actions* (Oxford) 1987.
6   Defined by the Damages Act 1996, s 1.
7   *Cookson v Knowles* [1979] AC 556.
8   [1998] 3 All ER 481, 485.

been fifteen or sixteen. However, the multiplier applied will, to a certain extent, depend on the rate of return that the plaintiff can expect to obtain from his lump sum.

The use of the multiplier has been criticised and the use of actuarial evidence advocated.[9] In times of high inflation the value of the return on the investment is reduced and the plaintiff under-compensated. However, the courts refused to make an allowance for future inflation, relying instead on the 'sound investment' policy and that the victims of a tort are entitled to no better protection than others who rely on capital for their support.[10] This, however, goes against the principle of restoring the victim to his pre-accident position, as he would have been better protected from inflation as an income earner rather than relying on capital.

In *Wells v Wells*,[11] the House of Lords ruled that the plaintiff is entitled to be compensated on the basis that they would invest in index-linked government securities (ILGS).[12] The average rate of return on ILGS is 3% and therefore, as a matter of guidance rather than precedent, the discount rate should be 3%. This would result in a higher multiplier and a larger lump sum.

The Damages Act 1996, s 1 gives the Lord Chancellor the power to give general guidance on rates of return. In the light of the decision in *Wells*, it appears likely that the rate will be fixed at 3%.[13]

The effect of the decision and the increase in multipliers can be seen in the fact that the application of a 3% discount rate resulted in increases in the awards of £300,000 to a six year old; £186,000 to a twenty-eight-year-old; and £108,000 to a fifty-eight-year-old.

Particular problems are caused by what are known as the lost years. Where the plaintiff's life expectancy has been reduced by an accident, it may be that the plaintiff should not be compensated for loss of earnings during these lost years. The argument against such compensation is that the plaintiff will not be alive to suffer financial loss or to enjoy the money. The damages will therefore benefit his dependants and not himself. But the dependants would have a claim under the Fatal Accidents Act 1976, unless the plaintiff had already accepted damages or settlement in respect of his claim.

English law has taken an objective approach to this question. Damages for loss of earnings are assessed on the plaintiff's life expectancy before the accident,[14] subject to a deduction for the amount the plaintiff would have spent pro rata on his own support during the lost years.[15] Generally, no award is given to a young child for the lost years.[16]

Where the plaintiff has not lost earnings but is likely to suffer future handicap in the labour market, he can be compensated for loss of earning capacity.[17] The multiplier is inappropriate, and a lump sum is awarded. The same method can be used to compensate a child who has not yet entered the labour market and has had his job prospects reduced.[18]

(b)   *Expenses*   The plaintiff is entitled to recover all expenses reasonably incurred as a result of the treatment of his injuries. Where the plaintiff is treated by the National

9   See Kemp (1985) 101 LQR 556.
10   See *Lim Poh Choo v Camden and Islington Area Health Authority* [1980] AC 174.
11   [1998] 3 All ER 481.
12   As recommended by the Law Commission Report 224 (1994) paras 2.25 - 2.28.
13   See Lewis (1997) 60 MLR 230, 234.
14   *Pickett v British Rail Engineering Ltd* [1980] AC 136 overruling *Oliver v Ashman* [1962] 2 QB 210.
15   *Harris v Empress Motors Ltd* [1983] 3 All ER 561.
16   *Croke (a minor) v Wiseman* [1981] 3 All ER 852.
17   *Smith v Manchester Corpn* (1974) 17 KIR 1.
18   *Joyce v Yeomans* [1981] 2 All ER 21, [1981] 1 WLR 549.

Health Service, the living expenses which he saves are set off against his loss of earnings.[19] He has a free choice as to whether to be treated privately or not.[20]

Where a third party has incurred pecuniary loss in providing care for the plaintiff, this amount is recoverable as damages. One problem raised for the courts by this head of damages is, whose loss is it? Should it be regarded as the plaintiff's loss, based on his need for care, or are the damages to compensate the voluntary carer? The latter approach has been held to be correct and that those damages are to be held on trust to be paid to the person providing the services.[1] One effect of this approach is that an award cannot be made where the services are provided by the defendant, as in *Hunt v Severs* itself.[2]

(c)   *Other pecuniary losses*   Any pre-trial pecuniary loss is recoverable, provided it is not too remote. Damages may be recovered for the necessary cost of employing a housekeeper or the loss of income suffered by a person who gratuitously renders housekeeping services.[3]

(iv)   Non-pecuniary loss[3a]

(a)   *Loss of amenity*   The plaintiff may recover damages for the injury itself, and any consequent inability to enjoy life. Damages are calculated on an objective basis, irrespective of the plaintiff's inability to appreciate the disability. This means that an unconscious plaintiff may recover full damages for loss of amenity. Despite criticisms of this principle,[4] it is consistently upheld by the courts.[5]

Damages for loss of amenity can create difficulties, since it is impossible to estimate, in monetary terms, the loss to the plaintiff. Any figure arrived at by the court is bound to be arbitrary.[6] The courts work from a tariff laid down by the Court of Appeal as the norm for injuries of a particular type. This figure can be adjusted in the light of the circumstances of a particular plaintiff. Thus, if a person used to enjoy a particular physical amenity, such as dancing, before the accident, the figure can be increased.

(b)   *Pain and suffering*   Damages may be recovered for suffering attributable to the injury itself and any consequential surgical operations. Past and future pain can be claimed for. Likewise, an award may be made for compensation neurosis, a medically recognised condition caused by awaiting the outcome of legal proceedings. Damages for pain and suffering cannot be recovered if no pain has been suffered, for example, where the victim of an accident does not recover consciousness. A conscious patient may be able to recover damages for mental suffering caused by the knowledge that his life expectancy has been curtailed,[7] or that his ability to enjoy life has been diminished by his physical handicap.[8] However, damages are not recoverable for loss of expectation of life itself.[9]

---

19   Administration of Justice Act 1982, s 5.
20   Section 2(4) of Law Reform (Personal Injuries) Act 1948.
1   *Hunt v Severs* [1994] 2 All ER 385. See Kemp (1994) 110 LQR 524; Matthews & Lunney (1995) 58 MLR 395; Hoyano (1995) 3 Tort L Rev 63.
2   Ibid at 394 per LORD BRIDGE.
3   *Daly v General Steam Navigation Co Ltd* [1980] 3 All ER 696.
3a   See Law Com No 257 (1999).
4   Pearson Commission Report, Vol 1, paras 393–398; Atiyah *Accidents* p 188.
5   *H West & Son Ltd v Shephard* [1964] AC 326; *Lim Poh Choo v Camden Health Authority* [1980] AC 174.
6   See Ogus (1972) 35 MLR 1.
7   Administration of Justice Act 1982, s 1(1)(b).
8   *H West & Son Ltd v Shephard* [1964] AC 326.
9   Administration of Justice Act 1982, s 1(1)(a).

Nervous shock,[10] neurosis[11] and other psychic disorders[12] are compensated by damages for pecuniary loss and by general damages for loss of amenity and pain and suffering. The courts have not been particularly generous and seem concerned to keep damages low. The top rate is reserved for cases where the plaintiff will be affected for the rest of his life. A woman who suffered mental disorder and whose life became a misery, spent mostly in institutions, was awarded £22,500.[13]

(v)   Deductions

The aim of an award of damages for personal injuries is to compensate the plaintiff for losses incurred as a result of the injury. If the plaintiff makes financial gain as a result of his injury, deductions may be made. The gains concerned may come in the form of state benefits, payments under an insurance policy, payments by an employer or gratuitous payments by friends.

A number of factors underlie the courts' approach to deductions. They do not wish to punish the thrifty plaintiff who has paid for insurance cover for accidents, and they do not wish to deter benevolence. The effect of this is that a plaintiff may receive compensation from more than one source, including overlapping payments for the same loss.

The deduction of social security benefits, paid as a result of the injuries caused by the tortfeasor, from damages, is particularly controversial.[14] If no deduction is made the plaintiff will be over-compensated. If the amount of benefits received or payable is simply deducted from the damages paid by the torfeasor, then the defendant will receive a windfall. This was roughly the position at common law in 1988.[15] In 1989 Parliament intervened with a scheme whereby the 'compensator' (usually the defendant's insurer) had to obtain a certificate from the Department of Social Security of the benefits paid, or likely to be paid, over the five-year period from the accident which gave rise to the claim. This amount is deducted from the amount paid to the plaintiff and then paid to the Department of Social Security.[16] For cases where the compensation was less than £2,500 the scheme did not apply.

The scheme was amended in 1997[17] by more closely defining the relevant benefits to be deducted from from damages and relating the deducted benefit to the particular head of damages. Any benefit which makes up for loss of earnings is now only deducted from damages for loss of earnings. Benefits for the cost of care will likewise only be deducted from damages for cost of care. Once the particular head of damage is exhausted no further deduction can take place. No deduction can now be made from damages for pain and suffering as there is no equivalent social security payment. The legislation also abolishes the provisions relating to payments under £2,500.

Non-state benefits are generally non–deductible. Insurance policy money for personal injuries is non-deductible as the plaintiff has paid for the benefit and it would not be right to deprive him of it.[18] However, in cases of property damage the plaintiff would be obliged to reimburse the insurer. The House of Lords accepted the view that pensions,

---

10   *Alcock v Chief Constable of South Yorkshire Police* [1991] 4 All ER 907; *McLoughlin v O'Brian* [1983] 1 AC 410, [1982] 2 All ER 298; *Brice v Brown* [1984] 1 All ER 997; *Whitmore v Euroways Express Coaches Ltd* (1984) Times, 4 May. See also ch 8.
11   *Liffen v Watson* [1940] 1 KB 556.
12   *Whitmore v Euroways Express Coaches Ltd* (1984) Times, 4 May.
13   *Brice v Brown* [1984] 1 All ER 997.
14   See Lewis (1998) 18 LS 15; Law Commission No 147 (1997).
15   *Hodgson v Trapp* [1988] 3 All ER 870.
16   Social Security Administration Act 1992, Part IV.
17   Social Security (Recovery of Benefits) Act 1997.
18   *Bradburn v Great Western Rly Co* (1874) LR 10 Exch 1.

whether discretionary or not and whether contributory or not, should be non-deductible.[19] The House was invited to overturn *Parry v Cleaver* but refused to do so and confirmed that occupational pensions are to be regarded as benefits provided by the employee.[20] Occupational sick pay is deductible even if the employer has insured against his contractual liability to provide sick pay.[1] If the employer has taken out an accident insurance policy for the employees' benefit but this was not related to any contractual liability to provide sick pay, payments made under the policy to employees will be treated as non-deductible as being equivalent to personal benevolence.[2] Any wages or sick pay received by the plaintiff will be deducted, unless the employee is obliged to repay the sick pay from any damages he receives.[3]

(vi)   Mental distress[4]

Difficulties are experienced in English law when dealing with damages for mental distress which is not consequent on physical injury. The expression 'mental distress' covers grief, disappointment, fear or worry suffered as a result of the defendant's wrong. Mental distress has to be kept separate from illnesses such as nervous shock and neurosis, which are treated as personal injuries. Where damages are awarded for mental distress, they are similar to the subjective award of damages for pain and suffering to a plaintiff who has suffered personal injuries. Whether an award of such damages satisfies the plaintiff's status quo or expectation interest is arguable, but whichever view is taken, policy reasons in favour of proper compensation would dictate that such damages should be awarded.[5] The courts have taken a piecemeal approach to the question, sometimes disguising the damages as aggravated damages.

Where the defendant's wrong amounts to a tort, the courts have frequently awarded aggravated damages. This approach applies to torts involving infringement of personal integrity,[6] reputation,[7] and property rights.[8] There are now signs that the courts openly recognise the interest protected and specifically award damages for injured feelings,[9] mental distress[10] or disappointment.[11] Old rules continue to block the way to the general recovery of such damages. Where the distress is caused by injury to a third party and does not amount to nervous shock, no recovery is allowed. Unresolved is the effect of the contractual rules on damages for distress, where the negligent performance of a service causes economic loss.

Where the wrong is a breach of contract, the courts largely adhere to the rule in *Addis v Gramophone Co Ltd*[12] that damages are not recoverable for mental distress caused by a breach of contract. Exceptions to this principle have been developed where the

---

19   *Parry v Cleaver* [1970] AC 1.
20   *Smoker v London Fire & Civil Defence Authority* [1991] 2 AC 502. See also *Longden v British Coal Corpn* [1998] 1 All ER 289.
1   *Hussain v New Taplow Paper Mills* [1988] AC 514.
2   *McCamley v Cammell Laird Shipbuilders* [1990] 1 WLR 963.
3   *Smoker v London Fire & Civil Defence Authority* [1991] 2 AC 502.
4   See also ch 9.
5   Burrows *Remedies* p 231-2.
6   *White v Metropolitan Police Comr* (1982) Times, 24 April.
7   *McCarey v Associated Newspapers Ltd (No 2)* [1965] 2 QB 86.
8   *Bone v Seale* [1975] 1 All ER 787, [1975] 1 WLR 797, CA; *Drane v Evangelou* [1978] 2 All ER 437. But note the approach of LORD HOFFMANN in *Hunter v Canary Wharf Ltd* [1997] 2 All ER 426 at 451.
9   *Archer v Brown* [1984] 2 All ER 267.
10   *Perry v Sidney Phillips & Son (a firm)* [1982] 3 All ER 705, [1982] 1 WLR 1297.
11   *Bagley v North Herts Health Authority* [1986] NLJ Rep 1014.
12   [1909] AC 488. See also *Bliss v South East Thames Regional Health Authority* [1985] IRLR 308; *Hayes v Dodd* [1990] 2 All ER 815.

objective of the contract was to confer either enjoyment,[13] relief from distress,[14] or where the distress was consequent on physical inconvenience caused by the breach of contract.[15]

The present approach to such damages in contract seems to rest on whether the court can find an implied term that the purpose of the contract was to provide enjoyment or prevent distress. An alternative approach based on the 'consumer surplus' has opened up following the House of Lords decision in *Ruxley Electronics & Construction Ltd v Forsyth*.[16] The 'consumer surplus' is where the plaintiff places a value above the market value on correct performance of a contract. The approach in *Ruxley*, awarding damages for loss of amenity, could provide a route for the courts in the employment cases by finding that an employee places a value on his job above a pecuniary one.

(4)   THE EFFECT OF DEATH ON AN AWARD OF DAMAGES FOR PERSONAL INJURIES

Where the defendant in an action dies, the cause of action survives against his estate[17] and a new cause of action is created for his dependants.[18]

(i)   The estate's action

The common law rule that an action did not survive death was removed by the Law Reform (Miscellaneous Provisions) Act 1934. This followed the introduction of compulsory third-party insurance for the use of motor vehicles. It was thought unjust that the defendant's estate, and hence his insurers, were not liable where the victim was killed in a road accident.

The 1934 Act does not create liability, it merely preserves the deceased's subsisting action[19] for the benefit of his estate. The action is essentially that which the deceased would have brought had he lived. The action is not for death caused by the defendant, so the defendant need not be responsible for the death. The estate can recover those damages which the deceased would have recovered, from the date of his injury to the time of trial. But where the interval between injury and death was so brief as to be part of the death itself, there is no actionable head of damages for the estate.[20] Any pecuniary losses such as loss of income,[1] or medical expenses[2] are recoverable, as are non-pecuniary losses for pain, suffering and loss of amenity.[3] No damages may be recovered by the estate for loss of earnings for the lost years, that is after the death of the injured person.[4] This removes the possibility of the defendant having to pay large damages for post-death loss of earnings to both the estate and dependants where these are different entities. Normally, the estate and the dependants will be the same persons and will be able to recover damages for post-death loss of earnings under the Fatal Accidents Act 1976.

13   See *Jarvis v Swans Tours Ltd* [1973] QB 233.
14   *Heywood v Wellers* [1976] QB 446.
15   *Perry v Sidney Phillips & Son (a firm)* [1982] 3 All ER 705, [1982] 1 WLR 1297. See also *Watts v Morrow* [1991] 1 WLR 1421.
16   [1996] AC 344.
17   Law Reform (Miscellaneous Provisions) Act 1934, s 1(1).
18   Fatal Accidents Act 1976.
19   Law Reform (Miscellaneous Provisions) Act 1934, s 1(4).
20   *Hicks v Chief Constable of South Yorkshire Police* [1992] 2 All ER 65.
1   *Murray v Shuter* [1976] QB 972.
2   *Rose v Ford* [1937] AC 826.
3   Ibid. Cf Damages (Scotland) Act 1976, s 2(3).
4   Administration of Justice Act 1982, s 4(2) overruling *Gammell v Wilson* [1982] AC 27 and see Waddams (1984) 47 MLR 437; Cane and Harris (1983) 46 MLR 478.

Finally, no damages for bereavement or exemplary damages may be recovered by the estate.[5]

Where the defendant's wrong has caused the death, any losses or gains to the estate consequent on the death are ignored in calculating damages under the 1934 Act.[6] An example of such a loss is the termination of an annuity paid to the deceased. An example of such a gain is an insurance payment on the death. An exception to this rule is that the court may award the estate any funeral expenses incurred when the defendant was responsible for the death.[7]

(ii)   The dependants' action

(a)   *Who can claim?*   A detailed list of dependants is given by the Fatal Accidents Act 1976, section 1(3). Actions may be brought by spouses, former spouses, cohabitees as man and wife for two years,[8] parents and other ascendants, children, including those treated as children and other descendants,[9] siblings, uncles, aunts and their issue. The action is brought by the personal representatives of the deceased,[10] or after six months of the appointment of personal representatives, by any dependant on behalf of himself and others.[11]

The provision of such a list can be criticised as having possible arbitrary effects, and the definition of who is a dependant has been continually amended by legislation to take account of changing social views of family structure. It is hard to disagree with the view that anyone who can establish a non-business pecuniary loss should be able to recover, leaving the court to decide whether a real loss has been suffered.[12]

(b)   *Nature of the action*   The action is essentially one for the loss of a breadwinner. The majority of cases are brought by wives or children deprived of the husband's or father's earnings, or by husbands or children deprived of a housekeeper. Where the wife works, the husband and children have a claim for loss of pecuniary benefit from those earnings.

This is a new right of action given to dependants, not a survival of the deceased's action.[13] The dependants must show that the deceased had a right of action if they are to be able to claim.[14] If the deceased had settled his claim or had obtained judgment against the defendant, the dependants will have no claim. But, if the deceased has limited the amount he could claim, the dependants are not bound by that limitation.[15]

(iii)   The amount recoverable

The basis of the action is that, because of the death, the dependants receive compensation for their losses. The main head of damages is the pecuniary loss suffered as from the date of death. Where the deceased lived for a period after the accident, pecuniary losses suffered in this period will be awarded to the estate under the Law Reform (Miscellaneous Provisions) Act 1934.

5   Administration of Justice Act 1982, s 4(1) and (2).
6   Law Reform (Miscellaneous Provisions) Act 1934, s 1(2)(c).
7   Ibid.
8   Fatal Accidents Act 1976, s 1(3)(b).
9   Ibid, s 1(3)(e) and (f).
10   Ibid, s 1(1).
11   Ibid, s 2(2).
12   Burrows *Remedies* pp 209–210.
13   Fatal Accidents Act 1976, s 1(1).
14   Ibid.
15   *Nunan v Southern Rly Co* [1924] 1 KB 223.

Pecuniary damages awarded under the Fatal Accidents Act 1976 are assessed in two stages.[16] First, an award may be made from the date of death up to the date of trial, in which case actual earnings which would have been received by the deceased are calculated. A sum which the deceased would have spent on his own support is deducted. Secondly, an award may be made from the date of trial into the future. The court faces the difficulty of guessing what would have happened to the deceased had he not been killed. It must be determined how long he would have lived and worked, and his promotion prospects will have to be assessed. It is necessary to determine how much of the deceased's earnings would have gone to his dependants and what their dependancy would have been.

A discount will be made from the award if the plaintiff is a child and the deceased's parent would have provided poor care and might have left the family.[17] The independence of a child must be taken into account and a discount is therefore made for the later years, for example teenagers, who require less care.[18] Where a child has been adopted this terminates any claim of the child in respect of the death of the natural mother.[19] If a widow is unsalaried at the date of trial, it will have to be considered whether she might become employed in the future. If this is likely, it will have to be considered to what extent this reduces her financial dependancy on her deceased husband. The courts normally apply a multiplier in this regard. The deceased's net earnings are assessed, from which is deducted the amount he would have spent on his own living expenses. Promotion prospects may be taken into account to augment the starting figure. Subsequently, an appropriate multiplier will be applied. The aim is to award a lump sum which, when invested, will produce an income equal to the dependant's loss of income over the period of dependency. For example, let us assume that the deceased is thirty years old, married with two children and earns a net income of £20,000 per annum with no promotion prospects. If he spent £6,000 per annum on his own living expenses, the damages would be £14,000 x 15 (the appropriate multiplier).[20] This would give a figure of £210,000 available for the dependants for their pecuniary loss.

No claim is allowed for amounts flowing from a business relationship with the deceased. In *Malyon v Plummer*,[1] the widow received £600 per annum for services rendered to her husband's company. The value of her services was assessed at £200 per annum. The balance was attributable to her relationship to the deceased, and her loss of dependency was therefore £400 per annum.

In calculating the loss, the court must have regard to a reasonable expectation of pecuniary benefit as of right or otherwise from the continuance of life.[2] On this basis, the court is directed that, in the case of a cohabitee, they must take into account the fact that the dependant had no enforceable right to financial support by the deceased as a result of their living together.[3] But, strangely, in assessing a widow's claim in respect of her husband's death, the court is to take no account of her remarriage or prospects of remarriage.[4] The aim of this provision is to put an end to the 'cattle-market' approach whereby the court had to assess a widow's prospects of remarriage. However, the rule results in over-compensation when the widow has already remarried by the time of the

16   *Cookson v Knowles* [1977] QB 913.
17   *Stanley v Saddique* [1992] QB 1.
18   *Corbett v Barking, Havering and Brentwood Health Authority* [1991] 1 All ER 498.
19   *Watson v Willmott* [1991] 1 All ER 473.
20   The effect of *Wells v Wells* [1998] 3 All ER 481 will be to increase this multiplier.
1   [1964] 1 QB 330.
2   Fatal Accidents Act 1976, s 3.
3   Ibid, s 3(4).
4   Ibid, s 3(3).

trial. The pecuniary loss suffered by the death of the first husband may have been compensated by her right to support from her second husband.[5]

Certain dependants have a claim for damages for bereavement.[6] Only the spouse of the deceased or parents of an unmarried child can claim. Damages are awarded for mental distress at the death, and a fixed sum of £7,500 is awarded.[7] The provision is welcome, but it is doubtful whether a fixed sum or such a narrow range of claimants is necessary. Does a parent cease to grieve at the death of a child over the age of 18 or when he is married?

(iv) Deductions

Deductions are governed by the Fatal Accidents Act 1976, section 4. In assessing the damages in respect of a person's death, benefits which have accrued or may accrue to any person from his estate or otherwise as a result of death are disregarded.[8] The gratuitous services of the tortfeasor can be taken into account as reducing the plaintiff's loss and are not a benefit accruing as a result of the death.[9] The section is not confined to material benefits. Where an unreliable natural mother was killed, the child's claim for loss of services could not be reduced because she had been replaced by a much more reliable stepmother.[10]

The effect of section 4 is that insurance money, pensions, gratuities and damages for pain and suffering inherited as part of the deceased's estate are non-deductible. There is now no overlap in relation to pecuniary damages, as the estate's pecuniary damages cover the period from accident to death, and the dependant's damages run from death onwards.

The new section 4 was inserted by the Administration of Justice Act 1982, following criticism of the old provision by the Law Commission and the Pearson Commission.[11] These reports had in mind the expansion of non-deductible benefits in respect of non-pecuniary damages awarded to the estate and accelerated inheritance due to the death. The wording of the section appears to be much wider, and would appear to conflict with section 3(3) by ordering the court not to take account of a remarriage.[12]

The provisions for recoupment of social security benefits do not apply to claims under the Fatal Accidents Act.

2. DAMAGE TO PROPERTY RIGHTS

(1) INTRODUCTION

The defendant's breach of obligation may result in the destruction of, or damage to, the plaintiff's property. Alternatively, it may result in the plaintiff being deprived of the use of his property. In the case of destruction or damage, the basic principle is *restitutio in integrum*, that is, the plaintiff must be put into as good a position as if his property had not been damaged.[13] It must be asked whether the plaintiff is entitled to damages

---

5   Cf Pearson Commission Report, Vol 1, paras 409–412.
6   Fatal Accidents Act 1976, s 1A.
7   Ibid.
8   See *Pidduck v Eastern Scottish Omnibuses Ltd* [1990] 2 All ER 69.
9   *Hayden v Hayden* [1992] 1 WLR 986. See *Kemp* (1993) 109 LQR 173.
10   *Stanley v Siddique* [1992] 1 QB 1, CA. See also *R v Criminal Injuries Compensation Board, ex p K (minors)* [1999] QB 1131.
11   Law Commission Report No 56, paras 254–256; Pearson Commission Report, Vol 1, paras 537–539.
12   See Burrows *Remedies* pp 217–218.
13   *The Liesbosch Dredger* [1933] AC 449 at 459 (per LORD WRIGHT).

representing the reduction in value of the property, or the cost of curing the defect. Pecuniary losses consequential on the damage or destruction may also be awarded. Where the plaintiff is deprived of the use of his property by the defendant's wrongful occupation of the land or misappropriation of a chattel, the courts are concerned with losses caused to the plaintiff and any unjust enrichment obtained by the defendant. The courts tend to distinguish between harm to real property and harm to chattels. However, it can be argued that there is no logical distinction between damage to a building and damage to a chattel.[14]

(2)   REAL PROPERTY

(i)   Damage

In *Dodd Properties (Kent) Ltd v Canterbury City Council*,[15] it was said that the assessment of damages for property damage is achieved by applying one or other of two quite different measures or, occasionally, a combination of the two. The first is to take the capital value of the property in an undamaged state and to compare it with its value in a damaged state. The second is to take the cost of repair or reinstatement. Which is appropriate will depend on a number of factors, such as the plaintiff's future intentions as to the use of the property and the reasonableness of those intentions. If he reasonably intends to sell the property in its damaged state, clearly the diminution in capital value is the true measure of damage. If he reasonably intends to continue to occupy it and repair the damage, clearly the cost of repairs is the true measure. And there may be in-between situations.[16]

The court's decision whether to award the difference in value or the cost of correction will turn on a number of factors. Where the property is required by the plaintiff for residential or commercial purposes, cost of correction will normally be the appropriate measure. This is reinforced by the plaintiff's obligation to take reasonable steps to mitigate his loss. If a factory is damaged, the plaintiff will need to effect the repairs as soon as possible to return the property to an operating condition and mitigate his consequential loss of profits. In *Harbutt's Plasticine Ltd v Wayne Tank and Pump Co Ltd*,[17] the plaintiffs' factory was burned down as a result of the defendant's breach of contract in installing an unsuitable heating system insulated with unsafe material. By the time of trial, the plaintiffs had already had the factory rebuilt, and were awarded £146,581 as the cost of rebuilding rather than £116,785 as the reduction in value. The fact that the plaintiffs had acquired a more modern factory did not require any deduction from their damages.[18] A similar principle also applies where the plaintiff uses the premises as his residence and has already had them repaired.[19] This is known as the 'betterment' principle whereby the court will not make deductions since the plaintiff would not be over-compensated, unless he were to sell the property.

Where the plaintiff intends to use the land as an economic asset by selling it, his damages should be based on the reduction in selling price. In *Taylor (Wholesale) Ltd v Hepworths Ltd*,[20] the plaintiff's billiard hall was destroyed by fire. The hall was disused, and the plaintiff intended to sell the site for redevelopment. Damages for reinstatement

---

14   Ogus *The Law of Damages* (1973) p 163.
15   [1980] 1 All ER 928.
16   Ibid at 938 (per DONALDSON LJ).
17   [1970] 1 QB 447.
18   Ibid at 472–473 (per WIDGERY LJ) See also *Dominion Mosaics & Tile Co Ltd v Trafalgar Trucking Co Ltd* [1990] 2 All ER 246.
19   *Hollebone v Midhurst and Fernhurst Builders Ltd* [1968] 1 Lloyd's Rep 38. See also *Bacon v Cooper (Metals) Ltd* [1982] 1 All ER 397. Cf Ogus *Law of Damages* (1973) p 134.
20   [1977] 1 WLR 659.

were refused, as the £2,500 reduction in value of the site was offset by saving the expense of clearing the site. A similar principle applies where the plaintiff is a reversioner.[1]

What if the plaintiff intended to stay where he was? In *Hussey v Eels*[2] the plaintiff bought a bungalow from the defendant for £53,000. The defendant had misrepresented that the bungalow did not suffer from subsidence. The plaintiff was unable to afford the £17,000 cost of rectifying the defects and had the bungalow demolished. Two years later planning permission was granted for two new bungalows and the plaintiff sold the site to a builder for £78,000. The plaintiff was awarded damages based on the difference (ie £17,000) between market value at time of the initial sale and the actual value of the premises. As the resale was not part of a continuous transaction commencing with the original purchase, the profit on the resale did not have to be taken into account. If the plaintiff lost an opportunity as a result of the defendant's breach of duty, such as the opportunity to acquire a statutory tenancy, then this loss may be recovered if the plaintiff had intended to remain in the premises.[3]

Where the plaintiff has already reinstated the property at the time of trial and has acted reasonably in doing so, he is entitled to damages. However, if the plaintiff is awarded damages for reinstatement when he has not yet carried out the work, he may choose not to have the work done. In *Tito v Waddell (No 2)*,[4] MEGARRY VC considered that a probable intention to do the work would be sufficient, and that the court could ask for an undertaking.[5] There is a contrary line of authority to the effect that what the plaintiff does with the damages is of no concern to the defendant.[6] LORD JAUNCEY in *Ruxley Electronics & Construction Ltd v Forsyth*[7] sought to reconcile the two lines of authority by saying that the intention to reinstate was only relevant to reasonableness and the loss sustained. Once the loss was established, intention as to use of the damages was irrelevant.

It is possible that the breach of obligation does not result in a reduction in the market value of the property and that the cost of reinstatement would be unreasonable. This was the situation in *Ruxley*.[8] The defendant builders had contracted to build a swimming pool 7ft 6in deep for the plaintiff but in breach of contract the pool was only 6ft 6in deep. There was no reduction in market value as the finished pool was safe for diving and the cost of construction would clearly be a waste of resources as it would cost the same as the original pool. The House of Lords awarded damages of £2,500 for loss of amenity based on the consumer surplus. This type of award recognises the plaintiff's subjective value of the thing contracted for, where that valuation exceeds the objective market value of the subject matter of the contract.[9]

(ii)   Wrongful interference with land

Where the defendant has wrongly occupied the plaintiff's land, the plaintiff is entitled to the *mesne* profits he would have made by using the land.[10] He is also compensated for loss of his use and enjoyment. This is calculated by awarding him the rent he would

1   *Moss v Christchurch RDC* [1925] 2 KB 750.
2   [1990] 1 All ER 449.
3   *Murray v Lloyd* [1990] 2 All ER 92.
4   [1977] Ch 106 at 317.
5   See also *Radford v de Froberville* [1977] 1 WLR 1262.
6   *Joyner v Weeks* [1891] 2 QB 31; *James v Hutton & Cook Ltd* [1950] 1 KB 9; *Darlington BC v Wiltshier Northern Ltd* [1995] 1 WLR 68, 80 per STEYN LJ.
7   [1996] 1 AC 344, 372–3. See Poole (1996) 59 MLR 272; Beale (1995) 111 LQR 54.
8   Ibid.
9   See Harris, Ogus and Phillips (1979) 95 LQR 581. See Mental Distress, above.
10   *McArthur & Co v Cornwall* [1892] AC 75.

have received from a lawful tenant.[11] These heads of damage can be regarded as status quo losses. But problems are caused where the defendant has made a profit from the land during his occupation and the plaintiff would not have put the land to such use.[12] These damages are better viewed as a reversal of the defendant's unjust enrichment, and not as compensation for the plaintiff.

If the plaintiff is unable to use his land as a result of the defendant's activities, the plaintiff will recover any lost profits, subject to rules on remoteness and mitigation. Illustrations can be found in nuisance cases consisting of a highway obstruction which results in a loss of custom,[13] and the unreasonable operation of building works resulting in lost custom.[14] Such damages can be properly regarded as restoring the status quo between the parties.

(3) DAMAGE TO CHATTELS

(i) Destruction of chattels

Destruction includes constructive total loss whereby damage is so great that it would not be reasonable to repair a chattel. Where a chattel has been destroyed, there is no difference between its reduction in value and the cost of repair. The court must apply the principle of *restitutio in integrum*. The plaintiff will recover a sum which represents the replacement value and places him in the same position as if the loss had not been inflicted.[15]

The majority of cases on destruction of chattels concern ships, but similar principles are applied to other chattels.[16] The difficulty is to determine what the plaintiff has lost. Early cases assessed the value of the chattel itself by reference to its selling price, and then added on consequential losses.[17] Consequential losses would include expenses and profits to be earned from charterparties entered at the time of collision,[18] but not loss of general future profits.[19]

A more flexible approach was advocated in *The Liesbosch Dredger*.[20] What had to be calculated was the value of the chattel.[1] This value is not the market value of the chattel, but its value to the owner 'as a going concern'.[2] The court had to reach a capitalised value of the vessel as a profit earning machine.[3] Based on this measure, the plaintiffs were able to recover the market price of a replacement dredger, the cost of adapting it to their use and transporting it to its place of use. Loss of profits incurred until a replacement could be bought and put into use should be recoverable.[4] The plaintiff may also recover for the cost of hiring a substitute until the replacement is available.[5]

---

11   *Hall v Pearlberg* [1956] 1 All ER 297n.
12   See *Whitwham v Westminster Brymbo Coal and Coke Co* [1896] 2 Ch 538.
13   *Fritz v Hobson* (1880) 14 Ch D 542.
14   *Andreae v Selfridge Ltd* [1938] Ch 1.
15   *The Liesbosch Dredger* [1933] AC 449 at 459 (per LORD WRIGHT).
16   *The Argentino* (1888) 13 PD 191 at 201 (per BOWEN LJ).
17   *The Clyde* (1856) Sw 23 at 25 (per DR LUSHINGTON).
18   *The Racine* [1906] P 273.
19   *The City of Rome* (1887) 8 Asp MLC 542n.
20   [1933] AC 449.
1   Ibid at 462–463 (per LORD WRIGHT).
2   Ibid at 464 (per LORD WRIGHT).
3   Ibid.
4   Ibid.
5   *Moore v DER Ltd* [1971] 3 All ER 517.

(ii)   Damage to chattels

The basic measure of damage is restitution, which can be effected either by repair of the existing article or by the purchase of a comparable article.[6] The normal method of assessment involves payment of the cost of repair, unless there is 'constructive total loss'. In *Darbishire v Warran*,[7] the cost of repairs to the plaintiff's car including hire charges, was £192. The cost of a replacement vehicle was £85. The plaintiff had his car repaired, but was only allowed the market value of £85. He should have mitigated his loss by purchasing a substitute vehicle. In contrast, in *O'Grady v Westminster Scaffolding Ltd*,[8] the plaintiff was allowed the cost of repairs to his almost unique car, although a replacement would have been cheaper. The court took into account the plaintiff's attachment to the vehicle, which he had carefully maintained, and the difficulties of obtaining a similar vehicle on the open market.[9] In *Darbishire,* the court distinguished *O'Grady,* stressing the uniqueness of the car rather than the attachment of the owner.[10] The consumer surplus value is recognised in cases like *O'Grady.* The principle would appear to be that the cost of repairs is the appropriate measure of damages, unless this exceeds the replacement value when the latter only is recoverable. There is an exception where the buyer of goods could have obtained specific performance. The plaintiff may have the repairs effected, although they exceed the replacement value.

Consequential losses recoverable include hiring a substitute until replacement or repair,[11] and any profits which the chattel would have earned.[12] Where the repair or replacement of the chattel results in the 'betterment' of the plaintiff in the sense that the chattel is worth more than it was before the accident, no deduction is made.[13] It is arguable that this represents over-compensation. It has been argued that an amount should be deducted to represent the plaintiff's 'betterment'.[14] However, the preferred view is that the plaintiff obtains no advantage unless the chattel is sold, and it should be for the defendant to show that the plaintiff will be over-compensated.[15]

(iii)   Wrongful interference with chattels

Wrongful interference with a chattel is actionable in the tort of conversion, trespass to goods and negligence.[16] The court will consider the value of the chattel in assessing damages.[17] In order to achieve the compensation objective, the court will also consider whether the plaintiff has suffered temporary or permanent deprivation. In the case of temporary deprivation, the plaintiff should not recover the full value of the chattel.

If deprivation is permanent, the court must determine the value of the chattel. Because of the plaintiff's duty to mitigate his loss, the appropriate value will normally be the market price of a replacement. Where there is no market for the type of chattel under consideration, the court will determine whether the chattel is required for sale or use. If it is intended to sell the chattel, the resale[18] or the market value[19] of the chattel will

6   *Darbishire v Warran* [1963] 1 WLR 1067.
7   Ibid.
8   [1962] 2 Lloyd's Rep 238.
9   Ibid at 239–240.
10   *Darbishire v Warran* [1963] 1 WLR 1067 at 1077–8. See also *The World Beauty* [1970] P 144.
11   *Darbishire v Warran* [1963] 1 WLR 1067 at 1077–8.
12   *The Argentino* (1888) 13 PD 191 at 201 (per BOWEN LJ).
13   *Bacon v Cooper (Metals) Ltd* [1982] 1 All ER 397.
14   Ogus *The Law of Damages* (1973) p 134.
15   Burrows *Remedies* pp 144–145.
16   See Torts (Interference with Goods) Act 1977, s 3.
17   Ibid.
18   *France v Gaudet* (1871) LR 6 QB 199.
19   *The Arpad* [1934] P 189.

determine the *quantum* of damages. If the chattel is intended to be used, the *quantum* of damages will be assessed by reference to the cost of manufacturing a replacement.[20] Where deprivation is temporary, the plaintiff will receive damages for loss of use. This could be assessed by reference to the cost of hiring that chattel for the period of deprivation.[1]

3.   DAMAGE TO ECONOMIC INTERESTS

(1)   ECONOMIC LOSS NOT CONSEQUENT ON DAMAGE TO PERSON OR PROPERTY

Damages are assessed on a compensatory basis. This raises the difficult question of compensation for what? English law has adopted an interests approach based on expectation, status quo and restitution.[2] Traditional analysis insists that the expectation interest is only protected in contract law, and that a tort action will only protect the status quo interest. This approach stems from a seminal law journal article which argued that contract damages should protect the reliance (status quo) interest rather than the expectation interest.[3] One effect of this approach would be to assimilate contract and tort damages on the basis that contract damages are forward-looking and tort damages backward-looking. Reliance damages would therefore put the plaintiff in his pre-contract position. Whether this premise was correct or has had practical effect is controversial[4] and the very description 'expectation interest' has been described as inappropriate in that it should be the 'performance interest.'[5] If this view is correct then the purpose of contract damages should be to secure performance of the contract rather than simply to secure the economic end result of performance.[6] If a builder contracts to build a pool 7ft 6in deep for £20,000 and builds one 6ft 6in deep, then on the former view damages should reflect the cost of complying with the contract, the cost of making the pool the contract depth. On the latter view it would be necessary to look at any economic loss to the plaintiff resulting from the breach of contract.[7]

The approach used by the courts is that of securing the economic result of performance.[8] The usual function of damages is therefore compensation. In contract the plaintiff must be put in the economic position he would have been in if the contract had been performed.[9] The plaintiff will be compensated for losses caused and gains prevented by the breach of duty. Where the plaintiff has saved money or has made a gain as a result of the breach, this should be taken into account in calculating his damages. In *British Westinghouse v Underground Electric Railways Ltd,*[10] the defendants contracted to supply turbines which proved to be defective. The plaintiff purchased replacement turbines which were more efficient and more profitable. The gain made on the new turbines exceeded the loss suffered as a result of those supplied by the defendants.

20   *J & E Hall Ltd v Barclay* [1937] 3 All ER 620.
1   *Hillesden Securities Ltd v Ryjak Ltd* [1983] 2 All ER 184.
2   See *Surrey County Council v Bredero Homes Ltd* [1993] 1 WLR 1361 at 1369 per STEYN LJ.
3   Fuller and Perdue (1936/37) 46 Yale LJ 52 and 373. See also Burrows (1983) 99 LQR 217.
4   Friedmann (1995) 111 LQR 628; Stapleton (1997) 113 LQR 257; Friedmann (1997) 113 LQR 424; Smith (1997) 113 LQR 426.
5   Friedmann (1995) 111 LQR 628 at 634.
6   Coote (1997) CLJ 537.
7   See the approaches to *Ruxley Electronics & Construction Ltd v Forsyth* by the Court of Appeal ([1994] 3 All ER 801) and the House of Lords ([1996] 1 AC 344).
8   *British Westinghouse v Underground Electric Railways Ltd* [1912] AC 673, 689 per VISCOUNT HALDANE LC. Cf *Linden Gardens Trust Ltd v Lenesta Sludge Disposals* [1994] 1 AC 85, 96–97 per LORD GRIFFITHS.
9   *Robinson v Harman* (1848) 1 Exch 850 at 855 (per PARKE B).
10   [1912] AC 673.

Accordingly, the plaintiff was only entitled to nominal damages. In tort, the plaintiff must be put in the position he would have been in if no tort had been committed.[11] In either case, if the plaintiff has suffered no loss he is not entitled to compensatory damages.[12]

Where contract and tort are called upon to protect the same right, there should be no difference in the assessment of damages.[13] In a contract for services the right is usually to have the service performed with reasonable care. This is also the tortious right and where there is concurrent liability there should be no difference in the measure of damages. The plaintiff should be put in the position he would have been in if the defendant had used reasonable care. This explains cases in negligence where the plaintiff's expectation interest is satisfied. If a solicitor negligently executes a will with the result that the plaintiff loses a bequest, what is lost is an expectation. However, the right was to have the service rendered with reasonable care and the remedy reflects this failure.[14] If, unusually, the service provider contracts to produce a result, there is no negligence action and the contractual remedy will reflect the contracted for service.

Whether the expectation interest should be protected is a matter of acute academic controversy,[15] but for present purposes, it will suffice to say that such protection depends on there being a bargain promise. Where there is a contract which does not result from a bargain promise, there is no clear reason for the expectation interest to be protected. This would appear to be true of contractual statements that a particular fact is accurate, as there is no incentive to make the promisor perform.[16]

It should be emphasised that the plaintiff has an action for losses caused and gains prevented, whether he pursues a claim for harm to his expectation interest or his status quo interest.

To illustrate the interests protected, suppose that A contracts to buy widgets from B for £100 and agrees to sell them to C for £120. If B fails to deliver the widgets, in theory, A can recover his lost profit of £20 on the sale to C, thereby protecting his expectation interest. He can recover any expenses incurred in carrying out the contract as status quo or reliance losses. If he pays B the £100, he can recover this in a restitution action. This example assumes that limiting factors, such as remoteness and mitigation, are satisfied.

The above example deals with the problem of non-performance. Where there is a defective performance, there may be different problems. Suppose that B tells A that the widgets are 'Gresley' widgets, worth £120, and they transpire to be plastic widgets worth £10. If B's statement is a contract term, A must be placed in the position he would have occupied had the statement been true. He will recover the difference between the actual value of the widgets (£10) and their stated value (£120), thereby protecting his expectation interest. If the statement is a misrepresentation, A will recover status quo damages only. These represent the difference between the price (£100) and the value (£10).

In some cases, particularly those of a commercial nature, expectations of profit are recoverable in an award of damages. This is a recognition of imperfect market conditions, since in a perfect market, the loss of profit on one contract would be exactly the same as the lost opportunity of making a similar contract with someone else. It follows that, in a perfect market, the expectation loss of the plaintiff is exactly the same as his status

---

11   *Livingstone v Raywards Coal Co* (1880) 5 App Cas 25,35 per LORD BLACKBURN.
12   *Surrey County Council v Bredero Homes Ltd* [1993] 1 WLR 1361.
13   Although there may be differences in the remoteness test. See ch 16.
14   See *White v Jones* [1995] 1 All ER 691.
15   See ch 6.
16   See *Dick Bentley Productions Ltd v Harold Smith (Motors) Ltd* [1965] 1 WLR 623 and Beale *Remedies for Breach of Contract* (1980) ch 9.

quo loss.[17] Given that market conditions are not perfect, losses of profit can and do occur. If a seller of goods is forced to find another buyer because the defendant has failed to take delivery of the goods, or if the buyer of goods is forced to find a replacement because the defendant refuses to deliver, the plaintiff may have suffered a loss of profit. Ordinarily, the measure of damages is represented by the loss directly and naturally resulting in the ordinary course of events from the breach of contract.[18] This loss can be represented by the profit the plaintiff would have made if the contract had been performed. In *Thompson (WC) Ltd v Robinson (Gunmakers) Ltd*[19] the defendant refused to take delivery of a new car, which the plaintiffs were unable to return to their suppliers without suffering any penalty. Under the Sale of Goods Act 1979, section 50(2), they were able to recover the £61 profit they would have made on the sale to the defendant. The plaintiffs were compensated for their lost volume, that is the loss of profit on a sale which they would have made but for the breach of contract. By contrast, in *Charter v Sullivan*[20] the seller was able to resell the car which the defendant had refused to accept and suffered no loss in the process. In these circumstances it was held that although it would be difficult to say that there was an available market, the plaintiffs had suffered no loss, even though it was argued that they had been deprived of the profit on the sale of one car due to the defendant's breach. If there had been an available market, the measure of damages would have been the difference between the market price at the date of breach and the contract price.[1]

A suggested distinction between the two cases is that in *Thompson*, supply of the vehicles exceeded demand, whereas in *Charter*, demand exceeded supply,[2] but it must also be considered that in each case the seller has sold one less car than he would otherwise sell.

It seems that lost volume claims are rare,[3] and that *Thompson v Robinson* must be regarded as exceptional. Generally, the plaintiff's measure of damages is the difference between the contract price and the lower resale price.[4]

(2) THE EXPECTATION INTEREST

(i) Methods of protecting expectations

The expectations referred to in this context are those engendered in the plaintiff by the defendant. While there is some dispute to the effect that expectations should not be protected, the common law does provide a limited degree of protection. The expectation interest is protected in three ways. A decree of specific performance, the award of an agreed sum and an award of damages placing the plaintiff in the position he would have occupied if the defendant's promise had been performed, all protect this interest.

Damages compensating for damage to the expectation interest largely concern loss of profit. Other pecuniary losses are recoverable under the status quo interest, and contract law places severe restrictions on non-pecuniary losses such as grief and distress. The plaintiff's action will be for any net profit he would have made on the contract. In practice, the courts have placed numerous obstacles in the way of the plaintiff who wishes to claim such loss.

---

17 Fuller and Perdue (1936/37) 46 Yale LJ 52 and 373 at 62.
18 Sale of Goods Act 1979, ss 50(2), 51(2).
19 [1955] 1 All ER 154.
20 [1957] 2 QB 117.
1 See Sale of Goods Act 1979, s 50(3). Cf *Charter v Sullivan* [1957] 2 QB 117.
2 *Charter v Sullivan* [1957] 2 QB 117 at 130 (per JENKINS LJ).
3 See *Beale, Bishop and Furmston* p 585.
4 See *Lazenby Garages Ltd v Wright* [1976] 2 All ER 770.

(ii)   Exceptions to the rule allowing recovery of expectation losses

A failure to pay money will not be compensated, and the only remedy is the award of an agreed sum.[5] A repudiatory breach of contract on the part of a buyer of goods is more than a failure to pay money, with the result that the seller can still sue for non-acceptance of the goods. The rule has two effects on the plaintiff. One is that he will be unable to put the money to use. This has been sidestepped by the decision in *Wadsworth v Lydall,*[6] which distinguished between general damages, which are not recoverable, and special damages, which are recoverable. Where the plaintiff merely claims that he could have put the money to use, he has no action. But, where he can show that he would have put the money to use and the defendant knew this, he can recover.[7] In *Wadsworth,* the defendant knew that the plaintiff intended to use the money as a deposit for the purchase of land. By delaying in making payment, the defendant was liable for interest which the plaintiff had to pay on a loan taken out to cover the deposit. The second disadvantage is that debts do not carry interest, unless the parties expressly or impliedly agree that they shall. However, where proceedings are commenced for the recovery of the debt, the court can award interest on judgment where the proceedings are settled.[8] The debtor can still avoid paying interest by settling before proceedings are commenced.

(iii)   Practical limitations on the recovery of expectation losses

The theory that expectation damages are recoverable for loss of profit resulting from breach of contract is, in practice, limited by the rules on remoteness and mitigation. A sub-contract loss may be too remote unless the defendant was aware of the sub-contract at the time he entered the contract with the plaintiff. In certain cases, the remoteness principle may be avoided where the defendant is deemed to be aware of a sub-sale by virtue of trade practice. In *Re Hall Ltd & Pim Junior & Co's Arbitration,*[9] the plaintiffs bought a cargo of wheat from the defendant and resold it to a third party before delivery. As it was common practice in the trade to resell cargoes whilst still afloat, the defendants were liable to the plaintiffs for loss of profit.

The plaintiff is also obliged to take reasonable steps to mitigate his loss by entering the market to purchase substitute goods or services. Where the price paid for the alternative is equal to the contract price, no action for loss of profit will lie other than for loss of the use of the profit while attempting to find a substitute on the market.

Where A agrees to buy widgets from B for £100 and subsequently agrees to resell them to C for £120, the loss of profit suffered by A if B refuses to sell will normally be too remote to be recovered. A is obliged to mitigate his loss by purchasing widgets from an alternative source, and his damages will be the difference between the market price and the contract price with B. If the market price and the contract price are the same, A will recover no damages for loss of profit. Where the market price is higher than the contract price, the damages awarded will protect A's status quo interest. The only occasion on which the full loss of profit will be awarded is where there is no available market for widgets, when the resale price will be assumed to be the market price.

---

5   *London, Chatham and Dover Rly Co v South Eastern Rly Co* [1893] AC 429.
6   [1981] 1 WLR 598. Approved in *President of India v La Pintada Compania Navigacion SA* [1985] AC 104 at 125–127.
7   See *Hadley v Baxendale* (1854) 9 Exch 341, r 2.
8   Administration of Justice Act 1982, s 15.
9   (1928) 33 Com Cas 324. See also *Koufos v Czarnikow Ltd, The Heron II* [1969] 1 AC 350.

A further difficulty encountered by a plaintiff seeking to recover loss of profit is that he must prove that he would have made a profit had the contract been performed. Where he can show that he would have made a profit but is unable to show what it would have been, he will recover for loss of the chance. In *Chaplin v Hicks*,[10] the defendant, in breach of contract, failed to give the plaintiff the opportunity to attend an audition, where twelve people out of 50 auditioned were to be given a theatrical engagement. The plaintiff could recover no damages for loss of a theatrical engagement, as she could not prove she would have been one of the twelve, but recovered £100 for loss of the chance.

If the plaintiff cannot prove that he would have made a profit had the contract not been broken, difficulties may arise. In *CCC Films (London) Ltd v Impact Quadrant Films Ltd*,[11] CCC were granted a licence to promote and exploit three films. $12,000 was paid to IQF but, in breach of contract, the films were lost. CCC had to abandon their claim for the profit lost through their inability to promote the films, as they could not prove they would have made a profit. Instead, they brought a successful action for status quo loss in respect of their wasted expenditure of $12,000. It was not necessary to show that they would have recovered the $12,000 but for the breach of contract by IQF. An action for status quo loss may appear to have practical advantages over an action for expectation losses.

(3) THE STATUS QUO INTEREST

In contract cases where the plaintiff has relied, to his detriment, on the defendant's promise, he should be compensated for that detrimental reliance. An award of status quo damages puts the plaintiff in the position he would have occupied had he not entered the contract. Such an award equates with the compensatory objective of tortious damages in seeking to put the plaintiff in the position he would have been in had the wrong not been committed.

The status quo interest in a contractual action can operate either as an alternative to expectation damages or as a complement to it.[12] There has been little discussion of this interest in English contract cases[13] compared to that in the United States.[14]

(i)   The status quo interest as a contractual alternative to the expectation interest

Where the plaintiff is unable to recover his expectation losses for the reasons considered above, he may elect to bring an action for his reliance or status quo losses.[15] In *Anglia Television Ltd v Reed*,[16] a television company incurred preliminary expenses of £2,750 for the purposes of making a film. The defendant was engaged as the leading actor, but later repudiated the contract. The potential profits likely to be made from the production of the film could not be ascertained, but the £2,750 was recoverable as a reliance loss. The plaintiffs had relied on their contract with the defendant, not in incurring the

---

10   [1911] 2 KB 786. See also *Manubens v Leon* [1919] 1 KB 208; *Allied Maples v Simmons & Simmons* [1995] 4 All ER 907. Contrast *Hotson v East Berkshire Health Authority* [1987] AC 750.

11   [1985] QB 16, [1984] 3 All ER 298. See also *McRae v Commonwealth Disposals Commission* (1950) 84 CLR 377. *Anglia Television Ltd v Reed* [1972] 1 QB 60 and see chs 6 and 7.

12   Ogus *The Law of Damages* (1973) pp 346–347.

13   Cf *Cullinane v British Rema Manufacturing Co* [1954] 1 QB 292, *Anglia Television Ltd v Reed* [1972] 1 QB 60.

14   Fuller and Perdue (1936/37) 46 Yale LJ 52.

15   *CCC Films (London) Ltd v Impact Quadrant Films Ltd* [1984] 3 All ER 298.

16   [1972] 1 QB 60.

expense, but in causing it to be wasted by not looking for someone else to play the part.

Since the plaintiff has a choice between claiming for lost profit or wasted expenditure, this might mean that he can escape from a bad bargain by seeking to recover wasted expenditure. English courts have tended to follow the United States' approach that this is not possible.[17] If the defendant can prove that the plaintiff would not have recouped his expenses had the contract been performed, no reliance damages are recoverable.[18] Suppose that A contracts to supply B with house building materials worth £8,000 and B spends £10,000 in preparation. If the market price of the house falls so that B would have made a loss of £5,000 on the sale of the house, B's expectation losses are nil, but his reliance loss is £8,000 if A fails to deliver. On the above principle, B will be limited to reliance damages of £3,000.

Contractual status quo damages will normally be for money spent in reliance on the contract in preparing or attempting to perform. A controversial issue concerns expenses incurred before the contract was made. If the purpose of status quo damages is to put the plaintiff in the position he would have been in if no contract had been made, such damages should properly be denied. In the United States, such damages are not recoverable,[19] but in England they are.[20] The answer to the problem is determined by asking when an obligation comes into existence. A contractual obligation traditionally arises upon acceptance of an offer. However, the difficulties of slotting all contract cases into the rules of offer and acceptance have meant that the courts must take a pragmatic approach. The defendant may be under an obligation when the plaintiff has relied on his words or actions. This reliance may arise in tort through negligent misstatement or through a unilateral or a collateral contract. Any expenses incurred after this reliance should be recoverable, provided the reliance is sufficient to found a legal obligation. Expenditure not required by the contract which would have been recouped if the contract had been performed, such as the cost of advertising the goods for resale, may also be recovered.[1] Where money has been paid to the defendant, it may be recovered as restitution loss.[2] Where money has been paid to a third party, or where services have been performed in reliance on the contract, these may be recovered, subject to the rules on remoteness and mitigation.[3]

(ii)   The status quo interest as a contractual complement to the expectation interest

Where the plaintiff claims both loss of profits and wasted expenditure, it might appear that he will be over-compensated. There are judicial statements to the effect that this is the case,[4] but these are misleading, as it is important to determine how profits are calculated. Where gross profits are recovered, the recovery of wasted expenditure will result in over-compensation. But where net profits only are allowed, there is no over-compensation.[5] However, in *Cullinane v British Rema Manufacturing Co Ltd*,[6] recovery of

---

17   See *Albert & Son v Armstrong Rubber Co* 178 F 2d 182 (1949).
18   *CCC Films (London) Ltd v Impact Quadrant Films Ltd* [1984] 3 All ER 298; *C & P Haulage v Middleton* [1983] 3 All ER 94.
19   *Chicago Coliseum Club v Dempsey* 256 Ill App 542 (1932).
20   *Anglia Television Ltd v Reed* [1972] 1 QB 60.
1   See *Foaminol Laboratories Ltd v British Artid Plastics* [1941] 2 All ER 393.
2   See ch 18.
3   See *Hydraulic Engineering Co v McHaffie* (1878) 4 QBD 670.
4   *Cullinane v British Rema Manufacturing Co Ltd* [1954] 1 QB 292 at 303 (per LORD EVERSHED MR).
5   See *Hydraulic Engineering Co v McHaffie* (1878) 4 QBD 670.
6   [1954] 1 QB 292 (MORRIS LJ dissenting).

net profits and wasted expenditure was refused but this decision is subject to some criticism.[7]

(4)   CLAIMS IN TORT FOR PURE ECONOMIC LOSS

Pure economic loss means economic loss not consequent on personal injuries, including death, or damage to or misappropriation of property. The matter of damages for misrepresentation, including misstatement and deceit, is dealt with elsewhere.

Traditionally, economic losses are recoverable in a tort action where the defendant had wrongfully interfered with the plaintiff's business or contract. This may be achieved through the economic torts of injurious falsehood, intimidation, conspiracy and inducement to breach of contract.[8] The damages awarded seek to put the plaintiff in the position he would have been in if the tort had not been committed. This will usually involve the recovery of expenses incurred,[9] or profits lost.[10]

Where the defendant negligently interferes with the plaintiff's business, no English case has allowed an action to succeed. The archetypal case arises where the defendant negligently severs a cable carrying power to the plaintiff's business, thereby causing loss of profit. In *Spartan Steel and Alloys Ltd v Martin & Co Ltd*,[11] the Court of Appeal held that an action for loss of profit would fail, unless that loss was consequential on damage to property. This decision was in some doubt following *Junior Books Ltd v Veitchi Co Ltd*,[12] but the Privy Council reaffirmed the rule that such losses are irrecoverable.[13] Such an action has succeeded in Australia,[14] where damages were assessed by compensating the plaintiff for expenditure caused and gains lost. The question of allowing such a claim raises problems in relation to the creation of obligations, but poses no problem in assessment of damages, as the plaintiff will be placed in the position he would have been in had the tort not been committed.

Other cases on pure economic loss in negligence involve situations where the defendant has negligently performed a service with resulting damage to the plaintiff. The objective of the damages award will be to place the plaintiff in the position he would have been in if the defendant had used reasonable care. Where a surveyor negligently surveys a house and the survey is relied upon by the plaintiff, damages will represent the difference between the purchase price and the market value of the house.[15]

One exception is where a surveyor has carried out a valuation for a lender. In these cases the duty owed by the surveyor is to give information as to the value of the property. Where the property is negligently overvalued, with resulting loss to the lender, the lender's damages are capped at the difference between what the property was valued at and what it should have been valued at. Any losses which are due to a fall in the property market are not recoverable unless they fall within this cap.[16]

Where the parties are not in a contractual relationship and the action is allowed, the status quo measure of damages is again awarded. The plaintiff is put in the position he would have been in if the defendant had used reasonable care. In *Junior Books v Veitchi*,[17]

7   See MacLeod (1970) JBL 19.
8   See Heydon *Economic Torts* (2nd edn, 1978).
9   *British Motor Trade Association v Salvadori* [1949] Ch 556.
10   *Goldsoll v Goldman* [1914] 2 Ch 603.
11   [1973] QB 27.
12   [1983] 1 AC 520.
13   *Candlewood Navigation Corpn Ltd v Mitsui OSK Lines Ltd* [1985] 2 All ER 935.
14   *Caltex Oil (Australia) Property Ltd v Dredge 'Willemstad'* (1976) 136 CLR 529.
15   *Perry v Sidney Phillips & Son (a firm)* [1982] 1 All ER 1005.
16   *South Australia Asset Management Corpn v York Montague Ltd* [1996] 3 All ER 365.
17   [1983] 1 AC 520.

the defendant negligently installed a sub-standard floor in the plaintiff's factory and the plaintiff was awarded the expense of having a new floor laid and the cost of paying employees, plus profits lost during the time the factory was not operating.

(5)   DAMAGES FOR MISREPRESENTATION, MISSTATEMENT AND DECEIT

Where the plaintiff has entered a contract in reliance on the defendant's misrepresentation or has incurred detrimental reliance loss as a result of a misstatement or deceit, the measure of damages is assessed by restoring the status quo. The plaintiff will be placed in the same position he would have been in if the statement had not been made rather than if it were true.

If A purchases a car for £17,000 in reliance on B's statement that it is worth £20,000 and it has a market value of £15,000, A's damages for misrepresentation will be £2,000. If the statement were a contractual term, his damages would be £5,000. If the plaintiff can establish that he would have used his resources in another way and made a profit, he can recover for the 'opportunity cost' of reliance. In *East v Maurer*[18] a hairdressing salon was bought on the basis of a fraudulent misrepresentation. Damages were awarded for the profit the plaintiff might have made had he bought a different hairdressers in the same area, although he could not recover for the profit he would have made had the misrepresentation been true. Similarly, where a loan is made on the basis of a misrepresentation, the representee cannot recover for interest which would have been paid under the contract but damages can be awarded for loss of use of the money while it was locked up in that contract.[19]

In claims for deceit, it is well established that the status quo measure is appropriate.[20] In *Archer v Brown*,[1] the plaintiff was induced to enter a partnership with the defendant by the latter's deceit. The plaintiff was held entitled to the amount he had paid for his shares, and interest on a loan taken out to buy the shares. His claim for loss of earnings was reduced to £2,500, as the claim for £16,000 was dependent upon the success of the firm. Where a claim is made for negligent misrepresentation under the Misrepresentation Act 1967, section 2(1), damages will put the plaintiff in the position he would have been in if the statement had not been made.[2] In view of the decision in *Royscot Trust Ltd v Rogerson*[3] it would appear that there is no advantage to the plaintiff in suing in deceit.

The Misrepresentation Act 1967, section 2(2), gives the court the discretionary power to award damages in lieu of rescission for innocent misrepresentation. There is no right to damages under section 2(2) and a representee cannot both rescind and claim damages. The discretion is a broad one to do what is equitable and will usually be exercised where the representee has entered a bad bargain but the cost of rescission to the representor would be prohibitive.[4] It is difficult to state what the measure of damages is but it may be that it is the loss in value of what has been bought under the contract.[5]

---

18   [1991] 2 All ER 733.
19   *Swingcastle v Alastair Gibson* [1991] 2 All ER 353.
20   *Smith New Court Securities Ltd v Scrimgeour Vickers Ltd* [1996] 4 All ER 769; *Doyle v Olby (Ironmongers) Ltd* [1969] 2 QB 158; *Smith Kline & French Laboratories Ltd v Long* [1989] 1 WLR 1.
1   [1984] 2 All ER 267.
2   *André et Cie SA v Ets Michel Blanc & Fils* [1977] 2 Lloyd's Rep 166; *Royscot Trust Ltd v Rogerson* [1991] 3 All ER 294.
3   Ibid.
4   *William Sindall plc v Cambridgeshire County Council* [1994] 1 WLR 1016.
5   *Thomas Witter Ltd v TBP Industries Ltd* [1996] 2 All ER 573.

Thus, where a vendor of land innocently fails to disclose that there is a private foul sewer running across the land, the measure would be the difference between the actual value received and the value which the property would have had if the representation had been true.

Where the plaintiff alleges misstatement resulting in financial loss, the principles are similar. In *Esso Petroleum Co Ltd v Mardon*,[6] the respondent took a lease on a petrol station in reliance on a negligent misstatement by Esso's representative as to the prospective throughput of the station. In assessing the respondent's damages for negligent misstatement, the court held that he was not to be compensated for his loss of bargain.[7] Esso had not warranted that the throughput would be a particular amount, they had undertaken to use reasonable care in its calculation. However, the amount awarded appears to have exceeded the true reliance loss.

6   [1976] QB 801.
7   Ibid at 820 (per LORD DENNING MR).

Chapter 18

Restitutionary remedies

1. INTRODUCTION

Damages are normally assessed on a compensatory basis. The plaintiff is compensated for the loss he has suffered as a result of the defendant's breach of duty. The award of damages may protect the plaintiff's expectation or status quo interests. However, the common law also protects a third interest, namely, the plaintiff's restitutionary interest.[1] Where the plaintiff has conferred a benefit on the defendant, the court may require the defendant to disgorge that benefit. In these cases, the court looks at the benefit to the defendant rather than the loss to the plaintiff. In some cases, the same result might be achieved where the plaintiff sues for damages to protect his status quo or expectation interests. For example, if X contracts to buy a car from Y for £1,000 and pays Y but Y does not deliver the car, X may maintain an action for damages for breach of contract. But X has also conferred a benefit on Y by giving him the £1,000 and may seek to bring an action for money had and received, to protect his restitution interest. Similarly, where there is a contract to perform a service where no price is fixed, there is a contractual obligation to pay a reasonable amount,[2] or a restitutionary remedy can be sought for the value of the work done.

In simple terms the victim of a tort may have the option of proceeding for a restitutionary remedy such as an action for money had and received. The victim of a breach of contract does not have this option and the contract must have 'failed' before the plaintiff has the option of seeking a restitutionary remedy such as quantum meruit. More contentiously, within tort and contract themselves, there may be restitutionary damages. These are damages which look to the defendant's gain.

A note of caution should be sounded here. The entire concept of 'restitutionary remedies' is a contentious one. Unjust enrichment is a very recent development in English law and was only officially recognised in 1991.[3] Judicial and academic concentration has been on rights as opposed to remedies. There is a fear that remedialism is closely associated with procedural formalism, in that legal claims should be channelled through

---

1   See ch 11. See also Goff and Jones *The Law of Restitution* (5th edn, 1998) and Birks *Introduction to the Law of Restitution* (1985).
2   Supply of Goods and Services Act 1982, s 15.
3   *Lipkin Gorman v Karpnale* [1991] 2 AC 548

prescibed forms of action. That this is not correct can be illustrated by the United States Restatement of the Law of Restitution (1983), which explicitly differentiates remedies from procedural forms.[4] What is clear is that the distinction between right and remedy is less clear in this area than in other subjects.

2.   UNJUST ENRICHMENT BY WRONGS

A wrong includes a tort, a breach of contract and breaches of statutory duty and equitable duties.[5] However, for the present purposes, only breaches of contractual and tortious duties are relevant. Where the defendant has been unjustly enriched as a result of his wrong, he may have made a positive gain or he may have saved some expense. In either case, normal rules of causation will apply, and it must be shown that, but for the wrong, the defendant would not have been unjustly enriched.

For the purposes of this chapter the distinction between unjust enrichment for wrongs and autonomous unjust enrichment will be adopted but this may cause difficulties. For example, when a tort is committed and the plaintiff has an election between tortious and restitutionary remedies, the question arises as to whether the restitutionary claim exists independently or is parasitic and dependant on the tortious action. It has been argued that the restitutionary claim is independent and that identification with tort has distorted our understanding of the nature of the restitutionary claim by isolating it from other such claims such as equitable ones.[6] Suppose that the defendant has induced the plaintiff to give him £5,000 by deceit. A tort action will lie in deceit for the £5,000 based on the defendants' tortious wrong. However, it is arguable that an action would lie in autonomous unjust enrichment for a restitutionary remedy for the return of the money, which was paid under an induced mistake of fact. Here, the fact that the defendant has lied to the plaintiff, causing the plaintiff loss, is irrelevant.

(1)   TORTIOUS WRONGS

(i)   Introduction

The overlap between tort and restitution arises where the defendant has interfered with the plaintiff's property. In such cases there is authority for the argument that an award of damages may be made to deprive the defendant of any gain which he may have made as a result of his tort where there is no loss to the plaintiff. There are also certain torts where the plaintiff has an election between suing for tortious damages, or, where it is more favourable, seeking a restitutionary remedy.

The approach taken here separates restitutionary damages in tort from other restitutionary remedies, such as an action for money had and received and an account of profits. This distinction could be regarded as artificial but it is argued that on the present state of the law it is justifiable.

(ii)   Electing between compensatory and restitutionary remedies

In most cases where the plaintiff is the victim of a tort, he will sue for compensatory damages or an injunction. The plaintiff may show that the tort gives rise to both a compensatory and a restitutionary remedy. Where this is the case, it would appear that he can choose to pursue his restitutionary remedy.

---

4   See K. Barker (1998) CLJ 301.
5   See *Birks* ch X.
6   Beatson 206–242.

In *United Australia Ltd v Barclays Bank Ltd*,[7] a cheque payable to the appellants was fraudulently endorsed by an employee to a company in which he was interested. Barclays collected and paid the cheque. An action against the endorsee was commenced, but later dropped. This action was for money had or received or money lent. An action for conversion was subsequently brought against Barclays. The House of Lords held that the prior claim for restitution had not extinguished the tort, and would not have done so, even against the same defendant.

(iii)   Restitutionary damages in tort

An award of damages in tort will normally reflect the plaintiff's loss caused by the tort. However, where there is no loss to the plaintiff but the defendant has made a gain or saved expense as a result of his wrong, it is possible that the court may award damages protecting the restitutionary interest. Although the idea of restitutionary damages may be heretical, it is clear that they are awarded in tort cases where anti-enrichment is one of the purposes of the tort action in question. This method may be used to avoid the narrowness of the restitutionary remedy of *quantum meruit*. In *Penarth Dock Engineering Co Ltd v Pounds*,[8] damages were awarded where the defendants committed a trespass by failing to remove their pontoon from the plaintiffs' dock. The plaintiffs suffered no loss, but damages were assessed by reference to the cost to the defendants of anchoring their pontoon in a dock of that kind. Similarly, in *Strand Electric and Engineering Co Ltd v Brisford Entertainments Ltd*,[9] the defendants had committed the tort of detinue by keeping and using the plaintiff's theatre equipment. Damages were assessed as the cost to the defendants of hiring similar equipment for the period in question. Again, there was no loss to the plaintiff. However, the majority in this case clearly regarded the damages as compensatory and not restitutionary.[10]

It has also been suggested that these cases are in fact compensating the plaintiff for his loss of opportunity to bargain.[11] The Court of Appeal has also sought to restrict these cases within a 'user' principle which did not extend to the tort of nuisance and regarded a gains based remedy as a troubling innovation.[12]

In cases of trespass to land restitutionary damages have been recognised. There are two possible measures of damages. The first is the loss to the plaintiff and the second is the value of the benefit which the occupier has received. These two bases are mutually exclusive and the plaintiff must elect. The value of benefit claim (mesne profits) is a claim for restitution.[13] In *Ashman*, the defendant tenant wrongfully refused to quit Royal Air Force married quarters after her husband left her. The Court of Appeal accepted that the plaintiffs were entitled to the benefit to the defendant of the accommodation, assessed on what it would have cost her to rent alternative local authority accommodation. It should be noted that the approach taken here does not comply with that of the majority in *Phillips v Homfray*.[14]

It should be noted that there is a connection between restitutionary damages and exemplary damages. In *Rookes v Barnard*,[15] LORD DEVLIN laid down the guidelines for the recovery of exemplary damages. One of the categories was where the defendant's

---

7   [1941] AC 1.
8   [1963] 1 Lloyd's Rep 359.
9   [1952] 2 QB 246.
10   See also *Ministry of Defence v Ashman* (1993) 66 P & CR 195.
11   Sharpe & Waddams (1982) 20 JLS 290.
12   *Stoke-on-Trent City Council v W & J Wass Ltd* [1988] 1 WLR 1406.
13   *Ministry of Defence v Ashman* (1993) 66 P & CR 195.
14   (1883) 24 Ch D 439. See below.
15   [1964] AC 1129.

conduct was calculated to make a profit for himself which might exceed the profit which was payable to the plaintiff. The award of such damages has been largely restricted by the English courts to cases of libel and actions by landlords against tenants.[16]

(iv) Torts giving rise to a restitutionary action

Discussion of this issue is clouded by the failure of the courts always to distinguish between restitution for wrongs and restitution on some other ground. The majority in *Phillips v Homfray*[17] took the view that a restitutionary remedy was only available where the defendant's gain consisted of taking the plaintiff's property or the proceeds of that property. Where the defendant had saved expense by using the plaintiff's land, no restitutionary remedy was available. However, the minority thought that, so long as a benefit had been acquired by the breach of duty, it should be recoverable.[18]

On the approach of the majority, a restitutionary remedy is available in respect of the tort of conversion. An action can be brought to recover the benefit conferred on the defendant in the form of the plaintiff's property or its proceeds.[19] If the market price of the property has risen since the time of conversion, the plaintiff can ignore the tort and sue for the price the defendant received for the goods when he sold them. A similar principle would apply to cases of trespass to goods[20] and trespass to land, where the defendant has extracted minerals from the land.[1]

It may be the case that although an action for money had and received is not available beyond these limitations, where the plaintiff seeks to remedy an unjust enrichment for a wrong, a wider principle exists. Tort actions can be divided into those which partly serve to prevent enrichment and those which do not. Clearly, where a tort action is set against enrichment, the remedies available should facilitate the reversal of the enrichment.[2] On this basis, for example, conversion, trespass to goods, trespass to land and breach of confidence can be regarded as anti-enrichment torts. Although no such distinction is explicitly articulated by English courts, it is reflected in the award of damages to protect the restitution interest and the equitable remedy of account of profits.

The equitable remedy of account[3] requires the defendant to provide the plaintiff with an account of the dealings between them, and to pay any balance found to exist. Whereas damages are to compensate for wrongly inflicted loss, the remedy of account requires the giving up of wrongfully obtained gains. Because it is an equitable remedy, little use has been made of it in tort actions, and it is restricted to cases of infringement of intellectual property rights. The action is available, for example, in copyright actions,[4] breach of confidence cases,[5] and where the tort of passing off has been committed.[6] One way forward in restitution would be to extend the remedy to any anti-enrichment tort. Breach of copyright cases are complicated by the fact that information may be regarded as property and may therefore fall within the *Phillips v Homfray* principle. In *Seager v Copydex (No 2)*,[7] the measure of damages for non-special information was said

---

16 See ch 15.
17 (1883) 24 Ch D 439.
18 Ibid at 471–472 (per BAGGALLY LJ).
19 *United Australia Ltd v Barclays Bank Ltd* [1941] AC 1.
20 *Oughton v Seppings* (1830) 1 B & Ad 241.
1 *Powell v Rees* (1837) 7 Ad & El 426.
2 *Birks* p 328.
3 See Burrows *Remedies* pp 263–269.
4 Copyright, Designs and Patents Act 1988, s 96(2) .
5 *Peter Pan Manufacturing Corpn v Corsets Silhouette Ltd* [1963] RPC 45.
6 *Lever v Goodwin* (1887) 36 Ch D 1.
7 [1969] 1 WLR 809.

to be based on the fee the defendant had saved by not employing a consultant to obtain that information.

Is it possible for non-proprietary torts to trigger a restitutionary remedy? It has been argued that deliberately committed torts should give rise to restitution.[8] This view, however, was not adopted by the Court of Appeal in *Halifax Building Society v Thomas*[9] T obtained a 100% mortgage from the plaintiffs by fraudulently misrepresenting his identity and creditworthiness. T defaulted and the property was sold by the plaintiffs. The proceeds of sale exceeded the advance and the plaintiffs applied for a declaration that they were entitled to retain the surplus on the basis that they had a personal restitutionary claim (secured by mortgage) or a proprietary restitutionary claim (through a constructive trust) to T's gains from his deceit. If made out, these claims would have defeated the competing claims of the Crown Prosecution Service to confiscate the surplus in execution of a criminal confiscation order. The Court of Appeal held that the plaintiff's restitutionary claims failed. Not every action for an account of profits from a wrongdoer, even where there has been use of the plaintiff's property, will be allowed, and it may be barred where there has been an election for another remedy (in this case a tortious one). Also, it would have been incorrect to regard T's unjust enrichment as having been gained at the expense of the plaintiffs. The wrong itself is not always in itself a sufficient factor to call for restitution. The argument for a proprietary remedy was defeated as Parliament had intervened to prevent a criminal retaining of ill-gotten gains and it was not for the courts to use the constructive trust to prevent a fraudster benefiting from his wrong. It is unfortunate that the issue came up on these facts as the claim by the Crown Prosecution Service was sufficient to strip Thomas of the profits from his fraud. Had this not been the case, could an award of restitutionary damages have been justified in the case or could exemplary damages have been claimed?

It is clear is that, at present, no action for money had and received is available in respect of a tort which results in the defendant not exploiting the plaintiff's property. For example, a pharmaceutical company may make large profits from marketing a drug which causes damage to some of its users. Although the affected users may have a negligence action for compensatory damages, they cannot claim a restitutionary remedy based on the profits made by the defendant. However, the *Phillips v Homfray* approach, while it may still hold for actions for money had and received, does not appear to hold in actions for restitutionary damages or account of profits. The key factor in all cases where a restitutionary remedy has been awarded is that they involve an interference with the plaintiff's property.

(2)   BREACH OF CONTRACT

Generally, where there is a breach of a valid contract, the appropriate monetary remedy is an award of damages to protect the plaintiff's expectation or status quo interest. Only where the contract has been validly terminated or where there has been a total failure of consideration will the plaintiff be able to recover on a restitutionary basis

Historically the restitution interest was not protected where there was no overlap with the expectation or status quo interest. If the defendant had made a profit or saving as a result of breaking his contract, he would not be compelled to disgorge that profit.[10] If X contracted to invest £10,000 with Y but invested it with Z at a greater profit, Y's damages were assessed on the basis of Y's loss, not X's gain.

---

8   Birks 573.
9   [1996] CL 217.
10   *Tito v Waddell (No 2)* [1977] Ch 106 at 332 (per MEGARRY VC).

To this general principle there was an exception. In *Wrotham Park Estate Co Ltd v Parkside Homes Ltd*,[11] the defendants built houses resulting in an infringement of a restrictive covenant intended to benefit the plaintiffs' land. An application for an injunction requesting the demolition of the houses was refused, and damages were awarded instead. The amount awarded represented the sum which the owner of the benefited land might have accepted for relaxing the covenant. In assessing this figure, the court took into account the profit made by the defendants from the houses. As the plaintiffs would not have relaxed the covenant, it is unlikely that damages were compensatory and can be regarded as restitutionary.

However, this case was distinguished in *Surrey County Council v Bredero Homes Ltd*[12]. The council sold a plot of land on the express agreement that it would be developed in accordance with the planning permission which had been granted earlier. After the sale, the purchasers obtained planning permission for a new scheme which was more profitable to them and proceeded to build in breach of their agreement with the council. The council knew of the breach but took no action. When the building was complete, the council brought an action for damages for breach of contract. As the council had suffered no loss as a result of the breach of contract the Court of Appeal awarded only nominal damages. *Wrotham Park* was distinguished on the ground that damages had been awarded under Lord Cairn's Act (per DILLON and ROSE LJJ) and that the court had been protecting a property interest (per STEYN LJ). In the view of STEYN LJ, restitutionary damages were available at common law where the defendant has made use of the defendant's property and thereby saved expense.[13]

The Court of Appeal has now recognised that, '[I]f the court is unable to award restitutionary damages for breach of contract, then the law of contract is seriously defective.'[14]

In *Attorney-General v Blake*,[15] the convicted spy George Blake had published his autobiography using information gained from his employment in the Secret Intelligence Service. A public law claim to restrain Blake from receiving any further royalties on the book was successful. A claim for account of profits based on a breach of fiduciary duty was rejected as the information was no longer secret or confidential. No claim was made for compensatory damages as the Crown declined the Court of Appeal's invitation to argue for restitution for breach of contract. However, the Court of Appeal laid down a test for such a claim.

There must be a breach which attracts 'inadequate' compensatory damages. The mere fact that the defendant's breach enabled him to enter into a more profitable contract with someone else will not suffice,[16] nor will the defendant's motives, however deliberate and cynical, normally be sufficient.[17]

Two situations were given where compensatory damages could be regarded as inadequate. The first was 'skimped performance,' where the defendant failed to provide the full extent of the services he had contracted to provide and for which he had charged the plaintiff. An example would be *City of New Orleans v Firemen's Charitable Association*[18] where the defendant was paid the full price for fire fighting services but saved expense by not providing the stipulated services but had not failed to extinguish any fires. The

11   [1974] 1 WLR 798. See also *Carr-Saunders v Dick McNeil Associates Ltd* [1986] 1 WLR 922.
12   [1993] 3 All ER 705.
13   See A Burrows [1993] LMCLQ 453. See also *Jaggard v Sawyer* [1995] 1 WLR 269.
14   *Attorney-General v Blake* [1998] 1 All ER 833, 845 per LORD WOOLF MR.
15   Ibid.
16   *Taylor v Caldwell* [1899] AC 451.
17   Adapting an observation by LORD KEITH in a different context in *Attorney-General v Guardian Newspapers Ltd (No 2)* [1988] 3 All ER 545, 643.
18   (1891) 9 So 486.

decision was that the plaintiff had not suffered any loss and could only recover nominal damages. The Court of Appeal in *Blake* felt that justice demanded that substantial damages should have been awarded based on the amount of expenditure the defendant had saved.

The second case is where the defendant has obtained his profit by doing the very thing which he contracted not to do, such as in *Blake* itself.

Both cases raise difficulties. How does 'skimped performance' differ from defective performance and where does the 'consumer surplus' point fit?[19] In the second case, all breaches of contract arguably involve the defendant doing something he had contracted not to do. This would make restitutionary damages fully available for breach of contract. This was clearly not the intention of the Court of Appeal, so it could be that only a breach of a negative promise would trigger such a claim.

Whatever the difficulties in ascertaining which breaches give rise to restitutionary damages, the Court of Appeal was clear that causation and remoteness would have to be satisfied and that only those gains occasioned directly by the breach and not those the breach simply gave the opportunity for, would be recoverable.[20] It is, however, far from clear which measure is applicable and how it would be calculated. In *Blake,* the full profit was recoverable, whereas in *Wrotham Park* only 5% was awarded.

The significance of *Blake* is that it indicates the willingness of the judiciary to develop claims for restitutionary damages. Whether this is the right route, if the rationale is 'inadequacy' of damages, is open to question. The problems created by compensatory damages for breach of contract are well known but they might be better solved by increasing the availability of specific performance or damages for cost of cure.[1]

3.   AUTONOMOUS UNJUST ENRICHMENT

Just as an action for damages is founded on a breach of contract or a tort, a restitutionary action may lie independently of a wrong, where it is based solely on an unjust enrichment of the defendant.

The law on this subject extends beyond the confines of a book of this nature, by incorporating equitable principles. Discussion is limited to the situation in which a contract fails rather than the wider ambit of restitution. For these purposes, a contract may fail for three reasons. The contract may be vitiated or qualified by a later event, or the parties may not have successfully concluded a contract. In all three situations, money or goods may be transferred or services rendered. If the contract fails, no action for damages will lie, and the plaintiff will be confined to a restitutionary remedy where this is available. As regards money paid, there is a common law action for money had and received. For services rendered, there is an action for a *quantum meruit*. In the case of frustrated contracts, there is statutory provision for the allocation of losses.[2]

(1)   VITIATION

A contract may be rendered void or voidable by a vitiating event. The parties may believe that they have made a valid contract, and may perform accordingly. If it later transpires

---

19   See *Ruxley Electronics & Construction Ltd v Forsyth* [1996] AC 344.
20   M Chen-Wishart [1998] LQR 363, 366.
1   See Coote [1997] CLJ 537. See also G Jones (1983) 99 LQR 442; J Beatson, *The Use and Abuse of Unjust Enrichment* (1991), 15–17.
2   Law Reform (Frustrated Contracts) Act 1943.

that the contract is vitiated because of a mistake,[3] a misrepresentation,[4] duress or undue influence,[5] it is necessary to determine the position of the parties in relation to their performance.

(i)   Mistake

Where the contract is held to be void, for example where there is a fundamental common mistake, the decision is a negative response and, in respect of the contract itself, does not produce a restitutionary solution. No title is passed *in rem*. Any money transferred may be recovered by means of an action for money had and received and, if any benefit has been conferred on the defendant by a purported performance, an action for a *quantum meruit* may lie. The independence of the restitutionary claim is illustrated by the fact that the plaintiff in such a claim is not limited to the amount that could have been claimed if the contract had not been void.[6] But note that a restitutionary claim will not be allowed to undermine the rule that a director must not make an unauthorised profit from his position as director.[7]

If the mistake is actionable in equity, any relief granted may not be restitutionary. Equity may grant relief on terms which amount to the creation of a new relationship. The modern application of this jurisdiction stems from *Solle v Butcher*[8] in which a lease was made under the mistaken belief that the rent payable was restricted by legislation. The contract was rescinded on terms that a new lease should be granted, allowing the landlord to recover additional sums in respect of improvements carried out on the premises subject to the lease. There is some doubt as to when this equitable jurisdiction will be exercised. It appears that it will only be exercised if enforcement of the original contract would cause hardship to the party who is mistaken. But, as the effect of mistake in equity is to render the contract voidable, the courts' power to set the contract aside is restitutionary in relation to the contractual rights themselves.[9]

(ii)   Rescission for misrepresentation

If the contract is voidable for misrepresentation, the appropriate restitutionary remedy is normally that of rescission.

Different uses of the word rescission have created a degree of terminological confusion.[10] Here, the word is used in what is submitted to be its correct sense, that is, where a contract is set aside because of a flaw in its formation. The expression rescission is also used when a contract is said to be rescinded for breach resulting from a defective performance.[11]

The distinction between these meanings of the word rescission is that a person cannot rescind for misrepresentation and recover damages under the contract, whereas he can rescind for breach and claim damages. It is preferable to say that in the event of a breach of contract the innocent party is discharged from further performance and that the contract survives for certain purposes.

---

3   See ch 23.
4   See ch 10.
5   See ch 24.
6   *Rover International Ltd v Cannon Film Sales Ltd (No 3)* [1989] 1 WLR 912.
7   *Guinness plc v Saunders* [1990] AC 663.
8   *Solle v Butcher* [1950] 1 KB 671; *Grist v Bailey* [1967] Ch 532; *Magee v Pennine Insurance Co Ltd* [1969] 2 QB 507 and see ch 23.
9   Birks p 163.
10   *Mersey Steel & Iron Co v Naylor Benzon & Co* (1882) 9 QBD 648 at 671 per BOWEN LJ; *Photo Production Ltd v Securicor Transport Ltd* [1980] AC 827 at 844 per LORD WILBERFORCE.
11   See *Bunge Corpn v Tradax SA* [1981] 1 WLR 711 at 723–724 per LORD ROSKILL.

The effect of a misrepresentation is to render the contract voidable at the option of the representee, who may affirm or rescind the contract. The contract is affirmed if the representee declares his intention to go ahead with the contract, or if he does some act from which such an intention can be inferred. The contract is rescinded if the representee institutes legal proceedings or gives notice to the other party. Rescission takes effect from the time such notice is given and the contract is terminated *ab initio*. Where notification to the representor is difficult, for example where a crime is involved, notice to the police or other body may suffice. In *Car and Universal Finance Co Ltd v Caldwell,*[12] a cheque tendered as payment for a car was dishonoured. The vendor informed the police and the Automobile Association before the crook sold the vehicle to a third party. This was held to be sufficient notification of an intention to rescind.

One effect of rendering the contract voidable is possible prejudice to third party rights. Where the contract has been rescinded before the sale to the third party, the third party acquires no title.[13] Conversely, if the property is sold before the contract is rescinded, the third party acquires good title and the original owner loses his title.

Where a misrepresentation has become incorporated as a term of the contract, the right to rescind survives.[14] There is some difficulty in determining whether the representee can rescind the contract and claim damages for breach of the term. It is possible that a court could use the Misrepresentation Act 1967, section 2(2), which gives the court a discretion to declare the contract subsisting, and award damages in lieu of rescission. Damages under section 2(2) are not the same as damages for breach of contract but, if the contract subsists, there may be a right to claim damages for breach of contract.

(iii)   Bars to rescission

(a)   *Affirmation of the contract*   Once the representee discovers the truth about the misrepresentation, he must rescind or lose the right to do so. If he continues to use the subject matter of the contract, then he will have affirmed the contract unless he was unaware of his right to rescind.[15]

(b)   *Lapse of time*   If the representor is guilty of fraud, lapse of time does not amount to a bar to rescission in itself. However, it may be evidence of affirmation. Time does not run until discovery of the truth. Where the misrepresentation is innocent or negligent, lapse of time, itself, may be a bar. In *Leaf v International Galleries,*[16] the plaintiff bought a painting on the strength of an innocent misrepresentation that it was by John Constable. Five years later, he discovered the painting was by another artist, but was held to have lost the right to rescind. It would appear that, in cases of innocent misrepresentation, simple lapse of time is a bar to rescission.

(c)   *Restitution impossible*   If the parties cannot be returned to their pre-contractual positions, rescission is not possible. Both parties must be able to give back what they received under the contract.

Where the benefit conferred by the representee is in monetary form, the plaintiff's restitution measure is the value received.[17] The plaintiff need not identify the money held by the defendant in order to obtain restitution. Where the subject matter of the contract is not money, the effect of rescission is to ignore the contract and leave a right

---

12   [1965] 1 QB 525.
13   Ibid and see Law Reform Committee 12th Report (1966) Cmnd 2958.
14   Misrepresentation Act 1967, s 1(a).
15   *Peyman v Lanjani* [1984] 3 All ER 703.
16   [1950] 2 KB 86; cf in mistake *Re Garnett* (1885) 31 Ch D 1.
17   *Birks* 171.

in rem in favour of the property transferred. In these cases, third–party rights will defeat the remedy.

There is provision for damages for misrepresentation, both by statute and at common law.[18]

Precise restitution is not necessary, provided the representee can account for any profits or make an allowance for any deterioration in the subject matter. A person who has taken possession under a contract to sell or lease land can rescind, provided he pays rent for the period of possession.[19]

(d)   *Injury to third parties*   Where an innocent third party acquires, for value, an interest in the subject matter of the contract, before rescission, the right to rescind is lost.

(iv)   Indemnity

Where the representee exercises a right to rescind the contract, he loses the right to claim damages under the contract. He may still claim damages for fraud, as these are damages in deceit, not under the contract. Alternatively, he may claim damages under the Misrepresentation Act 1967, section 2 (1).

The party seeking rescission must be compensated for money expended or obligations necessarily created by the contract. Such compensation is known as an indemnity.[20]

(2)   QUALIFICATION BY LATER EVENTS

Where the plaintiff has transferred wealth and a condition precedent to liability to pay has failed, there is a total failure of consideration. A failure of consideration may arise where the defendant does not fulfil his primary contractual obligations by reason of a breach of condition or an anticipatory repudiation. In such cases, an action will lie for damages or for restitution. Alternatively, the contract may be frustrated, in which case no action for damages will lie.

(i)   Breach of condition and anticipatory repudiation

Where the plaintiff has paid money but has not received the promised contractual performance, he has a choice between damages and a restitutionary remedy. Suppose that A contracts to buy B's car for £2,000 and A pays the price but B fails to deliver. If the market price at the agreed date of delivery is £1,750, A's damages will be £1,750. But, if A were to bring a restitutionary action for money had and received, his claim would be for £2,000. An additional factor in favour of claiming the restitutionary remedy is that it is for a liquidated sum which is usually resolved more quickly and cheaply than an action for damages.

The main obstacle to a restitutionary award is the insistence that the plaintiff must have received nothing under the contract. A partial failure of consideration does not give rise to a restitutionary remedy,[1] unless the contract is severable or easily apportionable.[2] Where goods are paid for in advance and there is a shortfall in delivery, the plaintiff can argue in favour of recovering a proportion of the money he has paid.[3]

---

18   See ch 17.
19   *Hulton v Hulton* [1917] 1 KB 813 at 826. Cf *Redgrave v Hurd* (1881) 20 Ch D 1.
20   See *Whittington v Seale–Hayne* (1900) 82 LT 49.
1   *Whincup v Hughes* (1871) LR 6 CP 78. Cf *Rover International Ltd v Cannon Film Sales Ltd (No 3)* [1989] 1 WLR 912.
2   *Ebrahim Dawood Ltd v Heath (Est 1927) Ltd* [1961] 2 Lloyd's Rep 512.
3   Cf Law Commission Report No 121 (1983) Part III.

Can the plaintiff claim damages for breach of contract and in restitution? In the *Mikhail Lermontov*[4] the High Court of Australia held that this was not possible. The plaintiff had booked a cruise on the defendant's vessel, which sank part way through the cruise. She recovered damages under various heads but failed in her claim for restitution of the fare as there had been no total failure of consideration. It was not possible to combine the two actions as restitution of the contractual consideration removes the basis on which the plaintiff is entitled to call on the defendant to perform his contractual obligations. Also, in most cases, the plaintiff will usually be protected by an award of damages for breach of contract, which may include an amount for substitute performance.[5]

Where the plaintiff has performed work for the defendant, he may claim for a *quantum meruit*. In *Planché v Colburn*,[6] the plaintiff was engaged to write a book for the defendant. The defendant terminated the contract after the plaintiff had carried out some research and had started to write the book. The plaintiff was awarded a sum as a *quantum meruit* for the work done, although the defendant had obtained no benefit.

Where the plaintiff has entered into a bad bargain, it will be to his advantage to claim on a *quantum meruit* if the defendant is in breach. In *Boomer v Muir*,[7] the plaintiff had justifiably terminated a contract to build a dam, and received $258,000 as the value of his work in part-building it. This was more than he would have received had he finished the work and received the contract price. There is no direct English authority which has decided whether a plaintiff can recover more on a *quantum meruit* than he could had he brought an action in contract. The New Zealand case of *Slowey v Lodder*[8] suggests that the contract price is not the limit as the Privy Council accepted, without further discussion on the point, that as the contract was lawfully treated as at an end by the plaintiff, he was entitled to sue for work and labour done.[9] In the context of void contracts KERR LJ was of the opinion that the quantum meruit was not subject to a ceiling determined by the contract price as the quantum meruit only arose because of the non existence of the contract.[10] However, where the reason why a party is unjustly enriched is the contract failure itself, the ceiling should be fixed at the amount set by the contract. In the complex case of *Banque Financière de la Cité v Parc (Battersea) Ltd*[11] there was a failed contract, in the sense that the party impoverished on making an advance to a third party mistakenly thought that they were obtaining a binding commitment from the party enriched that the latter would not enforce a loan owed by the third party. The relief sought was a declaration and did not seek to quantify the enrichment. Logically, however, the party impoverished should be no better off than if the contract had bound the enriched party as the unjust enrichment arose as a result of contract failure.

What is the position where the person seeking restitution is the person in breach? It is, of course, always necessary that the contract has been discharged and to this end it is necessary that the innocent party has accepted the breach and treated the contract as at an end. The party in breach may recover money paid as a deposit, provided this money is not security for performance.[12] This is a matter of construction of the contract but, once it does appear that the condition for retaining the money has failed, the fact

4   *Baltic Shipping Co v Dillon* (1993) 176 CLR 344.
5   For criticism of this part of the decision see K Barker [1994] LCMLQ 291, 294–6.
6   (1831) 8 Bing 14. See also *Slowey v Lodder* (1900) 20 NZLR 321; affd [1904] AC 442 (Privy Council).
7   24 P 2d 570 (California 1933).
8   (1900) 20 NZLR 321: affd [1904] AC 442.
9   But see Goff and Jones pp 532. See also Beatson pp 13–5.
10   *Rover International Ltd v Cannon Film Sales Ltd (No 3)* [1989] 1 WLR 912 at 926–928.
11   [1998] 1 All ER 737. See M Bridge [1998] JBL 323.
12   *Dies v British and International Mining and Finance Corpn Ltd* [1939] 1 KB 724.

that it failed in response to the payer's own breach does not matter.[13] However, where the innocent party has performed work or incurred expenses in performance of the contract, so that there is no total failure of consideration, the amount paid would be irrecoverable, as it provides a fund from which the payee can meet expenses.[14]

Where the party in breach claims for work done and the contract is divisible, he will be able to claim under the contract in respect of each divisible obligation that has been completely performed. Where the contract is entire, the party in breach cannot generally claim for work done under the contract. In *Sumpter v Hedges*,[15] a builder who abandoned a contract was unable to claim for the work he had performed, as either there was no free acceptance or a failure of consideration. This problem was addressed by the Law Commission[16] who proposed a remedy in such cases but this was never implemented, perhaps because of the strong dissenting report by Brian Davenport QC to the effect that non-payment was the only effective remedy that a consumer had.

(ii)   Frustration[17]

Where the contract is frustrated, no claim for damages can be maintained. The settlement of the parties' rights falls within the law of restitution. If money has been paid or a benefit has been conferred under the contract before the date of the frustrating event, it must be decided if that money can be recovered, and if restitution can be obtained in respect of the benefit.

(a)   *The common law rule*   The position at common law was that, if money was paid or payable before the date of the frustrating event, it was irrecoverable, unless there was a total failure of consideration. The contract had to be void *ab initio*. In *Chandler v Webster*,[18] the defendant contracted to hire a room which overlooked the route of the coronation procession of King Edward VII. The contract provided for payment in advance, some of which had been paid. The contract was frustrated when the procession was cancelled. It was held that the hirer could not recover his payment and remained liable for the balance due, as there had been no total failure of consideration.

This decision, in so far as it related to total failure of consideration, was overruled in *Fibrosa v Fairbairn*,[19] where it was held that it was not necessary to show that the contract was void *ab initio* in order to prove a total failure of consideration. The defendants had partially manufactured machinery under a contract which provided for an advance payment of £1,600. £1,000 of this amount had actually been paid. Delivery of the machinery was not desirable on policy grounds, due to the German occupation of Poland. Accordingly, the contract was held to be frustrated. It was held that the £1,000 paid was recoverable, as there had been a total failure of consideration because no machinery had been delivered.

Problems still remained after this decision. The defendants were unable to recover anything for the value of the work done, and the rule only applied where the consideration had wholly failed. If the plaintiff had received some benefit under the contract, the rule was inapplicable.

---

13   *Birks*, 238; quoted with approval in *Baltic Shipping Co v Dillon* (1993) 176 CLR 344, 390–1.
14   *Hyundai Heavy Industries Co Ltd v Papadopoulos* [1980] 1 WLR 1129.
15   [1898] 1 QB 673.
16   Law Commission 121 (1983).
17   See ch 23.
18   [1904] 1 KB 493.
19   *Fibrosa Spolka Akcyjna v Fairbairn, Lawson, Combe, Barbour & Co Ltd* [1943] AC 32.

(b)   *Statutory remedies*[20]   In response to the problems of the common law rule, the Law Reform (Frustrated Contracts) Act 1943 was passed. The Act applies to contracts governed by English law,[1] subject to a number of exceptions.[2]

Section 1(2) of the Act provides:

> All sums paid or payable to any party in pursuance of the contract before the time when the parties were discharged ... shall, in the case of sums paid, be recoverable from him as money received by him for the use of the party by whom the sums were paid, and, in the case of sums so payable, cease to be so payable.
>
> Provided that, if the party to whom the sums were so paid or payable incurred expenses before the time of discharge in, or for the purpose of, the performance of the contract, the court may, if it considers it just to do so having regard to all the circumstances of the case, allow him to retain or, as the case may be, recover the whole or any part of the sums so paid or payable, not being an amount in excess of the expenses so incurred.

The first part of section 1(2) gives a right to a party to recover sums paid or payable before the frustrating event, subject to the operation of the proviso. There need be no total failure of consideration for such sums to be recoverable or to cease to be payable. This prevents the enrichment of the defendant who, if he has conferred a benefit on the plaintiff, must seek to recover under the proviso or under section 1(3). The proviso to section 1(2) provides a means of compensating a defendant payee who has suffered reliance expenditure. The proviso allows the value of the defendant's part-performance to be set off against money already paid to the defendant. However, the defendant will have a claim, in his own right, where money was payable before the date of the frustrating event and which remains unpaid. Only where this money has been paid, whether under the contract or fortuitously, or is payable, will the defendant be able to maintain such an action. In any event, the defendant will not be able to recover more than his actual expenditure.

The basis of the proviso is uncertain, since the expense incurred by the defendant may confer no enrichment on the plaintiff. For example, in *Fibrosa v Fairbairn*,[3] the machinery contracted for was not delivered, with the result that the buyer was not enriched. However, if this case were to be considered in the light of the proviso to section 1(2), the seller would be able to recover in respect of his performance expenses.

If A has paid £10,000 to B under a contract which is later frustrated, and B has incurred performance expenses of £5,000, it must be decided how much B can retain. If the £10,000 was payable before the occurrence of the frustrating event and appropriate expenditure had been incurred, the proviso to section 1(2) is applicable. However, a number of possible solutions as to the *quantum* of recovery may be suggested. First, it might be argued that A should recover the £10,000 and B should recover nothing.[4] This would be consistent with basic principles of unjust enrichment, as there is no incontrovertible benefit to A. However, such an approach is inconsistent with the wording of the proviso. A second solution is to allow A to recover £5,000 on the basis that B has changed his position in reliance on the payment.[5] However, difficulties may arise if the £10,000 was not payable under the contract but had been paid gratuitously by A in advance. The proviso allows B to set off some of this money against his expenses, but it would be difficult to say that the expense was incurred in reliance on the payment.

20   See Haycroft and Waksman (1985) JBL 207.
1   Law Reform (Frustrated Contracts) Act 1943, s 1.
2   Ibid, s 2(5).
3   [1943] AC 32.
4   See *Gamerco SA v ICM/Fair Warning (Agency) Ltd* [1995] 1 WLR 1226.
5   *BP Exploration Co Ltd v Hunt (No 2)* [1979] 1 WLR 783 at 800 (per GOFF J).

The third solution is to allow A to recover £7,500 and thereby apportion B's loss equally between A and B. As the proviso appears to be a pragmatic device for adjusting losses in frustration cases rather than a direct application of principles of unjust enrichment, this would appear to be the preferred approach.

Section 1(3) of the Act provides:

> Where any party to the contract has, by reason of anything done by any other party thereto in, or for the purpose of, the performance of the contract, obtained a valuable benefit (other than a payment of money …) before the time of discharge, there shall be recoverable from him by the said party such sum (if any), not exceeding the value of the said benefit to the party obtaining it, as the court considers just, having regard to all the circumstances of the case and, in particular,
>
> (a)   the amount of any expenses incurred before the time of the discharge by the benefited party, in or for the performance of the contract, including any sums paid or payable by him to any other party in pursuance of the contract and retained or recoverable by that party under the last foregoing subsection, and
> (b)   the effect, in relation to the said benefit of the circumstances giving rise to the frustration of the contract.

Section 1(3) deals with non-monetary benefits acquired by a party to a frustrated contract prior to the frustrating event. It is illustrative of some of the problems posed by the law of restitution. The event gives rise to a restitutionary solution, as the contract has come to an end by reason of frustration. The major difficulty is to identify the benefit to the recipient and the value of that benefit. In *Appleby v Myers,*[6] a contract for the installation of machinery in a factory was frustrated when the factory was destroyed by fire. At the time, the machinery had been partly manufactured. As the contract provided for no payment until completion, nothing was recoverable under the law applicable at the time. If section 1(3) were to be applied to these facts, it would be necessary to determine whether the factory owner had acquired a valuable benefit.

The operation of section 1(3) has been considered in *BP Exploration Co (Libya) Ltd v Hunt (No 2).*[7] The defendant was granted a concession to explore for oil in Libya. He did not have the resources to do this himself, so he sold a half share in the concession to BP, on condition that they would do the exploration. The contract was frustrated when the Libyan government expropriated BP's share of the concession in 1971 and the defendant's share in 1973. The details of the agreement were complex, but provided that the risk of no oil being found lay with BP. If oil were to be found, BP's exploration expenses were to be paid out of the defendant's receipts. Oil came on stream in 1967, and BP claimed in respect of benefits allegedly conferred on the defendant. The problem was that BP had been paid from 1967 onwards, but the payments only covered two-thirds of their initial expenditure. Everything received by the defendant was profit, once the concession had been paid for.

GOFF J adopted a two-stage approach. First, it was necessary to value the benefit. Secondly, the court would have to award a just sum to take account of the benefit conferred. For the purposes of section 1(3), a benefit was said to consist of the end product of a service rather than the service itself. Section 1(3) distinguishes between the plaintiff's performance and the defendant's benefit, and section 1(3)(b) relates to the product of the plaintiff's performance.[8] In building cases, the court would have to value that part of the building completed at the date of the frustrating event, not the cost to the plaintiff of erecting the building.

---

6   (1867) LR 2 CP 651.
7   [1979] 1 WLR 783; affd [1982] 1 All ER 925, HL.
8   *BP Exploration Co Ltd v Hunt (No 2)* [1979] 1 WLR 783 at 801 (per GOFF J).

This approach creates difficulties in cases where the end product is eccentric, where work has no end product, and where the end product is destroyed by the frustrating event. Where the end product is eccentric in the sense that the recipient values it but it would be valueless on the market, the contract price should be used as a guide. Where a lucrative contract for the decoration of a house in execrable taste is frustrated before completion, the decoration might have lowered the value of the property. However, the benefit conferred may have to be valued by reference to the contract price.[9]

The effect on cases such as *Appleby v Myers*, where the end product is destroyed, is also unclear. The interpretation of section 1(3)(b) is crucial. If the effect of the circumstances giving rise to the frustrating event must be considered only in relation to the maximum award and not in the calculation of the just sum, the plaintiff will recover nothing. But, if section 1(3)(b) can be considered at the discretionary phase of calculating the just sum, an award could be made.

Once the benefit has been identified, this fixes the maximum amount of an award under section 1(3). The benefit to the defendant in *BP Exploration v Hunt* was not the day-to-day work done by BP in looking for and extracting the oil. It was the end product, namely, the enhancement of the defendant's concession.[10] Applying section 1(3)(b), the benefit to be valued was the oil actually obtained by the defendant from the time the field came on stream, and half of the compensation paid by the Libyan government, representing the enhanced value of Mr Hunt's share in the concession due to BP's efforts.

Valuation of the benefit poses problems where an inexpensive service confers a large benefit and vice versa. The court will value the benefit to the defendant at the time of the frustrating event. This sets the ceiling for the award, it does not determine the just sum to be paid.

The second stage requires the court to determine the just sum to be awarded. The approach adopted by GOFF J was to prevent unjust enrichment.[11] The party who had been enriched should give up such part of his enrichment as had been gained at the expense of the other. This is assessed by reference to the reasonable value of the plaintiff's performance, that is a *quantum meruit* action. What *Planché v Colburn*[12] allows for is a partial performance and discharge for breach, the statute allows for partial performance and frustration.

The value of the defendant's benefit in *BP Exploration v Hunt* under the first stage was assessed at $85 million. This was partly attributable to BP's efforts and partly due to the increased value of the concession. The just sum to be awarded was $34.5 million which represented the outstanding value of BP's work. As this did not exceed the maximum figure of $85 million, this was what BP received.

(iii)   No contract concluded[13]

Where the parties enter negotiations for a contract and the plaintiff commences work, for example in reliance on a letter of intent, no contract is completed. The common law has adopted a number of solutions to this problem,[14] but here we are concerned only with restitutionary remedies.

---

9   Ibid at 803 (per GOFF J).
10   Ibid at 802–803 (per GOFF J).
11   Ibid at 805 (per GOFF J).
12   (1831) 8 Bing 14.
13   See McKendrick (1988) 8 OJLS 197.
14   See ch 7.

Within the law of restitution, an action will depend on whether there has been a free acceptance of the benefit by the defendant or whether there is a total failure of consideration.[15] In *Peter Lind v Mersey Docks and Harbour Board*,[16] the parties commenced negotiations for the construction of a container dock. The negotiations failed on the issue of the price calculation formula. In the meantime, the plaintiffs had performed work worth more than £1 million and successfully claimed for this on a *quantum meruit*, as the defendants were left in possession of work which they had initially required.

The drawback of a restitutionary claim as far as the plaintiff is concerned is that he can only recover for the benefit he has conferred on the defendant. No claim for consequential losses or lost profits can be entertained. If the performance rendered by the plaintiff was defective then no effective counter-claim by the defendant can be made. In *British Steel Corpn v Cleveland Bridge and Engineering Co Ltd*,[17] Cleveland required nodes for use in construction. A letter of intent was sent to BSC but the parties failed to reach agreement on price or other contract terms. All but one of the nodes were delivered, although not on time and not in the right order. BSC claimed the price, either on a contract or on a quantum meruit and Cleveland counter-claimed damages for late delivery. It was held that no contract had been entered into but that BSC were entitled to a quantum meruit.

A restitutionary solution in these situations has problems. When parties negotiate over a proposed contract a party may be at risk of losing money expended in order to secure the contract and any expenditure may be 'subject to contract.'[18] It is difficult to find a satisfactory dividing line between when a party is at risk and where they are entitled to a quantum meruit claim. It has been suggested that by examining more precisely what the defendant requested (such as the order of delivery) it would be possible to say either that the buyer is not enriched or that the enrichment is not unjust.[19]

---

15   See ch 11.
16   [1972] 2 Lloyd's Rep 234. See also *British Steel Corpn v Cleveland Bridge and Engineering Co Ltd* [1984] 1 All ER 504.
17   [1984] 1 All ER 504.
18   *Regalian Properties plc v London Dockland Development Corpn* [1995] 1 WLR 212.
19   McKendrick (1988) 8 OJLS 197, 211–213.

Chapter 19

Limitation of actions

1. INTRODUCTION

It has been recognised by statute since 1623[1] that a defendant should not have the threat of an action hanging over him indefinitely. Successive statutes have therefore provided limitation periods, within which a claimant must serve his writ or forfeit his remedy. The present law is contained in the Limitation Act 1980, as amended by the Latent Damage Act 1986 and the Consumer Protection Act 1987. It should be noted that the law on limitation of actions is specifically a statutory development since there is no common law notion of a time bar. Reasons for imposing a time limit on pursuing a remedy are numerous. In the first place, it seems proper that defendants should be protected from the possibility of a stale claim. It has been said that a statute of limitations is an 'act of peace'[2] which is intended to prevent defendants from living in perpetual fear of the risk of legal action being brought against them, on the basis that litigation is not an intrinsically desirable activity.[3] Although it is in the public interest that there should not be protracted litigation, there is also a countervailing public interest that justice be done in appropriate circumstances. Accordingly, there are exceptional circumstances in which a claimant will be allowed to commence proceedings out of time, because the claimant suffers from some disability or has acted or failed to act due to some operative mistake or because the defendant has been guilty of fraud or concealment.

A second justification for limitation periods is that they are of benefit to claimants by encouraging them to bring proceedings promptly while relevant facts are still fresh in the memory of witnesses and while relevant documentation remains available.[4] Thirdly, rules on limitation of actions may be regarded as a reflection on the conduct of a dilatory claimant to the extent that such a claimant (or his lawyer) can only blame himself if declared to be out of time.[5]

---

1 Statute of Limitations 1623, 21 Jac 1, c 16. Although this is the earliest statute specifically called a statute of limitations, there had been earlier statutory intervention specific to property law issues.
2 *A'Court v Cross* (1825) 3 Bing 329 at 332 per BEST CJ.
3 See *Ampthill Peerage Case* [1977] AC 547 at 575 per LORD SIMON; *Donovan v Gwentoys Ltd* [1990] 1 All ER 1018 at 1024 per LORD GRIFFITHS.
4 *R B Policies at Lloyd's v Butler* [1950] 1 KB 76.
5 *Board of Trade v Cayzer Irvine & Co* [1927] AC 610 at 628 per LORD ATKINSON.

The advantages of short and rigid limitation periods for the defendant and the courts are obvious, but a plaintiff may be in the unfortunate position that he is unaware that he has suffered harm until after his remedy is barred. This situation arises where the plaintiff suffers latent damage in the form of personal injuries or unobservable damage to a building. In such cases, modern statutes have attempted the difficult task of allowing more flexible limitation periods.

Limitation provisions bar a remedy, but not the right to that remedy.[6] The effect of the expiry of a limitation period is to leave the plaintiff with an unenforceable claim. For example, a statute barred debt is still due, but cannot be enforced by action.[7] As the effect of limitation provisions is to create procedural rules, not substantive rules of law,[8] the defendant will be liable, unless he specifically pleads limitation.[9]

Although the Limitation Act 1980 applies only to actions at common law, there are parallel rules in equity based on the doctrine of laches or on the basis of acquiescence which also prevent the claimant from bringing an action at a very late stage. Where an equitable claim falls within the concurrent jurisdiction of equity, equity acts on the analogy of the Limitation Act.[10] A claim in equity to recover a simple contract debt is therefore barred after the lapse of six years.

In the case of purely equitable claims within its exclusive jurisdiction, equity applies the doctrine of laches. As laches is an equitable doctrine, no precise rule can be laid down as to when laches will or will not bar a claim, and each case depends upon the degree of diligence which might reasonably have been expected from the plaintiff. The plaintiff must show himself to be prompt and eager to assert his rights.[11] Thus it has been observed that 'A court of Equity requires that those who come to it to ask its active interposition to give them relief should use due diligence, after there has been such notice or knowledge as to make it inequitable to lie by...'[12] The court will consider the length of the delay, the acquiescence of the plaintiff, and the effect on the defendant of granting the order sought.[13] The concepts of laches and acquiescence are difficult to define and appear to be confusingly applied according to the facts of each case. Generally, whichever set of rules is applied, it is necessary to consider a range of factors including the period of delay, the extent to which the defendant's position has been prejudiced by the delay and the extent to which that delay has been caused by the actions of the claimant.[14] Thus, in general terms, the defendant may rely on the equitable defence if it can be shown that the claimant, by failing to institute proceedings, has or may be deemed to have either acquiesced in the defendant's conduct or has failed to bring suit in the knowledge that the defendant has infringed the claimant's rights. In a typical case where the claimant stands by in the knowledge that his rights have been infringed, it can be said that the claimant is estopped from proceeding against the defendant, usually because the latter has changed his position because of the delay.[15] A further reason for declining to assist a dilatory claimant is that the defendant or his witnesses may have difficulty in recalling relevant events. Thus in *Nelson v Rye*[16] the claimant, a

6   *Ronex Properties Ltd v John Laing Construction Ltd* [1982] 3 WLR 875 at 879 (per DONALDSON LJ).
7   *Curwen v Milburn* (1889) 42 Ch D 424 at 434–435 (per COTTON LJ).
8   Cf Limitation Act 1980, s 3.
9   *Dismore v Milton* [1938] 3 All ER 762.
10   *Knox v Gye* (1872) LR 5 HL 656 at 674 (per LORD WESTBURY).
11   *Milward v Earl of Thanet* (1801) 5 Ves 720n. Cf *Lazard Bros & Co Ltd v Fairfield Properties Co (Mayfair) Ltd* (1977) 121 Sol Jo 793.
12   *Erlanger v New Sombrero Phosphate Co* (1878) 3 App Cas 1218 at 1279 (per LORD BLACKBURN).
13   *Lindsay Petroleum Co v Hurd* (1874) LR 5 PC 221 at 239 (per LORD SELBORNE).
14   *Nelson v Rye* [1996] 2 All ER 186 at 200–201 (per LADDIE J).
15   See *Lamshed v Lamshed* (1963) 109 CLR 440 (no action for six years after initiating proceedings for specific performance, after which the defendant contracted to sell the land to a third party).
16   [1996] 2 All ER 186.

musician, sued his business manager for an account of moneys received during the period 1980 to 1990. Although the relationship arose out of contract, it was considered to be fiduciary in nature and therefore not governed by the provisions of the Limitation Act 1980. Nevertheless, the doctrine of laches applied and a refusal to allow the action to proceed was justified on the ground that the business manager might find it very difficult to recall the minutiae of what expenses were incurred and for what purpose during the period 1980 to 1985.

The doctrines of laches and acquiescence will apply to equitable claims or remedies to which the Limitation Act does not apply expressly or by analogy. It is expressly enacted that the Act will not apply to any claims for specific performance of a contract, injunctions or other equitable relief.[17] An example of a remedy falling within 'other equitable relief' would be where the plaintiff applied for rescission of a contract, for example on the ground of a misrepresentation. Similarly, it would appear that other analogous remedies such as Mareva injunctions and Anton Piller orders would also fall into this category. However, the Limitation Act 1980 can apply 'by analogy' on the basis that 'equity follows the law'.[18] This is a desirable position to adopt, since it would be unacceptable for a person seeking a legal remedy to be subject to a time bar when, in analogous circumstances, no such limitation is placed on a claimant seeking an equitable remedy. Thus an action against a fiduciary requiring him to account for a bribe is analogous to a common law action for moneys had and received and should be subject to a six-year limitation period[19] and an action by the beneficiary of a trust to recover payments made to another beneficiary can be likened to a common law action for the recovery of moneys paid under a common mistake of fact.[20] However, it should be noted that there may be circumstances in which an action in equity may have more than one analogue. For example, some actions may appear to be similar to one for moneys had and received[1] and one for a claim to the personal estate of a deceased person.[2] In such a case, it may be necessary to apply the more generous limitation period to the claimant.[3]

2.   CAUSES OF ACTION

The concept of a cause of action is a crucial consideration in all aspects of limitation of actions since time will not start to run against a claimant until his cause of action has accrued. When a cause of action accrues will differ according to the type of action under consideration. In contract actions time will start to run against the claimant when there is a breach of contract.[4] In contrast, in a tort action, the cause of action will not generally accrue until such time as damage has been caused, where damage is the gist of the action.[5] The difficulty for the common law is that the Limitation Act 1980 does not immediately appear to make provision for actions other than those which lie in contract or in tort. Accordingly special attention needs to be given to restitutionary claims and those which are based on statutory interventions which may not be

---

17   Limitation Act 1980, s 36(1).
18   *Knox v Gye* (1872) LR 5 HL 656.
19   *Metropolitan Bank v Heiron* (1880) 5 Ex D 319.
20   *Re Robinson* [1911] 1 Ch 502.
1   Subject to a six-year limitation period under the Limitation Act 1980, s 5.
2   Subject to a 12-year limitation period under the Limitation Act 1980, s 22.
3   *Re Diplock* [1948] Ch 465.
4   Limitation Act 1980, s 5.
5   Limitation Act 1980, s 2.

immediately classifiable as actions in tort or in contract, such as claims under the Misrepresentation Act 1967.

What constitutes a cause of action is not defined in the Limitation Act 1980.[6] In general terms, a cause of action has been judicially defined as 'every fact which it would be necessary for the plaintiff to prove, if traversed, in order to support his right to the judgment of the court.'[7] The problem which this definition throws up is that it deals with no more than the position of the claimant, but in order to ascertain whether there is a cause of action, regard must also be had to the position of the defendant. It follows that it is probably better to define a cause of action in broader terms. Thus in *Cooke v Gill*[8] it was stated that, 'Cause of action has been held from the earliest time to mean every fact which is material to be proved to entitle the plaintiff to succeed – every fact which the defendant would have a right to traverse.'

3.   ACCRUAL OF THE CAUSE OF ACTION IN CONTRACT

For the purposes of the Limitation Act 1980 there is an important distinction between a simple contract governed by section 5 and a specialty governed by section 12. In the case of simple contracts, time will start to run against the claimant from the date of breach for a period of six years, whereas in the case of a specialty, such as a contract under seal, the relevant period, running from the date of breach, is 12 years. The rationale behind this choice of starting date for the running of time is that the gist of an action in contract is that a promise has been given but not fulfilled, accordingly time should start to run as from the date on which the promisor fails to fulfil his promise. Simply stating that the gist of the claimant's cause of action is the promisor's breach of contract does not resolve the problem of identifying when time begins to run, since there may be acute difficulties in determining when the relevant breach actually occurred. What has to be asked is what has been promised and when has the promisor failed to fulfil that promise? Sometimes it is possible that a court may determine that the date on which a particular promise should be fulfilled is subject to a contingency. For example in contracts for the provision of credit facilities, the obligation of the debtor to repay the debt is often said to be subject to the requirement that the creditor should supply the debtor with written copies of the agreement between the parties.[9] Accordingly, there will be no breach of contract on the part of the debtor if he fails to repay the debt in accordance with the repayment schedule until he has been supplied with copies of the agreement by the creditor. Furthermore, in determining whether there has been a breach of contract, regard may be had to other terms of the contract. For example, in a contract for the sale of goods, normally the seller's obligation to deliver and the buyer's obligation to accept and pay for the goods are regarded as concurrent conditions.[10] However, if the buyer has been granted a period of credit in which to pay for the goods, the seller will not be able to complain of a breach on the part of the buyer until the period of credit has expired. In terms of the running of time, this means that the limitation period will not commence until the later date of a failure to pay following the expiry of the period of credit.

---

6   There is a definition of an 'action' which is stated to include proceedings in a court of law and an ecclesiastical court (s 38(1)) and arbitration proceedings (s 34(1)).

7   *Read v Brown* (1888) 22 QBD 128 at 131 (per LORD ESHER MR).

8   (1873) LR 8 CP 107.

9   *Bentworth Finance Ltd v Lubert* [1968] 1 QB 680.

10   Sale of Goods Act 1979, s 28.

(1)   CONTINUING BREACHES OF CONTRACT.

Some breaches of contract may be continuing in nature with the result that it may be difficult to identify precisely when the relevant breach occurred. For example, some contracts may involve the giving of a warranty that continues to be effective over a considerable period of time. This will be particularly the case where there has been an undertaking to perform some specific task which remains unperformed, such as the obligation of a solicitor to register an option to purchase identified property. While ever the option remains unregistered and there is no other bar to registration, such as a final disposition of the property to a third party, the warranty will continue to be operative.[11] Of course the difficulty with this line of reasoning is that it may produce a high degree of uncertainty as to the date on which time will begin to run against the claimant and later authorities seem to point to a preference for fixing a once-and-for-all date on which time should begin to run, if the terms of the contract permit this.[12]

(2)   AWARENESS OF LOSS.

The main problem presented by the rule that the cause of action accrues on breach is that a claimant may be out of time before he realises that he has a cause of action. Thus in *Lynn v Bamber*[13] the plaintiff purchased 240 'Purple Pershore' plum trees in 1921 but only discovered that the trees were of a different variety when they reached maturity in 1928. However, by that time the plaintiff was time barred in the absence of fraud or concealment on the part of the seller, despite the fact that it was unlikely that the buyer could have discovered the truth at the time of the contract, or even shortly afterwards.

(3)   ANTICIPATORY BREACH OF CONTRACT.

In some instances the promisor may be guilty of an anticipatory breach of contract, in which case, the breach occurs before the date on which performance is expected. Despite the fact that the promisee may wait until the agreed date of performance before commencing his action, the rule for the purposes of limitation of actions is that time will begin to run as from the date of the anticipatory breach, otherwise the claimant's action would never become time barred until such time as he chose to accept the defaulting party's repudiation.[14]

(4)   CONCURRENT CONTRACTUAL AND TORTIOUS LIABILITY.

A single set of facts may produce the result that a claimant may sue in both contract and tort. This has particular consequences for rules on limitation of actions, since the starting date for the running of time differs according to whether the action is framed in contract or in tort. These different starting dates may produce the anomalous result that a claimant is better off if he frames his action in tort rather than in contract. In a tort action for negligence, the gist of the claimant's action is that he has suffered damage, whereas the gist of an action for breach of contract is that there has been a breach of contract. In *Midland Bank Trust Co Ltd v Hett, Stubbs and Kemp (a firm)*,[15] the plaintiff was given an option to purchase a farm. The defendant solicitor negligently failed to register the option and, more than six years later, the farm was sold to a third party. It

---

11   *Midland Bank Trust Co v Hett, Stubbs, Kemp* [1979] Ch 384.
12   *Bell v Peter Browne & Co* [1990] 3 All ER 124 at 126 (per NICHOLLS LJ)
13   [1930] 2 KB 72. See also *Battley v Faulkner* (1820) 3 B & Ald 288.
14   See *Bell v Peter Browne & Co* [1990] 3 All ER 124 at 127 (per NICHOLLS LJ).
15   [1979] Ch 384, [1978] 3 All ER 571.

was held that the cause of action in negligence accrued when the farm was sold, as the plaintiff then suffered damage by losing his option to purchase. Accordingly, the action was not statute barred. The contract action was also allowed to proceed, as the breach of contract was not an act but an omission, which continued until the farm was sold. This form of continuing obligation could be limited by the Supply of Goods and Services Act 1982, section 14(1), which implies a term in contracts for the supply of services to the effect that a service is to be carried out within a reasonable time.

The fortunate effect of the reasoning adopted by OLIVER J in *Hett* was that the cause of action in contract and in tort accrued at the same time, but this will not resolve the problem where the breach of contract is considered to occur on an earlier date than the date on which damage is caused. Since the decision in *Hett* it has been recognised that there are circumstances in which a tortious duty of care may be owed despite the fact that this may outflank the contractual structure set up by the parties.[16] What is increasingly apparent is that there needs to be much more specific guidance from the House of Lords as to when the contractual structure argument must be taken into account and when it may be ignored. A more sensible approach to this issue has been adopted in Canada where it has been held that a concurrent tortious liability should not be imposed if its effect would be to allow the claimant to circumvent a contractual exclusion of liability for an act which would constitute the commission of a tort. Otherwise, the claimant ought to be allowed to assert the cause of action most advantageous to him.[17]

(5) CONTRACTUAL AND RESTITUTIONARY CLAIMS.

The early Statutes of Limitation on which the present Limitation Act 1980 is based recognised only that civil actions could lie in tort or in contract or could be based on a property interest. As a result of this restitutionary claims must be dealt with within the existing structure of the Limitation Act. It has been observed that the provisions of section 5 (contractual actions) must,

> be taken to cover actions for moneys had and received, formerly actions on the case ... though the words used cannot be felicitous.[18]

From this it follows that a restitutionary claim will be barred six years after the date on which the cause of action accrued, but, clearly, this cannot be the same date as that which applies to an action for breach of contract, since there may be no breach of contract at all. In addition, restitutionary claims may arise out of the commission of a wrong on the part of a defendant, in which case the contractual limitation period is clearly inapplicable. Furthermore, the general effect of a restitutionary claim is that it is for a specific sum of money. In contrast a claim for contractual and tortious damages is for an unliquidated amount

An important consideration is that the gist of the cause of action should be identified, since the occurrence of this event is the date from which time will run. For the purposes of a restitutionary claim it is arguable that the gist of the claimant's cause of action is that the defendant has unjustly retained a benefit at the claimant's expense.[19] This might lead to the conclusion that a claimant should only be time barred after he has given an

---

16 See eg *Henderson v Merrett Syndicates Ltd* [1994] 3 All ER 506. Moreover, following *Marc Rich & Co v Bishop Rock Marine Ltd* [1995] 3 All ER 307 it cannot now be argued that there should be a distinction drawn between physical harm and economic loss in determining whether a duty of care is owed to the claimant.

17 See *Central Trust Co v Rafuse* (1986) 31 DLR (4th) 481 at 522 (per LE DAIN J).

18 *Re Diplock* [1948] Ch 465 at 514 (per LORD GREENE MR).

19 See McLean (1989) 48 CLJ 472.

indication that he has waived his rights or has delayed excessively or where the passage of time is such as to prejudice the defendant's ability to establish a defence.[20] In all other circumstances, it seems logical to conclude that the injustice of allowing the defendant to retain the benefit will continue to constitute an unjust enrichment and that the claimant should not be time barred while that unjust enrichment continues.

(6)   CONTRACTUAL CLAIMS AND LATENT DAMAGE.

Difficulties may arise where a claimant who is neither mistaken nor adversely affected by fraud or deliberate concealment on the part of the defendant, is not reasonably able to discover the facts which allow him to commence proceedings after the date on which it is determined that he has suffered significant damage as a result of the defendant's acts or omissions. Primarily this problem of latent damage is viewed as one that impinges on tortious liability for negligence, since the gist of that cause of action turns on the date on which damage is caused. In order to counteract the injustice which might otherwise be caused by the problem of latent damage, legislation was introduced in the form of the Latent Damage Act 1986, at a time when the substantive law of tort seemed to recognise a much wider scope for the tort of negligence in the field of claims for economic loss than is presently the case following the decision in *Murphy v Brentwood DC*.[1] The problem of latent damage is viewed, primarily, as one to be dealt with through principles of tort law, despite the fact that there may be circumstances in which an action may exist concurrently in contract and tort. As a result the question has arisen whether the provisions of the Latent Damage Act can apply to an action based upon an alleged breach of contract. The primary difficulty is that the Latent Damage Act 1986[2] only applies to an 'action for damages for negligence'. This has given rise to the question whether such an action encompasses one for a contractual failure to exercise reasonable care. Subsequent case law suggests that all the 1986 Act envisaged was an action for negligence framed in tort and that 'contractual negligence' remains uncovered.[3] What confirms that this is the correct position is that there are specific provisions in section 14A which override the provisions of the Limitation Act 1980 section 2, but there is nothing which purports to override the provisions of section 5.[4] Moreover, while the Limitation Act 1980, section 11 makes a specific reference to 'contractual negligence', section 14A refers simply to 'negligence'.

4.   ACCRUAL OF THE CAUSE OF ACTION IN TORT

The Limitation Act 1980, section 2 provides that in a tort action, time will run for six years from the date on which the cause of action accrues. Accrual will depend on the nature of the tort committed by the defendant, since the gist of the cause of action differs according to whether the tort in question requires proof of damage or whether it is actionable per se. Special considerations also apply to torts of a continuing nature.

---

20   See *Lindsay Petroleum Co v Hurd* (1874) LR 5 PC 221 at 239–240 (per LORD SELBOURNE).
1   [1991] 1 AC 398.
2   Which inserted s 14A in the Limitation Act 1980.
3   *Iron Trade Mutual Insurance Co Ltd v JK Buckenham Ltd* [1990] 1 All ER 808; *Société Commerciale de Réassurance v ERAS (International) Ltd* [1992] 2 All ER 82 (note).
4   *Société Commerciale de Réassurance v ERAS (International) Ltd* [1992] 2 All ER 82 (note) at 85 (per MUSTILL LJ).

(1)   TORTS ACTIONABLE PER SE

In the case of torts actionable per se, the date of the defendant's act is the relevant point of time for the purposes of the accrual of the cause of action.[5] From this it follows that in an action for libel and some varieties of slander, trespass to the person and trespass to land, what matters is the date on which the wrongful act is committed.

(2)   CONTINUING TORTS

Some torts such as nuisance are continuing in nature and as a result, a fresh cause of action accrues on a day-to-day basis while ever the tort continues to be committed.[6] For the purposes of rules on limitation of actions this means that the plaintiff will be time barred in respect of the whole of his claim six years after the last date on which the tort was committed. If, however, an action is brought within six years of the last date on which the tort was committed, the claimant's action will be limited to those occasions which fall within the limitation period and the claim will be barred in respect of those occasions on which the tort was committed more than six years before the date on which the writ was issued. A practical consequence of the rule on continuing torts is that since the claimant will have successive actions in respect of a single state of affairs, while it continues to exist, the courts are unlikely to award prospective damages since there is a possibility that further actions may be brought.[7]

(3)   SINGLE-ACT TORTS REQUIRING PROOF OF DAMAGE

In single-act torts actionable upon proof of damage, such as the tort of negligence, the cause of action accrues on the earliest date on which the claimant has suffered actionable damage. The major difficulty is to determine when the claimant has suffered damage sufficient to found an action. A narrow construction of this requirement means that the claimant's cause of action is complete when he has suffered more than minimal damage as a result of the defendant's breach of duty,[8] but this fails to take account of the fact that in such circumstances, the claimant may be unaware of the fact of damage at that stage. As a result of this there have been suggestions that an alternative test should be applied to the effect that time should not begin to run against the claimant until, with reasonable diligence, he could have discovered that actionable damage had been suffered.[9] This second test, while disposing of the problem of unfairness to the claimant, does raise difficult policy issues concerning the desirability of open-ended liability. Eventually, it was determined by the House of Lords that the first of these tests, based on the mere fact of damage, should prevail,[10] leaving Parliament to legislate for difficult cases such as latent property damage and latent personal injury.

(i)   The meaning of damage

What constitutes actionable damage is a crucial consideration, since if common law rules do not recognise a particular variety of damage as being actionable under the tort of negligence, the claimant will not have a cause of action. Particular difficulties arise in distinguishing between damage to property, which is actionable under the tort of

---

5   *Duke of Brunswick and Luneberg v Harmer* (1849) 117 ER 75.
6   See *Darley Main Colliery Co v Mitchell* (1886) 11 App Cas 127; *Crumbie v Wallsend Local Board* [1891] 1 QB 503.
7   *Battishill v Reed* (1856) 18 CB 696.
8   *Cartledge v E Jopling & Sons Ltd* [1963] AC 758.
9   *Sparham–Souter v Town & Country Developments Ltd* [1976] QB 858.
10   *Pirelli General Cable Works v Oscar Faber & Partners* [1983] 2 AC 1.

negligence and merely defective property which, as a general rule, is not actionable. Where property is merely defective, all the claimant has suffered is pure economic loss, and, for reasons considered elsewhere, it is unlikely that any action under the tort of negligence will lie.[11]

Perhaps the greatest confusion in this area was created by the House of Lords in *Pirelli General Cable Works v Oscar Faber & Partners*[12] in which it was held that in a negligence action the claimant's cause of action accrues when damage is caused, but which went on to treat damage suffered by the owner of a building as a result of defects in plans prepared by a firm of architects as damage to property. In truth, what the owner of the building had received was a building that was not worth the amount he had paid for it. In the light of the decisions in *Murphy v Brentwood DC*[13] and *D & F Estates v Church Comrs for England*[14] it would appear that the kind of loss suffered by the owner of a building in cases of this kind should be reclassified as pure economic loss on the basis that a building is little more than a large scale product and that since the defectiveness of the building has resulted in no damage to anything other than the building itself what has been suffered is a mere decrease in value.

The effect of *Murphy* and *D & F Estates* is therefore to restrict the claimant's remedies in a significant way, despite the fact that much of what is contained in the Latent Damage Act 1986 is premised upon the existence of a duty of care in circumstances where the claimant suffers undiscoverable economic loss. If *Pirelli* is to be explained as a negligence case, it cannot be regarded as one involving physical harm to property. Instead, it seems that it must be regarded as a case of negligent advice that has resulted in economic loss in the form of diminution in the value of the building as a result of that advice. This, in turn, means that the requirements of *Hedley Byrne & Co Ltd v Heller & Partners Ltd*[15] will have to be complied with in order to establish liability on the part of the architects.

Where the loss suffered by the claimant results from a negligent act, the general principle of limitation of actions is that time will run from the date of damage. This may result in the claimant being out of time before he realises that he has suffered significant damage. Following the decision in *Murphy v Brentwood DC* there may be very limited circumstances in which economic loss caused by an negligent act remains actionable, but in these circumstances, the limitation problems may be even more complex. In cases such as *Junior Books Ltd v Veitchi Co Ltd*[16] which apparently survives the *Murphy* onslaught, it is arguable that the limitation period may run from one of two possible dates. In the first place, the loss suffered in cases like *Junior Books* is pure economic loss in the form of diminution in value, in which case it can be said that there is no damage to property. As a result it can be argued that one possible date from which time will run is the date on which the claimant first acquired an interest in the defective property, since this is the date on which he will bear the financial cost of putting right the defect in the property he has acquired. In most cases this will mean that the claimant is out of time well before any date on which he could possibly become aware of the nature of the damage suffered. Another view of the same argument is that it is the defect resulting from the negligent work which causes the expenditure incurred by the claimant rather than the mere existence of the faulty elements in the design of the

---

11   See chs 8, 10 and 25 considering the effect of the decision of the House of Lords in *Murphy v Brentwood DC* [1990] 2 All ER 908. It should be noted that this position does not prevail in other parts of the common law world, as to which see *Invercargill City Council v Hamlin* [1996] 1 All ER 756 (New Zealand); *Bryan v Maloney* (1995) 128 ALR 163 (Australia).
12   [1983] 2 AC 1.
13   [1990] 2 All ER 269.
14   [1988] 2 All ER 992.
15   [1964] AC 465.
16   [1983] 1 AC 520.

building, in which case time ought to run from the date on which the negligent work was completed.[17] An alternative argument is that since the kind of damage suffered is represented in the form of economic loss, time will not run against the claimant until it would be obvious to a reasonable person that the property concerned is not worth its unharmed market value.[18] The difficulty with this last approach is that it is at odds with the requirement in *Pirelli* that there should be physical damage to the claimant's property before the cause of action can accrue.[19] However, despite the fact that this argument is purely academic while the restrictions on the recovery of economic loss via the tort of negligence remain in place, LORD LLOYD in *Invercargill City Council v Hamlin* has provided a credible alternative starting date for the running of time, and, in the same process, has exposed the deficiencies of the decision in *Pirelli* by recognising that the existence of physical damage is a complete irrelevance in diminution in value claims. Instead, it has to be appreciated that diminution in value does not occur immediately and that the date of transfer of an interest in property should not be the date on which the cause of action accrues.

Under the present state of English law, the majority of claims for economic loss will have to be dealt with as cases of negligent misstatement, thereby falling within the principles laid down in *Hedley Byrne & Co Ltd v Heller & Partners Ltd.*[20] Sadly this distinction is very difficult to explain, even if there is a tenable distinction which can be drawn. The difficulty of distinguishing between the two can be witnessed in the reclassification of *Pirelli v Faber* as one of economic loss caused by negligent advice, despite the fact that the members of the House of Lords who decided the case quite clearly regarded it as a case involving material property damage resulting from a negligent act.

Where damage results from the giving of negligent advice, the date on which time will run against a claimant may depend on the nature of the advice given. In general terms, damage is caused by reliance on negligent advice, since this will be the date on which there will be financial detriment to the claimant. Accordingly, in the case of advice given by an architect or consultant engineer, the date of damage is likely to be the date on which the plans submitted by the professional are accepted by the claimant, despite the fact that, at this stage, the claimant is unlikely to have a possessory interest in the property yet to be built. In contrast, where a surveyor or a solicitor gives advice, it is likely to relate to existing property in which the claimant may already have an interest.

The precise position on the matter of limitation of actions relating to advice given by 'pure' service providers such as solicitors, accountants, stockbrokers, bankers and other financial service providers is complex. A number of possible dates may be suggested from which time should run against the claimant, which include the date on which advice is given; the date on which advice is acted upon; the date on which loss, as a result of acting upon the advice, is inevitable (sometimes called the 'no turning back' date) and the date on which financial loss is caused as a result of reliance on the advice.[1] An application of the decision in *Pirelli v Faber* would suggest that the last of these four possibilities is the appropriate date for the running of time, but in financial loss cases, the reliance of the claimant on the advice given by the defendant usually makes it

---

17 *London Congregational Union Incorporated v Harriss & Harriss (a firm)* [1988] 1 All ER 15 at 25 (per RALPH GIBSON LJ).

18 See *Invercargill City Council v Hamlin* [1996] 1 All ER 756.

19 Unfortunately, whenever the problem of the conflict between *Junior Books Ltd v Veitchi* and *Pirelli v Faber* has arisen, the court responsible for facing the conflict has side stepped the issue. See *Ketteman v Hansel Properties Ltd* [1985] 1 All ER 352; *Tozer Kemsley & Millbourn (Holdings) Ltd v Jarvis* (1983) 1 Const LJ 79.

20 [1964] AC 465

1 See eg *UBAF Ltd v European American Banking Corpn* [1984] QB 713.

inevitable that loss will be suffered, in which case, the 'no turning back' date may be more appropriate for the running of time against the claimant.

Part of the difficulty with negligent advice cases is that, in the past, the view was taken that liability should rest on the existence of a contract, in which case, it was assumed that the date of accrual of the cause of action should be the date on which the breach of contract occurred.[2] Accordingly, what became important was whether or not the claimant had relied on the advice given by the defendant rather than the date on which it became obvious that financial loss had been suffered. Thus in the case of a negligent failure by a solicitor to acquire a freehold interest in property, time ran from the date of the claimant acquiring an interest in the property rather than from the date on which the claimant sought to sell the property, despite the fact that the latter date was probably the earliest on which the claimant could have realised the consequences of the solicitor's negligence.[3] The difficulty with this line of reasoning, in the light of the later decision in *Pirelli*, is that the date of damage is not necessarily the date on which the breach of duty occurred and it was suggested that the decision in *Forster v Outred* could not survive. Despite this, later cases have confirmed the correctness of *Forster* on the basis that the date of breach will often be the date on which damage has been caused, since it is a question of fact in each case whether actual damage has been established.[4]

In the case of negligent advice on the part of a solicitor, the date of execution of the relevant document will not always be the relevant date for the purposes of the running of time. For example, a solicitor may give negligent advice with the result that his client's will becomes ineffective and an intended beneficiary is eventually denied a bequest which was otherwise intended. In such a case, the date of execution of the ineffective will may not be the appropriate starting point for the limitation period, since the claimant's action is not likely to be complete at that stage, since it is quite possible that the testator may change his mind at a later stage and alter the terms of his will. The logical answer seems to be that time will run against the beneficiary from the date of the testator's death, but this produces the unsatisfactory spectre of indeterminate liability,[5] subject only to a possible 15–year long-stop cut off date if the damage suffered is regarded as latent damage.[6]

Apart from solicitors, other professionals such as insurance brokers and surveyors may also give advice. In the case of advice given by an insurance broker, a particular problem may be that there has been a failure by the broker to reveal material facts to the insurer at the time of submitting a proposal for insurance. In these circumstances, the date on which the insured's cause of action seems to accrue is when a voidable insurance contract is procured, despite the fact that it will not usually be the case that the insured will realise that any harm has been suffered until he seeks to make a claim on the policy.[7] Surveyors are also capable of giving negligent advice, either in the form of an inaccurate survey report or in the form of a negligently prepared valuation. So far as inaccurate surveys are concerned, the position seems to be that damage is caused when the report is relied upon which will usually be the date on which the client irrevocably commits himself to acquiring an interest in the property which is the subject

2   See eg *Forster v Outred* [1982] 2 All ER 753; *Secretary of State for the Environment v Essex, Goodman and Suggitt* [1986] 2 All ER 69, [1986] 1 WLR 1432; *Bell v Peter Browne & Co* [1990] 3 All ER 124.
3   *Baker v Ollard & Bentley* (1982) 126 Sol Jo 593. See also *Sullivan v Layton, Lougher & Co* [1995] 2 EGLR 111.
4   *DW Moore & Co v Ferrier* [1988] 1 All ER 400 at 409 (per NEILL LJ).
5   *White v Jones* [1993] 3 All ER 481 at 492 (per SIR DONALD NICHOLLS V-C).
6   Limitation Act 1980, s 14B.
7   *Iron Trade Mutual Insurance Co Ltd v JK Buckenham Ltd* [1990] 1 All ER 808; *Islander Trucking Co Ltd v Hogg Robinson & Gardener Mountain (Marine) Ltd* [1990] 1 All ER 826.

matter of the report.[8] Prior to that date, the claimant will be in a position to avoid the expense of having to repair the defective building he subsequently acquires. Precisely what the relevant date is has given rise to some concern. In most of the cases to have considered the point, it has not been material to distinguish between the date of exchange of contracts and the date of completion,[9] with the result that it has made no difference whether the cause of action accrues when the property 'is bought' or when 'a deposit is paid on exchange'. However, the issue was directly in point in *Byrne v Hall Pain & Foster (a firm)*[10] in which the plaintiffs commissioned from the defendants a valuation report on a property they had an interest in purchasing. The report contained inaccuracies which were sufficient to establish an action for negligence. The writ was issued on 18 July 1994, completion having taken place on 22 July 1988 and exchange of contracts having taken place on 8 July 1988. Given the six-year time bar, it was crucial to determine whether the date of exchange or the date of completion was the relevant date for the purposes of the running of time. For these purposes, it was held that the cause of action accrued when contracts were exchanged rather than on completion, since that was the date on which the claimants had irrevocably committed themselves to acquiring an interest in a property which was worth less than the valuation led them to believe. According to Simon Brown LJ it was necessary to look for some 'detriment, liability or loss' including those which 'may arise on a contingency'.[11] For these purposes, once there was an exchange of contracts that detriment was intact.

In the case of negligent valuation, a financial institution may claim that loss has been suffered due to an inability to employ funds on other transactions since the negligence of the valuer has caused the commitment of funds to the transaction in respect of which the valuation was given. Moreover, it is likely that such a financial institution will lend more on the security of the property than they might otherwise lend, in the light of an over-valuation. If the date of the valuation is regarded as the date on which damage is caused, it is possible that the lender might be out of time before realising that they have an ineffective security for the funds they have lent. However, since the date on which damage is caused is a question of fact in each case, there may be other variables, which need to be taken into account. In the first place, it will be necessary for the lender to show that he would have used the money in the alternative manner suggested.[12] Accordingly, if the negligent valuer cannot prove that other transactions which could have been entered into during the relevant period would not have been of greater value than the transaction actually entered into, the losses suffered by the lender as a result of the inability to commit the funds are likely to be treated as actionable losses falling within the limitation period.[13]

(ii)   Latent damage

A particular problem concerning limitation periods is that of latent damage. This may consist of either personal injury or property damage that remains dormant for some years, only revealing itself in the form of some physical consequences well after the normal limitation period has expired. The issue of personal injury is considered in more detail below. The extension of tort law to negligently constructed buildings raised

---

8   *Secretary of State for the Environment v Essex, Goodman and Suggitt* [1986] 2 All ER 69, [1986] 1 WLR 1432.
9   See *Nykredit Mortgage Bank plc v Edward Erdman Group plc (No 2)* [1997] 1 WLR 1627 at 1630 (per Lord Nicholls).
10   [1999] 1 WLR 1849.
11   Ibid at 1857.
12   *Swingcastle Ltd v Alastair Gibson (a firm)* [1990] 3 All ER 433, affd [1991] 2 AC 223.
13   *First National Commercial Bank plc v Humberts (a firm)* [1995] 2 All ER 673.

problems of limitation where the building suffered from latent damage. The Latent Damage Act 1986 now governs the position in relation to defective buildings, and is dealt with elsewhere.[14]

Although the Latent Damage Act 1986 was introduced because of concern over the limitation periods in respect of defective buildings, it may have a wider application. The relevant provision is stated to apply to any action for damages for negligence, but this will not include an action in contract.[15] It seems that the reason for the exclusion of claims in contract is that the phrase 'any action for damages in negligence' in section 14A denotes circumstances in which there is a tortious duty of care. On this reasoning an action based on the tort of nuisance because no common law duty of care can be established or any action for the breach of a strict tortious duty, such as some actions in trespass or under the Animals Act 1971, ought also to fall outside the scope of the Latent Damage Act 1986. Personal injuries are specifically excluded but, as the Act does not define damage, it could be construed to apply to economic loss as well as physical damage.

Ordinarily time will start to run against a claimant for six years from the date on which damage is caused. However, as has been noted previously, in cases of latent damage this may mean that the claimant is out of time before he realises that he has suffered any damage. In order to meet this situation in circumstances in which a tortious duty of care is owed, the Limitation Act 1980, s 14A and s 14B provide for two possible limitation periods. The first of these runs for six years from the date on which damage is caused,[16] thereby preserving the principle established in *Pirelli General Cable Works v Oscar Faber & Partners*, but it seems unlikely that this will ever be the relevant starting date in cases of latent damage. The second, and alternative, starting date is based on the claimant's knowledge of facts relevant to his cause of action which allows the claimant to commence his action within three years of the date on which he acquired or should reasonably have acquired the necessary knowledge.[17] For practical purposes, however, the combined effect of section 14A(4)(a) and (b) is that there is a single limitation period which runs for six years from the date on which damage is caused, but which is capable of extension for a period of three years under section 14A(4)(b).[18] This analysis seems sensible, since the three year period in section 14A(4)(b) only comes into play if the period prescribed in section 14A(4)(a) has expired. Moreover, section 14A(3) refers to the 'applicable period' in the singular.[19] This analysis may prove to be particularly important in cases such as *Busby v Cooper* where the primary limitation period has already expired before the date on which the claimant could reasonably be aware that damage has been suffered.

Under section 14A(4)(b) the relevant starting date is the 'date of discoverability'. For these purposes, the claimant must have knowledge of two factors, namely, (a) of the material facts about the damage in respect of which damages are claimed and (b) of other facts relevant to the current action.[20] This covers not just actual knowledge, but also encompasses facts which a reasonable person suffering similar damage would regard as sufficiently serious to justify the institution of proceedings against a defendant who does not dispute liability and is in a position to satisfy a judgment.[1] For these purposes, it is necessary to consider what circumstances might persuade a reasonable person not

14   See ch 28.
15   Limitation Act 1980, s 14A(1); *Iron Trades Mutual Insurance Co Ltd v JK Buckenham Ltd* [1990] 1 All ER 808; *Société Commerciale de Réassurance v ERAS (International) Ltd* [1992] 2 All ER 82n.
16   Limitation Act 1980, s 14A(4)(a).
17   Limitation Act 1980, s 14A(4)(b).
18   *Busby v Cooper* [1996] CLC 1425.
19   Ibid at 1428–1429 (per HIRST LJ).
20   Limitation Act 1980, s 14A(6).
1   Limitation Act 1980, s 14A(7).

to commence proceedings. It has been held that it would not be reasonable for a claimant to delay the commencement of proceedings because of a fear that he might be exposed as an illegal immigrant,[2] since a reasonable person is taken to be someone who obeys the law. The requirement of knowledge on the part of the claimant will include knowledge acquired as a result of any expert advice he might have received.[3] Accordingly, it will be necessary to consider whether the claimant ought to have sought expert advice, and it will be no defence for a person to argue that he is ignorant of the damage suffered because he has failed to consult an expert, when in similar circumstances, a reasonable person would have sought advice. In some cases it may be that only minor damage is thought to have been suffered, but that this is later discovered to be much more serious. If the claimant is aware of the minor damage from the start, this may affect his claim, since a reasonable person might have been persuaded to sue at the earlier stage.[4] More specifically, the claimant must be aware that (a) the damage was attributable in whole, or in part to the act or omission which is alleged to constitute negligence; (b) of the identity of the defendant and (c) if it is alleged that the act or omission was that of a third party, of the identity of that person and the additional facts supporting the bringing of an action against the defendant.[5] From this, it follows that even if the claimant is aware that he has suffered significant damage, time will not run against him until he is aware that he may sue the defendant in respect of that damage. Also in the case of a claim against an employer alleging that he is vicariously liable for the acts of an employee, the effect of section 14A(8)(c) is that until the identity of the employee is known to the claimant, time will not start to run. Finally, a distinction is drawn between knowledge of facts and knowledge that, as a matter of law, an act or omission involves negligence, the last of these matters being irrelevant. Thus it will not be open to a claimant to extend the limitation period by arguing that he did not realise, as a matter of law, that there was a relevant breach of duty on the part of the defendant.

The main danger with a limitation period based on the knowledge of the claimant is that it is capable of producing the undesirable prospect of indeterminate liability. In order to counteract this danger, there is a long-stop provision in section 14B which runs not from the date of damage nor the date of knowledge, but from the date on which the relevant breach of duty occurred. In cases of latent damage covered by section 14A, the long-stop period runs for 15 years from the date of breach and can result in a claimant being time barred before his cause of action has even accrued under the 'date of discoverability' test.

(4) DAMAGES FOR PERSONAL INJURY AND DEATH

Special provisions on limitation of actions apply to cases of personal injury, since it has been recognised that the application of normal tort time limits may cause injustice where a person is deemed to be out of time before he could have been aware that any actionable damage had been suffered.

(i) The Definition of Personal Injury Actions

What amounts to an action for personal injury requires close consideration, since there are a number of instances in which it may be claimed that there has been an injury of a personal nature which does not fall within the precise language of the Limitation Act

---

2 *Coban v Allen* [1997] 8 Med LR 316.
3 Limitation Act 1980, s 14A(7).
4 See *Horbury v Craig Hall & Rutley* (1991) 7 PN 206; *Hamlin v Edwin Evans (a firm)* (1996) 29 HLR 414.
5 Limitation Act 1980, s 14A(8).

1980, section 11. Section 11(1) of that Act indicates that where a claimant or any other person suffers personal injury and may bring an action for negligence, nuisance or breach of duty (including a contractual or statutory duty), the provisions of the Act in respect of personal injuries shall apply.[6] Strictly construed, the language of section 11(1) does not cover simply an action *for* personal injury, but one where the damages claimed *consist of or include damages in respect of personal injury*. This will include both disease and impairment of mental condition[7] and almost certainly psychiatric damage and mental distress.[8]

Despite the fact that section 11 is couched in terms of 'damages in respect of personal injuries', it does not follow that all actions for damages in any way related to one for personal injuries fall within the scope of section 11. For example, where a person is injured in an accident but is denied compensation because of the negligence of his solicitor, section 11 does not apply, because the personal injury suffered by the claimant is not caused by the solicitor's negligence.[9] Similarly, there are actions which might, initially, appear to involve an element of personal injury, but which are, in fact, actions for economic loss. For example, where the claimant brings an action for 'wrongful conception' as a result of a failed sterilisation operation, the gist of the action is that the claimant has incurred extra expenditure in maintaining an unwanted child.[10] However, careful drafting of a claim may turn such an action into one for personal injury, since if the first sterilisation fails, the claimant may have to undergo a second sterilisation which inevitably involves a degree of pain and suffering. Moreover, the delivery of the unwanted child will also involve pain and suffering on the part of the mother and may result in an 'impairment' of the mother's condition.[11] The language used in section 11 indicates that an action for personal injury can emanate from the breach of a contractual duty. Thus the sale of a defective product, giving rise to a breach of the implied condition of satisfactory quality under the Sale of Goods Act 1979, section 14(2), which results in personal injury, would appear to fall within the scope of section 11. The fact that this involves the breach of a strict contractual obligation makes no difference.[12]

A particular problem which appears to arise from cases of 'wrongful conception' and cases involving the breach of a strict contractual obligation is that the claimant may have a choice between suing for different kinds of loss. As can be seen, a claimant suing for wrongful conception may frame his action in terms of either economic loss or in terms of personal injury. The decision in *Walkin v South Manchester Health Authority*[13] suggests that if the essence of the action is that personal injury has been suffered, it may be pleaded as such. The same may also be said of an action for breach of a strict contractual obligation to supply goods which are of satisfactory quality. In these circumstances, it would seem to be the case that where different kinds of loss have been suffered and they are sufficiently closely related, they may be treated as forming part of the same claim, since what matters is the underlying reality of the action brought by the claimant.[14]

---

6   However, the personal injury provisions do not apply to an action under the Protection from Harassment Act 1997, s 3: Limitation Act 1980, s 11(1A).
7   Limitation Act 1980, s 38(1).
8   See *Archer v Brown* [1985] QB 401; *Ichard v Frangoulis* [1977] 1 WLR 556.
9   *Ackbar v Green & Co* [1975] QB 582. Cf *Paterson v Chadwick* [1974] 1 WLR 890.
10   *Naylor v Preston Area Health Authority* [1987] 2 All ER 353.
11   *Walkin v South Manchester Health Authority* [1995] 4 All ER 132. Evidently, the same argument could not be applied to an action brought by the male parent of the unwanted child, since his loss would be purely financial.
12   *Howe v David Brown Tractors (Retail) Ltd* [1991] 4 All ER 30.
13   [1995] 4 All ER 132.
14   *Howe v David Brown Tractors (Retail) Ltd* [1991] 4 All ER 30 at 41 (per NICHOLLS LJ); *Walkin v South Manchester Health Authority* [1995] 4 All ER 132 at 142 (per AULD LJ).

Where the claimant is the victim of a deliberate act of violence, it is self-evident that there may have been personal injury, but it does not follow from this that the action will fall within the scope of section 11. In *Stubbings v Webb*[15] the House of Lords ruled that the victim of child sexual abuse in the 1970s, who had subconsciously attempted to forget her traumatic experience and did not commence proceedings until August 1987, having reached the age of majority in January 1975, was out of time. The reason given was that the normal six-year limitation period applied, which, in the case of intentional torts, runs from the date of the wrongful act. It had been argued for the victim that her subconscious attempt to forget the incident meant that she had no knowledge of the facts relevant to her cause of action until a much later date, in which case the 'date of knowledge' test under section 11 should apply. However, the court concluded that the Tucker Committee Report of 1949,[16] on whose recommendations special rules applicable to personal injury cases were based, had made it clear that intentional torts should not fall within the scope of the special rules, subsequently adopted, applicable to actions for damages for personal injury. Arguably, this might have been a correct stance to adopt in 1949 when there was no discretion to extend the limitation period in personal injury cases, but the law has moved on since that time. Nevertheless, the basis of the decision in *Stubbings v Webb* is that where there is a deliberate breach of duty, section 11 does not apply, since it is concerned only with accidental harm. Against this, it may be argued that in cases of battery, what is required is that the defendant should merely intend to commit the act which results in harm to the claimant, but there is no requirement that the defendant should intend to cause personal injury.[17] Sadly, the effect of the decision in *Stubbings v Webb* is to place the victim of a deliberate battery in a weaker position than the person who is the victim of accidentally inflicted harm. All of this does not mean that, in every case in which the claimant is the victim of a deliberate action, the claimant will be denied the opportunity to bring his case within the special provisions on personal injuries. It is important to ascertain what is the gist of the claimant's action against the defendant. In some instances, the gist of the action may be that there has been a failure to exercise reasonable care. For example, if there is an allegation of deliberate sexual abuse by a male relative coupled with an allegation that the mother of the victim failed to take reasonable care to protect the victim from exposure to the risk of injury, section 11 may apply.[18]

(ii)   Limitation periods applicable to actions for personal injury

Where the damages claimed by the plaintiff consist of or include a claim for damages for personal injuries, the limitation period runs for three years from the date of accrual of the cause of action or from the date on which the claimant had the knowledge of facts relevant to the cause of action.[19] This three-year period applies to actions for negligence, nuisance or breach of duty, whether the duty arises by virtue of a contract, or by virtue of a provision made by or under a statute, or independently of any such contract or any such provision.[20]

The reference to the date of knowledge is designed to deal with injustice caused by latent damage. In *Cartledge v E Jopling & Sons Ltd*,[1] the House of Lords had held that, in a pneumoconiosis case, time started to run as soon as damage occurred which, in this

---

15   [1993] AC 498.
16   *Report of the Committee on the Limitation of Actions*, Cmd 7740, 1949, para 23.
17   See eg *Wilson v Pringle* [1986] 2 All ER 440.
18   *Seymour v Williams* [1995] PIQR P470.
19   Limitation Act 1980, s 11(4).
20   Ibid, s 11(1).
1   [1963] 1 All ER 341.

case, was the date on which the lung tissue was scarred. However, a medical examination might not have revealed the damage at that stage.

The date of knowledge test requires the court to consider when the claimant first knew of certain facts relevant to the cause of action.[2] Although the language of section 14 is couched in terms of the knowledge of the claimant, the relevant knowledge may be that of another person, such as a parent who has taken over effective management of the claimant's affairs in the capacity of an agent.[3]

Knowledge is also a very difficult word to define. At one extreme it can be said that a person does not have knowledge until he is certain that a particular state of affairs exists, but on the other hand it can be argued that a person has knowledge of a fact where there is a reasonable suspicion that a relevant state of affairs exists. Accordingly, there is an important distinction to be drawn between 'knowledge' and mere 'belief'. For example, it may be the case that a claimant consults a medical expert regarding worrying symptoms which are believed to have been caused by negligence and is given medical advice that there is no cause for concern. In such a case, there may have been a belief that harm had been caused, but the subsequent advice may serve to allay fears and prevent the claimant from having the necessary knowledge to allow time to run against the claimant.[4] Alternatively, a 'fault principle' may be applied. For example, if a hospital trust is guilty of giving negative information, it is quite likely that a claimant will be treated as someone who has not been given the requisite information regarding the nature of his possible claim.[5] Clearly, it is a question of fact, in each case, whether the claimant has the necessary knowledge, since in some cases, the claimant will not have the required knowledge until he has consulted an expert, but in other cases, the degree of harm suffered may be sufficient to suggest to the reasonable person that there are grounds for concern without the need to seek expert advice. On this basis the mere fact that there is a firm belief that injury has been suffered will not necessarily mean that the claimant has knowledge of the fact that he has suffered actionable damage. Certainly, something which amounts to no more than a vague suspicion that harm has been suffered should not suffice to allow time to run against a claimant. However, if the claimant has a strong belief that he has sufficient grounds for seeking legal advice, even in the face of medical advice which might suggest the contrary, he may be taken to have the knowledge required for the purposes of section 11.[6]

Section 14 (1) sets out a number of factors which should be considered in determining whether the claimant has the knowledge necessary to allow time to run against him. These include knowledge that the injury was significant[7] in that the plaintiff would have reasonably considered it sufficiently serious to justify instituting proceedings against a defendant who did not dispute liability and was able to satisfy a judgment.[8] The wording of section 14(1)(a) indicates that it is concerned with both the person injured and the personal representatives of that person. Either party must have reasonable grounds for believing that the injury suffered is sufficient to justify the commencement of legal proceedings. For these purposes, section 14(3) provides that if it is reasonable to consult an expert, the injured person may be taken to have the knowledge of that expert. The

2   Limitation Act 1980, s 14.
3   *O' Driscoll v Dudley Health Authority* [1996] 7 Med LR 408.
4   *Stephen v Riverside Health Authority* [1990] 1 Med LR 261; *Nash v Eli Lilly & Co* [1993] 4 All ER 383. The difficulty with this line of argument is that if a person has 'knowledge' but is then disabused of that knowledge by subsequent advice, the required 'knowledge' may have existed. In this case, once time starts to run, it cannot be prevented from doing so.
5   *Bentley v Bristol & Weston Health Authority* [1991] 2 Med LR 359.
6   *Nash v Eli Lilly & Co* [1993] 4 All ER 383 at 396 (per PURCHAS LJ).
7   Ibid, s 14(1)(a).
8   Ibid, s 14(2).

difficulty of interpretation presented by the combination of the language used in sections 14(1) and 14(2) is that there are both subjective and objective elements comprised in the joint test created by these provisions. Inevitably, where subjective elements play a part, the end result is that each case will turn on its own particular facts. As a result, it may be necessary to consider 'would this plaintiff have considered the injury sufficiently serious'?[9] The difficulty with the interaction between section 14(1) and section 14(2) is that the latter requires consideration of the injured person's individual circumstances, whereas section 14(1) is couched in much more objective terms. Accordingly, a person of 'modest intellectual capacity' may be judged differently from one with a 'higher intellectual capacity.'[10] Nevertheless there are objective elements in the test posited by section 14(2) since the court must consider the seriousness of the injury and the value which can be placed upon it, although this must be set against the fact that the notional defendant adverted to in section 14(2) is one who is solvent and admits liability. For this reason, the central emphasis should be on the quantum of the injury rather than the claimant's subjective valuation of it, so that time should not run against a claimant if he could reasonably have accepted the injury as a fact of life which is not worth bothering about.[11]

Also to be considered is that the injury should be attributable, in whole or in part, to the alleged wrongful act or omission.[12] For these purposes, it may be sufficient that the claimant has no more than a general knowledge that his injuries are attributable to the defendant's act even if he is not aware of the specific act or omission which forms the basis of the action.[13] However, this broad test may have been undermined by more recent authority. In *Broadley v Guy Clapham & Co*[14] the plaintiff underwent an operation for the removal of a foreign body from her knee in 1980. After the operation her condition did not improve and later examinations revealed that she was suffering from left foot drop and nerve palsy. In 1983 she consulted a surgeon who advised that the 1980 operation might have been conducted negligently, but no further legal action was taken until 1990 when the plaintiff consulted a second firm of solicitors. The plaintiff's present action was against the first firm of solicitors employed by her in the 1980s. The Court of Appeal concluded that the words in section 14(1)(b) 'which is alleged to constitute...breach of duty' do no more than identify the facts of which the claimant should be aware before time begins to run, but the claimant does not need to be aware that those facts point to the existence of a breach of a rule of law or other code of behaviour.[15] Unfortunately for claimants, this line of reasoning means that injury is caused as soon as the relevant operation is carried out, but a possible resultant argument is that every time a successful operation is carried out, the claimant has suffered injury. However, the Court of Appeal in *Dobbie v Medway Health Authority*[16] has rejected this view on the ground that the hypothetical instance would not fall within the definition of personal injury in the Limitation Act 1980, section 38(1). It seems, therefore, that injury is suffered

9   *McCafferty v Metropolitan Police District Receiver* [1977] 1 WLR 1073 at 1081 (per GEOFFREY LANE LJ).
10 *Davis v City & Hackney Health Authority* [1991] 2 Med LR 366. Cf the treatment of 'trivial' injury in *Miller v London Electrical Manufacturing Co Ltd* [1976] 2 Lloyd's LR 284 at 287 (per LORD DENNING MR).
11 *Dobbie v Medway Health Authority* [1994] 4 All ER 450 at 457 (per SIR THOMAS BINGHAM MR).
12 Ibid, s 14(1)(b).
13 See *Wilkinson v Ancliff (BLT) Ltd* [1986] 3 All ER 427, in which the plaintiff was aware, in broad terms, that his working conditions had exposed him to danger and that his employers had not taken reasonable care to protect him.
14 [1994] 4 All ER 439.
15 Ibid at 448 (per HOFFMANN LJ). See also the distinction drawn in the same case between broad knowledge and specific knowledge which are covered by s 14(1)(b) and qualitative and detailed knowledge which are not at 446–447 (per BALCOMBE LJ). See also *Dobbie v Medway Health Authority* [1994] 4 All ER 450 at 456 (per SIR THOMAS BINGHAM MR).
16 Ibid.

at the time of an operation which many years later may reveal grounds for complaint. This line of argument may not apply in all cases, especially where there has been a negligent omission which results in a necessary medical procedure being delayed. In the case of an omission it would be difficult to say that the claimant is immediately aware that there has been negligence on the part of the defendant. For example if there is a delay on the part of a surgeon in carrying out a procedure which would have prevented the subsequent amputation of the claimant's leg, there is no immediate knowledge on the part of the claimant that damage has been suffered *as a result of the defendant's negligence*, since, usually, this can only be confirmed by subsequent advice from an independent expert.[17] In these circumstances, there is a difference between cases in which there is an operation (an act) followed by a deterioration in condition which should be immediately noticeable, and cases of omission based on negligent advice where it is not immediately obvious that any damage has been caused.[18] On this basis, it is clear that section 14(1)(b) is concerned with causation rather than with attributability to the defendant's breach of duty.[19]

The claimant must also be aware of the identity of the defendant[20] . From this it follows that in the case of a 'hit-and-run' traffic accident, the claimant cannot be time barred until such time as he becomes aware of the identity of the driver. Other problems associated with this provision may arise where an employee is injured at work, but the 'employer' is part of a larger group of companies, the identity of which is not immediately ascertainable.[1] However, it is always possible that an employee might have constructive knowledge of the identity of the defendant if he can make enquiries of a relevant regulatory agent.[2]

If the act or omission alleged to amount to an actionable breach of duty was that of a person other than the defendant, the claimant must also be aware of the identity of that other person and the additional facts supporting the bringing of an action against the defendant.[3] Ordinarily this will cover cases of vicarious liability and the claimant will have to be aware that the person responsible for his injuries is an employee of the defendant so that proceedings against the latter may be commenced.

Section 14(3) makes it clear that the claimant's knowledge of relevant facts does not have to be actual knowledge, since a court may take account of facts which he could have ascertained with the assistance of expert advice. Consideration may also be given to 'facts which are observable or ascertainable by the plaintiff.' What is ascertainable or observable seems to require consideration of objective factors only, although the courts do not seem to be agreed on this issue. One view is that although the general test to be applied is objective, it may be necessary to consider the position, circumstances and character of the individual claimant.[4] On this view, a patient who suffers injury during the course of an operation but does not immediately seek a second opinion due to his lack of intellect would appear to be in a better position than the patient who does seek a second opinion and is, thereby, taken to have the knowledge of the expert. Moreover, a further consequence of this approach is that a defendant could be exposed to a stale claim many years after the event to which it relates and which would be

---

17   See *Forbes v Wandsworth Health Authority* [1996] 4 All ER 881.
18   Ibid at 886 (per STUART-SMITH LJ).
19   See also *Spargo v North Essex District Health Authority* [1997] 8 Med LR 125.
20   Limitation Act 1980, s 14(1)(c).
1   *Simpson v Norwest Holst Southern Ltd* [1980] 1 WLR 968.
2   *Nash v Eli Lilly & Co* [1993] 4 All ER 383, applying Limitation Act 1980, s 14(3)(a). Other difficult cases may arise where there are two possible defendants in which case the claimant should sue each in the alternative: *Halford v Brookes* [1991] 3 All ER 559 at 574 (per LORD DONALDSON MR).
3   Ibid, s 14(1)(d).
4   *Nash v Eli Lilly & Co* [1993] 4 All ER 383 at 399 (per PURCHAS LJ).

difficult to contest. However, in *Forbes v Wandsworth Health Authority*,[5] a majority of the Court of Appeal found it difficult to agree with this proposition.[6] Since both are decisions of the Court of Appeal, the earlier decision ought to have been regarded as binding, however, the language of section 14(3) suggests an objective test, which would seem to support the majority view in *Forbes*. In support of *Nash v Eli Lilly,* policy considerations operate against the approach in *Forbes* as was admitted by the majority,[7] since if a claimant has to act quickly, this might encourage 'ambulance chasing' on the part of lawyers, which, in turn, could damage the doctor–patient relationship. Moreover, it should be noted that special cases which deserve consideration of subjective factors can be dealt with by way of the discretion to extend time under section 33. In any case, there may also be circumstances in which the relevant facts are plainly ascertainable by the claimant himself, without the need to consult an expert, in which case, the claimant will be taken to have the required knowledge despite the fact that there has been a delay in ascertaining the relevant facts on the part of a legal advisor. Thus in *Henderson v Temple Pier Co Ltd*[8] the claimant was injured when she slipped on entering a moored boat which had been converted as a restaurant. Her argument was that her solicitors had not ascertained the identity of the owners by the time the limitation period expired, but this was considered to be a fact which could have been ascertained by the claimant herself, without the need to resort to expert advice.

In cases such as *Forbes* it is possible to adopt one of two different approaches. On the one hand, the claimant can simply accept the fact that the operation has gone wrong, keep faith with his medical advisor, and do nothing. Alternatively, he may become suspicious and seek a further opinion. In this latter event, the claimant will be taken to be aware that he has suffered significant injury, but the same may not be true of the patient who does nothing. In *Forbes* it was considered to be unfair to the defendant to allow a stale claim to be heard many years later and that a claimant should be fixed with constructive knowledge at a relatively early date, subject to one possible exception where the initial injury is of no great significance, but which later develops into a much more serious complaint.[9] Under section 14(3)(b) where a claimant has no knowledge, or claims to have no knowledge of relevant facts, he can be treated as having constructive knowledge of those facts where the assertion of lack of knowledge is not realistic. This would appear to be the case where the victim of childhood sexual abuse argues that, subconsciously, he or she attempted to forget the distasteful experience.[10] The most likely circumstance in which the constructive knowledge rules will come into play is where the claimant ought to have made enquiries, has failed to do so and those enquiries would have readily provided the claimant with the necessary knowledge.[11] Other relevant considerations under section 14(3) are that a claimant may have been aware of a relevant fact at one stage, but his memory has subsequently failed. A logical response to this is that if a person has knowledge of a fact, he cannot later claim to have lost that knowledge, since relevant provisions of the Limitation Act 1980 refer to the date on which a person *first* had knowledge of a relevant fact.[12] However, the claimant's amnesia may result from a disability, in which case the Limitation Act 1980, section 28 will prevent time from running against him while the disability lasts. This will apply to a child under the

---

5   [1996] 4 All ER 881.
6   Ibid at 891 (per STUART-SMITH LJ.).
7   Ibid at 890 (per STUART-SMITH LJ).
8   [1998] 3 All ER 324.
9   Ibid (per STUART-SMITH LJ).
10   *Stubbings v Webb* [1993] 2 WLR 120 at 126 (per LORD GRIFFITHS).
11   See eg *Farmer v National Coal Board* (1985) Times, 27 April, CA; *Boynton v British Steel plc* [1997] CLY 655.
12   *Nash v Eli Lilly & Co* [1993] 4 All ER 383 at 395 (per PURCHAS LJ).

age of majority (a legal disability) who acquires factual knowledge, but, subsequently, genuinely forgets the matters in question and does not recall them until after achieving the age of majority.[13] Finally, it should be observed that the proviso to section 14(3) indicates that a claimant will not be fixed with constructive knowledge ascertainable with the advice of an expert so long as all reasonable steps have been taken to obtain that advice and, where appropriate, act on that advice. For these purposes, subjective considerations are important, so that the resources, intelligence and state of health of the claimant may be taken into account. Moreover, it will also be relevant to consider any omissions in a report to the claimant by his expert, since these omissions may relate to facts which the claimant would have needed to be aware of before being able to commence his action.[14]

Where the action relates to the death of a relative and is brought under the Law Reform (Miscellaneous Provisions) Act 1934, the limitation period runs for three years from the date of death or the date of the personal representative's knowledge, whichever is later.[15] If the action is brought under the Fatal Accidents Act 1976, the limitation period runs for three years from the date of death or the date of knowledge of the person for whose benefit the action is brought, whichever is later.[16] In either case, if the deceased himself was time barred, the estate or the dependants will have no action.

(iii)   Discretionary extension of the limitation period

The court is given a discretion to allow an action to be commenced after the statutory limitation period has expired, provided the circumstances justify this, whether the action is brought under section 11 by a surviving claimant or under section 12 by the representatives of a deceased person.[17] The discretion may be exercised where the court considers it equitable to do so, having regard to any prejudice caused to the plaintiff by adhering to the time limits, and any prejudice caused to the defendant by extending them. It follows from this that the definition of the word 'prejudice' is crucial to the operation of the discretion and it should be noted that prejudice may affect both the claimant and the defendant. Clearly, the prejudice to the claimant will be based upon the fact that there may have been circumstances, not covered by other provisions of the Limitation Act 1980, which act as an impediment to the bringing of an action. In contrast, the prejudice to the defendant will lie in the fact that he will have to defend an action which, in other circumstances, would have been regarded as time barred. A particular factor which will be taken into account is the relative strength or weakness of the claimant's case, since the stronger his case is, the greater the prejudice will be if his action is ruled to be out of time. On the face of it, the fact that the claimant's action is ruled to be out of time will always cause prejudice. However, if the strength of the claim is so weak that to allow it to progress would do no more than to give it a nuisance value, there would be no prejudice to the claimant.[18] In contrast, by allowing the action to proceed, the defendant inevitably suffers prejudice through the denial of his 'windfall' limitation defence. Moreover, in cases where the claimant's case against the defendant is very strong, there is arguably even greater prejudice to the defendant because of the increased likelihood of success on the part of the claimant. Thus, paradoxically, the prejudice to the defendant is at its lowest in cases where the claimant's chances of success are the weakest.

13   *Colegrove v Smyth* [1994] 5 Med LR 111 at 116 (per BUCKLEY J).
14   *Marston v British Railways Board* [1976] ICR 124.
15   Limitation Act 1980, s 11(5).
16   Ibid, s 12(2).
17   Ibid, s 33(1).
18   *Thompson v Brown* [1981] 1 WLR 744 at 750 (per LORD DIPLOCK).

Although the issue of prejudice to both parties is a relevant factor, there are other considerations set out in section 33 which must be taken into account since, judicially, they are regarded as mandatory requirements, where relevant.[19] However, other considerations may also be relevant[20] and it is clear that an appellate court will not lightly interfere with a decision taken by the trial judge on the facts of a particular case.[1] Moreover, it is important to bear in mind that the main reason for the development of the discretion was to deal with cases of 'long maturing industrial diseases' resulting from the negligence or breach of statutory duty of an employer[2] and that courts might be less sympathetic in other cases.

Where the discretion is exercised in favour of the claimant, there is undoubtedly prejudice to the defendant and that prejudice is all the greater where the defendant has no defence other than his reliance on the fact that the claimant is out of time. This may be a very relevant consideration where the defendant and his insurers have gone through a process of slowly increasing offers of settlement over a protracted period of time with the result that the claimant's writ is issued out of time.[3] Perhaps the most important consideration in assessing the meaning of prejudice is the extent of the claimant's delay. In cases where there is a considerable delay there will be very great prejudice to the defendant in having to defend a stale claim, but where the claimant is only a few days late and the defendant has little chance of successfully defending the action, there can be little prejudice to the defendant in real terms.

Another cause of possible prejudice to the defendant is that the claimant may have a strong case against another possible defendant, such as a legal advisor responsible for the delay. Even though the case against the legal advisor may be strong, there are other countervailing circumstances which ought to be taken into account. In the first place, there will still be some uncertainty over the likely success of the possible action against the advisor, there will be a need to instruct new legal advisors[4] and the defendant legal advisors will also have a detailed knowledge of the facts relating to the claimant's action.[5]

Public policy considerations may also be relevant, since it needs to be asked how far a defendant's insurers should be allowed to shift responsibility when they have received the payment of insurance premiums.[6]

Apart from the specific factors dealt with in section 33(3), the court must take account of 'all the circumstances of the case'. This will allow the court to consider the insurance position of the defendant, since if the action is allowed to proceed out of time, he will not have to absorb the full cost of compensating the claimant. As a result of this the defendant and his insurer can be satisfactorily regarded as a 'composite unit', but this can work to the disadvantage of a claimant, since an insurer is entitled to be placed in the same position as an uninsured defendant and claim the benefit of the limitation defence when the claimant's action is out of time.[7] On similar lines, the court may also take account of the legal position in determining where the balance of prejudice lies, especially since this can produce an additional prejudice for the defendant as he is unlikely to recover costs against a legally aided claimant should his defence succeed.[8]

19 *Halford v Brookes* [1991] 3 All ER 559 at 566 (per RUSSELL LJ).
20 For example the size of any possible award of damages.
1   Ibid.
2   *Thompson v Brown* [1981] 1 WLR 744 at 747 (per LORD DIPLOCK).
3   See *Hartley v Birmingham City District Council* [1992] 2 All ER 213 (writ one day late).
4   *Thompson v Brown* [1981] 1 WLR 744 at 750 (per LORD DIPLOCK).
5   See *Hartley v Birmingham City District Council* [1992] 2 All ER 213.
6   See *Firman v Ellis* [1978] QB 886 at 905 (per LORD DENNING MR). Although the position may be different where there is more than one insurer and there are two potential defendants: *Deerness v John R Keeble & Son (Brantham) Ltd* [1983] 2 Lloyd's Rep 260 at 264 (per LORD DIPLOCK).
7   See *Kelly v Bastible* [1997] 8 Med LR 15.
8   *Hartley v Birmingham City District Council* [1992] 2 All ER 213 at 577 (per LORD DONALDSON MR).

Section 33(3) sets out a specific check-list of relevant considerations which a court must take into account, where relevant. These include the length of delay, the reasons for the delay, the effect of the delay on the cogency of the evidence, and the conduct of the claimant and defendant. The delay adverted to in section 33(3)(a) is that which occurs between the date on which the primary limitation period expires and the date on which the claimant asks the court to exercise its discretion in favour of the claimant. Strictly, the delay which runs from the date on which the cause of action accrued is irrelevant, except that it may be regarded as one of the overall circumstances of the case.[9] A second consideration is the extent to which the defendant's evidence is likely to lack cogency in the light of the claimant's delay.[10] This would appear to cover cases in which the defendant or his insurers may have disposed of paperwork relating to the claimant's action or vital witnesses may have lost recollection of events relating to the claim. Nevertheless, there may be circumstances in which this argument loses its force, such as where the relevant evidence can be obtained from another source or where there has been a public inquiry into the events surrounding a particular accident. Also relevant to the exercise of the discretion is the conduct of the defendant after the cause of action arose.[11] In this respect it seems to be relevant to consider whether the defendant has responded reasonably and swiftly to any requests for the supply of information or whether he has acted in an obstructive manner or has attempted to delay a possible settlement. Also relevant to the possible exercise of the discretion is the duration of any disability suffered by the claimant after the date of accrual of the cause of action.[12] Disability, for these purposes, will not include legal disabilities such as unsoundness of mind or minority present before the date of accrual of the cause of action, since these will prevent time from running at all against the claimant until the disability has abated.[13] Where there is a supervening disability, which appears to include both unsoundness of mind and physical disability,[14] the court may override the time bar if it appears right to do so. This appears to be justified on the ground that the disability may make it difficult for the claimant to recall relevant events. A further consideration under section 33 is the extent to which the claimant has acted promptly and reasonably once he is aware that he has an action for damages against the defendant.[15] This will involve an enquiry as to blame on the part of the claimant, which will necessarily involve consideration of subjective factors. Thus it may be relevant to consider the claimant's emotional state and whether there is a desire not to prejudice an existing relationship with another person. Finally, regard may also be had to the steps taken by the claimant to obtain expert advice and the nature of that advice.[16] Here it will be relevant to consider whether the claimant has consulted an advisor but has been given bad advice with the result that his action is commenced out of time.[17] Provided the claimant has acted swiftly once the misapprehension has been corrected, it is likely that a court will allow an action to begin out of time.

The discretion is wide, since it is not limited to the factors stated in section 33 and has been stated to be unfettered.[18] However, this view may not be entirely accurate

9   *Donovan v Gwentoys Ltd* [1990] 1 All ER 1018.
10   Limitation Act 1980, s 33(3)(b).
11   Ibid s 33(3)(c).
12   Ibid s 33(3)(d).
13   Ibid s 28.
14   *Pilmore v Northern Trawlers Ltd* [1986] 1 Lloyd's Rep 552. This is despite the fact that the Limitation Act 1980, s 38(2) is supposed to be a complete definition of disability and does not include physical disability.
15   Limitation Act 1980, s 33(3)(e).
16   Ibid s 33(3)(f).
17   See *Halford v Brookes* [1991] 3 All ER 559.
18   *Firman v Ellis* [1978] QB 886, [1978] 2 All ER 851; *Donovan v Gwentoys Ltd* [1990] 1 WLR 472.

since there are certain limits to the discretion where the claimant has commenced proceedings and then discontinued them. In this case the discretion will only be exercised in the claimant's favour in the most exceptional circumstances. For example, in *Walkley v Precision Forgings Ltd*[19] a distinction was drawn between a claimant who had failed to issue a writ within the primary three-year limitation period and one who had done so, but failed to continue the action and then asked for permission to issue a second writ out of time. The reason given for this approach was that other than in very exceptional circumstances the claimant could not be said to have been prejudiced by the operation of either section 11 or section 12 since the true cause of any prejudice would be the claimant's own delay. Furthermore, in such circumstances there must always be inevitable prejudice to the defendant in having to defend the action, incur expenditure and face the risk of liability.[20] The rationale behind these cases, then, is that the first action would have been struck out for want of prosecution or because the claimant has of his own volition given up the claim, and whichever way the matter is viewed, the wounds are self-inflicted.[1] The exceptional cases adverted to in *Walkley* seem to include cases in which there has been misrepresentation or improper conduct on the part of the defendant,[2] cases where the first writ was invalid,[3] cases in which the validity of the first writ is extended and cases in which it can be said that the claimant did not have the required knowledge of relevant facts for the purposes of section 14. In this last case, the necessary prerequisites for the running of time will not be in place.[4] The difficulty with this view is that if the claimant has gone to the trouble of issuing the first writ this might suggest that he does have the required knowledge, except, perhaps, in cases of omission on the part of the defendant.

5. MISCELLANEOUS TIME LIMITS

(1) DEFECTIVE PRODUCTS

An action under the Consumer Protection Act 1987 must be brought within three years of suffering the relevant damage, or within three years of acquiring the necessary knowledge if this is later.[5] No action may be brought more than ten years after the product was first put into circulation.[6] The latter provision provides a longstop similar to the fifteen-year period under the Latent Damage Act 1986.

(2) FRAUD, CONCEALMENT AND MISTAKE

Where the claimant's action is based on the defendant's fraud, or where any fact relevant to his right of action is deliberately concealed by the defendant, the limitation period does not begin to run until the claimant has, or ought with reasonable diligence to have discovered, the fraud or concealment.[7] The provisions on fraud or concealment

19   [1979] 1 WLR 606. See also *Forward v Hendricks* [1997] 2 All ER 395.
20   Ibid at 618–619 per LORD DIPLOCK.
1   Ibid.
2   Here the defendant appears to be estopped from denying the justice of the claimant's action and from relying on ss 11 and 12, but there must be an unequivocal waiver of any intention to rely on the limitation defence and not just an apparent acceptance of liability: *Forward v Hendricks* [1997] 2 All ER 395 at 403 (per WALLER LJ).
3   Here the first writ is treated as a nullity, in which case the ability to serve a second writ may be barred by the operation of ss 11 or 12.
4   See *Stephen v Riverside Health Authority* [1990] 1 Med LR 261.
5   Consumer Protection Act 1987, s 5(5) and Sch 1. See also ch 25.
6   Ibid.
7   Limitation Act 1980, s 32(1).

apply to both tort and contract actions. What is required is that the claimant should have acted diligently, with the result that he will not be required to have taken all possible steps to discover the fraud or concealment, but must have acted as would a reasonable person.[8]

For the purposes of section 32, an allegation of fraud must be an essential element in the claimant's action against the defendant.[9] Accordingly, in actions in which an allegation of fraud is not essential, section 32 can have no application. Moreover, what must be undiscoverable is the fraud of the defendant rather than the damage suffered by the claimant.[10]

The concept of concealment is wide, encompassing circumstances in which a defendant is aware that he is guilty of a breach of duty and has taken steps to hide that fact. Strictly construed, the language of section 32 appears to be confined to cases in which the deliberate concealment predates the accrual of the cause of action; as a result it may not apply to cases of 'subsequent concealment'.[11] If this is correct, it could cause serious problems in cases of latent damage to buildings, since it is often the case that damage is not discovered for some considerable time after there has been a breach of duty by the defendant. The case law on defective buildings seems to suggest that the mere fact that negligent work has been covered up by the defendant is not, per se, sufficient to give rise to an inference of fraud,[12] and that it is important to have regard to the nature of the relationship between the parties. For example, it may be that a commercial organisation is expected to be able to employ specialists in order to discover attempts to cover up defects.

In professional negligence cases, the situation may arise in which incorrect advice is given, but the not corrected. In such a case the question may arise whether there has been an act of concealment. Generally, it is accepted that the initial negligent act or omission is not to be regarded as deliberate concealment. Instead what is required is some additional act amounting to concealment of the breach of duty. It has been observed that one construction of section 32 is that it cannot apply once time has started to run against the claimant, which resulted in some courts taking the view that the act of concealment was an additional breach of duty, thereby founding a new cause of action,[13] but this avoided the issue whether subsequent deliberate concealment fell within the scope of section 32. In *Sheldon v RHM Outhwaite (Underwriting Agencies) Ltd*[14] the matter was considered directly and a bare majority of the House of Lords ruled that section 32 could apply where the claimant's action had already accrued at the time of the act of concealment. In *Sheldon,* Lloyd's names commenced proceedings in 1992 against a firm of member agents, alleging negligence which had occurred in 1982. It was also alleged that members of the firm of agents had deliberately concealed important facts relating to its conduct after the alleged act of initial negligence. Part of the argument for the claimants was that a new limitation period, based on the concealment, came into operation under section 32. A bare majority of the House of Lords held that there had been a deliberate concealment and that it did not matter whether this occurred before or after the date of breach of duty on the part of the defendants. The basis of the decision appears to have been policy driven rather than being based strictly upon the wording of section 32, since it seems to be clear from the language of the section

8   *Peco Arts Inc v Hazlitt Gallery Ltd* [1983] 1 WLR 1315.
9   *Beaman v ARTS Ltd* [1949] 1 KB 550.
10   *RB Policies at Lloyd's v Butler* [1950] 1 KB 76.
11   *Tito v Waddell (No 2)* [1977] Ch 106 at 245 (per MEGARRY V-C).
12   *William Hill Organisation Ltd v Bernard Sunley & Sons Ltd* (1982) 22 BLR 1.
13   *Kitchen v Royal Air Forces Association* [1958] 2 All ER 241. Another possible approach is to treat a professional advisor as a fiduciary who is under an obligation to disclose the true facts.
14   [1995] 2 All ER 558.

that if time has started to run against a claimant, whatever the defendant does later cannot affect the running of time.[15] The majority in *Sheldon* appear to have taken the view that section 32 should be interpreted as a protective mechanism to prevent the defendant from covering up his wrongdoing by subsequent conduct. The view expressed by MEGARRY V-C in *Tito v Waddell* was taken to refer to the specific wording of the Limitation Act 1939 and did not take account of the change in the Limitation Act 1980 section 1(2) which allows for the 'extension or exclusion' of ordinary time limits under Part II of the Act.[16] The difficulty with this interpretation is that section 32(1)(b) serves to exclude the primary limitation period whether the concealment occurs one day or five years and 11 months after the date on which the primary limitation period would otherwise have started to run. Moreover as LORD KEITH observes, if the effect of concealment is to *exclude* the primary limitation period, an act of concealment some twenty years or more after the initial damage caused by the breach of duty ought to have the same effect. To the contrary, it may be argued that while section 28 of the Act is concerned with *extending* time limits in the case of disability, and section 33 allows time limits to be *excluded altogether*, section 32 only refers to *postponement* of a limitation period, which ought to be effected only by a prior act of concealment rather than a subsequent attempt to conceal relevant facts.[17]

A mistake on the part of the claimant may also affect the running of time under section 32(1)(c), but this must be a mistake which relates to the basis of the cause of action. It follows that the types of mistake which will suffice seem to be confined to an operative mistake of fact which renders a contract void or a mistake which allows for restitutionary recovery of moneys paid, including a mistake of law.[18] In contrast, a mistake as to some lesser matter such as to the quality of the subject matter of the contract will not suffice.[19] However, this view appears to be inconsistent with that taken in *Re Diplock*[20] in which a mistake on the part of the personal representative in distributing the estate of the deceased could postpone the running of time against the next of kin, despite the fact that the mistake was not an essential ingredient in the action.

Perhaps the most important distinction is between cases in which both parties are mistaken and those in which there is no more than a unilateral mistake. In the former case, the effect of the mistake is to render a contract void, in which case time will start to run as soon as the mistake is operative.[1] Thus where money is paid under a mistake, time will run from the time of payment. Claims of this kind are restitutionary in nature and are concerned with restoration to the claimant of benefits which the defendant is not, in conscience, entitled to receive. Unlike claims in tort and contract which raise issues of compensation for loss suffered by the claimant, a restitutionary claim is concerned with the unjust enrichment of the defendant. If the claimant is unaware of the enrichment, then it would seem to make sense that time should not run against him until he has become aware of that fact. In these circumstances, simple receipt of a benefit by the defendant ought to be an irrelevance.[2] Plainly, the injustice of allowing a defendant to keep the benefit of a payment made under a mistake remains intact while ever the

---

15   *Tito v Waddell (No 2)* [1977] Ch 106 at 245 (per MEGARRY V-C).
16   *Sheldon v RHM Outhwaite (Underwriting Agencies) Ltd* [1995] 2 All ER 558 at 564 (per LORD KEITH). A different way of putting this is that the words 'shall not begin to run' should be interpreted to mean 'shall not run': [1995] 2 All ER 558 at 576 (per LORD NICHOLLS).
17   *Sheldon v RHM Outhwaite (Underwriting Agencies) Ltd* [1995] 2 All ER 558 at 569–570 (per LORD LLOYD, dissenting).
18   *Kleinwort Benson Ltd v Lincoln City Council* [1998] 4 All ER. 513.
19   *Phillips-Higgins v Harper* [1954] 1 QB 411 at 418 (per PEARSON J).
20   [1948] Ch 465.
1   *Baker v Courage & Co* [1910] 1 KB 56.
2   Unfortunately, *Maskell v Horner* [1915] 3 KB 106 appears to decide otherwise.

claimant is unaware of the enrichment. Only when the claimant becomes aware of the enrichment does it become truly unjust, in which case the cause of action ought to be tied to the claimant's awareness of the fact of enrichment. The most detailed analysis of section 32(1)(c) is to be found in *Peco Arts Inc v Hazlitt Gallery Ltd*[3] in which the issue was whether the claimant could, with reasonable diligence, have been aware of a mistake as to the history of a work of art purchassd from the defendant. Both parties believed the work to be an original by Ingres. Applying *Baker v Courage*, time would have run from the date of the operative common mistake, but the decision of WEBSTER J appears to give other possibilities. It was considered that if there had been a condition or warranty as to attribution, only the seller of the painting could have been mistaken, in which case, the buyer will not have paid money under a mistake. Moreover, there is even a suggestion that if there is a bona fide mistake which amounts to a term of the contract, section 32 will not apply, although this is difficult to square with the wording of section 32.

Section D

Negation of liability

CONTENTS

Chapter 20

Fault of the plaintiff

1. INTRODUCTION

It is understandable that the fault of the plaintiff should be taken into account at common law in a system which based liability on individual fault.[1] However, the extent to which the fault of the plaintiff was taken into account in negating the liability of a defendant appeared to go too far. The general common law rule was that, if the plaintiff was considered to be contributorily negligent, he was denied a remedy altogether. In *Butterfield v Forrester*,[2] the plaintiff was unsuccessful where he violently rode his horse into a visible pole which the defendant had wrongly placed across the road. It was held that, if the plaintiff had used ordinary care, the accident would not have happened. But it is equally arguable that, if the defendant had not left the pole across the road, the plaintiff would not have come to any harm.

The justification for the 'all or nothing' approach adopted at common law is obscure. Nineteenth-century lawyers may have preferred to think in terms of absolutes and, logically, either the plaintiff or the defendant must have been wholly the cause of the harm suffered. Alternatively, there may have been an unwillingness to put in the hands of a jury the difficult task of comparing the relative fault of the two parties. The theory which has received most academic attention is that this approach served to protect emerging industries from potential tort liability, and thereby served to enhance the developing capitalist economy of the nineteenth century. Contributory negligence has been stated to be a form of subsidy to economic enterprise, which amounted to a 'cunning trap' set by the courts for nineteenth-century accident victims.[3] However, a detailed study of nineteenth-century court decisions in two American states has found that they were distinctly plaintiff-orientated, and that the defence of contributory negligence was rarely successful.[4] The large number of nineteenth-century English cases in which an employee failed to succeed in an action for negligence against his employer may provide some evidence for the industrial subsidy theory. However, the legal grounds

---

1   See *Reeves v Metropolitan Police Commissioner* [1999] 3 WLR 363 at 368 (per LORD HOFFMANN) and at 374 (per LORD JAUNCEY).
2   (1809) 11 East 60.
3   Friedman *A History of American Law* (1973) and Horwitz *The Transformation of American Law 1780—1860* (1977).
4   Schwartz (1981) 90 Yale LJ 1717.

for their failure extended beyond contributory negligence to the defences of assumption of risk and common employment.[5]

The seemingly excessive rigours of the common law rule became apparent to the courts, and there developed a rule to the effect that the loss would lie with the person who had the 'last opportunity' or the 'effective last chance' to avoid the harm suffered. The rule was said to emanate from *Davies v Mann*,[6] although none of these phrases was actually used in that case. One view is that the rule was an academic creation of Salmond,[7] but an American writer[8] has revealed that it first appeared in a book review,[9] and was later used in a United States case where a railroad engineer failed to notice a person sleeping on the track![10] The last opportunity rule became highly strained when the Privy Council introduced the notion of the 'constructive last opportunity'.[11] This meant that, if the defendant would have had the last opportunity to avoid the accident but for his negligence, he was deemed to be in the same position as if he did have the last opportunity. Understandably, no one was too sure what the rule imported.[12]

Subsequently, a power to apportion damages was permitted in cases of collision at sea by the Maritime Conventions Act 1911. A general power to apportion damages was permitted in non-Admiralty cases when the Law Reform (Contributory Negligence) Act 1945 was passed. Section 1(1) of the 1945 Act provides:

> Where any person suffers damage as the result partly of his own fault and partly of the fault of any other person or persons, a claim in respect of that damage shall not be defeated by reason of the fault of the person suffering the damage, but the damages recoverable in respect thereof shall be reduced to such an extent as the court thinks just and equitable having regard to the claimant's share in the responsibility for the damage.

2.   THE SCOPE OF THE 1945 ACT

In relation to types of damage suffered by the plaintiff, section 4 of the 1945 Act provides that the damage suffered by the plaintiff referred to in section 1(1) includes loss of life and personal injury. Property damage would also appear to be included, as this was the case before the passing of the 1945 Act. To the extent that economic loss is recoverable in the tort of negligence, it would be consistent to assume that this is also relevant damage for the purposes of the Act.

The scope of the Act is affected by the meaning of 'fault'. Section 1(1) makes it clear that both the plaintiff and the defendant should be partly 'at fault' in relation to the damage caused to the plaintiff. Section 4 of the Act defines 'fault' as:

> negligence, breach of statutory duty or other act or omission which gives rise to a liability in tort or would, apart from the Act, give rise to the defence of contributory negligence.

The word 'fault', therefore, is used in two contexts, namely the fault of the defendant and the fault of the plaintiff. The fault of the defendant is covered by the words 'negligence, breach of statutory duty or other act or omission which gives rise to a liability

---

5   See ch 27.
6   (1842) 10 M & W 546, 12 LJ Ex 10.
7   See *Salmond, Heuston & Buckley* pp 500–501 citing the 3rd edition (1912).
8   White *Tort Law in America—An* Intellectual History (1980) p 46.
9   (1886) 2 LQR 506 (Wills).
10   *Pickett v Wilmington* 117 NC 616 (1895).
11   *British Columbia Electric Rly Co Ltd v Loach* [1916] 1 AC 719.
12   Glanville Williams *Joint Torts and Contributory Negligence* (1951) p 234.

in tort'. This alludes to the 'original liability' of the defendant based on his fault.[13] The fault of the plaintiff is adverted to by the closing words of section 4, with the reference to an act or omission which would, apart from the Act, give rise to the defence of contributory negligence. Furthermore, the first part of the definition is also relevant to the fault of the plaintiff in cases where the plaintiff's contributory negligence constitutes a breach of duty owed to the defendant, for example where two drivers collide at a cross-roads when both have failed to exercise reasonable care.[14]

The definition of fault has given rise to difficulties in determining whether the apportionment provisions of the Act apply to all torts, including those which require proof of intention on the part of the defendant, and whether the defence is available in the event of a breach of contract on the part of the defendant.

(1) APPLICATION OF THE 1945 ACT TO BREACHES OF CONTRACT[15]

Whether or not the 1945 Act applies to a breach of contract so as to reduce the plaintiff's damages by reason of his contributory fault is a matter which has attracted much attention.[16] Where a contract term requires the exercise of reasonable care, a breach of that duty may be actionable in both contract or tort.[17] If the action is framed in tort, the contributory negligence of the plaintiff may be considered so as to reduce his damages. But if the 1945 Act does not apply to a breach of contract, the plaintiff can avoid a reduction of his damages in the event of disregard for his own interests by choosing to sue for the breach of a contractual duty of care rather than for the tort.

The cases which have considered this issue have indicated that three types of contractual duty must be distinguished in deciding whether contributory negligence is a defence in an action for breach of contract.[18] In the first instance, there are strict contractual duties, such as the duty of a seller to supply goods of the desired quality and fitness. Secondly, there are contractual duties of care which are higher than the duty owed in the ordinary law of negligence, such as an express or implied undertaking to exercise care to avoid causing losses which would not be recoverable in a tortious action, for example, many varieties of economic loss. Thirdly, there are duties of care which sound concurrently in contract and tort, such as an implied undertaking on the part of an occupier of land to take care in avoiding possible physical injury to a contractual visitor.

Other categorisations are also possible, for example a distinction can be made between contractual and tortious duties *simpliciter*, which leads to the conclusion that contributory negligence is only a defence to an action framed in tort.[19] Alternatively, it would be possible to distinguish between fault-based and strict duties whether framed in contract or in tort.[20]

---

13 *Barclays Bank plc v Fairclough Building Ltd* [1995] 1 All ER 289 at 301 (per BELDAM LJ).

14 *Forsikringsaktieselskapet Vesta v Butcher* [1988] 2 All ER 43 at 49 (per O'CONNOR LJ). Affd on other grounds in [1989] 1 All ER 402, HL.

15 Burrows *Remedies* pp 80–87; Palmer and Davies (1980) 29 ICLQ 45; Stanton (1981) 55 ALJ 278; Chandler (1989) 40 NILQ 152; Law Comm No 219, 1993.

16 See Law Comm No 219, 1993.

17 *Esso Petroleum Co Ltd v Mardon* [1976] QB 801; *Midland Bank Trust Co Ltd v Hett, Stubbs & Kemp (a firm)* [1979] Ch 384.

18 The trichotomy is derived from *Forsikringsaktieselskapet Vesta v Butcher* [1986] 2 All ER 488 at 508 (per HOBHOUSE J). Affd in [1988] 2 All ER 43, CA and on other grounds in [1989] 1 All ER 402, HL.

19 *Sole v W J Hallt Ltd* [1973] 1 All ER 1032 at 1040 (per SWANWICK J); *Acrecrest Ltd v Hattrell & Partners* [1983] 1 All ER 17 at 31 (per DONALDSON LJ); *Basildon District Council v J E Lesser (Properties) Ltd* [1985] 1 All ER 20; *A B Marintrans v Comet Shipping Ltd* [1985] 3 All ER 442.

20 See Law Commission WP 114 (1990) para 3.13.

The view that contributory negligence is a defence in some actions for breach of contract is desirable in terms of policy, but it may be difficult to square with the wording of the definition of 'fault' in section 4 of the 1945 Act. It has been observed that the definition of fault in section 4 of the Act possesses two limbs, one of which refers to the fault of the defendant, and one of which refers to the contributory negligence of the plaintiff.[1] Fault in relation to the defendant's conduct or the plaintiff's cause of action is defined as 'negligence, breach of statutory duty or other act or omission which gives rise to a liability in tort ...'. It follows that, before the contributory negligence of the plaintiff can be pleaded as a defence, the defendant must have been guilty of fault within the meaning of the first limb of section 4.

(i)　The fault of the defendant

Where there is a breach of a strict contractual duty, the apportionment provisions of the 1945 Act do not apply[2] for reasons discussed below in relation to the fault of the parties. In such cases, the defendant is not guilty of 'fault', and no apportionment of liability is made. Thus where a seller is in breach of the implied terms as to quality or fitness in a supply of goods transaction, the 1945 Act will not apply.[3] Likewise, if the defendant is an insurer in breach of a duty of utmost good faith, the 1945 Act will be inapplicable.[4] As SIMON BROWN LJ observed in *Barclays Bank plc v Fairclough Building Ltd*[5] the imposition of strict liability on a defendant is inconsistent with an apportionment of loss, since a plaintiff can expect strict performance of the defendant's obligations. Moreover, there is no general duty on a person to check that a strict warranty has been complied with.[6] Accordingly, in *Barclays Bank plc v Fairclough Building Ltd*, there was no obligation on the bank to ensure that the defendants had properly performed their obligations to ensure that standards of workmanship were the best of their kind, as required by the contract.

Where there is a breach of a purely contractual duty to take care which does not give rise to liability in tort, one interpretation of section 4 is that the word 'negligence' in the definition of the defendant's fault is not qualified by the words 'which gives rise to liability in tort'. On this interpretation, the breach of a contractual duty of care by the defendant can constitute negligence in this wider sense.[7] However, there is no such a thing as a negligent breach of contract,[8] and the manner in which a contract term is broken would appear to be immaterial.[9]

1　*Rowe v Turner, Hopkins & Partners* [1980] 2 NZLR 550 at 555–556 (per PRITCHARD J); *Basildon District Council v J E Lesser (Properties) Ltd* [1985] 1 All ER 20 at 30 (per JUDGE NEWEY QC); *Forsikringsaktieselskapet Vesta v Butcher* [1988] 2 All ER 43 at 48–49 (per O'CONNOR LJ).

2　*Forsikringsaktieselskapet Vesta v Butcher* [1986] 2 All ER 488 at 508–509 (per HOBHOUSE J); *Tennant Radiant Heat Ltd v Warrington Development Corporation* [1988] 1 EGLR 41 at 43 (per DILLON LJ); *Bank of Nova Scotia v Hellenic Mutual War Risks Association (Bermuda) Ltd, The Good Luck* [1989] 3 All ER 628 at 672 (per MAY LJ) (reversed on other grounds in [1991] 3 All ER 1 in which the issue of contributory negligence was not pursued); *Barclays Bank plc v Fairclough Building Ltd* [1995] 1 All ER 289 at 301 (per Beldam LJ).

3　*Basildon District Council v J E Lesser (Properties) Ltd* [1985] 1 All ER 20.

4　*Banque Keyser Ullmann SA v Skandia (UK) Insurance Co Ltd* [1987] 2 All ER 923 at 958–959 (per STEYN J). Affd in *Banque Financière de la Cité SA v Westgate Insurance Co Ltd* [1989] 2 All ER 952 at 1024 (per SLADE LJ).

5　[1995] 1 All ER 289.

6　Ibid at 302 (per BELDAM LJ), applying *Lambert v Lewis* [1982] AC 225 at 276 (per LORD DIPLOCK).

7　*De Meza and Stuart v Apple, Van Straten, Shena and Stone* [1974] 1 Lloyd's Rep 508.

8　*Grein v Imperial Airways Ltd* [1937] 1 KB 50 at 71 (per GREER LJ); Glanville Williams *Joint Torts and Contributory Negligence* (1951) pp 330–331. See also Swanton (1981) 55 ALJ 278 at 287–288.

9　*Quinn v Burch Bros (Builders) Ltd* [1966] 2 QB 370 at 379 (per PAULL J).

The presence of the word 'other' in section 4 suggests that 'negligence' and 'breach of statutory duty' are qualified by the words 'which gives rise to liability in tort'.[10] Since the breach of a purely contractual duty to take care gives rise only to liability in contract, it seems to follow that the 1945 Act should not apply in these cases.

Where the defendant is in breach of a contractual duty which is capable of giving rise to liability in the tort of negligence the defence is applicable.[11] This is the case because the content of the contractual obligation to exercise reasonable care is the same as the corresponding tortious duty requiring the exercise of reasonable care and the position of the plaintiff would remain the same even if there had been no contract with the defendant.[12] Thus where loss is caused by the professional negligence of a solicitor[13] or valuer,[14] but the client is in part to blame for that loss, it will be possible to reduce the plaintiff's damages whether the action is framed in contract or in tort. The position is also the same where a misleading statement made in the course of contractual negotiations can give rise to tortious liability for negligent misrepresentation or may be construed so as to give rise to contractual liability on the basis of a collateral warranty. Likewise in *Forsikringsaktieselskapet Vesta v Butcher*[15] it was considered, obiter, that insurance brokers had failed to exercise reasonable care in relation to the rearrangement of an insured risk. In defence, it was argued that the insured had failed to confirm that an earlier request for deletion of a 24-hour watch on their premises had been deleted. As events turned out, there was no need to proceed with the action against the brokers, since an action against the reinsurers succeeded. However, it was clear from the language used by the court that the plaintiffs would have had their damages reduced on the grounds of contributory negligence had the action against the brokers proceeded.

What is meant by concurrent liability is not entirely clear since it appears to have been assumed in *Vacwell Engineering Ltd v B D H Chemicals*[16] that if the plaintiff can sue for negligence and breach of contract, the 1945 Act can apply.[17] However, this view was expressed in a case in which the plaintiff could and did sue independently in contract for breach of the implied term as to fitness for purpose and in tort for breach of a duty to take reasonable care. In cases of this kind, it does not follow that there is concurrent liability, since the nature of the seller's obligation is different in each case. The action in contract is based on the seller's obligation to supply goods of a particular standard of fitness. The action in tort, on the other hand, is based on the supplier's duty to exercise reasonable care.[18] It follows that the plaintiff will only be able to sue the retailer for negligence if it can be shown that the latter has acted or omitted to act in some way which unreasonably results in the product becoming defective. What is important to emphasise is that just because a strict contractual duty is negligently performed, it does not follow that there has been fault on the part of the defendant.[19]

---

10   *Basildon DC v J E Lesser (Properties) Ltd* [1985] 1 All ER 20; *A B Marintrans v Comet Shipping Co Ltd* [1985] 3 All ER 442.
11   *Sayers v Harlow UDC* [1958] 1 WLR 623 at 624 (per LORD EVERSHED MR); *Quinn v Burch Bros Ltd* [1966] 2 QB 370 at 380–381 (per PAULL J); *Forsikringsaktieselskapet Vesta v Butcher* [1988] 2 All ER 43 at 52 (per O'CONNOR LJ); affd on other grounds in [1989] 1 All ER 402, HL; See also *Youell v Bland Welch & Co Ltd, The 'Superhulls Cover' Case (No 2)* [1990] 2 Lloyd's Rep 431 at 460 (per PHILLIPS J).
12   *Henderson v Merrett Syndicates Ltd* [1995] 2 AC 145 at 193.
13   See *Bristol & West BS v Mothew* [1998] Ch 1 at 26.
14   *First National Provincial Bank Ltd v Humberts* [1995] 2 All ER 673.
15   [1988] 2 All ER 43. Applied in *Birmingham Midshires Mortgage Services v David Parry & Co* (1996) 51 Con LR 1; *Platform Home Loans Ltd v Oyston Shipways Ltd* [1999] 1 All ER 833.
16   [1971] 1 QB 88.
17   Ibid at 110 (per REES J).
18   See Law Commission, WP 114 (1990) para 3.33(iii).
19   *Quinn v Burch Bros (Builders) Ltd* [1966] 2 QB 370 at 379 (per PAULL J).

Despite the fact that it is possible for there to be concurrent liability in contract and tort, it is still important to have close regard to the terms of the contract. In some cases, the terms of the contract may be inconsistent with the imposition of liability in tort which is greater than could have been imposed under the contract between the parties, in which case, the intentions of the parties should prevail.[20]

The remaining difficulty is that if the plaintiff sues for a breach of contract, what results is liability in contract regardless of the fact that concurrent liability in tort also exists. However, it has been argued that section 4, in so far as it relates to the defendant's fault, may be interpreted to cover an act or omission which normally or potentially produces tort liability.[1] From this, it follows that in any case where the defendant, potentially, could have been sued in tort, the defence of contributory negligence should be available. However, the terms of the contract still have to be considered since it may be apparent from those terms that the parties intended to exclude such liability in the event of the breach of contract and this may remain the case even where there is concurrent contractual and tortious liability.[2]

(ii)   The fault of the plaintiff

The definition of the plaintiff's fault in section 4 also suggests that the 1945 Act may not apply to an action for breach of contract. Section 4 refers to an act or omission which would, apart from the Act, give rise to a defence of contributory negligence. One interpretation of these words is that the plaintiff's conduct should be of a type which would have given rise to the common law defence of contributory negligence prior to the enactment of the 1945 legislation.[3] It seems this was not the case,[4] since one contracting party is not bound to guard against a breach of contract on the part of the other.

An alternative and better view is that if the defendant is concurrently liable in tort and contract and, if the plaintiff's conduct would have amounted to a total defence at common law had the action been framed in tort, then the 1945 Act applies, even though the action is, in fact, one for breach of contract.[5]

(iii)   Alternatives to contributory negligence as a defence to breach of contract

Even if contributory negligence does not apply as a defence to a breach of contract, the law of contract has adopted a number of devices which may limit the liability of a defendant to compensate the careless plaintiff. These consist of the rules on mitigation and causation, those cases in which it is held that the defendant has committed no breach of contract and instances in which it is held that a condition precedent to liability has failed.

---

20 See *Henderson v Merrett Syndicates Ltd* [1995] 2 AC 145 at 194 and *Barclay's Bank plc v Fairclough Building Ltd* [1995] 1 All ER 289 at 305 (per SIMON BROWN LJ).
1   Palmer and Davies (1980) 29 ICLQ 415 at 445. See also *Rowe v Turner, Hopkins & Partners* [1980] 2 NZLR 550 at 555–556, approved in *Forsikringsaktieselskapet Vesta v Butcher* [1988] 2 All ER 43 at 52 (per O'CONNOR LJ).
2   See *Barclays Bank plc v Fairclough Building Ltd* [1995] 1 All ER 289 at 305 (per SIMON BROWN LJ).
3   For criticism of the application of 1945 law to 1990s facts see *Youell v Bland Welch & Co Ltd, The 'Superhulls Cover' Case (No 2)* [1990] 2 Lloyd's Rep 431 at 460 (per PHILLIPS J).
4   *Forsikringsaktieselskapet Vesta v Butcher* [1988] 2 All ER 43 at 61 (per SIR ROGER ORMROD); *Tennant Radiant Heat v Warrington Development Corpn* [1988] 1 EGLR 41 at 43 (per DILLON LJ). Cf Glanville Williams *Joint Torts and Contributory Negligence* (1951) pp 214–222.
5   Palmer and Davies (1980) 29 ICLQ 415 at 445; Swanton (1981) 55 ALJ 278 at 280–281.

(a)   *Contributory negligence and mitigation of damage*[6]   Both these devices serve to limit the damages recoverable by the plaintiff, but they are not identical in effect. Contributory negligence involves fault on the part of the plaintiff in helping to bring about the loss or the event which causes it.[7] If the plaintiff's actions are to amount to contributory negligence, they will usually take place before or at the time of the breach. The doctrine of mitigation requires the plaintiff to take reasonable steps to minimise his loss and to refrain from taking unreasonable steps which increase his loss. Thus a buyer of goods who is aware that they cannot be used safely cannot pass the risk of loss to the seller.[8] The requirement of mitigation, therefore, arises after the breach. However, both a failure to mitigate and contributory negligence require fault on the part of the plaintiff, and can result in a reduction in an award of damages. What is required of the plaintiff by way of mitigation is similar to the standard he is required to reach in order to avoid the application of the defence of contributory negligence.

(b)   *Contributory negligence and causation*   Where the plaintiff's failure to exercise reasonable care is substantial, that failure can be treated as the cause of the loss suffered. In such a case, the defendant will not be liable for his alleged breach of contract, since it would be inequitable to allow the plaintiff to recover damages at all. If the defendant is in breach of a strict contractual duty, he is not at fault, but if the plaintiff has failed to take care for his own interests, he may be regarded as the author of his own loss. In *Lambert v Lewis*,[9] a retailer sold a defective towing hitch to the plaintiff, a farmer who continued to use it after becoming aware of its dangerous condition. When the defective hitch was the cause of an accident it was held that the plaintiff's action should fail because his own negligence in continuing to use the towing hitch was sufficient to sever the chain of causation. Essentially, the defendant's argument in a case of this kind is that the harm to the plaintiff is not such as would have been within the defendant's reasonable contemplation as a serious possibility, had all the relevant facts been known to him at the time the contract was made.[10]

Similar reasoning may also be used in cases where the defendant is in breach of a contractual duty to take care and the plaintiff has carelessly contributed to the loss he has suffered. In *Sole v W J Hallt Ltd*,[11] the plaintiff, an entrant to the defendant's premises, was owed an implied contractual duty of care.[12] The defendant had failed to exercise reasonable care in leaving a stairwell unguarded, but the plaintiff had also contributed to his own injury by walking backwards in the direction of the unguarded well. It was held that, if the action was based on a breach of the implied contractual term, the plaintiff's contributory negligence would break the chain of causation. However, the plaintiff was given the option to sue in tort, which allowed the recovery of reduced damages on the grounds of contributory negligence. This reasoning is suspect to say the least. If the plaintiff was the sole cause of his injuries for the purposes of the contract action, why was he not the sole cause when the action was framed in tort? If apportionment is only permitted when both parties are at fault, how could apportionment take place where one party was considered to be the sole cause of his own loss?

Generally, the application of causation principles will produce an all-or-nothing result. Either the plaintiff's fault is the whole cause of the loss he suffers or the defendant's

---

6   See ch 16 and Bridge (1989) 105 LQR 866.
7   Cf Glanville Williams *Joint Torts and Contributory Negligence* (1951) p 214.
8   *British Oil and Cake Ltd v Burstall* (1923) 39 TLR 406; *Compania Financiera Soleada SA v Hamoor Tanker Corporation Inc, The Borag* [1981] 1 All ER 856.
9   [1981] 1 All ER 1185. See also *Quinn v Burch Bros (Builders) Ltd* [1966] 2 QB 370.
10   See also ch 16.
11   [1973] QB 574. See also *O'Connor v B D B Kirby & Co* [1972] 1 QB 90.
12   Occupiers' Liability Act 1957, s 5.

breach of contract is the operative cause. Thus in *O'Connor v BDB Kirby & Co*,[13] the Court of Appeal described as novel the trial judge's decision that a client who had failed to check statements in an insurance proposal form, made on his behalf by a broker, was one third the cause of the loss suffered. However, a different approach can be applied where the plaintiff and defendant are both in breach of legal duties owed to each other. For example, in *Tennant Radiant Heat Ltd v Warrington Development Corporation*,[14] the plaintiff tenant's goods and the defendant landlord's warehouse were damaged partly by the tenant's breach of a strict covenant to repair and partly by the landlord's failure to exercise reasonable care in maintaining the property. In the event each party could recover against the other to the extent that the legal wrong of the other was the cause of the damage complained of. The landlord was considered to be 90% the cause of the damage to the goods and the plaintiff's damages were reduced accordingly, but only because each party was in breach of a legal duty owed to the other.[15]

(c)   *Defendant not in breach*   The conduct or inadvertence of the plaintiff may modify or exclude the defendant's contractual duty. For example in bailment cases, carelessness on the part of the bailor may qualify the bailee's duty to exercise reasonable care in attending to the bailed property.[16] Similarly, a seller of goods will not be liable for a breach of the implied term as to quality where, after examination of the goods, the buyer has failed to notice a patent defect.[17] Likewise, a pork chop which causes illness because it has not been cooked properly is not necessarily of unsatisfactory quality since the issue of quality must be judged by reference to a piece of meat which has been cooked according to accepted standards.[18]

Similar results may also be achieved where the court regards it as a condition precedent to the defendant's liability that the plaintiff should exercise reasonable care in his conduct. If that condition precedent is broken, the defendant is not guilty of a breach of contract. It may be a condition precedent to the liability of an occupier that his contractual visitor takes care in attending to his own safety.[19] The same may also be true in sale of goods cases. It would appear that, in *Lambert v Lewis*,[20] it was a condition precedent to the liability of the defendant that the owner of the vehicle with the attached towing hitch would exercise reasonable care by not using the hitch when he was aware of its defectiveness.[1] It followed that there was no breach of the implied condition of fitness for purpose.

It is also important to examine the wording of a contract to identify those losses for which the defendant is responsible in the event of the carelessness of the plaintiff. For example a contract for the sale of traveller's cheques which obliges the issuing bank to reimburse the value of stolen cheques requires reimbursement even in the event of negligent handling by the purchaser.[2] Conversely, if the reimbursement provision is

---

13   [1972] 1 QB 90 at 99.
14   [1988] 1 EGLR 41. Doubted in *Bank of Nova Scotia v Hellenic Mutual War Risks Association* [1989] 3 All ER 628 at 672 (per MAY LJ) revsd on other grounds in [1991] 3 All ER 1 but where the House of Lords agreed with the Court of Appeal's conclusions on causation: ibid at 19 (per LORD GOFF).
15   *Tennant Radiant Heat Ltd v Warrington Development Corporation* [1988] 1 EGLR 41 at 44 (per CROOM-JOHNSON LJ).
16   *Mayfair Photographic Ltd v Baxter Hoare* [1972] 1 Lloyd's Rep 410.
17   Sale of Goods Act 1979, s 14(2C)(b).
18   *Heil v Hedges* [1951] 1 TLR 512 at 514–515 (per McNAIR J).
19   *Hall v Brooklands Auto–Racing Club* [1933] 1 KB 205 at 213 (per SCRUTTON LJ); *Harper v Ashton's Circus Pty Ltd* [1972] 2 NSWLR 395 at 405 (per HOPE JA).
20   [1981] 1 All ER 1185.
1   Ibid at 1191 (per LORD DIPLOCK).
2   *El Awadi v Bank of Credit and Commerce International SA* [1989] 1 All ER 242.

subject to an express term to the effect that the customer should safeguard cheques against theft, negligence on the part of the customer will relieve the issuing bank of liability on the contract.[3]

(2)   APPLICATION OF THE 1945 ACT TO TORTS[4]

The important question in this regard is whether the definition of fault in section 4 limits the scope of the apportionment provisions. The defendant's conduct must amount to 'negligence, breach of statutory duty or other act or omission which gives rise to a liability in tort'. This should cause no great problem, since a defendant can be said to be at fault whenever he commits a tort.

So far as the fault of the plaintiff is concerned, generally, this will consist of a failure to take care on the part of the plaintiff, but the question may also arise, in a limited number of cases, whether there is also a defence of 'contributory intention.'[5] Generally, where a plaintiff has committed a deliberate act, that act will be regarded as the cause of any harm suffered with the result that the defendant will not be liable on the basis that there is a *novus actus interveniens.*[6] However, there is a limited number of cases in which the defendant is under a specific duty to guard against the commission of a deliberate act by the plaintiff, in which case both a failure to take care and a deliberate act on the part of the plaintiff may be pleaded in defence. If the plaintiff's deliberate act were to fall outside the scope of the defence, there might be exceptional circumstances in which that act was not regarded as a cause of the harm suffered, in which case, the plaintiff would recover in full. But as LORD JAUNCEY observes in *Reeves v Metropolitan Police Commissioner,*[7] this conclusion could produce unacceptable results. For example if A were to stand next to a vat of boiling liquid and is injured when he inadvertently lets his hand come into contact with the liquid, his damages could be reduced on the grounds of contributory negligence. In contrast, if the defence did not apply to deliberate acts, B who put his hand in the liquid as a dare to see how long he could withstand the pain, might be able to recover damages in full. Such a conclusion would be absurd.[8] In contrast, it might be argued that in cases in which the plaintiff deliberately causes harm to himself, he should be regarded as the primary cause of that harm, on the basis that the principle of autonomy of individuals means that the plaintiff should accept full responsibility for his actions. However, that argument is flawed because the plaintiff's own act must be 'outwith the contemplated scope of events to which the defendant's duty of care is directed.'[9] Accordingly, in *Reeves* a deliberate act on the part of a man held in police custody, in taking his own life was regarded as a substantial cause of his death, sufficient to allow a 50/50 apportionment of damages in the light of the failure of the police to properly protect the man who was known to have suicidal tendencies.

The plaintiff's conduct must constitute an act or omission which would, apart from the Act, give rise to the defence of contributory negligence. On a narrow view, this can be interpreted to mean that, if the defence of contributory negligence was not available at common law in respect of a particular tort, then it will not be available as a

---

3   *Braithwaite v Thomas Cook Travellers Cheques Ltd* [1989] 1 All ER 235.
4   Glanville Williams *Joint Torts and Contributory Negligence* (1951) pp 318–319; Hudson (1981) 4 Leg Stud 332.
5   See Williams, *Joint Torts & Contributory Negligence,* 1951, p 199.
6   *Reeves v Metropolitan Police Commissioner* [1999] 3 WLR 363 at 369 (per LORD HOFFMANN).
7   [1999] 3 WLR 363.
8   Ibid at 376 (per LORD JAUNCEY).
9   Ibid at 374 (per LORD JAUNCEY). It should also be noted that the self-determination argument only applies to duty issues rather than those concerned with breach of duty.

defence under the 1945 Act. An alternative view is that, where the conduct of the plaintiff is such as would have given rise to the defence at common law if he were suing for a tort such as negligence, the defence may be raised.

On the narrow view, the defence of contributory negligence will not apply to the torts of deceit,[10] and intentional interference with goods[11] and the same may also be true of other claims in respect of dishonesty such as an action for conspiracy to induce a breach of contract.[12] The defence certainly does not apply to conversion or intentional trespass to goods as a result of the Torts (Interference with Goods) Act 1977, section 11.[13] The position regarding trespass to the person is not wholly clear, but applying the wider view above, the case law seems to suggest that the defence can apply to cases of serious conduct amounting to intentional battery.[14] However, an application of the narrower view will allow a different conclusion since, before 1945, the defence was thought not to apply to torts requiring proof of intention.[15]

Where negligence is an element in the tort committed by the defendant, the defence would have been available at common law. Accordingly, the plaintiff's damages may be reduced where the defendant has committed a breach of statutory duty, even where the duty is absolute.[16] The defence also applied to nuisance, under the common law rule, but there were doubts as to whether the degree of contributory negligence required on the part of the plaintiff in a negligence action would be necessary in an action for nuisance.[17] Furthermore, certain statutory provisions expressly state that the torts they create are subject to the defence of contributory negligence.[18]

It is arguable that the defence should not apply to cases of negligent misstatement, if an essential requirement in such cases is reasonable reliance by the plaintiff on the defendant's statement. However, recent case law on negligent misstatements suggests that reasonable reliance may not always be a requirement, especially in cases based on a voluntary assumption of responsibility. Thus there are instances in which the provider of a reference has voluntarily undertaken responsibility towards the subject of the reference even though reliance by the subject of the reference is difficult to identify.[19] Likewise, in *White v Jones*[20] evidence of reliance by the intended beneficiaries of a will which proved to be ineffective due to the negligent advice of the defendant solicitor, was very tenuous. In the circumstances, the beneficiaries might have known of the testator's intentions, in which case there could have been reliance, but it was more likely that the beneficiaries were unaware of that intention. However, the case was expressly decided on the basis that proof of reliance was not necessary.

Where reliance is a necessary element, a number of questions arise. If the plaintiff has reasonably relied on the defendant's advice, how can there have been a failure to take steps to protect oneself from the consequences of the defendant's negligence?[1] Conversely, if the plaintiff has failed to take reasonable care in protecting his own interests, can his reliance on the defendant's statement be regarded as reasonable? It seems that

---

10   *Redgrave v Hurd* (1881) 20 Ch D 1. See also *Alliance & Leicester BS v Edgestop Ltd* [1994] 2 All ER 38.
11   *Corporacion National de Cobre del Chile v Sogemin Metals Ltd* [1997] 1 WLR 1396.
12   Ibid.
13   Cf Banking Act 1979, s 47.
14   *Murphy v Culhane* [1977] QB 94; *Barnes v Nayer* (1986) Times, 19 December.
15   *Horkin v North Melbourne Football Club Supporters Club* [1983] 1 VR 153.
16   *Caswell v Powell Duffryn Associated Collieries Ltd* [1940] AC 152.
17   *Trevett v Lee* [1955] 1 WLR 113 at 122 (per LORD EVERSHED MR); *Dymond v Pearce* [1972] 1 QB 496.
18   Animals Act 1971, ss 10 and 11; Consumer Protection Act 1987, s 6.
19   *Spring v Guardian Assurance plc* [1995] 2 AC 296.
20   [1995] 2 AC 207.
1   *JEB Fasteners Ltd v Marks, Bloom & Co (a firm)* [1981] 3 All ER 289 at 297 (per WOOLF J); *Mariola Marine Corp v Lloyd's Register of Shipping, The Morning Watch* [1990] 1 Lloyd's Rep 547 at 566–567 (per PHILLIPS J).

there may be exceptional circumstances in which a person is influenced by what the defendant has said but is at fault in failing to verify the accuracy of what has been said. Thus in *Gran Gelato Ltd v Richcliff (Group) Ltd*[2] the defence was applied to an action for negligent misstatement and one brought under the Misrepresentation Act 1967, section 2(1) on the basis that liability under the latter is founded on negligence,[3] although the reasonable reliance issue was not pursued.[4] In that case, a solicitor acting on behalf of the defendants had incorrectly asserted in inquiries before lease that there were no rights in favour of others which might adversely affect enjoyment of the property. It was accepted that the statement made on the defendant's behalf was relied on by the plaintiff and was intended to be so relied upon.[5] Accordingly the lessor had a cause of action under both the Misrepresentation Act and at common law for negligent misstatement. But the plaintiff was considered to have been contributorily negligent in not asking to see the head leases before going ahead. It was ultimately held that it will need to be a very special case before a person who is intended to rely on a statement should have his damages reduced[6] and that this was not such a case. The restriction on the applicability of the defence of contributory negligence was achieved not by saying that the defence never applies but that it will hardly ever be just and equitable to apportion damages on the ground that a person has too implicitly relied on the truth of that which is asserted.[7] The difficulty which remains with this analysis, particularly in relation to contributory negligence as a defence in an action under the Misrepresentation Act 1967, section 2(1) is that recent cases have increasingly applied rules relevant to an action for deceit due to the use in that section of the 'fiction of fraud'.[8] If, by analogy, rules on deceit also apply to the issue of defences as well as remedies this would seem to suggest that the defence of contributory negligence should not be available.[9]

3.   THE ELEMENTS OF CONTRIBUTORY NEGLIGENCE

Contributory negligence consists of a failure, by the plaintiff, to take reasonable care for his own safety or interests. The onus of proving contributory negligence lies on the defendant.[10] The same standard of care is required of the plaintiff as is applied to a defendant when considering the issue of breach of duty,[11] namely an objective standard, although some subjective criteria may be relevant.[12] It is not necessary to show that the plaintiff owed the defendant a duty of care,[13] but the defendant must prove that the plaintiff has unreasonably failed to attend to his own interests, thereby increasing the risk of loss. It follows that, while a motorcyclist owes no duty to other road users to

---

2   [1992] 1 All ER 865.
3   Ibid at 875 (per NICHOLLS VC).
4   Ibid at 874 where it was unhelpfully asserted without explanation, that contributory negligence is 'clearly' a defence to a common law action for negligent misstatement.
5   Ibid at 871–872.
6   Ibid at 876. For possible exceptional cases see Marshall & Beltrami (1991) LMCLQ 416.
7   Ibid and see also *Redgrave v Hurd* (1881) 20 Ch D 1 at 14 (per LORD JESSEL MR).
8   Eg *Royscot Trust Ltd v Rogerson* [1991] 3 All ER 294 at 300 (per BALCOMBE LJ) in relation to the measure of damages.
9   *Redgrave v Hurd* (1881) 20 Ch D 1; *Alliance & Leicester BS v Edgestop Ltd* [1994] 2 All ER 38.
10   *Heranger SS Co v Diamond SS Co* [1939] AC 94 at 104 (per LORD WRIGHT).
11   See ch 11.
12   See Fagelson (1979) 42 MLR 646.
13   Although this may be the case, for example fellow road users owe a duty of care to each other: *Nance v British Columbia Electric Rly Co* [1951] AC 601 at 611 (per VISCOUNT SIMON). Cf the arguably incorrect analysis in *Tremayne v Hill* [1987] RTR 131 at 134 (per SIR ROGER ORMROD) that the only question is whether the plaintiff owes a duty of care to himself or other road users.

wear a crash helmet, by failing to do so, he is guilty of contributory negligence if he is injured in a road accident while not wearing such a helmet.[14]

(1) FORESEEABILITY

Just as actionable negligence requires foreseeability of harm to others, so contributory negligence requires foreseeability of harm to oneself.[15] It follows that a person is guilty of contributory negligence if he ought reasonably to have foreseen that, if he did not act as a reasonable man would have acted, he might be harmed.[16] This has led to the view that the appropriate test is objective and impersonal.[17] However, this may not necessarily be true. For example, the fact that a finding of contributory negligence does not depend upon any breach of duty of care as between the plaintiff and the defendant has been held up as evidence that the test of contributory negligence is subjective.[18] Furthermore, subjective considerations will be taken into account when assessing the alleged contributory negligence of children,[19] and possibly persons suffering from some disability or deformity,[20] although regard should be had to the fact that children, generally, have a less full understanding of what they are doing than adults, so that an adult who takes his own life ought to be considered to know what he is doing.[1] Where a defendant is under a duty to prevent the plaintiff from deliberately inflicting injury on himself and that person is unaware of the risks to which he will expose himself or is too young to appreciate the risk,[2] or is of unsound mind to the extent that he might do something which a rational person would not or where the risk of deliberate self-harm is the result of something done by the defendant to the plaintiff, subjective considerations may have to be considered.[3]

The same subjective considerations would appear not to apply to someone incapable of making a rational judgment through self-induced intoxication.[4] It may be said that contributory negligence is synonymous with personal fault on the part of a workman.[5] For example, in *Caswell v Powell Duffryn Associated Collieries Ltd*,[6] it was said that the standard of care expected of an employee is affected by all the circumstances prevailing at the time of the accident, and that one must judge the issue of contributory negligence from the point of view of the reasonable workman, if he were to be exposed to the pressures and distractions to which the plaintiff was subject.

It is also relevant to consider the particular circumstances of the case in determining what degree of want of care on the part of the plaintiff will amount to contributory negligence. For example in cases of actionable economic loss, it may be relevant to

---

14   *O'Connell v Jackson* [1972] 1 QB 270. Similarly if he wears the helmet but fails to fasten the chin strap: *Capps v Miller* [1989] 2 All ER 333; or if a car passenger fails to wear a seat belt: *Froom v Butcher* [1976] QB 286.
15   *Jones v Livox Quarries Ltd* [1952] 2 QB 608 at 615 (per DENNING LJ).
16   Ibid.
17   *Rogers, Winfield and Jolowicz on Tort* p 238. See also *Billings v Riden* [1958] AC 240.
18   *McHale v Watson* (1964) 111 CLR 384.
19   *Gough v Thorne* [1966] 1 WLR 1387; *Yachuk v Oliver Blais Co Ltd* [1949] AC 386. Cf *Morales v Eccleston* [1991] RTR 151 (75% reduction in damages for 11-year-old playing football in the middle of a busy street).
20   *Reeves v Metropolitan Police Commissioner* [1999] 3 WLR 363 at 379 (per LORD HOPE).
1   Ibid at 371 (per LORD HOFFMANN).
2   See *Yachuk v Oliver Blais Ltd* [1949] AC 386; *Hughes v Lord Advocate* [1963] AC 837.
3   *Reeves v Metropolitan Police Commissioner* [1999] 3 WLR 363 at 379 (per LORD HOPE).
4   *Owens v Brimmell* [1977] QB 859.
5   Fagelson (1979) 42 MLR 646. See also Williams *Joint Torts and Contributory Negligence* (1951) p 253. Cf *Staveley Iron and Chemical Co v Jones* [1956] AC 627 at 642 (per LORD REID).
6   [1940] AC 152.

consider whether the plaintiff was insured against that loss in determining whether he has behaved with reasonable prudence.[7]

(i)   Conduct which may foreseeably result in harm to the plaintiff

A plaintiff may act in one of three ways, with the result that he may foreseeably suffer harm.[8] First, the plaintiff's failure to take care for his own safety may be a cause of the accident which results in his injury. This would appear to be the case where two motorists are equally to blame for an accident in which the plaintiff is injured.[9] Likewise, it may be said that a person who plies a driver with drinks and then accepts a lift with that person is a cause of a subsequent accident resulting from the driver's impaired ability to drive.[10]

The second variety of relevant conduct arises where the plaintiff places himself in a dangerous position thereby exposing him to the risk of involvement in the accident which causes the harm. Here, it is foreseeable that the plaintiff's failure to take care may result in injury. Thus, if an employee stands on the side-steps of a lorry and is killed when the lorry and an overtaking vehicle collide due to the negligence of both drivers, it is foreseeable that the employee will suffer some harm.[11] Similarly, in *Jones v Livox Quarries Ltd*,[12] the plaintiff rode on the towbar of a moving machine and, in so doing, foreseeably exposed himself to some risk of injury, albeit not the exact injury suffered. Foreseeability of harm was regarded as a relevant factor, but it is not the decisive test of causation.[13]

A variant on this type of case may also arise where a plaintiff does not place himself in a position which is dangerous per se, but is aware of circumstances which might render him more likely to suffer harm. This would appear to cover cases in which a plaintiff accepts a lift from a defendant who is incapable of driving safely due to his intoxication.[14] It might also cover cases where a person is aware of the inability of an inexperienced driver to drive safely,[15] or where a person accepts a lift in a vehicle which he realises is not roadworthy.[16] In each such event, the plaintiff's action can be seen as consisting of an unreasonable disregard for personal safety.

A third variety of foreseeably suffered harm arises where the plaintiff takes up a position which is not, in itself, dangerous, but where his failure to take precautions increases the likelihood that harm will ensue. This would seem to cover car passengers who fail to wear a seat belt,[17] and motorcyclists who fail to wear a crash helmet,[18] who stand a chance of being more seriously injured in an accident than would have been the case if the safety device had been used.

---

7   See *Banque Bruxelles Lambert SA v Eagle Star Insurance Co Ltd* [1995] 2 All ER 769 at 820 (per PHILLIPS J).
8   Gravells (1977) 93 LQR 581.
9   *Harvey v Road Haulage Executive* [1952] 1 KB 120; *Rouse v Squires* [1973] QB 889. See also *Fitzgerald v Lane* [1988] 2 All ER 961 at 970 (per LORD ACKNER).
10   *Owens v Brimmell* [1977] QB 859 at 867 (per TASKER WATKINS J); *Poole v Stewart* [1969] NZLR 501.
11   *Davies v Swan Motor Co (Swansea) Ltd* [1949] 2 KB 291.
12   [1952] 2 QB 608.
13   Ibid at 616 (per DENNING LJ).
14   *Owens v Brimmell* [1977] QB 859. The same could also be said of *Dann v Hamilton* [1939] 1 All ER 59. See LORD ASQUITH (1953) 69 LQR 317 (note).
15   *Nettleship v Weston* [1971] 3 All ER 581 at 587 (per LORD DENNING MR). See also Goodhart (1953) 69 LQR 184 (note).
16   This would be a more satisfactory explanation of *Dawrant v Nutt* [1960] 3 All ER 681. See also *Gregory v Kelly* [1978] RTR 426.
17   *Froom v Butcher* [1976] QB 286.
18   *O'Connell v Jackson* [1971] 3 All ER 129; *Capps v Miller* [1989] 2 All ER 333.

(ii)   The dilemma produced by the defendant's negligence

Allowance should be made for the fact that the court is enquiring into what is reasonable for the plaintiff's own safety. Accordingly, if the defendant's negligence has placed the plaintiff in a dilemma, the plaintiff may not be regarded as contributorily negligent if he acts in a manner which carries with it a slight risk of harm, if this is to avoid some greater inconvenience.[19] Conversely, if a person unreasonably reacts to a dilemma created by the defendant's negligence a finding of contributory negligence will probably follow.[20] In some instances, the plaintiff's reaction to the negligence of the defendant may have some considerable social value, as where a person intervenes to rescue another from the consequences of that negligence. In such a case, contributory negligence will not normally be found to exist, since danger invites rescue, and it would not be wise for the defendant to criticise the conduct of the rescuer.[1] Provided the rescuer has acted reasonably, there should be no bar to recovery.[2]

While it is true that a plaintiff should guard against the possibility that others might be careless,[3] the plaintiff's conduct in an emergency is not to be considered with the benefit of hindsight. If a person elects to act in a way which later proves to have been the wrong course of action, he may still be able to recover against the defendant in full. So long as the plaintiff's response is reasonable in the circumstances, he will not be guilty of contributory negligence. In *Jones v Boyce*,[4] a passenger on the defendant's coach was considered not to be guilty of contributory negligence when he jumped from a moving carriage which was in danger of overturning, despite the fact that had he remained on the coach, he would have come to no harm.

(2)   CAUSATION[5]

The concept of causation and the defence of contributory negligence are impossible to divorce from one another, since, to constitute a defence, the plaintiff's contributory fault must be a legal and factual cause of the harm suffered.[6] In determining whether a plaintiff's conduct is the cause of the damage suffered, it is necessary to ask first, whether the plaintiff has been negligent and secondly, whether that negligence contributed to his injury.[7] There are two possible explanations of a finding that contributory negligence is a cause of the harm suffered. One is that all features of the plaintiff's conduct should be causally relevant. Thus, if a plaintiff is involved in a collision while not licensed to drive, the absence of a licence is not to be regarded as a cause of the plaintiff's injury.[8] An alternative explanation of a finding of contributory negligence is that the plaintiff's injury is within the area of risk created by his negligent conduct. Thus, if a person places himself in a dangerous position but is injured by some other occurrence which falls outside the area of risk, he may not be regarded as contributorily negligent. For

---

19   *Jones v Boyce* (1816) 1 Stark 493.
20   See eg *Sayers v Harlow UDC* [1958] 1 WLR 623.
1   *Brandon v Osborne, Garrett & Co* [1924] 1 KB 548. Cf *Harrison v British Railways Board* [1981] 3 All ER 679.
2   *Haynes v Harwood* [1935] 1 KB 146. See also Glanville Williams *Joint Torts and Contributory Negligence* (1951) pp 360–364. Cf *Cutler v United Dairies* [1933] 2 KB 297; *Harrison v British Railways Board* [1981] 3 All ER 679.
3   *Jones v Livox Quarries Ltd* [1952] 2 QB 608 at 615 (per DENNING LJ).
4   (1816) 1 Stark 493. The principle would appear to apply to fear of property damage as well as harm to the person: *Wilson v United Counties Bank Ltd* [1920] AC 102 at 105.
5   See Hart and Honoré *Causation in the Law* (2nd edn, 1985) pp 207–225.
6   *Caswell v Powell Duffryn Associated Collieries Ltd* [1940] AC 152 at 165 (per LORD ATKIN).
7   See also *American Restatement, Torts* (2d) 463.
8   *Mandell v Dodge-Freedman Poultry Co* (1946) 163 ALR 1370. Cf *Johnson v Boston and Maine Rly* (1928) 61 ALR 1178.

example, a workman who exposed himself to a risk of falling off a working platform by moving to a slippery, unguarded area has been held not to have contributed to his injuries where a wall collapsed on top of him.[9]

Too refined an approach to the issue of causation should not be adopted, since the court has a power to apportion damages rather than treat one or other of the parties as wholly to blame for the harm suffered. Thus a plaintiff can be guilty of contributory negligence where he is harmed by some event which is not the most immediately obvious source of damage. In *Jones v Livox Quarries Ltd*,[10] the plaintiff was riding on the towbar of an earth removing machine when another vehicle negligently drove into the back of that machine, injuring the plaintiff. The most obvious risk of injury was that of being thrown off the towbar, but the harm suffered was still said to be caused by the plaintiff's failure to have regard for his own safety. Some older cases concerning the issue of contributory negligence may have adopted an excessively sympathetic attitude towards plaintiffs,[11] especially employees injured at work, since under the law prior to 1945, contributory negligence was a complete defence. In the light of the apportionment provisions in the 1945 Act the courts can adopt a more realistic approach to the issue of causation and even in cases in which the defendant is under a duty to guard against a deliberate act on the part of the plaintiff, that deliberate act may be regarded as a partial cause of the harm suffered, since the plaintiff has some responsibility for the harm suffered.[12]

In a causal analysis, it is necessary to ask whether the alleged consequence would have occurred but for the negligent act.[13] If the plaintiff's alleged contributory negligence fails the 'but for' test, one need go no further. The relevant alleged consequence is the harm suffered by the plaintiff, not the accident which results in that harm.[14] This much is clear from the wording of section 1(1) of the 1945 Act, which requires the necessary causal connection between the damage suffered and the plaintiff's negligence. If the plaintiff sits on the towbar or stands on the side steps of a moving vehicle and is injured in a collision between that vehicle and another, he is not the cause of the accident, but he may be the cause of the injury he suffers.[15]

If the plaintiff's fault is irrelevant to the harm suffered, it has no causative potency. For example, failure to wear a seat belt does not always contribute to the injury suffered by the plaintiff.[16] Likewise, if the plaintiff's fault consists of riding on the towbar of a moving vehicle, that fault is a cause of the harm suffered if the plaintiff falls off, but is completely irrelevant if the plaintiff is shot by a negligent sportsman.[17]

(3)   APPORTIONMENT

The apportionment principle is stated in the Law Reform (Contributory Negligence) Act 1945, section 1(1) which allows the reduction of damages '...to such extent as the court thinks just and equitable having regard to the claimant's share in the responsibility for the damage ...'.

---

9   *Smithwick v Hall and Upson Co* (1890) 59 Conn 261.
10   [1952] 2 QB 608.
11   See eg *Hutchinson v LNER Co* [1942] 1 KB 481 at 488 (per GODDARD LJ).
12   *Reeves v MPC* [1999] 3 WLR 363 at 371 (Per LORD HOFFMANN). See also *Environment Agency v Empress Car Co (Abertillery) Ltd* [1998] 2 WLR 350 at 358 (Per LORD HOFFMANN).
13   See ch 16.
14   *Capps v Miller* [1989] 2 All ER 333 at 340 (per CROOM-JOHNSON LJ).
15   *Davies v Swan Motors (Swansea) Ltd* [1949] 2 KB 291 at 324–326 (per DENNING LJ); *Jones v Livox Quarries Ltd* [1952] 2 QB 608 at 615 (per DENNING LJ). Cf Fagelson (1979) 42 MLR 646 at 655–656.
16   *Owens v Brimmell* [1976] 3 All ER 765 at 769 (per TASKER WATKINS J).
17   *Jones v Livox Quarries Ltd* [1952] 2 QB 608 at 616 (per DENNING LJ).

Section 1(1) directs the court to consider the plaintiff's share in the responsibility for the damage. In order to determine what this responsibility is, it is necessary to consider both the causative potency and the comparative blameworthiness of the conduct of both parties.[18] The reference to the 'share' in the responsibility for the damage would seem to suggest that the court must compare the degree of responsibility of both parties. However, in some cases, it would appear that the courts consider the fault of the plaintiff alone.

(i)   Causative potency

The causative potency of the plaintiff's contributory negligence appears to be a relevant factor in determining the plaintiff's share in the responsibility for the damage he suffers, especially in those cases where the plaintiff's negligence can be regarded as a cause of the accident in which he is harmed. In *Stapley v Gypsum Mines Ltd*,[19] two miners ignored instructions to bring down an unsafe mine roof which presented a danger to all those working in the area. When the roof collapsed and one of the men was killed, it was held that the disobedience of the two miners and their decision to return to normal work were causes of the accident. However, the conduct of the deceased contributed more immediately to the accident than anything.[20] Accordingly, the damages awarded to the widow of the deceased were reduced by 80%. There are also other cases in which the plaintiff's act is a primary cause of the harm suffered, for example where he takes his own life or does some act of self-mutilation. If this act is done while the plaintiff is in police custody, regard must be had to the fact that the police are under a duty to guard against such deliberate acts and whether they have failed to take the necessary steps to guard against injury or death, in which case, there may not be the same degree of reduction in the plaintiff's damages. Thus in *Reeves v Metropolitan Police Commissioner*[1] a 50/50 apportionment was considered appropriate on the basis that his deliberate act meant that he was in part responsible for his death.

The main difficulty with a comparison of the causative potency of the plaintiff's and the defendant's conduct is that a particular fact is either a cause of an event or it is not. It would appear to be meaningless to enquire which of two acts is more a cause of the harm suffered. If the harm suffered by the plaintiff would not have occurred but for the defendant's negligence and the plaintiff's contributory negligence, then both must be causes of that harm. Accordingly, an enquiry based solely on causative potency should result in a 50/50 apportionment in every case.[2]

However, it may be said that the lawyer's concept of causation diverges from the philosophic doctrine of causation,[3] and that public policy and commonsense considerations may be taken into account to determine what is the effectiveness of a particular cause of harm.[4] By comparing the causative potency of the plaintiff's and defendant's conduct, the court appears able to come to something other than a 50/50 apportionment, but this may be due to the use of the criterion of blameworthiness.

---

18   *Davies v Swan Motors (Swansea) Ltd* [1949] 2 KB 291 at 326 (per Denning LJ); *Stapley v Gypsum Mines Ltd* [1953] AC 663 at 682 (per Lord Reid); *Miraflores (Owners) v George Livanas (Owners)* [1967] 1 AC 826 at 845 (per Lord Pearce).
19   [1953] AC 663.
20   Ibid at 682 (per Lord Reid) and at 685 (per Lord Tucker).
1   [1999] 3 WLR 363.
2   See *Collins v Hertfordshire County Council* [1947] KB 598. Cf *Rouse v Squires* [1973] QB 889.
3   *Stapeley v Gypsum Mines Ltd* [1953] AC 663 at 687 (per Lord Asquith). See also Gravells (1977) 93 LQR 581.
4   See ch 16.

(ii)   Blameworthiness

Apparently in the interests of fairness, the blameworthiness of both parties is to be considered. However, it should be noted that a finding of contributory negligence on the part of a plaintiff differs substantially from a finding of negligence on the part of a defendant since at least part of the loss suffered is concentrated on the plaintiff himself, whereas losses caused by a negligent defendant will often be spread through insurance. Accordingly, while a negligent defendant may not bear the cost of his negligence, someone who has been contributorily negligent must face the consequences of that negligence through a financial penalty.[5]

The adoption of a test of comparative blameworthiness has been criticised.[6] For example, a comparison of the blameworthiness of the parties appears meaningless if the defendant is in breach of a strict liability duty, since the defendant may be liable regardless of his fault, although it can be argued that a person is at fault for the purposes of the 1945 Act wherever he commits a tort. If blameworthiness alone were to be considered, a minimal degree of negligence on the part of the plaintiff might lead to the plaintiff recovering nothing at all. For example, it has been found possible to reduce the plaintiff's damages by 100% where the defendant was 'innocently' in breach of a strict statutory duty.[7] Moreover similar results have also been achieved in cases of breach of statutory duty where the plaintiff's conduct was described as 'a crazy thing to do.'[8] On the other hand, in cases involving negligence on both sides, it has been said, obiter that to hold the plaintiff entirely responsible for the damage would be to defeat the purpose of the 1945 Act. If the plaintiff is 100% to blame there is no shared responsibility for the damage.[9] To reach any other conclusion is surely inconsistent with the wording of section 1(1) of the 1945 Act, which states that there '*shall*' be an apportionment where the damage to the plaintiff is suffered partly as a result of the fault of both parties. Moreover, where both parties are at fault justice and equity would not be served if the plaintiff were to be denied damages altogether.[10] Furthermore, in cases in which the defendant owes a duty to guard against some specified act of self-mutilation, it would be wrong to ignore the fact that the policy of the law is to require the defendant to take care to guard against that act, and to hold that the plaintiff is entirely to blame for his own injuries would be tantamount to saying that the defendant owes the plaintiff no duty of care at all.[11]

An alternative approach might be to ignore the defendant's degree of blameworthiness, since his responsibility for the harm suffered is established by the fact of the commission of a tort. Instead, where blameworthiness is considered, it should be that of the plaintiff alone. The proper test requires the court to consider the degree to which the plaintiff has departed from the standard set by the reasonable man.[12] This test would also appear to apply satisfactorily to those cases where the plaintiff has placed himself in a dangerous position or where he has failed to take necessary precautions for his own safety. While it may be difficult to apply a test of causation to a person who sits on the towbar of a moving vehicle or who fails to wear a seat belt, it can be said, in each case, that the plaintiff has acted in a way in which the reasonable man would not

5   Cane, *Atiyah's Accidents* pp. 47–48.
6   Payne (1955) 18 MLR 344; Cane, *Atiyah's Accidents* pp 50–52.
7   *Lavender v Diamints Ltd* [1948] 2 All ER 249 (reversed on the facts in [1949] 1 KB 585).
8   *Jayes v IMI (Kynoch) Ltd* [1985] ICR 155.
9   *Pitts v Hunt* [1990] 3 All ER 344 at 357 (per BELDAM LJ). See also *Reeves v MPC* [1999] 3 WLR 363 at 372 (per LORD HOFFMANN).
10   *Boyle v Kodak Ltd* [1969] 2 All ER 439.
11   *Reeves v MPC* [1999] 3 WLR 363 at 372 (per LORD HOFFMANN).
12   See Payne (1955) 18 MLR 344 at 347. See also Gravells (1977) 93 LQR 581 at 597.   .

have acted. Accordingly, it can be said that the plaintiff is to blame for the injury he suffers, and the court can assess the appropriate amount by which his damages should be reduced according to his degree of blameworthiness.

Seeking to compare the blameworthiness of the plaintiff and the defendant can be difficult where the plaintiff is injured due to his failure to wear a seat belt. Here, the plaintiff is in no way to blame for the accident,[13] although he has failed to take reasonable care for his own safety and has departed from the standards set by the reasonable man. For example, in *Froom v Butcher*,[14] it was held that, if the plaintiff's injury would have been avoided altogether if he had worn a seat belt, his damages should be reduced by 25%, but if he would have been injured in any case, albeit less severely, an appropriate reduction would be 15%, but if the damage suffered by the plaintiff would have occurred whether the safety device was worn or not, then no reduction would be appropriate.[15] Since a reduction will only be made in respect of an injury which is causally related to the failure to wear a seat belt, injuries caused by the facia of a car being forced into a passenger should not result in a reduction as these are likely to result whether the passenger is wearing a seat belt or not.[16]

Concentrating upon the blameworthiness of the plaintiff alone may cause problems in some instances where the plaintiff places himself in a dangerous position. It may be concluded that a man who sits on the towbar of a moving vehicle has an unreasonable disregard for his own safety. But it may be more difficult to determine the reasonableness or otherwise of the conduct of a person who accepts a lift from a drunken driver. The difference between the two cases is that a test of plaintiff-blameworthiness in drunken driver cases requires the court to consider the plaintiff's knowledge of the state of affairs which places him in danger. It has been observed that, if a driver were to be excused according to the knowledge of his passengers, injustice might follow if one passenger wrongly, but reasonably believed the driver to have had only two drinks, while another knew he had consumed a dozen drinks.[17] The defendant's negligence in either case is the same, but he will be liable in full if the plaintiff believes reasonably that he has had only two drinks, but his liability in damages will be reduced if the plaintiff knows that he has consumed considerably more. In such circumstances the court may consider how negligent was the driving of the defendant. For example, it has been said that the driver who controls the car has it in him to do, whilst under the influence of drink, great damage and therefore he must accept a far greater responsibility.[18]

Once there is a finding of contributory negligence on the part of the plaintiff, the court must make an apportionment, unless it can be waived under the *de minimis* principle. There is no discretion to excuse a plaintiff who has been contributorily negligent.[19] On the other hand, where the blameworthiness of the plaintiff is minute, for example less than 10%, it may be ignored under the *de minimis* principle,[20] although this rule may

---

13   Which in any case, is irrelevant to the issue of culpability in relation to the damage caused: *Capps v Miller* [1989] 2 All ER 333 at 340 (per CROOM-JOHNSON LJ).
14   [1976] QB 286. See also *Capps v Miller* [1989] 2 All ER 333.
15   Ibid at 295 (per LORD DENNING MR). These are guidelines only, not rigid rules: *Salmon v Newland* (1983) Times, 16 May.
16   Similar problems arose in *Owens v Brimmell* [1977] QB 859.
17   *Nettleship v Weston* [1971] 2 QB 691 at 700 (per LORD DENNING MR). See also Symmons (1977) 40 MLR 350.
18   *Owens v Brimmell* [1977] QB 859 at 867 (per TASKER WATKINS J).
19   *Boothman v British Northrop Ltd* (1972) 13 KIR 112 at 121–122 (per STEPHENSON LJ). Cf *Hawkins v Ian Ross (Castings) Ltd* [1970] 1 All ER 180 at 188 (per FISHER J).
20   *Johnson v Tennant Bros Ltd* [1954] CA Transcript 329.

not apply where the plaintiff is in breach of a statutory regulation.[1] The fact that there appears to be no single judicial test to determine the level of reduction of damages would appear to be consistent with the wording of the 1945 Act, which requires a reduction which is just and equitable in the circumstances. Sometimes, it makes sense to give greater emphasis to the causative potency of a particular action, but due regard must also be given to the blameworthiness or the culpability of the plaintiff's and defendant's conduct.

(iii)   Multiple defendants

Considerable problems can arise in determining the plaintiff's responsibility for his loss where there are a number of defendants, each of which has contributed to the damage suffered. If the plaintiff is faultless, he will be able to recover his full loss against any of the defendants, and the person proceeded against will have to seek a contribution from the other defendants under the Civil Liability (Contribution) Act 1978. In the contribution proceedings it will be necessary to consider the extent to which each defendant is a cause of the harm suffered and in this respect a distinction can be drawn between a defendant who is merely negligent and one who is reckless. The recklessness of the second defendant may be such that the first defendant is not a cause of a substantial proportion of the damage suffered by the plaintiff. Thus in *Wright v Lodge & Shepherd*[2] the plaintiffs were injured in a dual-carriageway accident when D1 recklessly swerved on to the westbound carriageway after striking D's car which was negligently parked on the eastbound carriageway. D2 was considered 10% the cause of injury to the passenger in her own car but not at all the cause of harm suffered by drivers on the westbound carriageway. While D2's conduct did present a danger, it was not a relevant danger where the reckless driving of D1 was concerned.[3]

Where the plaintiff has contributed to his injuries, it is necessary to balance the plaintiff's contributory negligence against each defendant separately. In *Fitzgerald v Lane*,[4] the plaintiff had stepped out into the traffic on a busy road. He was struck by D1's car being driven negligently in one direction and was deflected into the path of an oncoming vehicle negligently driven by D2. The trial judge held that all three parties were equally to blame and allocated a third of the share of responsibility to each of the parties, and reduced the plaintiff's damages by one-third. In the House of Lords, the apportionment of blame was varied, the plaintiff being found twice as much to blame as either of the defendants. Moreover, it was held that the two distinct and separate stages in the decision-making process should be kept apart. It is necessary to distinguish between the contributory negligence of the plaintiff and the extent to which his damages should be reduced, on the one hand, and the amount of contribution recoverable between the two defendants based on the extent of their responsibility for the damage, on the other hand.[5] Where the plaintiff's fault is a cause of the accident, his damages are to be reduced by the same amount as against any other person whose fault is a cause of the accident.[6] In this instance, the important factor was the plaintiff's degree of culpability in setting the scene for the collision or creating the initial danger, and the response of the defendants to this dangerous situation then had to be assessed.[7] What is contrasted is the plaintiff's

---

1   *Capps v Miller* [1989] 2 All ER 333 at 340 (per CROOM-JOHNSON LJ).
2   [1992] NLJR 1269.
3   Ibid at 1270 (per PARKER LJ).
4   [1988] 2 All ER 961.
5   Ibid at 966 (per LORD ACKNER).
6   *Davies v Swan Motor Co (Swansea) Ltd* [1949] 2 KB 291 at 325 (per DENNING LJ).
7   *Fitzgerald v Lane* [1988] 2 All ER 961 at 970 (per LORD ACKNER).

conduct and the totality of the tortious conduct of the defendants. Accordingly, the plaintiff was considered to be just as much to blame for his injuries as the two defendants, and his damages were reduced by 50%.

Chapter 21

Illegality and public policy

The role of policy in shaping the common law is frequently obscured by the formalism of judgments. When a judge applies a legal principle to the facts of a case, he is apparently performing a mechanical function. However, existing principles are modified and qualified, and new principles formulated. When this process occurs, one of the factors at work may be explicitly or implicitly a policy factor. The extent to which the judiciary admit to policy factors affecting their judgments varies, but in one area, the policy is reasonably clear. It is a policy of the law that a person should not be able to benefit from his misdeeds and it is often expressed in the maxim *ex turpi causa non oritur actio*.

The principal difficulty with public policy considerations is where the line should be drawn in determining whether a contract should be declared illegal and when a person may be denied compensation, following the commission of a tort by the defendant, on the ground that the plaintiff's action is tainted with illegality. It has been observed that public policy 'is a very unruly horse' and that 'once you get astride it you never know where it will carry you.'[1] However, the dangers of relying on public policy considerations can be reduced when 'there is a good man in the saddle' so that the court can 'come down on the side of justice.'[2]

The case law on illegal contracts suggests that there are degrees of illegality, since in some cases the contract is void altogether, whereas in other cases, it may be possible to sever illegal aspects of the contract from the remainder. In other cases, the degree of illegality may be insufficient to have any effect on the contract at all. For example, in *St John Shipping Corp v Joseph Rank Ltd*[3] the commission of a statutory offence of overloading a ship did not prevent the owner from recovering his carriage costs since the object of the statutory provision was considered to be to prevent overloading of ships rather than the prohibition of contracts. What this illustrates is that in the case of infringement of a statutory provision, close regard must be had to the particular mischief aimed at by the statute. Regard must also be had to the nature of the rule of law that has been violated. Some authorities seem to suggest that it is more likely that a contract will be declared illegal on the ground that a statutory provision has not been complied with,

---

1   *Richardson v Mellish* (1824) 2 Bing 229 at 252 (per BURROUGHS J).
2   *Enderby Town Football Club Ltd v Football Association Ltd* [1971] Ch 591 at 606–607 (per LORD DENNING MR).
3   [1957] 1 QB 267.

whereas, it is less likely that a similar stance will be taken in relation to violation of a common law rule.

The courts, in their role as the residual guardians of public morality, may strike down a contract when its purpose is illegal or it otherwise offends public morality. A further group of cases, namely those concerned with restraint of trade, is often included in a consideration of public policy. In this instance, while the restrictive provision is *prima facie* void, subject to proof of reasonableness, the reason for judicial intervention is more concerned with the protection of a person in a weak bargaining position than with issues of public morality. Finally, in actions between strangers the court may refuse to grant a remedy to a person injured in the course of an illegal act.

1.   CONTRACTS CONTRARY TO PUBLIC POLICY[4]

In theory there is a positive rule of policy that a person is free to make whatever contract he likes,[5] but some limitations on that rule must be entertained. The range of contracts that may offend public policy is vast and is difficult to classify. Some contracts may be invalid by reason of a statutory provision; in other cases, the intended mode of performance is illegal, and others may be invalid for general reasons of public policy.

(1)   STATUTORY INVALIDITY

In determining whether a statutory provision renders a contract illegal, it is important to have regard to the precise wording of the relevant statutory provision. Clearly, there must have been a breach of the relevant statutory provision, but even if there has, it does not follow that this will have civil law consequences, since some statutes expressly provide that a breach of their provisions are not to give rise to a civil law action.[6]

Some statutory provisions declare contracts of a particular genre to be illegal and therefore void. For example, the Gaming Act 1845 and various other statutes passed since that date have the effect of rendering void, gaming and wagering contracts.[7] Such contracts provide no rights on either side. Furthermore, restrictive trading agreements may be invalid under the provisions of the Competition Act 1998, based on the EC Treaty, Articles 81 and 82 (formerly Arts 85 and 86) and pyramid selling is invalid under the provisions of the Fair Trading Act 1973. If Parliament has expressly or impliedly forbidden a certain type of contract, the courts will refuse to enforce it. Here the intent of the parties is irrelevant. What matters is that Parliament has chosen to prohibit the making of certain types of contract and the sole enquiry is whether or not the contract under consideration falls within the forbidden class.[8]

Where a statute expressly declares a type of contract to be illegal, the statute is directed at both parties to the contract. Thus in *Re Mahmoud & Ispahani*[9] relevant Regulations forbade the sale of purchase of linseed oil without a licence issued by the Food Controller. In the circumstances there was no need to delve into the intention of Parliament, since it was plain from the wording of the Regulations that only licensed transactions were legal. The transaction in question clearly fell outside that category and, as a result, was

4   See *Treitel* ch 11; *Beale, Bishop and Furmston* chs 36, 37 and 38.
5   *Printing and Numerical Registering Co Ltd v Sampson* (1875) LR 19 Eq 462 at 465 (per Jessel MR).
6   See Trade Descriptions Act 1968, s 35; Fair Trading Act 1973, s 26. See also Trading Schemes Act 1996.
7   See *Treitel* ch 12; Furmston (ed), *The Law of Contract* (Butterworths) ch 5.16 et seq.
8   *Anderson Ltd v Daniel* [1924] 1 KB 138 at 149 (per Atkin LJ); *St John Shipping Corpn v Joseph Rank Ltd* [1957] 1 QB 267 at 283 (per Devlin J).
9   [1921] 2 KB 716.

held to be void from the start. In contrast, there may be circumstances in which the prohibition is only directed at one of the parties. In these circumstances, it does not automatically follow that the contract itself is prohibited.[10]

In other instances, a relevant statutory provision may do no more than impliedly prohibit a particular variety of contract. In these circumstances ascertainment of the intention of Parliament is paramount.[11] Moreover, it is also important to look at the state of mind of the parties. For example, if the parties deliberately set out to break the law, normally their contract will not be supported by the courts,[12] but there may be a different response where the law has been unwittingly infringed.[13]

(2)   CONTRACTS TO COMMIT A WRONG

In some instances, the mere making of a contract may amount to a wrong in law. This is particularly the case where a statutory provision makes it unlawful to enter into a particular type of contract or where the making of a contract, in itself, amounts to the commission of the crime and tort of conspiracy. Thus it is illegal to sell offensive weapons,[14] certain types of restricted drugs and to sell human organs or tissue for transplantation purposes.[15] A contract to commit a crime or a tort is generally illegal, the former amounting to participation in a conspiracy. Thus, a contract to defraud the Inland Revenue or to evade exchange controls will be invalid. Similarly, a contract may be regarded as illegal if it is envisaged that it will be performed in some illegal manner, provided the type of contract made is contrary to the public interest. In this last respect it is considered that if a contract is entered into with the object of committing an unlawful act, it is unenforceable by either party if there is a mutual intent to break the law.[16] If the necessary intent is unilateral, the person with that intent will not be able to maintain an action on the contract.[17] What matters here is whether the intent to break the law was contemplated at the time the contract was entered into. At one stage, an agreement entered into by a solicitor and his client providing that the solicitor would be paid his fees if litigation was successful, was regarded as illegal on the grounds that it was champertous. However, more recent legislataion has rendered such arrangements acceptable.[18]

A contract may also be illegal on the ground that it amounts to the commission of a civil wrong. Thus, a contract entered into by an insolvent debtor to pay one of his creditors may be declared illegal on the ground that it would amount to a fraud on other creditors, thereby involving the commission of the tort of deceit. However, it is important to consider the state of mind of the parties since if both parties are unaware that their contract amounts to the commission of a civil wrong, the contract will not be declared illegal. Where one of the parties is unaware of the illegality, the position is less clear, but it seems sensible to adopt the view that the party who is unaware of the illegality ought to be able to enforce the contract to the extent that he has performed what was required of him.[19]

---

10   *Phoenix General Insurance Co of Greece SA v Halvanon General Insurance Co* [1988] QB 216. See also *Group Josi v Walbrook Insurance* [1996] 1 WLR 1152.

11   See Buckley (1975) 38 MLR 535.

12   *St John Shipping Corpn v Joseph Rank Ltd* [1957] 1 QB 267 at 288 (per DEVLIN J).

13   Ibid (per DEVLIN J).

14   Restriction of Offensive Weapons Act 1959, s 1.

15   Human Organ Transplants Act 1989, s 1.

16   *St John Shipping Corpn v Joseph Rank Ltd* [1957] 1 QB 267 at 283 (per DEVLIN J).

17   Ibid.

18   See Courts and Legal Services Act 1990, s 58; Conditional Fee Agreements Order 1998 (SI 1998/1860).

19   See *Clay v Yates* (1856) 1 H & N 73 at 80 (per MARTIN B).

(3)   CONTRACTS CONTRARY TO PUBLIC POLICY GENERALLY

Certain types of contract may be disapproved of on general policy grounds. For example, contracts prejudicial to the administration of justice, such as an agreement to oust the jurisdiction of the court, are illegal. Similarly, those which promote corruption or tend to prejudice relations with a friendly foreign country may be unenforceable. Likewise, a contract to trade with the enemy in war time may be declared illegal. Contracts entered into for an immoral purpose have also been declared illegal.

Sexual immorality[20] has tended to be a dominant issue in this area, but there is no reason why other heads of immorality cannot be recognised. The doctrine of public policy is variable, depending on changing conditions and morals, but there is also a fear that unfettered use of the doctrine would create uncertainty. Accordingly, it has been stated that new heads of public policy cannot be created.[1] Although contracts which promote sexual immorality have been declared illegal in the past, the traditional view has been steadily eroded in cases concerned with arrangements between unmarried partners. Thus a licence agreement under which an unmarried couple occupied a furnished house has been held not to be contrary to public policy.[2] Similarly, where a couple become the parents of an illegitimate child, there would be nothing contrary to public policy in an agreement between the parents relating to the maintenance of the child and the mother.[3]

(4)   THE EFFECT OF CONTRACTUAL ILLEGALITY

There are two broad effects of contractual illegality. In the first place, a contract tainted with illegality may become unenforceable and secondly, if benefits have been received under an illegal contract there may be a restitutionary claim for recovery of those benefits.

In general, the plaintiff will not succeed in an action on an illegal contract or where the illegality in performance has to be pleaded in order to support his claim. The general reason given for this being that the court is not prepared to give assistance to the plaintiff, rather than for the protection of the defendant.[4] Thus if a contract to lend money is entered into in breach of restrictive legislative controls, the lender will not be able to recover the amount of the loan.[5] However, regard must be had to whether the whole contract is illegal and void or whether the illegality simply affects a term of the contract, as is usually the case where there is an illegal covenant in restraint of trade. In this latter case, the illegal covenant may be regarded as void, insofar as it has not been performed, without affecting the remainder of the contract.[6]

In a second group of cases the plaintiff will not succeed where he would benefit from his own illegal conduct.[7] In addition to these general rules, recent authorities suggested a pragmatic approach to the public policy defence which required it to be asked whether it would be an affront to public conscience to give the plaintiff relief.[8] On the face of it, this might be regarded as a residual test which can apply over and above the general principles stated above.[9] Thus it has been possible for a person to

---

20   See *Pearce v Brookes* (1866) LR 1 Exch 213.
1   *Janson v Driefontein Consolidated Mines Ltd* [1902] AC 484 at 491 (per LORD HALSBURY).
2   *Somma v Hazlehurst* [1978] 1 WLR 1014.
3   *Horrocks v Forray* [1976] 1 WLR 230.
4   See *Holman v Johnson* (1775) 1 Cowp 341.
5   *Spector v Ageda* [1973] Ch 30.
6   *Rock Refrigeration Ltd v Jones* [1997] ICR 938; *O'Sullivan v Management Agency & Music Ltd* [1985] QB 428.
7   *Euro-Diam Ltd v Bathurst* [1988] 2 All ER 23 at 28–29 (per KERR LJ).
8   Ibid and see also *Thackwell v Barclays Bank plc* [1986] 1 All ER 676 at 687 (per HUTCHISON J).
9   *Howard v Shirlstar Container Transport Ltd* [1990] 3 All ER 366 at 373 (per STAUGHTON LJ).

benefit from the commission of a crime, where to do so served to save the plaintiff's life.[10] However, the House of Lords has rejected this 'public conscience' test on the basis that it produces too many uncertainties in its application.[11]

If the plaintiff's illegal or immoral act is the very cause of the loss he suffers, it will usually be an affront to the public conscience to allow his action to succeed. On the other hand, if the plaintiff has participated in an illegal or immoral act, but the illegality does not contribute to the loss suffered by the plaintiff and that loss would have been the same whether he had engaged in the illegal conduct or not, the plaintiff's action should not be barred.[12] Thus the purchaser of a lease who participates in a deception as to the amount of the purchase price in order to avoid having to pay stamp duty is not to be denied an action for damages for fraud on the part of the vendor.[13] In this case, the vendor's fraud is the cause of the plaintiff's loss and the purchaser's participation in tax evasion was purely incidental, not contributing to the loss suffered.[14] It should be observed here that the plaintiff was not seeking to enforce the illegal contract,[15] but was permitted to sue the defendant for his independent tort of deceit.

It may be important to establish who is a guilty party for the purposes of ascertaining whether that person's action is affected by the illegality. For these purposes, if there is illegality in the performance of a contract, it may not follow that the contract is tainted, since the illegal performance may have occurred unwittingly.[16]

Generally, the 'innocent' party will be in a stronger position than the 'guilty' party. However it does not always follow that the 'innocent' party will always be able to enforce the illegal contract. For example, a mistake of law appears not to be a sufficient excuse.[17] In contrast, a mistake of fact may be sufficient to allow the 'innocent' party to enforce the contract. Thus a printer may be able to recover his charges where he unwittingly publishes defamatory material.[18] However, the case law is not entirely consistent on this issue, since there have been instances in which an innocent party having made a mistake of fact has been denied the right to enforce the contract, but this may be because the variety of contract entered into was considered to have been expressly prohibited by statute.[19]

2.   ILLEGALITY AS A DEFENCE IN A TORTIOUS ACTION

Public policy considerations operate across the common law, with the result that an action for breach of a tortious obligation may be denied on the ground of illegality, but only rarely. There is some controversy as to whether the maxim *ex turpi causa* is properly applicable to an action in tort brought by a wrongdoing plaintiff. If the plaintiff's action in tort is dependent upon establishing the validity of a contract tainted with illegality, his action will fail.[20] However, if his action in tort is based on the consequence of an

---

10   Ibid.
11   *Tinsley v Milligan* [1994] 1 AC 340.
12   *Saunders v Edwards* [1987] 2 All ER 651 at 665 (per NICHOLLS LJ).
13   Ibid.
14   Ibid at 665 (per NICHOLLS LJ).
15   Had he been permitted to do so this would have involved the enforcement of a contract to deceive a public authority: *Alexander v Rayson* [1936] 1 KB 169.
16   See *St John Shipping Corpn v Joseph Rank Ltd* [1957] 1 QB 267 (considered above); *Skilton v Sullivan*, [1994] 21 LS Gaz R 41 (unwitting submission of a false VAT invoice).
17   *Mohamed v Alaga & Co* [1998] 2 All ER 720.
18   *Clay v Yates* (1856) 1 H & N 73.
19   See *Re Mahmoud & Ispahani* [1921] 2 KB 716.
20   See *Taylor v Chester* (1869) LR 4 QB 309.

illegal contract but does not necessitate proof of the validity of that contract, an action in tort may still be maintained.[1]

Where the plaintiff's complaint is that the harm he has suffered arises out of his involvement in an illegal act, the plaintiff's wrongdoing may serve to bar his action. The difficulty is to determine what sort of illegality will suffice. Certainly, the commission of a crime will suffice for this purpose and it seems that non-criminal, but immoral conduct on the part of the plaintiff may also serve to deny the plaintiff's claim.[2]

Precisely what test should be applied so as to determine whether the plaintiff's action should be barred is not clear. It has been suggested on occasions that an appropriate test would be to ask whether it would be an affront to public conscience to allow the plaintiff's action to succeed. However, this test has not gained full support on the ground that it is particularly difficult to apply. An alternative, which seems to provide greater ease of application, is to ask whether the plaintiff's involvement in the illegal or immoral enterprise is such that it is impossible to ascertain the standard of care required of the defendant.

Two separate situations require consideration. One is where the plaintiff's illegal or immoral behaviour is independent of the defendant's tort and the second is where the plaintiff and the defendant are involved in a joint enterprise.

(1)   WRONGS INDEPENDENT OF THE DEFENDANT'S TORT

The mere fact of the commission of a tort by the plaintiff, of itself, will not be sufficient to bar his action. To say otherwise would mean that a trespasser would not be owed a duty of care by an occupier of premises, and a negligent driver would be denied recovery against another driver who is equally or more to blame for a traffic accident. Thus in *Revill v Newberry*[3] a duty of care was owed by the owner of premises to a burglar where he negligently discharged the contents of his gun knowing that the burglar was in the vicinity. However, in the circumstances, the burglar's damages were reduced by two-thirds, on the grounds of contributory negligence, so as to represent his responsibility for the injuries suffered. In contrast, where a burglar is actively involved in the commission of a crime, the position may be different. For example, it appears that a burglar can expect no sympathy if he is bitten by a guard dog[4] since his unlawful presence gives the dog the opportunity to bite. But the commission of a crime by the plaintiff will not always bar a claim. For example, a breach of statutory duty on the part of an employee may also constitute the commission of a criminal offence, but this is not likely to bar his civil claim against his employer.[5]

In order to have an effect on the plaintiff's action, the wrong he commits must be related to the loss he suffers. Thus a motorist who has failed to display a valid road tax disc at the time of a traffic accident caused by the defendant's negligence, will not be denied damages despite the fact that he has infringed road traffic law. Conversely, a widow has been denied success in an action for loss of support under the Fatal Accidents Act 1976 where her deceased husband's support was assumed to come from the proceeds of crime.[6] The widow, herself, was not a participant in any illegal act, yet she and her children were denied support. It may be objected that this result is the same as denying

---

1   *Bowmakers Ltd v Barnet Instruments Ltd* [1945] KB 65.
2   *Kirkham v Chief Constable of Greater Manchester Police* [1990] 3 All ER 246 at 251 (per LLOYD LJ).
3   [1996] QB 567.
4   *Cummings v Granger* [1977] 1 All ER 104 at 109 (per LORD DENNING MR).
5   *National Coal Board v England* [1954] AC 403.
6   *Burns v Edman* [1970] 2 QB 541.

a person recovery under the narrow rule in *Donoghue v Stevenson*[7] where the bottle of ginger beer has been stolen.[8]

In some instances, on policy grounds, it may be possible for the court to exercise a discretion in favour of denying the plaintiff's action against the defendant. In *Meah v McCreamer (No 2)*,[9] the defendant's negligence was the cause of a traffic accident in which the plaintiff was injured. A consequence of these injuries was that the plaintiff suffered a personality change that resulted in the plaintiff becoming a rapist. This in turn rendered the plaintiff liable in damages to the victims of the acts of rape. It was held that it would not be in the public interest to allow the plaintiff to be indemnified against the consequences of his criminal acts. A similar approach can be adopted where an award of damages might serve to encourage people to engage in criminal misconduct. Thus in *Clunis v Camden & Islington Health Authority*[10] the plaintiff had been convicted of manslaughter on the grounds of diminished responsibility and sought to recover from the defendants on the ground that they had failed to carry out an adequate mental health assessment. Had this been done, it was argued, the plaintiff might not have gone on to kill his victim. The court, nevertheless, concluded that the plaintiff was responsible for his actions and concluded that it would be contrary to public policy to allow the plaintiff to benefit from the commission of a crime.

(2)   JOINT ENTERPRISES

It is arguable that the principle *ex turpi causa* applies where the plaintiff's wrongful act involves a step in the execution of a common illegal purpose.[11] It follows that it may be possible to apply the defence where a participant in an affray gets more than he bargained for and is killed or seriously injured by another participant.[12] On the other hand, it is necessary not to use the *ex turpi causa* principle so as to deny all wrongdoing plaintiffs a right of action. The difficulty is to determine where the public interest lies. While it is in the public interest not to encourage crime, it is also in the public interest that a plaintiff harmed by the tortious conduct of another should be compensated especially where the defendant's wrong is disproportionate to that of the plaintiff.[13]

In the case of a joint unlawful enterprise, where the plaintiff sues for negligence, the court's reaction may be that it is impossible to recognise the existence of a duty of care.[14] For example in *Ashton v Turner*,[15] the plaintiff and the defendant were participants in a burglary. The plaintiff was injured when the intoxicated defendant negligently crashed the get-away vehicle. The plaintiff, who was also aware of the defendant's intoxication, was denied damages both on the grounds of public policy and, incorrectly, because he was *volens* to the risk of harm. In this case, the plaintiff and defendant were engaged in a joint criminal enterprise, but the public policy defence is not confined to behaviour on the part of the plaintiff which is criminal *per se*. In *Pitts v Hunt*[16] the plaintiff, a pillion passenger, had encouraged and supported an under-age, uninsured and drunken driver of a motorcycle in using the vehicle to frighten other road users. His conduct was sufficiently serious to justify the conclusion that the hazards inherent in the enterprise

---

7   [1932] AC 562.
8   See Yale [1970] CLJ 17.
9   [1986] 1 All ER 943.
10 [1998] 3 All ER 180.
11 *National Coal Board v England* [1954] AC 403 at 428–429 (per LORD ASQUITH).
12 *Murphy v Culhane* [1977] QB 94 at 98 (per LORD DENNING MR).
13 *Lane v Holloway* [1968] 1 QB 379; *Barnes v Nayer* (1986) Times, 19 December.
14 *Pitts v Hunt* [1990] 3 All ER 344 at 359 (per BALCOMBE LJ) and at 366 (per DILLON LJ).
15 [1981] QB 137.
16 [1990] 3 All ER 344.

were such that it was impossible to determine the appropriate standard of care required of the defendant,[17] with the result that the injuries suffered by the plaintiff in a traffic accident went uncompensated.

In cases of joint illegal enterprise, it is necessary to look at the degree of responsibility which the plaintiff has undertaken in the light of his participation in an illegal or immoral act. It is important that the public policy defence is confined to cases in which the plaintiff has done something illegal or immoral. In this respect it has been argued that the public policy defence should not be used as a means of introducing the defence of *volenti* via the back door in cases in which the plaintiff is aware that he is engaged in a risky enterprise.[18]

(3)   THE COMPETING TESTS

The difficulty with the reduced standard of care test, used in the cases considered above, is that while it may be a useful tool in respect of potential negligence liability, it cannot be an answer in all cases. It is true that it is a helpful test in some instances, for example, where the standard of care expected of a police driver is lowered when he is involved in a high-speed chase to apprehend an offender, since the stressful circumstances have to be considered.[19] But the test is less helpful in other cases because there are torts in which the standard of care required of the defendant is not a relevant issue. Moreover, there are negligence actions in which the appropriate standard of care is clear. For example, in cases of alleged medical negligence, the defendant must reach the standard of an ordinary skilled man exercising and professing the special skill of the defendant. But where the alleged medical negligence prevents the plaintiff from considering the possibility of an illegal abortion, it would be contrary to public policy to allow an action for damages for negligence since seeking the abortion would have involved breaking the law.[20] Furthermore, doubts have also been expressed that it is not good policy to encourage the belief that the duty to behave responsibly is diminished in circumstances in which the defendant's conduct is highly dangerous to others.[1]

An alternative test requires the court to consider whether it would be an affront to public conscience to grant relief.[2] This test is considered to be discredited in the context of an action for breach of an allegedly illegal contract,[3] but it seems that it may still have some currency in tort actions. For these purposes, it is relevant to consider whether granting relief might encourage others to behave in a similar manner or if the success of the plaintiff's action would serve to shock the ordinary citizen.[4] The difficulty in this regard is to identify those varieties of misconduct which are capable of invoking the public policy defence. These difficulties have been sufficient to persuade a majority of the Court of Appeal that a 'public conscience' test is unworkable[5] on the ground that the test depends, in large measure, on matters of an emotional nature[6] which might lead to a graph of illegalities according to the moral turpitude of the plaintiff.[7] The

---

17   Applying *Jackson v Harrison* (1978) 138 CLR 438 at 455 (per MASON J).
18   Kidner (1991) 11 Legal Studies 1 at 20.
19   *Marshall v Osmond* [1983] 2 All ER 225.
20   *Rance v Mid-Downs Health Authority* [1991] 1 All ER 801.
1   *Pitts v Hunt* [1990] 3 All ER 344 at 355–356 (per BELDAM LJ).
2   See *Euro-Diam Ltd v Bathurst* [1988] 2 All ER 23 at 28–29 (per KERR LJ); *Thackwell v Barclays Bank plc* [1986] 1 All ER 676 at 687 (per HUTCHISON J); *Howard v Shirlstar Container Transport Ltd* [1990] 3 All ER 366 at 373 (per STAUGHTON LJ).
3   See *Tinsley v Milligan* [1994] 1 AC 340, discussed above in relation to the effects of contractual illegality.
4   *Kirkham v Chief Constable of Greater Manchester Police* [1990] 3 All ER 246 at 251 (per LLOYD LJ).
5   *Pitts v Hunt* [1990] 3 All ER 344 at 358 (per BALCOMBE LJ) and at 362–363 (per DILLON LJ).
6   Ibid at 362 (per DILLON LJ).
7   Ibid at 363 (per DILLON LJ).

difficulty created by this graph, it seems, is that it will be necessary to create some mechanism whereby serious wrongs and immoral conduct may be distinguished from those which are not so serious and which do not justify the denial of a claim.[8] While this may be a criticism of the test, it has not prevented members of the judiciary from examining moral turpitude and drawing conclusions.[9] For example, it seems there is a distinction between a person who commits suicide while suffering from a serious mental instability and one who commits suicide when wholly sane.[10] The decision of the House of Lords in *Reeves v Metropolitan Police Commissioner*[11] indicates that what the Court of Appeal was saying in *Kirkham* was that the police should not owe a person of sound mind a duty of care to prevent him from committing suicide.[12] However LORD HOFFMANN expresses some disquiet with this view in the context of a case in which the police were under a duty to guard against the possibility of a prisoner taking his own life, whether he was sane or not.[13] Moreover, in the Court of Appeal in *Reeves* it was considered that the public would not regard it as shocking if the plaintiff were to recover damages in these circumstances.[14]

---

8   *Jackson v Harrison* (1978) 138 CLR 438 at 455 (per MASON J).
9   *Saunders v Edwards* [1987] 2 All ER 651 at 660 (per KERR LJ; *Pitts v Hunt* [1990] 3 All ER 344 at 358–359 (per BALCOMBE LJ).
10   *Kirkham v Chief Constable of Greater Manchester Police* [1990] 3 All ER 246 at 255 (per FARQUHARSON LJ).
11   [1999] 3 WLR 363. For further discussion of this case see ch 20.
12   Ibid at 368 (per LORD HOFFMANN).
13   Ibid.
14   See [1998] 2 All ER 381.

Chapter 22

Negation of liability by consent

Consistent with classical emphasis upon voluntary choice as the basis for the creation of common law obligations, it is not surprising that the consent of the plaintiff was, at one time, a dominant feature in determining when a wrongdoing defendant should be able to escape liability for his wrong. More recently, the importance of consent as a defence has been downgraded through legislative and judicial restrictions which have, in particular, sought to recognise inequality of bargaining power in exchange relationships and the compensation objective in non-exchange relationships. The declining importance of consent as a defence can be seen particularly in the context of negligently inflicted harm to the person where it seems inherently improbable that the plaintiff would consent to the harm inflicted by the defendant,[1] except in the most extreme circumstances. Moreover, if what is required is consent in advance, then this may be said to be inconsistent with the legal concept of negligence since it would be difficult to say that a plaintiff can appreciate the risks associated with a failure to take reasonable care until that act or omission has occurred.[2] However, it may be counter-argued that this view is based on negligence consisting of inadvertence on the part of the defendant. In contrast, where the defendant is guilty of deliberate misconduct, the case law indicates that the courts have little difficulty in treating a plaintiff who knows of and understands the potential risk as having consented to the risk which is subsequently created.[3]

In the case of exchange relationships of a commercial nature it is proper for the businesses concerned to allocate a risk of loss by determining who is in the best position to absorb it. This allocation of risk may be effected by means of an exclusion clause the presence of which is said to be consented to by the parties.

The issue of consent as a defence can arise in three main ways: where a wrongdoer in a non-exchange relationship expressly disclaims liability; where the plaintiff in a tort action is met with the defence of *volenti non fit injuria* — to one who is willing, no harm is done; and where there is an exclusion, restriction or limitation of the liability of one of the parties to an exchange relationship. On a strict construction of the doctrine of privity of contract, such clauses should only affect the parties to the contract. However, when it is considered that exclusion clauses are a suitable means of risk-allocation, it

---

1   See Fleming *Introduction* p 138; Jaffey (1985) CLJ 87.
2   See Cane *The Anatomy of Tort Law,* Hart Publishing, 1997, p 61.
3   Ibid and see *Morris v Murray* [1991] 2 QB 6.

will be the case, especially, following the enactment of the Contracts (Rights of Third Parties) Act 1999, that a third party can claim the benefit of an exclusion clause in a contract to which he is not a party.

In much more limited circumstances, a third party may also be subject to the burden imposed by an exclusion clause in a contract between two other parties, but such exceptional cases as there are have been developed at common law. The Contracts (Rights of Third Parties) Act 1999 has no application to contractual terms which impose burdens. Whichever set of rules applies, the view that the exclusion has been consented to may be entirely illusory.

1. NINETEENTH, TWENTIETH AND TWENTY-FIRST CENTURY ATTITUDES TO CONSENT AS A DEFENCE

(1) THE NINETEENTH CENTURY

For the greater part of the nineteenth century, the dominant philosophy was that of *laissez-faire*, which promoted a judicial emphasis upon the freedom of the individual to do as he pleased. One effect of this emphasis upon individualism was that exclusion clauses in contracts were tolerated, and the defence of *volenti non fit injuria* flourished, even in areas where, logically, it had no place at all.

Imprecision of thought led to the confusion of the issues of consent, contributory negligence and causation. The result was that, in the nineteenth century, the doctrine of *volenti* came to be implied in virtually all cases where the plaintiff appreciated a risk and chose to face it rather than stop what he was doing. This confusion did not really matter prior to the enactment of the Law Reform (Contributory Negligence) Act 1945, since *volenti* and contributory negligence were both total defences. Following the 1945 Act the court has a power to apportion damages in the light of the plaintiff's contributory negligence,[4] whereas *volenti* remains an absolute defence to liability. Furthermore, since it has been said, obiter, that it is statutorily impossible for a person to be 100 per cent contributorily negligent,[5] the distinction between the two defences becomes even more important.

The nineteenth-century attitude to the issue of consent in relation to matters of compensation can be illustrated by reference to the issues of workmen's compensation and of rescue. Employees were assumed to consent to the risks inherent in the work they did. Thus an employee engaged to work in a railway tunnel could be expected to guard against the risk of being struck by a train.[6] Since the employee was taken to be aware of the risk, when he carried on working he was expected to abide by the consequences. The employee was assumed to be in a position of equal bargaining power[7] since he was absolutely free to work elsewhere if he so desired. What this approach failed to consider was that an employee's consent almost certainly emanated from his poverty rather than his will.[8]

A similarly robust attitude was also taken in rescue cases. The emphasis upon individualism resulted in a general view that everyone acted in his own interests and that, if a person indulged in altruism by assisting another in an emergency, he did so at his own risk. However, what this ignores is that danger invites a rescue attempt and

---

4   See ch 20.
5   *Pitts v Hunt* [1990] 3 All ER 344.
6   *Woodley v Metropolitan District Rly Co* (1877) 2 Ex D 384.
7   See *Crichton v Keir* (1863) 1 M 407.
8   *Thrussel v Handyside* (1888) 20 QBD 359 at 364 (per HAWKIN J).

that, in a more caring society, consideration of the plight of others is a virtue to be encouraged.

The same emphasis on individualism was also applied to exclusion clauses in exchange relationships. Because these devices were part of a contract, it was said that men of full age and competence should have the utmost liberty of contracting, and that their contracts, when entered into freely and voluntarily, should be held sacred.[9] Applying principles of this type to exclusion clauses contained in standard form documents can lead to the view that the receiver of the document is content to deal on the terms referred to, whether he has read the document or not.[10] It should be emphasised that exhortations in favour of self-reliance did not go without qualification, even in the nineteenth century. It was recognised that persons not of full age and competence required protection, and it was later recognised that economic freedom could often create injustices which necessitated judicial or legislative intervention.

(2)   LATER DEVELOPMENTS

Before the end of the nineteenth century, it was recognised that a person might not always be in a position to truly consent to a risk of harm. In the case of the employer/employee relationship, it was accepted that mere knowledge of a risk was not sufficient to invoke the doctrine of *volenti non fit injuria*, with the result that a distinction was drawn between carelessness and intelligent choice.[11] Ultimately, the House of Lords in *Smith v Baker*[12] disposed of the idea that an employee could be presumed to consent to the risk of injury inherent in his employment simply because certain risks were apparent. It might be the case that an employee consents to certain risks where, for example, he is paid 'danger money'.[13] However, the general rule is now that a person cannot be said to be truly willing unless he is in a position to choose freely. This freedom of choice requires not only full knowledge of all the circumstances, but also the absence of any feeling of constraint upon the mind of the employee.[14] Accordingly, economic constraints such as the fear of losing one's job will serve to exclude the defence of *volenti*.

Similar views were also to be found in relation to rescue attempts. The Good Samaritan who consciously faces a risk of injury in an attempt to save the victim of the defendant's negligence will not be met by the defence of *volenti*.[15] In some instances, a rescuer who acts unreasonably may be denied recovery in full or in part, but, in such cases, the better view is that the rescuer is guilty of contributory negligence or is the cause of his own injury. However, it is now clear that, even in the twentieth and twenty-first centuries, policy considerations may also be relevant, even in the context of an altruistic act of rescue. Following the decision of the House of Lords in *White v Chief Constable of South Yorkshire Police*[16] there may be circumstances in which professional rescuers (in this case members of the South Yorkshire police force at the scene of the Hillsborough football ground disaster) are not regarded as foreseeable primary victims of the negligence of their employers. However, it should be noted that this decision was heavily influenced

9   *Printing and Numerical Registering Co v Sampson* (1875) LR 19 Eq 462 at 465 (per SIR GEORGE JESSEL MR). See also ch 24.

10   See *Parker v South Eastern Railway* (1877) 2 CPD 416 at 427 (per BRAMWELL LJ) (dissenting); *L'Estrange v F Graucob Ltd* [1934] 2 KB 394. See also Spencer (1973) CLJ 104.

11   *Thomas v Quartermaine* (1887) 18 QBD 685 at 698 (per BOWEN LJ).

12   [1891] AC 325.

13   Ibid at 362–363 (per LORD HERSCHELL).

14   *Bowater v Rowley Regis Corpn* [1944] KB 476 at 479 (per SCOTT LJ).

15   *Haynes v Harwood* [1935] 1 KB 146 at 157 (per GREER LJ). See also *Baker v TE Hopkins & Sons Ltd* [1959] 1 WLR 966.

16   [1999] 1 All ER 1 sub nom *Frost v Chief Constable of South Yorkshire Police*. Cf *Chadwick v British Transport Commission* [1967] 2 All ER 945.

by policy considerations on the basis that the House of Lords had previously held that members of the families of supporters killed or injured at the Hillsborough Disaster were unable to recover damages in respect of psychiatric harm suffered by them.

Towards the end of the nineteenth century, a more realistic attitude came to be adopted in respect of the use of contractual exclusions. The earlier part of that century had seen a substantial increase in mass produced articles, which heralded mass distribution of those products. In order to cope with this increased production, businesses began to use standardised contracts, known as standard form contracts or contracts of adhesion. Such contracts fall into one of two categories.[17] Some standard form contracts set out the terms of long-established mercantile transactions and their content is regarded as a fair and reasonable representation of standard business practice by all parties. Examples include policies of marine insurance, charterparties and bills of lading. More recently, trade associations have prepared standard form contracts, taking into account problems commonly occurring in the context of a particular trade or business.[18] In contrast, other types of standard form contract have developed out of the concentration of business in a relatively small number of hands. Such standard form contracts are invariably not the subject of negotiation between the parties, and have not been approved by the representatives of the weaker party. Standard form contracts which fall within this second category have been described as a weapon of consumer oppression.[19] One view, known as the 'exploitation theory', is that such terms tend to be used by businesses with near monopolistic or oligopolistic power against a person who is in no position to shop around for alternative sources of supply.[20] In contrast, it has been argued that the proliferation of standard form contracts is not the result of monopoly power, but is an attempt by businesses to reduce transaction costs.[1] The fact that such contract terms are offered on a 'take it or leave it' basis is because it does not suit the interests of either party to incur the costs involved in separately negotiating every transaction.[2]

The weaker party faced with the prospect of contracting under standard terms is frequently a consumer. The consumer contract is something which was not often encountered in the earlier part of the nineteenth century, when the classical rules of contract law were formulated. At that time, a contract was essentially a consensual transaction entered into by businesses of roughly equal bargaining power. Such contracts could be regarded as democratic, in the sense that the parties' obligations were based on mutual agreement. The same cannot be said of the modern consumer contract entered into on standard terms. It has been objected that such contracts are not democratic, since consumers may not read the terms of the contract and, even if they have been read, it is likely that the consumer will not understand their import. Furthermore, even if the consumer does understand the terms and objects to their presence, it is likely that he would be told that he could take the contract terms as stated or look elsewhere for an alternative source of supply.[3] In this case, it is difficult to argue that the consumer has agreed to the presence of an exclusion clause presented in such a manner. Control of such clauses can be justified on the ground of information asymmetry.

---

17   See *A Schroeder Music Publishing Co v Macaulay* [1974] 3 All ER 616 at 624 (per LORD DIPLOCK).
18   See *British Crane Hire Corpn Ltd v Ipswich Plant Hire Ltd* [1975] QB 303.
19   Yates p 2.
20   See Kessler 43 Col LR 629 (1943).
1   Trebilcock 'An Economic Approach to Unconscionability' in *Studies in Contract Law* (eds Reiter & Swan) (1981) pp 381–421.
2   Ibid. See further ch 24.
3   Slawson (1975) 84 Harv LR 529.

Because the consumer was assumed to have unequal bargaining power, both judicial and legislative responses attempted to redress the balance.[4] At one stage, a general doctrine of inequality of bargaining power appeared to commend itself to certain members of the judiciary,[5] and this could have encompassed unconscionable exclusion clauses.[6] However, the need for a general doctrine of this nature has been doubted in the House of Lords,[7] and it would appear that any general reform in this direction will have to come from Parliament or the European Commission. A partial legislative solution has been adopted in the form of the Unfair Contract Terms Act 1977. This introduces the concept of the reasonable exclusion clause and forbids outright certain types of exclusion or notice, particularly those which seek to exclude or restrict the rights of consumers and those which purport to restrict liability for negligently caused death or bodily injury. Moreover, the European Commission has included the issue of unfair terms in consumer contracts in its general consumer policy. This in turn has led to the adoption of the Directive on Unfair Terms in Consumer Contracts[8] which, in turn, has resulted in the adoption of the Unfair Terms in Consumer Contracts Regulations 1994,[9] now subsumed into the Unfair Terms in Consumer Contracts Regulations 1999.[10] These Regulations contain a non-exclusive list of terms which may be regarded as unfair to consumers, but have no application to purely business arrangements. However, it should be noted that these Regulations only create a presumption of unfairness and do not render any particular contract term automatically void.

2.   INDICATIONS OF CONSENT

(1)   *VOLENTI NON FIT INJURIA*

The maxim, which has its origins in Roman law,[11] is said to apply to both intentional and accidental harm. Insofar as it relates to intentional acts, the defence manifests itself in the form of consent, whereas, in relation to accidental harm, it is referred to as assumption of risk.

A person can consent to an act that would otherwise amount to the commission of a tort. Thus it will be a defence to an alleged trespass to land or goods for the defendant to show that the plaintiff consented to the invasion of his interest.[12] In this context, the defence manifests itself as a form of licence. In the context of trespass to the person, similar considerations also apply to the extent that a willing participant in a sport which involves the possibility of injury may be taken to consent to injuries suffered. Thus, one who engages in a sport such as boxing or cricket licences those injuries he receives in the course of participation, provided the rules of the game have been adhered to.

In like terms, a mentally handicapped woman whose pregnancy is terminated may maintain an action for battery unless it can be shown that she impliedly consents to the medical procedure,[13] although in a case such as this it may also be argued that the doctor who acts in an emergency is justified in doing what is in the best interests of the patient

---

4   See ch 24.
5   *A Schroeder Music Publishing Co Ltd v Macaulay* [1974] 3 All ER 616; *Lloyds Bank Ltd v Bundy* [1975] QB 326.
6   *Levison v Patent Steam Carpet Cleaning Co Ltd* [1978] QB 69.
7   *National Westminster Bank plc v Morgan* [1985] AC 686 at 708–709 (per Lord Scarman).
8   93/13. EEC, OJL 95/29.
9   SI 1994/3159.
10   SI 1999/2083.
11   The maxim was used to validate the voluntary act of a free man in selling himself into slavery.
12   *Willian Leitch & Co Ltd v Leydon* [1931] AC 90 at 109.
13   See *T v T* [1988] 1 All ER 613 at 625 (per Wood J).

on the ground that this is necessary in order to save life, to ensure improvement or to prevent deterioration in physical or mental health.[14] Moreover, where the patient is a child, the court has an inherent jurisdiction to decide what is in the best interests of the child patient, subject to obtaining any necessary consent. It follows that if a medical specialist reasonably believes that a particular medical procedure designed to prolong life would be cruel to the child, it should be withheld, despite the fact that the guardian and other medical experts may wish action to be taken.[15] More difficult questions may arise where the child patient is older and has expressed a clear choice. But if the child has elected to pursue a course of action which might endanger her health, such as seeking to cure herself of *anorexia nervosa*, the court may override that decision in the interests of the child and in order to prevent probable death.[16] The question of consent can also arise where an adult patient elects not to undergo a medical procedure on the basis of religious convictions. It seems that even where a clear objection has been expressed, clinical judgment may override that choice if the failure to provide the medical treatment might endanger the potential for life of an unborn child.[17] Moreover, even though an adult has the right to decline medical treatment even when this risks the possibility of permanent injury or premature death, the capacity of the patient to give that consent has to be considered. Thus, if the capacity of the patient to give a rational consent has been overborne by others or where that capacity is otherwise impaired, medical experts have the power to exercise their own clinical judgment in the best interests of the patient.[18] Where an adult patient is insensate and further treatment would be futile, withdrawal of medical treatment which will result in certain death is lawful provided it is in the patient's best interests.[19]

It should also be appreciated that the self-determination argument only applies to the denial of a duty of care and has no relevance where a duty is owed and the question of liability turns on whether there has been a breach of duty.[20]

Different considerations may apply where the defendant is guilty of deceit. For example, a dentist who carries out wholly unjustifiable work on the teeth of a patient with a view to recovering remuneration from a statutory body may be guilty of a battery.[1] However, the courts may be more lenient in other areas. For example, it has been held that where a defendant falsely offers money or induces the plaintiff to marry him by means of a false representation that he is not married to another person and subsequently engages in sexual intercourse, he is neither guilty of battery nor rape.[2]

Special problems may also arise in relation to persons in lawful custody. The general rule appears to be that, subject to special statutory considerations, even a prisoner has the same power as anyone else to give or withhold consent to medical treatment.[3] However, it should be noted that, in this context, a prison doctor is in a position to influence the decisions made by the prisoner.[4] Moreover, there may be circumstances in which prison or police authorities are under an express duty to guard against the risk of harm which results in the death of the prisoner. In these circumstances it is unlikely that the defence of *volenti* will succeed where, for example, the prisoner takes his own

---

14   *F v West Berkshire Health Authority* [1989] 2 All ER 545 at 565–566 (per LORD GOFF).
15   *Re J (a minor)* [1992] 4 All ER 614.
16   *Re W (a minor)* [1992] 4 All ER 627.
17   *Re S (adult, refusal of medical treatment)* [1992] 4 All ER 671.
18   *Re T (adult, refusal of medical treatment)* [1992] 4 All ER 649.
19   *Airedale NHS Trust v Bland* [1993] 1 All ER 821, HL. See also *St George's Healthcare Trust v S* [1999] Fam 26.
20   *Reeves v Metropolitan Police Commissioner* [1999] 3 WLR 363 at 374 (per LORD JAUNCEY).
1   See *Appleton v Garrett* (1995) 34 BMLR 23.
2   *R v Linekar* [1995] QB 250.
3   *Secretary of State for the Home Department v Robb* [1995] Fam 127.
4   *Freeman v Home Office (No. 2)* [1984] QB 524.

life.[5] In *Reeves v MPC*[6] the House of Lords held that a deliberate and informed act by a prisoner to take his own life did not negative causation where the police were under a duty to guard against that act.

However, there may be circumstances in which the defence of *volenti* may apply. For example there may be circumstances in which the police are required to guard against negligent or accidental harm to the claimant and the claimant does some act which causes himself injury. Provided the claimant has full knowledge of the risk, in which case the police will still owe a duty of care.[7] In *Reeves*, however, the duty was to guard against the deliberate act which resulted in death.

Medical trespass cases and those concerned with prisoners in custody apart, it has been held, obiter, that the various defences to an alleged trespass to the person, including that of consent, can be rationalised under one general exception embracing all physical contact which is generally acceptable in the ordinary conduct of daily life.[8] Thus, where two people inadvertently make contact in the street or where schoolboys engage in acceptable 'horseplay', the contact is not hostile and therefore not a trespass. In contrast, a rugby player who deliberately bites off the ear of an opponent is guilty of battery, because his conduct is hostile and unacceptable. In each case, the issue of consent is immaterial, and artificial distinctions between express and implied consent can be avoided.

In the case of accidental harm, the maxim *volenti non fit injuria* applies where the plaintiff has assumed the legal risk of injury in circumstances in which the defendant's act would otherwise amount to negligence. This requires the plaintiff to have voluntarily agreed that the defendant be exempt from liability for breach of a duty of care which would otherwise have been owed.[9] It follows from this that, before the issue of *volenti* can arise, a tort must have been committed. If there is no tort, there is no legal risk to which a person can consent. It follows from this that the defence of *volenti* can only apply so as to deny the existence of a duty and will have no effect where a duty exists and it is alleged that there is a breach of duty.[10] Moreover, if, for other reasons, it is determined that there is no breach of duty either, no tort is committed and the defence of *volenti* becomes irrelevant. Thus, if the court determines that a defendant has exercised reasonable care, any attempt to explain the defendant's non-liability in terms of *volenti* is misfounded.[11] In other instances, the plaintiff's actions may lower the standard of care required of the defendant,[12] in which case the lower standard may have been complied with, but this is not synonymous with an assumption of risk, since the issue is whether there has been a breach of duty, not whether there has been an assumption of risk.

---

5   See also *Kirkham v Chief Constable of Greater Manchester Police* [1990] 2 QB 283 at 295 (per FARQUHARSON LJ); *Reeves v Metropolitan Police Commissioner* [1999] 3 WLR 363 at 375 (per LORD JAUNCEY) and at 379 (per LORD HOPE).
6   [1999] 3 WLR 363.
7   Ibid at 379–380 (per LORD HOPE).
8   *Wilson v Pringle* [1986] 2 All ER 440 at 447 (per CROOM-JOHNSON LJ) applying *Collins v Wilcock* [1984] 3 All ER 374 at 377–378 (per ROBERT GOFF LJ).
9   *Buckpitt v Oates* [1968] 1 All ER 1145 at 1148; *Titchener v British Railways Board* [1983] 1 WLR 1427 at 1434. But cf *Wooldridge v Sumner* [1963] 2 QB 43 at 69 where it is suggested that the law of negligence assumes the principle of *volenti non fit injuria* to be inapplicable.
10   *Reeves v Metropolitan Police Commissioner* [1999] 3 WLR 363 at 374 (per LORD JAUNCEY).
11   *Smith v Baker* [1891] AC 325 at 366 (per LORD HERSCHELL). For an example of a judicial mistake of this kind, see *Titchener v British Railways Board* [1983] 1 WLR 1427.
12   *Hall v Brooklands Auto-Racing Club* [1933] 1 KB 205; *Murray v Harringay Arena Ltd* [1951] 2 KB 529. See also Kidner (1991) 11 Legal Studies 1.

(2) DISCLAIMERS OF LIABILITY

A person may disclaim responsibility for harm suffered by a person who comes into contact with his activities by issuing a notice to this effect. Under the Unfair Contract Terms Act 1977, section 2(1), such a term is ineffective if it seeks to exclude liability for death and bodily injury. Moreover, such a clause must also be reasonable in relation to types of damage other than death or bodily injury[13] if it is to affect the defendant's liability. Sometimes a plaintiff may have agreed that the defendant should not be liable for a failure to take care. This may be the case where an occupier of premises excludes the common duty of care owed under the Occupiers' Liability Act 1957, section 2(1) by means of a contractual exclusion clause. However, where the visitor is a trespasser of a sufficient age to understand the risk created by entering premises to which he has no invitation, such as an open-air swimming pool, no duty of care will be owed, on the ground that the trespasser ought to realise the risk involved, and can be taken to have accepted the risk.[14]

It is also possible to have an agreement to exonerate in the absence of a contract. Such was the position in *Hedley Byrne & Co Ltd v Heller*[15] where, but for an express disclaimer of liability, the plaintiff's reliance upon the defendant's advice would have given rise to a duty situation. In the circumstances, it would have been unfair to allow the plaintiff to succeed where the defendant would not have done the act which caused the damage if the plaintiff had not undertaken to forgo his claim. In a sense, the undertaking to forgo the legal right operates as a form of estoppel.[16] Moreover, given the high cost of domestic dwellings and the rates of interest charged to mortgage borrowers, it is not reasonable for a surveyor to use a disclaimer to impose the risk of economic loss arising from the valuer's own negligence in preparing his valuation report.[17] The same considerations will not necessarily apply to commercial purchasers, whose expectations may be such that it is reasonable for the valuer to disclaim liability for negligence.[18]

(3) EXCLUSION AND LIMITATION CLAUSES

Exclusion and limitation clauses are exclusively contractual terms and are distinct from the defence of *volenti*[19] since in most instances these manifestations of consent as a defence raise different issues.

There are numerous varieties of exclusion and limitation clause.[20] These include definition clauses which provide that certain acts or omissions are not to be regarded as a breach of contract at all. If there is no breach of contract, there is no liability against which the *proferens*, the person who seeks to rely on the clause, requires protection.[1] For example, a clause which provides that a warehouseman should take no greater care of perishable goods than is appropriate to imperishable goods means that, if the warehouseman exercises the care appropriate to imperishable goods, he has committed no breach of contract.[2]

13 Unfair Contract Terms Act 1977, s 2(2).
14 *Ratcliff v McConnell* [1999] 1 WLR 670.
15 [1964] AC 465.
16 See Jaffey (1985) 44 CLJ 87 at 88.
17 *Smith v Eric S Bush (a firm)* [1989] 2 All ER 514.
18 Ibid at 532 (per LORD GRIFFITHS).
19 See Unfair Contract Terms Act 1977, s 2(3); *Burnett v British Waterways Board* [1973] 1 WLR 700 at 705 (per LORD DENNING MR) and see Lowe (1974) 37 MLR 218.
20 See Yates & Hawkins, *Standard Business Contracts: Exclusions and Related Devices* (1986) pp 5–11.
1   *Photo Production Ltd v Securicor Transport Ltd* [1980] AC 827 at 851 (per LORD DIPLOCK). See also *Anglo-Continental Holidays Ltd v Typaldos Lines (London) Ltd* [1967] 2 Lloyd's Rep 61; cf Unfair Contract Terms Act 1977, s 3(2)(b)(ii) and see ch 24.
2   *Kenyon, Son & Craven v Baxter Hoare & Co Ltd* [1971] 1 WLR 519 at 522 (per DONALDSON J).

Other clauses may have the effect of shielding the *proferens* from an action for damages for breach of contract, or for repudiation of the contract. Here, there is a breach of contract, but liability for breach is in some way restricted. Limitations of this type should be distinguished from liquidated damages clauses, which fix a maximum limit on what can be recovered. A liquidated damages clause is a genuine attempt at estimating in advance the likely loss flowing from a breach of contract. A limitation clause is designed to protect one party against the legal consequences of other terms of the contract. The liquidated damages clause, in contrast, is for the benefit of both parties.[3]

Some clauses can have the effect of restricting the availability of a particular remedy, whether it be the right to damages, the right to reject or the right to set-off a debt owed by the *proferens*.[4] Others may have the effect of modifying procedural or evidential rules. For example, in building contracts, the final certificate is often regarded as conclusive evidence that the work has been completed in all respects, in accordance with the contract. In other cases, a clause may have the effect of imposing a limit on the time during which a remedy is available, as in the case of a notification of claims clause in an insurance policy. Yet another type, commonly found in shipping contracts might prohibit litigation per se requiring contractual disputes to be resolved by resort to arbitration.

In short, it can be observed that the effect of some exclusion and limitation clauses is to exclude liability where breach is admitted but, in other cases, it would appear that there is no breach of contract, because the clause operates at a stage prior to a breach of contract. This distinction is important when the relationship between exclusions, disclaimers and *volenti* is considered.

(4)   THE RELATIONSHIP BETWEEN *VOLENTI*, DISCLAIMERS AND CONTRACTUAL EXCLUSIONS

At first sight, the defence of *volenti* and the use of a disclaimer of liability or a contractual exclusion would seem to operate in the same way. However, there are significant differences in the effect of each of these devices.[5]

A successful plea of *volenti* means that the plaintiff has consented to the risk of actual damage for which there will be no redress in law.[6] It follows that *volenti* is a denial of duty on the part of the defendant, with the result that what would otherwise be regarded as tortious conduct on the part of the defendant is no longer so as a result of the plaintiff's consent. Non-contractual disclaimers and warning notices displayed by an occupier of premises also have a similar effect in that they displace the existence of a duty on the part of the defendant. It is necessary to ask whether a disclaimer of liability has prevented the court from inferring an undertaking to exercise reasonable care.[7] Similarly, a notice or series of notices displayed on premises may enable a visitor to be reasonably safe, or may lay down conditions on which a visitor may enter the occupier's premises.[8] If the notice is said to enable a visitor to be reasonably safe, the occupier is not negligent. If the notice is regarded as a condition of entry, its effect is to absolve the defendant from liability for the consequences of his breach. In other words, there is an admission of a

---

3   *Suisse Atlantique Société d'Armement Maritime SA v NV Rotterdamsche Kolen Centrale* [1967] 1 AC 361 at 420 (per LORD UPJOHN). Cf penalty clauses and see ch 14.
4   *Gill (Stewart) Ltd v Horatio Myer & Co Ltd* [1992] 2 All ER 257.
5   *White v Blackmore* [1972] 3 All ER 158 at 172 (per ROSKILL LJ).
6   Glanville Williams *Joint Torts and Contributory Negligence* (1951) p 308.
7   *Hedley Byrne & Co Ltd v Heller & Partners Ltd* [1964] AC 465 at 492 (per LORD REID).
8   See *White v Blackmore* [1972] 3 All ER 158; *Roles v Nathan* [1963] 2 All ER 908 at 913 (per LORD DENNING MR).

breach of duty, but there is a denial of liability in respect of the consequences of that breach. In *White v Blackmore*,[9] a notice at a car race track stated:

> It is a condition of admission that all persons having any connection with the organisation of the meeting ... are absolved from liability arising out of incidents causing damage or personal injury howsoever caused to the spectators.

It was held that this notice was sufficient to exclude the organisers' liability in respect of an accident caused by their failure to take care.[10]

It is possible that a sufficiently clearly worded notice could raise the defence of *volenti*. But if the dangerous state of affairs exists already, it may not be proper to regard the plaintiff as having consented to the risk. If a visitor is fully aware of the risk involved in entering premises, it might be the case that he assents to the legal risk that he may suffer damage. However, it is unlikely that a generally worded notice which seeks to exclude liability for damage, howsoever caused, would have this effect.

It has been observed that the effect of a disclaimer, a notice and a successful plea of *volenti* is to negative the existence of a duty on the part of the defendant. Exclusion and limitation clauses, for the most part, have a different effect. They operate in a manner similar to the notice in *White v Blackmore*, namely as a form of confession and avoidance. The generally accepted view of an exclusion clause is that it excludes a duty which would otherwise have flowed from the contract.[11] Accordingly, there is a breach of contract, but the exclusion or limitation operates after the breach, and negatives or reduces the liability of the *proferens*. It should also be appreciated that, in some instances, an exclusion clause may be drafted in such a way that it operates in a manner similar to the defence of *volenti*, by preventing an act or omission from amounting to a breach of contract. But here it may be better to regard a clause of this type as one setting the parameters of the contractual duty owed rather than one referring to the extent of prospective liability.

3.   EXPRESS ASSUMPTION OF RISK

While the defence of *volenti* and contractual exclusions of liability will generally operate in different ways, both defences are based broadly on the notion of consent. It should be appreciated that the issue of consent now tends to be judged objectively, although this tendency may result in a decision to the effect that a plaintiff has objectively consented to a risk of harm when, subjectively, this may not be immediately apparent. It is suggested that a distinction can be drawn between relational and non-relational settings, in that a more subjective test of consent is applied to the latter when deciding whether or not the defence of *volenti* should succeed. Moreover, in relational settings, it seems that a more rigid test of what constitutes consent may be applied to consumer transactions than to purely business relationships.

(1)   THE MEANING OF CONSENT

What constitutes consent for the purposes of the defence of *volenti* and what amounts to the necessary consent to the presence of an exclusion clause in a contract appears to be quite different. It is submitted that the proper view of the defence of *volenti* is that

---

9   Ibid.
10   Cf Unfair Contract Terms Act 1977, s 2(1).
11   *Hedley Byrne & Co Ltd v Heller & Partners Ltd* [1964] AC 465 at 492 (per LORD REID).

the plaintiff should have voluntarily assumed the risk of harm resulting from the defendant's negligence and that this requires an express agreement before that risk arises. For reasons discussed below, unless sanctioned by statute, the defence of *volenti* should have no application to cases where the alleged assumption of risk comes after the defendant has created the risk of harm. If what is required on the part of the plaintiff is a *full* appreciation of the risk of harm before it arises, it would seem to follow that the defence will rarely be relevant in cases of negligently inflicted injury, unless there is some strong policy reason which suggests otherwise.

In contrast, where there is an exchange relationship between the parties, the issue of consent seems to be judged more objectively. Accordingly, a person may be deemed to have assented to the allocation of a risk of damage through his acceptance of an exclusion clause, even though he may not be fully aware of its effect. For example, a person who signs a document without reading its contents cannot, in any real sense, be said to have agreed to the presence of an exclusion clause in the contract. However, by signing the document, the signatory is bound,[12] in the absence of fraud or misrepresentation.[13] In this latter event, the *proferens* is estopped from denying the misrepresented effect. In exceptional circumstances, it may be possible to argue that the common law defence of *non est factum* (not my deed) applies but this would render the contract void from the start.

Furthermore, even in the absence of a signature, a person may be bound where the *proferens* has taken sufficient steps to communicate the presence of an exclusion clause to a reasonable person. Thus, a person who is blind, illiterate,[14] or unable to understand English[15] may still be bound by an exclusion of liability if reasonable steps have been taken by the *proferens*.

(2) EXPRESS CONSENT IN NON-RELATIONAL SETTINGS

Where there is a non-exchange relationship between the parties, it is possible that the plaintiff may consent to run the risk of harm created by the defendant's conduct, in which case consideration of the defence of *volenti* is relevant. In the case of intentional torts such as trespass to the person, the defence of consent manifests itself in the form of a licence to inflict harm upon the plaintiff. But this appears to be limited to the infliction of harm which does not offend public morals.[16] Where the defendant is guilty of negligence, the defence takes the form of an assumption of risk, but, the apparent consent of the plaintiff is often better described as contributory negligence, or as a cause of the harm complained of. Alternatively, it may be that the defendant's conduct does not amount to the commission of a tort.

(i)   The requirements of the defence of *volenti non fit injuria*[17]

In determining whether the defence of *volenti* is available, it must be assumed that a tort has been committed by the defendant. In the absence of tortious conduct on the part of the defendant, it is immaterial whether the plaintiff has consented. On the assumption that there is tortious misconduct, further issues may arise. First, the plaintiff's acceptance of the risk must be voluntary. Secondly, it must be asked whether the plaintiff's

12   *L'Estrange v F Graucob Ltd* [1934] 2 KB 394.
13   *Curtis v Chemical Cleaning & Dyeing Co Ltd* [1951] 1 KB 805. See also *AEG (UK) Ltd v Logic Resource Ltd* [1996] CLC 265 at 277.
14   *Thompson v LMS Railway* [1930] 1 KB 41.
15   *The Luna* [1920] P 22.
16   *R v Brown* [1994] 1 AC 212.
17   See Jaffey (1985) 44 CLJ 87.

acceptance of the risk created by the defendant's breach of duty can come after the
negligent act has taken place, or is it the case that the defence is restricted to an agreement
in anticipation of future negligence? It must also be asked whether express or implied
agreement is required at all.

It is clear that before the plaintiff can be met by the defence of *volenti* he must have
voluntarily accepted the risk of harm created by the defendant's negligence. For this to
be the case, he must not be subject to any constraint which affects his free will. Thus,
if an employee is compelled by his economic circumstances to accept a job which
involves danger, his choice is not voluntary. Similarly, if a workman is required to work
in dangerous conditions created by the defendant, the fact that he has been compelled
by his employer to work for that other will be sufficient to rebut the suggestion that
his actions were voluntary.[18] But it has been held in *Johnstone v Bloomsbury Health
Authority*[19] that where a junior doctor contracts to work on average 88 hours per week,
the implied term of the contract that the employer will have reasonable regard for the
health of employees, based on the employer's duty to provide a safe system of work[20]
must be read subject to the express agreement to work the specified number of hours.[1]
This remains the case despite the fact that in order to qualify, a junior doctor is most
likely to work for the National Health Service, a near-monopoly employer, in which
case, the same terms are likely to prevail wherever the doctor elects to work.[2] This last
point is compelling but the decision of the majority, regrettably, suggests that, subject
to the express and implied terms being capable of reconciliation, the express term can
invoke something akin to the defence of *volenti* in circumstances in which the employee's
consent is not truly voluntary.

The issue of voluntariness also arises where *volenti* is set up as a defence against a
person of unsound mind. In this case, it is unlikely that the defence will be available
since the plaintiff's unsoundness of mind will prevent him from being able to form a
rational judgment.[3] Conversely, a person of sound mind who is capable of forming a
rational judgment may be met with the defence of *volenti* where he commits or attempts
to commit suicide.[4] The same issue may also arise where a drunken passenger takes a
lift with someone who is incapable of driving safely by virtue of alcoholic impairment.
It may be argued that the passenger is not capable of making a rational judgment, in
which case, it might be better to invoke the defence of contributory negligence[5]
especially since the defence of *volenti* is statutorily excluded in such circumstances.[6]

There appears to be a divergence of opinion over the question of whether agreement
is required at all. At one extreme, it has been held that nothing short of agreement will
suffice.[7] Thus it is argued that there must be an express or implied bargain under which
the plaintiff gives up his right to sue.[8] That a consent-based defence would otherwise
be recognised in English law is clear from the Unfair Contract Terms Act 1977 which

---

18   *Burnett v British Waterways Board* [1973] 2 All ER 631.
19   [1991] 2 All ER 293.
20   Based on the decision in *Wilsons & Clyde Coal Co Ltd v English* [1938] AC 57 and see ch 27.
1   *Johnstone v Bloomsbury Health Authority* [1991] 2 All ER 293 at 303 (per LEGGATT LJ) and at 304 (per
     BROWNE-WILKINSON VC); cf STUART SMITH LJ at 299.
2   Ibid at 299–300 (per STUART SMITH LJ) (dissenting).
3   *Kirkham v Chief Constable of Greater Manchester Police* [1990] 3 All ER 246 at 250 (per LLOYD LJ) and at
     254 (per FARQUHARSON LJ). See also *Reeves v Metropolitan Police Commissioner* [1999] 3 WLR 363.
4   Ibid. But when is suicide ever truly rational?
5   *Owens v Brimmell* [1977] QB 859.
6   Road Traffic Act 1988, s 149(3). Cf *Morris v Murray* [1990] 3 All ER 801 where the Road Traffic Act
     does not apply.
7   *Nettleship v Weston* [1971] 2 QB 691 at 701 (per LORD DENNING MR). See also *Baker v T E Hopkins &
     Son* [1959] 1 WLR 966 at 976 (per MORRIS LJ).
8   Williams *Joint Torts and Contributory Negligence* (1951) p 308.

provides that a person cannot by reference to a contract term or notice exclude or restrict liability for death or bodily injury caused by negligence.[9] Moreover, in the context of motor vehicle accidents, where the compulsory insurance provisions of the Road Traffic Act 1988 operate,[10] Parliament has considered it necessary to protect passengers from notices purporting to exclude the liability of the user of the car.[11]

It follows from the requirement of express prior agreement that the defence of *volenti* will not be available where a risk is created by the defendant's negligence and the plaintiff subsequently encounters the consequence of that negligence with knowledge of the risk involved. Thus a doctor who is aware that others have been placed in danger of carbon monoxide poisoning through the negligence of their employer in asking them to work in a confined space is not to be met by a plea of *volenti* if he attempts to rescue them and is overcome by the fumes. In this instance, the doctor only plays his part after the defendant has been negligent and cannot be considered to have agreed to the risk.[12] It is submitted that a contractual analogy can be drawn from the rules on the communication of exclusion clauses considered below. It is clear that a person will not be bound by an exclusion clause when it is brought to his attention after the contract has been entered into.[13] Thus, the willing acceptance of the relevant term must come before the defendant's breach of contract which gives rise to the plaintiff's claim. Applying similar principles to the defence of *volenti*, it seems only proper that the plaintiff's consent should come before the events which first give rise to the risk that the plaintiff might be injured, unless there is some other policy motive at work.

An alternative view is that no agreement is necessary, and that the defence can extend to cases where the plaintiff voluntarily encounters a risk already created by the defendant's negligence.[14] This view also has some judicial support[15] in circumstances in which the activity in which the plaintiff and defendant engage is heavily fraught with danger from the first,[16] so much so that the danger to the plaintiff is so extreme or glaring that the plaintiff's acceptance of the risk is like intermeddling with an unexploded bomb.[17]

Certain statutory provisions also suggest that a plaintiff may be met with a defence of *volenti* where he knowingly encounters an existing risk of harm.[18] Such cases cannot be said to involve agreement, since a person cannot be treated as having agreed to run a particular risk after it has already arisen. In contrast, if the agreement comes before the risk arises, the plaintiff may be met with the defence of *volenti*, because the defendant might not have committed the tort but for that agreement.

9   Unfair Contract Terms Act 1977, s 2(1). This provision appears to apply to an express contractual term which raises the defence of *volenti: Johnstone v Bloomsbury Health Authority* [1991] 2 All ER 293.
10   Road Traffic Act 1988, s 143.
11   Road Traffic Act 1988, s 149(3) and see *Pitts v Hunt* [1990] 3 All ER 344.
12   *Baker v T E Hopkins & Son* [1959] 1 WLR 966 at 976 (per MORRIS LJ). See also *Wooldridge v Sumner* [1963] 2 QB 43 at 70 (per DIPLOCK LJ).
13   See *Olley v Marlborough Court Hotel Ltd* [1949] 1 KB 532.
14   Clerk & Lindsell *Torts* (16th edn, 1989) pp 1–174. *Salmond, Heuston amd Buckley*, pp 490–491.
15   *Dann v Hamilton* [1939] 1 KB 509 at 517 (per ASQUITH J); *Nettleship v Weston* [1971] 2 QB 691 at 704 (per SALMON LJ).
16   *Morris v Murray* [1990] 3 All ER 801 at 805 (per FOX LJ).
17   *Dann v Hamilton* [1939] 1 KB 509 at 518 (per ASQUITH J). See also *Imperial Chemical Industries Ltd v Shatwell* [1965] AC 656 (experimenting with detonators).
18   Occupiers' Liability Act 1957, s 2(5); Animals Act 1971, s 5(2); Unfair Contract Terms Act 1977, s 2(3). Cf Occupiers' Liability Act 1957, s 2(1) and Unfair Contract Terms Act 1977, s 2(1), both of which deal with agreement rather than acceptance of risk.

(ii)   *Volenti* and other explanations of the plaintiff's conduct

Occasionally, *volenti*, as a consent-based defence is used in circumstances in which there is a better alternative explanation. These alternatives are, first, that there is a reduced standard of care; secondly that the plaintiff is guilty of contributory negligence or is the cause of the harm he suffers and thirdly that the public policy defence of *ex turpi causa non oritur actio* applies.

(a)   Reduced standard of care[19]

In some instances, the relationship between the parties is such that a reduced standard of care is required of the defendant. This reduced standard may arise because of the conduct of the plaintiff or from the circumstances in which the parties find themselves. It might appear that the conduct of the plaintiff constitutes an indication of consent, but since it is a requirement of the defence of *volenti* that a tort should have been committed before the defence has any relevance, the reduction in the standard of care required of the defendant may mean that no tort has been committed. This situation may arise where a person engages in a sporting activity in which there is a known risk of injury, even when the rules of the sport are complied with. However, the position may be different where there is a reckless tackle, since, even if there is a reduced standard of care, the defendant may still be liable on the basis that he has failed to satisfy that reduced standard of care.[20] It would appear, however, that there is some difficulty in ascertaining what is meant by the word 'reckless' in this context. For example it has been held that recklessness should not be equated with 'conscious advertence to the risk'. Thus it may be said that professional footballers consent to the risk of injury from fouls, even those committed intentionally.[1] In contrast, the referee at a football match does owe a duty of care to the players.[2]

The problem may also manifest itself where a spectator attends a sporting event which creates a risk of injury to those present, with the result that in an action by the spectator against either a participant[3] in or the organiser[4] of the event, the standard of care may be reduced to such an extent that there is no breach of the duty of care which would otherwise be owed. While some judgments do speak in terms of the spectator taking the risk of injury resulting from acts of performers in the course of the game, this should not be taken to be an application of the defence of *volenti*. Instead, the better view of these cases is that the standard of care required of the organiser and the participants must be related to what can reasonably be expected to occur and the extent to which an ordinary spectator can be expected to appreciate the risk of injury created by the activity in question.[5] Assent rather than consent may be the better word to use in these circumstances, in which case the spectator assents to the risk of injury but not to the lack of reasonable care which produces that risk.[6] It must be accepted that where professional sportsmen play in a competitive fashion, considerable risks to spectators may be created, but unless that activity constitutes something in the nature of a reckless disregard for the safety of a spectator[7] or an error of judgment that a reasonable

19   See Kidner (1991) 11 Legal Studies 1.
20   See *Condon v Basi* [1985] 1 WLR 866.
1   *McCord v Swansea City AFC* (1997) Times, 11 February, per Kennedy J.
2   *Smoldon v Whitworth* [1997] ELR 115.
3   *Wooldridge v Sumner* [1963] 2 QB 43.
4   *Murray v Harringay Arena Ltd* [1951] 2 KB 529.
5   *Hall v Brooklands Auto–Racing Club* [1933] 1 KB 205 at 214 (per SCRUTTON LJ).
6   *Wooldridge v Sumner* [1963] 2 QB 43 at 68–69 (per DIPLOCK LJ).
7   Ibid at 72 (per DIPLOCK LJ). Cf Goodhart (1962) 78 LQR 490.

competitor would not have made,[8] it is unlikely that there will be a breach of the duty of care owed to the spectator.

(b)   Contributory negligence[9]

Contributory negligence consists of the failure by the plaintiff to take reasonable care for his own safety. This may be a better explanation of some of the cases in which the issue of *volenti* has been raised. For example, where a person takes a lift in a car from a person who is known to be unfit to drive because of intoxication, it can be said that the passenger has failed to take care for his own safety.[10] In such cases, it would seem inappropriate to deny the plaintiff recovery altogether on the ground that he was *volens* since his fault is usually much less than that of the driver, but it may be appropriate to reduce the plaintiff's damages on the ground of contributory negligence.

Similar considerations will also apply to rescue cases. In a case where a person reasonably attempts to rescue a third person endangered by the defendant's negligence, the defence of *volenti* can hardly be appropriate, since danger invites rescue.[11] In contrast, if the rescuer has acted unreasonably so as to place himself in danger as a result of the defendant's negligence, occasionally, it may be appropriate to reduce his damages on the ground of contributory negligence.[12] Exceptionally, there have been cases in which contributory negligence has been used to deny the defendant's liability altogether by allowing a 100 per cent apportionment. Usually this has occurred where the plaintiff's blameworthiness is substantially greater than that of the defendant, for example where the defendant is in breach of a strict statutory duty.[13] However, this approach has been declared to be inconsistent with the spirit of the 1945 Act which requires an apportionment to be made, thus suggesting that the plaintiff should receive something by way of an award of damages.[14]

(c)   Causation

In some instances, a person may have acted so unreasonably as to be a cause of his own injuries. For example, if a rescuer takes an unnecessary risk, it may be that his conduct is regarded as a *novus actus interveniens*, thereby rendering the consequence of the defendant's negligence too remote. Sometimes, it may be suggested that the rescuer, in such a case, is *volens* to the risk created by the defendant.[15] However, the better view in cases of unnecessary rescue is that the plaintiff is the cause of his own injury.[16]

(d)   Ex turpi causa non oritur actio[17]

Occasionally, the plaintiff in a tort action may be guilty of criminal or immoral wrongdoing to the extent that it is seen proper to deny the recovery of damages.[18] This misconduct on the part of the plaintiff can be confused with implied consent,[19] with the result

---

8   *Wilks v Cheltenham Home Guard Motor Cycle and Light Car Club* [1971] 2 All ER 369 at 374 (per EDMUND DAVIES LJ).

9   See ch 20.

10   *Owens v Brimmell* [1977] QB 859. See also Lord Asquith's views on the appropriateness of a plea of contributory negligence in *Dann v Hamilton* [1939] 1 KB 509 cited in (1953) 69 LQR 317.

11   *Haynes v Harwood* [1935] 1 KB 146. See also *Brandon v Osborne, Garrett & Co* [1924] 1 KB 548; *Baker v T E Hopkins & Son* [1959] 1 WLR 966; *Videan v British Transport Commission* [1963] 2 QB 650.

12   *Harrison v British Railways Board* [1981] 3 All ER 679.

13   *Jayes v IMI (Kynoch) Ltd* [1985] ICR 155.

14   *Pitts v Hunt* [1990] 3 All ER 344. Cf *Baddeley v Earl Granville* (1887) 19 QBD 423.

15   *Cutler v United Dairies (London) Ltd* [1933] 2 KB 297.

16   *Haynes v Harwood* [1935] 1 KB 146 at 163 (per MAUGHAM LJ).

17   See ch 21.

18   See Kidner (1991) 11 Legal Studies 1.

19   *Ashton v Turner* [1981] QB 137.

that an award of damages may be refused. But it is important to realise that in these circumstances the courts are denying recovery for reasons of public policy not because the plaintiff has assented to the risk of harm. Thus, just as the presence of a spectator at a sporting event may suggest a reduced standard of care on the part of the defendant, so also illegal or immoral conduct on the part of the plaintiff may have the same effect.[20] In the case of torts which do not require a consideration of the standard of care required of the defendant, a more appropriate test might be to consider whether the plaintiff's actions are such that the public conscience demands that he should go uncompensated.[1] However, there are criticisms of this test on the ground that it may be unworkable.[2]

(3)   EXPRESS CONSENT IN EXCHANGE RELATIONSHIPS

Where there is an exchange relationship between the parties, it may be that the plaintiff is unable to secure a remedy against the defendant due to the presence of an exclusion clause or some other disclaimer of liability. In either event, it may be said that some element of agreement is involved. As a matter of policy, a person will rarely be considered to have run the risk of personal injury. Furthermore, where a person seeks to exclude his liability towards a consumer, it is often the case that an exclusion clause or related device will be regarded as ineffective. However, in business relationships, exclusion clauses may form part of a long-established pattern of commercial risk-allocation, and may be regarded as perfectly reasonable in the circumstances.

(i)   Exclusion of liability for personal injuries and death

Generally, English law takes the view that a person should not be able to exclude liability for personal injury caused to others. While it might be the case that a person may wish to reallocate a risk of harm to another, it should be appreciated that a person in a weak bargaining position may have no choice at all in deciding whether to accept or reject terms offered to him by another party. The control of onerous exclusion clauses is perceived as the function of Parliament rather than that of the courts, with the result that the use of exclusion clauses in certain circumstances has been prohibited by statute. Thus the operator of a public service vehicle,[3] railway and waterway operators[4] and private carriers[5] cannot contract to limit their liability in respect of the death of, or bodily injury to passengers. This trend against the use of exclusion clauses in relation to death or bodily injury was generalised in the Unfair Contract Terms Act 1977, which provides that a person acting in the course of a business cannot, by reference to a contract term or notice, exclude or restrict liability for death or personal injury resulting from negligence.[6]

---

20   *Pitts v Hunt* [1990] 3 All ER 344 at 358–359 (per BALCOMBE LJ) and at 365 (per DILLON LJ) applying *Jackson v Harrison* (1978) 138 CLR 438 at 456 (per MASON J).

1   *Thackwell v Barclays Bank plc* [1986] 1 All ER 676 at 687 (per HUTCHISON J). See also *Saunders v Edwards* [1987] 2 All ER 651; *Euro Diam Ltd v Bathurst* [1988] 2 All ER 23 and see ch 21.

2   See *Pitts v Hunt* [1990] 3 All ER 344 at 355–356 (per BELDAM LJ). See also *Tinsley v Milligan* [1994] 1 AC 340.

3   Public Passenger Vehicles Act 1981, s 29.

4   Transport Act 1962, s 43(7).

5   Road Traffic Act 1988, s 149(2).

6   Unfair Contract Terms Act 1977, s 2(1). Cf The Unfair Terms in Consumer Contracts Regulations 1999 which do not render such terms void, but merely regard them as prima facie unfair. See further ch 24.

(ii)   Exclusion of liability in consumer transactions

Where the person affected by an exclusion clause deals as a consumer,[7] there are a variety of statutory provisions and judicial techniques which serve to invalidate or restrict the application of such purported exemptions of liability. Any attempt by a person acting in the course of a business to exclude or restrict liability for a breach of the implied terms in a consumer contract for the supply of goods is rendered void.[8] Furthermore, in the case of all other contracts made with consumers, a purported exclusion of liability must satisfy a test of reasonableness,[9] as must any indemnity clause used in a consumer contract.[10]

The Unfair Terms in Consumer Contracts Regulations 1999 also make provision for a variety of terms wider than those covered by the Unfair Contract Terms Act 1977. However, it should be noted that, in certain respects, the 1977 Act operates in a broader arena than that occupied by the 1999 Regulations, especially in the sense that some contractual terms are rendered void by the 1977 Act, whereas the effect of the 1999 Regulations is simply to create a presumption of unfairness. Moreover, the Unfair Contract Terms Act 1977, despite its title, extends to cover some non-contractual relationships. Details of these provisions are spelt out elsewhere.[11]

Quite apart from statutory restrictions on the use of exclusion clauses in relation to consumers, the courts have adopted a number of rules of construction which make it difficult to treat a consumer as having agreed to the presence of an exclusion clause.[12]

(a)   Construction of the contractual document

If it is alleged that a consumer has agreed to a limitation or exclusion of the liability of the *proferens*, it may be possible for the court to treat the document containing the exclusion as non-contractual. Since contractual terms must be communicated at or before the time the contract is made, any term communicated at a later stage will be ineffective.[13] This is particularly important given the widespread use of standard form contracts under which the consumer has little choice whether or not to accept the terms proposed by the *proferens*. If the consumer is presented with a ticket which contains language which purports to exclude the contractual liability of the *proferens*, the exclusion is effective only if the ticket is a contractual document. For example, where the relevant document is a receipt for payment, which, by its nature, is delivered after a contract has been concluded, any purported exclusion of liability will not affect the consumer.[14] Similarly, a signature on an employee's time sheet is not sufficient to amount to a contractual document binding a third party with the employer.[15] Generally the test to apply will be whether a reasonable person would regard the document as contractual.[16]

A document will have contractual effect if the person to whom it is handed, and persons generally, are aware that it contains contractual terms.[17] It can be assumed that the device of treating a document as a receipt is more likely to be applied in favour of a consumer rather than a business contractor, since the latter is more likely to have understood the importance of the proposals of the other party.

---

7   Ibid, s 12.
8   Ibid, ss 6(1) and (2); ss 7(1) and (2).
9   Ibid, ss 3(1) and (2).
10   Ibid, s 4(1).
11   See ch 24.
12   Yates chs 2 and 4; Chin *Excluding Liability in Contracts* (1985) ch VI.
13   *Olley v Marlborough Court Ltd* [1949] 1 KB 532.
14   *Chapelton v Barry UDC* [1940] 1 KB 532.
15   *Grogan v Robin Meredith Plant Hire Ltd* (1996) 15 Tr LR 371.
16   Ibid at 375 (per AULD LJ).
17   *Parker v South Eastern Rly Co* (1877) 2 CPD 416 at 424 per MELLISH LJ. Cf *Alexander v Railway Executive* [1951] 2 KB 882.

(b)   The reasonable notice rule
If it is decided that a document containing an exclusion clause is contractual in nature, a second rule of construction may be employed to mitigate the effects of the purported exclusion of liability. A person will only be deemed to have agreed to the exclusion of liability if the *proferens* has given reasonable notice of its existence and, perhaps, its content. While it used to be sufficient to communicate to the reasonable man the mere existence of an exclusion clause,[18] it would now appear, particularly in consumer contracts, that it would be advisable to communicate the effect of the purported exclusion.[19] The contractual document contains the terms of the *proferens'* offer and in accordance with normal rules of offer and acceptance, any exempting terms must be drawn to the plaintiff's attention in the most explicit way.[20] This would seem to suggest that what is required is sufficient communication of the effect of the exclusion in question. This might imply that the presence of an exclusion clause has been insufficiently communicated unless it appears in the larger contract between the parties, rather than being communicated by some extraneous method. In some cases this will be possible, for example where the terms proposed by a tour operator can be reproduced in the brochure describing a holiday,[1] but in other cases this requirement would seem to go too far, as its practical effect would make standard form contracts excessively bulky, and would detract from the cost-reducing advantages of the widespread use of standard form contracting.

The approach adopted in later cases contrasts sharply with the fiction employed in the nineteenth-century ticket cases,[2] that if a customer took a ticket without objection, he had accepted the terms referred to therein. What must be appreciated is that consumers rarely read such conditions, and that, if the *proferens* wishes to rely on an exclusion clause in such a case, he must take reasonable steps to ensure that it has been properly communicated.

What is reasonable depends on two factors, namely the steps taken to communicate the existence of the exclusion clause, and the nature of the purported exclusion. In considering the steps taken by the *proferens*, it should be appreciated that consumers may be aware that the type of contract they make is sometimes subject to exclusions of liability.[3] Sometimes, it will be sufficient to refer to standard terms in a contractual document without reproducing them in full. But if there is no reference to the exclusion,[4] if the reference to it has been obliterated,[5] or if it is hidden amongst advertisements,[6] it is unlikely that the term will have been properly communicated. Likewise, reference to a set of terms in the course of a telephone conversation will not suffice if the other party has no means of knowing what the terms of the contract are.[7] Furthermore, if the front of a faxed document refers to a set of terms , but as with all faxed messages,

---

18   *Thompson v London, Midland & Scottish Rly* [1930] 1 KB 41. Cf *The Mikhail Lermontov* [1990] 1 Lloyd's Rep 579 at 594.
19   *Thornton v Shoe Lane Parking Co Ltd* [1971] 1 All ER 686.
20   Ibid at 690 (per LORD DENNING MR). See also *Olley v Marlborough Court Ltd* [1949] 1 KB 532.
1   See *Hollingworth v Southern Ferries Ltd, The Eagle* [1977] 2 Lloyd's Rep 70. See also *White v Blackmore* [1972] 3 All ER 158 at 165–168 (per LORD DENNING MR).
2   See *Parker v South Eastern Rly* (1877) 2 CPD 416; *Thompson v London, Midland & Scottish Rly* [1930] 1 KB 41.
3   Ibid at 422–423 (per MELLISH LJ). See also *McCutcheon v David MacBrayne Ltd* [1964] 1 WLR 125 at 129 (per LORD HODSON).
4   *Richardson, Spence & Co v Rowntree* [1894] AC 217.
5   *Sugar v London, Midland & Scottish Rly* [1941] 1 All ER 172.
6   *Stephen v International Sleeping Car Co Ltd* (1903) 19 TLR 621.
7   *Jayaar Impex Ltd v Toaken Group Ltd* [1996] 2 Lloyd's Rep 437.

the back is blank, there will be an insufficient attempt at communication unless the back of the original is also sent to the other contracting party.[8]

The characteristics of the consumer may also affect what is reasonable, with the result that additional steps may be required to communicate the presence of the exclusion. For example, it has been taken into account that a passenger was of a class of people not expected to read contractual small print.[9] Likewise, it may be necessary to translate contractual terms for the benefit of a person who cannot speak English.[10] However, the test is objective, with the result that erroneous or unjustified misunderstanding will be no defence.[11]

The nature of the purported exclusion is important, since the effect of onerous or unusual terms must be very carefully communicated if they are to be effective. While the reasonable notice rule applies broadly to the set of terms on which the *proferens* proposes to contract, a special rule may apply to individual terms which are of an onerous nature. It has been observed that some exclusions are so wide and destructive of rights that they could only be properly communicated if printed in red ink with a red hand pointing in their direction.[12]

(iii)   Exclusion of liability in business transactions

In the case of business relationships, the effect of an exclusion clause or some other disclaimer of liability is to operate as a risk-allocation device. In consumer transactions, one party may be in a position of unequal bargaining power in relation to the other. This is less likely to be the case in business relationships.

It is common to find that businesses may wish to establish relations with others only on conditions which modify the normal allocation of risks in favour of the person seeking to exclude liability. This method of risk-allocation, in most cases, can be said to represent the reasonable expectations of the parties and may provide for the most efficient allocation of resources. For example, one party may be in a better position than the other to insure against the potential risk of loss, in which case it is better that the risk of loss rests with him.[13] That one party rather than the other is a better cost-avoider is often recognised in standard form business contracts. Some standard form contracts have developed out of mercantile business practice, such as bills of lading, charterparties and policies of marine insurance, all of which contain exclusions of liability. It has been observed that the content of these standard form documents is regarded as fair and reasonable, because they have been worked out in detail by representatives of the businesses which engage in such transactions.[14] As such, it can be readily said that the content of such contracts has been agreed to.

While an express exclusion of liability will frequently be found in the form of a contract term, it is also possible for a person to disclaim liability for what would otherwise amount to the breach of a tortious duty of care in a non-contractual relationship of close proximity. For example, a banker giving a financial reference,[15] or a surveyor

---

8   See *Poseidon Freight Forwarding Co Ltd v Davies Turner (Southern) Ltd* [1996] 2 Lloyd's Rep 388.
9   *Richardson, Spence & Co v Rowntree* [1894] AC 217. Cf *Thompson v London, Midland & Scottish Rly* [1930] 1 KB 41.
10 *Geier v Kujawa, Weston and Warne Bros (Transport) Ltd* [1970] 1 Lloyd's Rep 364. Cf *JH Saphis (Merchants) Ltd v AL Zissimos Ltd* [1960] 1 Lloyd's Rep 490.
11 See *Bennett v Tugwell* [1971] 2 QB 267.
12 *J R Spurling Ltd v Bradshaw* [1956] 1 WLR 461 at 466 (per DENNING LJ); *Thornton v Shoe Lane Parking Co Ltd* [1971] 2 QB 163 at 170 (per LORD DENNING MR). See also *Interfoto Picture Library Ltd v Stiletto Visual Programmes Ltd* [1988] 1 All ER 348 at 350 (per DILLON LJ) and see MacDonald (1988) JBL 375.
13 *Photo Production Ltd v Securicor Transport Ltd* [1980] AC 827 at 851 (per LORD DIPLOCK).
14 *A Schroeder Music Publishing Co Ltd v Macaulay* [1974] 1 WLR 1308 at 1316 (per LORD DIPLOCK).
15 *Hedley Byrne & Co Ltd v Heller & Partners Ltd* [1964] AC 465.

compiling a valuation report which he knows will be passed on to a potential purchaser of the property surveyed,[16] may disclaim liability for negligence. This practice may indicate that such reliance as there is on the advice given is not reasonable and in some instances that the adviser does not voluntarily assume responsibility for the accuracy of that advice, with the result that (subject to the operation of the Unfair Contract Terms Act 1977) no duty of care is owed.

4. IMPLIED ASSUMPTION OF RISK

Where the circumstances so warrant, assumption of risk may be implied. This is most likely to occur in business relationships, where acceptance of an exclusion of liability is often inferred. It is much less likely that a similar approach will be adopted in relation to consumers and it is improbable that a plaintiff would be impliedly held *volens* to a risk of personal injury. Strong policy reasons, however, may dictate a contrary approach.

(1) IMPLIED CONSENT IN NON-RELATIONAL SETTINGS

(i) Implied consent and public policy

Sometimes, there may be strong policy reasons for implying an agreement to run a risk. Often this will be related to the misconduct of the plaintiff, with the result that a wrongdoing plaintiff may be denied recovery on the ground that he has impliedly consented to the negligence of the defendant which gives rise to the risk of injury. The wrongdoing of the plaintiff may be so grave as to invoke the maxim *ex turpi causa non oritur actio*, particularly where it is impossible for the court to be able to identify the standard of care required of the defendant.[17] In other instances, where the plaintiff's conduct is reprehensible, the court may resort to an explanation of his conduct in terms of implied assumption of risk.[18] Whichever approach is taken, the policy basis for the court's decision remains strong, namely that a plaintiff guilty of doing something bad, such as deliberately disobeying instructions,[19] encouraging a motorcyclist to endanger other road users[20] or taking a flight in an aeroplane with a pilot who is so intoxicated as to be unable to fly safely[1] should be denied damages altogether.[2]

In *Imperial Chemical Industries Ltd v Shatwell*,[3] the plaintiff and his brother were experienced shotfirers, engaged to carry out controlled explosions in the workplace. Statutory regulations required them to take certain safety precautions, which they chose to ignore, as a result of which the plaintiff was injured. The plaintiff sued the defendants vicariously for the negligence and breach of statutory duty of his brother. The question which arose for decision by the House of Lords was whether an employer who was under no statutory duty himself could be vicariously liable for an employee's breach of statutory duty towards another employee where the two employees had combined to produce the accident.

The court faced the dilemma that, if the plaintiff had been injured while acting alone, there would have been no action, as the employers were not subject to the

---

16 *Smith v Eric S Bush (a firm)* [1989] 2 All ER 514.
17 See ch 20.
18 *Imperial Chemical Industries Ltd v Shatwell* [1965] AC 656; *Ashton v Turner* [1981] QB 137; *Morris v Murray* [1990] 3 All ER 801.
19 *Imperial Chemical Industries Ltd v Shatwell* [1965] AC 656.
20 *Pitts v Hunt* [1990] 3 All ER 344 and see ch 21.
1   *Morris v Murray* [1990] 3 All ER 801. Cf *Dann v Hamilton* [1939] 1 KB 509.
2   *Weir* p 247.
3   [1965] AC 656.

statutory duty, but because the plaintiff had combined with his brother, the defendants faced the prospect of being liable in damages. In order to escape from this position, the House of Lords held that the plaintiff was *volens* to the risk of harm, thereby denying the defendants' liability altogether. An employee who deliberately disobeyed orders could be said to be *volens* to the risk in the fullest sense. If the plaintiff had sued his brother, there would have been no difficulty in finding an agreement to assume the risk of loss. Applying a variant of the 'officious bystander' test, it could be said that there was an implied agreement that the plaintiff would not sue his brother for any injury he might suffer.[4] The benefit of this implied agreement could be transferred to the defendants, with the result that they were not liable.

The close relationship between this and contributory negligence is also clear. Indeed, distinguishing between *Shatwell* and *Stapeley v Gypsum Mines*,[5] where the plaintiff was able to recover only 20% of her damages due to a successful plea of contributory negligence, is difficult. One possible point of distinction is that in *Stapeley*, the relevant statutory duty rested on the employer and that, in such circumstances, the employer cannot avoid liability by pleading *volenti*.[6] However, in both cases, the employees acted deliberately, with full knowledge of the risk involved. It has been pointed out that such behaviour is worse than negligence, and is deserving of a complete denial of liability.[7]

Similar policy considerations also apply where the plaintiff knowingly encounters a risk of considerable magnitude. In *Morris v Murray*[8] the plaintiff was considered *volens* where he surprisingly survived after taking a flight in a private aeroplane piloted by the defendant who had consumed the equivalent of 17 measures of whisky, took off in adverse weather conditions, downwind and uphill and flew the craft as if it were a model plane. The difficulty with applying the defence of *volenti* in these circumstances is that it creates the danger of equating consent (*volens*) with knowledge (*sciens*), but it should also be appreciated that where the defence is used it is founded on good sense and justice.[9] This would seem to suggest a strong policy basis for the defence, justifying its use where there is a high degree of risk which can be anticipated by the plaintiff in circumstances in which he is free from compulsion.[10] To allow the plaintiff in a case like *Morris v Murray* to walk away with even reduced damages for his contributory negligence would seem to defy common sense. But to talk of consent on the part of the plaintiff is probably misleading, certainly in cases where the risk is present before the plaintiff's acceptance of it.

(ii)   Statutory *volenti*

There are certain statutory provisions[11] which suggest that a plea of *volenti* may succeed where the risk of harm is already in existence when the plaintiff encounters it. If this is the case, the defence cannot be based upon the notion of express agreement. Instead, the defence becomes one of voluntary acceptance of the risk of injury in which there

---

4   Ibid at 688 (per LORD PEARCE).
5   [1953] AC 663 and see ch 19.
6   *Baddeley v Earl Granville* (1887) 19 QBD 423; *Wheeler v New Merton Mills Ltd* [1933] 2 KB 669. But cf *Jayes v IMI (Kynoch) Ltd* [1985] ICR 155.
7   *Imperial Chemical Industries Ltd v Shatwell* [1965] AC 656 at 672 (per LORD REID).
8   [1990] 3 All ER 801.
9   *Smith v Baker & Sons* [1891] AC 325 at 360 (per LORD HERSCHELL).
10   *Morris v Murray* [1990] 3 All ER 801 at 806 (per FOX LJ) and see also *Bowater v Rowley Regis Corpn* [1944] KB 476 at 479 (per SCOTT LJ).
11   Occupiers' Liability Act 1957, s 2(5); Animals Act 1971, s 5(2); Unfair Contract Terms Act 1977, s 2(3).

is no agreement at all. Generally, on the basis that it offends logic, it is undesirable that a person can be deemed to 'agree' to a risk of harm which has already arisen. In most cases of this kind, the defence of contributory negligence is more appropriate.

(a)   The Occupiers' Liability Act 1957, section 2(5)
This provision states that an occupier does not owe any obligation to a visitor in respect of risks willingly accepted as his by that person. The equivalent provision in Scottish law[12] has been interpreted by the House of Lords to extend to voluntary encounter with an already existing danger.[13] This view is also consistent with other provisions of the Occupiers' Liability Act 1957 which show that negation of liability by agreement is already catered for. Section 2(1) specifies that the common duty of care may be restricted, modified or excluded by agreement or otherwise. Where section 2(1) operates, the visitor is deemed to have agreed in advance to forgo his claim against the occupier where he has been warned adequately of any danger that might exist and that the occupier accepts no responsibility.[14] If section 2(5) is to add anything, it must cover something other than agreement, and would seem to apply to a voluntary encounter with an existing danger. Thus, if a person enters a dangerous building site at the invitation of the occupier and has been warned of the conditions of entry by an adequately positioned notice, his awareness of those conditions of entry may be sufficient to absolve the occupier of liability should the visitor be injured.

(b)   The Animals Act 1971, section 5(2)
It has been said that section 5(2) is distinct from the defence of *volenti* and covers the situation in which a person voluntarily enters premises where he knows there is a guard dog,[15] with the result that the defendant is not liable under the Animals Act 1971, section 2.

(c)   The Unfair Contract Terms Act 1977, section 2(3)
This sub-section provides that a person's agreement to or awareness of an excluding term or notice is not of itself to be taken as indicating his voluntary acceptance of any risk. The vital words are 'of itself' since they may be taken to suggest that simple awareness of a risk together with some other relevant factor may negative liability. This other factor might include a genuine willingness to surrender a right of action. Thus if X enters Y's land, mindful of a notice which purports to exclude liability for bodily injury caused by negligence, section 2(3) prevents Y from raising a complete defence to liability, not on the basis that the exclusion clause is valid, as that is void under section 2(1), but because of X's agreement or awareness, unless there is other evidence which makes it reasonable to absolve Y of liability.

(2)   IMPLIED CONSENT IN EXCHANGE RELATIONSHIPS

Where there is an exchange relationship between the parties, the court may be willing to infer acceptance of the presence of an exclusion clause on the basis of previous dealings between the parties. It is more likely that inferred agreements of this type will arise in business transactions rather than where one of the contracting parties is a consumer.

---

12   Occupiers' Liability (Scotland) Act 1960, s 2(3).
13   *Titchener v British Railways Board* [1983] 1 WLR 1427 at 1434 (per LORD FRASER).
14   *Ashdown v Samuel Williams* [1957] 1 QB 409; *White v Blackmore* [1972] 2 QB 651.
15   *Cummings v Grainger* [1977] QB 397 at 408 (per ORMROD LJ).

(i)   Implied consent in consumer transactions

Two issues arise in this context. First, it must be considered whether a consumer is bound by an exclusion clause because of previous dealings he may have entered into with the *proferens*. Secondly, it should be enquired whether a third party is entitled to the protection of an exclusion clause in a contract between a consumer and the *proferens*.

(a)   Previous course of dealing

If there has been a consistent course of dealing between the parties, knowledge of an exclusion clause can be implied. In consumer contracts, this is an unlikely event, although it is a possibility.[16] It is clear that the course of dealing must be consistent and variations in business practice on the part of the *proferens* are likely to result in a decision that the relevant term has not been properly communicated.[17] If the course of dealing is sporadic, as is likely in the case of consumer contracts, it is unlikely that the court will decide, as a matter of fact, that there is a consistent course of dealing.[18] Furthermore, where the plaintiff is a consumer, he is invariably not in a position of equal bargaining power,[19] with the result that it is unlikely that knowledge of the exclusion clause will be inferred.

(b)   Exclusion clauses and third parties

Sometimes, it may be necessary to decide whether an exclusion clause extends to protect a person who is not a party to the contract of which it forms a part. This situation gives rise to the issue of vicarious immunity. The classical response to this problem is that the third party remains unprotected due to the operation of the doctrine of privity of contract. In consumer transactions, the doctrine of privity of contract has been used as a means of controlling undesirable exclusion clauses. Thus in *Adler v Dickson*,[20] the plaintiff was a passenger on board the *SS Himalaya*. Her ticket contained a term to the effect that passengers were carried at their own risk, and that the company was not responsible for injuries suffered by passengers as a result of the negligence of the company's servants. When the plaintiff was injured as a result of the negligence of two crew members it was held that the exclusion clause served to protect the company but no-one else on the ground that the employees of the company were not parties to the contract.

In some instances, it may be possible for the *proferens* to intervene by seeking to stay an action in order to prevent the consumer from proceeding against the employee. In *Gore v Van der Lann*,[1] the plaintiff was an old-age pensioner in receipt of a free bus pass. The pass purported to be a licence issued on the terms that the plaintiff would not seek to make the issuing transport authority or its servants liable for any injury that might be suffered whilst travelling on the corporation's buses. The plaintiff was injured because the conductor caused the bus to move off while the plaintiff was boarding. The plaintiff proceeded against the conductor personally, and the transport authority sought to stay the proceedings on the ground that the plaintiff was bound by the condition in her bus pass that she would not seek to make servants of the corporation liable for her injuries. It was held, obiter, that because the corporation was not legally obliged to indemnify their employee and because there was no express promise by the plaintiff not to sue the employee, the corporation did not have a sufficient interest in the proceedings to have them stayed.

---

16   *Mendelssohn v Normand Ltd* [1970] 1 QB 177 at 182 (per LORD DENNING MR).
17   *McCutcheon v David MacBrayne Ltd* [1964] 1 WLR 125.
18   *Hollier v Rambler Motors (AMC) Ltd* [1972] 2 QB 71.
19   *British Crane Hire Ltd v Ipswich Plant Hire Ltd* [1975] QB 303 at 310 (per LORD DENNING MR).
20   [1955] 1 QB 158.
1   [1967] 1 All ER 360.

(ii)   Implied consent in business relationships

The use of exclusion clauses in business relationships is an obvious example of a deliberate allocation of risks. The *proferens* may be unwilling or unable to assume the risk of a particular loss and it may be that the most efficient solution is to seek to transfer that risk to the other party. Generally, there will have been express provision for one party to assume a risk of loss, but it is also possible for such agreement to be inferred from previous dealings as a result of generally accepted commercial practice. The process of inferring acceptance of an exclusion of liability is most clearly illustrated in cases where a third party can sue on or be sued on a contract between others.

(a)   Previous course of dealing

If the *proferens* has failed properly to communicate the existence of an exclusion clause to the other party, this is not necessarily fatal, if there is an established course of dealing between the parties. Where two businesses use apparently conflicting standard form contracts, giving rise to a 'battle of the forms',[2] one way of resolving the dispute is to refer to any previous dealings between the parties in order to identify the terms of the contract forming the basis of the dispute.[3]

For the previous dealings rule to apply, it must be shown that there has been a long and consistent course of dealings on terms which include the exemption clause. If this is the case, even if no steps have been taken on the occasion under consideration to give the other party actual notice of the clause, knowledge may be inferred.[4] It is essential that a consistent course of dealing is established, with the result that inconsistent business practice may prove fatal.[5] However, the fact that on one occasion out of 82 previous transactions there was a failure to communicate the standard terms of contracting does not mean that there is an inconsistent course of dealing.[6]

What is consistent is a question of fact. It is established that a course of dealing three or four times a month for three years is consistent.[7] But dealings described as isolated will not be sufficient.[8] In business transactions, it is more likely that a consistent course of dealing will be found to exist than in the case of consumer contracts.[9] However, it is established that, usage apart, no-one can contend that he has usual trading terms if he has never used them or brought them to the attention of anyone.[10]

What has been considered so far is the case where an exclusion is incorporated into a contract by reference to previous dealings between the two parties in dispute. However, it is also possible for an exclusion clause to be impliedly communicated by reference to another contract made contemporaneously with the transaction under consideration. For example, a bill of lading may provide that the exceptions contained in the charterparty with which it is associated are deemed to be incorporated in the bill of lading. Such a process of purported incorporation by reference is intended to minimise the time and cost of reproducing the terms twice over. However, the question will regularly arise

---

2   See *Butler Machine Tool Co Ltd v Ex-Cell-O Corp* [1979] 1 All ER 965 and see ch 7.
3   *Hardwick Game Farm v Suffolk Agricultural Assoc*, sub nom *Henry Kendall & Sons v William Lillico & Sons* [1969] 2 AC 31.
4   Ibid. See also *J R Spurling Ltd v Bradshaw* [1956] 2 All ER 121. Cf *McCutcheon v David MacBrayne Ltd* [1964] 1 WLR 125 at 134.
5   *McCutcheon v David MacBrayne Ltd* [1964] 1 WLR 125.
6   *SIAT di dal Ferro v Tradax Overseas SA* [1978] 2 Lloyd's Rep 470; affd [1980] 2 Lloyd's Rep 53.
7   *Henry Kendall & Sons v William Lillico & Sons Ltd* [1969] 2 AC 31.
8   *Metaalhandel JA Magnum BV v Ardfields Transport Ltd* [1988] 1 Lloyd's Rep 197.
9   Cf *Hollier v Rambler Motors (AMC) Ltd* [1972] 2 QB 71 (consumer contract) with *The Havprins* [1983] 2 Lloyd's Rep 356 (business transaction).
10   *Salsi v Jetspeed Air Services Ltd* [1977] 2 Lloyd's Rep 57 at 61 (per DONALDSON LJ).

whether the wording of the bill of lading is sufficiently clear to incorporate the terms contained in the charterparty.[11]

(b)   Common understanding

The parties to a contract may share some common basis which justifies the presumption that the parties have a common understanding of the terms of their contract. The common basis will usually be provided by the fact that both parties are familiar with the terms of a particular trade or type of contract. In *British Crane Hire Ltd v Ipswich Plant Hire Ltd*,[12] the parties had made an oral contract for the hire of earth moving equipment. At the time, nothing was said about the conditions of hire. Later, the owners sent a set of terms which were a variation of a set of terms prescribed by the Contractors Plant Association, and which were similar in effect to terms normally used by the hirers when they hired out machinery to others. Because of the common understanding of the parties, the trade association conditions were deemed to be part of the contract, even though there was no consistent course of dealings and despite non-communication of the relevant terms at the time of contracting.

A similar approach is also adopted in relation to conventions applicable to the carriage of goods and passengers by sea, road and air.[13] It should be noted that these conventions have the force of rules of law and, as such, obligations they create are legally imposed rather than impliedly agreed to. However, they do represent standard or conventional practice in relation to the type of carriage concerned.

(c)   Exclusion clauses and third parties[14]

Many commercial transactions, particularly those involving international trade, are multipartite ventures. Sometimes, they are not readily capable of analysis in terms of traditional rules of the law of contract which appear to treat the bilateral contract as typical. Since, in the field of commercial transactions, the law of contract is regarded as the servant of the needs of the business community, it is not surprising to find exceptional cases where the traditional rules of the law of contract fail adequately to explain commercial practice. One such exception arises in relation to exclusion clauses and third parties. A straightforward application of the doctrine of privity of contract would suggest that a third party cannot claim the benefit of, or be subject to, the burden of an exclusion clause contained in a contract between two other parties.

In relation to the benefit of an exclusion clause, a typical problem which may arise is that a firm of stevedores may have negligently damaged goods carried under the terms of a contract made between two other parties to a series of contracts intended to facilitate the international transport of those goods to the purchaser. The question which arises in this context is whether the stevedore can claim the benefit of an exclusion clause in the contract between the consignor and the carrier which purports to protect both the carrier and the stevedore. It is possible that holding the stevedore liable for negligence in unloading the cargo might undermine a valid allocation of risks in a commercial venture. In order to avoid this possibility, it is possible for the benefit of an exclusion clause to extend to a third party under a general doctrine of vicarious immunity.

---

11   See *Thomas & Co v Portsea SS Co Ltd* [1912] AC 1; *The Miramar* [1984] 2 All ER 326. Cf *The Merak* [1965] P 223.
12   [1975] QB 303.
13   Hague-Visby Rules (as amended) imposed by the Carriage of Goods by Sea Act 1971, s 1(2); Convention on the Contract for the International Carriage of Goods by Road imposed by the Carriage of Goods by Road Act 1965; Warsaw Convention as amended at the Hague in 1955 imposed by the Carriage by Air Act 1961, s 1.
14   See Yates & Hawkins *Standard Business Contracts* (1986) ch 7 E & F.

In *Elder Dempster & Co v Paterson, Zochonis & Co Ltd*,[15] the contract between the plaintiff cargo owners and the carriers of a cargo provided that the owner of the chartered ship carrying the cargo should not be liable for negligent stowage. Although there was no contract between the plaintiffs and the defendant shipowners, it was held that the shipowners were entitled to the protection of the exclusion clause. The only reason given for the decision was that it was consistent with commercial reality in that it circumvented the absurd conclusion that a negligent charterer could avoid liability but the shipowner could not.

One interpretation of the decision is that, if a person employs an agent to perform a contract, that agent is entitled, in performing the contract, to any immunity from liability which the contract confers on the principal.[16] This doctrine of vicarious immunity clearly flies in the face of the doctrine of privity of contract. However, the doctrine of vicarious immunity was later rejected by the House of Lords in *Scruttons Ltd v Midland Silicones Ltd*.[17] In this case, the defendants, a firm of stevedores, negligently damaged a drum of chemicals and sought the immunity offered by a limitation clause contained in the bill of lading which governed the relationship between the plaintiffs and the carrier. The relevant clause provided that the 'carrier' included any person bound by the bill of lading, whether acting as carrier or bailee. The House of Lords held that, since the stevedores were not parties to the contract of carriage, they could not rely on the limitation clause. They disposed of the doctrine of vicarious immunity by holding that it did not represent the ratio of the *Elder Dempster* case. Furthermore, since the limitation clause did not mention the stevedores by name, they were not entitled to its protection.

The result of this decision was that the effectiveness of exemption clauses became severely restricted, and the doctrine of privity of contract could be used to allow a successful action against a third party. It should be appreciated that this approach to exclusion clauses was employed when there was no direct statutory control of such devices in the form of the Unfair Contract Terms Act 1977. Denying the effectiveness of an exemption clause which protected an employee of the *proferens* might well be appropriate where the action was brought by a consumer suffering physical injuries,[18] but the same approach was hardly appropriate to commercial relationships, particularly in view of the fact that it is normal commercial practice for the owner of the cargo to insure in respect of losses of this kind. It seems strange that the owner should be allowed to hold the carrier's employees and contractors liable when they may not carry insurance in respect of the risk of loss in question. A strict application of the doctrine of privity of contract may leave third parties in a position in which they face risks considerably greater than those undertaken by the contracting parties. While the parties to the contract can calculate the possible risks of loss and insure accordingly, the same cannot be said of third parties, such as stevedores. Furthermore, one effect of the application of the doctrine of privity in these circumstances is that the insurer of the injured party could recover from the third party, in a tortious action, the amount he would have paid out under a policy covering the risk in question. Because of this state of affairs, other means of avoiding the effect of the decision in *Scruttons v Midland Silicones Ltd*[19] have been employed. These methods may take one of two courses. One is to find some means of circumventing the doctrine of privity of contract, and the other is to seek to limit the tortious duty owed by the third party.

---

15   [1924] AC 522.
16   See *Treitel* p 553
17   [1962] AC 446.
18   See *Adler v Dickson* [1955] 1 QB 158; *Genys v Matthews* [1965] 3 All ER 24; *Gore v Van der Lann* [1967] 2 QB 31.
19   [1962] AC 446.

One method of avoiding the effects of the doctrine of privity of contract is to treat one of the contracting parties as an agent for his employees or sub-contractors, but this requires an appropriately worded contractual provision. Such a provision should make it clear that a stevedore, for example, is intended to be protected by the limitation, that the carrier, in addition to contracting on his own behalf, also contracts as agent for the stevedore, and that the carrier has authority from the stevedore to contract in this way.[20] If there is no evidence that the carrier contracts on behalf of the stevedore, the benefit of the exclusion will not extend to that person.[1]

In *New Zealand Shipping Co Ltd v Satterthwaite*,[2] machinery belonging to the consignees was damaged by the defendant stevedores in the course of unloading a ship. The defendants sought the protection of a limitation clause contained in the bill of lading which formed the basis of a contract between the carriers and the consignors. Accordingly, the dispute arose between two litigants, neither of whom was a party to the contract of carriage. The relevant clause provided that no servant or agent, including an independent contractor of the carrier, was to be liable for any act or default while acting in the course of his employment. Furthermore, the clause provided that every limitation available to the carrier should also be available to specified third parties; that the carrier should be deemed to act as agent and trustee for such persons, and that such persons should be deemed to be parties to the contract. All members of the Privy Council agreed that an appropriately worded clause could protect a third party, and a majority held that this clause did serve to protect the stevedore. The process of constructing a contract between two litigants not party to the main contract proved to be tortuous, and it became evident that contracts can be created where they do not readily allow for analysis in terms of the common law rules of offer, acceptance[3] and consideration.[4] The Privy Council were prepared to treat the presentation of the bill of lading by the consignee as a unilateral offer of exemption which was capable of creating mutual obligations when the stevedores performed services for the benefit of the consignee by discharging the goods.[5]

While the decision in *Satterthwaite* may be difficult to explain on conceptual grounds, it does represent commercial reality in that those engaged in the carriage business are aware that agents and sub-contractors are used, and that such persons are likely to operate on the basis that their liability is limited. Accordingly, the decision has been followed in other jurisdictions,[6] and it would seem to represent English law in these circumstances, provided the third party is engaged only in performance of the contract in which the exclusion clause is contained.[7]

The assumption in *Satterthwaite's* case was that the stevedores were liable in tort to the consignee. However, an alternative strategy is to use the terms of the contract in order to structure a duty of care which might otherwise be owed.[8] In *Junior Books v Veitchi*,[9] the question arose whether a sub-contractor could rely on an exclusion clause

20 Ibid at 474 (per LORD REID).
1   *The Suleyman Stalskiy* [1976] 2 Lloyd's Rep 609. See also *Southern Water Authority v Carey* [1985] 2 All ER 1077 at 1085 (per JUDGE SMOUT), Official Referee.
2   [1975] AC 154. See also Reynolds (1974) 90 LQR 301; Coote (1974) 37 MLR 453; Palmer (1974) JBL 101 & 220.
3   See ch 7.
4   See ch 6.
5   [1975] AC 154 at 167–168 (per LORD WILBERFORCE).
6   *Miles International Corp v Federal Commerce & Navigation Co* [1978] 1 Lloyd's Rep 285; *Port Jackson Stevedoring Pty Ltd v Salmond & Spraggon (Australia) Pty Ltd* [1980] 3 All ER 257. Cf *Lummus Co Ltd v East African Harbours Corp* [1978] 1 Lloyd's Rep 317.
7   *Raymond Burke Motors Ltd v Mersey Docks & Harbour Co* [1986] 1 Lloyd's Rep 155.
8   See *Leigh & Sillivan Ltd v Aliakmon Shipping Co Ltd* [1985] 2 All ER 44 at 76 (per ROBERT GOFF LJ) and *Muirhead v Industrial Tank Specialities Ltd* [1985] 3 All ER 705 at 717 (per ROBERT GOFF LJ).
9   [1983] 1 AC 520.

in the building contract between the main contractors and the building owner. If the exclusion clause served to limit the duty of care, this would indirectly provide the sub-contractors with a defence to the action in the tort of negligence. LORD ROSKILL drew an analogy with the disclaimer used in *Hedley Byrne v Heller*,[10] and held, obiter, that the exclusion clause, if properly worded, might serve to limit the duty of care owed by the sub-contractor.[11] A similar approach has also been adopted in *Southern Water Authority v Carey*,[12] in which the agency argument used in *Satterthwaite's* case was inapplicable because there was no previous connection between the sub-contractor and the main contractor sufficient to give rise to an agency relationship. However, the terms of the building contract between the main contractor and the owner were held sufficient to negative the duty of care which would otherwise have been owed by the sub-contractor, probably because those terms were contained in a trade association standard form with which both parties would have been familiar.

The process of fitting contractual obligations into an action for negligence is regarded by some as too complex[13] and that, accordingly, in such borderline cases there should be no tortious liability at all. The reasoning employed in these circumstances is typified by that of LORD BRANDON in *Leigh & Sillavan Ltd v Aliakmon Shipping Co Ltd*,[14] that because the exclusion clause is contained in a contract to which one of the litigants is a party and to which the other is not, it cannot govern the relationship between the two. This is similar to the privity of contract reasoning which was adopted in *Scruttons Ltd v Midland Silicones Ltd*,[15] which caused so much difficulty in commercial relationships. However, there is a very important point of distinction between *Junior Books* and *The Aliakmon*. The former involves the question whether a third party is entitled to the benefit of an exclusion clause contained in a contract made between others, whereas *The Aliakmon* concerns the question whether a third party can be subject to the burden of a contract made by others, thereby raising the issue of vicarious entitlement.[16] In this second instance, it is perhaps more difficult, as a matter of policy, to render a person bound by the provisions of a contract when there is no implied inference of consent. But where the question is whether a sub-contractor's liability in negligence is restricted by the terms of a contract between the building owner and the consultant engineer, the absence of a contractual relationship between the sub-contractor and the building owner does not deprive the sub-contractor of protection, provided the main contract forms the basis of the duty of care owed by the sub-contractor to the building owner.[17] Thus the relevance of the exclusion clause is to qualify the duty of care which might otherwise be owed by the sub-contractor[18] or his employees.[19] In *Norwich City Council v Harvey*[20] the contract between the main contractor and the building owner required the owner to insure the building against fire damage. Due to the defendant sub-contractor's negligence, the building was damaged by fire, but the insurance provision in the main contract was considered to be a matter of which the defendant would have been aware and which served to negative any duty of care which would otherwise have been owed. The building owners were taken to have assumed the risk of damage

---

10   [1964] AC 465.
11   [1983] 1 AC 520 at 546.
12   [1985] 2 All ER 1077.
13   *Junior Books Ltd v Veitchi Co Ltd* [1983] 1 AC 520 at 552 (per LORD BRANDON) (dissenting).
14   Sub nom *The Aliakmon* [1986] AC 785 at 817. See also Adams & Brownsword [1990] JBL 23.
15   [1962] AC 446.
16   See *Beale, Bishop & Furmston* pp 831–833.
17   *Pacific Associates Inc v Baxter* [1989] 2 All ER 159 at 179 (per PURCHAS LJ).
18   Ibid at 187–188 (per RALPH GIBSON LJ).
19   *Norwich City Council v Harvey* [1989] 1 All ER 1180 at 1184 (per MAY LJ).
20   Ibid.

by fire and the sub-contractor was taken to have contracted with the main contractor on that basis.[1] The decision makes sound commercial sense in that it clearly identifies the best insurer and orders the liabilities of the other parties accordingly, but at the expense of the doctrine of privity of contract.

The general rule, illustrated by *The Aliakmon*,[2] is that the burden of an exclusion clause in a contract between, for example, sellers of goods and a carrier, does not bind a third party, such as the buyer of goods under shipment. However, there are some exceptional instances. For example, in *Pyrene Co Ltd v Scindia Navigation Co Ltd*,[3] a contract for the sale of goods provided that the buyer should arrange shipment. Arrangements were made and the contract between the buyer and carrier contained terms which excluded the carrier's liability. While the goods were still at the seller's risk, they were damaged due to the carrier's negligence. It was held that the seller was bound by the exclusion on the ground that the buyer was the seller's agent.[4] An alternative explanation is that an implied contract arose between the carrier and the seller when the goods were accepted for loading.[5]

A second exception arises in cases of bailment, where a sub-bailee's terms may sometimes bind the customer who has contracted with the principal bailee. In *Johnson Matthey Ltd v Constantine Terminals Ltd*,[6] the consignors arranged for the shipment of a quantity of silver. The carriers arranged for it to be stored, pending shipment, during which time it was stolen. The sub-bailee's contract with the carriers contained exclusions of liability which were held to be binding on the consignors, because the consignors could not prove that a bailment existed unless they were prepared to rely on the terms of the storage contract between the carriers and the sub-bailees.

1   Ibid at 1187 (per MAY LJ).
2   [1986] AC 785.
3   [1954] 2 QB 402.
4   Ibid at 423–425.
5   See *New Zealand Shipping Co Ltd v AM Satterthwaite & Co Ltd* [1975] AC 154. Cf *The Aliakmon* [1986] AC 785 at 808 (per LORD BRANDON).
6   [1976] 2 Lloyd's Rep 215. Cf *Morris v C W Martin & Sons Ltd* [1966] 1 QB 716.

Chapter 23

Risk–allocation

1. INTRODUCTION

Where a legal relationship fails to satisfy the expectations of the parties, losses may be incurred and it is necessary to determine where these are to fall. This process of risk–allocation may be carried out by the parties themselves, by the court or by Parliament.

(1) EXCHANGE RELATIONSHIPS

In an exchange relationship, it is for the parties to determine where a particular risk of loss is to fall. Those who are 'risk averse' will seek to pass risks to another wherever possible. This may be effected by taking out market insurance, but the same result can be achieved by securing a promise from the other party to the contract, in which case the promisor becomes an insurer of that risk of loss. Thus risks of loss may be allocated by the use of exclusion clauses or other related devices, although the law may intervene where strong policy reasons dictate that risks should not be allocated in this manner.[1] Similarly, where a risk of loss is foreseen by the parties, it may be provided for in the form of an agreed damages clause which stipulates how much is to be paid by way of compensation in the event of the breach giving rise to that risk of loss.[2]

Since the intentions of the parties are so important in determining where a risk of loss should fall, the parties might be expected to expressly provide for all those losses which will be actionable and for a valuation of each risk in terms of damages payable. But this would not be feasible since the transaction costs involved would be prohibitive. Instead, the law lays down a set of rules, namely those on remoteness of damage,[3] to determine which losses will be actionable. Under these rules, a defendant will be liable for normal losses and those remote losses of which he was made aware by the plaintiff at the time of contracting. This emphasises the importance of the parties' intentions in the process of risk-allocation. It seems right, in principle, that the defendant should accept the risk of normal loss caused by his broken promise. Moreover, the rules on remote losses encourage the exchange of information between the parties, with the

---

1 See chs 22 and 24.
2 See ch 14.
3 See ch 16.

result that transaction costs are reduced. This exchange of information is particularly important in relation to an efficient allocation of risk since a person cannot hope to make a rational decision unless he is as fully informed as possible.

If the contract does not provide for an event which produces a risk of loss the law can treat contractual obligations as absolute and allow the loss to lie where it falls. In this case, a promisor is bound to carry out his promise, even when subsequent events render this impossible.[4] But this would be unrealistic, therefore a legal rule is required in order to allocate that risk. As far as possible, the court will have regard for the presumed intention of the parties as reasonable men, but other factors will also play a part. For example it may be necessary to identify the person who is in the best position to avoid or minimise the risk or to allocate the risk to the person who is most likely to be able to insure against it.

(2)   NON-EXCHANGE RELATIONSHIPS

Problems of risk-allocation may also arise beyond the boundaries of exchange relationships. For example, where an accident is negligently caused, it is necessary to determine where the risk of injury should fall. There is a significant difference between tort and contract actions. In contract actions, risk-allocation is generally a matter for the parties whereas since tort plaintiffs and defendants rarely have the opportunity to communicate and exchange information, rules on the allocation of risk in tort actions have to be legally imposed.

The main problem in non-exchange relationships is to determine how a risk of loss should be allocated. This is largely a matter of social justice based on the need to compensate a person for the harm he has suffered. Where the defendant is shown to be at fault, common sense dictates that he should be held responsible for his actions, but it is also necessary to balance the risk created against matters such as the utility of his conduct and the precautions necessary to guard against the risk of harm.[5]

Occasionally, tort law imposes strict liability, requiring the risk creator (such as one who carries on an extra-hazardous activity) to compensate the plaintiff even in the absence of fault.[6] In other instances, a business carrying on an activity which creates a risk of harm may be liable in the absence of fault for the reason that such losses are regarded as the normal risks of that business.[7]

These rules beg the question, who is the risk creator? It could be argued that the pedestrian injured in a road traffic accident is the risk creator because he chooses to walk the streets. Likewise a person killed in consequence of an escape of ionising radiations from a nuclear processing plant could be the risk creator because he chose to live in that area, but this is generally not the case. It follows that tests need to be formulated which will allow the identification of the person who should accept the risk of loss.

(3)   PRINCIPLES OF RISK-ALLOCATION

It can be seen from the foregoing that the issue of risk-allocation arises in a number of different situations. This chapter is concerned mainly with the issue in the context of the broad notion of impossibility of performance in contractual dealings.

---

4   See *Paradine v Jane* (1647) 82 ER 897 and ch 11.
5   See ch 12.
6   See Nuclear Installations Act 1965; *Rylands v Fletcher* (1868) LR 3 HL 330 and see ch 29.
7   See Atiyah *Vicarious Liability* pp 22–24; Atiyah *Accidents* p 482.

Where the risk created by a breach of contract is insignificant, it can be left to lie where it falls. Thus in simultaneous exchanges such as most consumer contracts, the risk that a supermarket will reduce the price of bread the day after a consumer has purchased a loaf is one which can be borne by the consumer. In long-term commercial contracts, changes may occur which fundamentally affect the position of the parties. In determining where the risk should fall, the courts will take into account a number of factors. Of primary importance are the intentions and reasonable expectations of the parties, but it is also possible to consider who is the least cost-avoider or who is the best insurer against the risk of loss.[8]

(i)   The intentions and reasonable expectations of the parties

If a contract provides for the event which creates the risk of loss, determining the intentions and reasonable expectations of the parties is a matter of judicial construction of the contract. For example, the parties may have included a *force majeure* clause in the contract, stipulating the effect of certain contingencies affecting performance, such as delays or strikes. Thus it is important to construe the language of the contract, whether the problem is one of frustration or mistake. For example, if the parties make provision for an event which would not otherwise be regarded as a frustrating event, the court must ask whether the relevant provision is worded so as to cover the event in question.[9] Similar issues also arise in relation to mistakes provided for in the contract. Thus in *William Sindall plc v Cambridgeshire CC*[10] it was held that where a seller of land had limited his liability for defects in title *known to him,* he would not be liable in respect of an easement of which he had no knowledge.

The reasonable expectations of the parties do not cover just the risk of loss, but also chances of gain generated by some unexpected occurrence. Both gains and losses can be analysed in the same way, with the result that a person who stands to gain from a contract in a manner that is beyond his reasonable expectations may be denied that gain. Typically, such problems are dealt with by rules on mistake, which provide that the gainer ought to have been aware of the unilateral mistake of the other.[11]

(ii)   The least cost-avoider and the best insurer

Sometimes an attempt to ascertain the intentions of the parties is futile, as in cases to which the doctrine of frustration applies. Generally, a frustrating event is uncontemplated by either party, in which case they cannot be said to have any intentions as to how the risk of loss should be allocated. However, they may have reasonable expectations in retrospect. Accordingly, the court will attempt to find a just solution by considering what the response of the parties as fair and reasonable men would have been in the light of the change of circumstances.

In order to find an appropriate solution, the court may consider which of the parties is the superior risk-bearer. One possible solution is to ask if one party is in a better position than the other to prevent the risk of loss from materialising. Such a person is the least cost-avoider. Accordingly, a person who brings about a frustrating event,[12] or

---

8   See Posner and Rosenfield (1977) 6 JLS 83 (reproduced in Kronman and Posner *The Economics of Contract Law* (1979)).
9   See *Hoecheong Products Ltd v Cargill (Hong Kong) Ltd* [1995] 1 Lloyd's Rep 584; *The Kriti Rex* [1996] 2 Lloyd's Rep 171.
10   [1994] 1 WLR 1016.
11   *Hartog v Colin and Shields* [1939] 3 All ER 566. See also *Sherwood v Walker* 33 NW 919 (1887).
12   *Maritime National Fish Ltd v Ocean Trawlers Ltd* [1935] AC 524; *J Lauritzen AS v Wijsmuller BV, The Super Servant Two* [1990] 1 Lloyd's Rep 1.

one who could have performed his contractual obligations by some other reasonable method without having to encounter an alleged frustrating event,[13] may be required to accept the risk of loss.

Prevention is not the only way of dealing with a risk of loss. It is also possible to insure against risk. Accordingly, the court may seek to discover which of the parties is the best insurer. For these purposes, insurance includes both market insurance and self-insurance, whereby a business may decide to spread costs between its customers through a minimal increase in the price of the product or service it provides. When the best insurer has been identified, he may be expected to absorb an unexpected risk of loss. For example, it seems to be generally accepted that a tenant is in a better position to insure against possible interruption of a lease than is the landlord.[14] Also, in cases involving the shipment of goods, an event such as the closure of the Suez Canal may not frustrate a contract,[15] since the shipper is probably in the best position to appreciate the magnitude of the expected loss and the probability of the unexpected event. Furthermore, such a person is in the best position to spread possible losses by means of insurance.

(4)   METHODS OF RISK-ALLOCATION

The issue of judicial risk-allocation generally arises where a contract is silent on a matter relevant to a dispute between the parties. What the court must do is to fill the gaps left by the parties so as to determine where the risk of loss is to fall.

The court may interpret the terms of the contract so as to produce a satisfactory solution, with the result that the contract is enforced. Alternatively, the contract may be declared void or voidable, or the parties may be discharged from their obligations to perform, with the result that the risk of loss is apparently shared between the parties.

(i)   Interpretation of the terms of a contract

A contract can be enforced by one of two means. Either its express terms can be interpreted so as to cover the event creating the risk of loss, or a term may be implied to cover the event in question. Each of these approaches is capable of giving effect to the intentions and reasonable expectations of the parties. The process of implying a contractual term often appears to operate as a form of judicial legislation, not really connected with the intentions of the parties at all.[16] While interpretation of contract terms will usually result in the enforcement of the contract against one of the parties, it is also possible that the terms can be interpreted in such a way as to discharge the parties from their obligations.

(a)   Enforcement by interpretation

In the case of an oral contract, the process of construction will involve hearing the evidence of the parties followed by identification of the obligations to which the parties are subject. Where the contract is written, the parol evidence rule states that only the written document may be considered by the court, and extrinsic evidence will not be admitted as an aid to interpretation. While the rule provides for certainty, it is subject to so many exceptions that its effect must now be regarded as minimal.[17] For example,

---

13   *Blackburn Bobbin Co Ltd v Allen* [1918] 2 KB 467; *Tsakiroglou & Co Ltd v Noblee Thorl GmbH* [1962] AC 93.

14   *National Carriers Ltd v Panalpina (Northern) Ltd* [1981] AC 675.

15   *Ocean Tramp Tankers Corpn v V/O Sovfracht, The Eugenia* [1964] 2 QB 226; *Tsakiroglou & Co Ltd v Noblee Thorl GmbH* [1962] AC 93.

16   See ch 7.

17   Law Commission No 154 (1986) Cmnd 9700, para 2.7.

extrinsic evidence may be admitted where the contractual document does not cover the entire agreement.[18] Similarly, extrinsic evidence may be admitted to show the existence of a related collateral contract.[19] Furthermore, when deciding if a written instrument should be rectified, the court may hear the oral evidence of the parties, indicating that the written document does not represent what was agreed. The rule and its exceptions seem to be based squarely on the desire to give effect to the intentions and reasonable expectations of the parties. If the written document is intended to contain all the terms of the agreement, there is nothing wrong in applying the parol evidence rule.[20] But if the parties differ in their interpretation of what has been agreed, it is necessary to consider whether the written document has the appearance of a complete agreement.[1] On this basis, where parol evidence is either admitted or excluded, the court is applying an objective test of agreement.[2]

There is a general rule that a contractual document should be construed according to the ordinary grammatical meaning of the words used in it,[3] with the result that evidence of prior negotiations will be inadmissible.[4] However, there are exceptions, for example, if the contractual document is ambiguous, evidence of prior negotiations may be admitted to show that the parties had reached an agreement.[5]

Pre-contractual statements are important in the process of risk-allocation, where one party has relied on a statement made by the other. Risk of loss may be allocated to the person making the statement which induces reliance. The devices used to do this include construing the statement as a misrepresentation, an express term of the contract, or as forming the basis of a collateral contract between the parties.[6]

(b)   Discharge by interpretation

In some instances, the terms of a contract may be interpreted in such a way as to discharge the parties from further performance of their obligations. Normally, the process of discharge will be effected by means of rules on mistake or frustration of contract. But it is possible to encounter cases which do not satisfactorily comply with the conventional rules associated with these doctrines. Applying the typical pragmatic approach of English courts to such problems, it may be possible to interpret the terms of a contract so as to facilitate discharge of the parties' performance obligations. In *Staffordshire Area Health Authority v South Staffordshire Waterworks Co*,[7] a contract made in 1929 for the supply of water provided for a fixed price equivalent to 2.9 pence per 1,000 gallons, payable at 'all times hereafter'. By 1975, the normal rate charged by the defendants had risen to 45 pence per 1,000 gallons, thereby rendering uneconomic the supply of water under the 1929 terms. A majority of the Court of Appeal held that, as a matter of construction, the words 'at all times hereafter' meant that the obligations imposed were intended to survive only during the continuance of the agreement, and that the agreement was determinable at any time by the giving of reasonable notice. Accordingly, the defendants could terminate the agreement of 1929 and replace it with new terms as to payment, provided they gave reasonable notice. The decision seems to be confined to contracts of infinite duration, with the result that had the contract been for a specified period of

18   *Allen v Pink* (1838) 4 M & W 140; *J Evans & Son (Portsmouth) Ltd v Andrea Merzario Ltd* [1976] 2 All ER 930.
19   *City and Westminster Properties (1934) Ltd v Mudd* [1959] Ch 129.
20   Law Commission No 154 op cit, paras 1.7 and 2.7.
1   See Treitel p 178.
2   Law Commission No 154 op cit, paras 2.14 and 2.17.
3   *Lovell and Christmas Ltd v Wall* (1911) 104 LT 85 at 88 (per COZENS-HARDY MR).
4   *Prenn v Simmonds* [1971] 3 All ER 237.
5   *The Karen Oltman* [1976] 2 Lloyd's Rep 708.
6   See *McRae v Commonwealth Disposals Commission* (1950) 84 CLR 377 and see also ch 26.
7   [1978] 3 All ER 769. Cf *Watford DC v Watford RDC* (1987) 86 LGR 524.

50 years, the price could not have been varied by giving notice unless there was a term making provision for price variation.[8]

An alternative strategy may be to imply into the contract a term permitting discharge. For example, in *Sainsbury Ltd v Street*,[9] the defendant agreed to supply 275 tons of cattle feed barley to be grown on the defendant's land. Adverse weather conditions caused the land to produce only 140 tons which the defendant sold to another person at a higher price per ton than that agreed with the plaintiffs. McKenna J implied a term to the effect that the defendant would be excused if his land did not produce the quantity contracted for, but that term did not release him from the obligation to deliver what he had produced. While the contract was not frustrated, as there remained an obligation to deliver the barley grown, the term implied served to provide an appropriate solution.

(ii)   Mistake

It would be misleading to take the view that English law has a coherent doctrine of mistake. A person may be mistaken over a matter of some importance, but the law will not always provide relief. It is important to appreciate that, if a mistake is said to be operative, it will have the effect of discharging the parties from their contract, which may not accord with the rule of commercial convenience that contracts should be enforced. Furthermore, since a contract is void at common law in the event of an operative mistake, the result may have a catastrophic effect on a third party. If a sale of goods contract is declared void on the ground of mistake, the common law rule dictates that no contract ever existed. Property in the goods does not pass to the buyer and, if he has sold the goods to a third party, that person will, subject to the operation of the rule *nemo dat quod non habet*,[10] acquire no right to the goods in question.

The effect of the common law rule is such that it is rarely used,[11] although where it is pleaded and the contract is void it would appear to render irrelevant the rules on mistake in equity.[12] In equity, rules on mistake have a wider scope, which allow the court to render a contract voidable at the instance of the mistaken party and to order rescission of the contract on terms that attempt to do justice to both parties and to take account of the position of third parties.

The common law and equitable rules on mistake must be considered alongside other methods of risk-allocation, with the result that the contract itself must be considered in order to determine where the risk of loss should fall. Thus a plea of mistake will fail in any case where the contract expressly or impliedly provides for the allocation of risk.[13] In some instances, even if common law and equitable rules provide no assistance, it may be possible to have a contract set aside under the provisions of a relevant statute.[14]

---

8   See *Kirklees MBC v Yorkshire Woollen District Transport* (1978) 77 LGR 448. Cf *Wates v Greater London Council* (1983) 25 BLR 1.
9   [1972] 3 All ER 1127. See Hudson (1968) 31 MLR 535.
10   See Atiyah *Sale* ch 19; Bridge, *The Sale of Goods* (OUP, paperback edn, 1998) ch 4.
11   To such an extent that it has been suggested that the common law rule should merge with that applied in equity. See Phang (1989) 9 Legal Studies 291.
12   *Associated Japanese Bank (International) Ltd v Crédit du Nord SA* [1988] 3 All ER 902 at 912 (per Steyn J); Cf *Solle v Butcher* [1950] 1 KB 671 at 691 (per Denning LJ).
13   *Associated Japanese Bank (International) Ltd v Crédit du Nord SA* [1988] 3 All ER 902 at 912 (per Steyn J).
14   See *Re Goldcorp Exchange* [1995] 1 AC 74 at 103, possibly referring to the New Zealand Contractual Mistakes Act 1977.

(iii)   Frustration

Where after a contract is concluded, an event occurs which renders further performance impossible or impractical, the role of the court is to determine where risks of loss caused by that event should fall. The common law doctrine which permits this process of risk-allocation is that of frustration. Where a contract is frustrated, it is not void *ab initio*, but the parties are discharged from the need for further performance of their contractual obligations as from the date of the frustrating event. A number of consequential problems arise from the operation of the doctrine of frustration. For example, one of the parties may have paid in advance for the product or service to be provided under the contract, or one of the parties might have partly performed his obligations, thereby conferring a valuable benefit on the other. Common law rules proved to be inadequate to deal with such issues, which are now provided for in the Law Reform (Frustrated Contracts) Act 1943.[15]

2.   MISTAKE

(1)   TYPES OF MISTAKE

Where a mistake operates, it serves to negative or, in some cases, to nullify consent.[16] A mistake which negatives consent is one which prevents the formation of an agreement and is relevant to the issue of ascription of responsibility.[17] Accordingly, if the parties are at cross-purposes,[18] or if a party is mistaken as to the identity of the person with whom he has contracted,[19] it is said that no agreement has been reached. The test of agreement is objective,[20] with the result that the subjective intentions of the parties are irrelevant. Not all of these cases involve the issue of risk-allocation.

In other instances, rules on mistake, such as those concerned with mistake as to identity, considered above and the operation of the rule *non est factum*[1] may serve to protect third party rights. In these cases A has contracted with B who has resold goods to C. A now wishes to recover his property from C, a *bona fide* purchaser, on the ground that he has been misled by B. Where B is guilty of fraud or misrepresentation, A will have a remedy against B in damages. B will acquire a voidable title to property passing under the contract[2] and, if A acts quickly enough, he may be able to prevent a good title passing to C.[3] Where B's misrepresentation is such that A is truly mistaken and the rules as to mistake as to identity or *non est factum* apply, the contract between A and B is void and C acquires no better title than B.

In cases of mistake as to identity the person with whom A contracts is a rogue (X) who claims to be B. For these purposes, A must think he has contracted with B in the belief that X, with whom he is negotiating is B; X must be aware of this misapprehension and it must be established by A that the identity of B is a matter of crucial importance.[4] If the mistake merely relates to the ability of X (or B) to pay, it is unlikely that the

---

15   See ch 18.
16   *Bell v Lever Bros Ltd* [1932] AC 161 at 217 (per LORD ATKIN).
17   See ch 7.
18   See *Scriven Bros & Co v Hindley & Co* [1913] 3 KB 564; *Raffles v Wichelhaus* (1864) 2 H & C 906.
19   *Cundy v Lindsay* (1878) 3 App Cas 459; *Ingram v Little* [1961] 1 QB 31. Cf *King's Norton Metal Co Ltd v Edridge Merrett & Co Ltd* (1897) 14 TLR 98; *Lewis v Averay* [1972] 1 QB 198.
20   *Smith v Hughes* (1871) LR 6 QB 597. See chs 4 and 7.
1   Literally 'not my deed' and see *Gallie v Lee*, sub nom *Saunders v Anglia Building Society* [1971] AC 1004.
2   *Phillips v Brooks Ltd* [1919] 2 KB 243; *Lewis v Averay* [1972] 1 QB 198.
3   *Car and Universal Finance Co Ltd v Caldwell* [1965] 1 QB 525.
4   *Cundy v Lindsay* (1878) 3 App Cas 459; *Ingram v Little* [1961] 1 QB 31.

mistake will be sufficiently serious.[5] Moreover, the mistake must relate to the identity of the person with whom A contracts. Thus a mistake as to the identity of a messenger will not be sufficient to render void a contract made with the person to whom the message should have been delivered.[6]

A mistake which nullifies consent is one which is shared by both parties and gives rise to a common misunderstanding which is fundamental to the decision of the parties to enter into the agreement. Whether such mistakes affect the validity of a contract is essentially a matter of risk-allocation. These are sometimes called common mistakes and they will materially affect the decision of the parties to make the contract. They are also referred to as expectation mistakes,[7] in that the parties are mistaken about certain assumptions made prior to entering into the contract. The position may be further complicated by the chance that during the negotiations, one party has stated his understanding of certain facts. If that state of facts proves to be untrue, the statement may be treated as a warranty or as a misrepresentation[8] thereby obviating the need to plead mistake.

(2)   FUNDAMENTAL MISTAKES

(i)   What mistakes are fundamental?

To be operative, a mistake must be fundamental and should relate to a matter of fact which existed at the time of contracting. The early cases on shared mistakes drew inspiration from the civilian notion of errors *in substantia*, seeking to distinguish a mistake as to the substance of the subject matter of the contract from a mere mistake as to motive.[9] In *Bell v Lever Bros Ltd*,[10] the type of mistake required at common law was variously described as one which relates to an assumption that both parties regard as essential,[11] or one which makes the thing supplied essentially different from the thing as it was believed to be.[12] In other words, one person is unable to supply the very thing, whether goods or services, that the other party has contracted to take,[13] and the new state of facts destroys the identity of the subject matter of the contract as it was in the original state of facts.[14]

These statements may be taken to mean that the mistake must relate to a matter, the accuracy of which is a condition precedent to liability. If that condition precedent fails and the contract is executory, the contract is unenforceable.[15] If the contract is executed, the party who has paid money can recover it on the ground that there has been a total failure of consideration.[16] In equity too, it appears that there must be a common, fundamental misapprehension which leads to the failure of some condition on which the existence of the contract depends.[17] However, there are judicial statements to the

---

5   *Phillips v Brooks Ltd* [1919] 2 KB 243; *Lewis v Averay* [1972] 1 QB 198.
6   *Citibank NA v Brown Shipley & Co Ltd* [1991] 2 All ER 690. Cf *Lake v Simmonds* [1927] AC 487.
7   See *Beale, Bishop and Furmston* ch 18.
8   See ch 10.
9   *Kennedy v Panama New Zealand and Australian Royal Mail Co Ltd* (1867) LR 2 QB 580 at 588 (per BLACKBURN LJ).
10   [1932] AC 161.
11   Ibid at 235 (per LORD THANKERTON).
12   Ibid at 218 (per LORD ATKIN).
13   Ibid at 222 (per LORD ATKIN).
14   Ibid at 227 (per LORD ATKIN).
15   Ibid at 225 (per LORD ATKIN).
16   Ibid and see ch 11.
17   *Solle v Butcher* [1950] 1 KB 671 at 693 (per DENNING LJ).

effect that there is a category of actionable mistake in equity which is wider than that at common law.[18]

Established examples of mistakes sufficiently important to justify the invalidation of a contract include mistakes as to the possibility of performing the contract, and possibly some mistakes as to the quality of the thing contracted for. If two persons enter into a contract for the sale of goods which, unknown to them, have been destroyed before the time of contracting, the contract is void.[19] In *Associated Japanese Bank (International) Ltd v Crédit du Nord SA*[20] a bank guarantee of repayments under a leaseback of non-existent machinery was held to be void. This was not because the parties assumed the machines to exist but because the machines were the guarantor's security, with the result that the mistake made the subject matter of the contract of guarantee essentially different from what was reasonably believed.[1] The difficulty with this view is that the non-existent machines were not the subject matter of the contract of guarantee, but if the guarantee and the leaseback are regarded as part of a composite transaction, an analogy can be drawn with those cases in which the subject matter of the void contract is non-existent.[2] What seems to matter is whether the parties think they are dealing with one thing, but discover that they are dealing with something very different. For example in *Grains & Fourrages SA v Huyton*[3] the price for two lots of goods was agreed under the common misapprehension that the correct quality certificates had been exchanged. However, unknown to the parties the certificates had been interchanged and related, respectively, to the wrong lot of goods.

Sometimes a contract is either physically[4] or legally incapable of performance. For example, a contract to take a lease of land is void if, unknown to the parties, the lessee is already the owner of the land.[5] Finally, in rare cases, it may be possible for a mistake as to the quality of the thing contracted for to satisfy the requirements of a fundamental mistake. That such a mistake can be fundamental is not ruled out by the decision of the House of Lords in *Bell v Lever Bros Ltd*,[6] but it would appear that a mistake as to the value of the thing contracted for, no matter how large a mistake that might be, does not render the contract void. In *Bell v Lever Bros Ltd*,[7] two executive officers of a subsidiary of Lever Bros were offered substantial compensation in return for the termination of their contracts, thus allowing the subsidiary company to amalgamate with another. In fact, the two officers had committed breaches of their duties as directors, which would have justified dismissal without compensation. It was argued that there was a fundamental mistake which rendered the compensation agreement void. The House of Lords held, by a majority, that the mistake related only to a quality of the service contract, and that Lever Bros had got exactly what they had contracted for.[8]

Generally, it can be said that a mistake as to quality will not be fundamental since, in the case of a contract for the sale of goods, the buyer gets what he contracted for, albeit of a different quality. Thus, a contract for the sale of a painting, believed by the parties to be by Constable but which turns out to be by some other artist, is not void.[9]

---

18 *William Sindall plc v Cambridgeshire CC* [1994] 3 All ER 932 at 959 (per EVANS LJ.)
19 Sale of Goods Act 1979, s 6.
20 [1988] 3 All ER 902.
1 Ibid at 913 (per STEYN J). See also *Scott v Coulson* [1903] 2 Ch 249.
2 Ibid.
3 [1997] 1 Lloyd's Rep 628.
4 *Sheikh Bros Ltd v Ochsner* [1957] AC 136.
5 *Cooper v Phibbs* (1867) LR 2 HL 149.
6 [1932] AC 161 at 218 (per LORD ATKIN).
7 Ibid.
8 Ibid at 223 (per LORD ATKIN).
9 *Leaf v International Galleries* [1950] 2 KB 86 at 89.

It may be said that the contract is for a painting, not for a painting by Constable. In any case, it would appear that in the art world, if the buyer wishes to be assured that the painting he buys is by *John* Constable, he should contract to that effect if he can find a dealer who is prepared to stand by his attribution.[10] Likewise, a mistake as to the valuation of property is unlikely to attract even the attention of a court applying equitable principles. Thus in *William Sindall plc v Cambridgeshire County Council*[11] a mistake relating to the presence of a sewer beneath land purchased for £5 million which would require £18,000 worth of work to rectify was not considered fundamental. The cost of repairing the sewer equated to the loss of one house on an intended development of 60 houses and 30 flats.

In some cases there may be assumptions made by both parties about the quality of the subject matter which assist in identifying it. In this case, a mistake as to the quality of the subject matter of the contract may be sufficiently fundamental for the contract to be void. Thus if both parties to a contract for the sale of table linen believe it to be a genuine relic of Charles I, the contract is void if the linen is merely Georgian.[12]

Despite the apparent rule that a mistake of quality will rarely be regarded as fundamental, there are, nevertheless, a number of cases in which the courts have granted relief on the ground of an operative mistake as to quality or have found some alternative means of avoiding the consequences of the views expressed in *Bell v Lever Bros*. For example, in *Griffiths v Brymer*[13] the parties entered into a contract to hire a room overlooking the route of the Coronation procession of King Edward VII, but unknown to the parties, the Coronation celebrations were cancelled due to the King's illness. Unlike most of these 'Coronation cases' in which the contract was entered into before it was discovered that the King was ill, this contract was concluded after the news had been broken, but before the contracting parties became aware of the news. According to WRIGHT J, the contract was void on the ground that the parties were under a misconception with regard to the existing state of facts about which they were contracting. The difficulty with this view is that the mistake inevitably related to a quality of the subject matter of the contract and it would be difficult to fit these facts into any of the identified categories of fundamental mistake at common law.

In other circumstances the courts may contrive to use alternative doctrines in order to get round the problem of mistake as to quality. For example in *Gamerco SA v ICM/ Fair Warning Ltd*[14] the court dubiously applied the doctrine of frustration so as to allow the use of the apportionment provisions of the Law Reform (Frustrated Contracts) Act 1943 as opposed to allowing losses to lie where they fell, which is the consequence of an application of common law rules on mistake. In *Gamerco* the plaintiffs agreed to promote a rock concert to be staged by the defendants in Madrid. Shortly before the date of the performance, but after conclusion of the contract, the venue was discovered to be unsafe due to the use of high alumina cement in its construction. As a result, the Spanish authorities banned the use of the venue and no alternative stadium was available. While the problem could have been dealt with through the use of rules on mistake, the court contrived to treat it as a case of frustration. As a case on mistake, the court would have had to grapple with the category known as mistake as to quality and the difficulty of fitting the facts of the case within the restrictive analysis of this category in *Bell v Lever Bros*.

---

10   *Harlingdon & Leinster Enterprises Ltd v Christopher Hull Fine Art Ltd* [1990] 1 All ER 737 at 746 (per NOURSE LJ).
11   [1994] 3 All ER 932.
12   *Nicholson & Venn v Smith Marriott* (1947) 177 LT 189.
13   (1903) 19 TLR 434.
14   [1995] 1 WLR 1226.

(ii) Fundamental mistakes and risk-allocation

Judicial emphasis on the concept of fundamental mistake is misleading. The only point it illustrates on risk-allocation is that small risks can normally be allowed to lie where they fall, but greater risks may need to be appropriately allocated. It is therefore necessary to look for other reasons why a court chooses to allocate a risk of loss to one party rather than the other. It has been argued that the fact that a mistake is fundamental is only a starting point and is not a sufficient ground, on its own, to justify relief.[15] In any case, the existence of a fundamental mistake is not always necessary to invalidate a contract. A mistake as to the terms of a contract does not have to be fundamental. In *Smith v Hughes*,[16] it was said that a sale of oats believed by one party to be warranted to be old but not intended to be so warranted by the other may be void for mistake. Similarly, in equity, relief may be granted in some cases where the mistake is not fundamental in the narrow common law sense. Thus, equitable relief has been given for a mistake as to value,[17] for a mistake of law[18] and for mistaken inference.[19] Also, a mistake does not have to be fundamental to allow rectification of a written document that fails to represent the intentions of the parties.

Important factors in the risk-allocation process are the intentions of the parties and their reasonable expectations, whether the mistake has been induced, and whether the mistake might result in an unjust enrichment.

(3) THE PROTECTION OF REASONABLE EXPECTATIONS

(i) Impossibility

Most of the cases in which a contract is void at common law appear to involve an element of impossibility of performance. If the contract cannot be performed on one side, for example where the subject matter of the contract has been destroyed, neither party can sue the other. In this instance, the parties cannot have any reasonable expectation of performance and since there has been a total failure of consideration, money paid under the contract can be recovered. The party prevented from performing cannot reasonably expect the other party to pay for something which is valueless.

(ii) Interpretation of the contract

In some instances, an apparently fundamental mistake will not cause the contract to be avoided. This may be because, on a construction of the contract, the reasonable expectations of the parties have been expressed or may be implied, and the risk of loss can be allocated accordingly. For example, if a contract of marine insurance provides for payment of the policy moneys whether the ship insured is lost or not lost, the parties are bound by the contract whether or not the ship insured had perished at the time the contract was made. Accordingly, the insured is bound to pay the premium, and the insurer is bound to pay the policy moneys in the event of loss, unless the insured knew the ship had perished at the time of making his proposal.[20]

---

15 See Swan 'The Allocation of Risk in the Analysis of Mistake and Frustration' in Reiter and Swan *Studies in Contract Law* (1981) p 187.
16 (1871) LR 6 QB 597.
17 *Re Garnett* (1885) 31 Ch D 1.
18 *Allcard v Walker* [1896] 2 Ch 369. See also *Kleinwort Benson Ltd v Lincoln CC* [1998] 4 All ER 513 (money paid under a mistake as to the legal powers of the local authority was recoverable).
19 *Solle v Butcher* [1950] 1 KB 671; *Grist v Bailey* [1967] Ch 532.
20 Marine Insurance Act 1906, Sch 1, r 1.

In *Couturier v Hastie*,[1] the parties entered into a contract for the sale of a quantity of corn. Unknown to the parties, the corn had already been sold because it had begun to overheat on board the ship which was carrying the cargo. The judgments do not mention that the contract was void, nor do they refer to a mistake having been made. Instead, it was stated that, on a true construction of the contract, the parties contemplated that there was an existing something to be sold and bought,[2] and that, if that thing did not exist, the buyer was not liable for the price. Whether this means that the risk lay on the seller is doubtful, because it is unlikely that, had the buyer sued the seller for non-delivery, he would have succeeded. Accordingly, this case may be properly regarded as one which was void, in that neither party could sue the other.

The process of interpretation will involve an examination of the express terms of the contract and, if these are not conclusive, such terms which by necessary implication, serve to provide for an appropriate allocation of risk. In *Associated Japanese Bank (International) Ltd v Crédit du Nord SA*[3] there was an express term that the guarantee would not be effective unless the machines, which were the subject of the associated leaseback agreement, existed. But even if this was not the case, it was possible to imply a condition precedent to the liability of the guarantor that the machines should exist.[4] Such a term is implied because it gives effect to the expectation of both parties as reasonable men that the machines existed at the time the contract of guarantee was entered into.[5]

(iii)   Rectification of written instruments

Where the parties to a contract mistakenly fail to include all the terms of the contract in the written document, it may be possible to have the document rectified so that it accords with the agreement made between the two parties. It is important to stress that it is the document that is rectified. This equitable remedy does not apply to the rectification of contracts.[6] Where the remedy is granted, it gives effect to the intentions of the parties and properly expresses their reasonable expectations. Sometimes, it may not be necessary to resort to the remedy of rectification, since the court may be able to repair the mistake, if trivial, as a matter of construction.[7]

The remedy of rectification is normally only available where the document fails to record the common intention of both parties.[8] Thus the remedy is available where one of the parties intends to sign a document in one capacity, but in fact signs in another capacity.[9] However, the same will not be true of a failure to express the intention of only one of the parties. Thus, if a lease states the rent payable and this accords with the intentions of one of the parties but not the other, generally, rectification will not be granted. However, a mistake by one person may result in a successful application for rectification if the other party knows of the mistake, fails to notify the other party and would derive some inequitable benefit from the mistake.[10] If a person knows the other

---

1   (1856) 5 HL Cas 673.
2   Ibid at 681 (per LORD CRANWORTH).
3   [1988] 3 All ER 902.
4   Ibid at 908–909 (per STEYN J). The term is implied under the 'officious bystander' test in *Shirlaw v Southern Foundries (1926) Ltd* [1939] 2 KB 206 at 227 (per MACKINNON LJ) and see also ch 7.
5   Ibid at 909 (per STEYN J).
6   *McKenzie v Coulson* (1869) LR 8 Eq 368; *Frederich E Rose (London) Ltd v William H Pim Jnr & Co Ltd* [1953] 2 QB 450.
7   *Porteus v Element Brooks Ltd* [1996] CLY 1029; *Nittan UK Ltd v Solent Steel Fabrications Ltd* [1981] 1 All ER 633.
8   *Riverlate Properties Ltd v Paul* [1975] Ch 133.
9   *Druiff v Parker* (1865) LR 5 Eq 131 (drawer/payee on a bill of exchange). Cf *Co-operative Bank plc v Tipper* [1996] 4 All ER 366 (guarantor/borrower).
10   *A Roberts & Co Ltd v Leicestershire County Council* [1961] Ch 555; *Thomas Bates & Son Ltd v Wyndham's (Lingerie) Ltd* [1981] 1 All ER 1077.

is mistaken, no injustice is done to him by ordering rectification, since he could not have had any reasonable expectations that he would gain from the contract. In the circumstances, the expectations he has are unreasonable. The fact that the party not mistaken might derive some inequitable benefit is relevant to the issue of unjust enrichment, which is another factor to take into account in the process of risk-allocation.

A further consideration is that if a contracting party is to succeed in an application for rectification, he should not be aware of the mistake made by the other party. At one stage, the courts appeared to require actual awareness of the mistake, but more recent authorities suggest that awareness may be implied, especially in circumstances in which the party seeking relief has been guilty of misleading the other. In *Commission for the New Towns v Cooper (Great Britain) Ltd*[11] the view was expressed that if A intends B to be mistaken and diverts B's attention from discovering the mistake by making false or misleading statements and B makes the mistake which A intends then even if A does not know of the mistake, but merely suspects that B is mistaken, this will be sufficient to allow rectification. Thus in *Cooper*, A arranged a meeting with B reasonably leading B to believe that the meeting was to discuss an issue different to A's intended motive, namely, to secure the transfer of an option which B enjoyed over commercial property assigned to A. In the course of this meeting A gave the impression that he was looking to expand the business run from those premises, when, in fact, he wished to close the business down, provided he was able to secure the transfer of B's option to himself. As a result of the meeting B transferred the option to A, but later sought rectification of the written document when A's real motives were discovered. At first instance it was held that since A did not have actual knowledge of B's mistake, rectification was not possible. However, the Court of Appeal reversed this ruling on the ground that the contract should be performed in accordance with B's understanding as to what had been agreed. Accordingly, the contract was rectified in the light of A's unconscionable conduct.

Where a document is rectified, it does not need to be preceded by a binding contract. For example, a continuing common intention[12] or some outward expression of accord[13] will suffice, and the document failing to fully record the extent of that accord may be rectified.

(iv)   Unexpected gain

Just as the court must decide where to allocate a risk of loss which is not contractually provided for, so also it must decide if a person is entitled to the benefit of an unanticipated windfall that comes his way. If the gain is a matter beyond the reasonable expectations of the parties, it may be decided that the benefit cannot be retained. In some instances, such a gain may constitute an unjust enrichment.[14]

If one of the contracting parties is aware of the unilateral mistake of the other and fails to so inform that other, if the person with knowledge of the mistake stands to gain, the contract may be invalidated. The gain he would otherwise have made cannot be treated as a reasonable expectation. The principle applies equally to mistakes at common law and in equity.

In *Smith v Hughes*,[15] the buyer purchased oats believing them to be old when they were, in fact, new oats. The seller brought an action for the price when the buyer

11   [1995] Ch 259.
12   *The Olympic Pride* [1980] 2 Lloyd's Rep 67.
13   *Joscelyne v Nissen* [1970] 2 QB 86.
14   See chs 11 and 18.
15   (1871) LR 6 QB 597.

refused to take delivery. It was held that, if the seller believed that the buyer was contracting to purchase old oats, the court would have found in favour of the buyer and he could have raised an action for the price. Sometimes, knowledge of a mistake can be presumed by reference to a custom. For example, in *Hartog v Colin and Shields*,[16] a contract to sell hare skins was made at an agreed price per pound. Negotiations had proceeded on the basis that the price payable was per piece, and there was a trade custom to fix the price in the same manner. Accordingly, the buyer was taken to have known of the mistake of the seller and the mistake was operative.

The equitable remedy of rectification operates on the same basis. Rectification of a document is normally ordered only where the document fails to record the common intention of both parties. However, if the document fails to record the intention of one person only and the other is aware of this but fails to inform the mistaken party and would otherwise stand to gain, the contractual document may be rectified. For example, in *Thomas Bates & Son Ltd v Wyndham's (Lingerie) Ltd*,[17] the tenants of premises leased from the plaintiffs, on previous occasions, had contracted for an option to renew the lease at a rental to be fixed by arbitration. The new lease failed to include any provision for arbitration, a fact which was noted by the tenants, but was not drawn to the attention of the plaintiffs. It was held that rectification could be ordered because of the tenants' knowledge of the mistake and because there was a chance of some inequitable benefit to the party aware of the other's mistake.

In other instances, the evidence may show that a person has no reasonable expectation of the gain he makes. For example, in *Grist v Bailey*,[18] the plaintiff contracted to sell a freehold house to the defendant for £850, subject to the rights of a sitting tenant. In fact, there was no sitting tenant, and with vacant possession, the property was worth £2,250. The defendant's agent assumed there was a protected tenant and gave evidence to the effect that he would not have expected to acquire the property for anything like £850 if there was vacant possession. It was held that, although the mistake was not one which would invalidate the contract at common law, the contract could be rescinded in equity, subject to the imposition of new terms. The plaintiff was required to give the defendant the opportunity to buy the house for a proper vacant possession price.[19]

In *Grist v Bailey*, it was clear from the evidence that the defendant did not entertain any reasonable expectation of making the gain. In contrast, where there is no evidence as to the expectations of the parties, it may be assumed that the person making the gain entertained the possibility that he might make a profit out of the transaction. In such a case, principles of risk-allocation would seem to suggest that the sanctity of contracts should be observed. It follows that a mistake as to the value of the thing contracted for will not usually have any effect on the contract.[20] *Sherwood v Walker*[1] provides an example of a contract which has been wrongly invalidated in such circumstances. The plaintiff paid $70 to a commercial cattlebreeder for a cow which both parties believed to be barren. In fact, the cow proved to be fertile and was in calf, with the result that its value was $750. The court held the contract void on the basis of a fundamental mistake. The decision was justified on the assumption that the plaintiff had not intended to buy a cow that might breed. However, there appears to be no evidence that this was the case, and it is arguable that the plaintiff might have hoped to make a profit. The fact that both parties believed the cow to be barren may have been significant, but the

---

16   [1939] 3 All ER 566.
17   [1981] 1 All ER 1077. See also *A Roberts & Co Ltd v Leicestershire County Council* [1961] Ch 555.
18   [1967] Ch 532.
19   Ibid at 543 (per GOFF J).
20   *Bell v Lever Bros Ltd* [1932] AC 161.
1   66 Mich 568, 33 NW 919 (1887).

mistake was as to the quality of the thing contracted for which normally indicates that the contract should not be held void.

(v)   Presumed knowledge of risk

It might be argued that the defendant in *Sherwood v Walker*[2] was lucky, and that the plaintiff was wrongly denied the chance of a gain he might have expected. Generally, in contracts of a speculative nature, the loss will lie where it falls unless it can be said that the parties had reasonable expectations as to how the risk should be allocated. For example, in *Amalgamated Investment and Property Co Ltd v John Walker & Sons Ltd*,[3] a property developer purchased a warehouse which, unknown to the parties, had been listed as a building of special architectural and historical interest. As a consequence of listing, the building could only be developed under very strict conditions, with the result that its value dropped from £1,710,000 to £210,000. It was held that equity would not grant relief for a mistake which related merely to the expectations of the parties, and that the risk of property being listed is one which every owner and purchaser must recognise that he is subject to.[4] The purchaser was taken to have known the risk that obtaining planning permission might prove difficult. It may be argued that the purchaser knows more about his business than the vendor, and that the risk should rest with him. This decision contrasts with that in *Grist v Bailey*,[5] considered above, in which relief was granted to the inexperienced vendor of a domestic dwelling. A similar approach to valuation mistakes is taken in equity, whether the mistake is made by one of the parties or by a third party.[6]

(4)   INDUCED MISTAKE

Where a mistake results from reliance upon what the other party has said or done, it is often reasonable to return the parties to the position they were in before the mistake, thereby allocating the risk of loss to the person who has induced the mistake. In this respect, there is an obvious overlap between the law on mistake and that relating to misstatement.[7]

In the case of a mistake as to the subject matter of the contract, namely a mistake which supposedly negatives consent, a person misled by the other party may not be bound by the contract. For example, in *Scriven Bros & Co v Hindley & Co*,[8] the buyer at an auction, due to an ambiguous catalogue, mistakenly believed that he was bidding for a lot which consisted of hemp. In fact, it consisted of hemp and tow. It was held that a contract cannot arise where the person seeking to enforce it has negligently caused or contributed to the mistake.[9] If the mistake relates to the terms of the contract, a similar principle also applies. For example, if a person warrants that he is selling old oats and supplies new oats, the contract may be void for mistake.[10]

The relationship between mistake and breach of warranty is also important in cases of apparent shared mistake. The common law rule is that a fundamental shared mistake will render the contract void *ab initio*, but this can produce harsh results, particularly

2   Ibid.
3   [1977] 1 WLR 164. See Brownsword (1977) 40 MLR 467.
4   Ibid at 175 (per BUCKLEY LJ).
5   [1967] Ch 532.
6   See *Campbell v Edwards* [1976] 1 WLR 403; *Macro v Thompson* [1996] BCC 707.
7   See ch 18.
8   [1913] 3 KB 564.
9   Ibid at 569 (per A T LAWRENCE J).
10   *Smith v Hughes* (1871) LR 6 QB 597.

where one of the parties has incurred pre-contractual expenditure in reliance on the state of affairs he believes to exist.

Where the mistake has been induced by a statement of the other party, it might be possible to allocate the risk of loss to the maker of that statement. For example, in *McRae v Commonwealth Disposals Commission*,[11] the defendants purported to sell salvage rights in a wrecked vessel, stating where the wreck could be found. The plaintiff incurred expense in setting up the salvage operation, only to discover that there was no wreck at the location given. The High Court of Australia held that, because the defendants were seriously at fault by recklessly asserting the existence of the wrecked ship, they could be taken to have warranted its existence. Accordingly, the plaintiff was entitled to recover his reliance loss in an action for breach of warranty.[12]

In equity, the reliance principle is also relevant. Some mistakes as to quality may be remediable in equity where common law rules on shared mistakes do not apply. An explanation of this equitable jurisdiction is that one of the parties may have been induced to make the mistake by the other party. For example, in *Solle v Butcher*,[13] the defendant acquired a house and converted it into a number of flats, one of which he proposed to lease to the plaintiff, his business partner. Rent control legislation limited the rent payable on certain properties to £140 per annum, but after obtaining advice, the plaintiff informed the defendant, incorrectly, that the flat which he proposed to lease was unaffected by the £140 limit. Accordingly, an annual rent of £250 was agreed. The plaintiff sought to recover the amount he had paid in excess of the statutory limit of £140. The Court of Appeal held that the lease could be rescinded on the terms that the defendant would offer the plaintiff a new lease on the premises at a rent not exceeding £250 per annum. An important factor in this decision was that of reliance. It was observed that the lease was probably induced by an innocent but material misrepresentation by the plaintiff which amounted to an unambiguous statement as to private rights.[14]

(5)   THE PREVENTION OF AN UNJUST ENRICHMENT

If a person mistakenly confers a benefit on the other party to the contract, it may be that the benefit is recoverable on the basis of an unjust enrichment. The type of mistake which will permit such recovery is rare. Many apparent mistakes are no more than mispredictions or miscalculations, such as where a person mistakenly values the thing he purchases. But, some mistakes are operative and, unless their effect is reversed, an unjust enrichment might follow. For example, it is possible to recover a payment made under the mistaken belief that one is *liable* to pay. Thus if a party enters into a contract with an unformed company, payments under the contract are made under the mistaken belief that the contract is valid and may be recovered.[15] Similarly, in *Norwich Union Fire Insurance Society Ltd v William H Price Ltd*,[16] an insurer mistakenly paid the value of a lost cargo in the belief that one of the perils insured against had caused the loss. In fact, the loss was caused by an event which was not covered by the policy. If the effects of the mistake had not been reversed, the insured would have been unjustly enriched.

11   (1950) 84 CLR 377.
12   Ibid at 407. See also ch 6.
13   [1950] 1 KB 671. See also *Magee v Pennine Insurance Co Ltd* [1969] 2 QB 507 and see Cartwright (1987) 103 LQR 594.
14   Ibid at 695 (per DENNING LJ).
15   *Rover International Ltd v Cannon Films Sales Ltd (No 3)* [1989] 3 All ER 423.
16   [1934] AC 455.

In considering whether a mistake might give rise to an unjust enrichment, it is necessary to consider the conduct and the knowledge of the person who stands to gain. It has been observed already that relief from the consequences of a unilateral mistake may be granted on the ground that the other party is aware of the mistake.[17] In such a case, the gain which might otherwise be made is not a matter within the reasonable expectations of the parties. A further explanation of these cases is that, if the mistake were not to be remedied, an unjust enrichment would also follow. Similar principles apply where the mistake of one party has been induced by the fraud or misrepresentation of the other. To allow the gain to be kept would amount to an unjust enrichment of the defendant.

While a liability mistake may be remedied, the same cannot be said of a causative mistake such as that which arose in *Bell v Lever Bros Ltd*.[18] The facts of this case have been partially considered already, but to analyse it in the context of unjust enrichment, further factors must be taken into account. Bell was paid £30,000, £17,000 of which was taken to represent his salary had the contract run its full course. Accordingly, the balance of £13,000 must have been paid for a reason unconnected with the contract. The payment appears to have been made because Lever Bros were grateful for what Bell had done and they wanted to reward him for his valuable services.[19] Accordingly, this was a gratuitous payment which could not be recovered by the donor. If Bell was disentitled to his salary of £17,000, payment of that sum might amount to an unjust enrichment. However, there is nothing to suggest that the enrichment was unjust. The mistake was not as to Lever Bros' liability to pay. The payment was made because Lever Bros thought it desirable to terminate Bell's contract upon the amalgamation of one of their subsidiary companies with another company. Furthermore, Bell had not acted fraudulently, and he did not have his breaches of duty in mind when he made the termination agreement, with the result that he could not be said to have known of Lever Bros' mistake.

A decision which is difficult to reconcile with *Bell v Lever Bros Ltd* is that of the Court of Appeal in *Magee v Pennine Insurance Co Ltd*.[20] In the latter a compromise agreement to pay the insured the value of an accident-damaged car was rescinded because the insurers mistakenly believed that the insurance policy was valid. In fact, it was voidable for misrepresentation, although the insured was unaware of the misstatement made on his behalf in the proposal form. Applying objective principles, if a person signs a document without reading it, he will be bound by its contents on the basis of his fault.[1]

The difficulty presented by *Magee* is that the insurers were allowed to avoid the insurance policy after four years, with the result that they kept the insurance premiums paid during that period. At first sight, this might appear to constitute an unjust enrichment of the insurers. Furthermore, it has been said that the facts of *Magee* and *Bell* are indistinguishable,[2] with the result that relief should not have been granted in *Magee*.

---

17   See eg *Hartog v Colin and Shields* [1939] 3 All ER 566; *Thomas Bates & Son Ltd v Wyndham's (Lingerie) Ltd* [1981] 1 All ER 1077.
18   [1932] AC 161.
19   Ibid at 181 (per LORD BLANESBURGH).
20   [1969] 2 QB 507.
1   See *Gallie v Lee* [1971] AC 1004; *L'Estrange v F Graucob Ltd* [1934] 2 KB 394. See also Adams and Brownsword (1987) 7 LS 205 at 211 and see ch 7.
2   [1969] 2 QB 507 at 516 (per WINN LJ).

3.   FRUSTRATION

(1)   INTRODUCTION

(i)   Frustration and risk-allocation

A frustrating event is generally regarded as one which is sufficiently fundamental to destroy the foundation of the contract,[3] or which renders performance of the contract radically different from that which was originally agreed.[4] As in most cases of mistake, the common law rule on frustration of a contract emphasises the fundamental nature of the frustrating event. However, this disguises the important risk-allocation function of the doctrine. It will be necessary to identify the superior risk-bearer under the general principles of risk-allocation considered above, although unlike the position in relation to mistake, it is possible to split losses caused by a frustrating event between the contracting parties.

(ii)   Development and theory of the doctrine of frustration

(a)   Frustration theory

At one time, it was believed that contractual obligations were absolute,[5] but this is no longer the case. In appropriate circumstances, the court may discharge the parties from further performance of their contractual obligations on the occurrence of some event not provided for in the contract. The notion of absolute liability fitted with classical contract theory, but when the judges came to fashion a doctrine of frustration in the nineteenth and twentieth centuries, they were faced with an ideological riddle. If they were simply to act as umpires to give effect to the parties' wishes, how could they intervene to alter the balance of the contract?

The apparent rule of absolute liability remained essentially intact until the decision in *Taylor v Caldwell*,[6] where BLACKBURN J drew on some exceptions to *Paradine v Jane*, and stated that, where the parties expect a particular thing to continue to exist so that the contract can be performed, there is an implied condition[7] that the parties shall be excused if that thing is destroyed without the fault of either party. The justification for judicial intervention on the basis of an implied term was also employed in cases of frustration of purpose, particularly where performance of a voyage charterparty was rendered futile by the temporary unavailability of the ship.[8] The general approach in these cases was to say that inordinate delay was sufficient to frustrate the common purpose of the parties, as the charterparty was subject to an implied condition that the ship should arrive in time for the definite voyage. By the early twentieth century, the courts were able to combine implied conditions and frustration of adventure into a doctrine linked to the notion of consensus by means of a pure fiction.[9] To courts wedded to the idea of contractual obligations based on agreement, the new doctrine required some sort of explanation.

A difficulty with the use of implied conditions is that in strict theory, the court will only imply a term in order to give effect to the presumed intention of the parties. The problem with frustrating events is that they are usually beyond the contemplation of the parties, in which case it is difficult to say whether or not the parties intended their

---

3   *Krell v Henry* [1903] 2 KB 740 at 751 (per VAUGHAN WILLIAMS LJ).
4   *Davis Contractors Ltd v Fareham UDC* [1956] AC 696 at 728–729 (per LORD RADCLIFFE).
5   *Paradine v Jane* (1647) 82 ER 897.
6   (1863) 122 ER 309.
7   See also *FA Tamplin SS Co v Anglo-Mexican Petroleum Products Co* [1916] 2 AC 397 at 404 (per EARL LOREBURN).
8   *Jackson v Union Marine Insurance Co Ltd* (1874) LR 10 CP 125; *Freeman v Taylor* (1831) 8 Bing 124.
9   Simpson (1975) 91 LQR 247 at 271–273. See *Krell v Henry* [1903] 2 KB 740.

contractual obligations to be absolute or whether they intended the performer to be excused performance on the occurrence of the event in question. It is difficult to imagine how a frustrating event could be impliedly within the contemplation of the parties, since, if it had been contemplated, it would have been provided for in the contract. As an extreme example, there would be an implied term in a contract between a consumer and a milkman that should the milkman be attacked by a tiger, performance will be required on all but 'tiger days'.[10] Furthermore, the parties to a contract are unlikely to view a frustrating event in the same way — for example the party in the stronger position will prefer to keep the contract in existence.[11]

In *Davis Contractors v Fareham UDC*,[12] LORD RADCLIFFE adopted the view of LORD WATSON in *Dahl v Nelson* that:[13] 'The meaning of the contract must be taken to be, not what the parties did intend, but that which the parties as fair and reasonable men would have agreed upon if, having such possibility in view, they had made express provision as to their rights and liabilities in the event of its occurrence.'

Applying this test of construction, it is possible to treat frustration as an attempt to find a just and reasonable solution.[14] What is apparent is that this view represents a move away from consensus theory towards a judicial policy of intervention to impose a fair or just solution where a frustrating event occurs. Furthermore, the outside event or change of circumstances must have occurred without fault or default on either side.[15] This indicates that a fault-based principle has been imported into the doctrine of frustration. If one of the parties has brought about the frustrating event or has failed to take steps which might have avoided the effects of the subsequent frustrating event, he may be regarded as the most appropriate risk-bearer.

(b)   Development of the doctrine

The doctrine covers two types of event, namely cases of impossibility of performance and cases involving frustration of the purpose of a contract. In cases of impossibility of performance, one party to the contract claims that his own performance of the contract has become impossible or so burdensome that he should no longer be obliged to fulfil his part of the bargain. In contrast, in cases of frustration of purpose, one party claims that, while performance of the contract may be physically possible, the value of the other party's performance is so diminished by the frustrating event that he should no longer be obliged to pay for that performance. This will be the case where a state of facts assumed to form the basis of the contract fails to materialise.

At one time, it was thought that the doctrine of frustration did not apply to all contracts. However, in *National Carriers Ltd v Panalpina (Northern) Ltd*,[16] the House of Lords held that the doctrine is of general application to all contracts, although there may be some contracts which are more difficult to frustrate than others. For example, leases creating a legal estate in land and other contracts involving long-term speculation will rarely be subject to the doctrine.[17] The principal difficulty in this regard is that the longer the contract has to run the more difficult it becomes to say whether an alleged frustrating event will have a serious effect on the performance obligations of the parties.

10   *Davis Contractors v Fareham UDC* [1956] 2 All ER 145 at 153 (per LORD REID). See also *James Scott & Sons Ltd v R & N Del Sel* 1922 SC 592 at 597 (per LORD SANDS).

11   Ibid.

12   Ibid at 160.

13   (1881) 6 App Cas 38 at 59.

14   *Joseph Constantine Steamship Line Ltd v Imperial Smelting Corpn Ltd* [1942] AC 154 at 186 (per LORD WRIGHT).

15   See *Paal Wilson & Co A/S v Partenreederei Hannah Blumenthal, The Hannah Blumenthal* [1983] 1 All ER 34 at 44 (per LORD BRANDON). See also *F C Shepherd & Co Ltd v Jerrom* [1987] QB 301.

16   [1981] AC 675.

17   Ibid at 692 (per LORD HAILSHAM).

The position may be different so far as contracts for the sale of land are concerned even though the contract may have the effect of creating an equitable interest in the land.[18]

(c)   Law and fact

The doctrine of frustration is said to involve mixed questions of fact and law. It is inevitable that factual issues will play an important part, as it cannot be said that a particular event will always be sufficient to frustrate a contract. The distinction between issues of fact and issues of law might appear, at first sight, confusing, since cases of this type are heard by a judge sitting alone. However, the distinction is important where an appellate court considers the findings of an arbitrator or a court of first instance.

A suggested distinction between the issues is that events which are capable of frustrating a contract are a matter of law, and whether a particular event did frustrate the contract under consideration is a matter of fact.[19] As a result of this, if an arbitrator correctly directs himself on the issues of law, an appellate court will generally not interfere with his decision on the facts, unless he has reached a decision which no reasonable arbitrator would reach.[20]

(2)   INTERPRETATION OF THE CONTRACT

(i)   Events provided for in the contract

The starting point in any process of risk-allocation must be the terms of the contract. Where the contract provides for the occurrence of an alleged frustrating event and allocates the risk, the provision must generally be enforced, as to do otherwise would defeat the reasonable expectations of the parties. The contract may provide that one person or the other should bear the risk of loss, or it may provide some solution. For example, in some of the 'cancelled coronation' cases, the contract provided that the ticket holder was entitled to use his ticket on the day the coronation actually took place.[1] Sometimes, the nature of the contract suggests a solution, and the court may imply a term to the effect that the contract is not frustrated. This can happen where the contract is made long before the date of performance, in which case the contract is treated as speculative in nature, with the result that losses will lie where they fall.[2]

Implying contractual terms which modify the parties' obligations is something which the courts, generally, will not do. This is particularly so where the contract is contained in an elaborately drafted commercial document. However, on occasions, such a possibility has been suggested,[3] and a similar result can also be achieved by means of an interpretation of the language used in the contract.[4]

---

18 See *Wong Lai Ying v Chinachem Investment Co Ltd* (1979) 13 Build LR 81(unforeseen landslip frustrated contract of sale where development would have been delayed for 30 months). Cf *E Johnson & Co (Barbados) Ltd v NSR Ltd* [1997] AC 400 (contract for the sale of land not frustrated by a threat of compulsory purchase).

19 *Pioneer Shipping Ltd v BTP Tioxide Ltd, The Nema* [1982] AC 724 at 753 (per Lord Roskill). See also *Universal Cargo Carriers Corpn v Citati* [1957] 2 QB 401 at 435 (per Devlin J).

20 Ibid.

1 *Clark v Lindsay* (1903) 19 TLR 202.

2 *Larrinaga & Co v Société Franco-Américaine des Phosphates de Médulla* (1923) 92 LJKB 455.

3 See *The Maira (No 2)* [1985] 1 Lloyd's Rep 300 at 311 (per Kerr J) affd on other grounds [1986] 2 Lloyd's Rep 12.

4 See *Staffordshire Area Health Authority v South Staffordshire Waterworks Co* [1978] 3 All ER 769.

(ii)   Construction of the contractual provision

Where a contractual provision is sufficiently wide to cover the frustrating event, it does not always follow that the doctrine of frustration is inapplicable. For example, in *Metropolitan Water Board v Dick Kerr & Co Ltd*,[5] a firm of building contractors agreed to construct a reservoir over a period of six years. The contract further provided that, in the event of delays, 'however occasioned', the contractors would be given an extension of time to complete construction. A government order required the contractors to stop work and sell all their equipment. The House of Lords held that the provision in respect of delays was intended to apply only to temporary difficulties such as bad weather or labour shortages. It could not have been intended to apply to a change in conditions which the parties could not possibly have contemplated at the time the contract was made.[6] Accordingly, the contract was held to be frustrated. A similar method of construction can be applied to a provision which covers some events but not others. For example, a term in a charterparty which relates to the availability of the ship will have no effect if the cargo is not available.[7]

(iii)   Incomplete provisions

Where a frustrating event is partially provided for in the contract, the doctrine of frustration may still apply. In *Bank Line Ltd v A Capel & Co Ltd*,[8] a term in a charterparty allowed the charterer to cancel in the event of requisition of the ship for government service, but there was no similar right in favour of the shipowner. When the ship was requisitioned, it was held that the contract was frustrated. The provision in the contract was not full and complete and, in any event, was intended to deal only with the effect of requisition where the contingency did not frustrate the contract.

(3)   THE REASONABLE EXPECTATIONS OF THE PARTIES

Where it is impossible to perform a contract, it would not be fair for the reasonable man to hold the parties to their contract. The same can also be said of cases in which there is a total failure of consideration, for example, where the purpose of the contract is frustrated. The expectations of the reasonable man, or the court, can be treated as the expectations of the parties, and an appropriate allocation of risks can be made.

(i)   Impossibility

(a)   Destruction of the subject matter of the contract

Generally, a contract will be frustrated if the thing contracted for is destroyed. In *Taylor v Caldwell*,[9] a music hall which was the subject of a licence agreement was destroyed by fire before the date on which it was to be used. Because the main purpose of the contract was defeated, the contract was held to be frustrated. Likewise, in a contract for the sale of specific goods, commercial destruction of specific goods will normally result in the frustration of the contract.[10] For these purposes, the goods do not have to be totally destroyed, but they must have become something other than that which was

---

5   [1918] AC 119.
6   Ibid at 126.
7   *Pioneer Shipping Ltd v BTP Tioxide Ltd, The Nema* [1982] AC 724.
8   [1919] AC 435.
9   (1863) 3 B & S 826.
10   Sale of Goods Act 1979, s 7.

contracted for. Thus, if without fault on the part of the seller, a buyer is supplied with sewage-contaminated dates the contract is properly regarded as frustrated.[11]

If the thing destroyed is not the subject matter of the contract, but is nonetheless essential to the performance of the contract, the court may still apply the doctrine of frustration. For example, in *Appleby v Myers*,[12] a contract to install machinery in an identified factory was held to be frustrated when the factory was destroyed. This remained the case despite the fact that the subject matter of the contract, namely the machinery, was unharmed.

Because it is important to consider the reasonable expectations of the parties in the process of risk-allocation, it is possible for a contract to survive the destruction of its subject matter. This illustrates the importance of considering an alleged frustrating event in its factual context. In *The Maira (No 2)*,[13] a contract to manage a ship was held not to be frustrated by the destruction of the ship. Other management functions, such as the repatriation of the crew and the payment of wages, remained after the ship had been destroyed. Accordingly, a term was implied to the effect that the managers should be remunerated at a reduced rate according to the proportion of work still left to be performed.

(b)   Death and incapacity

The death of a person who has contracted to provide a service will frustrate the contract.[14] Similarly, personal incapacity caused by illness[15] and the imprisonment of the performer[16] are both capable of frustrating a contract to provide a service. In the case of imprisonment, the person imprisoned would not be able to plead frustration because of his fault. The death or incapacity of the recipient of the service is also capable of frustrating the contract. However, these principles will not apply to all contracts. For example, contracts for the sale of goods do not require performance by a specific individual, with the result that the death of the seller will not prevent performance of the contract. Even where the contract is of a type that may be frustrated by reason of personal incapacity, it is important to consider the event in its context. For example, in deciding whether a contract to provide personal services is frustrated by incapacity, the court will have to consider the nature and expected duration of the contract and the likely duration of the incapacity. It may be that there is still a reasonable expectation that the contract will be capable of later performance. Apart from the doctrine of frustration there may be other means of dealing with death or serious illness. For example, where a consumer becomes ill to the extent that he cannot go on a pre-booked package holiday, there is statutory provision which will allow him to transfer the benefit of the holiday to a suitably qualified person, thereby avoiding the possibility of discharge.[17]

(c)   Impossibility of performance

If the contract provides for performance in a specific way and that method of performance becomes impossible, the parties may be discharged from performance. For example, if a particular ship is nominated to carry a cargo and that ship becomes unavailable, the contract may be frustrated.[18] However, it is important that the contract should be

---

11   *Asfar & Co Ltd v Blundell* [1896] 1 QB 123.
12   (1867) LR 2 CP 651.
13   Sub nom *Glafki Shipping Co SA v Pinios Shipping Co No 1* [1985] 1 Lloyd's Rep 300; affd on other grounds [1986] 2 Lloyd's Rep 12.
14   *Stubbs v Holywell Rly Co* (1867) LR 2 Exch 311.
15   *Condor v Barron Knights Ltd* [1966] 1 WLR 87.
16   *F C Shepherd & Co Ltd v Jerrom* [1986] 3 All ER 589.
17   Package Travel, Package Holidays & Package Tours Regulations 1992 (SI 1992/ 3288), reg 13.
18   *Nickoll and Knight v Ashton Edridge & Co* [1901] 2 KB 126.

construed as allowing performance only in the manner stipulated. For example, in *Lauritzen AS v Wijsmuller BV, The Super Servant Two*,[19] a contract to carry an oil rig to its site was held not to be frustrated when the transportation unit intended to be used was lost at sea. The reason for this was that the contract provided that it was to be performed by either *Super Servant One* or *Super Servant Two*, identical vessels owned by the defendants and *Super Servant One* was still available.

There is a fine line between impossibility and impracticability. It has been said that the doctrine of frustration is not lightly to be invoked to relieve contracting parties of the normal consequences of imprudent commercial bargains.[20] Accordingly, the parties to a contract may have to endure events such as normal price fluctuations, depreciations in currency and unexpected obstacles to completion where they render performance impracticable rather than impossible. For example, in *Tsakiroglou & Co Ltd v Noblee Thorl GmbH*,[1] a contract for the sale of goods at a price which included the cost of the goods, insurance and carriage to Hamburg was rendered too expensive to perform due to the closure of the Suez Canal. Both parties expected the cargo to be shipped via the canal, but the contract made no express provision for this. It was held that the contract was not frustrated, as performance was still possible using the alternative, but much longer, route via the Cape of Good Hope. Even if the contract had provided that the expected route was via the Suez Canal, it is unlikely that the contract would have been frustrated.[2] The increased expense, it seems, is an ordinary incident of commercial bargaining which the seller was expected to bear,[3] although increased cost alone will not excuse performance.[4] Furthermore, the discharge solution may have resulted in the unjust enrichment of the seller for reasons to be considered below.

The problems of increased cost are illustrated in *Davis Contractors Ltd v Fareham UDC*,[5] in which a firm of building contractors agreed to build an estate of houses in eight months for £94,000. Due to labour shortages, the work took 22 months and cost the contractors £115,000. The contractors attempted to use the doctrine of frustration as a sword rather than a shield by asking for discharge of the contract so that they could recover on a *quantum meruit* the reasonable value of the work done. The House of Lords held that the delays were within the normal range of commercial contemplation, and that there was no significant change in the obligation undertaken. Accordingly, the contract was not frustrated.

In some instances, it appears that impracticability does serve to frustrate a contract. For example, wartime conditions may fundamentally change the conditions in which a contract is to be performed, so that the new circumstances are beyond the contemplation of the parties. In such a case, although performance of the contract may be physically possible, the impracticability of performance can be said to be one reason why the parties are discharged.[6] However, the same result can be achieved by an interpretation of the express terms of the contract.

In other cases, it may be argued that severe inflation serves to frustrate a contract.[7] However, this result is likely to be exceptional, as a wholly abnormal rise or fall in prices

---

19   [1990] 1 Lloyd's Rep 1.
20   *Pioneer Shipping Ltd v BTP Tioxide Ltd, The Nema* [1982] AC 724 at 752 (per LORD ROSKILL).
1   [1962] AC 93. See also *Ocean Tramp Tankers Corpn v V/O Sovfracht, The Eugenia* [1964] 2 QB 226.
2   Ibid at 112 (per LORD SIMONDS). See also *Palmco Shipping Inc v Continental Ore Corpn* [1970] 2 Lloyd's Rep 21.
3   Contrast the position in the USA where extreme and unreasonable difficulty, expense, injury or loss may serve to discharge a contract: *American Restatement Contracts*, 2d para 261 comment d.
4   *UCC* s 2–615 comment 4.
5   [1956] AC 696.
6   See *Metropolitan Water Board v Dick Kerr & Co Ltd* [1918] AC 119.
7   See *National Carriers Ltd v Panalpina (Northern) Ltd* [1981] AC 675 at 712 (per LORD ROSKILL).

is usually treated as one of the ordinary incidents of commercial bargaining.[8] Furthermore, the parties can employ a device such as a price-escalation clause to allow for such events. However, even these may be inadequate where inflation increases not at a trot or a canter, but at a gallop.[9] Even so, it is unlikely that inflation will serve to discharge a contract. In *Staffordshire Area Health Authority v South Staffordshire Waterworks Co*,[10] LORD DENNING MR treated as frustrated by reason of fifty years of continuing inflation, a contract to supply water at a fixed price of seven old pence per 1,000 gallons. The difficulty with this view is that, on a traditional analysis, it would be necessary to specify the date on which inflation became so intolerable that the contract was frustrated. The view of the majority, in this case, is preferable, namely that an agreement of indefinite duration is capable of termination by giving reasonable notice. If the contract had been for a fixed term, the parties would have been taken to have agreed to the allocation of risks created by the contract which would include possible price fluctuations.[11]

(d)   Unavailability

If a thing required for performance of the contract becomes unavailable, the contract may be frustrated. The reasonable expectations of the parties may be defeated if the contract cannot be performed in the way originally intended. Thus the unavailability of a ship[12] or a cargo[13] or the expropriation of mineral exploration rights by government action[14] may serve to frustrate a contract.

The unavailability of a thing will not always frustrate a contract, because the factual circumstances of the case must be considered when identifying the reasonable expectations of the parties. It may be that mere temporary unavailability will have no effect, but this must be considered in the light of the terms of the contract. For example, the temporary unavailability of a ship for ten weeks will frustrate a voyage charterparty if the period of unavailability coincides exactly with an anticipated nine-week voyage. Conversely, the same period of unavailability is unlikely to affect a time charter extending over a period of five years.

In *Jackson v Union Marine Insurance Co Ltd*,[15] a ship was chartered to carry a cargo from Newport to San Francisco in January. The ship ran aground one day after it had departed from Newport, and was not likely to be available until the following August. Ordinarily, this would have amounted to a breach of contract on the part of the shipowner, but for a clause in the contract which exempted him from liability for delays caused by the perils of navigation. It was held that the charterer was entitled to treat the contract as being at an end and engage another person to carry his cargo. The delay was said to have frustrated the contract. The issue in this case is similar to that which arises in instances of frustration of purpose, namely, was the defect in performance by one party sufficient to justify refusal to perform by the other party? The reason why one party is discharged from performance is that there has been a total failure of consideration. The plaintiff should not be expected to perform when the other party has completely failed to perform what is required of him. Accordingly, cases of this type are not strictly cases of impossibility at all,[16] although judicial language may treat them as such.

8   See *British Movietonews Ltd v London and District Cinemas Ltd* [1952] AC 166 at 185 (per VISCOUNT SIMON).
9   *Wates Ltd v Greater London Council* (1983) 25 BLR 1 at 34.
10   [1978] 3 All ER 769.
11   See *Kirklees MBC v Yorkshire Woollen District Transport Co Ltd* (1978) 77 LGR 448.
12   *Bank Line Ltd v A Capel & Co* [1919] AC 435.
13   *Pioneer Shipping Ltd v BTP Tioxide Ltd, The Nema* [1982] AC 724.
14   *BP Exploration Co (Libya) Ltd v Hunt* [1983] 2 AC 352.
15   (1874) LR 10 CP 125. See Stannard (1983) 46 MLR 738.
16   See McElroy and Williams *Impossibility of Performance* (1941); Stannard (1983) 46 MLR 738 at 741.

Where the contract is for a specified period, as in the case of a time charterparty, delay may still frustrate the contract. One issue is whether a full performance of the contract should be rendered when the delay comes to an end. In *Bank Line Ltd v A Capel & Co*,[17] a time charterparty which was expected to run for 12 months from April 1915 was held to be frustrated when the ship did not become available from government requisition until September 1915. The reasonable expectation of the parties was that the contract should run from April 1915 and a September to September charter would have amounted to a totally different thing to that originally contemplated.

A second issue in cases of delay is whether the balance of the contract should be performed, for example where delay prevents the use of a ship for the first three years of a five-year time charter. Here difficulties may arise where the court must speculate as to the likely length of delay. In *FA Tamplin SS Co Ltd v Anglo-Mexican Petroleum Products Co Ltd*,[18] a ship was chartered for five years from December 1912 until December 1917. The ship was requisitioned in February 1915. It was held that the contract was not frustrated, as there might have been many months during which the ship would have been available. Clearly, the House of Lords had to speculate on the likely duration of the war which resulted in requisition and, with hindsight, they were perhaps optimistic as to how quickly hostilities would come to an end.

The decision in *Tamplin* should not be taken to mean that long-term contracts of this type cannot be frustrated. What matters here is the ratio which the interruption bears to the contract as a whole. For example, where a ship was trapped in the course of the Gulf war between Iran and Iraq, the charterparty to which the ship was subject could be treated as discharged on the ground that there was little likelihood of the ship becoming available for use before the end of the agreed period of hire.[19]

(ii)   Public policy/ Illegality

There may be circumstances in which an event supervenes after the making of the contract that has the effect of rendering further performance of the contract impossible or futile. In one sense, the doctrine of discharge on the ground of illegality is broader than the doctrine of frustration, since the court must have regard to the interests of the public as well as factors relating to the parties themselves.[20] Such will be the case where the contract involves trading with the enemy after the outbreak of war.[1]

More difficult are cases in which performance of the contract becomes illegal without the involvement of the public interest issues necessarily relevant in cases involving trading with the enemy. There may be circumstances in which subsequent legislation strikes at the very root of the agreement between the parties, in which case the contract will be frustrated. Thus if there is a contract for the sale of pine wood, but subsequent legislation renders it illegal to sell at the price agreed between the parties and to import timber of the kind contracted for, the contract is frustrated.[2] Likewise, if it becomes clear that the venue for a rock concert cannot be used because it is unsafe and will not be licensed

17   [1919] AC 435.
18   [1916] 2 AC 397.
19   *Kodros Shipping Corpn of Monrovia v Empresa Cubana de Fletes, The Evia (No 2)* [1983] 1 AC 736; *International Sea Tankers Inc v Hemisphere Shipping Co Ltd, The Wenjiang (No 2)* [1983] 1 Lloyd's Rep 400. See also *Pioneer Shipping Ltd v BTP Tioxide Ltd, The Nema* [1982] AC 724.
20   See *Treitel*, p 826.
1   See *Fibrosa Spolka Akcyjna v Fairbairn Lawson Combe Barbour Ltd* [1943] AC 32.
2   *Denny Mott & Dickson Ltd v James B Fraser & Co Ltd* [1944] AC 265.

by the appropriate authorities as a venue for a public performance it would appear that the supervening illegality is best regarded as the basis for discharge of the contract.[3]

(iii)   Frustration of purpose

It has been noted already that a distinction should be drawn between cases in which one person claims that his own performance has become impossible and those in which the performance of the other party is so bereft of value that the contract should be discharged. Cases of frustration of purpose fall within this second category. The coronation cases illustrate the problem.

In *Krell v Henry*,[4] the parties had made a contract for the hire of rooms overlooking the route of King Edward VII's coronation procession. The procession was cancelled as a result of the king's illness. The plaintiff sued the defendant for the balance of the hire charges due under the contract. However, it was held that the contract was frustrated because of the cessation of the state of affairs which was essential to the performance of the contract.[5]

In terms of appropriate risk-allocation, this decision might appear suspect. If the procession had gone ahead and it had rained, with the result that participants wore waterproof clothing, much of the pageantry would have been lost, but it is likely that such a risk would have been borne by the defendant. So also where the procession is called off altogether, it would appear logical to expect the defendant to protect himself in some way against that risk of loss, as is normally expected of a tenant under a lease.[6]

The decision in *Krell v Henry* should be contrasted with that in *Herne Bay Steam Boat Co v Hutton*[7] which concerned a contract to hire a pleasure boat for the purpose of viewing the Royal review of the fleet and for a day's cruise round the fleet. The review, one of the proposed coronation festivities, was cancelled when the king fell ill. It was held that the contract was not frustrated. One distinction between the two cases appears to be that there was still a fleet to observe in the *Herne Bay* case,[8] whereas there was nothing to see in *Krell*. Furthermore, the evidence in *Krell* suggested that the room was hired to watch something happening on that particular day. One other point of distinction is that the coronation procession was an event likely to be restaged, as was the case. If the contract had not been discharged, it is likely that the plaintiff would have had the advantage of hiring the room twice at a suitably enhanced price. In contrast, it is unlikely that the fleet would wait off Spithead pending the convalescence of the king, given that the fleet also had an important defence commitment.

Krell is an unusual case, which is not generally followed. If a person finds that he cannot put the subject matter of the contract to its intended use, that is a risk he will have to bear. Thus, if a property developer discovers that he can only develop a building within strict limits and that property has diminished substantially in value as a result of this, the contract is still not likely to be discharged on the ground of frustration.[9]

---

3   See *Gamerco SA v ICM/Fair Warning Ltd* [1995] 1 WLR 1226. To argue that it was the state of the stadium which frustrated the contract would raise questions as to whether the appropriate legal mechanism is the doctrine of frustration or that of mistake, since the defect in the stadium must have been present at the time the contract was made.

4   [1903] 2 KB 740.

5   Ibid at 748 (per Vaughan Williams LJ).

6   See *National Carriers Ltd v Panalpina (Northern) Ltd* [1981] AC 675.

7   [1903] 2 KB 683.

8   Ibid at 692 (per Sterling LJ).

9   *Amalgamated Investment and Property Co Ltd v John Walker & Son Ltd* [1977] 1 WLR 164; *William Sindall plc v Cambridgeshire CC* [1994] 1 WLR 1016.

(4) THE LEAST COST-AVOIDER

In determining who is the superior risk-bearer, one solution may be to discover which of the parties is in the best position to take reasonable steps to avoid the risk of loss. A variety of fault doctrine would appear to have evolved, with the result that a person who has brought about a frustrating event will not be able to plead that event in order to secure a discharge from the contract. Similar principles may also apply where one of the parties could have taken steps to prevent the risk of loss from arising and where the risk of loss is foreseeable.

(i) Foreseeable risks

If the risk of loss has been foreseen by the parties, the assumption is that the parties have contracted with that risk in mind. Accordingly, the loss should lie where it falls.[10] The same principle also applies to events which could have been foreseen by the parties.[11] Accordingly, in the case of a long-term requirements contract at a fixed price, the risk of loss caused by increased raw material costs will lie on the supplier, unless he has provided for indexation of the price to an appropriate cost-indicator.

The foresight test applied is stringent and is certainly not the same as the remoteness test applied in cases of physical harm.[12] An event, which for other purposes might be regarded as foreseeable, is sometimes capable of frustrating a contract. In *Tatem Ltd v Gamboa*,[13] a ship was chartered expressly for the purpose of evacuating civilians from northern Spain during the course of the Spanish Civil War. The hire charges were stated to be payable until redelivery. The ship was seized by the Nationalists and was eventually released so that the charterer could redeliver it to the owner six weeks after the expiry of the agreed period of hire. The owners claimed hire charges for the full period, including the time during which the ship was under the control of the Nationalists. GODDARD J held that the contract was frustrated. Although detention of the ship was probably foreseeable, the duration of that detention was not. The decision does seem strange in that the parties had foreseen and provided for another event, namely, the loss of the ship. In that event, the charterer was under no further obligation to pay the hire charges. This would seem to suggest that the parties may have intended the risk of loss caused by detention to lie where it fell.

(ii) Reasonable risk-avoidance steps

Where performance of the contract is rendered impracticable, one of the parties may be better placed to take steps to mitigate the effects of the alleged frustrating event. In *Tsakiroglou & Co Ltd v Noblee Thorl GmbH*,[14] the seller could have taken the step of arranging for shipment by an alternative route. The same principle would also seem to explain cases where the alleged frustrating event defeats the purpose of one of the parties only. That person, for the most part, will be treated as having an appreciation of the risks involved, and will be expected to take steps to avert the risk or provide for it in the contract. In *Blackburn Bobbin Co Ltd v Allen & Sons Ltd*,[15] a contract for the sale of Finnish birch timber was entered into. The buyer was unaware that the timber had to

---

10 *Krell v Henry* [1903] 2 KB 740 at 752 (per VAUGHAN WILLIAMS LJ).
11 *Davis Contractors Ltd v Fareham UDC* [1956] AC 696 at 731 (per LORD RADCLIFFE).
12 See ch 16.
13 [1939] 1 KB 132. See also *Ocean Tramp Tankers Corpn v VO/ Sovfracht, The Eugenia* [1964] 2 QB 226 at 239 (per LORD DENNING MR).
14 [1962] AC 93.
15 [1918] 1 KB 540. See also *Walton Harvey Ltd v Walker and Homfrays Ltd* [1931] 1 Ch 274.

be imported from Finland. At the time of the contract, exports of timber from Finnish ports was prevented by a blockade, but timber could have been shipped from other Scandinavian ports, provided it was first carried overland to Sweden. The seller chose not to adopt this course of action, and sought to have the contract discharged on the ground of frustration. It was held that, since the buyer was unaware that the timber had to be imported from Finland, he could have made any one of a number of assumptions. For example, he might have believed that the timber was already stockpiled in the United Kingdom, or he might have believed that stocks were easily obtainable from other Scandinavian countries. Accordingly, since the event did not frustrate the common intentions of both parties at the time the contract was made, the risk of loss lay with the seller. He was the best risk-avoider in that he could have taken steps at an earlier stage to secure performance of the contract.

(iii)   A doctrine of fault

One of the requirements of the doctrine of frustration is that the frustrating event should occur without the fault of either party to the contract.[16] The problem is to determine what is meant by the use of the word 'fault'. On a narrow interpretation, it can be argued that a person will only be prevented from relying on the doctrine of frustration where he has acted deliberately or in breach of an actionable duty. Conversely, a wider view requires the supervening event to be something over which the party seeking to treat the contract as frustrated has no control.[17] What matters is whether the party seeking to rely on an event as discharging him from a contractual promise was responsible for the occurrence of that event.[18]

The default that matters is that of the person seeking to treat the contract as discharged. Thus the party in default cannot seek to treat the contract as frustrated, but his default will not affect the position of the innocent party.[19] Accordingly, if an employee is sentenced to imprisonment, his default will prevent him from relying on the doctrine of frustration, but it will have no effect on the position of the employer.[20]

The fault principle is described as the rule against 'self-induced frustration'. In terms of risk-allocation, the person at fault is the least cost-avoider and, if he suffers loss through his own fault, it will lie where it falls. For these purposes, fault seems to consist of three varieties. First, the person seeking discharge may have made a deliberate choice which amounts to a breach of contract and which brings about the frustrating event. In *The Eugenia*,[1] the charterer of a ship deliberately diverted the ship into a war zone in direct contravention of an express term of the contract. Accordingly, the alleged frustrating event was self-induced and the charterer was viewed as the least cost-avoider.

A second variety of fault exists where the person seeking discharge has deliberately and freely chosen to act in a way which brings about the frustrating event. In *Maritime National Fish Ltd v Ocean Trawlers Ltd*,[2] the appellants wished to use on five boats a type of net known as an 'otter trawl' for which a government licence was required. Only three licences were granted. One of the boats they chose not to license was the subject of a charterparty which the appellants argued was discharged on the ground of frustration. The Privy Council rejected the claim. If the appellants had so wished, they could have elected to license the chartered boat.

---

16   *Paal Wilson & Co A/S v Partenreederei Hannah Blumenthal, The Hannah Blumenthal* [1983] 1 AC 854.
17   Ibid at 882 (per GRIFFITHS LJ).
18   *J Lauritzen AS v Wijsmuller BV, The Super Servant Two* [1990] 1 Lloyd's Rep 1 at 10 (per BINGHAM LJ).
19   *FC Shepherd & Co Ltd v Jerrom* [1986] 3 All ER 589 at 603 (per MUSTILL LJ).
20   Ibid.
1   Sub nom *Ocean Tramp Tankers Corpn v V/O Sovfracht, The Eugenia* [1964] 2 QB 226.
2   [1935] AC 524.

In *Maritime National Fish* the decision was based on the free election of the appellants, in circumstances in which the allegedly frustrated contract could have been performed, but there are cases where one of the parties is faced with 'Hobson's choice'. For example, what would have been the position if the appellants had chartered two ships from the respondents and had been granted only one licence?[3] Here it is arguable that there has been no election, although it is also possible to say that the risk that only one licence might be granted is one the charterer takes. In *The Super Servant Two*,[4] the defendants contracted to carry a drilling rig using either of two ships, *The Super Servant One* or *The Super Servant Two*. The latter sank and it was claimed that the contract with the plaintiffs was frustrated since the *Super Servant One* was committed to the performance of another contract. Since a frustrating event must radically change the nature of the contractual rights and obligations of the parties as they were contemplated at the time of contracting,[5] it could be assumed that performance of this contract using either of the two ships was contemplated. On this basis it was not open to the defendants to argue that the contract was frustrated.[6] Moreover, since the alleged frustrating event was based on the election of the defendants not to perform the contract with the rig owners, it was a matter within the defendants' control to which the doctrine of frustration does not apply.[7]

The third possible variety of fault is negligence. Thus if a person acts in a manner which amounts to an actionable breach of a duty to exercise reasonable care and which brings about the alleged frustrating event, that person will not be able to rely upon the doctrine of frustration.[8] Conversely, it has been suggested that an opera singer who goes out in the rain and catches cold might be able to plead frustration of a contract to appear in an opera production, provided she did not deliberately seek to avoid the engagement.[9] The answer to the problem seems to lie in the notion of control.[10] If a person is in control of the alleged frustrating event and could have prevented it from happening, the least cost-avoider rule suggests that he is the person who should bear the risk.

In any event, the problem may be solved by the incidence of the burden of proof. In *Joseph Constantine SS Line Ltd v Imperial Smelting Corpn Ltd*,[11] it was held that the onus of proving self-induced frustration lies on the party not in default. If he is unable to show, on a balance of probability, that the frustrating event was caused by the negligence of the other party, the parties may still be discharged from performance.

(5)   THE BEST INSURER

Insurance is an alternative to prevention as a means of risk-avoidance. One of the parties to a contract may be able to spread his costs so as to cover a risk of loss or obtain market insurance in respect of that risk more easily than the other party. Some of the unavailability cases illustrate the role of insurance. For example, in *Tsakiroglou & Co Ltd v Noblee Thorl GmbH*,[12] the seller of goods would have had a wide range of customers and by raising the cost of his product could have taken steps to cover the possibility that the Suez

---

3   See *Treitel* p 805.
4   Sub nom *J Lauritzen AS v Wijsmuller BV* [1990] 1 Lloyd's Rep 1.
5   *National Carriers Ltd v Panalpina (Northern) Ltd* [1981] AC 675 at 700 (per LORD SIMON OF GLAISDALE).
6   *J Lauritzen AS v Wijsmuller BV, The Super Servant Two* [1990] 1 Lloyd's Rep 1 at 9 (per BINGHAM LJ).
7   Ibid at 10 (per BINGHAM LJ).
8   *J Lauritzen AS v Wijsmuller BV, The Super Servant Two* [1990] 1 Lloyd's Rep 1 at 10 (per BINGHAM LJ).
9   *Joseph Constantine SS Line Ltd v Imperial Smelting Corpn Ltd* [1942] AC 154 at 166–167 (per LORD SIMON)
10 *Paal Wilson & Co A/S v Partenreederei Hannah Blumenthal, The Hannah Blumenthal* [1983] 1 AC 854 at 882 (per GRIFFITHS LJ).
11 [1942] AC 154.
12 [1962] AC 93.

Canal might be closed. In other words, he could have self-insured against the risk of loss in question.

In some instances, a person may take the view that he will find it difficult to obtain market insurance in respect of a particular risk. In these circumstances, he will contract around that possibility. The problems of obtaining market insurance may serve as a ground for criticising the decision in *Tatem Ltd v Gamboa*,[13] in which the contract expressly provided that, should the ship be lost, the charterers would not be responsible for the payment of hire charges. However, no similar provision was made for the foreseeable possibility that the ship might be detained. An explanation of this is that the shipowners might have found it easier to insure against loss than detention, and that they expected the charterers to insure against that risk. If this was the case, the decision to treat the contract as frustrated would appear to be misfounded.

Where the contract is a lease, the best insurer rule also seems to be relevant. At one time, it would appear that the tenant was treated as an absolute insurer against all risks of disruption to the lease.[14] The result of this was that a rule developed to the effect that the doctrine of frustration did not apply to lease. This produced the anomaly that some long-term contracts such as charterparties were subject to the doctrine, whereas leases were not.

In *National Carriers Ltd v Panalpina (Northern) Ltd*,[15] it was held that a lease could be frustrated, although this would rarely be the case. The difficulties which arise in the context of leases are that, because a lease is generally for a long period of years, it is a form of speculation. In speculative ventures, the parties must appreciate that circumstances will change and that they must be deemed to accept the risks which may arise over a period of time.[16] Also, because a lease is a long-term venture, a temporary interruption may not be important in relation to the number of years yet to run. Accordingly, in *National Carriers*, a twenty-month interruption of a ten-year lease was insufficient to allow the contract to be frustrated.

If a lease were to be frustrated, the effect would be to throw the whole burden of disruption upon the landlord, who would be deprived of his rent and would bear the cost of possible destruction by fire and the cost of reletting the premises. In contrast, if the lease is not frustrated, the tenant still bears the burden of paying rent for premises he cannot use and is obliged to insure the premises and keep them under repair. If, as is normally the case, a lease is not frustrated, this constitutes judicial acceptance that the tenant is the best insurer against a risk of disruption.

In some instances, a lease may be frustrated, although much will depend on the length of the letting. For example, the lease of a holiday cottage over a few months might be frustrated if the cottage were to be totally destroyed. Likewise, coastal erosion or some other convulsion of nature which causes land to fall into the sea would serve to frustrate a lease.[17] Furthermore, the apparent harshness of the rule may be mitigated by the express terms of the lease. For example, it is common to find provision for the termination of the lease upon the happening of specified events.

---

13   [1939] 1 KB 132.
14   *Paradine v Jane* (1647) 82 ER 897.
15   [1981] AC 675.
16   See *Amalgamated Investment and Property Co Ltd v Walker & Son Ltd* [1977] 1 WLR 164 discussed above.
17   *Cricklewood Property and Investment Trust Ltd v Leighton's Investment Trust Ltd* [1945] AC 221 at 229 (per VISCOUNT SIMON LC).

(6)   PREVENTION OF UNJUST ENRICHMENT

A contract is terminated automatically as from the time of the frustrating event.[18] This may lead to the unjust enrichment of one of the parties. For example, payment may have been made in advance, or one of the parties may have partly performed his obligations under the contract prior to the date of discharge, in which case he may have conferred a valuable, but unpaid for, benefit on the other party. These problems were not dealt with very well at common law,[19] and legislation in the form of the Law Reform (Frustrated Contracts) Act 1943 was passed. Since, in these circumstances, the contract is discharged, any solution provided is restitutionary in nature, and is considered in more detail elsewhere.[20]

Apart from remedies after discharge, the principle against unjust enrichment, in its widest sense, may operate at an earlier stage to justify a refusal to treat the contract as frustrated. Occasionally, it is possible that discharge of the contract will result in a gain to one of the parties. For example, if a shipowner elects to treat a charterparty as frustrated in the event of requisition, despite the charterer's willingness to continue paying hire charges, this may be because government compensation on requisition exceeds the income from hire charges. In *FA Tamplin SS Co Ltd v Anglo-Mexican Petroleum Products Co Ltd*,[1] the decision not to treat the contract as frustrated may well have been explicable on these grounds. Similar considerations may also have applied to *Tsakiroglou & Co Ltd v Noblee Thorl GmbH*,[2] as the market price of the goods which were the subject matter of the contract had risen substantially between the date of contract and the closure of the Suez Canal. Had the contract been held frustrated, the seller would have been able to resell the cargo at the increased price and would not have had to pay the extra cost of transporting the cargo via the Cape of Good Hope.

---

18   *Hirji Mulji v Cheong Yue SS Co Ltd* [1926] AC 497 at 505.
19   See *Chandler v Webster* [1904] 1 KB 493; *Fibrosa Spolka Akcyjna v Fairbaim, Lawson, Combe, Barbour Ltd* [1943] AC 32.
20   See ch 18.
1   [1916] 2 AC 397.
2   [1962] AC 93.

Chapter 24

Unconscionability

1. INTRODUCTION

(1) JUSTICE, CERTAINTY AND PUBLIC POLICY

In contract law, there are, theoretically, two opposing values, namely justice or fairness on the one hand, and certainty or predictability on the other hand.[1] Common law rules of the law of contract developed in the nineteenth century are said to epitomise the value of certainty. For example, it has been said that:

> No man of *ripe years* and of *sound mind*, *acting freely and with his eyes open*, ought to be hindered, with a view to his advantage, from making such bargain, in the way of obtaining money, as he thinks fit, nor ... anybody hindered from supplying him upon any terms he thinks proper to accede to.[2]

This might seem to suggest a bias in favour of unbridled free enterprise, but examination of the emphasised words reveals that judicial intervention is permitted on the grounds of justice or fairness and relief may be granted where one of the contracting parties is at a disadvantage because of his age, or because he is not of sound mind, or where he is not acting freely.[3]

While the value of certainty is particularly important in business relationships because it promotes commercial stability, it is important not to associate it with rigidity. Legal rules should be predictable in the sense that they do not defeat the reasonable expectations of the parties and should provide a reasonable regularity of result.[4]

The value of justice or fairness dictates that the parties to a contract may be relieved of their obligations on the grounds of unconscionability, unfairness or inequality of bargaining power. Most of the rules designed to operate in this way are equitable in origin, and can be said to be concerned with either procedural fairness or substantive

---

1   See Reiter (1981) 1 OJLS 347; Atiyah *Rise and Fall* pp 324–332. Cf Tiplady (1983) 46 MLR 601.
2   *Printing and Numerical Registering Co v Sampson* (1875) LR 19 Eq 462 at 465 (per LORD JESSEL MR).
3   For an explanation of rules on formation mistakes, misrepresentation, duress, undue influence and abuse of bargaining position in terms of inequality of bargaining see Cartwright *Unequal Bargaining* (1991).
4   Llewellyn *The Common Law Tradition* (1960) p 215.

fairness.[5] Procedural fairness requires that a person should not be allowed to keep the benefits of a contract which has been unfairly brought into existence, for example one extracted by fraud, force or other unfair conduct.[6] In contrast, the terms of a contract are sometimes said to be unfair, in the sense that they favour one party over another. In such cases, equity will not intervene to grant relief unless the substantive unfairness or contractual imbalance is such as to raise a presumption of procedural unfairness.[7]

Rules concerned with unfairness or unconscionability are largely based on policy grounds. Two major policies are of particular importance. The first is the protection of the public interest epitomised by the rules on illegal contracts. The second is the protection of weaker parties. Much of modern consumer protection law and the rules on duress, undue influence, restraint of trade and the control of exclusion clauses would appear to be based on this policy ground. While it is evident that many rules of the law of contract are concerned with policing the bargain and its possible undesirable effects, it would appear that English law has no general principle which can be used to explain these rules.

(2) A GENERAL PRINCIPLE OF UNCONSCIONABILITY

In some jurisdictions, an express attempt has been made to state a generalised principle of unconscionability. For example, in the United States, it is provided that:

> If the court as a matter of law finds the contract or any clause of the contract unconscionable at the time it was made, the court may refuse to enforce the contract, or it may enforce the remainder of the contract without the unconscionable clause, or it may so limit the application of any unconscionable clause as to avoid any unconscionable result.[8]

The nearest English law has come to such a generalised principle is to be found in the minority judgment of LORD DENNING MR in *Lloyds Bank Ltd v Bundy*,[9] where he stated that the law:

> gives relief to one who, without independent advice, enters into a contract or transfers property for a consideration which is grossly inadequate, when his bargaining power is grievously impaired by reason of his own needs or desires, or by his own ignorance or infirmity, coupled with undue influences or pressures brought to bear on him by or for the benefit of the other.[10]

Subsequently, it was held by the House of Lords in *National Westminster Bank plc v Morgan*[11] that there is no need to erect a general principle of relief against inequality of bargaining power, since Parliament has undertaken the task, particularly in the form of modern consumer protection legislation, and that if restrictions are required upon the freedom of contract, the responsibility should be that of Parliament, not the courts.[12] However, it is submitted that a generalised principle of the type suggested by LORD DENNING might be a fruitful source of development, provided its parameters are

---

5   See Atiyah *Essays*, Essay No 11; Leff (1967) 115 U Pa LR 485.
6   *Hart v O'Connor* [1985] 2 All ER 880 at 887 (per LORD BRIGHTMAN).
7   Ibid.
8   *UCC* § 2–302. See also *Commercial Bank of Australia v Amadio* (1983) 46 ALR 402.
9   [1975] QB 326.
10 Ibid at 339.
11 [1985] 1 All ER 821.
12 Ibid 830 (per LORD SCARMAN).

sufficiently well defined. Moreover, various members of the judiciary have, at times, expressed sympathy for the more generalised approach suggested in *Bundy*.[13]

(i) The content of a general principle

LORD DENNING's general principle in *Lloyds Bank Ltd v Bundy* is based on four essential requirements, namely, lack of advice, disparity of consideration, exploitability and pressure or influence. Exploitability would appear to be a constant factor in cases falling within the principle, but, on occasions, the other factors may be absent.[14]

It was not envisaged that the principle should apply to all cases of apparent imbalance or unfairness. It has been argued that the basis for intervention is that there has been an abuse of a position of bargaining strength, not just because the parties start off in an unequal position.[15] Thus it was said that the principle would not be relevant to contracts which are the result of the ordinary interplay of forces.[16] Conversely, it might apply to cases of duress and other cases in which an unfair advantage has been obtained by an unconscientious use of power, cases involving undue influence and undue pressure, and cases of marine salvage. The principle could also be applied to the renegotiation of a contract,[17] the settlement of a tort claim,[18] onerous exclusion clauses[19] and contracts in restraint of trade.[20] Furthermore, it has been argued[1] that a general principle of unconscionability can extend to encompass rules on equitable relief against forfeiture, penalty clauses, the withholding of discretionary remedies such as specific performance and injunctions, and the issue of adequacy of consideration. Furthermore, unconscionability also seems to play an important role in determining whether a gratuitous promise is enforceable under the equitable doctrine of estoppel.

(a) *Procedural unfairness* Rules on procedural fairness require that a person should not be allowed to keep the benefits of a contract extracted by fraud, misrepresentation, force, threats or other illegitimate means. In a traditional analysis, cases of this kind are concerned with the reality of consent. Accordingly, the issue of unconscionability can be disguised by saying that there is no agreement.

The common law rule is that the court will not enquire into the adequacy of the consideration for a promise,[2] which suggests that courts should not be concerned with procedural fairness. However, unconscionability seems to play an important role in determining whether a promise to perform an existing duty is enforceable. Where such performance is a good consideration, it will invariably be found that it is not contrary to public policy to enforce the promise.[3] However, where it is said that performance of an existing duty does not amount to a good consideration, an element of unconscionability may be found. For example, it may be that one party has sought to exert improper pressure on the promisor.[4] Similarly, where a person has promised to

---

13   See *Lloyds Bank v Bundy* [1975] QB 326 at 347 (per SIR ERIC SACHS); *Crédit Lyonnais Bank Nederland NV v Burch* [1997] 1 All ER 144 at 151 (per NOURSE LJ).
14   See Tiplady (1983) 46 MLR 601 at 611–612.
15   Cartwright, *Unequal Bargaining*, (1991) p 218.
16   *Lloyds Bank Ltd v Bundy* [1975] QB 326 at 336 (per LORD DENNING MR).
17   *D and C Builders Ltd v Rees* [1966] 2 QB 617.
18   *Arrale v Costain Civil Engineering Ltd* [1976] 1 Lloyd's Rep 98.
19   *Levison v Patent Steam Carpet Cleaning Co Ltd* [1978] QB 69.
20   *A Schroeder Music Publishing Co Ltd v Macaulay* [1974] 3 All ER 616, [1974] 1 WLR 1308.
1   See Waddams (1976) 39 MLR 369.
2   See chs 3 and 6.
3   See *Ward v Byham* [1956] 1 WLR 496 at 498 (per DENNING LJ); *Williams v Williams* [1957] 1 WLR 148 at 151 (per DENNING LJ).
4   See *Harris v Watson* (1791) Peake 102 at 103 (per LORD KENYON).

take less than the full amount of a debt owed to him, the traditional rule states that there is no consideration for the promise.[5] However, this may result in the court striking down a perfectly reasonable business adjustment or settlement. But the traditional rule does serve to protect a person who has been subjected to unconscionable pressure. For example, in *D and C Builders v Rees*,[6] a builder agreed to take less than the full amount owed to him in respect of work he had carried out on the defendant's behalf. The defendant knew the builder was in financial difficulty and seemingly took advantage of this impecuniosity in an unconscionable fashion by offering less than the agreed value of the work on a take it or leave it basis.

(b) *Substantive unfairness* Rules of substantive fairness require that a fair result is achieved in a particular case. In classical analysis, rules of this kind were regarded as anomalous because they interfered with a distribution agreed upon by the parties. Unconscionable behaviour by one of the parties may serve to justify intervention in a number of instances. For example, the use of unreasonable exclusion clauses is controlled by the Unfair Contract Terms Act 1977, The Unfair Terms in Consumer Contracts Regulations 1999[7] and common law rules of construction in the interests of substantive fairness of exchange. Where the purported exclusion of liability is wholly unreasonable, it can be said that the *proferens* is seeking to take advantage of his unequal bargaining position. Likewise, the view that 'Chancery mends no man's bargain'[8] is misleading, as there are undoubtedly cases where equity does intervene, apparently on the ground of unconscionability. Equitable rules on undue influence, penalties, forfeitures and mistake[9] are all examples of mending a bargain.

As the traditional concern of equity is the prevention of an unconscionable insistence upon otherwise enforceable legal rights, the equitable doctrines of estoppel may serve to protect the promisee against an unconscionable change of mind by the promisor. The doctrines of estoppel have been used to modify or suspend an existing legal right of the promisor.[10] However, where there is no existing legal right, the situation is not clear cut. Enforcement of an otherwise unenforceable contractual promise may not be possible,[11] but equitable intervention may be justified due to the promisor's unconscionable conduct.[12] For example, a court might prevent a person from denying the existence of a contract he has led another to believe will be entered into.[13] One view of this is that it undermines the role of contract law, but equitable intervention prevents the promisee from suffering as a result of the promisor's unconscionable refusal to keep his word.

Equitable rules on forfeiture are also based on the notion of unconscionability. The general common law rule is that a party in breach of contract cannot recover property which, in fulfilment of his contractual obligations prior to breach, he has transferred to the other party.[14] However, in equity, relief against forfeiture can be granted where it

---

5   *Foakes v Beer* (1884) 9 App Cas 605.
6   [1966] 2 QB 617.
7   SI 1999/2083.
8   *Maynard v Mosely* (1676) 3 Swan 651 at 655 (per LORD NOTTINGHAM).
9   See ch 23.
10 See ch 6.
11 *Combe v Combe* [1951] 2 KB 215.
12 See *Amalgamated Investment and Property Co Ltd (in liquidation) v Texas Commerce International Bank Ltd* [1982] QB 84 at 105–108 (per ROBERT GOFF J); *Pacol Ltd v Trade Lines Ltd, The Henryk Sif* [1982] 1 Lloyd's Rep 456 at 467–468 (per WEBSTER J).
13 See *Hoffman v Red Owl Stores* 133 NW 2d 267 (1965); *Waltons Stores (Interstate) Ltd v Maher* (1988) 76 ALR 513 and see Duthie (1988) 104 LQR 362.
14 *Hirji Mulji v Cheong Yue SS Co Ltd* [1926] AC 497 at 510 (per LORD SUMNER).

is unfair for a person to use his legal right to take advantage of another.[15] But this may amount to no more than giving time to pay outstanding sums due under the contract.[16]

Whether equity will go further than to extend the time for payment is not clear. It has been suggested that wider relief is available if the forfeiture provision is penal in nature and it is unconscionable for a deposit of money to be retained.[17] But a very narrow view of the jurisdiction to give relief against forfeiture has been taken and it does not extend to the recovery of hire payments in a charterparty terminated by the hirer's breach because the forfeiture does not relate to a possessory or proprietary right.[18] The result of this is that very fine distinctions have been made in order to justify the granting of relief. For example, a contractual licence to use trade mark rights does not allow relief from forfeiture[19] whereas a contract to assign a patent right does, because it involves the forfeiture of a proprietary right.[20]

The emphasis on the penal nature of forfeiture provisions is consistent with the approach adopted in relation to penalty clauses providing for the payment of an agreed sum or the transfer of property to the party not in default.[1] The courts apply a test which distinguishes between a penalty clause which operates *in terrorem* over the party in breach and a genuine pre-estimate of damage flowing from a breach.[2] However, this disguises the role of unconscionability in the court's decision. An important factor is whether the amount stipulated in the agreed damages clause is unreasonable, unconscionable, extravagant or extortionate.[3] If this is the case, the relevant provision of the contract can be struck down.

(ii) The parameters of a general principle

The difficulty presented by a general principle of unconscionability is that if it is applied without restrictions, it will result in perfectly reasonable business risk-allocations being upset.

Accordingly, it is necessary to set limits on the circumstances in which a court may intervene on the grounds of unconscionability or unfairness. Without such limits, the general principle would produce intolerable uncertainty in the law. The doctrine of inequality of bargaining power as enunciated in *Lloyds Bank Ltd v Bundy*[4] suffers from a lack of explanation of its limits. It does not distinguish between legitimate and illegitimate forms of advantage-taking. The elements of the general principle are sometimes present and sometimes absent. For example, absence of advice will not always be fatal. The use of influence or pressure by one party is not always a requirement of judicial intervention. What is clear is that, without clear elucidation, a general principle of unconscionability may be described as nothing more than an emotionally satisfying incantation which is devoid of real content and a licence to decide cases by instinct.[5]

---

15 For example, the rules against there being a 'clog on the equity of redemption' and against forfeiture of leases. See Cheshire and Burn *Modern Law of Real Property* (14th edn, 1988) pp 638–651.
16 *Kreglinger v New Patagonia Meat and Cold Storage Co Ltd* [1914] AC 25 at 56 (per LORD PORTER).
17 *Stockloser v Johnson* [1954] 1 QB 476 at 476, 483, 485, 489–490 (per SOMERVELL and DENNING LJJ). Cf *Hyundai Shipbuilding and Heavy Industries Co Ltd v Pournaras* [1978] 2 Lloyd's Rep 502.
18 *Scandinavian Trading Tanker Co AB v Flota Petrolera Ecuatoriana, The Scaptrade* [1983] 2 AC 694.
19 *Sport International Bussum BV v Inter-Footwear Ltd* [1984] 2 All ER 321.
20 *BICC plc v Burndy Corpn* [1985] 1 All ER 417.
1   See ch 14.
2   *Dunlop Pneumatic Tyre Co Ltd v New Garage and Motor Co Ltd* [1915] AC 79.
3   Ibid at 87 (per LORD DUNEDIN); at 97 (per LORD WRIGHT) and at 101 (per LORD PARMOOR).
4   [1975] QB 326.
5   Leff (1967) 115 U Pa LR 485 at 527.

2. DURESS

The classical view of duress is that it is a variety of procedural unfairness which prevents a valid agreement from being reached. But, where a person contracts under the pressure of a threat, it is arguable that his consent is real, albeit a case of 'Hobson's choice'. But the impropriety or otherwise of the threatener is just as important as the consent given by the person under threat. Thus it is arguable that by considering impropriety, the courts are more concerned with the substantive fairness of the result in a particular case.[6] In this regard, it is important to consider whether the consent of the 'innocent' party has been vitiated and whether the conduct of the threatening party is illegitimate.[7] For these purposes, the mere application of commercial pressure will not suffice, even where the party applying such pressure has taken advantage of a monopoly situation.[8]

(1) THREATS SUFFICIENT TO CONSTITUTE DURESS

The narrow common law rule that a contract is voidable if made under duress was restricted to actual or threatened physical violence to the person or unlawful constraint of the person.[9] Thus a threat of lawful imprisonment[10] and a threat to levy distress on a man's goods[11] did not amount to common law duress. However, it will be seen that the more modern approach to the question of duress concentrates on whether the defendant's threat is legitimate and on whether the claimant's will has been coerced and that these tests taken together are capable of covering cases of 'duress of goods'.[12] Thus there is actionable duress where the Iraqi government threatened to detain dredgers owned by the claimants unless the latter agreed to the government's terms for their release.[13]

In equity and through the application of restitutionary principles there is a wider basis for intervention. For example, a threat of lawful imprisonment was sufficient in equity to render a contract voidable for undue pressure.[14] Furthermore, money paid under duress of goods could be recovered in a restitutionary action for moneys had and received.[15] However, strangely, the rule did not extend to agreements to pay if made under duress which has been criticised on the ground that in the case of a payment, there must have been a stage at which there was also an agreement to pay.[16]

Subsequently, the common law rule on duress of goods was the subject of much criticism on the ground that a threat to property could be just as coercive as a threat to the person. In *The Siboen and The Sibotre*,[17] it was thought that a threat to burn a man's house or to slash a valuable painting would be sufficient to invalidate a contract made as a result of the threat.[18]

---

6   Atiyah *Essays* Essay No 11, pp 345–346.
7   See *Atlas Express Ltd v Kafco* [1989] QB 833 at 839 (per TUCKER J). See also *CTN Cash and Carry Ltd v Gallagher Ltd* [1994] 4 All ER 714.
8   *CTN Cash and Carry Ltd v Gallagher Ltd* [1994] 4 All ER 714 at 718 (per STEYN LJ).
9   *Barton v Armstrong* [1976] AC 104.
10 *Cumming v Ince* (1847) 11 QB 112.
11 *Skeate v Beale* (1840) 11 Ad & El 983. Cf *Vantage Navigation Corp v Suhail, The Alev* [1989] 1 Lloyd's Rep 138 at 145 (per HOBHOUSE J).
12 See *Pao On v Lau Yiu Long* [1980] AC 614.
13 *Royal Boskalis Westminster NV v Mountain* [1997] 2 All ER 929.
14 *Williams v Bayley* (1866) LR 1 HL 200.
15 *Maskell v Horner* [1915] 3 KB 106.
16 Beatson *The Use and Abuse of Unjust Enrichment* (1991) pp 106–109.
17 Sub nom *Occidental Worldwide Investment Corpn v Skibs A/S Avanti* [1976] 1 Lloyd's Rep 293.
18 Ibid at 335 (per KERR J). See also *Royal Boskalis Westminster NV v Mountain* [1997] 2 All ER 929.

That a threat to property might constitute duress at common law spawned the view that a threat to interfere with a contract might also suffice. This has led to the emergence of a general theory of economic duress.[19] This form of duress may arise in a number of different contexts. For example, during the course of re-negotiation of a contract one party may suggest that he is unable to fulfil his contractual obligations unless the other party is prepared to pay extra. If the threat of non-performance is illegitimate, the judicial response may come in one of two forms. Either the threat might be regarded as duress or it might be decided that the promise to make extra payment is not supported by consideration. In the light of the apparent dismantling of the requirement of strict sufficiency of consideration,[20] the difficulty is to determine when a threat crosses the dividing line between duress and hard bargaining. In *The Siboen and The Sibotre*, it was said that a protest by the victim or his apparent acceptance of the transaction as concluded would be important issues in determining whether a threat constitutes economic duress. In *The Atlantic Baron*,[1] the defendants threatened not to complete the construction of an oil tanker unless the plaintiffs were prepared to pay an additional 10% on top of the contract price. Unknown to the defendants, the plaintiffs had arranged a profitable charter of the ship on completion. The plaintiffs were advised that the defendants had no legal entitlement to the extra 10%, with the result that they agreed to pay, without prejudice to their legal rights. Eight months after completion of the ship, the plaintiffs sought to recover the excess payment. It was held, in principle, that the threat not to complete construction constituted economic duress, but the delay in commencing proceedings and the absence of any protest constituted an affirmation of the contract. This affirmation meant that the plaintiff was no longer entitled to relief from the duress of the defendant.

The decision in *The Atlantic Baron* does not mean that any threat to break a contract will amount to economic duress. In *Pao On v Lau Yiu Long*,[2] the plaintiffs agreed to sell a partly-constructed building to the defendants. The arrangement involved a transfer of shares in a subsidiary company which owned the building. It was subsequently realised by the plaintiffs that, by agreeing to sell the shares at a fixed price, the defendants might make a considerable profit if the shares were to rise in value. The plaintiffs threatened to pull out of the deal unless the defendants were prepared to abandon the original contract and replace it with a contract of indemnity which would protect the plaintiffs from a fall in value of the shares, but would allow them to benefit from any rise in value prior to the date of the final transfer of ownership of the building. The defendants feared adverse publicity which might affect public confidence in the company if the contract were not performed. Under pressure, they complied with the plaintiffs' demands. Subsequently, the shares fell in value, and the plaintiffs sought to recover their loss under the indemnity contract. It was held that there was no duress, as the defendants had carefully considered their position and, after advice, chose to avoid litigation for commercial reasons. In determining whether a threat constitutes duress, it is necessary to consider whether the victim protested; whether there was any alternative course of action open to the victim such as the pursuit of an adequate legal remedy; whether the victim was independently advised, and whether, after making the contract, the victim took sufficient steps to avoid it.

Regard also has to be had to the source of the decision to renegotiate. It should be noted that in *The Atlantic Baron* the request for additional payment came from the party

---

19   See, generally, Phang (1990) 53 MLR 107.
20   *Williams v Roffey Bros & Nicholls (Contractors) Ltd* [1990] 1 All ER 512 and see ch 6.
1   Sub nom *North Ocean Shipping Co Ltd v Hyundai Construction Co Ltd* [1979] QB 705. Adams (1979) 42 MLR 57.
2   [1980] AC 614.

who had encountered difficulty in fulfilling his contractual obligations. In contrast, in *Williams v Roffey Bros & Nicholls (Contractors) Ltd*[3] the offer of extra payment, if the sub-contractor could complete his contract on time, was initiated by the surveyor acting on behalf of the main contractors. In this last event the evidence of duress is non-existent and the offer of extra payment may be said to have been made voluntarily.

It is also relevant to consider the reasons for the making of the 'threat'. For example, a contracting party cannot be criticised for acting against the interests of the other party where he has legitimate fears over the liquidity of that party. Thus in *CTN Cash and Carry Ltd v Gallagher Ltd*[4] it was perfectly acceptable conduct for the defendants to refuse to grant further credit facilities when they became worried about the continued ability of the other party to pay under the terms of the contract. Similarly, there is nothing wrong in a contracting party threatening to enforce the terms of an existing contract. Thus in *Westpac Banking Corporation v Cockerill*[5] the bank was owed money by a customer and sought to agree a settlement, partly by means of a threat to appoint a receiver should the customer not agree to the terms of the settlement. In the circumstances, there was nothing illegitimate in what the bank had done, since they were perfectly entitled to use legal means to recover the debt owed to them.

(2) THE EFFECT OF DURESS

(i) Contract void or voidable

It is generally supposed that a contract is voidable at the instance of the victim of a threat constituting duress.[6] This is also consistent with the decision in *The Atlantic Baron*[7] to the effect that a plea of duress can be met by a defence of affirmation of the contract.

(ii) The effect of duress on the victim and the legitimacy of the threat

The classical view of duress was that it should overbear the will of the victim.[8] But this is subject to the particular criticism that it overplays the reaction of the person who is threatened. Moreover, if the will of the party seeking relief is overborne, the sole reason for entering the contract will have been the duress of the other party. But it is clear from the decision in *Barton v Armstrong*[9] that the coercive pressure must be a reason for making the contract—not the reason or even the *predominant* or *clinching* reason.[10] Despite this, recent decisions have paid lip-service to the overborne will theory, saying that duress must constitute a coercion of the will so as to vitiate consent.[11] However, it may

---

3   [1990] 1 All ER 512.
4   [1994] 4 All ER 714.
5   (1998) 152 ALR 267.
6   *Pao On v Lau Yiu Long* [1980] AC 614 at 634 (per LORD SCARMAN); *Universe Tankships Inc of Monrovia v International Transport Workers Federation* [1982] 2 WLR 803 at 812 (per LORD DIPLOCK); *Dimskal Shipping Co SA v International Transport Workers Federation, The Evia Luck (No 2)* [1992] 1 Lloyd's Rep 115 at 120 (per LORD GOFF). Cf *Barton v Armstrong* [1976] AC 104 at 120—contract void (per LORD CROSS). See also Lanham (1966) 29 MLR 615.
7   [1979] QB 705.
8   Described as an unhelpful approach in *Dimskal Shipping Co SA v International Transport Workers Federation, The Evia Luck (No 2)* [1992] 1 Lloyd's Rep 115 at 120 (per LORD GOFF).
9   [1976] AC 104.
10 Ibid at 119 (per LORD CROSS).
11 *Pao On v Lau Yiu Long* [1980] AC 614 at 636 (per LORD SCARMAN). See also *The Siboen and The Sibotre* [1976] 1 Lloyd's Rep 293 at 336 (per KERR J); *Vantage Navigation Corp v Suhail, The Alev* [1989] 1 Lloyd's Rep 138 at 145 (per HOBHOUSE J); *Atlas Express v Kafco (Importers and Distributors) Ltd* [1989] 1 All ER 641 at 645 (per TUCKER J).

be argued that duress does not result in an overborne will, in a literal sense, since the victim does know what he is doing and intends to submit to the duress.[12]

The fallacy of the overborne will theory has been exposed in *The Universe Sentinel*[13] in which it was stated that the victim of a threat of duress is fully aware of the nature and terms of the contract into which he enters. A proper enquiry into the issue of unconscionability does not concentrate upon the mind of the victim, instead it should concentrate on the nature of the threat and the legitimacy of the demand[14] which applied pressure to the victim. LORD SCARMAN seemed to reject the overborne will theory altogether, preferring to describe duress as involving:

> not the lack of will to submit [*sic*] but the victim's intentional submission arising from the realisation that there is no practical choice open to him.[15]

It follows from this that there are two elements in cases of alleged duress. First, there must be an illegitimate threat and, secondly, there must be an absence of practical choice available to the victim.

It must be determined what constitutes illegitimate pressure. For these purposes, there appears to be a distinction between pressure which is wrongful in the sense that it is a threat to commit a crime, tort or breach of other legal or equitable duty and illegitimate pressure which involves no threat to break a duty owed in law.[16] It is necessary to identify some sort of a threat on the part of the defendant. In most instances of economic duress this will be a threat to break a contract.[17]

Typically, duress will be relevant where there is an attempt at renegotiation of the terms of an existing contract. If one of the parties is unable to proceed for financial reasons, it may make sense to go to the other party to explain the position. But does telling the truth amount to an implied threat? The economic torts have drawn a distinction between threats, warnings and inducements and a threat requires an intimation that unless the addressee acts in a particular way, something will be done which the addressee will not like.[18] It follows that merely passing on information will not be a threat.[19] If a similar test is applied to cases of duress, it would seem to follow that it should be implicit in what the defendant says that unfortunate consequences might result from a failure to comply with the demand.

The nature of the demand also matters.[20] Duress has been found where the demand was connected with a threat to terminate performance,[1] to withhold[2] or to 'black'[3] property belonging to the other party. The more unreasonable the demand, the more likely it is that the threat will be regarded as illegitimate.

The second issue is whether the victim has any practical choice available to him. The presence or absence of practical choice may be established by reference to any

12   See Atiyah (1982) 98 LQR 197; (1983) 99 LQR 353. Cf Tiplady (1983) 99 LQR 188.
13   Sub nom *Universe Tankships Inc of Monrovia v International Transport Workers Federation* [1982] 2 WLR 803. See also Carty and Evans (1983) JBL 218.
14   Ibid at 820 (per LORD CROSS) and at 822 (per LORD DIPLOCK).
15   Ibid at 828. Should 'submit' read 'resist': *B & S Contracts and Design Ltd v Victor Green Publications Ltd* [1984] ICR 419 at 428 (per KERR LJ).
16   Ibid at 814 (per LORD DIPLOCK).
17   But not always: *B & S Contracts and Design Ltd v Victor Green Publications Ltd* [1984] ICR 419 (threat to allow a workers' strike to take place).
18   *Hodges v Webb* [1920] 2 Ch 70 at 89 (per PETERSON J).
19   Ibid at 87.
20   *The Universe Sentinel* [1982] 2 WLR 803 at 828–829 (per LORD SCARMAN).
1   *The Atlantic Baron* [1979] QB 705. Cf *Pao On v Lau Yiu Long* [1980] AC 614.
2   *Vantage Navigation Corp v Suhail, The Alev* [1989] 1 Lloyd's Rep 138.
3   *The Universe Sentinel* [1983] 1 AC 366; *Dimskal Shipping Co SA v International Transport Workers Federation, The Evia Luck (No 2)* [1992] 1 Lloyd's Rep 115.

protest made by the victim, and the fact that the victim has received legal advice before deciding what to do. However, silence alone does not necessarily mean acceptance of the state of affairs. It is also relevant to consider whether the victim could reasonably be expected to pursue an alternative remedy. If the practical effect of the pressure is to give the victim no choice, then the pressure is likely to amount to duress. Thus if the chances of obtaining an injunction to avert the threat are minimal or non-existent[4] or if the practicality of seeking an alternative remedy is too risky or disruptive to the victim's business,[5] the threat is still likely to be illegitimate. In contrast, the fact that there has been a protest is not conclusive evidence of duress for the simple reason that 'grumbling is a way of business life'.[6]

Also relevant to the question whether a person had any practical choice open to him is whether the available alternative is reasonable.[7] Thus, it may not be reasonable to call the bluff of the party issuing the threat if to wait and see whether the threat is carried out might be damaging to business. Likewise, waiting to see if the threat is carried out might also prejudice the performance of a contract with a third party, thereby causing a loss of business reputation on the part of the person subject to the threat. Thus in *Atlas Express Ltd v Kafco*[8] the threat by a carrier not to deliver the defendant's goods to a major retail supplier unless the defendant was prepared to pay twice the contracted rate amounted to duress. An important consideration in the decision appears to have been that the defendant was unable to find an alternative carrier and that failure to fulfil the contract with the retail supplier would have damaged the defendant's business reputation.

At present, the rule is stated in terms of the illegitimacy rather than the wrongfulness of the threat, which could mean that threats of lawful action may fall within the rule. This would mark a significant departure from the orthodoxy that it is not duress to do what there is a legal right to do.[9] Nevertheless there are cases which accept that a threat can be illegitimate where it threatens lawful action.[10] But this does not mean that any threat to do that which is lawful will constitute duress, because the nature of the demand must be balanced against what is threatened and it may require a particularly unconscionable threat of lawful action to tip the scales. For example, it has been argued that the threat of lawful action should be malicious and unrelated to any legitimate interest and be intended only to acquire the thing demanded.[11]

(iii) Duress as a tort

Although the main issue is whether a threat amounting to economic duress constitutes the commission of a tort, it should be noted that a threat of a personal nature may also amount to a tort. If the threat causes a person, reasonably, to fear for his own safety, the tort of assault may have been committed. Moreover, less direct threats may amount to the tort of harassment under the Protection from Harassment Act 1997. For this Act to apply, there must have been conduct on at least two occasions which a reasonable person would regard as harassment.

---

4   As in *Dimskal Shipping Co SA v International Transport Workers Federation, The Evia Luck (No 2)* [1992] 1 Lloyd's Rep 115.

5   *Vantage Navigation Corpn v Suhail, The Alev* [1989] 1 Lloyd's Rep 138 at 146 (per HOBHOUSE J).

6   *Huyton SA v Peter Cremer GmbH & Co* [1999] 1 Lloyd's Rep 620.

7   Ibid (per HOBHOUSE J).

8   [1989] QB 833.

9   Dawson (1947) 45 Mich LR 253 at 287; *Smith v Charlick Ltd* (1924) 34 CLR 38 at 56 (per ISAACS J).

10   *The Universe Sentinel* [1983] 1 AC 366 at 401 (per LORD SCARMAN); *Dimskal Shipping Co SA v International Transport Workers Federation, The Evia Luck (No 2)* [1992] 1 Lloyd's Rep 115 at 121 (per LORD GOFF).

11   Beatson *The Use and Abuse of Unjust Enrichment* (1991) p 134.

The economic torts are intimately concerned with issues of fair and unfair trading. But what is unfair will often depend on what political position a commentator takes. While political policies may come and go, a decision of the House of Lords may stand for decades due to the doctrine of precedent.

An unlawful threat may constitute economic duress, but the fact that the threat is unlawful may also constitute the commission of the tort of intimidation. It has been seen that the effect of duress is to make a contract voidable, but if duress also amounts to the commission of a tort, an award of damages might be granted.

It has been said that a person who hinders another in his trade or livelihood is liable to an action.[12] But the principle has not taken root in English law. In particular, there are two decisions of the House of Lords, based firmly on the policy of freedom of competition, which have made the development of the economic torts very difficult.[13]

Despite the non-interventionist stance indicated above, it seems that an innominate tort of causing loss by unlawful means may be in the process of development[14] of which the specific economic torts such as inducement to breach of contract, conspiracy and intimidation are merely examples.[15] This would leave the courts with the daunting task of defining an unlawful act.[16] For these purposes, it is not sufficient that the defendant has acted unfairly, but it must be shown that he had an intention to do a wrongful act which would foreseeably injure the plaintiff.

It has been seen that duress consists of illegitimate pressure which will include threats of an unlawful nature, but whether this means that duress is a tort is a different matter. It may be that the threat of a debtor to pay nothing unless the creditor is willing to accept less than the amount he is owed constitutes intimidation.[17] Moreover, there are *dicta* in *Universe Tankships Inc of Monrovia v International Transport Workers Federation*[18] which seem to suggest an extension of the boundaries of the tort of intimidation. It was said that, if duress causes loss or damage to the victim, the duress is actionable as a tort.[19] Loss or damage can be caused without there being an intention to injure the plaintiff. Furthermore, if merely illegitimate, as opposed to unlawful pressure is sufficient to constitute duress, it would appear that the tort of intimidation might be committed in circumstances in which there is no unlawful act.

3. UNDUE PRESSURE AND UNDUE INFLUENCE

A contract or a gift may be set aside in equity on the grounds of influence expressly used by the donee for the purpose of securing a benefit, or where the relationship between the parties gives rise to a presumption of influence by the donee over the donor.[20] However, it should also be appreciated that there is a general reluctance on the part of the courts to exercise this discretionary power, since, in commercial transactions, proper regard should be had to the issue of commercial certainty.[1] Where the court does choose to intervene, it would appear to do so on grounds of substantive fairness of the result in a particular case, and does so in cases of undue pressure and

---

12   *Keeble v Hickeringill* (1706) 11 East 574n (per HOLT CJ).
13   *Allen v Flood* [1898] AC 1 (trade union threat of lawful industrial action not a tort); *Mogul Steamship Co v McGregor, Gow & Co* [1892] AC 25 (trade protectionism by trading association not a tort).
14   See Carty (1988) 104 LQR 250.
15   *Merkur Island Shipping Corpn v Laughton* [1983] 2 AC 570 at 608 (per LORD DIPLOCK).
16   See Elias and Ewing [1982] CLJ 321; Carty (1988) 104 LQR 250.
17   *D and C Builders Ltd v Rees* [1966] 2 QB 617 at 625 (per LORD DENNING MR).
18   [1982] 2 WLR 803.
19   Ibid at 828 (per LORD SCARMAN).
20   *Allcard v Skinner* (1887) 36 Ch D 145 at 171 (per COTTON LJ).
1   *Banco Exterior Internacional v Mann* [1995] 1 All ER 936 at 945 (per HOBHOUSE LJ).

undue influence. What seems to matter is the effect of the conduct of the party exerting or presumed to exert influence over the other. In some instances, the party exerting the influence may have a particular motive, but that motive is actually irrelevant in determining whether the court will grant relief.

Generally the influence exerted on the weaker party must be substantial, but need not amount to domination,[2] and there is no requirement that the weaker party should have blindly acquiesced in everything done by the other party.[3] Moreover, the mere existence of the required element of influence will suffice to allow a contract to be impugned. There is no need to prove the effect of the influence. This differs from the position so far as misrepresentation is concerned, since it is a legal requirement that a misrepresentation must induce the misrepresentee to enter into the contract with the misrepresentor.[4]

It should be noted, however, that the rules on undue influence operate on the basis of a presumption and that the defendant can rebut the presumption by showing that the claimant entered the contract freely and independently of any influence which might have been presumed to exist.

The varieties of undue influence have been classified in two separate groups, namely actual undue influence (class 1 undue influence) and presumed undue influence (class 2 undue influence).[5] The second of these is further divided into two sub-groups, namely, cases where the inference of undue influence arises from the class of relationship existing between the parties (class 2A) and cases in which the inference is drawn from the particular relationship between the parties (class 2B).

(1) ACTUAL UNDUE PRESSURE

A person seeking relief in equity in respect of alleged undue pressure is required to prove affirmatively[6] that the other party did exert undue influence on the weaker party so as to persuade the weaker party to enter into the transaction in respect of which relief is sought.[7] This onus of proof will require the person seeking relief to show that the transaction entered into is wrongful in the sense that the person seeking relief has been forced, tricked or misled into parting with property.[8] For the purposes of this particular category, it will not be possible for a court to draw an inference of influence from the relationship between the parties.

Equity has been prepared to intervene in cases in which the common law was not prepared to give relief. For example, a threat of lawful imprisonment[9] has been held sufficient to justify setting the contract aside on the ground of unfair and improper conduct, provided the influenced party had a legitimate interest in preventing the prosecution. It has also been held that there is actual undue influence where a husband uses 'moral blackmail' to persuade his wife that the continuation of their marriage depends on her entering into the impugned transaction.[10] Furthermore, cases of dependency may be found in other relationships. For example it has been held to amount to class 1

2   *Bank of Commerce and Credit International SA v Aboody* [1990] 1 QB 923 at 969 (per Slade LJ).
3   *Bank of Scotland v Bennett* [1997] 1 FLR 801.
4   See *Goldsworthy v Brickell* [1987] Ch 378.
5   *Barclays Bank plc v O'Brien* [1994] 1 AC 180 at 189 (per Lord Browne-Wilkinson).
6   See *Howes v Bishop* [1909] 2 KB 390.
7   *Barclays Bank plc v O'Brien* [1994] 1 AC 180 at 189 (per Lord Browne-Wilkinson).
8   *Allcard v Skinner* (1887) 36 Ch D 145 at 182–183 (per Lindley LJ).
9   *Williams v Bayley* (1866) LR 1 HL 200.
10   *Bank of Scotland v Bennett* [1997] 1 FLR 801.

undue influence for a young carer to threaten to cease caring for an elderly relative if that relative did not enter into the transaction under consideration.[11]

For the purposes of class 1 undue influence, it used to be a requirement that before relief could be granted, the party seeking relief had suffered some manifest disadvantage.[12] This requirement is troublesome in one respect. While it is understandable that the courts may wish to look for evidence of disadvantage when they are merely presuming undue influence, it is not so clear why this should be a requirement in cases of actual pressure. It has been argued that this insistence is at odds with the position in respect of other vitiating factors such as duress and misrepresentation where there is no requirement of manifest disadvantage.[13] In line with this criticism, the House of Lords has now held that in cases of actual pressure there is no requirement of 'manifest disadvantage.'[14] The reasoning underlying this change of direction seems to be that since the party against whom relief is sought has exerted actual pressure, his behaviour is unacceptable in using his improper influence to bring about the contract. As LORD BROWNE-WILKINSON observed in *CIBC Mortgages plc v Pitt*[15] actual undue influence is a species of fraud with the result that the party subject to that influence is entitled to have the transaction set aside as of right.[16]

As in the case of common law duress, the main difficulty is to determine what sort of pressure is not acceptable. For these purposes, it seems that there is no need to intend to cause detriment and there can be undue pressure even where the person applying the pressure believes he has acted in a justifiable manner.[17] What matters is whether the mind of the person subject to the pressure becomes nothing more than a channel through which the will of the other party operates.[18]

(2) PRESUMED UNDUE INFLUENCE

Undue influence may be presumed because of the type of relationship which exists between the parties (class 2A undue influence) or because the elements of the actual relationship between two people suggests that one of them has reposed trust and confidence in the other (class 2B undue influence). It has been suggested that the basis of relief is that one party has been guilty of the victimisation of the other,[19] although this requirement has been the subject of criticism. Nevertheless, the rule is based on the principle that the unconscionable behaviour of one party has led to his receipt of an unfair advantage or to the conferment of some advantage on another.

(i) Relationships to which the presumption applies

It has been asserted that there is no transaction to which the presumption of undue influence cannot apply.[20] But it is necessary to divide cases of presumed undue influence into two groups. First, there are those relationships to which it is readily assumed the presumption will apply, in the absence of evidence to the contrary (class 2A). This

---

11   *Langton v Langton* [1995] 2 FLR 890.
12   *Bank of Credit and Commerce International SA v Aboody* [1990] 1 QB 923 at 969–970 (per SLADE LJ).
13   Cartwright *Unequal Bargaining* (1991) p 176.
14   *CIBC Mortgages plc v Pitt* [1994] 1 AC 200.
15   Ibid.
16   Ibid at 209.
17   *Bank of Credit and Commerce International SA v Aboody* [1990] 1 QB 923 at 970 (per SLADE LJ).
18   Ibid at 969.
19   *National Westminster Bank plc v Morgan* [1985] AC 686 at 706 (per LORD SCARMAN).
20   *Goldsworthy v Brickell* [1987] 1 All ER 853 at 865 (per NOURSE LJ).

group appears to include the relationship between religious adviser and disciple,[1] doctor and patient,[2] guardian and ward,[3] trustee and beneficiary,[4] solicitor and client[5] and parent and child.[6] So far as the parent/child relationship is concerned, it is likely that such influence as exists will dissipate when the child reaches the age of 21 or perhaps 18 in modern circumstances. Moreover, it is clear that the roles may become reversed in later life, so that the emancipated child is able to exert influence over an ageing parent, although such cases are likely to be treated as falling within class 2B.[7]

The second group of cases (class 2B) requires a close analysis of the nature of the relationship. As has been observed, judicially, there must be a 'meticulous examination of the facts' before it can be classified as one to which the presumption of undue influence will apply.[8]

Generally, cases falling within class 2B require the party seeking relief to have reposed trust and confidence in the wrongdoer before the presumption will apply.[9] The types of relationship to which the presumption has been held to apply have included young employee and charming employer,[10] naïve customer and bank manager,[11] elderly man and younger neighbour,[12] elderly lady and her niece,[13] wife and husband[14] and fiancée and fiancé.[15] It should be noted that merely because a particular relationship has been recognised as falling within class B on a particular occasion, it will not follow that all such relationships will be treated in the same way. The important consideration is the particular relationship in a given case. Thus it has been held that the presumption does not apply to the ordinary relationship of employer and employee,[16] that of husband and wife, where there has been a lack of influence[17] or that of parent and emancipated child.[18]

At one time, it was assumed that the husband/wife relationship would fall within class 2A, but that is no longer the case. It is clear, following *Barclays Bank plc v O'Brien*, that the husband/wife relationship should not, automatically, lead to a presumption that influence has been exercised by one partner over the other. Nevertheless, it has been observed that the courts have always shown a 'special tenderness' towards wives on the ground that 'the sexual and emotional ties' that exist between the parties to a marriage provide a 'ready weapon for undue influence'.[19] Plainly, the same can also be said of other 'partnership' relations, in which case the presumption can also be applied to unmarried partners,[20] including a young man who was no longer living under the same roof as his more dominant elder brother.[1]

---

1   *Allcard v Skinner* (1887) 36 Ch D 145.
2   *Dent v Bennett* (1839) 4 My & Cr 269.
3   *Taylor v Johnston* (1882) 19 Ch D 603.
4   *Beningfield v Baxter* (1886) 12 App Cas 167.
5   *Wright v Carter* [1903] 1 Ch 27.
6   *Bullock v Lloyds Bank* [1955] Ch 317.
7   See *Avon Finance Co Ltd v Bridger* [1985] 2 All ER 281 (son a chartered accountant); *Mahoney v Purnell* [1996] 3 All ER 61 (son-in-law/ father-in-law).
8   *National Westminster Bank plc v Morgan* [1985] AC 686 at 709 (per LORD SCARMAN).
9   *Barclays Bank plc v O'Brien* [1994] 1 AC 180 at 190 (per LORD BROWNE-WILKINSON).
10 *Crédit Lyonnais v Burch* [1997] 1 All ER 144.
11 *Barclays Bank plc v O'Brien* [1994] 1 AC 180.
12 *Goldsworthy v Brickell* [1987] 1 All ER 853.
13 *Re Craig* [1971] Ch 95.
14 *Barclays Bank plc v O'Brien* [1994] 1 AC 180 at 190 (per LORD BROWNE-WILKINSON).
15 *Zamet v Hyman* [1961] 1 WLR 1442.
16 *Matthew v Bobbins* [1980] 2 EGLR 97.
17 *Howes v Bishop* [1909] 2 KB 390.
18 *Bainbridge v Browne* (1881) 18 Ch D 188. See also *Lancashire Loans Ltd v Black* [1934] 1 KB 380.
19 *Barclays Bank plc v O'Brien* [1994] 1 AC 180 at 190–191 (per LORD BROWNE-WILKINSON).
20 *Massey v Midland Bank plc* [1995] 1 All ER 929.
1   *Bank of Baroda v Shah* [1988] 3 All ER 24.

The presumption may apply to any relationship, provided the necessary degree of trust and confidence can be found. In *Lloyds Bank Ltd v Bundy*,[2] four guidelines were established to indicate the circumstances in which a relationship might be subject to the presumption.[3] The relationship is usually one in which one person relies on the advice or guidance of another; the person giving the advice or guidance is aware of that reliance; the person relied upon will usually obtain some benefit or have some interest in the conclusion of the transaction, and the relationship is one of confidence out of which influence naturally grows. In *Bundy*, the defendant was an elderly farmer whose son's business was in financial difficulty. He had already guaranteed his son's debts to the extent of £7,500, securing the guarantee on his own house. A representative of the bank advised the defendant that the bank could only continue to support the son's business if the defendant would increase the charge on his house to £11,000. The defendant's position was not explained to him by the bank, nor did the defendant obtain any independent advice. The Court of Appeal held that the defendant had placed confidence in the bank and that, since it was in the interest of the bank that the guarantee should be executed, the transaction could be set aside.

The decision in *Bundy* should not be taken to mean that the relationship of banker and customer will always be classified as one of confidence and trust. Indeed, *Bundy* has been referred to as a special case which turned on its own facts.[4] It would appear that, normally, the banker/customer relationship is not one of confidentiality, and that the presumption of undue influence does not apply. In *National Westminster Bank plc v Morgan*,[5] the respondent's husband's business was in deep financial trouble and he was unable to keep up payments due under the mortgage on the family home. The bank agreed to refinance the debt in order to avoid threatened foreclosure by the original mortgagees. The bank took a legal charge on the property. The respondent only agreed to this after having been assured by the bank that the arrangement covered no more than the amount of the original loan. In fact, this assurance was inaccurate, as the mortgage extended to cover all of the husband's liabilities to the bank. However, no further liabilities were incurred. The husband died, and the question arose whether the mortgage could be set aside on the ground of undue influence. In the circumstances, it was held that the bank had not crossed the line which distinguished a normal business relationship from one in which the bank was able to exert influence over their customer.

In other cases, it is necessary to determine how great is the confidence placed by one person in another. For example, the necessary relationship may exist between an ageing farmer and his neighbour where the neighbour agrees to take a tenancy and does so on terms highly advantageous to himself, with apparently little given in return.[6] Likewise, an impressionable young performer may be able to rely on the presumption where he engages a manager on terms which are very one-sided in favour of the manager.[7]

While the formulation in *Bundy* concentrates on the degree of trust reposed in the defendant by the claimant, a more controversial suggestion is that the principle is capable of extending to onerous contract terms, in general.[8] Thus in *Credit Lyonnais v Burch*[9] it was observed that there might be circumstances in which a person could have a contract

2   [1975] QB 326. See Carr (1975) 38 MLR 463; Sealy [1975] CLJ 17.
3   Ibid at 347 (per Sir Eric Sachs) approved in *National Westminster Bank plc v Morgan* [1985] AC 686 at 709 (per Lord Scarman).
4   *National Westminster Bank plc v Morgan* [1985] AC 686 at 698 (per Lord Scarman).
5   Ibid.
6   *Goldsworthy v Brickell* [1987] 1 All ER 853.
7   *O'Sullivan v Management Agency and Music Ltd* [1985] QB 428.
8   See *Crédit Lyonnais Bank Nederland v Burch* [1997] 1 All ER 144 at 152–153 (per Millett LJ).
9   Ibid.

set aside on the ground that its terms were harsh and oppressive and that the other party had imposed those terms in a 'morally reprehensible manner.'

(ii) Domination

In *National Westminster Bank plc v Morgan*,[10] it was held that one reason why the respondent should not succeed was that the bank had not exercised a dominating influence over her. While it is true that domination may be a relevant factor, it is not the only matter to be considered. In *Goldsworthy v Brickell*,[11] it was held that the relationship between two people can produce an abuse of confidence which falls short of domination and that, in such cases, the presumption can still apply.[12] However, if the evidence shows that the transaction would have been entered into regardless of the influence of the other party, then it is unlikely that relief will be granted.[13]

The requirement of domination has been criticised. One view is that in *Morgan*, LORD SCARMAN was over-influenced by the decision in *Poosathurai v Kannappa Chettiar*[14] which was specifically based on the content of the Indian Contract Act 1872, section 16. That provision specifically refers to a requirement of domination, but such a requirement has been specifically rejected in the English Court of Appeal.[15]

(iii) Manifest disadvantage

In *National Westminster Bank plc v Morgan*,[16] the purpose of intervention on the ground of presumed undue influence (classes 2A and 2B) was said to be to prevent the victimisation of one party by the other. This requires proof that the transaction entered into is to the manifest disadvantage of the person seeking relief.[17] In *Morgan* the transaction was advantageous to the respondent because it served to save her from losing the matrimonial home. It is important to distinguish between gifts and commercial transactions. In the case of a gift, the disadvantage is plain to see and does not have to be proved since the donor has given away something of his own. This remains the case where the gift is small.[18] But in commercial transactions like *Morgan*, no immediate disadvantage may be discernible. It is necessary for the person seeking to invoke the presumption of undue influence to prove that he has suffered some disadvantage in order to justify intervention.

What constitutes a sufficient disadvantage is not wholly clear. It has been seen that in the case of a substantial gift, there is immediate evidence of disadvantage, but it would appear that the requirement of manifest disadvantage can be satisfied in other ways. For example, it may be that the party seeking relief has paid for a benefit at too high a price. In *Cheese v Thomas*[19] it was held that there had to be a 'clear and obvious' disadvantage to the party claiming relief.[20] Thus in *Cheese,* the claimant, aged 80, jointly purchased a house together with his great nephew, who intended to occupy the property with the

---

10   [1985] AC 686.
11   [1987] 1 All ER 853.
12   Ibid at 868 (per NOURSE LJ).
13   *Bank of Credit and Commerce International SA v Aboody* [1990] 1 QB 923 at 971 (per SLADE LJ).
14   (1919) LR 47 Ind App 1.
15   *Goldsworthy v Brickell* [1987] 1 All ER 853. See also *Barclays Bank plc v Coleman* [2000] 1 All ER 385 at 398 (per NOURSE LJ).
16   [1985] AC 686.
17   Ibid at 706 (per LORD SCARMAN).
18   *Bank of Credit and Commerce International SA v Aboody* [1990] 1 QB 923 at 958–959 (per SLADE LJ).
19   [1994] 1 All ER 35.
20   Ibid at 39 (per NICHOLLS V-C. See also *Barclays Bank plc v Coleman* [2000] 1 All ER 385 at 399 (per NOURSE LJ).

old man. The claimant paid half the purchase price, the remainder being secured on a mortgage acquired by the great nephew. Unknown to the claimant, the terms of the mortgage were such that, in the event of default, both occupants could be ejected. The Court of Appeal concluded that the terms of the contract were manifestly disadvantageous to the claimant on the basis that he had used up all of his money in acquiring a right which was seriously insecure and which tied him to the property in question.[1]

It has been seen that the requirement of manifest disadvantage does not apply to cases of class 1 undue pressure. Moreover, the requirement in relation to class 2 cases has also been doubted (obiter) on the ground that other varieties of equitable relief are not subject to a similar requirement.[2] It should also be noted that no English case prior to the decision in *Morgan* has insisted that English law requires proof of manifest disadvantage. In the light of this criticism, it may be that the House of Lords will be called upon, at some future stage, to rule on the correctness of the decision in *Morgan* in relation to cases of class 2 presumed undue influence. Moreover, the Court of Appeal in *Barclays Bank plc v Coleman*[3] has taken the view that for disadvantage to be 'manifest' it must be clear and obvious and has to be more than just *de minimis*, but that does not mean that it has to be large or even medium-sized.[4] In *Coleman* the claimant's husband acquired a property using a loan secured on the matrimonial home in which the claimant had an interest. The charge over the matrimonial home extended to all moneys owed by the husband to the bank, including future borrowings. As a result, unknown to the claimant, her interest in the matrimonial home was seriously prejudiced. This was held to be sufficient to constitute a manifest disadvantage, although the claimant's action failed for other reasons related to the nature of the legal advice she had received prior to entering into the transaction.

(iv) Vicarious undue influence[5]

In some instances, influence may be exerted by someone other than the person with whom the contract is made. This may often happen where a relative of the person seeking relief has acted on behalf of the lender of money. Here the question is whether the person for whose benefit the contract is made can be in any better position than the person who exerts influence. In *Chaplin v Brammall*,[6] the defendant's husband was left to persuade her to guarantee debts owed by the husband to the plaintiff. Since the defendant was not independently advised and, since her husband was regarded as the agent of the plaintiff, the latter was deemed to be aware of the techniques of persuasion used to secure the defendant's agreement. The rule can also apply to other relationships, such as parent and emancipated child.[7] For the agency principle to apply, the lender does not need to be aware of the method intended to be used by his agent to procure the agreement of the debtor.[8] However, the creditor will only be liable for the acts of someone deemed to be his agent, with the result that he will not be liable for unauthorised intervention.[9] In such a case, the unconscionable conduct of the intermediary will not be regarded as the conduct of the creditor. The difficulty is to decide where the line is to be drawn, and on this the cases are not clear. It appears that

---

1   Ibid.
2   See *CIBC Mortgages plc v Pitt* [1994] 1 AC 200 at 209 (per LORD BROWNE-WILKINSON).
3   [2000] 1 All ER 385.
4   Ibid at 399 (per NOURSE LJ).
5   See MacDonald (1990) JBL 469; Chandler (1991) JBL 333.
6   [1908] 1 KB 233.
7   See *Avon Finance Co Ltd v Bridger* [1985] 2 All ER 281.
8   *Kingsnorth Trust Ltd v Bell* [1986] 1 All ER 423.
9   *Coldunnell Ltd v Gallon* [1986] 1 All ER 429.

there is no duty to ensure that independent advice has been received. Moreover a person is not to be regarded as an agent simply because he has been left to secure the signature of the party claiming relief.[10] The use of the notion of agency in undue influence cases has proved highly artificial and, in the absence of a contractual or ostensible authority, this artificial concept should be abandoned.[11] Conversely, it appears that there is still some strength left in the policy argument that especially vulnerable people should be afforded protection.[12] It follows that if a creditor knows of the relationship between the debtor and the surety and has failed to take reasonable steps to ensure that the surety's consent is true and informed, the transaction may be set aside. It seems that there is a duty to ensure that the surety is given an understandable explanation of the precise effect of relatively straightforward transactions in circumstances in which the surety is the victim of undue pressure, material misrepresentation or otherwise lacks an adequate understanding of the transaction entered into.[13]

An important feature in cases of vicarious undue influence is that the contract in respect of which relief is sought is between the person exerting the influence and another party (usually a bank or other financial institution). If the contract was between the person exerting the influence and the party seeking relief, it is unnecessary that the latter is aware of the influence of the other, but the same is not true of cases in which a party seeks relief in respect of a contract made with a third party. In these cases of vicarious undue influence, an important requirement is that the party against whom relief is sought has notice of the undue influence. The important factor in such cases is that the party against whom relief is sought was sufficiently aware of the possibility of influence and has failed to do anything about it.[14]

In *Britannia Building Society v Pugh*[15] a husband and wife team of property developers borrowed over £1 million, which was partly secured on their matrimonial home. The wife later sought to have the transaction set aside, so far as it related to the matrimonial home, on the ground that her husband had exerted undue influence of which the lenders could be taken to be aware. She relied on the facts that the amount of the loan was more than twice the value of the matrimonial home and that the development business was primarily that of her husband. Accordingly it was argued that the Building Society had notice of the 'possible existence' of undue influence. This line of argument was rejected on the basis that in the 1980s it could not be said that just because a husband takes the lead in the running of a family business there should be an automatic inference that he might exert improper pressure on his wife.[16] Accordingly, so far as the lenders were concerned, it could not be said that they had notice that the transaction amounted to any more than a normal advance of money to a husband and wife for their joint benefit. To arrive at any other conclusion would result in banks and building societies having to make arrangements to meet all wives separately from their husbands so as to advise her of the nature of any transaction involving the creation of a charge over a matrimonial house.[17] What seems to matter is whether the nature of the relationship between the parties is such that it is capable of developing into one of trust and confidence or if the transaction entered into is extravagantly improvident, such that

---

10   *Barclays Bank plc v O'Brien* [1992] 4 All ER 983 at 1009 (per SCOTT LJ). See also Berg (1993) LMCLQ 101.
11   *Barclays Bank plc v O'Brien* [1992] 4 All ER 983 at 1013 (per PURCHAS LJ).
12   Ibid at 1008 (per SCOTT LJ).
13   Ibid.
14   See *Banco Exterior Internacional v Mann* [1995] 1 All ER 936 at 944 (per MORRITT LJ).
15   [1997] 2 FLR 7.
16   Ibid at 20 (per WARD LJ).
17   *CIBC Mortgages plc v Pitt* [1994] 1 AC 200 at 211 (per LORD BROWNE-WILKINSON).

the third party may be taken to have notice of the possibility of influence by one party over the other.[18]

(v) Rebutting the presumption of undue influence

The presumption of undue influence is rebuttable. If it can be shown that the person alleging undue influence has gone into the transaction with his eyes open, it will not be unconscionable to enforce the arrangement he has made. The easiest way of establishing that a person has made the contract with a free and independent mind is to show that he has received advice from another person, although this will not always be the case. For example, there have been instances in which a court has observed that whatever advice might have been received, the character of the person to whom the advice was given was such that he probably would have ignored it.[19]

Where advice is taken, it seems that the person claiming relief must have had the nature and consequences of his proposed actions explained to him.[20] In such a case, any influence which might have been presumed has not affected the decision to enter into the contract.[1] If the advice given is not independent the presumption will not be upset. This may occur where a solicitor acting for the person exercising influence also advises the person seeking relief.[2]

The absence of advice is not necessarily fatal, since the influence of the other party may be weak, or there may be some other reason, independent of the influence, which has persuaded a person to make a contract.

Where advice is taken, it must have been given by someone who is independent and technically qualified to give that advice. For these purposes, independence does not mean that the adviser cannot be the agent of, for example, the lender of money or the person alleged to have exerted the influence. Thus, there have been cases in which a solicitor acting on behalf of the lender or the person exerting influence has been regarded as independent, since the solicitor ceases to be the agent of the person employing him and owes a duty to the signatory alone.[3] This view, may, however, be questionable, since a solicitor employed by the lender has been delegated the duty of giving independent advice with the result that the lender becomes responsible for the discharge of that duty.[4]

The requirement of technical competence may raise interesting questions, such as whether the adviser must be a fully qualified lawyer. In *Barclays Bank plc v Coleman*[5] the relevant advice was tendered by a legal executive rather than a solicitor. The Court of Appeal had regard for the realities of a modern legal practice and concluded that legal advice had, nonetheless, been given, provided it was given with the authority of the legal executives principal. Provided this advice was given from the relevant practice address, it could be assumed that the legal executive had been authorised to act in the way he did. Accordingly, in *Coleman,* independent legal advice had been given which led to the conclusion that the lending bank did not have constructive notice of the wife's rights in relation to the matrimonial home subject to their charge. Other factors to consider will include the extent of the adviser's knowledge of all material

---

18 *Crédit Lyonnais Bank Nederland NV v Burch* [1997] 1 All ER 144 at 154–155 (per MILLETT LJ).
19 See *Re Brocklehurst* [1978] Ch 14.
20 *Re Coomber* [1911] 1 Ch 723 at 729–730.
1   See *Inche Noriah v Shaik Allie Bin Omar* [1929] AC 127 at 135.
2   See *Powell v Powell* [1900] 1 Ch 243.
3   *Barclays Bank plc v Thompson* [1997] 1 FLR 156 at 166 (per SIMON BROWN LJ). Cf *Royal Bank of Scotland v Etridge* [1997] 3 All ER 628.
4   *Royal Bank of Scotland v Etridge* [1997] 3 All ER 628 at 635 (per HOBHOUSE LJ).
5   [2000] 1 All ER 385.

circumstances. Thus there may be instances in which the adviser is unaware of important facts relating to the transaction, in which case, his advice may not be sufficiently informed to displace the presumption of undue influence.[6]

Plainly, the advice given must relate to the nature of the document to be signed, but the advice may have to go further before it can be classified as fully independent.[7] In particular, it may be necessary for the adviser to be aware of the possibility that influence could be exercised so that advice can be given as to the extent of liability and the degree of risk undertaken.[8]

An additional relevant factor is the extent to which the party against whom relief is sought has taken steps to encourage the other party to seek advice. If no such steps are taken, it might be readily assumed that the lender may still have reasonable grounds for suspecting that influence has been exerted.[9] Moreover, there are judicial suggestions that a bank ought to persuade the party who might be subject to influence to attend a private meeting, in the absence of the party who could assert influence, at which the extent of possible liability is explained and at which the importance of taking independent legal advice is emphasised.[10]

There may be circumstances in which the party seeking relief does not seek independent advice and the lending bank is aware of this. In such circumstances, the bank comes under an obligation to insist that advice is taken.[11] Mere encouragement to seek advice will not rebut the presumption that the bank remains aware that the other party may not have contracted with an independent mind. Thus in *Midland Bank plc v Kidwai*[12] the bank arranged a private meeting with the claimant, and advised her of the importance of seeking independent advice. Despite this, the claimant was prepared to sign the document at the meeting, indicating to the bank that they were aware that she had not been independently advised. It followed that the bank could not assert that they believed she had entered the transaction with an independent mind. However, the court concluded that, on the facts, the claimant was sufficiently aware of the nature of the transaction and dismissed her claim for relief. Unfortunately it is difficult to follow the reasoning, since the court also expressed the view that any advice given by the bank could not be regarded as independent.[13] As a result, it would seem to follow that the bank had not discharged their duty to ensure that the claimant entered the transaction with an independent mind. In contrast, if the claimant has received clear advice, but chooses to ignore it, he cannot later be heard to complain. Thus in *Crédit Lyonnais Bank Nederland NV v Burch*[14] the fact that the claimant had received two letters from a solicitor advising that the relevant security was unlimited in terms of time and amount, both of which she ignored, was regarded as sufficient to displace the presumption of undue influence.

Where advice has been sought, the advice given must satisfy certain criteria. In *Royal Bank of Scotland plc v Etridge*[15] a number of rules of guidance were laid down, so that, provided they are followed, the transaction only stands to be impugned if its terms are so harsh and unconscionable that no reasonable legal adviser could advise the claimant

---

6   See *Inche Noriah v Sheik Allie bin Omar* [1929] AC 127 (failure to appreciate that the gift encompassed the whole of the donor's property).
7   *Banco Exterior Internacional v Mann* [1995] 1 All ER 936 at 947 (per HOBHOUSE LJ).
8   *Barclays Bank plc v O'Brien* [1994] 1 AC 180 at 196–197 (per LORD BROWNE-WILKINSON).
9   *Crédit Lyonnais Bank Nederland NV v Burch* [1997] 1 All ER 144 at 156 (per MILLETT LJ).
10 *Barclays Bank plc v O'Brien* [1994] 1 AC 180 at 196 (per LORD BROWNE-WILKINSON). Cf *Royal Bank of Scotland v Etridge (No 2)* [1998] 2 FLR 843.
11 *Crédit Lyonnais Bank Nederland NV v Burch* [1997] 1 All ER 144 at 156 (per SWINTON THOMAS LJ).
12 [1995] 4 Bank LR 227.
13 Ibid at 307–308 (per MORRITT LJ).
14 [1997] 1 All ER 144.
15 [1997] 3 All ER 628.

to go through with it. The guidelines provide that if the claimant has dealt with the bank through the medium of a solicitor, whether acting for the claimant alone or for the claimant and the party who might exert influence, it can be assumed that the solicitor has considered the possibility of a conflict of interest and has advised accordingly.[16] For these purposes, it makes no difference whether the solicitor is acting on behalf of both the claimant and, for example, her husband, since it can be assumed that the solicitor will regard himself as being under a duty to advise the claimant appropriately.[17] From this, it follows that the bank will not be taken to have imputed knowledge of what the solicitor learns from the claimant in the course of the interview, since he is acting in the capacity as the claimant's legal adviser.[18] Secondly, if there is evidence that the claimant is not represented by a solicitor, it will suffice if the bank has urged the claimant to seek independent advice before entering into the transaction.[19] Thirdly, the bank is entitled to assume that because the solicitor has undertaken the task of advising the claimant of the nature of the transaction, he regards himself as an independent adviser. Accordingly, there will be no need for the bank to question the issue of independence, even where the solicitor also acts on behalf of the person in a position to exert influence.[20] Fourthly, the bank cannot be expected to question the value of the advice given, so that even if the solicitor is asked only to explain the nature of the transaction and not to ensure that the claimant was sufficiently independent of the party capable of exerting influence, the bank will not be fixed with constructive notice. Moreover, if the solicitor confirms that he has explained the nature of the transaction, but does not confirm that the claimant understood it, this will not be taken as evidence sufficient to support the view that the bank has constructive notice of the claimant's rights.[1] In contrast, if the solicitor is asked to explain the nature of the transaction to the claimant, but fails to confirm that he has done so, this should put the bank on guard, creating the risk that the transaction may be set aside at a later date.[2] A final possibility is that the claimant is made fully aware of the nature of a particular transaction at its outset, but fails to receive independent advice on a later occasion when the extent of possible liability is increased. In these circumstances, the courts have taken the view that they may apply the doctrine of severance, familiar in the case of the doctrine of restraint of trade. Accordingly, it is possible that the lending bank may be taken to have no notice of the claimant's rights in relation to the initial transaction, but may have constructive notice of those rights on a later occasion if the claimant has failed to received the advice necessary to fully inform him on that later occasion.[3]

Sometimes, the fact that independent advice has been taken may not suffice to remove the possibility that the lending bank is charged with constructive notice of the claimant's rights. This may be the case where the evidence of undue influence is very strong, to the extent that even if the claimant is given advice, he may not have regard for it. In *Crédit Lyonnais Bank Nederland NV v Burch*[4] there was strong evidence of influence by an employer over a junior employee, which was accentuated by the onerous nature of the terms of the contract. In the circumstances, the judge was prepared to accept that if the transaction was concluded, it was because the claimant had not been

16   See *Bank of Baroda v Reyerel* [1995] 2 FLR 376.
17   *Barclays Bank plc v Thompson* [1997] 1 FLR 156.
18   *Halifax Mortgage Services Ltd v Stepsky* [1996] 2 All ER 277.
19   *Massey v Midland Bank plc* [1995] 1 All ER 929.
20   *Banco Exterior Internacional v Mann* [1995] 1 All ER 936.
1   *Royal Bank of Scotland plc v Etttridge* [1997] 3 All ER 628 at 635 (per HOBHOUSE LJ). See also *Cooke v National Westminster Bank plc* [1998] 2 FLR 783.
2   *Cooke v National Westminster Bank plc* [1998] 2 FLR 783.
3   *Barclays Bank plc v Caplan* [1998] 1 FLR 532. But cf *Dunbar Bank plc v Nadeem* [1998] 2 FLR 457.
4   [1997] 1 All ER 144.

properly advised or because, despite receiving advice, the employer had influenced her to ignore the advice she had received.

4. UNCONSCIONABLE BARGAINS

(1) EQUITABLE RELIEF

A further group of cases may justify equitable intervention to achieve a fair result where one party is in a position to exploit the weakness of the other. For example, an agreement made with an expectant heir[5] in anticipation of his expectancy can be set aside. It is not sufficient that the expectancy is sold at an undervalue,[6] but if the undervalue is so gross as to constitute fraud, the transaction may be set aside.[7]

Transactions in which advantage has been taken of a poor or ignorant person or any other person in need of special protection may also be set aside. In *Cresswell v Potter*,[8] a wife, in the course of divorce proceedings, transferred her interest in the matrimonial home for an inadequate consideration. As she had not been advised, the transaction could be set aside since advantage was taken.

(2) BARS TO EQUITABLE RELIEF

In all cases in which equitable relief may be granted, including unconscionable bargains, cases of alleged undue influence and possibly duress, a number of bars may prevent relief.

A person who expressly or impliedly[9] affirms a contract may be denied relief. A similar result may obtain where the party seeking relief has acquiesced by giving an unequivocal representation that a right will not be enforced, with the intention that the representation be relied on and that the other party has acted to his detriment upon the representation.[10] The bar is apparently a variety of promissory estoppel.

Equitable relief can also be denied if it is impossible to restore the parties to the position they were in before the contract was made. Although precise restitution may not be possible, rescission may still be granted if a practical and just solution can be achieved. Third-party rights are also relevant since the grant of equitable relief must not affect rights already accrued.[11]

(3) CONSUMER PROTECTION

Much modern consumer protection legislation is designed to counteract the effect of an inequality of bargaining power on the part of consumers. In the field of consumer credit law, the courts have a power to re-open an agreement on the ground that it constitutes an extortionate credit bargain. A bargain is extortionate if it requires payments which are grossly exorbitant or if the bargain grossly contravenes ordinary principles of fair dealing.[12]

---

5   *Earl of Aylesford v Morris* (1873) 8 Ch App 484.
6   Law of Property Act 1925, s 174.
7   *Fry v Lane* (1888) 40 Ch D 312.
8   [1978] 1 WLR 255n. Cf *Backhouse v Backhouse* [1978] 1 All ER 1158, [1978] 1 WLR 243.
9   For example by inaction. See *The Atlantic Baron* [1979] QB 705.
10   *Goldsworthy v Brickell* [1987] 1 All ER 853 at 872–873 (per NOURSE LJ).
11   See *Coldunell Ltd v Gallon* [1986] 1 All ER 429; *Bainbrigge v Browne* (1881) 18 Ch D 188.
12   Consumer Credit Act 1974, s 138(1).

5. JUDICIAL AND STATUTORY CONTROL OF UNFAIR CONTRACT TERMS

(1) INTRODUCTION

The use of exclusion clauses and other unfair terms, especially in consumer contracts may produce a substantively unfair result, particularly where the contractual term operates in favour of a business. For this reason, the courts, Parliament and the European Community, have intervened in order to ensure that exclusion clauses and other varieties of contractual term in consumer contracts are not unreasonable or unconscionable or contrary to the requirement of good faith.

Judicial techniques, in relation to exemption clauses, have tended to rely on the process of interpretation, but it has been admitted that the driving force behind these techniques of interpretation is a test of reasonableness.[13] Much of the need for this apparent judicial subterfuge has gone with the open provision for a test of reasonableness in the Unfair Contract Terms Act 1977. Moreover, the Unfair Terms in Consumer Contracts Regulations 1999[14] introduce important restrictions on the use of a much wider range of terms in consumer contracts and give the power to object to the use of such terms to not just Government organisations, but also those concerned with the representation of consumers.[15]

The Unfair Contract Terms Act 1977 applies to both consumer contracts and to contracts between businessmen and renders some contract terms totally invalid while others are subject to a requirement of reasonableness. It may be reasonable to exercise control over exclusion clauses in consumer contracts where there is likely to be disparate bargaining power, but the same approach is not necessarily applicable to all business contracts and may produce unacceptable levels of uncertainty and an economically inefficient result. In contrast, the Unfair Terms in Consumer Contracts Regulations 1999[16] apply only to consumer contracts in the circumstances specified in the Regulations.

Efficiency evaluation of a rule is based on the assumption that there is a perfectly competitive market, and that participants in market transactions are roughly equal in terms of bargaining power. Bargaining power is not always equal, and a firm in a monopoly position may choose to incorporate exclusion clauses in its standard contract terms which primarily serve its own interests to the prejudice of contracting parties in a weaker position. Exclusion clauses used in this way are instruments of consumer oppression.[17] But exclusion clauses are also useful tools of commercial convenience.[18] A business will deal with large numbers of customers and suppliers, and it may not make sense to negotiate a fresh contract on each occasion. The use of standard form contracts containing exclusion clauses reduces transaction costs by dispensing with the need for experienced negotiators, by obviating the need for repeated drafting of contracts and by placing the process of concluding a contract in the hands of junior personnel who do not need drafting and negotiation skills.[19] In this light, exclusion clauses are often reasonable means of allocating risks. To subject all such clauses to a requirement of reasonableness may have the effect of producing uncertainties which are not warranted in the circumstances.

---

13   *Gillespie Bros & Co Ltd v Roy Bowles Transport Ltd* [1973] QB 400 at 415 (per LORD DENNING MR).
14   SI 1999/2083.
15   See Unfair Terms in Consumer Contracts Regulations 1999 (SI 1999/2083) regs 11 & 12 and Sch 1.
16   SI 1999/2083.
17   *Yates* p 2.
18   Ibid.
19   Macaulay (1966) 19 Vanderbilt LR 1051. See also Trebilcock 'An Economic Approach to Unconscionability' in *Studies in Contract Law* (eds Reiter and Swan) (1981) pp 381–421.

(2) JUDICIAL CONSTRUCTION OF EXCLUSION CLAUSES

The types of exclusion employed by contractual draftsmen are numerous,[20] ranging from the outright exclusion of liability to terms which seek to restrict the remedies available to the other party and those which seek to define the obligations of the parties. It should be appreciated that the varieties of exclusion will increase as the courts develop techniques to deal with known standard terms. The common law method of controlling exclusion clauses is the weapon of interpretation. A document containing an exclusion may be regarded as non-contractual or the court may say that insufficient notice has been given to incorporate the exclusion in the contract.[1] A further interpretative device includes enquiring whether the clause, as drafted, covers the breach of contract under consideration.

(i) Primary and secondary obligations

The conventional view of an exclusion clause is that it serves as a shield to liability in damages or for repudiation of the contract. As such, it relates to a secondary obligation under the contract, for example the obligation to pay damages in the event of breach of one of the primary obligations of the contract. Viewed in this way, the contract will be construed so as to determine what was agreed, and the exclusion clause will be construed separately to determine whether it applies to the primary obligations of the *proferens*. However, such a view of exclusion clauses can be misleading. Undoubtedly, there are many exclusion clauses which do serve to excuse a person from liability in the event of a breach of a primary obligation, but there are others which serve to define that which has been promised.[2] For example, in *Photo Production Ltd v Securicor Transport Ltd*,[3] an employee of a security firm started a small fire which spread, thereby destroying a factory. The security firm relied on an exclusion clause which provided that under no circumstances were they to be responsible for any injurious act or default of any employee, unless that act or default could have been foreseen and avoided by the exercise of diligence. LORD WILBERFORCE found a breach of contract which was covered by the exclusion clause.[4] However, a different view of the clause was that it modified the terms of the promise, with the result that the security firm was offering a much lower standard of performance than might, at first, have been expected.[5]

Suppose X agrees to sell a blue Ford Focus 1600, but the contract provides that X accepts no responsibility should the car be of a different colour, model, make and engine capacity. If the seller delivers a white Rover 25, it is arguable that there is no breach of contract. The relevant provision is not an exclusion clause, but one that defines the extent of the undertaking by converting the promise to one to supply a car of any description.

(ii) Strict interpretation

A person who seeks to rely on an exclusion clause will be able to do so only if it covers the breach of contract complained of. If the clause is interpreted strictly, it may be found not to cover the breach where the language used by the *proferens* is vague. The Unfair Terms in Consumer Contracts Regulations 1999 also contain a statutory version

---

20   See ch 22.
1   See also ch 22.
2   See *Yates* pp 123–133.
3   [1980] AC 827.
4   Ibid at 846.
5   Ibid at 851 (per LORD DIPLOCK).

of this common law rule of construction in as much as they provide that where there is doubt about the meaning of a written term, the interpretation which is most favourable to the consumer shall prevail.[6] However, it should be noted that these Regulations operate against the background of a general requirement of 'fairness' and it may be that the rule of strict interpretation will only apply to terms which are classified as unfair within the meaning of the Regulations.

In the process of interpretation it has been said that a distinction should be drawn between indemnity clauses and clauses purporting to exclude liability altogether on the one hand and, on the other hand, clauses seeking to limit or reduce the liability of the *proferens*. The House of Lords has observed that exclusion clauses and indemnity clauses which alter the primary obligations which would otherwise arise under the contract must be rigidly and strictly construed.[7] In contrast, a limitation clause which alters the *proferens'* secondary liability to pay damages in the event of a breach of contract should be given its natural meaning.[8] It is important that the court should not strain to read an ambiguity into a limitation clause where none exists. In *George Mitchell (Chesterhall) Ltd v Finney Lock Seeds Ltd*,[9] the defendants had supplied a quantity of cabbage seed which produced cabbages with no heart, with the result that the entire crop had to be ploughed into the ground. A clause in the contract limited the liability of the seller to a refund of the cost of the seed or to replacement of the seed. The plaintiffs claimed damages of £61,000, which represented their lost profits. In the Court of Appeal, it was held, applying the so-called 'peas and beans cases',[10] that what was delivered was not cabbage seed.[11] The House of Lords held that such a strained interpretation of a limitation clause was not warranted, and that, on a literal interpretation, the clause did serve to limit the liability of the sellers to either replacement of the seed or to a refund of the price. What had been delivered was defective seed, not the wrong seed altogether. How far this distinction should be maintained is difficult to see, since a clever draftsman should not have too much difficulty in creating a limitation clause which does not fall far short of amounting to an outright exclusion of the remedies available in the event of a breach of contract. It should be noted that the distinction drawn by the House of Lords has been rejected in Australia.[12] Moreover, at least one member of the House of Lords has impliedly expressed doubts as to the correctness of the decision by asserting that all contractual terms should be subject to 'common sense principles by which any serious utterance would be interpreted in ordinary life.'[13]

(iii) **The** *contra proferentem* **rule**

Ambiguities in the term of the contract on which the *proferens* seeks to rely will be construed against that person and in favour of the other party to the contract. For example, in *Houghton v Trafalgar Insurance*,[14] an insurance policy purported to exclude liability for damage caused while 'the vehicle is carrying a load in excess of that for which it is constructed'. A four-seater car was involved in an accident when it was carrying five people. The exclusion was held not to be effective because people do

---

6   UTCCR 1999, reg 7(2).
7   *Ailsa Craig Fishing Co Ltd v Malvern Fishing Co Ltd* [1983] 1 All ER 101 at 105 (per LORD FRASER).
8   Ibid. See also *George Mitchell (Chesterhall) Ltd v Finney Lock Seeds Ltd* [1983] 2 AC 803, [1983] 2 All ER 737.
9   Ibid.
10   See *Chanter v Hopkins* (1838) 4 M & W 399; *Smeaton Hanscomb & Co Ltd v Sassoon I Setty & Co* [1953] 1 WLR 1468.
11   [1983] QB 284 at 305–306 (per OLIVER LJ).
12   See *Darlington Futures Ltd v Delco Australia Pty* (1986) 68 ALR 385.
13   See *Investors Compensation Scheme v West Bromwich BS* [1998] 1 All ER 98 at 114 (per LORD HOFFMANN).
14   [1954] 1 QB 247.

not constitute a 'load'. Similarly, an exclusion clause in a written contract can be construed *contra proferentem* where the wording of the clause is not sufficiently clear to abrogate a separate oral collateral agreement.[15]

It has also been held that a clause which purports to exclude liability for a breach of warranty will not extend to cover liability for a breach of condition,[16] and a clause which seeks to exclude liability for a breach of the implied terms in a sale of goods contract will have no effect upon an express term of the contract.[17]

It is perhaps significant that most of the case law on the *contra proferentem* rule predates the passing of the Unfair Contract Terms Act 1977. Since that Act was passed, the courts have tended to frown on an over-strict interpretation of contractual terms.[18]

(iv) Exclusion of liability for negligence

An important aspect of the *contra proferentem* rule is that it may be used to prevent the use of a contract term as a means of limiting a source of liability other than a breach of the contract. This process of interpretation is particularly important where the alternative source of liability lies in the tort of negligence. While the purported exclusion of liability for negligence is now governed by statute,[19] judicial interpretation may serve to prevent the term from being relied upon at all.

In order to exclude liability for negligence, clear words must be used, since it is inherently improbable that one party to a contract should absolve the other from the consequences of his negligence.[20] Accordingly, the *proferens* can only be sure of success if he uses the word negligence, or some acceptable alternative, in the contract.[1] The difficulty with the express use of the word negligence in the terms of the contract is that this may have the effect of discouraging customers from entering into a contract.[2]

The more likely event is that a contract term will be drafted in more general language with the use of words such as 'no liability is accepted for loss or damage.' Ordinarily, language of this kind will not be sufficient to exclude liability for negligence. This is particularly the case where there is some alternative basis for liability. For example, in *White v John Warwick & Co Ltd*,[3] a contract for the hire of a bicycle purported to exclude the liability of the owner for personal injuries suffered by the hirer. The Court of Appeal held that the clause served only to exclude the contractual liability of the owner and did not extend to exclude liability in the tort of negligence. When dealing with the issue of excluding liability for negligence, a distinction can be drawn between cases where the only possible liability is for negligence and those cases in which there is some alternative basis of liability.

(a) *Proferens only liable for negligence* If the only possible liability of the *proferens* lies in the tort of negligence, the use of general words would appear to suffice. In *Alderslade v Hendon Laundry Ltd*,[4] the defendants laundered the plaintiff's handkerchiefs, but limited

---

15   *Webster v Higgin* [1948] 2 All ER 127; *J Evans & Son (Portsmouth) Ltd v Andrea Merzario Ltd* [1976] 2 All ER 930, [1976] 1 WLR 1078.

16   *Wallis, Son and Wells v Pratt and Haynes* [1911] AC 394.

17   *Andrews Bros (Bournemouth) Ltd v Singer & Co Ltd* [1934] 1 KB 17.

18   See eg *Photoproduction Ltd v Securicor Transport Ltd* [1980] AC 827 at 851 (per LORD DIPLOCK). See also *Thomas Witter Ltd v TBP Industries Ltd* [1996] 2 All ER 573 at 598 (per JACOB J).

19   See Unfair Contract Terms Act 1977, s 2.

20   *Gillespie Bros Ltd v Roy Bowles Transport Ltd* [1973] QB 400 at 419 (per LORD DENNING MR).

1   *Smith v South Wales Switchgear Ltd* [1978] 1 WLR 165 at 172 (per VISCOUNT DILHORNE)

2   *EE Caledonia Ltd v Orbit Valve plc* [1994] 2 Lloyd's Rep 239 at 246: "The draftsman on the underground ... would say 'one does not want to frighten off one or other of the parties'".

3   [1953] 2 All ER 1021.

4   [1945] KB 189.

their liability for lost or damaged articles to twenty times the cost of laundering. It was held that the defendants' only duty was to exercise reasonable care in keeping the handkerchiefs in safe custody. Accordingly, the limitation clause would have been redundant if it were to be held to apply to liability other than that for negligence. This decision was taken to mean that, wherever the only possible liability is for negligence, a generally worded exclusion will always apply. However, this interpretation is not strictly accurate, since a clause must still make it clear that liability for negligence is intended to be excluded. An exclusion clause can be interpreted as a warning that the *proferens* is not to be considered liable in the absence of negligence. In *Hollier v Rambler Motors (AMC) Ltd*,[5] the defendants sought to rely on a clause which provided that they were not to be responsible for fire damage to vehicles kept on their premises. It was held that this served merely as a warning that the defendants were not to be responsible for fire damage caused otherwise than by their own negligence. Since the damage to the plaintiff's vehicle resulted from the negligence of the defendants, the exclusion clause did not protect them. But if the car had been damaged by fire in the course of an attempted burglary, the clause would have protected the defendants, provided that the break-in was not attributable to the defendants' want of care.

(b) *Proferens liable independently of negligence* Where the *proferens'* liability may be for negligence or for breach of a strict liability duty, the requirement of clarity becomes very important. The failure to use clear words can be interpreted so that the exclusion applies only to breach of the strict liability duty. For example, in *White v John Warwick & Co Ltd*,[6] the defendants might have been alternately liable for negligence or for the failure of the bicycle to comply with the strict requirement of fitness for purpose. The generally worded exclusion of liability was taken to apply to breach of the strict contractual duty, but not to the alternative liability in negligence. What is necessary is that the *proferens* should make it clear that liability for negligence is excluded. For example, the use of language such as 'the owner shall not be liable for any damage howsoever caused'[7] or 'the owner shall be indemnified against all claims and demands whatsoever'[8] is considered sufficient to exclude liability for negligence. Furthermore, since the issue is one of interpretation, it is important to give effect to the intentions of the parties.[9] Thus, if it is clear that liability for negligence is not accepted, even in the absence of an express reference to negligence, that intention will be given effect. For example, a term which states that shipowners are to be liable only for negligent stowage and personal default, means what it says and the owners are not liable for the negligence of their crew in causing the ship to become stranded.[10]

(v) Repugnancy

Where an exclusion clause is repugnant or inconsistent with the main object and intention of the transaction as disclosed by the other terms of the contract,[11] it may be inoperative. Here the court is effectively applying a judicial test of reasonableness. The problem with the repugnancy rule is that it appears to require an exclusion clause to be construed separately from the rest of the contract, when the modern tendency is to construe an

5   [1972] 2 QB 71. Cf *Spriggs v Sotheby Parke Bernet & Co* [1986] 1 Lloyd's Rep 487.
6   [1953] 2 All ER 1021.
7   *Joseph Travers & Sons Ltd v Cooper* [1915] 1 KB 73; *White v Blackmore* [1972] 2 QB 651.
8   *Gillespie Bros Ltd v Roy Bowles Transport Ltd* [1973] QB 400.
9   *The Golden Leader* [1980] 2 Lloyd's Rep 573 at 574.
10   Ibid.
11   See *Sze Hai Tong Bank Ltd v Rambler Cycle Co Ltd* [1959] AC 576 at 587 (per LORD DENNING). See also *J E Evans & Son (Portsmouth) Ltd v Andrea Merzario Ltd* [1976] 1 WLR 1078.

exclusion clause along with the rest of the contract so as to ascertain the intentions of the parties. It may be that looking at the main purpose of the contract is more appropriate to standard form consumer contracts and that, in commercial transactions, the better approach is to look at the exclusion clause in the context of the other terms of the contract.[12] For the most part, a repugnant exclusion clause in a consumer contract is unlikely to satisfy the statutory requirement of reasonableness.

(vi) Seriousness of the breach

(a) *Fundamental terms and fundamental breaches* Before the passing of the Unfair Contract Terms Act 1977, the courts were prepared to strike out an exclusion clause where its effect would have been to exclude liability for a particularly serious breach of contract, such as virtual non-performance of the contract. Two main techniques were employed to deal with serious breaches. First, it was assumed that an exclusion clause was not intended to excuse non-performance of a fundamental term of the contract. Thus, an exclusion clause would be construed very narrowly so as not to apply to breaches of such terms. Examples of breaches of a fundamental term included substantial deviation from an agreed route in shipping cases,[13] and the failure of the seller of goods to supply the thing contracted for.[14] It was said that a breach of a fundamental term would arise where what had been done or omitted to be done did not fall within the 'four corners' of the contract,[15] and the breach was treated as being more serious than a breach of a condition of the contract.

The second technique involved treating an exclusion clause as inapplicable, as a matter of law, to serious or 'fundamental' breaches of contract. These were breaches which had the effect of depriving the party not in default of substantially the whole benefit which it was intended that he should obtain from the contract.[16] The view developed that, as a matter of law, both a breach of a fundamental term and a fundamental breach of contract could not be excluded.[17] This might have made sense, at the time, in consumer contracts, but the rule of law approach had the effect of defeating a seemingly reasonable allocation of risks in many commercial contracts.

The rule of law approach was ultimately rejected,[18] and it was established that whether or not an exclusion clause applied to a fundamental breach or the breach of a fundamental term was a matter of construction of the contract. This resulted in the overruling of a few cases based on the substantive rule of law approach.[19]

---

12 See *Photo Production Ltd v Securicor Transport Ltd* [1980] AC 827 at 843 (per LORD WILBERFORCE) and see Yates and Hawkins *Standard Business Contracts* (1986) p 85.

13 See for example *Glynn v Margetson & Co* [1893] AC 351; *Thorley Ltd v Orchis SS Co Ltd* [1907] 1 KB 660.

14 *Chanter v Hopkins* (1838) 4 M & W 399 at 404 (per LORD ABINGER); *Smeaton Hanscomb & Co Ltd v Sassoon I Setty & Co* [1953] 1 WLR 1468.

15 See *Gibaud v Great Eastern Rly Co* [1921] 2 KB 426 at 435 (per SCRUTTON LJ) and see also Chin *Excluding Liability in Contracts* (1985) ch 2.

16 *Wathes (Western) Ltd v Austins (Menswear) Ltd* [1976] 1 Lloyd's Rep 14 at 19 (per MEGAW LJ).

17 See eg *Karsales (Harrow) Ltd v Wallis* [1956] 1 WLR 936.

18 *UGS Finance Ltd v National Mortgage Bank of Greece* [1964] 1 Lloyd's Rep 446 at 450 (per PEARSON LJ); *Suisse Atlantique Société d'Armement Maritime SA v NV Rotterdamsche Kolen Centrale* [1967] 1 AC 361; *Photo Production Ltd v Securicor Transport Ltd* [1980] AC 827; *George Mitchell (Chesterhall) Ltd v Finney Lock Seeds Ltd* [1983] 2 AC 803.

19 *Charterhouse Credit Co Ltd v Tolley* [1963] 2 QB 683; *Harbutt's Plasticine Ltd v Wayne Tank and Pump Co Ltd* [1970] 1 QB 447; *Wathes (Western) Ltd v Austins (Menswear) Ltd* [1976] 1 Lloyd's Rep 14.

(b) *The rule of construction* The decision of the House of Lords in the *Suisse Atlantique*[20] case gave rise to a number of difficulties. While it was supposed to have laid to rest the view that there was a substantive rule of law which rendered invalid an exclusion clause in the event of a fundamental breach of contract, the decision was not conclusive. First, whatever was said about exclusion clauses was strictly *obiter*, as the House of Lords determined that they were concerned with a limitation clause. Furthermore, there were a number of statements which allowed the Court of Appeal to continue to apply the rule of law approach.

Any doubts on the status of the doctrine of fundamental breach were disposed of in *Photo Production Ltd v Securicor Transport Ltd*.[1] It was made abundantly clear that the doctrine of fundamental breach is a rule of construction only; that an exclusion clause can survive a fundamental breach of contract; that a fundamental breach is the same as a breach of condition or a serious breach of an innominate term, with the result that, while the contract itself is not discharged, performance of the primary contractual obligations are discharged, while secondary obligations, such as the duty to pay damages and the provisions of an exclusion clause, remain in existence.

It is crucial, as a matter of construction, that the exclusion clause is said to apply to the breach of contract under consideration. The decision in *Photo Production* should not be taken to mean that the doctrine of fundamental breach is now irrelevant, for there may be cases in which an exclusion clause is construed so as not to apply to a particular breach. While the Unfair Contract Terms Act 1977 may have rendered the doctrine obsolete in certain respects, there are contracts to which the Act does not apply, in which case the doctrine can play a constructive part.

Because the doctrine is based on a construction of the words of an exclusion clause in the context of the breach of contract, it can be regarded as an illustration of the *contra proferentem* rule. If the clause purports to exempt a person from liability for a non-performance which defeats the reasonable expectations of the parties, that clause may be struck out. It would be reasonable to assume that the common law rule of construction may still be used where the thing delivered is fundamentally different from that which was contracted for. As a matter of construction, the courts may treat as devoid of contractual content a clause which permits a substantial deviation from the primary obligations of one of the parties. This approach could well be taken in relation to a breach of a so-called fundamental term and in relation to the deviation cases. However, in construing exclusion and limitation clauses, it is important that the court does not apply a strained construction to the words of the exclusion in the context of the alleged breach of contract.[2] Particularly in the field of commercial transactions, where risks are normally borne by insurance, there would appear to be some justification for leaving the parties free to apportion risks as they think fit, and for the court not to intervene.[3]

(3) STATUTORY CONTROL OF EXCLUSION CLAUSES AND RELATED DEVICES

The most direct attack on exclusion clauses and related devices has come from Parliament in the form of the Unfair Contract Terms Act 1977,[4] and through the introduction of

---

20   Sub nom *Suisse Atlantique Société d'Armement Maritime SA v NV Rotterdamsche Kolen Centrale* [1967] 1 AC 361.
1   [1980] AC 827.
2   See *Ailsa Craig Fishing Co Ltd v Malvern Fishing Co Ltd* [1983] 1 All ER 101; *George Mitchell (Chesterhall) Ltd v Finney Lock Seeds Ltd* [1983] 2 AC 803.
3   *Photo Production Ltd v Securicor Transport Ltd* [1980] AC 827 at 843 (per LORD WILBERFORCE).
4   See Coote (1978) 41 MLR 312; Sealy [1978] 37 CLJ 15; Palmer and Yates [1981] 40 CLJ 108.

the Unfair Terms in Consumer Contracts Regulations 1999,[5] although there are other statutes which may render purported exclusions of liability ineffective.

(i) The scope of the Unfair Contract Terms Act 1977

Despite its title, the Act applies to the purported exclusion of tortious and contractual liability. Furthermore, its effect is not restricted to exclusions employed in an exchange relationship, since a notice, purportedly excluding the liability of an occupier to his lawful, contractual or non-contractual visitors is equally subject to some of the provisions of the Act. The title of the Act is also misleading insofar as it refers to 'unfair terms'. What should be appreciated is that it only applies to terms that exclude or limit liability, yet as the 1999 Regulations demonstrate, there is a much wider range of unfair terms which may operate against the consumer interest.

(a) *Business liability* The 1977 Act states that, subject to exceptions, its provisions apply only to business liability. This covers liability arising from things done or to be done by a person in the course of his own or an employer's business or from the occupation of premises used for the business purposes of the occupier.[6]

The difficulty is to determine what is meant by a business purpose. The Act states that a business includes a profession and the activities of government departments or local or public authorities.[7] However, excluded from the provisions of the Act is the granting of access for recreational or educational purposes, unless the granting of such access falls within the business purposes of the occupier.[8] The purpose of this last provision is said to be to allow farmers and owners of countryside areas to exclude liability to day-trippers. However, where the granting of access is incidental to business use, a purported exclusion of liability falls within the provisions of the Act. For example, it may be that a lecturer who provides tutorials at home cannot exclude liability should the student fall downstairs. Furthermore, the definition of business liability gives rise to uncertainty in other respects. For example, it is not clear whether a function put on to raise money for charity would constitute a business activity,[9] or whether the occasional use of one's home for part-time work would bring the private dwelling within the provisions of the Act. It can also be argued on a strict reading of section 1(3) that the partial use of premises for business purposes might result in the application of the Act to the premises in all their uses. If this were to be the case, the use of a church hall for the purposes of a jumble sale might render the Act applicable to its use as the venue for a Sunday School.

The Act generally applies only to business liability so that a purely private contractual arrangement will not be regulated. However, the provisions of the Act in relation to the implied terms in supply of goods contracts extend to some private transactions.[10] The extent of this exception is limited since the statutory terms as to quality and fitness are only implied in cases of business supply. For the purposes of the Sale of Goods Act 1979, a person acts in the course of a business even where he does not regularly supply goods of the type sold,[11] so that a sale of stock in trade may still be one made in the course of a business.

5   SI 1999/2083. These Regulations consolidate and add to the Unfair Terms in Consumer Contracts Regulations 1994, SI 1994/3159, which are now revoked.
6   Unfair Contract Terms Act 1977, s 1(3).
7   Ibid, s 14.
8   Ibid, s 1(3)(b) added by the Occupiers' Liability Act 1984, s 2.
9   See eg *White v Blackmore* [1972] 2 QB 651. See also Bragg and Brazier (1986) 130 Sol Jo 251 and 274.
10 Unfair Contract Terms Act 1977, s 6(4).
11 *Ashington Piggeries Ltd v Christopher Hill Ltd* [1972] AC 441 at 494 (per Lord WILBERFORCE); *Stevenson v Rogers* [1999] 2 WLR 1064.

In *Stevenson v Rogers*[12] it was accepted that a person sells in the course of a business in three different sets of circumstances. First a seller sells goods in the course of a business where the sale is in the nature of trade carried out with a view to profit, even if this is a one-off venture. Secondly, a sale is made in the course of a business if it is integral to the business carried on by the seller and thirdly, there is a sale in the course of a business where the transaction is incidental to the business carried on by the seller, but the type of transaction concerned is undertaken with a degree of regularity.[13] However, a different approach may apply to the Unfair Contract Terms Act 1977, since it has been held that a company can 'deal as a consumer' where the purchase is merely incidental to the business carried on by the buyer and where there is no degree of regularity in the type of purchase concerned.[14] If a similar interpretation is applied to the notion of business liability in the 1977 Act, it would serve to reduce the number of contracts subject to its provisions. Moreover, what ought to matter is the nature of the business carried on so that a buyer's reason for making a purchase or a visitor's reason for visiting premises should be irrelevant. However, it is implicit in comments made by in *Stevenson v Rogers* that the correctness of the decision in *R & B Customs Brokers Ltd v United Dominions Trust Ltd* might need to be called into question, since in that case, the court did not have the power to consider the legislative history of a piece of legislation following the decision of the House of Lords in *Pepper v Hart*.[15] Had the court been able to consider law reform proposals on which the Supply of Goods (Implied Terms) Act 1973 was based, it would have been clear that it was intended that the phrase 'supply in the course of a business' should be interpreted in the manner adopted by the court in *Stevenson v Rogers*.[16]

(b) *Excluding or restricting liability* The Act is mainly concerned with contract terms or notices which exclude or restrict liability. This reference to liability will normally cover the secondary obligations of the *proferens*, such as the obligation to pay damages in the event of a breach of duty. The Act also controls clauses which operate in an analogous manner, such as those which limit the time within which a claim must be brought; those which restrict the right to a remedy[17] and those which restrict or exclude relevant rules of evidence.[18] By concentrating on terms which exclude or restrict liability, the Act appears not to apply to provisions which potentially extend the liability of the *proferens*. It follows that a valid agreed damages clause will not be covered since the sum agreed may exceed the actual damage suffered by the injured party. Nor does the Act apply to an arbitration clause.[19]

Subject to exceptions, the Act appears not to apply to clauses which purport to modify the primary obligations of the *proferens*. A convenient distinction is that the Act prevents a person from excluding or restricting liability, but does not affect the exclusion or restriction of a primary duty. The two exceptions to the rule are that a person's ability to exclude the duty of care giving rise to liability in negligence[20] and the duties

---

12   Ibid.
13   Ibid at 1069 (per POTTER LJ).
14   *R & B Customs Brokers Co Ltd v United Dominions Trust Ltd* [1988] 1 All ER 847. See Brown (1988) JBL 386.
15   [1993] AC 593.
16   *Stevenson v Roger* [1999] 2 WLR 1064 at 1076–1077 (per POTTER LJ).
17   Such as the right of set-off: *Stewart Gill Ltd v Horatio Myer & Co Ltd* [1992] 2 All ER 257; *Schenkers Ltd v Overland Shoes Ltd* [1998] 1 Lloyd's Rep 498.
18   Unfair Contract Terms Act 1977, s 13(1); *Thomas Witter Ltd v TBP Industries Ltd* [1996] 2 All ER 573 and see MacDonald (1992) 12 Legal Studies 277.
19   Unfair Contract Terms Act 1977, s 13(2).
20   Unfair Contract Terms Act 1977, ss 13(1), 2 and 5.

arising out of the terms implied by law in supply of goods contracts[1] are affected by the provisions of the Act. Apart from these exceptions, the primary obligations of the parties form the basis of an agreement, and it would amount to judicial rewriting of a contract if the courts were to intervene in relation to such obligations. Accordingly, the Act will not apply to a clause which provides that a horse is warranted sound except for hunting.[2] The seller is not seeking to exclude liability should the horse not be suitable for hunting, he is agreeing to sell a horse which is suitable for purposes other than hunting, and the buyer has no reasonable expectation of acquiring a hunter.

The difficulty thrown up by the wording of section 13(1) is that it appears to have been inserted with a view to prevent the Act from being side-stepped by a draftsman who is able to word a contract term so as to appear to relate to a primary obligation. This appears to require a 'form and substance' distinction,[3] but the Act gives no indication as to how that distinction is to be made. It may be that the appropriate test to apply is the 'but for' test,[4] familiarly used in negligence cases when addressing the issue of factual causation. In the context of the 1977 Act it appears that what has to be asked is whether there would have been any obligation and resultant liability had the relevant term not been incorporated in the contract. If such liability would have existed, but for the presence of the term, then the term, in essence, is one that excludes or restricts liability.

The distinction between primary and secondary obligations is important, since some commentators take the view that an exclusion clause must be considered along with the rest of the terms of a contract in order to determine what has been agreed.[5] Considered in this way, an exclusion clause will, in many cases, serve to define the primary obligations of the parties. But rigid adherence to this view would emasculate the Unfair Contract Terms Act[6] by allowing a tortfeasor to opt out of the Act, not recognising his own answerability to the plaintiff.[7] Accordingly, a disclaimer notice which seeks to exclude the duty to exercise reasonable care must be considered only after it has been asked whether such a duty would have existed but for the presence of the disclaimer.[8] This approach must be qualified in relation to other primary obligations since if it is held that all such purported modifications are covered by the provisions of the Act, perfectly valid allocations of risk would be subject to the reasonableness provisions of the Act.

(c) *The inapplicability of the Act* The Act does not apply in certain circumstances, in which case, common law rules will still apply. Exclusions to which the Act will not apply fall within two categories, namely, cases specifically excepted and cases which do not fall within the general scheme of the Act. The latter category covers cases not involving the purported exclusion of business liability. Moreover, an exclusion of business liability is not covered by the Act where it is not made on written standard terms of business, and the person subject to the exclusion is not a consumer.[9]

Certain varieties of contract are specifically excepted from some or all of the provisions of the Act. The Act does not apply to contracts for the international supply of goods.[10] Sections 2–4 and section 7 do not apply to contracts of insurance, contracts relating to

1   Ibid, ss 13(1), 6 and 7.
2   See Coote (1978) 41 MLR 312 at 317.
3   *Johnstone v Bloomsbury HA* [1991] 2 All ER 293 at 301 (per STUART SMITH LJ).
4   *Phillips Products Ltd v Hyland* [1987] 2 All ER 620 at 625 (per SLADE LJ).
5   Coote *Exception Clauses* (1964) ch 1; *Yates* pp 123–133. See also *Photo Production Ltd v Securicor Transport Ltd* [1980] AC 827 at 851 (per LORD DIPLOCK).
6   *Smith v Eric S Bush (a firm)* [1989] 2 All ER 514 at 523 (per LORD TEMPLEMAN).
7   Cf *Harris v Wyre Forest DC* [1988] 1 All ER 691 at 697 (per NOURSE LJ).
8   See also *Phillips Products Ltd v Hyland* [1987] 2 All ER 620 at 625 (per SLADE LJ).
9   Unfair Contract Terms Act 1977, s 3(1).
10 Ibid, s 26(2).

interests in land, contracts relating to intellectual property, contracts relating to the formation, dissolution or the constitution of a company, and contracts relating to securities.[11] Contracts of marine salvage, charterparties and contracts of carriage of goods by sea are subject to the provisions of section 2(1), but not to the remaining provisions of sections 2–4 or section 7, except where the person affected deals as a consumer.[12] In relation to employment contracts, the employer cannot seek to restrict or exclude his liability for negligence to the employee,[13] but it is possible for the negligence liability of the employee to be excluded,[14] whether to the employer or to a third party. This is important since an individual working for another does fall within the definition of business liability in section 1(3).

(ii) Exclusion of liability for negligence

The 1977 Act applies to an attempt by the *proferens* to exclude or restrict his liability for negligently caused harm. For the purposes of the Act, negligence includes the breach of a contract term requiring the exercise of reasonable care and skill,[15] the breach of any common law duty to exercise reasonable care and skill,[16] and a breach of the common duty of care imposed by the Occupiers' Liability Act 1957.[17] It does not matter whether the breach of duty was inadvertent or intentional[18] with the result that the commission of torts such as trespass to the person[19] and nuisance,[20] insofar as they require the exercise of reasonable care involve negligence liability. Conversely, the breach of a strict statutory duty or a breach of the rule in *Rylands v Fletcher*[1] would not constitute negligence liability.

If the *proferens* admits to a breach of duty which amounts to negligence, a purported exclusion will relate to his secondary liability to pay damages. But the exclusion may be worded in such a way as to prevent the duty from arising in the first place.[2] In order to deal with this situation section 13(1) provides that:

> To the extent that this part of the Act prevents the exclusion or restriction of any liability
> ... sections 2 and 5 to 7 also prevent excluding or restricting liability by reference to terms
> and notices which exclude or restrict the relevant obligation or duty.

It has been held that the effect of this provision is to prevent a building surveyor from providing in a valuation report supplied to a consumer purchaser that he accepts no responsibility for the content of the report.[3] In this respect, it is important to distinguish between the compilation of the report itself and the work which leads up to its compilation since if the preparatory work is done without fault, there should be no

---

11   Ibid, Sch 1 para 1 and see *Micklefield v SAC Technology Ltd* [1991] 1 All ER 275.
12   Ibid, Sch 1 para 2.
13   Ibid, Sch 1 para 4.
14   Ibid.
15   Ibid, s 1(1)(a).
16   Ibid, s 1(1)(b).
17   Ibid, s 1(1)(c). But there is no reference to the duty owed to trespassers under the Occupiers' Liability Act 1984 which is best regarded as a minimum, non-excludable standard. See ch 28.
18   Ibid s 1(4).
19   *Fowler v Lanning* [1959] 1 QB 426; *Letang v Cooper* [1965] 1 QB 232.
20   See *Bolton v Stone* [1951] AC 850; *Goldman v Hargrave* [1967] 1 AC 645; *Leakey v National Trust for Places of Historic Interest or Natural Beauty* [1980] QB 485.
1   (1868) LR 3 HL 330.
2   This was the way in which the disclaimer in *Hedley Byrne & Co Ltd v Heller & Partners Ltd* [1964] AC 465 operated.
3   *Smith v Eric S Bush (a firm)* [1989] 2 All ER 514. See also MacDonald (1992) 12 Legal Studies 277.

misstatement.[4] The question to ask is whether but for an exclusion or disclaimer of liability, a duty of care would have been owed. If the answer is in the affirmative, that exclusion or disclaimer is subject to the provisions of the Act. The true effect of the exclusion has to be considered. If in substance it excludes liability, the 1977 Act will apply.[5] Similarly, if the effect of a contract term is, in substance, to raise the common law defence of *volenti non fit injuria*, this amounts to a restriction of liability for negligence and the 1977 Act is capable of applying.[6]

(iii) Statutory invalidity

Certain types of exclusion are rendered totally ineffective by the Act.

(a) *Negligently inflicted death or personal injury* By section 2(1) of the Act, a person cannot, by means of any contract term or notice, exclude or restrict his own liability for death or personal injury caused by negligence.[7] Section 2(1) also extends to notices which purport to exclude liability for death or bodily injury. Accordingly, the occupier of business premises cannot erect a notice stating that visitors enter at their own risk. In the light of the interpretation of section 13, considered above, the effect of section 2(1) is that a person cannot seek to exclude or restrict the duty which gives rise to negligence liability for death or bodily injury. Thus, a notice which has the effect of denying the existence of a duty of care, in the first place, will be subject to the total invalidity provision.

Section 2(1) merely prevents a person from excluding or restricting his own liability for negligence. If the effect of the relevant term or notice is to exclude or restrict the liability of another person,[8] or if it serves to specify that someone else should accept responsibility, section 2(1) does not apply. Accordingly, an indemnity clause in a plant hire agreement which shifts responsibility for injury suffered by the plaintiff from the owner of the plant to the hirer is not a clause which excludes or restricts liability.[9]

Where the liability which results in physical harm to the plaintiff is strict, section 2(1) does not apply. However, other statutory provisions[10] and other provisions of the 1977 Act may apply.

(b) *Defective products and guarantees of consumer goods* Section 5 of the Act provides that liability for loss of or damage to consumer goods arising from the goods proving to be defective while in use and which results from defective manufacture cannot be excluded or restricted by a provision in a manufacturer's guarantee. Section 5 does not affect the relationship between the consumer and the retailer. It is designed to cover the manufacturer/consumer relationship. The fact that there may not be a contractual relationship between the manufacturer and the consumer does not matter, since the relevant provision can be treated as a notice within the meaning of the Act.

Where a product proves to be defective within the meaning of the Consumer Protection Act 1987, Part I, the producer's liability for death or personal injury and damage to consumer property cannot be excluded by means of a contract term, notice

---

4   Ibid at 524 (per LORD TEMPLEMAN).
5   *Phillips Products Ltd v Hyland* [1987] 2 All ER 620 at 626 (per SLADE LJ); approved in *Smith v Eric S Bush (a firm)* [1989] 2 All ER 514 at 530 (per LORD GRIFFITHS).
6   *Johnstone v Bloomsbury Health Authority* [1991] 2 All ER 293 at 301 (per STUART-SMITH LJ).
7   Other comparable provisions can be found in the Transport Act 1962, s 43(7) and the Public Passenger Vehicles Act 1981, s 29.
8   *The Chevalier Roze* [1983] 2 Lloyd's Rep 438.
9   *Thompson v T Lohan (Plant Hire) Ltd* [1987] 2 All ER 631.
10 See Defective Premises Act 1972, s 1(1); Consumer Protection Act 1987, ss 5 and 7.

or other provision.[11] Unfortunately, a notice is defined as a notice in writing, which may leave it open for such liability to be restricted by means of an oral notice.

(c) *Implied terms in consumer contracts for the supply of goods*[12] In a contract for the sale of goods or a contract of hire purchase, any attempt to exclude or restrict liability for breach of the implied terms as to title[13] is ineffective.[14] This provision is not confined to consumer contracts, and will apply in a business relationship. In relation to the implied terms as to description, quality, fitness for purpose and correspondence with sample,[15] it is provided that, where a person deals as a consumer, liability for breach cannot be excluded or restricted.[16] Similar provisions to those which apply to sale of goods and hire-purchase contracts also apply to other consumer contracts for the transfer of ownership in goods[17] by virtue of the Unfair Contract Terms Act 1977, section 7(2). However, where ownership is not transferred, as in the case of a contract of hire, an attempt to exclude or restrict liability for want of title is subject only to a requirement of reasonableness.[18]

An important requirement in relation to section 6(2) and section 7(2) is that a person affected by the purported exclusion should deal as a consumer and it is for the *proferens* to prove this.[19] Dealing as a consumer imports three elements, namely that the buyer should be an individual not acting in a business capacity, that the seller should deal in the course of a business and that the goods supplied should be of a type ordinarily supplied for private use or consumption.[20] For these purposes, a person who purchases goods at an auction sale or by way of competitive tender is deemed not to deal as a consumer.[1]

The general tenor of section 12 is that a consumer is a non-business purchaser of goods. But this does not mean that purchases made by a company always fall outside the scope of the 1977 Act, as currently interpreted. In broad terms, every time a company enters into a contract, it does so in the course of a business, since if this were not the case, the transaction would be *ultra vires*.[2] But if the purchase is not for a definite business purpose and is one which is not regularly made by the corporate buyer it may be regarded as a 'consumer' purchase. In *R & B Customs Brokers Ltd v United Dominions Trust Ltd*[3] a freight forwarding business purchased a car for both business use and the private use of its directors. The suppliers sought to rely on a contractual exclusion clause when the vehicle proved to be unfit for its intended use. The Court of Appeal held that since the purchase was not an integral part of the purchaser's business as a freight forwarder and as there was no degree of regularity in the type of purchase concerned, the buyer had dealt as a consumer with the result that the exclusion clause was ineffective.[4] This decision is subject to criticism on two grounds. First, the intention of Parliament appears

11   Consumer Protection Act 1987, ss 5 and 7. See also ch 24.
12   See ch 24.
13   See Sale of Goods Act 1979, s 12; Consumer Credit Act 1974, Sch 4, para 35.
14   Unfair Contract Terms Act 1977, s 6(1).
15   See Sale of Goods Act 1979, ss 13–15; Consumer Credit Act 1974, Sch 4, para 35.
16   Unfair Contract Terms Act 1977, s 6(2).
17   See Supply of Goods and Services Act 1982, ss 2–5, 7–10.
18   Unfair Contract Terms Act 1977, s 7(4) as amended by the Supply of Goods and Services Act 1982, s 17(3).
19   Unfair Contract Terms Act 1977, s 12(3).
20   Ibid, s 12(1).
1   Ibid, s 12(2).
2   *R & B Customs Brokers Ltd v United Dominions Trust Ltd* [1988] 1 All ER 847 at 853 (per DILLON LJ).
3   [1988] 1 All ER 847.
4   See also *Rasbora Ltd v J C L Marine Ltd* [1977] 1 Lloyd's Rep 645; *Peter Symmons & Co v Cook* (1981) 131 NLJ 758.

to have been to make a simple distinction between business and non-business purchases as a literal reading of section 12(1)(a) reveals.[5] Moreover, the Law Commission report on which the Unfair Contract Terms Act 1977 was based recommended that in the case of business purchases, exclusion clauses related to the implied terms in the Sale of Goods Act 1979 should be subject to a requirement of reasonableness but not that they should be rendered void.[6] Secondly, the reason for intervention in favour of consumers is their apparent inequality of bargaining power, but the same cannot be said of many business purchasers. Indeed, in *R & B Customs Brokers* it was said that had the issue of reasonableness been up for consideration, the exclusion clause would have satisfied the test laid down by the Act[7] which suggests that the parties were in a position of equal bargaining strength.

The second and third requirements of 'dealing as a consumer' are that the supplier must act in the course of a business and that the goods should be of a type ordinarily supplied for private use or consumption. The latter requirement may cause problems in relation to goods which can be put to both business and private uses, such as a word processor or a car. If a business purchases something of a type which is normally put to private use, an exclusion clause in the contract will not necessarily be void since the buyer may be purchasing in a business capacity. But the problem, considered in reverse, may be more serious since if a consumer purchases an item normally regarded as the subject of a business purchase, an exclusion clause may still stand despite the unequal bargaining power of the parties.

(iv) Exclusions subject to a requirement of reasonableness

Some exclusions of liability may be permitted if the *proferens* can prove that the relevant term or notice satisfies the statutory test of reasonableness.[8]

(a) *Negligently inflicted harm other than death or personal injury* Where a person seeks to exclude or restrict liability for harm other than death or personal injury, he may do so, provided the exclusion satisfies a test of reasonableness.[9] Thus a notice displayed by an occupier of premises or a term in a contract for the supply of services which seeks to exclude liability for a breach of the implied term requiring the exercise of reasonable care and skill[10] must be reasonable if the breach causes property damage or economic loss.

(b) *Residual consumer contracts* By virtue of section 3(1), a purported exclusion or restriction of liability must satisfy the test of reasonableness where one of the parties deals as a consumer. This section applies to those consumer contracts not covered by the statutory invalidity provisions considered above and includes consumer contracts for the supply of services.

(c) *Contracts entered into on the written standard terms of the other party* If one person, who need not be consumer, deals on the written standard terms of the other, a purported exclusion or restriction of liability must satisfy the requirement of reasonableness.[11] This provision applies where the bargaining strength of the parties is unequal and the contract

---

5   See also the criticisms of the decision in *R & B Customs Brokers* in *Stevenson v Rogers* [1999] 2 WLR 1064, considered above.
6   Law Comm No 24 (1969) paras 90–95.
7   *R & B Customs Brokers Ltd v United Dominions Trust Ltd* [1988] 1 All ER 847 at 855 (per DILLON LJ).
8   Ibid, s 11(5).
9   Unfair Contract Terms Act 1977, s 2(2).
10   Supply of Goods and Services Act 1982, s 13 and see ch 25.
11   Unfair Contract Terms Act 1977, s 3(1).

is based on a set of written standard terms. Written standard terms are not defined in the Act, but the meaning of the comparable Scottish provision 'standard form contract' has been judicially considered.[12] The phrase 'standard form contract' does not indicate a wholly written set of standard terms and a part-written, part-oral contract may fall within this provision.[13] Furthermore, a set of terms may be regarded as standard if they are applied in a particular case without material variation. Thus, where a set of terms is substantially altered, they may cease to be standard terms, in which case the Act will not apply.

Where section 3(1) does apply, whether the contract is a consumer contract or one made on written standard terms, a purported exclusion or restriction of liability must satisfy the test of reasonableness, if it operates in one of three ways specified in section 3(2). The first of these is where a person who is in breach of contract seeks to exclude or restrict any liability of his in respect of that breach.[14] This provision refers specifically to liability, therefore there must be a breach of contract. Accordingly, an exclusion which modifies the primary obligations of the *proferens*, with the result that a particular act or omission is not a breach of contract, will not be affected. Section 3(2)(a) is concerned solely with a purported exclusion or restriction of a secondary obligation, such as that to pay damages in the event of a breach of contract. Section 3(2)(a) covers any liability, and will therefore apply to a purported exclusion of a strict contractual liability.

Secondly unless it is reasonable to do so, the *proferens* cannot claim to be entitled to render a performance substantially different from that which was reasonably expected of him.[15] If this is to add anything to section 3(2)(a), it must cover something other than a breach of contract. For example, it might cover a stipulation that a particular method of performance is not to be regarded as a breach of contract, such as a clause in a tour operator's standard form contract enabling him to change the advertised route, the nature of the accommodation provided or the time of travel.[16]

Section 3(2)(b)(i) assumes that it is possible to identify a reasonably expected performance. The difficulty is to determine from whose point of view the performance must be assessed. The relevant expectations may be those of the reasonable man who reads all the terms of the contract, the man who reads nothing before he makes a contract or a person who knows what the contract says but expects the purported exclusion to be applied fairly. If the last of these views is applied, the relevant test is, effectively, the main purpose of the contract rule employed in relation to breaches of a fundamental term in deviation cases.[17]

The third type of clause caught by section 3 is one which allows the *proferens* to claim to be entitled, in respect of the whole or any part of his contractual obligation, to render no performance at all.[18] This would appear to add nothing to the protection already given at common law. If a person renders no performance at all, surely there is a total failure of consideration, in which case the contract will fail. Furthermore, where there is a non-performance of part of that which is promised, section 3(2)(b)(i) would appear to be relevant in that performance may be regarded as substantially different from that which was reasonably expected.

---

12   *McCrone v Boots Farm Sales* 1981 SLT 103.
13   See *British Crane Hire Ltd v Ipswich Plant Hire Ltd* [1975] QB 303.
14   Unfair Contract Terms Act 1977, s 3(2)(a).
15   Ibid, s 3(2)(b)(i).
16   See *Anglo-Continental Holidays Ltd v Typaldos (London) Ltd* [1967] 2 Lloyd's Rep 61. See also Law Commission No 69 (1975) paras 143–146.
17   See *Glynn v Margetson & Co* [1893] AC 351.
18   Unfair Contract Terms Act 1977, s 3(2)(b)(ii).

(d) *Non-consumer contracts for the supply of goods* An attempt to exclude liability for a breach of the implied terms concerning description, sample, quality and fitness in contracts for the supply of goods,[19] where the buyer deals otherwise than as a consumer, is subject to a requirement of reasonableness.[20]

(e) *Indemnity clauses* An indemnity clause in a consumer contract must satisfy the test of reasonableness,[1] but the same requirement does not extend to indemnity clauses in business contracts.[2] An indemnity clause may work in one of two ways.[3] First, it may require a contracting consumer to indemnify the other party to the contract in respect of that other's liability to the consumer.[4] For example, a contract for the removal of the consumer's personal effects to another house may provide that the consumer will indemnify the carrier against all claims and demands in excess of £500 in the event of the carrier's negligence or other breach of contract.[5] Alternatively, the contract term may require the consumer to act as an insurer in respect of the other party's liability to third parties.[6] Thus a term in the removal contract, above, to the effect that the consumer agrees to indemnify the carrier in respect of damage caused to a third party in the course of unloading the vehicle would have to satisfy the test of reasonableness. Here much will turn on who is in the best position to insure against such liability.

(f) *Misrepresentation* The 1977 Act amends[7] the Misrepresentation Act 1967, section 3, which also required a purported exclusion of liability for misrepresentation to satisfy a test of reasonableness. Section 3 is intended to cover clauses which exclude liability and restrict remedies, but is restricted to representations rather than terms of the contract.[8] However, if a clause can be drafted in such a way that it appears to do neither, it may escape an application of the reasonableness test.[9] One way of doing this might be to provide that the misrepresentee does not rely on the misrepresentor's statement, in which case there would appear to be no actionable misrepresentation because of the absence of reliance. However, the court would be unlikely to allow such a clause to evade the provisions of section 3 in a case where the reference to absence of reliance is a pure sham.[10]

(v) The tests of reasonableness[11]

(a) *The general test* Section 11(1) provides that, in relation to contractual terms falling within the Act, the appropriate test is whether the clause is fair and reasonable, having regard to the circumstances which were, or ought reasonably to have been known to, or in the contemplation of the parties when the contract was made. It is important to note that the test is applied at the time the contract is made, not at the time of breach,

---

19 Sale of Goods Act 1979, ss 13–15; Consumer Credit Act 1974, Sch 4, para 35; Supply of Goods and Services Act 1982, ss 3–5, 8–10.
20 Unfair Contract Terms Act 1977, ss 6(3) and 7(3).
1 Ibid, s 4(1).
2 See *Thompson v T Lohan (Plant Hire) Ltd* [1987] 2 All ER 631.
3 See Adams and Brownsword (1988) JBL 200.
4 Covered by s 4(2)(a).
5 See *Gillespie Bros & Co Ltd v Roy Bowles Transport Ltd* [1973] QB 400.
6 Covered by s 4(2)(b).
7 Unfair Contract Terms Act 1977, s 8
8 See *Thomas Witter Ltd v TBP Industries Ltd* [1996] 2 All ER 573; *WRM Group v Wood* [1998] CLC 189.
9 See *Overbrook Estates Ltd v Glencombe Properties Ltd* [1974] 1 WLR 1335.
10 See *Cremdean Properties Ltd v Nash* (1977) 244 Estates Gazette 547 at 551 (per BRIDGE LJ).
11 See Adams and Brownsword (1988) 104 LQR 94; James (1987) JBL 286.

with the result that subsequent events including the nature of the breach are not to be considered, except in so far as they were within the contemplation of the parties at the time the contract was made.[12] Moreover, the reasonableness of the whole term must be considered, not just that part of it which is relied on by the *proferens*,[13] since the other party could not have had it in mind, at the time the contract was made, which part of the term might be invoked.[14] It follows that if the term unreasonably restricts a right to a remedy in circumstances which have not arisen, it may still be held ineffective.

For the purposes of a non-contractual notice, there is a similar test, requiring consideration of what was fair and reasonable having regard to the circumstances obtaining when the liability arose or would have arisen but for the notice.[15] The person seeking to rely on the term or notice bears the onus of proving reasonableness[16] under this test and the special tests referred to below.

What is reasonable is not defined in the Act, since this is a factual matter that will vary from case to case. A number of factors help in the identification of a reasonable exclusion of liability and if relevant should be considered in every case.[17] These include the relative bargaining strength of the parties; whether it is reasonably practicable to obtain goods or services from another source, taking into account cost and time factors; how difficult is the task undertaken by the *proferens* and the practical consequences flowing from the court's decision. The reference to bargaining strength means that where the party affected by the exclusion is a consumer, the courts are more likely to regard it with suspicion than would be the case in a commercial transaction.[18] Inevitably the reasonableness requirement will involve consideration of the insurance position, in particular, which of the two parties could reasonably be expected to insure against the loss suffered.[19] Generally, it would appear that the larger the amount involved, the more likely it is that adequate insurance cover will not be available, with the result that an exclusion or limitation of liability to the extent of insurance cover will be reasonable.[20] Another relevant factor may include the complexity and comprehensibility of the exclusion,[1] which is particularly important where consumers are concerned since they are unlikely to have access to independent legal advice. Furthermore, the guidelines which apply to exclusion of liability for breach of the implied terms in supply of goods contracts[2] are likely to be tacitly, if not overtly, taken into account when applying the general test of reasonableness.[3]

(b) *Limitation clauses* Where a clause purports to limit the liability of the *proferens* to a specified sum of money, the Act does provide some guidance on the meaning of reasonableness. Section 11(4) directs the court to have particular regard to the resources available to the *proferens* to meet his liability and whether insurance in respect of the risk was readily available. Thus, it would seem to follow that, if a manufacturer or supplier can obtain insurance without materially raising the cost of his product or service an

---

12   Cf *George Mitchell (Chesterhall) Ltd v Finney Lock Seeds Ltd* [1983] 2 AC 803 based on the Sale of Goods Act 1979, s 55 (as amended) which refers to 'all the circumstances of the case'.
13   *Stewart Gill Ltd v Horatio Myer & Co Ltd* [1992] 2 All ER 257 at 262 (per STUART-SMITH LJ).
14   Ibid.
15   Unfair Contract Terms Act 1977, s 11(3).
16   Unfair Contract Terms Act 1977, s 11(5).
17   *Smith v Eric S Bush (a firm)* [1989] 2 All ER 514 at 531–532 (per LORD GRIFFITHS).
18   Ibid at 532 (per LORD GRIFFITHS).
19   Ibid at 531; *Photo Production Ltd v Securicor Transport Ltd* [1980] AC 827 at 843 (per LORD WILBERFORCE).
20   *Smith v Eric S Bush (a firm)* [1989] 2 All ER 514 at 532 (per LORD GRIFFITHS).
1   *Stag Line Ltd v Tyne Shiprepair Group Ltd, The Zinnia* [1984] 2 Lloyd's Rep 211 at 222 (per STAUGHTON J).
2   Unfair Contract Terms Act 1977, Sch 2.
3   *Phillips Products Ltd v Hyland* [1987] 2 All ER 620 at 628 (per SLADE LJ). See below.

attempt to limit liability is likely to be regarded as unreasonable.[4] But a bailee who is asked to store goods, the value of which is known only by the owner, can reasonably limit his liability since the owner is in the best position to insure the goods at minimal cost.[5] It should be observed that section 11(4) is inapplicable to those terms which seek to exclude liability.[6]

(c) *The special test applicable to non-consumer contracts for the supply of goods* Section 11(2) of the Act specifies that, in determining whether an attempt to exclude liability for breach of the implied terms as to description, quality and fitness in a non-consumer contract for the supply of goods is reasonable, regard should be had to the guidelines stated in Schedule 2 to the Act. The factors referred to in the guidelines include the relative strength of the bargaining positions of the parties; whether there was any inducement to agree to the exclusion; whether any condition as to the enforcement of liability could practicably be complied with; whether the buyer could have bought elsewhere without being subject to the exclusion, and whether the goods were made to the special order of the buyer.

The list of guidelines is not exclusive, and other factors may be considered, if appropriate. An examination of decided cases will not be particularly helpful, since what is reasonable will differ from case to case. For this reason it is arguable that the Act has allowed for the exercise of judicial discretion with all the attendant uncertainty this may create.[7] Moreover, this also runs against the general view that in commercial transactions, the parties should be left to decide what is best for themselves.[8]

The courts are keen to discourage appeals on the issue of reasonableness and it has been observed that an appellate court should treat the decision of the court of first instance with the greatest respect and that, in reaching a decision in a particular case, there may be room for differences of judicial opinion.[9] Moreover, the decision of the trial court on the facts will not be a binding precedent in other cases.[10]

Where an exclusion clause is reasonable, it will be given effect, even where performance of the primary obligations of the parties to the contract of which it forms a part have been discharged.[11] This sets apart the issues of reasonableness and discharge from performance. Where a contract has been affirmed following a breach which would justify discharge from performance, the court is not precluded from holding that an exclusion clause is unreasonable within the meaning of the 1977 Act.[12]

(vi) Evasion of the Unfair Contract Terms Act 1977

Section 10 of the Act is designed to prevent evasion of the provisions of the Act by means of a secondary contract. Thus, it is provided that a person is not bound by a contract term which prejudices or takes away rights which arise under or in connection with the performance of another contract. The wording of section 10 envisages a contract between P and X which purports to take away rights which P has under a contract with D. Accordingly, section 10 will not apply to a contract between P and D which

---

4   *George Mitchell (Chesterhall) Ltd v Finney Lock Seeds Ltd* [1983] 3 WLR 163 at 172 (per LORD BRIDGE).
5   *Singer (UK) Ltd v Tees & Hartlepool Port Authority* [1988] 2 Lloyd's Rep 164.
6   See *Flamar Interocean Ltd v Denmac Ltd, The Flamar Pride* [1990] 1 Lloyd's Rep 434 at 438 (per POTTER J).
7   See Adams and Brownsword (1988) 104 LQR 94.
8   See *Photo Production Ltd v Securicor Transport Ltd* [1980] AC 827. See also *Stag Line Ltd v Tyne Shiprepair Group Ltd, The Zinnia* [1984] 2 Lloyd's Rep 211.
9   *George Mitchell (Chesterhall) Ltd v Finney Lock Seeds Ltd* [1983] 2 AC 803 at 815–816 (per LORD BRIDGE).
10   *Phillips Products Ltd v Hyland* [1987] 2 All ER 620 at 630 (per SLADE LJ).
11   Unfair Contract Terms Act 1977, s 9(1).
12   Ibid, s 9(2).

purports to take away rights conferred under another contract between the same two parties.[13] It follows that section 10 has no application to the terms of a subsequent compromise agreement between the parties to an existing agreement. The wording of section 10 also means that a term which takes away the right to sue in tort would not be affected, since this is not a right conferred under a contract.[14]

Unfortunately, the language used in section 10 differs from that used in the rest of the Act. Instead of dealing with terms which exclude or restrict liability, it refers to terms which prejudice or take away rights, so that the interpretative provisions of section 13 will not apply to section 10 as they are concerned with terms which exclude or restrict liability. Moreover, since section 10 is concerned with secondary evasion which takes away rights it would appear not to apply to a term which allows a person to render a performance substantially different to that which is reasonably expected of him under section 3(2). These are terms which define the contractual obligations of the parties and cannot be said to take rights away since they have not been given in the first place.

(vii) The Scope of the Unfair Terms in Consumer Contracts Regulations 1999[15]

The Regulations apply a test of fairness[16] in contracts between consumers and those who sell or supply to the consumer.[17] The Regulations are further restricted in their application to terms which have not been individually negotiated.[18] For the purposes of the Regulations, a term is regarded as unfair if it is contrary to the requirement of good faith and causes a significant imbalance in the parties' rights and obligations arising under the contract, to the detriment of the consumer.[19] Should a term be classified as unfair, the consumer will not be bound by it,[20] but if the rest of the contract is capable of subsisting, following removal of the unfair term, it will continue to bind the parties.[1]

The Regulations have no application to certain types of term. Most important amongst these is the so-called 'core' term, except insofar as they are required to be written in 'plain intelligible language'.[2] Moreover, some of the examples[3] of unfair terms listed in Schedule 2 are stated not to have an effect on financial services contracts. The Regulations also contain a list of terms which may be regarded as unfair,[4] although it should be appreciated that this is merely indicative and non-exhaustive, so that terms other than those listed may also be considered. An important distinction between the Unfair Contract Terms Act 1977 and the 1999 Regulations is that despite its title, the 1977 Act is not concerned with a very wide variety of unfair terms, being restricted in its application to terms which exclude or restrict liability. In contrast, the list of potentially unfair terms in Schedule 2 to the 1999 Regulations is much wider. However, in some respects, the Regulations have a narrower scope than the 1977 Act, since the latter is capable of applying to more than just consumer contracts. Furthermore, while the 1977 Act applies a test of reasonableness to the majority of exemption clauses and notices covered by it, the appropriate test to apply under the Regulations is one of fairness. Furthermore,

---

13   *Tudor Grange Holdings Ltd v Citibank NA* [1991] 4 All ER 1 at 13 (per Browne-Wilkinson VC).
14   *The Chevalier Roze* [1983] 2 Lloyd's Rep 438 at 442 (per Parker J).
15   SI 1999/2083, replacing the Unfair Terms in Consumer Contracts Regulations 1994 (SI 1994/3159).
16   Unfair Terms in Consumer Contracts Regulations 1999, reg 5.
17   Ibid, reg 4(1).
18   Ibid, reg 5.
19   Ibid, reg 5(1).
20   Ibid, reg 8(1).
1   Ibid, reg 8(2).
2   Ibid, reg 6(2).
3   Particularly those in Sch 1(g), (j) and (l) relating to termination and variation.
4   Ibid, Sch 2(1)(a) to (q).

some terms are automatically ineffective under the 1977 Act, whereas under the Regulations any term will survive if it satisfies the test of fairness, regardless of its specific content. It follows, for example, that there might be circumstances in which it is fair to seek to exclude liability for negligently caused death or bodily injury or to exclude liability for breach of the implied term in a sale of goods contract that goods should be of satisfactory quality.

Since it is clear that the 1999 Regulations only apply in favour of 'consumers', it is important to examine the definition of this protected class. It has been seen that the way in which the definition of 'dealing as a consumer' under the 1977 Act has been interpreted, it is possible for a limited company to challenge the reasonableness of an exemption clause. However, this would not be possible under the 1999 Regulations, since a consumer is defined as 'a natural person who in making a contract ... is acting for purposes which are outside his business, trade or profession'.[5] Moreover, unlike the 1977 Act, there is nothing in the Regulations to prevent a purchaser at auction from relying on their provisions.

The 1994 Regulations defined the words 'seller' and 'supplier' in terms of those who sell or supply goods and services, which led to the belief that, as drafted, they might not apply to transactions involving land. The 1999 Regulations, in contrast reflect what was probably intended in the EC Unfair Terms Directive,[6] namely, that transactions involving land should be covered.[7]

(viii) Enforcement of the Unfair Terms in Consumer Contracts Regulations 1999

The underlying assumption in the Unfair Contract Terms Act 1977 is that the provisions of the Act may be used to challenge an exemption clause in the course of civil proceedings brought by the consumer. This presupposes that the consumer is in a position to be able to afford to litigate. However, it may not be economically worthwhile for a consumer to risk the expense of civil litigation. In contrast, the 1999 Regulations give powers to the Director General of Fair Trading and other 'qualifying bodies' to seek an injunction to prevent the continued use of unfair terms.[8] For these purposes 'qualifying bodies' include most of the statutory regulators of public utility companies, the Data Protection Registrar, all weights and measures authorities and the Consumers' Association.[9] In addition to the power to apply for an injunction, the Director General of Fair Trading is also under a general duty to consider non-vexatious and non-frivolous complaints to the effect that a particular trader is using unfair terms in contracts with consumers,[10] and in order to facilitate this process, special powers relating to the obtaining of information are conferred under regulation 13. Should it be determined that the use of a particular type of term is unfair, the Director or a qualifying body may seek an undertaking from the trader that the use of such terms will be discontinued.[11] Once an undertaking has been given, the Director is under a duty to arrange for publication of details of the undertaking, so that others may become aware of the adjudication of

---

5   Ibid, reg 3.
6   (1993)OJL95/29.
7   UTCCR 1999, reg 3(1).
8   Unfair Terms in Consumer Contracts Regulations 1999, reg 12. The power of a 'qualifying body' to seek an injunction is limited to circumstances in which the body has given 14 days notice to the Director General of Fair Trading of its intention: reg 12(2).
9   Ibid, Sch 1.
10 Ibid, reg 11.
11 Ibid, reg 14.

unfairness.[12] In general terms, the way in which this last objective has been achieved has been through the regular publication of bulletins by the Office of Fair Trading indicating the reasons why a particular type of term is regarded as unfair.

(ix) Terms not individually negotiated

An important provision in the 1999 Regulations is that a term which is not individually negotiated shall be regarded as unfair if, contrary to the requirement of good faith, it causes a significant imbalance in the parties' rights and obligations arising under the contract, to the detriment of the consumer.[13] For these purposes, a term is always to be regarded as not having been individually negotiated if it has been drafted in advance and the consumer has not been able to influence the substance of the term.[14] This provision raises the question of what the term should have been drafted in advance of. The assumption seems to be that if the term was drafted prior to any negotiations leading to a contract it will fall within the scope of regulation 5(2). Accordingly, terms contained in the supplier's standard terms of business which are applied, without alteration, to all consumer contracts would fall within this provision.

(x) Core terms

The Regulations do not apply to a term which relates to the definition of the main subject matter of the contract, if the term is written in plain and intelligible language.[15] Moreover, the Regulations also provide that they have no application to terms that relate to the adequacy of the price or remuneration, as against the goods or services supplied in exchange.[16] The difficulty, here, is to ascertain what constitutes a 'core' term, although some guidance can be found from the language of the Directive on which the Regulations are based. This gave the example of an insurance contract which contains terms clearly defining or circumscribing the risk insured against and which are relevant to the calculation of the premium payable by the consumer.

While there may be good reasons for including the 'core' term exemption, since to apply the provisions of the Regulations, in these circumstances, would interfere with the essence of the contract entered into, there are still some difficulties in ascertaining the boundaries of the exception. Although it would appear that the only requirement of 'core' terms is that they should be written in 'plain and intelligible language', there is a further requirement. The Director General of Fair Trading has taken the view that to be consistent with the requirement of fairness, even core terms have to be adequately communicated to the consumer.[17]

The difficulty with the 'core' terms exception is that if it is interpreted in a broad sense, this could have the effect of undermining the purpose of the Regulations, since draftsmen may be able to use language that takes an otherwise unfair term outside the scope of the Regulations. One way in which the scope of the exception may be limited would be to restrict it to terms relating to the main subject matter of the contract, so that terms relating to the periphery remain regulated. However, this would appear not to be confirmed by the insurance example given in the Directive, since the terms relating

---

12   Ibid, reg 15.
13   Ibid, reg 5(1).
14   Ibid, reg 5(2).
15   Ibid, reg 6(2)(a).
16   Ibid, reg 6(2)(b).
17   OFT Bulletin 4, para 11.

to delimitation of risk and adjustment of the premium are technical matters which may be buried in the detailed wording of an insurance policy.[18]

Whatever else may be said about 'core' terms, they must be written in 'plain and intelligible language' in order to completely avoid the application of the Regulations.[19] Arguably, this requirement, itself, is not written in 'plain and intelligible language', since there is no obvious consequence in the event of a failure to comply, other than a provision to the effect that if there is doubt about the meaning of a written term, the interpretation of that term which is most favourable to the consumer will prevail.[20] This would seem to suggest a *contra proferentem* construction, which according to common law rules should mean that the term is unenforceable against the consumer otherwise than in accordance with a reasonable consumer's interpretation of the term. The Regulations also fail to state from whose perspective the requirement of plain and intelligible language is to be assessed. If assessed on an objective basis, this would seem to suggest an 'ordinary consumer' test and on this matter the Office of Fair Trading considers that the 'ordinary consumer' should be someone acting without legal advice.[1] According to the Office of Fair Trading, this would require the relevant term to avoid the use of 'lawyers' language' such as phrases as 'consequential loss', 'time being of the essence of the contract' and '*force majeure*', unless these phrases are explained in language the consumer can understand.

(xi) The test of unfairness

The Regulations provide that the unfairness of a term is to be assessed taking account of the nature of the goods or services for which the contract was concluded and by referring, at the time of conclusion of the contract, to all the attendant circumstances and the other terms of the contract (or other contract on which it is dependent).[2] As with the Unfair Contract Terms Act 1977, the relevant date for assessment is the time of conclusion of the contract, rather than the time of alleged breach. It is also clear from the language of regulation 6(1) that regard must be had to the terms of a secondary contract on which the principal contract is dependent. However, even if the secondary contract is not one on which the primary contract is dependent, its terms could still be considered as other 'circumstances attending the conclusion of the contract'. However subsequent events, such as a breach of contract, including its seriousness, will not be relevant considerations unless they could have been foreseen at the time the contract was concluded.

For the purposes of the unfairness test, there are two primary considerations, namely whether the term fails to satisfy the requirement of good faith and secondly whether it causes a significant imbalance in the parties' rights and obligations to the detriment of the consumer.[3] What this provision fails to state is where the burden of proof lies. In the absence of any statement placing the onus of proving absence of good faith and insignificant imbalance on the party seeking to rely on the term, it must be assumed that the onus of proof lies on the consumer. This differs substantially from the approach adopted in the Unfair Contract Terms Act 1977, which places the onus of proving reasonableness on the *proferens*.[4]

In order for a term to cause a significant imbalance in the parties' rights and obligations, it must be contrary to the requirement of good faith. The notion of good faith in

18   See *Butterworth's Common Law Series, Law of Contract*, Furmston, (ed) para 3.104.
19   Ibid, reg 7(1).
20   Ibid, reg 7(2).
1   OFT Bulletin 3, para 19.
2   Ibid, reg 6(1).
3   Ibid, reg 5(1).
4   UCTA 1977 s. 11(5).

contracting is more familiar to lawyers from a civil law background than to those from a common law background. In general terms, what the requirement of good faith does is to ask the parties to a contract to 'play fair' or to 'come clean'.[5] For the purposes of the 1994 Regulations, there was guidance as to the meaning of good faith in Schedule 2. This indicated that regard was to be had to the strength of the bargaining positions of the parties, whether the consumer had received an inducement to agree to the term, whether the goods or services were supplied to the special order of the consumer and the extent to which the supplier had dealt fairly and equitably with the consumer. However, this guidance is absent from the 1999 Regulations, although the guidelines in the 1994 Regulations appear broadly similar to the factors which guide a decision on whether an exemption clause is reasonable for the purposes of the Unfair Contract Terms Act 1977. The least familiar of the 1994 guidelines is the requirement of 'fair and equitable dealing'.

In addition to the general requirement of good faith, the 1999 Regulations contain a 'grey list' of terms which may be regarded as unfair. The fact that a type of term is listed does not mean that all such terms will be treated as unfair, since the list is 'indicative and non-exhaustive'.[6] These include terms which have the object of:

(a) excluding or limiting the legal liability of a seller or supplier in the event of the death of a consumer or personal injury to the latter resulting from an act or omission of that seller or supplier;

(b) inappropriately excluding or limiting the legal rights of the consumer *vis-à-vis* the seller or supplier or another party in the event of total or partial non-performance or inadequate performance by the seller or supplier of any of the contractual obligations, including the option of offsetting a debt owed to the seller or supplier against any claim which the consumer may have against him;

(c) making an agreement binding on the consumer whereas provision of services by the seller or supplier is subject to a condition whose realisation depends on his own will alone;

(d) permitting the seller or supplier to retain sums paid by the consumer where the latter decides not to conclude or perform the contract without providing for the consumer to receive compensation of an equivalent amount from the seller or supplier where the latter is the party cancelling the contract;

(e) requiring any consumer who fails to fulfil his obligation to pay a disproportionately high sum in compensation;

(f) authorising the seller or supplier to dissolve the contract on a discretionary basis where the same facility is not granted to the consumer, or permitting the seller or supplier to retain the sums paid for services not yet supplied by him where it is the seller or supplier himself who dissolves the contract;

(g) enabling the seller or supplier to terminate a contract of indeterminate duration without reasonable notice except where there are serious grounds for doing so;

(h) automatically extending a contract of fixed duration where the consumer does not indicate otherwise, when the deadline fixed for the consumer to express this desire not to extend the contract is unreasonably early;

(i) irrevocably binding the consumer to terms with which he had no real opportunity of becoming acquainted before the conclusion of the contract;

(j) enabling the seller or supplier to alter the terms of the contract unilaterally without a valid reason which is specified in the contract;

(k) enabling the seller or supplier to alter unilaterally without a valid reason any characteristics of the product or service to be provided;

5   See *Interfoto Picture Library Ltd v Stiletto Visual Programmes Ltd* [1989] QB 433 at 439 (per BINGHAM LJ).
6   UTCCR 1999, Sch 2.

(l)   providing for the price of goods to be determined at the time of delivery or allowing a seller of goods or supplier of services to increase their price without in both cases giving the consumer the corresponding right to cancel the contract if the final price is too high in relation to the price agreed when the contract was concluded;

(m) giving the seller or supplier the right to determine whether the goods or services supplied are in conformity with the contract, or giving him the exclusive right to interpret any term of the contract;

(n)   limiting the seller's or supplier's obligation to respect commitments undertaken by his agents or making his commitments subject to compliance with a particular formality;

(o)   obliging the consumer to fulfil all his obligations where the seller or supplier does not perform his;

(p)   giving the seller or supplier the possibility of transferring his rights and obligations under the contract, where this may serve to reduce the guarantees for the consumer, without the latter's agreement;

(q)   excluding or hindering the consumer's right to take legal action or exercise any other legal remedy, particularly by requiring the consumer to take disputes exclusively to arbitration not covered by legal provisions, unduly restricting the evidence available to him or imposing on him a burden of proof which, according to the applicable law, should lie with another party to the contract.

How useful this list is may be doubted. Since it is only indicative, it has no obvious status. Moreover there is nothing in the Regulations to place on the party seeking to rely on a particular term a duty to prove that the term is prima facie fair. On the other hand, it does give some guidance on the meaning of fairness in the context of the Regulations.

To date, most attempts at enforcement of the Regulations have come through the Office of Fair Trading which has sought assurances from traders that they will cease to use terms regarded as unfair. As a result, there has been little case law other than the decision of the Court of Appeal in *Director General of Fair Trading v First National Bank plc*.[7] Here the defendants sought to rely on a clause in their standard loan agreement that provided for interest payments in the event of default, covering both the outstanding principal amount and accrued unpaid interest. The effect of the term was to leave debtors with a substantial liability for interest even after the debt had been discharged. At first instance, the injunction sought by the Director General was refused on the ground that there had been no substantive or procedural unfairness. However, the Court of Appeal disagreed, mainly on the ground that the trial judge had adopted an over-subjective view of what was fair or unfair. As PETER GIBSON LJ observes:

> The test of unfairness is not to be judged from personal concepts of inherent fairness apart from the requirements of the Directive and Regulations, and we are far from convinced that a borrower would think it fair that when he is taken to court and an order for payment by instalments has been tailored to meet what he could afford and he complied with that order, he should then be told that he has to pay further sums by way of interest.

In particular, PETER GIBSON LJ thought that the term created 'an unfair surprise' and for that reason could be regarded as unfair.

Perhaps the most significant aspect of the decision rests in the willingness of the Court of Appeal to overturn the decision of the trial judge. It may be noted that under the Unfair Contract Terms Act 1977, the Court of Appeal has been very reluctant to disagree with the court of first instance on the matter of reasonableness of an exemption clause.

7   [2000] 2 WLR 353, reversing the decision of EVANS-LOMBE J, [2000] 1 All ER 240.

Part II

Specific obligations

CONTENTS

Chapter 25

Liability for defective products

1. THE CONTRACT/TORT DICHOTOMY

Where a person is harmed by a defective product, his action may lie in contract or tort, or both, according to the type of damage suffered and the nature of the relationship between the person harmed and the person responsible for the harm.

Suppose X buys from Y a television made by Z. If, due to the use of defective components or poor design, the television explodes injuring both X and A (X's son) and damages other property belonging to X, a number of possible actions may lie. Z the manufacturer, may owe a tortious duty to both X and A in respect of his failure to take reasonable care and may be in breach of the apparently strict duty imposed by the Consumer Protection Act 1987. Since the primary focus of tortious rules in the context of a product liability action is the safety of the product supplied, these duties are likely to extend only to death, personal injuries and damage to property other than the television itself. X may be able to sue Y for breach of the contractual implied terms as to satisfactory quality and fitness for purpose, breach of which will allow an action for both personal injuries and damage to property other than the television, as items of consequential loss. But since contractual rules on product liability are also concerned with qualitative defects, X may also be able to reject the television and recover the amount paid for it under the contract on the basis that he has been deprived of a product of the quality and fitness he could reasonably expect. Moreover, Y, in turn, may be able to sue on the contract he has with Z, in respect of his liability to X. But no contractual action will be available to A, since he has no contractual relationship with anyone and will be precluded from bringing an action in contract by virtue of the operation of the doctrine of privity of contract.

From this, it can be seen that the tortious duties owed to the user of a product are more concerned with product safety than with product quality,[1] the purpose of which is to compensate the plaintiff to the extent to which he is out of pocket by returning him to the position he was in before the harm was suffered.

---

1 See *Junior Books Ltd v Veitchi Co Ltd* [1983] 1 AC 520 at 549 (per LORD BRANDON) (dissenting); *D & F Estates Ltd v Church Comrs for England* [1988] 2 All ER 992 at 995 (per LORD BRIDGE); *Murphy v Brentwood District Council* [1990] 2 All ER 908 at 925 (per LORD BRIDGE) and see also Cane (1979) 95 LQR 117; Clarke (1985) 48 MLR 325.

Rules of the law of contract, while capable of dealing with unsafe products, also provide a remedy where the product itself is qualitatively defective, in the sense that the product is not worth the amount paid for it by the purchaser. Thus in an action for breach of the implied terms of quality and fitness, the purchaser may recover damages for personal injury[2] or harm to property[3] as items of consequential loss.[4] Moreover, where the product is not worth the amount paid for it, the purchaser is entitled to damages in respect of its decrease in value so as to represent the harm to the purchaser's expectations of quality.

An often cited distinction between contractual and tortious remedies has been that tort law remedies are meant to protect the plaintiff from wrongful harm rather than to protect the plaintiff's expectations. However, this distinction may be problematic since there are instances in which a tortious remedy has been provided where the protected interest of the plaintiff appears to relate to his expectations of proper performance by the defendant.[5] Moreover, in the context of a product liability action, it should also be noted that the definition of defectiveness in the Consumer Protection Act 1987 is based on general expectations of safety,[6] but these are not the same expectations as those protected by the Sale of Goods Act 1979.

2.   PLAINTIFFS AND DEFENDANTS

(1)   PRIVITY OF CONTRACT AND ITS ATTENDANT DIFFICULTIES

Common law liability for defective products is dominated by the doctrine of privity of contract, which dictates that only the parties to a contract can acquire rights and be subject to obligations under the contract. The doctrine can be divided into two categories – 'vertical' and 'horizontal' privity.[7] Vertical privity is that which exists between one person and his immediate predecessor or successor in a descending chain of distribution from the producer to the retailer. Horizontal privity is the privity which exists between the retailer and the consumer who buys from him.

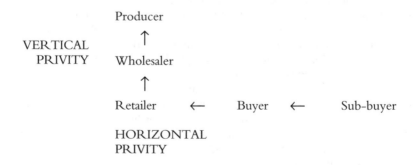

2   *Godley v Perry* [1960] 1 WLR 9 (injury to purchaser); *Preist v Last* [1903] 2 KB 148 (injury to purchaser's spouse, but only that loss suffered by the purchaser was actionable).
3   *Wilson v Rickett Cockerell* [1954] 1 QB 598.
4   Cf Waddams (1974) 37 MLR 154.
5   See *Junior Books Ltd v Veitchi Co Ltd* [1983] 1 AC 520 (expectation of product quality) and *White v Jones* [1995] 2 AC 207 (expectation of gain as an intended beneficiary of a will). See also Stapleton (1997) 113 LQR 257.
6   Consumer Protection Act 1987, s 3.
7   Law Commission Working Paper No 64 (1975) para 120.

In cases where there is no vertical privity, the buyer's problems may be resolved by the use of third- and fourth-party proceedings. For example, in *Dodd & Dodd v Wilson & McWilliam*[8] the plaintiff employed the defendant, a veterinary surgeon, to inject his cattle with a serum which later proved to be unfit for its intended use, and the cattle became ill. The veterinary surgeon sought an indemnity from his supplier who, in turn, brought in the manufacturers as fourth parties to the proceedings. The end result was that the manufacturers had compensated the plaintiff without there being any need to establish the negligence of the former. However, such a result can only be achieved if all parties remain solvent and there are no exemption clauses breaking the chain of liability through to the manufacturer.[9]

In the absence of privity of contract, the ultimate consumer may proceed against the producer of a defective product either in negligence or under Part I of the Consumer Protection Act 1987. Thus, a donee,[10] a member of the buyer's family,[11] or a bystander[12] injured by a defective product would fall outside the requirements of the doctrine of privity. Their action, if any, would have to be in tort against the manufacturer or producer of the defective product.

Arguably, there is nothing wrong in treating a contractual plaintiff more favourably than an outsider to the contract, since the former has provided consideration. But the requirements of fitness and quality under the Sale of Goods Act 1979, section 14 are legally imposed obligations which all purchasers of products can expect to be complied with. Also, while the law of contract continues to allow the consumer to recover damages for personal injuries[13] and property damage, one can expect the courts to adopt a more liberal attitude to the doctrine of privity.

(2)   CIRCUMVENTION OF THE DOCTRINE OF PRIVITY OF CONTRACT

There are numerous circumstances in which it is apparent that goods have been bought on behalf of someone other than the purchaser. For example, the buyer of a present may ask for it to be gift-wrapped, or a parent may buy a toy obviously intended for the use of a child. Food may be purchased in such quantities that it is obviously intended for consumption by an entire family, or a vehicle may be acquired, the supplier knowing that it is to be used by persons other than the immediate transferee. In all such cases, a non-contractual plaintiff may well be affected, but a strict application of the doctrine of privity of contract would deny such a person a contractual action. To deal with some of these difficulties, a number of devices have been developed at common law.

(i)   The collateral warranty[14]

The user of a defective product may have an action against its manufacturer on the basis of a collateral warranty. Although the greatest use of this device, in the past, has been in cases where the so-called parol evidence rule might prevent the use of extrinsic evidence to show that an oral statement which is not incorporated in a written contractual

---

8   [1946] 2 All ER 691.
9   See *Lambert v Lewis* [1980] 1 All ER 978, CA; revsd [1981] 1 All ER 1185, HL.
10   *Donoghue v Stevenson* [1932] AC 562.
11   *Daniels and Daniels v R White & Sons Ltd and Tabard* [1938] 4 All ER 258; *Preist v Last* [1903] 2 KB 148.
12   *Stennett v Hancock and Peters* [1939] 2 All ER 578.
13   This places the contractual plaintiff in a highly privileged position, in that the retailer is strictly liable for the consequences of supplying defective products. Normally, the plaintiff in an action for personal injury will have to base his action in negligence and prove fault on the part of the defendant.
14   See Wedderburn [1959] CLJ 58.

document is nevertheless a term of the contract,[15] it may also be used in other circumstances. For example, there are 'floating warranties'[16] under which the principal contract is one to which either the maker or the recipient of the warranty is not a party. Thus in the case of a product liability action, the warranty may have been made by the manufacturer of a product, but the buyer purchases the product from some other wholesale or retail outlet. In these circumstances, although the apparent basis of liability is contractual, the court will reflect on the words and conduct of the defendant and decide whether the plaintiff has relied to his detriment on what the defendant has said or done. In the majority of collateral warranty cases, the statement made by the defendant will induce an act of detrimental reliance resulting in out of pocket loss on the part of the plaintiff. Accordingly, an award of damages will not protect the plaintiff's full expectation interest in the sense that he will not be placed in the position he would have been in had the statement been true.[17] However, in the case of 'floating warranties' by manufacturers, the buyer may be able to show that the manufacturer has guaranteed his product or has made some other statement with the intention that it should be acted upon in the form of a purchase of the product from another supplier. In these circumstances, the buyer may have the benefit of an action for breach of a collateral warranty against the manufacturer should the product prove to be qualitatively defective so that he is placed in the same position as if he had brought an action for breach of one of the implied terms in the Sale of Goods Act 1979 against the retailer.[18] In the foregoing example, the collateral contract is used as a means of creating liability on the part of the manufacturer, but it should also be noted that in some instances the dealings between the parties may be such that the collateral contract operates so as to deny the liability of the defendant both in contract and in the tort of negligence.[19]

In strict theory, the courts should look for a contractual intent before holding the defendant liable on a collateral contract.[20] But, there is no justification for this requirement in the early development of the warranty doctrine, the origins of which actually lie in the law of tort. Moreover, there are a number of cases which show that convincing proof of a contractual intent has not always been sought.[1]

Due to the present contractual basis of collateral warranties, the courts will search for consideration for the guarantee of quality, which can be found in the act of purchasing the guaranteed goods from a retail supplier.[2] But could consumer use of an extravagantly described product satisfy the requirement of consideration? In *Carlill v Carbolic Smoke Ball Co*[3] BOWEN LJ observed that an offer can be made to the whole world which can ripen into a contract with anyone who performs the specified condition contained in

---

15   See eg *Esso Petroleum Co Ltd v Mardon* [1976] QB 801.

16   See Beatson *Anson's Law of Contract* (27th edn, 1998) p 129.

17   See eg *Esso Petroleum Co Ltd v Mardon* [1976] QB 801.

18   *See Shanklin Pier Ltd v Detel Products Ltd* [1951] 2 KB 854; *Wells (Merstham) Ltd v Buckland Sand and Silica Ltd* [1965] 2 QB 170.

19   *Greater Nottinghamshire Co-operative Society Ltd v Cementation Piling and Foundation Ltd* [1988] 2 All ER 971; *Norwich City Council v Harvey* [1989] 1 All ER 1180.

20   *Heilbut Symons & Co v Buckleton* [1913] AC 30; *Lambert v Lewis* [1980] 1 All ER 978 (decision reversed on other grounds), [1981] 1 All ER 1185, HL; *Independent Broadcasting Authority v EMI Electronics* (1980) 14 BLR 1. Cf Williston (1913) 27 Harv LR 1, and see also Waddams (1969) 19 Univ Tor LJ 157 and (1974) 37 MLR 154.

1   *De Lassalle v Guildford* [1901] 2 KB 215; *Schawel v Reade* [1913] 2 IR 64; *Couchman v Hill* [1947] KB 554; *Dick Bentley Productions v Harold Smith (Motors) Ltd* [1965] 2 All ER 65; *Andrews v Hopkinson* [1957] 1 QB 229.

2   *Shanklin Pier Ltd v Detel Products Ltd* [1951] 2 KB 854 at 856 (per McNAIR J).

3   [1893] 1 QB 256. See also *Wood v Letrik* (1932) Times, 12 January; *Bowerman v ABTA Ltd* [1995] NLJR 1815.

the advertisement.[4] However, in *Lambert v Lewis*[5] the view was expressed that the advertisers in *Carlill* were not saying, 'If you acquire our product, we promise it is safe and merchantable . . .'.[6] They were simply expressing confidence in their wares and backing this confidence with an offer to compensate the plaintiff.

While the majority of product liability cases in which a collateral warranty has been recognised have involved express statements, there is no reason why the same device could not be extended to implied warranties, which are logically indistinguishable.[7] Indeed, it has been suggested that it might be possible to imply warranties of quality and fitness from the simple presence of goods on the market.[8] This is a step which has been taken in the United States where the law has not been dogged by the requirement of a contractual intent in order to find a collateral warranty. In *Henningsen v Bloomfield Motors Inc*[9] it was observed that the layman does not have the opportunity or the capacity to inspect or to determine the fitness of a car for use and must rely on the manufacturer who has control of the construction of the vehicle and, in most cases, the dealer who supplies the vehicle. In these circumstances the 'demands of social justice' are that the manufacturer should be taken to impliedly warrant the fitness of the vehicle supplied to the customer.

(ii) Third-party proceedings

If a person other than the buyer of defective goods can sue the supplier, the harsher effects of the horizontal privity requirement may be avoided. Thus if one person can be said to have contracted on behalf of others, in limited circumstances, those others may be able to maintain an action against the supplier of the defective product. For example, in *Lockett v A & M Charles Ltd*,[10] it was held that where two people enter a restaurant and order a meal, regardless of who actually pays for the meal, there is a contract between the restaurant owner and each of the diners so that the person who has not paid is still a contracting party and can sue for breach of contract if the food served is unfit for human consumption. TUCKER J rejected the defendant's argument that the contract was with the husband who had made the booking, preferring to hold that each person who goes into a hotel and orders food is making himself liable to the proprietor for what he orders, no matter what the private arrangements between the diners regarding the matter of payment might be.[11] The position might be different where a host hires a room in a hotel in order to hold a party for friends and requests that the hotel caterers provide a finger buffet. In these circumstances the host is the sole contracting party and it is highly unlikely that the hotelier could sue the guests should the host decline to pay for the hire of the room and buffet facilities.

Whether this principle could be used to allow bystanders, members of the purchaser's family or other persons not in horizontal privity with the retailer to sue remains doubtful, since it is not always immediately obvious in cases involving the purchase of defective products that the buyer is acting on behalf of others. It is arguable that where one person purchases large quantities of food in a weekly or monthly 'shop' that the substantial amount purchased suggests that someone other than the purchaser will consume at

---

4 Ibid at 268.
5 [1980] 1 All ER 978 reversed on other grounds in [1981] 1 All ER 1185, HL.
6 Ibid at 1002 (per STEPHENSON LJ).
7 See Simpson *History* pp 241–242.
8 Miller and Lovell *Product Liability* (1977) p 65. Cf Atiyah *Sale of Goods* p 238.
9 161 A 2d 69 (NJ, 1960). See also Miller and Lovell *Product Liability* (1977) pp 15–18.
10 [1938] 4 All ER 170. Cf *Buckley v La Reserve* [1959] Crim LR 451 and see also *Jackson v Horizon Holidays Ltd* [1975] 3 All ER 92.
11 Ibid at 172 (per TUCKER J).

least a proportion of the amount purchased, but there is no authority supporting recovery on the part of the non-purchaser in the absence of a presumed agency.[12]

(iii)   Non-contractual solutions

(a)   Manufacturers and producers
The doctrine of privity of contract merely provides that a third party cannot sue on a contract to which he is not privy. It does not prevent an action in tort against a negligent manufacturer, provided there is a sufficient relationship of proximity between the parties.[13] Alternatively, there may be an action under Part I of the Consumer Protection Act 1987.

The rule of manufacturer's liability in *Donoghue v Stevenson*[14] has not been confined to food and drink causing physical harm, but covers all defectively manufactured products. Thus, a duty of care is owed by a manufacturer of clothing to those who wear his product,[15] and a stonemason owes a duty of care in respect of a badly erected tombstone.[16]

The rule in *Donoghue v Stevenson* is couched in terms of manufacturer's liability, but it is better to regard the rule as extending to anyone responsible for putting into circulation a product which is not reasonably safe. Accordingly, liability has been extended to negligent retailers,[17] wholesalers,[18] repairers,[19] assemblers,[20] and those who hire or lease products.[1] The rule of liability can also extend to donors.[2]

The Consumer Protection Act 1987[3] imposes strict liability upon the producer[4] of a defective product. The term 'producer' covers the manufacturer of a finished article or a component, or the producer of raw materials. The effect of the Act is to make a producer liable for a defect by virtue of the fact that he has supplied the finished product.[5] Consequently, where the producer is not liable for defects in the finished product, for example where it is excluded from the provisions of the Act, the producer cannot be made liable for a defect in any constituent part supplied by another person.[6]

The term 'producer' is also extended to cover 'own-branders', that is, retailers who apply their own name or trade mark to a product manufactured by some other person. By doing so, own-branders hold themselves out as producers.[7] Importers are also regarded as producers for the purposes of the Act, if, in the course of a business, they bring a

---

12   *Heil v Hedges* [1951] 1 TLR 512.
13   *Donoghue v Stevenson* [1932] AC 562.
14   Ibid.
15   *Grant v Australian Knitting Mills Ltd* [1936] AC 85.
16   *Brown v Cotterill* (1934) 51 TLR 21.
17   *Fisher v Harrods Ltd* [1966] 1 Lloyd's Rep 500; *Andrews v Hopkinson* [1957] 1 QB 229.
18   *Watson v Buckley, Osborne, Garrett & Co Ltd* [1940] 1 All ER 174.
19   *Haseldine v CA Daw & Son Ltd* [1941] 2 KB 343; *Herschtal v Stewart and Ardern Ltd* [1940] 1 KB 155; *Stennett v Hancock and Peters* [1939] 2 All ER 578.
20   *Malfroot v Noxal Ltd* (1935) 51 TLR 551; *Howard v Furness Houlder Argentine Lines Ltd* [1936] 2 All ER 781.
1   *White v John Warrick & Co Ltd* [1953] 2 All ER 1021.
2   *Hawkins v Coulsden and Purley UDC* [1954] 1 QB 319; *Griffiths v Arch Engineering Co (Newport) Ltd* [1968] 3 All ER 217. See also Miller and Lovell *Product Liability* (1977) pp 308–309.
3   See Merkin *A Guide to the Consumer Protection Act 1987* (1987).
4   Consumer Protection Act 1987, s 2(2)(a). There can be more than one producer of a product, in which case liability is joint and several: s 2(5).
5   Ibid, s 1(3).
6   Ibid.
7   Ibid, s 2(2)(b).

defective product into the EC from outside.[8] This is a particularly useful provision in relieving the consumer of the need to sue out of jurisdiction where the manufacturer of a defective product is located outside a European Community member state. For example in *G v Fry Surgical International Ltd*[9] the plaintiff was injured in the course of surgery when a pair of surgical scissors broke during an operation and became embedded in his knee joint. The defect was clearly due to negligent manufacture, but the scissors had been manufactured in Sweden, which was outside the EC at the time. Instead proceedings were brought against the importer, who readily settled for £1,700.

In limited circumstances, a retail supplier may be subject to the strict liability regime imposed by the Act. If, within a reasonable period of the date of damage, a consumer requests the supplier of a defective product to identify the producer, and the supplier fails to comply within a reasonable time of that request, the supplier may be held responsible.[10] Thus if a retailer is unable or unwilling to provide evidence as to the identity of the producer or neglects to respond to a request made by the consumer he may be held responsible for the value of the claim which would otherwise have been made against the producer.[11]

The Act is lacking in one respect, in that it does not identify when damage is caused to the consumer, with the result that it is difficult to determine when the 'reasonable period' commences. If the date of damage is the date on which it begins to occur,[12] the consumer may be out of time before he is even aware that he has grounds for complaint. On the other hand, if the relevant date is when the consumer became aware, or ought to have become aware, of the damage, the reasonable period will run from a much later date. Some guidance is provided in relation to property damage, which is suffered when it is reasonably discoverable,[13] but nothing is said about personal injury.

(b)   Consumers

Initially, the negligence-based manufacturer's liability was confined to purchasers[14] and immediate donees.[15] However, after a short period of judicial conservatism, the 'narrow rule' was extended to include employees of the user,[16] passengers in a vehicle,[17] commercial users,[18] borrowers[19] and mere bystanders.[20] Thus, any person reasonably likely to be endangered by the product in its defective form came to be protected by the fault-based rule.

While the 1987 Act is entitled The Consumer Protection Act, it gives no definition of the term 'consumer'. Furthermore, it is clear that any person who suffers damage is entitled to proceed against the producer.[1] Also, many 'consumer' complaints may actually be excluded from the Act, because there is a lower limit on the liability of the producer

---

8   Ibid, s 2(2)(c).
9   Case settled, but referred to in the First European Commission Review of the operation of the Product Liability Directive, 85/374/EEC (13.12.95, COM (95) 617 Final.)
10   Consumer Protection Act 1987, s 2(3).
11   Such a result has been achieved in Germany (882) LG Lübeck 3.9.91 (50 197/91).
12   See *Pirelli General Cable Works Ltd v Oscar Faber and Partners* [1983] 2 AC 1.
13   Consumer Protection Act 1987, s 5(5), (6).
14   *Grant v Australian Knitting Mills Ltd* [1936] AC 85.
15   *Donoghue v Stevenson* [1932] AC 562.
16   *Taylor v Rover* [1966] 1 WLR 1491.
17   *Malfroot v Noxall* (1935) 51 TLR 551.
18   *Vacwell Engineering Co Ltd v BDH Chemicals Ltd* [1971] 1 QB 111n; *Barnett v H and J Packer & Co Ltd* [1940] 3 All ER 575.
19   *Griffiths v Arch Engineering Co (Newport) Ltd* [1968] 3 All ER 217.
20   *Stennett v Hancock and Peters* [1939] 2 All ER 578; *Brown v Cotterill* (1934) 51 TLR 21; *Makin v T W Hand Fireworks Co* (1962) 37 DLR (2d) 455.
1   Consumer Protection Act 1987, s 2(1).

of £275 in respect of damage to property.[2] Damage is defined in section 5, and the major exclusion consists of damage to commercial property.[3] The general scheme of the Act is to compensate individuals rather than companies.

The type of harm suffered by the consumer is a relevant factor in determining the liability of the defendant. The negligent manufacturer whose product causes physical harm must generally accept responsibility for the failure of his product to reach desired standards of safety. If the product merely causes economic loss, then the plaintiff's likelihood of success in a negligence action is diminished. Such losses are seen as the province of the law of contract, although they may be recovered in a tortious action if there is a sufficient degree of proximity between the parties, but this is an increasingly unlikely event in product liability actions.[4] Under the Consumer Protection Act 1987, Part I, there is no prospect of recovering economic losses, since the loss recoverable is confined to physical injury and some varieties of property damage.[5]

(iv)   Reform of the doctrine of privity of contract

What seems clear, at present, is that under English law there is little prospect of any escape from the unfortunate effects of the doctrine of privity of contract. This remains the case following the referral of the doctrine of privity to the Law Commission[6] which has resulted in the enactment of the Contracts (Rights of Third Parties) Act 1999. The Law Commission made a number of recommendations to the effect that contracts made for the benefit of a third party should become enforceable, but these recommendations were based largely on giving effect to the express or implied intent of the contracting parties.[7] Of course the difficulty with product liability actions is that a large number of buyers of goods are consumer purchasers who are unlikely to contract in a manner which will express the combined intention of both parties that the contract is made for the benefit of a third person. It might be the case that a commercial buyer of goods who has in mind the rights of a third person, such as a potential sub-buyer, might contract expressly for the benefit of that third party or name the third party in such a way that it is the implied intention of the contracting parties that the third person is an intended beneficiary. Moreover, as the Law Commission demonstrate, there may even be occasions when a consumer purchaser makes it sufficiently clear that he is contracting on behalf of another. For example, it is possible that invitees to a relative's wedding may choose to buy a three-piece suite as a wedding gift, indicating to the retailer that the article purchased is intended to be a gift and that the suite should be delivered to a specified third party, the delivery slip bearing the name of the intended recipient. In these circumstances, the Law Commission considered that there would be sufficient evidence of an intent to benefit a third party to allow the third party to sue should the gift prove not to be of satisfactory quality.[8] In contrast, the same would not be true where the retailer is not informed that the article purchased is not intended as a gift and the present is delivered directly to the purchaser's address.[9]

---

2   Ibid, s 5(4).
3   Ibid, s 5(3).
4   See *Murphy v Brentwood DC* [1990] 2 All ER 908 but cf the position in New Zealand where different economic conditions suggest a different approach, at least in relation to defective buildings: *Invercargill City Council v Hamlin* [1996] 1 All ER 756.
5   Ibid, s 5(1).
6   *Privity of Contract: Contracts for the Benefit of Third Parties* (Law Comm Rep No 242, 1996. See also Adams, Beyleveld & Brownsword (1997) 60 MLR 238).
7   Ibid para 7.6. and see also ch 6 for discussion of the detailed provisions of the 1999 Act.
8   Ibid para 7.41.
9   Ibid para 7.42.

In the light of the special position of consumers, the Law Commission did consider whether it would be appropriate to legislate for a special test of enforceability for consumers,[10] but, in the end, they decided it would not be desirable to take the step of recommending that third parties should be able to enforce a contract made for their benefit in the absence of an express or implied intention by the contracting parties to do so. This remained the case even where the third party had justifiably and reasonably relied on the contract made by those others. This decision seems to have been arrived at on the policy ground that individual special cases might need to be considered, but that a general reforming measure should not be allowed to introduce conflicting results.[11] On these recommendations, it seems unlikely that where, for example, a manufacturer contracts with a wholesaler or retailer, there would be any express or implied identification of the ultimate consumer so as to allow the latter to sue as a third party. However, it will be seen below that there is a European Commission proposal to introduce a European consumer guarantee which might substantially improve the position of consumer purchasers of defective products.

3. PRODUCTS

(1) THE CONTRACT OF SALE AND OTHER TRANSACTIONS

If the plaintiff is an immediate transferee, his most likely action will be one for breach of one of the implied terms of his contract with the supplier. For the purposes of the sale of Goods Act 1979, s 2(1) a contract for the sale of goods is defined as one under which the seller transfers or agrees to transfer the property in goods to the buyer for a money consideration, called the price. For the purposes of these contracts, the issue of product quality is addressed by the implied terms contained in sections 12 to 15 of the 1979 Act.

One of the essential requirements of the 1979 Act is that some money is paid by way of consideration. Thus a contract of part-exchange can still be a sale of goods contract,[12] However, it may be more convenient to regard the part-exchange relationship as involving two separate contracts of sale, namely a principal contract under which a garage, for example, sells a new car to the buyer and a secondary contract under which the part-exchange vehicle is purchased by the garage from the buyer.[13] If the goods are given away as part of a promotional exercise,[14] or if there is a barter agreement,[15] the contract is not one which falls within the definition of a sale of goods contract, since in each case, there is no money consideration. Furthermore, if performance of the contractual obligations substantially involves the exercise of skill or the performance of a service[16] by the supplier, it is no longer governed by the Sale of Goods Act 1979 since the substance of the contract is the performance of the service or the exercise of skill rather than the transfer of ownership in the end product. In all of these cases in which a material article changes hands, but in which the definition of a sale of goods contract is not satisfied, the relevant implied terms for the purposes of the goods supplied

---

10 Ibid para 7.54–7.56.
11 Ibid para 7.55. Possible special cases might include consumer guarantees and the rights of subsequent purchasers or tenants to sue in respect of defective construction work.
12 *Aldridge v Johnson* (1857) 7 E & B 885, 119 ER 1476.
13 *G J Dawson (Clapham) Ltd v H and G Dutfield* [1936] 2 All ER 232; *Flynn v Mackin and Mahon* [1974] IR 101.
14 *Esso Petroleum Ltd v Customs and Excise Comrs* [1976] 1 All ER 117, [1976] 1 WLR 1.
15 *Chappell & Co Ltd v Nestlé Co Ltd* [1960] AC 87 at 109 (per LORD REID). See also Trading Stamps Act 1964 (as amended).
16 *Robinson v Graves* [1935] 1 KB 579; *Young and Marten Ltd v McManus Childs Ltd* [1969] 1 AC 454.

are contained in the Supply of Goods and Services Act 1982.[17] Where the contract is one of hire or is one of hire purchase the contract ceases to be one for the sale of goods, since in each case there is no transfer of or agreement to transfer property in the goods. The essential feature of these contracts is that there is a bailment under which possession may be transferred, but there is no obligation on the bailee to become the legal owner of the subject matter of the contract. So far as the issue of product liability is concerned, however, implied terms similar to those found in the Sale of Goods Act 1979 will form part of the contract.[18] A second feature of the definition of a contract for the sale of goods, and for that matter, any other contract involving the supply of goods is that the subject matter of the contract must fall within the definition of the word 'goods'. It has been seen above that there are certain varieties of contract which may involve a mixture of both supply of goods and the exercise of skill or the provision of labour.[19] In this case, it is important to distinguish between the supply of goods element under which the supplier is a guarantor of the quality of the goods supplied and the supply of services element under which the supplier is liable only on proof of fault.[20]

Inter alia, goods are defined as all personal chattels other than things in action and money, including industrial growing crops, things attached to or forming part of land (if there is an agreement to sever them from the land before sale).[1] It follows from this that merely because trees etc. may grow on land they may still be regarded as the subject matter of a contract of sale if there is an agreement to sever the growing trees from the land so as to facilitate the supply of timber, however, the contract must consist of something more than a mere licence to take from the land at will.[2] If something is attached to land, such as a wall or some variety of electrical fitting, it may originally be regarded as part of the land, but it can become the subject matter of a contract of sale, if it is agreed that the stones making up the wall be sold or if it is agreed that the fitting be removed and sold. By their nature, goods are tangible articles, which explains the exclusion from the definition of goods of intangible items of personal property such as debts and shares in a company. The definition is particularly broad, but must be considered in the light of the underlying function of the Sale of Goods Act 1979, namely to facilitate trade in goods. As a result of this, it is arguable that any tangible article which is not the ordinary subject of trade may not be treated as goods. This restriction would seem to apply to sales of body parts, some of which are illegal by statute.[3] However, a more difficult question is whether there would be a contract for the sale of goods in respect of human blood products, especially those which are hepatitis or HIV-infected. Judicial decisions on the point are not conclusive,[4] but the general trend has been to reach decisions which tend to support the position of the blood supplier.[5]

A further problem case is that intellectual products such as information contained in computer software or ideas expressed in a book may or may not be regarded as 'goods'. The Sale of Goods Act 1979 would apply if a book supplied though a retail outlet was discovered to have 50 pages missing or if a floppy disk was discovered to be so badly

---

17   Supply of Goods and Services Act 1982, ss 1–5.
18   Supply of Goods and Services Act 1982, ss 6–10 (contracts of hire);Supply of Goods (Implied Terms) Act 1973, s 10 (contracts of hire purchase).
19   For example a contract under which a plumber agrees to supply and install a central heating system.
20   See further ch 26.
1   Sale of Goods Act 1979, s 61(1).
2   *Morgan v Russell & Sons* [1909] 1 KB 357.
3   Human Organ Transplant Act 1989, s 1 which makes it an offence to make or receive payment for human organs whether from a corpse or a living person.
4   *Perlmutter v Beth David Hospital* 123 NE 2d 792 (1954) (supply of services); *Reilly v King County Central Blood Bank Inc* 492 P 2d 246 (1972) (sale of goods).
5   For example by holding that there is no money consideration.

damaged that it could not be used in a computer drive. However, different considerations may apply where the information given by the author of a book or the computer program recorded on the disk is defective to the extent that a user suffers damage in trying to follow those instructions or in attempting to use the software for its intended purpose. For example, would the author of a recipe book be regarded as the supplier of a defective product if a recipe for chilli con carne using unprocessed red kidney beans failed to point out that the beans should be boiled for a substantial period before use in order to remove toxins naturally present in the beans? Authors would be extremely worried if they were to be regarded as guarantors of the accuracy of every statement made in a book and might be tempted to disclaim liability for reliance on the written word. In the past it has ordinarily been the case that a supplier of information is liable only on proof of fault, yet there are dicta in *St Albans City & District Council v International Computers Ltd*[6] which suggest that the supply of information in computer disk form can be regarded as a sale of goods, despite the fact that if it is the program which is defective, the complaint relates to the provision of information. In the *St Albans* case, SIR IAIN GLIDEWELL appears to distinguish between 'off the shelf' computer software and that which is designed to special order, which he suggests involves the supply of a service.[7] It seems illogical to regard a computer program as goods when it is supplied in disk form, yet regard the same information as involving the supply of a service when it is transferred to the user's computer system without the user being supplied with a tangible article.

It is true to say that information supplied with goods can be relevant in deciding whether a product is of the desired standard of quality. In determining whether goods are of satisfactory quality or fit for the particular purpose for which the buyer requires them under section 14 of the Sale of Goods Act 1979, regard will be had to the effectiveness and intelligibility of any instructions supplied with the goods.[8] In these circumstances, however, the problem is that the product cannot be used if the instructions supplied are unintelligible or inadequate. In contrast if computer software contains inaccurate information this does not stop the computer disk from being used, but merely means that the information supplied by the software provider is inaccurate. If the conventional view of information provision has been swept aside, is the next logical step that a solicitor could be sued under the Sale of Goods Act for supplying a negligently drafted letter of advice (a material article containing information)?[9]

(2)   PRODUCTS AND THE RULE IN *DONOGHUE v STEVENSON*

If there is no relevant contract for the supply of goods, the injured consumer may turn to the law of tort. He must show that the article about which he complains is one to which the rule in *Donoghue v Stevenson*[10] applies. The plaintiff had supposedly consumed the contents of a bottle of ginger beer which included a decomposed snail. As a result, she suffered gastro-enteritis. The House of Lords, by a majority, held that the manufacturer of goods owes a duty to exercise reasonable care towards all those foreseeably likely to come into contact with the defective product. It might have been possible in the immediate aftermath of *Donoghue v Stevenson* to confine the application of the rule to food and drink. However, such a narrow interpretation was rejected by the Privy Council in *Grant v Australian Knitting Mills Ltd*,[11] in which the rule was applied to woollen

6   [1996] 4 All ER 481.
7   Ibid at 493 and see ch 26.
8   *Wormell v RHM Agriculture (East) Ltd* [1987] 3 All ER 75; *Amstrad plc v Seagate Technology Inc* (1997) 86 BLR 34.
9   Bridge *The Sale of Goods* (paperback edition, 1998) Foreword p vi.
10   [1932] AC 562. See also Heuston (1957) 20 MLR 1.
11   [1936] AC 85.

undergarments which were impregnated with excessive quantities of sulphites, thereby causing the plaintiff to suffer from dermatitis.[12] The result of this decision was that the rule could be applied to all manufactured products, including cleaning fluids,[13] lifts,[14] motor vehicles and repairs done to them,[15] hair dye,[16] tools used in the workplace,[17] chemicals,[18] and disinfectants.[19] The rule also applies to containers in which goods are supplied,[20] as do the implied terms of fitness and merchantability in contracts for the supply of goods.[1]

(3)   PRODUCTS AND THE CONSUMER PROTECTION ACT 1987

The Act defines a product as including goods, electricity, component parts and raw materials.[2] Since goods include substances, growing crops, things comprised in land by virtue of being attached to it, ships, aircraft and vehicles,[3] it is difficult to imagine anything which cannot be regarded as a product. Arguably, human body parts and blood products and possibly intellectual products such as ideas expressed in a book[4] will fall within the provisions of the Act provided they cause personal injury or property damage. Thus it is arguable that a recipe book which contains defective information and causes the consumer to suffer illness through eating inadequately cooked food might fall within the provisions of the Act. Similarly computer software can reasonably be regarded as a product for the purposes of the Act, although it might be necessary to distinguish between 'off the shelf' products and those which are designed to special order which may be better regarded as involving the supply of information services.[5] Just as the provision of information by a retailer or manufacturer of goods is relevant in determining whether goods are of the desired standard of quality or fitness under the Sale of Goods Act, so also will it be relevant under the Consumer Protection Act 1987. It will be seen in determining whether a product is defective, a court will have regard to instructions as to use issued with the product.[6] It is likely that this provision will involve similar considerations to those which apply in a fault-based enquiry as to whether there has been a breach of the duty of care owed by a manufacturer of an allegedly unsafe product, in which it is clear that badly worded instructions may render a manufacturer liable for negligence.[7]

---

12   The manufacturer was liable despite evidence suggesting that the plaintiff had worn the same garment for at least a week without ever removing it during that period.
13   *Fisher v Harrods Ltd* [1966] 1 Lloyd's Rep 500.
14   *Haseldine v C A Daw & Son Ltd* [1941] 3 All ER 156.
15   *Andrews v Hopkinson* [1957] 1 QB 229; *Malfroot v Noxal* (1935) 51 TLR 551; *Herschtal v Stewart and Ardern* [1940] 1 KB 155.
16   *Kubach v Hollands* [1937] 3 All ER 907; *Watson v Buckley, Osborne, Garrett & Co Ltd* [1940] 1 All ER 174; *Parker v Oloxo Ltd* [1937] 3 All ER 524.
17   *Taylor v Rover Co* [1966] 1 WLR 1491; *Mason v Williams and Williams* [1955] 1 WLR 549.
18   *Vacwell Engineering Co Ltd v BDH Chemicals Ltd* [1971] 1 QB 88.
19   *British South Africa Co v Lennon Ltd* (1915) 113 LT 935; *Grant v Cooper* [1940] NZLR 947.
20   *Fisher v Harrods Ltd* [1966] 1 Lloyd's Rep 500; *Hill v James Crowe (Cases) Ltd* [1978] 1 All ER 812.
1   *Geddling v Marsh* [1920] 1 KB 668; *Morelli v Fitch and Gibbons* [1928] 2 KB 636.
2   Consumer Protection Act 1987, s 1(2).
3   Ibid, s 45(1).
4   See Whittaker (1989) 105 LQR 125 and see also *St Albans City & District Council v International Computers Ltd* [1996] 4 All ER 481 considered above.
5   Ibid. But see the discussion of this issue and *St Albans City & District Council v International Computers Ltd* [1996] 4 All ER 481 in relation to the Sale of Goods Act above.
6   Consumer Protection Act 1987, s 3(2)(a).
7   *Vacwell Engineering Co Ltd v BDH Chemicals Ltd* [1971] 1 QB 88; *Watson v Buckley, Osborne, Garrett & Co Ltd* [1940] 1 All ER 174.

There are some specific exclusions from the provisions of the Act. For example, a building disposed of by the creation of an interest in land is not a product,[8] although, the materials used to construct the building will be subject to the Act if they prove to be defective.

Further important exceptions relate to nuclear power[9] and agricultural produce which has not undergone an industrial process.[10] This last exception has been abolished in the light of recent food scares concerning salmonella in eggs, BSE contamination of beef products and more recently genetically modified organisms. The consumer interest in safe food has made it a priority to reconsider the continued viability of this particular exception, so that for the future the Product Liability Directive will apply to primary agricultural produce.[11]

Under the present state of the law, however, it is necessary to determine what amounts to an industrial or initial process. For example, fresh fruit, vegetables and meat would seem to escape the provisions of the Act if it is decided that harvesting or slaughtering is not an industrial process. But frozen poultry and canned vegetables would be regarded as products for the purposes of the Act. The difficulty would appear to be to decide what is an industrial process.[12] For example, would the spraying of growing crops with pesticides constitute an industrial process? Likewise, it would appear to be difficult, on the present wording of the 1987 Act and the Product Liability Directive to determine whether recent experiments involving the cloning of sheep involve an industrial process sufficient to take the end product of the process out of the strict liability regime created by the Act.[13] These problems of interpretation apart, there is also an argument that the 1987 Act has not given proper effect to the wording of the EC Directive, which refers to an initial process,[14] but if the terms 'initial' and 'industrial processing' are inconsistent with each other, the wording of the Directive should prevail over that contained in the Act,[15] although this may not produce a satisfactory answer since the language used by the Directive is itself equivocal.

By virtue of the inclusion of ships, aircraft and vehicles in the definition of a product, it seems likely that major transport disasters will now fall within the provisions of the Act, if caused by the defectiveness of the vehicle.

4.   DEFECTIVENESS

English product liability law has two principal aims – product safety and product quality. The appropriate standard required of the producer or supplier appears to differ according to whether an action is brought in the tort of negligence, under the Consumer Protection Act 1987 or under the Sale of Goods Act 1979. Generally, the role of tortious rules in relation to defective products is to achieve an acceptable standard of safety, whereas contractual rules are predominantly concerned with expectations of product quality. However, it will be seen below that there has been a considerable blurring of the edges

---

8   Ibid, s 46(4).
9   Ibid, s 6(8).
10   Ibid, s 2(4).
11   See Directive 99/34 EC amending Directive 85/374/EEC concerning liability for defective products.
12   See Merkin *The Consumer Protection Act 1987* (1987) ch 3.3; Bradgate and Savage (1987) NLJ 929 at 931.
13   See McLeish (1997) 147 NLJ 682.
14   Council Directive 85/374/EEC art 2. Cf the third recital which refers to an industrial process.
15   Geddes *Product and Service Liability in the EEC* (1992) para 2.3.1.2.

of the boundary between contract and tort. For example, the new definition of satisfactory quality in the sale of Goods Act 1979, s 14(2B) makes it clear that an aspect of the quality of goods is whether or not they are safe. Moreover, as would be expected, the requirement of satisfactory quality is defined in terms of the expectations of reasonable people, but it is also significant that the standard of safety required to satisfy the definition of defectiveness in the Consumer Protection Act 1987, s 3(1) is also defined in terms of consumer expectations.

The standard of safety applied in cases of negligence is that which is expected by the reasonable man. If ginger beer is not as safe as the reasonable man would expect, the manufacturer is negligent. This involves a cost-benefit analysis of the defendant's conduct balanced against the value of his product to society. Thus, the court will take into account matters such as the likelihood of the product causing harm, the severity of harm, the benefit to be obtained from running the risk of harm and the practicability of taking precautions to avoid harm.[16]

In cases falling within the provisions of the Sale of Goods Act 1979, the test applied to the issue of product quality is one of consumer expectations. The Act provides that goods are of satisfactory quality if they:

> meet the standard that a reasonable person would regard as satisfactory, taking account of any description of the goods, the price (if relevant) and all other relevant circumstances.[17]

Implicit in this test is the assumption that reasonable people, if aware of all relevant circumstances, will agree about the defective quality of a product according to a common standard. Clearly there is no such thing as a common standard of quality, since the required quality of an article will depend on the terms of the contract and other surrounding circumstances. For example, a higher standard can be expected of an expensive motor car than can be expected of a budget family car,[18] and more can be expected of a comparatively expensive second-hand car such as a sports car than of a vehicle of lower specification.[19] However, if the reasonable man is aware of the attendant circumstances of a contract, an appropriate standard of quality can be ascertained.

In a contractual action, the required standard of quality is ascertainable by reference to the terms of the contract. But, since the seller's obligation to supply goods of the required quality is legally imposed and not voluntarily assumed, the expectations concerned could be said to be those of the average consumer.[20] However the wording of the definition of satisfactory quality in section 14(2A) might appear to make the test more objective than this since it refers not to the expectations of a reasonable consumer, but to the expectations of a reasonable person, which would seem to include not just consumers, but also expectations as to use which a reasonable retailer or producer might have. Nonetheless, what the average consumer might have in mind will still be a relevant consideration so that it may be relevant to consider whether such a person might have been influenced, *inter alia*, by the advertising and reputation of the manufacturer.

The boundary between tort and contract in the field of product liability law appears to have been considerably blurred by the provisions of the Consumer Protection Act 1987. This defines product safety in terms of a test of general expectations, thereby combining elements common to both tortious and contractual actions. The Act provides

---

16   See ch 12.
17   Sale of Goods Act 1979, s 14(2A).
18   *Rogers v Parish (Scarborough) Ltd* [1987] 2 All ER 232.
19   *Shine v General Guarantee Corpn* [1988] 1 All ER 911.
20   See Clarke (1985) 48 MLR 325 at 336. Cf *Junior Books Ltd v Veitchi Co Ltd* [1983] 1 AC 520 at 552 (per LORD BRANDON (dissenting)).

that a product is defective if, 'the safety of the product is not such as persons generally are entitled to expect . . .'[1] The Act renders a producer strictly liable for his defective products, but it would appear, on closer examination, that the provisions of the Act add little to the protection already provided by an action in negligence.[2]

It has been observed that determining whether or not a manufacturer is negligent involves a cost-benefit analysis. The same can be said of a general expectations test, particularly when it is expressly qualified by a state of the art defence.[3] In order to decide whether general expectations of safety have been met, the court will have to consider the benefits of a product balanced against the costs it imposes on the consumer and society generally.[4]

5. FAULT-BASED LIABILITY FOR DEFECTIVE PRODUCTS

The 'narrow rule' in *Donoghue v Stevenson*[5] provides that,[6]

> A manufacturer of products, which he sells in such form as to show that he intends them to reach the ultimate consumer in the form in which they left him with no possibility of intermediate examination and with the knowledge that the absence of reasonable care in the preparation or putting up of the products will result in an injury to the consumer's life or property, owes a duty to the consumer to take reasonable care.

It has been seen above that perhaps the least difficult aspect of the rule in *Donoghue v Stevenson* is to establish that a particular person is a manufacturer and that the person who uses his end product is a consumer so that the latter is owed a duty of care by the former. More difficult is the problem of proving fault on the part of the manufacturer. The essential requirement of the rule is that the manufacturer should have failed to exercise reasonable care in the preparation of his product, with the result that the ultimate consumer suffers injury. The failure to take care can occur in the process of production, at design stage or in the failure of the producer to give adequate directions as to the manner of use of a product.

(1) FAILURE TO TAKE REASONABLE CARE

(i) The production process

Many things can go wrong in the course of the production process, but it should be emphasised that under the common law principle in *Donoghue v Stevenson,* the key issue is whether the manufacturer has acted in such a way that his conduct may be regarded as negligent in the sense that he has failed to take reasonable care to ensure that the end product is in a reasonably safe state so as to be fit for consumption. It should be noted that product defects which result from a breakdown in the production process usually present the smallest number of problems in establishing fault on the part of the manufacturer, since the end product has failed to reach the standard of safety set by the manufacturer himself.

1   Consumer Protection Act 1987, s 3(1).
2   See Stapleton (1986) 6 OJLS 392; Newdick (1987) 103 LQR 288. In this regard much turns on what is understood by a system of strict liability for defective products. For discussion of the various theories of strict product liability see Stapleton, *Product Liability* (1994) chs 5–9.
3   Consumer Protection Act 1987, s 4(1)(e).
4   Stapleton (1986) 6 OJLS 392.
5   [1932] AC 562.
6   Ibid at 599.

The end product may be defective because of the introduction of impurities, such as unwanted foreign objects in food intended for human consumption as in *Donoghue v Stevenson*.[7] Furthermore, the negligence of the manufacturer may take the form of failing to remove impurities or substances naturally present, such as a bone in a chicken sandwich,[8] or where chemicals used to bleach clothing have not been thoroughly washed away before the product is put into the public domain.[9]

The production process may break down due to inadequate construction.[10] Alternatively inadequate materials may have been used in the manufacture of the product.[11] The court will not concentrate solely on the end product since, if the packaging supplied with the product is defective, this, too, can amount to a breach of duty of care on the part of the manufacturer.[12] Additionally, it is not always the package alone which causes the harm, as where a bung comes out of a bottle,[13] a beer keg explodes,[14] or a glass ampoule breaks[15] and a person is injured because of the subsequent spillage or reaction, then the manufacturer will be considered to be at fault if there is more he could have done to avoid the presence of the defect.

Sometimes, the end product is defective because of the use of inadequate component parts supplied by someone else. Undoubtedly the manufacturer of the component can be held responsible for injuries which can be traced to the component, although difficulties arise on the issue of causation, since it could be argued that the assembler should have tested the component before using it. However, in these circumstances, the producer of the end product is under a duty to give thought to the suitability of the component for its intended use and cannot just rely on the component manufacturer to produce a good design.[16]

(ii)   Design defects

Design defects also fall within the general rule on manufacturer's liability.[17] A product produced as intended but which because of defective design or planning causes injury is capable of falling within the rule. It is arguable that design defects are more serious than production defects, since an entire range of products will be defective. But there is the problem that while proof of fault will be a simpler matter in the case of production defects, since the defective end product fails to meet the standard of safety set by the manufacturer, the same is not true in the case of design defects. In these circumstances, the end product is in accordance with the manufacturer's design, but because the design itself is defective, anything produced in accordance with that design will also be defective, but this could be due to factors beyond the manufacturer's control, such as the state of technological development at the time the product was first put into circulation. In these circumstances, if no reasonable manufacturer could have been

---

7   [1932] AC 562. See also *Chaproniere v Mason* (1905) 21 TLR 633.
8   *Tarling v Nobel* [1966] ALR 189.
9   *Grant v Australian Knitting Mills Ltd* [1936] AC 85. See also *Watson v Buckley, Osborne, Garrett & Co* [1940] 1 All ER 174.
10   *White v John Warrick & Co* [1953] 1 WLR 1285; *Herschtal v Stewart and Ardern Ltd* [1940] 1 KB 155; *Walton v British Leyland (UK) Ltd* (1978) Product Liability International (August 1980) pp 156–160.
11   *Taylor v Rover* [1966] 1 WLR 1491; *Mason v Williams and Williams* [1955] 1 WLR 549; *Andrews v Hopkinson* [1957] 1 QB 229.
12   *Barnett v H and J Packer & Co Ltd* [1940] 3 All ER 575; *Hill v James Crowe (Cases) Ltd* [1978] 1 All ER 812.
13   *Fisher v Harrods Ltd* [1966] 1 Lloyd's Rep 500.
14   *Fehr Brewing Co v Corley* 96 SW 2d 860 (Ky, 1936).
15   *Vacwell Engineering Co Ltd v BDH Chemicals Ltd* [1971] 1 QB 111.
16   See *Winward v TVR Engineering Ltd* [1986] BTLC 366 (car manufacturer adjudged negligent for not testing engines supplied by another producer).
17   *Hindustan SS Co v Siemens* [1955] 1 Lloyd's Rep 167 at 177 (per WILLMER J).

expected to be aware of the possibility of the design error, persons injured by such products are unlikely to be able to prove fault on the part of the manufacturer.

Examples of design defects include instances in which a whole range of products made with materials which are not sufficiently strong or durable result in a defective range of goods. In these circumstances, if the manufacturer could reasonably be expected to have been aware of the faults in the components used, he will be liable.[18] Similarly, if through inadvertence, a product has been planned in such a way that it is dangerous, or creates health hazards, the producer is negligent. Finally, defective design may be established where a product lacks certain essential safety features, which the manufacturer could, reasonably, have been expected to incorporate into the finished design. For example, in *Griffiths v Arch Engineering*,[19] the design defect consisted of a failure to provide a grinding machine with an adequate guard for the protection of the user.

The standard set is one of reasonable safety, not absolute safety, and it has been suggested that the standard is the same as that required by the Sale of Goods Act 1979, section 14(2) in respect of the quality of the goods supplied.[20] However, it should be observed that the nature of liability under the Sale of Goods Act is such that the retailer guarantees the quality if the goods supplied, whereas the nature of liability under the rule in *Donoghue v Stevenson* is that there is a defence based on proof that reasonable care has been taken by the manufacturer. Thus although it will be no defence under the Sale of Goods Act 1979 for the retailer to argue that he could not have avoided the presence of defect in the goods supplied, even through the exercise of reasonable care,[1] the same defence may be available to the manufacturer of goods under the 'narrow rule' in *Donoghue v Stevenson*.

A convenient illustration of the problems caused by design defects is the tragic 'Thalidomide' incident. A drug had been developed for the purposes of treating 'morning sickness' in pregnant women. The design stage of the product failed to reveal that one of the side effects of the drug was to cause physical deformities in the fetus. The difficulty with a case like this is that it is almost impossible to prove fault. The drug manufacturer can always argue that the state of scientific and technical development, at design stage, is such that no one could have foreseen the side effects. The only way that liability can be brought home is to impose strict liability for product defects. However, the system of strict liability for defective products contained in the Consumer Protection Act 1987 contains a 'state of the art' defence, which allows a manufacturer to escape liability if he can prove that he could not have avoided the presence of a defect in the light of scientific development at the time his product was put into circulation.

A second possibility with design defects is that the manufacturer may not be aware, initially, of the nature and extent of the defect built into his product, but does become aware of the defect at a later stage after the product has been put into circulation. In these circumstances, a reasonable manufacturer will take such steps as are necessary to ensure that consumers of his product are kept reasonably safe. How far this duty extends is subject to some doubt, since it has to be appreciated that in a negligence enquiry, a manufacturer cannot be judged by reference to technological developments which occur after his product has been put into circulation. Certainly if a product is put into circulation with a design defect of which the manufacturer later becomes aware, there is a breach of duty if further products of the same kind and subject to the same defect are later put into circulation[2]. Moreover, if after putting a product into circulation there

---

18   *Adelaide Chemical and Fertiliser Co Ltd v Carlyle* (1940) 64 CLR 514.
19   [1968] 3 All ER 217.
20   Miller and Lovell *Product Liability* (1977) p 209 and see also *Godley v Perry* [1960] 1 WLR 9.
1   See *Frost v Aylesbury Dairy Co Ltd* [1905] 1 KB 608.
2   See *Wright v Dunlop Rubber Co Ltd* (1972) 13 KIR 255.

is some reasonable step which could be taken to guard against the risk of injury to consumers then it should be taken so long as the cost associated with implementing those safety precautions is not excessive. In *Walton v British Leyland (UK) Ltd*[3] the defendants manufactured a motor vehicle which proved, later, to suffer from design defects relating to the axle, which were known to be capable of causing the wheel to become detached during use. Despite the known danger, the manufacturers took a 'commercial decision' not to make it widely known that the particular range of cars concerned suffered from the defect, choosing instead to advise main dealers to look out for the defect when vehicles of the range concerned were brought in by owners for service or repair. In the circumstances, it was quite likely that there might be owners who did not use a main dealer for the purpose of service or repair so that there might be a significant number of defective vehicles which were not inspected for safety. In the light of this failure on the part of the manufacturers, WILLIS J held that, at the very least, there was a breach of the duty of care owed by the manufacturer to users of this type of vehicle based on their failure to fit a safety device to the range of cars after they became aware of the defect. However, WILLIS J was also unprepared to rule out the possibility that there might also be a breach of duty in failing to warn the public of the defect after the range of vehicles had been put on the market.[4] Accordingly, there would appear to be a duty to warn consumers of newly discovered dangers and possibly to recall defective products. For example, it has been observed that,

> . . . a manufacturer's duty of care does not end when the goods are sold. A manufacturer who realises that omitting to warn customers about something which might result in injury to them must take reasonable steps to attempt to warn them, however lacking in negligence he might have been at the time the goods were sold.[5]

Clearly, the effect of this is that manufacturers must monitor their products while they are in circulation and be aware of later scientific and technological developments so as to be able to warn users of dangers which come to light at a late stage. Thus in *Hollis v Dow Corning Corp*[6] due to internal research, a manufacturer of breast implants became aware, after the product had been put into circulation, that there was a possibility that the implants might rupture. No warning was given to doctors until 1985, but the plaintiff had undergone breast-implant surgery in 1983. Although the risk of rupture was small, it was nevertheless considered to be negligent for the manufacturer not to have made the medical profession aware of the risks associated with their product, since the manufacturer is in the best position to ensure that his product is safe for normal use by being aware of the risks attendant on the use of that product.[7]

(iii)   Warnings and instructions for use

The presence or absence of a warning or instructions is important in two respects. The failure to give an adequate warning may, of itself, amount to a breach of duty, but where a suitable warning is given, the consumer's injury may have been caused by someone other than the manufacturer.

If the supplier of a car allows it on the road with a steering defect which would be noticed by a competent mechanic, his failure to warn the consumer of the dangers

---

3   (1978) Product Liability International (August 1980) pp 156–160.
4   Although comments in this respect are purely obiter.
5   *E Hobbs (Farms) Ltd v Baxenden Chemical Co Ltd* [1992] 1 Lloyd's Rep 54 at 65.
6   (1995) 129 DLR (4th) 609.
7   Ibid at 623 per LA FOREST J.

involved amounts to negligence.[8] A false representation is also capable of constituting negligence. Thus, in *Watson v Buckley, Osborne, Garrett & Co Ltd*,[9] the defendants were liable where they represented a dangerous hair dye to be harmless, particularly since they had not carried out adequate tests. A warning is also inadequate for what it fails to say. For example, in *Vacwell Engineering Co Ltd v BDH Chemicals Ltd*,[10] an irrelevant warning informed the user of a chemical that it had a harmful vapour, but it did not reveal that it had explosive tendencies. Such a warning could have the effect of lulling the user into a false sense of security.

A number of relevant factors will have to be considered in deciding whether the presence or absence of a warning of itself constitutes a breach of duty. First, it is necessary to take into account the nature of the danger presented by the product. Generally, the duty to warn will arise where the danger is latent and it is a practicable step to issue a warning. The most common cases insisting on a duty to warn involve explosives,[11] inflammable substances,[12] substances harmful to the skin[13] and pharmaceutical products, although in this last case, the warning is often given to a 'learned intermediary' such as a doctor rather than directly to the consumer which is likely to raise issues of causation.[14]

A second consideration is the obviousness of the danger. It seems that it is not necessary to warn of dangers of which everyone ought to be aware.[15] Thus, there is no need to warn that a knife can cut the user, or that a match can ignite.[16] However, it is sometimes difficult to draw the dividing line between what is and what is not an obvious defect. For example, in *Andrews v Hopkinson*,[17] the defendant was required to warn in respect of a 'patent steering mechanism defect' which was only patent to mechanics, but not to consumers.

The cases considered thus far concentrate upon warnings prepared before the product goes into circulation but it is also possible that a defect only becomes apparent after the product goes into circulation. Here the manufacturer would certainly need to issue a warning in respect of all future supplies of the product,[18] but it is not entirely clear whether English law requires the manufacturer to recall defective products which have already been supplied. In *Wright v Dunlop Rubber Co Ltd*,[19] the second defendants, ICI, put on the market an anti-oxidant which it was later discovered had carcinogenic properties. No warning was issued at any time, and the first defendants used the product with the result that the plaintiff, one of their employees, contracted cancer. The Court of Appeal held that ICI had failed in its duty by not keeping up with new developments and in failing to take sufficiently prompt action in response to the new information.[20] This could be seen as creating either a duty to warn of subsequently discovered dangers, or a duty to ensure that supplies affected after the discovery of the new information

8   *Andrews v Hopkinson* [1957] 1 QB 229. But cf *Hurley v Dyke* [1979] RTR 265 in which there are suggestions that if a car is sold 'as seen and with all its faults' the warning will suffice to discharge the duty owed by the supplier even if he is aware of a specific defect which renders the car dangerous and the existence of which has not been communicated to the buyer. NB both cases were based on facts which occurred before the Unfair Contract Terms Act 1977 was passed, as to which see ch 24.

9   [1940] 1 All ER 174.

10   [1971] 1 QB 88 and 111n.

11   Ibid.

12   *Norton Australia Pty Ltd v Streets Ice Cream Pty Ltd* (1968) 120 CLR 635.

13   *Fisher v Harrods Ltd* [1966] 1 Lloyd's Rep 500; *Devilez v Boots Pure Drug Co* (1962) 106 Sol Jo 552.

14   See *Buchan v Ortho Pharmaceuticals (Canada) Ltd* (1986) 25 DLR (4th) 658.

15   *Farr v Butters Bros & Co Ltd* [1932] 2 KB 606.

16   Prosser *Law of Torts* (4th edn, 1971) p 649.

17   [1957] 1 QB 229.

18   Consumer Protection Act 1987, s 13(1)(b).

19   (1972) 13 KIR 255.

20   Ibid.

should be accompanied by an appropriate warning.[1] More recently, the Divisional Court has held in *Walton v British Leyland (UK) Ltd*[2] that a car manufacturer who knows of a defect which puts users at risk owes a duty to recall all affected cars, so far as is possible, and to remedy the defect. In this case, Allegro cars manufactured by the defendants had an alarming habit of shedding the occasional wheel. This was later discovered to be due to defective hub bearings. The defendants took a commercial decision that product recall would be too expensive in terms of direct cost and possible damage to the reputation of the range of vehicles concerned, and thus decided not to recall. WILLIS J had some doubts as to whether he had set too high a standard, but concluded that there is also a lesser duty to ensure that a known defect does not affect subsequently supplied products. Since the plaintiff had bought his car after the defendants were aware of the problem, the manufacturer was in breach of this less stringent duty of care.

(2)   PROOF OF NEGLIGENCE

As a general rule, English law adopts the rule that 'he who affirms must prove',[3] with the result that a plaintiff must show that the defendant was negligent. In product liability cases, this requires the consumer to establish that his injury was caused by the product, that the product was defective, that the injury was caused by the defect, and that his injuries resulted from the manufacturer's failure to exercise reasonable care.

This may appear to impose a substantial burden on the consumer, particularly when the strict duties imposed upon the retailer under the Sale of Goods Act 1979 and other related statutes are compared. However, there are certain evidential devices which can come to the aid of the consumer. First, under the Civil Evidence Act 1968, section 11, the burden of disproving negligence is cast upon the defendant if he has been convicted of a criminal offence arising out of the facts which form the basis of the product liability action. Thus, if a manufacturer supplies food unfit for human consumption, or has supplied goods which contravene safety regulations, thereby committing a criminal offence under the Food Safety Act 1990 or under the Consumer Protection Act 1987, Part II, the Civil Evidence Act might well be of use in a subsequent negligence action.

The second evidential device which is to the consumer's assistance is the principle of *res ipsa loquitur*[4] (the facts speak for themselves). While there is a *dictum* in *Donoghue v Stevenson*[5] to the effect that *res ipsa loquitur* does not apply to product liability cases, however, this has been explained on the basis that the decision in *Donoghue v Stevenson* marked a substantial change in the law and that LORD MACMILLAN was merely expressing the view that a tort of strict liability was not emerging.[6] In contrast, there are also very persuasive statements which suggest that precise particulars of negligence do not always have to be identified. In *Grant v Australian Knitting Mills Ltd*[7] it was said that:

> The appellant is not required to lay his finger on the exact person in all the chain who was responsible or to specify that he did wrong. Negligence is found as a matter of inference from the existence of the defects, taken in connection with all the known circumstances.[8]

---

1   Miller and Lovell *Product Liability* (1977) p 248.
2   Product Liability International (August 1980) pp 156–160 and see also *Hobbs (Farms) Ltd v Baxenden Chemical Co Ltd* [1992] 1 Lloyd's Rep 54, considered above.
3   *Abrath v North Eastern Rly* (1883) 11 QBD 440.
4   See ch 11.
5   [1932] AC 562 at 622 (per LORD MACMILLAN).
6   *Carroll v Fearon* (1998) Times, 26 January per JUDGE LJ.
7   [1936] AC 85.
8   Ibid at 101 (per LORD WRIGHT).

Thus in *Carroll v Fearon*[9] the plaintiff was injured when a car driven by the first defendant went out of control. Evidence established that the accident occurred as a result of the disintegration of a tyre manufactured by the second defendants, Dunlop. It was shown that this disintegration happened because of inadequate rubber penetration of the cords which made up the tyre. While it was not possible to point to any particular individual responsible for this defect, it was still possible to infer negligence on the part of Dunlops since, '...if the manufacturing process had worked as intended that defect would not have been present.'[10]

Where there is an inference of this kind, the manufacturer will be required to show that he was not negligent in using an improper system, and secondly that his employees have not been careless.[11] It has been suggested that this almost amounts to the imposition of strict liability[12] and that, in practical terms, the manufacturer is turned into an insurer[13] since if evidence is called that there is an adequate manufacturing system, this will raise a strong inference of fault on the part of an employee, in which case the manufacturer will be vicariously liable for harm cause by employee fault. So far as the general policy of the common law is concerned, this shifting of the burden of proof is not at all surprising. It has the effect of mitigating the hardship caused by a strict application of the doctrine of privity of contract, and by providing a remedy for those plaintiffs who would otherwise fall outside the protection provided by strict contractual liability.

(3) CAUSATION

The rule in *Donoghue v Stevenson* states that the manufacturer should intend the products to '. . . reach the ultimate consumer in the form in which they left him with no reasonable possibility of intermediate examination'. This raises two closely connected issues: is there another independent cause of the plaintiff's injury, and is some other person expected to test or examine the goods before they reach the ultimate consumer? If the answer to either question is yes, the manufacturer will be relieved of responsibility for the defective product.

(i) Alternative cause

The defendant will only be liable for the condition of the goods when they leave him. However, this is not to be construed literally. For example, the underwear in *Grant v Australian Knitting Mills Ltd*[14] did not need to remain in the packing cases in which it was sent out by the manufacturer. It was observed that,[15] 'The decision in *Donoghue's* case did not depend on the bottle being stoppered and sealed.' What is important is that the product is subject to the same defect at the time of both circulation and consumption.

Other factors, such as wear and tear, inadequate repair or consumer misuse, may be regarded as the cause of the harm suffered. Particular problems can arise in the case of lengthy chains of distribution and assembled products containing component parts manufactured by others. For example, in *Evans v Triplex Safety Glass Ltd*,[16] the plaintiff

---

9   (1998) Times, 26 January.
10 Ibid per Judge LJ.
11 *Grant v Australian Knitting Mills Ltd* [1936] AC 85. Cf *Daniels and Daniels v R White & Sons Ltd and Tabard* [1938] 4 All ER 258.
12 *Winfield and Jolwicz* p 334; Fleming *Torts* p 486.
13 Fleming *Torts* p 486.
14 [1936] AC 85.
15 Ibid at 106–107 (per Lord Wright).
16 [1936] 1 All ER 283.

bought a car which was fitted with a windscreen manufactured by the defendants. The windscreen shattered and injured passengers in the car. It was held that, while the plaintiff did not have to eliminate every possible cause of injury, he did have to show that it was more probable than not that the injury was due to faulty manufacture. This he had not done, because it was possible that the disintegration of the windscreen was due to faulty fitting by the manufacturer of the car or due to some cause unrelated to defective manufacture. Moreover there had also been a lapse of time of more than a year between the date of supply and the date of the accident.

In the case of allegedly defective pharmaceutical products, there may be difficult problems of causation, since there may be several possible explanations of how the harm suffered by the plaintiff came about. In these circumstances, it is possible that the plaintiff will fail on the ground that he has not discharged the burden of establishing a causal link between the defendant's breach of duty and the harm suffered by the plaintiff. For these purposes, it seems to be insufficient to show that there is an increased risk of injury, particularly where the range of drugs produced by the manufacturer suffers from a design defect.[17] However, a different approach appears to be taken in relation to production defects, where the product complained of is not in line with others of the same variety produced by the defendant. In *Best v Wellcome Foundation Ltd*[18] the defendants had supplied a batch of pertussis vaccine which was more potent and toxic than the product which they normally supplied. The Supreme Court of Ireland was prepared to infer a causal link between the defective vaccine and the brain damage provided there was evidence that the first convulsion suffered by the child occurred shortly after the first occasion on which the drug was administered. Strictly, there should not be a difference between design defects and production defects so far as the matter of causation is concerned, since the question in each case is whether, in fact, the defendant's breach of duty has caused the harm complained of. However, consistent with the approach adopted under other aspects of the 'narrow rule' it seems that it is easier to establish the elements of a negligence action where the manufacturer has failed to reach the standards he has set for himself.

A further matter which should be considered is whether the user of the product is the cause of his own injury. If, for example, the plaintiff uses goods in a manner which was never intended, such as eating pork sausages without properly cooking them,[19] or using a step ladder as a working platform,[20] the manufacturer may be able to avoid liability. One explanation of these cases is that if the plaintiff is aware of the defectiveness of the manufacturer's product that knowledge precludes liability on the part of the manufacturer. However, if there are no practical steps which the plaintiff can take to avoid the risk created by the defendant, the latter will remain the cause of the harm suffered.[1]

Misuse by the plaintiff may have one of two effects. On the one hand, it is possible that the plaintiff's damages will be reduced on the grounds of contributory negligence[2] or it may be that the consumer misuse absolves the manufacturer from liability altogether. Where the consumer misuse is blatant, the product is not being used as the manufacturer

---

17   *Loveday v Renton* [1990] 1 Med LR 117 (plaintiff unable to prove that pertussis vaccine can cause brain damage in children).
18   [1994] 5 Med LR 81.
19   *Heil v Hedges* [1951] 1 TLR 512.
20   *Campbell v O'Donnell* [1967] IR 226.
1   *Rimmer v Liverpool City Council* [1984] 1 All ER 930 at 938 per STEPHENSON LJ; *Targett v Torfaen BC* [1992] 3 All ER 27 at 37 per SIR DONALD NICHOLLS VC.
2   Cf *Farr v Butters* [1932] 2 KB 606 and *Griffiths v Arch Engineering Co (Newport) Ltd* [1968] 3 All ER 217 as representations of the position before and after the Law Reform (Contributory Negligence) Act 1945. See also ch 20.

intended, in which case it may be said that the product is not defective and that there is no breach of duty on the part of the manufacturer.[3]

(ii) Intermediate examination

Whether or not there is an opportunity to examine goods before they reach the consumer raises an issue of causation since the person who is expected to make the examination may be regarded as the cause of the harm suffered. However, this should not be used as a reason for saying that the original manufacturer owes no duty of care in respect of the product he puts into circulation. The 'narrow rule' refers to a 'possibility' of an intermediate examination, but it is better to refer to this as a probability of such examination.[4] The mere fact that someone has a chance to examine goods does not, of itself, exonerate the manufacturer. It was said in *Griffiths v Arch Engineering*[5] that the 'defence' of intermediate examination is only available if the manufacturer could:

> . . . reasonably have expected the person to whom he had passed the article would use the opportunity for inspection in such a way as to give him an indication of the risk . . . .[6]

Accordingly, in *Grant v Australian Knitting Mills Ltd*,[7] the Privy Council was able to reject the argument that the plaintiff should have washed the underwear before he wore it for the first time. There was nothing in the evidence which showed that the manufacturer could reasonably expect that precaution to be taken.

One way in which a manufacturer can reasonably expect an examination to take place is by issuing a warning to the consumer or some other intermediary. Since a retail supplier profits from selling the goods, it is often reasonable to expect him to inspect a chattel before supply. If it turns out to be defective for some reason of which the supplier ought to have been aware, then the supplier himself is negligent.[8]

In *Kubach v Hollands*,[9] the second defendants supplied to a school a substance which purported to be manganese dioxide. It was used in an experiment, and caused an explosion because of the presence of impurities. The second defendants had acquired the compound from a third party under instructions that the goods had to be examined and tested before use. These instructions had not been passed on by the second defendants. Accordingly, they were liable, because they knew of the intended use, but the warning served to exonerate the third party. There was no breach of duty, since an appropriate warning had been given.

An intermediate examination is also capable of breaking the chain of causation, thereby exonerating the manufacturer. Thus, in *Taylor v Rover Co Ltd*,[10] a foreman employed by the first defendant discovered a defect in a chisel but failed to withdraw the chisel from use, or at least report the matter, as was his duty. This failure was a break in the chain of causation, with the result that the manufacturer of the chisel was not liable.

(4) INJURY

A defective product is capable of causing physical damage to the person, physical damage to property other than the defective product; financial loss consequent upon injury to

---

3   *Aswan Engineering Establishment Co v Lupdine Ltd* [1987] 1 All ER 135 at 154 per LLOYD LJ.
4   *Paine v Colne Valley Electricity Supply Co Ltd* [1938] 4 All ER 803.
5   [1968] 3 All ER 217.
6   Ibid at 222 (per CHAPMAN J).
7   [1936] AC 85.
8   *Andrews v Hopkinson* [1957] 1 QB 229.
9   [1937] 3 All ER 907; *Holmes v Ashford* [1950] 2 All ER 76.
10   [1966] 1 WLR 1491.

the person or property; physical damage to the defective product itself; the cost of repairing defects in the product which have not yet caused physical loss; loss of profit caused by taking the defective product out of service and diminution in the value of the product resulting from its defectiveness.[11]

The *Donoghue v Stevenson* principle refers to negligence on the part of the manufacturer resulting in an injury to the consumer's life or property. This is consistent with the traditional view that a tortious action should be in respect of unsafe or dangerous chattels causing harm to the person or to property. Thus, the narrow rule presents no bar to the recovery of damages for illness caused by defective food,[12] skin diseases caused by defects in clothing,[13] and damage to buildings caused by a failure to warn of the explosive nature of a chemical.[14] If economic loss suffered by the consumer is directly consequent on personal injury[15] or damage to other property owned by the consumer[16] it is recoverable on ordinary tort principles.

A requirement of physical damage does not apply to cases of negligent misstatement under the rule in *Hedley Byrne v Heller*, which allows the recovery of economic loss suffered in consequence of reliance upon the defendant's words or advice. A product liability action may be based on a negligent act or a negligent misstatement, with the result that such cases fall between the neighbour principle and the rule in *Hedley Byrne v Heller*.[17] For example, a manufacturer may be guilty of allowing a breakdown in his production process which will constitute a negligent act or he may have supplied misleading instructions, which could be regarded as a misstatement. Similarly, if it can be established that a consumer has relied on a manufacturer's national advertising that a product is suitable for a particular purpose,[18] and that the manufacturer is aware of the nature and extent of that reliance, it may be argued that a duty of care could still be owed. This reliance is often said to be evidence of the strong degree of proximity required to justify the recovery of damages for economic loss. If there is a very strong relationship of proximity between the parties, falling marginally short of a contractual relationship, such losses may be recoverable. In consumer terms, if this relationship of proximity were said to exist between a manufacturer and a consumer, the consumer could recover the cost of remedying defects in the product, the cost of replacement, if necessary, and anything spent by the consumer in repairing the goods or hiring a replacement. However, it would appear that the necessary relationship of proximity will probably not exist as between consumer and manufacturer.[19]

Difficult issues arise in cases of economic loss in the form of damage to the defective product itself or diminution in the value of the product. Traditionally, the solution to the question of recovery has been based on consideration of the manner in which the economic loss was caused. This has resulted in the view that losses caused through reasonable reliance on negligently uttered words may be recovered,[20] but that, as a general rule, pure economic loss in the form of qualitative defectiveness in a product

---

11   See Cane (1979) 95 LQR 117.
12   *Donoghue v Stevenson* [1932] AC 562.
13   *Grant v Australian Knitting Mills Ltd* [1936] AC 85.
14   *Vacwell Engineering Co Ltd v BDH Chemicals Ltd* [1971] 1 QB 111.
15   For example medical expenses and lost earnings, and see ch 16.
16   Provided there is a sufficiently close relationship of proximity between the consumer and the manufacturer: *Muirhead v Industrial Tank Specialties Ltd* [1985] 3 All ER 705.
17   [1964] AC 465. See Craig (1976) 92 LQR 213.
18   See Palmer and Murdoch (1983) 46 MLR 213; Oughton (1987) JBL 370.
19   *Junior Books Ltd v Veitchi Co Ltd* [1983] 1 AC 520 at 533 and 547 (per LORDS FRASER and ROSKILL). See also *Muirhead v Industrial Tank Specialties Ltd* [1985] 3 All ER 705 and *Simaan v Pilkington Glass Co Ltd (No 2)* [1988] 1 All ER 791.
20   *Hedley Byrne & Co Ltd v Heller & Partners Ltd* [1964] AC 465.

purchased by a consumer is not recoverable.[1] This emphasis on the manner in which the loss was caused has been criticised on the ground that it misses the key issue which is whether there is any justifiable policy ground for restricting the liability of the tortfeasor.[2] Such policy reasons may be found in the form of the 'floodgates' argument that the imposition of a duty to exercise reasonable care might result in an excessive volume of potential claimants or in liability in an indeterminate amount. But, in the case of qualitative defects there is unlikely to be such a problem[3] with the result that it is probably better only to impose liability for qualitatively defective products where the consumer has no reasonable alternative means of protection.[4] Since the consumer will normally have the protection of the Sale of Goods Act conditions of quality and fitness there will usually be an adequate alternative remedy provided the retailer remains solvent and in the case of commercial transactions, there is not an effective exclusion of liability.

As indicated above, the courts prefer to approach the issue of economic loss by considering the means by which the loss was caused. In the case of qualitative defects, the generally held view is that since the product is not dangerous but is merely valueless, such loss may be recovered in an action for breach of contract against the supplier of the product.[5] Great emphasis was placed on the judgment of LORD BRANDON in *Junior Books v Veitchi*[6] and *East River SS Corpn v Transamerica Delaval Inc*[7] both of which proceeded on the basis that loss due to repair costs, decreased value and lost profits consist of the failure of the consumer to receive the benefit of a bargain.

The 'one-sided'[8] application of a United States' court decision may be criticised on the ground that in some states, the doctrine of privity of contract which retains a stranglehold in English law, has all but collapsed with the result that a contractual action may be maintained by plaintiffs who would not be allowed to succeed in English law. A contractual action may be brought by some American consumers against a manufacturer on the basis of a transferable warranty. Accordingly, restrictions on the ability of a consumer to recover economic losses in a tort action are not as serious in the context of the law of the United States.

The argument that claims in respect of the quality of goods are exclusively the province of the law of contract is one which requires justification. At one stage it was argued that it would be too difficult to ascertain the required standard of quality, given the very general nature of liability in tort.[9] But this is not acceptable. The standard of quality applicable in English sales law differs according to the circumstances of price, condition and description of the goods and other relevant considerations,[10] yet there has been little difficulty in identifying the standard applicable to a given case. The process employed in these circumstances seems to differ little from that used in establishing whether there has been a breach of a duty to exercise reasonable care – relevant surrounding circumstances are considered and an appropriate balance subsequently reached.

---

1   *D and F Estates v Church Comrs for England* [1988] 2 All ER 992 at 1006–1007 (per LORD BRIDGE). See also *Aswan Engineering Establishment Co v Lupdine Ltd* [1987] 1 All ER 135 and *Murphy v Brentwood District Council* [1990] 2 All ER 908.
2   See Stapleton (1991) 107 LQR 249 at 259.
3   *Junior Books Ltd v Veitchi Co Ltd* [1983] 1 AC 520 at 532–533 (per LORD FRASER) and at 545–546 (per LORD ROSKILL).
4   Stapleton (1991) 107 LQR 249 at 271–274.
5   *D and F Estates v Church Comrs for England* [1988] 2 All ER 992 at 1006 (per LORD BRIDGE).
6   [1983] 1 AC 520 at 551–552 (dissenting).
7   106 S Ct 2295 at 2300–2302 ((1986) per BLACKMUN J).
8   See Fleming (1990) 106 LQR 525 at 530 and see also Cooke (1991) 107 LQR 46 at 58–63.
9   See *Junior Books v Veitchi* [1983] 1 AC 520 at 551–552 (per LORD BRANDON).
10   Sale of Goods Act 1979, s 14(2A).

More recent decisions in the House of Lords have sought to justify their refusal to allow the recovery of damages in tort in defective quality cases on other grounds. In particular, it has been argued that defective quality claims will frequently involve issues of consumer protection, which are best left to Parliament to decide where appropriate limits should be placed.[11] Moreover, it has also been argued that to impose a duty of care in a situation in which the parties are not in privity of contract would be contrary to principle in introducing the obligations of a contractual relationship in the form of a transmissible warranty of quality.[12] But it may be argued that these criticisms apply equally to other established authorities in the law of negligence.[13] For example, the argument that consumer protection is the province of the legislature has been conveniently ignored where necessary and the House of Lords itself has felt able to work out appropriate limits to the duty imposed.[14] Furthermore, the argument that the introduction of 'contract-like obligations' through the medium of a tortious duty to take reasonable care is contrary to principle suggests the re-introduction of the 'privity of contract fallacy'[15] which was so convincingly disposed of in *Donoghue v Stevenson*. What matters more than anything in cases of defective quality is whether there is some alternative source of redress in the form of readily available insurance[16] or an action in contract against another supplier in the chain of distribution.

One way in which the difficulties of the economic loss problem have been resolved in the past has been to categorise actionable losses as a variety of physical damage,[17] particularly where there is some danger to the consumer which can be averted only by repairing the defective product. The status of this 'imminent danger' test is in some doubt. LORD BRIDGE in *D and F Estates* seems to say that the test no longer applies, LORD OLIVER in the same case, suggests otherwise.[18] If the test is still relevant, it seems to follow that a defective product may be repaired in order to avert an imminent danger to the health or safety of the consumer and the cost of those repairs may be recovered from the manufacturer provided the damage arises from a use of the product which could have been reasonably foreseen.

A further possibility briefly existed, namely that some products are complex structures, part of which may cause damage to another part of the same product.[19] In such instances, it was believed that the damage caused by one part of the structure to the other part could be recovered in tort as a variety of damage to other property. Many consumer purchases could be regarded as complex structures. For example, a defective part in a motor vehicle may have the effect of damaging the engine with the result that the engine requires replacement. Difficulties in satisfactorily defining the notion of a complex structure appear to have led to the demise of the test.[20]

---

11   *D and F Estates v Church Comrs for England* [1988] 2 All ER 992 at 1007 (per LORD BRIDGE); *Murphy v Brentwood DC* [1990] 2 All ER 908 at 923 (per LORD KEITH); at 931 (per LORD BRIDGE); at 938 (per LORD OLIVER).

12   *Murphy v Brentwood DC* [1990] 2 All ER 908 at 921 (per LORD KEITH); at 925–926 (per LORD BRIDGE); at 935 (per LORD OLIVER).

13   See Stapleton (1991) 107 LQR 249 at 268–273.

14   See *Donoghue v Stevenson* [1932] AC 562; *Smith v Eric S Bush (a firm)* [1989] 2 All ER 514.

15   See *Winterbottom v Wright* (1842) 10 M & W 109 and see ch 2.

16   See eg *Reid v Rush & Tompkins Group plc* [1989] 3 All ER 228; *Van Oppen v Clerk to the Bedford Charity Trustees* [1989] 3 All ER 389.

17   *Anns v Merton London Borough Council* [1978] AC 728; *Batty v Metropolitan Property Realisations Ltd* [1978] QB 554.

18   *D and F Estates v Church Comrs* [1988] 2 All ER 992 at 1014.

19   Ibid at 1006–1007 (per LORD BRIDGE).

20   *Murphy v Brentwood DC* [1990] 2 All ER 908 at 922 (per LORD KEITH); at 926–928 (per LORD BRIDGE) and at 932–933 (per LORD OLIVER).

6.   STRICT LIABILITY FOR DEFECTIVE PRODUCTS

(1)   THE CONSUMER PROTECTION ACT 1987, PART I[1]

Part I of the Act is intended to apply to the producer of a defective product a regime of strict liability.[2] However, it is possible that the new regime adds little to the protection already afforded by the Sale of Goods Act 1979, except that there is no requirement of a contractual relationship. Moreover the common law negligence liability of a manufacturer differs little from that imposed under the 1987 Act except that there is no longer a need for the plaintiff to show that there has been a breach of any duty of care. Conversely, many of the elements of the concept of defectiveness, which forms the cornerstone of the 1987 legislation, seem to import features well recognised in common law tort actions concerning the breach of duty issue.

(i)   The Act and the European Community Directive

The provisions of the Consumer Protection Act in relation to product liability are a direct result of a European Community Directive,[3] which was intended to produce a uniform code on product liability within the EC. The Consumer Protection Act is intended to do no more than give effect to the requirements of the EC Directive[4] and is not intended to subject a producer to any greater liability. Since section 1(1) of the Act specifically refers to the Directive by name, a court should be able to consider the provisions of the Directive in order to determine the effect of the Act. This, in turn, is likely to lead to the employment of rules of construction influenced by mainland European traditions which may not be familiar to the common lawyer.

The rationale underlying the Product Liability Directive was examined by ADVOCATE-GENERAL TESAURO in *EC Commission v United Kingdom*[5] in which he expressed the view that many of the calls for the introduction of a system of strict liability for defective products were stimulated by a desire to see that consumers injured as a result of the growth of industrial activity in the production sector were adequately compensated.[6] As has been documented in academic literature and law reports, there have been too many occasions in the past when a consumer has been injured by a defective product but has been unable to ask for an effective remedy since it has proved very difficult procedurally to prove negligence on the part of the producer.[7] Relying on academic literature, TESAURO A-G identified a number of propositions which justified the introduction of a regime of strict liability in relation to defective products. These were that producers tend to have greater contractual and economic power compared with consumers; that producers are better able to internalise costs associated with the production process through insurance and that by reducing administrative costs the producer can bring about an improvement in social benefits.[8] As TESAURO A-G points out, the wording of the Product Liability Directive as finally agreed differed substantially from earlier drafts. In particular, it was originally intended to introduce a system of absolute liability under which there would be no defence available to a producer once

---

1   See Merkin *Guide to the Consumer Protection Act 1987* (1987); Clark (1987) 50 MLR 614; Savage and Bradgate (1987) 137 NLJ 929, 953, 1025 and 1049.
2   Consumer Protection Act 1987, s 2(1).
3   Directive 85/374/EEC (25 July, 1985). See Schuster (1998) Consum LJ 195 for a review of the effect of the Product Liability Directive in various European member states.
4   Consumer Protection Act 1987, s 1(1).
5   Case C300/95 [1997] All ER (EC) 481.
6   Ibid at 486.
7   Ibid at 487.
8   Ibid.

it was shown that a product he had put into circulation was defective.[9] In contrast, the final wording of the Directive made it clear that member states could choose not to apply the new law to certain types of product and that there should be an option to include a development risks defence. This last defence had the effect of introducing a system of strict rather than absolute liability, but was intended to take account of the principle of fair apportionment of risk as between the injured consumer and the producer by subjecting the producer only to liability for quantifiable risks.[10]

(ii)   The Act and the common law

The Consumer Protection Act is intended to supplement existing common law rules and not to replace them.[11] Accordingly, there is nothing to prevent an injured consumer from suing a manufacturer for his negligence or a retailer for a breach of the implied terms in the Sale of Goods Act 1979. Indeed, there may be circumstances in which the common law route is to be preferred or is the only route available. For example, the losses recoverable under the Act are limited, with the result that an action for economic loss or damage to the defective product itself[12] will have to be based on the appropriate common law rule. Moreover, due to the definition of the word 'producer',[13] it appears that the 1987 Act will not apply to persons involved in the process of approval and certification of, for example, pharmaceutical products.[14] Also, limitation periods under the Act appear to be less generous than those which apply to common law contract and tort actions.

(iii)   Defectiveness[15]

By concentrating upon the defectiveness of a product as the basis of liability, the Consumer Protection Act 1987 may have introduced a regime which differs little from a common law negligence action. A regime of 'full strict liability'[16] would impose liability on a producer whose product causes any harm after it has been used in the manner intended. A consequence of this approach is that liability would be imposed on the producer whether or not the defect in the product was discoverable or avoidable.

The regime introduced under the Consumer Protection Act is not one of full strict liability because it is based on the concept of defectiveness and because of the presence of the development risks defence considered below. By adopting this approach, it is likely that the same difficult questions which have affected negligence liability will also apply to the Act. For example, the role of warnings will have to be considered, as will the state of scientific and technological development at the time the product is put into circulation.

(a)   The elements of defectiveness
Section 3(1) of the Act provides that a product is defective if its safety is not such as persons generally are entitled to expect. The emphasis is upon safety, with the result that the Act has no application to safe but useless products, which will continue to be covered by the Sale of Goods Act 1979.

9   Ibid at 488.
10   Ibid.
11   CPA 1987, s 2(6).
12   Ibid, s 5(2).
13   Ibid, s 2(2).
14   See *N v United Kingdom Medical Research Council* [1996] 7 Med LR 309.
15   See Stoppa (1992) 12 LS 210.
16   See Stapleton (1986) 6 OJLS 392 at 400.

The level of safety required of a product is supposed to be based on objective standards, namely the safety expected by persons generally. But ascertaining what persons generally are entitled to expect may prove to be an excessively vague test. In one sense, the test is identical to that applied in cases of negligence, in that it requires the court to consider the overall social costs created by a product balanced against the social benefits conferred by the use of the product. For example, a vaccine for whooping cough might produce harmful side-effects but, if these costs do not outweigh the benefits of providing an immunity against the disease, the vaccine will not be considered defective. This approach is remarkably similar to that adopted at common law in determining whether a person is in breach of his duty of care.[17] In the case of production defects, the definition should make little difference to the existing law, since there is an objective basis for assessing general expectations, namely the rest of the line of products produced by the manufacturer. Moreover, since, in the case of production defects the offending product has failed to reach the standards set by the manufacturer himself, it seems likely that there will be little argument that the product concerned has failed to reach the standard which persons generally would expect of that particular product.

In contrast, greater difficulty will be encountered in relation to design defects, since as the product will not have been marketed previously, it will be difficult or impossible to ascertain what people generally would expect.[18]

Section 3(2) of the Act specifies a number of factors which may be taken into account in determining what persons generally are entitled to expect. These include the manner of marketing the product, its get up and instructions or warnings issued with the product.[19] Furthermore, expectations about use[20] and the time of supply[1] may be considered.

In considering the marketing of the product, the court may take into account factors such as the reason for manufacture and the way the product has been promoted, as well as instructions for use and appropriate warnings about the manner of use. Thus it will be relevant to consider the producer's intended market, since what is safe for use by adults may not always be safe for use if the intended market is the child population. Likewise, food products intended for use by persons with a particular infirmity may need to adhere to higher standards than those intended to be marketed to persons generally.

Just as an appropriate warning can relieve a manufacturer of liability in the tort of negligence, so also, it seems, a producer may be able to argue that his product is not defective because of the materials supplied with it. The court can also consider expectations about use, especially in the light of the provisions of section 3(2)(b) which require the court to consider what might reasonably be expected to be done with or in relation to the product. The Act is silent on whose expectations are to be considered, but it is reasonable to assume that since the Act refers to persons generally, it will not be merely the expectations of a reasonable consumer, but also those of reasonable producers and other persons generally. A markedly different result might be achieved according to whether the relevant expectations are those of the producer, the actual consumer, consumers generally or persons (including producers) generally. The effect of this provision would seem to cover extreme cases of unexpected use, such as the

---

17 See eg *Watt v Hertfordshire County Council* [1954] 2 All ER 368, [1954] 1 WLR 835; *Roe v Minister of Health* [1954] 2 QB 66 and see ch 11.
18 See Stoppa (1992) 12 Legal Studies 210.
19 Consumer Protection Act 1987, s 3(2)(a). Cf Art 6(1)(a) of the Directive which refers simply to 'presentation'.
20 Ibid, s 3(2)(b).
1 Ibid, s 3(2)(c).

attempted warming of a poodle in a microwave oven, or where industrial alcohol clearly marked as a fuel is used as the base for a party cocktail.[2] The time of supply is also relevant, with the result that accepted safety standards at the time the product is put into circulation will be taken into account. This is further emphasised by the provisions of section 3(2) to the effect that a product should not be regarded as defective by virtue of the fact that safer products are developed after the time a product is put into circulation. Nor is a producer liable for defects arising after the time of supply,[3] for example those caused by wear and tear.

It should be emphasised that the matters referred to in section 3(2) are not the only factors which may be considered. For example, it has been suggested that economic considerations might be taken into account, with the result that a manufacturer could argue that his product is so cheap that safety cannot reasonably be expected.[4] But since the Act is concerned with safety rather than quality, it is anticipated that the courts will seek to establish certain minimum standards of safety below which no producer may fall.[5]

(b)   Development risks

In determining whether a product is defective, the Act provides that it is a defence for a producer to show that:

> the state of scientific and technical knowledge at the relevant time was not such that a producer of products of the same description as the product in question might be expected to have discovered the defect if it had existed in his products while they were under his control.[6]

The likely effect of the defence is that it will relieve the pharmaceutical and aerospace industries from liability in the majority of cases. Both of these industries are more likely than most to produce products with design defects, and it is design defects which are primarily protected by the development risks defence. The defence has the effect of removing one positive effect the Act might have had, namely to impose liability on producers for unknowable risks or risks knowable only by extraordinary means. The main practical difference between this and a negligence standard is that the burden of proof rests on the producer rather than the consumer.

The presence of the defence may be said to have advantages. For example, it is said to encourage research and development in new products. Furthermore, its presence has cost implications. Since there is less likelihood of a successful action against a producer, product liability insurance premiums can be kept manageably low, with the result that the cost of products should not rise excessively.

For the purposes of this defence, the 'relevant time' is the date on which the defendant supplied the product to another,[7] ie the date on which the product was first put into circulation, even though, at that stage, it had not reached the hands of a consumer. This provision in the 1987 Act seems to differ from the requirements of the EC Directive,[8] which appeared to lay down a purely objective test enquiring what was the state of knowledge at the time the product was put into circulation. However, the European

---

2   *Barnes v Litton Industrial Products* 409 F Supp 1353 (1976).
3   Consumer Protection Act 1987, s 4(1)(d).
4   Merkin *Guide to the Consumer Protection Act 1987* (1987) p 31.
5   Cf the minimum standard imposed by the Occupiers' Liability Act 1984 based on the non-excludable standard of common humanity, and see ch 28.
6   Consumer Protection Act 1987, s 4(1)(e). See also Newdick (1988) 47 CLJ 455.
7   Ibid s 4(2)(a).
8   Directive 85/374/EC Art 7(e).

Court of Justice has taken a different view,[9] possibly based on the fact that there was no objective evidence of the failure of English courts to misinterpret s 4(1)(e).[10] At one stage, it was thought that the wording of section 4(1)(e) had the effect of extending the defence further than that proposed in the Directive by allowing subjective considerations, peculiar to the individual producer, to be taken into account. For example, on the wording of s 4(1)(e) there was room to argue that a small-scale producer might not have the resources to keep up with technological advances of which others could be aware. Conversely, it could also be argued that the real intention behind the defence is to require the producer to prove that the defect in his product could not reasonably have been discovered, in which case the wording of section 4(1)(e) more accurately represents the real purpose of the defence,[11] but also has the effect of making the strict liability regime almost identical to the fault-based regime under the narrow rule in *Donoghue v Stevenson*.

The effect of the defence has been considered by the European Court of Justice in *EC Commission v United Kingdom*[12] in which the European Commission brought proceedings under the EC Treaty, art 169 for a declaration to the effect that the United Kingdom had failed to take the measures necessary to implement Council Directive EEC 85/374. The argument presented by the EC Commission was that through the use of wording in section 4(1)(e) which differed from the language used in the Product Liability Directive the United Kingdom had introduced a defence which had to be applied on a partially subjective basis. However, the Court was of the opinion that since section 4(1)(e) requires a domestic court to consider the most advanced level of scientific and technical knowledge at the time the product was put into circulation, this will raise a presumption that that knowledge is possessed by the producer at the time his product is put into circulation with the result that the test applied under section 4(1)(e) is still an objective one.[13] However, in determining what the relevant state of knowledge is, the court will have to have regard to whether any particular knowledge is accessible at the time of putting the product into circulation. Thus it will be necessary for a domestic court to determine, as a matter of fact, whether a scientific discovery or speculation amounts to knowledge. It should be observed that many scientific experiments may be initially dismissed as not making any particular discovery, only to become mainstream scientific belief at a later stage. A court will have the difficult task of ascertaining what amounts to knowledge at any given time. Furthermore, a domestic court will also have to determine whether particular knowledge is accessible or in circulation. For example, TESAURO A-G opines that a significant discovery by a Manchurian scientist which is published only in his home state in the Chinese language might not be regarded as knowledge for the purposes of a UK manufacturer, whereas the same might not be true of research in the USA published in a mainstream American scientific journal in the English language.[14]

It has been noted already that there is no current English case law relevant to this defence, but there have been developments in other parts of the European Community which might be relevant in the interpretation of the defence. For example, the German Supreme Court has held that the defence does not apply to manufacturing defects and will be confined to design defects.[15] On the reasoning employed in the German court

9   See *EC Commission v United Kingdom* Case C–300/95 [1997] All ER (EC) 481 and see Hodges (1998) 61 MLR 560; Mildred & Howells (1998) 61 MLR 570.
10   Due to the fact that there have been no English cases in which s 4(1)(e) has been considered.
11   See Newdick (1988) 47 CLJ 455 at 459–460.
12   Case C300/95 [1997] All ER (EC) 481.
13   Ibid at 494.
14   Ibid at 489.
15   See *Product Liability International*, May 1996, p 73.

even undiscoverable manufacturing defects cannot be regarded as development risks.[16] This would seem to suggest that the defence is not the same as that found in much consumer protection legislation in the form of a defence of exercising reasonable precautions and acting with due diligence.

(iv)   Losses recoverable

Since the Act is concerned with the safety of the consumer, it follows that personal injury and death are actionable.[17] It is also possible to recover in respect of damage to property other than the defective product itself,[18] subject to restrictions. The Act provides that a producer will not be liable for damage to property which is not of a type ordinarily intended for private use, occupation or consumption[19] and not intended by the person suffering harm mainly for his own private use, occupation or consumption.[20] It follows from this that damage to consumer property is actionable, but damage to property used purely for commercial purposes falls outside the Act. Beyond these types of harm, the Act has no application, with the result that damage to the defective product itself and damage to something supplied with the product, such as a container, is not recoverable.[1] Also, there is no provision in the Act for the recovery of purely economic loss.

(v)   Causation

Under section 2(1) of the Act, the consumer of a defective product still bears the onus of proving that there is a defect in the product, and that the defect is the cause of the injury or damage he has suffered. Difficulties may arise in this regard if the consumer has put a product to an unexpected use, since that use might be regarded as the cause of the injury. In negligence actions, intermediate examination creates problems of causation,[2] but these would seem not to exist for the purpose of the 1987 Act. If someone other than the producer of the finished product is also regarded as its producer this will merely raise the issue of contribution between joint tortfeasors,[3] and will not affect the consumer's likelihood of success.

(vi)   Limitations on liability

(a)   *Financial limits*

The EC Directive gave the option to fix an upper limit on liability,[4] but this option was not taken up, principally on the ground that any limit imposed would be arbitrary. However, there is a minimum loss requirement for the purposes of property damage of £275.[5] No such minimum is applied to personal injury claims.

---

16   In the German case, the defence was held not to apply to a bottle of mineral water which exploded as a result of either a hairline crack in the glass bottle or an undiscoverable hollow in the glass from which the bottle was made.
17   Consumer Protection Act 1987, s 5(1).
18   Ibid.
19   Ibid, s 5(3)(a).
20   Ibid, s 5(3)(b).
1   Ibid, s 5(2).
2   See *Griffiths v Arch Engineering Co Ltd* [1968] 3 All ER 217.
3   Consumer Protection Act 1987, s 2(5).
4   Directive 85/374/EC Art 16.
5   Consumer Protection Act 1987, s 5(4).

(b)   Time limits[6]

In the case of personal injuries and property damage, it is generally the case that an action must be brought within three years of the date on which damage occurred.[7] In cases of latent damage the relevant limitation period runs for three years from the date of the plaintiff's knowledge of harm.[8] Furthermore, there is a long-stop provision which prevents any action from being commenced in respect of a defective product ten years after it was first put into circulation.[9]

(c)   Exclusion and limitation of liability

Generally, no exclusion of liability is permitted by means of any contract term or notice.[10] It has been pointed out that, in respect of notices, there is a drafting error,[11] in that notice is defined as 'a notice in writing'.[12] This may mean that an oral notice might be used to exclude the liability of a producer unless the words 'any other provision' in section 7 cover this situation.

(d)   Defences

If a defect is due to compliance with a statutory provision or European Community obligation, the producer will not be liable.[13] Furthermore, a consumer who contributes to the harm he suffers may be met with the defence of contributory negligence.[14]

(2)   BREACH OF STATUTORY DUTY

In the field of product liability, there would appear to be two categories of statute which impose duties on producers and retailers of goods. There are those which lay down minimum standards for food and drugs,[15] and those which lay down standards for other manufactured goods.[16] Whether a civil action for breach of statutory duty lies in respect of these statutes and regulations is dependent upon a judicial construction of the intention of Parliament. For the most part, the general view is that 'consumers' are too wide a class of people to be protected by an action for breach of statutory duty. If an Act is passed for the protection of the public as a whole, and not for the benefit of a particular class of people, then the court may conclude that no action for breach of statutory duty will be available.[17] Conversely, it has also been said that it would be strange if a less important duty owed to a section of the public may be enforced by action, while a more important duty owed to the public at large cannot be enforced.[18] The more restrictive view has been accepted so far as food legislation is concerned, on the ground that consumers of food are such a large class as to be identifiable only with the whole community.[19]

---

6   See also ch 18.
7   Limitation Act 1980, s 11A(4)(a).
8   Ibid, s 11A(4)(b). For the meaning of knowledge see chs 18 and 28.
9   Ibid, s 11A(3).
10   Consumer Protection Act 1987, s 7.
11   Merkin *Guide to the Consumer Protection Act 1987* (1987) p 43.
12   Consumer Protection Act 1987, s 45(1).
13   Ibid, s 4(1)(a).
14   Ibid, s 6(4) and see ch 19.
15   For example, the Food Safety Act 1990, the Medicines Act 1968 and regulations made thereunder.
16   Consumer Protection Act 1987, Part II.
17   *Solomons v R Gertzenstein Ltd* [1954] 2 QB 243.
18   *Phillips v Britannia Laundry* [1923] 2 KB 832 at 841 (per ATKIN LJ). This has since been approved in *Monk v Warbey* [1935] 1 KB 75.
19   *Buckley v La Reserve* [1959] Crim LR 451.

A second factor to consider in deciding whether an action for breach of statutory duty lies in respect of the supply of a defective product is the nature of the penalty provided,[20] and whether there is an adequate civil remedy. So far as food is concerned, it is likely that contravention of the Food Safety Act 1990 also constitutes a breach of one of the Sale of Goods Act implied terms. The result of this is that it has been held in *Square v Model Farm Dairies (Bournemouth) Ltd*[1] that, because adequate civil remedies exist, no action for breach of statutory duty will lie in respect of the offence of supplying food not of the nature, substance or quality demanded.

The same difficulties of ascertaining the intention of Parliament do not exist in respect of the Consumer Protection Act 1987, which contains express provision to the effect that the failure of a person to fulfil an obligation owed by him under the Act is an actionable breach of statutory duty, subject to the normal incidents of the tort.[2]

(i)   The nature of the obligations imposed under the Consumer Protection Act 1987

The Act specifies that safety regulations may be made in respect of goods,[3] and that failure to comply with such a regulation amounts to the commission of an offence.[4] Suspension orders can be made which suspend the supply of goods or component parts.[5] Prohibition notices may be served on a specific person to prevent him from supplying particular goods,[6] and a notice to warn may be issued requiring a person to warn consumers of unsafe goods.[7] Failure to comply with any notice amounts to the commission of an offence.[8] The Act imposes a new general safety requirement, breach of which constitutes the commission of an offence.[9] For the purposes of civil action, all that matters is whether the defendant is guilty of a breach of safety regulations,[10] since no action for breach of statutory duty will lie in respect of the breach of the general safety requirement, a prohibition notice, a suspension notice or a notice to warn.[11]

(ii)   The incidents of an action for breach of statutory duty[12]

The duty must be owed to the plaintiff. Section 41(1) provides that the duty is owed by the person under the obligation to 'any other person who may be affected by . . .' the breach. In order for the plaintiff to succeed, he must show that he has been affected by the failure to comply with the safety regulation. In particular, it is necessary that the injury suffered is one which the Act is intended to prevent.[13] The Consumer Protection Act is concerned with the safety of consumers. Thus it is doubtful whether economic loss, such as lost profits suffered by a retailer, could be recovered. In any case, the retailer may also fail on the ground that he is not a consumer. The other essential requirements

20   *Groves v Lord Wimbourne* [1898] 2 QB 402.
1   [1939] 2 KB 365.
2   Consumer Protection Act 1987, s 41(1).
3   Ibid, s 11(1).
4   Ibid, s 12(1).
5   Ibid, s 14.
6   Ibid, s 13(1)(a).
7   Ibid, s 13(1)(b).
8   Ibid, ss 13(4), 14(6).
9   Ibid, ss 10(1).
10   Ibid, s 41(1).
11   Ibid, s 41(2).
12   See Cane (1979) 3 JPL 315.
13   *Gorris v Scott* (1874) LR 9 Exch 125.

of the tort are that the defendant must be in breach of his duty and that breach must have caused the harm suffered by the plaintiff.

One difficulty is whether the tort is one of strict liability or not. It might be argued that, in the light of the statutory defence of due diligence,[14] it is open to a defendant sued for a breach of statutory duty to avoid civil liability by showing that he has exercised reasonable care. However, there are *dicta* in *Harrison v National Coal Board*[15] to the effect that a reasonable care defence to a criminal prosecution may not be available in a civil action for breach of statutory duty. However, in *Harrison*, the relevant statute did not provide for a civil action, and it may be that, where the Act specifically provides for a civil remedy and there is a no-negligence defence, the liability created is fault-based rather than strict, but the onus of disproving negligence would lie on the defendant. Certainly it would appear to be sufficient for a plaintiff to show that the defendant's conduct has materially contributed to the risk of injury,[16] particularly if the defendant's conduct amounts to an omission to do something. If a product is not safe, it should not be too difficult to establish that it has materially contributed to the injury suffered by the consumer.

(3)   *CAVEAT EMPTOR*

In contractual actions, the general common law rule was one of *caveat emptor* but, as has been seen, this rule was not always adhered to, even before the passing of the Sale of Goods Act 1893. This Act, which in many respects has remained unaltered, is based substantially on giving effect to the intentions of the parties, particularly in the context of business transactions. However, there have been substantial inroads into the *caveat emptor* rule in relation to consumer transactions. For example there have been important changes applicable to the use of exemption clauses, and more recently there has been an overhaul of the old requirement that goods should be of merchantable quality following the introduction of a new requirement of satisfactory quality at the request of the consumer lobby. Increasingly the impression is given that, for the purposes of consumer transactions, there has been an effective abandonment of the rule *caveat emptor*. However, the same appears not to be true of purely commercial transactions. For example it has been observed by LORD STEYN in *Slater & Slater Co Ltd v Finning Ltd* that,[17]

> Outside of private sales, the shift from *caveat emptor* to *caveat venditor* in relation to the implied condition of fitness for purpose has been a notable feature of commercial law. But to uphold the present claim would be to allow *caveat venditor* to run riot.

The most important provisions of the Sale of Goods Act[18] for the purposes of product liability are the implied terms relating to description, quality and fitness.

One of the greatest difficulties which faces a court attempting to apply the implied terms in the Sale of Goods Act 1979 is that they have to be applied to both consumer and commercial transactions. The provisions of the Sale of Goods Act 1893 were originally intended as a fall-back position for commercial buyers and sellers in the event that they had failed to deal expressly with some important aspect of their contract of sale. However

---

14   Consumer Protection Act 1987, s 39(1).
15   [1951] AC 639 at 657–658.
16   *McGhee v National Coal Board* [1972] 3 All ER 1008. Cf *Wilsher v Essex Area Health Authority* [1988] 1 All ER 871.
17   [1996] 3 All ER 398 at 410. See also *Harlingdon & Leinster Enterprises v Christopher Hull Fine Art Ltd* [1990] 1 All ER 737.
18   Other related statutes include the Supply of Goods (Implied Terms) Act 1973 (hire purchase) and the Supply of Goods and Services Act 1982 (contracts for the supply of goods other than sale).

as the twentieth century has progressed and mass-produced consumer goods have become more widely available to individual consumers with increased purchasing power following the more widespread availability of credit facilities, the implied terms in the Sale of Goods Act 1979 have increasingly come to be regarded as instruments of consumer protection. This development has culminated in the introduction of a new requirement of satisfactory quality to replace the former implied condition that goods supplied will be of merchantable quality. In general terms, the word 'merchantable' was considered to be too much of a commercial contractors' term to be fully representative of the needs of consumer buyers. Instead, it was thought that the words 'acceptable' or 'satisfactory' quality would be more understandable by the majority of consumer buyers who have come to rely, increasingly, on this implied term. Unfortunately the interests of consumer buyers and commercial buyers are very different, yet the same set of rules have to be applied in each case. In the light of these perceived differences between consumer and commercial transactions, it is becoming increasingly attractive to introduce a cast-iron distinction between the two in the form of a 'Consumer code' and a 'Commercial code' given the difference of emphasis between the two types of transaction highlighted in the discussion which follows.

(4)   THE IMPLIED CONDITION THAT GOODS MUST CORRESPOND WITH THEIR DESCRIPTION

The Sale of Goods Act 1979, section 13(1) provides:[19]

> Where there is a contract for the sale of goods by description, there is an implied condition that the goods supplied will correspond with that description.

It is a little perplexing as to why statements made by the seller which relate to the description of the goods sold should be regarded as appropriate material for an implied term, since by their nature these statements which identify the subject matter of the contract must surely form the basis of the contract and be, in their own right, express terms of the contract of sale.

The phrase 'sale by description' seems to cover a very wide range of transactions. It will cover transactions in which the buyer does not see the goods but relies on a written or oral description, such as a contract to sell generic or future goods,[20] or one to sell unascertained goods.[1] Section 13(3) also provides that a sale will still be by description if the goods are exposed for sale and are selected by the buyer. What seems to matter is that an article should be sold as a thing corresponding to a particular description,[2] and that the buyer has relied on that description.[3] Thus, sales in a retail shop are sales by description where the buyer states generally what he wants and the seller provides something which purports to accord with the buyer's request.[4] Even the purchase of a second-hand car which has been carefully examined by the buyer before the sale has been held to be a sale by description, because there was partial reliance on an

19   See also Supply of Goods (Implied Terms) Act 1973, s 9(1), and Supply of Goods and Services Act 1982, ss 3(2), 8(2).
20   See Sale of Goods Act 1979, s 61(1).
1   Section 61(1) of the Sale of Goods Act 1979 defines specific goods as those which are identified and agreed on at the time of the contract. It follows that anything which is not so identified will be treated as an item of unascertained goods.
2   *Grant v Australian Knitting Mills Ltd* [1936] AC 85.
3   *Joseph Travers & Son Ltd v Longel Ltd* (1947) 64 TLR 150; *Harlingdon & Leinster Enterprises v Christopher Hull Fine Art Ltd* [1990] 1 All ER 737.
4   *Grant v Australian Knitting Mills Ltd* [1936] AC 85.

advertisement.[5] These developments have had the effect of treating virtually all contracts for the sale of goods as sales by description, even where the goods are specific. Probably the only contracts which are not made by description are those for the sale of unique or individual, unmarked items which are purchased on a 'take it or leave it' basis.[6] In these circumstances there is nothing said by the seller on which the buyer is able to rely. Thus it follows that in any case where it is established that the buyer places no reliance at all on the seller's description, the implied condition in section 13 will not apply.[7]

(i)   The designation of description as an implied undertaking

By designating section 13 as an implied term, the draftsman of the Sale of Goods Act treated as a legally imposed obligation something which, in fact, goes to the very root of the agreement between the parties. If a person fails to supply goods which correspond with their description, he has fundamentally failed to perform the contract.[8] One possible consequence of this designation might have been to allow a seller to contract out of his responsibilities under section 13 in much the same way as was possible with the conditions of quality and fitness before the passing of the Unfair Contract Terms Act 1977. However, the courts tend to treat the implied condition in section 13 as a fundamental obligation and refuse to allow it to be too easily defeated by an exclusion clause.[9]

(ii)   The status of descriptive statements

Not every descriptive word will take effect as a term of the contract. Some descriptive words such as mere advertising puffs will have no legal effect at all. Similarly, there may be other words of description which are regarded as mere labels which do not fundamentally affect the substance of what has been contracted for,[10] and others may amount to representations rather than terms, thereby giving rise to an action for rescission or damages for misrepresentation but not to one for breach of contract.

In some instances, a statement, although expressed as a condition of the contract, will not be regarded as such, since the consequences of its breach are not sufficiently serious.[11] The implied terms in the Sale of Goods Act are stated by Parliament to be conditions, with the result that it will not be open to a court to make use of the common law development of the intermediate term.[12] Section 15A of the Sale of Goods Act 1979 now allows the court to treat a breach of an implied condition as giving rise only

---

5   *Beale v Taylor* [1967] 1 WLR 1193. It is arguable that this decision ignores the traditional common law distinction between terms and representations, on the basis that the actionable statement was one made by a private individual with no particular skill. The decision in *Beale* may be regarded as a policy decision which sought to provide the buyer with a remedy in damages for misrepresentation at a time when damages for misrepresentation were not generally available. Cf the approach in *Oscar Chess Ltd v Williams* [1957] 1 All ER 325.

6   This begs the question why the car in *Beale v Taylor* (above) was not regarded as an item of specific goods.

7   *Harlingdon & Leinster Enterprises Ltd v Christopher Hull Fine Art Ltd* [1990] 1 All ER 737 at 744 (per NOURSE LJ) and at 751 (per SLADE LJ).

8   *Chanter v Hopkins* (1838) 4 M & W 399. See also Sale of Goods Act 1979, s 30.

9   *Vigers Bros v Sanderson Bros* [1901] 1 KB 608.

10   See *Reardon Smith Line Ltd v Yngvar Hansen-Tangen* [1976] 1 WLR 989.

11   See the development of the notion of the innominate term in *Hong Kong Fir Shipping Co Ltd v Kawasaki Kisen Kaisha Ltd* [1962] 1 All ER 474 and *Cehave NV v Bremer Handelsgesellschaft mbH, The Hansa Nord* [1976] QB 44 discussed in ch 13.

12   *Ashington Piggeries Ltd v Christopher Hill Ltd* [1972] AC 441 at 503 (per LORD DIPLOCK); *Cehave NV v Bremer Handelsgesellschaft mbH, The Hansa Nord* [1976] QB 44 at 56 (per LAWTON LJ) .

to an action for damages where the breach is so slight that it would be unreasonable for the buyer to reject the goods. However, this option is only available where the buyer deals otherwise than as a consumer so that in consumer sales, no matter how insignificant the breach of condition may be, the buyer still has the right to reject, yet in commercial transactions for the sale of goods, the court may deny the buyer's right of rejection on the ground that the seller's breach does not warrant such extreme action. At first sight, this discretion might appear to be similar to the operation of the common law *de minimis* rule, however, the latter has taken on such a narrow meaning as to be almost unworkable. The new section 15A avoids the complications of the *de minimis rule* and instead concentrates on the materiality of the breach and the reasonableness of allowing the buyer to pursue his common law right of rejection for a breach of condition.

Where a descriptive statement is made, it will be necessary to determine whether it is a contractual term or a representation. At first sight, section 13 would seem to suggest that any failure to correspond with a descriptive statement will constitute a breach of condition. But this approach would have the effect of wiping away the common law distinction between representations and terms of the contract. There are cases which suggest that the traditional distinction still stands,[13] but there are also others in which the distinction appears to have been ignored. For example, in *Beale v Taylor*,[14] the defendant advertised for sale a motor car which purported to be a 'Herald, Convertible, White, 1961'. It was an 'amalgam' of parts of two cars which had been welded together. The Court of Appeal held that the words '1961 Herald' constituted part of the description of the car, although they could easily have been treated as an external inducement and therefore a mere representation.[15] A possible justification for the decision in *Beale* is that the statement was one made by a seller and these tend to be more strictly construed than the misleading utterances of the consumer purchaser in *Oscar Chess v Williams*. Moreover, *Beale* was decided at a time when damages for misrepresentation were not widely available and may be an example of the desire of the courts to compensate for losses suffered as a result of reasonable reliance.

Although not a specific requirement of section 13, for all practical purposes the buyer must reasonably rely on the seller's description of the goods since the description must have sufficient influence to become an essential term of the contract.[16] If this were not to be the case, the sale would not be *by* description.[17] Moreover, without this requirement, virtually all descriptive words would amount to conditions of the contract of sale, whereas it has been held that in the absence of reliance by the buyer the descriptive words would not be incorporated into the contract.[18]

In order to form part of the contract description, the words must identify the goods supplied.[19] The appropriate test is to ask whether the buyer got what he bargained for according to the standards of the relevant market.[20] Because the standards of different markets will vary, it is likely that apparently contradictory decisions will result. For example, a mixture of hemp and rape oil did not satisfy the description 'foreign refined rape oil',[1]

---

13   *Heilbut Symons v Buckleton* [1913] AC 30.
14   [1967] 1 WLR 1193.
15   As in *Oscar Chess Ltd v Williams* [1957] 1 WLR 370.
16   *Harlingdon & Leinster Enterprises Ltd v Christopher Hull Fine Art Ltd* [1990] 1 All ER 737 at 744 (per NOURSE LJ).
17   *Berger & Co Inc v Gill & Duffus SA* [1984] AC 382 at 394 (per LORD DIPLOCK).
18   *Harlingdon & Leinster Enterprises Ltd v Christopher Hull Fine Art Ltd* [1990] 1 All ER 737 at 744 (per NOURSE LJ) and at 752 (per SLADE LJ).
19   *Ashington Piggeries Ltd v Christopher Hill Ltd* [1972] AC 441 at 503–504 (per LORD DIPLOCK).
20   Ibid at 489 (per LORD WILBERFORCE).
1   *Nicol v Godts* (1854) 10 Exch 191. See also *Robert A Munro & Co Ltd v Meyer* [1930] 2 KB 312.

but herring meal contaminated by a toxin generated by an internal chemical reaction is still herring meal.[2]

In seeking to determine whether words identify the goods sold, it is necessary to enquire whether those words identify an essential part of the description of the subject matter. It follows that words which merely identify the location of the goods will not normally form part of the description.[3] Conversely, words which identify the nature of the thing purchased will form part of the description. Thus a car dealer asked to supply a Ford Sierra cannot get away with supplying a Ford Ka.

(5) THE IMPLIED CONDITION OF SATISFACTORY QUALITY

The Sale of Goods Act 1979, section 14(2) provides:[4]

> Where the seller sells goods in the course of a business, there is an implied condition that the goods supplied under the contract are of satisfactory quality.[5]

However, this condition has no application where the matter which renders the quality of the goods has been specifically drawn to the buyer's attention before the contract is made[6] or where the buyer has examined the goods before the contract is made and that examination ought to have revealed the defects of which the buyer later complains.[7]

(i) Sale in the course of a business

Section 14 requires the seller to sell the goods in the course of a business.[8] A particular problem which has surfaced is that the scope of a number of different statutory provisions is limited to circumstances in which a seller sells or supplies goods in the course of a trade or business, or some other similar circumstances. Likewise there are other statutory provisions which operate in different ways according to whether a buyer deals otherwise than as a consumer. All of these provisions, to some extent, are influenced by the manner in which the phrase 'dealing in the course of a business' (or some similar phrase) is interpreted.

For the purposes of the Sale of Goods Act 1979, there are dicta to the effect that a person may be regarded as a business seller even where he has no habit of selling goods of the type under consideration.[9] However, a different approach is applied to the Trade Descriptions Act 1968, s 1,[10] under which the emphasis is on whether the offending supply may be regarded as integral to the business carried on by the defendant. For these purposes it seems that a person may be regarded as supplying goods in the course of a trade or business only if there is some degree of regularity in the course of dealing in question. Thus a doctor who disposes of an unwanted typewriter will not be seen to have sold the article in the course of a business, since it is not incidental to the business of a doctor to sell typewriters. In contrast, the sale by a car hire company of its older

2   *Ashington Piggeries Ltd v Christophre Hill Ltd* [1972] AC 441.
3   *Reardon Smith Line Ltd v Yngvar Hansen-Tangen* [1976] 1 WLR 989.
4   See also Supply of Goods (Implied Terms) Act 1973, s 10(2); Supply of Goods and Services Act 1982, s 9(2), (3); Supply of Goods and Services Act 1982, s 4(2), (3).
5   Sale of Goods Act 1979, s 14(2).
6   Ibid s 14(2C)(a).
7   Ibid s 14(2C)(b).
8   Sale of Goods Act 1979, s 61(1) defines a business as including a profession and the activities of any government department or a local or public authority.
9   *Ashington Piggeries Ltd v Christopher Hill Ltd* [1972] AC 441 at 494 (per LORD WILBERFORCE).
10 *Davies v Sumner* [1984] 1 WLR 405; affd [1984] 3 All ER 831; *Havering London Borough Council v Stevenson* [1970] 1 WLR 1375.

cars may be regarded as a sale in the course of a business if sales of that kind are completed on a regular basis.[11] Perhaps oddly, and almost certainly with a view to adopting a consistent line of definition of the phrase 'dealing in the course of a business', a similar line of reasoning has been adopted under the Unfair Contract Terms Act 1977, section 12.[12] However, it does not follow that the same approach should be adopted for each piece of legislation which uses the same or similar language. In *Stevenson v Rogers*[13] the defendant had operated as a self-employed fisherman for a period of 20 years and sold his boat to the plaintiffs. Subsequently, it was discovered that the boat suffered from defects rendering it unmerchantable, but the question arose whether the Sale of Goods Act 1979, section 14(2) applied to someone whose business was that of a fisherman rather than a boat seller. POTTER LJ accepted that there are three broad categories used to identify when a person sells in the course of a business. First, a seller sells goods in the course of a business where the sale is in the nature of trade carried out with a view to profit, even if this is a one-off venture. Secondly, the sale is made in the course of a business if it is integral to the business carried on by the seller and thirdly, there is a sale in the course of a business where the transaction is incidental to the business carried on by the seller, but the type of transaction concerned is undertaken with a degree of regularity. What this means is that unlike the more restrictive approach taken under the Trade Descriptions Act 1968, a sale is made in the course of a business under the 1979 Act wherever the seller agrees generally, or in a particular case, to supply the goods ordered. POTTER LJ could see the value of adopting a consistent definition of a single phrase across a range of statutory provisions, but also observed that different purposes are served by the Sale of Goods Act 1979, section 14 and the Trade Descriptions Act 1968, section 1. The latter imposes criminal liability and if there is an ambiguity in a statutory provision imposing criminal liability, it is right that it is construed in favour of a person charged with the commission of an offence. In contrast, the changes to the requirement of merchantable quality (and more recently, the introduction of a statutory requirement of satisfactory quality) brought about by statutory intervention make it clear that its primary purpose is the protection of consumers against sub-standard quality in the goods they buy. As such, it is important that as wide a net as possible is cast so as to adequately protect consumers. It is also implicit in comments made by POTTER LJ that the correctness of the decision in *R & B Customs Brokers Ltd v United Dominions Trust Ltd*[14] might need to be called into question, since in that case, the court did not have the power to consider the legislative history of a piece of legislation following the decision of the House of Lords in *Pepper v Hart*.[15] Had the court been able to consider law reform proposals on which the Supply of Goods (Implied Terms) Act 1973 was based, it would have been clear that it was intended that the phrase 'supply in the course of a business' should be interpreted in the manner adopted by the court in *Stevenson v Rogers*.

The requirement in section 14(2) that the seller should sell in the course of a business also applies to the condition of fitness for purpose in section 14(3), but is not present in section 13 of the same Act. Thus, the implied condition that goods must correspond with their description can be broken by a private seller.[16]

---

11   See *Havering London Borough Council v Stevenson* [1970] 1 WLR 1375.
12   See *R and B Customs Brokers Ltd v UDT* [1988] 1 All ER 847.
13   [1999] 2 WLR 1064.
14   [1988] 1 All ER 847. However, it should be noted that in this case the court was concerned not with the definition of the phrase 'selling in the course of a business' but with the complementary issue whether a person 'deals as a consumer'.
15   [1993] AC 593.
16   See *Beale v Taylor* [1967] 1 WLR 1193.

(ii)   Goods supplied under the contract

Since sections 14(2) and (3) apply to all goods supplied under the contract, anything supplied pursuant to the agreement must be of satisfactory quality or fit for the buyer's intended purpose, as the case might be. Thus, if a person supplies a solid fuel which explodes due to the presence of a detonator, the goods as a whole supplied are not of satisfactory quality, even though the lumps of fuel might be of the appropriate quality on their own.[17] Likewise, if goods are supplied in a container, both the container and its contents must satisfy the requirements of section 14(2) and (3). Thus, if a bottle of mineral water injures the buyer due to a defect in the container, there is a breach of both section 14(2) and (3).[18] Moreover, since instructions supplied with goods are capable of rendering them useless, these too would appear to fall within the general scope of section 14.[19]

(iii)   Disclosed defects and examination by the buyer

Section 14(2C)(a) provides that the condition of satisfactory quality has no application to defects which have been disclosed to the buyer. It is likely that this provision will be most relevant in the case of the sale of secondhand goods, to which section 14 does apply.[20] However, it is not clear from section 14 how much information should be provided. For example, it is not clear from the wording of the 1979 Act whether it is sufficient to describe goods as 'seconds' without identifying the particular defect from which the goods suffer. Arguably, a provision which is intended to protect consumer purchasers ought to be interpreted so as to require the seller to specifically identify the defect from which goods suffer so that the buyer may be said to have been fully informed as to the nature of his purchase prior to the date of contracting.

Under section 14(2C)(b), the condition is also inapplicable where the buyer has examined the goods and that examination has, or ought to have, revealed the defect to which the goods are subject. It is clear that there must have been an examination and if there is a present and obvious defect, the buyer purchases subject to it. Conversely, the exception does not apply to latent defects, such as the presence of arsenic in beer, which are not reasonably discoverable upon any examination.[1]

The wording of section 14(2C)(b) has given rise to difficulties in conditional sale agreements, where the buyer may take possession of goods before the contract is legally concluded. In such cases, the buyer may be aware of a defect and request repair, but since the defect is discovered before the contract is legally concluded, the buyer may have had a chance to inspect the goods and may have to purchase subject to that defect[2] unless the court is prepared to treat an undertaking to effect a repair as forming the basis of a collateral warranty.

(iv)   The nature of the obligation

Section 14(2) implies a condition of 'satisfactory quality'. The word 'satisfactory' is now defined in section 14(2A) in the following manner:

---

17   *Wilson v Rickett, Cockerell & Co Ltd* [1954] 1 QB 598.
18   *Geddling v Marsh* [1920] 1 KB 668; *Morelli v Fitch and Gibbons* [1928] 2 KB 636.
19   See *Wormell v RHM Agriculture* [1987] 3 All ER 75 at 77 (per DILLON LJ).
20   *Bartlett v Sidney Marcus Ltd* [1965] 1 WLR 1013.
1   See *Wren v Holt* [1903] 1 KB 610.
2   See *R and B Customs Brokers Ltd v UDT* [1988] 1 All ER 847.

Goods are of satisfactory quality if they meet the standard that a reasonable person would regard as satisfactory taking account of any description of the goods, the price (if relevant) and all the other relevant circumstances.

Additionally, section 14(2B) now gives a non-exclusive list of factors which may be taken into account by the court in determining whether particular goods are of the required standard of quality. Section 14(2B) provides:

For the purposes of this Act, the quality of goods includes their state and condition and the following (among others) are in appropriate cases aspects of the quality of goods—
(a)   fitness for all the purposes for which goods of the kind in question are commonly supplied;
(b)   appearance and finish;
(c)   freedom from minor defects;
(d)   safety, and
(e)   durability.

In some respects, the introduction of this new standard of satisfactory quality may be criticised, but it may also go a long way towards satisfying the requirements of the consumerist lobby who have long taken the view that the old requirement of merchantability was openly based on the needs of the business community. While it is true that the requirement of merchantable quality was developed at a time when consumer purchases were not as common as they are at the turn of the century, it must be noted that the case law on the requirement of merchantable quality had shown that the courts were mindful of the needs of consumer purchasers, taking account of matters such as safety, durability, minor defects and appearance and finish. Moreover, it is arguable that since 100 years of common law jurisprudence on the meaning of the requirement of merchantability has been wiped away, it will take a long time to discover the true ramifications of the 1994 changes. On the other hand, it seems likely that courts will continue to employ the reasoning under the old law, as appropriate, especially in cases where it is considered that the present wording of section 14(2) does not differ from that used in earlier definitions of merchantable quality. However, it is also arguable that the introduction of the new definition will allow courts to approach the issue of quality on a 'clean slate' and develop the law in new directions, where appropriate.

One problem which does remain is that the standard of quality provided for in section 14(2) is applicable to consumer and business contracts alike and that a development in a particular direction (for example one which favours consumer purchasers) could have adverse effects if applied to a purely commercial contract for the sale of goods. As a result it may be necessary for the courts to have close regard to the developments which they unleash, which, in turn, could encourage somewhat conservative decision-making. Perhaps the answer lies in the development of separate codes for consumer and business purchasers of goods. Finally, it must be noted that the 1994 changes will not be the last word on the standard of quality to be expected by consumer purchasers, since the European Community Directive on the Sale of Consumer Goods and Associated Guarantees has recently been adopted[3] which is intended to introduce a Europe-wide consumer guarantee of the quality of goods purchased within the Community. At first sight many of the provisions of the Directive appear to impose obligations on the seller of goods which are similar to those contained in the Sale of Goods Act 1979, but the remedies provided for in the Directive go beyond the English options of damages or repudiation. The main provisions of the Directive require, as a minimum basic standard

---

3   Directive 99/44 EC.

of quality, that goods sold to consumer purchasers should 'be in conformity with the contract of sale'. For these purposes, goods are considered to be in conformity with the contract if they comply with the description given by the seller; are fit for a particular purpose for which the consumer requires them, made known to the seller by the consumer; are fit for the purposes for which the goods in question are normally used and show the quality and performance normal in goods of the same type.[4]

The 1994 legislation was not the first attempt to provide a statutory definition of the expected standard of quality, since there had been an earlier attempt at definition in the Supply of Goods (Implied Terms) Act 1973 which contained many of the elements now included in the 1994 changes in the law. Prior to 1973 there was no statutory definition of the requirement of merchantable quality, and the courts had proceeded on the basis of two distinct tests of merchantability which applied according to the circumstances of the case. In general terms one of these tests was more appropriate to the needs of the business community, being based upon the saleability or useability of the goods in the light of the defect from which they suffered, whereas, the second test, based on acceptability, was more appropriate to the needs of buyers who did not purchase for resale, but for use or consumption. Clearly the latter test was more appropriate when dealing with consumer complaints about the quality of the goods purchased.

In *Henry Kendall & Sons v William Lillico & Sons Ltd*[5] the majority adopted a test of acceptability,[6] whereas the minority applied a test of usability. The acceptability test required the goods to be in such a state that the buyer, with knowledge of any defect in them, would buy them without any substantial abatement of the price obtainable for such goods when in a reasonable, sound condition and without special terms.[7] By contrast, the usability test required that goods should be usable for at least one of the purposes for which goods of the same description are commonly used. Goods were treated as being unmerchantable under this test if they could not have been used by a reasonable man for any purpose, for which goods which complied with the description under which those goods were sold, would normally be used.[8]

Of these two tests, the 1973 definition of merchantable quality seemed to place more emphasis on usability rather than acceptability. This could be regarded as unfortunate, given the use of section 14 in a consumer context, since the acceptability of goods supplied would appear to be more important to the consumer purchaser. Given the criticisms applied to the outmoded notion of merchantability, pressure for reform of the law led to the more detailed definition of satisfactory quality in the 1994 legislation.[9]

For the most part, the requirement of satisfactory quality relates to the physical characteristics of the goods supplied, as the elements emphasised in the statutory definition in section 14(2A) and (2B) seem to suggest, concentrating on matters such as safety, durability, freedom from minor defects and appearance and finish. However, just as under the law on merchantable quality, this will not be exclusively the case, as regard

---

4   Ibid.
5   [1969] 2 AC 31.
6   See also *Bristol Tramways Co Ltd v Fiat Motors Ltd* [1910] 2 KB 831 at 841 (per FARWELL LJ) and *Grant v Australian Knitting Mills Ltd* (1933) 50 CLR 387 at 418 (per DIXON J).
7   *Australian Knitting Mills Ltd v Grant* (1933) 50 CLR 387 at 418 (per DIXON J).
8   *Henry Kendall & Sons v William Lillico & Sons* [1969] 2 AC 31 at 77 (per LORD REID). See also *Cammell Laird & Co Ltd v Manganeze Bronze and Brass Co Ltd* [1934] AC 402 at 430 (per LORD WRIGHT).
9   The Sale & Supply of Goods Act 1994, which abolished the requirement of merchantable quality and introduced into the Sale of Goods Act 1979, s 14 the novel requirement of satisfactory quality, based on the recommendations of the Law Commission No 160 Cm 137 (1987).

may be had to the state or condition of the goods[10] and goods may be of unsatisfactory quality because their legal state is such that they cannot be used, for example where goods fail to comply with legal export requirements or contravene the intellectual property rights of a third party.[11] Whether section 14(2) applies to non-physical defects was also considered by the Court of Appeal in *Harlingdon & Leinster Enterprises Ltd v Christopher Hull Fine Art Ltd*[12] where the court was divided on the issue whether a mistake as to authorship of a painting rendered it unmerchantable. A majority appears to have reached the conclusion that a defect of this kind does relate to quality[13] since a painting may be purchased for its aesthetic qualities.

The statutory definition now gives a list of factors which may be considered, together with all other relevant factors, in determining whether particular goods reach the desired standard of quality. It is important to emphasise that not all of these factors will be relevant in a given case and it may be necessary to give greater weight to some of these considerations than to others. All of this serves to demonstrate the elusive nature of a requirement of quality. While it may be possible to lay down minimum safety standards, the problem with quality is that what is acceptable in qualitative terms will depend upon a whole range of different factors such as the description of the goods, their price and the area of the market at which the goods are aimed.

(a)   *The standard a reasonable person would regard as satisfactory*[14]

This phrase, used in the definition of the requirement of satisfactory quality, is perhaps the clearest message that section 14(2) has become a primary instrument of consumer protection. It has been seen already that the judicial definitions of merchantable quality prior to 1973 had different emphases. On the one hand the test of saleability or usability was singularly more appropriate to the needs of commercial buyers who purchased goods for the purposes of resale. In contrast, the second test, based on acceptability, was more attuned to the needs of buyers such as ordinary consumers who purchased goods for use or consumption. It was generally accepted that the 1973 definition was more concerned with usability than with acceptability, but the definition of satisfactory quality now appears to be more specifically concerned with the expectations of reasonable people and, thus, with the acceptability of the goods sold. This may be the proper approach in relation to purely consumer contracts, but over-emphasis on the needs of consumers could prove counter-productive in relation to commercial contracts. The requirement of satisfactory quality turns upon whether the goods supplied reach the standard that a reasonable person would regard as satisfactory which might be interpreted in such a way that goods are treated as being unsatisfactory even though the buyer can use those goods or can resell them, albeit at a reduced price.[15] In these circumstances, but only in non-consumer contracts, it is now provided that the court may refuse to allow the buyer to reject the goods if the seller's breach of the implied terms as to description, quality or fitness is so slight that it would be unreasonable to allow rejection.[16] It should be noted that this modification of the buyer's remedies does not apply to consumer transactions, but if the goods supplied are not in such a state that they would

---

10   Sale of Goods Act 1979, s 14(2B).
11   *Niblett Ltd v Confectioners Materials Co Ltd* [1921] 3 KB 387. Cf *Sumner Permain & Co v Webb & Co* [1922] 1 KB 55.
12   [1990] 1 All ER 737.
13   Ibid at 745 (per NOURSE LJ) and at 750 (per STUART-SMITH LJ).
14   Sale of Goods Act 1979, s 14(2A).
15   See eg *Cehave NV v Bremer Handelsgesellschaft MbH, The Hansa Nord* [1976] QB 44, based on the old requirement of merchantable quality.
16   Sale of Goods Act 1979, s 15A(1).

be acceptable to a reasonable person, it would seem to follow that virtually all consumers would also be so minded, and would want to reject those goods.

In determining whether particular goods reach the standard that a reasonable person would regard as satisfactory, it should be remembered that all the surrounding circumstances must be taken into account. Thus even if goods are delivered in a defective state, for example suffering from some minor or cosmetic defects, it does not automatically follow that they will be regarded as unsatisfactory, since other factors such as the price or the way in which the goods have been described may lower the standard of quality expected by a reasonable person. For example, a reasonable person would almost certainly expect a car described as secondhand to suffer from some minor defects, a matter reflected in the lower price charged for secondhand cars when compared with their brand new counterparts.[17]

The standard of quality is based on the expectations of a reasonable *person* rather than a reasonable buyer. In the light of this it is arguable that the relevant test should take on board the expectations of reasonable sellers as well as the expectations of the purchaser. From this it should follow that if a buyer unreasonably misuses goods in a manner which could not have been expected by a reasonable seller, the buyer should not be later heard to complain. Thus if a buyer purchases goods which have clearly set out instructions for storage and use which the buyer chooses to ignore, the seller should be able to argue that the goods have been used in a manner which could not reasonably have been expected.[18] It might also be argued that a court could take into account how other buyers might have reacted to goods suffering from the same defect as those which are the subject matter of the dispute. However, this will not always be an appropriate consideration. For example in *Amstrad plc v Seagate Technology Inc*[19] computer equipment sold to the buyer did not operate within the range of temperatures indicated by the seller. In the light of the description given, the equipment was held to be unmerchantable despite the fact that other purchasers of the same equipment had been able to use it without any ill effects. Here the crucial factor was the description given rather than the fact that others could still use it as expected.

(b)   Description[20]

A description applied to the goods is relevant, since it indicates to the buyer the standard he can expect. In *Bartlett v Sydney Marcus Ltd*,[1] a secondhand car was sold at a £25 reduction because it had a defective clutch, which it was understood the buyer would repair. As described, the car was merchantable (and would also satisfy the requirement of satisfactory quality) even though it cost considerably more than £25 to repair. What is important about a description is that it will influence what a reasonable person might expect in terms of quality. Thus, as in *Bartlett* a reasonable person would not expect a secondhand car to be absolutely faultless. However, it should also be appreciated that even though goods may have been used before, this will not reduce the standard of quality to be expected by a reasonable person to nothing.

---

17   See *Thain v Anniesland Trade Centre* 1997 SCLR 991 (Noted Consum LJ (1998), 69 (6-year-old car with 80,000 miles on the clock sold for £2,995 developed an irremediable gearbox fault after two weeks' use but was still of satisfactory quality in the light of the age and price of the car).

18   See eg *Heil v Hedges* [1951] 1 TLR 512 (failure to cook meat properly).

19   (1997) 86 BLR 34.

20   Ibid.

1   [1965] 1 WLR 1013.

(c)   Price[2]

The price paid for goods is also relevant in that a low price may indicate a lower standard of quality. Conversely, if goods are only saleable at a price which is substantially lower than the contract price it would seem to follow that they are not of satisfactory quality.[3] The reference to 'a price substantially lower than the contract price' represents a watering down of the acceptability test originally stated in *Grant v Australian Knitting Mills Ltd,*[4] which did not permit any abatement in price. As a result of this, goods have been held to be merchantable even where they were defective.[5] This watering down seems to have been carried through to the 1973 statutory definition of merchantable quality especially in regard to cosmetic defects. The first statutory definition of merchantable quality required goods to be 'as fit for the purpose . . . for which goods of that kind are commonly bought as it is *reasonable* to expect.' Likewise, the present definition of satisfactory quality requires goods to 'meet the standard a reasonable person would regard as satisfactory...'. It could be argued that complicated manufactured goods, such as cars, can be reasonably expected to suffer from minor teething problems. Likewise, a reasonable person might also expect some goods to suffer from some minor defects, especially where the goods have been purchased very cheaply.

(d)   *Fitness for all the purposes for which goods of the kind in question are commonly supplied*[6]

Perhaps the most important change brought about in the 1994 definition of satisfactory quality is that the goods supplied must be for all purposes for which goods of the kind in question are commonly supplied. Thus if a particular type of goods is commonly supplied for more than one normal purpose, it will not be sufficient for the seller to supply goods which are fit for one such normal purpose but not others. This stands in contrast to the position before 1994 when it was enough for the seller to supply goods which were fit for any of the purposes for which goods of that kind were commonly supplied.[7] Even after the statutory definition of merchantable quality was introduced in 1973, the position remained the same, it being enough that the goods supplied were fit for any purpose regarded as normal for that type of goods.[8] The apparent justification for this approach seems to have been that since the requirement of merchantable quality was imposed regardless of any communication between the parties, the seller could not know which one of several possible uses the buyer might have in mind. Thus provided the goods were fit for any of their normal uses, the seller could be taken to have satisfied his obligations under the Sale of Goods Act.

The new requirement of satisfactory quality is different in this respect since it is now clear that in order for goods to reach the required standard they must be fit for all normal uses. While this might appear to represent a substantial change in the law, it should be appreciated that the list of factors in section 14(2B) are stated to be indicators of the required standard of quality *in appropriate cases*. Thus, if one of the elements listed in section 14(2B) is not complied with, it will not follow automatically that the goods supplied are not of satisfactory quality since a court may regard other factors as more important in determining whether the appropriate standard of quality has been reached.

---

2   Sale of Goods Act 1979, s 14(2A).
3   *BS Brown & Sons Ltd v Craiks Ltd* [1970] 1 All ER 823.
4   (1933) 50 CLR 387 at 418 (per DIXON J).
5   *Cehave NV v Bremer Handelsgesellschaft MbH, The Hansa Nord* [1976] QB 44.
6   Sale of Goods Act 1979, s 14(2B)(a).
7   See *Henry Kendall & Sons v William Lillico & Sons Ltd* [1969] 2 AC 31; *BS Brown & Son Ltd v Craiks Ltd* [1970] 1 All ER 823.
8   See *Aswan Engineering Co v Lupdine Ltd* [1987] 1 WLR 1.

Nevertheless, the fact that goods should be fit for all common uses may cause problems since in commercial transactions, if a seller supplies goods which are fit for one normal use but not another, there is a potential breach of section 14(2), but if the buyer seeks to use this breach to escape from what is in effect a bad bargain he may be able to seek rejection of the goods even where he is able to use those goods for the particular purpose he had in mind. For example in *Cehave NV v Bremer Handelsgesellschaft MbH, The Hansa Nord*[9] the buyer purchased citrus fruit pellets which were considered not to be of merchantable quality, but were nonetheless fit for the particular purpose which the buyer had in mind. However, because of the technical breach of the requirement of merchantable quality, the buyer intended to reject the goods, thereby casting them on to the local market at a much reduced price which would allow him to buy them back at the lower market price. In the event, the Court of Appeal was able to make use of the common law doctrine of innominate terms on the basis that there was also an express term to the effect that the pellets would be of good quality. But for this eventuality, the buyer would have been left in the position of being able to take advantage of the fact that the goods could still be used for the purpose he had in mind but were, nevertheless, not of merchantable quality. There is an answer to problems of this kind where, as in *The Hansa Nord,* the buyer and seller are both commercial contracting parties, since the 1994 changes to the Sale of Goods Act mean that a court now has the discretion to downgrade the right of rejection to an action for damages if the seriousness of the breach is not sufficiently great to warrant rejection.[10] However, this approach will have no application to consumer purchasers who will be in a position to be able to reject the goods should they fail to function satisfactorily in relation to any normal use.

In the light of this change in the law, it is possible that the courts may adopt a more stringent view of what is a common or normal use for a particular variety of goods, thereby casting on the buyer the responsibility of making it clear to the seller, at the time of contracting, what particular use he has in mind and, thereby, bringing the requirement of fitness for purpose in section 14(3) into play. The danger created by section 14(2B)(a) is that where goods can be put to a number of different uses, the price charged may differ according to the particular use intended by the buyer. In such cases, it would be unreasonable to allow the buyer to reject goods where they are unfit for a common use while still being fit for the particular use which the buyer had in mind.

What is a 'common' purpose is difficult to define since the decision will depend on the context in which the case arises. It is clear that goods will not have to be fit for immediate use since it is often the case that something has to be done to goods in order to render them fit for use. For example, furniture may have to be assembled or food cooked.

(e)   *Appearance and finish and freedom from minor defects*[11]

There were a number of decisions prior to the introduction of the statutory definition of merchantable quality demonstrating that cosmetic defects could render a product unmerchantable.[12] However, it was never entirely clear whether a consumer purchaser could reject goods simply on the ground that they suffered from a number of small, but irritating minor defects. The main problem in this regard seems to have been that a car, for example, with minor running problems or cosmetic defects could still be driven,

---

9   [1976] QB 44.
10   Sale of Goods Act 1979, s 15A.
11   Sale of Goods Act 1979, s 14(2B)(b) and (c).
12   *Jackson v Rotax Motor and Cycle Co Ltd* [1910] 2 KB 937.

in which case it was possible that such goods would be regarded as being of the required standard of quality, especially if the defects could be repaired at a relatively low cost.[13] Decisions of this kind raise doubts as to the reason for including a specific reference to appearance, finish and minor or cosmetic defects in the definition of satisfactory quality. It should be emphasised that the list of factors in section 14(2) are merely elements to be considered in determining whether particular goods are of satisfactory quality or not. Thus other factors such as description or price may prove to be more important than the presence of some minor defect.

Whether or not a specific reference to minor defects was actually necessary may be doubted in the light of the decision in the Court of Appeal in *Rogers v Parish (Scarborough) Ltd*.[14] In this case, the plaintiff bought a new Range Rover which suffered from a number of minor defects, including a misfiring engine, an oil leak, a noisy gearbox and unacceptable paintwork. The vehicle was still capable of being driven, but the plaintiff wished to reject it. It was held that a defect which is capable of being repaired may still render goods unsatisfactory. Furthermore, a car is purchased not only to move from one point to another, but also for its appropriate degree of comfort, ease of handling, reliability and appearance. What is appropriate depends on the price paid.[15] Thus the purchaser who had paid a high price for the vehicle could reject it on the ground that it was not of satisfactory quality.[16] Conversely, this would also suggest that the less a person pays, the lower the standard of quality he can expect.

(f)   Safety[17]

It is clear from section 14(2B)(d) that the safety of goods is a factor which may be considered in deciding whether goods are of satisfactory quality. This was not explicit under the old law, but there are decisions on the meaning of merchantable quality which indicate that safety was always a relevant consideration. Thus it has been held that a new car which cannot be safely used is not of merchantable quality.[18]

(g)   Durability

The condition of merchantable quality only had to be satisfied at the time of delivery of the goods[19] and generally that position will remain the same for the purposes of the requirement of satisfactory quality. However, this does not mean that defects which manifest themselves after delivery leave the buyer unprotected, since a defect can be present at the time of sale without revealing itself until much later on. Also, in the case of perishable goods, it is necessary that they be shipped in such a state that they will arrive in an acceptable condition. Thus, if potatoes are shipped in apparently good condition but are found to be rotten when unloaded, there is a breach of section 14(2).[20]

These cases do not suggest that there is a condition of durability, although there are *dicta* in *Lambert v Lewis*[1] to the effect that there is a continuing warranty that goods will continue to be fit for a reasonable time after delivery, so long as the goods remain in

---

13   *Millars of Falkirk v Turpie* 1976 SLT (Notes) 66. See also *Thain v Anniesland Trade Centre* 1997 SCLR 991.
14   [1987] 2 All ER 232. See also *Shine v General Guarantee Corpn* [1988] 1 All ER 911.
15   Ibid at 237 (per MUSTILL LJ).
16   Contrast the position in the art world where *caveat emptor* seems to prevail: *Harlingdon & Leinster Enterprises v Christopher Hull (Fine Art) Ltd* [1990] 1 All ER 737.
17   Sale of Goods Act 1979, s 14(2B)(d).
18   See *Bernstein v Pamson Motors (Golders Green) Ltd* [1987] All ER 220 at 226 (per ROUGIER J). See also *Bartlett v Sidney Marcus Ltd* [1965] 1 WLR 1013.
19   *Crowther v Shannon Motors* [1975] 1 WLR 30.
20   *Mash and Murrell v Joseph I Emmanuel* [1961] 1 All ER 485 (reversed on the facts [1962] 1 All ER 77), and see also *Beer v Walker* (1877) 46 LJQB 677.
1   [1981] 1 All ER 1185 at 1191 (per LORD DIPLOCK).

the same apparent state as that in which they were delivered. Now it is clear from section 14(2B)(e) that a factor to consider in determining whether goods are of satisfactory quality is whether or not they are sufficiently durable. The inclusion of a specific reference to durability may not make a lot of difference to the position of the buyer who wishes to reject the goods and recover the purchase price since it is likely in most cases that before the problem of durability is discovered, the buyer will be deemed to have accepted the goods[2] and will be confined to an action for damages only.

Special considerations seem to apply to 'supply and fit' contracts for example where a manufacturer agrees to manufacture equipment and instal it at the buyer's premises. In such a case, it seems that the seller is to be allowed a reasonable time in which to make necessary adjustments to the equipment for the purpose of ensuring that the goods are in conformity with the contract. Accordingly, the buyer will not be entitled to reject immediately on discovery that the goods do not correspond with the contract specification. Instead, he must wait for the expiry of a reasonable period before seeking to reject.[3]

(6)   THE IMPLIED CONDITION OF FITNESS FOR PURPOSE

The Sale of Goods Act 1979, section 14(3) provides:[4]

> Where the seller sells goods in the course of a business and the buyer expressly, or by implication, makes known—
> (a)   to the seller, or
> (b)   where the purchase price or part of it is payable by instalments and the goods were previously sold by a credit broker to the seller, to that credit broker,
> any particular purpose for which the goods are being bought, there is an implied condition that the goods supplied under the contract are reasonably fit for that purpose, whether or not it is a purpose for which such goods are commonly supplied, except where the circumstances show that the buyer does not rely, or that it is unreasonable for him to rely, on the skill or judgment of the seller or the credit broker.

It has been observed already that section 14(3), like section 14(2), applies only where the seller sells in the course of a business, and that section 14(3) also applies to all goods supplied under the contract, including instructions supplied with the goods, with the result that misleading instructions may render the goods unfit for their intended use.[5]

(i)   The purpose

Section 14(3) requires the goods to be fit for the particular purpose for which the buyer requires them. This can be a normal purpose or a special purpose. If the goods are requested for their normal purpose, it would appear that, for the most part, both section 14(2) and (3) will apply. This overlap is inevitable when one considers that satisfactory quality is defined in section 14(2B)(a) in terms of fitness for purpose. However, it would appear that there might be circumstances where goods are fit for the buyer's intended purpose, but are not of satisfactory quality. For example, a car may be capable of being driven but might be unsatisfactory due to the presence of a large number of cosmetic defects. Also, goods might be satisfactory but unfit for the buyer's intended purpose.

2   Sale of Goods Act 1979, ss 11(4) and 35 and see *Bernstein v Pamson Motors (Golders Green) Ltd* [1987] 2 All ER 220.
3   See *Burnley Engineering Products Ltd v Cambridge Vacuum Engineering Ltd* (1994) 50 Con LR 10.
4   See also Supply of Goods (Implied Terms) Act 1973, s 10(3); Supply of Goods and Services Act 1982, s 9(4), (5) and s 4(4), (6).
5   See *Wormell v RHM Agriculture* [1987] 3 All ER 75 at 77 (per DILLON LJ).

For example, in *Ashington Piggeries Ltd v Christopher Hill Ltd*,[6] had the animal feed supplied been fit for animals in general, although not fit for mink in particular, there might have been a breach of section 14(3) without there being a breach of section 14(2).

If goods have only one purpose, then it will be assumed that the buyer requires them for that purpose. Thus, there is no need to state that you wish to use a hot water bottle for the purpose of keeping warm and without fear of being covered with its contents.[7]

If the goods can be used for more than one purpose, the required use must be made known to the seller, or someone having authority to receive such communication. Thus, if the buyer of coal specifies that it should be fit for use on a particular type of ship, then failure to supply coal of the required standard will constitute a breach of section 14(3), since there is no such thing as a normal ship, and coal merchants should be aware of this.[8] However, if a buyer fails to reveal that he or she suffers from some physical peculiarity which makes use of the goods unsafe, the buyer may be considered to require the goods for a special purpose. In *Griffiths v Peter Conway Ltd*,[9] the plaintiff failed to reveal that she had an unusually sensitive skin which made her particularly prone to dermatitis. It was shown that the tweed coat she purchased would not have harmed a normal person. Accordingly, the sensitivity of the plaintiff was treated as rendering her use of the coat a special use, which had not been communicated to the seller. This begs the question, if there is no such thing as a normal ship, why is there a normal person? However, the difference between *Griffiths v Conway* and *Manchester Liners v Rea* may also be explained on the basis that the coal merchant in the latter case had dealt with the buyer on previous occasions and was probably taken to be aware of the buyer's needs. Moreover, the approach of the Court of Appeal in *Griffiths* has also been confirmed by the House of Lords in *Slater & Slater v Finning Ltd*[10] in which it was held that if goods fail to serve the purpose required by the buyer because of the failure of the buyer to advise the seller of some abnormality affecting himself or his property, the buyer cannot be heard to complain. Moreover, it would appear that this remains the case even where the buyer is unaware of the abnormality in question. In *Slater* the buyer's fishing vessel had an unusual engine which meant that three 'off-the-shelf' camshafts fitted by the seller caused the engine to malfunction. The sellers were held to be entitled to assume that that the camshafts would be used in a 'normal' engine and that if this was not the case, the onus was on the buyer to make known to the seller any idiosyncrasy in their property which might affect performance.

(ii)   Reliance on the seller's skill and judgment

The implied condition in section 14(3) is inapplicable where the buyer does not rely upon the seller's skill and judgment. If the seller knows the purpose for which the goods are required, reliance is usually inferred as a matter of course, particularly if the buyer is a consumer. For example, in *Grant v Australian Knitting Mills Ltd*,[11] it was observed that reliance will be assumed from the fact that the buyer goes into a shop confident that the tradesman has selected his stock with skill and judgment.[12] This assumed reliance upon the retailer is often a pure fiction and in some cases, the buyer has, in fact, relied on the manufacturer. In such a case, it would not be impossible, in theory, to imply on

---

6   [1972] AC 441.
7   *Preist v Last* [1903] 2 KB 148.
8   *Manchester Liners Ltd v Rea* [1922] 2 AC 74.
9   [1939] 1 All ER 685.
10   [1996] 3 All ER 398.
11   [1936] AC 85.
12   Ibid at 99 (per Lord WRIGHT).

the part of the manufacturer a warranty of fitness, provided the manufacturer is not subject to any greater liability than the seller of the goods. Other factors which may assist in determining whether reliance is reasonable include the relative expertise of the parties,[13] whether instructions for use have been provided either before or after making the contract[14] and whether the supplier is also the manufacturer.[15] Furthermore, evidence of reliance may also be derived from the fact that the parties have dealt with each other on some previous occasion in relation to the type of goods purchased.[16]

If the buyer relies totally on his own skill and judgment, he can have no recourse to section 14(3). Similarly, if it is unreasonable for the buyer to rely on the seller's skill and judgment, section 14(3) is of no assistance. The concept of unreasonable reliance is one which was introduced by the Supply of Goods (Implied Terms) Act 1973 and is now embodied in the 1979 Act. One effect of this introduction is that it is now for the seller to prove that the buyer did not rely on him, or that it was unreasonable to expect the buyer to rely upon him. Prior to the 1973 Act, the onus of proving reliance lay on the buyer.[17] Reliance may be unreasonable if the seller informs the buyer that he has no expertise in some particular respect,[18] or where the buyer ought to know that the seller has no such expertise. For example, if a person were to enter an 'off-licence', ask for a bottle of brown ale and declare, 'It's hair wash night', one might expect the retailer to have some knowledge of the taste but not necessarily of the suitability of the product for washing hair. Likewise, the 'idiosyncrasy' cases considered above[19] may also be explained in terms of the unreasonableness of the buyer's reliance on the seller. In each case it can be said that until the buyer has informed the seller of the skin complaint or the unusual variety of engine he cannot expect the seller to exercise any skill and judgment in selecting suitable goods. In contrast the buyer in *Manchester Liners Ltd v Rea* could be said to have placed reasonable reliance on the seller's skill and judgment in the light of their previous dealings with each other. Accordingly, the cornerstone of liability under section 14(3) would appear to be the express or implied provision of information by the buyer as to the purpose he has in mind.

While section 14(3) has no application in the absence of reasonable reliance, there is nothing to preclude the buyer from partially relying on the seller. In such a case, the loss suffered by the buyer must arise out of the reliance he has placed on the seller's skill and judgment. In *Ashington Piggeries Ltd v Christopher Hill Ltd,*[20] the appellants were mink-farmers who had asked the respondents to supply a mink food according to a formula prepared by them. The respondents had never previously produced a feed for mink, but had prepared foods for other types of farm animal. The respondents made some suggestions which resulted in an alteration to the appellants' formula. Subsequently, farmers to whom the feed was supplied complained that mink were dying. This was discovered to be due to the generation of a toxic substance (DMNA) resulting from a chemical reaction between some of the ingredients included at the respondents' suggestion. The appellants claimed that the feed was not fit for its intended purpose, namely being fed to the mink.

The House of Lords held that, while the appellants relied on their skill and judgment to ensure that no peculiarities of the mink made the food unsuitable for feeding mink, they had also relied on the respondents to exercise skill in obtaining proper ingredients,

13   *Henry Kendall & Sons v William Lillico & Sons* [1969] 2 AC 31.
14   *Wormell v RHM Agriculture (East) Ltd* [1987] 3 All ER 75.
15   *Henry Kendall & Sons v William Lillico & Sons* [1969] 2 AC 31 at 84 (per LORD REID).
16   *Manchester Liners Ltd v Rea* [1922] 2 AC 74.
17   Ibid.
18   *Ashington Piggeries Ltd v Christopher Hill Ltd* [1972] AC 441.
19   See *Griffiths v Peter Conway Ltd* [1939] 1 All ER 685; *Slater & Slater v Finning Ltd* [1996] 3 All ER 398.
20   [1972] AC 441. See also *Cammell Laird v Manganeze Bronze* [1934] AC 402 and *Medway Oil and Storage Co Ltd v Silica Gel Corpn* (1928) 33 Com Cas 195, HL.

mixing them properly and ensuring that they were safe to feed to animals in general. The respondents had failed in this regard and accordingly, since the loss suffered arose out of the buyer's reliance on the seller's area of expertise, there was a breach of section 14(3).

(iii)   Strictness of the duty

Contractual duties are said to be strict. However, section 14(3) requires the buyer to have reasonably relied on the seller's skill and judgment. This might suggest that the seller can only be held liable if he has failed to do something which could reasonably be expected of him. But it is now clear that the seller must accept responsibility for harm caused by latent defects which are undiscoverable by the exercise of any skill or judgment. In *Frost v Aylesbury Dairy Co Ltd*,[1] the seller sold milk contaminated with typhoid bacteria. This defect could not have been discovered by taking any sort of reasonable precautions, yet there was still held to be a breach of the implied condition of fitness. The argument that section 14(3) does not apply to latent defects has now been laid to rest by the House of Lords in *Henry Kendall & Sons v William Lillico & Sons Ltd*,[2] where it was said that the law has gone further than compensating the plaintiff only where there has been a failure to exercise skill and judgment. The buyer now has an assurance that the goods will be *reasonably* fit for his intended use, and that covers defects which are latent and could not have been discovered.[3] On the other hand the duty of the seller is only to supply goods which are reasonably fit for the purpose required by the buyer[4] and this means that regard must be had to the preciseness with which the buyer has specified his requirements. The proper question to ask is, 'were these goods reasonably fit for the specified purpose?'[5] Thus if the buyer fails to reveal salient information which is exclusively within his knowledge, the seller cannot be expected to anticipate this and section 14(3) will not assist the buyer.[6]

---

1   [1905] 1 KB 608. See also *Ashington Piggeries Ltd v Christopher Hill Ltd* [1972] AC 441.
2   [1969] 2 AC 31.
3   Ibid at 84 (per LORD REID).
4   See Atiyah, *Sale of Goods* p 188.
5   *Henry Kendall & Sons v William Lillico & Sons Ltd* [1969] 2 AC 31 at 115 (per LORD PEARCE).
6   *Griffiths v Peter Conway Ltd* [1939] 1 All ER 685 at 691 (per LORD GREENE MR).

Chapter 26

Defective services

1. INTRODUCTION

(1) THE RANGE OF SERVICES PROVIDED

The range of services which may be provided is so wide that any attempt to list them all would be futile, although most services do fall into one of two broad categories.[1] It may be a pure service, or it may be a service linked to a transfer of ownership in goods or materials.

Pure services are those in which nothing other than the skill or expertise of the supplier is endowed upon the consumer. The professional services of a doctor, lawyer, surveyor or financial adviser fall within this category. Apart from advice givers, pure services are also provided by a window cleaner, a refuse collector or a hairdresser through the exercise of his own labour or skill. Leisure services such as those provided by a cinema, a theatre or a travel agent, transport services and bailment services such as those provided by a furniture remover or a repairer will also fall within this category. Services which are coupled with a supply of goods or materials form the second category and will usually be provided by a skilled tradesman. Typical examples include the work of plumbers and electricians who will supply the materials necessary to effect a repair.

Whatever the type of service may be, the industry has its fair share of 'cowboys', who may develop undesirable practices which give reasonable ground for complaint. Problems arising from the supply of services include shoddy performance, late completion and over-charging.[2]

(2) THE BASIS OF LIABILITY

Services can be provided by way of contract between the provider and the recipient or independently of a contract. For example, there is no contractual relationship between

---

1 See Woodroffe *Goods and Services — The New Law* (1982) pp 97–98; Lawson *The Supply of Goods and Services Act 1982* (1982) pp 104–105.
2 See Lantin and Woodroffe *Service Please — Services and the Law: A Consumer View* (1981); Dugdale and Stanton *Professional Negligence* (3rd edn, 1998); 'Car Servicing and Repairs: A Discussion Paper' (OFT 1980).

a barrister and his client,[3] therefore such duties as the barrister may owe must lie in tort. Bankers, solicitors, accountants and surveyors may give advice both within and without a contractual relationship. The contract is subject to an implied term that the adviser will exercise reasonable care and skill, but there is also an independent tortious duty to exercise reasonable care which may be owed to a third party. In solicitor–client cases there are also fiduciary duties on the solicitor. In the case of National Health Service medical treatment there is no contract between the patient and the surgeon, the regional health authority or the hospital trust. In such a case, the regional health authority or hospital trust may be vicariously liable for the negligent failure of the surgeon to take reasonable care. The area of building services also provides its fair share of non-contractual duties of care. Services provided by way of bailment will often involve a contractual relationship, but where the bailment is gratuitous, the duty owed by the bailee is still one to take reasonable care of the property in his possession or to effect repairs with reasonable care and skill. It follows that the repairer of a motor vehicle is in breach of a duty to take care if a wheel flange he has negligently repaired comes loose and strikes a pedestrian.[4]

(i)   Contractual liability

Unlike the requirement of the Sale of Goods Act 1979 that there should be a money consideration, any consideration will suffice for the purposes of a contract for services.[5] Thus an exchange of goods for services will still fall within the provisions of the Act. The contractual obligations owed by the parties may be expressed by the contract, or may be implied by the 1982 Act or at common law.

The 1982 Act implies three terms. In all contracts to which the Act applies,[6] the charge for the service may be expressed by the contract or, if no charge is fixed, a reasonable charge must be paid by the recipient.[7] Furthermore, a person who supplies a service in the course of a business impliedly undertakes to perform the service with reasonable care and skill,[8] and will perform the service within a reasonable time, where the contract is silent as to the date for performance.[9] These provisions are supposed to constitute an accurate codification of the common law prior to the Act.[10] However, there are other common law rules relevant to contracts for the supply of a service which are not contained within the Act.[11]

Not all services come within the provisions of the Supply of Goods and Services Act 1982. Consistent with the view that the Act gives effect to the common law, a distinction is drawn between contracts for the supply of a service and a contract of service or apprenticeship. The former are subject to the provisions of the Act, whereas the latter are not.[12] Accordingly, contracts of employment do not fall within the scope of the 1982 Act. The distinction between a contract of service and a contract for services

3   *Kennedy v Broun* (1863) 13 CBNS 677; *Swinfen v Lord Chelmsford* (1860) 5 H & N 890.
4   *Stennett v Hancock and Peters* [1939] 2 All ER 578.
5   Supply of Goods and Services Act 1982, s 12(3).
6   These include all contracts under which the supplier agrees to carry out a service by virtue of section 12(1), including one in which goods are transferred or bailed.
7   Supply of Goods and Services Act 1982, s 15.
8   Supply of Goods and Services Act 1982, s 13. See *Wilson v Best Travel Ltd* [1993] 1 All ER 353.
9   Ibid, s 14.
10   Law Commission No 156 (1986) Cmnd 9773, para 2.43.
11   The Supply of Goods and Services Act 1982, s 16(3)(a) provides that the Act does not prejudice any rule of law which imposes a stricter duty on the supplier of a service. Furthermore, s 16(4) provides that the Act is subject to the provisions of any other enactment relating to the provision of services. See eg Merchant Shipping Act 1894, s 503(1) and Defective Premises Act 1972, s 1.
12   Supply of Goods and Services Act 1982, s 12(2).

is often difficult to make and has spawned a variety of tests, which are discussed elsewhere, to differentiate between the two.[13]

Under the Supply of Goods and Services Act 1982, section 12(4), there is a power to exempt certain services from the provisions of the Act. So far, exemptions have been made in respect of advocates,[14] company directors providing services for their company,[15] directors of building societies providing services to the society[16] and arbitrators.[17] All of these exemptions are intended to give effect to the position which existed at common law before the Act was passed. The result is that the professions concerned are not affected by section 13 of the Act, which imposes a contractual duty to exercise reasonable care and skill.

Many contracts for the provision of services also involve a supply of goods. For example, a skilled tradesman such as a plumber may supply a shower unit and exercise skill in installing the equipment. In these circumstances, it is important to be able to identify the source of any complaint made by the customer. If the shower unit is defective, the strict obligations relating to quality and fitness which apply to sale of goods contracts will be relevant.[18] If the complaint is that the work has not been carried out to the customer's satisfaction, then subject to any express agreement, the supplier of the service is only liable for a failure to exercise reasonable care.

Distinguishing between a contract for the supply of a service and one for the supply of goods is not easy. Some contracts are primarily contracts for the supply of a service which only incidentally involve the supply of a material article. For example, the supply of medicines or blood by a hospital is probably best regarded as purely incidental to the service provided by a doctor.[19] Conversely in *Dodd & Dodd v Wilson & McWilliam*[20] the plaintiff's cattle were harmed when the defendant, a veterinary surgeon, used a serum which was not fit for its intended use. It was established that there was no fault on the part of the defendant, but he was nonetheless liable. It is difficult to distinguish between these cases, but it is possible to argue that a substance such as human blood is not normally the subject of a commercial transaction.[1]

The test employed to distinguish between a supply of goods and a supply of services is to enquire what is the substance of the contract. If the contract is substantially one for the exercise of some skill, it is likely to be regarded as a supply of services. For example, an artist engaged to paint a portrait undoubtedly supplies a material article when the painting is handed over, but it is the skill of the artist which is the essential ingredient of the contract.[2] But a contract made with a restaurant owner for the supply of a meal is one for the sale of goods despite the skill exercised by the chef.[3]

---

13   See further ch 27.
14   SI 1982/1771, art 2(1). But cf *Arthur JS Hall v Simons* (2000) Times, 21 July, HL, overruling *Rondel v Worsley* [1969] 1 AC 191. See also ch 8.
15   SI 1982/1771, art 2(2). See also *Re City Equitable Fire Insurance* [1925] Ch 407 and *Lagunas Nitrate Co v Lagunas Syndicate* [1899] 2 Ch 392.
16   SI 1983/902.
17   SI 1985/1. See also *Sutcliffe v Thackrah* [1974] AC 727 and *Arenson v Casson, Beckman, Rutley & Co* [1977] AC 405.
18   See ch 25.
19   *Perlmutter v Beth David Hospital* 123 NE 2d 792 (1955); *Roe v Minister of Health* [1954] 2 QB 66.
20   [1946] 2 All ER 691.
1   Atiyah *Sale of Goods* pp 25 26. Cf Consumer Protection Act 1987, s 45(1) and see ch 25.
2   *Robinson v Graves* [1935] 1 KB 579.
3   *Lockett v A & M Charles Ltd* [1938] 4 All ER 170. See also Supply of Goods and Services Act 1982, s 12(3)(a).

(ii)   Tortious liability

A person who supplies a service in the absence of a contract is not immune from liability, since he may be liable in tort for a failure to exercise reasonable care. It follows that, if defective services have been provided for no reward, or if the performance of a service adversely affects a bystander,[4] the provider of that service may be liable to compensate the plaintiff due to his failure to take reasonable care. Much will depend on the kind of harm suffered by the recipient of the service. For example it is more likely that physical harm to the person or property will be actionable than pure economic loss.

Even where there is a contractual relationship, the consumer of a service may choose to sue for breach of a tortious duty, since it is now established that contractual and tortious duties of care may exist concurrently.[5] In order for concurrent liability to apply it is necessary for the contract and tort duties to be concurrent, although they need not be co-extensive. There must also be a free standing duty in tort. A builder who has a contract with the client will not be concurrently liable in tort for economic loss as there is no such tortious duty.[6] There is no concurrent liability where the contractual duty is stricter than reasonable care[7] but it is possible for wider duties to be imposed in negligence than in contract, as the duty in tort is imposed by the general law, whereas the contractual duty is said to arise from the common intention of the parties.[8]

Whether a plaintiff chooses to sue in contract or tort has practical implications.[9] For example, there are different rules on limitation of actions,[10] jurisdiction, contributory negligence[11] and remoteness of damage according to whether the case is one for breach of contract or for a breach of tortious duty. Although there are different rules on assessment and remoteness of damage according to whether the action is based in tort or contract,[12] the distinction makes no difference in the case of the supply of services. The measure of damages the plaintiff will receive is the same in either case.[13] Where a service is provided, there is a pre-existing relationship between the parties and, as a result, there is no need to apply a remoteness principle which is primarily designed to govern disputes which arise between strangers.

(iii)   The European dimension

The position of the supplier of a service seems set to change in the light of the intervention of the European Community. It has long been recognised that the Community has paid more attention to the position of the consumer of goods at the expense of the consumer of services. The first attempt at regulation proposed a fault-based regime under which the supplier of services was required to prove that he was not at fault after the consumer had established that actionable damage had been caused by the performance of the service under consideration.[14] The services directive was strongly criticised for a number of reasons. In particular, its definition of fault was unclear

---

4   See *Stennett v Hancock and Peters* [1939] 2 All ER 578.
5   *Henderson v Merrett Syndicates Ltd* [1995] 2 AC 145.
6   *D & F Estates Ltd v Church Comrs for England* [1989] AC 177.
7   See ch 12.
8   *Holt v Payne Skillington* (1995) 77 BLR 51; Whittaker (1997) 17 LS 169.
9   See Poulton (1966) 82 LQR 346; Fridman (1977) 93 LQR 422; Holyoak (1983) 99 LQR 591: Burrows (1995) CLP 103.
10   See ch 19.
11   See ch 20.
12   See ch 16.
13   See ch 17.
14   Proposal for a Council Directive on the liability of suppliers of services COM(90) 482 final (OJ C12/8, 18 January 1991).

and it was difficult to ascertain what types of service would fall within its provisions. The effect of the reversal of the burden of proof would have been to require the supplier of an allegedly defective service to prove a negative and there were also fears that the cost of insurance to service suppliers might prove to be prohibitive.

In the light of the various criticisms, the directive was withdrawn and replaced by new proposals.[15] These have the aims of improving information for consumers (based on voluntary codes) and intend to introduce specific legislation dealing with particular areas of the services sector;[16] and simplify guarantees, after-sales service and the settlement of disputes. There is already legislation in respect of package holiday travel.[17]

2.   THE GENERAL DUTIES OF THE SUPPLIER OF SERVICES

(1)   THE DUTY TO EXERCISE REASONABLE CARE AND SKILL

(i)   Privity of contract and tortious proximity

Whether the action is brought in contract or in tort, the duty of care owed by the supplier of a service is the same, that is, to take reasonable care. As a general rule, the relationship between the consumer and the supplier of a service will be very close since performance of the service will have been specifically requested. Even where there is no contractual relationship, the supplier of a service is often aware that someone in the class of persons to which the consumer belongs will rely on the service provided. For example, a surveyor knows that his survey report will be relied upon by the purchaser of a house, thus the duty to take care exists, both where there is a contractual relationship between the two,[18] and where the survey is provided for the benefit of a building society and later passed on to the prospective purchaser of whose existence the surveyor must be aware.[19] A solicitor also owes a duty of care to his client,[20] and to a third party to whom the solicitor has voluntarily assumed responsibility.[1]

Where a service is provided in the absence of a contract, it is necessary to establish a sufficiently close relationship of proximity between the supplier and the consumer. Where the consumer suffers physical harm, that relationship of proximity should not be too difficult to find unless there are awkward policy considerations.[2] Thus a car repairer owes a duty of care to not only the owner of the vehicle and his passengers[3] but also to any other person who comes into contact with the repaired vehicle.[4]

The position is more difficult where financial harm is suffered by the plaintiff, which often will be the case where the supply of services is concerned.[5]

(ii)   The degree of care and skill required

Section 13 of the Supply of Goods and Services Act 1982 provides that:

---

15   Com (94) 2640.
16   The medical service and construction sectors are currently under consideration.
17   EC Directive 90/314.
18   *Perry v Sydney Phillips & Sons* [1982] 1 WLR 1297.
19   *Yianni v Edwin Evans & Sons* [1982] QB 438; *Smith v Eric Bush (a firm)* [1989] 2 All ER 514.
20   *Midland Bank Trust Co Ltd. v Hett & Stubbs, Kemp (a firm)* [1979] Ch 384.
1   *White v Jones* [1995] 2 AC 207.
2   As may be the case where the provision of medical services is concerned.
3   *Haseldine v CA Daw & Son Ltd* [1941] 2 KB 343; *Herschtal v Stewart and Ardern Ltd* [1940] 1 KB 155.
4   *Stennett v Hancock and Peters* [1939] 2 All ER 578.
5   See ch 10 for a discussion of the issues surrounding actions for negligently inflicted economic loss.

In a contract for the supply of a service where the supplier is acting in the course of a business, there is an implied term that the supplier will carry out the service with reasonable care and skill.

By referring to an implied term rather than a condition, section 13 allows the court to apply the common law development of the intermediate term.[6] This will permit consideration of the seriousness of the supplier's breach in determining what remedy should be awarded.

The appropriate standard of liability is generally that of the reasonable man[7] whether the action is framed in contract or tort. How the reasonable man behaves is largely a matter of policy, but the court will be able to refer to trade norms in determining what standard of care and skill is appropriate. In general terms, the standard is that of the reasonably competent member of the relevant trade.[8] Thus a jeweller piercing a client's ears is expected to reach the standard of an ordinary skilled jeweller, but he does not have to conform to the standards of a surgeon.[9] Regard must also be had to the nature of the work undertaken. For example, the work done by an auctioneer in valuing a painting by an unknown artist is very inexact in its nature, involving the giving of an opinion which might be fallible. Accordingly, provided the auctioneer has acted honestly and diligently, his failure to spot a potentially very valuable piece of work does not constitute negligence.[10] Conversely, where the work done is subject to acceptable trade norms, they must be adhered to. Thus a hairdresser who fails to read instructions printed on a bottle of hair dye,[11] or a carpet layer who leaves his work in a condition whereby a person can trip up[12] both fail to perform their service in a safe and workmanlike manner.[13] The supplier may be liable if he impliedly warrants that he possesses the skill necessary to perform the service.[14]

A relevant factor in determining whether there has been a breach of duty is that of general and approved practice in the relevant trade.[15] Compliance with such a practice is some evidence of the exercise of reasonable care.[16] Thus a solicitor who inadvertently repudiates his client's contract is not negligent if he has adhered to general conveyancing practice.[17] Evidence of adherence to such practices is not conclusive since as a matter of policy, a court may wish to disapprove of the practice if it has become out-dated.[18] Moreover there is some evidence that courts are prepared to ignore common practices and substitute a higher standard of care where the issue before the court is one of general or legal knowledge, where no particular skill is needed to see that the practice is wrong and where there is extrinsic evidence which suggests the general practice should be changed.[19]

---

6   See *Hong Kong Fir Shipping Co Ltd v Kawasaki Kisen Kaisha Ltd* [1962] 1 All ER 474 and *Cehave NV v Bremer Handelsgesellschaft mbH, The Hansa Nord* [1976] QB 44.

7   See further ch 12.

8   *Bolam v Friern Hospital Management Committee* [1957] 1 WLR 582 at 586 (per MCNAIR J).

9   *Phillips v William Whiteley Ltd* [1938] 1 All ER 566. See also *Wells v Cooper* [1958] 2 QB 265.

10   *Luxmoore-May v Messenger May Baverstock (a firm)* [1990] 1 All ER 1067 at 1076 (per SLADE LJ).

11   *Watson v Buckley, Osborne, Garrett & Co* [1940] 1 All ER 174.

12   *Kimber v William Willett Ltd* [1947] 1 All ER 361.

13   Ibid at 362 (per TUCKER LJ).

14   *Harmer v Cornelius* (1858) 5 CBNS 236. See also Law Commission No 156 (1986) Cmnd 9773, para 2.44 and Supply of Goods and Services Act 1982, s 16(3)(b).

15   See further ch 12.

16   *Morris v West Hartlepool Steam Navigation Co Ltd* [1956] AC 552.

17   *Simons v Pennington & Sons* [1955] 1 WLR 183. But see *Edward Wong Finance Co Ltd v Johnson Stokes & Master* [1984] AC 296; *G & K Ladenbau v Crawley & De Reya* [1978] 1 WLR 266.

18   *Brown v Rolls Royce Ltd* [1960] 1 WLR 210; *Bolitho v City & Hackney HA* [1997] 4 All ER 771.

19   See Holyoak (1990) 10 LS 201, 209; *Edward Wong Finance Co Ltd v Johnson Stokes & Master* [1984] AC 296.

Unless otherwise provided by contract the objective standard requires only the exercise of reasonable care. Thus perfection is not warranted[20] nor, generally, is there any guarantee that the service will achieve a particular result.[1] Even an error of judgment on the part of a doctor[2] or a commodity broker[3] may be excused. But, errors of judgment which would not have been made by a reasonable man exercising the skill under consideration are actionable.[4] Where a person acts to the best of his ability but fails to reach the standard of the reasonable man he is still liable since inexperience is irrelevant.[5] A novice who has just started in a particular trade is expected to reach the same standard as a person with thirty years' experience.[6]

It has been argued that in consumer transactions, the standard of reasonable care and skill is too low and that it can give rise to uncertainty as to what can be expected.[7] But the consumer of a service will often give exact details of his requirements so that the standard can be set by reference to the customer's instructions.[8] Moreover, the standard presently applied is flexible and decided cases do supply guidance on how the principle is to be applied in particular cases.[9] What this fails to recognise is that consumers frequently do not specify the standard of work required, particularly where professional services are concerned. It is arguable that, in many cases, the recipient of a service is insufficiently informed to demand a particular level of performance.

(2)   GUARANTEEING A RESULT

As a general rule, the supplier of a service does not guarantee a particular result. Thus a solicitor does not warrant the success of legal action pursued on his client's behalf, nor does a doctor guarantee the success of an operation.[10] Where a supplier is taken to have given a guarantee of service suitability this will usually be the result of an express contractual term. Thus in *G K Serigraphics (a firm) v Dispro Ltd*,[11] the appellants contracted to stick a laminated surface on printed boards. When the lamination failed to work the appellants were held to have expressly taken on an absolute obligation to properly laminate the boards.[12]

Occasionally, the circumstances in which a service is provided may justify the implication of a standard higher than that of reasonable care, so that a service supplier may be required to achieve a particular outcome. In *Greaves & Co (Contractors) Ltd v Baynham Meikle & Partners*,[13] the defendants, acting as the plaintiff's sub-contractors, were the designers of a warehouse floor intended to be suitable for the use of fork-lift trucks carrying barrels of oil. The floor proved to be inadequate when it cracked due to vibrations caused by the moving of fork-lift trucks. The plaintiffs, as main contractors, admitted liability to the owner, and sought an indemnity from the defendants for breach

20 *Duchess of Argyll v Beuselinck* [1972] 2 Lloyd's Rep 172 at 185 (per MEGARRY J).
1   *Thake v Maurice* [1986] 1 All ER 497.
2   *Whitehouse v Jordan* [1981] 1 All ER 267.
3   *Stafford v Conti Commodity Services* [1981] 1 All ER 691.
4   *Whitehouse v Jordan* [1981] 1 All ER 267 at 281 (per LORD FRASER).
5   *Jones v Bird* (1822) 5 B & Ald 837.
6   *Nettleship v Weston* [1971] 2 QB 691. Cf *Wilsher v Essex Area Health Authority* [1986] 3 All ER 801.
7   National Consumer Council Paper (1985) (Stephenson and Clark).
8   'Consumer Safety: A Consultative Document' (Cmnd 6398, 1976) p 22.
9   Law Commission No 156 (1986) Cmnd 9773, para 2.24.
10 Cf Trade Practices Act 1974, s 74(2) (Australia) under which the supplier of some services (but not the professional services of an architect or engineer) impliedly warrants that the service will be reasonably fit for the purpose made known to him by the consumer and that the service is of such a quality that it might reasonably be expected to achieve the desired result.
11 [1980] CA Transcript 916.
12 Ibid at 23 (per GRIFFITH LJ).
13 [1975] 3 All ER 99.

of an implied term that the warehouse would be fit for its intended purpose. It proved crucial that there was a warning from the British Standards Institution that traffic vibration might result in the cracking of a floor of the type recommended by the defendants. The Court of Appeal concluded that, in the circumstances, there was an implied term in fact[14] that the floor would be reasonably fit for the use of fork–lift trucks.[15] It might be argued from this that all professional people may be taken to warrant a particular result. However, this view was rejected in the Court of Appeal on the ground that the implication of the warranty was justified because of the special facts of the case.[16]

The decision in *Greaves* suggests that design services fall into a distinct category in which the courts are prepared to imply very high standards. The justification for this is that design services have an end-product which may place the supplier in a position similar to that of the supplier of goods provided there is no term of the contract which negates the liability of the designer.[17] Thus, a contract to build a house will contain implied terms to the effect that the best materials will be used, that the best workmanship will be applied to those materials, and that the end product will be fit for human habitation.[18]

What the supplier has contracted to provide is an essential consideration. It would be unreasonable to expect the supplier of a service to have to comply with the unstated desires of the consumer. Thus if a carpet layer lays a carpet with a medallion design in such a way that the medallion is not placed in the middle of the room, this does not mean that reasonable care and skill has not been exercised. If the medallion has to be centrally located, the likely response of the carpet layer is that considerably more carpet would need to be purchased.[19] What is clear is that the consumer cannot expect perfection unless he contracts and accordingly pays for perfection. At the same time, if the client engages the services of an expert, the fee he pays should reflect the standard of performance and he may be entitled to expect something more than the standard of the reasonably competent.[20]

(3)   PERFORMANCE OBLIGATIONS

(i)   Personal performance

It has been argued that since the Supply of Goods and Services Act 1982, section 13 provides that, '... the supplier will carry out the service', it imposes three separate requirements.[1] First it requires the supplier to perform the contract in person. Secondly, that the supplier will actually perform the work contracted for and thirdly that in so performing, he will exercise reasonable care and skill. If this interpretation is correct, it would mean that the statutory implied term has effected a change to the position at common law, since delegation is permitted at common law where the circumstances of the case allow this.[2] The Law Commission believes that section 13 will not be construed so as to compel personal performance,[3] but on the wording of the provision,

---

14   See ch 7.
15   [1975] 3 All ER 99 at 104 (per LORD DENNING MR).
16   Ibid at 106 (per GEOFFREY LANE LJ).
17   *Independent Broadcasting Authority v EMI Ltd* (1980) 14 BLR 1 at 47-48 (per LORD SCARMAN).
18   *Miller v Cannon Hill Estates Ltd* [1931] 2 KB 113; *Perry v Sharon Development Co Ltd* [1937] 4 All ER 390; *Basildon District Council v JE Lesser (Properties) Ltd* [1985] 1 All ER 20. Cf *Lynch v Thorne* [1956] 1 All ER 744. See also ch 7.
19   *CRC Flooring v Heaton* (1984) 3 Tr L 33.
20   *Duchess of Argyll v Beuselinck* [1972] 2 Lloyd's Rep 172 at 183 (per MEGARRY J).
1   Palmer (1983) 46 MLR 619.
2   *Davies v Collins* [1945] 1 All ER 247.
3   Law Commission No 156 (1986) Cmnd 9773, para 2.25.

such a construction is possible. In some instances, delegation is not permitted, as it is the essence of the contract that it should be personally performed. This is so in cases of bailment, where the bailee has been selected for his special skill.[4]

(ii)   Time of performance

(a)   *Time of performance fixed*   Where a contract stipulates a date for performance of the service, it becomes necessary to decide whether the stipulation is of the essence of the contract or not.[5] If it is, a failure to complete a service on time will be regarded as a breach of condition which will allow the intended recipient to repudiate the contract and employ someone else to carry out the necessary work.[6]

Time will be of the essence of a contract if this is clearly stated,[7] or if it can be implied from the surrounding circumstances.[8] If a person asks for building work to be completed in time for guests arriving at Christmas, the importance of keeping to the deadline is sufficiently emphasised. Similarly, the circumstances surrounding a contract to purchase shares by a specified date will normally suggest that time is of the essence of the contract because of the volatility of the subject matter.[9]

Generally, where there is a mercantile contract for the provision of a service, stipulations as to the time of performance will be deemed to be of the essence of a contract.[10] If the contract is one for the provision of building services, serious problems of delay may be caused where a nominated sub-contractor drops out prior to performance. In such a case, it would appear that the main contractor is not responsible for such delay unless there is an express provision which makes the main contractor liable.[11]

Where the time of performance is not of the essence of the contract, there is nonetheless a breach of contract, and the plaintiff can sue for damages.[12] For example, a person may ask for an extension to a house to be completed by a specified date. If, as a result of late completion, that person is unable to take in as many paying guests as would otherwise have been the case then, provided the loss of custom is not too remote, it may be recovered through an award of damages.

Where the time of performance is not, at first, of the essence of the contract, the customer may make it so by giving reasonable notice. In *Charles Rickards Ltd v Oppenheim*,[13] in which a car chassis was not delivered on time, the purchaser pressed for delivery and subsequently asserted that, unless the chassis was delivered within four weeks, he would not accept it. Failure to deliver within that four-week period was held to amount to a breach of condition, as the buyer had made the time of performance the essence of the contract by giving reasonable notice. The requirement that the notice be reasonable emanates from contracts for the sale of land in which time would be needed to complete title, but it has been observed that the rule should not be extended in the case of purely commercial contracts so as to allow a party in breach yet more

---

4   *Edwards v Newland* [1950] 2 KB 534. And see further Palmer *Bailment* (1979) pp 514–517.
5   *Cheshire and Fifoot* pp 567–568; *Treitel* pp 739–741.
6   See ch 13.
7   *Steedman v Drinkle* [1916] 1 AC 275.
8   *United Scientific Holdings Ltd v Burnley Borough Council* [1978] AC 904 at 958 (per LORD FRASER).
9   *British and Commonwealth Holdings plc v Quadrex Holdings Inc* [1989] 3 All ER 492 at 504 (per BROWNE-WILKINSON VC).
10   *Bunge Corpn v Tradax SA* [1981] 2 All ER 513.
11   *Percy Bilton Ltd v Greater London Council* [1982] 2 All ER 623.
12   *Raineri v Miles* [1981] AC 1050.
13   [1950] 1 All ER 420.

time to perform his contractual obligations.[14] Moreover, later authority suggests that where appropriate the innocent party may serve notice making time of the essence as soon as there has been any delay at all.[15]

(b)   *No time for performance fixed*   The Supply of Goods and Services Act 1982, section 14(1) provides that where the contract fails to fix the time of performance or does not provide a mechanism by which it can be fixed, there is an implied term that the supplier will carry out the service within a reasonable time.

Section 14(2) provides, that what is a reasonable time is a question of fact. Consequently, regard will be had to such matters as the nature of the work to be done, the availability of any necessary materials and the general conditions or customs of the relevant trade. The test applied is objective, requiring the court to consider the time which, ordinarily, would have been taken by a reasonably competent tradesman to complete the type of work in question. In *Charnock v Liverpool Corpn*,[16] a garage took eight weeks to effect repairs to the plaintiff's vehicle when a competent mechanic would have completed the work in five weeks. Accordingly, the defendant had failed to comply with the implied term that the work would be completed within a reasonable time. It was considered to be no excuse that the car was taken in when the summer holidays were approaching and the garage was under-staffed, and that the garage was engaged in other work for an important commercial customer. If the garage had communicated these circumstances to the plaintiff and he had still allowed the work to proceed, he might not have had any ground for complaint.

If the delay is due to something or someone beyond the control of the supplier, he will not be liable. Thus, if the customer is responsible for the delay,[17] or if a strike by workmen renders performance impossible,[18] the provider of the service will not have to accept responsibility.

If the service has not been carried out within a reasonable time, there is a breach of contract, whether or not the time of performance is of the essence of the contract.[19] Accordingly, the customer will always be entitled to recover damages if he has suffered actionable harm.

(4)   THE DUTY TO PAY A REASONABLE AMOUNT

(i)   Consideration fixed by the contract

If the contract specifies what is to be given in return for the service,[20] the general rule is that the customer is bound by the contract he has made. The rule at common law is that a court will not mend a bad bargain and will not interfere so as to reopen a contract which has already been made.[1] This is particularly so where businessmen are concerned. It may be wise to allow such contracting parties to negotiate for themselves the best possible deal and not to intervene in cases where it is alleged that a bad bargain has been entered into.[2]

---

14   *British and Commonwealth Holdings plc v Quadrex Holdings Inc* [1989] 3 All ER 492 at 504–505 (per BROWNE-WILKINSON VC).
15   *Behzadi v Shaftesbury Hotels Ltd* [1991] 2 All ER 477.
16   [1968] 3 All ER 473.
17   See eg *Ford v Cotesworth* (1868) LR 4 QB 127 at 133–134 (per BLACKBURN J).
18   *Hick v Raymond and Reid* [1893] AC 22.
19   *Raineri v Miles* [1981] AC 1050.
20   Unlike the Sale of Goods Act 1979, the Supply of Goods and Services Act 1982, s 15 does not require a money consideration.
1   See ch 6.
2   *Photo Production Ltd v Securicor Transport Ltd* [1980] AC 827 at 843 (per LORD WILBERFORCE).

The same attitude is not necessarily appropriate in the case of consumer users of a service. Generally, the consumer will be aware of the price payable for goods he may choose to purchase, but this is often not the case where services are supplied.[3] Some suppliers of services will display set charges, but others may wish to wait to see what quantity of work the job entails before valuing its cost. In rare cases, the court has a power to reopen an agreement where the amount charged for the service is considered extortionate.[4] But as a general rule, if the consumer has agreed to pay an identifiable amount, he will be bound, even if that amount later proves to be excessive.[5]

A consumer can protect himself by obtaining from the supplier a quotation rather than a mere estimate of price. The former is a binding promise to do the work at a fixed price, with the result that the supplier of the service will be bound even if the work takes much longer than was anticipated.[6] In contrast, an estimate is a non-binding prediction.[7] In some instances, the supplier of a service may be under a duty to take reasonable care to ensure that he supplies an accurate estimate which would appear to fall within the rule in *Hedley Byrne & Co v Heller & Partners Ltd.*[8]

In rare instances, the court may be able to construe the terms of a contract in such a way as to re-write the terms of payment.[9] It may also be possible to strike out a term as to payment if it imposes onerous requirements. In *Interfoto Picture Library Ltd v Stiletto Visual Programmes Ltd,*[10] a term in a contract to hire photographic transparencies stipulated that, should the hirer retain the transparencies for longer than agreed, he would pay a charge of £5 per transparency per day in respect of over-retention. The Court of Appeal recognised the need of the owner to ensure speedy return of the transparencies, but held that the amount charged was excessive. Furthermore, since no steps had been taken to communicate the existence of the onerous provision to the hirer, the court felt able to strike it out and impose a *quantum meruit* payment of £3.50 per transparency per week of over-retention. In other cases, the doctrines of duress and undue influence may be employed to the aid of a person who has made an improvident bargain.[11]

The Supply of Goods and Services Act 1982, section 15 implies a term that a reasonable charge will be made where no price is fixed by the parties. However, it is clear from section 15 that the implied term will not operate if the consideration is fixed by the contract, determinable in a manner agreed by the parties or determinable by reference to a course of dealing. Thus, if it is agreed that the price payable for a service should be determined by an independent third party, or if the service in question is regularly provided for the recipient by the supplier on standard terms and a course of dealing can be identified, then the charge payable may already be determinable.

Apart from legal rules, there may also be non-legal pressures on the parties which ensure that a fair price is paid. In the case of business dealings, there may be a need to

3   National Consumer Council *Services and the Law: A Consumer View* (1981) p 17.
4   Consumer Credit Act 1974, ss 137–139. See also Solicitors Act 1974, s 61 (contentious business), s 57(5) and Solicitors' (Non-Contentious Business) Remuneration Order 1994 SI 1994/2616 (non-contentious business) and the Consumer Protection (Cancellation of Contracts Concluded away from Business Premises) Regulations 1987 (SI 1987/2117) implementing the EC Council Directive on Doorstep Selling (85/577/EEC) (as subsequently amended).
5   *Kennedy v Broun* (1863) 143 ER 268; *Pao On v Lau Yiu Long* [1980] AC 614 at 629 (per LORD SCARMAN).
6   *Gilbert & Partners (a firm) v Knight* [1968] 2 All ER 248.
7   *Croshaw v Pritchard and Renwick* (1899) 16 TLR 45. See also Law Commission No 156 (1986) Cmnd 9773, para 4.28.
8   [1964] AC 465. See ch 9. See also *Kidd v Mississauga Hydro-Electric Commission* (1979) 97 DLR (3d) 535 and *J & JC Abrams Ltd v Ancliffe* [1981] 1 NZLR 244.
9   See *Staffordshire Area Health Authority v South Staffordshire Water Works Co* [1978] 3 All ER 769. See also ch 22.
10 [1988] 1 All ER 348. See also ch 24.
11 See ch 24.

secure the client's business in the future,[12] in which case it is important to keep charges at an economically acceptable level. This position may not apply in consumer cases, where services are often supplied on a 'one-off' basis.

(ii)   No consideration fixed

Where there is no provision, express or implied for the charge payable for a service, the Supply of Goods and Services Act 1982, section 15(1) implies that a reasonable charge shall be paid. What is a reasonable charge is treated as a question of fact.[13] Where the implied term does operate, it has the effect of ordering a *quantum meruit* for services rendered.[14] A similar result may be achieved where there is an agreement to pay but no figure has been fixed. In such a case, the court may order that a reasonable amount be paid.[15]

What is a reasonable price will depend on the circumstances of the case. It may be that the market price will be treated as a reasonable price.[16] But this is not necessarily so, and the court must select a charge which is fair and just to both parties.[17] Sometimes, it may be the case that the market price in one country is artificially depressed due to government restrictions, in which case the court might elect to treat a reasonable price as one which is somewhat higher, so as to take account of world market conditions.[18]

3.   SPECIFIC TYPES OF SERVICE

(1)   MEDICAL SERVICES

(i)   Who is responsible if medical services fail?

Where a plaintiff has a legitimate complaint concerning the provision of medical services his action may lie either in contract or in tort.[19] The doctor's situation implies skill in surgery,[20] with the result that the same standard of care is applicable whether the action lies in contract or tort. Indeed, there are strong policy reasons for making a surgeon liable in the absence of a contract. For example, the patient might be too young or too ill to give a valid consent. Also, a surgeon might be employed by a large number of subscribers to a hospital, in which case there might be difficulties in establishing a contractual relationship.[1]

(a)   *Personal liability of the doctor*   Where there is a contractual relationship between a doctor and his patient, then the doctor will be personally liable according to the terms of the contract. If the patient is treated under the National Health Service, there will be no contractual liability, although the patient will have made some payment by virtue of his payment of direct taxes and national insurance contributions.[2]

---

12   See Beale and Dugdale (1975) 2 Brit J of L & S 45.
13   Supply of Goods and Services Act 1982, s 15(2).
14   *Paynter v Williams* (1833) 1 Cr & M 810; *Way v Latilla* [1937] 3 All ER 759.
15   *Sir Lindsay Parkinson & Co Ltd v Comrs of Works and Public Buildings* [1949] 2 KB 632.
16   *Sellars v Andrews Labrador Fisheries Ltd* (1951) 28 MPR 189 (Newfoundland).
17   *Acebal v Levy* (1834) 10 Bing 376.
18   *Glynwed Distribution Ltd v S Koronka & Co* 1977 SLT 65.
19   *Thake v Maurice* [1986] 1 All ER 497.
20   *Shiells and Thorne v Blackburne* (1789) 1 Hy Bl 159 (per Heath J).
1   *Pippin v Sheppard* (1822) 11 Price 400.
2   *Pfizer Corpn v Minister of Health* [1965] AC 512.

Generally, the doctor will only be liable for a breach of the implied term that he will exercise reasonable care and skill,[3] and a court will not imply a term to the effect that the doctor has guaranteed a particular result.[4] However, if the doctor supplies goods in the course of providing his service, he may be subject to a stricter form of liability which is also tied to the service he provides. A doctor may supply goods where he gives an injection, supplies drugs, fits a prosthesis or lends a pair of crutches. If the product supplied is not of satisfactory quality,[5] or is not fit for the purpose intended by the recipient,[6] there is a breach of contract. Of particular importance is the requirement of fitness for purpose. It is arguable that medical materials might be required to be suited to one of three possible purposes.[7] They might be required to be fit for use in the treatment of human beings, or they might be required to be suitable for curing the ailment diagnosed by the doctor, or they might have to be fit for curing the ailment suffered by the patient. If the first of these possibilities is accepted, all the doctor would have to ensure is that the drugs are not harmful. The second possibility would allow the doctor to avoid liability if he were to give an adequate explanation to the patient of what he was doing. If the doctor were to explain that he had diagnosed a disease by the name of Cooke's complaint and that Oughton's ointment was appropriate to the patient's needs, the doctor would not be in breach of the implied term, so long as the ointment was a suitable cure for the disease diagnosed.[8] The third possible interpretation of fitness for purpose might result in the imposition of strict liability in respect of the service supplied if a diagnosis is inaccurate. But the doctor could qualify his potential liability by a suitable explanation to the effect that a medicament will only be effective if the diagnosis is correct.

(b)   *The liability of health authorities and trusts*[9]   A medical injury may be caused by any one of a number of people within the employment of a health authority or trust (hereafter health authority). If such a person is acting within the scope of his employment, the health authority may be held vicariously liable for the tort causing the injury to the patient.[10] Health authorities are now liable on the principle of *respondeat superior,*[11] (let the principal answer) which now means that they may be liable for the acts of their employees acting under contracts of service,[12] and more senior medical staff such as anaesthetists[13] and special consultants.[14] The position of part-time consultants is not quite so clear, and there are *dicta* to the effect that a health authority may not be vicariously liable for their acts.[15] Until 1990, an agreement between the Ministry of Health and the medical defence societies[16] allowed for the costs of any action to be shared between the two parties. Since January 1990, under a scheme known as Crown Indemnity, the entire costs of a negligence action have been borne by the National Health Service.

3   Supply of Goods and Services Act 1982, s 13.
4   *Thake v Maurice* [1986] 1 All ER 497.
5   Supply of Goods and Services Act 1982, ss 4(2), (9), 9(2), (9) and see also ch 25.
6   Supply of Goods and Services Act 1982, ss 4(4), (5), 9(4), (5).
7   See Bell (1984) 4 Legal Studies 175.
8   See also *Dodd and Dodd v Wilson and McWilliam* [1946] 2 All ER 691.
9   Newdick, *Who Should We Treat* (Oxford, Clarendon Press 1994) ; Montgomery, *Health Care Law* (Oxford, OUP 1997) , ch 4.
10 See also ch 27.
11 *Roe v Minister of Health* [1954] 2 QB 66.
12 This would cover radiographers (*Gold v Essex County Council* [1942] 2 All ER 237); assistant medical officers (*Cassidy v Minister of Health* [1951] 1 All ER 574), and house surgeons (*Collins v Hertfordshire County Council* [1947] 1 All ER 633).
13 *Roe v Minister of Health* [1954] 2 QB 66.
14 *Albrighton v Royal Prince Alfred Hospital* [1980] 2 NSWLR 542.
15 See eg *Collins v Hertfordshire County Council* [1947] 1 All ER 633.
16 Who provide indemnity insurance for doctors.

Apart from vicarious liability, a health authority may sometimes attract a form of direct liability for failure to take reasonable care of its patients.[17] The basis of this liability is that the health authority is under a personal, non-delegable duty to take care.[18] In *Kondis v State Transport Department*,[19] it was said that where a non-delegable duty of care is imposed, it is because the relationship between the parties is such that it is appropriate to require the defendant to ensure that reasonable care is taken to provide for the safety of the plaintiff.[20] A hospital undertakes to care for, supervise, control and treat patients who are in special need.[1] This view has been relied upon in the Court of Appeal in *Wilsher v Essex Area Health Authority*,[2] in which a child suffered sight impairment as a result of the alleged negligence in supervision of a senior registrar. The health authority was held vicariously liable, but, both BROWNE-WILKINSON VC and GLIDEWELL LJ thought that there was no reason why a health authority could not be directly liable, in appropriate circumstances, for a failure to provide sufficient or properly qualified and competent medical staff, if their organisation was at fault.[3] On the facts, it was thought that requiring a doctor to work every other night and every other weekend on top of his normal working week whilst making him responsible for all paediatric care in the hospital did not constitute a breach of the defendant's duty.

The existence of a primary duty to provide a safe and effective care regime was firmly established in *Bull v Devon Area Health Authority*.[4] An action was brought against the health authority over its decision to operate a split site service. The plaintiff alleged that this was a cause of her son's brain damage when there was a delay in summoning a doctor from the other site. It was held that the hospital owed a duty to provide a reasonable standard of services for mother and baby and that they had failed to do this.[5]

The extension of the hospital's duty of care in this way does have its attendant difficulties, particularly if the hospital is funded by the area health authority. It might be the case that a hospital is under-staffed as a result of a policy decision of the health authority, based on inadequacy of resources. According to the House of Lords in *Anns v Merton London Borough Council*,[6] no action will lie for the negligent formulation of policies as opposed to the negligent performance of an operational decision.[7] For policy reasons, a court might feel inclined to deny the liability of the authority in such a case.[8]

(ii)   What tort — trespass or negligence?

Identifying what tort, if any, has been committed is particularly significant in cases involving consent to medical procedures.[9] If a patient is not given proper information

17   See Bettle (1987) 137 NLJ 573; Montgomery (1987) 137 NLJ 703.
18   The notion of the non-delegable duty was first used in the context of the employer–employee relationship. See *Wilsons and Clyde Coal Co Ltd v English* [1937] 3 All ER 628 and *McDermid v Nash Dredging and Reclamation Co Ltd* [1987] 2 All ER 878 and see ch 27.
19   (1984) 58 ALJR 531.
20   Ibid at 537 (per MASON J).
1   Ibid. See also *Gold v Essex County Council* [1942] 2 KB 293 and *Cassidy v Ministry of Health* [1951] 2 KB 343.
2   [1986] 3 All ER 801. Reversed on other grounds in [1988] 1 All ER 871.
3   Ibid at 833 (per BROWNE-WILKINSON VC). See also at 831 (per GLIDEWELL LJ).
4   [1993] 4 Med LR 117.
5   See also *Ogden v Airedale Health Authority* [1996] 7 Med LR 153.
6   [1978] AC 728.
7   Ibid at 754 (per LORD WILBERFORCE). This problem would not affect private hospitals which are run with a view to profit.
8   For observations along these lines in relation to the standard of care required of a prison hospital see *Knight v Home Office* [1990] 3 All ER 237 at 243 (per PILL J). ('The duty is tailored to the act and function to be performed.')
9   See Skegg *Law, Ethics and Medicine* (1984) ch 4; Mason and McCall-Smith *Law and Medical Ethics* (4th edn, 1994) ch 10; Tan Keng Feng (1987) 7 LS 149; Teff (1985) 101 LQR 432; Robertson (1985) 97 LQR 102.

about a proposed operation, this may vitiate his consent so that a battery is committed. At the same time, failure to ensure that the patient is properly advised may, in some cases, amount to negligence.

(a)   *Battery*   A battery is committed where a person is touched in a hostile manner and without his express or implied consent.[10] There is no need to prove that the touching caused harm and if successful, the plaintiff will receive damages assessed on the principle of directness rather than that of reasonable foresight of harm applicable to cases of negligence.

A battery is committed where a surgeon carries out an operation other than one to which the patient consented.[11] Conversely, where the patient's consent is real, no action for battery will lie. Thus where a patient agrees to a pain-relieving injection, but is not informed that a possible side-effect is numbness and immobility, the consent to the medical procedure is nonetheless real.[12] Instead the action, if any, will lie in negligence[13] which requires proof of damage caused by the defendant. In order for the consent to be 'real' the patient must understand the 'nature, purpose and effects' of the treatment.[14]

In some instances, it may not be possible to obtain the necessary consent. For instance, a patient may be unconscious or legally or mentally incapable of giving consent. In the case of the unconscious patient, it may be argued that, for example, a life-saving operation is performed with implied consent on the fictitious ground that the majority of patients would consent in such circumstances. Alternatively, such operations may be better justified on the grounds of necessity, provided there is no known objection to the medical procedure and it would be unreasonable to postpone the operation until a later date. On the other hand, the necessity argument cannot be used to justify a medical procedure carried out for the convenience of the doctor. Thus, the sterilisation of a woman in the course of performing a Caesarian section is a battery where performed out of convenience rather than to save life.[15]

Sometimes, a member of the patient's family will be present in which case, proxy consent may be given to a necessary medical procedure. In law, this consent is not of value unless the patient has authorised the relative to give or withhold it.

Particular problems surround the issue of consent by minors. The minor may want treatment which the parent does not wish the child to have, or the minor may refuse treatment which the parent desires. In the latter case a tension between individual autonomy and paternalism is raised. By statute, the consent of a minor aged 16 years or more is effective and there is no need for parental consent.[16] Where the minor is under 16 years of age, the courts have adopted a test of understanding. The child must have significant understanding and the intelligence to fully understand the proposed medical treatment.[17] If the child is 'Gillick competent' in this sense, then the doctor does not need to obtain parental consent for the proposed treatment. If the child is incapable of giving a valid consent then parental consent should be sought. If this is not possible,

10   In medical trespass cases absence of consent is the preferred basis for liability: *F v West Berkshire HA* [1989] 2 All ER 545 at 564 (per LORD GOFF). Cf the hostility test in *Wilson v Pringle* [1986] 2 All ER 440 at 447 (per CROOM-JOHNSON LJ) and see ch 22.

11   *Cull v Surrey Royal County Hospital* [1932] 1 BMJ 1195 (consent to abortion, hysterectomy performed). See also Skegg (1974) 90 LQR 512.

12   *Chatterton v Gerson* [1981] QB 432 at 442 (per BRISTOW J). See also *Hills v Potter* [1983] 3 All ER 716; *Davis v Barking, Havering & Brentwood Health Authority* [1993] 4 Med LR 85.

13   Ibid at 444 (per BRISTOW J).

14   *Re C (Adult: Refusal of Treatment)* [1994] 1 WLR 290; *Re MB (Medical Treatment)* [1997] 2 FLR 426, See Gunn (1994) 2 Med LR 8.

15   *Murray v McMurchy* [1949] 2 DLR 442. Cf *Marshall v Curry* [1933] 3 DLR 260 (removal of testicle for the protection of health).

16   Family Law Reform Act 1969, s 8(1).

17   *Gillick v West Norfolk and Wisbech Area Health Authority* [1985] 3 All ER 402.

then the doctor should initiate care proceedings[18] or invite the court to exercise its inherent jurisdiction.[19] In emergency cases the doctor can proceed with life saving treatment, provided this is in the child's best interests.[20]

Where the minor refuses treatment, the courts have leaned heavily and controversially in favour of paternalism. In the case of a child under 16 years, the child can be made a ward of court and the court can order treatment to be carried out, against the child's wishes, if the court thinks this is in the child's best interests.[1] The powers of the court extend to overriding the refusal of a 16-year-old and it may be that a parent can override a competent minor's refusal, although the refusal is an important factor to be taken into account when making clinical judgments as to what is in the child's best interests.[2]

Difficult issues may also arise where the patient is above the age of majority but where his or her judgment is impaired through, for example, mental handicap. The problem has arisen in the context of the proposed sterilisation of an incompetent adult woman. It has been held that, in such circumstances, to operate without consent would be a tortious act and that consent cannot be implied, but that the sterilisation could be justified on the basis of good medical practice in the interests of the patient's health.[3] Moreover, the House of Lords in *F v West Berkshire HA*[4] has held that a doctor has the power at common law to give treatment to an adult patient who is incapable of giving consent provided the treatment is in the patient's best interests. Such treatment will be in the patient's best interests if it is designed to save life or to ensure improvement or prevent deterioration in the patient's physical or mental condition.[5] The best interests test, in extreme cases, may also justify the withdrawal of medical treatment, so that the patient dies.[6]

(b)   *Negligence*   The distinction between battery and negligence may be troublesome. In general battery is concerned with acts done without the consent of the patient, whereas negligence is concerned with acts done by a doctor in the absence of reasonable care. While battery may be the relevant tort where the nature of a particular treatment has not been communicated to the patient, an action in negligence is more likely where there is a failure to advise on the risks attendant to an operation.[7]

Problems may arise in ascertaining which is the relevant tort since a failure to inform a patient of certain consequences of an operation could be said to manifestly affect the real consent of the patient and should be treated as a case of battery especially where the degree of non-disclosure is sufficiently great to affect the ability to give an informed consent.[8] However, English law remains that if a patient has consented, in general terms, to a procedure, he must bring an action for negligence if the advice he has been given is defective.[9]

---

18   *Re R (a minor)* [1993] 2 FCR 544.
19   *Re O (a minor)* [1993] 2 FLR 149.
20   *F v West Berkshire Health Authority* [1989] 2 All ER 545.
1   *Re R (a minor)* [1991] 4 All ER 177.
2   *Re W (a minor)* [1992] 4 All ER 627.
3   *T v T* [1988] 1 All ER 613 at 621 (per WOOD J).
4   [1989] 2 All ER 545.
5   Ibid at 551 (per LORD BRANDON) and at 565–566 (per LORD GOFF). See also *Re T (adult: refusal of medical treatment)* [1992] 4 All ER 649.
6   *Airedale NHS Trust v Bland* [1993] 1 All ER 821, HL.
7   *Chatterton v Gerson* [1981] QB 432. See also *Reibl v Hughes* (1980) 114 DLR (3d) 1 at 10 (per LASKIN CJC).
8   See Tan Keng Feng (1987) 7 LS 149 at 154–160.
9   *Sidaway v Board of Governors of Bethlem Royal Hospital* [1984] 1 All ER 1018, CA, affd on other grounds in [1985] 1 All ER 643, HL.

(iii)   Medical negligence

In any action for negligence, there are three elements. The defendant must owe the plaintiff a duty of care,[10] there must be a breach of duty of care[11] and the plaintiff must suffer damage as a result of that breach which is not too remote.[12]

(a)   *Duty of care — the rights of the foetus*   While the existence of a duty of care as between doctor and patient is well established, some difficulty has been encountered where a child is harmed prior to its birth. If the child is harmed by the wrongful act of a third party whilst it is *in utero*, then an action may be brought both by statute[13] and at common law.[14]

Under the 1976 Act, the protection extended to the child covers harm caused by events occurring prior to conception. Thus, if a mother is adversely affected by a defective birth control device with the result that a child, subsequently conceived, is born disabled, an action may lie. The position at common law is that a child is deemed to be born whenever its interests so require, with the result that the child is clothed with all the rights of action it would have had if it had existed at the time of the alleged negligent act.[15]

Neither the common law nor the Congenital Disabilities (Civil Liability) Act 1976 permits an action for 'wrongful life', that is a complaint to the effect that the child should not have been born. The Act provides that an action will only lie where, but for the conduct giving rise to the disabled birth, the child would have been born normal,[16] not that it would not have been born at all. The result of this is that the Act permits no action by the child for 'wrongful life'.[17] Such an action would be contrary to the public interest in the sanctity of life by imposing on a doctor a duty towards the child to take away its life.[18] Furthermore, permitting such an action would mean that the law regarded the life of a handicapped child as so much less valuable than that of a normal child that it would not be worth preserving.[19] To the contrary, there is the argument that it should be for the child, not the court, to decide whether existence is to be preferred to non-existence and that the court should not decide this issue.

While there may not be an action for 'wrongful life' on the part of the child, there is nothing to prevent an action brought by the parents of the child for 'wrongful birth'. If a child is born after one of its parents has been sterilised, damages may be awarded for disturbance to family finances,[20] and other expenses incurred as a result of the doctor's negligence. In *Emeh v Kensington and Chelsea and Westminster Area Health Authority*,[1] it was held that damages may be awarded for wrongful conception so as to cover pre-natal and post-natal medical expenses, pain and suffering, loss of consortium and the

---

10   See ch 8.
11   See ch 12.
12   See also ch 16.
13   Congenital Disabilities (Civil Liability) Act 1976, s 1(1) and (2). See also Pace (1977) 40 MLR 141.
14   *Burton v Islington HA* [1992] 3 All ER 833.
15   Ibid at 838 (per DILLON LJ).
16   Congenital Disabilities (Civil Liability) Act 1976, s 1(2)(b) and s 4(5). Cf Fortin [1987] J Soc Welfare Law 306.
17   See Tedeschi (1966) Israel LR 513. The existence of such an action at common law has been denied in *McKay v Essex Area Health Authority* [1982] QB 1166. See Robertson (1982) 45 MLR 697; Weir [1982] CLJ 225.
18   *McKay v Essex Area Health Authority* [1982] 2 WLR 890 at 902 (per STEPHENSON LJ).
19   Ibid (per STEPHENSON LJ).
20   *Udale v Bloomsbury Area Health Authority* [1983] 2 All ER 522; *Allen v Bloomsbury Health Authority* [1993] 1 All ER 651.
1   [1984] 3 All ER 1044. See also *Thake v Maurice* [1986] 1 All ER 497.

reasonable cost of rearing the unplanned child. A deduction from these damages may be made in respect of the value of the child's aid, comfort and society.[2]

(b)   *Breach of duty*[3]   Whether a person is in breach of a duty of care is determined objectively. The court will take into account the degree of foreseeability that harm will be caused rather than the probability that damage will be caused. For example, while it is probable that leakage of a phenol solution into an anaesthetic will cause paralysis, it is not foreseeable that such leakage will occur where the medical profession has not been alerted to the possibility of invisible cracks in the container in which the anaesthetic is stored.[4] A foreseeable event is one which may be discovered by a reasonable man possessed of the knowledge and experience available at the time in question.[5]

Other factors considered in determining whether there has been a breach of duty include the magnitude of the risk involved balanced against the utility of the defendant's conduct and in the light of the cost of any precautions considered necessary to guard against the risk created. In the context of medical negligence, it should be remembered that medical science has conferred considerable benefits upon society, but those benefits bring with them a number of risks. It would not be reasonable to take all of those benefits without also accepting some of the risks involved.[6]

Doctors possess special skills which ordinary people do not hold. Accordingly, the appropriate test of liability is that of the ordinary skilled man exercising and professing to have the special skill under consideration, otherwise known as the 'Bolam test'.[7] The doctor cannot be judged by the man on the Clapham Omnibus, because such a hypothetical being does not possess the skills of a doctor.

Since the standard of care required is that of the ordinary skilled person exercising and professing to have the skill under consideration, an inexperienced doctor is to be judged at the same level as his more experienced colleagues, but the duty must be determined by reference to the post which the doctor occupies rather than according to the rank or status of the person filling a particular post.[8] In *Wilsher v Essex Area Health Authority*,[9] it was recognised that junior doctors have to gain experience by dealing with live patients and that the appropriate standard to require is that of the well-informed junior houseman in a unit offering a highly specialised service.[10] While this might appear to be fairly onerous, the junior doctor can discharge his duty of care by seeking the advice of a superior,[11] as the junior houseman did in this case.

In assessing the degree of skill appropriate to a doctor, the court will consider any general and approved practice relevant to his particular skill and that of any other relevant practitioner.[12] If a doctor fails to comply with a general practice, this will raise an inference of negligence on his part. Conversely, if a doctor does comply with generally approved practice, this will not rule out a finding of negligence if the practice itself is defective. If a doctor acts in a way which would be approved of by a responsible body of medical

2   Ibid at 1056 (per PURCHAS LJ). To deny an action for damages in such a case might lead to a decision to apply for a late abortion, (per WALLER LJ) at 1050–1051.
3   See also ch 12.
4   *Roe v Minister of Health* [1954] 2 All ER 131.
5   It was observed by DENNING LJ ibid at 137 that the events of 1947 should not be looked at with 1954 spectacles.
6   Ibid.
7   *Bolam v Friern Hospital Management Committee* [1957] 2 All ER 118 at 121 (per MCNAIR J).
8   *Wilsher v Essex Area Health Authority* [1986] 3 All ER 801 at 813 (per MUSTILL LJ).
9   [1986] 3 All ER 801. Reversed on other grounds in [1988] 1 All ER 871. See ch 16.
10   Ibid at 813 (per MUSTILL LJ). Cf BROWNE-WILKINSON VC at 832–833.
11   Ibid at 831 (per GLIDEWELL LJ).
12   *Rance v Mid-Downs Health Authority* [1991] 1 All ER 801 at 821 (per BROOKE J).

opinion, he is not guilty of negligence. The reason for this, particularly in the realm of treatment and diagnosis, is that there is ample scope for a genuine difference of opinion.[13] It follows that, even if there is a body of medical opinion opposed to the course of action followed by a doctor, the doctor is not guilty of negligence so long as there are others who would have acted in the same way as he acted.

One complaint about the 'Bolam test' is that it effectively enables the medical profession to set its own standards, as it is the expert evidence given at trial that will determine whether the doctor is negligent. Although such evidence will not normally be challenged by the court, it has been stressed by the House of Lords that the exponents of a body of professional opinion must demonstrate that their opinion had a logical basis and that they had directed their minds to the question of comparative risks and benefits and had reached a defensible conclusion.[14] In general, judges will not choose between responsible bodies of medical opinion.[15]

The doctor's duty to his patient encompasses three varieties of medical practice: diagnosis, treatment and advice. All three matters are subject to the same test of liability, namely, did the doctor act as an ordinary skilled man exercising and professing to have the special skill under consideration? In *Whitehouse v Jordan*,[16] it was held that where the defendant caused the plaintiff to suffer brain damage in an attempted trial by forceps delivery, he was not guilty of negligence. It was accepted that the defendant had not pulled too long and too hard, and that he had acted in the same way as others would have acted in the circumstances. Moreover, it was thought that an error of judgment on the part of a professional man does not amount to negligence.[17] However, in the House of Lords, this view was criticised on the ground that an error of judgment may constitute negligence if it is glaringly below proper standards.[18] Moreover, whether a particular practice is professionally acceptable is for the court to decide. Thus the law will not hand over to the medical profession the entire question of the scope of the duty.[19]

The 'Bolam test' also applies to alleged negligence in diagnosis. In *Maynard v West Midlands Regional Health Authority*,[20] two consultants thought the plaintiff was suffering from tuberculosis, but there were unusual complications which suggested the possibility of Hodgkins' Disease. A test had been taken which would determine the plaintiff's complaint, but the results were not likely to be available for some time. The defendants decided to conduct an exploratory operation, which revealed that the plaintiff was suffering from tuberculosis and not Hodgkins' Disease. A result of the operation was that the plaintiff's vocal cords were damaged, causing a speech impediment. Such damage was an inherent risk of the operation in question. It was alleged that the defendants were negligent in carrying out the operation before the result of the earlier test was known. However, there was a body of medical opinion which would have acted in the same way as the defendants, since Hodgkins' Disease needed to be treated at a very early stage, otherwise the plaintiff might have died. Accordingly, the defendants were not negligent, even though there were others who would have acted differently and for reasons which the trial judge preferred.

13   *Hunter v Hanley* 1955 SLT 213 at 217 (per LORD PRESIDENT CLYDE).
14   *Bolitho v City & Hackney Health Authority* [1997] 3 WLR 1151. See also *Joyce v Meron, Sutton & Wandsworth Health Authority* [1996] 7 Med LR 1.
15   But see *De Freitas v O'Brien* [1993] 4 Med LR 281.
16   [1981] 1 All ER 267.
17   [1980] 1 All ER 650 at 658 (per LORD DENNING MR).
18   [1981] 1 All ER 267 at 280–281 (per LORD FRASER); at 276 (per LORD EDMUND-DAVIES); at 284 (per LORD RUSSELL).
19   *Sidaway v Board of Governors of Bethlem Royal Hospital* [1985] 1 All ER 643 at 663 (per LORD BRIDGE); *Bolitho v City & Hackney Health Authority* [1997] 3 WLR 1151.
20   [1985] 1 All ER 635.

The same approach is also taken in respect of advice given by a doctor to his patient, whether the advice relates to a potential cure or if it is non-therapeutic in nature, such as advice given prior to a face-lift or a sterilisation.[1] In *Sidaway v Board of Governors of Bethlem Royal Hospital*,[2] the defendant, a neurosurgeon, failed to warn the plaintiff of a small percentage chance of damage to the spinal cord if she were to undergo an operation to relieve her of a persistent pain in her neck and shoulders. It was alleged that the defendant had broken his duty to warn the plaintiff of all possible risks inherent in the operation, so that she was unable to give an informed consent to the operation. A majority of the House of Lords held that the 'Bolam test' applied, and that, since the defendant had acted as other neurosurgeons might act, there was no negligence. It was said to be important that, in some cases, a patient might be alarmed by a full disclosure, and that it might not be in the best interests of the patient to be aware of all possible consequences of a proposed operation.

In defence of the 'Bolam test', it should be remembered that it is not static, as it must take account of advances resulting from clinical and technological research.[3] To this extent, it may be regarded as a reasonably flexible test of liability. However, it is important that a patient should be in a proper position to make an informed decision whether or not to undergo a particular operation. It has been questioned whether medical judgment should determine whether, and in what circumstances, a patient should be warned by his doctor of the risks inherent in the doctor's proposed course of treatment.[4]

In *Sidaway v Board of Governors of Bethlem Royal Hospital*,[5] a second contention of the plaintiff was that she had a right to decide for herself whether to submit to the proposed operation, and that this right was independent of the 'Bolam test'. In effect, she had sought to rely on the doctrine of 'informed consent', which has commended itself to a number of United States jurisdictions.[6] The most far-reaching statement of the doctrine is to be found in *Canterbury v Spence*,[7] in which four propositions were put forward. These are, first, that every human being of adult years and of sound mind has a right to determine what shall be done with his own body. Secondly, that consent is the informed exercise of a choice and that entails an opportunity to evaluate knowledgeably the options available and the risks attendant on each. Thirdly, the doctor must disclose all risks material to a prudent patient. Fourthly, a doctor has a therapeutic privilege which enables him to withhold information as to a risk if it can be shown that a reasonable medical assessment of the patient would indicate to the doctor that disclosure would pose a serious threat of psychological detriment to the patient.[8]

The doctrine proved attractive to one member of the House of Lords in *Sidaway* because it invokes a test which can be determined by the court, namely that of the prudent patient. Under this test, the doctor may be said to have failed to exercise reasonable care where he does not warn of a risk which a reasonable person, in the position of the patient, would regard as material or significant.[9] This is not to say that medical evidence would be unimportant, because such evidence would have to be

---

1   *Gold v Haringey Health Authority* [1987] 2 All ER 888.
2   [1985] 1 All ER 643.
3   Ibid at 657 (per LORD DIPLOCK).
4   Ibid at 649 (per LORD SCARMAN (dissenting)).
5   Ibid.
6   See *Salgo v Stanford University Board of Trustees* 154 Cal App 2d 560 (1957).
7   464 F 2d 772 (DC Circ, 1972).
8   As explained in *Sidaway v Board of Governors of Bethlem Royal Hospital and the Maudsley Hospital* [1985] 1 All ER 643 at 653 (per LORD SCARMAN). See also Robertson (1981) 97 LQR 102; Teff (1985) 101 LQR 432; Brazier (1987) 7 LS 169.
9   *Sidaway v Board of Governors of Bethlem Royal Hospital and the Maudsley Hospital* [1985] 1 All ER 643 at 653–654 (per LORD SCARMAN). See *Rogers v Whittaker* (1992) 175 CLR 479 for the Australian position.

heard to determine whether a risk is material and whether the doctor was justified in withholding all relevant information.

The majority of the House of Lords were not persuaded by the doctrine of informed consent and held that the 'Bolam test' should be applied. Particular difficulties with the doctrine of informed consent were seen to be the imprecise nature of the objective test, and that the doctrine seems to ignore the realities of the doctor/patient relationship.[10] The question remains whether the 'Bolam test' suffices to protect the patient's right to make an informed consent to medical treatment. The danger is that, while it may be appropriate for the medical profession to decide on matters relevant to treatment and diagnosis, the principle of self-determination dictates that the patient should be as fully informed as possible. Leaving the medical profession to decide what information should be given would appear to disregard this principle.

It seems that a failure to provide some information is capable of contravening the 'Bolam test'. If a patient of sound mind asks specific questions about the risks involved in a particular treatment, the doctor must answer truthfully and as fully as is required by the patient.[11] But this would require the patient to have some knowledge of possible risks in order to ask the appropriate questions. Furthermore, there are some risks which no reasonable member of the medical profession would fail to mention, particularly where they are special in kind or magnitude or special to the patient.[12] In *Reibl v Hughes*,[13] a surgeon was held to have been negligent where he failed to reveal that a proposed operation on the brain carried with it a four per cent chance of death and a ten per cent chance that a stroke might result from the operation. Without this information, the patient was unable to make a balanced decision. If the risk to the patient is not of such a magnitude, then provided there is a body of responsible medical opinion which would withhold the information, the doctor will not be guilty of negligence.

(c)   *Proof of negligence*   In cases of medical negligence the plaintiff must bear the burden of proving that the defendant failed to take care. The proportion of successful plaintiffs in medical negligence cases appears to be substantially lower than in other cases involving personal injury.[14] This might suggest that doctors are more careful than other people, or it might indicate that it is more difficult for a patient to prove negligence. The latter view would appear to have some foundation, particularly when one encounters statements to the effect that an error of professional judgment does not constitute negligence on the part of a doctor.[15] Furthermore, since the standard of care is set by reference to general and approved practice, the plaintiff will have to find expert medical evidence to the effect that a doctor has failed to act as others in the profession would have acted in the circumstances under consideration. In some instances, the patient is harmed because of some risk inherent in the treatment he has undergone. Where this is the case, the courts are reluctant to hold the doctor to be negligent, particularly if the accident was unavoidable.[16] What seems to be behind this reluctance is that

---

10   Ibid at 662 (per LORD BRIDGE).
11   Ibid at 661 (per LORD BRIDGE) and at 665 (per LORD TEMPLEMAN). See also *Rogers v Whittaker* [1992] 3 Med LR 331.
12   Ibid at 663 (per LORD BRIDGE) and at 665 (per LORD TEMPLEMAN).
13   (1980) 114 DLR (3d) 1 (Can SC).
14   Royal Commission on Civil Liability and Compensation for Personal Injury (The Pearson Report) (1978) Cmnd 7054, Vol 1, para 1326 reveals that payment was made in 30%–40% of cases of alleged medical negligence, whereas the corresponding figure in other cases of personal injury is 86%.
15   *Whitehouse v Jordan* [1980] 1 All ER 650 at 658 (per LORD DENNING MR) (disapproved [1981] 1 All ER 267).
16   *Hatcher v Black* (1954) Times, 2 July.

expanding liability might produce an increase in the practice of defensive medicine whereby doctors take steps to protect themselves from possible legal action.

It was thought at one time that there might be circumstances in which the burden of proof shifted to the doctor. This was particularly so if the defendant had done some act which involved an element of risk to the plaintiff. In such a case, it was thought appropriate to ask the defendant to justify his conduct.[17] This view has been disapproved of in *Wilsher v Essex Area Health Authority*,[18] with the result that the burden of proof will ordinarily rest on the plaintiff.

Easing of the onus of proof on the patient might be achieved by an application of the principle of *res ipsa loquitur*.[19] If the circumstances of the case are such that an inference of negligence can be made, the defendant may be called upon to give an explanation of what has happened. The test which the courts appear to apply is that of the common experience of mankind,[20] but a problem with this test is that what goes on in the operating theatre is beyond the scope of common experience.[1] However, it is clear now that the doctrine may be used,[2] albeit sparingly. The difficulty with medical malpractice cases is that injuries may be caused by unavoidable risks, and the courts are reluctant to apply *res ipsa loquitur* except in extreme cases. Where the doctrine does apply, it does not shift the burden of proof to the defendant, but merely requires him to give an explanation which is capable of balancing the probabilities.[3]

(2)   PROFESSIONAL ADVISORY SERVICES

(i)   Liability in contract or in tort?[4]

Where a professional advisor has a contract with the client, the client has the option of suing either in contract or in negligence.[5] There must be an independent duty in negligence and the duties in contract and negligence must be concurrent. Thus, a solicitor can be sued in contract or negligence by the client, who may take advantage of the more favourable limitation period in negligence.[6] A financial advisor is also concurrently liable, as are surveyors, architects and accountants.

The basis of the negligence action is the principle in *Hedley Byrne v Heller*,[7] which is an assumption of voluntary responsibility by a person having special skill or knowledge to the client. The existence of the contract between advisor and client would appear to establish such an assumption of responsibility[8] and where the contract is silent on a particular matter, but the advisor has assumed responsibility for it, there can be liability

---

17   *Clark v MacLennan* [1983] 1 All ER 416 at 427 (per PETER PAIN J), purportedly applying *McGhee v National Coal Board* [1972] 3 All ER 1008.

18   [1986] 3 All ER 801 at 815 (per MUSTILL LJ). See also ch 16.

19   See ch 12.

20   See Ellis-Lewis [1951] 11 CLJ 74 at 80.

1   *Mahon v Osborne* [1939] 2 KB 14.

2   *Cassidy v Ministry of Health* [1951] 2 KB 343 at 365 (per DENNING LJ), where it was observed that if a person goes into hospital with two stiff fingers and emerges from an operation with four stiff fingers, then he is entitled to an explanation of what has happened. See also *Roe v Minister of Health* [1954] 2 QB 66.

3   This is consistent with the view expressed in *Colvilles Ltd v Devine* [1969] 1 WLR 475. See also *The Kite* [1933] P 154. Cf *Moore v R Fox & Sons Ltd* [1956] 1 QB 596. See further ch 12.

4   See Kaye (1984) 100 LQR 680.

5   *Henderson v Merrett Syndicates Ltd* [1995] 2 AC 145.

6   *Midland Bank Trust Co Ltd v Hett, Stubbs & Kemp* [1979] Ch 384. Approved by the Court of Appeal in *Forster v Outred & Co (a firm)* [1982] 1 WLR 86. Although in *Midland Bank* the limitation period was held to be the same in either action.

7   [1964] AC 465.

8   *Barclays Bank plc v Fairclough Building Ltd (No 2)* (1995) 76 BLR 1.

in negligence.[9] An estate agent who is retained for a particular purpose by contract but who holds himself out as competent to advise on local planning requirements may be liable in negligence even though the contract says nothing about planning requirements.[10]

The practical consequence of concurrent liability is that the limitation period may now run from the date damage is caused rather than from the date of the breach of contract, since the liability of the solicitor may lie in tort independent of the contract with the client. However, in *Hett*, the two relevant dates were said to be the same.

The position of the advocate presents different problems. At common law, there is no contract between a barrister and his client,[11] so any liability which does exist must lie in tort. However, for reasons of public policy,[12] this tortious liability is severely restricted. Thus an advocate[13] used not to be liable for the conduct of litigation.[14] This immunity has now been removed by a seven-man House of Lords in *Arthur JS Hall & Co (a firm) v Simons*[15] thus overruling the decision in *Rondel v Worsley*[16]. In *Arthur JS Hall & Co (a firm) v Simons* it was accepted that there was no longer any public interest justification for the immunity. The 'cab rank' principle based on the view that a barrister has no choice whether or not to represent a client was dismissed as having no substance. The 'divided loyalty' argument, based on the obligation owed by a barrister to his client and to the court, was considered to have become unsustainable in the light of changes to the civil justice system following the Civil Procedure Rules 1998. While the strongest argument in favour of the immunity was considered to be the prospect of re-litigation, it was considered to be subject to sufficient control by the courts through their power to strike out vexatious litigation.

The policy arguments which favoured the immunity of advocates are not entirely convincing and have not commended themselves to all common law jurisdictions.[17] Furthermore, the whole basis of the immunity is subject to the criticism that the quality of legal services might improve if an advocate could be sued for his negligence.[1] The removal of this immunity might well be of particular value if the effect is to increase the level of communication and the flow of information from lawyer to client.

The increasing impact of the European Convention on Human Rights and the impending implementation of the Human Rights Act 1998 are already having an effect on policy immunities in negligence and it appears likely that blanket policy immunities will not survive as is now confirmed by the decision in *Hall v Simons*.[2]

(ii) Measure of damages[3]

Despite the problems which could arise from concurrent contractual and tortious liability, the guiding principle on the measure of damages for negligent professional advice is

---

9   *Holt v Payne Skillington* (1995) 77 BLR 51. Cf *Reid v Rush and Tompkins Group plc* [1990] 1 WLR 212 at 229 per RALPH GIBSON LJ.

10   Ibid.

11   *Kennedy v Broun* (1863) 13 CBNS 677; *Swinfen v Lord Chelmsford* (1860) 5 H & N 890. See also art 2(1) of Supply of Services (Exclusion of Implied Terms) Order 1982 (SI 1982/1771).

12   See ch 8.

13   The immunity covered both barristers and solicitors: Courts and Legal Services Act 1990, s 62. Cf *Somasundaram v M Julius Melchior & Co* [1989] 1 All ER 129.

14   *Rondel v Worsley* [1969] 1 AC 191.

15   (2000) Times, 21 July

16   [1969] 1 AC 191.

17   *Demarco v Ungaro* (1979) 95 DLR (3d) 385. See also Zander *Legal Services for the Community* (1978) ch 4.

1   Veljanovski and Whelan (1983) 46 MLR 700.

2   See ch 8 for a discussion of this topic.

3   See ch 15.

that the plaintiff should be placed in the position he would have been in had he not suffered the wrong complained of,[4] or, put another way the plaintiff should be put in the position he would have been in had the defendant exercised reasonable care.[5]

In the case of negligent professional advice, particularly where property damage is suffered, there are two possible ways of compensating the plaintiff. First he may be given the 'cost of cure' and secondly he may be compensated by reference to the diminution in value of his property. Which is the more appropriate measure will depend on the circumstancres of the case. Awarding the diminution in value will allow the plaintiff to recover the difference between the market value of the property on the day it was purchased and the purchase price paid in reliance on the advice.[6]

(iii)   Liability to third parties

Until recently, a professional person's duty was owed only to his client. Thus it followed that no action could be maintained against a solicitor by a third party.[7] However, this rule has since been side-stepped in relation to the liability of a solicitor,[8] with the result that a duty of care may be owed to third party.[9] It is also clear that accountants[10] and surveyors[11] may be held liable to a third party for a failure to exercise reasonable care.

Since the loss caused by negligent advisers is often economic, the important restrictions on negligence liability for such losses, considered above[12] must be taken into account. What is clear is that foresight of harm alone is no longer the relevant criterion. There are now two possible approaches. The conventional approach to negligence duty of ca. In *Hall v Simons*re is that laid down in *Caparo Industries plc v Dickman*.[13] There must be proximity between the parties and that it must be just and equitable in all the circumstances to, thereby overruling the decision in impose a duty of care. In advice cases, it is necessary that there exists a 'special relationship' between the parties which is generally identifiable by reference to four criteria.[14] First, the advice must be required by the plaintiff for a specific or generally identified purpose made known to the adviser at the time the advice is given. Secondly, the adviser must be aware that his advice will be communicated to the plaintiff, either specifically or as a member of an identifiable class (for example, domestic house purchasers). Thirdly, the adviser must know that the advice will be relied upon by the plaintiff for the particular purpose in contemplation without further inquiry. Finally, the plaintiff must act upon the advice to his detriment. There must be a very close relationship of proximity, for example, where accounts are prepared specifically for submission to a potential investor in a company,[15] such a duty

4   *Dodd Properties (Kent) Ltd v Canterbury City Council* [1980] 1 All ER 928 at 938 (per DONALDSON LJ).
5   *Perry v Sidney Phillips & Son* [1982] 3 All ER 705 at 708 (per LORD DENNING MR).
6   *Smith v Eric S Bush (a firm)* [1989] 2 All ER 514 at 524 (per LORD TEMPLEMAN). See also *Esso Petroleum Co Ltd v Mardon* [1976] QB 801.
7   *Robertson v Fleming* (1861) 4 Macq 167, HL.
8   *White v Jones* [1995] 2 AC 207. (1995) 111 LQR 357; [1995] CLJ 238.
9   Including, it seems, the spouse of a client: *Al-Kandari v J R Brown & Co* [1988] 1 All ER 833. See Markesinis (1987) 103 LQR 346.
10   *JEB Fasteners Ltd v Marks, Bloom & Co (a firm)* [1981] 3 All ER 289; *Galoo v Bright Grahame Murray* [1995] 1 All ER 16.
11   *Yianni v Edwin Evans & Sons* [1981] 3 All ER 592; *Roberts v J Hampson & Co* [1989] 2 All ER 504.
12   See 'The duty to exercise reasonable care and skill'.
13   [1990] 1 All ER 568.
14   *Caparo Industries plc v Dickman* [1990] 1 All ER 568 at 587 (per LORD OLIVER;) see also at 576 (per LORD BRIDGE).
15   *Caparo Industries plc v Dickman* [1990] 1 All ER 568 at 598 (per LORD OLIVER) and at 579 (per LORD BRIDGE). See also *JEB Fasteners Ltd v Marks, Bloom & Co (a firm)* [1981] 3 All ER 289 and *Morgan Crucible Co plc v Hill Samuel Bank Ltd* [1991] 1 All ER 148; *Galoo v Bright Grahame Murray* [1995] 1 All ER 16. Cf *James McNaughton Paper Group Ltd v Hicks Anderson & Co* [1991] 1 All ER 134.

may be found. Likewise, an insurance broker will owe a duty of care to the future assignee of a policy arranged by the broker, especially if the assignee, to the broker's knowledge, has participated in giving instructions.[16]

It is clear from the '*Caparo*' analysis that, for the most part, there must be some form of direct reliance by the plaintiff on the advice given by the defendant. However, an alternative analysis has emerged founded on 'voluntary assumption of responsibility,' which makes it possible to avoid the direct reliance principle.[17] On this basis it is possible for the giver of a reference to be liable to the subject of the reference[18] and for a solicitor to be liable to a beneficiary under a will.[19]

Determining the extent of a solicitor's liability to a third party depends on the capacity in which the third party acts. The problem is that the third party's interests may be at variance with those of the solicitor's client. Clearly the solicitor's primary duties are owed to his own client, and it may be the case that a solicitor has best served his client's interests by acting in a hostile manner to a third party.[20] Before a solicitor is held to owe a duty of care to a third party, normally it must be shown that the solicitor has voluntarily assumed responsibility to the third party or that the third party has reasonably relied on the solicitor's actions or statements. It seems that the latter may be difficult to show, particularly where a third party might be expected to obtain legal advice himself in order to safeguard his own interests.

Where a solicitor is given instructions which are intended to benefit a third party it is often difficult to establish reliance by the third party upon the solicitor but, because the solicitor is required by his contract with his client to confer the benefit upon the third party, a duty of care may exist. For example, where a solicitor has been instructed to prepare a will leaving a legacy to a particular person and those instructions have been executed badly, or not executed at all,[1] the solicitor may have broken the duty of care he owes to the intended beneficiary. In these cases the only person who suffers loss is left without a claim unless the law is prepared to fashion a remedy for breach of a duty owed to the client.[2] The assumption of responsibility by the solicitor in the wills cases is to the testator and there is thus no conflict between the solicitor's contractual duty to the client and the duty to the third party. The remedy to the beneficiary is granted as the beneficiary is the only person who has suffered loss and the testator's wishes are carried out. The duty owed by the solicitor does not extend to cover a failure to advise the testator that an *inter vivos* transaction is misconceived and might harm the interests of a potential devisee.[3] What distinguishes this last case is that the potential devisee is not someone in a sufficiently close relationship of proximity with the solicitor, since the solicitor would not have had him in mind as a person likely to be affected at the time the transaction was entered into, and that transaction did not have as its object the intention to benefit the devisee.[4] Furthermore, if a duty were to be owed, it could not be limited to a person in the position of the devisee. It would also have to extend to any other person to whom the property might be passed.[5] This, of course, would then raise the spectre of indeterminate liability.

---

16   *Punjab National Bank v de Boinville* [1992] 3 All ER 104 at 118 (per STAUGHTON LJ).
17   See ch 8.
18   *Spring v Guardian Assurance* [1994] 3 All ER 129.
19   *White v Jones* [1995] 2 AC 207.
20   *Ross v Caunters* [1980] Ch 297 at 322 (per MEGARRY VC).
1   *White v Jones* [1995] 2 AC 207; *Gartside v Sheffield, Young and Ellis* [1983] NZLR 37.
2   Ibid at 259 per LORD GOFF.
3   *Clarke v Bruce Lance (a firm)* [1988] 1 All ER 364.
4   Ibid at 369–370 (per BALCOMBE LJ).
5   Ibid at 370 (per BALCOMBE LJ).

It would appear that there is no direct assumption of responsibility to the third party as a solicitor does not owe a duty when responding to questions on behalf of his client[6] and the solicitor does not owe a duty if the estate[7] or the client[8] has an effective remedy, as the need to do justice which underpinned *White v Jones* is not present.

(3)   BAILMENTS[9]

The supply of a service may frequently give rise to a bailment relationship. Wherever a customer's goods are handed over to another for the purposes of safekeeping, repair or service or some kind of processing, a bailment comes into existence. Likewise, where it is arranged that goods should be carried by land, sea or air, the carrier is a bailee of the goods.

(i)   The creation of bailments

It would be misleading to equate the creation of a bailment relationship with the law of contract. It is true that many bailments do arise out of a contractual relationship, as where a service has been specially contracted for, but there may also be a bailment in the absence of a contract. For example, a person who is contractually incapable may still be a party to a bailment,[10] as may a person who is not in privity of contract.[11] So also a person who has not furnished consideration may be a party to a gratuitous bailment.

In most cases of bailment, there will be a delivery of goods by the bailor to the bailee, as for example, where goods are entrusted to a carrier, a film processor or a cleaner. However, it is still possible to have a bailment without delivery. For example, the bailee may come into possession of the bailor's property through the hands of an intermediary.

Not every person who takes possession of personal property belonging to another will necessarily be treated as a bailee. It may be that a person must, at least, voluntarily assume possession of that property. But a person who is unknowingly in possession of property belonging to another will not be treated as a bailee.

(ii)   Enforcement of bailments

Because a bailment may exist independently of the law of contract, the view has been expressed that the duties of a bailee lie in tort. For example, it has been stated that the common law duties of a bailee are to take proper care of the goods in his possession and to refrain from converting the chattel.[12] However, there are a number of ways in which the duty of a bailee differs from the duty of care owed generally under the tort of negligence. First, the bailee's duty is owed only to the bailor, whereas an ordinary tortious duty is owed to people generally. Secondly, a bailee is under a number of special duties which would not be imposed on persons generally. For example, a bailee is under a duty to guard the bailor's property against theft whereas the normal tort rule is that a

---

6   *Gran Gelato v Richcliff (Group) Ltd* [1992] Ch 560. See also *Williams v Natural Life Health Foods* [1998] 2 All ER 577.

7   *Carr-Glynn v Frearsons* [1997] 2 All ER 614.

8   *Hemmens v Wilson Browne* [1993] 4 All ER 826.

9   See Palmer *Bailment* (1991).

10   *Martin v LCC* [1947] KB 628.

11   *Morris v C W Martin & Sons Ltd* [1965] 2 All ER 725 at 733 (per Lord Denning MR); *Cia Portorafti Commerciale SA v Ultramar Panama Inc, The Captain Gregos (No 2)* [1990] 2 Lloyd's Rep 395 at 404–406 (per Bingham LJ); *The Pioneer Container* [1994] 2 AC 324.

12   *Morris v C W Martin & Sons Ltd* [1965] 2 All ER 725 at 738 (per Salmon LJ). See also *Hedley Byrne & Co Ltd v Heller & Partners Ltd* [1964] AC 465 at 526 (per Lord Devlin).

defendant does not have to guard against the actions of a third party.[13] There are also circumstances in which it is difficult to say that the bailee has been negligent in the ordinary sense of the word but, because he is a bailee, he is liable for the loss suffered by the bailor.[14]

(a)   *The duty to take reasonable care*   The bailee's duty is to take reasonable care of chattels in his possession. In *Houghland v R R Low (Luxury Coaches) Ltd*,[15] the defendants' coach had broken down and a replacement had been sent for. The passenger's luggage was transferred to the new coach but, when the coach arrived at its destination, one of the plaintiff's cases was missing. The Court of Appeal held that, since there had been no supervision of the luggage transfer, the defendants had failed to exercise reasonable care.[16]

The comparison between the duty owed by a bailee and the duty owed by persons generally in the tort of negligence is not exact. It should be noted that the burden of proof in ordinary negligence actions lies on the plaintiff. However, in the case of bailments, the bailee is under a duty to prove that he has exercised reasonable care, or that his failure to take care did not contribute to the bailor's loss.[17] Reasons for this include the view that only the bailee knows what care has been taken, and that the bailee may be tempted to cut corners by paying as little as possible for security measures.[18]

(b)   *The standard of care*   The standard of care required of a bailee appears to be based on ordinary principles of the law of negligence. At one time, it was thought that there was a clear-cut distinction between gratuitous bailments and bailments for reward. While the fact that payment may have the effect of raising the standard required by a bailee, a gratuitous bailee is still subject to ordinary rules on the standard of care.[19] Accordingly, a bailee must exercise the degree of skill appropriate to an ordinary person of his particular calling.

---

13   For example *P Perl (Exporters) Ltd v Camden LBC* [1984] QB 342.
14   See *Lee Cooper Ltd v C H Jeakins & Sons Ltd* [1967] 2 QB 1. Cf Weir [1965] CLJ 1.
15   [1962] 1 QB 694.
16   See also *Sutcliffe v Chief Constable of West Yorkshire* [1996] RTR 86.
17   *Joseph Travers & Sons Ltd v Cooper* [1915] 1 KB 73.
18   *British Road Services Ltd v Arthur Crutchley Ltd* [1968] 1 All ER 811 at 822 (per SACHS LJ).
19   *Birch v Thomas* [1972] 1 All ER 905 (gratuitous carriage of passengers).

Chapter 27

Employers' liability

This chapter concerns the legal liability of employers for injuries sustained by employees at work. The terminology employer and employee is used, but many of the older cases in particular use the terminology master and servant. Public insurance plays an important part in workmen's compensation, but a detailed consideration of the subject should be sought elsewhere.[1]

1. HISTORICAL DEVELOPMENT OF EMPLOYERS' LIABILITY

Judicial responses to employees' actions against their employers were initially hostile. The issue tended to be seen in terms of contractual duties. If no such duty was owed by the employer, there would normally be no liability. Although the personal liability of the employer was admitted, the courts erected an 'unholy trinity' of defences of common employment, *volenti non fit injuria* and contributory negligence.

The doctrine of common employment stems from *Priestley v Fowler*,[2] in which it was held that an employer would not be liable where the employee was injured by the negligence of a fellow employee. The justification for the rule was said to be that the contractual relationship between employer and employee impliedly stipulated that the employee had voluntarily accepted the risk of injury in such circumstances. The idea of voluntary acceptance of risk was extended, through the defence of *volenti*, to any hazard, not just those created by fellow employees.[3] The final barrier was that any contributory negligence on the part of the employee would be fatal to his claim.[4] The reality of working conditions in industry meant that most injuries were caused by the negligence of fellow employees rather than directly by the employer. The doctrine of common employment was usually an insurmountable obstacle to the plaintiff, even if the other two defences did not apply.

A change in judicial opinion is noticeable from the end of the nineteenth century onwards, possibly motivated by the passing of the Employers' Liability Act 1880. An

1   See Atiyah *Accidents* chs 13 and 14.
2   (1837) 3 M & W 1.
3   *Clarke v Holmes* (1862) 7 H & N 937.
4   *Senior v Ward* (1859) 1 E & E 385; *Alsop v Yates* (1858) 27 LJ Ex 156.

action by an employee for breach of statutory duty was permitted.[5] This was not subject to the doctrine of common employment. The defence of *volenti* was emasculated by the House of Lords for the purposes of most actions against an employer by an employee.[6]

Later, the standard of care for employees was set low, thus reducing the impact of the then full defence of contributory negligence.[7] Subsequently, the Law Reform (Contributory Negligence) Act 1945 treated contributory negligence as a partial defence only, and allowed the damages according to responsibility for the harm suffered. The doctrine of common employment seemed to lose some of its effect when the House of Lords restated the employer's personal duty in broad, non-delegable terms.[8] The doctrine was eventually abolished by the Law Reform (Personal Injuries) Act 1948, which sealed the fate of a 'highly artificial and now unfashionable fiction'.[9]

Despite the relaxation of judicial attitudes towards workmen's compensation, the most significant contribution towards this matter has been through insurance. This first emerged in the Workmen's Compensation Act 1897. The significance of the Act was that it enabled an employee to recover compensation without having to prove fault. The Act made the employer an insurer for injuries received in accidents arising 'out of, and in the course of employment'.[10] The scheme was subjected to prolonged criticism and many amendments, and the Beveridge Report[11] recommended a national insurance scheme, whereby benefits were payable to victims of industrial accidents and sufferers from prescribed industrial diseases. This was implemented in the National Insurance (Industrial Injuries) Act 1946.[12]

2.   COMMON LAW LIABILITY

(1)   INTRODUCTION

England and Wales operate a dual system of compensation for industrial injuries. The employee may obtain compensation through the National Insurance scheme, but this does not prevent him from bringing a civil action against his employer for damages. In many cases, the employee will obtain a higher amount in damages than through social security, however some benefits paid may be recouped from a damages award or settlement.[13]

The abolition of the doctrine of common employment and the reduction in significance of *volenti* and contributory negligence has improved the prospect of a successful action. The fact that most employers must insure against such an action also ensures that an award of damages will be met.[14] However, directors are not personally liable in damages for failure to comply.[15] Such actions are now amongst the most numerous to be dealt with by the courts, but to put this into perspective, only 10%–

---

5   *Groves v Lord Wimborne* [1898] 2 QB 402.
6   *Smith v Baker* [1891] AC 325 and see ch 21.
7   *Caswell v Powell Duffryn Associated Collieries Ltd* [1939] 3 All ER 722.
8   *Wilsons and Clyde Coal Co Ltd v English* [1938] AC 57.
9   *Dorrington v London Passenger Transport Board* [1947] 2 All ER 84 (per Hilberry J).
10   Workmen's Compensation Act 1897, s 1(1).
11   Royal Commission on Workmen's Compensation (1945) Cmnd 6588.
12   See Atiyah *Accidents*, ch 13.
13   See ch 17.
14   The Employers' Liability (Compulsory Insurance) Act 1969 makes such insurance mandatory except for nationalised industries, local authorities and the police.
15   *Richardson v Pitt-Stanley* [1995] QB 123.

15% of industrial injuries are compensated through the tort damages system.[16] The major objection to the use of the tort system as a means of personal injury compensation is that compensation is made to depend not simply on the accident victim's losses, his need or the merits of his conduct, but largely on the fortuitous circumstance of whether he can blame anyone.

An employee may bring an action against his employer on the grounds of the employer's personal negligence, breach of statutory duty and his vicarious liability for the negligence of another employee.

(2)   THE EMPLOYER'S PERSONAL DUTY OF CARE

The duty is one to take reasonable care for the safety of employees in the course of their employment. It is personal in the sense that its performance cannot be delegated, and is discharged by the exercise of due skill and care. In many respects, it is merely a specialised form of the general duty of care in negligence.

The authoritative version of the duty was laid down in *Wilsons and Clyde Coal Co Ltd v English.*[17] It requires the employer to provide 'a competent staff of men, adequate material, and a proper system and effective supervision'.[18] The definition is useful for the purposes of exposition, but it is not satisfactory to regard the employer's duty as a series of separate obligations. This approach causes problems when trying to fit new situations into existing categories, and it is preferable to observe the duty as a single duty to take reasonable care for the safety of employees in the course of their employment.[19]

(i)   The nature of the duty

The duty is personal to the employer, and its performance cannot be delegated to another person,[20] including an independent contractor.[1]

The extent of the duty is to provide for the safety of his servant in the course of his employment.[2] In this branch of the law, the phrase 'in the course of his employment' has a broader definition than elsewhere. The duty is not restricted to cases when the employee is at his place of work, and covers both ingress and egress, and is not restricted to actual performance of the work.[3] The employer, for example, may be liable where the employee is on a frolic of his own,[4] or where the employee is sent to work on the premises of a third party.[5]

Much of the case law is concerned with accidents at work but there is now an increasing awareness of health risks which is reflected in the case law[6] and the duty

---

16   Royal Commission on Civil Liability and Compensation for Personal Injuries (1978) Cmnd 7054, Vol 1, Table 5.
17   [1938] AC 57.
18   Ibid at 78 (per LORD WRIGHT).
19   *Wilson v Tyneside Window Cleaning Co* [1958] 2 QB 110 at 113 (per PEARCE LJ) and at 123–124 (per PARKER LJ).
20   *Wilsons and Clyde Coal Co Ltd v English* [1938] AC 57 at 78 (per LORD WRIGHT); *McDermid v Nash Dredging & Reclamation Co Ltd* [1987] AC 906.
1   *Davie v New Merton Board Mills Ltd* [1959] AC 604 at 645 (per LORD REID). See now Employers' Liability (Defective Equipment) Act 1969.
2   *Priestley v Fowler* (1837) 150 ER 1030 at 1032 (per LORD ABINGER).
3   *Davidson v Handley Page Ltd* [1945] 1 All ER 235 at 237 (per LORD GREENE).
4   *Allen v Aeroplane and Motor Aluminium Castings* [1965] 1 WLR 1244.
5   *Thomson v Cremin* [1953] 2 All ER 1185.
6   See *Thompson v Smith's Shiprepairers (North Shields) Ltd* [1984] QB 405—noise; *Jameson v CEGB* [1997] 3 WLR 151—asbestos.

now extends to the avoidance of negligently caused stress to the employee.[7] Most actions are brought in tort but there is also a contract between the employer and employee. This may raise problems where the terms of the contract conflict with the duties imposed on the employer by tort law.[8] Any implied terms in the contract to take reasonable care for the health and safety of the employee are subject to express terms which require the employee to work specified hours.[9] However, unless the employer has reserved an absolute right to compel the employee to work specified hours, the express term giving a discretion has to be exercised in such a way as not to breach the implied term to take reasonable care for the employee's health and safety.[10]

In the absence of an express or implied term in the contract of employment, the employer does not owe a duty to protect the employee against economic loss.[11]

(ii) Standard of care

The duty is to guard against foreseeable risks, but only those which he can guard against by any measure, the convenience and expense of which are not entirely disproportionate to the risks involved.[12]

The rule that the employer need not guard against all foreseeable risks is illustrated by *Latimer v AEC Ltd*.[13] In this case, heavy rain flooded the defendants' factory floor and the floor became slippery. The defendants took all possible precautions to dispose of the effects of the flood, but the plaintiff was still injured. He argued that the factory should have been closed. This argument was rejected by the House of Lords, as the risk involved did not justify such an onerous precaution.

The standard of care is that of the reasonable, prudent employer. Evidence of general practice is relevant, but not conclusive. There are *dicta* to suggest that, where a particular employee is skilled and experienced at a particular kind of work, the employer may rely on his skill in avoiding the risks.[14] Conversely, where an employee has a weakness or susceptibility which the employer knew, or ought to have known about, the employer will need to take extra precautions.[15]

(iii) Competent staff

The abolition of the doctrine of common employment has rendered this branch of the duty of comparatively little importance. The employer may be liable where he uses an employee with insufficient experience or training for a particular job,[16] and a fellow employee is injured as a result.

One area of continuing importance is where an employee indulges in violent conduct or practical jokes or bullying and another employee is injured, either physically or mentally. The employer is unlikely to be held vicariously liable,[17] but, if he were aware

---

7   *Walker v Northumberland County Council* [1995] 1 All ER 737.
8   *Johnstone v Bloomsbury Health Authority* [1991] 2 All ER 293; *Scally v Southern Health and Social Services* [1992] 1 AC 294.
9   *Johnstone v Bloomsbury Health Authority* [1991] 2 All ER 293.
10 Ibid.
11 *Reid v Rush & Tompkins Group plc* [1989] 3 All ER 228. See *Scally v Southern Health and Social Services Board* [1992] 1 AC 294 where the court was prepared to imply such a term.
12 *Harris v Brights Asphalt Contractors Ltd* [1953] 1 QB 617 at 626 (per SLADE J). See also *Morris v West Hartlepool Steam Navigation Co Ltd* [1956] 1 All ER 385.
13 [1953] AC 643.
14 *Smith v Austin Lifts Ltd* [1959] 1 All ER 81 at 85; *Withers v Perry Chain Co Ltd* [1961] 1 WLR 1314.
15 *Paris v Stepney Borough Council* [1951] AC 367 at 375 (per LORD SIMONDS).
16 *Butler v Fife Coal Co* [1912] AC 149.
17 *O'Reilly v National Rail and Tramways Appliances Ltd* [1966] 1 All ER 499.

of the employee's propensity towards this kind of behaviour, he may be liable under his personal duty of care.[18]

(iv)   Adequate material

The duty is to provide the necessary plant and equipment and to take reasonable care to maintain it in a proper condition. The employer does not guarantee the safety of the equipment and, at common law, could not be held liable for a latent defect in the equipment which could not have been discovered with reasonable care.[19] The Employer's Liability (Defective Equipment) Act 1969 now provides that, if an employee suffers personal injury as a result of a defect in equipment supplied by the employer and the defect is due to the fault of a third party, the injury is deemed attributable to the negligence of the employer. This relieves the employee of the necessity of identifying and suing the manufacturer of the defective equipment. The word 'equipment' has been given a broad meaning and includes a merchant ship[20] and a flagstone which an employee was working on.[1]

(v)   Safe place of work

Where the employee is working on the employer's premises, the employer must act in the same manner as would the reasonably prudent employer. Reasonable care must be taken for the employee's safety.[2] The duty applies where the employee is working on other premises, but the standard of care varies with the circumstances.[3]

(vi)   Safe system

This is the most commonly invoked branch of the employer's duty, and the most difficult to define. It has been said that the employer must devise a suitable system, to instruct his men in what they must do[4] and supply any implements that may be required.[5] In this case, a window cleaner was injured when standing on a window sill whilst cleaning the exteriors of windows, as instructed by his employers. The sill of one window was not securely attached to the premises, and the plaintiff fell when it gave way. The employer was held liable, as he had failed to instruct the plaintiff to test the sill before entrusting his weight to it.

In devising a safe system, the employer should be aware that workmen are often careless for their own safety, and his system must, as far as possible, reduce the effects of an employee's own carelessness.[6] He must also take reasonable care to ensure that his system is complied with, but he is not obliged 'to stand over workmen of age and experience at every moment they are working ... to see that they do what they are supposed to do'.[7]

There is also a close connection between safe system of working and breach of statutory duty. In many instances, there are detailed statutory regulations governing the

18   *Hudson v Ridge Manufacturing Co Ltd* [1957] 2 QB 348.
19   *Davie v New Merton Board Mills Ltd* [1959] AC 604.
20   *Coltman v Bibby Tankers Ltd* [1988] AC 276.
1   *Knowles v Liverpool City Council* [1993] 4 All ER 321.
2   *Latimer v AEC Ltd* [1953] AC 643.
3   *Wilson v Tyneside Window Cleaning Co* [1958] 2 QB 110; *Cook v Square D Ltd* [1992] ICR 262
4   *Pape v Cumbria CC* [1992] 3 All ER 211.
5   *General Cleaning Contractors v Christmas* [1953] AC 180 at 194 (per LORD REID). See also *McDermid v Nash Dredging and Reclamation Co Ltd* [1987] 2 All ER 878 at 887 (per LORD BRANDON).
6   *General Cleaning Contractors Ltd v Christmas* [1953] AC 180 at 189–190 (per LORD REID).
7   *Woods v Durable Suites Ltd* [1953] 1 WLR 857 at 862 (per SINGLETON LJ).

organisation of the workplace. Safe system of working usually covers the avoidance of accidents to employees but it also now encompasses an employee's mental health. Safe system includes a duty to take reasonable care not to damage an employee's mental health by using a system of work that creates a foreseeable risk of mental breakdown.[8] In *Walker v Nothumberland County Council*[9] the plaintiff suffered a breakdown as a result of his stressful work as a social worker. He recovered, returned to work and suffered a second breakdown. Breach having been established, it was held that the first breakdown made the second foreseeable and a duty was owed by the employer.[10]

(3)   BREACH OF STATUTORY DUTY

(i)   Introduction

The tortious action for breach of statutory duty extends beyond the area of industrial safety, although the majority of cases fall in this area. The tort has been used in relation to business losses, company law, consumer protection, restrictive practices, copyright, employment law, liability of public authorities and welfare rights.[11]

The role of breach of statutory duty in industrial injury compensation stems from protective legislation passed in the nineteenth century. The modern form of such legislation dates from the Factories Act 1844, which dealt not only with safety, but also health and welfare. Enforcement of industrial safety legislation was primarily effected by means of criminal penalties. In some cases, the 1844 Act provided for increased penalties, all or part of which could be paid to the victim, at the discretion of the Secretary of State, and in other cases, free legal aid was provided. The free legal aid cases, which were based on the employer's duties at common law, were subject to the doctrine of common employment. As the operation of that doctrine spread, so the effectiveness of the provisions diminished.

The source of the modern private remedy for breach of statutory duties is the Court of Appeal decision in *Groves v Lord Wimborne*.[12] The action was brought under the Factory and Workshop Act 1878, which made an occupier of a factory who did not properly fence dangerous machinery liable to a fine of £100. The whole or part of the fine, at the discretion of the Secretary of State, could be paid to the person injured. The plaintiff lost his arm in an unfenced cogwheel, and was entitled to recover £150. The Court of Appeal was of the opinion that, as there was no certainty that any part of the fine would be awarded to him and Parliament could not have intended £100 to be exclusive compensation, he should have an action in tort.[13] The reasoning on the inadequacy of the fine should be regarded as suspect in view of an earlier decision.[14] The case is best viewed as a policy decision based on changing views on the compensation of victims of industrial accidents, which may have been prompted by the passing of the Workmen's Compensation Act 1897. The decision also distinguished the new action from negligence, as the defence of common employment provided no defence to an action for breach of statutory duty.[15] The decision did not provide an analysis of the

---

8   *Petch v Customs & Excise Comrs* [1993] ICR 789.
9   [1995] 1 All ER 737. Dolding & Mullender (1996) 59 MLR 296; Sprince (1995) 17 Liverpool Law Rev 189.
10   See also *Frost v Chief Constable of South Yorkshire Police* [1997] 1 All ER 540.
11   See Stanton *Breach of Statutory Duty in Tort* (1986).
12   [1898] 2 QB 402.
13   [1898] 2 QB 402 at 408 (per A L SMITH LJ); at 414 (per RIGBY LJ) and at 416–7 (per VAUGHAN-WILLIAMS LJ).
14   *Atkinson v Newcastle and Gateshead Waterworks Co* (1877) 2 Ex D 441.
15   *Groves v Lord Wimborne* [1898] 2 QB 402 at 410 (per A L SMITH LJ). See also *Baddeley v Earl of Granville* (1887) 19 QBD 423. *Dictum* of LORD CHELMSFORD in *Wilson v Merry* (1868) LR 1 Sc & Div 326 rejected.

theory of the new action,[16] but by establishing the availability of such an action, it provided the basis for the conclusion that protective industrial legislation is invariably construed as providing a civil remedy.

Until 1974, industrial safety legislation followed a pattern of penal sanction, and the courts were prepared to infer tortious liability on the basis of *Groves v Lord Wimborne*.[17] The Robens Committee on Safety and Health at Work[18] found that existing law was too detailed and fragmented to be understandable, even to those who were responsible for industrial safety. Their major recommendations were complemented by the Health and Safety at Work etc Act 1974. The Act differs from previous legislation in that it gives express guidance on whether a civil action is available. Sections 2 to 7 of the Act impose general duties on employers. Section 2, for example, requires the employer to ensure, as far as is reasonably practicable, the health, safety and welfare at work of his employees. The general duties are not actionable in tort,[19] and rely upon penal sanctions for their enforcement. Existing regulations, such as the Factories Act 1961, were retained, but the 1974 Act provided a procedure to replace these by regulations and codes of practice. Section 15 gives the Secretary of State power to make regulations for any of the general purposes of the Act. A breach of any such regulations is actionable in tort unless otherwise provided. Initially progress was slow but was accelerated by a series of EC Directives[20] implemented by a series of Regulations, the major one being the Management of Health and Safety at Work Regulations 1992,[1] which does not give rise to civil liability but the other Regulations do. The major change is an attempt to provide unified regulations which govern different aspects of employment, rather than the old system of having regulations for each trade.[2]

In relation to industrial safety, the Act has been a success, as it has concentrated the minds of both sides of industry on the issue of safety. Lawyers tend to be obsessed by the issue of compensation, but accidents can be reduced more effectively by abatement notices, penal sanctions and codes of practice provided by the 1974 Act and regulations. This proactive approach is emphasised by the requirement placed on employers to carry out a risk assessment of the risks to which employees are exposed.

The Regulations do not provide a comprehensive code of compensation as their primary purpose is not to provide for civil liability for injured workers. The English system therefore continues to be industrial safety legislation attracting civil sanctions, combined with common law liability for negligence.

(ii)   Elements of the tort

The action for breach of statutory duty is sometimes referred to as 'statutory negligence'.[3] It is preferable to treat the action as distinct from negligence.[4] Negligence connotes a failure to act with reasonable care, whereas the standard of conduct that will amount to breach of statutory duty varies from statute to statute.[5] Once the plaintiff has established the availability of a civil action under a statute, he faces difficulties similar to those which apply for an action for negligence. He must show that the duty to prevent

---

16   Fricke (1960) 76 LQR 240 and Williams (1960) 23 MLR 233.
17   [1898] 2 QB 402. Cf *Uddin v Associated Portland Cement Manufacturers Ltd* [1965] 2 QB 582.
18   1972 (Cmnd 5034).
19   Health and Safety at Work Act 1974, s 47(1)(a).
20   89/391; 89/654; 89/655; 89/656; 90/269; 90/270; 91/383.
1   SI 1992/2051. Implementing Directive 89/391.
2   Eg Factories Act 1961 and Mines and Quarries Act 1954.
3   *Lochgelly Iron and Coal Co Ltd v M'Mullan* [1934] AC 1 at 23 (per Lord Wright).
4   Cf Stanton *Breach of Statutory Duty* (1986) p 25.
5   See *Caswell v Powell Duffryn Associated Collieries Ltd* [1940] AC 152 at 177–178 (per Lord Wright) and *Murfin v United Steel Companies Ltd (Power Gas Corpn Ltd Third Party)* [1957] 1 WLR 104.

the injury suffered was owed to him, and that the injury was caused by the defendant's breach of duty.

(a)   *Duty*   Before considering whether a duty is owed to a particular plaintiff, it is necessary to discover whether the statutory provision in question gives rise to a civil action for damages. This is said to depend on the intention of Parliament, which is discerned by interpretation of the statute. The statute may give express guidance on the question, either by precluding an action, or by attempting to grant one. Preclusion of an action is normally evidenced by words such as 'nothing in the Act shall be construed as conferring a right of action in any civil proceedings.'[6]

A statute may also create a tortious action by express words. This action may be a substitute for a common law action,[7] or it may exist with a common law action.[8] Where the statute provides for industrial safety, there is usually no problem, as the jurisprudence of this area is sufficiently well developed. The formula usually used is that breach of the duty shall be actionable.[9]

Major difficulties arise where the statute provides for a criminal sanction in the event of breach of its provisions, but is silent as to civil liability. The courts must attempt to give effect to the intention of Parliament[10] on a matter which Parliament probably gave no thought to at all.[11] The courts have used various tests to determine parliamentary intention. One is whether the statute was passed for a defined class of persons[12] or for the public at large.[13] A second test is whether the statute was passed to prevent the type of harm the plaintiff suffered.[14] A third test is whether the remedy provided by the statute was adequate.[15] None of these tests is of much use, as they can produce contrary results and conceal the policy factors which lie behind the decision. The decision in *Phillips v Britannia Hygienic Laundry Co*[16] can be explained as a reluctance by the courts to introduce strict liability for road accidents in the absence of compulsory insurance.[17] There are few examples outside of industrial safety where an action has been allowed in the absence of a common law duty.[18]

Alternatives to the fictitious intention test have been proposed. The Law Commission[19] has proposed that, if the statute provides no remedy for its enforcement, there should be a presumption in favour of an action. However, this approach conflicts with the ability of the court to take into account policy factors and an enquiry whether the civil action furthers the aims of the legislation.[20] In the United States and Canada, breach of statutory duty has been regarded as a species of negligence, usually called

6   Health and Safety at Work Act 1974, s 47(1)(a); Guard Dogs Act 1975, s 5(2)(a); Medicines Act 1968, s 133(2)(a). Cf Consumer Credit Act 1974, s 170(1).
7   Nuclear Installations Act 1965.
8   Mineral Workings (Offshore Installations) Act 1971, s 11.
9   See Health and Safety at Work Act 1974, s 47(2).
10   *Hague v Deputy Governor of Parkhurst Prison* [1991] 3 All ER 733.
11   See *Cutler v Wandsworth Stadium Ltd* [1949] AC 398 at 410 (per LORD DU PARQ).
12   *Issa v Hackney LBC* [1997] 1 WLR 956.
13   *Solomons v R Gertzenstein Ltd* [1954] 2 QB 243; *X v Bedfordshire CC* [1995] 2 AC 633, 671. Cf *Phillips v Britannia Hygienic Laundry Co* [1923] 2 KB 832 and *McCall v Abelesz* [1976] QB 585.
14   *Monk v Warbey* [1935] 1 KB 75 and see Motor Insurers Bureau Scheme 1972. Cf *Phillips v Britannia Hygienic Laundry Co* [1923] 2 KB 832. Cf *Hague v Deputy Governer of Parkhurst Prison* [1991] 3 All ER 733; *Richardson v Pitt-Stanley* [1995] ICR 303.
15   *Groves v Lord Wimborne* [1898] 2 QB 402. Cf *Atkinson v Newcastle and Gateshead Waterworks Co* (1877) 2 Ex D 441.
16   [1923] 2 KB 832.
17   Atiyah *Accidents* p 79. Cf *London Passenger Transport Board v Upson* [1949] AC 155.
18   *Read v Croydon Corpn* [1938] 4 All ER 631.
19   Law Commission No 21 (1969) para 38 and Appendix A(4).
20   See Buckley (1984) 100 LQR 204 at 232–234.

statutory negligence.[1] This is said to have the advantage that, while the usual standard of reasonable care leaves doubts as to what precautions are required, the standard set by the statute is clearly indicated and removes uncertainty. There are two approaches to this. The first is that breach of the statutory requirement constitutes negligence *per se*. The second is that breach only provides *prima facie* evidence of negligence. The latter approach was preferred in *The Queen in Right of Canada v Saskatchewan Wheat Pool*,[2] on the ground that not every minor breach of statute should be regarded as negligence.[3] In England the view is that the careless performance of a statutory duty does not in itself give rise to an action in the absence of a right of action for breach of statutory duty simpliciter or a common law duty of care.[4] Adoption of the statutory negligence approach should not be welcomed in this country, as it would confine actions to existing tort law, and, in particular, would reproduce all the difficulties which have been encountered with liability for omissions at common law.

Modern judicial approaches can be divided into those which favour the presumption approach and those which favour the discretionary approach.[5] The discretionary approach is illustrated in *Ex p Island Records Ltd*,[6] where LORD DENNING MR laid down a broad rule, not depending on the scope and language of the statute. When a lawful business suffers damage as the result of a breach of a statutory prohibition, there is a right of action.

> The truth is that in many cases the legislature has left the point open … . The dividing line between the pro-cases and the contra-cases is so blurred and ill defined that you might as well toss a coin to decide it.[7]

The presumption approach is best illustrated in *Lonrho Ltd v Shell Petroleum Co Ltd*:[8]

> One starts with the presumption … that where an Act creates an obligation, and enforces the performance in a specified manner … that performance cannot be enforced in any other manner … . (T)here are two classes of exception to this general rule. The first is where on the true construction of the Act it is apparent that the obligation or prohibition was imposed for the benefit or protection of a particular class of individuals, as in the case of the Factories Acts and similar legislation … . The second exception is where the statute creates a public right … and a particular member of the public suffers … particular, direct and substantial damage other and different from that which was common to all the rest of the public.[9]

Where presumptions create a result that is contrary to the intention of the statute, the presumptions must give way. The difficulty with this approach is that the presumptions are so easily displaced that it is difficult to determine a unifying practice. In particular the courts are reluctant to find that breach of a statute which gives administrative discretion to a public body creates a right of action in tort.[10]

Most pieces of industrial safety legislation have been construed so as to provide a civil remedy in damages.[11] The presumption approach justifies this view by reference to LORD DIPLOCK's first exception, that it is apparent that the obligation is imposed for the protection of a class of individuals.

---

1   *American Restatement, Torts* (2d) para 288(B).
2   (1983) 143 DLR (3d) 9.
3   Cf Buckley (1984) 100 LQR 204, 206–210 and Matthews (1984) 4 OJLS 429.
4   *X v Bedfordshire CC* [1995] 2 AC 633.
5   Stanton *Breach of Statutory Duty* (1986) p 31.
6   [1978] Ch 122.
7   Ibid at 135 (per LORD DENNING MR).
8   [1981] 2 All ER 456.
9   Ibid at 461 (per LORD DIPLOCK).
10   *X v Bedfordshire CC* [1995] 2 AC 633; *O'Rourke v Camden LBC* [1997] 3 WLR 86.
11   Cf *Uddin v Associated Portland Cement Manufacturers Ltd* [1965] 2 QB 15.

In *Rickless v United Artists Corpn*[12] LORD DENNING's broad statement of principle concerning interference with a lawful business interest was treated as wrong by the Court of Appeal as it conflicted with the *ratio* of the *Lonrho* case. The action was brought by the widow of Peter Sellers for the unauthorised use of clips from the *Pink Panther* films. The Court held that section 2 of the Dramatic and Musical Performers' Protection Act 1958 fell within LORD DIPLOCK's first exceptional case.

(b)   *Duty to the plaintiff to prevent the type of injury which occurred*   In an action for breach of statutory duty in the field of industrial safety, it will not normally be necessary for the plaintiff to show that the statute confers a right to sue for a breach of statutory duty. Precedents based on older legislation such as the Factories Act 1961 will serve this purpose. Furthermore, the Health and Safety at Work Act 1974 specially creates such an action.

The plaintiff must show that the duty was owed to him. Factory legislation confers the right to sue on 'person's employed'. It follows that a fireman fighting a fire at a factory which is not his place of employment is not able to sue for breach of statutory duty.[13]

The plaintiff must also show that the type of injury he suffered was the type the legislation sought to prevent. In *Gorris v Scott*,[14] the defendant broke a statutory duty to provide pens for cattle carried on his ship. He was held not liable when the plaintiff's sheep were swept overboard as the purpose of the statute was to lessen the risk of disease. In industrial safety cases, this requirement does not normally present a problem, as most actions are for personal injuries, and it has been held that it does not matter if the injury occurred in a way not contemplated by the statute.[15]

(c)   *Breach of duty*   Whether the duty imposed by the statute has been broken is a question of interpretation. No single standard exists, and liability may be strict or, in rare cases, absolute. Strict liability is a standard higher than that of reasonable care, but which admits of qualifications. Absolute liability admits of no qualification. Difficulties are caused by the fact that there is no single recognised method of statutory interpretation, and the legislation in industrial safety cases may have both penal and compensatory objectives. Usually, the court will take the ordinary meaning of the words used in the context of the statute. However, it is sometimes possible to make alterations to the words of a statute in order to avoid unacceptable results. If the statute is penal in nature, the courts have to be careful to avoid creating a strict liability criminal offence in the absence of clear parliamentary language.[16]

A strict statutory interpretation may have the effect of imposing absolute liability on the employer. In *John Summers and Sons Ltd v Frost*,[17] the defendants were held liable in damages when the plaintiff's hand came into contact with a moving grinding wheel. The Factories Act 1961, section 14(1) required 'every dangerous part of any machinery to be securely fenced'. A literal interpretation of these words required the wheel to be completely fenced off. The court refused to read in the unexpressed words 'so far as reasonably practical'. The employer unsuccessfully argued that, if the machine was securely fenced, it would be unusable.

---

12   [1988] QB 40 at 54.
13   *Hartley v Mayoh & Co* [1954] 1 QB 383. See also *Knapp v Railway Executive* [1949] 2 All ER 508.
14   (1874) LR 9 Exch 125. See also *Wentworth v Wiltshire CC* [1993] 2 WLR 175.
15   *Donaghey v Boulton and Paul Ltd* [1968] AC 1. Cf *Close v Steel Co of Wales Ltd* [1962] AC 367.
16   *Haigh v Charles W Ireland Ltd* [1973] 3 All ER 1137, [1974] 1 WLR 43.
17   [1955] AC 740, [1955] 1 All ER 870.

Such liability was unusual, although some regulations are so specific as to exclude any qualification. For example, in *Chipchase v British Titan Products Co Ltd*,[18] statutory regulations provided that a working platform from which a person is likely to fall more than 6ft 6in had to be at least 34 inches in width. The defendants were held not liable when the plaintiff fell from a 9 inch wide platform 6 feet above the ground. However, it is common to find the standard of liability qualified by the statute. Such qualification may include the practicability of precautions. The onus of proving the impracticability of precautions rests on the employer, and the courts have not generally allowed the qualification to be easily invoked. If the precaution is possible, it must be taken, even if the risks involved in taking it outweigh the benefits conferred by it.[19] The standard of liability can therefore be said to be strict.

Another qualification is that of 'reasonable practicability'. This qualification allows the balancing of the expense and time involved in taking the precaution set against the risk of injury. In this sense, it is similar to negligence, but the burden of proof is on the employer, who must advance evidence rather than conjecture. If the employer has failed to consider the precaution, he will fail. In *Marshall v Gotham Co Ltd*,[20] regulations required a mine roof to be made secure so far as reasonably practicable. The roof collapsed due to a rare geological fault which had not occurred for twenty years and could not be predicted in advance. The House of Lords held that the known risk had to be balanced against safety measures, and the defence was established.[1]

The Regulations brought in under the EC 'framework' Directive[2] also impose a mixture of obligations and old case law will probably still be relevant to interpretation on questions such as 'reasonably practicable.'[3] The replacement for section 14 of the Factories Act 1961 is regulation 11 of the Provision and Use of Work Equipment Regulations 1992, which provides a series of precautions according to practicability.[4] If practicable there have to be fixed guards on machinery. If this is not practicable then other guards or protection devices must be provided. The last in the series is that failing all else, the employer must at least provide information, training and supervision.

Given the strict standards of many statutory duties, it is normally easier for the plaintiff to prove breach of such duties as opposed to a common law duty, but this is not always the case. In *Bux v Slough Metals Ltd*,[5] an action for breach of statutory duty failed when the plaintiff did not wear safety goggles provided by his employer. A negligence action succeeded, as the evidence showed that the plaintiff would have worn the goggles if he had been firmly instructed to do so and supervised.

Although the Regulations are designed to be proactive, providing an administrative framework backed up by the Health and Safety Executive enforcement powers, it may be that a failure comply with the Regulations by, eg not carrying out a risk assessment, could be evidence of a failure to take care to provide a safe system of work. It has been suggested that the Regulations may come to represent what is required under the common law and that this will blur the line between statutory and common law liability.[6]

---

18   [1956] 1 QB 545.
19   *Boyton v Willment Brothers Ltd* [1971] 1 WLR 1625; *Sanders v F H Lloyd & Co Ltd* [1982] ICR 360. Cf *Jayne v National Coal Board* [1963] 2 All ER 220.
20   [1954] AC 360, [1954] 1 All ER 937.
1   Approving *Edwards v National Coal Board* [1949] 1 All ER 743 at 747 (per AsQUITH LJ).
2   89/391.
3   Eg Workplace (Health Safety and Welfare) Regulations SI 1992/3004 reg 12 (3). To keep floors free from obstructions or substances which may cause a fall so far as is reasonably practicable.
4   SI 1992/2932.
5   [1974] 1 All ER 262, [1973] 1 WLR 1358.
6   *Winfield* p 276.

(d) *Causation* It is necessary for the plaintiff to prove that the employer's breach of statutory duty was a cause of his injuries.[7] Causation involves two issues. One is a factual enquiry to discover who is the cause in fact of harm suffered. This is resolved by hearing evidence and drawing inferences from that evidence. The second issue is to identify the legal or proximate cause of the harm. This involves policy issues and value judgments in determining what legal consequences should attach to the defendant's conduct.

Causation is of particular importance in industrial safety cases since, once it is shown that the employer has broken a strict liability duty, it may be the only defence available to him.

In general, there is no distinction between actions for breach of statutory duty and those for common law negligence. The plaintiff must show that but for the defendant's breach of statutory duty, the plaintiff would not have suffered the injury.[8] In *McWilliams v Sir William Arrol,*[9] the employer was in breach of his statutory duty by removing safety belts from a building site. The action failed, as it was shown that the deceased steelworker would not have worn a belt, even if it had been provided.

Where there is more than one possible cause and both parties have contributed towards the injury, the issue of contributory negligence arises.[10] However, it may be that, although the breach of duty is part of the chain of causation which produces the injury, the plaintiff's own act is the legal cause of the injury.[11]

Breach of statutory duty raises one specialised issue of causation. The act or omission of the plaintiff himself may have the result in law that both plaintiff and defendant are in breach of statutory duty. In *Ginty v Belmont Building Supplies Ltd,*[12] the plaintiff was an experienced workman employed by the defendant roofing contractors. Statutory regulations binding on both parties required crawling boards to be used on fragile roofs. The boards were provided by the defendants, but were not used by the plaintiff, who fell through a roof. Both parties were in breach of their statutory duty. The plaintiff's claim failed, as the employer had done everything possible to ensure that the statutory duty was complied with, and the sole reason for the breach was the plaintiff's omission. It is difficult for the employer to succeed in this 'defence' as, if any causal responsibility rests with the employer, he will be liable. Where the plaintiff establishes the defendant's breach of duty, he has a *prima facie* case. The defendant can escape liability if he is able to show that the only act or default which caused the breach was that of the plaintiff. But, if some blame can be attached to the defendant, for example if he has asked the employee to do a job beyond his competence, the plaintiff may recover.[13]

(iii) Defences

(a) *Contributory negligence*[14] The Law Reform (Contributory Negligence) Act 1945 applies to breach of statutory duty actions, since fault is defined so as to include breach of statutory duty.[15] By section 1(1) of the Act, the court may reduce the plaintiff's damages by the proportion for which he is responsible for his injuries. This defence causes particular problems in relation to industrial safety legislation. The purpose of such legislation is to safeguard employees, and this often includes safeguarding them against

---

7   *McWilliams v Sir William Arroll* [1962] 1 WLR 295; *Pickford v ICI* [1998] 3 All ER 462.
8   See ch 16.
9   [1962] 1 WLR 295. Cf *McGhee v National Coal Board* [1973] 1 WLR 1.
10   See ch 20.
11   *Moir-Young v Dorman Long (Bridge and Engineering) Ltd* (1969) 7 KIR 86.
12   [1959] 1 All ER 414. Cf *Ross v Associated Portland Cement Manufacturers Ltd* [1964] 2 All ER 452.
13   *Boyle v Kodak Ltd* [1969] 2 All ER 439, [1969] 1 WLR 661.
14   See ch 20.
15   Law Reform (Contributory Negligence) Act 1945, s 4.

the consequences of their own carelessness. The rationale of contributory negligence as a defence is that it requires people to take care for their own safety, and acts as a deterrent to careless conduct. It is unlikely that an employee will alter his behaviour because of the existence of the contributory negligence defence, and it is not surprising that the courts have no settled rules for apportionment. They do take account of the difficulties of monotony and tiredness, and *dicta* show that the courts will be slow to find contributory negligence on the part of an employee.[16] The cases reveal an inconsistency of approach, for example, deductions of one-third may be made for 'momentary errors',[17] but no deduction may be made for momentary inadvertence.[18]

(b)   *Volenti non fit injuria*[19]   This defence can be raised when a person has full knowledge of a risk and freely undertakes to run it at his own expense. Since the end of the nineteenth century, the defence has had scarcely any role in employer–employee cases, on the ground that there is no freedom of choice on the part of the employee.[20] Even where the employee is aware of the risk, economic factors detract from his freedom of choice. The defence is normally regarded as inappropriate in cases of breach of statutory duty where the employer is in breach of the duty,[1] as it would be contrary to public policy to allow the employee to exempt the employer from his statutory duties. The defence is available where the employee is in breach of statutory duty, and the employer is sued on the grounds of his vicarious liability. In *ICI Ltd v Shatwell*,[2] two brothers employed as shotfirers by the defendants were injured whilst testing detonators. They were in breach of their statutory duty in failing to take shelter. The House of Lords held that the brothers were *volens* to the risk, and had no action against the defendants in respect of the employer's vicarious liability for negligence or breach of statutory duty.

(4)   VICARIOUS LIABILITY[3]

(i)   Introduction

An employer is vicariously liable at common law for torts committed by an employee in the course of his employment. This liability protects anyone injured by the tort, including a fellow employee. Liability is strict in the sense that the employer is liable in the absence of personal fault on his part, and the fault of the employee is imputed to the employer.

Various reasons have been advanced for the imposition of vicarious liability, so as to excuse its departure from the fault system. It has been suggested that the employer is in control of the behaviour of his employee,[4] or that the employer is liable on the basis of causation.[5] The modern common law approach is essentially pragmatic. It has been said that the doctrine has not grown from any clear, logical or legal principle, but from social convenience and rough justice.[6] The imposition of liability is based on the

---

16   *Caswell v Powell Duffryn Associated Collieries Ltd* [1939] 3 All ER 722; *Staveley Iron and Chemical Co Ltd v Jones* [1956] AC 627.
17   *Mullard v Ben Line Steamers Ltd* [1970] 1 WLR 1414.
18   *Johns v Martin Simms (Cheltenham) Ltd* [1983] 1 All ER 127.
19   See ch 22.
20   *Smith v Baker & Sons Ltd* [1891] AC 325.
1   *Baddeley v Earl of Granville* (1887) 19 QBD 423; *Wheeler v New Merton Board Mills Ltd* [1933] 2 KB 669.
2   [1965] AC 656.
3   Atiyah *Vicarious Liability in the Law of Torts* (1967).
4   *Honeywill and Stein Ltd v Larkin Bros (London's Commercial Photographers) Ltd* [1934] 1 KB 191 at 196.
5   *Hutchinson v York, Newcastle and Berwick Rly Co* (1850) 5 Exch 343 at 350, 155 ER 150.
6   *ICI v Shatwell* [1965] AC 656 at 685 (per LORD PEARCE).

employer's greater ability to pay and to spread losses that might be caused. Loss-spreading or distribution can be achieved by passing on the cost to customers directly in the form of higher prices and by insurance. It is compulsory for employers to insure against their liability for personal injuries to their employees.[7] If losses are incurred in pursuit of the employer's business interests, the doctrine can be justified on moral grounds.[8] Damages awarded or higher insurance premiums can be regarded as production costs which should be internalised.[9] It is also arguable that the doctrine may have a deterrent effect in pressuring the employer to effect accident prevention procedures, particularly in the selection, supervision and disciplining of personnel.[10]

(ii)   Liability rules

Before liability can be imposed on the employer, it must be shown that a tort has been committed by one of his employees in the course of his employment.

(a)   *Who is an employee?*   A legal distinction is drawn between an employee for whom the employer is liable and an independent contractor for whom he is not liable.

Various tests have been put forward to determine the distinction. Traditionally, a distinction was drawn between a contract of service made with an employee and a contract for services made with an independent contractor. However, this distinction does not explain how we determine which is which. Other tests include that of control. If the employer retained control over the performance of the work by telling a person what to do and how to do it, that person was an employee.[11] This test is now outdated, as it reflected a society where ownership of the means of production coincided with the possession of technical knowledge and skill.[12] Most employees are now skilled, and the employer will not have all or any of those skills. An accountant or a lawyer working for an organisation may be told what to do, but his method will be beyond the comprehension of an employer, who will probably be an administrator. This quickly became apparent in the case of doctors, when the courts wished to make their employers vicariously liable.[13] When hospitals were organised on a charitable or voluntary basis, the courts were reluctant to open their funds to legal action.[14] Once medical services were on a more assured financial footing after the introduction of the National Health Service, the courts found it feasible to make health authorities vicariously liable.

The deficiencies of the control test led the courts to search for alternatives. An integration test was suggested, whereby a person was an employee when his work was an integral part of the business. An independent contractor worked for the business, but as an accessory, not an integral part of it. It was thus possible to distinguish between a chauffeur and a taxi driver, a staff reporter and a newspaper contributor.[15] Even this test does not solve all problems and attempts have been made to put forward more complex criteria.

---

7   Employers' Liability (Compulsory Insurance) Act 1969; Employers' Liability (Compulsory Insurance) General Regulations 1971, SI 1971/1117.
8   See Cane (1980) 2 OJLS 30 at 34.
9   Cf BRAMWELL B's letter to Sir Henry Jackson QC reprinted in Ogus and Veljanovski *Readings in the Economics of Law and Regulation* (1984) pp 125–127.
10   See *Morgans v Launchbury* [1973] AC 127 for an example of incentive.
11   *Honeywill and Stein Ltd v Larkin Bros (London's Commercial Photographers) Ltd* [1934] 1 KB 191 at 196.
12   Kahn-Freund (1951) 14 MLR 504 at 505.
13   *Gold v Essex County Council* [1942] 2 KB 293; *Cassidy v Ministry of Health* [1951] 2 KB 343.
14   *Hillyer v St Bartholomew's Hospital (Governors)* [1909] 2 KB 820.
15   *Stevenson, Jordan and Harrison Ltd v MacDonald and Evans* [1952] 1 TLR 101. See also *Market Investigations Ltd v Minister of Social Security* [1969] 2 QB 173.

In *Ready Mixed Concrete (South East) Ltd v Minister of Pensions and National Insurance,*[16] the following criteria for the determination of a contract of service were put forward. First, the employee should agree that, in consideration of a wage or other remuneration, he will provide his own work and skill in the performance of some skill for his employer. Secondly, the employee agrees expressly or impliedly to be subject to his employer's control. Thirdly, the other provisions of the contract should be consistent with its being a contract of employment or service.[17]

The courts may take into account a number of tests, but the weight attached to each will depend on the facts of the case. If the parties have designated status in the contract by reference to words such as 'self-employed', and if the terms of the contract genuinely reflect self-employed status, the court will regard the contract as a contract for services. However, the parties cannot alter the truth of their relationship by the label they choose to place upon it.[18] It has been suggested that liability should be based on economic factors such as the relative risk-bearing capacity of the parties and the solvency of the employee.[19] As the objective of vicarious liability is to enable the plaintiff to satisfy his judgment, this would appear to supply a suitably pragmatic approach.

(b)   *Lending an employee*   The principles applicable where an employee is loaned to another employer were laid down in *Mersey Docks and Harbour Board v Coggins and Griffiths (Liverpool) Ltd.*[20] A employed B as a mobile crane driver and hired B and the crane to C. The contract between A and C provided that B should be the employee of C, but B was paid by A, who also had the power to dismiss. A person was injured because of B's negligent handling of the crane. The question was whether A or C was vicariously liable for B's negligence. The House of Lords laid down that a contract term is not decisive, and that the burden was on A as the permanent employer to show that C was B's employer. Where labour only is lent, the control test makes it easier to infer that the hirer is the employer. Where labour and plant is hired, it is more difficult to rebut the presumption, as the hirer may not have control of the way the plant is used. On the facts, A had failed to rebut the presumption, and remained B's employer for the purposes of vicarious liability.[1]

(c)   *Course of employment*   The employer will only be responsible for torts committed by the employee in the course of his employment. Whether a tort is committed in the course of employment is a question of fact which can produce irreconcilable cases. The courts have frequently used Salmond's definition that an act is in the course of employment:

> if it is either (1) a wrongful act authorised by the master, or (2) a wrongful and unauthorised mode of doing some act authorised by the master.[2]

On the basis of this definition, it is possible for an employer to be liable for an act which he has prohibited, if the prohibition applies to the way in which the job is done rather than the scope of the job itself. It follows that an employer of a bus driver is liable when the driver of the bus races other buses contrary to instructions.[3] A dairy

---

16   [1968] 2 QB 497.
17   [1968] 2 QB 497 at 515 (per MACKENNA J). See also *O'Kelly v Trusthouse Forte plc* [1983] 3 All ER 456.
18   *Massey v Crown Life Insurance Co* [1978] 2 All ER 576; *Ferguson v John Dawson & Partners (Contractors) Ltd* [1976] 3 All ER 817.
19   Sykes (1984) 17 Yale LJ 1231.
20   [1947] AC 1.
1   See Atiyah *Vicarious Liability in the Law of Torts* (1967) pp 171–285.
2   *Salmond and Heuston* p 521.
3   *Limpus v London General Omnibus Co Ltd* (1862) 1 H & C 526.

company is vicariously liable when a milkman, contrary to orders, carries on his milk float a child who is injured as a result of the milkman's negligent driving.[4] The employer of the driver of a petrol tanker is liable for a fire caused by the driver throwing a lighted match on the floor while delivering petrol.[5] In contrast, a bus conductor who attempts to drive a bus acts outside the scope of his employment.[6]

The modern trend is to interpret the scope of employment broadly, which creates difficulty in reconciling some of the older cases. For example, in two cases, it was held that a driver who carried an unauthorised passenger had acted outside the scope of his employment.[7] However, in *Rose v Plenty*,[8] a similar act was held to be within the scope of the employee's employment. The older cases could be distinguished as, in *Rose v Plenty*, the employee's act was in furtherance of the employer's business.[9]

Similar problems are encountered where a driver deviates from his prescribed route and is involved in an accident. In such a case, the employee may be on a 'frolic of his own'.[10] This test is inconclusive, as it does not say how a 'frolic' is to be determined. It also illustrates that the test is purely factual. If the employee merely uses an unauthorised route but is still on the employer's business, he is within the scope of his employment.[11] If the employee is on an unauthorised journey, this may take him outside the scope of his employment.[12]

Most journeys to and from work will be outside the course of employment unless the employee is on the employer's business. In *Smith v Stages*,[13] Stages and another employee were travelling to their homes in the Midlands after working in South Wales. Their car crashed and both men were injured. The House of Lords held that the men were in the employer's time and therefore within the course of employment. The employers paid travelling expenses and the men were paid for the day they travelled.

(d) *Employee's criminal conduct* Most examples of vicarious liability involve negligent conduct by the employee. But it is well established that an employer may be liable for the employee's criminal conduct. The original rule was that the employer would be liable where the crime was committed on his employer's behalf, but not where it was committed for the employee's benefit.[14] This restriction was rejected in *Lloyd v Grace, Smith & Co*,[15] where a solicitor's clerk was found to have acted within the scope of his employment when he fraudulently induced a client to convey properties to him. The crime was committed solely for the employee's benefit. Such liability will only attach where the employee acts within his actual or apparent authority.

(e) *Employer's indemnity* Employers and employees are treated as joint tortfeasors. The plaintiff may sue both of them, but in practice, it will normally be the employer who is proceeded against. By statute, the employer has the right to recover a complete indemnity from the employee for the damages he has had to pay to the plaintiff.[16] The

---

4   *Rose v Plenty* [1976] 1 All ER 97, [1976] 1 WLR 141.
5   *Century Insurance Co Ltd v Northern Ireland Road Transport Board* [1942] 1 All ER 491.
6   *Beard v London General Omnibus Co* [1900] 2 QB 530.
7   *Twine v Bean's Express Ltd* (1946) 62 TLR 458; *Conway v George Wimpey & Co Ltd* [1951] 2 KB 266.
8   [1976] 1 WLR 141.
9   Ibid at 144 (per LORD DENNING MR).
10 *Joel v Morrison* (1834) 6 C & P 501 at 503 (per PARKE B).
11 *A & W Hemphill Ltd v Williams* [1966] 2 Lloyd's Rep 101; *General Engineering Services Ltd v Kingston and Saint Andrew Corpn* [1988] 3 All ER 867.
12 *Storey v Ashton* (1869) LR 4 QB 476.
13 [1989] AC 928.
14 *Barwick v English Joint Stock Bank* (1867) LR 2 Exch 259.
15 [1912] AC 716. Cf *Morris v C W Martin & Sons Ltd* [1966] 1 QB 716.
16 Civil Liability (Contribution) Act 1978, s 1(1).

House of Lords has also created a common law right of indemnity on the basis of an implied contractual term. In *Lister v Romford Ice and Cold Storage Co Ltd*,[17] a driver knocked over his father who was acting as his mate on a lorry. The father recovered damages on the basis of the employer's vicarious liability for the driver's negligence. The damages were paid by the employer's insurers who, exercising their right of subrogation, brought proceedings against the driver for an indemnity. The House of Lords held, by a majority, that there was an implied term in the driver's contract of employment that he would perform his contractual duties with due care. No term could be implied that the driver was entitled to the benefit of any insurance taken out by his employer. The common law right to an indemnity will be lost where the employer is personally liable, or where he is liable due to the acts of other employees.[18] The employee may be able to recover a contribution in such a case.

The employer's right to an indemnity can be said to provide an incentive to employees to be safety conscious. However, it would also appear to conflict with the overall purposes of vicarious liability. There can be little point in placing the insurance burden on the employer and then allowing the insurer to recover the damages paid from the employee, who is not in such a favourable position to insure. The indemnity rule is also unlikely to lead to good industrial relations. These factors have been recognised in a 'gentleman's agreement' by employer's liability insurers that they will not pursue their rights to an indemnity under the *Lister* principle, unless there is evidence of collusion or misconduct. It would appear that the agreement is limited to the common law right of indemnity, and there is nothing to prevent an insurer from exercising his statutory right to an indemnity. The courts have demonstrated their hostility to subrogation in an industrial setting, and have gone to extremes to prevent its use.[19]

(f)   *Independent contractors*   An employer, generally, is not liable for the torts of his independent contractor. He can be liable if he has authorised the commission of a tort, in which case liability would be joint and not vicarious. The employer is also liable if he has failed to exercise due care in the selection of a contractor, or has failed to check that the work is properly performed.[20] The employer is also liable where he is in breach of a non-delegable duty. This may arise in relation to the tort of nuisance, the rule in *Rylands v Fletcher*[1] or in negligence. In *McDermid v Nash Dredging & Reclamation Co Ltd*,[2] the plaintiff was instructed by his employer, the defendant, to work on a tug owned by the defendant's parent company. Due to the negligence of the tug-master, the plaintiff suffered personal injuries. The House of Lords held that the defendant company was under a personal duty to provide a safe system of work and to operate it. This duty could not be delegated even to a person whom the defendant believed to be competent.

---

17   [1957] AC 555, [1957] 1 All ER 125. See Jolowicz [1957] CLJ 21.
18   *Jones v Manchester Corpn* [1952] 2 QB 852.
19   *Morris v Ford Motor Co Ltd* [1973] QB 792, [1973] 2 All ER 1084.
20   See Occupiers' Liability Act 1957, s 2(4)(b) and ch 28.
1   (1868) LR 3 HL 330.
2   [1987] AC 906; McKendrick (1990) 53 MLR 770.

Chapter 28

Liability arising out of land ownership and occupation I — premises

1. OCCUPIERS' LIABILITY TO ENTRANTS TO DEFECTIVE PREMISES

(1) INTRODUCTION

Until the late nineteenth century, land ownership was regarded as a source of rights rather than of obligations. An obligation was owed to neighbours through the law of nuisance, but a person who entered the land of another did so at his own risk. The occupier's only obligation was to refrain from wilfully injuring an entrant and, after the Peterloo Riots in 1819, the judiciary reluctantly conceded that he could not set mantraps for trespassers.

Reform came in the mid-nineteenth century[1] but, because of suspicion of juries who might not share the same conceptions of land ownership, a large degree of judicial control was retained. This was achieved by dividing entrants onto land into categories, each of which was owed a different duty. These categories included contractual entrants, invitees, licensees and trespassers. The strength of the duty was determined by the advantage which the entrant could bring to the occupier. The most favoured were contractual entrants, who had paid a price for their entry and were protected by a requirement of positive action on the part of the occupier.

Subsequently, the courts became entangled in the complexities of a set of fine distinctions intended to determine who was a lawful entrant. The courts seemed unable to adapt to changing social conditions, and were unable to bring this sub-category of negligence within the broad Atkinian principle of reasonable care.[2]

The inability of the House of Lords to reverse its own previous decisions until 1966 was partly responsible for the confusion. Following the Third Report of the Law Reform Committee,[3] Parliament passed the Occupiers' Liability Act 1957,[4] which now governs the law relating to entrants on premises, except for trespassers.

---

1   See *Indermaur v Dames* (1866) LR 1 CP 274 at 288 (per WILLES J).
2   See Fleming *Introduction* p 70.
3   (1954) Cmnd 9305.
4   This necessitated the reversal of the House of Lords' decisions in *Cavalier v Pope* [1906] AC 428; *London Graving Dock Co Ltd v Horton* [1951] AC 737 and *Thomson v Cremin* [1956] 1 WLR 103n.

(2)   LIABILITY TO VISITORS UNDER THE OCCUPIERS' LIABILITY ACT 1957

(i)   Scope of the Act

The Act applies not only to land and buildings, but also to fixed and moveable structures, including any vessel, vehicle or aircraft.[5] The Act has been held to apply to a digging machine used to construct a tunnel.[6] As well as applying to personal injuries suffered by the visitor, the Act extends to damage to property, including the property of persons not themselves visitors.[7]

Prior to the 1957 Act, a distinction had been drawn between the occupier's 'occupancy' duty and his 'activity' duty.[8] The courts had tended to confine the distinction between the various kinds of entrants to damage suffered as a result of the static condition of the premises. If the accident was caused by the occupier's activity, such as driving a vehicle, the ordinary law of negligence applied.[9] There is considerable controversy as to whether or not this distinction has been abolished by the Act.[10] Section 1(1) refers to 'dangers due to the state of the premises or things done or omitted to be done on them'. But section 1(2) refers to harm suffered 'in consequence of a person's occupation or control of premises'. The dispute is unlikely to be particularly significant, as the application of general negligence rules or the specific statutory rules is unlikely to produce a different result in the case of activity duties. If an occupier drives his car on his land, under ordinary negligence rules, he owes a duty to take reasonable care to all foreseeable victims of his negligent driving. Under the Act, he owes a duty to visitors to take 'such care as in all the circumstances of the case is reasonable ...'.[11] As one problem to be dealt with by the Act was the different duties owed to different classes of entrant, and this problem only arose in relation to the 'occupancy' duty, the view that the distinction survives is to be preferred.

(ii)   Who owes the duty?

The duty under the Act is imposed on the occupier, but there is no statutory definition of an occupier. The term occupier is misleading, since the duty rests on the person who controls the premises rather than on the physical occupier.

In *Wheat v E Lacon & Co Ltd*,[12] the defendants were the owners of a public house, which was run by a manager who had a licence to live on the first floor and take in paying guests for his own profit. The ground floor was used to sell alcohol. A paying guest was killed when he fell down an unlit staircase with a defective handrail. The House of Lords considered who was in occupation of that part of the premises by a construction of the agreement between the defendants and their manager. On the facts, the common duty of care was held not to have been broken, but it was also considered that the defendants had not divested themselves of control of any part of the building, and that they and the manager were both occupiers of a structure or part of it,[13] although

---

5   Occupiers' Liability Act 1957, s 1(3)(a).
6   *Bunker v Charles Brand & Son Ltd* [1969] 2 QB 480.
7   Occupiers' Liability Act 1957, s 1(3)(b). Cf Occupiers' Liability Act 1984, s 1(8).
8   See Newark (1954) 17 MLR 102 at 109.
9   *Slater v Clay Cross Co Ltd* [1956] 2 QB 264.
10   *Winfield and Jolowicz* pp 291–292; North *Occupiers' Liability* (1971) pp 80–82 and Odgers [1957] CLJ 39–40. Cf *Salmond and Heuston* pp 266–267. See also *British Railways Board v Herrington* [1972] AC 877 at 929 and 942.
11   Occupiers' Liability Act 1957, s 2(2).
12   [1966] AC 552.
13   See also *Fisher v C H T Ltd (No 2)* [1966] 2 QB 475.

the duty required of each might be different.[14] An owner in possession is an occupier, but it is not necessary for a person to have an estate in the land to be treated as such.[15] In contrast, a landlord who parts with possession on a demise will normally relinquish control, but if he retains control of a common staircase or entrance hall, he will owe a duty of care.[16]

Physical possession of the premises is not necessary. In *Harris v Birkenhead Corpn*,[17] the local authority had served a notice to treat and a notice of entry before making a compulsory purchase order on the premises in question. The property was damaged by vandals before the authority had taken steps to secure it, and a child was injured on the premises. The local authority, not the previous owner, was held to be the occupier, as control had passed to the authority. The emphasis on control is justified on the ground that the controller of premises is in the best position to prevent accidents.

(iii)   A duty to whom?

(a)   *Lawful visitors*   The common duty of care is owed to all the occupier's lawful visitors.[18] The distinction between invitees and licensees is therefore abolished,[19] and the common duty of care will now be owed to a contractual entrant who is owed no express contractual duty of care.[20] Trespassers were excluded from the provisions of the Act, and continued to be dealt with by common law rules and now by the Occupiers' Liability Act 1984.

Persons who enter premises under a right conferred by law, such as policemen or firemen, are treated as visitors, whether or not they have the occupier's permission to enter.[1] Employees of public utility companies also come within this category of entrant. However, a person who exceeds his power of entry may be regarded as a trespasser.[2] A person using a public right of way was not treated as a licensee or invitee, and it was held in *Greenhalgh v British Railways Board*[3] that section 2(6) of the 1957 Act had not extended the range of persons who could be treated as lawful visitors.[4] A user of a private right of way is now owed a duty under the Occupiers' Liability Act 1984.

(b)   *Implied permission*   At the time when the obligation owed to a trespasser was minimal, the success of the plaintiff's action would frequently depend on whether or not he was classified as a trespasser. In marginal cases, the courts would be prepared to find an implied permission to enter. In *Lowery v Walker*,[5] people regularly used the defendant's unfenced land as a short-cut. The defendant took no serious steps to prevent this, as most were his customers. Subsequently, the defendant allowed on his land a wild horse, which attacked the plaintiff who was taking the short-cut. The plaintiff was held not to be a trespasser and was able to recover.

14   See *A M F International Ltd v Magnet Bowling* [1968] 1 WLR 1028.
15   *Humphreys v Dreamland (Margate) Ltd* (1930) 144 LT 529.
16   *Liverpool City Council v Irwin* [1976] QB 319.
17   [1975] 1 WLR 379. See also *Bunker v Charles Brand & Sons Ltd* [1969] 2 QB 480.
18   Occupiers' Liability Act 1957, s 1(2).
19   See Law Reform Committee (1954) Cmnd 9305, para 78(1) and (1958) 21 MLR 359 at 360.
20   Occupiers' Liability Act 1957, s 5(1). A contractual entrant can frame his action in tort *Sole v W J Hallt & Co Ltd* [1973] QB 574. Cf Winfield [1973] CLJ 209.
1   Occupiers' Liability Act 1957, s 2(6).
2   *Darling v A-G* [1950] 2 All ER 793.
3   [1969] 2 QB 286; *McGeown v Northern Ireland Housing Executive* [1995] 1 AC 233. See Barker & Parry (1995) LS 335.
4   The provisions of the Occupiers' Liability Act 1984 apply to National Park entrants and to persons entering land in pursuance of an access agreement (s 1(1)(a)) but not to persons using the highway (s 1(7)).
5   [1911] AC 10. Cf *Great Central Rly v Bates* [1921] 3 KB 578.

This willingness to find an implied licence or permission was particularly strong in the case of children,[6] but signs of judicial caution had appeared before the law on trespassers was altered in 1972.[7]

The effect of the Occupiers' Liability Act 1984 on the law relating to trespassers is to reduce to insignificance the number of cases where implied permission will be necessary. There is now very little difference between the position of a child trespasser, whom the occupier knows or ought to know to be present, and a child visitor. What is clear is that a person has an implied licence to walk up to the door of premises and state his business. The occupier may revoke his licence by asking him to leave within a reasonable time. After this, the entrant becomes a trespasser.[8] This would apply to salesmen, political canvassers or Jehovah's Witnesses. The presumption of an implied licence could be rebutted by displaying a notice specifically prohibiting entry.[9]

Finally, it is clear that the duty is only owed in respect of those parts of the building which the visitor is permitted to enter. If he goes beyond his permission, he will become a trespasser.[10] Any usage incidental to that permitted will be covered. Thus a person entering a public house will be entitled to use the toilet.

(iv)   What is the duty?

The common duty of care is owed by the occupier to all lawful visitors. Section 2(2) provides:

> The common duty of care is a duty to take such care as in all the circumstances of the case is reasonable to see that the visitor will be reasonably safe in using the premises for the purposes for which he is invited or permitted by the occupier to be there.

Whether this duty has been broken is a question of fact in each case, and factors applicable to the standard of care in ordinary cases of negligence will be applicable.[11] It is the visitor and not the premises that must be made reasonably safe. If a football stadium has loose concrete lying around and this is thrown at police officers by football hooligans, then the occupier may be liable as this is a foreseeable result of the occupier's breach of duty.[12] The Act gives specific guidance on two special factors.

(a)   *Persons entering in the exercise of a calling*   Section 2(3)(b) provides that:

> an occupier may expect that a person, in the exercise of his calling, will appreciate and guard against any special risks ordinarily incident to it, so far as the occupier leaves him free to do so.

In *Roles v Nathan*,[13] two chimney sweeps were killed by carbon monoxide gas while attempting to seal a sweep hole in the chimney of an operating coke-fired boiler. The occupier was held not liable for the deaths, as section 2(3)(b) applied. In *General Cleaning Contractors Ltd v Christmas*,[14] the occupier was held not liable to a window cleaner who

---

6   See *Cooke v Midland Great Western Rly of Ireland* [1909] AC 229.
7   *Edwards v Railway Executive* [1952] AC 737; *Phipps v Rochester Corpn* [1955] 1 QB 450.
8   *Robson v Hallett* [1967] 2 QB 939.
9   *Christian v Johannesson* [1956] NZLR 664 at 666. See also Law Reform Committee (1954) Cmnd 9305, para 67.
10   See *The Calgarth* [1927] P 93 at 110 (per SCRUTTON LJ) and the Occupiers' Liability Act 1957, s 2(2).
11   See ch 12.
12   *Cunningham v Reading Football Club Ltd* [1992] 1 PIQR P141.
13   [1963] 1 WLR 1117.
14   [1953] AC 180.

was injured through the insecurity of part of the exterior of the premises. The window cleaner was expected to guard against the special risks ordinarily incident to his calling.

The calling of a visitor is not, in itself, a defence where the occupier has failed to exercise the required standard of care. For example, a fireman who has exercised reasonable care in an attempt to extinguish a fire negligently started by the occupier of premises will still be able to recover against the occupier if he is injured in the course of exercising his calling.[15]

(b)   *Children*   Section 2(3)(a) provides: 'an occupier must be prepared for children to be less careful than adults.'
If an occupier allows a child to enter his premises, he must take the child's characteristics into account. In *Moloney v Lambeth London Borough Council*,[16] a four-year-old child fell through the bars of a ballustrade. An adult could not have squeezed through the gap but, because of the child's age and size, the occupier was held not to have discharged his duty of care. In *Glasgow Corpn v Taylor*,[17] a seven-year-old child died after eating poisonous berries from a tree in a public park. The tree was not fenced and no warning was given. The defendants were held liable.

In the case of very young children, an occupier may discharge the duty by ensuring that the premises are safe for a child accompanied by the sort of guardian whom the occupier is, in the circumstances, entitled to expect him to have. In *Phipps v Rochester Corpn*,[18] the five-year-old plaintiff was injured while out with his seven-year-old sister. The plaintiff was injured in circumstances which an adult could have avoided. As the occupier was entitled to expect a five-year-old to be accompanied by an adult, he was not liable. If the child's injury can be attributed to the negligence of both the occupier and the guardian, the occupier will be able to recover a contribution from the guardian.[19]

(c)   *Warnings*   Section 2(4)(a) provides:

> where damage is caused to a visitor by a danger of which he had been warned by the occupier, the warning is not to be treated without more as absolving the occupier from liability, unless in all the circumstances, it was enough to enable the visitor to be reasonably safe.[20]

It is clear from this section that a warning of a danger, given to the visitor, may discharge the duty if it enables him to be reasonably safe. Whether a warning has this effect is a question of fact in each case, and the warning will not automatically discharge the duty.[1]
For example, a notice at a railway station ticket office which warns passengers that repair work is being carried out on the roof may not serve to discharge the duty. However, if part of the concourse is roped off and a notice is prominently displayed which requires passengers not to enter that area, the duty may have been discharged. It may be that the danger is so obvious that no warning is necessary. An adult does not have to be warned that it is dangerous to go near to the edge of an obvious cliff.[2] The warning may discharge the duty of care, or it may exclude liability for the consequences of its breach.[3]

15   *Salmon v Seafarer Restaurants* [1983] 1 WLR 1264; *Ogwo v Taylor* [1988] AC 431.
16   (1966) 198 Estates Gazette 895.
17   [1922] 1 AC 44.
18   [1955] 1 QB 450.
19   *Simkiss v Rhondda Borough Council* (1982) 81 LGR 460.
20   Reversing *London Graving Dock Co Ltd v Horton* [1951] AC 737.
1   *Roles v Nathan* [1963] 1 WLR 1117; *Bunker v Charles Brand & Sons Ltd* [1969] 2 QB 480.
2   *Cotton v Derbyshire Dales DC* (1994) Times, 20 June.
3   See *White v Blackmore* [1972] 2 QB 651. See also ch 21.

(d)   *Independent contractors*   A problem frequently arises where injury is caused to a visitor by contractors working on other people's premises. The contractor may be an occupier if he has sufficient control of the premises. Furthermore, he may be liable under ordinary principles of negligence to a foreseeable victim of his negligence. The issue is whether the occupier can discharge his common duty of care by entrusting work to an independent contractor. Section 2(4)(b) provides:

> Where damage is caused to a visitor by a danger due to the faulty execution of any work of construction, maintenance or repair[4] by an independent contractor employed by the occupier, the occupier is not to be treated without more as answerable for the danger if in all the circumstances he had acted reasonably in entrusting the work to an independent contractor and had taken such steps (if any) as he reasonably ought in order to satisfy himself that the contractor was competent and the work had been properly done.[5]

In order to discharge the common duty of care, the occupier must have acted reasonably in entrusting the work to an independent contractor, and have selected the particular contractor with reasonable care.[6] If possible, the work must be properly supervised and checked when it is completed. If the job is of a technical nature, the occupier may have discharged the duty by entrusting it to a competent contractor. In *Haseldine v CA Daw & Son Ltd*,[7] the plaintiff visited a tenant in a block of flats belonging to the defendant, and was injured when a lift fell to the bottom of its shaft. The accident happened as a result of the negligence of a firm of engineers employed by the defendant to maintain and repair the lift. By employing a reputable firm of engineers, the defendant was held to have discharged the common duty of care owed to the plaintiff. Because of the technical nature of the work, the defendant could not have been expected to check its satisfactory completion. However, in *AMF International v Magnet Bowling*,[8] it was suggested that, if the work is complex as in the case of the construction of a large building or a ship, the occupier may be required to have the contractor's work supervised by a properly qualified professional, such as an architect or surveyor. Likewise in *Woodward v Hastings Corpn*,[9] the defendants were liable where a school cleaner left an icy step in a dangerous condition. It would have been possible for the job to have been checked.[10]

(v)   Defences

There are three possible defences to an action under the 1957 Act. Although the Act does not specifically mention contributory negligence, it is implicit in section 2(3) that, where the occupier is in breach of the common duty of care and the visitor fails to take reasonable care for his own safety, damages will be reduced under the Law Reform (Contributory Negligence) Act 1945.[11]

Section 2(5) provides that, while knowledge of a danger does not, of itself, deprive the visitor of a remedy, the occupier will not be liable in respect of risks willingly accepted by the visitor.[12]

---

4   See *AMF International Ltd v Magnet Bowling Ltd* [1968] 1 WLR 1028 at 1043 (per MOCATTA J).
5   Reversing *Thomson v Cremin* [1953] 2 All ER 1185.
6   See *Ferguson v Welsh* [1987] 3 All ER 777.
7   [1941] 2 KB 343.
8   *AMF International Ltd v Magnet Bowling Ltd* [1968] 1 WLR 1028 at 1044 (per MOCATTA J).
9   [1945] KB 174.
10   Ibid at 183 (per DU PARCQ LJ).
11   *Stone v Taffe* [1974] 1 WLR 1575
12   See *Roles v Nathan* [1963] 1 WLR 1117; North *Occupiers' Liability Act* (1971) p 115.

By section 2(1), an occupier can extend, exclude, restrict or modify the extent of his liability[13] by a contract term or by a properly worded notice.[14] Liability may also be restricted by bye-laws and by statutory authority.

There are now three occasions on which the occupier of premises cannot exclude the common duty of care. The first is where a visitor enters premises under a right conferred by law.[15] Secondly, a contract with one person, for example a builder, cannot limit the duty owed to others,[16] such as the builder's employees. Thirdly, the Unfair Contract Terms Act 1977 significantly restricts the ability to exclude liability where premises are used in the course of a business.[17] The 1977 Act renders void a purported exclusion of liability for negligence causing death or bodily injury,[18] and subjects to a requirement of reasonableness any purported exclusion of liability in respect of harm other than death or bodily injury.[19] An occupier of premises is also provided with a defence where the visitor has voluntarily encountered an existing risk of injury.[20]

Finally, it should be noted that, where an occupier succeeds in discharging the common duty of care by means of a warning, the 1977 Act would appear to have no application, as section 2 of the Act is limited to notices excluding liability for breach. With an effective warning, there has been no breach.

(3)   LIABILITY TO TRESPASSERS

(i)   Introduction

The ownership of land used to be regarded as a source of privilege but, due to changing social attitudes in the twentieth century, land-ownership has now become a source of duties. This change is well illustrated by the issues of an occupier's liability towards trespassers.

The traditional hostility of the common law towards trespassers is illustrated in *Robert Addie & Sons (Collieries) Ltd v Dumbreck*,[1] which represented the law until 1972 and in which it was held that a trespasser entered the property of another at his own risk. The sole duty of the occupier was not to intentionally or recklessly harm a trespasser known to be on the land. Judicial ingenuity managed to avoid the harshness of the rule in the case of child trespassers by treating many of them as lawful visitors through the rules on implied licences and allurements, that is, something inherently attractive such as poisonous berries.[2] A later judicial development was to apply a test of foreseeability to current activities as opposed to the static condition of the property,[3] but this was disapproved of by the Privy Council.[4]

The House of Lords reconsidered the issue in *British Railways Board v Herrington*,[5] taking into account changing social conditions, such as increased dangers, particularly

---

13   *Simms v Leigh Rugby Football Club Ltd* [1969] 2 All ER 923; *Bunker v Charles Brand & Son Ltd* [1969] 2 QB 480 at 488–489. See also ch 21.

14   Giving statutory authority to *Ashdown v Samuel Williams & Sons Ltd* [1957] 1 QB 409. See also Gower (1956) 19 MLR 536.

15   See *Winfield and Jolowicz* p 307.

16   Occupiers' Liability Act 1957, s 3(1).

17   Unfair Contract Terms Act 1977, ss 1(3), 14. See Mesher (1979) Conv 58; Jones (1984) 47 MLR 713 at 726 and see also ch 24.

18   Unfair Contract Terms Act 1977, s 2(1).

19   Ibid, s 2(2).

20   Ibid, s 2(3).

1   [1929] AC 358.

2   See *Glasgow Corpn v Taylor* [1922] 1 AC 44.

3   *Videan v British Transport Commission* [1963] 2 QB 650.

4   *Railways Comr v Quinlan* [1964] AC 1054.

5   [1972] AC 877, [1972] 1 All ER 749.

to children, resulting from industrialisation. They held that an occupier owes a duty of common humanity to trespassers which, in the case of child trespassers, appeared to be indistinguishable from a duty to exercise reasonable care. The common humanity test granted a remedy to a child trespasser injured on an inadequately fenced railway line,[6] to a child burned while playing on an unsupervised building site,[7] to a child electrocuted by a power line passing within five feet of an embankment,[8] and to a child injured whilst playing in an unsecured and unoccupied house.[9]

The gist of the duty was that the trespasser had to take the occupier, rather than the land, as he found him. A subjective standard of care was imposed, based on the gravity of the danger, the likelihood of the trespasser's presence and the occupier's wealth and resources.

Herrington's case was speedily referred to the Law Commission, who concluded that, as no clear principle emerged from it, legislative action was necessary.[10] This conclusion is puzzling, as the courts do not appear to have had any difficulty applying the decision. However, the Occupiers' Liability Act 1984 was passed, which now governs the legal position of trespassers.

(ii)   The parties to the action under the Occupiers' Liability Act 1984[11]

The Occupiers' Liability Act 1984, section 1(1)(a) provides that the duty is owed by the occupier of premises, who is defined as a person who owes the common duty of care as defined for the purposes of the Occupiers' Liability Act 1957.[12]

The duty is owed to persons other than visitors.[13] These include trespassers, persons exercising private rights of way,[14] and persons exercising public rights of access, including entrants to national parks. The duty is not owed to persons exercising a public right of way, and persons using a publicly maintained highway will continue to be governed by the ordinary rules of negligence.[15] If the highway is not publicly maintained, the highway owner is liable for poor repairs but not for failure to repair.[16]

(iii)   When does the duty exist?

Once the relationship of occupier and visitor is established, the common duty of care under the Occupiers' Liability Act 1957, section 2(2) is owed. But, if the relationship of occupier and trespasser is established, there is no automatic duty owed under the 1984 Act, section 1(3) of which provides that an occupier of premises owes a duty of care to a trespasser if:

(a)   he is aware of the danger or has reasonable grounds to believe it exists;

(b)   he knows or has reasonable grounds to believe that the other is in the vicinity of the danger concerned or that he may come into the vicinity of the danger (in either case, whether the other has lawful authority for being in that vicinity or not); and

---

6   *British Railways Board v Herrington* [1972] AC 877.
7   *Pannett v P McGuiness & Co Ltd* [1972] 2 QB 599, [1972] 3 All ER 87.
8   *Southern Portland Cement Ltd v Cooper* [1974] AC 623, [1974] 1 All ER 87.
9   *Harris v Birkenhead Corpn* [1975] 1 All ER 1001, [1976] 1 WLR 279.
10   Law Commission No 75 (1976) Cmnd 6428; see also Royal Commission on Civil Liability and Compensation for Personal Injuries (1978) Cmnd 7054, Vol 1, ch 28.
11   See Buckley (1984) Conv 413.
12   Occupiers' Liability Act 1984, s 1(2). See also *Wheat v Lacon* [1966] AC 552.
13   Ibid, s 1(1)(a).
14   *Holden v White* [1982] QB 679.
15   Occupiers' Liability Act 1984, s 1(7).
16   See Highways Act 1980.

(c)   the risk is one against which, in all the circumstances of the case, he may reasonably
       be expected to offer the other some protection.

The Occupiers' Liability (Scotland) Act 1960 which covers visitors and trespassers
contains no similar provision, and no problems appear to have been encountered with
its operation. It must be asked whether any cases are excluded by the operation of
section 1(3), which would have been covered by a straightforward application of the
duty to take reasonable care.[17]

The duty owed to trespassers covers only death and personal injuries,[18] whereas the
duty owed to a visitor also encompasses loss of, or damage to, property. The scope of
the duty owed to trespassers is governed by the Occupiers' Liability Act 1984, section
1(1)(a), which covers risk of injury caused by reason of a danger due to the state of the
premises or things done or omitted to be done on them. It is not clear whether this
covers the occupancy duty to the exclusion of the activity duty,[19] although it has been
said that the duty is confined to the liability of an occupier as an occupier and would
therefore not apply to a case where an occupier shot a burglar.[20] However, the factors
involved in determining the scope of the duty owed should be the same as those in
section 1. Since the same uncertainty applies to the Occupiers' Liability Act 1957, the
same must also be said of the 1984 Act. The duty owed to trespassers can be discharged
by an appropriate warning or by discouraging people from incurring the risk.[1] Whether
such a warning is effective will depend on the age of the entrant, the character of entry
and the nature of the risk. A warning notice or an oral warning would normally be
sufficient for adults but, in the case of children, obstacles to entry may have to be erected.

(iv)   What is the duty?

If a duty is owed, the standard of reasonable care in all the circumstances of the case
applies.[2] The circumstances will include the nature and character of the entry, the age
of the entrant, the nature of the premises and the extent of the risk. The precautions
to be taken by the occupier will be objectively measured against whether the risk
justified the cost. This contrasts with the 'common humanity' standard which was
subjective in that the occupier only had to take precautions which, with his particular
skill and resources, he could be expected to take.

Most of the decided cases on trespassers involve children, but the Act applies equally
to adults, for example a burglar. In *Revill v Newbery*[3] the defendant occupier shot the
plaintiff who was trying to break into his shed. Previous thefts had occurred, which
was why the defendant was waiting in the shed. The Court of Appeal decided that the
Act did not apply and proceeded at common law but on the same lines as section 1.
They held that the plaintiff satisfied section 1(3)(b) but they did not address section
1(3)(c) as to whether it was a risk against which, in all the circumstances of the case, the
defendant might reasonably be expected to offer the burglar some protection. The
fact that the plaintiff was a burglar did not mean that he was an outlaw and therefore
ex turpi causa did not apply. Damages were reduced by two-thirds for contributory
negligence. The extreme facts in *Revill* undoubtedly affected the decision and it is unlikely

---

17   Law Commission No 75 (1976) Cmnd 6428, para 28.
18   Occupiers' Liability Act 1984, s 1(8).
19   Law Commission No 75 (1976) Cmnd 6428, para 23 concludes that the 1957 Act does not apply to
      the activity duty.
20   *Revill v Newbery* [1996] QB 567.
1   Occupiers' Liability Act 1984, s 1(5).
2   Ibid, s 1(4).
3   [1996] 1 All ER 291.

that protection would be given to a burglar who broke his leg by falling through a defective floorboard.

(v)   Defences

(a)   *Volenti non fit injuria*   Section 1(6) of the 1984 Act provides that *volenti* is a defence. In the case of trespassers, an objective test of agreement is applied, with the result that an adult who enters premises with knowledge of the risk of harm will be considered to be *volens* to the risk.

(b)   *Exclusion*   The 1984 Act is silent on the matter of exclusion of liability, despite suggestions that provisions for this should have been made.[4] There was some doubt as to whether the Unfair Contract Terms Act 1977 applied to the common humanity test, as that could be regarded as a minimum non-excludable duty.[5] The wording of the Unfair Contract Terms Act indicates that it cannot apply to the Occupiers' Liability Act 1984,[6] with the result that a lawful visitor to business premises may be in a worse position than a trespasser if the duty to the latter is not capable of exclusion.[7]

2.   OWNERS' AND OCCUPIERS' LIABILITY TO NEIGHBOURS

(1)   INTRODUCTION

Expanding negligence liability has raised the question whether a landowner owes a duty of care to an adjoining occupier to secure his land against the entry of trespassers who may damage the neighbour's property. The problem is part of the wider question whether a person owes a duty of care to prevent third parties causing damage.[8]

(2)   UNSECURED PREMISES

If the defendant's premises are left unsecured and thieves enter in order to gain access to the plaintiff's property, a duty of care may not be owed. In *P Perl (Exporters) Ltd v Camden London Borough Council*,[9] the defendants were aware of the lack of security and burglaries had taken place on their own premises, but they had taken no steps to provide security. The Court of Appeal held that the plaintiff should fail. Although it was foreseeable that thieves might gain access to the plaintiff's property through the defendants' property, the defendants were not bound to foresee that, as a natural and probable consequence of their failure to secure, persons over whom they had no control would steal the plaintiff's goods. If the defendants did have control over the trespasser, the result might have been different. A second problem arises where empty premises are entered by trespassers and damage is caused to the plaintiff's property by fire or flood resulting from the trespasser's activities. In *King v Liverpool City Council*,[10] the plaintiff was a tenant in a block of flats owned by the defendants. The flat above the plaintiff's became vacant and, despite his requests for it to be boarded up, nothing was done.

---

4   Law Commission No 75 (1976) Cmnd 6428, Appendix A, Draft Bill Clause 3.
5   Ibid, para 60; Coote (1975) 125 NLJ 752.
6   Unfair Contract Terms Act 1977, s 1(1)(b) and (c) refer to 'common law duties' and 'the statutory duty' under the Occupiers' Liability Act 1957.
7   Jones (1984) 47 MLR 714 at 724.
8   See *Home Office v Dorset Yacht Co Ltd* [1970] 2 All ER 294 and ch 8.
9   [1983] 3 All ER 161.
10   [1986] 3 All ER 544, [1986] 1 WLR 890.

Vandals broke in and damaged water pipes on three occasions, and the water escaped to the plaintiff's flat, causing damage. The defendants were held not liable, as it was not possible to take effective steps to defeat the vandals' actions, therefore no duty of care was owed. These cases were reconsidered by the House of Lords in *Smith v Littlewoods Organisation Ltd.*[11] The defendants had purchased a cinema with the intention of demolishing it and building a supermarket. The building was left empty and unattended, and a fire started in it, which seriously damaged the plaintiff's property. The plaintiff's action failed. Cases in which a duty of care would exist in these circumstances were said to be rare. Each case would turn on its own circumstances and on socially accepted standards of behaviour, but here, the defendants had not known of the previous acts of vandalism, and the cinema itself did not present an obvious fire risk.

The cases show a judicial unwillingness to place on occupiers a heavy burden of responsibility to secure premises. A comparable situation which has received a different response can be found in the law of nuisance, where an occupier may be liable for nuisances created by trespassers or acts of nature.[12] However, before nuisance law is applicable, there must be a state of affairs on the defendant's land which amounts to a nuisance. Where burglars are concerned, this is not the case, unless the occupier discovers their presence and fails to act. However, fire and similar hazards can constitute a nuisance. In *King v Liverpool City Council*,[13] nuisance was argued at first instance, but failed because no reasonable precautions could avoid the problem.

A strong policy issue underlies these cases, namely that persons in the position of the plaintiffs should be insured against the consequences of a burglary.[14] If such persons are not insured, it is reasonable to allow them to take the risk of loss. Only in rare cases of obvious neglect by the defendant will a duty of care be said to exist. In cases like *King v Liverpool City Council*,[15] the plaintiff was much less likely to be insured against the type of loss which was suffered, but the difficulties faced by the defendants in counteracting vandalism persuaded the court that no such duty should be owed.[16]

3.   BUILDERS' LIABILITY

(1)   INTRODUCTION

(i)   Plaintiffs and defendants

The liability of an occupier of premises to his visitors is based on his control of those premises. However, it may be the case that harm is caused by a defect in a building created by the builder, who does not have the same control.

The term 'builder' includes all persons involved in the construction and sale of buildings, such as the builder and his sub-contractor, development companies, suppliers of materials, architects, surveyors, engineers and local authorities.

The process of house construction normally involves the purchase of land by a development company which engages a builder to construct the properties. The buildings may be designed by an architect, and the site may be subjected to a geological survey to determine suitability for building purposes. Plans must be lodged with the local authority, who have powers to reject, approve or alter them, and to carry out on-site

---

11   [1987] AC 241.
12   *Sedleigh-Denfield v O'Callaghan* [1940] 3 All ER 349; *Goldman v Hargrave* [1967] 1 AC 645; *Leakey v National Trust for Places of Historic Interest or National Beauty* [1980] 1 All ER 17.
13   [1986] 3 All ER 544.
14   *Lamb v Camden London Borough Council* [1981] QB 625.
15   [1986] 3 All ER 544.
16   Ibid at 522 (per PURCHAS LJ).

inspections to ensure conformity with the plans. Building Regulations prescribe minimum standards of public health and safety. Once completed, the house will be sold by the development company, but there may also be subsequent purchasers from the first buyer. There may be variations on this pattern. For example, there might not be a development company if the builder sells the house himself, or a house may be built to the special order of the purchaser on the purchaser's own land.

If a building is dangerous, the owner, his family and guests, as well as neighbours and passers-by may be injured. If the property is simply defective, the only person to suffer damage will be one with a property interest, but this damage is pecuniary in nature. The damage suffered may be remediable in an action for breach of contract. Thus, the first purchaser can proceed against the development company or builder in this way, so long as the writ is issued within the appropriate limitation period, which runs for six years from the date of the breach of contract.[17] Other participants in the building process will not be parties to a contract with the purchaser, who must seek any possible remedy elsewhere. Likewise, subsequent purchasers will be denied an action for breach of contract due to the doctrine of privity of contract. The subsequent purchaser is also unlikely to have any action against the person who sold him the property because, in relation to the state of the building, the doctrine of *caveat emptor*[18] retains a tight hold. A further problem with a contractual action is that the development company or builder may have gone into liquidation.[19]

The most important protection for purchasers of new houses is probably the National House Building Council scheme. The NHBC scheme applies to registered builders and developers. Once registered, the builder must construct to NHBC standards and allow the work to be inspected. For a consideration of five pence, the purchaser receives the House Purchasers' Agreement from the vendor. This warrants that the dwelling has been or will be built in an efficient and workman-like manner and of proper materials so that it will be fit for human habitation. Substance is given to this by the vendor agreeing to remedy, at his own expense, any defect reported within the first two years, where the defect arises from a breach of the NHBC standards. The buyer and subsequent purchasers also receive the benefit of the NHBC insurance policy which covers the case where the vendor fails to remedy the defect. The policy also covers major damage to the dwelling which occurs between two and ten years of the date of completion. The scheme has the dual advantage of ensuring high building standards and that a reasonably speedy remedy is available when those standards are not met.

(ii)   Historical development of liability

The history of liability for defective premises has been dominated by the law of contract and the supposed rule emerging from *Winterbottom v Wright*,[20] that only a party to a contract could sue on it and that the only duties created by the contract were between the contracting parties.[1] In *Bottomley v Bannister*,[2] it was held that the builder of a house is liable only for breach of contract. The view that there was no liability in tort was justified on the basis that there was no 'duty in the air ... a duty to undertake that no one shall suffer from one's carelessness'.[3] The House of Lords subsequently held that

---

17   Limitation Act 1980, s 5. See also ch 19.
18   See ch 3.
19   See the remarks on the instability of the building trade in *Dennis v Charnwood Borough Council* [1983] QB 409 at 423 (per LAWTON LJ).
20   (1842) 10 M & W 109.
1   See *Dutton v Bognor Regis UDC* [1972] 1 QB 373 at 392–393 (per LORD DENNING MR).
2   [1932] 1 KB 458.
3   Ibid at 476.

there was such a duty in connection with defective products,[4] but this decision was held not to apply to realty.[5]

The steady advance of the tort of negligence rendered this situation untenable. It was held that a building contractor who was not an occupier was liable on ordinary negligence principles to a lawful visitor.[6] In the case of trespassers, it was held that the status of the plaintiff was irrelevant to an action against a contractor.[7] *Dicta* in *British Railways Board v Herrington*[8] pointed to the removal of the distinction between occupiers and non-occupiers in this respect. But it is submitted that the Occupiers' Liability Act 1984, section 1(2)(a) preserves the previously stated view. In *Sharpe v ET Sweeting & Sons Ltd,*[9] it was decided that a builder would owe a duty of care as long as he had not been the owner of the property.

At this stage, a builder could be held liable to a foreseeable victim of his negligent work who suffered personal injuries, but not if he had been the owner of the land, when he enjoyed immunity. The problem was referred to the Law Commission,[10] which led to the passing of the Defective Premises Act 1972.

(2) MODERN BUILDERS' LIABILITY

(i)   Contractual liability

In the case of an ordinary sale between individuals, the maxim, *caveat emptor*, retains a firm hold. The onus lies on the purchaser to discover faults in the property before exchanging contracts by commissioning a survey. It is possible to seek an express assurance of fitness, but such contract terms are rare and, in any case, a purported exclusion of liability in this respect is not covered by the Unfair Contract Terms Act 1977.[11] Alternatively, an action may lie for the misrepresentation of the vendor or his agent, in which case purported exclusions of liability are subject to the Unfair Contract Terms Act.[12]

In some instances, the vendor is also the builder of the property. There may be express terms in the contract but, normally, there is no detailed specification of the dwelling. Where the house has yet to be completed, it is well established that there is a three-part warranty on the part of the builder, namely, that the house will be built in a good and workman-like manner; that the house will be built of proper materials and that the house will be fit for human habitation.[13] In the case of commercial buildings, the warranty of fitness does not apply, but it would appear that the remaining parts of the warranty are applicable, and a term will be implied that the building will be reasonably fit for any purpose known to be intended.[14]

The implied term which imposes strict liability[15] will only avail the first purchaser. Similarly, the first purchaser is the only person able to take advantage of the six-year limitation period running from the date the defective work was carried out.

4   *Donoghue v Stevenson* [1932] AC 562.
5   *Otto v Bolton and Norris* [1936] 2 KB 46.
6   *AC Billings & Sons Ltd v Riden* [1958] AC 240.
7   *Buckland v Guildford Gas Light and Coke Co* [1949] 1 KB 410.
8   *British Railways Board v Herrington* [1972] AC 877 at 914, and 943.
9   [1963] 1 WLR 665.
10 Law Commission Report on Civil Liability of Vendors and Lessors for Defective Premises (1970) Law Com No 40.
11 Unfair Contract Terms Act 1977, Sch 1, para 1(b).
12 Misrepresentation Act 1967, s 3 (as substituted by the Unfair Contract Terms Act 1977, s 8). See also ch 24.
13 *Miller v Cannon Hill Estates Ltd* [1931] 2 KB 113.
14 *IBA v EMI Electronics Ltd* (1980) 14 BLR 1.
15 *Hancock v B W Brazier (Anerley) Ltd* [1966] 1 WLR 1317; *Young and Marten Ltd v McManus Childs Ltd* [1969] 1 AC 454.

(ii)   Statutory liability

The Defective Premises Act 1972 applies only to dwellings and not to commercial or industrial properties. Section 1(1) imposes on builders, sub-contractors, architects and other professional persons a duty to ensure that building work is done in accordance with the three implied terms of workman-like manner, proper materials and fitness for habitation. The section applies to nonfeasance as well as to misfeasance.[16] Failure to fit a damp course would result in the dwelling being unfit for human habitation, as would a flat conversion with no gas or electricity.[17] This duty is owed to the person to whose order the building is provided, and every person who acquires an interest in the dwelling. The section sweeps aside the contractual privity limitation previously applicable at common law. Subsequent purchasers now have a theoretical action against the builder/ developer. However, the duty does not apply where the dwelling is protected by an 'approved' scheme.[18] In practice this meant the NHBC scheme which applied to nearly all new houses and thereby limited section 1 to alterations and conversions.[19]

However, it now appears that the scheme has not been effective since 1988 as a result of changes made to the scheme by the NHBC.[20] This means that if a house was built after 1987 under the NHBC scheme owners may take proceedings under section 1.

The advantages of section 1, where it does apply, are that liability is strict, and that the duty cannot be excluded.[1] The test for causation is whether the breach is a significant cause of, or factor in, the buildings' unfitness.[2] The measure of damages is all losses naturally consequent on the breach, not merely the diminution in value or cost of cure.[3] The relevant limitation period runs for six years from the date on which the dwelling was completed,[4] which means that in most cases the plaintiff will be out of time before any defect is discovered. Section 3 of the Act serves to remove the builder's immunity from a negligence action but, by the time the Act was in force, the courts had already taken this step.

(iii)   Tortious liability

In the 1970s the courts embarked on an extension of the builder's liability in negligence.[5] It was held that a duty of care was owed by builders and local authorities to foreseeable victims of their negligence, such as persons acquiring an interest in the property.

The typical case brought under this head of negligence was where the purchaser of a house discovered that the house had defective foundations. The purchaser could sue the builder for negligence if the foundations were too shallow or made from the wrong materials. Alternatively, an action could be brought against the local authority for negligently approving defective plans or for negligent inspection of work in progress.

One difficulty posed to the common law by these cases was, for what kind of loss was the defendant being made liable? Was it physical damage or pure economic loss?

---

16   *Andrews v Schooling* [1991] 3 All ER 723.
17   *Smith v Drumm* [1996] EGCS 192.
18   Defective Premises Act 1972, s 2.
19   See Spencer [1974] CLJ 307; [1975] CLJ 48.
20   Duncan Wallace (1991) 107 LQR 228 at 242-3, citing *Halsbury's Statutes*, annotation to Section II of the 1972 Act. Noter-up service, November 1990.
1   Defective Premises Act 1972, s 2.
2   *Bayoumi v Protim Services Ltd* (1996) 30 HLR 785.
3   Ibid.
4   Ibid, s 1(5).
5   *Dutton v Bognor Regis UDC* [1972] 1 QB 373; *Anns v Merton London Borough Council* [1978] AC 728, [1977] 2 All ER 492.

In *Anns v Merton London Borough Council,*[6] the damage in such cases was described as physical damage to the house itself[7] and the amount recoverable was the amount required to ensure that the building was not a danger to the health or safety of the occupier.[8] The quantum of damages represented the amount required to make the house safe.

A number of problems emerged from the case law. Because of the financial instability of the building trade many, if not most actions, were brought against local authorities. Local authority funding became a serious political issue in the 1980s and it was questioned whether the losses in defective building cases should fall on them. In some cases developer/builders could persuade local authority officers to accept economical designs and then deflect responsibility elsewhere if the design failed. This would be done either by substituting the local authority for the real defaulter or by reducing the defaulter's liability through contributions.

The *Anns v Merton* doctrine also opened the difficult question of liability for omissions in negligence. A further problem was that if the liability in question was insured, was it right that the insurer should use the doctrine of subrogation to recover moneys paid under an insurance policy?

The jurisprudence developed by the courts after *Anns v Merton* raised questions as to which defects would qualify for liability. Eventually almost any defect appeared to qualify apart from pure amenity defects. Some cases came close to a tortious warranty of quality and there was clearly scope for extension into cases of defective chattels.

(a)   *The present law*   The courts began to restrict liability for negligence in 1984 when the House of Lords prevented a developer from subsidising his losses by recovering damages from a local authority.[9]

In *D & F Estates Ltd v Church Commissioners for England,*[10] the House of Lords held that in the absence of a contractual relationship between the parties, the cost of repairing a structure, which was discovered before the defect had caused personal injury or physical damage to other property, was not recoverable in a negligence action. The cost of effecting such repairs amounted to compensation for economic loss which was not recoverable in a negligence action except within the *Hedley Byrne & Co Ltd v Heller & Partners Ltd*[11] principle of reliance or on the unique proximity of *Junior Books v Veitchi.*[12]

The effect of the decision was, subject to a difficulty over a possible loophole based on the 'complex structure' theory,[13] to render the builder immune from a negligence action in respect of the cost of repairs.

The decision left an apparent anomaly, in that the builder, who was the real defaulter, could not be sued, whereas the local authority could. This anomaly was swiftly cured when a seven judge House of Lords used the 1966 Practice Direction to overrule *Anns v Merton* in *Murphy v Brentwood District Council.*[14]

The plaintiff purchased a pair of semi-detached houses from a construction company in 1970. The houses had been built on a concrete raft on an infilled site in 1969. The raft was defective and settlement occurred, causing serious cracks in the houses. It was alleged that the defendant council had negligently approved plans for the construction

---

6   [1977] 2 All ER 492.
7   Ibid at 504–505.
8   Ibid.
9   *Governors of the Peabody Donation Fund v Sir Lindsay Parkinson & Co Ltd* [1984] 3 All ER 529.
10   [1988] 2 All ER 992; Wallace (1989) 105 LQR 46.
11   [1964] AC 465.
12   [1983] 1 AC 520.
13   [1988] 2 All ER 992 at 1006 (per LORD BRIDGE); at 1012 (per LORD OLIVER).
14   [1990] 2 All ER 908; Duncan Wallace (1991) 107 LQR 228; Cooke (1991) 107 LQR 46; Hayes (1992) 12 OJLS 112; *Murphy's Law*, National Consumer Council, November 1991.

of the raft. The plaintiff's case was based on the argument that repair was necessary in order to avert a present or imminent danger to the health or safety of the occupant. Gas and drainage pipes had broken as a result of the settlement and there was a risk of further breaks.

The House of Lords held that the council was not liable for the plaintiff's loss, which was economic and not within the accepted categories. The decision brings local authorities' liability into line with that of builders. They are not liable for the cost of remedial measures caused by a defect in a building's construction.

The complex structure theory put forward in *D & F Estates* was essentially rejected as regards buildings. A building or product cannot be regarded as a complex structure if it has been wholly constructed or manufactured by one person so as to form a single indivisible unit. Therefore damage to a building caused by defective foundations cannot be regarded as damage to other property. A distinction was however drawn between an integral part of the structure and a distinct item incorporated into the structure where equipment was manufactured by different suppliers. If the central heating system in a house built by A is fitted negligently by B and causes damage to the house, then that damage may be treated as damage to 'other' property and recovered in a negligence action against B by the house owner.[15] This example, however, has nothing to do with complex structure theory as B would have been liable for negligently damaging the building even before *Anns*. This is simply a question of which contractor erected the particular piece of equipment.[16]

A number of points remain unclear after *Murphy*. Does a local authority owe a duty of care in respect of personal injuries or property damage to the occupant of the house? Counsel for the local authority was happy to accept that such a duty was owed but the House preferred to reserve opinion on this point. It may be that the local authority is under no liability whatsoever but a more likely view is that there would be liability for personal injuries.[17] Where the local authority is also the designer and builder a duty is owed in respect of a design defect which causes personal injury to the occupant even though the occupant was aware of the defect.[18] However, no duty is owed by a local authority in respect of property damage where plans for a shopping centre were negligently approved.[19]

(b)   *Critique*   The clear intention of the House of Lords in *Murphy* was to close off what had become a troublesome area of law which had generated considerable litigation.

The decision has been attacked as hostile to consumers.[20] This was not the view taken by the court,[1] which was of the opinion that most litigation was between insurance companies. The idea seemed to be that the risk would be covered by standard insurance policies and the insurance company was simply recouping its losses from the builder/local authority. In fact most household insurance policies exclude pre-existing risks, which will include faulty workmanship, defective materials and damage caused by either. The reason for insurance companies being involved in the litigation appeared to be the competitive nature of this market. Where a third party was legally liable to their insured,

---

15   *Murphy v Brentwood District Council* [1990] 2 All ER 908 at 922 (per LORD KEITH); at 928 (per LORD BRIDGE); at 932 (per LORD OLIVER).

16   See *Nitrigin Eireann Teoranta v Inco Alloys Ltd* [1992] 1 All ER 854; *Jacobs v Morton* (1994) 72 BLR 92.

17   Duncan Wallace (1991) 107 LQR 228 at 223–224.

18   *Targett v Torfaen BC* [1992] 3 All ER 27. Applying *Rimmer v Liverpool City Council* [1984] 1 All ER 930.

19   *Tesco Stores Ltd v Wards Construction (Investment) Ltd* (1995) 76 BLR 94. Applying *Marc Rich & Co v Bishop Rock Marine Co Ltd* [1995] 3 All ER 307.

20   *Murphy's Law*, National Consumer Council, November 1991; Hayes (1992) 12 OJLS 112.

1   [1990] 2 All ER 908 at 923 (per LORD KEITH).

to maintain customer loyalty, the insurance company compensated for the damage and took over the claim. As there is no longer any such liability, it is unlikely that the insurance companies will now take such an approach. A person discovering faulty foundations will obtain no help from his insurance company and has no recourse in negligence either.

The decision in Murphy has not proved popular with Commonwealth courts. In Australia it has been held that a purchaser of a house could recover in respect of quality defects which presented no danger,[2] in Canada that a remote purchaser could recover the cost of remedying dangerous defects against the builder.[3] In New Zealand, the Court of Appeal imposed liability on a local authority for negligent inspection of a building under construction.[4]

The House of Lords emphasised the importance of the Defective Premises Act 1972 in this area and said the courts should not be seen to go beyond the protection provided by the Act. If the NHBC scheme has ceased to be an approved scheme within section 2, then this will extend the ambit of the Act considerably. However, to provide genuine protection for the consumer, the limitation period will require amendment so as to provide a discoverability period.

A distinct anomaly is shown by the House of Lords' approach to organising economic loss cases according to how the loss was caused. If A wishes to purchase a house and a valuation is obtained for the building society from a surveyor, then A is entitled to rely on the valuation to establish a duty of care owed to him by the surveyor. However, if A purchases a house which was built with defective foundations as a result of a negligent report given to the builder by a surveyor, would A be allowed to sue the surveyor or does this case fall within the no-liability principle established by *Murphy* for defectively constructed realty? If it does not fall within the no-liability principle, then the risks arising from defectively constructed buildings will be moved from builders to professional advisors.

There is some evidence that such an approach could be taken. LORD KEITH has observed that *Pirelli General Cable Works Ltd v Oscar Faber & Partners*[5] is more like *Hedley Byrne* than *Anns v Merton*.[6] In other words negligent professional advice which causes a person to purchase defective property could be actionable. If the case is subject to no liability because it falls within the defectively created realty 'pocket' of cases on economic loss, then it draws a line between identical behaviour leading to identical loss in the two examples.[7] In both cases the surveyor has given negligent professional advice and A has suffered economic loss as a result of acquiring defective realty.

(3)   LIMITATION OF ACTIONS[8]

Given the longevity of buildings as opposed to other products, and the fact that defects in their construction may take some time to manifest themselves, the question of limitation of actions is crucial. The problem is to steer a course between the Scylla of indefinite liability for builders and the Charybdis of leaving the plaintiff with no remedy. In an action for breach of contract, the plaintiff has six years from the date of breach in

---

2   *Bryan v Maloney* (1995) 128 ALR 163.
3   *Winnepeg Condominium Corpn No 36 v Bird Construction Co Ltd* (1995) 121 DLR (4th) 193.
4   *Invercargill City Council v Hamlin* [1994] 3 NZLR 513: affd; [1996] AC 624. (Privy Council). See also (1996) 112 LQR 396; (1997) 60 MLR 94.
5   [1983] 2 AC 1.
6   *Murphy v Brentwood DC* [1990] 3 WLR 414 at 427.
7   Stapleton (1991) 107 LQR 249 at 283.
8   See ch 19.

which to issue a writ.[9] However, in the case of deliberate concealment of a defect, the limitation runs from the date on which the defect was discovered or could have been discovered with reasonable diligence.[10] In the case of an action under the Defective Premises Act 1972, section 1, the relevant limitation period runs for six years from the date on which the dwelling was completed.[11] These periods operate to the advantage of the defendant, as the plaintiff may be non-suited before he even knows he has an action.

In a tort action, the limitation period runs for six years from the date of the accrual of a right of action.[12] It is difficult to decide when a right of action accrues in a building case. Case law suggests two possible alternatives. One is the date on which the damage is discovered,[13] and the other is the date on which the damage occurred.[14] The former test is advantageous to the plaintiff, but leaves open the possibility of indeterminate liability on the part of the defendant. An architect may have designed a building in the 1940s, but the damage may not be discovered until the 1980s. By this stage, the architect may be retired, and may have problems with his insurance. The latter test raises the same problem as the contract limitation period, namely that the plaintiff may be non-suited before he is aware he has a cause of action. Both tests are dependent on the date on which the damage is caused. These problems resulted in the passing of the Latent Damage Act 1986. This Act applies where the starting date for calculating the limitation period falls after the date on which the cause of action has accrued. There are three major provisions dealing with limitation periods.

Initially, the decision in *Pirelli General Cable Works Ltd v Oscar Faber & Partners*[15] was confirmed, and the limitation period ran for six years from the date of the damage.[16] What constitutes damage is a question of fact which varies according to the circumstances of each case. In cases of negligent advice, damage is caused when the advice is relied upon. *Pirelli General Cable Works Ltd v Oscar Faber & Partners* suggests that, in order to come within the latent damage rule, the damage must be physical.[17] However, the 1986 Act gives no definition of damage, and it may be interpreted to include economic loss, if the court so desires, in which case such damage is recoverable.

The second possible limitation period runs for three years from the earliest date on which the plaintiff or his predecessor first knew, or could have known, of the facts required to commence proceedings.[18] This introduces a discoverability test similar to that advocated in *Sparham-Souter v Town and Country Developments*.[19] Such a test requires the plaintiff to be aware of all the relevant facts before the limitation period begins to run, with the result that he must be aware of the defect, or ought reasonably to be aware of it.[20] The standard applied is that of the reasonable man. The owner is not endowed with the knowledge of an expert, and the damage must be sufficiently serious to justify the institution of legal proceedings.[1]

The third provision operates as a longstop, which is designed to prevent the discoverability test from creating indefinite liability. No action may be commenced in

9   Limitation Act 1980, s 5.
10   Ibid, s 32(1)(b). See also *King v Victor Parsons & Co* [1973] 1 All ER 206, [1973] 1 WLR 29.
11   Defective Premises Act 1972, s 1(5).
12   Limitation Act 1980, s 2.
13   *Sparham-Souter v Town and Country Developments (Essex) Ltd* [1976] QB 858, [1976] 2 All ER 65.
14   *Pirelli General Cable Works Ltd v Oscar Faber & Partners* [1983] 2 AC 1, [1983] 1 All ER 65.
15   Ibid.
16   Limitation Act 1980, s 14A(4)(b).
17   [1983] 2 AC 1 at 16 (per LORD FRASER).
18   Limitation Act 1980, s 14A(4)(b).
19   [1976] QB 858.
20   Limitation Act 1980, s 14A(10).
1   Ibid, s 14A(7).

cases of latent damage beyond fifteen years of the breach of duty which causes the damage.[2] In cases of negligent construction, the appropriate breach occurs on the date the construction is completed. In negligent inspection cases, it occurs at the date of the inspection and, in negligent advice cases, it occurs when the report is completed.

In cases of deliberate concealment of a defect, none of the above rules apply, and the limitation period runs for six years from the date on which the plaintiff discovers the concealment of the defect.[3]

4. LANDLORDS' LIABILITY

(1) INTRODUCTION

(i) Common law and statutory protection

The occupier of premises and the owner may not be the same person, as the premises may be let by a landlord to a tenant. The tenancy may be private or public. Common law rules initially determined who was responsible for maintaining the premises in a safe condition. But, in the late nineteenth century, Parliament intervened to impose on some landlords an obligation to repair. This occurred mainly in the types of tenancies where the landlord was likely to be in a better position financially to effect repairs, that is in short-term residential tenancies.

In some cases, statutory intervention assisted tenants in obtaining compensation for damage suffered as a result of dilapidated premises, but was of no assistance to third parties. The Byzantine structure of the common law meant that the tenant's family and guests were left with no remedy because of the doctrine of privity of contract. But, if a person was injured on the highway or on neighbouring premises, there was a possibility of a nuisance action against the landlord. If the tenant's mother resided with him and was injured in the house, she had no remedy against the landlord. But, if she was walking on the highway past the house and was injured by falling masonry, she might succeed in an action for public nuisance.[4]

(ii) Common law development

At common law, landlords, like builders and vendors, used to be immune from liability towards persons on their premises. There was generally no law against letting a tumbledown house.[5] The key authority was *Cavalier v Pope*,[6] in which it was held that the landlord owed no duty outside of his contract with the tenant. This immunity survived *Donoghue v Stevenson*,[7] which was not thought to apply to realty.[8]

Surprisingly, the approach to persons not on the premises was more generous. The law of public nuisance gave a remedy to passers-by on the highway, and neighbours affected by dilapidated premises might succeed in an action for private nuisance.

Statutory reform was provided by the Defective Premises Act 1972,[9] but the position of the landlord who does not create the defect in his premises is seemingly still covered

---

2   Ibid, s 14B.
3   Ibid, s 32(5).
4   See now the Defective Premises Act 1972, s 4.
5   *Robbins v Jones* (1863) 15 CBNS 221 at 240 (per ERLE CJ).
6   [1906] AC 428.
7   [1932] AC 562.
8   *Davis v Foots* [1940] 1 KB 116.
9   See Law Commission No 40 (1970) para 45.

by the old immunity, and it will require a decision of the House of Lords to remove it.[10]

(2)   LIABILITY FOR DEFECTS AT THE TIME OF LETTING

(i)   Common law liability

Liability may arise through an express contractual term in the lease, or through the torts of negligence or nuisance.

(a)   *Contractual liability*   An express term in the lease may render the landlord liable to his tenant. For example, the tenant in *Cavalier v Pope*[11] could have maintained an action against the landlord. However, if one tenant acts perfectly reasonably, another tenant will have no reasonable grounds for complaint.[11a]

(b)   *Negligence*   Where a landlord is an occupier within the meaning of the Occupiers' Liability Act 1957, he will owe the common duty of care.[12] A landlord who is not an occupier will owe no duty of care in negligence unless he played an active part in creating the defect.

In *Rimmer v Liverpool City Council*,[13] the plaintiff was a tenant in a council flat which had been designed and built by the defendants. He was injured when he slipped and put his hand through a glass panel which was a standard feature in the flats. He sued the council for negligence in letting a flat with a dangerous feature. The Court of Appeal held that there was no duty of care on landlords to ensure that the premises were reasonably safe at the time of letting. The defendants did owe a duty of care to the plaintiff as designers and builders of the flat to take reasonable care in relation to its design and construction, and had broken that duty.

Until the House of Lords considers a case on defects present at the time of letting, which the landlord did not create, *Cavalier v Pope* remains good law.

(c)   *Nuisance*   The general rule in nuisance is that the landlord is not liable for a nuisance on his premises, as he is not in occupation. An exception to this rule exists in regard to nuisances existing at the time of the letting, where the landlord will be liable if he knew, or ought to have known of the nuisance before letting.[14] The landlord is also liable if he is said to have authorised the nuisance,[15] especially if he has knowledge of the activities of licensees on his land. [15a]

(ii)   Statutory liability

The Defective Premises Act 1972, section 3, which applies to premises,[16] was intended to abolish the lessor's immunity, but failed to do so. The wording of the section means that a duty only exists where the defect is created by workings carried out before the letting. It does not apply to a failure to do work, or to defective works carried out after the letting.[17] A provision which was intended to reverse *Cavalier v Pope*[18] by creating,

---

10   See *Rimmer v Liverpool City Council* [1985] QB 1, [1984] 1 All ER 930.
11   [1906] AC 428.
11a See *Southwark LBC v Tanner* [1999] 3 WLR 939, HL
12   Occupiers' Liability Act 1957, s 2(2).
13   [1985] QB 1, [1984] 1 All ER 930. See also *Targett v Torfaen BC* [1992] 3 All ER 27.
14   *Gandy v Jubber* (1864) 5 B & S 78.
15   *Harris v James* (1876) 45 LJQB 545. Cf *Smith v Scott* [1973] Ch 314.
15a See *Lippiatt v South Gloucestershire Council* [1999] 3 WLR 137. Cf *Hussain v Lancaster City Council* [1999] 2 WLR 1142 regarding more remote activities.
16   Cf Defective Premises Act 1972, s 1 which applies to dwellings.
17   Cf *Rimmer v Liverpool City Council* [1985] QB 1.
18   [1906] AC 428.

on the part of vendors and lessors, a duty to warn of known defects in the property failed to be enacted because of the effect it would have had on vendors of property.[19]

(3)   LIABILITY FOR DEFECTS DURING THE COURSE OF LETTING

Once the property has been let, the issue of responsibility for the repair and maintenance of the premises is primarily governed by the lease. Express terms as to the condition of the premises at the time of letting are rare.[20] However, the landlord may expressly covenant to repair the exterior and structure of the premises. In the absence of an express covenant to repair, the common law is reluctant to impose one. However, a relevant term may be implied where the landlord lets off property as flats and retains control of the landings, stairs and other common parts. Here, he is obliged to take reasonable care to keep these parts in good repair.[1]

The reluctance of the courts to intervene led to legislative measures from 1885 onwards. Presently, the most important terms implied by statute are contained in the Landlord and Tenant Act 1985, sections 11–14. This Act implies into every lease of a dwelling for less than seven years a covenant on the part of the lessor to repair the structure and exterior of the property. Exclusion of liability is not permitted.

(i)   Statutory liability

The Defective Premises Act 1972, section 4[2] creates a statutory duty on landlords in connection with repair of the premises after their demise.[3] This section applies to premises, not just dwellings, and applies where premises are let under a tenancy or right of occupation given by contract or an enactment.[4]

For the section to apply, the landlord must be under an obligation to the tenant for the maintenance or repair of the premises,[5] or he must have an express or implied right or power to enter the premises to carry out any description of maintenance or repair.[6] If the landlord knows, or ought to know, of the relevant defect,[7] he owes a duty of care to all persons who might reasonably be expected to be affected by the defects in the state of the premises.[8] This duty is to take such care as is reasonable to see that such persons are reasonably safe from personal injury or damage to their property.[9] A relevant defect is one which would have constituted a failure by the landlord to carry out his obligation to the tenant to maintain or repair the premises.[10] The duty is owed to the tenant, residents, visitors and trespassers, neighbours and passers-by on the highway, and is effected by giving to third parties the benefit of the tenant's contractual rights.

19   Hansard HC 830–1823, 11 February 1972; Hansard HL 330–1371, 16 May 1972. See also *Bowen v Paramount Builders (Hamilton) Ltd* [1977] 1 NZLR 394 at 415.
20   Cf *Cavalier v Pope* [1906] AC 428.
1   See *Liverpool City Council v Irwin* [1977] AC 239.
2   See *McAuley v Bristol CC* [1992] 1 All ER 749.
3   Replacing the Occupiers' Liability Act 1957, s 4.
4   Defective Premises Act 1972, s 4(6).
5   Ibid, s 4(1).
6   Ibid, s 4(4).
7   Ibid, s 4(2).
8   Ibid, s 4(1).
9   Ibid.
10   Ibid, s 4(3).

(ii)   Common law liability

Liability may arise at common law either through the lease or in the torts of negligence or nuisance. Because of the peculiar piecemeal development of this area of the common law, it is convenient to divide liability according to the status of the plaintiff.

(a)   *The tenant*   The tenant will have a potential action for breach of contract against the landlord. This may arise from the breach of an express or implied covenant to repair. He will also have a statutory action under the Defective Premises Act 1972, section 4.

(b)   *Tenant's family, visitors and trespassers*   The previous reluctance to grant a remedy to persons falling into this category[11] has now been remedied. Statutory rights under the Defective Premises Act 1972, section 4 exist, and the wider common law duty of care in negligence will also apply where the family or visitors are injured due to the landlord's negligence.[12]

The position of trespassers has not yet been subjected to judicial consideration. It would appear that a trespasser who has an action against the occupier under the Occupiers' Liability Act 1984 may also be a foreseeable victim of the landlord's breach of duty under the Defective Premises Act 1972, section 4.

(c)   *Neighbours and passers-by*   Historically, liability exists in nuisance. In the case of neighbours, the liability would be in private nuisance, provided they had an interest in land. Passers-by would have a potential action in public nuisance if they could show special damage. The normal person to sue would be the occupier of the premises from which the nuisance emanated, but the landlord would also be liable under certain conditions.

The law in this area is confused, but the following principles have emerged. A landlord will be liable for a nuisance if he has reserved the right to enter and repair, or has the implied right to do so.[13] Where the lease obliges the tenant to repair the premises, only the tenant is liable.[14] But, if the defect existed at the commencement of the tenancy and the landlord knew, or ought to have known, of it, he will be liable. If the landlord has covenanted to repair the premises, both he and the tenant are potential defendants in a nuisance action.[15]

The problem in this area can now be avoided where the Defective Premises Act 1972, section 4 applies, and the landlord is sued on the basis of his statutory duty. However, there may be circumstances in which section 4 has no application but common law nuisance rules apply.

---

11   *Cavalier v Pope* [1906] AC 428. See also *Malone v Lasky* [1907] 2 KB 141.
12   *AC Billings & Son Ltd v Riden* [1958] AC 240; *Cunard v Antifyre Ltd* [1933] 1 KB 551.
13   *Wilchick v Marks* [1934] 2 KB 56; *Heap v Ind Coope and Allsop Ltd* [1940] 2 KB 476; *Mint v Good* [1951] 1 KB 517.
14   *Brew Bros Ltd v Snax (Ross) Ltd* [1970] 1 QB 612.
15   *Wringe v Cohen* [1940] 1 KB 229. See also Landlord and Tenant Act 1985, ss 11–14.

Chapter 29

Liability arising out of land ownership and occupation II — disputes between neighbours

1. INTRODUCTION

In any society, there are bound to be disputes between adjacent land-owners. English law deals with these by means of the tort of nuisance and the rule in *Rylands v Fletcher.*[1] It might seem more appropriate to deal with this issue through the medium of property law, as is the case in most civilian systems, but English law has tended to concentrate on providing remedies rather than upon conferring property rights. This emphasis serves to explain why the law of tort has been employed in this respect.

The tort of nuisance is of ancient origin,[2] and has three roots. The first was the assize of nuisance which allowed an action for loss of profit arising from the defendant's interference with incorporeal rights, such as rights to water and rights of way. The second was common or public nuisance, which constituted an interference with the neighbourhood, usually interference with the highway. Thirdly, gaps in the law were filled by the action on the case in the fifteenth and sixteenth centuries. A remedy was given to non-freeholders who could not proceed under the assize. This was done by extending the meaning of interferences with enjoyment from disseisement to those involving noxious trades. A remedy was also given to those who suffered special damage as a result of common or public nuisance.

During the sixteenth and seventeenth centuries, the action on the case supplanted the assize and covered three very different kinds of loss. The confusion caused by this development is still evident in modern law.

The modern law of nuisance was shaped in the nineteenth century, and was influenced by two factors. In legal procedure, jury influence declined, and the court acquired greater power to shape the law. Secondly, the nature of land changed with the industrial revolution.[3] Nuisance acquired a public law function. In the absence of detailed planning law and environmental protection legislation, the courts used private law as an instrument for zoning land for particular purposes such as industrial or residential, and to set permissible standards of noise and air and water pollution. The drawback with this technique was that the courts had to wait for litigants to proceed. As a method

---

1   (1868) LR 3 HL 330.
2   For the early history, see Winfield [1930–32] 4 CLJ 189; Newark (1949) 65 LQR 480.
3   See Brenner (1974) 3 J Leg Stud 403; McLaren (1983) 3 OJLS 155.

of environmental control, nuisance law has largely been supplanted by legislation and, in any case, is an inefficient method of achieving such control.[4]

Nuisance retains importance in dealing with the innumerable problems that arise between neighbouring landowners. Apart from problems caused by the unfortunately named public nuisance, the subject is best understood if it is realised that nuisance is concerned with invasions of a person's interest in the use or enjoyment of his land. The gist of a nuisance lies in the kind of harm caused, not in the type of conduct used in causing it. Conduct may be relevant in determining whether a particular kind of damage amounts to a nuisance.

The second tort protecting a person's use of land is a judicial creation stemming from the nineteenth century, and is a legal product of the industrial revolution. *Fletcher v Rylands*[5] governs liability for escapes from land, caused by its non-natural use, resulting in damage.

2. NUISANCE

Nuisance is divided into three categories, public, private and statutory. The attachment of the term 'nuisance' to the former is confusing, as it has no necessary connection with land usage, and originates in the criminal law. Statutory nuisances have been created by Parliament where the common law has proved to be too slow or ineffective.

(1)   PUBLIC NUISANCE[6]

Every public nuisance is a crime, but acquires its tortious character by virtue of the rule allowing a person who suffers special damage to bring an action for damages.

A public nuisance was defined in *A-G v PYA Quarries Ltd*[7] as 'One which materially affects the reasonable comfort and convenience of life of a class of Her Majesty's subjects.'[8] Whether the number of persons affected constitutes a class is a question of fact in each case.[9]

Acts which are capable of amounting to a public nuisance are difficult to define with any precision. Two groups are identifiable, consisting of abuses of the highway[10] and the carrying on of trades creating discomfort to others, such as those producing noise or smells. There is also a third group which consists of a selection of assorted wrongs, such as holding a badly organised pop festival, keeping a brothel or making a hoax alarm call or making hundreds of obscene phone calls to women.[11]

The mere commission of an act classed as a public nuisance is a crime, but not everyone affected by the nuisance can sue for damages. In order to do this, a member of the class affected must show that he suffered special damage over and above that suffered by the class. Special damage in the context of nuisance differs from special, as opposed to general damages, in the quantification of damage. Special damage in nuisance may be general damage provided it is substantial, direct, and not consequential.[12] Whether the

4   See Ogus and Richardson [1977] 36 CLJ 284; Steele (1995) LS 236. Cf McLaren (1972) Osgoode Hall LJ 505.
5   (1865) 3 H & C 774, 159 ER 737 (Court of Exchequer); (1866) LR 1 Exch 265 (Court of Exchequer Chamber); sub nom *Rylands v Fletcher* (1868) LR 3 HL 330 (House of Lords).
6   Spencer [1989] 48(1) CLJ 55.
7   [1957] 2 QB 169.
8   Ibid at 169 (per ROMER LJ).
9   *R v Madden* [1975] 1 WLR 1379.
10   See *Jacobs v LCC* [1950] AC 361 at 375 (per LORD SIMONDS).
11   *R v Johnson* [1997] 1 WLR 367.
12   *Walsh v Ervin* [1952] VLR 361.

damage must be different in kind, or merely in extent, to that suffered by the general public is obscure and undecided.[13] Damages may be recovered for personal injuries,[14] damage to property[15] or economic loss.[16]

(2) STATUTORY NUISANCES

Much of common law nuisance has been supplanted by statutory powers which are designed to control environmental damage. The major provision is the Environmental Protection Act 1990, which defines various matters as statutory nuisance and imposes a duty on local authorities to serve an abatement notice. Failure to comply without reasonable excuse is a criminal offence.

Detailed consideration of this topic is not possible, but it can be noted that the concept of statutory nuisance marks an encroachment of public law into a traditional private law area, and removes many of the difficulties of expense and delay associated with private actions. Compensation is not normally available for a statutory nuisance, but this is not normally a problem, as the most appropriate private law remedy is the injunction.

(3) PRIVATE NUISANCE

A private nuisance can be defined as an 'unlawful interference with a person's use or enjoyment of land, or some right over, or in connection with it'.[17] This definition divides private nuisances into those affecting the use or enjoyment of land, and those affecting servitudes. Servitudes include rights of way and rights to light, and are more appropriately dealt with in books on property law.

(i)   Plaintiffs

The question as to who has locus standi to bring a nuisance action defines the nature of the tort as it defines the interest that is protected. That the tort protected interests in property was underlined in *Malone v Lasky*.[18] The wife of the tenant of premises was injured by a cistern dislodged by vibrations on the defendant's premises. As she had no interest in the land, she was unable to sue in private nuisance. Some relaxation of this rule was seen in *Khorasandjian v Bush*[19] where the court of Appeal held that a plaintiff with no proprietary interest could obtain an injunction to restrain a private nuisance in the form of harassment by telephone calls.[20] Doctrinal purity was restored, however, by the House of Lords in *Hunter v Canary Wharf Ltd*.[1] Actions in nuisance brought by spouses and children of tenants, whose television reception was interfered with, and who were affected by dust, were denied. The only person who can bring a private nuisance action is someone with a proprietary or possessory interest in land. This includes owners, tenants and reversioners, where there is permanent damage to the reversion. A licensee with exclusive possession and a person with exclusive possession who is unable

---

13   See Buckley *Law of Nuisance* (1981) p 62.
14   *Castle v St Augustine's Links Ltd* (1922) 38 TLR 615.
15   *Halsey v Esso Petroleum Co Ltd* [1961] 1 WLR 683. See also *The Wagon Mound (No 2)* [1967] 1 AC 617.
16   *Rose v Miles* (1815) 4 M & S 101; *Fritz v Hobson* (1880) 14 Ch D 542; *Benjamin v Storr* (1874) LR 9 CP 400.
17   *Winfield and Jolowicz* p 494. See also *Read v J Lyons & Co Ltd* [1945] KB 216 at 236 (per Scott LJ).
18   [1907] 2 KB 141, Kodiliny (1989) 9 J Leg Stud 284.
19   [1993] 3 WLR 476.
20   Applying *Motherwell v Motherwell* (1976) 73 DLR (3d) 62.
1   [1997] 2 All ER 426. Overruling *Khorasandjian v Bush* and reversing the Court of Appeal, [1996] 1 All ER 482. See Cane (1997) 113 LQR 515; O'Sullivan [1997] CLJ 483; Oliphant (1998) 6 Tort L Rev 21.

to prove title will also have actions but not mere licensees or family members of the owner or tenant. Even possession under the Matrimonial Homes Act 1983 which gives such a person a right of occupation in the matrimonial home, which can be registered in order to give protection against third parties, will have no action unless the right to exclusive possession has been formally granted by a court.[2]

The rationale for the decision in *Hunter* is clearly a desire to return nuisance to its property based roots, although several practical reasons are given for the rule.[3] The strict rule can be objected to on the grounds that the scope of any meaningful protection offered to plaintiffs is reduced and that the tort of nuisance is stultified.[4] The opposing view expressed by LORD COOKE in his dissenting speech on this point is that nuisance is an obligations based tort and should not deny relief to those in substantial occupation of the property.

Any hope that the strict rule will be straightforward to apply appears likely to be short-lived. The first problem that is likely to surface is, when will a spouse who does not hold a legal interest but who claims a equitable interest behind a trust, be able to assert a sufficient proprietary interest?[5]

The strict rule has an effect on the damages which can be claimed in nuisance. What is protected by nuisance is the plaintiff's interest in the land affected. Normal damages will represent the depreciation in value of the land but what if the claim is for loss of amenity, such as discomfort, smells or loss of sleep? Generally, an allegation of negligence is essential in an action for damages for personal injuries.[6] There is no authority on nuisance where an action for personal injuries has succeeded where a negligence action would have failed. LORD HOFFMANN was of the view that loss of amenity damages in nuisance could not be assessed by reference to personal injuries cases and should be assessed on the basis of diminution in capital value of the land.[7] Assessment of damages on this basis is likely to prove difficult but it must be remembered that the primary remedy in nuisance is the injunction ordering the defendant to cease his activity.

(ii) Defendants

(a) *Occupiers* In most nuisance actions, the defendant will be the owner or occupier of the land from which the nuisance emanates. An occupier may be vicariously liable for nuisances created by his servants as well as those he creates himself. An occupier may be liable for a nuisance created by an independent contractor, if the occupier owes a non-delegable duty to the plaintiff.[8] This imposes on the defendant a duty to take reasonable care. No question of strict liability arises in such circumstances. What is classed as a non-delegable duty is not clear. An owner of land enjoys the right to support from adjoining land. In *Bower v Peate*,[9] the defendant was held liable in nuisance where a contractor engaged to do construction work on his land undermined support for the plaintiff's adjoining land. That the principle does not just apply to cases involving material damage to the plaintiff's land is illustrated by *Matania v National Provincial Bank Ltd*,[10] where the defendant was held liable when his contractor created noise and dust, constituting a nuisance to the occupiers of higher floors in the same building. However,

---

2   Ibid at p 453 per LORD HOFFMANN.
3   LORD HOFFMANN at p 453; LORD GOFF at p 439.
4   See LORD COOKE (dissenting on this point) and Cane (1997) 113 LQR 515.
5   See *Lloyds Bank v Rossett* [1990] 1 All ER 1111.
6   *Read v J Lyons & Co Ltd* [1947] AC 156 at 170–1 (per LORD MACMILLAN).
7   *Hunter v Canary Wharf Ltd* [1997] 2 All ER 426 at 451.
8   *Winfield and Jolowicz* pp 515–517.
9   (1876) 1 QBD 321.
10   [1936] 2 All ER 633.

if the contractor has taken over occupation of the land to the exclusion of the owner, the owner will only be liable in a nuisance action if he knows, or ought to have known, of the creation of the nuisance.[11]

An owner of land may also be liable in a nuisance action if his contractor's operations on the highway endanger passers-by on the highway.[12] But, if the work is merely carried on close to the highway, the employer will not be liable for injuries to passers-by.[13]

(b)   *Occupiers' liability for nuisances created by other causes*   The most significant development in twentieth-century nuisance law has been the shift in emphasis from land ownership as a source of rights to its being a source of duties. It has long been established that the occupier is liable for nuisances created by himself and by persons under his control. This rule was extended to nuisances created by a predecessor in title, where the occupier knew, or ought to have known, of the defect.[14]

If a nuisance was created by a person not under the occupier's control, such as a trespasser, or where it resulted from an act of nature, the occupier enjoyed immunity in private, but not in public nuisance.[15] This immunity was lost in the case of trespassers creating a nuisance in *Sedleigh-Denfield v O'Callaghan*.[16] The occupier was considered liable if he adopted the nuisance for his own purposes, or continued it by failing to take steps to avoid it once he had actual or constructive knowledge of its existence. The rule also extends to cases where a trespasser causes a nuisance without any alteration to the plaintiff's land, for example where trespassing gypsies constitute a nuisance.[17]

The rule on trespassers was extended to nuisances created by acts of nature in *Goldman v Hargrave*.[18] Lightning struck a tree on the defendant's land and the tree caught fire. The defendant chopped the tree down and left the intense fire to burn out. Three days later, the fire spread to the plaintiff's land. The Privy Council held the defendant liable for failing to abate the nuisance and imposed a subjective standard of care on the defendant, based on the cost of abatement and the financial means and age or fitness of the defendant.[19]

The principle in *Goldman* was incorporated into English law, and extended by *Leakey v National Trust*.[20] Damage was caused by the land itself, when natural weathering and the nature of the soil caused parts of a hill to fall on the plaintiff's land. The principle in this case has also been extended to cover dry rot spreading from one property to another,[1] apparently circumventing the rule that the owner of a servient tenement subject to an easement of support owes no duty to incur expenditure.

The basis of liability in these cases lies not in the use of land, but in the failure to abate something which might damage a neighbour.[2]

(c)   *Creators*   The creator of a nuisance may always be sued, even if he is no longer in occupation of the land from which the nuisance originates.[3] This principle is subject

---

11   *Gourock Ropework Co v Greenock Corpn* 1966 SLT 125.
12   *Tarry v Ashton* (1876) 1 QBD 314; *Holliday v National Telephone Co* [1899] 2 QB 392.
13   *Salsbury v Woodland* [1970] 1 QB 324.
14   *St Anne's Well Brewery Co v Roberts* (1928) 140 LT 1.
15   *Job Edwards v Birmingham Navigation Co* [1924] 1 KB 341.
16   [1940] AC 880.
17   *Page Motors Ltd v Epsom and Ewell Borough Council* (1981) 80 LGR 337.
18   [1967] 1 AC 645. See also Harris [1967] CLJ 24–26.
19   Ibid at 663 (per LORD WILBERFORCE). See Gearty [1989] 48(2) CLJ 214.
20   [1980] QB 485. See also Buckley (1980) 96 LQR 185.
1   *Bradburn v Lindsay* [1983] 2 All ER 408. See Jackson [1984] Conv 54.
2   *Goldman v Hargrave* [1967] 1 AC 645 at 661 (per LORD WILBERFORCE).
3   *Thompson v Gibson* (1841) 7 M & W 456.

to *Cambridge Water Co v Eastern Counties Leather plc*,[4] in that a defendant must be able to foresee damage of the type which occurred at the time when the chemicals which polluted the water system were released. The defendants could not be liable for damage which they could foresee but at which point they were unable to rectify as the chemicals had been irretrievably lost below ground.

In cases where the cause of action originates on a public highway,[5] or from the sea,[6] it is not clear whether the action lies in public or private nuisance. In *Southport Corpn v Esso Petroleum Co Ltd*,[7] there was a divergence of judicial opinion on this issue, but DEVLIN J's view, at first instance, that the action lies in private nuisance, appears to be supported by *Hubbard v Pitt*,[8] where picketing of the plaintiff's premises from the public highway was held to be a private nuisance.

(iii)   Interference with use and enjoyment

The basis of the plaintiff's case in a private nuisance action is that the defendant has caused a substantial interference with his use or enjoyment of land. The interference may take numerous forms, such as smell, noise, vibrations, dust or other emission. No account is taken of trivialities, and the approach of the courts is 'not merely according to elegant or dainty modes of living, but according to plain and sober and simple notions among the English people'.[9] The House of Lords' decision in *Hunter v Canary Wharf Ltd*[10] may have affected the whole basis of nuisance. The balancing act had the effect of marking out the place of nuisance in the law of obligations and, in particular, differentiating it from negligence. The effect of *Hunter* may be that nuisance is effectively removed from obligations and becomes an adjunct of property law.[11]

The court has to perform the task of balancing the defendant's right to use his land as he chooses, with the plaintiff's right to enjoy his land without interference. The test applied by the court to determine this balance is the reasonableness test, namely, has the defendant used his land in a reasonable manner?[11a]

(iv)   The reasonableness test

(a)   *Historical introduction*   The modern law of private nuisance was largely shaped in the late nineteenth century in response to the forces generated by the Industrial Revolution. Until the end of the eighteenth century, nuisance was characterised by the idea that, once the plaintiff established interference with his use and enjoyment of land then, unless the interference was trivial, liability would follow. It was no defence that the defendant had acted reasonably or that he acted for the public benefit.[12]

The advent of the Industrial Revolution raised the problem of balancing the interests of land conservationists with those of industrial exploitation. The conservationists' view insisted upon natural rights to clean air and water,[13] whereas the exploitationists' view would permit industrial activity if carried on in a reasonable location and in a reasonable

---

4   [1994] 2 WLR 53.
5   *Midwood & Co Ltd v Manchester Corpn* [1905] 2 KB 597.
6   *Esso Petroleum Co Ltd v Southport Corpn* [1956] AC 218, [1953] 3 WLR 773.
7   Ibid.
8   [1976] QB 142, [1975] 3 All ER 1.
9   *Walter v Selfe* (1851) 4 De G & Sm 315 at 322 (per KNIGHT-BRUCE VC). Cf *Andreae v Selfridge & Co Ltd* [1937] 3 All ER 255.
10   [1997] 2 All ER 426.
11   Cane (1997) 113 LQR 515.
11a   *Southwark LBC v Tanner* [1999] 3 WLR 939, HL.
12   *William Aldred's Case* (1610) 77 ER 816 at 821.
13   *Bamford v Tunley* (1862) 122 ER 27; *A-G v Birmingham Corpn* (1858) 70 ER 220.

manner.[14] The latter view appears to accord with the doctrine of reasonableness in negligence cases.

The conflict between these issues was resolved in *St Helens Smelting Co v Tipping*.[15] The plaintiff had purchased an estate in the heavily industrialised area of St Helens. The fumes from the defendant's copper works caused physical damage to his garden, and also generally interfered with his use and enjoyment of his land. The House of Lords upheld the plaintiff's claim and granted an injunction, closing down the works. A key factor for the later development of the tort of nuisance was the distinction between material damage to property and personal discomfort. In the case of discomfort only, locality was a relevant issue.[16] Although the decision favoured the plaintiff, it has been suggested that it was sympathetic to land exploitation, and left nuisance as a 'broken reed' in controlling pollution.[17] However, it can also be argued that the common law was already irrelevant as a means of pollution control, since the cost of pursuing an action, the difficulties in establishing cause and effect and the social obstacles to a legal action arising from the profitability of land ownership all worked against a successful suit.[18]

It would therefore be incorrect to regard the common law as having failed doctrinally to operate as an effective weapon against pollution. Because of its essentially reactive nature and the institutional factors mitigating against its effectiveness, this was a task it was never equipped to achieve. This task was increasingly taken over by regulation, with an increasing parliamentary concern for public health, and the common law was left to deal primarily with 'ad hoc disputes between neighbours'.[19]

(b) *Material damage[20] to property* The rule in *St Helen's Smelting Co v Tipping*[1] provided that a person who, by his activities on land, causes material damage to the plaintiff's land, will be liable in nuisance, unless the plaintiff is shown to be over-sensitive or if one of the defences to nuisance applies. This rule can be criticised on the ground that it is difficult to define what is meant by material damage to property. If a factory produces emissions which do not damage the land but make living on it uncomfortable and disagreeable, the value of residential land may well be diminished. This may be classified as material damage, but the plaintiff could be defeated by the locality factor.[2]

In *Hunter v Canary Wharf Ltd*,[3] LORD HOFFMANN emphasised that there are not separate torts of causing injury to land and discomfort to people, or between property damage and personal injuries, there is simply a tort against property.[4] An article by Professor Newark which argued that nuisance should not be a tort guarding against personal injuries was cited with approval.[5] The emphasis in either material damage or interference with use and enjoyment will therefore be on the land rather than the owner and interest in the land becomes 'a qualifying condition or a springboard which entitles him to sue for injury to himself.'[6]

---

14   *Hole v Barlow* (1858) 140 ER 1113.
15   (1865) 11 HL Cas 642.
16   Ibid at 651–652 (per LORD WESTBURY).
17   Brenner (1974) 3 J Leg Stud 403.
18   MacLaren (1983) 1 OJLS 155.
19   Buckley *Law of Nuisance* (1981) p 9. But see Gearty [1989] 48(2) CLJ 214.
20   See Buckley *Law of Nuisance* (1981) ch 7.
1   (1865) 11 HL Cas 642.
2   See Ogus and Richardson [1977] 36 CLJ 284 at 299.
3   [1997] 2 All ER 426.
4   Ibid at 452.
5   (1949) 65 LQR 480. See [1997] 2 All ER 426 at 435 per LORD GOFF.
6   [1997] 2 All ER 426 at 451 per LORD HOFFMANN.

In order to prove actionable loss, the plaintiff must therefore show either a reduction in the capital value of the land or a diminution in its amenity value. [7]

The major development in cases of material damage has been from liability for positive misfeasance to liability for an omission to act. The courts have been guided by policy factors similar to those governing the development of modern negligence liability. As the occupier of the land acquires a benefit from his occupation, so he also has to shoulder the burdens which his land may impose on neighbours. The concept of loss-distribution is also relevant. It is possible to insure against risks created by land occupation, and the best insurer in these cases will usually be the occupier.

In *Sedleigh-Denfield v O'Callaghan*,[8] a trespasser laid a drainage pipe in a ditch on the defendants' land. The defendants were aware of the presence of the pipe and allowed it to become blocked with leaves, thereby causing flooding to the plaintiff's land. The House of Lords held the defendants liable in nuisance on the basis of continuing or adopting the nuisance. Subsequently, occupiers were held liable for nuisances caused naturally by lightning and by defects in soil.[9]

Although a duty to take positive action is imposed on occupiers, the standard by which they are judged is not the ordinary objective negligence standard of the reasonable man, but a subjective standard, based on the cost of abating the nuisance or the physical effort required, balanced against the defendant's financial resources or his age and fitness.[10] As policy dictates that the duty should be imposed on the occupier, it would be unjust to impose too onerous a burden where the hazard is not created by his fault.

(c)   *Interference with use and enjoyment*   Where the interference does not cause material damage to the property but interferes with the plaintiff's use and enjoyment of it, the defendant's use of his property is assessed by the reasonableness test. This test reflects the give and take nature of nuisance law, and involves a balancing process. A number of factors individually or collectively are used to determine the reasonableness of the defendant's conduct. These include locality, duration of the nuisance, sensitivity, public utility, malice and degree of fault.

(d)   *Locality*   The effect of the compromise reached in *St Helen's Smelting Co v Tipping*[11] was that locality was a relevant factor in determining the reasonableness of the defendant's activity. Those who lived in an industrial area would have to put up with more in the way of discomfort from noise and smells than those who lived in residential areas. It has been said that what would be a nuisance in Belgrave Square would not necessarily be so in Bermondsey.[12] The effect of this rule was to make actions in respect of discomfort virtually impossible in industrial areas.[13] However, even if the defendant's activity is carried out in an industrial area, he will not be immune solely because that activity is typical of that area. In *Rushmer v Polsue and Alfieri Ltd*,[14] the plaintiff, a milkman, obtained an injunction in respect of noise at night caused by printing presses, even though he lived in the printing area of London. However, it may be objected that, since the plaintiff

---

7   See O'Sullivan [1997] CLJ 483; Oliphant (1998) 6 Tort L Rev 21.
8   [1940] AC 880.
9   *Goldman v Hargrave* [1967] 1 AC 645; *Leakey v National Trust for Places of Historic Interest or Natural Beauty* [1980] QB 485.
10   Cf the duty imposed on occupiers to trespassers by *British Railways Board v Herrington* [1972] AC 877 prior to the Occupiers' Liability Act 1984.
11   (1865) 11 HL Cas 642.
12   *Sturges v Bridgman* (1879) 11 Ch D 852 at 865.
13   Brenner (1973) 3 J Leg Stud 403 at 413.
14   [1906] 1 Ch 234; affd [1907] AC 121.

was the only resident in the area, the granting of the injunction was economically inefficient in terms of cost-abatement.[15]

The effect of the locality test is to introduce a form of judicial zoning. When the character of an area is established, this will pose little problem but, where an area is in transition, the balance may be difficult to achieve.[16]

(e)   *Duration*   The duration of an interference may be crucial in determining its potential as a nuisance. Building works often interfere with the use and enjoyment of land but, if they are carried on with reasonable care and skill, using modern methods and such interference as there may be is minimised, no actionable nuisance is committed.[17]

Some difficulty is caused where there is a state of affairs on the defendant's land likely to cause damage to the plaintiff. The actual interference may only occur once or very occasionally. It is clear that, if the state of affairs is foreseeably likely to cause harm to the plaintiff's land, a nuisance is committed.

In *Spicer v Smee*,[18] defective electrical wiring was installed in the defendant's premises. This caused a fire, which caused the destruction of the plaintiff's adjoining bungalow. The defendant was held liable in nuisance as 'private nuisance arises out of a state of things on one man's property whereby his neighbour's property is exposed to danger.'[19] Similarly in *Midwood v Manchester Corpn*,[20] a badly insulated electrical cable laid under the highway caused a fire which damaged the plaintiff's house. It was held that the defective condition of the wiring threatened substantial harm, and that a nuisance had been committed.

(f)   *Sensitivity*   A relevant factor in the process of balancing the parties' interests is the abnormal sensitivity of the plaintiff or his property. In *Robinson v Kilvert*,[1] paper stored by the plaintiff on his own premises was damaged by the defendant's activities. It was held that, because the damage was caused principally because of the sensitivity of the paper, no nuisance was committed.

An important qualification to the rule is that, if the defendant's activities are classified as a nuisance, the plaintiff may recover in respect of harm to sensitive property, such as an orchid.[2] However, before such loss is recoverable, remoteness of damage requirements must be satisfied.

The sensitivity rule is also useful to illustrate the common law approach to new technology. In *Bridlington Relay Co v Yorkshire Electricity Board*,[3] the plaintiff used an aeriel mast to boost television pictures into Bridlington. Television reception was adversely affected by the defendant's overhead power line. The plaintiff applied for a nuisance injunction, requiring the defendant to bury the line. The application failed on the ground that the plaintiff's activity was sensitive, and that television as a leisure activity, of little benefit to its users, was not protected by the law of nuisance. However, in *Nor-Video*

---

15   Ogus and Richardson [1977] 36 CLJ 284.
16   See *Allen v Gulf Oil Refining Ltd* [1981] 1 All ER 353 at 357 (per LORD WILBERFORCE).
17   *Harrison v Southwark and Vauxhall Water Co* [1891] 2 Ch 409; *Andreae v Selfridge & Co Ltd* [1938] Ch 1.
18   [1946] 1 All ER 489.
19   Ibid at 493 (per ATKINSON J).
20   [1905] 2 KB 597. See also *Bolton v Stone* [1951] AC 850; *SCM (UK) Ltd v WJ Whittall & Son Ltd* [1970] 1 WLR 1017; *British Celanese Ltd v AH Hunt (Capacitors) Ltd* [1969] 1 WLR 959; *Castle v St Augustine's Links Ltd* (1922) 38 TLR 615.
1   (1889) 41 Ch D 88. See also *Heath v Brighton Corpn* (1908) 98 LT 718.
2   *McKinnon Industries Ltd v Walker* [1951] 3 DLR 577.
3   [1965] Ch 436.

Services Ltd v Ontario Hydro,[4] on similar facts, it was stated that television viewing is an important incident of ordinary enjoyment of property and should be protected as such.

It would appear that *Hunter v Canary Wharf Ltd*[5] leaves open the question of whether nuisance can be committed by interference with a recreational amenity. The approach of the majority to nuisance as being based on property interest, rather than personal harm, will make it difficult to make such a claim unless the plaintiff can show amenity damage. With regard to *Hunter* itself and television, the ratio is that no action will lie where the interference with reception is caused by the erection of a building. If a landowner has the right to block light by erecting a building then he has the right to block television signals.[6] However, LORD GOFF[7] refused to accept that television viewing was a purely recreational activity and LORD COOKE[8] suggested exceptions to the presumption of non-actionability in cases where the the building was erected maliciously. However, this view of malice seems to go against *Bradford Corpn v Pickles*.[9] If a person has a right to do something then his motive is irrelevant.

(g)   *Public utility*   Sometimes, there can be a conflict between the public utility of the defendant's activity and the interests of the plaintiff. For example, the activities of the defendant may provide employment or recreational facilities whilst also interfering with the plaintiff's enjoyment of his own land. Whether or not the utility of the defendant's activity is relevant depends, to a large extent, on the remedy sought by the plaintiff. In many cases, the plaintiff will seek an injunction in order to terminate or curtail the defendant's activities. In other cases, damages may be sought, in which case the defendant has effectively bought the right to continue his activity.

Unsurprisingly, nineteenth-century cases placed emphasis firmly on private rights. A striking example is provided by *A-G v Birmingham Borough Council*,[10] in which an injunction was granted to restrain the defendants from discharging raw sewage into a river which flowed through the plaintiff's property. This was ordered, despite the argument that the town would be converted into a vast cess pool if the injunction was granted. Likewise, an injunction has been granted to prevent Ireland's only cement factory from operating, at a time when building was of urgent public necessity.[11]

A movement towards the greater recognition of public utility was apparent in *Miller v Jackson*.[12] In practice, a large industrial concern can obtain the benefit of an Act of Parliament giving it statutory authority as a defence to a nuisance action.[13] The traditional respect paid to private rights by the common law can be circumvented by the legislature giving greater weight to factors such as employment.

(h)   *Malice*   The question may arise whether an otherwise lawful activity may become a nuisance because it is motivated by malice. As English law tends to concentrate on the issues of causation, to the exclusion of the rights of individuals, the law is somewhat confused.[14]

---

4   (1978) 84 DLR (3d) 221.
5   [1997] 2 All ER 426.
6   Ibid at 454 per LORD HOFFMANN; at 470 per LORD HOPE.
7   Ibid at 431.
8   Ibid at 463.
9   [1895] AC 587.
10   (1858) 70 ER 220.
11   *Bellew v Irish Cement Ltd* [1948] IR 61.
12   [1977] QB 966, [1977] 3 All ER 338. Cf *Kennaway v Thompson* [1981] QB 88.
13   See *Allen v Gulf Oil Refining Ltd* [1981] 1 All ER 353.
14   Cf the position in French law. See Catalia and Weir (1964) 38 Tulane LR 221.

In *Bradford Corpn v Pickles*,[15] the defendant extracted percolating water in undefined channels, with the result that the water supply to the plaintiffs' reservoir was reduced. The defendant's motive was to compel the plaintiffs to buy his land at his price. The plaintiffs' action failed, because motive was said to be irrelevant to liability.[16] In contrast, in *Christie v Davey*,[17] it was held that, where the defendant blew whistles, banged trays and hammered on the plaintiff's wall, a nuisance was committed. The plaintiff was a music teacher and the defendant had maliciously reacted in response to the musical sounds he could hear from next door. Similarly in *Hollywood Silver Fox Farm Ltd v Emmett*,[18] the defendant committed a nuisance when he maliciously discharged guns on his own land, close to the boundary with the plaintiff's land. The plaintiff's silver foxes, which he bred commercially, were in season and the defendant was aware that they were sensitive to noise. An injunction was granted to restrain the defendant. Whether these cases can be reconciled is a matter of academic debate.[19] The position would appear to be that, where material damage is caused to the plaintiff's land, the defendant's motive is irrelevant as is also the case where the act constitutes a nuisance to a servitude. Where the nuisance constitutes an interference with the use or enjoyment of land, the preferable view is that, in determining the reasonableness of the defendant's act, his motive is an important factor. *Pickles* case is best regarded as a case *sui generis* with servitudes, where motive is irrelevant. What is relevant in this case is whether the servitude existed or not. Once the court had decided that a landowner, in this case the corporation, had no right to receive water percolating in undefined channels,[20] the issue was decided.

(v)   Fault[1]

For the purposes of tort law, fault generally means intention, recklessness or negligence.[2] Whether fault is a necessary ingredient in the tort of nuisance is a matter of some complexity. In the late nineteenth century and early twentieth century, the fault principle of tortious liability became dominant. The key tort in modern law is the tort of negligence, in which liability is conduct-based. Many types of interest can be defended in negligence, but the only common thread is that the defendant's conduct must be labelled negligent before liability can be imposed. The only exception to this is the doctrine of *res ipsa loquitur*, which can be regarded as a back-door method of imposing strict liability.[3] Earlier forms of tortious liability, such as nuisance, were not based on the defendant's conduct. Instead, the interest of the plaintiff invaded was the focal issue. This led to the view that torts such as trespass and nuisance were torts of strict liability and that, in nuisance, once a sufficient degree of interference and causation were established, then liability followed. The predominance of the fault principle in the twentieth century led to older forms of tortious liability being examined in terms of fault.

Obligations in nuisance are based on the mutual interdependence of occupiers of land. An occupier may use his land as he pleases, until this usage causes material damage to, or unreasonably interferes with his neighbour's land. What is at issue in most cases

---

15   [1895] AC 587.
16   Ibid at 594 (per LORD HALSBURY LC).
17   [1893] 1 Ch 316.
18   [1936] 2 KB 468.
19   *Winfield and Jolowicz* pp 504–5050; Fridman (1958) 21 MLR 484.
20   See also *Stephens v Anglian Water Authority* [1987] 1 WLR 1381; *Home Brewery Co Ltd v William Davis & Co (Leicester) Ltd* [1987] QB 339.
1   See Dias [1967] CLJ 62; Buxton (1966) 29 MLR 676; Newark (1954) 17 MLR 579; Gearty [1989] CLJ 48(2) 214.
2   See ch 12.
3   See ch 12.

is not whether the defendant was at fault, but whether he should abandon his activity. In many cases, the defendant will act intentionally and foresee some interference with the plaintiff's land, but consider the activity to be within the bounds of legality. If the plaintiff applies for an injunction, the defendant will normally be aware of the effect of his activity before the date of the trial. However, he may still claim to have acted legally. It has been stated that, in such circumstances, consideration of the strictness of the duty is out of place, because all the court is concerned with is whether the defendant should be told to stop his interference with the plaintiff's rights.[4] Cases such as *Rapier v London Tramways Co*,[5] in which it was said that whether or not the defendant had taken reasonable care was irrelevant must be viewed in the light of the fact that an injunction had been applied for.

If the action is for damages, a distinction is sometimes drawn between liability for continuing or adopting a nuisance and creating a nuisance. In the case of continuance or adoption, liability is said to be fault-based, whereas a stricter standard may apply, according to the factual situation under consideration, in the case of nuisance creation. The reason for this distinction is historically based. The imposition of liability for continuing or adopting a nuisance only occurred at a time when the tort of negligence was well developed.

The distinction between continuance and creation is not helpful, as it is difficult to define what is meant by strict liability. In some cases, fault, in the sense of want of reasonable care and attention, is not an essential requirement in the determination of liability. This includes cases involving nuisance to servitudes and interference with a natural right incident to ownership of land. Likewise, in *Wringe v Cohen*,[6] strict liability was imposed on the owner of premises adjoining the highway where highway users or adjoining occupiers were injured as a result of a failure to repair the premises. However, this rule is subject to a number of exceptions. For example, there will be no liability where the defect in the premises is due to the secret or unobservable process of nature, or the act of a trespasser unless it can be shown that the owner was at fault.

In some cases of nuisance, fault is an essential requirement. It has been observed that this is so in the case of continuation or adoption of a nuisance. The same can be said of states of affairs which lead to an isolated act causing damage to the plaintiff.

In *The Wagon Mound (No 2)*,[7] it was said that the foreseeability of damage test applies equally to actions for damages in both nuisance and negligence. It follows that, before a defendant can be liable in nuisance, he must have been able to foresee the kind of damage which the plaintiff suffered. Therefore fault, in the sense of foreseeability, may be essential to the issues of remoteness of damage, if not to initial liability. This may explain the difficult and rather obscure *dictum* that:

> Nuisance is a term used to cover a wide variety of tortious acts or omissions and in many, negligence in the narrow sense is not essential ... And although negligence may not be necessary, fault of some kind is almost always necessary and fault generally involves foreseeability.[8]

Some of these statements may suggest that a plaintiff may succeed in a nuisance action when an action in negligence might fail. For example, if an industrialist establishes a cooking oil processing plant, the process may produce noxious smells. The industrialist

---

4   Law Commission No 32 (1970) p 25.
5   [1893] 2 Ch 588.
6   [1940] 1 KB 229.
7   Sub nom *Overseas Tankship (UK) Ltd v Miller SS Co Pty* [1967] 1 AC 617. See also *Cambridge Water Co v Eastern Counties Leather plc* [1994] 2 AC 264.
8   Ibid at 639 (per LORD REID).

may employ expert advice in installing the latest equipment to avoid such problems. If the factory still produces unpleasant smells, a negligence action may fail if the magnitude of harm is outbalanced by the precautions taken to avoid such harm. If the industrialist has complied with modern practice, he has exercised reasonable care. However, if the action is brought in private nuisance, the court does not consider the defendant's conduct, but investigates the plaintiff's interest and enquires how it is affected by the defendant's activity. If this is classed as an unreasonable interference, an injunction will be granted. The court determines that, if the activity cannot be carried on without the interference, it must not be pursued at all. The fact that all reasonable care has been exercised is irrelevant.

This distinction between nuisance and negligence is sufficient to justify the distinction between the two torts. It was said in *Leakey v National Trust*[9] that the difficulty of distinction is not disposed of by transmuting liability in nuisance (however occasioned) into a duty to do what can reasonably be done in the circumstances of a particular case to prevent or diminish the consequences of a nuisance. This formulation may ... create fresh problems, and the derivative problems may defy resolution.[10]

(vi) Remedies

(a) *Injunction*[11] The injunction is the most powerful weapon in nuisance cases. Frequently, the plaintiff will have as his objective the cessation of the defendant's activity. The court may, at its discretion, grant a perpetual injunction terminating the activity, or limit the activity to certain times. In order to lessen the impact on the defendant, the court may suspend the injunction to give him the opportunity to eliminate the source of the complaint.[12] Even a perpetual injunction may not terminate the activity, as it may force the defendant to pay a high price to the plaintiff for the right to carry it out.[13]

Where the plaintiff proves the nuisance, the court must determine the relevant circumstances in which the injunction may or may not be granted. In *Shelfer v City of London Electric Lighting Co*,[14] the defendant's operations caused vibration and noise. The defendant claimed that the plaintiff should be limited to damages as, to award an injunction would deprive Londoners of the provision of electricity. In cases of continuing and actionable nuisances, it was said that the discretion not to grant an injunction should be exercised only in very exceptional circumstances.[15] If the injury to the plaintiff's legal rights is small and capable of being compensated by a small monetary payment and it would be oppressive to grant an injunction, damages may be awarded.[16] The basis of the decision is that the defendant cannot buy the right to commit a nuisance.[17]

The award of an injunction will not follow automatically where the conditions in *Shelfer's* case are not satisfied. An injunction can be refused on general equitable grounds in the case of unreasonable or unmeritorious plaintiffs.[18]

9   [1980] QB 485.
10   Ibid at 529 (per SHAW LJ).
11   See also ch 14.
12   See *Pride of Derby v British Celanese Ltd* [1953] Ch 149; *Halsey v Esso Petroleum Co Ltd* [1961] 2 All ER 145.
13   See Ogus and Richardson [1977] 36 CLJ 284.
14   [1895] 1 Ch 287.
15   Ibid at 316–317 (per LINDLEY LJ).
16   Ibid at 322–323 (per A L SMITH LJ).
17   See also *Wood v Conway Corpn* [1914] 2 Ch 47; *Cowper v Laidler* [1903] 2 Ch 337; *Pride of Derby v British Celanese Ltd* [1953] Ch 149.
18   *Behrens v Richards* [1905] 2 Ch 614.

The *Shelfer* principle may be criticised on the ground that it fails to take account of the implications for the general public of the award of an injunction. In the United States, it has been advocated that industry should internalise the costs of its interference with amenity.[19] One way of doing this is to provide statutory compensation or common law damages for the victims of industrial nuisances.[20] Recent English authorities have been mainly concerned with nuisances caused by social rather than industrial concerns. In *Miller v Jackson*,[1] balls struck from a cricket ground had interfered with the plaintiff's enjoyment of her garden. The Court of Appeal held that the interference amounted to a nuisance, but refused to grant an injunction because the defendant's activities were reasonable and beneficial as a social focus to the village, and because the plaintiff had come to the nuisance.

This is a case which clearly departs from the *Shelfer* principles, by putting public interest above private rights.[2] However, this does not represent a trend towards upgrading the public interest. In *Kennaway v Thompson*,[3] the plaintiff was disturbed by power-boat racing. The nuisance was admitted and damages were awarded at first instance on public interest grounds. The plaintiff successfully appealed against the refusal of an injunction and the Court of Appeal discounted the merits of the defendant's activities.

(b)   *Damages*   In public nuisance cases, the plaintiff must prove damage in order to succeed. In private nuisance, damage is normally a necessary requirement, but this may be presumed.[4] Actions in respect of a nuisance to easements or *profits à prendre* are actionable per se.[5]

The damage in a nuisance case will normally be a depreciation in the value of the land affected. Where the nuisance constitutes an interference with personal comfort or convenience the assessment will be more difficult. One approach taken in *Bone v Seale*[6] was that damages could be assessed on a comparative basis with damages for loss of amenity in personal injuries cases, such as loss of smell. However this approach was dissaproved by LORD HOFFMANN in *Hunter,* as nuisance is primarily a tort against land, not the person and damages should be assessed by reference to the diminution in the capital value of the property.[7]

Damages for economic loss are common in public nuisance cases, but authority on this point is scarce in private nuisance. In *Dunton v Dover District Council*,[8] it was held that losses due to a downturn in bookings caused by a nuisance were recoverable by a hotel proprietor. The problems which affect economic loss recovery in negligence are not usually present in nuisance cases. Before liability can be established in nuisance, it must be shown that the plaintiff's property interest has been damaged. An attempt to use nuisance to recover economic loss failed in *SCM (UK) Ltd v W J Whittall & Son Ltd*,[9] when it was held that an isolated escape damaging an electric power cable was not a nuisance.

---

19   *Boomer v Atlantic Cement Co* 257 NE (2d) 870 (1970).
20   See Fleming *Introduction* pp 188–189. Cf *Markesinis & Deakin* p 447.
1   [1977] QB 966.
2   Ibid at 981–982 (per LORD DENNING).
3   [1981] QB 88, [1980] 3 All ER 329.
4   *Fay v Prentice* (1845) 1 CB 828.
5   *Nicholls v Ely Beet Sugar Factory Ltd* [1936] Ch 343.
6   [1975] 1 All ER 787.
7   [1997] 2 All ER 426 at 451.
8   (1977) 76 LGR 87.
9   [1970] 2 All ER 417; affd [1970] 3 All ER 245.

(c)   *Abatement*   Nuisance is one of the rare instances in English law when the plaintiff may use self-help. The remedy of abatement has been referred to as one which the law does not favour, and it is not usually advisable.[10] The remedy can be exercised by cutting branches from overhanging trees,[11] and the stopping up of drains.[12] If the abatement requires entry to another person's land, notice must usually be given,[13] or the abator will be a trespasser.

(vii)   Defences

The three principal defences are those of prescription, contributory negligence and statutory authority. However, there are also three matters which might appear to constitute a defence to nuisance, but will not normally be treated as such.

(a)   *Coming to the nuisance*   Generally, the defendant cannot plead that he was carrying on his activity before the plaintiff moved to the area and that the plaintiff was aware of the nuisance when he moved.[14] A recent attack on this principle was made by LORD DENNING MR in *Miller v Jackson*,[15] but the majority of the Court of Appeal rejected this argument as far as the establishment of a nuisance was concerned. It did, however, affect the decision not to grant the injunction.

(b)   *That the nuisance was due to many*   If the nuisance is caused by several persons, it is no defence that the contribution of the defendant would not, in itself, constitute a nuisance.[16]

(c)   *Usefulness*   An argument that the defendant's activity is useful is no defence. In *Adams v Ursell*,[17] a fish and chip shop in a residential area was held to be a nuisance, even though it was of great utility to its clientele.

(d)   *Prescription*   In cases of private nuisance, if the nuisance has been actionable for a period of twenty years and the plaintiff was aware of this during the relevant period, the defence of prescription applies. In *Sturges v Bridgman*,[18] the defendant had used an industrial pestle and mortar for a period of twenty years. A neighbour, who had built consulting rooms in his garden, complained when the noise and vibration caused by the defendant's activities substantially interfered with his medical practice. The defence of prescription failed on the ground that the nuisance had not been actionable for the whole of the preceding twenty-year period.

(e)   *Contributory negligence*[19]

(f)   *Statutory authority*   The emphasis on private rights in nineteenth-century nuisance cases raised a conflict between the need of industrialists to inflict sometimes inevitable harm, and the rights of neighbouring landowners. The construction and operation of

10   *Lagan Navigation Co v Lambeg Bleaching, Dyeing and Finishing Co* [1927] AC 226 at 244 (per LORD ATKINSON). See also *Burton v Winters* [1993] 1 WLR 1077.
11   *Lemmon v Webb* [1895] AC 1.
12   *Charles v Finchley Local Board* (1883) 23 Ch D 767.
13   *Jones v Williams* (1843) 11 M & W 176.
14   *Bliss v Hall* (1838) 4 Bing NC 183; *Sturges v Bridgman* (1879) 11 Ch D 852.
15   [1977] QB 966.
16   *Thorpe v Brumfitt* (1873) 8 Ch App 650.
17   [1913] 1 Ch 269.
18   (1879) 11 Ch D 852.
19   See ch 20.

railways was a potential source of nuisance litigation, and companies strengthened their position by obtaining statutory authority to operate their railways. The courts interpreted such legislation as an authority to cause interference by smoke, noise and vibration, provided there was no negligence on the part of the company.

If a statute orders something to be done, there will be no liability for performing the duty and for any inevitable consequences. Similar principles apply where the statute confers a power rather than a duty. Difficulties may arise in determining what is an inevitable consequence. An inevitable consequence is one which cannot be avoided by the use of due care and skill.[20] The implied reference to negligence is not always appropriate in cases of nuisance. In such cases, the appropriate enquiry is whether the authorised activity could have been carried out without causing a nuisance. In *Metropolitan Asylum District Managers v Hill*,[1] a local authority with a statutory power to build a smallpox hospital was restrained from erecting it in a place which would have been a source of danger to local residents. However, the power could have been carried out without committing a nuisance, by siting the hospital in a less populated area.

There are other cases where the activity authorised will inevitably infringe on individuals' rights. For example, where a railway is authorised on a prescribed route, or where a refinery is to be built in a prescribed place.[2] The just solution to this problem is to provide a compensation scheme in the statute.[3] The provision of such a scheme would be strong evidence that a person's common law rights have been removed by the statute.

National interest may also prove to be a relevant factor in determining the availability of the defence of statutory authority. In *Allen v Gulf Oil Refining Ltd*,[4] the defendants were statutorily empowered to compulsorily purchase land in a rural area and build an oil refinery, a jetty and railways. The plaintiff alleged a nuisance consisting of smell, noise and vibration, but statutory authority was pleaded as a defence. The plaintiff argued that the relevant Act[5] authorised construction but not use of the refinery. Because of the public demand for oil products, the House of Lords held that Parliament must have intended the development to be built and operated unless there was evidence of negligence on the part of the defendants.

The decision can be criticised, as it authorised a substantial intrusion upon the life of local residents, while leaving them with no legal redress. A preferable approach would have been to allow an action for damages, while still allowing the operations to continue, as the public interest would have been satisfied whilst catering for private rights.

The granting of planning permission does not authorise the commission of a nuisance, although such permission may change the nature of a locality.[6] Whether it does so change the nature of the locality is important in determining whether the defendant's actions constitute a nuisance.[7] It should be noted that the granting of planning permission should be irrelevant where there is physical damage to the plaintiff's property, although statutory authority will be a defence if the damage is an inevitable result of the authorised activity.

---

20   See *Geddis v Bann Reservoir (Proprietors)* (1878) 3 App Cas 430 at 455–456 (per LORD BLACKBURN).
1   (1881) 6 App Cas 193.
2   *Allen v Gulf Oil Refining Ltd* [1981] AC 1001, [1981] 1 All ER 353. See Davis (1974) 90 LQR 361.
3   See *Marriage v East Norfolk Rivers Catchment Board* [1950] 1 KB 284. See also Land Compensation Act 1973, s 1.
4   [1981] AC 1001, [1981] 1 All ER 353.
5   Gulf Oil Refining Act 1965, s 5.
6   *Gillingham BC v Medway (Chatham) Dock Ltd* [1993] QB 343.
7   *Wheeler v JJ Saunders Ltd* [1995] 2 All ER 697. See Tromans [1995] CLJ 494.

3.   **THE RULE IN** *RYLANDS V FLETCHER*

(1)   INTRODUCTION

A species of tortious strict liability was introduced by the decision in *Rylands v Fletcher*.[8] The rule provides that a person who, for his own purposes, brings on his land, and collects and keeps there anything likely to do mischief if it escapes, must keep it at his peril, and, if he does not do so, he is prima facie answerable for all the damage which is the natural consequence of its escape.[9] The defendant had employed contractors to build a reservoir on his land to supply water for his factory. The contractors negligently failed to stop up a disused mine shaft. When the reservoir was filled, the plaintiff's adjoining mine was flooded.

None of the existing forms of tortious liability applied to the case. The flooding was not trespass, as it was not a direct and immediate consequence of the defendant's activity. It was not a nuisance, as, at that time, no liability attached for an isolated escape. There was no negligence, because an employer was not liable for the negligence of his independent contractors.[10] BLACKBURN J, in the Court of Exchequer Chamber, held that the defendant was liable under his rule, seemingly formulated from existing analogies such as cattle trespass, nuisance and filth from a privy.[11] The House of Lords approved the decision and the rule, subject to the addition of the requirement that the defendant's user of his land should be 'non-natural'.[12] The development of a novel principle of law was cloaked by BLACKBURN J's application of a general principle to existing rules of strict liability in English tort law. That new law was created is undisputable, and policy reasons for the decision have been asserted.[13] It is unlikely that the decision represented an attack on industrial interests by a judiciary representing the landed classes, as the competing interests in the case were both industrial. What it does represent is a recognition that industrial enterprise could inflict serious damage on neighbouring landowners, and that the preferable solution to a fault-based system of liability, was that the damage inflictor should internalise costs by accepting liability for the damage caused.

The fact that the decision came as the tort system was moving strongly towards fault-based liability to protect emergent industrial concerns should cause no great surprise. Although this era was regarded as the high point of *laissez-faire*, the period was also one of conflicting opinions and attitudes. Conflict existed between the classical economists and the utilitarians,[14] and the judiciary were also divided in their approach to the problems created by new industry and commerce.[15] Differing philosophies give rise to differing judgments, and the opinions in *Rylands* represent just one strand of judicial thinking in relation to a particular problem.

Whether the rule was intended by its author to mark the beginning of a new principle, based on strict liability, governing all extra-hazardous activities, will never be known. What is known is that, by a process of judicial misunderstanding and hostility, the principle has been emasculated to the point where it plays very little part in practical modern

---

8   (1865) 3 H & C 774, 159 ER 737 (Court of Exchequer); (1866) LR 1 Exch 265 (Court of Exchequer Chamber); (1868) LR 3 HL 330 (House of Lords).
9   (1866) LR 1 Exch 265 at 279 (per BLACKBURN J).
10   *Bower v Peate* (1876) 1 QBD 321 appears to be the first attack on this principle.
11   *Tenant v Goldwin* (1704) 2 Ld Raym 1089.
12   (1868) LR 3 HL 330 at 338–339.
13   Bohlen (1911) 59 U Pa LR 298; Molloy (1942) U Chic LR 266; Pound (1940) 53 HLR 365; Simpson (1984) J Leg Stud 208. Cf Prosser *Selected Topics in the Law of Torts* (1953) ch 3.
14   See ch 2.
15   Atiyah *Rise and Fall* pp 359–383.

law. This is evidenced by the dearth of modern law on the subject.[16] The process of emasculation commenced with the requirement that the use of the land should be non-natural, and continued in the House of Lords' decision in *Read v Lyons*[17] that there should be an escape from the premises on which the 'thing' was accumulated, and that personal injury should not be compensated. Furthermore, great damage was done to the principle through the definition of what constituted a non-hazardous activity,[18] and the steady encroachment of fault principles into the rule, particularly where the escape was due to the act of a stranger or by virtue of statutory authority.

The modern view is that the rule is a species of nuisance concerned with isolated escapes. In *Cambridge Water Co v Eastern Counties Leather plc*[19] the defendants used a solvent in their tannery which was spilt onto the floor and, unknown to the defendants, seeped into the ground through a concrete floor and was then carried by percolating water to the plaintiff's borehole where water was extracted. The water, which was for domestic purposes, was contaminated. The House of Lords accepted the view of Professor Newark,[20] that all that the rule does is to apply strict liability in nuisance to claims for damages in cases of isolated escapes and as the type of damage suffered was not foreseeable, the defendants were not liable. However, throughout the judgments the rule is treated separately from nuisance and will continue to be so here.[1] The remaining advantage that the rule has over negligence is that provided the damage is foreseeable, it does not matter whether the defendant has acted with all reasonable care.

(2)   PARTIES TO THE ACTION

The basis of a *Rylands v Fletcher* action is that a neighbouring landowner should not be exposed to an unreasonably high degree of risk from the defendant's use of his land. It follows from this that the plaintiff will normally be an occupier of adjacent land. The defendant must control or occupy the premises from which the thing escapes. In *Smith v Scott*,[2] the defendant corporation let a house to an anti-social family. The corporation incurred no liability under the rule as it did not exercise sufficient control over the premises. An exception to this rule exists where a dangerous thing is brought on to the highway or where an already present danger causes damage to adjacent property.[3] The exception applies where two companies use the same highway. In *Charing Cross Electricity Supply Co v Hydraulic Power Co*,[4] the rule in *Rylands v Fletcher* applied where water escaped from the defendant's water main and damaged the plaintiff's electric cables.

One consequence of *Cambridge Water*[5] is that the moving of *Rylands* closer to nuisance probably means that a proprietary interest in the land affected is required, as in nuisance.

---

16   Cf the position in American law which eventually accepted strict liability for ultra-hazardous activities. See Gregory (1951) 37 Virg LR 359.
17   [1947] AC 156.
18   *Shiffman v Grand Priory in British Realm of Venerable Order of the Hospital of St John of Jerusalem* [1936] 1 All ER 557.
19   [1994] AC 264.
20   (1949) 65 LQR 480.
1   The rule has effectively been abolished in Australia. *Burnie Port Authority v General Jones Pty Ltd* (1994) 120 ALR 42.
2   [1973] Ch 314.
3   *Midwood v Manchester Corpn* [1905] 2 KB 597; *Rigby v Chief Constable of Northamptonshire* [1985] 2 All ER 985.
4   [1914] 3 KB 772.
5   [1994] AC 264.

(3)   REQUIREMENTS OF THE RULE

(i)   Things likely to do mischief if they escape[6]

The rule has not been confined to things with an intrinsically dangerous quality, such as chemicals and explosives. The thing complained of is examined in the context of its surroundings. However, the concept of non-natural user appears to have been used in an attempt to confine liability to extra-hazardous activities. However, following the decision in *Cambridge Water*[7] the damage must be foreseeable. It may not be necessary for the courts to to examine whether the thing was dangerous, as this will come within the foreseeability of damage test. If the thing in question is not dangerous then it is unlikely to cause damage if it escapes.

The rule has been held to apply to accumulations of water,[8] electricity,[9] fire,[10] explosives,[11] gas,[12] slag heaps,[13] chair-o-planes,[14] caravan dwellers who foul and damage nearby property[15] and things giving off noxious gases and fumes.[16]

(ii)   Accumulation

The 'thing' must have been accumulated or brought on to the defendant's land. This means that there will be no liability for things naturally on the land. In *Smith v Kenrick*,[17] the defendant was not liable for the escape of water by gravitation or percolation where it was naturally on the defendant's land and he was not actively responsible for its presence there.

The requirement of an accumulation distinguishes the action from nuisance, where there need be no tangible accumulation to found liability.[18]

(iii)   Non-natural user[19]

It was unclear at one stage whether the word natural should be equated with non-artificial use, or whether it meant ordinary and usual. Adopting the first meaning might have given the rule a very wide application, but in *Rickards v Lothian*,[20] the narrower meaning was adopted. A non-natural user was defined as:

> some special use bringing with it increased danger to others and must not merely be the ordinary use of the land or such use as is proper for the general benefit of mankind.[1]

---

6   See Stallybrass [1929] 3 CLJ 376 at 382–385.
7   [1994] 2 AC 264.
8   *Rylands v Fletcher* (1868) LR 3 HL 330.
9   *National Telephone Co v Baker* [1893] 2 Ch 186.
10   *Jones v Festiniog Rly Co* (1866) LR 3 QB 733; *Musgrove v Pandelis* [1919] 2 KB 43.
11   *Miles v Forest Rock Granite Co (Leicestershire) Ltd* (1918) 34 TLR 500; *Rainham Chemical Works Ltd v Belvedere Fish Guano Co Ltd* [1921] 2 AC 465.
12   *Batcheller v Tunbridge Wells Gas Co* (1901) 84 LT 765.
13   *A-G v Cory Bros and Co Ltd* [1921] 1 AC 521.
14   *Hale v Jennings Bros* [1938] 1 All ER 579.
15   *A-G v Corke* [1933] Ch 89. Cf *Matheson v Board of Governors of Northcote College* [1975] 2 NZLR 106. See also *Smith v Scott* [1973] Ch 314.
16   *West v British Tramways Co* [1908] 2 KB 14.
17   (1849) 7 CB 515, 137 ER 205. See also *Ellison v Ministry of Defence* (1996) 81 BLR 101.
18   See *Goldman v Hargrave* [1967] 1 AC 645; *Leakey v National Trust for Places of Historic Interest or Natural Beauty* [1980] QB 485.
19   Newark (1961) 24 MLR 557.
20   [1913] AC 263 (Privy Council).
1   Ibid at 279–280 (per Lord Moulton), approved in *Read v Lyons* [1947] AC 156 at 169 (per Viscount Simon).

The adoption of this test means that there is no objective test for what constitutes a non-natural user. It was possible for the use of land as a munitions factory to be declared a non-natural user in 1921 and a natural use in 1946.[2] The test, however, is not whether the activity is of benefit to the community, such as the creation of employment, or that it is common in a particular industry. The trial judge in *Cambridge Water* used this reasoning but it was rejected by the House of Lords 'as the storage of substantial quantities of chemicals is an almost classic example of non-natural user.'[3]

The modern test is close to the negligence test in that the courts balance the seriousness of the harm threatened against the utility of the defendant's conduct. This approach is illustrated by *Mason v Levy Auto Parts of England Ltd*,[4] where the defendants stored large quantities of inflammable materials on their land. The materials ignited in mysterious circumstances. In determining whether the defendants were liable under *Rylands v Fletcher*, it was stated that regard must be had to the quantities of materials stored, the way in which they were stored, and the character of the neighbourhood. It was recognised that these considerations would also justify a finding of negligence.[5]

LORD GOFF in *Cambridge Water*[6] was of the opinion that non-natural user was similar to reasonable user in nuisance, as both operate as control devices.[7]

Although the concept of non-natural user should be flexible in order to deal with changing social and economic conditions, it is submitted that it is wrong to equate it with negligence and introduce the idea of reasonable user as a concept. The key factor in a strict liability regime is that it should be applied where the defendant's use of his land is legal, but presents a threat to his neighbours which they should not have to countenance. If damage occurs despite the exercise of reasonable care on the part of the defendant, the cost should be borne by the defendant through the imposition of strict liability. There is no reason why his neighbours should have to insure against the risk of harm when the defendant benefits from his activities.

(iv)   Escape

The decision of the House of Lords in *Read v Lyons*[8] placed a considerable restriction on the capacity of *Rylands v Fletcher* to deal with the problem of extra-hazardous activities. The plaintiff worked in a munitions factory and was injured on the premises in an explosion. The argument of counsel that escape meant escape from control was rejected in favour of the rule that the escape must be from the defendant's land.

The decision moved *Rylands v Fletcher* closer to nuisance as an action governing the relations between neighbouring landowners,[9] and creates a distinction between those outside the premises and those inside. This is illustrated by the Abbeystead Pumping Station disaster.[10] A party of local residents were invited to tour the pumping station by the North West Water Authority. While they were on the premises, an explosion caused by the build-up of methane in the pipes killed some and injured others. The victims were put to the test of showing negligence against the defendants, as they were on the premises at the time of the explosion.

---

2   *Rainham Chemical Works Ltd v Belvedere Fish Guano Co Ltd* [1921] 2 AC 465; *Read v J Lyons & Co Ltd* [1947] AC 156.
3   [1994] 2 WLR 53 at 83 per LORD GOFF.
4   [1967] 2 QB 530.
5   Ibid at 542–543 (per MACKENNA J).
6   [1994] 2 WLR 53 at 83.
7   See also *Ellison v Ministry of Defence* (1996) 81 BLR 101.
8   [1947] AC 156.
9   *Newark* (1949) 65 LQR 480 at 488.
10   *Eckersley v Binnie* (1988) 18 Con LR 1, CA.

(v)   Damage

The plaintiff must prove that he has suffered damage. In *Cambridge Water*,[11] the House of Lords held that it was an essential element that the type of harm suffered by the plaintiff was foreseeable by the defendant, even though the defendant could be liable in the absence of reasonable care. As contamination of the plaintiff's water supply was not foreseeable at the time of the spillages, the defendants were not liable. The test endorsed was that the defendant is only liable for that damage which the reasonable bystander would have foreseen. The escape itself must be foreseeable. This is different to assuming the escape and then asking, following the escape, what type of damage the reasonable bystander would have foreseen.[12] The latter test is closer to BLACKBURN J's judgment, as otherwise it is difficult to argue that the keeper of a dangerous thing does so at his peril and *Rylands* itself would have been decided differently had the escape had to be foreseeable.[13]

Damages are recoverable where there is harm to the land or to chattels on the land. The position with regard to personal injuries is not clear. LORD MACMILLAN, in *Read v Lyons*,[14] denied that such damages were recoverable. There is, however, earlier authority to the effect that they may be recovered,[15] and later Court of Appeal *dicta* to suggest that they are recoverable.[16] Since *Read v Lyons*, the position has been that an occupier of land may recover for personal injuries, thereby confirming the correctness of *Hale v Jennings*.[17] But earlier cases, such as *Shiffman v Order of St John*,[18] which allowed a non-occupier to succeed must be regarded as incorrectly decided. The House of Lords' decision in *Hunter v Canary Wharf Ltd*[19] that the plaintiff must have an interest in the land affected, would appear to settle this point in relation to non-occupiers, even assuming they still have locus standi to claim. The combination of *Cambridge Water*, bringing *Rylands* closer to nuisance, and *Hunter*, with its emphasis on nuisance being a tort against land, may mean that damages for personal injuries cannot be recovered at all.

Whatever the scope of the present law, it is a matter for regret that proprietary interests continue to receive greater protection than physical interests.[20]

The position with regard to damages for economic loss is equally unclear. In *Weller v Foot and Mouth Disease Research Institute*,[1] it was held that cattle auctioneers who suffered a loss of income as a result of the escape of a virus from the defendant's premises could not recover under *Rylands v Fletcher*, as they had no interest in any land to which the virus escaped.[2] It is possible that economic loss could be recovered in a *Rylands v Fletcher* action. However, given the tendency to equate *Rylands v Fletcher* with nuisance and proprietary interests, the problem would usually be approached from a different angle to that in negligence.

11   [1994] 2 AC 264.
12   Wilkinson (1994) 57 MLR 799.
13   Fleming (1995) 3 Tort L Rev 56, 58.
14   [1947] AC 156 at 170–171.
15   *Hale v Jennings Bros* [1938] 1 All ER 579; *Shiffman v Grand Priory in British Realm of Venerable Order of the Hospital of St John of Jerusalem* [1936] 1 All ER 557.
16   *Perry v Kendricks Transport Ltd* [1956] 1 WLR 85 at 92 (per PARKER LJ).
17   [1938] 1 All ER 579.
18   [1936] 1 All ER 557.
19   [1997] 2 All ER 426.
20   Cf *Aldridge and O'Brien v Van Patter* [1952] 4 DLR 93.
1   [1966] 1 QB 569.
2   [1966] 1 QB 569 at 588.

(4)   DEFENCES

The liability under *Rylands v Fletcher* is strict and not absolute, and certain exceptions to liability have been developed by the courts.

(i)   Consent of the plaintiff

Invoking the defence of consent may be unnecessary in some cases because of the judicial approach to the meaning of non-natural user. For example, if a bath overflows and damages property belonging to the occupier of another floor in the same building, the case may be disposed of by treating the water supply as a natural use of the property, or by invoking the defence of common benefit.

Where the consent of the plaintiff is relevant, this is an illustration of the general defence of *volenti non fit injuria*.[3]

(ii)   Common benefit

An extension of the idea of consent is that the source of the danger is maintained for the benefit of both parties. In *Carstairs v Taylor*,[4] roof water was collected in a box. A rat gnawed through the box and water leaked and damaged the plaintiff's goods. As the box was maintained for the common benefit of the plaintiff and defendant, no action lay.

At one time, it was thought that the defence did not apply to utility companies in an action brought by the consumer, since the consumer had no choice as to his source or conditions of supply. However, in *Dunne v North Western Gas Board*,[5] common benefit was considered to be an important factor, as supplies such as gas and electricity are brought to places where they are required by the community.[6] Furthermore, it was thought that a nationalised industry did not accumulate a substance for its own purposes. Whether a similar approach is adopted in favour of a privatised monopoly remains to be seen!

(iii)   Act of a stranger

In some cases, the escape will occur because of the act of a third party. In *Rickards v Lothian*,[7] the waste pipe of a lavatory basin was deliberately blocked up by a third person. As a result, water flooded the plaintiff's premises, The defendant occupier was not liable, as the escape was caused by the wrongful act of a stranger.

The occupier will not be liable for the acts of a trespasser, but may be responsible for the acts of his servants, independent contractors and lawful visitors over whom he has sufficient control. The basis of the defence is the absence of control by the defendant over the act of a stranger on his land.[8] The effect of the defence, once raised, is to convert the action ostensibly based on strict liability into one for negligence. If the defendant was not at fault, the plaintiff will not succeed. This subverts the original purpose of the rule, which was intended to place liability for exceptional risks on the person who creates the risk. Instead, the use of this defence makes liability dependent on a negligent failure to control the risk.

---

3   See ch 22.
4   (1871) LR 6 Exch 217.
5   [1964] 2 QB 806.
6   Ibid at 832 (per SELLERS LJ).
7   [1913] AC 263.
8   *Perry v Kendricks Transport Ltd* [1956] 1 WLR 85 at 90 (per JENKINS LJ).

(iv)   Act of God

This defence is available where the escape is caused by natural forces, in circumstances which no human foresight can provide against, and of which human prudence is not bound to recognise the possibility.[9] The defence succeeded in *Nichols v Marsland*,[10] where the defendant created ornamental lakes by damming a stream. An exceptionally heavy rainfall caused the embankment to collapse and the escaping water damaged four bridges. The decision was criticised in *Greenock Corpn v Caledonian Railway*,[11] and there has been a tendency to restrict its application. It was possible that the defence would apply to lightning strikes, tornadoes or earthquakes, but, as in the case of the defence of act of a stranger, the effect is to shift attention towards the culpability of the defendant and whether he ought to have foreseen the possibility of the event. The effect of *Cambridge Water*[12] ruling that the damage must be reasonably foreseeable, is that unforeseeable natural occurrences will not give rise to actions.

(v)   Default of the plaintiff

If the escape is due to the act or default of the plaintiff, he will have no action.[13] If this amounts to contributory negligence, then his damages will be reduced in proportion to his responsibility for the harm suffered.[14]

(vi)   Statutory authority

Whether statutory authority is a defence to *Rylands v Fletcher* depends on a construction of the statute.

In *Green v Chelsea Waterworks Co*,[15] the defendants were under a statutory duty to maintain a continuous supply of water through their pipes. They were held to be immune from action in the absence of negligence when one of their pipes burst, causing flooding. In *Charing Cross Electricity Supply Co v Hydraulic Power Co*,[16] the defendants had a power to supply water, but were not under a duty to do so. The plaintiff, on similar facts to *Green*, succeeded in his claim. In *Green*, it was inevitable that pipes would rupture as a result of the defendants' performance of their statutory duty. In the latter case, only permissive authority was given.

Whether local authorities can take advantage of statutory authority was considered in *Smeaton v Ilford Corpn*.[17] UPJOHN J did not consider it necessary to decide whether a local authority exercising statutory duties is completely outside the rule.

(5)   THE FUTURE OF THE RULE IN *RYLANDS v FLETCHER*

It is not clear whether the original purpose of the rule was to impose strict liability for extra-hazardous activities, or whether it was viewed as a pragmatic extension of the law of private nuisance. In modern times, there has been a tendency for the courts to interpret

---

9   *Tennent v Earl of Glasgow* (1864) 2 M 22 at 26–27, HL (per LORD WESTBURY), approved by the House of Lords in *Greenock Corpn v Caledonian Rly Co* [1917] AC 556.
10   (1876) 2 Ex D 1.
11   [1917] AC 556.
12   [1994] 2 AC 264.
13   *Rylands v Fletcher* (1868) LR 3 HL 330 at 340.
14   See ch 20.
15   (1894) 70 LT 547.
16   [1914] 3 KB 772.
17   [1954] Ch 450.

Rylands v Fletcher as a species of nuisance.[18] In some cases, the plaintiff may succeed in both torts, but there are differences between the two. In nuisance, there is no requirement of accumulation or non-natural user, but the tort is limited to persons with an interest in land. *Rylands v Fletcher* is a tort originating from land usage, but it is not clear whether the plaintiff need have an interest in land to sue.[19]

The strongest attack on the rule has come in the form of the infiltration of a fault requirement. This is apparent in the application of the requirement of non-natural user, the requirement of foreseeability of the escape and type of damage and the defences of act of a stranger, act of God and statutory authority. The effect of this has been to remove a remedy from the plaintiff when he most needs it, that is, when he has been injured by the defendant's activities which have exposed him to risk. For example, in *Pearson v North Western Gas Board*,[20] the plaintiff was seriously injured and her husband was killed in a gas explosion. It was impossible to prove fault and the rule in *Rylands v Fletcher* did not apply, because the gas supply was deemed to be a common benefit. In a heavily industrialised society with widely available insurance, justice is not always done by requiring an injured person to prove fault.[1]

The prevalence of the fault principle in the compensation debate and the restriction of the rule to escapes makes it difficult to introduce a cohesive system of strict liability for damage resulting from extra-hazardous activities.[2] The Law Commission[3] made some proposals based on liability for 'dangerous things' and 'dangerous activities', but made no recommendation for reform until the whole fault principle had been examined. The proposals made a reappearance in the Pearson Commission's Report.[4] The Commission envisaged a statutory scheme limited to death and personal injuries, with a parent statute empowering a minister to list dangerous things and activities by statutory instrument. The Commission does not appear to have attached any great importance to this part of their proposals, and the scheme is not particularly well thought through.[5] The rule would not appear to have any significant role to play as one of the toxic torts in the protection of the environment. This is because of the restrictive meaning given to non-natural user by the courts. However the view in *Cambridge Water* on non natural user was in favour of expansion, albeit limited by the foreseeability rule.

The conclusion must be that, for the foreseeable future, the courts are wedded to the fault structure of compensation, and that any change will have to come through legislation. At present, there is no political impetus for such change, although there are statutes which impose strict standards of liability for some hazards.[6]

---

18   *Read v J Lyons & Co Ltd* [1947] AC 156 or 183 (per LORD SIMONDS). *Cambridge Water Co v Eastern Counties Leather plc* [1994] 2 AC 264.
19   West (1966) 30 Conv 95 at 101.
20   [1968] 2 All ER 669.
1   See *Benning v Wong* (1969) 122 CLR 249 at 304 (per WINDEYER J).
2   See *Cambridge Water Co v Eastern Counties Leather plc* [1994] 2 WLR 53 at 79 per LORD GOFF.
3   Law Commission No 32 (1970).
4   Royal Commission on Civil Liability and Compensation for Personal Injury (1978) Cmnd 7054, Vol 1, ch 31.
5   See Atiyah *Accidents* p 144.
6   Nuclear Installations Act 1965. See *Merlin v British Nuclear Fuels plc* [1990] 3 All ER 711. Civil Aviation Act 1982, s 7 – things falling from aircraft. Environmental Protection Act 1990, Part II – poisonous waste. Water Industry Act 1991, s 209 - escapes from water mains.

Index